South Africa, Lesotho & Swaziland

Mary Fitzpatrick, Becca Blond, Gemma Pitcher,
Simon Richmond, Matt Warren

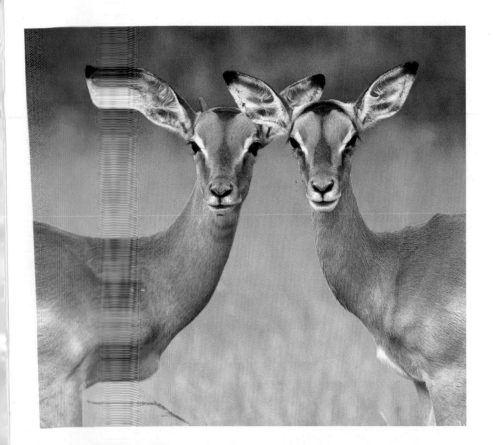

Contents

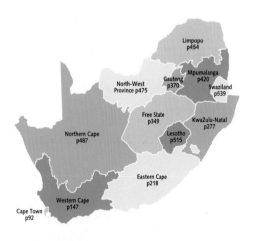

Limpopo
p454

Mpumalanga
p420

Gauteng
p370

North-West
Province p475

Swaziland
p539

Free State
p349

KwaZulu-Natal
p277

Northern Cape
p487

Lesotho
p515

Eastern Cape
p218

Western Cape
p147

Cape Town
p92

Lonely Planet books provide independent advice. Lonely Planet does not accept advertising in guidebooks, nor do we accept payment in exchange for listing or endorsing any place or business. Lonely Planet writers do not accept discounts or payments in exchange for positive coverage of any sort.

Destination South Africa, Lesotho & Swaziland

Whether you're after wildlife and wilderness, or relaxation and refinement, South Africa, Lesotho and Swaziland are bound to please. Together, they offer something for everyone: rural rhythms and urban beats, low-key backpacker hostels and luxurious lodges, on-the-edge adventure and laid-back lounging. All this is set against the backdrop of one of the most stunning topographies on the planet, rimmed by the pounding surf and sublime seascapes of South Africa's 2800km coastline.

Behind the incredible natural beauty, South Africa's soul – ravaged and scarred, beautiful and hope-filled – is the stage for the daily drama of one of the world's greatest experiments in racial harmony. Glittering cities with abundant amenities and first-world infrastructure rub shoulders with sprawling townships, where vast numbers of South Africans are stalked by the shadows of hunger, poverty and one of the highest HIV/AIDS infection rates in the world. While it's easy to travel around focusing on the former, you'll only discover the country's heart by seeing the latter. And there's never been a better time than now – just over a decade since South Africa's first free, multiracial elections – as the colours of the 'rainbow nation' finally begin to fuse.

Travel in South Africa is easy: the road network is excellent, there's a wide array of good-value accommodation and dining options, and costs are reasonable. Topping things off is the chance to detour to rugged Lesotho – a hiking and pony-trekking paradise – or to easy-going Swaziland, where the vibrant traditional culture will envelop you at every turn.

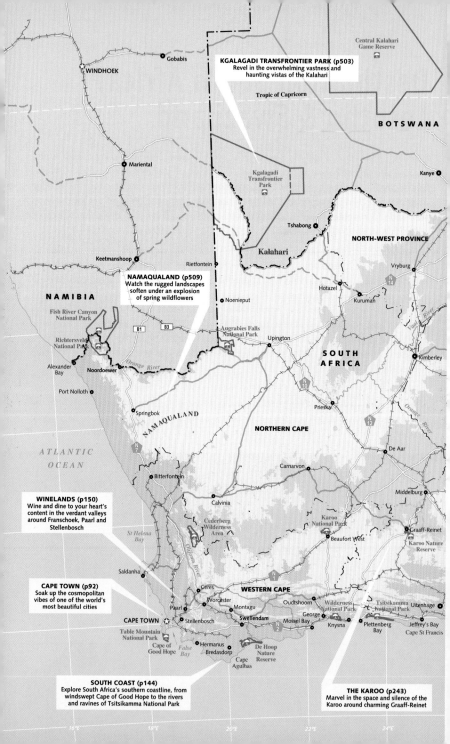

WINDHOEK

Gobabis

KGALAGADI TRANSFRONTIER PARK (p503)
Revel in the overwhelming vastness and haunting vistas of the Kalahari

Central Kalahari Game Reserve

Tropic of Capricorn

BOTSWANA

Mariental

Kanye

Kgalagadi Transfrontier Park

Keetmanshoop

Rietfontein

Tshabong

NORTH-WEST PROVINCE

Vryburg

NAMAQUALAND (p509)
Watch the rugged landscapes soften under an explosion of spring wildflowers

Noenieput

Hotazel

NAMIBIA

Fish River Canyon National Park

Richtersveld National Park

Alexander Bay

Noordoewer

Orange River

B1

B3

Augrabies Falls National Park

Upington

Kuruman

SOUTH AFRICA

Kimberley

Port Nolloth

Springbok

NAMAQUALAND

NORTHERN CAPE

Prieska

Orange River

De Aar

ATLANTIC OCEAN

Bitterfontein

Carnarvon

Middelburg

N7

WINELANDS (p150)
Wine and dine to your heart's content in the verdant valleys around Franschoek, Paarl and Stellenbosch

Calvinia

Cederberg Wilderness Area

Karoo National Park

Beaufort West

Graaff-Reinet

Karoo Nature Reserve

St Helena Bay

Olifants River

Saldanha

Ceres

Worcester

WESTERN CAPE

Oudtshoorn

Wilderness National Park

Tsitsikamma National Park

Uitenhage

CAPE TOWN (p92)
Soak up the cosmopolitan vibes of one of the world's most beautiful cities

CAPE TOWN

Paarl

Stellenbosch

Montagu

Swellendam

George

Mossel Bay

Knysna

Plettenberg Bay

Jeffrey's Bay

Cape St Francis

Table Mountain National Park

Cape of Good Hope

False Bay

Hermanus

Bredasdorp

De Hoop Nature Reserve

Cape Agulhas

SOUTH COAST (p144)
Explore South Africa's southern coastline, from windswept Cape of Good Hope to the rivers and ravines of Tsitsikamma National Park

THE KAROO (p243)
Marvel in the space and silence of the Karoo around charming Graaff-Reinet

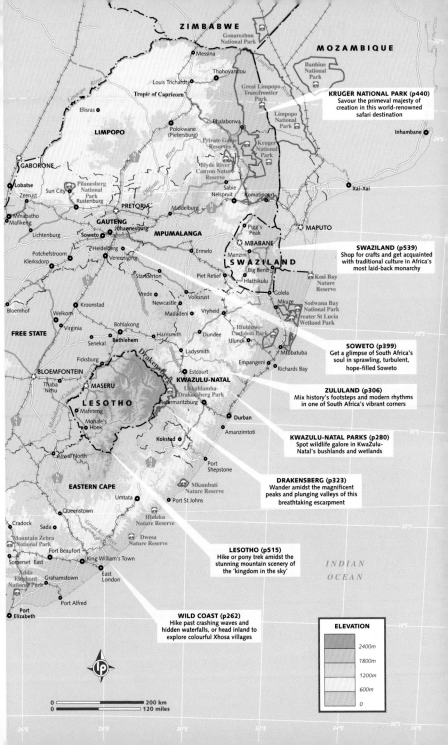

ZIMBABWE

MOZAMBIQUE

KRUGER NATIONAL PARK (p440)
Savour the primeval majesty of creation in this world-renowned safari destination

Tropic of Capricorn

LIMPOPO

Inhambane

GABORONE

Lobatse
Zeerust

Mmabatho
Mafikeng

Lichtenburg

Potchefstroom
Klerksdorp

GAUTENG

PRETORIA

Johannesburg

Soweto

Middelburg

MPUMALANGA

MAPUTO

Heidelberg

Vereeniging

Ermelo

Manzini

MBABANE

SWAZILAND (p539)
Shop for crafts and get acquainted with traditional culture in Africa's most laid-back monarchy

S W A Z I L A N D

Standerton

Vrede

Newcastle

Volksrust

Piet Retief

Big Bend

Hlathikulu

Kosi Bay Nature Reserve

Bloemhof

Kroonstad

Welkom

Madadeni

Vryheid

Golela

Mkuze

Sodwana Bay National Park Greater St Lucia Wetland Park

Virginia

Bohlakong

Harrismith

Dundee

Hluhluwe-Umfolozi Park

FREE STATE

Senekal

Bethlehem

Ladysmith

Ulundi

Mtubatuba

SOWETO (p399)
Get a glimpse of South Africa's soul in sprawling, turbulent, hope-filled Soweto

Ficksburg

Estcourt

Empangeni

Richards Bay

BLOEMFONTEIN

MASERU

KWAZULU-NATAL

Thaba 'Nchu

Ukhahlamba-Drakensberg Park

Pietermaritzburg

ZULULAND (p306)
Mix history's footsteps and modern rhythms in one of South Africa's vibrant corners

LESOTHO

Mafeteng

Mohale's Hoek

Durban

Amanzimtoti

KWAZULU-NATAL PARKS (p280)
Spot wildlife galore in KwaZulu-Natal's bushlands and wetlands

Aliwal North

Kokstad

Port Shepstone

DRAKENSBERG (p323)
Wander amidst the magnificent peaks and plunging valleys of this breathtaking escarpment

EASTERN CAPE

Umtata

Mkambati Nature Reserve

Port St Johns

LESOTHO (p515)
Hike or pony trek amidst the stunning mountain scenery of the 'kingdom in the sky'

Cradock

Sada

Hlodeka Nature Reserve

Mountain Zebra National Park

Fort Beaufort

Dwesa Nature Reserve

Somerset East

Addo Elephant National Park

Grahamstown

King William's Town

East London

Port Alfred

WILD COAST (p262)
Hike past crashing waves and hidden waterfalls, or head inland to explore colourful Xhosa villages

Port Elizabeth

INDIAN OCEAN

ELEVATION

2400m

1800m

1200m

600m

0

0 — 200 km
0 — 120 miles

Wild, woolly and wonderful, South Africa's unparalleled collection of animals, large and small, is the country's biggest attraction. The **Greater St Lucia Wetland Park** (p315) gives you coastal sunrises and serenity, and opportunities to hang out with hippos and crocodiles. The adjoining **Mkhuze Game Reserve** (p320) boasts hides and pans galore, and has some of South Africa's best birding. More off-the-beaten-path are the dramatic desertscapes of **Augrabies Falls National Park** (p507). At Swaziland's tiny **Mkhaya Game Reserve** (p560), you're more likely to meet a black rhino in the wild than anywhere else in Africa.

For wilderness, few places surpass **Tsitsikamma National Park** (p222) with its rivers, ravines and evergreens; **Ukhahlamba-Drakensberg Park** (p325) and the jagged peaks of the Drakensberg range; or Lesotho's rugged and remote **Sehlabathebe National Park** (p537).

TIM ROCK

Delight in the abundant wildlife of Hluhluwe-Imfolozi Park (p313)

Marvel at over 500 species of birdlife in Kruger National Park (p440)

CAROL POLICH

Ponder the vast expanses of Kgalagadi Transfrontier Park (p503)

ANDREW MACCOL

RICHARD I'ANSON

Admire the world's largest land mammal at Addo Elephant National Park (p235)

KIM WILDMAN

Look up at a curious giraffe

Watch the sun set in Kruger National Park (p440)

CAROL POLICH

Travelling in Africa doesn't have to be rough, and there's no better proof of this than South Africa. Sip fine wines in some of the many wineries throughout the Western Cape's **Winelands** region (p150); enjoy top-notch cuisine in cosmopolitan **Cape Town** (p127); luxuriate in some of the continent's finest wildlife lodges in the **private wildlife reserves** (p451) around Kruger National Park; indulge yourself on the classic **Blue Train** (p606); or float in a hot-air balloon above the vast lowveld plains near **Sabie** (p425).

ARIADNE VAN ZANDBERGEN

Sample local produce at the Cape Peninsula wineries (p114)

Stay at an over-the-top hotel in Sun City (p479)

RICHARD I'ANSON

Lounge in one of Cape Town's atmospheric accommodation options (p123)

ARIADNE VAN ZANDBERGEN

On the outskirts of unabashedly urban Johannesburg, **Soweto** (p399) exposes South Africa's soul, pulsing with hope and determination. Graceful and genteel – at least on the surface – **Cape Town** (p92) boasts a stunning setting; yet away from the centre, apartheid's scars run deep. **Durban** (p281) is fringed by an overdeveloped coastline, and is a hot spot for surfers and party-goers. **Bloemfontein** (p352), staid and stately by day, offers one of South Africa's liveliest music and pub scenes; while **Graaff-Reinet** (p246) – urban in contrast to the vast Karoo spaces surrounding it – has a superb architectural heritage and small-town charm.

RICHARD I'ANSON

Visit Durban for a whiff of the East (p281)

Embrace big and brash Johannesburg (p374)

ANDREW BURKE

NIC BOTHMA

Check out Cape Town's nightlife scene (p133)

Explore Cape Town's City Bowl and colourful Bo-Kaap area (p100)

ARIADNE VAN ZANDBERGEN

Travelling in South Africa, Lesotho and Swaziland is anything but pedestrian. Try rafting the white-water rapids on the **Usutu River** (p560), saddling up in the area around **Haenertsberg** (p469), paragliding over the **Kalahari** (p498) around Kuruman, or peddling your mountain bike up into the mists at Lesotho's **Sani Pass** (p531). Want to keep your feet on *terra firma*? Hike in the rugged **Cederberg Wilderness Area** (p214); trek along the Free State's **Sentinel Hiking Trail** (p364); or walk on Swaziland's wild side in **Malolotja Nature Reserve** (p557).

PAUL KENNEDY

Catch a wave

Hike or mountain bike through Table Mountain National Park (p100)

SIMON RICHMOND

TIM ROCK

Head out on a dive at Sodwana Bay (p318)

Take advantage of the beach life along Cape Town's Atlantic Coast (p110)

MANFRED GOTTSCH...

What tiny Lesotho lacks in urban sophistication, it makes up for with one of Southern Africa's most vibrant traditional cultures, best experienced on a **pony trek** (p534) through local villages. South Africa's vibrant traditions pervade the mystical **Venda region** (p466), where ancestral beings abound, and **Zululand** (p306), home to one of the country's best-known and enigmatic cultures.

History comes to life at the unmissable shrine to the struggle, **Robben Island** (p110), and at the **Nelson Mandela Museum** (p272), a tribute to freedom's triumph.

DI JONES

Experience Lesotho's Basotho culture (p529)

ARIADNE VAN ZANDBERGEN

Feel the beat of a Zulu festival (p309)

RICHARD I'ANSON

Witness a sacred Swazi ceremony (p550)

Travel through colourful Xhosa villages in the Transkei region of the Wild Coast (p262)

DENNIS JONES

South Africa's boasts 2800km of stunning coastline. The verdant **Garden Route** (p188), with its dunes, lagoons and woodlands, stretches into the shorelines claimed by Eastern Cape – arguably the most beautiful in the country, especially along the Transkei **Wild Coast** (p262). North of here is sultry and subtropical, with the long beaches of Durban sliding into the estuaries and coral reefs beyond **Cape Vidal** (p315), and off into the wilds of the stunning **Kosi Bay Nature Reserve** (p320).

ARIADNE VAN ZANDBERGEN

Stand at the tip of the Cape Peninsula (p144)

Visit the African continent's southernmost point, Cape Agulhas (p172)

CAROL POLICH

JANE SWEENEY

Laze on the beach at relaxed and friendly Plettenberg Bay (p203)

Watch whales parade offshore at Hermanus (p168)

TIM RC

Getting Started

South Africa's infrastructure is well developed. Outside school holidays (when accommodation in popular areas fills up) it's possible to visit almost on the spur of the moment. Swaziland and (especially) Lesotho have less-developed infrastructure than South Africa, but are small and easily navigated, and you can sort things out as you go. In all three countries, though, you'll get more out of your visit with some advance planning.

Travellers flying in from Europe, North America or Australasia will find South Africa to be reasonably good value, notable in particular for the generally high quality of accommodation and food. However, the increasing strength of the rand means that it's not the bargain that it once was. For overland travellers, South Africa is more expensive than places such as Malawi or Zimbabwe, yet with a bit of effort it's possible to get by on a close-to-shoestring budget. Among the best deals are national parks and reserves, which offer excellent and accessible wildlife-watching at significantly less cost than you would pay in some parts of East Africa.

Getting around between major towns is easy and comfortable by bus or private car. Away from major routes, you'll need a car, or plenty of time to wait for public transport connections. Car travel is also a good way to go in Lesotho and Swaziland, although public transport will take you almost everywhere in these countries cheaply and with a minimum of hassle.

WHEN TO GO

South Africa can be visited comfortably any time. However, depending on what you plan to do, it's worth paying attention to the seasons, which are the reverse of those in the northern hemisphere. Winter (June to September) is cooler, dry and ideal for hiking and outdoor pursuits. Because vegetation is less dense, and thirsty animals congregate around rivers and other permanent water sources, winter is also the best time for wildlife-watching. In the eastern highveld, nights are often crisp and clear, with occasional frosts, so come prepared with a jacket.

Summer (late November to March) brings rain, mists and – in the lowveld, including much of eastern Swaziland – some uncomfortably hot

Although accommodation in South Africa isn't quite as full or pricey during other school holidays as during the main December–January break, prices rise and reservations are recommended. See p578 for holiday periods.

See Climate Charts (p572) for more information.

DON'T LEAVE HOME WITHOUT...

- binoculars for wildlife-watching and a zoom lens for taking great wildlife shots
- an appetite for biltong, boerewors and mealie pap
- making room in your schedule to visit at least one township
- your yellow fever vaccination card, if you've been travelling elsewhere in Southern Africa
- reading the Malaria section of the Health chapter (p610) in this book if you'll be travelling in malarial areas
- a torch (flashlight) and warm, waterproof clothing for those cold, black, starry nights in the Lesotho highlands
- a sleeping bag if you're planning on camping
- a good book for long bus rides

days. Along the Indian Ocean coast, conditions are sultry and tropical, with high humidity. Spectacular summer thunderstorms are common in Swaziland and Lesotho, and in Lesotho flooding can wash out some sections of road.

More of a consideration than weather is school holidays. From mid-December through January, waves of vacation-hungry South Africans stream out of the cities for their annual holidays. Visitors from Europe and North America add to the crush. The absolute peak is from Christmas to mid-January, followed by Easter. Accommodation in tourist areas and national parks is heavily booked, and prices can more than double. If you visit Cape Town, the Garden Route or other popular areas during this time, it's essential to book accommodation in advance. On the plus side, the high summer months offer some great festivals, including the Cape Town Minstrel Carnival, and Swaziland's Incwala ceremony. See p576 for more information on festivals.

Spring (mid-September to November) and autumn (April and May) are ideal almost everywhere. Spring is also the best time to see vast expanses of Northern Cape carpeted with wildflowers.

COSTS & MONEY

Travelling in South Africa is not as cheap as in many less-developed African countries. However, it usually works out to be less expensive than travelling in Europe or North America, and the quality of facilities and infrastructure is generally high. At the budget level, it's quite possible to get by on about R200 per day with a bit of effort, by camping or staying in hostels or self-catering accommodation, and using public transport.

For mid-range travel – where South Africa's best value is to be found – plan on about R300 per person per day, more if you hire a vehicle and less if you stay in self-catering places (many of which are extremely comfortable).

Life in the luxury lane starts at about R1500 per person per day, and can climb to more than five times this if you decide to ensconce yourself in some of the continent's top wildlife lodges.

Costs in Lesotho and Swaziland are the same as, or somewhat less than, in South Africa, with savings coming from cheaper local transport, inexpensive food and (in Lesotho) plentiful opportunities to stay with locals or camp.

HOW MUCH?

Bottle of wine
R60

Car hire per day
R250

Kilo of mangoes
R6

Kruger National Park
entry per person
R120

Surfboard
R1600

LONELY PLANET INDEX

Litre of petrol
R3.80

Litre of bottled water
R5

Can of Black Label beer
R6

Souvenir T-shirt
R60

Street snack – roasted
mealie
R2

CUTTING COSTS

In popular tourist areas, it's easy to pay much more than the averages listed under Costs & Money if you don't keep a watch on expenses. Cape Town in particular has a long history of enticing travellers, showing them a good time and emptying their wallets. However, there are also plenty of excellent-value options, both in accommodation and dining, that won't break your budget. Some ways to save include:

- avoid travelling during school-holiday periods
- always ask about midweek or weekend discounts, as well as reduced rates for children
- take advantage of self-catering facilities and camping grounds
- save your receipts to reclaim your value-added tax (VAT; see p581)
- focus on just one or two areas of the country, and don't try to cover too much distance
- use public transport, or try to travel in a group to share car-rental costs

TOP 10S
CLASSIC BOOKS

South Africa's struggles have produced an unsurpassed collection of literature – essential reading to get into the heart of the country. The following titles have been chosen for the broad spectrum of perspectives that they reflect.

- *Long Walk to Freedom* Nelson Mandela
- *The Marabi Dance* Modikwe Dikobe
- *My Traitor's Heart* Rian Malan
- *Singing Away the Hunger: Stories of a Life in Lesotho* Mpho 'M'atsepo Nthunya
- *A Burning Hunger: One Family's Struggle Against Apartheid* Lynda Schuster
- *The Mind of South Africa* Allister Sparks
- *Let My People Go* Albert Luthuli
- *The Heart of Redness* Zakes Mda
- *Cry, The Beloved Country* Alan Paton
- *The Lying Days* Nadine Gordimer

GREAT VIEWS

Towering escarpments, vast expanses and a spectacular coastline have bestowed this part of the continent with some breathtaking views. Some not-to-miss vistas:

- Cape Town, Robben Island and Table Bay from the top of Table Mountain (p100)
- Lepaquoa Valley, from the waterfall near the entry to Lesotho's Bokong Nature Reserve (p533)
- Namaqualand's vast expanses of spring flowers (p509)
- the convergence of two oceans at Cape of Good Hope (p144)
- Kruger National Park's seemingly endless tracts of bushland and savanna (p440)
- stark and solitary landscapes of shifting sun-seared sands in Kgalagadi Transfrontier Park (p503)
- the Wild Coast around Port St Johns (p268)
- dawn over a pan at Mkhuze Game Reserve (p320)
- the stunning panorama from the top of the Amphitheatre in Royal Natal National Park (p326)
- northwestern Swaziland's mountain panoramas near Piggs Peak (p557)

ARCHITECTURAL LANDMARKS

South Africa's history is written in its architecture. Hunt up these landmarks, and watch the story unfold before you.

- Regina Mundi Church in Soweto (p401)
- Cape Dutch houses along Church St in Tulbagh (p176)
- Robben Island prison, where Mandela was incarcerated (p110)
- Alayam Hindu Temple in Durban (p288)
- traditional villages in Zululand around Eshowe (p309)
- Auwal Mosque and Cape Town's Bo-Kaap area (p96)
- small, brightly coloured Xhosa houses in the villages inland from the Wild Coast (p262)
- Johannesburg's new Constitutional Court (p382)
- Pretoria's Church Sq and Voortrekker Monument (p409)
- Linton Panel in Cape Town's South African Museum (p105)

TRAVEL LITERATURE
While not 'travel literature', Nelson Mandela's superb and inspirational autobiography *Long Walk to Freedom* is one of the best ways to prepare for a South Africa trip. To pick up where Mandela leaves off, try the less profound but insightful and eminently readable *Somewhere Over the Rainbow: Travels in South Africa* by British journalist Gavin Bell.

South from the Limpopo: Travels through South Africa chronicles inveterate Irish writer Dervla Murphy on her bicycle journey through the rainbow nation before, during and after the 1994 elections. Booker Prize–winning author Justin Cartwright's *Not Home Yet* is a slim but illuminating study of the expat South African's trips home between 1994 and 1996.

In the readable, but ultimately forgettable *Swahili for the Broken-Hearted*, author Peter Moore brings you with him to Cape Town, with brief forays into Lesotho and Swaziland, as part of his longer African sojourn. Paul Theroux's *Dark Star Safari* is a more cynical chronicle of African travels, with the final episodes set in South Africa.

INTERNET RESOURCES
Linx Africa (www.linx.co.za) Links to almost everywhere, including enough hiking and mountain-bike trails to keep you busy for months.

See p584 for regional tourism websites.

Lonely Planet (www.lonelyplanet.com) South Africa travel tips, the Thorn Tree bulletin board, and heaps of helpful links at the SubWWWay.

Mail & Guardian Online (www.mg.co.za) All the latest breaking national news.

South Africa Info (www.safrica.info) Everything you want to know about South Africa on the country's official gateway.

South African National Parks (www.parks-sa.co.za) The best place to start your safari.

South African Tourism (www.southafrica.net) South Africa's very helpful official site.

Itineraries

CLASSIC ROUTES

CAPE & COAST

two weeks / Cape Town to Oudtshoorn

This is the South Africa of the tourist brochures, but with good reason – boasting beautiful natural scenery, excellent infrastructure and amenities. The loop can be done by public transport, but is better by car to take advantage of the many worthwhile detours. See p596 for information on getting around.

After a few days in **Cape Town** (p92), including a stay at a **township B&B** (p145), tear yourself away from this beautiful city and head to the fertile valleys of the Winelands, with a night or two in shady **Stellenbosch** (p151) or **Franschhoek** (p159) with its fine wining and dining. From here, head east to the artists' enclave of **Montagu** (p183), and then via the scenic Rte 62 through the Little Karoo to **Oudtshoorn** (p186), South Africa's ostrich capital. Possible detours along the way include **Hermanus** (p168) for whale-watching, if the season is right; **Cape Agulhas** (p172) for the thrill of standing at Africa's southernmost point; or **De Hoop Nature Reserve** (p173) for some hiking or mountain biking.

Oudtshoorn makes a good springboard for heading into the Karoo via the spectacular **Swartberg Pass** (p206) and on to charming **Prince Albert** (p206), from where it's a straight ride on the N1 back to Cape Town. Alternatively, make your way south, joining the N2 along the Garden Route, near **Knysna** (p197), with its serene sylvan setting, and **Plettenberg Bay** (p203), a classic beachside resort town. From here, make your way back to Cape Town via Oudtshoorn and Rte 62, or directly along the N2.

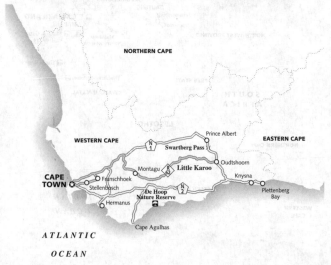

Exploring Cape & Coast – from Cape Town to Oudtshoorn to the Garden Route and back – will take you 1000km on good roads through some of the most beautiful country in Southern Africa. You could whizz along in about 10 days, or relax along the way and stretch things out to three weeks or more.

WILD WANDERINGS   one–two weeks / Johannesburg to KwaZulu-Natal

Johannesburg (Jo'burg; p374) is the gateway to some of the best wildlife and culture in Southern Africa. Everything is within easy reach on public transport, though you'll need a car (or organised tour) to explore inside the parks (see p596 for information on getting around and p605 for details on tours). After spending time becoming acquainted with the city, including at least an overnight set aside for visiting **Soweto** (p399), make your way east via Nelspruit to **Kruger National Park** (p440). The teeming wildlife here and in the neighbouring **private wildlife reserves** (p451) will undoubtedly hold you captivated for at least several days. Time permitting, there are also several good detours from Nelspruit that you could do before or after visiting Kruger, including **Sabie** (p425), which has pine forests and mountain biking and rafting opportunities nearby.

From Kruger National Park, continue south into Swaziland, where you can spend a few days hiking in the beautiful **Malolotja Nature Reserve** (p557) before heading on to **Mbabane** (p545). From there, it's an easy drive to the excellent **Mkhaya Game Reserve** (p560) for some more wildlife watching. Return to Jo'burg, or head south into KwaZulu-Natal where **Mkhuze Game Reserve** (p320), **Hluhluwe-Imfolozi Park** (p313) and several other top-notch wildlife-watching areas await you. With three weeks, you would have time to continue into **Lesotho** (p516), and from there back to Jo'burg.

Seven to 10 days is the minimum you'll need to cover this 1600km loop taking in Jo'burg, Kruger National Park and bits of Swaziland. Roads are good throughout, except for the occasional patch of gravel in Swaziland and Kruger. To do the route justice, or to include KwaZulu-Natal, Mpumalanga and/or Lesotho, plan on at least three weeks.

THE BIG TRIP

two months / Cape Town to Cape Town

Starting in **Cape Town** (p92), head eastwards following either Rte 62, the Garden Route or bits of both (see Cape & Coast, p17), through to Eastern Cape. If you enter Eastern Cape from Prince Albert via the Karoo, stop at **Graaff-Reinet** (p246) to enjoy its architecture, striking setting, and the nearby **Karoo Nature Reserve** (p249). Entering via the coast, good stops include **Tsitsikamma National Park** (p222) for hiking, **Addo Elephant National Park** (p235) for elephants and **Jeffrey's Bay** (p225) for surf breaks. Moving eastwards, spend some time in **Amatola** (p251), before making your way to the **Wild Coast** (p262). From here, it's off along the coast to **Durban** (p281) and then inland, up and over the **Sani Pass** (p531), for a detour into **Lesotho** (p516).

From Lesotho, head back to KwaZulu-Natal, and spend as much time as possible in the **Greater St Lucia Wetlands** (p315) and nearby **KwaZulu-Natal parks** (p315). **Sodwana Bay** (p318) is an ideal spot to chill out and do some diving before heading to **Swaziland** (p540), **Kruger National Park** (p440) and on to **Jo'burg** (p374), **Pretoria** (p404) and possibly **Sun City** (p478).

Leave the city lights behind and head southwest to **Kimberley** (p492), gateway to South Africa's vast, open northwest. Explore the **Kalahari** (p498), including the starkly beautiful **Augrabies Falls National Park** (p507), before swinging down towards **Namaqualand** (p508) to catch the explosion of spring flowers. Finish up relaxing in the **Winelands** (p150) before returning to Cape Town.

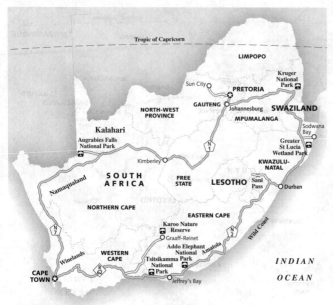

This 4700km jaunt on generally good roads will give you an excellent overview of South Africa, Lesotho and Swaziland. Six weeks (more via public transport) is the bare minimum, but it's better to allow at least two months to explore along detours, and to get into the pulse of this corner of the continent.

ROADS LESS TRAVELLED

TRADITIONAL TRAILS   one month / Swaziland to Johannesburg

If it's traditional culture you're after, leave Cape and coast behind and head east. **Swaziland** (p540) – easily reached from both Jo'burg and Maputo (Mozambique) – makes an excellent introduction, especially if you can time things to be there for the annual **Umhlanga (Reed) Dance** (p550) or the **Incwala** (p550). Swaziland's crafts are top-notch and another way to step into the culture. Selection is especially good in the **Malkerns Valley** (p553) and the **Ezulwini Valley** (p549). From Swaziland, head south into the Zulu heartland of KwaZulu-Natal. In **Zululand** (p306), you'll find many traditional Zulu villages and with luck be able to catch a **Zulu festival** (p309). Make your way down to **Durban** (p281), and then west into **Lesotho** (p516) where a **pony trek** (p534) or hike through Basotho villages is an excellent way to get acquainted with local life and culture. Crafts here are also worthwhile, with **Teyateyaneng** (p527) the unofficial craft centre. From Lesotho, make your way south into Eastern Cape's **Transkei region** (p262). Away from the coast, you'll find rolling hills dotted with Xhosa villages, and life going at the same pace that it has for centuries. From here, make your way back to Durban (there's frequent public transport from Umtata, see p270) – maybe catching an **Indian festival** (p291) en route – and then back to Jo'burg.

Step into this pulsating 3000km loop, and leave the blandness of Western culture behind. It's easy to cover the distance in three weeks, but to really get into local rhythms, allow as much time as possible. In general, the rougher the road, the more vibrant the local cultures.

NORTHERN TRACKS   four–six weeks / Johannesburg to Cape Town

With time and transport, South Africa's northwest makes an excellent alternative to the well-trodden coast. The atmosphere is rugged, distances long and everything's pervaded by a wonderful sense of openness. From **Jo'burg** (p374) head southwest to **Bloemfontein** (p352), one of South Africa's more attractive cities with a rich history and surprisingly good nightlife. From Bloemfontein, it's a short hop to the diamond capital of **Kimberley** (p492) with its Anglo-Boer battlefields and many atmospheric pubs. Turn northwest to **Kuruman** (p498) – an unassuming town that has made a name for itself in paragliding circles – and on to **Kgalagadi Transfrontier Park** (p503), where at least four days are needed to do it justice. The next stops are **Upington** (p500) and the wonderful **Augrabies Falls National Park** (p507), which merits at least two or three days for hiking, rafting and canoeing. Then it's on to the rugged and remote **Richtersveld National Park** (p512) with its mountainous, desert landscapes, rocky peaks, ravines and gorges. Plan on three to four days here to take advantage of the excellent hiking. From Richtersveld, swing down to **Namaqualand** (p508) and try to catch the spring flowers before making your way to **Cape Town** (p92) to finish things up. With extra time, detour to the Hantam Karoo town of **Calvinia** (p514), enjoying the magnificent views en route along the road from **Vanrhynsdorp** (p490), continuing to Cape Town via **Clanwilliam** (p216) and **Citrusdal** (p215).

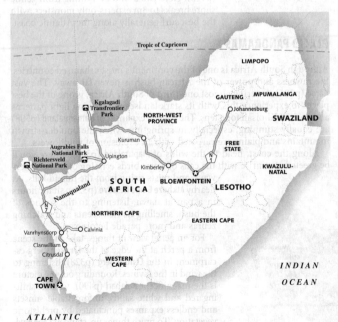

After travelling 2300km through South Africa's vast, open north, settling back into an urban lifestyle won't be easy. Consider a 4WD for Kgalagadi, Richtersveld and Augrabies Falls parks; elsewhere the roads are good. To include more hiking or rafting, allow six weeks for this itinerary.

TAILORED TRIPS

SURFING SAFARI

South Africa has some of the best and most consistent surfing in the world. **East London** (p256), with its quintessential beach lifestyle, makes a good first port of call. It's an ideal spot to make contacts before heading to the renowned **Jeffrey's Bay** (p225), Southern Africa's undisputed surfing capital, boasting what may be the world's best wave. It's a good place to buy cheap surf clothing and surfboards. For the thrill of the unknown, head to the **Wild Coast** (p262), with its spectacular coastline, point breaks and lure of the unknown.

Rivalling Eastern Cape as South Africa's surfing centre are **Durban** (p281) and the surrounding KwaZulu-Natal coast (see the boxed text on p290). Surf culture reigns supreme here – there's even a surfing museum (p290).

Western Cape's Garden Route holds its own with the Eastern Cape, especially around **Mossel Bay** (p189) which has several top surf spots. If conditions are right, **Plettenberg Bay** (p203) and **Still Bay Point** (p189) can also be rewarding.

Rounding out the picture is the **Cape Peninsula** (p118). Here you'll find everything from gentle shore breaks to 3m experts-only monsters, with the best surf generally along the Atlantic coast.

PLACID PANORAMAS

Although South Africa is one of the continent's most urbanised countries, the rawness and power of the African bush is never far away. The vast **Karoo** (p206), covering almost one-third of South Africa, is one of the best places to experience this, with its stark landscapes, striking light patterns and ancient Khoisan footsteps. The rugged expanses of **Namaqualand** (p508) are equally stunning, especially in springtime when the boulder-strewn mountains and plains are carpeted with an explosion of wildflowers.

Along the coast, head to the wilds of **Maputaland** (p306), where you'll be greeted at sunrise with the calls of water birds echoing over the waterways, and mists rising from the inland hills. At nearby **Mkhuze Game Reserve** (p320), sit for hours in a pan at dawn, listening to the sounds of the bush, smelling its rich scents and watching zebras and more parade before you

For an aerial view of things, take in the scene from a perch at the edge of the Drakensberg escarpment in the **Central Berg** (p328), listening to the wind in the ravines. Rounding out the picture is the magnificent **Kalahari** (p490), with its shifting red and white sands, unforgettable sunsets and endless expanses punctuated by prehistoric vegetation. To finish things up, stand at **Cape Agulhas** (p172) under spray from the crashing seas, and revel in being at Africa's southern tip.

HIKER'S PARADISE

South Africa has hikes to suit every taste. Ranging from several hours to several days, they're a superb way to experience the country's stunning, diverse topography. Hard-core hikers should head to **Tsitsikamma National Park** (p222) or the **Wild Coast** (p262): both offer outstanding sea views and challenging terrain. Inland, try the **Cederberg Wilderness Area** (p214), with its weathered sandstone formations and San rock paintings, or any of the central Drakensberg hiking areas, such as **Royal Natal National Park** (p326), with its dramatic cliffs and valleys, and **Golden Gate Highlands National Park** (p363), with beautifully coloured sandstone outcrops and plenty of animals.

For something a bit tamer, try the Cape Peninsula, where the **Cape of Good Hope Nature Reserve** (p144) offers unsurpassed walking against a backdrop of wind-whipped sea and spray. Cape Town's **Table Mountain** (p100) is rewarding, and tougher than it looks, thanks to temperamental weather.

The **Blyde River Canyon Nature Reserve** (p429) provides wide vistas and dramatic drop-offs over the edge of the Klein Drakensberg escarpment. **Lesotho** (p516) is a country seemingly created with hiking in mind, where you can set off into the hills and walk at will. Swaziland's **Malolotja Nature Reserve** (p557) is one of Southern Africa's premier walking destinations, with a wonderful wilderness atmosphere and intriguing flora and birdlife.

IN THE FOOTSTEPS OF MANDELA

Tracing the renowned statesman's footsteps provides an excellent overview of recent South African history. Starting in Cape Town, **Robben Island** (p110) is the essential stop. Nearby in Paarl is **Victor Verster Prison** (now Drakenstein Prison; p557), from where Mandela walked to freedom.

The Eastern Cape contains the moving **Nelson Mandela Museum** (p272) in Umtata, Qunu (Mandela's boyhood home and current residence), and tiny Mveso village (his birthplace). From here, head to **Soweto** (p378), passing near Sharpeville (site of the Sharpeville Massacre). It was in Soweto that African National Congress (ANC) resistance to apartheid discovered its soul, with Mandela among the leadership. The ANC's Freedom Charter was declared in Soweto's Kliptown (Freedom) Sq, and the Soweto Uprising was ignited here (at Orlando West Secondary School on Vilakazi St). It was also to Soweto that Mandela returned after being released from prison.

Jo'burg (p382) is indelibly marked with Mandela's footprints, including the law office he shared with Oliver Tambo (on Fox St, just off Ghandi Sq), **City Hall** (p378) and various jails, including the notorious **Old Fort** (p382). **Museum Africa** (p381) is worthwhile for its exhibit on the 1956–61 Treason Trials in which Mandela testified. Pretoria's **Palace of Justice** (p381) is where the Rivonia Trial, which sentenced Mandela to life imprisonment, was held.

The Authors

MARY FITZPATRICK

Mary first glimpsed the Johannesburg skyline over a decade ago. Since then, South Africa's beauty, turmoil and indomitable spirit have lured her back dozens of times. In between, she's made numerous forays into Lesotho and Swaziland. Her most cherished moments include witnessing South Africa's first multiracial elections; being driven from the Cape of Good Hope in a police paddy wagon on Christmas Eve; trying to make a can of tuna last for more than one meal while hiking in Lesotho; and gazing over rolling-hill panoramas in northwestern Swaziland. Mary works as a full-time travel writer from her home base in Cairo, on the northern end of the African continent.

My Favourite Trip

If I could go from place to place without thinking about transport in between, I'd try to include the following in my next Southern Africa journey: hiking at Cape of Good Hope Nature Reserve (p144) in Table Mountain National Park, for the wind, spray and incredible vistas; wandering around the Lesotho highlands near Oxbow (p530); spending an afternoon perched above one of the valleys of the Golden Gate Highlands National Park (p363), taking in the silence and the scenery; and as much time as possible in KwaZulu-Natal's parks, especially Mkhuze Game Reserve (p320) and Hluhluwe-Imfolozi Park (p313). Johannesburg (p374) is my favourite city, and Swaziland (p540) the most enjoyable detour.

BECCA BLOND

As hard as she tried Becca couldn't cope with a 9-to-5 job, so she traded reporting on rock stars, wildfires and homicides for wandering the world. She was lucky enough to travel to South Africa twice in one year – first to update parts of *Africa on a Shoestring* and next to research the Northern and Western Cape chapters of this book. Becca first got the African travel bug while studying in Zimbabwe during her university days. She's been back five times in the last six years. When she's not living out of a backpack she calls Boulder, Colorado, home where she lives with her best friend and a large collection of wooden giraffes.

GEMMA PITCHER

Gemma Pitcher grew up in Buckinghamshire with her nose buried in books with titles like *Across the Dark Continent* and *Safari Adventure*. This prompted her to disappear to Africa at age 17, travelling through six countries from Nairobi down to Harare. She returned to Britain to read English at Exeter University, writing her final-year thesis on South African nationalism. She followed this with a spell researching Xhosa history on the Wild Coast, before returning home once more to become a safari consultant, then ultimately a freelance travel writer. She has completed several other assignments for Lonely Planet in Southern and East Africa. She lives in London when Africa's not calling.

SIMON RICHMOND

Simon Richmond was instantly bitten by the Cape Town bug when he arrived in the Mother City in 2001 to research both Lonely Planet's *South Africa, Lesotho & Swaziland* 5 guide and the *Cape Town* 3 city guide. Three years later, the award-winning travel writer returned to research the Cape Town chapter of this guide, setting up home in Rondebosch for a month, shopping for groceries at the local Woolworths and roaming from Cape Point to the Winelands in a shiny red Tazz.

MATT WARREN

Matt first travelled to Africa as a student from Edinburgh University, driving into Kenya's far north and sailing from Mombasa to Zanzibar on a cargo dhow. He never looked back, making numerous trips across the continent and discovering a particular affinity for the ever-changing face of South Africa. He is now planning a solo motorcycle journey from London to Cape Town. When not updating Lonely Planet guides, Matt works as a journalist, filing stories from locations as far afield as Kosovo, Cambodia and Japan.

CONTRIBUTING AUTHORS

Jane Cornwell wrote the Music chapter (p54). Jane is an Australian-born, London-based journalist writing on music for publications including the *Evening Standard, Guardian, Songlines* and *Jazzwise*. Her articles also appear regularly in the *Australian* newspaper. She holds a postgraduate honours degree in anthropology and has worked for the Institute of Contemporary Arts; Real World Records; World of Music, Arts and Dance (WOMAD); and Sydney's Ignite Festival.

Sally Sara wrote the Culture chapter (p45). Sally spent more than four years living and working in South Africa as a foreign correspondent with the Australian Broadcasting Corporation (ABC). Sally has reported from more than 20 countries on four continents, and has been a finalist in the prestigious Walkley Awards for excellence in journalism. She is the winner of an Australian national radio award, the Dalgety Award for Rural Journalism, and was South Australian Young Journalist of the Year in 1997. In 1999 she won the British Prize for Journalism.

Charlene Smith wrote the Snapshot chapter (p26). Charlene is a multiaward-winning South African journalist and documentary filmmaker. She is the author of six books, covering such subjects as Nelson Mandela, Robben Island, Soweto and HIV and AIDS. She has lived in Zambia, Japan and Argentina and has travelled to more than 80 countries around the world. Charlene lives and works in Johannesburg.

Dr Caroline Evans wrote the Health chapter (p607). Caroline studied medicine at the University of London and completed general-practice training in Cambridge. She is the medical adviser to the Nomad Travel clinic, a private travel health clinic in London, and is also a GP specialising in travel medicine. She has been an expedition doctor for Raleigh International and Coral Cay expeditions.

Snapshot

**FAST FACTS:
SOUTH AFRICA**

Population: 44.8 million
(2001 census)

Official languages: 11
(English, Afrikaans,
isiNdebele, isiXhosa,
isiZulu, Sepedi, Sesotho,
Setswana, siSwati,
Tshivenda and Xitsonga)

Surface area:
1,219,900km

Area suitable for
agriculture: 12.13%
(0.77% for permanent
crops)

Literacy rate: 86.4%
(87% for males and
85.7% for females)

National fish: the galjoen
(*Coracinus capensis*)

Phones in entire African
continent owned by
South Africans: 40%
(including 7 million
mobile phones)

Age of South Africa's
wine industry:
320 years – the oldest
anywhere outside Europe

Successive test wins by
the Springboks rugby
team from August 1997
to November 1998:
17 (equalling a world
record)

In 1994, South Africa attained democracy but not freedom, claims Pieter Dirk Uys, the country's most beloved satirist. In 2002, the Medical Research Council reported that a young man aged 16 to 29 in the Western Cape was more likely to be shot dead than to die from any other cause but from HIV/AIDS. An estimated one in two women would get raped in her lifetime.

In 2004, politicians battled to coerce a disillusioned electorate out of their apathy and to the polls. A decade after the end of apartheid, 42% of the population was unemployed; more people had electricity but few had the capacity to pay for it; and more than a million homes had been built, yet shacks crawled across urban landscapes.

Before the election the finance minister, Trevor Manuel, set aside two billion rand to fight HIV/AIDS – South Africa has one of the world's highest rates of infection – and six billion rand to promote Black economic empowerment, which cynics observed would probably go to the same small cadre of former liberation fighters who had become inordinately wealthy since 1994. President Thabo Mbeki promised a million new jobs – without a doubt the biggest voter issue, along with crime – but did not say how he would deliver on that promise to the 10 million seeking work.

And yet, despite its trials and tribulations, life is better – most South Africans would agree – than it was a decade ago. Contradictions abound, but the political violence that was threatening to engulf the country in the early '90s has now all but disappeared. In April 2004, the African National Congress (ANC), as expected, won a landslide victory in the country's third democratic elections. Paranoia and dogmatism are out, diversity is in. There are many solutions, lots of strategies, and different ways to approach an issue. Corporate bankers build homes for and alongside the residents of the settlements that sprawl around South Africa's modern cities. Under the United Nations Habitat for Humanity (UNHH) programme, corporates don't just sign cheques, their executives get involved. Different worlds meet, and ever so slowly the 'better life for all' promised by the ANC is coming to be.

In tiny Swaziland, where the Eton-educated king has nine wives and each year selects another at the traditional reed dance for maidens, the average life expectancy is 27 because of AIDS. This has not deterred King Mswati III from crippling the nation's finances by buying a private jet for himself and tightly circumscribing civil rights. Yet Swaziland has remained immune to the racial animosities that exist in its larger neighbour, and cultural pride runs strong.

Lesotho, encircled by South Africa, has remained calm since South Africa led a Southern African Development Community raid in the late '90s to restore constitutional rule. While a corruption-riddled major dam project to feed South Africa's industrial heartland with water has not brought Lesotho the much-needed revenue it requires, the mood in the mountain kingdom is upbeat.

South Africa, too, is a place where hardship prevails in many communities, but an undercurrent of hope runs strong. South Africans long ago learnt – most powerfully under the racial segregation and discrimination of apartheid – that if you want the world to change, you do it yourself.

At Cape Town's beautiful Table Bay, tourists queue for the Robben Island ferry. They are going to see where Nelson Mandela spent two decades imprisoned. Former Robben Island prisoners now guide visitors and are often asked 'Why don't you hate?' The answer comes with a smile, 'We don't have time, there's too much to do.'

History

South Africa's turbulent history has been written and rewritten dozens of times – always a different version, depending on who was holding the pen. Yet it's only in the past decade that the full story has been told. As collaboration and reconciliation slowly begin to replace mistrust and suspicion, there's hope that in the coming decades the country's full potential will be realised.

THE FIRST SOUTH AFRICANS

See www.pbs.org/wgbh /evolution/humans /humankind/o.html for an overview of human evolution in Southern Africa.

The first people to see dawn at the southern tip of the African continent were likely the San – skilled hunter-gatherers who followed a nomadic lifestyle. Their respect for the land was great, and their lifestyle low impact – other than a series of striking rock paintings, they left few traces of their early culture for posterity. Attempts to date this rock art indicate that the San were living in what is now South Africa as early as 25,000 years ago, and possibly as early as 40,000 years ago. Small numbers still live in South Africa today, making theirs one of the world's oldest continuous cultures.

Prior to the San, the picture is murkier. A major archaeological find in 1998 at Sterkfontein near Johannesburg (Jo'burg) revealed that human-like creatures or 'hominids' roamed and hunted across the highveld at least three million years ago. By about one million years ago, these creatures – by then known as *homo erectus* – had come to closely resemble modern humans, and ranged well beyond Africa, including in Europe and Asia. Somewhere around 100,000 years ago, *homo sapiens*, or modern man, came onto the scene. Although it's still a topic of hot debate among archaeologists, fossils found in South Africa near the mouth of the Klasies River in Eastern Cape indicate that our *homo sapiens* ancestors may have been backpacking around South Africa as early as 90,000 years ago.

Beginning around 2500 years ago, some San groups acquired livestock from points further north. Gradually they laid their hunting-gathering traditions to the side and became pastoralists, tending to small herds of cattle and oxen. The arrival of livestock introduced the concepts of personal wealth and property ownership into San society. Community structures solidified and expanded, and chieftaincies developed. These pastoralist San, who were known as Khoikhoi (men of men), began to make their way south, reaching as far as the Cape coast. Along the way, they mixed and mingled with the hunter-gatherer San, to the point where drawing a clear line between the two groups became impossible – hence the use of the term 'Khoisan'. Over time, the Khoikhoi established themselves along the coast, while small groups of San continued to inhabit the interior.

THE ARRIVAL OF THE BANTU-SPEAKERS

At about this same time, Bantu-speaking peoples also began arriving in what is now South Africa. Originally from the Niger Delta area in West Africa, they had started to make their way south and eastwards about

TIMELINE	c 25,000 BC	100AD-500AD
	The San watch the sun rise in South Africa	Bantu speakers arrive in present-day KwaZulu-Natal

1000 BC, reaching present-day KwaZulu-Natal by AD 500. The Bantu speakers not only had domestic animals, but they farmed crops (particularly maize), were skilled iron workers, and lived in settled villages. They arrived in Southern Africa in small waves, rather than in one cohesive migration. Some groups – the ancestors of today's Nguni peoples (Zulu, Xhosa, Swazi and Ndebele) – sought out beach-front properties and settled near the coast. Others – now known as the Sotho-Tswana peoples (Tswana, Pedi, Basotho) – settled in the highveld, while today's Venda, Lemba and Shangaan-Tsonga peoples made their home in the northeast of present-day South Africa.

That the Bantu speakers and the Khoisan mixed is certain, as evidenced by rock paintings showing the two different groups interacting. The type of contact isn't known, although there's linguistic proof of integration, as several Bantu languages (notably Xhosa and Zulu) have incorporated the clicks characteristic of the earlier Khoisan languages. Numerous Khoisan artefacts have also been found at the sites of Bantu settlements.

EUROPEAN EXPEDITIONS

The first Europeans to reach Southern Africa were the Portuguese, who were drawn southwards in the hope of finding a sea route to India and the East. In 1487, the intrepid Bartholomeu Dias and a small band of adventurers rounded a rocky, windy cape. Dias named it Cabo da Boa Esperança (Cape of Good Hope). A decade later, in 1498, the equally intrepid Vasco da Gama rounded the same point of land, and then kept sailing northeastwards. En route, he called in at various ports along the South African and Mozambican coasts before finally reaching India.

Although the Portuguese basked in the nautical achievement of successfully negotiating the cape, they showed little interest in South Africa itself. Its fierce weather and rocky shoreline posed a threat to their ships, and many of their attempts to trade with the local Khoikhoi ended in violence. The Mozambican coast, further northeast, was altogether more to their liking, with appealing bays to use as way-stations, succulent prawns and links with the legendary gold fields of the interior.

The Portuguese had little competition in the region until the late 16th century, when the English and Dutch began to challenge them along their trade routes. Traffic around the continent's southern tip increased, and the Cape became a regular stopover for scurvy-ridden crews. In 1647 a Dutch vessel was wrecked in what is now Cape Town's Table Bay. The marooned crew – the first Europeans to attempt settlement in the area – built a fort and stayed for a year until they were rescued. Their letters back home must not have been all bad, as shortly thereafter, the Dutch East India Company (Vereenigde Oost-Indische Compagnie or VOC) decided to establish a permanent settlement. The VOC – one of the major European trading houses sailing the spice route to the East – had no intent of colonising the area. They simply wanted to establish a secure base where passing ships could shelter, and where hungry sailors could stock up on fresh supplies of meat, fruit and vegetables. To this end, a small VOC expedition, under the command of Jan Van Riebeeck, reached Table Bay in April 1652.

> 'Many attempts by the Portuguese to trade with the local Khoikhoi ended in violence'

1487	1652
Bartholomeu Dias successfully navigates the Cape of Good Hope	First Dutch settlement, at Table Bay, Cape Town

THE DUTCH SETTLE IN

While the new settlement traded (out of necessity) with the neighbouring Khoikhoi people, the relationship could hardly be described as warm, and there were deliberate attempts to restrict contact. Partly as a consequence, VOC employees found themselves faced with a labour shortage. To remedy this, they released a small group of Dutch from their contracts and permitted them to establish their own farms, from which they would then supply the VOC settlement with their harvests. The arrangement proved highly successful, producing abundant supplies of fruit, vegetables, wheat and wine; they later raised livestock. The small initial group of free burghers, as these farmers were known, steadily increased, and began to expand their farms further north and east into the territory of the Khoikhoi.

The majority of burghers were of Dutch descent, and members of the Calvinist Reformed Church of the Netherlands, but there were also numerous Germans. In 1688 the Dutch and the Germans were joined by French Huguenots, also Calvinists, who were fleeing religious persecution under King Louis XIV.

In addition to establishing the free burgher system, Van Riebeeck and the VOC also began to import large numbers of slaves, primarily from Madagascar and Indonesia. With this additional labour, the areas occupied by the VOC expanded further north and east where clashes with the Khoikhoi were inevitable. The beleaguered Khoikhoi were driven from their traditional lands, decimated by introduced diseases, and destroyed by superior weapons when they fought back – which they did in a number of major 'wars', and with guerrilla resistance which continued into the 19th century. Most survivors were left with no option but to work for Europeans in an exploitative arrangement that hardly differed from slavery. Over time, the Khoisan, their European overseers, and the imported slaves mixed, with the offspring of these unions forming the basis for today's Coloured population.

Among the best-known Khoikhoi groups were the Griqua, who had originally lived on the western coast between St Helena Bay and the Cederberg Range. In the late 18th century, they managed to acquire guns and horses and began trekking northeastwards. En route, they were joined by other groups of Khoisan, Coloureds and even White adventurers, and rapidly gained a reputation as a formidable military force. Ultimately, the Griquas reached the highveld around present-day Kimberley, where they carved out territory that came to be known as Griqualand.

BURGHERS MEET THE BUSH

As the burghers, too, continued to expand into the rugged hinterlands of the north and east, many began to take up a seminomadic pastoralist lifestyle, in some ways not so far removed from that of the Khoikhoi who they were displacing. In addition to its herds, a family might have had a wagon, a tent, a Bible and a couple of guns. As they became more settled, a mud-walled cottage would be built – frequently located, by choice, days of hard travel away from the nearest European. These were the first of the Trekboers (Wandering Farmers, later shortened to Boers) – completely independent of official control, extraordinarily self-sufficient and isolated. Their harsh lifestyle produced courageous

1658	c 1700
The first slaves are brought to South Africa	Trekboers (Boers) set off for the hinterlands (present-day Western Cape)

individualists, but also a backward people, whose only source of knowledge was often the Bible.

BRITS AT THE CAPE

As the 18th century drew to a close, Dutch mercantile power began to fade, and the British moved in to fill the vacuum. They seized the Cape to prevent it from falling into rival French hands, then briefly relinquished it back to the Dutch, before finally garnering recognition of their sovereignty of the area in 1814.

Awaiting the British at the tip of the continent was a colony with 25,000 slaves, 20,000 White colonists, 15,000 Khoisan and 1000 freed Black slaves. Power was restricted to a White elite in Cape Town, and differentiation on the basis of race was deeply entrenched. Outside Cape Town and the immediate hinterland, the country was populated by isolated Black and White pastoralists.

Like the Dutch before them, the British initially had little interest in the Cape Colony, other than as a strategically located port. One of their first tasks was trying to resolve a troublesome border dispute between the Boers and the Xhosa on the colony's eastern frontier. In 1820, about 5000 middle-class British immigrants – mostly traders and businesspeople – were persuaded to leave England behind and settle on tracts of land between the feuding groups with the idea of providing a buffer zone. The plan was singularly unsuccessful. By 1823, almost half of the settlers had retreated to the towns – notably Grahamstown and Port Elizabeth – to pursue the jobs they had held in Britain.

While doing nothing to resolve the border dispute, this influx of settlers solidified the British presence in the area, thus fracturing the relative unity of White South Africa. Where the Boers and their ideas had once been largely unchallenged, there were now two language groups and two cultures. A pattern soon emerged whereby English speakers were highly urbanised, and dominated politics, trade, finance, mining and manufacturing, while the largely uneducated Boers were relegated to their farms.

The gap between the British settlers and the Boers further widened with the abolition of slavery in 1833 – a move that was generally regarded by Boers as being against the God-given ordering of the races. Yet, the British settlers' conservatism and sense of racial superiority stopped any radical reforms and, in 1841, a Masters and Servants Ordinance was passed perpetuating White control. Meanwhile, British numbers

A CHOSEN PEOPLE?

Boer lifestyle and culture – both real and idealised – have had a major influence on South Africa's history. While many of the early members of the Dutch VOC expedition planned to ultimately return to Europe, the Boers soon began to develop a view of themselves as a distinct community who were permanently settled in South Africa. According to their Calvinist beliefs, they were God's chosen people, who had the duty to civilise their Black neighbours and thereby ensure their salvation. Some scholars also say that it was Calvinism, and especially its doctrine of predestination, that spawned the Afrikaner idea of racial superiority: the separation of the races had been divinely ordained, and thus justified all efforts to preserve the purity of the White race in its promised land.

1816	1820
Shaka Zulu becomes chief of the Zulu; the *difaqane* begins	British settlers arrive in Eastern Cape

increased rapidly in Cape Town, in the area east of the Cape Colony (present-day Eastern Cape), in Natal (present-day KwaZulu-Natal) and, after the discovery of gold and diamonds, in parts of the Transvaal (mainly around present-day Gauteng).

DIFAQANE & DESTRUCTION

Against this backdrop, the stage was being set for a time of immense upheaval and suffering among the African peoples of the region. This period is known as the *difaqane* (forced migration) in Sotho, and as *mfecane* (the crushing) in Zulu.

The roots of the *difaqane* are disputed, although certain events stand out. One of the most significant was the rise of the powerful Zulu kingdom. In the early 19th century, Nguni tribes in what is now KwaZulu-Natal began to shift from loosely organised collections of kingdoms into a centralised, militaristic state. The driving force behind this shift was Shaka Zulu, son of the chief of the small Zulu clan. At first something of an outcast, Shaka proved himself in battle, and was gradually able to consolidate power in his hands. He built large armies, shocking others in the clan by placing the armies under the control of his own officers, rather than the hereditary chiefs. Shaka then set out on a massive programme of conquest and terror. Those who stood in his way were either enslaved or decimated. Even his *impis* (warrior regiments) were subject to similar rigours – failure in battle meant death.

Not surprisingly, tribes in the path of Shaka's armies turned on their heels and fled, in turn becoming aggressors against their neighbours. This wave of disruption and terror spread throughout Southern Africa and beyond, leaving death and destruction in its wake. It also accelerated the formation of several states, notably those of the Sotho (present-day Lesotho) and Swazi (now Swaziland). See p518 and p543 for more.

In 1828, Shaka met his untimely end when he was killed by his half-brothers Dingaan and Umhlanga. The weaker and less-skilled Dingaan became king, relaxing military discipline yet continuing the despotism. Dingaan also attempted to establish relations with British traders on the Natal coast, but events were unfolding that were to see the demise of Zulu independence.

THE GREAT TREK

Meanwhile, the Boers were growing increasingly dissatisfied with British rule in the Cape Colony. The British proclamation of equality of the races was a particularly sharp thorn in their side. Beginning in 1836, several groups of Boers – together with large numbers of Khoikhoi and Black servants – decided to trek off into the interior in search of greater independence. North and east of the Orange River (which formed the Cape Colony's frontier) these Boers – or Voortrekkers (Pioneers) – found vast tracts of apparently uninhabited grazing lands. They had entered, so it seemed, their promised land, with space enough for their cattle to graze, and for their culture of antiurban independence to flourish. Little did they know that what they found – deserted pasture lands, disorganised bands of refugees and tales of brutality – were the result of the *difaqane*, rather than the normal state of affairs.

1836	1852
Start of the Great Trek	Boer Republic of Transvaal created

With the exception of the more powerful Ndebele, the Voortrekkers encountered little resistance among the scattered peoples of the plains. They had been dispersed by the *difaqane* and lacked horses and firearms. Their weakened condition also solidified the Boers' belief that European occupation meant the coming of civilisation to a savage land.

However, the mountains (where King Moshoeshoe I was forging the Basotho nation that was later to become Lesotho) and the wooded valleys of Zululand were a more difficult proposition. Resistance here was strong, and the Boer incursions set off a series of skirmishes, squabbles and flimsy treaties that were to litter the next 50 years of increasing White domination.

A RIVER RUNS RED

The Great Trek's first halt was at Thaba 'Nchu, near present-day Bloemfontein, where a republic was established. Following disagreements among their leadership, the various Voortrekker groups split apart. While some headed north, most crossed the Drakensberg into Natal, with the idea of establishing a republic there. As this was Zulu territory, the Voortrekker leader Piet Retief paid a visit to King Dingaan, and was promptly massacred by the suspicious Zulu. This massacre triggered others, as well as a revenge attack by the Boers. The culmination came on 16 December 1838 in the Battle of Blood River at the Ncome River in Natal. Several Boers were injured, while several thousand Zulus were killed, reportedly causing the Ncome's waters to run red.

After this victory (the result of superior weapons), the Boers felt that their expansion really did have that long-suspected stamp of divine approval. Yet their hopes for establishing a Natal republic were short-lived. The British annexed the area in 1843, and founded their new Natal colony at present-day Durban. Most of the Boers – feeling increasingly squeezed between the British on the one side and the African populations on the other – headed north, with yet another grievance against the British.

The British set about establishing large sugar plantations in Natal, but found few takers from the neighbouring Zulu areas for labour. They turned to India to resolve this labour shortage, and in 1860 the SS *Truro* arrived in Durban harbour with over 300 people on board. Over the next 50 years, 150,000 more indentured Indians arrived, as well as numerous free 'passenger Indians', building the base for what was to become one of the largest Indian communities outside India. As early as 1893, when Mohandas (Mahatma) Gandhi arrived in Durban, Indians outnumbered Whites in Natal.

THE BOER REPUBLICS

The Boers meanwhile plugged on with their search for land and freedom, ultimately establishing themselves at Transvaal (encompassing parts of Gauteng, Limpopo, Northwest and Mpumalanga provinces) and the Orange Free State. For a while it seemed that these republics were beginning to settle into stable states, despite having thinly spread populations of fiercely independent Boers, no industry and minimal agriculture. Then the Boers' world was turned on its head in 1869 with the discovery of diamonds near Kimberley. The diamonds were found on land belonging to the Griqua,

DID YOU KNOW?

Until 1994, 16 December was celebrated by Whites as the Day of the Vow, before being renamed the Day of Reconciliation.

1860	1869
SS *Truro* arrives in Durban with over 300 Indians for indentured service	Diamonds found near Kimberley

but to which both the Transvaal and Orange Free State laid claim. Britain quickly stepped in and resolved the issue by annexing the area for itself.

The discovery of the Kimberley diamond mines unleashed a flood of European and Black labourers to the area. Towns sprang up in which the 'proper' separation of Whites and Blacks was ignored, and the Boers were angry that their impoverished republics were missing out on the economic benefits of the mines.

THE ANGLO-BOER WARS

Long-standing Boer resentment turned into full-blown rebellion in the Transvaal, and the first Anglo-Boer War, known by Afrikaners (as the descendants of the early Boers became known; see p48) as the War of Independence, broke out in 1880. It was over almost as soon as it began, with a crushing Boer victory at the Battle of Majuba Hill in early 1881. The republic regained its independence as the Zuid-Afrikaansche Republiek (ZAR; South African Republic). Paul Kruger, one of the leaders of the uprising, became president of the ZAR in 1883.

Meanwhile, the British, who viewed their defeat at Majuba as an aberration, forged ahead with their desire to federate the Southern African colonies and republics. They saw this as the best way to come to terms with the fact of a White Afrikaner majority, as well as to promote their larger strategic interests in the area.

In 1879, Zululand came under British control. Then in 1886, gold was discovered in the Witwatersrand (the area around Jo'burg), accelerating the federation process and dealing the Boers yet another blow. Jo'burg's population exploded to about 100,000 by the mid-1890s, and the ZAR suddenly found itself hosting thousands of *uitlanders* (foreigners), both Black and White, with the Boers squeezed to the sidelines. The influx of Black labour was particularly disturbing for the Boers, many of whom were going through hard times and resented the Black wage-earners.

The enormous wealth of the mines soon became irresistible for British imperialists. In 1895, a group of renegades led by Captain Leander Jameson entered the ZAR with the intention of sparking an uprising on the Witwatersrand and installing a British administration. The scheme was a fiasco, but it was obvious to Kruger that it had at least the tacit approval of the Cape Colony government, and that his republic was in danger. He reacted by forming an alliance with Orange Free State.

The situation peaked in 1899, when the British demanded voting rights for the 60,000 foreign Whites on the Witwatersrand. (Until this point, Kruger's government had excluded all foreigners from the franchise.) Kruger refused, calling for British troops to be withdrawn from the ZAR's borders. When the British refused, Kruger declared war. This second Anglo-Boer war was more protracted and the British were better prepared than at Majuba Hill. By June 1900, Pretoria, the last of the major Boer towns, had surrendered. Yet resistance by Boer *bittereinders* (bitter enders) continued for two more years with guerrilla-style battles, which in turn were met by scorched-earth tactics by the British. By 1902, 26,000 people had died of disease and neglect in the camps (see p355). On 31 May 1902, a superficial peace came with the signing of the Treaty of Vereeniging. Under its terms, the Boer republics

DID YOU KNOW?

The Witwatersrand contains the world's largest gold deposit, thus far yielding roughly one-third of all the gold ever mined on earth.

1879	1881
Zululand comes under British control	First Anglo-Boer War ends; Transvaal becomes the South African Republic

acknowledged British sovereignty, while the British in turn committed themselves to reconstruction of the areas under their control.

PEACE & UNITY?

During the immediate postwar years, the British focused their attention on rebuilding the country, in particular the mining industry. By 1907, the mines of the Witwatersrand were producing almost one-third of the world's gold. But the peace brought by the treaty was fragile, and challenged on all sides. The Afrikaners found themselves in the ignominious position of being poor farmers in a country where big mining ventures and foreign capital rendered them irrelevant. They were particularly incensed by Britain's unsuccessful attempts to anglicise them, and to impose English as the official language in schools and the workplace. Partly as a backlash to this, Afrikaans came to be seen as the *volkstaal* (people's language) and a symbol of Afrikaner nationhood, and several nationalistic organisations sprang up.

Blacks and Coloureds were completely marginalised. Harsh taxes were imposed, wages were reduced and the British caretaker administrator encouraged the immigration of thousands of Chinese to undercut any resistance. Resentment was given full vent in the Bambatha Rebellion of 1906, in which 4000 Zulu lost their lives after protesting onerous tax legislation.

> He who hates, hates himself.
>
> ZULU PROVERB

The British meanwhile moved ahead with their plans for union. After several years of negotiation, the 1910 Act of Union was signed, bringing the republics of Cape Colony, Natal, Transvaal and Orange Free State together as the Union of South Africa. Under the provisions of the act, the Union was still a British territory, with home-rule for Afrikaners. The British High Commission Territories of Basotholand (now Lesotho), Bechuanaland (now Botswana), Swaziland, and Rhodesia (now Zimbabwe) continued to be ruled directly by Britain.

English and Dutch were made the official languages. (Afrikaans was not recognised as an official language until 1925.) Despite a major campaign by Blacks and Coloureds, the voter franchise remained as it was in the pre-Union republics and colonies, and only Whites could be elected to parliament.

REPRESSION, RESISTANCE & RAMPANT RACISM

The first government of the new Union was headed by General Louis Botha, with General Jan Smuts as his deputy. Their South African National Party (later known as the South African Party or SAP) followed a generally pro-British, White-unity line. More radical Boers split away under the leadership of General Barry Hertzog, forming the National Party (NP) in 1914. The NP championed Afrikaner interests, advocating separate development for the two White groups and independence from Britain.

There was no place in the new Union for Blacks, despite constituting over 75% of the population. Under the Act of Union, they were denied voting rights in the Transvaal and Orange Free State areas, and in Cape Colony were granted the vote only if they met a property ownership qualification. Coming on the heels of British wartime propaganda promising freedom from 'Boer slavery', the failure to grant the franchise was regarded by Blacks as a blatant betrayal. It wasn't long before a barrage of oppressive legislation

1886	1893
Gold discovered in the Witwatersrand	Mohandas (Mahatma) Gandhi arrives in Durban

was passed, making it illegal for Black workers to strike, reserving skilled jobs for Whites, barring Blacks from military service and instituting restrictive pass laws. In 1913, the Natives Land Act was enacted, setting aside 8% of South Africa's land for Black occupancy. Whites, who made up 20% of the population, were given over 90% of the land. Black Africans were not allowed to buy, rent or even be sharecroppers outside their designated area. Thousands of squatters were evicted from farms and forced into increasingly overcrowded and impoverished reserves, or into the cities. Those who remained were reduced to the status of landless labourers.

Black and Coloured opposition began to coalesce, and leading figures such as John Jabavu, Walter Rubusana and Abdullah Abdurahman laid the foundations for new nontribal Black political groups. Most significantly, a Columbia University–educated attorney, Pixley ka Isaka Seme, called together representatives of the various African tribes to form a unified national organisation to represent the interests of Blacks, and to ensure that they had an effective voice in the new Union. Thus was born the South African Native National Congress, known from 1923 onwards as the African National Congress (ANC).

Parallel to this, Mohandas Gandhi had been working with the Indian populations of Natal and the Transvaal to fight against the ever-increasing encroachments on their rights. See the boxed text below.

MAHATMA GANDHI

In 1893 Mohandas (Mahatma) Gandhi, a young Indian solicitor, set sail for Durban, South Africa, to take on a one-year legal contract in South Africa. Anti-Indian sentiment in Natal was high, and upon his arrival he was thrown out of a first-class train wagon at Pietermaritzburg because of his race.

The incident had a profound effect on Gandhi. He began schooling himself in methods of nonviolent resistance, and became increasingly involved with the local Indian community, working with them to safeguard their political rights. Within a short period, Gandhi had not only established himself as a successful attorney, but also as the leading spokesperson for Indian interests in South Africa.

In 1896, and again in 1901, Gandhi returned briefly to India where he lobbied extensively to bring attention to the plight of Indians in South Africa. Back in South Africa, Gandhi developed the thinking that was to guide his political activity for the rest of his life. He gave up the trappings of a successful attorney, began washing his own clothes, committed himself to a life of celibacy and nonpossession, and devoted himself fully to service. He also developed his defining philosophy of satyagraha (meaning, very loosely, truth through nonviolence).

In 1907, the Transvaal government passed the Asiatic Registration Act requiring all Indians to register with the Registrar of Asiatics, and carry a certificate of registration. Gandhi called on the Indian community to defy the act, and to offer no resistance if they should be arrested. Over the next seven years, numerous similar incidents followed, including a court decision nullifying all Hindu and Muslim marriages, which Gandhi and his followers also peacefully defied. In response, Gandhi – along with thousands of other Indians who had joined him in his satyagraha struggle – was repeatedly arrested.

Gandhi finally returned to India in 1914 – over 20 years after he first arrived in South Africa for a year-long stay. Apart from the profound global influence of Gandhi's life, his tactics in South Africa resulted in the 1914 passage of the Indian Relief Bill, which among other concessions restored recognition of Hindu and Muslim marriages.

1902	1910
Treaty of Vereeniging ends the second Anglo-Boer War	Union of South Africa created, with no voting rights for Blacks; Lesotho and Swaziland remain British protectorates

In 1924 the NP, under Hertzog, came to power in a coalition government, and Afrikaner nationalism gained a greater hold. Dutch was replaced by Afrikaans (previously only regarded as a low-class dialect of Dutch) as an official language of the Union, and the so-called *swart gevaar* (Black threat) was made the dominant issue of the 1929 election. Hertzog joined briefly in a coalition with the more moderate Jan Smuts in the mid-1930s, after which Smuts took the reins and – amid much controversy – led South Africa into WWII on the side of the Allies. However, any hopes of turning the tide of Afrikaner nationalism were dashed when Daniel François (DF) Malan led a radical breakaway movement, the Purified National Party, to the central position in Afrikaner political life. The Afrikaner Broederbond, a secret Afrikaner brotherhood that had been formed in 1918 to protect Afrikaner culture, soon became an extraordinarily influential force behind both the NP and other organisations designed to promote the *volk* ('people', the Afrikaners).

See www.anc.org.za for more on the African National Congress (ANC) and South African history.

Due to the booming wartime economy, Black labour became increasingly important to the mining and manufacturing industries, and the Black urban population nearly doubled. Enormous squatter camps grew up on the outskirts of Jo'burg and, to a lesser extent, outside the other major cities. Conditions in the townships were appalling, but poverty was not only the province of Blacks; wartime surveys found that 40% of White schoolchildren were malnourished.

THE WALLS OF APARTHEID GO UP

In the run-up to the 1948 elections, the NP campaigned on its policy of segregation, or 'apartheid' (an Afrikaans term for the state of being apart). It was voted in, in coalition with the Afrikaner Party (AP), and under the leadership of DF Malan.

Apartheid – long a reality of life – became institutionalised under Malan. Within short order, legislation was passed prohibiting mixed marriages, making interracial sex illegal, classifying every individual by race and establishing a classification board to rule in questionable cases. The noxious Group Areas Act of 1950 set aside desirable city properties for Whites, while banishing non-Whites into the townships. The Separate Amenities Act created, among other things, separate beaches, buses, hospitals, schools and even park benches.

The existing pass laws were further strengthened: Blacks and Coloureds were compelled to carry identity documents at all times and were prohibited from remaining in towns, or even visiting them, without specific permission. Couples were not allowed to live together (or even visit each other) in the town where only one of them worked, and children had to remain in rural areas.

In 1960, tensions came to a head in the Sharpeville Massacre (see p38). Soon thereafter, Prime Minister Hendrik Verwoerd, whose rabid racism earned him the unofficial title of 'architect of apartheid', announced a referendum on whether the country should become a republic. The change was passed by a slim majority of voters. Verwoerd withdrew South Africa from the Commonwealth, and in May 1961 the Republic of South Africa came into existence.

1912	1914
South African Native National Congress established (forerunner to the ANC)	National Party is formed

ACTION & ACTIVISM

These developments pushed the hitherto relatively conservative ANC into action. In 1949 they developed an agenda that for the first time advocated open resistance in the form of strikes, acts of public disobedience and protest marches. These continued throughout the 1950s, and resulted in occasional violent clashes. In June 1955, at a congress held at Kliptown near Jo'burg, a number of organisations, including the Indian Congress and the ANC, adopted a Freedom Charter. This articulated a vision of a nonracial democratic state, and is still central to the ANC's vision of a new South Africa.

In 1959, a group of disenchanted ANC members, seeking to sever all links with White government, broke away to form the more militant Pan African Congress. First on the PAC's agenda was a series of nationwide demonstrations against the hated pass laws. On 21 March 1960, police opened fire on demonstrators surrounding a police station in Sharpeville, a township near Vereeniging. At least 67 people were killed, and 186 wounded; most of those shot were shot in the back.

To many domestic and international onlookers, the struggle had crossed a crucial line at Sharpeville, and there could no longer be any doubts about the nature of the White regime. In the wake of the shooting, a massive stay-away from work was organised, and demonstrations continued. Verwoerd declared a state of emergency, giving security forces the right to detain people without trial. Over 18,000 demonstrators were arrested, including much of the ANC and PAC leadership, and both organisations were banned.

As Black activists continued to be arrested, the ANC and PAC began a campaign of sabotage through the armed wings of their organisations, Umkhonto we Sizwe (Spear of the Nation, MK) and Poqo ('Pure' or 'Alone'), respectively. In July 1963, 17 members of the ANC underground movement were arrested. Together with ANC leader Nelson Mandela, who had already been arrested on other charges, they were tried for treason at the widely publicised Rivonia Trial. In June 1964, Mandela and seven others were sentenced to life imprisonment. Oliver Tambo, another member of the ANC leadership, managed to escape South Africa and lead the ANC in exile.

> I have fought against White domination and I have fought against Black domination. I have cherished the ideal of a democratic and free society in which all persons live together in harmony and with equal opportunities. It is an ideal which I hope to live for and to achieve. But if needs be, it is an ideal for which I am prepared to die.
> *Nelson Mandela, 20 April 1964, Rivonia Trial*

Nelson Mandela's autobiographical *Long Walk to Freedom* offers an unparalleled recounting of South African and African National Congress (ANC) politics during the tumultuous 1960s, continuing up until his release from prison three decades later.

For more on Mandela, see www.pbs.org/wgbh /pages/frontline/shows /mandela, or check out the exhaustive *Mandela: the Authorised Biography* by Anthony Sampson.

DECADES OF DARKNESS

With the ANC banned, and Mandela and most of the rest of its leadership in jail or exile, South Africa moved into some of its darkest times. Apartheid legislation was enforced with increasing gusto, and the walls between the races were built ever higher. Most odious was the creation of separate 'homelands' for Blacks (see the boxed text on p39). In 1966, Verwoerd was stabbed to death, but his policies continued under BJ Vorster and, later, PW Botha.

1948	1955
National Party gains control of the government; apartheid is institutionalised	The Freedom Charter is drawn up by various organisations, including the ANC, in Klipstown

THE 'HOME'LANDS

In 1962 – two years before Nelson Mandela was sentenced to life imprisonment – the Transkei was born. It was the first of 10 so-called 'Bantustans' or 'homelands' that were intended to provide a home for all Black South Africans. On these lands – so went the White South African propaganda – Blacks would be self-sufficient, self-governing citizens, living together with others of their own tribe.

The realities were much different. The homeland areas had no infrastructure or industry, and were incapable of producing sufficient food for the burgeoning Black population. They were also completely disproportionate in size to the numbers of people they were supposed to host. All the homelands together constituted only 14% of South Africa's land, while Blacks made up close to 80% of the country's population. Tribal divisions were made arbitrarily, and once a person had been assigned to a homeland, they could not leave without a pass and permission. The resulting suffering was intense and widespread. Overpopulated farming lands were rapidly exhausted, and families were divided as men were forced to return alone to urban areas as guest workers without rights.

Following creation of the homelands, Blacks flooded to the cities seeking work: while life in urban squatter camps was bad, life in the homelands was worse. To stop this, the government banned Blacks from being employed as shop assistants, receptionists, typists and clerks. The construction of housing in the Black 'locations' (dormitory suburbs for Black workers) was halted, and enormous single-sex hostels were built instead.

The situation in the homelands was further worsened by internal political strife. In an effort to garner more power for themselves, some homeland leaders became collaborators with the government, accepting 'independence' while crushing all resistance to their control and to the South African government.

Although the homelands came to an end with the demise of apartheid, their legacies – including completely insufficient infrastructure and distorted population concentrations in the homeland areas – continue to scar the face of South Africa today.

During the 1970s, resistance again gained force, first channelled through trade unions and strikes, and then spearheaded by the South African Students' Organisation, under the leadership of the charismatic Steve Biko. Biko, a medical student, was the main force behind growth of South Africa's Black Consciousness Movement, which stressed the need for psychological liberation, Black pride and nonviolent opposition to apartheid.

Things culminated in 1976, when the Soweto Students' Representative Council organised protests against the use of Afrikaans (regarded as the language of the oppressor) in Black schools. On 16 June police opened fire on a student march, beginning a round of nationwide demonstrations, strikes, mass arrests, riots and violence that, over the next 12 months, took over 1000 lives.

In September 1977, Steve Biko was killed (see the boxed text on p253). Unidentified security police bashed him until he lapsed into a coma; he went without medical treatment for three days and finally died in Pretoria. At the subsequent inquest, the magistrate found that no one was to blame, although the South African Medical Association eventually took action against the doctors who failed to treat Biko. South Africa was never to be the same again. A generation of young Blacks committed themselves to a revolutionary struggle against apartheid ('Liberation before Education' was the catch-cry) and the Black communities were politicised.

1960	1961
Sharpeville massacre; ANC and Pan African Congress (PAC) banned	South Africa leaves the Commonwealth and becomes a republic

SOUTH AFRICA UNDER SIEGE

By 1980 South Africa was the only country in Africa with a White government and a constitution discriminating against the majority of its citizens. As international opinion turned decisively against the White regime, the government (and most of the White population) increasingly saw the country as a bastion besieged by communism, atheism and Black anarchy. Considerable effort was put into circumventing sanctions, and the government even developed nuclear weapons (which have since been destroyed).

Negotiating majority rule with the ANC was not considered an option (publicly, at least), which left the government to defend the country against external and internal threats through sheer military might. A siege mentality developed among Whites, and although many realised that a civil war against the Black majority could not be won, they preferred this to 'giving in' to political reform. Brutal police and military actions seemed entirely justifiable. Paradoxically, the international sanctions that cut Whites off from the rest of the world enabled Black leaders to develop sophisticated political skills, as those in exile forged ties with regional and world leaders.

Larry Schwartz recalls the realities of military service during South Africa's darkest days in The Wild Almond Line *– a memoir of growing up in a segregated country and being a conscript in the apartheid-era army.*

From 1978 to 1988 the South African Defence Force (SADF; now called the South African National Defence Force; SANDF) made a number of major attacks inside Angola, Mozambique, Zimbabwe, Botswana and Lesotho. All White males were liable for national service, and thousands fled into exile to avoid conscription. Many more were scarred mentally and physically by their participation in vicious struggles in the region, or in the townships of South Africa.

WINDS OF CHANGE

In the early 1980s, a new wind began to blow across South Africa. Whites constituted only 16% of the total population, in comparison with 20% 50 years earlier, and this number was continuing to fall. Recognising the inevitability of change, PW Botha told White South Africans to 'adapt or die'. Numerous reforms were instituted, including repeal of the pass laws. But Botha stopped well short of full reform, and many Blacks (as well as the international community) felt the changes were only cosmetic. Protests and resistance continued full force, as South Africa became increasingly polarised and fragmented, and unrest was widespread. A White backlash also arose, giving rise to a number of neo-Nazi paramilitary groups, notably the Afrikaner Weerstandsbeweging (AWB), led by Eugène Terre'Blanche. The opposition United Democratic Front (UDF) was also formed at this time. With a broad coalition of members, led by Archbishop Desmond Tutu and the Reverend Allan Boesak, it called for the government to abandon its proposed reforms, and instead to abolish apartheid and eliminate the homelands.

International pressures also increased, as economic sanctions began to dig in harder, and the value of the rand collapsed. In 1985, the government declared a state of emergency, which was to stay in effect for five years. The media was censored and, by 1988, 30,000 people had been detained without trial, with thousands tortured.

1964	1976
Nelson Mandela sentenced to life imprisonment	Soweto uprisings begin

STALKED BY A SHADOW

Amidst this turmoil, a perhaps even darker shadow had started to move across South Africa. In 1982, the first recorded death from AIDS occurred in the country. Within a decade, the number of recorded AIDS cases had risen to over 1000, and by the mid-1990s, it had reached 10,000. Yet, these officially recorded cases were only the tip of the iceberg, with some estimates placing the actual number of HIV-positive cases at close to one million in 1995. Fuelled by the entrenched migrant labour system at South Africa's mines, AIDS is estimated to have been spreading at the explosive rate of over 500 new cases per day.

In the late 1980s, the South African Chamber of Mines began an education campaign to try and stem the rise of cases. But without a change in

NELSON MANDELA

Nelson Rolihlahla Mandela is without doubt one of the global leaders of the millennium. Once vilified by South Africa's ruling Whites and sentenced to life imprisonment, he emerged from 27 years of incarceration calling for reconciliation and forgiveness, and was able to rally together all South Africans at the most crucial of times.

Mandela, son of a Xhosa chief, was born on 18 July 1918 in the small village of Mveso on the Mbashe River. When he was young the family moved to Qunu, south of Umtata in what is now Eastern Cape. Here he grew up living in a kraal (rural housing compound) such as those that still dot this landscape, living a typical rural life, while at the same time being groomed for a future position in the tribal leadership. After attending school at the University College of Fort Hare, Mandela headed to Jo'burg, where he soon became immersed in politics. He also finished his law degree and, together with Oliver Tambo, opened South Africa's first Black law firm. Meanwhile, in 1944, together with Tambo and Walter Sisulu, Mandela formed the Youth League of the African National Congress (ANC), which worked to turn the ANC into a nationwide grassroots movement. During the 1950s, Mandela was at the forefront of the ANC's civil disobedience campaigns, for which he was first arrested in 1952, tried and acquitted. Various arrests and detention followed. After the ANC was banned in the wake of the Sharpeville Massacre, Mandela advocated establishing its underground military wing, Umkhonto we Sizwe. In 1964, while serving time for an earlier arrest, Mandela was brought to stand trial for sabotage and fomenting revolution in the widely publicised Rivonia Trial. After brilliantly arguing his own defence, he was sentenced to life imprisonment, and spent the next 18 years in the infamous Robben Island prison, before being moved to Pollsmoor Prison on the mainland, and later to Victor Verster prison near Paarl, from which he was eventually released.

Throughout his incarceration, Mandela repeatedly refused to compromise his political beliefs in exchange for freedom, saying that only free men can negotiate. Among other things, he rejected offers of release in exchange for recognising the independence of the Transkei (and thereby giving tacit approval of the legitimacy of the apartheid regime).

On 18 February 1990, Mandela was released and in 1991 he was elected president of the ANC. From this position, he continued the negotiations (which had started secretly while he was in prison) to demolish apartheid and bring an end to minority rule. In 1993, Mandela shared the Nobel peace prize with FW de Klerk and, in the first free elections the following year, was elected president of South Africa. In his much-quoted speech, 'Free at Last!', made after winning the 1994 elections, he focused the nation's attention firmly on the future, declaring, 'This is the time to heal the old wounds and build a new South Africa'.

In 1997, Mandela – or Madiba, his traditional Xhosa name – stepped down as ANC president, although he continues to be actively involved in politics as an elder statesman.

1977	1982
Steve Biko murdered	The first recorded AIDS death in South Africa

the underlying conditions of mine workers – a major factor contributing to the epidemic – success could hardly be expected. Long periods away from home under bleak conditions, and a few days leave a month were the apartheid-induced realities of life under which thousands of miners and other labourers worked. Compounding the problem was the fact that as of the mid-1990s, many health officials were still focused more on the incidence of tuberculosis than of AIDS.

As South Africa began to take its first tenuous steps to dismantle the walls of apartheid, AIDS lay waiting to explode like a ticking time bomb.

THE WALLS BEGIN TO FALL

In 1986, President Botha announced to parliament that South Africa had 'outgrown' apartheid. The government started making a series of minor reforms in the direction of racial equality, while maintaining an iron grip on the media and on all antiapartheid demonstrations.

In late 1989, a physically ailing Botha was succeeded by FW de Klerk. At his opening address to the parliament in February 1990, de Klerk announced that he would repeal discriminatory laws and legalise the ANC, the PAC and the Communist Party. Media restrictions were lifted, and de Klerk released political prisoners not guilty of common-law crimes. On 11 February 1990, 27 years after he had first been incarcerated, Nelson Mandela walked out of the grounds of Victor Verster prison a free man.

From 1990 to 1991 the legal apparatus of apartheid was abolished. A referendum – the last Whites-only vote held in South Africa – overwhelmingly gave the government authority to negotiate a new constitution with the ANC and other groups.

A Burning Hunger: One Family's Struggle Against Apartheid by Lynda Schuster is an extraordinary recounting of a Black family's fight against apartheid, from the Soweto uprisings in 1976 until liberation in the early 1990s.

FREE ELECTIONS

In December 1991 the Convention for a Democratic South Africa (Codesa) began negotiations on the formation of a multiracial transitional government and a new constitution extending political rights to all groups. Months of wrangling finally produced a compromise and an election date, although at considerable human cost. Political violence exploded across the country during this time, particularly in the wake of the assassination of Chris Hani, the popular leader of the South African Communist Party. It's now known that elements within the police and army contributed to this violence. There have also been claims that high-ranking government officials and politicians ordered, or at least condoned, massacres.

In 1993, a draft constitution was published guaranteeing freedom of speech and religion, access to adequate housing and numerous other benefits, and explicitly prohibiting discrimination on almost any grounds. Finally, at midnight on 26–27 April 1994, the old national anthem 'Die Stem' (The Call) was sung and the old flag was lowered, followed by the raising of the new rainbow flag and singing of the new anthem, 'Nkosi Sikelele Afrika' (God Bless Africa). The election went off peacefully, amidst a palpable feeling of goodwill throughout the country.

The ANC won 62.7% of the vote, less than the 66.7% that would have enabled it to rewrite the constitution. As well as deciding the national

SOUTH AFRICA'S GOVERNMENT

In 1996, after much negotiation and debate, South Africa's parliament approved a revised version of the 1993 constitution that established the structure of the country's new, democratic government. Today, the national government consists of a 400-member National Assembly, a 90-member National Council of Provinces, and a head of state (the president), who is elected by the National Assembly. In addition, there are nine provincial governments, each headed by a premier and a 10-person executive council. The provinces (and their capitals) are: Western Cape (Cape Town), Eastern Cape (Bisho), Northern Cape (Kimberley), KwaZulu-Natal (Pietermaritzburg), Mpumalanga (Nelspruit), Gauteng (Johannesburg), Free State (Bloemfontein), Northwest Province (Mafikeng), and Limpopo (Polokwane (Pietersburg)).

A South African president has more in common with a Westminster-style prime minister than a US president, although as head of state the South African president has some executive powers denied most prime ministers. The constitution stands at the centre of the legal system, and is most notable for its expansive Bill of Rights.

Operating parallel to these Western-style institutions is a system of traditional leadership, under which all legislation pertaining to indigenous law, tradition or custom must be referred to the Council of Traditional Leaders. Although the council cannot veto or amend legislation, it can delay its passage.

National elections are held every five years, and are next due in 2009.

government, the election decided the provincial governments, and the ANC won in all but two provinces. The NP captured most of the White and Coloured vote and became the official opposition party.

REWRITING HISTORY

Following the elections, focus turned to the Truth & Reconciliation Commission (1994–99), which worked to expose crimes of the apartheid era under the dictum of Archbishop Desmond Tutu: 'Without forgiveness there is no future, but without confession there can be no forgiveness'. Many stories of horrific brutality and injustice were heard by the commission, offering some catharsis to people and communities shattered by their past.

The commission operated by allowing victims to tell their stories and perpetrators to confess their guilt, with amnesty on offer to those who made a clean breast of it. Those who chose not to appear before the commission would face criminal prosecution if their guilt could be proven. Yet, while some soldiers, police and 'ordinary' citizens have confessed their crimes, it seems unlikely that the human rights criminals who gave the orders and dictated the policies will present themselves (PW Botha is one famous no-show), and it has proven difficult to gather evidence against them.

FREE ELECTIONS – SECOND ROUND

In 1999, South Africa held its second democratic elections. In 1997 Mandela had handed over ANC leadership to his deputy, Thabo Mbeki, and there was speculation that the ANC vote might therefore drop. In fact, it increased to put the party within one seat of the two-thirds majority that would allow it to alter the constitution.

1997	1999
Nelson Mandela retires as ANC president, succeeded by Thabo Mbeki	ANC wins landslide victory in second democratic elections

The NP, restyled as the New National Party (NNP), lost two-thirds of its seats, as well as official opposition status to the Democratic Party (DP) – traditionally a stronghold of liberal Whites, with new force from conservatives disenchanted with the NP, and from some middle-class Blacks. Coming in just behind the DP was the KwaZulu-Natal-based Inkatha Freedom Party (IFP), historically the voice of Zulu nationalism. While the IFP lost some support, its leader, Chief Buthelezi, held onto power as the national Home Affairs minister.

INTO THE FUTURE

Beyond the Miracle: Inside the New South Africa by Allister Sparks is a realistic yet optimistic analysis of South Africa as it steps into the future, written by one of South Africa's most respected journalists.

Despite the scars of the past and the enormous problems ahead, South Africa today is an immeasurably more optimistic and relaxed country than it was a decade ago. While Mbeki is held in far less affection by the ANC grassroots than the beloved 'Madiba' (Mandela), he has proven himself a shrewd politician, maintaining his political preeminence by isolating or coopting opposition parties. In 2003, Mbeki skilfully manoeuvred the ANC to a two-thirds majority in parliament for the first time – giving it the power to rewrite the constitution if it chooses.

Yet, it has not been all clear sailing. In the early days of his presidency, Mbeki's effective denial of the AIDS crisis invited global criticism, and his conspicuous failure to condemn the forced reclamation of White-owned farms in neighbouring Zimbabwe unnerved both South African landowners and foreign investors.

In the coming years, attention is likely to focus overwhelmingly on crime, economic inequality, overhauling the educational system and, especially, AIDS. With an estimated 4.5 million South Africans affected – more than in any other country in the world – this scourge threatens to eclipse all of South Africa's other problems.

2003	2004
ANC gains a two-thirds majority in parliament for the first time, giving it the power to rewrite the constitution	An estimated 4.5 million AIDS cases in South Africa

The Culture

THE NATIONAL PSYCHE

A decade after the end of apartheid, South Africa is still finding its way. The bloodshed of the final days of apartheid has left its mark, but the optimism and determination of the liberation struggle are still there. Freedom has delivered a whole range of new challenges. Opinion polls show that unemployment is the number-one concern for South Africans. Crime comes second, followed by HIV/AIDS.

While the formal racial divisions of apartheid have dissolved, its shadows still exist. It's not unusual to hear Whites being automatically addressed as 'Madam' or 'Sir'. In some ways, it's become a society divided by class rather than colour: the gap between rich and poor is vast. Manicured suburbs and squalid townships are only minutes away from each other, and different groups are living separate, but parallel lives.

The 'new South Africa' is still very young. It can be an inspiring place, rich in forgiveness and spirit. But it's also soured by violence and selfishness. Despite some improvements since 1994, violent crime has stabilised at still unacceptably high levels. A generation grew up amid almost daily brutality and uncertainty and the nation is still setting its moral boundaries.

Archbishop Desmond Tutu delivered a rousing speech at the funeral of African National Congress (ANC) leader Walter Sisulu in May 2003. The crowd roared as he spoke out against violent crime: 'We wanted to be free, not so that we would become a nation of car hijackers and criminals.'

But while crime continues to grab headlines and undermine South Africa's reputation as a tourism destination, it's important to keep it in perspective. South Africa is a unique, refreshing and fascinating place to visit. It's physically beautiful and its people will be your biggest reward. The political history is so fresh that those who lived through it are there to guide you. It's a rare chance to experience a country that is rebuilding itself after profound change. The story of South Africa is a story of hope.

LIFESTYLE

It's difficult to give a single picture of everyday life in South Africa. For some Whites, there is still a sense of fear and loss now that the old regime has gone. For others it's almost a case of 'I told you so', displaying a gloomy sense of satisfaction from talking about South Africa's problems and shaking their heads about the government's performance.

Many middle-class and wealthy families live in heavily secured homes and spend their leisure time in equally fortified shopping centres. Visit an upmarket shopping mall and you'll see people dining alfresco-style, under umbrellas at cafés that are actually indoors. Guards patrol the walkways and shops to keep any criminals at bay.

Life is very different for the millions of South Africans who are still living in poverty. Tiny matchbox houses are home to large extended families and there's very little space and privacy.

Township life is vibrant and informal. People gather on street corners and in local bars known as 'shebeens'. Weddings and funerals are big events and are often open to anyone who wants to show up. Formal invitations are rare. Weddings often spill onto the street with plenty of dancing. If you're passing by, during a visit to the townships, stop and check it out. You'll more than likely be encouraged to join in. Don't miss it: it's great fun and a really interesting insight into family life.

DID YOU KNOW?

South Africa has the largest market share in the world for BMW, which runs special antihijacking courses for its customers.

DID YOU KNOW?

Seventy-three percent of South African households have a radio and 53% have a television. Less than 2% of Black households have a computer, compared to almost half of all White households.

Unfortunately, funerals are becoming one of the most frequent gatherings. Every Saturday the cemeteries are crowded with mourners. The AIDS epidemic is having a huge impact and many of those who are being buried are young people. South Africa has the largest HIV-positive population in the world.

Many women have formed burial societies to save money for the increasing number of family funerals. The spread of HIV from partner to partner means that people attend the funerals of one relative after the next. Thousands of households in South Africa, Lesotho and Swaziland are now headed by children, because their parents have died from AIDS. Sometimes the only survivors from an entire family are the eldest children, who were born before their parents became infected. A large number of grandparents who have nursed and lost their adult offspring to AIDS are also looking after their orphaned grandchildren, many of whom are also HIV-positive.

There's still a lot of stigma attached to HIV/AIDS. Many people are ashamed to admit that a relative died of AIDS. Family members will often tell you that their loved one passed away from tuberculosis or the flu.

Swaziland now has the highest HIV-infection rate in the world and Lesotho is also one of the worst-affected countries.

POPULATION & PEOPLE

South Africa, Lesotho and Swaziland are part of a delicate and complicated tapestry of cultures and ethnic groups.

South Africa's Gauteng province, which includes Johannesburg (Jo' burg) and Pretoria, is the economic engine of the country. It generates more than half of South Africa's wealth and is the most densely populated and urbanised province. At the other end of the scale, the rural and underdeveloped Eastern Cape is the poorest province, where up to 20% of adults have never received any formal schooling.

South Africa's economy attracts millions of immigrants from across the continent. Some come to the country legally, but many others take their chances. South Africa's Department of Home Affairs sends illegal immigrants from Zimbabwe back home on a train, but some simply jump out of the windows of the moving carriages before they reach the border. Many illegal immigrants live in Jo'burg's impoverished inner city. Their presence angers some South Africans who accuse outsiders of taking jobs and creating crime.

Swaziland has strong economic and social ties with South Africa. Almost three-quarters of Swazi exports go to South Africa and even more goods and services are imported. Up to 70% of Swazis live in rural areas and many rely on farming for survival. Swazi culture is very strong and quite distinct from South Africa. The atmosphere often feels more conservative and formal than across the border. The monarchy has an influence on many aspects of life, from cultural ceremonies to politics. Some Swazis are very proud of the royal traditions and are suspicious of those who call for greater democracy. But some human rights and opposition activists believe power should be transferred from the king to the people.

Lesotho's big connection with South Africa has been the mining industry. In the 1990s, up to 120,000 Basotho men were employed by South African mines. Up to one third of Lesotho's household incomes came from wages earned by the miners. But tens of thousands of jobs were lost when the mining industry underwent restructuring. Many former miners have returned home to Lesotho, to join the ranks of the unemployed.

DID YOU KNOW?

The Zulu word for grandmother is *gogo*. *Gogos* play a vital role in many families and their monthly pension is often the only regular source of income for the extended family.

Beyond economics, different regions and groups have complicated links. While much of the focus has been on Black and White relations in South Africa, there is also friction and distrust between Black, Coloured and South Africans of Indian descent.

In 2002, well-known performer and producer Mbongeni Ngema released a song called 'AmaNdiya' which translates as 'The Indians'. The lyrics accused Indians of trying to oppress Black South Africans. Human rights activists called for the song to be banned and it prompted a bitter debate.

The Black and White divide can still be a sensitive topic. But sometimes locals are surprisingly open when they talk about the stereotypes and prejudices that exist between various groups. Ask a Zulu what he or she thinks about Xhosas or quiz English-speaking Whites about their views on Afrikaners.

WOMEN

In South Africa, Lesotho and Swaziland, women play a vital role in society. South African women were at the centre of the antipass law demonstrations and bus boycotts of the '50s, protesting under the slogan 'You strike the woman and you strike the rock'. There is a strong representation of women in South Africa's parliament, and it's guaranteed in the constitution.

But the reality for many South African women is very different. Poverty, sexual violence and HIV are overshadowing progress. South Africa has among the highest incidence of rape in the world. In 2003, there were more than 52,000 cases of rape reported to the South African police service. Some women's groups say the real figures are much worse, because many women are too afraid to report the crime. Cape Town's Rape Crisis group estimates that on average a woman is assaulted in South Africa every 23 seconds.

Statistics show that women are more likely than men to be infected with HIV. Biologically, the virus spreads more easily from an infected man to a woman during intercourse. Many women become infected at an early age, because they are having sex with older men. The threat of sexual violence often undermines the ability of young women to ensure their partner is wearing a condom.

Swazi women have also made parliamentary gains in the 2003 elections. Swaziland's biggest urban centre, Manzini, is represented solely by female MPs. But traditions and the law are still lagging behind. Widows were disqualified from standing in the election. They were ordered to stay indoors at home, in line with local customs. Some Swazis believe that a widowed woman is 'unclean' because she still carries the spirit of her dead husband. Under Swazi law, women are given the same status as children. They can't own property in their own name, enter contracts or secure bank loans without the sponsorship of a male relative. Ironically, a government survey has found that more than 70% of small businesses in Swaziland are operated by women.

In Lesotho, women shouldered a big share of economic, social and family responsibilities, while their husbands and male relatives went to work in the mines in South Africa. Many of the mining jobs have now disappeared and the textile industry has become a big part of Lesotho's economy. Up to 90% of the new jobs have gone to women. Basotho women are often better educated that their male counterparts, as many boys in rural areas are forced to tend cattle, instead of spending time in the classroom.

DID YOU KNOW?

Minibus taxis have been named after former Olympic distance runner Zola Budd. The taxis were given her name because of their reputation for being fast and reliable.

Proud of Me, by Charlene Smith, is a truly frightening, honest and compelling account of rape. Smith is a highly respected journalist and activist who was sexually assaulted at her home in Johannesburg in 1999.

SOUTHERN AFRICA'S SLOWLY MELTING POPULATION POT Mary Fitzpatrick

There are few countries where racial and ethnic conflicts have been as turbulent, protracted and high-profile as in South Africa. The country's heart pulses with the blood of groups with a diversity that covers the ancient San and Khoikhoi, 17th-century Dutch settlers, 19th-century British traders, Bantu-speaking African peoples, Indians, Jews, Portuguese and more. Yet it is only since 1994, with the commitment of the African National Congress (ANC) to building a nonracial 'rainbow nation', that there has been any significant degree of collaboration and peace between the various groups.

During the apartheid era, the government attempted to categorise everyone into one of four major groups – easily enough said, perhaps, but disastrous to implement. The classifications – as African (at various times also called 'native' and 'Bantu', and sometimes now also 'Black'), Coloured, Asian or White – were often arbitrary and highly contentious. They were used to regulate where and how people could live and work, and became the basis for institutionalised inequality and intolerance.

Today, these times are slowly fading into history, although now discrimination based on wealth is threatening to replace racial discrimination. Yet the apartheid-era classification terms continue to be used. While we've also used these terms throughout this book, they work only to a certain extent, and within each of the four major categories are dozens of subgroups that are even more subjective and less clearly defined.

Lesotho and Swaziland were never subject to racial categorisation. This, plus the fact that both countries were for the most part formed around a single tribal group (the Basotho in Lesotho, and the Swazi in Swaziland), means that the constant awareness of racism that you'll encounter while travelling in South Africa is largely absent from these societies.

African

The vast majority of South Africans – about 77% – are Africans. Although subdivided into dozens of smaller groups, all ultimately trace their ancestry to the Bantu-speakers who migrated to Southern Africa in the early part of the first millennium AD. Due to the destruction and dispersal of the difaqane, and to the forced dislocations and distortions of the apartheid era, tribal affiliation tends to be much weaker in South Africa than in other areas of the continent.

Today, discussions generally focus on ethno-linguistic groupings. With the new constitution's elevation of 11 African languages to the status of 'official' language, the concept of ethnicity is also gaining a second wind. The largest ethno-linguistic group is the Nguni, which includes Zulu, Swazi, Xhosa and Ndebele peoples. Other major groups are the Sotho-Tswana, the Tsonga-Shangaan and the Venda.

The Zulu have maintained the highest profile ethnic identity over the years, centred in recent times around Chief Mangosotho Buthelezi's Inkatha Freedom Party and calls for an autonomous Zulu state. About 23% of South Africans speak Zulu as a first language. The second-largest group after the Zulu are the Xhosa, who have been extremely influential in politics. Nelson Mandela is Xhosa, as were numerous other figures in the apartheid struggle, and Xhosa have traditionally formed the heart of the Black professional class. About 18% of South Africa's population uses Xhosa as a first language. Other major groups include the Basotho (who live primarily in and around Lesotho and South Africa's Free State), the Swazi (most of whom are in Swaziland) and the Tswana (who live primarily in Limpopo and North-West Province, and in Botswana). The Ndebele and Venda peoples are fewer in number, but have maintained very distinct cultures. These and other groups have been profiled in the regional chapters throughout this book.

Coloured

During apartheid, 'Coloured' was generally used as a catch-all term for anyone who didn't fit into one of the other racial categories. Despite this, a distinct Coloured cultural identity has developed over the years – forged at least in part by Whites' refusal to accept Coloureds as equals and Coloureds' own refusal to be grouped socially with Blacks.

Among the diverse ancestors of today's Coloured population are Afrikaners and others of European descent, West African slaves, political prisoners and exiles from the Dutch East Indies and some of South Africa's original Khoisan peoples. One of the largest subgroups of Coloureds is the Griqua (see p30), most of whom are members of the Dutch Reformed Church. Another major subgroup is the Cape Malays, with roots in places as widely dispersed as India, Indonesia and parts of East Africa. Most Cape Malays are Muslims, and have managed to preserve their culture – especially evident today in Cape Town's Bo-Kaap district, in the *karamats* (tombs of Muslim saints) circling the city, and at the end of Ramadan, when you can see thousands of Muslims praying on Cape Town's Sea Point promenade.

Today, most Coloureds live in Northern Cape and Western Cape, with significant populations also in KwaZulu-Natal. About 20% speak English as their first language. The vast majority – about 80% – are Afrikaans speakers, and one of the oldest documents in Afrikaans is a Quran transcribed using Arabic script.

The most public secular expression of Cape coloured culture is the riotous Cape Minstrel Carnival (see the boxed text on p576).

White

Most of South Africa's approximately 5.5 million Whites (about 12% of South Africans) are either Afrikaans-speaking descendents of the early Dutch settlers or English speakers. The Afrikaners, who mix German, French, British and other blood with their Dutch ancestry, constitute only about 7% of the country's total population. Yet they have had a disproportionate influence on South Africa's history. Rural areas of the country, with the exception of Eastern Cape, KwaZulu-Natal and the former homelands, continue to be dominated by Afrikaners, who are united by the Afrikaans language, and by membership in the Dutch Reformed Church – the focal point of life in country towns.

While some Afrikaners still dream of a *volkstaat* (an independent, racially pure Boer state), the urbanised middle class tends to be considerably more moderate. Interestingly, the further the distance between the horrors of the apartheid era and the 'new South Africa', seemingly the more room there is for Afrikaners to be proud of their heritage. One expression of this is the growing popularity of the Klein Karoo National Arts Festival (see p576).

Important Afrikaner cultural organisations include the secret Afrikaner Broederbond, which is highly influential in National Party politics; the Federasie van Afrikaanse Kultuuvereninginge (FAK), which coordinates cultural events and movements; and the Voortrekkers, an Afrikaner youth organisation based on the scouting movement.

About two-thirds of South Africa's White English speakers trace their roots to the English immigrants who began arriving in South Africa in the 1820s, although they are far less cohesive as a group than the Afrikaners. Other White South Africans include about 100,000 Jews, many of whom immigrated from Eastern Europe, or fled Nazi Germany during the 1930s and 1940s; a sizeable Greek population; and about 50,000 Portuguese, most of whom came over from Mozambique during the 1970s.

Asian

About 98% of South Africa's roughly one million Asians are Indians. Many are descended from the indentured labourers brought to KwaZulu-Natal in the second half of the 19th century, while most of the others trace their ancestry to the free 'passenger Indians' who came to South Africa during the same time as merchants and business people. During apartheid, Indians were discriminated against by Whites, but were frequently seen as White collaborators by some Blacks.

Today's South African Indian population is primarily Hindu, with about 20% Muslims, and small numbers of Christians. Close to 90% live in Durban and other urban areas of KwaZulu-Natal, where Hindu temples, curries and Eastern spices are common parts of everyday life. Most speak English as a first language; Tamil or Hindi and Afrikaans are also spoken.

In addition to the Indians, there are about 25,000 Chinese, concentrated primarily in Johannesburg, and small numbers of other East Asians.

SPORT

Sport should almost be listed under 'Religion'. Many South Africans are passionate about it, and after decades of being shut out from international competition, the national teams are hunting for glory. The most popular spectator sports are football, cricket and rugby. The majority of football fans are Black, while cricket and rugby attract predominately White crowds, although things are slowly changing.

South African rugby is still struggling to shake its reputation as a Whites-only domain, despite the inclusion of Black players and officials. Victory in the 1995 Rugby World Cup was a turning point. The image of President Nelson Mandela celebrating while wearing a Springboks jersey became a symbol of reconciliation. South African fans adore their beloved 'Boks' and Springbok-fever runs high in the lead up to international rugby tournaments.

Development programmes are nurturing talent across the colour divides, and rugby and cricket are played regularly in Soweto and in some other townships.

The big local football match is the Soweto Derby between high-profile Jo'burg teams the 'Orlando Pirates' and the 'Kaizer Chiefs'. If a local invites you to a game, don't miss it. And if you're in the townships, keep an eye out for football stars cruising the streets in their expensive cars. Many of the top players are flamboyant and enjoy pop-star status among their fans.

The downfall of former South African cricket captain Hansie Cronje in a match-fixing scandal in 2000 was agonising for cricket fans. Cronje was revered as a hero and leader by his supporters, especially in his hometown of Bloemfontein. He died in a plane crash in 2002.

MEDIA

After decades of restrictions and repression, South Africa's media is in transition. The national broadcaster, SABC, is adjusting to its role as an independent voice. It is an important source of news for millions of South Africans. The three big topics of discussion are sport, business and crime. Investigative and political journalism are slowly evolving. SABC has 20 radio stations and four free-to-air TV channels.

Privately owned e-tv was launched in 1998. e-tv has a younger, funkier style. The presentation is smooth, while its field reporting is still developing.

Surf the radio airwaves and you'll get a sense of South Africa's diversity. Specialist stations broadcast in all of the 11 official languages. Jo'burg's Y-FM has been one of the big success stories. It's a youth station that broadcasts in a mixture of English and township slang. Tune into Y-FM 99.2 if you want to get a taste of the local version of hip-hop, known as Kwaito music.

The media industry has been the site of significant Black empowerment deals. Stations and publications have changed hands. Previously White-dominated radio station Jacaranda-FM is now one of the top rating Black stations.

The *Sowetan* is South Africa's biggest-selling English daily newspaper. It caters to a largely poorly educated audience but has a more sophisticated political and social outlook than most of the major White papers.

RELIGION

Christianity is the dominant religion in South Africa, Lesotho and Swaziland. More than 75% of South Africans identify themselves as Christians. The Zion Christian Church (ZCC) is the largest in South Africa, with

DID YOU KNOW?

The Australian Football League (AFL) has introduced 'Aussie Rules' football to South Africa. The game is still in its infancy. Keep a look out for local kids playing AFL; there are several teams in Mafikeng.

DID YOU KNOW?

South Africa's national football team is called Bafana Bafana, which means 'Boys Boys' in Zulu. The women's team is called Banyana Banyana, Zulu for 'Girls Girls'.

an estimated four million followers. Every year more than one million ZCC members gather at Zion city near Polokwane in Limpopo province during festivals at Easter and in September.

The Nederduitse Gereformeerde (NG) or Dutch Reformed churches have a national congregation of more than 3.5 million people. The NG Church is the largest, with more than 1200 churches across the country.

Muslims, Hindus and Jews combined make up less than 6% of South Africans. The rest of the population are atheist, agnostic and a small number of people who follow traditional African beliefs.

Most of the Hindus are South Africans of Indian decent. Up to two-thirds of South Africa's Indians have retained their Hindu faith. Islam has a small but growing following, particularly in the Cape. The Jewish community is estimated to be around 100,000, mostly in Jo'burg.

African traditional believers are a small group on their own. But their traditions and practices have a significant influence. The use of *muti*, or traditional medicine, is widespread, even among those who practise Christianity. Go for a walk near the entrance to Chris Hani Baragwanagth Hospital in Soweto and you will see hawkers selling all sorts of herbs, powders and liquid concoctions.

Religion plays an extremely important and personal role in many people's lives. If you're in Lesotho on a Sunday, you'll see families walking long distances through the mountains to go to church on even the most bitter winter morning. Faith is a source of hope for many who are enduring poverty and suffering.

ARTS
Literature
If you really want to get a sense of where South Africa has come from, and what makes its people tick, get into some local literature. The nation has a deep and diverse literary history.

Many of the first Black South African writers were missionary-educated. Solomon Thekiso Plaatje published his historical novel *Mhudi* in 1930. Plaatje was the first Secretary-General of the ANC.

In 1948, Alan Paton published his acclaimed novel, *Cry, the Beloved Country*. His tale of a Black priest who comes to Jo'burg to find his son, became an international best seller.

During the '50s, *Drum* magazine became the focal point of lively satire, fiction and comment. It gave a popular voice to urban Black culture, telling the stories of those who were trying to live their lives despite oppression. At the same time, renowned future Nobel laureate Nadine Gordimer began publishing her first stories. Her most famous novel, *July's People,* was released in 1981. It depicts the collapse of White rule.

In the '60s, Afrikaner writers were also getting their share of controversy. Breyten Breytenbach was jailed for becoming involved with the liberation movement. Andre Brink was the first Afrikaner writer to be banned by the apartheid government. His novel *A Dry White Season* told the story of a White South African who discovered the truth about a Black friend who died in police custody.

The '70s gave rise to several influential Black poets, including Mongane Wally Serote. Serote is a veteran of the liberation struggle. His work, such as *No Baby Must Weep,* gave an insight to the lives of Black South Africans under apartheid.

Zakes Mda made a successful transition from poetry and plays to become a novelist. *The Heart of Redness* won the 2001 Commonwealth Writers Prize and has become part of the school curriculum.

DID YOU KNOW?

Muti comes from the Zulu word *umuthi,* which literally means 'tree'. *Muti* is derived from hundreds of different sources including plants and animal parts.

The Good Doctor, by Damon Galgut, a talented novelist from Cape Town, was short-listed for the Booker Prize. It tells the story of a young doctor who arrives at a hospital in a neglected corner of rural South Africa and whose good intentions go horribly wrong.

John Maxwell (JM) Coetzee first went into print in the '70s. International success came two decades later. His powerful and brittle novel *Disgrace* was released in 1999 and won Coetzee his second Booker Prize. Coetzee also won the Nobel Prize for Literature in 2003.

South Africa's unique social and political history has generated a strong stable of writers. Local literature can take you back into the days of apartheid and can also take you inside the lives of characters experiencing the 'new South Africa'.

Architecture

The indigenous architecture of South Africa is impressive, including the Zulu 'beehive huts' and the elaborately painted Ndebele houses and kraals.

The colonial days were dominated by European design. Pretoria was home to some of the most conservative and stately creations. The English architect Sir Herbert Baker won acclaim for Pretoria's Union Buildings (p411).

Jo'burg grew quickly after the discovery of gold in 1886 and those who were making money were eager to show it off with palatial homes and grand offices. In Durban, the designs were more playful. Flamboyant buildings, with Art Deco influences, gave the city its own style. Cape Town's building boom in the 1930s left plenty of impressive Art Deco designs too; see p382.

The dour days of apartheid delivered many bland office blocks and public buildings and now architecture is playing catch-up. The White-dominated industry is gradually attracting more Black professionals, but it's a slow process and South Africa is still finding a sense of style that reflects the nation. Security is a big consideration for contemporary architects. South Africa's crime rate means that high walls, electric fences, boom gates and guard houses are part of the plans for many buildings.

The Constitutional Court in Jo'burg (p382) is an example of new South African architecture. It was officially opened by President Thabo Mbeki in March 2004. It's on the site of the old Jo'burg Fort, where many famous antiapartheid activists were jailed during the liberation struggle.

Visual Arts

South African art had its beginnings with tribal groups such as the San who left their distinctive designs on rock faces and cave walls. When European painters arrived, some of their early works were used to depict Africa to colonial enthusiasts back home.

Black artists were sidelined for many decades. *Yellow Houses* by Gerard Sekoto was the first work by a Black painter to be bought by the Jo'burg Art Gallery. During the apartheid era, racism, oppression and violence were common themes on canvas. Many Black artists who were unable to afford materials, adopted cheaper alternatives including lino prints. Artists played an important role in designing the logos for T-shirts, banners and posters during the liberation struggle. But, you'll notice there's only a limited amount of graffiti today, compared to cities in Australia, Europe or the United States.

Some Basotho women painted their houses in the gold, black and green colours of the ANC. The distinctive style of house decoration, known as *litema,* is an important part of Basotho culture. The tradition began with women painting symbols on their houses, to pray for rain and good fortune.

A lack of public funds for the arts sector has meant that it has become more reliant on corporate collectors and the tourism industry.

Age of Iron, by JM Coetzee, is the tale of a lone elderly woman who is confronted by unexpected bloodshed. Coetzee's writing is exquisite and gives a sense of the violence and isolation of apartheid South Africa.

Contemporary art ranges from vibrant crafts sold on the side of the road to high-priced paintings that hang in trendy galleries. Innovative artists are using everything from telephone wire, safety pins, beads, plastic bags and tin cans to create their works.

Local sculpture is also diverse. Artists including Jackson Hlungwane and Helen Martins have experimented with a range of styles and materials.

Theatre & Dance

The early colonial days were dominated by European and American plays, staged for local audiences. But homegrown playwrights, performers and directors gradually emerged. Theatre became popular in the townships in the 1930s. Herbert Dhlomo was one of the first Black South African writers to have his work published in English. The lively neighbourhood of Sophiatown also gave rise to numerous productions. But the apartheid regime's National Theatre Fund didn't provide support to Black theatre companies.

Writer and director Athol Fugard played a crucial role in developing and nurturing Black theatrical talent. He used his vast talents to establish several troupes in Port Elizabeth and Jo'burg during the '50s. By the '60s and '70s, theatre and politics were tangled together. Several artists were arrested and charged for their role in the fight against apartheid and others had their work banned. The innovative two-man show *Woza Albert!* won rave reviews and awards around the world. It portrayed Jesus Christ arriving in apartheid South Africa.

In 1974, rundown buildings at Jo'burg's old 'Indian' fruit market were converted to become the Market Theatre. Patrons and performers defied the apartheid government's notorious Group Areas Act to ensure that the theatre was an all-race venue. The Market Theatre (see p394) is still one of the best-known performance spaces in the country.

The end of apartheid took with it the powerful themes of racism and oppression, which had spawned decades of local creative output. But the performing arts are now enjoying a renaissance and exploring new topics.

African Footprint had its world premiere in 2000. The show has been a highly successful showcase of young South African dancers. The First National Bank (FNB) Dance Umbrella is an annual festival of dance and choreography. It brings together local and international artists and provides a stage for developing new work.

DID YOU KNOW?

Nelson Mandela has released a collection of sketches of Robben Island. Mandela took lessons from a young local artist before creating his work. The prints are sold to raise money for children's charities and AIDS projects.

Music

Nelson Mandela once declared that music would be the salvation of his people. Just as music fuelled the resistance to apartheid, it continues to sing out for freedom and justice, providing a soundtrack to everyday lives. Music is everywhere in South Africa, coming through every available medium, communicating in every imaginable style. Want a 'typical' South African sound? Forget it. South Africa has the greatest range of musical styles on the African continent, and more than any country of similar size anywhere in the world. Rock, jazz, classical, gospel, rap, reggae, maskanda, mbaqanga, kwaito. And much more. Here centuries-old traditions jostle with new genres that spring from old ones. Western styles are given an idiosyncratic stamp. The country's gargantuan recording industry – with its new crop of independent Black-owned labels – watches, ready to pounce. The country's government has pledged its unstinting support.

A decade's worth of freedom has proved that a recovering country can still produce sophisticated talent to the highest international standards. The music of the Rainbow Nation continues to address social concerns, express sadness and bring joy. No one sound will ever identify South Africa, which can only be a good thing. Part of what makes South African music so astounding is its range. What follows is a by-no-means definitive look at the major genres, with their major players. So get humming, swing your hips and dive in.

POTTED HISTORY OF SOUTH AFRICAN MUSIC

The Zulu, Xhosa and Sotho people have been singing and dancing for thousands of years – this is the music that attracted Paul Simon before he recorded his 1988 album *Graceland* – just as the Venda have been playing their mbiras (thumb pianos) and reed pipes. There are eight distinct 'tribal' traditions in South Africa, and a decade of democracy has seen a resurgence in traditional musicians making very traditional music. But from the earliest colonial times to the present day, South Africa's music has created and reinvented itself from a mixture of older local and imported styles. Most of the popular ones use either Zulu a-capella singing or harmonic mbaqanga as a vocal base, ensuring that whatever the instrument – the banjo, violin, concertina and electric guitar have all had a profound influence – the sound stays proudly, resolutely African.

Ever wondered why the chord sequences of many South African songs feel familiar? Blame the church: the Protestant missionaries of the 19th century developed a choral tradition that, in tandem with the country's first formal music education, South African composers would blend with traditional harmonic patterns – Enoch Sontonga's 1897 hymn 'Nkosi Sikelel, i Afrika' (God Bless Africa), originally written in Xhosa, is now the country's national anthem. Today the gospel movement is *the* major industry player. Gloria Bosman, Sibongile Khumalo, Pinise Saul and other top Black South African artists now working across a range of genres – classical, jazz, gospel, opera – started singing in mission-school choirs or in church. Others, such as redoubtable gospel superstar Rebecca Malope, crossed over from the shiny world of pop.

Zulu music's veteran exponents Ladysmith Black Mambazo – wrongly considered 'typical' South African music by many Westerners, who are

Featuring music and interviews by Abdullah Ibrahim, Hugh Masekela, Miriam Makeba among others, Lee Hirsch's *Amandla! A Revolution in Four-Part Harmony* (2003) explores the role of music in the fight against apartheid. Made over nine years, this is a deeply affecting film.

RECOMMENDED LISTENING

- **Marabi** – *From Marabi To Disco*, Various Artists (Gallo, South Africa)
- **Kwela** – *Spokes Mashiyane*, King Kwela (Gallo, South Africa)
- **Mbaqanga** – *Soul Brothers*, Kuze Kuse (Gallo, South Africa)
- **Jazz** – *Sheer Jazz*, Various Artists (Sheer Sound, South Africa)
- **Gospel** – *Joyous Celebration – Live in Cape Town*, Joyous Celebration (Gallo, South Africa)
- **Neotraditional Music** – *Phuzekhemisi*, We Baba (Gallo, South Africa)
- **Soul & Reggae** – *Prisoner*, Lucky Dube (Shanachie, USA)
- **Bubblegum, Kwaito & Current Trends** – *Bongolution*, Bongo Maffin (Sony/Lightyear Entertainment, USA)

---

familiar with their contribution to the *Graceland* phenomenon – exemplify the way indigenous harmonies were neatly mixed with the sounds of European and African church choirs (a vocal style known as mbube). And, similar to the way much contemporary South African art was born from oppression, Ladysmith's 'tip-toe' isicathimiya music, with its high-kicking, soft-stepping dance, has its origins in all-male miner's hostels in Natal province in the 1930s, with workers at pains not to wake their bosses. Isicathimiya choirs still appear in weekly competitions in Johannesburg (Jo'burg) and Durban.

Kwela music, like most modern styles, came out of the townships. Kwela, meaning 'jump up' was the instruction given to those about to be thrown into police vans during raids. Areas like Soweto, Sharpeville, District Six and Sophiatown, now infamous, gave rise to urban, pan-tribal genres, mostly inspired by music – jazz, swing, jive, soul – coming in (or back) from America. Black South Africans added an urban spin: kwela, with its penny whistles (an instrument evolved from the reed flutes of Black cattle herders) and one-string bass, became sax-jive, or mbaqanga. Marabi soul took off in the 1970s. Bubblegum pop dominated the 1980s. Kwaito, South Africa's very own hip-hop, exploded in the 1990s and remains, apart from gospel and a burgeoning R&B scene, the country's most popular genre.

America and Europe were the inspiration for White South African artists. Sixties phenomenon Four Jacks and a Jill were pure Western pop; British punk inspired 1970s working-class outfits à la Wild Youth. The 1980s saw a crossover of Black and White musicians: Johnny Clegg and Juluka (now Savuka)'s fusion of White rock and pop with traditional Zulu music challenged racist restrictions and set a precedent for others to follow. Grunge helped shape the likes of Scooters Union, the Springbok Nude Girls and other 1990s guitar bands. Rock continues to, well, rock the country today. Afrikaans music – Dozi, Lize Beekman, Dave Kramer, Amanda Strydom – is enjoying a renaissance. And then there's the huge cutting-edge dance music scene – house, techno, kwaito, hip-hop, acid jazz, broken beats, R&B, dancehall and all grooves in between, often with live elements thrown in.

Musicians such as jazz legend and former exile Hugh Masekela stress the need for continued vigilance over the effect of apartheid on lives and culture. In the meantime, the music of the resistance has kept its fire; post-1994, it simply changed its focus. Other scourges – HIV and AIDS, poverty, the abuse of women and children – are being written about, talked about and sung about. Opportunities abound in the current climate of cultural and artistic expression. Boundaries are down, there is a constant cross-pollination of styles and many genres, especially jazz, are booming.

Artists to watch out for include singer/songwriter Vusi Mahlasela, multi-instrumentalist and singer Neo Muyanga, masked kwaito star Mzekezeke, R&B force TK, jazz saxophonist Moses Khumalo, classical outfit Soweto String Quartet, rocker Arno Carstens, rappers Skwatta Kamp and producer and DJ Oscar 'Oskido' Mdlongwa. Others will swiftly become apparent. As will the fact that democracy, so bitterly won, has never sounded so sweet.

South African Music: A Century of Traditions in Transformation (2004) is a comprehensive handbook from ethnomusicologist Carol A Muller, who examines the way both Black and White South Africans have used music to express a sense of place in South Africa, on the continent and overseas.

MARABI

In the early 1900s travelling African-American minstrel shows, vaudeville acts, ragtime piano players and gospel groups impressed local audiences in the growing cities of Cape Town and Jo'burg. Urbanisation had a domino effect on musical styles: visiting American jazz artists and records by the likes of Louis Armstrong and Duke Ellington kick-started what would later become the South African jazz scene. By the 1920s and 1930s the urban ghettos were singing and swinging to a defining, dangerous (in Sotho it means 'gangster') small band sound: marabi.

Played on cheap pedal organs and keyboards with accompaniment from pebble-filled cans, marabi flooded illegal township shebeens and dancehalls. Its siren's call got people in and drinking, but it also offered some dignity and consolation to the oppressed working-class areas where it was played. Marabi's trancelike rhythms and cyclical harmonies had links to American Dixieland and ragtime; subsequent decades saw the addition of penny whistle, drums, banjo and a big-band swing, even bebop aesthetic.

Marabi made its way into the jazz-dance bands that produced the first generation of professional Black musicians: the Jazz Maniacs, Merry Blackbirds and Jazz Revellers. Often referred to, simply (and not always correctly), as 'African jazz' or 'jive', marabi reinforced these bands' distinctive South African style and raised their popularity among Black and White audiences. It also spawned other styles; one of these was kwela.

DID YOU KNOW?

South African Music Week is held in August every year.

KWELA

Kwela was the first popular South African style to make the world sit up and take notice. Initially played on acoustic guitar, banjo, one-string bass and, most importantly, the penny whistle, kwela was taken up by kids with no access to horns and pianos but keen to put their own spin on American swing. Groups of tin-flautists would gather to play on street corners in White areas, danger of arrest (for creating a 'public disturbance') upping the music's appeal and attracting hoards of rebellious White kids known as 'ducktails'. Rumours had it these groups were also lookouts for the shebeens.

Kwela combos gained a live following but little recording took place until 1954, when Spokes Mashinyane's Ace Blues became the smash African hit of the year and sent White producers scurrying towards the Black market. Artists such as Sparks Nyembe and Jerry Mlotshwa became popular; the hit 'Tom Hark' by Elias Lerole and His Zig-Zag Flutes even crossed over to Britain, where, probably because of its similarity to skiffle, it stayed in the (1958) charts for 14 weeks.

In the early 1960s Mashiyane introduced the saxophone to kwela with his song 'Big Joe Special', ending the penny-whistle boom and creating sax-jive. Sax-jive quickly became mbaqanga.

MBAQANGA

The saxophone became vital to jive music, which, much to the dismay of White kwela fans, was now limited to performances in the townships. Not everyone approved: jazz saxophonist Michael Xaba dismissed it as 'mbaqanga' (loosely translated as 'easy money') in response to its contingent of musically illiterate practitioners. The term stuck and became an endearment. The genre had its innovators, of course: Joseph Makwela and Marks Mankwane of celebrated session players the Makhona Tshole Band added electric guitars to the cascading rhythms – most notably a funky, muscular bass – while sax player/producer West Nkosi set the pace. This hugely popular electric sound backed singers whose vocal style was later christened mqashiyo (after a dance style), even though it wasn't really any different from mbaqanga.

Mbaqanga's idiosyncratic vocals came out of 1950s groups like the Manhattan Brothers and Miriam Makeba's Skylarks, groups who copied African-American doo-wop outfits but used Africanised five-part harmonies instead of four. In the 1960s Aaron Lerole of Black Mambazo added his groaning male vocals to the mix, but it was the growling bass of Simon 'Mahlathini' Nkabinde and his sweet-voiced Mahotella Queens (backed by the Makhona Tshole Band) who would inspire a generation – including Izintombi Zezi Manje Manje and the Boyoyo Boys (the latter being sampled by British producer/chancer Malcolm McClaren on the 1981 British number one 'Double Dutch').

Mbaqanga remains a dominant force in the music of South Africa today, its influence apparent in everything from soul and reggae to R&B, kwaito and, of course, jazz.

JAZZ

Structurally, harmonically and melodically distinctive, the force that is South African jazz started as an underground movement and became a statement of protest and identity. In the hands of such exiled stars as singer Miriam Makeba, pianist Abdullah Ibrahim (formerly Dollar Brand) and trumpeter Hugh Masekela, it was famously an expatriate music representing the suffering of a people. Dynamic outfit, the Blue Notes, led by pianist Chris McGregor and featuring sax player Dudu Pukwana, helped change the face of European jazz after relocating to the UK. Jazzers who stayed behind kept a low profile while developing new sounds and followings with, variously, jazz-rock fusion, Latin and even Malay crossovers.

World-renowned exiles who returned home after the end of the anti-apartheid cultural boycott had to work hard to win back local audiences. All now enjoy healthy followings – Masekela remains South Africa's most enduring musical ambassador – in what is a thriving mainstream scene. Frequent festivals, often featuring top overseas acts, are providing platforms (the Awesome Africa festival in Durban each September is a must) and the South African media is lending its support.

Well-known locals are moving jazz forward, working with DJs, artists, poets and dance companies. Saxophonist and arranger Zim Ngqawana is drawing on folk and rural traditions as well as Indian, avant-garde and classical music. Saxophonist Moses Khumalo is doing his best to ignore the 'bright new hope of South African jazz' tag and

Louise Meintjes' *Sound of Africa! Makin Music Zulu in a South African Studio* (2003) is a 1990s-set account of the making of a mbaqanga album by Izintombi Zesimanje, in a state-of-the-art recording studio in Johannesburg. Meitje deftly recaptures both personal and political contexts in this book, which has great photos too.

DID YOU KNOW?

Increasingly it's the independent labels, a burgeoning force on the South African music scene, which are discovering talent and taking the risk on new sounds.

South African Music (www.music.org.za) has links to local artists, performances and music news.

making glorious music. Guitarists Jimmy Dludlu and Lucky Ranku are lending their ringing chords to collaborations with music-school graduates. Female vocalists Gloria Bosman, Sibongile Khumalo, Tutu Puoane, Judith Sephumo and myriad others are making their mark. Many are enjoying further success in another genre with common roots: gospel.

GOSPEL

As ever, it's the African influences that make South African gospel unique. The music industry's biggest market – bolstered by the country's 80% Christian Black population – the country's gospel is an amalgam of European choral music, American influences, Zulu a-cappella singing and other African traditions incorporated within the (Zionist, Ethiopian, Pentecostal, Apostolic) church. All joy, colour and exuberance, rhythm, passion and soul, gospel choirs perform constantly across South Africa, lifting the roofs off big formal venues and community halls alike. Twenty-four–piece ensemble and overseas success story the Soweto Gospel Choir feature, like many big choirs, a band with drummers and dancers.

This vast genre tends to be divided into traditional gospel – as personified by the heavyweight International Pentecostal Church Choir (IPCC) – and modern gospel, as emoted by the tiny diva Rebecca Malope, a singer whose albums tend to go platinum within weeks (her latest, *Hlala Nami*, stole Best African Gospel Album at the 2004 South African Music Awards). Gospel acts to watch out for include stalwarts Amadodana Ase Wesile, rising stars Lusanda Spiritual Group, male vocalist Benjamin Dube, modernist Deborah Fraser (an erstwhile backing singer for Yvonne Chaka Chaka and Lucky Dube) and the jazz/gospel diva Pinise Saul, a former exile with the voice of an angel.

Gospel also comprises much of the oeuvre of Ladysmith Black Mambazo, whose sweet but rousing 10-part mbubu harmonies send their songs of praise soaring. Ladysmith's Zulu isicathimiya music, enjoying renewed popularity ever since the group guested on the *Graceland* song 'Homeless', is a prime example of the way traditional South African music used Western influences to produce unique musical styles.

Pascale Lamche's *Sophiatown* (2003) looks at Johannesburg's bustling Sophiatown, the Harlem of South Africa. Home to many artists and musicians, it was flattened for redevelopment in the 1950s. Archive footage and interviews with Nelson Mandela, Hugh Masekela and Dorothy Masuka make for compulsive viewing.

LADYSMITH BLACK MAMBAZO

South Africa's famed 10-man a-cappella group has been together for over 40 years, high-kicking and harmonising ever since their leader, Joseph Shabalala, divined the idea for their unique vocal style in a dream. Ladysmith Black Mambazo's most recent album, *Raise Your Spirit Higher* – full of songs praising God, Zulu traditions and honourable living – is, remarkably, their 44th. They still sound as fresh as the veldt after a rainstorm.

The eldest son of a healer and a soothsayer, Shabalala grew up believing in prophecies in a Zulu farming community near Ladysmith in Natal. In 1958 he heard radio for the first time. Determined to reinterpret traditional Zulu songs, he formed a group with his brother and cousins. They toured the provinces, won competitions and were harassed and admired in equal measure. In 1986 they burst onto the global mainstream when they sang, not uncontroversially, on Paul Simon's *Graceland* album. Shabalala understood the album to be a tool in breaking down apartheid by bringing the music of South Africa to the world.

Shabalala has plans to build an academy in Ladysmith that will foster the education and preservation of indigenous South African music and culture. Four of Shabalala's sons now feature in the Ladysmith Black Mambazo line-up; the entire group, however, can still touch their noses with their shins.

NEOTRADITIONAL MUSIC

Away from the urban life of the townships and the cities' recording studios, traditional musicians from the Sotho, Zulu, Pedi and Shangaan regions were creating dynamic social music. By the 1930s, many were mixing call-and-response singing with the dreamy 10-button concertina, an instrument that is currently making a comeback in Zulu traditional pop. The Sotho took up the accordion; the Pedi the German autoharp; and the Zulu embraced the guitar.

Maskanda is a form of rhythmic and repetitive guitar picking developed by the Zulu migrant workers of the 1950s and 1960s, who sang of life on the move. Many made do with an *igogogo*, an instrument fashioned from an oil can; maskanda stalwart Shiyani Ngcobo, whose 2004 debut album arrived after 30 years spent honing his craft, still uses the *igogogo* in his live sets. Today's top-selling maskanda acts include Amatshitshi Amhlophe, Bhekumuzi Luthuli, Imithente and Phuzekhemisi, whose shows can often include dozens of singers, dancers and instrumentalists.

Upbeat and vaguely Latin sounding, Tsonga (formerly Shangaan) music tends to feature a male leader backed by a female chorus, guitars, synths, percussion and an unabashed disco beat. Best-known acts include Thomas Chauke and the Shinyori Sisters, Elias Baloyi and the Mamba Queens and George Maluleke, whose album *Ri Orheli* triumphed at the 2004 South African Music Awards.

Young Xhosa artist Lungiswa is the only female South African musician to play the mbira in her traditional/urban crossovers. Veteran singer Bhusi Mhlongo fuses the Zulu traditional sound with hip-hop and kwaito. Roots are being mixed with every sound imaginable, from country, blues and house (check out DJ Gregory and the Africanism scene) to rock, reggae and soul.

SOUL & REGGAE

The American-led soul music of the 1960s had a huge impact on township teenagers, who crooned to tunes by Wilson Pickett, Percy Sledge and Booker T and the MGs. The local industry tried various cheap imitations, following suit a decade later with a local form of disco that wasn't really that much different from local soul. Neither genre was to last. The few South African 'soul' groups that made it did so on the back of a blend of soul and marabi, like the Movers, or soul and electric bass mbaqanga, like the Soul Brothers, a band who spawned dozens of imitators and are still going strong today. Contemporary South African soul is usually filed under mbaqanga: the genre from which reggae star Lucky Dube sprang into another style of music entirely.

After a few years as a mbaqanga artist Lucky Dube switched to reggae in 1984, becoming one of South Africa's biggest-selling recording artists in the process. His socially aware English lyrics and laid-back rhythms continue to command a huge following, even if African reggae has largely disappeared within ragga and been sucked, if you like, into kwaito. When reggae does surface it is often as part of something else: maverick trio Mike, Titi and Frank combine gruff ragga-voices with sweet harmonies, R&B, reggae, traditional and club sounds.

BUBBLEGUM, KWAITO & CURRENT TRENDS

The disco that surfaced in the 1970s came back – slick, poppy and Africanised – in the 1980s as 'bubblegum'. Vocally-led and aimed squarely at the young, this electronic dance sound owed as much to mbaqanga as it did to America. What the Soul Brothers started, superstars like

DID YOU KNOW?

Paul Simon's *Graceland* album has sold seven million copies worldwide and was vital in alerting the rest of the world to the music of South Africa.

Rage (www.rage.co.za) is an online magazine with music news, reviews and fashion.

One World (www.one world.co.za) is an independent music cyberstore selling South African music and a limited range of books and videos.

TOP 10 SOUTH AFRICAN ALBUMS

- *The Indestructible Beat of Soweto, Volumes 1–6*
  Various artists

- *Jazz in Africa, Volume 1*
  Jazz Epistles

- *The Best Of*
  Miriam Makeba and the Skylarks

- *Urban Zulu*
  Busi Mhlongo

- *Live at the Market Theatre*
  Sibongile Khumalo

- *Kwaito: South African Hip-Hop*
  Various artists

- *The Best Of*
  Mahlathini and the Mahotella Queens

- *Hope*
  Hugh Masekela

- *Shaka Zulu*
  Ladysmith Black Mambazo

- *The Voice*
  Vusi Mahlasela

DID YOU KNOW?

Over the past few years home-grown R&B is rivalling kwaito for radio play. Names making it big include KB, Loyiso, TK, Lira and more.

Brenda Fassie, Sello 'Chicco' Twala and Yvonne Chaka Chaka refined. Both Chicco (a renowned producer) and Chaka Chaka remain hugely popular; the sudden death of the outrageous and brilliant Fassie in May 2004 left South Africa reeling. Bubblegum, too, is moving on: long-term heartthrob Ringo Madlingozi marries romantic Xhosa lyrics with dance-floor grooves, gospel and jazz; the ever-bold Jabu Khaniyile is adding influences from the Congo and elsewhere.

Post-1994, kwaito (pronounced kwi-to, meaning 'hot') exploded onto the country's dance-club floors, the musical voice of young, Black, urban South Africa. A rowdy mix of everything they'd grown up on – bubblegum, hip-hop, R&B, ragga, mbaqanga, traditional, jazz and British and American house music – kwaito became a fashion statement, a state of mind, a lifestyle. Chanted or sung in township slang (usually over programmed beats and backing tapes), kwaito's lyrics range from the anodyne to the fiercely political. Acts such as Arthur, Mandoza, Zola and Bongo Maffin remain major players. Others – remix outfit Revolution, 1960s- and house-inspired group Mafikizolo, glamour girl Thembi – are catching up.

'Kwaito was born the year Nelson Mandela was released', said masked kwaito star Mzekezeke at the 2004 South African Music Awards. Freedom of expression used to be a luxury for Black youth living in a country torn apart by apartheid. Not any more. The first place this freedom became visible was the music scene. A scene that is thriving, creating and reinventing itself in ways far too numerous to mention here.

Environment

THE LAND

South Africa spreads over 1,233,404 sq km – five times the size of the UK – at the tip of the African continent. On three sides, it's edged by a windswept and stunningly beautiful coastline, winding down the Atlantic seaboard in the west, and up into the warmer Indian Ocean waters to the east.

Much of the country consists of a vast plateau averaging 1500m in height, and known as the highveld. To the east is a narrow coastal plain (the lowveld), while to the northwest is the low-lying Kalahari basin. The dramatic Drakensberg escarpment marks the point where the highveld plummets down towards the eastern lowlands.

Tiny Lesotho is completely surrounded by South Africa. It sits entirely above 1000m, perched on a 30,350 sq km patch of highland plateau and rugged peaks. Swaziland is almost half Lesotho's size, measuring only 17,363 sq km. Yet within its tiny borders it encompasses diverse ecological zones, ranging from rainforest in the northwest to savanna scrub in the east.

WILDLIFE

South Africa contains some of the most accessible and varied wildlife-watching found anywhere on the continent.

Animals
SOUTH AFRICA

South Africa is home to an unparalleled diversity of wildlife. It boasts the world's largest land mammal (the African elephant), as well as the second largest (white rhino) and the third largest (hippopotamus). It's also home to the tallest (giraffe), fastest (cheetah) and smallest (pygmy shrew). You probably have a better chance of seeing the Big Five – the black rhino, Cape buffalo, elephant, leopard and lion – in South Africa than anywhere else. There's also a lesser-known 'Little Five' – the rhinoceros beetle, buffalo weaver, elephant shrew, leopard tortoise and ant lion – if you're looking for a challenge. See the colour Wildlife Guide (p69) for a glimpse of some of these and other animals.

DID YOU KNOW?

Lesotho has the highest lowest point of any country in the world (1380m, in southern Lesotho's Orange River valley).

It's well worth hunting up a copy of *Field Guide to Mammals of Southern Africa* by Chris and Tilde Stuart before heading off on safari.

RESPONSIBLE TRAVEL

Tourism is a big industry in Southern Africa. Following are a few guidelines for minimising strain on the local environment:

- ask permission before photographing people
- don't give money, sweets or pens to children; donations to recognised projects or local charitable organisations are a better option
- support local enterprise
- avoid buying items made from ivory, skin, shells etc
- save natural resources
- inform yourself of South Africa's history, and be sensitive to it in your travels.

Also check the website of Fair Trade in Tourism South Africa (www.fairtourismsa.org.za).

The best time for wildlife-watching is the cooler, dry winter (June to September) when foliage is less dense, and animals congregate at water-holes, making spotting easier. Summer (late November to March) is rainy and hot, with the animals more widely dispersed and often difficult to see. However, the landscape turns beautiful shades of green around this time and birdlife is abundant.

South Africa hosts over 800 bird species, including the world's largest bird (the ostrich), its heaviest flying bird (Kori bustard), and vividly coloured sunbirds and flamingos. Also here in abundance are weavers, who share their huge city-like nests with pygmy falcons, the world's smallest raptors.

Bird-watching is good year-round, with spring (August to November) and summer the best.

Endangered Species

The black rhino is the highest profile entry on South Africa's threatened species list (good places to spot these include Mkhuze Game Reserve and Hluhluwe-Imfolozi Park), and the riverine rabbit the country's most endangered mammal. The wild dog (seen with luck in Hluhluwe-Imfolozi Park, p313) is also endangered, as is the roan antelope.

Endangered bird species include the graceful wattled crane and the blue swallow. The African penguin and the Cape vulture are considered threatened.

LESOTHO

Thanks primarily to its altitude, Lesotho is home to fewer animals than many Southern African countries. Those you may encounter include rheboks, jackals, mongooses, meerkats and elands.

Close to 300 species of birds have been recorded in Lesotho, notably bearded vultures, lammergeiers and bald ibises.

SWAZILAND

Tiny Swaziland boasts about 120 species of mammals – one-third of Southern Africa's nonmarine mammal species. Many (including elephants, rhinos and lions) have been introduced, and larger animals are restricted to nature reserves and private wildlife farms. Mongooses and large-spotted genets are common, and hyenas and jackals are found in the reserves. Leopards are present, but rarely seen.

Swaziland's varied terrain supports abundant bird life, including the blue crane, ground woodpecker and lappet-faced vulture.

Plants

Over 20,000 plant species sprout from South Africa's soil – an amazing 10% of the world's total, although the country constitutes only 1% of the earth's land surface.

DID YOU KNOW?

More bird species have been sighted in Swaziland than in the larger Kruger National Park.

DID YOU KNOW?

Rhinos aren't named for their colour, but for their lip shape: 'white' comes from *wijde* (wide) – the Boers' term for the fatter-lipped white rhino.

Contact the Johannesburg-based Endangered Wildlife Trust (www.ewt.org.za) for more on South Africa's endangered species.

THE CAPE FLORAL KINGDOM

The tiny Cape Floral Kingdom is the smallest of the world's six floral kingdoms, but unquestionably the most diverse. Here you'll find an incredible 1300 species per 10,000 sq km, some 900 more species than are found in the South American rainforests.

The Cape Floral Kingdom extends roughly from Cape Point east to Grahamstown and north to the Olifants River. Today, most of the remaining indigenous vegetation is found only in protected areas, such as Table Mountain and the Cape Peninsula.

The dominant vegetation is *fynbos* (fine bush), with small, narrow leaves and stems. The *fynbos* environment hosts nearly 8500 plant species, most of which are unique to the area.

Some members of the main *fynbos* families – heaths, proteas and reeds – have been domesticated elsewhere, but many species have a remarkably small range: clearing an area the size of a house can mean extinction.

Dozens of flowers that are domesticated elsewhere grow wild here, including gladiolus, proteas, birds of paradise and African lilies. South Africa is also the only country with one of the world's six floral kingdoms within its borders (see the boxed text, above).

In the drier northwest, there are succulents (dominated by euphorbias and aloes), and annuals, which flower brilliantly after the spring rains, and are one of Northern Cape's major tourist attractions (see p509).

In contrast to this floral wealth, South Africa has few natural forests. They were never extensive, and today only remnants remain. Temperate forests occur on the southern coastal strip between George and Humansdorp, in the KwaZulu-Natal Drakensberg and in Mpumalanga. Subtropical forests are found northeast of Port Elizabeth through the Transkei area, and in KwaZulu-Natal.

In the north are large areas of savanna, dotted with acacias and thorn trees.

Lesotho is notable for its high-altitude flora, including Cape alpine flowers and the spiral aloe (*Aloe polyphylla*).

Swaziland's grasslands, forests, savannas and wetlands host about 3500 plant species – or about 14% of Southern Africa's recorded plant life.

The spiral aloe is Lesotho's national flower. Look for its left- and right-handed (clockwise and anticlockwise) varieties on the slopes of the Maluti Mountains.

NATIONAL PARKS & RESERVES
South Africa

South Africa has close to 600 national parks and reserves, collectively boasting spectacular scenery, impressive fauna and flora, excellent facilities and reasonable prices. They'll likely be the highlight of your visit. The most famous feature wildlife, while others are primarily wilderness sanctuaries or hiking areas. The table on p66–7 lists some of the best, though all are well worth exploring.

The majority of the larger wildlife parks are under the jurisdiction of the **South African National (SAN) Parks Board** (☎ 012-343 9770; www.parks-sa.co .za), except for those in KwaZulu-Natal, which are run by **KZN Wildlife** (☎ 033-845 1000; www.kznwildlife.com). Several other provinces also have conservation bodies that oversee smaller conservation areas within their boundaries. **Komatiland Forests Ecotourism** (☎ 012-481 3615, 013-764 1392; ecoklf@mweb.co.za) oversees forest areas, promotes ecotourism and manages several hiking trails around Mpumalanga. Other useful contacts include:

Cape Nature Conservation (☎ 021-426 0723; www.capenature.org.za)
Eastern Cape Tourism Board (☎ 043-701 9600; www.ectourism.co.za)

Kenneth Newman's *Birds of Southern Africa* is an excellent field guide covering South Africa, Lesotho and Swaziland.

All South African national parks now charge a daily entry ('conservation') fee. Amounts vary; see individual park listings for details. If you are a South African resident or a national of a South African Development Community (SADC) country (this includes many of South Africa's neighbours), you are entitled to reduced rates. Another way to save is to consider purchasing a 'Wild Card' from SAN Parks. There are different versions of the card, including one for foreign tourists which gives you 10 days entry into any one park for R600 (R1000 per couple, R1500 per family). This isn't much of a saving for some of the less expensive parks, but if you're planning at least five days in Kruger National Park (where the daily entry fee is R120), it's well worth buying. For details on acquiring a Wild Card, see the SAN Parks website (www .parks-sa.co.za).

In addition to its national parks, South Africa is also party to several transfrontier parks joining conservation areas across international borders. These include Kgalagadi Transfrontier Park, combining Northern Cape's old Kalahari Gemsbok National Park with Botswana's Gemsbok National Park; and the ambitious Great Limpopo Transfrontier Park, which spreads nearly 100,000 sq km (larger than Portugal) across the borders of South Africa, Mozambique and Zimbabwe (see p489). Private wildlife reserves also abound.

In total, just under 7% of South African land has been given protected status. The government has started teaming up with private landowners to bring private conservation land under government protection, with the goal of ultimately increasing the total amount of conservation land to over 10%.

James Stevenson Hamilton's classic, *A South African Eden*, chronicles South Africa's early wildlife conservation efforts and the creation of Kruger National Park.

Lesotho

In part because of a land tenure system that allows communal access rights to natural resources, less than 1% of Lesotho's area is protected – the lowest protected area coverage of any nation in Africa. Remote Sehlabathebe National Park (p537) is the main conservation area, known for

---

SAFARI INFO

The best and cheapest (especially if you're in a group) way to visit the parks is usually with a hired car. A 2WD is perfectly adequate in most parks, but during winter when the grass is high, a 4WD or other high-clearance vehicle will enable you to see more. Organised safaris are readily arranged with all major tour operators, and with backpacker-oriented outfits, most of which advertise at hostels.

Several major parks (including Kruger, Hluhluwe-Imfolozi and Pilanesberg) offer guided wilderness walks accompanied by armed rangers. These are highly worthwhile, as the subtleties of the bush can be much better experienced on foot than in a vehicle. They should be booked well in advance with the relevant park authority (see contacts listed earlier in this section, and in the individual park listings in the regional chapters). Shorter morning and afternoon walks are also possible at many wildlife parks, and can generally be booked the day before. For overnight walks, it's necessary to get a permit in advance from the relevant park authority, and you'll generally be restricted to overnighting in official camp sites or huts.

Throughout South Africa, park infrastructure is of high quality. You can often get by without a guide, although you'll almost certainly see and learn more with one. All national parks have rest camps offering good-value accommodation, ranging from self-catering cottages to camp sites. Most also have restaurants, shops and petrol pumps. Advance bookings for camping and cottages are essential during holiday periods. Otherwise, it's generally possible to get accommodation at short notice.

Most park and reserve entrances close around sunset.

DON'T GET CHARGED

One of South Africa's major attractions is the chance to go on safari and to get 'up close and personal' with the wildlife. Remember, however, that the animals aren't tame and their actions are often unpredictable. Some tips to avoid getting charged (and to avoid other less dramatic perils of the bush):

■ heed the warnings of safari guides

■ don't move in too close to an animal – for good photos, invest in a telephoto lens

■ never get between a mother and her young, or between a hippo and the water

■ don't feed animals; baboons' canine teeth are sometimes larger than those of a lion

■ watch out for black rhinos, which will charge just about anything

■ brush up on your tree-climbing skills

■ avoid snake bites by wearing boots, socks and long trousers when walking through undergrowth, and taking care around holes, crevices and when collecting firewood

■ avoid ticks by wearing insect repellent when hiking; check your body and clothes if you've been walking through tick-infested areas (ie any scrubland, even in cities) or sitting under camel thorn trees (a favoured haunt for ticks).

its isolated wilderness setting. Others include Ts'ehlanyane National Park (p527), Bokong Nature Reserve (p533) and the Liphofung Cultural Site Reserve (p530). For more information, see p520.

Swaziland

About 4% of Swaziland is protected, and its conservation areas are particularly good value for your money. They are also quite low-key, with fewer visitors than many of their counterparts in South Africa. Among the best are the easily accessed Mlilwane Wildlife Sanctuary (p552), Mkhaya Game Reserve (p560), and the beautiful Malolotja Nature Reserve (p557), which is used primarily for hiking.

DID YOU KNOW?

The only place in the world to find the riverine rabbit is near rivers in the central Karoo (Northern Cape).

ENVIRONMENTAL ISSUES
South Africa

South Africa is the world's third most biologically diverse country. It's also one of Africa's most urbanised, with approximately 60% of the population living in towns and cities. Major challenges for the government include managing increasing urbanisation and population growth while protecting the environment. The picture is complicated by a distorted rural–urban settlement pattern – a grim legacy of the apartheid era (p37) – with huge population concentrations in townships that generally lack adequate utilities and infrastructure.

Land degradation is one of the most serious problems, with about one-fourth of South Africa's land considered to be severely degraded. In former Homeland areas (see the boxed text on p39), years of overgrazing and overcropping have resulted in massive soil depletion. This, plus poor overall conditions, is pushing people to the cities, further increasing urban pressures.

Water is another issue. South Africa receives an average of only 500mm of rainfall annually, and droughts are common. To meet demand, all major South African rivers have been dammed or modified. While this has improved water supplies to many areas, it has also disrupted local ecosystems and caused increased silting.

TOP PARKS & RESERVES

Park	Features	Activities	Best Time to Visit	Page
Cape Peninsula/Western Cape				
Cederberg Wilderness Area	mountainous & rugged; San rock paintings, bizarre sandstone formations, abundant plant life	hiking	year-round	p214
Table Mountain National Park	rocky headlands, seascapes; water birds, bonteboks, elands, African penguins	hiking, mountain biking	year-round	p100
Eastern Cape				
Addo Elephant National Park	dense bush, coastal grasslands, forested kloofs; elephants, black rhinos, buffaloes	vehicle safaris, walking trails, horse-riding	year-round	p235
Tsitsikamma National Park	coast, cliffs, rivers, ravines, forests; Cape clawless otters, baboons, monkeys, rich birdlife	hiking	year-round	p222
KwaZulu-Natal				
Hluhluwe-Imfolozi Park	lush, subtropical vegetation, rolling savanna; rhinos, giraffes, lions, elephants, lots of birds	wilderness walks, wildlife-watching	May-Oct	p313
Greater St Lucia Wetland Park	wetlands, coastal grasslands; elephants, birds, hippos	wilderness walks, vehicle/boat safaris	Mar-Nov	p315
Mkhuze Game Reserve	savanna, woodlands, swamp; rhinos & almost everything else; hundreds of bird species	guided walks, bird walks, vehicle safaris	year-round	p320
Ukhahlamba-Drakensberg Park	awe-inspiring Drakensberg escarpment; fantastic scenery & wilderness areas	hiking	year-round	p325

South Africa has long been at the forefront among African countries in conservation of its fauna. However, funding is tight, and will likely remain so as long as many South Africans still lack access to basic amenities. Potential solutions include public–private sector conservation partnerships, and increased contributions from private donors and international conservation bodies such as World Wide Fund for Nature.

See the World Wide Fund for Nature (WWF) South Africa website for an overview of conservation efforts in the country, at www.panda.org.za.

THE GREAT IVORY DEBATE

In 1990, following a massive campaign by various conservation organisations, the UN Convention on International Trade in Endangered Species (Cites) banned ivory trading in an effort to protect Africa's then-declining elephant populations. This promoted recovery of elephant populations in areas where they had previously been ravaged. Yet in South Africa – where elephants had long been protected – the elephant populations continued to grow, leading to widespread habitat destruction.

TOP PARKS & RESERVES

Park	Features	Activities	Best Time to Visit	Page
Free State				
Golden Gate Highlands National Park	spectacular sandstone cliffs & outcrops; zebras, jackals, rheboks, elands, birds	hiking	year-round	p363
Mpumalanga/Limpopo				
Kruger National Park	savanna, woodlands, thornveld; the Big Five & many more	vehicle safaris, guided wildlife walks	Jun-Oct	p440
Blyde River Canyon Nature Reserve	canyon, caves, river; stunning vistas	hiking, kloofing	year-round	p429
Northern Cape				
Augrabies Falls National Park	desert, river, waterfalls; klipspringers, rock dassies; striking scenery	hiking, canoeing, rafting	Apr-Sep	p507
Richtersveld National Park	mountainous desert; haunting beauty; klipspringers, jackals, zebras, plants, birds	hiking	Apr-Sep	p512
Lesotho				
Sehlabathebe National Park	mountain wilderness; bearded vultures, rheboks, baboons; wonderful isolation	hiking	Mar-Nov	p537
Swaziland				
Malolotja Nature Reserve	mountains, streams, water-falls, grasslands, forests; rich bird & plant life, impalas, klipspringers	hiking	year-round	p557

Solutions to the problem of elephant overpopulation have included creating transfrontier parks to allow animals to migrate over larger areas; relocating animals; small-scale elephant contraception efforts; and, most controversially, culling.

As a result of culling, South Africa has amassed significant ivory stockpiles. In 2002, after much pressure, Cites relaxed its worldwide ivory trading ban to allow ivory from legally culled elephants to be sold, with the idea that earnings could go towards conservation projects. However, the decision has been disputed by several other governments on the (quite plausible) grounds that resuming trade will increase demand for ivory, and thus encourage poaching.

Under the current plan, Cites will monitor things to see whether poaching does indeed increase after the ban is relaxed (early signs suggest that it will). Meanwhile, ivory's popularity is growing. In China – one of the main markets for the illegal ivory trade – ivory is now the rage in mobile phone ornamentation.

Lesotho

Environmental discussion in Lesotho centres on the controversial Highlands Water Project (see p532). Among the concerns are disruption of traditional communities, flooding of agricultural lands, and possible adverse ecological impact on the Senqu (Orange) River.

Other environmental issues include animal population pressure (resulting in overgrazing) and soil erosion. About 18 to 20 tonnes of topsoil per hectare is lost annually, with sobering predictions that there will be no cultivatable land left by 2040.

On a brighter note, Lesotho and South Africa recently combined forces in the Maluti–Drakensberg Transfrontier Conservation and Development Project to protect the alpine ecosystem of the Maluti and Drakensberg mountains.

Swaziland

Three of Swaziland's major waterways (the Komati, Lomati and Usutu Rivers) arise in South Africa, and Swaziland has been closely involved in South Africa's river control efforts. Drought is a recurring problem in eastern lowveld areas.

Other concerns include lack of community participation in conservation efforts, and insufficient government support.

For links on environmental issues in South Africa, see www-sul.stanford.edu /depts/ssrg/africa/south africa/rsaenviro.html and for a helpful overview, see www.botany.uwc.ac.za /inforeep/SA_enviro.htm.

Wildlife Guide

Any mention of Africa immediately evokes images of animals – more than any other continent, Africa is associated with its wildlife. Indeed, Southern Africa is home to of one of the richest wildlife communities on the planet – on even a short visit to the parks of South Africa you are guaranteed viewings of dozens of mammal species and hundreds of birds. An opportunity to view the fabled big cats and great herd animals is one of the prime attractions for visitors to the region.

South Africa's various landscapes, from woodland and savanna to dry shrubland, are a haven for wildlife not only abundant but diverse. Within the many parks and reserves, wildlife is also eminently viewable in that it's particularly used to the presence of human beings (in vehicles). Visitors can enjoy up-close encounters and the chance of sightings normally limited to specialists who live and work with animals. Every scale of experience is here, whether you want to see the epic seasonal migrations of huge zebra herds, watch solitary big cats closing in on a kill or enjoy the skittish antics of a troop of vervet monkeys.

Most significant wildlife populations in South Africa are enclosed within fences, intended to prevent conflict with the sizeable human populations that now exist around most of the parks. But bear in mind that most parks are vast and you'll only see fences when you drive through the gates – rest assured the animals that you encounter are wild.

Keep in mind, too, that wildlife tourism is one of the main sources of revenue for conservation efforts in Southern Africa. The money you spend in national parks and wildlife reserves is ploughed back into the parks, thus ensuring that future visitors will be able to spot a leopard stalking its prey or a white rhino pondering its solitude.

Zebra's skin detail.

PHOTO BY RICHARD I'ANSON

Both bushbaby species are often found in family groups of up to six or seven individuals.

PHOTO BY MITCH REARDON

PRIMATES

BUSHBABIES
GREATER BUSHBABY
Otolemur crassicaudatus (pictured);
lesser Bushbaby Galago moholi

Named for their plaintive wailing call, bushbabies are actually primitive primates. They have small heads, large rounded ears, thick bushy tails and the enormous eyes that are typical of nocturnal primates. The greater bushbaby has dark-brown fur, while the tiny lesser bushbaby is very light grey with yellowish colouring on its legs. Tree sap and fruit are the mainstay of their diet, supplemented by insects as well as, in the case of the greater bushbaby, lizards, nestlings and eggs.

Size: Greater bushbaby length 80cm, including a 45cm tail; weight up to 1.5kg; lesser bushbaby length 40cm; weight 150g to 200g. **Distribution:** Greater bushbaby is restricted to far northeast of region; lesser bushbaby to north of Limpopo. **Status:** Common but strictly nocturnal.

The male vervet monkey has a distinctive bright blue scrotum, an important signal of status in the troop.

PHOTO BY ABI

VERVET MONKEY
Cercopithecus aethiops

The most common monkey of the woodland-savanna, the vervet is easily recognisable by its speckled grey hair and black face fringed with white. Troops may number up to 30. The vervet monkey is diurnal and forages for fruits, seeds, leaves, flowers, invertebrates and the occasional lizard or nestling. It rapidly learns where easy pickings can be found around lodges and camp sites, but becomes a pest when it becomes habituated to being fed. Most park authorities destroy such individuals, so please avoid feeding them.

Size: Length up to 130cm, including a 65cm tail; weight 3.5kg to 8kg; male larger than female. **Distribution:** Widespread in woodland-savanna throughout much of the east and north of the region; absent from deserts, except along rivers. **Status:** Very common and easy to see.

The chacma baboon lives in troops of up to 150 animals, and there is no single dominant male.

PHOTO BY LUKE HUNTER

CHACMA BABOON
Papio ursinus

The snout of the chacma baboon gives it a more aggressive appearance than other primates, which have more humanlike facial features. However, when you see the interactions within a troop, it's difficult not to make anthropomorphic comparisons. It is strictly diurnal and forages for grasses, fruits, insects and small vertebrates. The chacma baboon is a notorious opportunist and may become a pest in camp sites, which it visits for hand-outs. Such individuals can be dangerous and are destroyed by park officials: don't feed them.

Size: Shoulder height 75cm; length up to 160cm, including a 70cm tail; weight up to 45kg; male larger than female and twice as heavy. **Distribution:** Throughout the region, except for the heart of deserts. **Status:** Common in many areas and active during the day.

RODENTS

SPRINGHARE
Pedetes capensis

In spite of its name and large ears, the springhare is not a hare but a very unusual rodent with no close relatives. With its powerful, out-sized hind feet and small forelegs, it most resembles a small kangaroo and shares a similar energy-efficient hopping motion. The springhare digs extensive burrows, from which it emerges at night to feed on grass and grass roots. Reflections of spotlights in its large, bright eyes often give it away on night safaris.

Although swift and able to leap several metres in a single bound, the springhare is preyed upon by everything from jackals to lions.

PHOTO BY NIGEL J DENNIS/NHPA

Size: Length 80cm, including a 40cm tail; weight 3kg to 4kg. **Distribution:** Widespread in the centre and north of the region; favours grassland habitats with sandy soils. **Status:** Common but strictly nocturnal.

CAPE PORCUPINE
Hystrix africaeaustralis

The Cape porcupine is the largest rodent native to Southern Africa. Its spread of long black-and-white banded quills from the shoulders to the tail makes it unmistakable. For shelter, it either occupies caves or excavates its own burrows. The porcupine's diet consists mainly of bark, tubers, seeds and a variety of plant and ground-level foliage. The young are born during the hot summer months, in litters of between one and four.

If attacked, a porcupine drives its rump into the predator – the quills are easily detached from their owner but can remain embedded in the victim, causing serious injury or death.

PHOTO BY DAVE HAMMAN

Size: Length 70cm to 100cm, including a 15cm tail; weight 10kg to 25kg. **Distribution:** Throughout the region. **Status:** Nocturnal but occasionally active on cooler days; difficult to see.

CAPE GROUND SQUIRREL
Xerus inauris

The Cape ground squirrel is a sociable rodent that lives in a colonial burrow system, usually containing up to a dozen individuals but sometimes as many as 30. It feeds on grass, roots, seeds and insects, but readily takes hand-outs from people in tourist camps. The ground squirrel is well adapted to dry surroundings – it does not need to drink, extracting all the moisture it requires from its food. It often stands on its hind legs to scan its surroundings, and erects its elegant fan-like tail when danger threatens. The tail is also used as a sunshade.

The burrows of the ground squirrel are often shared with meerkats.

PHOTO BY MITCH REARDON

Size: Length 45cm, including a 20cm tail; weight up to 1kg. **Distribution:** North-central South Africa. **Status:** Common; active throughout the day.

CARNIVORES

JACKALS
BLACK-BACKED JACKAL
Canis mesomelas (pictured);
side-striped jackal Canis adustus

This jackal relies heavily on scavenging but is also an efficient hunter, taking insects, birds, rodents and even the occasional small antelope. It also frequents human settlements and takes domestic stock. Pairs of black-backed jackals form long-term bonds, and each pair occupies an area varying from 3 to 21.5 sq km. Litters contain one to six pups; they are often looked after by older siblings as well as by their parents. The less-common side-striped jackal is grey in colour with a distinctive white-tipped tail.
Size: Shoulder height 35cm to 50cm; length 95cm to 120cm, including 30cm to 35cm tail; weight 12kg. **Distribution:** Black-backed throughout region; side-striped only in northeast. **Status:** Black-backed common, active night and day; side-striped less abundant, active night and early morning.

BAT-EARED FOX
Otocyon megalotis

The bat-eared fox eats mainly insects, especially termites, but also wild fruit and small vertebrates. It is monogamous and is often seen in groups comprising a mated pair and offspring. Natural enemies include large birds of prey, spotted hyenas, caracals and larger cats. It will bravely attempt to rescue a family member caught by a predator by using distraction techniques and harassment, which extends to nipping larger enemies on the ankles.
Size: Shoulder height 35cm; length 75cm to 90cm, including a 30cm tail; weight 3kg to 5kg. **Distribution:** Throughout western half of South Africa and open parts of Limpopo. **Status:** Common, especially in national parks; mainly nocturnal but often seen in the late afternoon and early morning.

WILD DOG
Lycaon pictus

The wild dog's blotched black, yellow and white coat, and its large, round ears, make it unmistakable. It is highly sociable, living in packs of up to 40, although 12 to 20 is typical. Great endurance hunters, the pack chases prey to the point of exhaustion, then cooperates to pull down the quarry. The wild dog is reviled for killing prey by eating it alive, but this is probably as fast as any of the 'cleaner' methods used by other carnivores. Mid-sized antelopes are the preferred prey, but it can kill animals as large as buffaloes.
Size: Shoulder height 65cm to 80cm; length 100cm to 150cm, including a 35cm tail; weight 20kg to 35kg. **Distribution:** Restricted to major parks of the extreme northeast. **Status:** Highly threatened, with numbers declining severely from a naturally low density.

HONEY BADGER
Mellivora capensis

Africa's equivalent of the European badger, the honey badger (also known as the ratel) has a reputation for a vile temper and ferocity. Mostly nocturnal, it is omnivorous, feeding on small animals, carrion, berries, roots, eggs, honey and especially on social insects (ants, termites and bees) and their larvae. Its

While stories of it attacking animals the size of buffaloes are probably folklore, the honey badger is pugnacious and very powerful for its size.

PHOTO BY MARTIN HARVEY/ANTPHOTO.COM

thick, loose skin is an excellent defence against predators, bee stings and snake bites. In some parks, honey badgers habitually scavenge from bins, presenting the best opportunity for viewing this animal.

Size: Shoulder height 30cm; length 95cm, including a 20cm tail; weight up to 15kg. **Distribution:** Widespread, although absent from central South Africa and from Lesotho. **Status:** Generally occurs in low densities; mainly nocturnal.

GENETS
SMALL-SPOTTED GENET
Genetta genetta; large-spotted genet
Genetta tigrina (pictured)

Relatives of mongooses, genets resemble long, slender domestic cats and have pointed foxlike faces. The two species in the region are very similar, but can be differentiated by the tail tips (white in the small-spotted genet, black in the large-spotted genet). They are solitary

Like many other mammals, genets deposit their droppings in latrines, usually in open or conspicuous sites.

PHOTO BY ARIADNE VAN ZANDBERGEN

animals, sleeping by day in burrows, rock crevices or hollow trees and emerging at night to forage. Very agile, they hunt well on land or in trees, feeding on rodents, birds, reptiles, nestlings, eggs, insects and fruits.

Size: Shoulder height 18cm; length 85cm to 110cm, including a 45cm tail; weight 1.5kg to 3kg. **Distribution:** Small-spotted genet is widespread in South Africa, but absent from the central east; large-spotted is common in eastern and southern coastal regions. **Status:** Very common but strictly nocturnal.

MONGOOSE

Although common, most mongooses are solitary and are usually seen only fleetingly. The slender mongoose (*Galerella sanguinea*; pictured) is recognisable by its black-tipped tail, which it holds aloft like a flag when running. A few species, such as the dwarf mongoose (*Helogale parvula*), the banded mongoose (*Mungos mungo*)

Social behaviour helps the mongoose when confronting a threat: collectively, they can intimidate much larger enemies.

PHOTO BY DAVE HAMMAN

and the meerkat (*Suricata suricatta*), are intensely sociable. Family groups are better than loners at spotting danger and raising kittens. Insects and other invertebrates are their most important prey.

Size: Ranges from 40cm and 400g (dwarf mongoose) to 120cm and 5.5g (white-tailed mongoose). **Distribution:** At least two or three species in most of region; the greatest diversity is in northeast. **Status:** Common where they occur; sociable species are diurnal, solitary species are nocturnal.

The male aardwolf assists the female in raising the cubs, mostly by babysitting at the den while the mother forages.

PHOTO BY MITCH REARDON

AARDWOLF
Proteles cristatus

The smallest of the hyena family, the aardwolf subsists almost entirely on harvester termites (which are generally ignored by other termite eaters because they are so noxious), licking over 200,000 from the ground each night. Unlike other hyaenids, it does not form clans; instead, it forages alone, and mates form only loose associations with each other. The aardwolf is persecuted in the mistaken belief that it kills stock, and may suffer huge population crashes following spraying for locusts (the spraying also kills termites).

Size: Shoulder height 40cm to 50cm; length 80cm to 100cm, including a 25cm tail; weight 8kg to 12kg. **Distribution:** Throughout the region, except for southern and western coasts. **Status:** Uncommon; nocturnal but occasionally seen at dawn and dusk.

Female spotted hyena are larger than, and dominant to, males and have male physical characteristics, the most remarkable of which is an erectile clitoris (which renders the sexes virtually indistinguishable).

PHOTO BY ARIADNE VAN ZANDBERGEN

SPOTTED HYENA
Crocuta crocuta

Widely reviled as a scavenger, the spotted hyena is actually a highly efficient predator with a fascinating social system. Clans, which can contain dozens of individuals, are led by females. The spotted hyena is massively built and appears distinctly canine, although it's more closely related to cats than to dogs. It can reach speeds of up to 60km/h and a pack can easily dispatch adult wildebeests and zebras. Lions are its main natural enemy.

Size: Shoulder height 85cm; length 120cm to 180cm, including a 30cm tail; weight 55kg to 80kg. **Distribution:** Occurs only in the northeast of the region. **Status:** Common where there is suitable food; mainly nocturnal but also seen during the day.

The caracal's long back legs power a prodigious ability to leap – it even takes birds in flight.

PHOTO BY JANE SWEENEY

CARACAL
Felis caracal

Sometimes also called the African lynx due to its long tufted ears, the caracal is a robust, powerful cat that preys predominantly on small antelopes, birds and rodents but is capable of taking down animals many times larger than itself. Like most cats, it is largely solitary. Females give birth to one to three kittens and raise them alone. The caracal is territorial, marking its home range with urine sprays and faeces. It occupies a range of habitats but prefers semiarid regions, dry savannas and hilly country; it is absent from dense forest.

Size: Shoulder height 40cm to 50cm; length 95cm to 120cm; weight 7kg to 18kg; male slightly larger. **Distribution:** Throughout the region except for much of KwaZulu-Natal and the western and southern coasts. **Status:** Fairly common but largely nocturnal and difficult to see.

LEOPARD
Panthera pardus

The leopard is the supreme ambush hunter, using infinite patience to stalk within metres of its prey before attacking in an explosive rush. It eats everything from insects to zebras, but antelopes are its primary prey. It is a solitary animal, except during the mating season when the male and female stay in close association for the female's week-long oestrus. A litter of up to three cubs is born after a gestation of three months and the females raise them without any assistance from the males.

The leopard is highly agile and hoists its kills into trees to avoid losing them to lions and hyenas.

PHOTO BY ABI

Size: Shoulder height 50cm to 75cm; length 160cm to 210cm, including a 70cm to 110cm tail; weight up to 90kg. **Distribution:** Absent from most of region except northeast and mountainous areas of south and east. **Status:** Common, but being mainly nocturnal they are the most difficult of the large cats to see.

LION
Panthera leo

The lion lives in prides of up to about 30, the core comprising four to 12 related females, which remain in the pride for life. Males form coalitions and defend the female groups from foreign males. The lion is strictly territorial, defending ranges of between 50 to 400 sq km. Young males are ousted from the pride at the age of two or three, entering a period of nomadism that ends at around five years old when they are able to take over their own pride. The lion hunts virtually anything, but wildebeests, zebras and buffaloes are the mainstay of its diet.

The lion spends much of the night hunting, patrolling territories and playing.

PHOTO BY LUKE HUNTER

Size: Shoulder height 120cm; length 250cm to 300cm, including a 100cm tail; weight up to 260kg (male), 180kg (female). **Distribution:** Restricted to major reserves of South Africa's northeast. **Status:** Common where it occurs; mainly nocturnal but easy to see during the day.

CHEETAH
Acinonyx jubatus

The world's fastest land mammal, the cheetah can reach speeds of at least 105km/h. The cheetah preys on antelopes weighing up to 60kg, as well as hares and young wildebeests and zebras. Litters may be as large as nine, but in open savanna habitats most cubs are killed by other predators, particularly lions. Young cheetahs disperse from the mother when aged around 18 months. The males form coalitions; females remain solitary for life.

The cheetah usually stalks prey to within 60m before unleashing its tremendous acceleration, as it becomes exhausted after a few hundred metres.

PHOTO BY ANDREW VAN SMEERDIJK

Size: Shoulder height 85cm; length 180cm to 220cm, including a 70cm tail; weight up to 65kg. **Distribution:** Kgalagadi Transfrontier Park, parts of Limpopo and reserves of South Africa's northeast. **Status:** Uncommon, with individuals moving over large areas; active by day.

The aardvark digs deep, complex burrows for shelter, which are also used by many other animals such as warthogs and mongooses.

PHOTO BY NIGEL DENNIS/ANTPHOTO.COM

UNGULATES (HOOFED ANIMALS)

AARDVARK
Orycteropus afer
Vaguely pig-like (its Afrikaans name translates as 'earth-pig') with a long tubular snout, powerful kangaroo-like tail and large rabbitlike ears, the aardvark is unique and has no close relatives. Protected by thick wrinkled pink-grey skin, aardvarks forage at night by sniffing for termite and ant nests, which they rip open with their astonishingly powerful front legs and large spadelike nails. Normally nocturnal, they occasionally spend cold winter mornings basking in the sun before retiring underground.
Size: Shoulder height 60cm; length 140cm to 180cm, including a 55cm tail; weight 40kg to 80kg. **Distribution:** Widely distributed throughout nearly the entire region. **Status:** Uncommon; nocturnal and rarely seen.

An adult African elephant's average daily food intake is about 250kg of grass, leaves, bark and other vegetation.

PHOTO BY ALEX DISSANAYAKE

AFRICAN ELEPHANT
Loxodonta africana
The African elephant usually lives in small family groups of between 10 and 20, which frequently congregate in much larger herds at a common water hole or food resource. Its society is matriarchal and herds are dominated by old females. Bulls live alone or in bachelor groups, joining the herds when females are in season. A cow may mate with many bulls during her oestrus. An elephant's life span is about 60 to 70 years, though some individuals may reach 100 or more.
Size: Shoulder height up to 4m (male), 3.5m (female); weight 5 to 6.5 tonnes (male), 3 to 3.5 tonnes (female). **Distribution:** Restricted to a few reserves in South Africa's northeast, east and south. **Status:** Very common in some parks.

Despite its resemblance to a large guinea pig, the dassie is actually related to the elephant.

PHOTO BY LUKE HUNTER

ROCK DASSIE
Procavia capensis
The rock dassie (also known as the hyrax) occurs practically everywhere there are mountains or rocky outcrops. It is sociable, living in colonies of up to 60 individuals. It feeds on vegetation, but spends much of the day basking on rocks or chasing other rock dassies in play. Where it's habituated to humans it is often quite tame, but otherwise it dashes into rock crevices when alarmed, uttering shrill screams. Rocks streaked white by dassies' urine are often a conspicuous indicator of a colony's presence.
Size: Length 40cm to 60cm; weight up to 5.5kg. **Distribution:** Throughout the region except the central eastern coast; absent from dense forest. **Status:** Common and easy to see, especially where they have become habituated to humans.

ZEBRAS
BURCHELL'S ZEBRA
Equus burchellii (pictured);
mountain zebra Equus zebra

Burchell's zebra has shadow lines between its black stripes, whereas the mountain zebra lacks shadows and has a gridiron pattern of black stripes just above its tail. Both species are grazers but occasionally browse on leaves and scrub. Stallions may hold a harem for as long as 15 years, but they often lose single mares to younger males, which gradually build up their own harems. Both types of zebras are preyed upon by all the large carnivores, with lions being their main predators.

Size: Shoulder height 140cm to 160cm; weight up to 390kg; mountain zebra smaller than Burchell's zebra; female of both species smaller than male. **Distribution:** Burchell's zebras in northeast of region; mountain zebras in a few reserves in Southern Africa. **Status:** Burchell's zebra common; mountain zebra less common.

The zebra social system centres around small groups of related mares over which stallions fight fiercely.

PHOTO BY MANFRED GOTTSCHALK

RHINOCEROSES
WHITE RHINOCEROS
Ceratotherium simum (pictured);
black rhinoceros Diceros bicornis

The white rhino is a grazer, preferring open plains, while the black rhino is a browser, living in scrubby country. The black rhino is prone to charging when alarmed – its eyesight is extremely poor and it has been known to charge trains or elephant carcasses. The white rhino is generally docile, and the more sociable species, forming cow-calf groups numbering up to 10. The black rhino is solitary and territorial, only socialising during the mating season.

Size: White rhino shoulder height 180cm; weight 2100kg to 1500kg; black rhino shoulder height 160cm; weight 800kg to 1200kg. **Distribution:** Restricted to protected areas, occurs naturally only in some reserves of KwaZulu-Natal. **Status:** White rhino threatened but well protected; black rhino endangered.

Aggressive poaching for rhino horn has made rhinos Africa's most endangered large mammals.

PHOTO BY CAROL POLICH

WARTHOG
Phacochoerus aethiopicus

The warthog's social organisation is variable, but groups usually consist of one to three sows with their young. Males form bachelor groups or are solitary, only associating with the female groups when a female is in season. The warthog feeds mainly on grass, but also eats fruit and bark. In hard times, it will burrow with its snout for roots and bulbs. It rests and gives birth in abandoned burrows or in excavated cavities of abandoned termite mounds.

Size: Shoulder height 70cm; weight up to 105kg, but averages 50kg to 60kg; male larger than female. **Distribution:** Restricted to the region's northeast. **Status:** Common and easy to see.

The distinctive facial warts can be used to determine the sex of warthogs – females have a single pair of warts under the eyes whereas males have a second set further down the snout.

PHOTO BY ABI

The hippo is extremely dangerous on land and kills many people each year, usually when someone inadvertently blocks the animal's retreat to the water.

PHOTO BY DAVID WALL

HIPPOPOTAMUS
Hippopotamus amphibius

The hippo is found close to fresh water, and spends the majority of its day submerged in water before emerging at night to graze on land. It can consume around 40kg of vegetable matter each evening. The hippo lives in large herds, tolerating close contact in the water but prefering to forage alone when on land. Adult bulls aggressively defend territories against each other, and most males bear the scars of conflicts (providing a convenient method of sexing hippos). Cows with calves are aggressive towards other individuals.

Size: Shoulder height 150cm; weight 1 to 2 tonnes; male larger than female. **Distribution:** Restricted to the region's northeast. **Status:** Common in major watercourses.

Despite the giraffe's incredibly long neck, it still has only seven cervical vertebrae – the same number as all mammals, including humans.

PHOTO BY JOHN HAY

GIRAFFE
Giraffa camelopardalis

The name 'giraffe' is derived from the Arabic word zarafah (the one who walks quickly). Both sexes have 'horns' – they are actually short projections of skin-covered bone. The giraffe browses on trees, exploiting a zone of foliage inaccessible to all other herbivores except elephants. Juveniles are prone to predation and a lion will even take down fully grown adults. The giraffe is at its most vulnerable at water holes and always appears hesitant when drinking.

Size: Height 4m to 5.2m (male), 3.5m to 4.5m (female); weight 900kg to 1400kg (male), 700kg to 1000kg (female). **Distribution:** Restricted to the region's northeast. **Status:** Common where it occurs and easy to see.

During the dry season the nyala is active only in the morning and evening, but during the rains they more often feed at night.

PHOTO BY LUKE HUNTER

NYALA
Tragelaphus angasii

The nyala is one of Africa's rarest and most beautiful antelopes. Males are grey with a mane and long hair under the throat and hind legs; they also have vertical stripes down the back and loin, lyre-shaped horns with white tips. Females are a ruddy colour with vertical white stripes and have no horns. The nyala browses on trees and bushes. Female nyala and their young live in small groups. The young may be taken by baboons and birds of prey.

Size: Shoulder height 115cm (male), 100cm (female); weight 100kg to 140kg (male), 60kg to 90kg (female); horns up to 85cm long. **Distribution:** Restricted to the region's northeast. **Status:** Common where it occurs, but well camouflaged.

BUSHBUCK
Tragelaphus scriptus

When startled, the bushbuck bolts and crashes loudly through the undergrowth.

PHOTO BY MITCH REARDON

A shy and solitary animal, the bushbuck inhabits thick bush close to permanent water and browses on leaves at night. It is chestnut to dark brown in colour and has a variable number of white vertical stripes on its body between the neck and rump, as well as a number of white spots on the upper thigh and a white splash on the neck. Normally only males grow horns, which are straight with gentle spirals and average about 30cm in length. It can be aggressive and dangerous when cornered.

Size: Shoulder height 80cm; weight up to 80kg; horns up to 55cm long; male larger than female. **Distribution:** Throughout the region's northeast and eastern and southern coastal areas. **Status:** Common, but difficult to see in the dense vegetation of their habitat.

GREATER KUDU
Tragelaphus strepsiceros

A strong jumper, the greater kudu readily clears barriers more than 2m high.

PHOTO BY LUKE HUNTER

The greater kudu is Africa's second-tallest antelope and the males carry massive spiralling horns much sought after by trophy hunters. It is light grey in colour with between six and 10 white stripes down the sides and a white chevron between the eyes. The kudu lives in small herds comprising females and their young, periodically joined by the normally solitary males during the breeding season. It is primarily a browser and can eat a variety of leaves, but finds its preferred diet in woodland-savanna with fairly dense bush cover.

Size: Shoulder height up to 150cm; weight 200kg to 300kg (male), 120kg to 220kg (female); horns up to 180cm long. **Distribution:** Throughout much of region's north, and with populations in central and southern South Africa. **Status:** Common.

ELAND
Taurotragus oryx

The eland normally drinks daily, but can go for over a month without water.

PHOTO BY DAVID WALL

Africa's largest antelope, the eland is massive. Both sexes have horns averaging about 65cm long that spiral at the base and sweep straight back. The male has a distinctive hairy tuft on the head, and stouter horns than the female. The eland prefers savanna scrub, feeding on grass and leaves in the early morning and from late afternoon into the night. It usually lives in groups of around six to 12, generally comprising several females and one male. Larger aggregations (up to a thousand) sometimes form at 'flushes' of new grass.

Size: Shoulder height 124cm to 180cm; weight 300kg to 950kg; horns up to 100cm long. **Distribution:** Small parts of north-central and northeastern South Africa and the Drakensberg. **Status:** Naturally low density, but relatively common in their habitat and easy to see.

The common duiker is capable of going without water for long periods, but it will drink whenever water is available.

PHOTO BY ROB DRUMMOND

COMMON (OR GREY) DUIKER
Sylvicapra grimmia

One of the most common small antelopes, the common duiker is usually solitary, but is sometimes seen in pairs. It is greyish light brown in colour, with a white belly and a dark-brown stripe down its face. Only males have horns, which are straight and pointed, and rarely grow longer than 15cm. This duiker is predominantly a browser, often feeding on agricultural crops. This habit leads to it being persecuted outside conservation areas, though it is resilient to hunting.

Size: Shoulder height 50cm; weight 10kg to 20kg; horns up to 18cm long; female slightly larger than male. **Distribution:** Very widespread throughout the region. **Status:** Common; active throughout the day, except where disturbance is common.

The waterbuck's oily hair has a strong musky odour – especially with mature males, potent enough that even humans can smell them.

PHOTO BY DAVID WALL

WATERBUCK
Kobus ellipsiprymnus

The waterbuck has a bull's-eye ring around its rump, and white markings on the face and throat. It's a solid animal with a thick, shaggy, dark-brown coat. Only males have horns, which curve gradually out before shooting straight up to a length averaging about 75cm. The small herds consist of cows, calves and one mature bull; younger bulls live in bachelor groups. This grazer never strays far from water and is a good swimmer, readily entering water to escape predators.

Size: Shoulder height 130cm; weight 200kg to 300kg (male), 150kg to 200kg (female); horns up to 100cm long. **Distribution:** Wet areas in northeastern South Africa. **Status:** Common and easy to see.

The whistling call of the reedbuck is often repeated when advertising territories, and is also given in alarm.

PHOTO BY ANDREW VAN SMEERDIJK

REEDBUCKS
COMMON REEDBUCK
Redunca arundinum (pictured); mountain reedbuck Redunca fulvorufula

The common reedbuck is found in wetlands and riverine areas. The rarer mountain reedbuck inhabits hill country and is the smaller, but is otherwise physically similar, with the underbelly, inside of the thighs, throat and underside of the tail white, and with males having distinctive forward-curving horns. However, their social systems differ: common reedbucks live in pairs on territories; female mountain reedbucks form small groups, the range of each encompassing the territories of several males.

Size: Common reedbuck shoulder height 90cm; weight 50kg to 90kg; mountain reedbuck shoulder height 70cm; weight 20kg to 40kg; male bigger in both species. **Distribution:** Common reedbucks in north and east of region; mountain reedbucks in region's east. **Status:** Common and easy to see.

ROAN ANTELOPE
Hippotragus equinus

The roan antelope is one of Southern Africa's rarest antelopes, and one of Africa's largest. A grazer, it prefers tall grasses and sites with ample shade and water. Its coat varies from reddish fawn to dark rufous, with white underparts and a conspicuous mane of stiff, black-tipped hairs from the nape to the shoulders. Its

Both sexes of roan antelope have long backward-curving horns.

PHOTO BY JASON EDWARDS

face is distinctively patterned black and white and its long, pointed ears are tipped with a brown tassel. Herds of normally less than 20 females and young are led by a single adult bull; other males form bachelor groups.
Size: Shoulder height 140cm; weight 200kg to 300kg; horns up to 100cm long. **Distribution:** Can be seen in Kruger NP. **Status:** One of the less common antelopes; although numbers are declining, they are not difficult to see where they occur.

SABLE ANTELOPE
Hippotragus niger

The sable antelope is slightly smaller than the roan antelope, but more solidly built. It is dark brown to black, with a white belly and face markings. Both sexes have backward-sweeping horns, often over 1m long; those of the male are longer and more curved. It occurs in habitat similar to, but slightly

Both the roan and sable antelopes are fierce fighters, even known to kill attacking lions.

PHOTO BY DENNIS JONES

more wooded than, that of the roan antelope. Females and young live in herds, mostly of 10 to 30. Mature males establish territories that overlap the ranges of female herds; other males form bachelor groups.
Size: Shoulder height 135cm; weight 180kg to 270kg; horns up to 130cm long. **Distribution:** Restricted to extreme northeastern South Africa. **Status:** Common and easy to see.

GEMSBOK
Oryx gazella

The gemsbok (or oryx) can tolerate arid areas uninhabitable to most antelopes. It can survive for long periods without drinking (obtaining water from its food) and tolerates extreme heat. A powerful animal with long, straight horns present in both sexes, it's well equipped to defend itself and some-

As a means of conserving water, the gemsbok can let its body temperature climb to levels that would kill most mammals.

PHOTO BY ANDREW MACCOLL

times kills attacking lions. Herds usually contain five to 40 individuals but aggregations of several hundred can occur. The gemsbok is principally a grazer, but also browses on thorny shrubs unpalatable to many species.
Size: Shoulder height 120cm; weight 180kg to 240kg; horns up to 120cm long; male more solid than female and with thicker horns. **Distribution:** North-central South Africa. **Status:** Common where it occurs, but often shy, fleeing from humans.

Bontebok and blesbok often stand about in groups facing into the sun with their heads bowed.

PHOTO BY LUKE HUNTER

BONTEBOK & BLESBOK
Damaliscus dorcas dorcas &
Damaliscus dorcas phillipsi

Closely related subspecies, the bontebok and the blesbok are close relatives of the tsessebe. The best way to tell them apart is to look at their colour – the blesbok has a dullish appearance and lacks the rich, deep brown-purple tinge of the bontebok. Both species graze on short grass, and both sexes have horns. As with many antelope, males are territorial, while females form small herds. The bontebok was once virtually exterminated and numbers have recovered to only a few thousand.

Size: Shoulder height 90cm; weight 55kg to 80kg; horns up to 50cm long. Female smaller than male.
Distribution: Endemic to South Africa; bontebok confined to southwest; blesbok widespread in central region. **Status:** Bontebok rare but easy to see where they occur; blesbok is common.

The tsessebe is a grazer, and although it can live on dry grasses, it prefers flood plains and moist areas that support lush pasture.

PHOTO BY ARIADNE VAN ZANDBERGEN

TSESSEBE
Damaliscus lunatus

The tsessebe is dark reddish-brown, with glossy violet-brown patches on the rear thighs, front legs and face. The horns, carried by both sexes, curve gently up, out and back. A highly gregarious antelope, it lives in herds and frequently mingles with other grazers. During the mating season, bulls select a well-defined patch, which they defend against rivals, while females wander from one patch to another. It is capable of surviving long periods without water as long as sufficient grass is available.

Size: Shoulder height 120cm; weight 120kg to 150kg (male), 75kg to 150kg (female); horns up to 45cm long. **Distribution:** Found in parts of northeastern South Africa. **Status:** Common where they occur.

The wildebeest is a grazer, and moves constantly in search of good pasture and water.

PHOTO BY LUKE HUNTER

BLUE WILDEBEEST
Connochaetes taurinus

The blue wildebeest is gregarious, forming herds of up to tens of thousands in some parts of Africa, often in association with zebras and other herbivores. In Southern Africa, numbers are much reduced and huge herds are a rarity. Males are territorial and attempt to herd groups of females into their territory. Because it prefers to drink daily and can survive only five days without water, the wildebeest will migrate large distances to find it. During the rainy season it grazes haphazardly, but in the dry season it congregates around water holes.

Size: Shoulder height 140cm; weight 200kg to 300kg (male), 140kg to 230kg (female); horns up to 85cm long. **Distribution:** The region's central eastern coast, northeast and central north. **Status:** Very common but mostly restricted to protected areas.

KLIPSPRINGER
Oreotragus oreotragus

Male and female klipspringers form long-lasting pair bonds and occupy a territory together.

PHOTO BY LUKE HUNTER

A small, sturdy antelope, the klipspringer is easily recognised by its curious tip-toe stance – its hooves are well adapted for balance and grip on rocky surfaces. The widely spaced short horns are present only on the male of the species. The klipspringer normally inhabits rocky outcrops; it also sometimes ventures into adjacent grasslands, but always retreats to the rocks when alarmed. This amazingly agile and sure-footed creature is capable of bounding up impossibly rough rock faces.

Size: Shoulder height 55cm; weight 9kg to 15kg; horns up to 15cm long; female larger than male.
Distribution: On rocky outcrops and mountainous areas throughout the region; absent from dense forests. **Status:** Common.

STEENBOK
Raphicerus campestris

If a potential predator approaches, the steenbok lies flat with neck outstretched, zigzagging away only at the last moment.

PHOTO BY ARIADNE VAN ZANDBERGEN

The steenbok is a very pretty and slender small antelope; its back and hindquarters range from light reddish-brown to dark brown with pale underpart markings. The upper surface of its nose bears a black, wedge-shaped 'blaze' useful for identification. Males have small, straight and widely separated horns. Although steenboks are usually seen alone it appears likely that they share a small territory with a mate, but only occasionally does the pair come together. The steenbok is active in the morning and evening.

Size: Shoulder height 50cm; weight up to 10kg to 16kg; horns up to 19cm long. **Distribution:** Apart from a large area of the central east and eastern coast, steenbok are widely distributed throughout the region in all habitats, except desert areas. **Status:** Common where it occurs.

SUNI
Neotragus moschatus

When surprised the suni will freeze, sometimes for prolonged periods, before bounding away with a barking alarm call.

PHOTO BY RICHARD I'ANSON

This tiny antelope, which vies with the blue duiker for the title of smallest in the region, is best looked for from observation hides at water holes. It is often given away by the constant side-to-side flicking of its tail (blue duikers wag their tails up and down). Suni are probably monogamous, living in pairs on their small territories, and use secretions from a large scent gland in front of their eye to mark their territories. They nibble selectively on leaves and fallen fruit.

Size: Shoulder height 35cm; weight 4kg to 6kg; horns up to 14cm long. **Distribution:** Wooded areas of the region's extreme northeast; can be seen in Kruger National Park and False Bay Park. **Status:** Difficult to see because it is small, shy and lives in thickets; active in the early morning and late afternoon.

The impala is known for its speed and its ability to leap – it can spring as far as 10m in one bound, and 3m into the air.

PHOTO BY ABI

IMPALA
Aepyceros melampus

Although it is often dismissed by tourists because it is so abundant, the graceful impala is a unique antelope that has no close relatives. Males have long, lyre-shaped horns averaging 75cm in length. The impala is a gregarious animal, and forms herds of up to 100 or so. Males defend female herds during the oestrus, but outside the breeding season they congregate in bachelor groups. It is the common prey of lions, leopards, cheetahs, wild dogs and spotted hyenas.

Size: Shoulder height 90cm; weight 40kg to 70kg; horns up to 80cm long; male larger than female. **Distribution:** Widespread in the northeast of the region. **Status:** Very common and easy to see.

The springbok is extremely common in arid areas, usually in herds of up to 100, whose social structure varies considerably.

PHOTO BY ARIADNE VAN ZANDBERGEN

SPRINGBOK
Antidorcas marsupialis

The springbok is one of the fastest antelopes (up to 88km/h) and has a distinctive stiff-legged, arched-backed bounding gait called 'pronking', which is commonly displayed when it sees predators. When pronking, it raises a white crest along the back (normally hidden within a skin fold) and the white hairs of the rump. It can survive for long periods without drinking, but may move large distances to find new grazing, sometimes congregating in herds of thousands when doing so. Both sexes have ridged, lyre-shaped horns.

Size: Shoulder height 75cm; weight 25kg to 55kg; horns up to 50cm long; male larger than female. **Distribution:** Northwestern and central-northern South Africa. **Status:** Very common and easy to see.

Although it is generally docile, the buffalo can be very dangerous and should be treated with caution.

PHOTO BY LUKE HUNTER

AFRICAN BUFFALO
Syncerus caffer

The African buffalo is the only native wild cow of Africa. Both sexes have distinctive curving horns that broaden at the base and meet over the forehead in a massive 'boss'; those of the female are usually smaller. It has a fairly wide habitat tolerance, but requires areas with abundant grass, water and cover. The African buffalo is gregarious and may form herds numbering thousands. Group composition is fluid and smaller herds often break away, sometimes rejoining the original herd later.

Size: Shoulder height 160cm; weight 400kg to 900kg; horns up to 125cm long; female somewhat smaller than male. **Distribution:** Restricted to some reserves of the region's northeast and east. **Status:** Common; can be approachable where they are protected.

Food & Drink

It's only since the dismantling of apartheid that anyone has talked of 'South African cuisine' as a unified whole. Earlier, the Africans had their mealie pap, the Afrikaners their boerewors, and the Indians and Cape Malays their curries. Today, along with divisions in other aspects of life, the culinary barriers are starting to fall.

Awaiting the visiting gastronome is a savoury melting pot reflecting a fusion of influences: hearty meat and vegetable stews that resulted when the Dutch encountered the African bush; a seemingly endless variety of maize dishes that have been at the centre of African family life for centuries; a sprinkling of *piri-piri* (hot pepper) from Mozambique; and scents of curry and coriander that have wafted over the Indian Ocean from Asia.

It can take some work to discover this diversity, and not get overwhelmed by the fast-food chains and homogenised, oversauced dishes that are easy to find anywhere. But if you're gastronomically inclined and willing to forage a bit for your food, South Africa offers a delectably rich culinary heritage that's just waiting to be discovered.

STAPLES & SPECIALITIES

Three meals a day is the norm for most South Africans, though what you'll be served at each mealtime is likely to be completely different, depending on where you are in the country. Afrikaners have developed breakfast into an art form, albeit unbelievably creamy and calorie-rich, featuring lots of meat, eggs and sugar. It's easier to keep the figure trim travelling in Swaziland, Lesotho or among South Africa's African population, where you'll be treated to a bowl of piping hot porridge, usually maize or sorghum based, sometimes sweetened, sometimes slightly fermented and sour. Breakfast buffets at many hotels keep up their loyalty to the queen, with classic British breakfasts of eggs, limp toast and grilled tomatoes. In Cape Town's Bo-Kaap area, or among Durban's Indian population, you're just as likely to be served a spicy curry or atchar (pickled fruits and vegetables).

In *Flavours of South Africa*, South African culinary guru Peter Veldsman traces the history of South African cuisine, with lots of information on ingredients and local specialities.

Biltong & Boerewors

Traditional Afrikaner cuisine traces its roots back to the early days of Dutch settlement in South Africa. Your first introduction is likely to be biltong (dried meat), which enjoys the unofficial status of national snack. Rusks (dried bread) are another common item, and come in just as handy on a trek today as they did for the Voortrekkers on their long journeys into the hinterlands. The appeal of spicy boerewors (farmer's sausage) is less apparent, though they have a loyal following. If you're having trouble getting used to them, it could be that you're eating *braaiwors* (barbecue sausage), an inferior grade. *Potjiekos* (pot food) kept Boer families well fed as their wagons rolled into the horizon. It features stewed meat and vegetables that have bubbled away for hours in a three-legged pot over hot coals.

Perhaps more than anything else, it's the braai (barbecue) – an Afrikaner institution that shows signs of breaking its way across race lines – that defines South African cuisine. It's as much a social event as a form of cooking, with the essential elements boerewors and beer.

Cape Cuisine

Cape cuisine (often referred to as Cape Malay cuisine) has its roots in the mixing of the 'Malay' slaves (many of whom were from Madagascar and

Indonesia) with the Dutch settlers. It's often stodgy and overly sweet, but – along with its close cousin Afrikaner cuisine – well worth trying. The central feature is an intriguing mixture of exotic Asian spices and local produce. Dishes to watch for (all described on p88) include bobotie, *waterblommetjie bredie* and *malva*. True Cape cuisine, which is strongly associated with the Muslim community, contains no alcohol.

DID YOU KNOW?

Real boerewors must be 90% meat, of which 30% can be fat. We can only imagine what goes into unregulated *braaiwors*...

Curries

Along with Mahatma Ghandi, India's other great export to South Africa's shores has been the curry. The place to go for the spiciest curries is Durban. This is also where you'll find *bunny chow* (half a loaf of bread, scooped out and filled with curry), a uniquely South African twist on traditional Indian cuisine. Curries are also popular in Cape cuisine, though they're usually not as spicy.

Mealie Pap

Mealie pap (maize porridge) is the most widely eaten food in South Africa, as well as in Swaziland and Lesotho. It's thinner or stiffer depending on where you eat it, bland and something of an acquired taste. However, it's ideal if you want something filling and economical, and can be quite satisfying served with a good sauce or stew.

Meat

There are few areas in the world where meat could be considered a 'staple', but certain parts of South Africa would certainly be among them. Anything that can be grilled is, with ostrich, crocodile, warthog and kudu only a few of the variants you'll find – along with the more traditional beef and lamb. Steaks in particular tend to be excellent value.

DID YOU KNOW?

A little-advertised treat of South Africa travel is the country's wide variety of excellent natural fruit juices, including passionfruit and *nartjie* (tangerine).

Seafood

Considering the fact that it's surrounded by two oceans, South Africa has a remarkably modest reputation as a seafood-lover's destination. Yet Cape Town, the west coast and the Garden Route have some of the best fish dishes you'll find anywhere. Among the highlights: lightly spiced fish stews, *snoekbraai* (grilled snoek), mussels, oysters and even lobster. Pickled fish is popular in Cape cuisine.

DRINKS

Beer

Beer is the national beverage. There are numerous reasonable brands, including Castle and Black Label and Namibia's all-natural Windhoek. In the Cape provinces try Mitchell's and Birkenhead's. Lager-style beer comes in cans or dumpies (small bottles) for around R9. Bars serve long toms (750ml bottles). Draught beers are uncommon. In Lesotho, watch for white or yellow cloths hung in front of houses to advertise homebrew.

DID YOU KNOW?

South African beer is around 5% alcohol – similar to Australian beer, but stronger than UK brews. Even Castle Lite has 4% alcohol.

Water

Tap water is safe throughout the country, except in rural areas. In Swaziland and Lesotho, stick to bottled water, and purify stream water.

Wine

South African wine debuted in 1659. Since then, it's had time to age to perfection, and is of a high standard and reasonably priced. Dry whites are particularly good – Sauvignon Blanc, Riesling, Colombard and Chenin

Blanc. Popular reds include Cabernet Sauvignon, pinotage (a local cross of Pinot and Cinsaut, which was known as Hermitage), Shiraz and Pinot Noir. No wine may use any estate, vintage or origin declaration on its label without being certified. No South African sparkling wine may be called champagne, although a number of producers use Chardonnay and Pinot Noir blends and the *méthode champenoise*.

Wine prices average from around R50 in a restaurant or bottle store. Most restaurants stock a few varieties in dinkies (250ml bottles).

WHERE TO EAT & DRINK

If you're after fine dining in cosy surroundings, head to the Winelands. Along the Western Cape coast, open-air beachside eateries serve fish braais under the stars. A highlight of visiting a township is experiencing family-style cooking in a B&B. In addition to speciality restaurants, every larger town has several places offering homogenised Western fare at homogenised prices (R40 to R60). Most restaurants are licensed, but some allow you to bring your own wine for minimal or no corkage charge.

Larger towns have cafés, where you can enjoy a cappuccino and sandwich or other light fare. In rural areas, 'café' usually refers to a small corner store selling soft drinks, chips and meat pies. Most places are open from about 8am to 5pm.

In the old days most South African pubs had a *kroeg* (bar) where White men would drink, a ladies' bar and lounge for White couples, and a hole in the wall where bottles would be sold to Blacks and Coloureds. Unofficial segregation is still the norm, and bars are heavily male-dominated. Johannesburg, Durban, Cape Town and Kimberly have the best selection of pubs. Reasonable but soulless franchised bars proliferate in urban areas, and most smaller towns have at least one hotel. In townships, things centre around shebeens – informal drinking establishments that were once illegal but are now merely unlicensed. Throughout South Africa, and in major towns in Lesotho and Swaziland, you can also buy alcoholic drinks at bottle stores and supermarkets.

VEGETARIANS & VEGANS

South Africa is a meat-loving society, but it's easy enough to find vegetarian offerings in larger towns, and to make do in rural areas by self-catering. In tourist areas and student towns, such as Grahamstown, you'll even find the occasional vegetarian restaurant. Otherwise, there's little that's specifically vegetarian. Cafés are good bets, as many will make veggie food to order. Indian and Italian restaurants are also good, although many pasta sauces contain animal fat. Major cities have health food stores selling tofu, soy milk and other staples, and can point you towards vegetarian-friendly venues.

Eating vegan is difficult: most nonmeat dishes contain cheese, and eggs and milk are common ingredients. Health-food shops are your best bet, though most are closed in the evenings and on weekends.

In Lesotho and Swaziland, it's more challenging to keep variety in a vegetarian diet; if possible stock up in South Africa.

Good vegetarian restaurants are recommended throughout this book.

WHINING & DINING

Children are well catered for in South Africa, and most restaurants are very family-friendly. Many have special children's meals, and it's easy to find menu items that are suitable for young diners. Highchairs are readily available at restaurants in tourist areas. Apart from curries and

For a unique South African experience, sip some red-coloured rooibos (red bush) tea – plain, with lemon or with milk. It's noncaffeinated, and consumed with gusto, especially by the health-conscious.

Tip from 10% to 15% in restaurants. In rural areas of Swaziland and Lesotho, it's more common to simply round up the bill.

Hungry for a quick bite? Try a roasted mealie (cob of corn) or Durban's filling *bunny chow* (curry-to-go).

other spicy dishes, there isn't anything in particular to avoid. Although tap water is fine to drink, if you've been giving your child bottled water at home or elsewhere on your travels, it's probably best to continue to do so here. Child-size boxes of fresh juice and beverages, such as carbonated apple juice, make good snacks. For more on travelling with children, see p571.

HABITS & CUSTOMS

In tourist areas, dining etiquette and customs are very Westernised. However, eating and snacking on the street is much less common than it is in Europe and the US.

For those who can afford it, three meals per day are the norm. Dinner is the main event, although lunch may be more filling in rural areas. Portions are usually large. In restaurants, for something light, a soup and salad (which often come with cheese) should more than suffice. The most popular snack is roasted mealies, sold along roadsides throughout the country.

In parts of KwaZulu-Natal, Eastern Cape and Limpopo province's Venda region, and sometimes in townships, you may also have the chance to try eating with your fingers. It's a bit of an acquired art: use your right hand only, work to ball up the staple (pap) with your fingers, dip it in the sauce or stew, and then eat it, ideally without dripping sauce down your elbow or having your ball of staple break up in the communal stew pot.

Braais are the main food-centred social event. If you're invited to one, dress is casual and the atmosphere very relaxed.

EAT YOUR WORDS

Want to know *phutu* from *umphokoqo*? A boerewor from a *braaiwor*? Get behind the cuisine scene, by getting to know the language. For pronunciation guidelines see p615.

Menu Decoder

It's unlikely that you'll see all of these items on the same menu, but they provide an insight into the diversity of South African cuisine.

FOOD

amadumbe – yam-like potato; a favourite staple in KwaZulu-Natal

atchar – a Cape Malay dish of pickled fruits and vegetables, flavoured with garlic, onion and curry

biltong – dried, salted meat, often spread with brown sugar and vinegar during the drying process

bobotie – a curried-mince pie topped with egg custard, usually served on a bed of rice with a dab of chutney

boerewors – spicy sausage, traditionally made of beef and pork plus seasonings and plenty of fat; an essential ingredient at any braai and often sold like hot dogs by street vendors

bredie – hearty Afrikaner pot stew, traditionally made with lamb and vegetables

bunny chow – South Africa's answer to Indian fast food: half a loaf of bread, scooped out and filled with curry; best eaten in Durban

curry – just as good as in India. Head to Durban if you like your curry spicy, and to Cape Town (Bo-Kaap) for a milder version

eisbein – pork knuckles

fetkoeks – literally, 'fat cakes'; deep-fried bread dough with a rich fruit or mince-meat filling

frikkadel – fried meatball

imbasha – a Swazi fried delicacy of roasted maize and nuts

imifino – Xhosa dish of mealie meal and vegetables

kingklip – an excellent firm-fleshed fish, usually served fried; South Africa's favourite fish

koeksesters – small doughnuts dripping in honey, which are very gooey and figure-enhancing

konfyt – fruit preserve

line fish – catch of the day

malva – delicious sponge dessert, sometimes called vinegar pudding, since it's traditionally made with apricot jam and vinegar

mashonzha – mopane worms, fried, grilled or served with *dhofi* (peanut sauce); common in Venda areas

mealie – cob of corn, popular grilled as a snack

mealie meal – finely ground maize

mealie pap – maize porridge; a Southern African staple, best eaten with sauce or stew

melktart – a rich, custard-like tart made with milk, eggs, flour and cinnamon

monkey gland sauce – a sauce made from tomato and Worcester sauces and chutney; often offered with steaks

mopane worms – caterpillars found on mopane trees; dried and served in spicy sauce as a crunchy snack

morogo – leafy greens, boiled, seasoned, and served with pap; *imifino* in Xhosa

Mrs Balls' Chutney – most famous brand of this sour-sweet condiment

pap & sous – maize porridge with a tomato and onion sauce

phutu – a Zulu dish of crumbly maize porridge, often eaten with soured milk; *umphokoqo* in Xhosa

piri-piri – hot pepper

potjiekos – meat and vegetables cooked for hours on a three-legged pot over a fire

rooster koek – griddle cake traditionally cooked on the braai

russian – a large red sausage, fried but often served cold (and revolting)

rusk – twice-cooked biscuit, usually served for breakfast or as a snack and much better than those given to teething babies

rystafel – Dutch/Afrikaner version of an Indonesian meal consisting of rice with many accompanying dishes

samosa – spicy Indian pastry

samp – mix of maize and beans; see *umngqusho*

slaphakskeentjies – a Cape Malay dish of onions poached in a milk and mustard sauce

smilies – slang term for boiled and roasted sheep's heads, often sold in townships and rural areas

snoek – a firm-fleshed migratory fish that appears off the Cape in June and July, served smoked, salted or curried

sosatie – lamb cubes, marinated with garlic, tamarind juice and curry powder, then skewered with onions and apricots, and grilled; originally Muslim, but now often made with pork fat

tincheki – boiled pumpkin cubes with sugar, common in Swaziland

ting – sorghum porridge, popular among the Tswana

umngqusho – samp (dried and crushed maize kernels), boiled, then mixed with beans, salt and oil, and simmered; a Xhosa delicacy (called *nyekoe* in Sotho)

umvubo – sour milk and mealie meal

venison – if you see this on a menu it's bound to be some form of antelope, usually springbok

vetkoek – deep-fried dough ball sometimes stuffed with mince; basically a heart attack on a plate. Called *amagwinya* in Xhosa

vienna – a smaller version of the *russian*

waterblommetjie bredie – Cape Malay stew mixing lamb with water-hyacinth flowers and white wine

DRINKS

Don Pedro – an alcoholic milkshake traditionally made with whiskey and ice cream, but also commonly available with other liquors

mampoer – home-distilled brandy made from peaches and prickly pear

rooibos – literally, 'red bush' (Afrikaans); herbal tea that reputedly has therapeutic qualities

spook & diesel – rum and Coke

springbok – a cocktail featuring crème de menthe topped with Amarula Cream (a South African version of Baileys Irish Cream)

steen – Chenin Blanc; most common variety of white wine

sundowner – any drink, but typically alcohol, drunk at sunset
umnqombothi – Xhosa for rough-and-ready, home-brewed beer
witblitz – 60-proof 'white lightning', a traditional Boer spirit distilled from fruit

Food & Drinks Glossary

FOOD

biefstuk	steak
biltong	dried, salted meat
boerewors	spicy farmer's sausage
brood	bread
groente	vegetables
hoender	chicken
kaas	cheese
vleis	meat
varkvlies	pork
vis	fish
vrugte	fruit

DRINKS

bier	beer
cool drink	canned soft drink
dinkies	250mL bottles of wine
dumpies	small bottles of beer
glas melk	glass of milk
koppie koffie	cup of coffee
long toms	750mL bottles of beer
tee	tea
wyn	wine

OTHER

braai	open-air barbecue; from braaivleis (grilled meat)
kroeg	bar
padkos	picnic
shebeen	unlicensed bar

South Africa

MITCH REARDON

Cape Town

Whichever way you look at it, Cape Town occupies one of the world's most stunning locations. Few other cities can boast of a 1073m-tall mountain slap-bang in their centre. As beautiful as the surrounding beaches and vineyards can be, it's this rugged wilderness, coated in a unique flora, that is the focus of everyone's attention.

You'll notice how vibrantly colourful everything is, from the beaded dolls and patterned shirts in the shops to the Victorian bathing chalets at St James' beach and the pastel-painted façades of the Bo-Kaap. The many different faces on the streets are proof of South Africa's rainbow nation and a reminder of the city's tumultuous, recorded history of over 350 years.

Apartheid allowed Whites to reserve some of the world's most spectacular real estate, and the stark contrast between poverty-stricken Crossroads and ritzy Clifton remains – black and white. And yet you must visit the ever-growing Cape Flats townships (home to about 1.5 million people) to truly understand this city and to glimpse its future. Not everything you see will appal you. On the contrary, it can be argued that a stronger sense of optimism and pride are found in the shacks of Khayelitsha than in the mansions of Tamboerskloof.

For all the city's contradictions you'll find Capetonians likeable, open-minded and ultra-relaxed. Like many ports, Cape Town is a master of showing visitors a good time. The range and quality of accommodation is brilliant (particularly the luxury guesthouses). Its restaurants and bars compare favourably with those of other cosmopolitan cities. There's a lively cultural scene, particularly when it comes to music, which pervades every corner of the city, and if outdoor activities and adrenaline buzzes are your thing, you've come to the right place.

HIGHLIGHTS

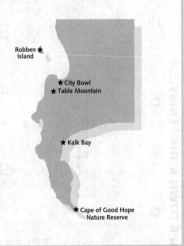

- Pondering the past, present and future of South Africa at **Robben Island**, its most infamous prison (p110)
- Getting on top of magnificent **Table Mountain** and looking down on the city (p100)
- Exploring the **City Bowl**, where you'll find museums, the Company's Gardens and wonderful Art Deco and Victorian architecture (p100)
- Heading to the **Cape of Good Hope Nature Reserve** for wide open spaces, wildlife, empty beaches and the dramatic scenery of the peninsula's rugged tip (p144)
- Browsing the fish market, antique shops and convivial cafés at **Kalk Bay** (p140)

Robben ★ Island

★City Bowl
★ Table Mountain

★ Kalk Bay

★ Cape of Good Hope Nature Reserve

| ■ TELEPHONE CODE: 021 | ■ POPULATION: 2.9 MILLION | ■ AREA: 2487 SQ KM |

CAPE TOWN

CAPE TOWN & THE PENINSULA

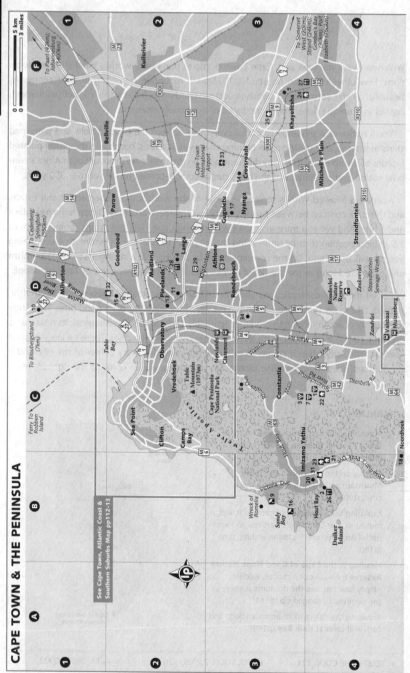

See Cape Town, Atlantic Coast & Southern Suburbs Map pp112–13

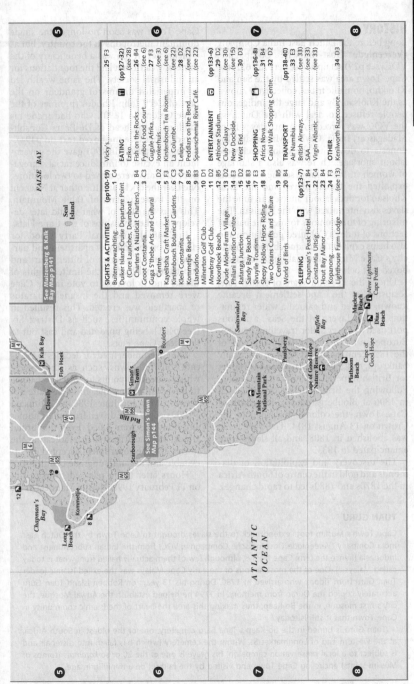

SIGHTS & ACTIVITIES (pp100–19)
Buitenverwachting...................1 C4
Duiker Island Cruise Departure Point
(Circe Launches, Drumboat
Charters & Nauticat Charters)...2 B4
Groot Constantia.....................3 C3
Guga S'thebe Arts and Cultural
Centre....................................4 D2
Kayelitsha Craft Market............5 F3
Kirstenbosch Botanical Gardens...6 C3
Klein Constantia......................7 C4
Kommetjie Beach.....................8 B5
Llandudno..............................9 B3
Milnerton Golf Club................10 D1
Mowbray Golf Club.................11 D2
Noordhoek Beach....................12 B5
Oude Molen Farm Village........13 D2
Philani Nutrition Centre...........14 E3
Ratanga Junction....................15 D2
Sandy Bay Beach....................16 B3
Sivuyile Tourism.....................17 E3
Sleepy Hollow Horse Riding.....18 B4
Two Oceans Crafts and Culture
Centre..................................19 B5
World of Birds........................20 B4

Vicky's.................................25 F3

EATING (pp127–32)
Eziko...................................(see 28)
Fish on the Rocks...................26 B4
Fynbos Food Court.................(see 6)
Gugule Afrika........................(see 3)
Jonkerhuis............................(see 3)
Kirstenbosch Tea Room...........(see 6)
La Colombe..........................(see 6)
Lelapa.................................28 D2
Peddlars on the Bend..............(see 22)
Spaanschemat River Café.........(see 22)

ENTERTAINMENT (pp133–6)
Athlone Stadium.....................29 D2
Club Galaxy..........................30 D3
New Dockside........................(see 15)
West End..............................30 D3

SHOPPING (pp136–8)
Africa Nova...........................31 B4
Canal Walk Shopping Centre.....32 D2

TRANSPORT (pp138–40)
Air Namibia..........................33 E3
British Airways.......................(see 33)
SAA....................................(see 33)
Virgin Atlantic.......................(see 33)

SLEEPING (pp123–7)
Chapman's Peak Hotel.............21 B4
Constantia Uitsig....................22 C4
Hout Bay Manor.....................23 B4
Kopanong.............................24 F3
Lighthouse Farm Lodge...........(see 13)

OTHER
Kenilworth Racecourse............34 D3

CAPE TOWN

HISTORY

Long before the Dutch East India Company (Vereenigde Oost-Indische Compagnie; VOC; see p29) set up a base here in 1652, the Cape Town area was settled by the San and Khoikhoi nomadic tribes, collectively known as the Khoisan. By and large the indigenous people refused to deal with the Dutch so the VOC was forced to import slaves from Madagascar, India, Ceylon, Malaya and Indonesia to deal with the colony's chronic labour shortage. There was also a shortage of women in the colony, so the Europeans exploited the female slaves and the local Khoisan for both labour and sex. In time the slaves also intermixed with the Khoisan. The offspring of these unions formed the basis of sections of today's Coloured population and also helps explain the unique character of the city's Cape Muslim population (also see the boxed text below).

Under the 150-odd years of Dutch rule, Kaapstad, as the Cape settlement became known, thrived and gained a wider reputation as the 'Tavern of the Seas', a riotous port used by every sailor travelling between Europe and the East. But by the end of the 18th century the VOC was practically bankrupt, making Cape Town an easy target for British imperial interests in the region. Following the British defeat of the Dutch in 1806 at Bloubergstrand, 25km north of Cape Town, the colony was ceded to the Crown on 13 August 1814. The slave trade was abolished in 1808, and all slaves were emancipated in 1833.

The discovery and exploitation of diamonds and gold in the centre of South Africa in the 1870s and 1880s led to rapid changes.

Cape Town was soon no longer the single dominant metropolis in the country, but as a major port it too was a beneficiary of the mineral wealth that laid the foundations for an industrial society. The same wealth led to imperialist dreams of grandeur on the part of Cecil John Rhodes (premier of the Cape Colony in 1890), who had made his millions at the head of De Beers Consolidated Mines (see the boxed text on p494).

Bubonic plague in 1901 gave the government an excuse to introduce racial segregation: Africans were moved to two locations, one near the docks and the other at Ndabeni on the western flank of Table Mountain. This was the start of what would later develop into the townships of the Cape Flats.

In 1948 the National Party stood for election on its policy of apartheid and narrowly won. In a series of bitter court and constitutional battles, the limited rights of Blacks and Coloureds to vote in the Cape were removed and the insane apparatus of apartheid was erected. This resulted in whole communities, such as District Six (see p101), being uprooted and cast out to the bleak Cape Flats.

The government tried for decades to eradicate squatter towns, such as Crossroads, which were focal points for Black resistance to the apartheid regime. In its last attempt between May and June 1986, an estimated 70,000 people were driven from their homes and hundreds were killed. Even this brutal attack was unsuccessful in eradicating the towns, and the government accepted the inevitable and began to upgrade conditions.

Hours after being released from prison on 11 February 1990, Nelson Mandela made

---

TUAN GURU

Cape Town's Muslim roots extend back to the slaves brought to Cape Town by the Dutch East India Company (Vereenigde Oost-Indische Compagnie; VOC) from the Indian subcontinent and Indonesia (hence the term Cape Malays, although few of them actually hailed from what is today called Malaysia). One of the most famous of the early Cape Malays was the exiled Islamic leader Tuan Guru from Tidore, who arrived in 1780. During his 13 years on Robben Island Tuan Guru accurately copied the Quran from memory. In 1794 he helped establish the Auwal Mosque, the city's first mosque, in the Bo-Kaap, thus making this area the heart of the Islamic community in Cape Town that it still is today.

Tuan Guru is buried in the Bo-Kaap's Tana Baru cemetery, one of the oldest in South Africa, at the western end of Longmarket St. Within the cemetery (which has fallen into disrepair and is subject to a local preservation campaign) his grave is one of the 20 or so *karamats* (tombs of Muslim saints) encircling Cape Town and visited by the faithful on a minipilgrimage.

his first public speech in decades from the balcony of Cape Town's City Hall, heralding the beginning of a new era for South Africa. Much has improved in Cape Town since – property prices are booming and the city centre is becoming a safer and more pleasant place to shop, work and live, with the development of ritzy loft-style apartments in grand old structures such as the Old Mutual Building and the old Board of Executors building.

Full integration of Cape Town's mixed population, however, remains a long way off, if it's achievable at all. The African National Congress (ANC) and the New National Party (NNP) are working together on the city council which, if ever there was a sign of the times, is headed up by mayor Nomaindia Mfeketo, a Black woman. Meanwhile the vast majority of Capetonians who live in the Cape Flats are still split along race lines and suffering horrendous economic, social and health problems. It is here, in areas such as Mitchell Plains, Langa, Crossroads and Khayelitsha, that Cape Town is having to deal with the AIDS pandemic and violent drug-related crime.

CLIMATE

Weather is not really a critical factor in deciding when to visit Cape Town. Great extremes of temperature are unknown, although it can be relatively cold and wet for a few months in winter (between June and August) when temperatures range from 7° to 18°C. From September to November the weather is unpredictable. December to March can be very hot, although the average maximum temperature is only 26°C and the strong southeasterly wind (known as the Cape Doctor) generally keeps things bearable. From March to April, and to a lesser extent in May, the weather remains good and the wind is at its most gentle.

For hourly updates on the weather check www.weathersa.co.za and for more information also see p572.

LANGUAGE

In the Cape Town area three of South Africa's 11 official languages (all equal under the law) are prominent: Afrikaans (spoken by many Whites and Coloureds), English (spoken by nearly everyone) and Xhosa (spoken mainly by Blacks).

ORIENTATION

Cape Town's commercial centre – known as the City Bowl – lies to the north of Table Mountain and east of Signal Hill. The inner-city suburbs of Tamboerskloof, Gardens and Oranjezicht are all within walking distance of it. Nearby Signal Hill, Green Point and Sea Point are other densely populated seaside suburbs.

The city sprawls quite a distance to the northeast (this is where you'll find the beachside district of Bloubergstrand and the enormous Canal Walk Shopping Centre, but little else of interest to visitors). To the south, skirting the eastern flank of the mountains and running down to Muizenberg at False Bay, are a string of salubrious suburbs including Observatory, Newlands and Constantia.

On the Atlantic coast, exclusive Clifton and Camps Bay are accessible by coastal road from Sea Point or through Kloof Nek, the pass between Table Mountain and Lion's Head. Camps Bay is a 10-minute drive from the city centre and can easily be reached by public transport, but as you go further south, the communities of Llandudno, Hout Bay and Noordhoek are better explored with your own car or bike.

The False Bay towns from Muizenberg to Simon's Town can all be reached by rail and are covered in the Around Cape Town section (p140), along with details on the spectacular Cape of Good Hope Nature Reserve (p144), 70km south of the city centre. You'll also find details here of the communities in the Cape Flats (p145), stretching along the N2 southeast of Table Mountain.

INFORMATION

BOOKSHOPS

The main mass-market bookshop and newsagent is CNA, with numerous shops around the city.

Clarke's Bookshop (Map pp102-3; ☎ 423 5739; www.clarkesbooks.co.za; 211 Long St, City Bowl) Stocks an unsurpassed range of books on South Africa and the continent, and has a great second-hand and antiquarian section.

Exclusive Books Waterfront (Map pp108-9; ☎ 419 0905; Victoria Wharf); Cavendish Sq Mall (Map pp112-13; Claremont); Lifestyles on Kloof (Map p106) Has an excellent range, including some books in French.

Travellers Bookshop (Map pp108-9; ☎ 425 6880; Victoria Wharf, Waterfront)

CAPE TOWN

CAPE TOWN IN...

Two Days

Start with a trip up **Table Mountain** (p100). After admiring the view return to the city and wander through the **Company's Gardens** (p107), nipping into the **South African National Gallery** (p105) to sample the best of the country's art. Get a taste of African cuisine at **Off Moroka Cafe Africaine** (p128), then go souvenir shopping at **Greenmarket Sq** (p136) and along **Long St** (p101).

Kick off day two with a half-day tour of the **Cape Flats townships** (p122). These generally include the **District Six Museum** (p100). Sail out to **Robben Island** (p110) in the afternoon; then hang out at the **Waterfront** (p107) in the evening, maybe taking in a jazz performance at the **Green Dolphin** (p134) or **Manenberg's Jazz Café** (p134).

Four Days

Follow the two-day itinerary and on day three explore the Southern Suburbs starting with a visit to the **Irma Stern Museum** (p115) and then a spot of wine tasting in **Constantia** (p114). An afternoon stroll around **Kirstenbosch Botanical Gardens** (p111) is recommended. You could have afternoon tea here or at the tearoom beside the nearby **Rhodes Memorial** (p115), with its sweeping view across the Cape Flats. Put on your dancing shoes in the evening and head over to the **Waterkant** to dine (p130), drink (p130) and bop (p134) the night away with the gorgeous guys and girls.

On day four explore the communities along False Bay, maybe surfing in **Muizenberg** (p140) or walking down the coast to St James. Have lunch at the **Olympia Café & Deli** (p140) and pick around Kalk Bay's many antique shops. Continue on to **Simon's Town** (p143) and magnificent **Cape Point** (p140). Returning to the city via the Atlantic Coast and **Chapman's Peak Drive** (p111) pause at **Camps Bay** for a sundowner cocktail (p133).

EMERGENCY

In an emergency call ☎ 107 or ☎ 112 if using a mobile phone. Other useful phone numbers:

Ambulance (☎ 10177)
Automobile Association (AA) emergency rescue (☎ 082-16111)
Fire brigade (☎ 535 1100)
Mountain Rescue Services (☎ 948 9900)
Police (☎ 10111)
Rape Crisis Centre (☎ 447 1467)
Sea Rescue (☎ 405 3500)

INTERNET ACCESS

Cape Town is one of the most wired cities in Africa. Most hotels and hostels have Internet facilities and in the city there are several handy Internet cafés, including one at Cape Town Tourism (p99); it charges R15 for the first 15 minutes and R48 per hour. Cheaper and quieter is the National Library (Map pp102–3) in the Company's Gardens which charges R10 per 30 minutes. Internet cafés line Long St and Main Rd at Sea Point (Map pp112–13) where you'll find some of Cape Town's cheapest access rates, as low as R10 per hour. Try **Café Erté** (Map pp112-13;

☎ 434 6624; 265A Main Rd, Sea Point) which is also a gay-friendly bar (also see the boxed text on p135). At the Waterfront, Cape Town Tourism again has Internet access at its office and there's also **Odyssey Internet** (Map pp108-9; ☎ 418 7289) above Cinema Nouveau in the Victoria Wharf shopping mall.

LEFT LUGGAGE

Main train station (Map pp102-3; per bag per day R6; ☒ 8am-3.30pm) Next to Platform 24.

MAPS

Lonely Planet's *Cape Town City Map* includes detailed transport information and a walking tour. Cape Town Tourism (p99) produces a free map that will serve most short-term visitors' needs. If you're staying for more than a week or so, and have a car, consider buying Map Studio's *Cape Town* street directory, available from most bookshops and newsagents (R75).

MEDIA

Cape Town's two newspapers the *Cape Times* (morning) and the *Cape Argus* (afternoon) print practically the same news. The weekly

Mail & Guardian, published Friday, includes excellent investigative and opinion pieces and a good arts review supplement with details of what's going on in Cape Town.

MEDICAL SERVICES

Medical services are of a high standard in Cape Town. Many doctors make house calls; they're listed under 'Medical' in the phone book and hotels and most other places to stay can arrange a visit.

Christiaan Barnard Memorial Hospital (Map pp102-3; ☎ 480 6111; 181 Longmarket St, City Bowl) The best private hospital; reception is on the 8th floor.

Groote Schuur Hospital (Map pp112-13; ☎ 404 9111; Main Rd, Observatory) In an emergency, you can go directly to the casualty department here. As every local will proudly tell you while driving past on the N2, this is where in 1967 the late Dr Christiaan Barnard made the world's first successful heart transplant.

SAA-Netcare Travel Clinic (Map pp102-3; ☎ 419 3172; Room 314, Fountain Medical Centre, Adderley St, City Bowl; ☟ 8am-5pm Mon-Fri, 9am-1pm Sat) For vaccinations and travel health.

MONEY

Money can be changed at the airport, most commercial banks and at Cape Town Tourism (see right). Rennies Travel (right), the local agent for Thomas Cook, has foreign-exchange offices (some of which have been renamed Thomas Cook offices).

There are ATMs all over town; read the boxed text on p574.

Amex City Bowl (Map pp102-3; ☎ 408 9700; Thibault Sq); Waterfront (Map pp108-9; ☎ 419 3917; Waterfront)

POST

Main post office (Map pp102-3; ☎ 464 1700; Parliament St, City Bowl; ☟ 8am-4.30pm Mon-Fri, 8am-noon Sat) Has a poste-restante counter.

TELEPHONE

At phone boxes a phonecard is useful; you can buy one at Cape Town Tourism, newsagents and general stores.

You can rent mobile phones from the Cell C, MTM and Vodacom desks at the airport and buy SIM cards from them for your own phones. Top-up cards for the pay-as-you-go SIM card packages are available all over town. In town, **Cellurent** (☎ 418 5656; www.cellurent.co.za) offers a good deal on rental phones; it will deliver one to you and pick it up from you before you leave.

TOURIST INFORMATION

Cape Town Tourism (www.tourismcapetown.co.za) City Centre (Map pp102-3; ☎ 426 4260; cnr Castle & Burg Sts, City Bowl; ☟ 8am-7pm Mon-Fri, 8.30am-2pm Sat, 9am-1pm Sun Dec-Mar, 8am-6pm Mon-Fri, 8.30am-1pm Sat, 9am-1pm Sun Apr-Nov); Waterfront (Map pp108-9; ☎ 405 4500; Clock Tower Centre, Waterfront; ☟ 9am-9pm) Very impressive and busy facility. Here you'll find advisers who can book accommodation, tours and rental cars. Western Cape Tourism has a desk here, and you can get advice on **Cape Nature Conservation Parks** (☎ 426 0723) and the **National Parks & Reserves** (☎ 423 8005). There's also an adviser for safari and overland tours, an Internet café, a Monkeybiz outlet and a foreign-exchange booth. The Waterfront office is a scaled-down version of the main city-centre office.

TRAVEL AGENCIES

Africa Travel Centre (☎ 423 5555; www.backpackers.co.za; the Backpack, 74 New Church St, Tamboerskloof) Located at the Backpack (see the boxed text on p125), books all sorts of travel and activities, including day trips; hire cars and offers extended truck tours of Africa.

Atlantic Tourist Information Centre (Map pp112-13; ☎ 434 2382; www.capetowntravel.co.za; 242 Main Rd, Three Anchor Bay) Gay-run tour company and travel agent. Also hires out bicycles.

Flight Centre (Map p106; ☎ 461 8658; Gardens Centre, Mill St, Gardens)

Rennies Travel City Bowl (Map pp102-3; ☎ 423 7154; 101 St George's Mall); Sea Point (Map pp112-13; ☎ 439 7529; 182 Main Rd, Sea Point); Waterfront (Map pp108-9; ☎ 418 3744; Victoria Wharf Shopping Centre) Agent for Thomas Cook travellers cheques and handles international and domestic bookings.

STA Travel (Map pp102-3; ☎ 418 6570; 31 Riebeeck St, City Bowl)

Wanderwomen (☎ 082-298 2085; www.wanderwomen.co.za) Female-run travel agent and tour company.

VISA EXTENSIONS

Department of Home Affairs (Map pp102-3; ☎ 462 4970; 56 Barrack St, City Bowl; ☟ 8am-3.15pm Mon-Fri)

DANGERS & ANNOYANCES

Cape Town remains one of the most relaxed cities in Africa, which can instil a false sense of security. People who have travelled overland from Cairo without a single mishap or theft have been known to be cleaned out in Cape Town – generally when doing something stupid like leaving their gear on a beach while they go swimming.

Paranoia is not required but common sense is. There is tremendous poverty on the peninsula and the 'informal redistribution of wealth' is reasonably common. The townships on the Cape Flats have an appalling crime rate and unless you have a trustworthy guide or are on a tour they are off-limits.

Care should be taken in Sea Point and quiet areas of the city centre, such as the Company's Gardens, at night. Walking to or from the Waterfront is not recommended at night either and you should take care during the day, sticking to the main route along the foreshore. The rest of Cape Town is reasonably safe. As always, listen to local advice. There is safety in numbers.

Swimming at all the Cape beaches is potentially hazardous, especially for those inexperienced in surf. Check for warning signs about rips and rocks and only swim in patrolled areas.

The mountains in the middle of the city are no less dangerous just because they are in the city. Weather conditions can change rapidly, so warm clothing, water and a good map and compass are always necessary; see the boxed text on p117.

Another hazard of the mountains is ticks, which can get onto you when you brush past vegetation (see p612).

SIGHTS
Table Mountain National Park
Formerly Cape Peninsula National Park, the newly renamed **Table Mountain National Park** (www.tmnp.co.za), covering some three quarters of the peninsula, stretches from flat-topped Table Mountain to Cape Point. Here we focus on the main attraction – the 1086m-high mountain itself. Most people will take the **cable car** (Map p106; ☎ 424 8181; www.tablemountain.net; adult one way/return R57/110, child R30/58; ⏰ 8.30am-7pm Feb-Nov, 8am-10pm Dec & Jan) up to the summit. The views from the cable car and on the summit are phenomenal. Once you're at the top there are souvenir shops, a café and some easy walks to follow. The cable cars (every 10/20 minutes in high/low season) don't operate when it's dangerously windy, and there's obviously not much point going up if you are simply going to be wrapped in the cloud known as the 'tablecloth'. Call in advance to see if they're operating. The best visibility and conditions are likely to be first thing in the morning or in the evening. For details of climbing the mountain see p117.

If you don't have your own transport, *rikkis* (see p139) will drop you at the cable car from the city centre for R10; a non-shared taxi will cost around R50.

City Bowl
The commercial heart of Cape Town, City Bowl is squeezed between Table Mountain, Signal Hill and the harbour. Immediately to the west is the Bo-Kaap and to the east Zonnebloem (once known as District Six).

DISTRICT SIX MUSEUM
If you see only one museum in Cape Town make it the **District Six Museum** (Map pp102-3; ☎ 461 8745; www.districtsix.co.za; 25A Buitenkant St, City Bowl; adult/child R10/5; ⏰ 9am-3pm Mon-Thu, 9am-4pm Fri). Note that almost all township tours stop here first to explain the history of the pass laws. The museum is as much for the people of the now-vanished District Six as it is about them. The displays are moving and poignant: a floor covered with a large-scale map of District Six, former residents having labelled where their demolished homes and features of their neighbourhood were; reconstructions of home interiors; faded photographs and recordings. Many of the staff, practically all displaced residents themselves, have heartbreaking stories to tell (see the boxed text opposite).

You can also arrange **walking tours** (☎ 466 7208; per person R50, 10 people minimum) of the old District Six.

CASTLE OF GOOD HOPE
Built between 1666 and 1679 to defend Cape Town, this stone-walled **castle** (Map pp102-3; ☎ 787 1200; www.castleofgoodhope.co.za; entrance on Buitenkant St, City Bowl; Mon-Sat adult/child R18/8, Sun R9/4; ⏰ 9am-4pm; tours 11am, noon & 2pm Mon-Sat) is commonly touted as the city's oldest building. It's worth coming for one of the tours (the noon tour on weekdays coincides with the changing of the guard, since the castle is still the headquarters for the Western Cape military command), although you can quite easily find your own way around. A key ceremony at the castle gate – when the keys to the gate are handed over in an orchestrated ceremony – is held at 10am Monday to Friday. There are extensive displays of militaria and some interesting ones on the castle's archaeology and

THE REBIRTH OF DISTRICT SIX

In 1966, the poor, but multiracial and vibrant inner-city area District Six was classified as a White area. Its 50,000 people, some of whose families had been there for five generations, were gradually evicted, and dumped in bleak and soulless townships on the Cape Flats where depressed and dispirited youths increasingly joined gangs and turned to crime. Friends, neighbours and even relations were separated. Such was the controversy of the government's move that even today District Six largely remains an open wasteland. Thankfully, this is beginning to change.

In November 2000 President Thabo Mbeki signed a document handing back the confiscated land to the former residents, and on 11 February 2004, 38 years to the day since it was declared a Whites-only area, keys to the first set of new homes being built here were handed over to 87-year-old Ebrahiem Murat and 82-year-old Dan Mdzabela. It will be impossible for all the 8000 or so forcibly removed families to return (new constructions such as the Cape Technikon college now occupy part of the area), but the District Six Beneficiaries Trust is planning on building 4000 homes in the next few years, repopulating this slice of prime real estate.

the reconstruction of the so-called Dolphin Pool. The highlight is the bulk of the **William Fehr Collection** (☼ 9.30am-4pm), including some fabulous bits of Cape Dutch furniture, such as a table seating 100, and paintings by John Thomas Baines.

HOUSES OF PARLIAMENT

One of the most interesting things you can do in Cape Town is visit the **Houses of Parliament** (Map pp102-3; ☎ 403 2537; www.parliament.gov.za; Parliament St, City Bowl; admission free; tours by appointment Mon-Fri). If parliament is sitting, fix your tour for the afternoon so you can see the politicians in action. Opened in 1885 and enlarged several times since, this is where British Prime Minister Harold Macmillan made his famous 'Wind of Change' speech in 1960. The articulate tour guides will proudly fill you in on the mechanisms and political make-up of their new democracy. You must present your passport to gain entry at the visitors entrance near the corner of Parliament and Roeland Sts.

MICHAELIS COLLECTION & GREENMARKET SQUARE

Donated by Sir Max Michaelis in 1914, the impressive **Michaelis Collection** (Map pp102-3; ☎ 481 3933; www.museums.org.za/iziko; Greenmarket Sq, City Bowl; admission by donation; ☼ 10am-5pm Mon-Fri) is in the Old Townhouse, which used to be the City Hall. The Dutch and Flemish paintings and etchings from the 16th and 17th centuries (including works by Rembrandt, Frans Hals and Anthony Van Dyck) have benefited from the re-cent bright repainting of the once-gloomy house.

While you're here you can also browse the lively souvenir market in cobbled **Greenmarket Sq** (p136) and inspect the striking Art Deco façades of the buildings (see p120) around the square.

LONG ST

The Victorian buildings with their iron lace balconies make **Long St** (Map pp102-3) the most attractive of the City Bowl's streets. Stacked with second-hand book shops, the street is also developing a reputation for its streetwear boutiques, a good complement to the host of bars and clubs that crank up at night. It's difficult to believe, given its hedonistic and utterly commercial (it even has its own website: www.longstreet.co.za) nature, that this was once part of the city's Islamic quarter. Several of the area's old mosques remain, including the **Noor el Hamedia Mosque** (1884) on the corner of Dorp St and the **Palm Tree Mosque** (185 Long St), the last 18th-century house on the street. Another remnant of the past are the **Long St Baths** (p119).

SIGNAL HILL & NOON GUN

Once also known as Lion's Rump, as it is attached to Lion's Head by a 'spine' of hills, **Signal Hill** (Map pp108-9) separates Sea Point from the City Bowl. There are magnificent views from the 350m-high summit, especially at night. Head up Kloof Nek Rd from the city and take the first turn-off to the right at the top of the hill.

CAPE TOWN

CITY BOWL & BO-KAAP

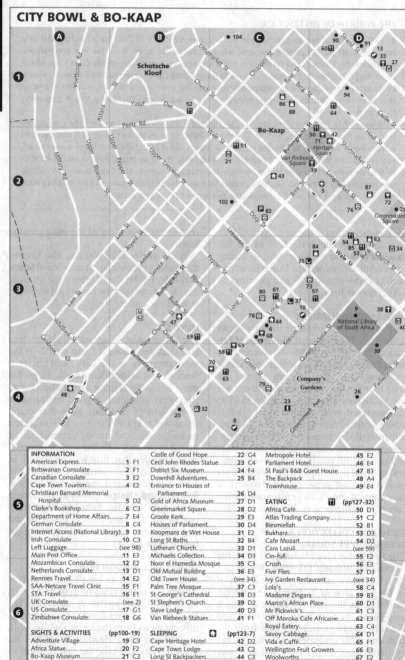

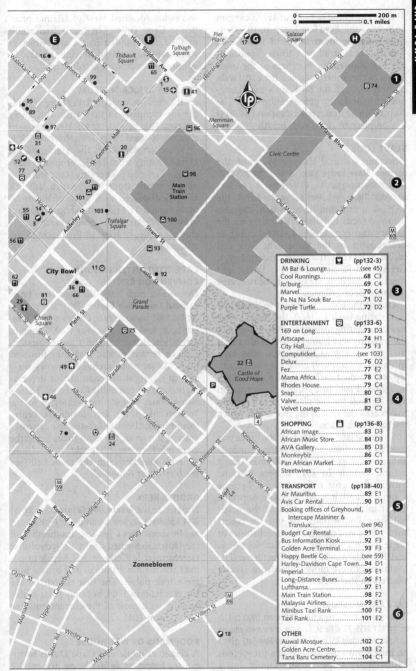

DRINKING (pp132-3)
M Bar & Lounge...................(see 45)
Cool Runnings........................**68** C3
Jo'burg..................................**69** C4
Marvel...................................**70** C4
Pa Na Na Souk Bar..................**71** D2
Purple Turtle.........................**72** D2

ENTERTAINMENT (pp133-6)
169 on Long...........................**73** D3
Artscape...............................**74** H1
City Hall................................**75** F3
Computicket.........................(see 103)
Delux....................................**76** D2
Fez.......................................**77** E2
Mama Africa..........................**78** C3
Rhodes House........................**79** C4
Snap.....................................**80** C3
Valve....................................**81** E3
Velvet Lounge.......................**82** C2

SHOPPING (pp136-8)
African Image.........................**83** D3
African Music Store.................**84** D3
AVA Gallery...........................**85** D3
Monkeybiz.............................**86** C1
Pan African Market..................**87** D2
Streetwires............................**88** C1

TRANSPORT (pp138-40)
Air Mauritius..........................**89** E1
Avis Car Rental.......................**90** D1
Booking offices of Greyhound,
    Intercape Maininer &
    Translux.........................(see 96)
Budget Car Rental...................**91** D1
Bus Information Kiosk..............**92** F3
Golden Acre Terminal..............**93** F3
Happy Beetle Co...................(see 59)
Harley-Davidson Cape Town......**94** D1
Imperial.................................**95** E1
Long-Distance Buses................**96** F1
Lufthansa..............................**97** E1
Main Train Station..................**98** F2
Malaysia Airlines....................**99** E1
Minibus Taxi Rank..................**100** F2
Taxi Rank.............................**101** E2

OTHER
Auwal Mosque.....................**102** C2
Golden Acre Centre...............**103** E2
Tana Baru Cemetery..............**104** C1

At noon Monday to Saturday, a cannon known as the **Noon Gun** (Map pp108–9) is fired from the lower slopes of Signal Hill. You can hear it all over town. Traditionally this allowed the burghers in the town below to check their watches. It's a stiff walk up here through the Bo-Kaap – take Longmarket St and keep going until it ends. The Noon Gun Tearoom & Restaurant (p128) is a good place to catch your breath.

SLAVE LODGE

Once the Cultural History Museum, the former **Slave Lodge** (Map pp102-3; ☎ 460 8240; www.museums.org.za/iziko; 49 Adderley St, City Bowl; adult/child R10/2; ⏰ 8.30am-4.30pm Mon-Sat) of the VOC is a museum in transition, the aim being to focus the displays directly on the history and experience of slaves and their descendants in the Cape. The bits and pieces in its collection from ancient Egypt, Greece and Rome and the Far East might stay here, but if so, are likely to be relegated to upper-floor galleries.

One of the oldest buildings in South Africa, dating back to 1660, the Slave Lodge has a fascinating history in itself. Until 1811 the building was home, if you could call it that, to as many as 1000 slaves, who lived in damp, unsanitary, crowded conditions. Up to 20% died each year. The slaves were bought and sold just around the corner on Spin St; look for the plaque in the ground that marks the spot of the tree under which the sales took place.

From the late-18th century the lodge was used as a brothel, a jail for petty criminals and political exiles from Indonesia, and a mental asylum. In 1811 it became Cape Town's first post office. Later it became a library, and it was the Cape Supreme Court until 1914. The walls of the original Slave Lodge flank the interior courtyard where you can find the tombstones of Cape Town's founder, Jan Van Riebeeck, and his wife Maria De La Queillerie. The tombstones were moved here from Jakarta where Van Riebeeck is buried.

BO-KAAP MUSEUM

This small but engaging **museum** (Map pp102-3; ☎ 481 3939; 71 Wale St, Bo-Kaap; www.museums.org.za/iziko; adult/child R5/2; ⏰ 9am-4pm Mon-Sat) gives an insight into the lifestyle of a prosperous 19th-century Cape Muslim family and a somewhat idealised view of Islamic practice in Cape Town. The house itself, built in 1763, is the oldest in the area which is worth strolling around (during the day) to admire the traditional architecture.

GOLD OF AFRICA MUSEUM

Established by Anglogold, the biggest gold-mining company in the world, this glitzy **museum** (Map pp102-3; ☎ 405 1540; www.goldofafrica.com; 96 Strand St, City Bowl; adult/child R20/10; ⏰ 9.30am-5pm Mon-Sat), in the Martin Melck House (dating from 1783), promotes African gold jewellery. There are some stunning pieces, mostly from West Africa, and it's all well displayed with a lot of historical background. The museum shop is worth a browse for interesting gold souvenirs, including copies of some of the pieces in the museum.

CAPE TOWN INTERNATIONAL CONVENTION CENTRE

Opened in mid-2003, the **Cape Town International Convention Centre** (CTICC; Map pp108-9; ☎ 410 5000; www.cticc.co.za; Convention Sq, 1 Lower Long St, City Bowl) provides over 10,000 sq m of exhibition space, a major theatre, modern African restaurant and a swanky business hotel. As far as its architecture goes it's a step in the right direction at this depressingly concrete end of the City Bowl. There's also a water-taxi station linking it to the Waterfront (p140). Step inside the centre to admire the bold and distinctive artworks gracing the foyer, the main focus being the giant relief sculpture *Baobabs, Stormclouds, Animals and People* in the main hall (see the boxed text opposite).

GROOTE KERK

Nip inside the **Groote Kerk** (Map pp102-3; ☎ 461 7044; Adderley St, City Bowl; admission free; ⏰ 10am-2pm Mon-Fri; services 10am & 7pm Sun), mothership of the Dutch Reformed Church (Nederduitse Gereformeerde Kerk, or NG Kerk), to admire the mammoth organ and ornate Burmese teak pulpit. The first church on the site was built in 1704, but only parts of this remain, with most of the current building dating from 1841.

KOOPMANS DE WET HOUSE

A classic example of a Cape Dutch townhouse, **Koopmans de Wet House** (Map pp102-3;

BRETT MURRAY

When Brett Murray's iconoclastic statue *Africa* (Map pp102–3) was placed in St George's Mall in 2000, Cape Town was fairly split between those who thought it fantastic and those who wondered what the hell it was. The giant African fetish object with a rash of Bart Simpson heads popping out. It still turns heads today and the artist's work has become so popular and prevalent around the city that it's almost as if Cape Town has caught the Brett Murray bug.

Murray's best known works are his 'Boogie Lights' series, which can be bought at various shops around the city including African Image (p137). There are also pieces by Murray in the South African National Gallery (p105), but to date his most significant work is the 6.5-tonne artwork *Baobabs, Stormclouds, Animals and People* that hangs at the Cape Town International Convention Centre (p100). This collaboration with the late San artist Tuoi Steffaans Samcuia of the !Xun and Khwe San Art and Cultural Project is astonishing in its scale and design – huge steel figures, animals and trees standing out against the maple wall panels.

☎ 464 3280; www.museums.org.za/iziko; 35 Strand St, City Bowl; adult/child R5/2; ☾ Mon only by appointment) is furnished with 18th- and early-19th-century antiques. It's an atmospheric place with ancient vines growing in the courtyard and floorboards that squeak just as they probably did during the times of Marie Koopmans de Wet, the socialite owner after whom the house is named.

LUTHERAN CHURCH

Converted from a barn in 1780, the first **Lutheran Church** (Map pp102–3; ☎ 421 5854; 98 Strand St, City Bowl; admission free; ☾ 10am-2pm Mon-Fri) in the Cape has a striking pulpit, perhaps the best created by the master German sculptor Anton Anreith, whose work can also be seen in Groote Kerk (p100) and at Groot Constantia (p111).

Gardens & Around   Map p106

Rising up Table Mountain's slopes are the ritzy suburbs of Gardens, Tamboerskloof, Oranjezicht and Vredehoek. Most of the major sights here are clustered around the Company's Gardens, which can also be approached from the City Bowl.

SOUTH AFRICAN NATIONAL GALLERY

There are always fascinating temporary exhibitions at this **gallery** (☎ 467 4660; www.museums.org.za/iziko; Government Ave, Gardens; adult/child R10/2, Sun free; ☾ 10am-5pm Tue-Sun), as well as permanent displays, including the wonderful sculpture of the *Butcher Boys* by Jane Alexander, looking like a trio of *Lord of the Rings* orcs who have stumbled into the gallery. Also check out the remarkable carved teak door in the courtyard, and a dinosaur

sculpture made from wire. There's a pleasant café and a good shop with some interesting books.

SOUTH AFRICAN MUSEUM & PLANETARIUM

At the time of research this **museum** (☎ 424 3330; www.museums.org.za/iziko; 25 Queen Victoria St, Gardens; adult/child R8/2, free Sun; ☾ 10am-5pm) was undergoing a major reorganisation of its collection. The first stage has largely been completed with a new Rock Art gallery showcasing the art and culture of the area's first peoples, the Khoi and San, and including the famous Linton Panel, an amazing example of San rock art.

Throughout the rest of the building there is a truly compelling collection of objects. Look out for the startlingly lifelike displays in the African Cultures Gallery of African people (which were cast from living subjects); the terracotta Lydenburg Heads, the earliest known examples of African sculpture (AD 500–700); the Whale Well, which is hung with giant skeletons of these mammals and is sometimes used as a venue for concerts; and the 2m-wide nest of the sociable weaver bird, a veritable avian apartment block. Attached to the museum is the **planetarium** (☎ 424 3330; www.museums.org.za/iziko; 25 Queen Victoria St, Gardens; adult/child R10/6; ☾ 10am-5pm). The displays and star shows here unravel the mysteries of the southern hemisphere's night sky. Shows are given on Tuesday (R20; 8pm including a 3D star show, and 2pm), Thursday (2pm) and Saturday (2.30pm). There are more frequent shows during school holidays.

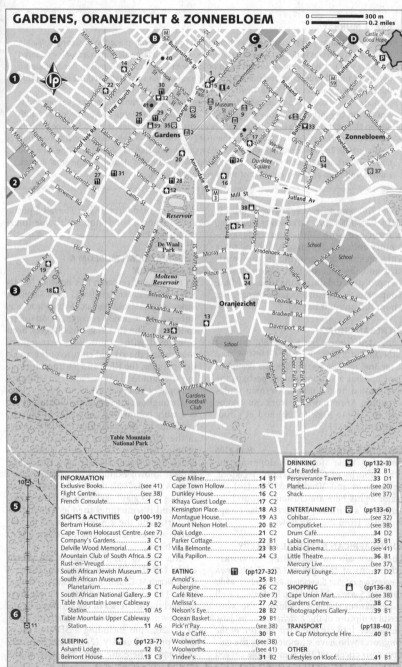

GARDENS, ORANJEZICHT & ZONNEBLOEM

SOUTH AFRICAN JEWISH MUSEUM & CAPE TOWN HOLOCAUST CENTRE

The **South African Jewish Museum** (☎ 465 1546; www.sajewishmuseum.co.za; 88 Hatfield St, Gardens; adult/ child R50/25; ☷ 10am-5pm Sun-Thu, 10am-2pm Fri) is one of the most imaginatively designed and interesting of the city's museums. Entry is through the beautifully restored **Old Synagogue** (1862), from where a wooden gangplank leads to state-of-the-art galleries with displays on the vibrant history of the nation's Jewish community, which today numbers around 90,000.

It's possible also to visit the beautifully decorated baroque **Great Synagogue** (guided tours 10am-2pm Mon-Thu, 10am-4pm Sun). The Gardens Shul, as it was known, was consecrated the same year that Cape Town elected its first Jewish mayor, Hyman Liberman.

In the same complex of buildings you also find the **Cape Town Holocaust Centre** (☎ 462 5553; www.museums.org.za/ctholocaust; 88 Hatfield St, Gardens; admission free; ☷ 10am-5pm Sun-Thu, 10am-1pm Fri). Although small, the centre packs a lot in with a considerable emotional punch. The history of anti-Semitism is set in a South African context with parallels drawn to the local struggle for freedom. Stop to watch the video tales of Holocaust survivors at the end.

COMPANY'S GARDENS

A lovely place to escape the bustle of the city are the **Company's Gardens**, what remains of Van Riebeeck's original 18-hectare vegetable garden. The main gates are at the south end of Adderley St next to St George's Cathedral and on Annandale Rd in Gardens. They once provided fresh produce for the VOC's ships, but as sources of supply were diversified, the grounds became a superb pleasure garden planted with a fine collection of botanical species from South Africa and the rest of the world. As pleasant as the grounds are, there are occasional reports of muggings (security has apparently been beefed up in response).

You'll pass through the Gardens on the way to the South African Museum (p105) and South African National Gallery (p105). Keep an eye out for statues designed by Sir Herbert Baker (p411) including the Delville Wood Memorial, honouring South African soldiers who fell during WWI, and the statue of Cecil Rhodes, hand held high and pointing north in his vainglorious imperialist dream of an empire from the Cape to Cairo.

RUST-EN-VREUGD

The delightful 18th-century mansion **Rust-en-Vreugd** (☎ 464 3280; www.museums.org.za/iziko; 78 Buitenkant St, City Bowl; ☷ Mon only by appointment) was once the home of the state prosecutor. It now houses part of the William Fehr collection of paintings and furniture (the major part is in the Castle of Good Hope, p100). Paintings by John Thomas Baines show early scenes from colonial Cape Town, while the sketches of Cape Dutch architecture by Alys Fane Trotter are some of the best you'll see. There's also a pleasant garden.

BERTRAM HOUSE

A minor diversion if you're at this end of the Company's Gardens is a visit to **Bertram House** (☎ 424 9381; www.museums.org.za/iziko; cnr Orange St & Government Ave, Gardens; ☷ Mon only by appointment), the only surviving Georgian-style brick house in Cape Town, dating from the 1840s. Inside it's decorated appropriately to its era with Regency-style furnishings and 19th-century English porcelain.

Green Point, Waterkant & Waterfront   Map pp108–9

Cape Town's prime Atlantic Coast suburbs start at the Waterfront. Near here you'll also find Green Point, inside of which is the trendy enclave of Waterkant.

VICTORIA & ALBERT WATERFRONT

Commonly referred to as just the Waterfront, this is one of Cape Town's most successful tourist areas with masses of shops, restaurants, bars, cinemas and other attractions, including cruises of the harbour (p116). Much of the Waterfront's charm derives from the fact that it remains a working harbour. Most of the redevelopment has been undertaken around the historic Alfred and Victoria Basins (constructed from 1860 and named after Queen Victoria and her son Alfred). Although these wharves are too small for modern container vessels and tankers, the Victoria Basin is still used by tugs, harbour vessels of various kinds and fishing boats. The new development around the pretty Clock Tower and the Nelson Mandela Gateway departure point

GREEN POINT, WATERKANT & WATERFRONT

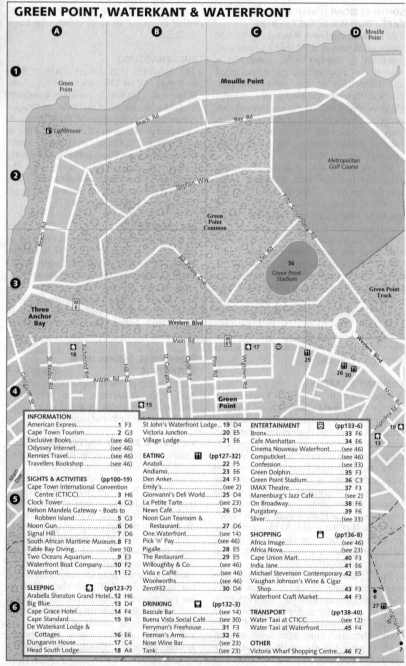

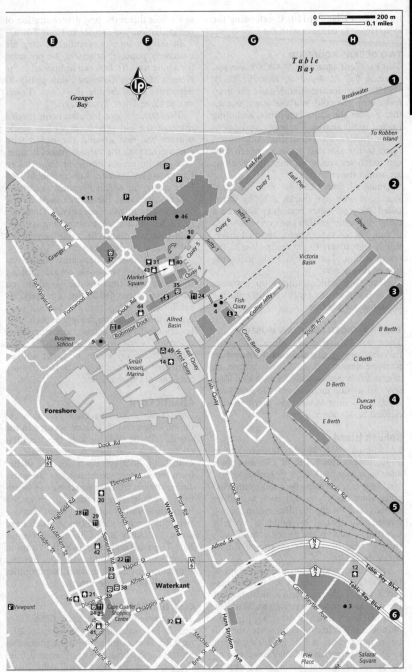

for Robben Island (p110) is extending the Waterfront to connect with the City Bowl.

TWO OCEANS AQUARIUM

This excellent **aquarium** (☎ 418 3823; www.aquarium.co.za; Dock Rd, Waterfront; adult/child R55/25; ⊙ 9.30am-6pm) features denizens of the deep from both the cold and the warm oceans that border the Cape Peninsula, including ragged tooth sharks. There are seals, penguins, turtles, an astounding kelp forest open to the sky and pools in which kids can touch sea creatures; these things alone are worth the entry fee.

Qualified divers can get into the tank; sharing it with five sharks, a 150kg short-tailed stingray, other predatory fish and a delightful turtle wouldn't be everyone's idea of fun, but for experienced, certified divers this is a great way to get really close to the ocean action. The cost is R400 including hire of diving gear.

Have your hand stamped on entrance and you can return again any time during the same day for free.

SOUTH AFRICAN MARITIME MUSEUM

There are lots of model ships and some full-sized ones at this marginally interesting **maritime museum** (☎ 405 2880; www.museums.org.za/iziko; Dock Rd, Waterfront; adult/child R10/3; ⊙ 10am-5pm). Admission includes entry to SAS *Somerset*, a wartime vessel now permanently docked beside the museum.

Robben Island

Proclaimed a UN World Heritage Site in 1999, **Robben Island** (☎ 419 4200; www.robben-island.org.za; adult/child R150/75; ⊙ hourly ferries 8am-3pm, sunset tours 5pm & 6pm Dec & Jan) is unmissable. Most likely you will have to endure crowds and being hustled around on a guided tour that at 2½ hours is woefully too short – such is the price of the island's infamy. Still, you must go to see this, a shrine to struggle.

Used as a prison from the early days of the VOC up until the first years of majority rule, Robben Island's most famous involuntary resident was Nelson Mandela. You will learn much of what happened to Mandela and other inmates, since one will be leading your tour. The guides are happy to answer questions you may have, and although some understandably remain bitter,

as a whole this is the best demonstration of reconciliation you can see in Cape Town.

Booking a tour is essential as they are extremely popular; otherwise be prepared for a long wait. Tickets can be booked at the Nelson Mandela Gateway (Map pp108-9) departure point beside the Clock Tower and at Cape Town Tourism (p99).

The standard tour includes being guided through the old prison, as well as a 45-minute bus ride around the island with commentary on the various places of note, such as the prison house of Pan-African Congress (PAC) leader Robert Sobuke, the lime quarry in which Mandela and many others slaved and the church used during the island's stint as a leper colony. There will be a little time for you to wander around on your own; you could check out the penguin colony near the landing jetty.

All tours have set departure and return times, but when you book, consider asking to extend your time on the island so you have time to see **Cell Stories**, a remarkable exhibition in the prison's A Section (and not on the regular tour). Here in each of 40 isolation cells is an artefact and story from a former political prisoner, such as chess pieces drawn on scraps of paper and an intricately patterned belt made from fishing nets and old shoe leather.

Atlantic Coast

Cape Town's Atlantic coast has some of the most spectacular coastal scenery in the world. The beaches include the trendiest on the Cape, and there is an emphasis on sunbaking. Although it's possible to shelter from the summer southeasterlies, the water comes straight from the Antarctic and swimming is exhilarating (ie freezing). From Sea Point (best visited for its excellent outdoor swimming pools; see p119), you can head down to Bantry Bay, Clifton and Camps Bay. The road continues over the rump of mountains past Llandudno to Hout Bay and continues through the small communities of Noordhoek and Kommetjie.

CLIFTON BEACHES

There are four linked beaches at **Clifton** (Map pp112-13), accessible by steps from Victoria Rd. They might be the trendiest beaches on the Cape, almost always sheltered from the wind, but the water is still cold. If you care about these things, Nos 1 and 2 beaches are for models and confirmed narcissists, No 3 is the gay beach, and No 4 is for families. Although vendors hawk drinks and ice creams along the beach, there are no shops down here, so bring your own food if you're out for a day of sunbaking.

CAMPS BAY BEACH

With the spectacular, giant buttresses of Table Mountain's Twelve Apostles as a backdrop, and soft white sand, **Camps Bay** (Map pp112–13) has one of the most beautiful beaches in the world. That it is within 15 minutes of the city centre also makes it very popular, particularly on weekends. The beach is often windy and the water is decidedly on the cool side. There are no life-savers and the surf is strong, so take care if you do swim. The strip of smart bars (p133) and restaurants (p131) here are very popular places for drinks at sunset or just general all-day lounging.

LLANDUDNO & SANDY BAY BEACHES

The surfing at **Llandudno** (Map pp94–5) on the beach breaks (mostly rights) is best at high tide with a small swell and a southeasterly wind. Nearby is **Sandy Bay** (Map pp94–5), Cape Town's nudist beach and gay stamping ground. It's a particularly beautiful stretch of sand and there's no pressure to take your clothes off if you don't want to. Like many such beaches, Sandy Bay has no direct access roads. From the M6, turn towards Llandudno, keep to the left at forks, and head towards the sea until you reach the Sunset Rocks parking area. The beach is roughly a 15-minute walk to the south. Waves here are best at low tide, with a southeasterly wind.

CHAPMAN'S PEAK DRIVE

After R150 million of safety work **Chapman's Peak Dr** (Map pp94–5) reopened to mixed reviews in 2003. Environmentalists were up in arms about what had been done to ensure that the dangerous rock slides that had closed the road in the first place wouldn't be a problem in the future. Plus there was the issue of the toll booths and the R20 toll that everyone now needs to pay to travel along this 5km road linking Hout Bay with Noordhoek. It remains, however, one of the most spectacular stretches of coastal road in the world and a thrilling drive.

WORLD OF BIRDS

Kids and bird fanciers will appreciate this **aviary** (Map pp94–5; ☎ 790 2730; www.worldofbirds .org.za; Valley Rd, Hout Bay; adult/child R40/28; 🕑 9am-5pm), South Africa's largest, with over 330 species of birds. A great effort has been made to make the aviaries large and natural with lots of tropical landscaping.

TWO OCEANS CRAFTS AND CULTURE CENTRE

On the road towards Kommetjie from Fish Hoek, beside the township of Masiphumelele, is the cheerful and creative **Two Oceans Craft and Culture Centre** (Map pp94–5; ☎ 785 3495; cnr Kommetjie & Chasmay Rds, Sun Valley) where you can buy excellent crafts made at a local training centre, such as the Bambanani bowls circled by figures holding hands. There's also the Sonwabile restaurant serving Xhosa food, and the Chakalaka jazz performances on the first Sunday of the month. See p122 for details of a walking tour starting from here.

NOORDHOEK BEACH

This magnificent 5km stretch of sand (Map pp108–9) is favoured by surfers and horse riders. It tends to be windy and dangerous for swimmers. The **Hoek**, as it is known to surfers, is an excellent right beach break at the northern end that can hold large waves (only at low tide); it's best with a southeasterly wind.

Southern Suburbs

Heading west around Table Mountain and Devil's Peak will bring you to the Southern Suburbs, beginning with the bohemian, edgy areas of Woodstock and Observatory and moving through to the increasingly more salubrious suburbs of Rondebosch, Newlands and Constantia, home to South Africa's oldest vineyards and wine estates.

KIRSTENBOSCH BOTANICAL GARDENS

Among the most beautiful gardens in the world, Cape Town's **botanical gardens** (Map pp94–5; ☎ 762 9120; www.nbi.ac.za; Rhodes Dr, Bishopscourt; adult/child R20/5; 🕑 8am-7pm Sep-Mar, 8am-6pm Apr-Aug) have an incomparable site on the eastern side of Table Mountain, overlooking False Bay and the Cape Flats. The 36-hectare landscaped section seems to merge almost imperceptibly with the 492 hectares of *fynbos* (fine bush) vegetation cloaking the mountain slopes.

CAPE TOWN, ATLANTIC COAST & SOUTHERN SUBURBS

INFORMATION
Atlantic Tourist Information Centre..**1** D2
Exclusive Books.......................(see 57)
Groot Schuur Hospital....................**2** G4
Rennies Travel.........................(see 56)

SIGHTS & ACTIVITIES   (pp100–19)
Camps Bay Beach..........................**3** C4
City Rock..................................**4** H3
Clifton Beaches..........................**5** C3
Graaff's Pool.............................**6** C2
Groote Schuur.............................**7** G5
Irma Stern Museum........................**8** H4
Lion's Head...............................**9** C3
Milton's Pool............................**10** C2
Mostert's Mill...........................**11** H4
Pro Divers...............................**12** D2
Rhodes Memorial.........................**13** G4
Riverclub................................**14** H3
Sanctuary Spa............................**15** B5
Sea Point Pavillion......................**16** C2
Transplant Museum......................(see 2)
University of Cape Town..................**17** G5
Woolsack.................................**18** G5

SLEEPING 🛏   (pp123–7)
Bay Hotel...............................**19** C4
Green Elelphant.........................**20** G3
Huijs Haerlem...........................**21** D2
Lion's Head Lodge & Aardvark
   Backpackers..........................**22** C2
Olaf's Guest House......................**23** C2
Planet Africa...........................**24** C2
Primi Royal.............................**25** C5
Stans Halt Youth Hostel.................**26** C4
Villa Rosa..............................**27** C2
Vineyard Hotel..........................**28** G6
Winchester Mansions Hotel...........**29** C2

EATING 🍴   (pp127–32)
Ari's Souvlaki..........................**30** C2
Blues...................................**31** C4
Buzbey Grill............................**32** D1
Café Ganesh.............................**33** H4
Diva....................................**34** H4
Gardener's Cottage....................(see 53)
La Perla................................**35** C2
New York Bagels........................**36** C2
Pick 'n' Pay..........................(see 31)
Rhodes Memorial Restaurant.......(see 13)
Sandbar.................................**37** C4
Woolworths............................(see 57)

DRINKING 🍷   (p132–3)
A Touch of Madness......................**38** H4
Bazara...............................(see 31)
Café Carte Blanche......................**39** H4
Cool Runnings...........................**40** H3
Eclipse.................................**41** C4
Forester's Arms.........................**42** G6
La Med..................................**43** B4

ENTERTAINMENT 🎭   (pp133–6)
Baxter Theatre..........................**44** H5
Café Erté...............................**45** D2
Cape Comedy Collective..................**46** H5
Cavendish Nouveau....................(see 57)
Computicket...........................(see 56)
Dizzy Jazz..............................**47** C5
Independent Armchair Theatre........**48** H4
Newlands Cricket Ground.................**49** H6
Newlands Ruby Stadium...................**50** H6
Royal Cape Yacht Club...................**51** F2

SHOPPING 🛍   (pp136–8)
Mnandi Textiles & Design................**52** H3
Montebello..............................**53** G6
Young Designers Emporium...........(see 57)

ATLANTIC
OCEAN

Three
Anchor
Bay

Green
Point
Lighthouse   Beach Rd
Mouille Point

Western Blvd

**Green
Point**

Rocklands
Beach

Rocklands
Bay

High Level Rd
**Three
Anchor
Bay**

Signal
Hill
(350m)

**Schotsche
Kloof**

Tamboerskloof

Boat
Bay

**Sea
Point**

Queens
Beach

Sea Point

Beach Rd

Fresnaye

Saunders
Rocks

**Bantry
Bay**

Kloof Nek Rd

Kloof St

Gardens

**Clifton
Bay**

Victoria Rd

Clifton

Kloof Rd

Kloof Nek

Glen Country
Club

Diep

River

**Camps
Bay**

Victoria Rd

Camps Bay

**Bakoven
Bay**

Bakoven

Camps Bay Dve

**Table
Mountain
(1073m)**

**Table Mountain
National Park**

Kasteelpoort

Rontree

River

Oudekraal

Victoria Rd

Twelve
Apostles

Hely-
Hutchinson
Reservoir
Woodhead

Victoria
Reservoir

Dommisse
Hut

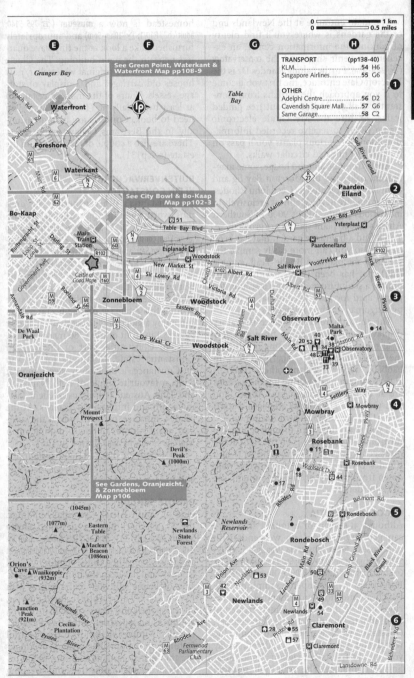

See Green Point, Waterkant &
Waterfront Map pp108-9

See City Bowl & Bo-Kaap
Map pp102-3

See Gardens, Oranjezicht,
& Zonnebloem
Map p106

The main entrance at the Newlands end of the gardens is where you'll find plenty of parking, the information centre, an excellent souvenir shop and the **conservatory** (☺ 9am-5pm). Further along Rhodes Dr is the Ryecroft Gate entrance, the first you'll come to if you approach the gardens from Constantia. Call to find out about free guided walks, or hire the My Guide electronic gizmo (R25) to receive recorded information about the various plants you'll pass on the three signposted circular walks.

Apart from the almond hedge, some magnificent oaks, and the Moreton Bay fig and camphor trees planted by Cecil John Rhodes, the gardens are devoted almost exclusively to indigenous plants. About 9000 of Southern Africa's 22,000 plant species are grown here. You'll find a fragrance garden that has been elevated so you can more easily sample the scents of the plants, a Braille Trail, a kopje (hill) that has been planted with pelargoniums, a sculpture garden and a section for plants used for *muti* (traditional medicine) by sangomas (traditional healers).

The atmosphere-controlled conservatory displays plant communities from a variety of terrains, the most interesting of which is the Namaqualand and Kalahari section, with baobabs, quiver trees and others. There is always something flowering but the gardens are at their best between mid-August and mid-October. The **Sunday afternoon concerts** (see p123) are a Cape Town institution.

If you're driving from the city centre, the turn-off to the gardens is on the right at the intersection of Union Ave (the M3) and Rhodes Dr (the M63). Alternatively, walk down from the top of Table Mountain; see p117 for details.

GROOT CONSTANTIA

Although it's a bit of a tourist trap (and can get very crowded on weekends with tour buses), **Groot Constantia** (Map pp94-5; ☎ 794 5128; www.grootconstantia.co.za; Groot Constantia Rd, High Constantia; tastings incl glass R20; ☺ 10am-6pm Dec-Apr, 10am-5pm May-Nov) is a superb example of Cape Dutch architecture and embodies the gracious lifestyle the wealthy Dutch created in their adopted country. In the 18th century, Constantia wines were exported around the world and were highly acclaimed; today you should try its Sauvignon Blanc, Riesling and pinotage. The beautifully restored

homestead is now a **museum** (☎ 795 5140; adult/child R10/1; ☺ 10am-5pm) and appropriately furnished; take a look at the tiny slave quarters beneath the main building. The Cloete Cellar, the estate's original wine cellar, now houses old carriages and a display of storage vessels. Tours of the modern cellar run at least twice daily at 11am and 3pm; you need to book. Concerts are held occasionally in the Bertrams Cellar tasting room. There are also a couple of restaurants on the estate (see p131).

BUITENVERWACHTING & KLEIN CONSTANTIA

Of Constantia's other wineries, the ones most worthwhile visiting are **Buitenverwachting** (Map pp94-5; ☎ 794 5190; www.buitenverwachting.co.za; Klein Constantia Rd; tastings free; ☺ 9am-5pm Mon-Fri, 9am-1pm Sat) and **Klein Constantia** (Map pp94-5; ☎ 794 5188; www.kleinconstantia.com; Klein Constantia Rd; tastings free; ☺ 9am-5pm Mon-Fri, 9am-1pm Sat). Buitenverwachting means 'beyond expectations' – certainly the feeling one gets on visiting this estate set on 100 hectares. You can enjoy a **picnic lunch** (bookings ☎ 794 1012; per person R85) in front of the 1786 manor house.

Klein Constantia, part of the original Constantia estate, is famous for its Vin de Constance, a deliciously sweet muscat wine, a favourite tipple of both Napoleon and Jane Austen. It has an excellent tasting room and informative displays. At the estate's entrance, pause to look at the *karamat* (saint's tomb) of Sheik Abdurachman Matebe Shah; he was buried in 1661.

For details of the hotel and restaurants at the Constantia Uitsig winery, see p127 and p131.

GROOTE SCHUUR

One of South Africa's seminal buildings, the Sir Herbert Baker–redesigned **Groote Schuur** (Map pp112-13; ☎ 686 9100; Groote Schuur Estate, Klipper Rd; admission R50; ☺ tours by appointment only) was bequeathed to the nation by Cecil Rhodes, and has been the home of a succession of Prime Ministers culminating with FW de Klerk. The recently restored interior, all teak panels and heavy colonial furniture, antiques and tapestries of the finest calibre, is suitably imposing. But its most beautiful feature is the colonnaded veranda overlooking the formal gardens slopping uphill towards an avenue of pine trees and sweeping views of Devil's Peak. The tour includes tea on this veranda. You must bring your passport to gain entry to this high security area; the entrance is unmarked but easily spotted on the left as you take the Princess Anne Ave exit off the M3.

RHODES MEMORIAL

In 1895 Cecil John Rhodes purchased the eastern slopes of Table Mountain for £9000 as part of a plan to preserve a relatively untouched section. After his death an impressive granite **memorial** (Map pp112–13) to Rhodes was constructed here, commanding a view of the Cape Flats and the mountain ranges beyond – and by implication, right into the heart of Africa. Despite the classical proportions of the memorial and the eight large bronze lions, Rhodes looks rather grumpy. Behind the memorial there's a pleasant tearoom (p131) in an old stone cottage nearby. The exit for the memorial is at the Princess Anne Interchange on the M3.

IRMA STERN MUSEUM

The most enjoyable **museum** (Map pp112-13; ☎ 685 5686; www.irmastern.co.za; Cecil Rd, Rosebank; adult/child R8/4; ☼ 10am-5pm Tue-Sat) of the Southern Suburb's, the pioneering 20th-century artist Irma Stern (1894–1966) lived in this charming house for 38 years and her studio has been left intact, as if she'd just stepped out into the verdant garden for some fresh air. Her ethnographic art and craft collection from around the world is as fascinating as her own expressionist art, which has been compared to Gauguin's. To reach the museum from Rosebank station walk a few minutes west to Main Rd, cross over and walk up Chapel St.

TRANSPLANT MUSEUM

This **museum** (Map pp112-13; ☎ 404 5232; www.gsh .co.za; Groote Schuur Hospital, Observatory; adult/child R5/3; ☼ 9am-1.45pm Mon-Fri) details the history of the world's first heart transplant in the very theatre in which it all happened in 1967. The displays have a fascinating Dr Kildare quality to them, especially given the heart-throb status of Dr Christiaan Barnard at the time. To reach the hospital from Observatory station, walk west along Station Rd for about 10 minutes. If you're driving from the city, take the Eastern Boulevard (N2), turn off at Browning Rd, and then turn right on Main Rd.

OUDE MOLEN FARM VILLAGE

Located in the once-abandoned buildings and grounds of part of the Valkenberg mental hospital, this **farm village** (Map pp94-5; Alexandra Rd, Mowbray) includes the only organic farm within Cape Town's city limits. You can volunteer to work here through the Willing Workers on Organic Farms scheme (www .wwoof.org) as well as stay at a backpackers lodge (p127). A horse trail leads from here, through the mental hospital grounds and Observatory up to Devil's Peak; for details of how to arrange rides see p118.

UNIVERSITY OF CAPE TOWN

For the nonacademic there is no real reason to visit the **University of Cape Town** (UCT; Map pp112–13), but it is an impressive place to walk around, with ivy-covered neoclassical façades, and a fine set of stone steps leading up to the temple-like Jameson building. Check out Smuts and Fuller Halls halfway up the steps. Visitors can usually get parking permits at the university – call at the information office on the entry road, near the bottom of the steps.

As you're following the M3 from the city, just after the open paddocks on Devil's Peak, you'll pass the old **Mostert's Mill** a real Dutch windmill dating from 1796, on the left. Just past the old windmill, also on the left, is the exit for the university. To get there, turn right at the T-intersection after you've taken the exit.

Alternatively, if you approach UCT from Woolsack Dr, you'll pass the **Woolsack**, a cottage designed in 1900 by Sir Herbert Baker for Cecil Rhodes. The cottage was the winter residence of Rudyard Kipling from 1900 to 1907 and it's said he wrote the poem *If* here.

ACTIVITIES

Cape Town offers a raft of activities that together constitute an outdoor-thrillseeker's charter.

Abseiling

Abseil Africa (☎ 424 4760; www.abseilafrica.co.za; R295) offers a 112m drop off the top off Table Mountain. Don't even think of tackling this unless you've got a head (and a stomach) for heights; this shimmy down a rope will give you a huge adrenaline rush. Take your time, because the views are breathtaking.

Bookings can also be made through **Adventure Village** (Map pp102-3; ☎ 424 1580; 229B Long St, City Bowl).

Amusement Park

The big African-themed amusement park, **Ratanga Junction** (Map pp94-5; ☎ 550 8504; www .ratanga.co.za; Century City, Milnerton; adult/child incl rides R90/45; ⏰ 10am-5pm Wed-Fri & Sun, 10am-6pm Sat) is next to Canal Walk Shopping Centre, around 5km north of the city centre along the N1. It's only open from the end of November to the beginning of May. For a 90-second adrenaline rush the 100km/h Cobra rollercoaster is recommended.

Cruises

DUIKER ISLAND CRUISES

From Hout Bay's harbour (Map pp94-5) you can catch regular daily cruises to Duiker Island, also known as Seal Island because of its colony of Cape fur seals. Three companies run these cruises daily, usually with guaranteed sailings in the mornings. The cheapest, with a none-too-spectacular glass-bottom boat, is **Circe Launches** (☎ 790 1040; www .circelaunches; adult/child R30/10); the others are **Drumbeat Charters** (☎ 791 4441; adult/child R45/20) and **Nauticat Charters** (☎ 790 7278; www.nauticat charters.co.za; adult/child R50/20). All are based at the harbour.

HARBOUR CRUISES

A cruise into Table Bay should not be missed. **Waterfront Boat Company** (Map pp108-9; ☎ 418 5806; www.waterfrontboats.co.za; Shop 7, Quay 5, Waterfront) offers a variety of cruises, including the highly recommended 1½-hour sunset cruises (R170) on its fabulous wood- and brass-fitted schooners *Spirit of Victoria* and *Esperance*. A jet-boat ride is R250 per hour.

Cycling

Also see the listing for **Day Trippers** (p121); some of its tours include cycling, including trips to Cape Point.

Downhill Adventures (Map pp102-3; ☎ 422 0388; www.downhilladventures.com; cnr Orange & Kloof Sts, Gardens) is a long-established outfit and offers a variety of cycling trips and adventures. Try a thrilling mountain-bike ride down from the lower cable car station on Table Mountain (R350), or ride through the Constantia winelands and the Cape of Good Hope (R500). You can also rent bikes here for R100 per 24 hours.

Diving

Cape Town offers a number of excellent shore and boat dives. The best time is from June to November, when the water on the False Bay side is warmer and visibility is greater. Diving anytime of the year off the Atlantic coast will require a 5mm-thick wetsuit.

Shark-cage diving is heavily promoted in Cape Town despite the fact that this actually happens at Gansbaai, some 150km southeast of city; see p168 for details of reliable operators. Alternatively if you want to get up close and personal with a shark, the Two Oceans Aquarium at the Waterfront (p107) offers a decent alternative.

A couple of good local dive operators:
Pro Divers (Map pp112-13; ☎ 433 0472; www.prodiver ssa.co.za; 88B Main Rd, Sea Point)
Table Bay Diving (Map pp108-9; ☎ 419 8822; Shop 7, Quay 5, Waterfront)

Flying & Paragliding

The are several legal ways to get high in Cape Town and all are guaranteed to give you a fantastic buzz. Paragliding is amazing but, if you want to do this, it's essential to make an inquiry on your first day in Cape Town. The weather conditions have to be just right and arranging flights at short notice is difficult, particularly if you want to fly off Lion's Head. For more information on aerial pursuits, see p566.

Civair (☎ 934 4488; www.civair.com) National charter operator offering both helicopter and small-plane tours of the Cape. Scenic flights kick off at R1800 for two people for 20 minutes and up to R5400 for an hour-long tour covering the whole cape.

Paragliding Cape Town (☎ 082-727 6584; flights from R750) This number puts you through to Ian Willis who is part of a collective of paragliding instructors and enthusiasts offering tandem flights in and around Cape Town. As well as launches off Lion's Head it also offers options to fly from Silvermine over False Bay and from the mountains overlooking Hermanus (p168).

Golf

Golf is a big deal on the Cape, with some 55 courses dotted around the city. Some are superb and many welcome visitors (but you should book). For more details of fees etc contact the **Western Province Golf Union** (☎ 686 1668; wpga@global.co.za).

Milnerton Golf Club (Map pp94–5; ☎ 434 7808; Tanglewood Cres, Milnerton) Around 12km north of the City Bowl along the R27, Milnerton has a magnificent position overlooking Table Bay with great views of Table Mountain. Wind can be a problem, though.

Mowbray Golf Club (Map pp94–5; ☎ 685 3018; Raapenberg Rd, Mowbray) Considered by some as the best in-town course for its rural setting and birdlife.

Riverclub (Map pp112–13; ☎ 448 6117; Observatory Rd, Observatory) The place to come if you just want to practise your swing as there's a driving range and lessons available.

Hiking & Rock Climbing

The mountainous spine of the Cape Peninsula is a hiker's and rock climber's paradise, but it's not without its dangers, chief of which are the capricious weather conditions; see the boxed text right. Numerous books and maps give details, including Mike Lundy's *Best Walks in the Cape Peninsula*, but to get the best out of the mountains hire a local guide.

City Rock (Map pp112–13; ☎ 447 1326; www.cityrock .co.za; cnr Collingwood & Anson Sts, Observatory) Popular new indoor climbing gym offering climbing courses. It also rents and sells climbing gear.

Mountain Club of South Africa (Map p106; ☎ 465 3412; www.cap.mcsa.org.au; 97 Hatfield St, Gardens) Serious climbers can contact the club, which can recommend guides. It has a climbing wall (R5) which is open 10am to 2pm Monday to Friday, 6pm to 9pm Tuesday and Wednesday.

Venture Forth (☎ 447 4672; www.ventureforth.co.za) Excellent guided hikes and rock climbs with enthusiastic, savvy guides that are tailored to your requirements and aim to get you off the beaten track. The fee of R400 includes all refreshments and city centre transfers.

CLIMBING TABLE MOUNTAIN

Over 300 routes up and down the mountain have been identified, perhaps indicating how easy it is to get lost. Bear in mind that the mountain is over 1000m high and conditions can become treacherous quickly. Thick mists can make the paths invisible, and you'll just have to wait until they lift. Unprepared and foolhardy hikers die here ever year; read our dos and don'ts (see right) before setting off.

None of the routes is easy but the **Platteklip Gorge** walk on the City Bowl side is at least straightforward. Unless you're fit, try walking down before you attempt the walk up. It takes about 2½ hours from the upper cableway station to the lower, taking it fairly easy. Be warned that the route is

---

TABLE MOUNTAIN DOS & DON'TS

Do:

- tell someone the route you're planning to climb up the mountain and take a map (or better still, a guide)
- take water and some food
- take a weatherproof jacket – the weather can change for the worst with lightning speed
- wear proper hiking boots or shoes and a sun hat
- take a mobile phone, if you have one

Don't:

- climb alone
- leave litter on the mountain
- make a fire on the mountain – they're banned

---

exposed to the sun and, for much of the way, a vertical slog.

Another option is the **Indian Windows** route that starts from directly behind the lower cableway station and heads straight up. The hikers you see from the cable car, perched like mountain goats on apparently sheer cliffs, are taking this route, and it's the one you'll end up on if you do the abseil from the summit.

The **Pipe Track** is a less steep route that runs along the west side of the mountain towards the Twelve Apostles. There are also two popular routes up the mountain from Kirstenbosch Botanical Gardens along either **Skeleton Gorge** (which involves negotiating some sections with chains) or **Nursery Ravine**. These can be covered in three hours by someone of moderate fitness. The trails are well marked, and steep in places, but the way to the gardens from the cableway and vice versa is not signposted.

LION'S HEAD

The 2.2km hike from Kloof Nek to the peak of **Lion's Head** (Map pp112–13) is one of the best you can do in Cape Town and is highly recommended on a full moon night when many people gather at the summit to watch the sun go down. The moonlight aids the walk back down, although you should always bring a torch (flashlight) with you.

HOERIKWAGGO HIKING TRAIL

At the time of research details were still to be finalised for the Hoerikwaggo Hiking Trail through Table Mountain National Park. The official launch will be in 2005, but this is already shaping up to be one of the top hikes in South Africa. It will start just south of the City Bowl in Vredehoek and run for five days and roughly 80km over Table Mountain, down the Atlantic Coast to Kommetjie and across Silvermine to culminate at the very tip of Cape Point.

Table Mountain National Park (www.tmnp.co.za) is constructing (and will be managing) the trail, and named it Hoerikwaggo after the ancient Khoi and San word for Table Mountain. Some 50 tonnes of local sandstone have had to be airlifted onto the mountain to bridge gaps in and shore up eroded parts of the planned footpath. There will be basic accommodation in existing structures on the mountain as well as camping allowed around designated areas with ecofriendly water and ablution facilities.

For more details, including the fee for the trail and registration system check the Park's website.

The track's start is clearly marked at the top of Kloof Nek Rd; it involves a little climbing but there are chains on the rocks.

Horse Riding

The **Oude Molen Farm Village** offers horse riding (per hour R100) trails at this ecovillage (see p111), including one running up to the Rhodes Memorial through the neighbouring Valkenberg Hospital.

Sleepy Hollow Horse Riding (Map pp94–5; ☎ 789 2341; ☎ 083-261 0104; Noordhoek) can arrange horse riding (per hour R100) along wide and sandy Noordhoek beach, as well as in the mountainous hinterland.

Kayaking

You'll get a discount on trips with **Sea Kayak Simon's Town** (Map p144; ☎ 082-501 8930; www.noord hoek.co.za; Wharf Rd, Simon's Town) if you're staying at Simon's Town Backpackers (p143), which it also runs. Paddles out to the penguins at Boulders cost R200.

Kloofing

Kamikaze Canyon is just one of the kloofs (cliffs or gorges) near Cape Town in which you can go kloofing (or 'canyoning'). This sport, which entails climbing, hiking, swimming and jumping, is great fun, but can be dangerous (so check out operators' credentials carefully before signing up). Two long-running operators are Abseil Africa/ Adventure Village (see p115) and Day Trippers (see p122). On the Abseil Africa tour the high jumps into pools are optional, but on the Day Trippers tour there's one 5m jump that you cannot avoid. The cost for a day trip is around R550.

Skydiving

Given the shaky rand, this is one of the cheapest places for you to learn to skydive or do a tandem dive. The view over Table Bay and the peninsula alone makes it worthwhile.

Skydive Cape Town (☎ 082-800 6290; www.sky divecapetown.za.net; skydives per person R1200) is an experienced outfit based about 20km north of the city centre in Melkbosstrand.

Surfing & Sandboarding

The Cape Peninsula has plenty of fantastic surfing possibilities, from gentle shore breaks ideal for beginners to 3m-plus monsters for experts only. In general, the best surf is along the Atlantic side, and there is a string of breaks from Bloubergstrand through to the Cape of Good Hope. Most of these breaks work best in southeasterly conditions. The water can be freezing (as low as 8°C) so a steamer wet suit and booties are required.

The focal point for surfing on the Cape, **Kommetjie** (Map pp94–5), pronounced Kommi-kee, offers an assortment of reefs that hold a very big swell. Outer Kommetjie is a left point out from the lighthouse. Inner Kommetjie is a more protected smaller left with lots of kelp (only at high tide). They both work best with a southeasterly or southwesterly wind.

On False Bay (Map p141), head to **Muizenberg** and **Kalk Bay**. The waves here tend to be less demanding in terms of size and temperature (up to 20°C), and work best in northwesterlies. For the daily surf report call ☎ 082-234 6353 or check www .wavescape.co.za.

And if you don't want to get wet there's always sandboarding, which is just like snowboarding except on sand dunes.

A couple of operators:

Downhill Adventures (Map p102-3; ☎ 422 0388; www.downhilladventures.com; cnr Orange & Kloof Sts, Gardens) As well as mountain-biking trips, these adrenaline-focussed guys run a surf school with introductory courses for R350. They got the craze for sandboarding going in the Cape and their trip to Betty's Bay is R500.

Gary's Surf School (Map p141; ☎ 788 9839; www .garysurf.co.za; Surfer's Corner, Muizenberg) Genial surfing coach Gary Kleinhan claims he can get anyone who can swim standing on a board within a day; if you don't get up, you don't pay for the two-hour lesson (R380). His shop, the focus of Muizenberg's surf scene, rents out boards and wetsuits for R100 each per day. The school also runs sandboarding trips (R250) to the dunes at Kommetjie.

Swimming

Although many accommodation options have swimming pools (or at least a plunge pool) to cool down in, if you're looking for a real swimming work out, there a couple of stand-out institutions. The **Sea Point Pavilion** (Map pp112-13; ☎ 434 3341; Beach Rd, Sea Point; adult/child R10/5; ⏰ 7am-6.50pm Oct-Apr, 8.30am-5pm May-Sep) is a huge outdoor pool complex with some lovely Art Deco decoration. It gets very busy on hot summer days – not surprisingly since the pools are always at least 10°C warmer than the ocean.

Long St Baths (Map pp102-3; ☎ 400 3302; cnr Long & Buitensingel Sts; pool only adult/child R8/5; ⏰ 7am-7pm Mon-Sat, 7am-6pm Sun) have been nicely restored with painted murals of city-centre

life on the walls. The pool is heated and very popular with the local community. You'll also find here the separate and good **Turkish steam baths** (R45; incl massage R60). Women are admitted from 8.30am to 7.30pm Monday and Thursday, 8.30am to 1pm Tuesday, and 9am to 6pm Saturday; men from 8am to 7.30pm Tuesday, 8am to 7.30pm Wednesday and Friday, and 8am to noon Sunday. Note, the massage is only available to women.

If you want to swim safely in the sea, Sea Point also has a couple of rock pools: at the north end, **Graaff's Pool** (Map pp112–13) is for men only and is generally favoured by nudists; just south of here is **Milton's Pool** (Map pp112–13), which also has a stretch of beach. Be warned though that the water here will be freezing.

Windsurfing & Kiteboarding

With all that summer wind it's hardly surprising that the Cape coast is a top spot for windsurfers and kiteboarders. Bloubergstrand, 25km north of the City Bowl on the Atlantic Coast, is a popular location and is where you'll find **Windswept** (☎ 082-961 3070; www.windswept.co.za) offering a three-hour beginners course for R450, or if you know the ropes you can hire a board from R250. Packages including accommodation are available. Another key place for these sports is Langebaan (p210); contact **Cape Sport Centre** (☎ 022-772 1114; www.capesport.co.za) for details of its windsurfing and kiteboarding rates.

SPA WARS

In the competitive environment of Cape Town's accommodation market, the latest star addition to the facilities at top-end hotels is the spa. All are open to nonguests for a fee (from around R100).

Leading the way is the sleek, contemporary **Altira Spa** at the top of the Arabella Sheraton Grand Hotel (p126). Floor to ceiling windows afford great views; you can swim laps looking out at the Waterfront or relax in the Jacuzzi while gazing up at Table Mountain.

Not to be outdone, the Cape Grace Hotel (p126) has also recently added the **Spa**. Decorated in vibrant, warm and earthy colours there are both African and spice-route themes going on here with some massages apparently incorporating traditional San methods.

The luxury Twelve Apostles Hotel at Ouderkraal goes for a radically different approach at its **Sanctuary Spa** (Map pp112-13; ☎ 437 9000; www.12apostleshotel.com; Twelve Apostles Hotel, Victoria Rd, Camps Bay; **P**) which is built underground in a mock cave that looks like it could be the set from a James Bond movie, a feeling that is compounded when you get a look at the state-of-the-art contraptions in the treatment rooms. It also has Cape Town's only Rasul chamber (a Middle Eastern sauna) as well as a flotation pool.

WALKING TOUR

Cape Town experienced a building boom in the 1930s. This walk takes you past prime examples of the grand Art Deco architecture from this era at the same time as introducing pieces of contemporary public art. There are plenty of opportunities to shop, eat, drink and rest along the way.

Starting from Cape Town's **Main Train Station (1)** look across to the corner of Adderley and Riebeeck Sts to view the **Colosseum Building (2)**. Designed by WH Grant, one of Cape Town's foremost Art Deco architects, this orange and cream building has striking 'Aztec-style' mouldings. Turn right onto the pedestrianised St George's Mall where, opposite Waterkant St, is **Africa (3)**, the controversial Bart-Simpson-meets-African-curio statue by Brett Murray (see the boxed text on p105).

Continue to the junction with Strand St, turn right, then take a left into Burg St where, at No 24, you'll see the blue and cream **New Zealand House (4)**, an example of a style known as Cape Mediterranean designed by Grant. Next door at No 26 the

elegant symmetry of **Hardware House (5)** lead you on to the more elaborate pink, grey and cream **Namaqua House (6)**, on the corner of Burg and Shortmarket Sts.

You're now in cobbled **Greenmarket Sq (7)**, created as a farmers' market in the early 18th century and filled Monday to Saturday with one of the city's best crafts and souvenir markets. Three quarters of the buildings surrounding the square hail from the 1930s, the main exception being the **Old Town House (8)**, completed in 1761, and now home to the Michaelis Collection (p101) of Dutch and Flemish masterworks.

Walking in a clockwise direction around the square, check out **Kimberley House (9)** at 34 Shortmarket St, built of sandstone with teak window frames and an attractive diamond theme design. **Market House (10)** fronting on to

Start/Finish: Cape Town Main Train Station/ Main Post Office
Distance: 2km
Duration: at least two hours

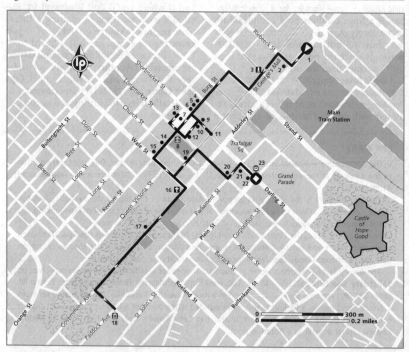

the square is the most elaborately decorated building of all with some majestic stone carved eagles and flowers on its façade. Nip into the building's entrance on Shortmarket St and climb up to the hair clinic on the first floor to see the equally impressive original Art Deco interior.

As you come out of Market House, before returning to Greenmarket Sq, spend a moment to admire a piece of modern art that is easily overlooked: set into the pavement at the junction of Shortmarket St and St George's Mall is **Come to Pass (11)** by Fritha Langerman and Katherine Bull, winners in 2002 of the Cape Town Public Sculpture Competition.

Back on the square, the dazzling, white **Protea Insurance Building (12)** was built in 1928 and renovated in 1990. Opposite is **Shell House (13)**, once the South African headquarters of Shell, now a hotel and restaurant. Exit the square on Burg St and take the next right on to the pedestrianised portion of **Church St (14)**. There's a flea market here Monday to Saturday and along the short street you'll find Cape Town's best collection of galleries and crafts shops.

On the corner of Burg and Wale Sts is the **Waalburg Building (15)**. Take a moment to admire the bronze and Table Mountain stone panels decorating the building's façade and depicting scenes of South African life, before turning left on Wale St and right onto Adderley St, passing **St George's Cathedral (16)** and entering the **Company's Gardens (17;** p105). It's a lovely place to rest and if you have time you should explore the country's best collection of contemporary art at the **South African National Gallery (18;** p105).

Returning to Wale St, turn into St George's Mall and continue to Longmarket St, passing **Newspaper House (19)** at No 122, another of Grant's buildings in the Cape Mediterranean style. Turn right down Longmarket St and keep on it until you get to the corner of Parliament St where you won't miss the glossy black chrome and glass façade of **Mullers Opticians (20)**, one of the best preserved Art Deco shop fronts in the city.

On the corner of Parliament and Darling Sts stands **Old Mutual (21)** the most impressive Art Deco building in all of Cape Town. This 18-storey building, built in 1939, was once the tallest structure in Africa bar the Pyramids. On its façade you'll find one of the longest continuous stone friezes in the world, while the side of the building on Parliament St is adorned with noble carvings of African races.

Next to Old Mutual, on the corner of Darling and Plein Sts is grey and blue **Scotts Building (22)** displaying yet again Grant's elegant designs. Finish up by taking a look inside the **Main post office (23)** across the road. Here you'll discover colourful painted panels of Cape Town scenes by GW Pilkington and Sydney Carter.

CAPE TOWN FOR CHILDREN

Cape Town, with its beaches, parks and fun family attractions, such as the **Two Oceans Aquarium** (p107) and the amusement park **Ratanga Junction** (p116), is a great place to bring the kids. South Africans tend to be family oriented, so most places cope easily with kids' needs. 'Family' restaurants, such as the Spur chain, offer children's portions, as do some of the more upmarket places.

Many of the sights and attractions of interest to parents will also entertain kids. The **Table Mountain cable car** (p100), the attractions at the **Waterfront** (p107; especially the seals, which can usually be seen at Bertie's Landing), the penguin colonies both at **Robben Island** (p110) and **Boulders** (p143), and **Cape Point** (p140) with its baboons and other animals, will delight kids. The **South African Museum** (p105) has plenty to offer the younger visitor, including special shows at the Planetarium.

At the beach you'll have to watch out for rough surf, but there are some quiet rock pools, as well as some sheltered coves. The **Sea Point Pavilion** (p119) has a great family swimming pool that is significantly warmer than the surrounding ocean. There's also a sheltered rock pool at **St James** (p140) on False Bay.

If you're looking for a childminder, contact either **Childminders** (☎ 788 6788) or **Super Sitters** (☎ 439 4985) who charge from R30 per hour (minimum of three hours), excluding transport expenses.

For tips on keeping children (and parents) happy on the road, check out Lonely Planet's *Travel with Children* by Cathy Lanigan.

TOURS

Cape Town Tourism (p99) should be your first stop to find out about all the many tours on offer in and around the city.

QUIRKY CAPE TOWN

- Learn about the world's first successful heart transplant carried out by heart-throb Christiaan Barnard at the Transplant Museum (p111).

- Clap along as the Cape Minstrel groups dance through the streets in their shiny satin suits in the Cape Town New Year Karnaval (p123).

- Inspect the unfinished highway (Map pp108–9), between the City Bowl and the Foreshore, where the Western Blvd (M6) crosses the N2, beloved by action-movie directors as a ready-made set.

- Join in the mad-hatter tea party and have your fortune told at Madame Zingara (p128), or the neighbouring restaurant Cara Lazuli (p128).

- Check out Brett Murray's iconoclastic *Africa* statue in St George's Mall (p105).

City & General Bus Tours

The double-decker bus tour **Cape Town Explorer** (☎ 426 4260) is good for a quick orientation on a fine day; it runs regularly on a circular route from the Waterfront via Cape Town Tourism and Camps Bay. A full trip (you can hop on and off) costs adult/child R90/40 and takes two hours.

For walking tours of the city try **Cape Town on Foot** (☎ 426 4260; tours R100), led by experienced guide Ursula Stevens, Monday to Friday at 11am, from Cape Town Tourism's office on Burg St.

The long-running and reliable **Day Trippers** (☎ 511 4766; www.daytrippers.co.za) brings mountain bikes on most of its trips, so you can do some riding if you want. Most tours cost around R350 and include Cape Point, the Winelands and, in season, whale-watching.

Special-Interest Tours

Plenty of companies offer day trips to the Winelands, but unless you're tight for time it's better to stay overnight closer by, say in Stellenbosch, and take a tour there. See p155 for details of a couple of operators.

Some recommendations:

Birdwatch Cape (☎ 762 5059; www.birdwatch.co.za; half-day tour R270) Offers informative tours pointing out the many unique species of the Cape bird kingdom.

Ferdinand's Tours & Adventures (☎ 421 1660; tours R335) A very popular option for backpackers. The tours take in at least four wineries and include lunch. Things can get pretty raucous as they do on its regular **booze cruises** (R245) on a catamaran out of Gordon's Bay on the False Bay side of the city.

Imvubu Nature Tours (☎ 706 0842; www.imvubu.co.za; tours adult/child R30/15) Based at the Rondevlei Nature Reserve (p140). Take one of its tours around the reserve and you might be lucky enough to see the elusive hippos. Increase your chances by arranging to stay in the island bush camp. Boat trips (per person R30), for a minimum of four people are held between August and February.

Township & Cultural Tours

Lots of operators offer township tours. The half-day tours are sufficient – the full-day tours tack on a trip to Robben Island that is best done separately and for which you don't need a guide. Consider asking the tour operator how much of what you spend actually goes to help people in the townships, since not all tours are run by Cape Flats residents.

Bookings for most tours can be made directly or via Cape Town Tourism.

Adventure Kalk Bay (☎ 788 2242, 788 5113; adventure@kalkbay.co.za; walking tours R100) Community-based tourism project offering guided walks around Kalk Bay that explain the fishing culture of the village. It can also arrange a homestay with one of the local families.

Bo-Kaap Community Guided Tours (☎ 422 1554; tours R100) Learn about the Cape Muslim and Cape Coloured experience on this good history-based walking tour of the Bo-Kaap district, which lasts around two hours.

Charlotte's Walking Tours (☎ 083-982 5692; walking tour R50) Good alternative to the standard bus tour of the townships is this walking tour of Masiphumelele, on the way to Kommetjie, led by the ebullient Charlotte and starting from the Two Oceans Crafts and Culture Centre (p110). The walk lasts for an hour and is arranged at a mutually agreed time with Charlotte.

Grassroute Tours (☎ 706 1006; www.grassroutetours.co.za; half/full day R290/450) One of the most experienced operators of townships tours. The guides are enthusiastic and knowledgeable and tours usually drop by Vicky's (p145) B&B for a chat with this Khayelitsha legend. It also runs other tours, including a walking tour of the Bo-Kaap to learn about Cape Muslims (R240).

New World Inc (☎ 790 8825; tours R250) Specialising in music tours of the townships. These can include workshops on African instruments or traditional dancing as well as visits to local shebeens (unlicensed bars) and clubs such as Duma's Falling Leaves and Yellow Door.

Sam's Cultural Tours (☎ 423 5417, 082-970 0564; half-day tour R250) Charming Sam Ntimba also works for Day Trippers on its township tours. His tours include visits to a dormitory and shebeen in Langa and a crèche project in Khayelitsha.

Tana Baru Cultural Tours (☎ 424 0719; tours R150) Offers a tour of the Bo-Kaap that focuses more on people, and includes tea at the guide's home. It can also arrange B&B accommodation in the Bo-Kaap for R150 per person.

Township Tours SA (☎ 083-719 4870; tours R75) Guide Afrika Moni takes you on a two-hour walking tour of the Hout Bay township Imizamo Yethu, including a visit to a sangoma, a shebeen and art projects.

FESTIVALS & EVENTS

Hardly a week goes by in Cape Town without some event or celebration happening somewhere in the city and immediate surroundings, from the outdoor arts performances of January to Carols by Candlelight in the Company's Gardens in time for Christmas. For a full run-down contact the **Cape Town's Events Office** (☎ 487 2764; www.capetownevents.co.za). Also see p576 for more festival listings.

JANUARY & FEBRUARY

Cape Town New Year Karnaval This colourful carnival is held on the streets of the City Bowl and Bo-Kaap on 1 January and the following three Saturdays at the Green Point (Map pp108–9) and Athlone (Map pp94-5) stadia. Cape Town's longest-running annual street party was first officially documented in 1907, but dates to the early 1800s when slaves enjoyed a day of freedom over the New Year period. The carnival was inspired by visiting American minstrels, hence the make-up and colourful costumes that are part of the song-and-dance parades. The highlight is the 1 January parade, which ends at Green Point Stadium.

J&B Met (☎ 426 5775) South Africa's biggest horse race, with a jackpot of R1.5 million, is a time for big bets and even bigger hats. Head to Kenilworth Racecourse (Map pp94–5) to catch the action. At the time of research it was moved to April due to an equine flu scare, but it's generally held the last Saturday of January.

Opening of Parliament A grand parade with military marching bands halts the traffic down Adderley and Parliament Sts when parliament opens in early February. Come to see the MPs and dignitaries in their finest outfits, to glimpse celebrities, such as Nelson Mandela, and to groove with the public at the pop concert traditionally held in Greenmarket Sq afterwards.

MARCH & APRIL

Cape Town Festival (☎ 082-899 8791; www.cape townfestival.co.za) Having started in 1999, this is becoming a major annual arts event held in the middle of March throughout the City Bowl and at the Waterfront. It includes comedy, drama, debates, an African short-film festival and a food festival in the Company's Gardens.

North Sea Jazz Festival (☎ 4122 5651; www.nsjfcape town.com) Cape Town's biggest jazz event, attracting all the big names from both South Africa and overseas. At the time of research it was held at the Cape Town International Convention Centre at the end of March.

MAY

Cape Gourmet Festival (☎ 465 0069; www.gourmet sa.com) For two weeks from early May, Cape Town celebrates with various food-focussed events. A highlight is the Tastic Table of Reconciliation and Unity where a table for 700 multiethnic diners is set up at the top of Table Mountain.

SEPTEMBER & OCTOBER

Smirnoff International Comedy Festival (☎ 685 7880) Featuring local talents as well as international comedians, this is a justly popular event held over a week at the end of September at the Baxter Theatre (p136) and a few other venues around town.

Cape Argus/Woolworths Gun Run (☎ 426 5775; www.gunrun.co.za) Starting from Beach Rd in Mouile Point this popular half-marathon is the only time that the Noon Gun on Signal Hill gets fired on a Sunday – competitors try to finish the race before the gun goes off. It's generally held at the end of September.

NOVEMBER & DECEMBER

Mother City Queer Project (☎ 426 5709; www.mcqp .co.za) Everyone is as queer as folk at this massive, must-attend gay dance party held in early December. Check out the theme and run yourself up a fabulous costume – they won't let you in unless you're dressed appropriately.

Kirstenbosch Summer Sunset Concerts (☎ 799 8782; www.nbi.ac.za; adult/child incl entry to the gardens R30/10; ☼ 5.30 or 6.30pm-end Nov-Apr) These Sunday afternoon concerts (usually held from 5pm) are a Cape Town institution. Bring a blanket, a bottle of wine and a picnic and join the crowds enjoying anything from an aria performed by local divas to a funky jazz combo. There's usually a special concert for New Year's Eve, too.

SLEEPING

There's somewhere in Cape Town to suit practically everyone's budget. Advance booking is recommended, especially during school holidays from mid-December to the end of January and at Easter – prices can double and many places are fully booked.

Think about what part of the city you might want to stay in. If you aim to hit the beaches then suburbs along the Atlantic or

False Bay coasts (see p140) will make better sense than, say, Gardens or the City Bowl. If you want easy access to nightlife, then anywhere within walking distance of Long St should be fine. If you have a car, then anywhere's fine, but remember to inquire about the parking options when you make a booking; city centre hotels can charge anything from R20 to R40 per day for parking.

City Bowl
Map pp102–3
BUDGET
Long St Backpackers (☎ 423 0615; www.longstreet backpackers.co.za; 209 Long St; dm/s/d with shared bathroom R70/110/180; ☐) First of the Long St hostels and still standing out from the pack. In a block of 14 small flats, with four beds and a bathroom in each, arranged around a leafy, quiet courtyard.

Parliament Hotel (☎ 461 6710; www.parliament hotel.co.za; 9 Barrack St; s/d with breakfast R250/350; ☐ ☒) One of the best inexpensive central hotels. It's a nonflash, but friendly, place with spotless, good-sized rooms and a café.

St Paul's B&B Guest House (☎ /fax 423 4420; 182 Bree St; s/d with shared bathroom R120/200) One of the best budget places with neat rooms and a quiet courtyard. The rates include breakfast.

MID-RANGE
Metropole Hotel (☎ 423 7247; www.metropolehotel .co.za; 38 Long St; s/d from R400/1100; ☐ ☒ ☐) The ancient cast-iron elevator is still in place, but otherwise the Metropole has been given a complete makeover to become a super-smooth boutique hotel, aimed at the gay and *Wallpaper**-reader market. Go for the larger superior rooms with their ostrich trimmed bedsteads. Its restaurant Veranda and its bar M Bar & Lounge (p132) also get top marks.

Townhouse (☎ 465 7050; www.townhouse.co.za; 60 Corporation St; s/d R471/866; ☐ ☒ ☐ ☒) Newly renovated rooms just add to the appeal of this often-recommended hotel with good service and high standards. The rates rise only slightly in summer. Ask for a room with a view of the mountain. It also has a small pool and gym.

Cape Town Lodge (☎ 422 0030; www.capetown lodge.co.za; 101 Buitengracht St; s/d from R795/895; ☐ ☒ ☐ ☒) There's some nice African craft touches to the interior décor of this well-located business hotel, which has a small plunge pool in a courtyard. Request a room with a mountain view.

Gardens & Around
Map p106
BUDGET
Ashanti Lodge (☎ 423 8721; www.ashanti.co.za; 11 Hof St, Gardens; camp sites per person/dm/d with shared bathroom R55/85/250; guesthouse d R320; ☐ ☒) Superpopular party hostel in a big, brightly painted old house with a fantastic view of Table Mountain from its deck. For something quieter opt for the excellent en suite rooms in two separate National Monument houses round the corner. There is a 5% discount for Hostelling International (HI) members and it also offers camping.

Oak Lodge (☎ 465 6182; oaklodge@intekom.co.za; 21 Breda St, Gardens; dm/d from R70/210) A hippy air still pervades this one-time commune, now the most chilled hostel in Cape Town. It's taken over nearly all the flats in the attached block, which represent a great long-term accommodation option with their own kitchens and bathrooms.

MID-RANGE
Dunkley House (☎ 462 7649; www.dunkleyhouse.com; 3B Gordon St, Gardens; d/ste with breakfast R750/990; ☒ ☐ ☒) Ultrastylish guesthouse close by the Company's Gardens. The rooms are in neutral tones, all with CD players and satellite TV, and there's a plunge pool in the courtyard.

Parker Cottage (☎ /fax 424 6445; www.parkercot tage.co.za; 3 Carstens St, Tamboerskloof; d with breakfast from R550; ☒ ☐ ☒) Elegant Victorian mansion with eight individually decorated double rooms, two with air-conditioning.

iKhaya Guest Lodge (☎ 461 8880; www.ikhayalo dge.co.za; Dunkley Sq, Gardens; s/d with breakfast R560/840, s/d apt R810/1140; ☐ ☒ ☐) Bag of African style at this excellent option in the trendy media district. The luxurious self-catering lofts are worth checking out, especially for the panoramic views across to Lion's Head.

Cape Town Hollow (☎ 423 1260; www.capetown hollow.co.za; 88 Queen Victoria St, Gardens; s/d with breakfast R480/780; ☐ ☒ ☐ ☒) Overlooking the Company's Gardens this recently upgraded and renamed mid-range hotel has pleasant rooms and good facilities for the price, including a pool, small gym, business centre and restaurant.

Belmont House (☎ 461 5417; www.capeguest.com /belmont/; 10 Belmont Ave, Oranjezicht; s/d with breakfast R220/440; ☒) The rooms in this smart guesthouse are small, but nicely decorated. There is a kitchen for guests' use and a garden.

CAPE TOWN

TOP FIVE CAPE TOWN SLEEPING

- **The Backpack** (Map pp102-3; ☎ 423 4530; www.backpackers.co.za; 74 New Church St, Tamboerskloof; dm/s/d with shared bathroom R85/220/285, d R360; P 🖳 🐾) Not too laid-back, not too loud, guests love the Backpack and it's easy to see why. For years it has stayed ahead of the crowd by constantly adapting, yet always offering top-notch accommodation for the price and wonderfully clued-up service from their travel desk.
- **Cape Heritage Hotel** (Map pp102-3; ☎ 424 4646; www.capeheritage.co.za; 90 Bree St; s/d from R725/1000; P 🔀 🖳) Enjoy the gracious Cape Dutch-meets-contemporary style of this delightful boutique hotel that's part of the Heritage Sq redevelopment of 18th-century buildings. Each of the 15 rooms is individually decorated and some have four-poster beds.
- **Head South Lodge** (Map pp108-9; ☎ 434 8778; www.headsouth.co.za; 215 Main Rd, Green Point; s/d with breakfast R595/695; P 🔀 🖳 🐾) A homage to the 1950s with its retro furnishings and fabulous collection of Vladimir Tretchikoff prints hung throughout the well-maintained building. The 15 rooms are spacious, the location good and there's a tiny plunge pool in the front garden.
- **Kensington Place** (Map p106; ☎ 424 4744; www.kensingtonplace.co.za; 38 Kensington Cres, Higgovale; d with breakfast R2400; P 🔀 🖳 🐾) Nestling discretely in the shelter of Table Mountain, Kensington Place has eight spacious and tastefully decorated rooms all with balconies, satellite TV and DVD players, free Internet access, fresh fruit and flowers. Add in a small pool and faultless service and you have Cape Town's ultimate boutique hotel.
- **Villa Papillon** (Map p106; ☎ 462 6850; www.villa-papillon.com; 7 Labouners St, Oranjezicht; s/d with breakfast R912/1140; 🔀 🖳 🐾) At this discrete guesthouse, the individually styled rooms have great themes including Japanese, funky 1950s and the silky, flowery papillon suite with a king-sized bed and oversized shower.

TOP END

Mount Nelson Hotel (☎ 483 1000; www.mountnelson hotel.orient-express.com; 76 Orange St; d/ste from R4660/6990; P 🔀 🖳 🐾) Pith-helmeted doormen greet you at Cape Town's most famous hotel, the sugar pink–coated 'Nellie'. Surrounded by seven acres of grounds and dating from 1899, the feel is very much end-of-Empire. The rooms are on the chintzy side but full of character. Even if you don't stay, drop by for afternoon tea or a meal (see p129).

Villa Belmonte (☎ 462 1576; www.villabelmonteho tel.co.za; 33 Belmont Ave, Oranjezicht; s/d from R970/1290; P 🔀 🖳 🐾) Top-class luxury accommodation is offered at this ornately Italianate villa with a huge pool and excellent facilities, including a good restaurant. Choose city or mountain views from the rooms.

Montague House (☎ 424 7337; www.montague house.net; 18 Leeuwenhof Rd, Higgovale; s/d with breakfast R995/1300; 🔀 🖳 🐾) Shakespeare's plays are the inspiration for the room design at this delightful boutique guesthouse on the lower slopes of Table Mountain.

Cape Milner (☎ 426 1101; www.threecities.co.za; 2A Milner Rd, Tamboerskloof; s/d with breakfast R1230/2460; P 🔀 🖳 🐾) Another old hotel goes all contemporary and minimalist. The monochrome décor is softened by the friendliness

of the staff and good views of the mountains from its terrace.

Green Point, Waterkant & Waterfront   Map pp108–9

BUDGET

Big Blue (☎ 439 0807; www.bigbluebackpackers.hostel .com; 7 Vesperdene Rd, Green Point; dm/d with shared bathroom R80/220, d R270; P 🖳 🐾) The most happening hostel in Green Point is a colourful, quirky affair with a grand hallway and Zen-style garden.

St John's Waterfront Lodge (☎ 439 1404; www .stjohns.co.za; 6 Braemar Rd, Green Point; dm/d with shared bathroom R80/180, d R220; P 🖳 🐾) This often-recommended hostel is a large, relaxed and friendly place with very good facilities, including a large garden and two pools.

MID-RANGE

Cape Standard (☎ 430 3060; www.capestandard.co.za; 3 Romney Rd, Green Point; s/d R550/700; P 🔀 🐾) At this appealing, secluded hotel choose from beach house–chic rooms downstairs or more edgy, contemporary rooms upstairs. All have big, mosaic tiled bathrooms.

Dungarvin House (☎/fax 434 0677; kom@mweb .co.za; 163 Main Rd, Green Point; s/d with breakfast R320/540; P) The German-speaking owner of this nicely restored Victorian mansion has young children and keeps plenty of cuddly toys on hand, making this a very child-friendly option.

Village Lodge (☎ /fax 421 1106; reservations@the villagelodge.com; 49 Napier St, Waterkant; s/d R350/550; ❂) Smart, small guesthouse with two locations – one close by the Waterkant clubs for party animals, the other higher on the hill. There's a cute café attached where you can take breakfast and a shop selling local ceramics and glass.

TOP END

Cape Grace Hotel (☎ 410 7100; www.capegrace.com; West Quay, Waterfront; s/d with breakfast from R4085/4200; P ❂ ⬛ ⬛) More like an exclusive, yet welcoming, club than a hotel. There's understated luxury in most rooms (go for the ones facing Table Mountain), an excellent restaurant (see p130) and a colourfully decorated spa (see p119).

De Waterkant Lodge & Cottages (☎ /fax 419 1097; www.dewaterkant.co.za; 20 Loader St, Waterkant; s/d with breakfast R550/900; apt R1200; ❂ ⬛ ⬛) Choose either the beautifully restored lodge with its magnificent rooftop views, or one of the self-catering cottages, each individually decorated with top-quality art and antiques.

Arabella Sheraton Grand Hotel (☎ 412 9999; www.arabellasheraton.com/capetown; Convention Sq, Lower Long St, Foreshore; d/ste with breakfast from R2960/4900; P ❂ ⬛ ⬛) Sleek, contemporary business-focussed hotel attached to the new Cape Town International Convention Centre (p100). The corporate feel is softened by warmer colours in the rooms and sweeping views of the city, mountains and sea. Excellent facilities include the roof-top Altira Spa (see p119).

Victoria Junction (☎ 418 1234; www.proteahotels .com; cnr Somerset St & Ebenezer Rd, Green Point; s/d with breakfast R965/1376, apt s/d R1526/1876; P ❂ ⬛ ⬛) Popular, arty hotel and serviced self-catering apartments that are part of the Protea chain. The rooms are loft-style with exposed brick walls.

Atlantic Coast

SEA POINT   Map pp112–13
Budget
Planet Africa (☎ 434 2151; www.planetafrica.co.za; 17 Kei Apple Rd, Fresnaye; dm/d/apt with breakfast R115/494/787; P ❂ ⬛ ⬛) Millions of rand have been spent on this stylish African-

themed complex which provides practically every variation of room from luxury dorms to well-equipped self-catering apartments. It's lacking atmosphere, but is clearly a place for backpackers who want to be pampered, with a pool that's large enough to swim in, and a huge bar and restaurant.

Lion's Head Lodge (☎ 434 4163; www.lions-head -lodge.co.za; 319 Main Rd, Sea Point; d R330; P ❂ ⬛) The rates at this decent, but old-fashioned budget hotel fall if you stay longer than one night. Sharing the hotel's facilities is **Aardvark Backpackers** (☎ 434 4172; dm/d R80/280), which has its dorms in converted flats. There's a useful travel centre and a 10% discount for HI members.

Mid-Range

Huijs Haerlem (☎ 434 6434; www.huijshaerlem.co.za; 25 Main Dr, Sea Point; s/d with breakfast R680/980; P ❂ ⬛ ⬛) Up one of the steeper slopes of Sea Point, this excellent gay-owned guesthouse comprises of two houses decorated in top-quality antiques joined by delightful gardens.

Olaf's Guest House (☎ 439 8943; www.olafs.co.za; 24 Wisbeach Rd, Sea Point; s/d with breakfast R590/810; ❂ ⬛ ⬛) A gorgeous place, with eight individually decorated rooms and a plunge pool in the front garden.

Villa Rosa (☎ 434 2768; www.villa-rosa.com; 277 High Level Rd, Sea Point; s/d with breakfast R410/615; P) Quaint guesthouse offering tastefully decorated rooms with high ceilings and huge bathrooms.

Top End

Winchester Mansions Hotel (☎ 434 2351; www .winchester.co.za; 221 Beach Rd, Sea Point; s/d with breakfast from R1150/1500; P ❂ ⬛ ⬛) This Cape Dutch–style beauty has recently added a top floor with more modern rooms, and a heated pool. You'll pay more for rooms with sea views, but the courtyard with a fountain is lovely, too. Sunday brunch with live jazz is held from 11am to 2pm for R125.

CAMPS BAY & HOUT BAY
Budget
Stan Halt Youth Hostel (Map pp112-13; ☎ /fax 438 9037; www.hisa.org.za/stanhalt.htm; the Glen, Camps Bay; dm R45; P) How much longer this HI hostel will remain at its idyllic location, in the one-time stables of the Round House hunting lodge, is anyone's guess. It's long

been slated to move to Deer Park in Vredehoek, but if it's still open the dorms here are among the cheapest and most peaceful in Cape Town. It's a steep 15-minute walk to the nearest shops and restaurants in Camps Bay. If you're coming by public transport the easiest way is to take a shared taxi to the top of Kloof Nek, then walk down Kloof Rd towards Camps Bay.

Mid-Range

Chapman's Peak Hotel (Map pp94-5; ☎ 790 1036; info@chapmanspeakhotel.co.za; Main Rd, Hout Bay; s/d with breakfast R500/700; P) Convivial inn at the start of Chapman's Peak Dr, with a good pub and restaurant. The rooms aren't huge but are nicely furnished and most have sea views.

Top End

Bay Hotel (Map pp112-13; ☎ 438 4444; www.the bay.co.za; 69 Victoria Rd, Camps Bay; d R2690-3860; P ✖ 🖳 😩) Hang-out for the well-heeled that's just a stone's toss from the beach. The rooms in white and earth tones are soothing and spacious, the ones with sea views being pricier.

Hout Bay Manor (Map pp94-5; ☎ 790 0116; www .houtbaymanor.co.za; Baviaanskloof Rd, Hout Bay; s/d with breakfast R925/1550; P ✖ 🖳 😩) The original building at this small luxury hotel dates from 1871. The rooms are big and attractively furnished with a floral motif, some with four-poster beds.

Primi Royal (Map pp112-13; ☎ 438 2741; www .primi-royal.com; 23 Camps Bay Dr, Camps Bay; d from R1500; P ✖ 🖳 😩) Sleek boutique hotel overlooking Camps Bay but set away from the main drag. Rose petals scattered across the bed linen in the individually decorated rooms on arrival is a nice touch.

Southern Suburbs

BUDGET

Green Elephant (Map pp112-13; ☎ 448 6359; green elephant@iafrica.com; 57 Milton Rd, Observatory; dm/s/d/tr with shared bathroom R75/160/280/295, d R250; 🖳 😩) Split over two houses, the Green Elephant is a deservedly popular alternative to the city-centre hostels. It's spacious, colourful and generally quiet, with a tree-climbing dog for entertainment.

Lighthouse Farm Lodge (Map pp94-5; ☎ /fax 447 9177; msm@mweb.co.za; Violet Bldg, Oude Molen Farm Village, Alexandria Rd, Mowbray; dm/d with shared bathroom R50/150; P) The nicer of the two hostels on

the grounds of the old hospital turned into a farm and alternative community of artists (see p111). It's a very simple but relaxed place and you can pay your way by working on the organic farm through the Willing Workers on Organic Farms scheme (www .wwoof.org). It's best if you have your own transport, but otherwise it's within walking distance of Pinelands train station, and there's good security around the complex.

TOP END

Constantia Uitsig (Map pp94-5; ☎ 794 6500; www .constantiauitsig.co.za; Spaanschemat River Rd, Constantia; s & d from R2300; P ✖ 🖳 😩) Suitably exclusive and salubrious hotel set within a vineyard with beautiful gardens, a pool and three top-notch restaurants to choose from.

Vineyard Hotel (Map pp112-3; ☎ 683 3044; www .vineyard.co.za; Colinton Rd, Newlands; s/d from R795/1095; P ✖ 🖳 😩) Handy for both Kirstenbosch Botanical Gardens (p111) and the cricket (p135), you want to choose a room at this very appealing hotel overlooking the lovely gardens and the mountains. It's also worth visiting for **tea** (R58) in the lounge (June to late-September only).

EATING

Cape Town's dining scene is impressive. There's a good variety of cuisines from around the globe on offer, and the quality of the ingredients is high, with the locally grown fruit, vegetables and seafood all being particularly fine. You shouldn't miss the opportunity to sample some traditional Cape Malay food, and there are several good African restaurants in Cape Town, too.

Most restaurants are licensed but some allow you to bring your own wine for little or no corkage charge. Call ahead to check the restaurant's policy. Several bars and pubs serve good food too; see p132.

Cape Town is a picnicker's and self-caterer's paradise. Among the spots to plan an alfresco meal are the Atlantic beaches (particularly Clifton and Camps Bay towards sunset), Lion's Head, Table Mountain, and Kirstenbosch Botanical Gardens. For provisions, check the large and cheap Pick 'n' Pay supermarkets first; there are branches at Victoria Wharf Shopping Centre (Map pp108–9), Gardens Centre (Map p106), Sea Point and Camps Bay (Map pp112–13). Woolworths also sells a fine range of high-quality foods; you'll find stores at Victoria Wharf Shopping Centre (Map pp108–9), in the City Bowl (Map pp102–3), Lifestyles on Kloof (Map p106), the Gardens Centre (Map p106), and Cavendish Sq (Map pp112–13) in Claremont. For specialist products check out the excellent delis, such as Gionvanni's Deli World (p131) in Green Point and Melissa's (p129) in Gardens.

Cafés and restaurants generally open daily, the former serving food from 7.30am to around 5pm. A few places (more usually in the City Bowl) will be closed on Sunday or occasionally Monday. If a restaurant opens for lunch it will generally be from 11.30am to 3pm, with dinner usually kicking off around 7pm with last orders at 10pm. Variations of more than half an hour from these times are listed in the review.

City Bowl & Bo-Kaap
CAFÉS & QUICK EATS
Cafe Mozart (Map pp102–3; ☎ 424 3774; 37 Church St, City Bowl; mains R30-50) Watch the world go by from the outdoor tables at this deservedly popular café serving good bistro-style food.

Crush (Map pp102–3; ☎ 422 5533; 100 St George's Mall, City Bowl; mains R20-30) Proving healthy eating need not be boring, Crush brings a splash of contemporary style and colour to

St George's Mall with its freshly squeezed juices, smoothies and tasty wraps.

Lola's (Map pp102-3; ☎ 423 0885; 228 Long St, City Bowl; mains R20-30) Long-established funky vegetarian café that is the most chilled place to hang out on Long St, with street tables and a gay-friendly vibe.

Mr Pickwick's (Map pp102-3; ☎ 424 2696; 158 Long St, City Bowl; mains R20-30; ☺ 8am-1am Mon-Thu, 8am-4am Fri) The place to recuperate after a night out clubbing. This licensed, deli-style café stays open very late for good snacks and meals. Try the foot-long rolls.

Cin-full (Map pp102-3; ☎ 424 5249; 38 Shortmarket St, City Bowl; mains R20-30) Yummy cinnamon buns, made on the premises and drenched in cream cheese icing, are a sticky delight here. It does a good range of inexpensive sandwiches, too.

RESTAURANTS
Africa Café (Map pp102-3; ☎ 422 0221; 108 Shortmarket St, City Bowl; meals R125; ☺ 6.30-11pm Mon-Sat) With fantastic décor, this is the best place in Cape Town to sample a range of African food. No fewer than 15 different dishes make up the pancontinental feast and you can have as much as you like of each.

Five Flies (Map pp102-3; ☎ 424 4442; 14-16 Keerom St, City Bowl; 2-/3-/4-course meals R100/135/155) In the

---

TOP FIVE CAPE TOWN EATING

■ **Aubergine** (Map p106; ☎ 465 4909; 39 Barnet St, Gardens; 3-course menu R210) Set in the convivial 19th-century home of the first Chief Justice of the Cape, Aubergine is one of Cape Town's outstanding restaurants. Chef Harald Bresselschmidt creates many memorable dishes, such as a puff pastry tart of aubergine and tomato or sesame-coated quail cutlets.

■ **Café Ganesh** (Map pp112-13; ☎ 448 3435; 38B Trill Rd, Observatory; mains R30-40) Junkyard décor and kooky wallpaper create the chic-shack atmosphere at this funky student hang-out, dishing up tasty falafel, roti, curries and the like. Call to find out about its monthly dance parties.

■ **Cara Lazuli** (Map pp102-3; ☎ 426 2351; 11 Buiten St, City Bowl; mains R70; ☺ 7.15-11pm Mon-Sat) Adjoining its sister restaurant Madame Zingara (above), this Moroccan-themed establishment offers up a similar party atmosphere with tarot-card readers and belly dancers to supplement the inventive menu of *tagines* (Moroccan style of cooking in a clay conical pot) and couscous. The fresh mint iced granitas are delicious and you can finish your meal off with a hookah.

■ **Off Moroka Cafe Africaine** (Map pp102-3; ☎ 422 1129; 120 Adderley St, City Bowl; mains R25-30; ☺ 6.30am-9pm Mon-Thu, 6.30am-midnight Fri, 8.30am-midnight Sat) The ultimate inner-city cultural melting pot, Off Moroka serves a fab range of African dishes and hosts live music and experimental DJs in the evenings. Always potentially interesting are the off-the-wall poetry and literary sessions on Monday at 8pm. There's a cover charge of R1 for performances.

■ **Savoy Cabbage** (Map pp102-3; ☎ 424 2626; 101 Hout St, City Bowl; mains R70-90) Long-running star performer on the city's contemporary dining scene is keeping up standards. The food (a terrine of local fois gras with citrus salad, the signature minced beef stuffed cabbage rolls) doesn't clobber you with strong flavours and the staff are equally soothing and professional.

wood-panelled Dutch Club building (1752), this is a wonderfully atmospheric place with a central cobbled courtyard. It offers course menus of inventive contemporary cooking.

Madame Zingara (Map pp102-3; ☎ 426 2458; 192 Loop St, City Bowl; mains R70; ☼ 7-11pm Mon-Sat) Known for its bohemian atmosphere, this is a confirmed crowd pleaser. Unless you're a committed carnivore we'd advise against its infamous whopper stack of beef fillets doused in chilli-chocolate sauce, but otherwise don't miss out on a fun night here, which can include tarot-card readings and dressing up in the hats hung on the walls.

Marco's African Place (Map pp102-3; ☎ 423 5412; 15 Rose Lane, Bo-Kaap; mains R60-70; ☼ noon-11pm) African restaurant striking all the right notes, with a good range of local dishes and drinks. Try Themba's meatballs, Zwelethu's chicken or Mqomboh beer. At night when the band starts (cover charge R10), expect to start dancing with the staff.

Bukhara (Map pp102-3; ☎ 424 0000; 33 Church St, City Bowl; mains R70) Considered by many to be Cape Town's best Indian restaurant. Enjoy its spicy, tasty food in a stylish setting.

Royal Eatery (Map pp102-3; ☎ 422 4536; 279 Long St, City Bowl; mains R60; ☼ noon-midnight Mon-Sat) We love the retro style of this gourmet burger bar that also serves good salads and pasta dishes. It also serves late into the night.

Ivy Garden Restaurant (Map pp102-3; ☎ 423 2360; Old Town House, Greenmarket Sq, City Bowl; mains R70) Delightful courtyard restaurant behind the Old Town House, serving both snacks and full meals. Try its platter of four Cape specialities for R70.

Biesmiellah (Map pp102-3; ☎ 423 0850; Wale St, Bo-Kaap; mains R50; ☼ noon-11pm Mon-Sat) Authentic Cape Malay and Indian food at this Bo-Kaap institution decorated with tapestries of the Taj. It's all halal and no alcohol is served.

Noon Gun Tearoom & Restaurant (Map pp108-9; ☎ 424 0529; 273 Longmarket St, Bo-Kaap; set menu R90; ☼ 10am-10pm Mon-Sat) After witnessing the noon blast of the cannon, slip into this homely family-run restaurant on Signal Hill to enjoy the view and Cape Malay dishes, such as bobotie. It can get busy with tour groups.

SELF-CATERING
Atlas Trading Company (Map pp102-3; ☎ 423 4361; 94 Wale St, Bo-Kaap; ☼ 8am-5.15pm Mon-Thu, 8am-12.15pm & 2-5.15pm Fri, 8.30am-1pm Sat) Since 1944

Atlas has provided the Cape Muslim community with over 100 different herbs and spices. It's a wonderfully atmospheric place and the proprietors will happily share some local recipes with you.

Wellington Fruit Growers (Map pp102-3; ☎ 461 7160; 96 Darling St; ☼ 8am-5pm Mon-Fri, 8am-1pm Sat) A Cape Town institution, this long, narrow shop sells a huge range of nuts, dried and glace fruit, deli items, tinned foods and *lots* of candies.

Gardens & Around   Map p106
Kloof St has the best selection of restaurants and cafés in Gardens. There are several good cafés in both the Lifestyles on Kloof and Gardens Centre malls.

CAFÉS & QUICK EATS
Mount Nelson Hotel (☎ 483 1000; 76 Orange St; afternoon tea R65; ☼ 2.30-5.30pm) For sheer indulgence drop by this hotel (p125) for a delicious afternoon tea, including the local delicacies, such as samosas (savoury fried pastry parcels), as well the usual finger sandwiches, cakes and scones.

Vida e Caffé (mains R20; ☼ 7.30am-5pm Mon-Fri) City Bowl (Map pp102-3; off Tulbagh Sq); Gardens (Map pp102-3; ☎ 426 0627; 34 Kloof St); Waterfront (Map pp108-9; ☎ 425 9440; Victoria Wharf Shopping Centre) Shaping up to be the Starbucks of Cape Town, Vida e Caffé does coffee, freshly squeezed orange juice, Portuguese-style pastries and beefy filled rolls with considerable panache, ideal for breakfast or a fast lunch.

Melissa's (☎ 424 5540; 94 Kloof St, Gardens; mains R30; ☼ 7.30am-8pm Mon-Fri, 8am-8pm Sat & Sun) Pay by the kilogram for the delicious lunch buffets at this superpopular place, then browse the shelves for goodies, such as handmade fudge, fig nougat, potato chips and muesli rusks for a picnic or gourmet gifts.

Café Riteve (☎ 465 1594; 88 Hatfield St, Gardens; mains R30; ☼ 9.30am-5pm Mon-Wed, 9.30am-10pm Thu & Sun, 9.30am-3pm Fri) Sample good Jewish cuisine, all kosher, at this contemporary bistro in the grounds of the South African Jewish Museum. It sometimes hosts live music, plays and comedy shows in the evenings (from R65 for meal and show).

RESTAURANTS
Arnold's (☎ 424 4344; 60 Kloof St, Gardens; mains R40-60; ☼ 9am-late) We've had some good reviews for this casual bistro-style place and it really

deserves them. The food is tasty and good value and the staff are very welcoming. Try the biltong salad or unique 'bushman's' game burger.

Yindee's (☎ 422 1012; 22 Camp St, Gardens; mains R50-60; ⏰ 6.30-10.30pm Mon-Sat) Fine Thai cuisine at this red-painted mansion on the corner of Kloof and Camp Sts. Inside you can either dine Western-style in an elegant deep-blue dining room or in the red room at low tables sitting on cushions.

Nelson's Eye (☎ 423 2601; 9 Hof St, Gardens; mains R80-100) Darkly atmospheric restaurant that gets most people's thumbs up as Cape Town's best steak house. Also a good place to try local game and ostrich.

Ocean Basket (☎ 422 0322; 75 Kloof St, Gardens; mains R60) The main branch of a chain restaurant that is beloved by families for its jolly decoration, good-value meals and fresh, simple approach to seafood. Eat in the patio garden at the back.

Green Point, Waterkant & Waterfront   Map pp108–9

Green Point and the Waterkant are riding high as the hot dining locations, the Cape Quarter in particular being the place to see and be seen. The Waterfront's plethora of restaurants and cafés offer up unrivalled variety, convenience and a lively atmosphere, but keep an eye on prices at what is essentially a giant tourist trap.

CAFÉS & QUICK EATS

La Petite Tarte (☎ 425 9077; Shop A11 Cape Quarter, 72 Waterkant St, Waterkant; mains R30-40; ⏰ 8am-4pm Mon-Fri, 8am-2pm Sat) Home-made savoury and sweet French-style tarts lead the way at this adorable café on the Dixon St–side of the Cape Quarter, where you can also savour Mariage Freres Teas.

News Café (☎ 434 6196; 83 Main Rd, Green Point; mains R40; ⏰ 7.30am-2am) Buzzy café-bar that's a good spot for anything from breakfast or a bistro-type meal to late-night drinks.

RESTAURANTS

One.Waterfront (☎ 418 0520; Cape Grace Hotel, West Quay, Waterfront; mains R70-100) The fishcakes are a winner at the Cape Grace's smart, yet casual, restaurant, as are many more of chef Bruce Robertson's inventive, not-to-be-tried-at-home dishes. Some exciting options for vegetarians here, too.

The Restaurant (☎ 419 2921; 51A Somerset Rd, Green Point; mains R90; ⏰ 11am-3pm Mon-Fri, 7-10pm Mon-Sat) The décor is jumble-sale chic, the food pared back to essentials and all the better for it. A lunch dish of fish of the day, string fries and salsa at R50 is a bargain.

Pigalle (☎ 421 434; 57A Somerset Rd, Green Point; mains R80-100; ⏰ noon-3pm Mon-Sat, 7pm-midnight) Pigalle brings the glamour of the dinner-dance back to Cape Town, in possibly the city's most dramatic interior. The menu features retro favourites, such as shrimp cocktail, with the seafood platter (R250) being outstanding value for what you get.

Willoughby & Co (☎ 418 6115; Shop 6132 Victoria Wharf, Waterfront; mains R60-70; ⏰ restaurant 11.30am-10.45pm, deli 9am-8.30pm) Huge servings of sushi are the standout from a good value fish-based menu at this casual eatery and deli, on the ground floor of Victoria Wharf. Commonly acknowledged as one of the better places to eat at the Waterfront.

Emily's (☎ 421 1133; Shop 202 Clock Tower Centre, Waterfront; mains R80) Justly renowned for its eclectic and artistic approach to modern South African cooking – imagine a marinated crocodile and avocado pizza and you get the brightly coloured picture. You're also sure to find something to your taste on its epic wine list.

Anatoli (☎ 419 2501; 24 Napier St, Green Point; dishes R60; ⏰ 7-11pm Tue-Sun) Wall-carpeted Anatoli has been here for years and with good reason: The delicious meze (cold/hot R18/26) brought round on enormous wooden trays make a great meal.

Andiamo (☎ 421 3687; Shop C2, Cape Quarter, Waterkant St, Waterkant; mains R60; ⏰ 8am-11pm) Deli, restaurant and bar that's one of the most popular in this hip shopping and dining centre. Lounge in one of its seagrass sofas while nibbling at antipasto, or cruise its well-stocked deli.

Den Anker (☎ 419 0249; Pierhead, Waterfront; mains R80; ⏰ 11am-11pm) One of the more charming of the Waterfront's many dining options, Den Anker offers a great range of authentic Belgian beers with which to wash down a menu heavy on mussels and other seafood.

Zero932 (☎ 439 6306; 79 Main Rd, Green Point; mains R70; ⏰ 9am-11pm) Trendy Belgian-beer restaurant serving locally grown mussels in 1kg pots or open-faced on platters; it has plenty of other dishes, too, and 26 different bottled beers plus three more on tap.

SELF-CATERING

Gionvanni's Deli World (☎ 434 6983; 103 Main Rd, Green Point; mains R20-30; ❂ 8.30am-9pm) Not as big as rival delis, but bursting with flavoursome products. The staff will make up any sandwich you fancy from all its provisions. If you can't wait to eat, there's a small café.

Atlantic Coast

There's no shortage of places to eat along Sea Point's Main Rd and Regent St, many of them at the budget-end of scale, reflecting the suburb's less-than-hip credentials. In contrast, Camps Bay, playground of the rich and beautiful, couldn't be hotter – and you'd be well advised to book ahead anywhere here if you wish to get a prime spot for sunset drinks and nibbles.

CAFÉS & QUICK EATS

New York Bagels (Map pp112-13; ☎ 439 7523; 51 Regent Rd, Sea Point; mains R30; ❂ 7am-11pm) As well as the deli there's the airy multilevel café next door where you wander around various stalls to choose a mix 'n' match meal of, say, a hot-beef-on-rye sandwich followed by a spicy stir-fry.

Sandbar (Map pp112-13; ☎ 438 8336; 31 Victoria Rd, Camps Bay; mains R30) One of Camps Bay's better value options is this less self-consciously fashionable café with street tables, serving good sandwiches and light meals.

Ari's Souvlaki (Map pp112-13; ☎ 439 6683; 83A Regent St, Sea Point; mains R25; ❂ 10am-midnight) Meze, kebabs and falafel are on offer at this Greek institution. It's nothing fancy, but it's honest.

Fish on the Rocks (Map pp94-5; ☎ 790 0001; Harbour Rd, Hout Bay; mains R25; ❂ 10.30am-8.15pm) Enjoy eating some of Cape Town's best fish and chips at a prime spot right at the end of Hout Bay Harbour Rd.

RESTAURANTS

Blues (Map pp112-13; ☎ 438 2040; the Promenade, Victoria Rd, Camps Bay; mains R85; ❂ noon-midnight) Overlooking the beach, Blues is a smart casual restaurant in the 'Californian tradition', which means the menu has something to please practically everyone.

Buzbey Grill (Map pp112-13; ☎ 439 5900; 14 Three Anchor Bay Rd, Sea Point; mains R60-70; ❂ 6-11pm Tue-Sat) Retro institution that attracts an older crowd who value a well-done steak or plate of seafood; the calamari is legendary.

La Perla (Map pp112-13; ☎ 439 9538; Beach Rd, Sea Point; mains R60-70; ❂ noon-11.30pm) Stylish operator with terrace seating and a comfy bar that is one of the few decent seaside options in this area. It serves some 30-plus pastas.

Southern Suburbs

Along Lower Main Rd in Observatory it's wall-to-wall restaurants, cafés and bars, most with menus slanted towards the tastes and budgets of the resident student population. More upmarket restaurants can be found in and around Constantia's wineries. Kirstenbosch Botanical Gardens (p111) also has several decent dining options in case you forgot your picnic basket.

CAFÉS & QUICK EATS

Gardener's Cottage (Map pp112-13; ☎ 689 3158; Montebello Craft Studios, 31 Newlands Ave, Newlands; mains R40) This cute café and tea garden in the grounds of the craft studios is worth visiting in its own right for its relaxed atmosphere and simple, hearty meals.

Kirstenbosch Tea Room (Map pp94-5; ☎ 797 4883; Kirstenbosch Botanical Gardens, Rhodes Dr, Bishopscourt; mains R20-30) New café proving popular with its high-roofed design and general menu of sandwiches, quiches and light meals, such as fish and chips. If you want some food to eat in the gardens, drop by the Fynbos Food Court, which also sells beer and wine.

Rhodes Memorial Restaurant (Map pp112-13; ☎ 689 9151; Groote Schuur Estate, Rondebosch; mains R40-60) This thatched, stone cottage is a fantastic spot for lunch or afternoon tea, on the side of Devil's Peak and right behind the memorial (p111). The scones are just enormous.

RESTAURANTS

Spaanschemat River Café (Map pp94-5; ☎ 794 3010; Constantia Uitsig, Spaanschemat River Rd; mains R60) Next to the wine shop at the entrance to the Constantia Uitsig wine estate, this relaxed restaurant is good value and serves huge portions, often made with organic and free-range products.

La Columbe (Map pp94-5; ☎ 794 2390; Constantia Uitsig, Spaanschemat River Rd; mains R90) If you want to go up-market at Constantia Uitsig, try the winery's celebrated, relaxed French restaurant. The menu – all written in French – changes daily.

Jonkerhuis (Map pp112-13; ☎ 794 4255; Groot Constantia, Constantia; mains R80; ☉ 9am-11pm Tue-Sat, 9am-5pm Sun & Mon) Staff dressed in 17th-century slave costumes serve up traditional Cape dishes such as bobotie and *bredies* (pot stews of meat or fish, and vegetables) at this pretty, atmospheric restaurant in the Groot Constantia winery (p111). Its Cape brandy tart is a tea-time treat.

Diva (Map pp112-13; ☎ 448 0282; 88 Lower Main Rd; mains R500) Best known for its tasty pizzas (the Mediterranean with wine-soaked aubergine is a favourite), Diva offers up plenty of other Italian goodies in a faded Venetian-style atmosphere.

Peddlars on the Bend (Map pp94-5; ☎ 794 7747; Constantia Uitsig, Spaanschemat River Rd; mains R50-60) If you don't fancy all that highfalutin wine-estate fodder, the hearty dishes such as chicken pie and *eisbein* (pork knuckle) served at this lively pub should suit you fine.

DRINKING

Long and Kloof Sts and the gay Waterkant district (see the boxed text on p135) are incredibly lively all night long on summer weekends, as is the Waterfront. Most bars open around 3pm and close after midnight, and much later Friday to Sunday. Alternative opening times are listed in the reviews below.

City Bowl   Map pp102-3

Marvel (☎ 426 5880; 236 Long St, City Bowl; ☉ 8pm-4am Mon-Sat) Groovy, understated bar that is (at the time of research) one of the best on Long St. There are cosy booths at the front, a pool table at the back and a selection of hot DJs throughout the week.

Jo'burg (☎ 422 0142; 218 Long St, City Bowl) Long St's most crowded hang-out, with live music on Sundays and a pool table at the back. Check out Brett Murray's highly aroused Bart Simpson on the wall (for more information on Brett Murray see the boxed text on p105).

M Bar & Lounge (☎ 423 7247; www.metropolehotel.co.za; 38 Long St, City Bowl) Like stepping into the sexiest tomato in town, this overwhelmingly red bar hides its charms at the back of the revamped Metropole Hotel. Versace-clad sofas just add to the glamour.

Pa Na Na Souk Bar (☎ 423 4889; Heritage Sq, 100 Shortmarket St, City Bowl; ☉ 11am-1am Mon-Sat) Welcome to the style kazbah at this sybaritic bar with balconies overlooking the restored courtyard of Heritage Sq.

Cool Runnings City Bowl (☎ 426 6584; 227 Long St); Observatory (Map pp112-13; ☎ 448 7656; 96 Station St) Reggae-theme bar brings a laid-back Caribbean atmosphere to Long St in the City Bowl, above Adventure Village. The popular branch in Observatory has a sand-covered courtyard for that beachside atmosphere.

Purple Turtle (☎ 423 6194; cnr Long & Shortmarket Sts, City Bowl) The antithesis of hip is this grunge and Goth centre. Dress right down or in black with purple make-up to feel at home. It's worth checking out for its alternative music gigs, too.

Gardens & Around   Map p106

Cafe Bardeli/Cohibar (☎ 423 4444; Darter's Rd, Gardens; ☉ 9am-1am Mon-Sat) In the Longkloof Studios building just off Kloof St, Bardeli is a reliable place to sink a Chardonnay or beer, grab something to eat and be seen with trendy media types. Adjoining it is Cohibar (see the boxed text on p135).

Planet (☎ 483 1864; Mount Nelson Hotel, 76 Orange St, Gardens) A fabulous mobile of the planets hangs above this delectable silver-coated champagne and cocktail bar, serving some 250 different bubblies and 50-odd alcoholic concoctions.

Perseverance Tavern (☎ 461 2440; 83 Buitenkant St, Zonnebloem) Cecil Rhodes called this pioneering pub his local. The flickering candles in the dim interior still give it plenty of atmosphere.

Shack (☎ 461 5892; 43-45 De Villiers St, Zonnebloem) Part of the complex of venues on the edge of District Six, this happening bar on several levels with a pool hall and table football packs an interesting, studenty crowd.

Green Point, Waterkant & Waterfront   Map pp108-9

Nose Wine Bar (☎ 425 2200; www.thenose.co.za; Cape Quarter, Dixon St, Waterkant) First-class wine bar where you can sip your way around some 35 of the Cape's best wines with 12 changing on a monthly basis. It also serves good food and runs wine-tasting courses.

Fireman's Arms (☎ 419 1513; 25 Mechau St, City Bowl) One of the few old-style pubs left in town – so old in fact that it still has the Rhodesian and old South African flags pinned up along side its collection of fireman's helmets. You can watch rugby on the

Groot Constantia homestead (p114),
Cape Town

Langa, Cape Flats (p145), Cape Town

Busker in St George's Mall (p120),
Cape Town

Cape Malay area (p96), Bo-Kaap, Cape Town

Jazz musician, the Green Dolphin (p134), Waterfront, Cape Town

ARIADNE VAN ZANDBERGEN

Clock tower (p107) at Victoria & Albert Waterfront, Cape Town

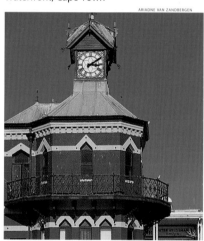

ARIADNE VAN ZANDBERGEN

ARIADNE VAN ZANDBERGEN

Market and Old Town House (p120), Grand Pde, Cape Town

Camps Bay (p111) with the Twelve Apostles in the background, Cape Peninsula

MANFRED GOTTSC

big-screen TV, grab some seriously tasty pizza or just down a lazy pint or two.

Ferryman's Freehouse (☎ 419 7748; East Pier Rd, Waterfront) Adjoining Mitchell's Waterfront Brewery, this traditional, wood-clad pub-restaurant serves a variety of freshly brewed beers and good-value meals.

Buena Vista Social Café (☎ 433 0611; Exhibition Bldg, 81 Main Rd, Green Point) Taking its inspiration from the famous CD of Cuban music, Buena Vista is *mucho sympatico*. A tapas menu supplements the mix of cigars, Bacardi and Cokes, and bronzed babes.

Bascule Bar (☎ 410 7100; Cape Grace, West Quay, Waterfront) The Grace's sophisticated earthtoned lounge bar specialises in whisky – over 400 of them! If you're feeling flush go for the 50-year-old Glenfiddich, just R15,200 a tot.

Tank (☎ 419 0007; Shop B15, Cape Quarter, Waterkant St, Waterkant) Pacific rim cuisine for the style set is offered at this uberchic lounge bar and restaurant. Most patrons seem to just hang by the luminous bar and fish tank practising their poses and pouts.

Atlantic Coast   Map pp112–13
Eclipse (☎ 438 0882; the Promenade, Victoria Rd, Camps Bay) There's a postcard-perfect view of the beach from this oh-so-trendy bar. Let wafer-thin, tattooed staff bring you something tall and chilled to enjoy on a chocolate leather ottoman as the sun slips beneath the horizon.

Baraza (☎ 438 1758; Victoria Rd, Camps Bay) Comfy seaside cocktail bar with a killer view – and you may have to kill to be able to admire it from one of the hotly contested cane chairs.

La Med (☎ 438 5600; Glen Country Club, Victoria Rd, Clifton) Perennially favourite spot for sunset drinks, although essentially it's just a bar with lots of outdoor tables and a good view.

Southern Suburbs   Map pp112–13
Café Carte Blanche (☎ 447 8717; 42 Trill Rd, Observatory) With bags of boho chic, this tiny café-bar plastered with art and on two cosy floors is the place for a secret assignation or late-night canoodlings.

Foresters' Arms (☎ 689 5949; 52 Newlands Ave, Newlands; ☺ 10am-11pm Mon-Sat, 9am-4pm Sun) Big mock-Tudor pub, affectionately known as Forries, which has been around over a century; it offers a convivial atmosphere and good pub meals.

A Touch of Madness (☎ 448 2266; 12 Nuttal Rd, Observatory) Now installed in roomier premises, this café-bar keeps its eclectic art-house atmosphere, dressed up in purple with lace trimmings.

ENTERTAINMENT
From drumming your hands numb at the Drum Café (p134) to dancing the night away at a Long St club, Cape Town certainly knows how to throw a party (or a 'jol' as they say in South Africa). The city has such a lively atmosphere (especially in summer) that many people put in some very long nights; most bars and clubs don't get going until after 11pm anyway.

Wednesday, Friday and Saturday are the biggest nights for drinking and clubbing. As well as the more commercial venues there's a range of informal places that come and go. Some started out as private parties that were just too good to stop. Among the hottest tickets in town are those for the monthly **Vortex trance parties** (☎ 794 4032; vortex@mweb.co.za).

For listings, see the weekly arts guide in the *Mail & Guardian* and the nightly entertainment section in the *Cape Argus*.

You can book seats for practically anything with **Computicket** (☎ 918 8910; www.computicket.com). There are outlets in the Golden Acre Centre (Map pp102–3), in the Gardens Centre (Map p106), in the Adelphi Centre in Three Anchor Bay (Map pp112–13) and at the Waterfront (Map pp108–9).

Cinemas
Cape Town has plenty of cinemas showing all the latest international releases. The big multiplexes can be found in the Victoria Wharf Shopping Centre at the Waterfront (Map pp108–9), Cavendish Sq (Map pp112–13) and Canal Walk Shopping Centre (Map pp94–5).

Labia (Map p106; ☎ 424 5927; www.labia.co.za; 68 Orange St, Gardens; tickets R25) Together with its two-screen **Labia on Kloof** (Map p106; ☎ 424 5727) in the Lifestyles on Kloof centre around the corner, this is the best cinema for 'mainstream alternative' films. It's named after the old Italian ambassador and local philanthropist Count Labia.

Cavendish Nouveau (Map pp112–13; ☎ 082-167 89; Cavendish Sq, Claremont; tickets Wed-Mon R35, Tue R18) With its sibling Cinema Nouveau Waterfront (Map pp108–9), this classy multiplex showcases the best of independent and art-house movies. It's worth booking seats in advance since it's very popular.

IMAX Theatre (Map pp108-9; ☎ 419 7365; BMW Pavilion, Waterfront) Offering the biggest screen entertainment in Cape Town, you might want to take the kids along here to see one of the eye-popping documentaries.

Live Music
BANDS
Drum Café (Map p106; ☎ 461 1305; www.drumcafe .co.za; 32 Glynn St, Gardens; admission plus drum hire Mon/ Wed & Fri R60/80) Learn to beat out a rhythm on *djembes* at the facilitated drum circles held every Monday, Wednesday and Friday from 9pm at this warehousey, inner-city hang-out. Huge fun and a refreshing breath of truly African entertainment. Check the café's website for details of events, lessons and kids' workshops.

Mama Africa (Map pp102-3; ☎ 426 1017; 178 Long St, City Bowl; mains R70) The buzzing atmosphere here, fuelled by the swinging African bands playing nightly, outpaces the variable food, which includes a tourist-pleasing range of game and African dishes. Bookings are essential at weekends unless you want to perch at the bar. There's a cover charge of R15, or R10 if you are dining.

Mercury Live (Map p106; ☎ 465 2106; www.mer curyl.co.za; 43 De Villiers St, Zonnebloem; cover free-R400) Top South African bands and overseas visitors belt their stuff out at this flexible venue with great sound quality and a laid-back student-union atmosphere.

CLASSICAL
The incredibly active **Cape Town Philharmonic** (www.ctpo.co.za) leads the way on the Mother City's classical music scene, performing concerts mainly at **City Hall** (Map pp102-3; ☎ 410 9809; Darling St, City Bowl) as well as at Artscape (below), the Waterfront and elsewhere around the Cape. It also teams up with **Cape Town Opera** (www.capetownopera.co.za) who has performed at the Waterfront's Aqua Opera season (on a floating stage in the harbour) and on Robben Island.

Artscape (Map pp102-3; ☎ 421 7695; www.artscape .co.za; 1-10 DF Malan St, Foreshore) Consisting of three different-sized auditoria, this performing-arts complex is the hub of classical and theatrical performances in Cape Town. You can catch regular classical concerts as well as bal-let, opera and theatre. Walking around this area at night is not recommended; book ahead for a nonshared taxi since there are none to be found on the streets. There's plenty of secure parking.

JAZZ
Dizzy Jazz (Map pp112-13; ☎ 438 2686; 41 the Drive, Camps Bay; cover R20) This convivial restaurant (specialising in seafood platters) and music venue has live jazz on Friday and Saturday and other types of music the rest of the week.

Green Dolphin (Map pp108-9; ☎ 421 7471; www .greendolphin.co.za; Waterfront; cover R20) Consist-ently good line-up of artists at this up-market jazz venue and restaurant serving decent food, with shows kicking off at 8pm daily. If you don't mind an obstructed view, the cover charge is a little lower.

Manenberg's Jazz Café (Map pp108-9; ☎ 421 5639; Clock Tower Centre, Waterfront; cover R30-80) Jazz and African jive is on the menu every night at this famed jazz club and restaurant newly relocated to the Waterfront. For the bands playing the sundowner set from 5pm to 7pm it's free, but a cover charge kicks in later.

West End (Map pp94-5; ☎ 637 9132; Cine 400 Bldg, College Rd, Ryelands Estate, Athlone; cover R30; ☽ 8pm-late Fri & Sat) One of Cape Town's top jazz venues, West End attracts international stars. You'll need to drive here but there's plenty of security.

Nightclubs
Most top nightclubs are concentrated in the City Bowl around Long St, but there are a few others worth checking out in Athlone, Milnerton, Waterkant and Zonnebloem.

Rhodes House (Map pp102-3; ☎ 424 8844; www .rhodeshouse.com; 60 Queen Victoria St, City Bowl; cover R50) Shimmy and pout with the glam set at this luxurious venue spread over a grand old house. The long queues and cooler-than-thou attitude can be a pain, but with the right party crowd it can be an awesome night out here.

Snap (Map pp102-3; 6 Pepper St, City Bowl; cover R20) The Cape Flats comes to the city at this urban African club with a welcoming, predominantly Black audience. Dance to music from across Africa.

169 on Long (Map pp102-3; ☎ 426 1107; 169 Long St, City Bowl) One of the best Long St ven-ues, where you're guaranteed to party with

GAY & LESBIAN CAPE TOWN

With a distinct and very high-profile gay area (the Waterkant) and a plethora of gay-friendly accommodation, drinking and dining establishments, Cape Town is the gay capital of South Africa, if not the whole continent. It's quite a lively scene – for the latest on where to go check out the *Pink Map* available from Cape Town Tourism and most of the venues listed here, the gay listings in the magazine *Cape Etc* and the website www.gaynetcapetown.co.za.

The **Mother City Queer Project** (p123) is a huge costume party held every year in December. The **Out in Africa Gay and Lesbian Film Festival** (☎ 465 9289; www.oia.co.za) hits town in February.

Most places of interest are clustered in a tight grid of streets in the Waterkant. **Bronx** (Map pp108-9; ☎ 419 9219; 35 Somerset Rd, Waterkant) is the city's premier gay bar attracting a mixed crowd. Next door are the excellent dance clubs **Sliver & Confession** (Map pp108-9; ☎ 421 4798; 27 Somerset Rd, Waterkant; cover R20). It's a predominantly gay crowd, particularly upstairs at the luminously painted Confession where hard House and bare chests are the go. Sliver gives it up to a more mixed crowd into happy clappy House. Chill out in the fairy light–festooned courtyard.

Cafe Manhattan (Map pp108-9; ☎ 421 6666; 74 Waterkant St, Waterkant) is generally credited with getting the Waterkant's gay scene up and running. The restaurant's not much cop, but it's certainly still a good bar with outdoor tables in just the right spot to catch the crowds.

Valve (Map pp102-3; ☎ 084-361 3321; Groote Kerk Arcade, Parliament St, City Bowl) is an atmospheric venue where a dance party for lesbian and lesbian-friendly folk is held on the first and third Friday of the month. Adjoining Cafe Bardeli (p132) is Cohibar, which hosts the Habit, a lesbian/women's night on the last Saturday of the month.

Out of the Waterkant area you could check out **Café Erté** (Map pp112-13; ☎ 434 6624; 265A Main Rd, Sea Point), a vibey Internet café and chilled hang-out for the late-night clubbing set; or the laid-back **Velvet Lounge** (Map pp102-3; ☎ 083-709 0419; 136 Bree St, City Bowl) with pool tables and a lot less pumped-up crowd than in the Waterkant.

The cabaret and supper venue On Broadway (p136) is popular with all Capetonians – the resident artists are dynamic drag duo Mince.

---

more Blacks and Coloureds than Whites. The funky R&B music, sometimes live, and long, cool balcony are a large part of the attraction.

Mercury Lounge (Map p106; ☎ 465 2106; www .mercuryl.co.za; 43 De Villiers St, Zonnebloem; cover R10) Very groovy, unpretentious club with the excellent Mercury Live upstairs (opposite). Get down to everything from classic Duran Duran to Motown hits.

Deluxe (Map pp102-3; ☎ 422 4832; Unity House, cnr Long & Longmarket Sts, City Bowl; cover R30) With a leaning towards the latest grooves in French House and tribal trance, Deluxe attracts a slightly older and more musically sophisticated mixed-gay crowd.

Fez (Map pp102-3; ☎ 423 1456; 38 Hout St, City Bowl; cover R40) The funky Moroccan theme is carried on at this sister venue to Pa Na Na Souk Bar (p132). Expect queues out the door at weekends and a lively, young crowd.

Club Galaxy (Map pp94-5; ☎ 637 9132; College Rd, Ryelands Estate, Athlone; cover R30) Long-time Cape Flats dance venue where you can get down to R&B, hip-hop and live bands with

a Black and Coloured crowd. The equally legendary West End jazz venue (opposite) is next door.

Purgatory (Map pp108-9; ☎ 421 7464; 8B Dixon St, Waterkant; cover R50) This is what you get if you spend R2 million on your venue. Terraces overlook the dance floor and giant paintings of nudes hang in the VIP bar downstairs at this ultrastylish place with a mainly straight crowd.

New Dockside (Map pp94-5; ☎ 552 2030; www .docksidesuperclub.com; Century City, Century City Blvd, Milnerton; cover R50) Mega club on four floors with state-of-the-art everything beside the mammoth Canal Walk Shopping Centre. International DJs such as Paul Van Dyk occasionally grace the decks.

Sports
CRICKET

Newlands Cricket Ground (Map pp112-13; ☎ 657 3300; ticket hotline ☎ 657 2099; Camp Ground Rd, Newlands) Venue for all international matches. The season runs from September to March with the day–night matches drawing the biggest crowds. Grab a spot on the grass bank to soak up the festive atmosphere. Tickets cost around R50 for local matches and up to R200 for internationals.

FOOTBALL

With tickets costing just R20, attending the footie in Cape Town is not only cheap but also a hugely fun and loud night out with Capetonian supporters taking every opportunity to blow their plastic trumpets. The season runs from August to May. Ajax Cape Town, affiliated with the Dutch club Ajax Amsterdam, plays matches at Newlands Rugby Stadium (below). Matches are sometimes also played at Green Point Stadium (Map pp108–9) off Beach Rd in Green Point, and Athlone Stadium (Map pp94–5), off Klipfontein Rd in Athlone. This last stadium is home to the 2002 national champions, Santos, as well as Hellenic. Tickets can be purchased through **Computicket** (☎ 918 8910; www.computicket.com).

RUGBY

Newlands Rugby Stadium (Map pp112-13; ☎ 659 4600; Boundary Rd, Newlands) This hallowed ground of South African rugby is home to the Stormers. Tickets for Super 12 games cost from R35 to R45 in the stands and R55 to R65 in seats. Tickets for international matches cost around R250 to R300.

YACHTING

Royal Cape Yacht Club (Map pp112-13; ☎ 421 1354; www.rcyc.co.za; Duncan Rd, Foreshore) Races known as the 'Wags' are held every Wednesday afternoon at the club. Get there at 4.30pm if you want to take part, otherwise it's a 6pm start.

Theatre, Cabaret & Comedy

Major productions are staged at Artscape (p134). On Broadway (below) has great cabaret shows and is popular with Capetonians (also see p135).

Baxter Theatre (Map pp112-13; ☎ 685 7880; www .baxter.co.za; Main Rd, Rondebosch) Three venues at this landmark venue in the Southern Suburbs, covering everything from kids' shows to Zulu dance spectaculars.

On Broadway (Map pp108-9; ☎ 418 8338; www .onbroadway.co.za; 21 Somerset Rd, Waterkant) This is a hugely popular cabaret and supper venue, so book ahead. There are shows nightly ex-

cept Monday and tickets cost around R50 to R60.

Cape Comedy Collective (Map pp112-13; ☎ 689 3000; the Grouse, Main Rd, Rondebosch) Every Thursday join the heckling student crowd at the Grouse pub for an evening of comedy from host Sean Wilson and some of the Cape's best wise crackers. For details of other comedy shows around town see www.samp .co.za and www.comedyclub.co.za.

Independent Armchair Theatre (Map pp112-13; ☎ 447 1514; 135 Lower Main Rd, Observatory) This bar and casual theatre-cum-lounge has an eclectic range of other events, including comedy, Japanese animated and quirky movie nights, and band gigs.

SHOPPING

You'll find most things you need at shops in the city centre and the Waterfront, but if you hunger for a suburban mall, try the stylish mall **Cavendish Sq** (Map pp112-13; ☎ 671 8042; www.cavendish.co.za; Cavendish St, Claremont; ☼ 9am-6pm Mon-Thu, 9am-9pm Fri, 9am-6pm Sat, 10am-4pm Sun) or **Canal Walk** (Map pp94-5; ☎ 555 3100; www .canalwalk.co.za; Ratanga Junction, Century City, Milnerton; ☼ 9am-9pm), the largest mall on the continent, about 5km north of the city centre. The **Gardens Centre** (Map p106; Mill St, Gardens) is another handy central shopping complex.

There are good craft and souvenir markets in **Greenmarket Sq** (p101; cnr Shortmarket & Burg Sts, City Bowl; ☼ 9am-4pm Mon-Sat), outside the **Green Point Stadium** (Map pp108-9; Western Blvd, Green Point; ☼ 8.30am-6pm Sun); and in Khayelitsha (p145).

Antiques & Art

For antiques and art, Church and Long Sts in the City Bowl are particularly worth a browse. There's a small market daily along the pedestrianised section of Church St between Long and Burg Sts, and this is where you'll also find several interesting commercial galleries. Along St George's Mall you'll find some very good (as well as some very ordinary) art by township artists.

AVA Gallery (Map pp102-3; ☎ 424 7436; 35 Church St, City Bowl) Exhibition space for the non-profit Association for Visual Arts (AVA), which shows some very interesting work by local artists.

Photographers Gallery (Map p106; ☎ 422 2762; 87 Kloof St, Gardens) Fabulous gallery upstairs from a classy interior-décor shop. In it you'll find classic prints by the likes of George Hallett, including photographs he took in District Six during the 1960s.

Michael Stevenson Contemporary (Map pp108-9; ☎ 421 2575; www.michaelstevenson.com; Hill House, De Smidt St, Green Point) One of the city's best exhibition spaces is put to good use displaying the works of up-and-coming and established South African artists such as Hilton Neil, Bernie Searle and Brett Murray.

Crafts

There are craft shops all over town but few of the traditional African items come from the Cape Town area itself. Great buys include the local township-produced items, such as beadwork dolls, toys made from recycled tin cans and wire sculptures.

African Image City Bowl (Map pp102-3; ☎ 423 8385; cnr Church & Burg Sts); Waterfront (Map pp108-9; ☎ 419 0382; Victoria Wharf Shopping Centre) Fab range of new and old craft and artefacts, at reasonable prices. You'll find a lot of township crafts here as well as wildly patterned shirts. The branch at Victoria Wharf stocks a more upmarket range.

Africa Nova Waterkant (Map pp108-9; ☎ 425 5123; Cape Quarter, 72 Waterkant St); Hout Bay (Map pp94-5; ☎ 790 4454; Main Rd) One of the most stylish, contemporary and desirable collections of African textiles, art and craft. It's known for its original potato print fabrics made by women in Hout Bay.

Mnandi Textiles & Design (Map pp112-13; ☎ 447 6814; 90 Station St, Observatory) Sells cloth from all over Africa and clothing printed with everything from ANC election posters to animals and traditional African patterns. You can have clothes tailor-made.

Monkeybiz (Map pp102-3; ☎ 426 0145; www.monkeybiz.co.za; 43 Rose St, Bo-Kaap) The colourful products, including long-legged dolls, animals and bags, all made by women in the townships are brilliant. Turn up on Friday morning here, its main showroom, to meet the women artists.

Montebello (Map pp112-13; ☎ 685 6445; 31 Newlands Ave, Newlands) Worthy development project promoting good local design and creating jobs in the craft industry. On Monday to Friday you can visit the artists studios and the good café the Gardener's Cottage (p131).

Pan African Market (Map pp102-3; ☎ 426 4478; www.panafrican.co.za; 76 Long St, City Bowl) A microcosm of the continent with a bewildering range of art and craft as well as a cheap café and music store packed into its three floors. On the 3rd floor you'll find **Wola Nani** (☎ 423 7385; www.wolanani.co.za), an NGO addressing the needs of those infected with HIV and AIDS. Buy one of its decorated light bulbs, papier-mâché bowls and frames, safety-pin bracelets with bead or wire detail.

Streetwires (Map pp102-3; ☎ 426 2475; www.streetwires.co.za; 77 Shortmarket St, Bo-Kaap) Watch wire sculpture artists at work at this social upliftment project for young Blacks and Coloureds. Stocks an amazing range, including working radios and chandeliers.

Waterfront Craft Market (Map pp108-9; ☎ 408 7842; Dock Rd, Waterfront) Also known as the Blue Shed, this eclectic arts and crafts market harbours some great buys. Search out African Guitars selling the all-electric township 'blik' guitars made from oil cans, wood and fishing wire, and the beautiful jewellery of Get Wired.

Fashion & Outdoor Gear

Cape Union Mart (Map pp108-9; ☎ 419 0019; Victoria Wharf, Waterfront) Set yourself up for everything from a hike up Table Mountain to a Cape-to-Cairo safari at this impressive outdoors shop. There are many other branches around the city, including at the Gardens Centre.

India Jane Waterkant (Map pp108-9; ☎ 421 3517; 125 Waterkant St); Claremont (Map pp112-13; 683 7607; Cavendish Sq, Cavendish St); Kalk Bay (Map p141; 788 3020; Main Rd) The sexy, silky clothes at India Jane's boutiques reflect the stylish, laid back atmosphere of the city and include the Indian-meet-African designs of local hot young designer Maya Prass. The menswear store A Suitable Boy is upstairs at the Cavendish Sq branch.

Young Designers Emporium (Map pp112-13; ☎ 683 6177; Shop F50, Cavendish Sq, Cavendish St, Claremont) Bit of a jumble but you'll most likely find something groovy to suit among the street clothes and accessories for both him and her by new South African designers.

Other

African Music Store (Map pp102-3; ☎ 426 0857; 134 Long St, City Bowl) The knowledgeable staff here can advise you on the big selection of local music, including all top jazz, kwaito, and dance and trance recordings.

Vaughan Johnson's Wine & Cigar Shop (Map pp108-9; ☎ 419 2121; vjohnson@mweb.co.za; Dock Rd, Waterfront) Sells practically every wine you could wish to buy (plus a few more) and is open, unlike most wine sellers, on Sunday.

GETTING THERE & AWAY
Air
Cape Town International Airport (Map pp94-5; ☎ 934 0407), 20km east of the city, is served by direct flights from many countries, although several will touch down first in Johannesburg (Jo'burg).

For domestic services the one-way fares quoted here are full economy but discounts are available (see p587). **South African Airways** (SAA; ☎ 0860 359 722, 011-978 1111; www.flysaa .com) flies between Cape Town and major centres, including Durban (R1620), East London (R1650), Jo'burg (R1740), Kimberley (R1660), Port Elizabeth (R1000) and Upington (R1665). For the cheapest fares to Jo'burg and Durban check with **Kulula** (☎ 0861 585 852; www.kulula.com). For details on other airlines, see p596.

International airlines with offices in Cape Town:
Air Mauritius (Map pp102-3; ☎ 421 6294; 11th fl, Strand Towers, 66 Strand St, City Bowl)
Air Namibia (Map pp94-5; ☎ 936 2755; Cape Town International Airport)
British Airways (Map pp94-5; ☎ 934 0292; Cape Town International Airport)
KLM (Map pp112-13; ☎ 082-234 5747; Slade House, Boundary Tce, 1 Mariendahl Lane, Newlands)
Lufthansa (Map pp102-3; ☎ 0861 266 554; 9th fl, Picbel Arcade, 58 Strand St, City Bowl)
Malaysia Airlines (Map pp102-3; ☎ 419 8010; 8th fl, Safmarine House, 22 Riebeeck St, City Bowl)
SAA (Map pp94-5; ☎ 936 1111; Cape Town International Airport)
Singapore Airlines (Map pp112-13; ☎ 674 0601; 3rd fl, Sanclaire, 21 Dreyer St, Claremont)
Virgin Atlantic (Map pp94-5; ☎ 683 2221; Cape Town International Airport)

Bus
The three major long-distance bus lines all operate out of Cape Town. Their booking offices and main arrival and departure points are at the Meriman Sq end of Cape Town train station (City Bowl).
Greyhound (☎ 505 6363; www.greyhound.co.za)
Intercape Mainliner (☎ 380 4400; www.intercape.co.za)
Translux (☎ 449 3333; www.translux.co.za)

There's little to choose between the prices, and each company's services and routes are similar. For more information on bus routes and fares, and on the Baz Bus, see p598.

Car & Motorcycle
Driving in Cape Town is on the whole a pleasure. The city has an excellent road and freeway system that, outside the late-afternoon rush hour (kicking off around 4pm), carries surprisingly little traffic. The only downside is getting used to the sometimes erratic breaking of road rules by fellow drivers.

Major local and international car and motorcycle hire companies in Cape Town:
Avis (Map pp102-3; ☎ 0861 021 111; www.avis.co.za; 123 Strand St, City Bowl)
Budget (Map pp102-3; ☎ 0860 016 622; www.budget .com; 120 Strand St, City Bowl)
Harley-Davidson Cape Town (Map pp102-3; ☎ 424 3990; www.harley-davidson-capetown.com; 45 Buitengracht St, City Bowl; ☻ 9am-5pm Mon-Sat) Rents a Harley 1340cc Big Twins or an MG-B convertible sports car for R1150 for 24 hours.
Imperial (Map pp102-3; ☎ 0861 131 000; www.imper ialcarrental.co.za; cnr Loop & Strand Sts, City Bowl)
Le Cap Motorcycle Hire (Map p106; ☎ 423 0823; www.lecapmotorcyclehire.co.za; 45 New Church St, Tamboerskloof; motorcycle hire per day from R200; ☻ 9am-5pm Mon-Fri, 10am-1pm Sat)

Smaller, cheaper companies come and go; you'll find plenty of brochures for them at Cape Town Tourism and all the hostels. The deals may look tempting, but read the small print (R99 per day is a rate that is seldom, if ever, available). If you're not looking for anything fancy try the **Happy Beetle Co** (Map pp102-3; ☎ 426 4170; info@thehappybeetleco .com), run by the people who operate Madame Zingara (p128), which rents out 1970s VW Beetles for R100 per day for up to 14 days and then R85 per day thereafter. It also has a few Vespa scooters for R125 per day.

Minibus Taxi
In Cape Town, most long-distance minibus taxis start picking up passengers in townships, especially Langa and Nyanga, perhaps also making a trip into the main train station if they need more people. The townships are not great places to be wandering around in the early hours of the

morning carrying a pack, so *do not* go into them without good local knowledge; it's preferable to go with a reliable local guide. Langa is relatively safe and long-distance taxis leave from the Langa shopping centre early in the morning. A local-area minibus taxi from Cape Town train station to Langa costs about R5. A taxi to Jo'burg costs about R250 (compared with R395 on Intercape) and departs at around 7am. The trip is long, uncomfortable and potentially dangerous because of driver fatigue. Between a few people, hiring a car would be cheaper.

Train

All trains leave from the main Cape Town train station. It can take a long time to get to the front of the queue at the **booking office** (☎ 449 4596; ☉ 7.30am-4.55pm Mon-Fri, 7.30-10.30am Sat).

There's a left-luggage facility next to Platform 24 (see p98).

For detailed information about train routes and fares, see p605.

GETTING AROUND
To/From the Airport

Several companies offer a shuttle service between the airport and the city. **Backpacker Bus** (☎ 082-809 9185; www.backpackerbus.co.za) picks up from hostels and hotels in the city and does airport transfers for R90 per person.

Nonshared taxis are expensive; expect to pay around R200.

Bicycle & Scooter

The Cape Peninsula is a great place to explore by bicycle, but there many are hills, and distances can be deceptively large – it's nearly 70km from the centre to Cape Point. Unfortunately, you aren't supposed to take bicycles on suburban trains. For bicycle hire, try Downhill Adventures (p116) or Atlantic Tourist Information Centre (p99).

Bus

Cape Town's Golden Arrow public bus network is reliable, if run-down. Most services stop running early in the evening. Buses are most useful for getting along the Atlantic Coast from the city centre to Hout Bay (trains service the suburbs to the east of Table Mountain). When travelling short distances people wait at the bus stop and take either a bus or a minibus taxi, whichever arrives first.

The main bus station, the **Golden Acre Terminal** (Map pp102-3; Grand Pde, City Bowl), has a helpful **bus information kiosk** (Map pp102-3; ☎ 0801 212 111, 461 4365; Castle St; ☉ 5.30am-7pm Mon-Fri, 7am-1.30pm Sat).

Destinations and off-peak fares (applicable from 8am to 4pm) from the city include the Waterfront (R2.50), Sea Point and Kloof Nek (R2.90), Camps Bay (R4.20) and Hout Bay (R6.70). Peak fares are about 30% higher. If you're using a particular bus regularly, it's worth buying 'clipcards', which give you 10 trips at a discount price.

Minibus Taxi

Minibus taxis cover most of the city with an informal network of routes and are a cheap way of getting around. Useful routes are from Adderley St (opposite the Golden Acre Centre) to Sea Point along Main Rd (R2.50) and up Long St to Kloof Nek (R2).

The main stop is on the upper deck of the main train station, accessible from a walkway in the Golden Acre Centre or from stairways on Strand St. It's well organised, and finding the right stop is easy. Anywhere else, you just hail minibus taxis from the side of the road. There's no way of telling which route a taxi will be taking except by asking the driver. For minibus taxi etiquette, see the boxed text on p604.

Rikki

Tiny, open vans, called **rikkis** (☎ 423 4888), provide Asian-style transport in the City Bowl and nearby areas for low prices. They operate from 7am to 7pm Monday to Friday, and until 2pm Saturday. They can be booked or hailed on the street and travel as far afield as Camps Bay and Observatory. A single-person trip from the main train station to Tamboerskloof costs R15; to Camps Bay it costs R25. A *rikki* from the City Bowl to Kirstenbosch Botanical Gardens costs R70 for the first four people and R10 for each extra person.

Although cheap and fun, *rikkis* may not be the quickest way to get around, as there is usually a certain amount of meandering as passengers are dropped off, and they can be notoriously slow to turn up to a booking.

Taxi

It's worth considering taking a nonshared taxi late at night or if you're in a group, but they're expensive (about R10 per kilometre). There is a taxi rank (Map pp102–3) on Adderley St in the city, or call **Marine Taxi** (☎ 434 0434) or **Unicab Taxis** (☎ 447 4402).

Train

Metro commuter trains are a handy way to get around, although there are few (or no) trains after 6pm Monday to Friday and after noon on Saturday. For information contact **Cape Metro Rail** (☎ 0800 656 463; www .capemetrorail.co.za).

Metro trains have 1st- and economy-class carriages only. The difference in price and comfort is negligible, although you'll find the 1st-class compartments to be safer on the whole.

The most important line for visitors is the Simon's Town line, which runs through Observatory and then around the back of Table Mountain through upper-income White suburbs, such as Rosebank, down to Muizenberg and along the False Bay coast. These trains run at least every hour from around 5am to 7.30pm Monday to Friday (to 6pm on Saturday), and from 7.30am to 6.30pm on Sunday. (*Rikki*s meet all trains and go to Boulders.) On some of these trains you'll find Biggsy's, a restaurant carriage and rolling wine bar. There's a small extra charge to use it.

Metro trains run some way out of Cape Town, to Strand on the eastern side of False Bay, and into the Winelands to Stellenbosch and Paarl. They are the cheapest and easiest means of transport to these areas; security is best at peak times.

Some 1st-/economy-class fares include Observatory (R5.50/4.20), Muizenberg (R8.50/ 5.50), Simon's Town (R12/7.30), Paarl (R14.50/ 8.50) and Stellenbosch (R12/7.50).

The **Spier Train** (☎ 419 5222) runs occasional trips to the Spier wine estate (p153) and Darling (p210).

Water Taxi

There is a water-taxi service between the Cape Town International Convention Centre (p104) and the Cape Grace Hotel (p126) at the Waterfront. The service runs every half-hour from 9am to 7pm and costs R20 one way.

AROUND CAPE TOWN

The communities hugging the coastal strip of the Cape Peninsula around False Bay – Muizenberg, St James, Kalk Bay and Simon's Town – have a distinct seaside-resort and village feel compared to Cape Town proper. Here you'll also find the natural wonders of the Rondevlei Nature Reserve at Zeekoevlei, the penguins at Boulders and the dramatic expanses of Cape Point, part of the Table Mountain National Park (p100).

The townships of the Cape Flats, spreading east from Table Mountain, are a whole other world entirely. They're best visited on a day trip from Cape Town (p120), although we'd recommend you stay at one of the B&Bs there to really experience the full extent of *ubuntu* – Xhosa hospitality.

RONDEVLEI NATURE RESERVE

This small **reserve** (Map pp94–5; ☎ 706 2404; Fisherman's Walk Rd, Zeekoevlei; adult/child R10/5; ☒ 7.30am-5pm Mar-Nov, 7.30am-7pm Mon-Fri, 7.30am-7pm Sat & Sun Dec-Feb) encompasses a picturesque wetlands with native marsh and dune vegetation. Hippos lived in the area 300 years ago and were reintroduced to the reserve in 1981. There are now six of them but it's very unlikely you'll spot them unless you stay overnight – for details contact Imvubu Nature Tours (p122) based at the reserve. Guided walks are available and you can spot some 230 species of birds from the waterside trail, two viewing towers and hides.

MUIZENBERG & KALK BAY

A popular holiday resort in the early 20th century, **Muizenberg**, 25km south of the City Bowl, is on the up again after a period in the economic doldrums. Properties are being renovated and new cafés and restaurants are opening. Muizenberg's broad white beach is popular with surfers – hire boards or get lessons from Gary's Surf School (p119) and there are free lockers in the pavilions on the promenade. Families love it here because the beach shelves gently and the sea is generally safer (and warmer) here than elsewhere along the peninsula. There's plenty of parking, and a pleasant **coastal walk** from the handsome train station to the neighbouring suburb of **St James**, where you'll find a tidal pool safe for children to swim in and the last of the much-photographed, colourfully painted Victorian bathing huts.

Kalk Bay's attractive fishing harbour is at its most picturesque in the late morning when the community's few remaining fishing boats pitch up with their daily catch and a lively quayside market ensues. This is an excellent place to buy fresh fish for a braai (barbecue). For an insight into the lives of the Kalk Bay's fisher folk sign up for a local walking tour (p122).

For more information about the area go to **Muizenberg Tourist Information Centre** (☎ 788 6193; the Pavilion, Beach Rd, Muizenberg; ☒ 9am-5.30pm Mon-Fri, 9am-1pm Sat).

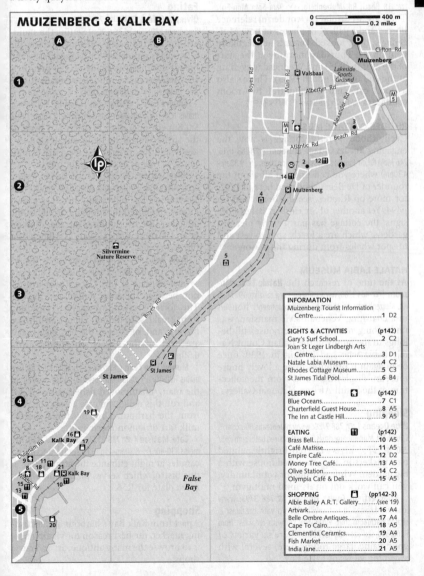

MUIZENBERG & KALK BAY

INFORMATION	
Muizenberg Tourist Information	
Centre................................	1 D2

SIGHTS & ACTIVITIES	(p142)
Gary's Surf School........................	2 C2
Joan St Leger Lindbergh Arts	
Centre...............................	3 D1
Natale Labia Museum.................	4 C2
Rhodes Cottage Museum.........	5 C3
St James Tidal Pool....................	6 B4

SLEEPING	(p142)
Blue Oceans................................	7 C1
Charterfield Guest House.........	8 A5
The Inn at Castle Hill.................	9 A5

EATING	(p142)
Brass Bell....................................	10 A5
Café Matisse...............................	11 A5
Empire Café................................	12 D2
Money Tree Café.........................	13 A5
Olive Station...............................	14 C2
Olympia Café & Deli....................	15 A5

SHOPPING	(pp142-3)
Albie Bailey A.R.T. Gallery............	(see 19)
Artvark..	16 A4
Belle Ombre Antiques.................	17 A4
Cape To Cairo..............................	18 A5
Clementina Ceramics..................	19 A4
Fish Market..................................	20 A5
India Jane....................................	21 A5

Sights

JOAN ST LEGER LINDBERGH ARTS CENTRE

The great granddaughter of the founder of the *Cape Times*, Joan St Leger was an artist and poet. She bequeathed her Sir Herbert Baker–designed home and the adjoining properties to the **Joan St Leger Lindbergh Arts Foundation** (☎ 788 2795; artcentre@linbergh-arts.co .za; 18 Beach Rd, Muizenberg; ⌚ 9am-5pm Mon-Fri). There are art displays, a wonderful reference library and a gallery of photos of how Muizenberg once looked. **Concerts** are regularly held on the Thursday morning at the start of the month (R35) and Wednesday evening at the end of the month (R85). There's also a good café and a delightful two-room **guesthouse** (s/d with breakfast R300/350; P).

RHODES COTTAGE MUSEUM

Cecil Rhodes' pretty cottage is now the engaging **Rhodes Cottage Museum** (☎ 788 1816; 246 Main Rd, St James; admission by donation; ⌚ 9.30am-4.30pm) where you can find out all about the founder of De Beers, who died here in 1902; for more on Rhodes, see the boxed text on p494. Yet another of Sir Herbert Baker's designs, the cottage has particularly pleasant gardens, which are a lovely spot to rest and to spot whales from during the season.

NATALE LABIA MUSEUM

At the time of research the **Natale Labia Museum** (☎ 464 3280; www.museums.org.za/iziko; 192 Main Rd, Muizenberg; ⌚ Mon only by appointment) housed in a charming Venetian-style mansion, was undergoing renovation. The house still belongs to the family of the Italian Count Natale Labia who had it built in 1930; once open again it promises to be a lovely house museum displaying works from the collection of the South African National Gallery.

Sleeping

Blue Oceans (☎ 788 9780; www.blueoceans.50g.com; 3 Church Rd, Muizenberg; dm/s & d with shared bathroom R65/200; P 💻) This is a relaxed, brightly painted backpackers in a spacious old house with a big garden. While waiting for your laundry, you can work out on its mini multigym.

Charterfield Guest House (☎ 788 3793; www .chartfield.co.za; 30 Gatesville Rd; s/d with breakfast & shared bathroom from R200/220, s/d with breakfast from R200/340, self-catering flat R200) There's a variety of good-value, large rooms here, several with sweeping views of False Bay.

The Inn At Castle Hill (☎ 788 2554; www.castlehill .co.za; 37 Gatesville Rd; s/d with breakfast R300/600; P) Some of the convivial rooms in this renovated Edwardian home overlook the bay and all are decorated with works by local artists.

Also see Joan St Leger Lindbergh Arts Centre (p142) for details of its guesthouse.

Eating

Olympia Café & Deli (☎ 788 6396; 134 Main Rd, Kalk Bay; mains R40-75; ⌚ 7am-9pm) Setting the standard for relaxed rustic cafés by the sea, the Olympia is renowned for its breakfasts, and breads and pastries made on the premises. Its Mediterranean-influenced main dishes are generally delicious, too.

Empire Café (☎ 788 1250; 11 York Rd, Muizenberg; mains R50; ⌚ 7am-4pm Tue-Sun, 6.30-10.30pm Thu & Sat) Superb operation that has fast become the surfies' favourite hang-out. It's on two levels and has interesting local art exhibitions, as well as excellent light meals.

Olive Station (☎ 788 3264; 165 Main Rd, Muizenberg; mains R30; ⌚ 8am-5pm Mon, 8am-9pm Wed-Sat, 8am-9pm Sun) The olives sold here are grown locally and cured in wooden barrels. In the attached café overlooking the sea, dine on tasty Lebanese dishes, such as kibbeh and filo pastry pies.

Brass Bell (☎ 788 5455; Kalk Bay Station, Main Rd, Kalk Bay; mains R60-70; ⌚ 10am-11.30pm) There are several options at this Cape Town institution between the train station and the sea. The formal restaurant serves everything from breakfast to dinner. There's an alfresco pizzeria and, of course, the bar. Fish braais are held on the terrace on Sunday from 6.30pm.

Money Tree Café (☎ 788 2242; Main Rd, Kalk Bay; mains R20-30; ⌚ 9am-4pm Tue-Sun) The wives of the many unemployed fishermen cook for and run this delightful café across the road from the harbour. Drop by for a slice of milk tart or lemon meringue.

Café Matisse (☎ 788 1123; 76 Main Rd, Kalk Bay; mains R30-40; ⌚ 8.30am-11pm) Eclectic décor and candles at night enhance the atmosphere at this bistro, which serves pizzas and a good meze plate for R56.

Shopping

Apart from Kalk Bay's harbour and its fishing market, the best reason for visiting here is to browse the many antique, art and curio shops.

Our pick of the bunch:

Artvark (☎ 788 5584; 48 Main Rd) For crafts.

Belle Ombre Antiques (☎ 788 9802; 19 Main Rd) For appealing Cape country antiques and African artefacts.

Cape to Cairo (☎ 788 4571; 100 Main Rd) An Aladdin's cave of interior-design goods.

Clementina Ceramics & Albie Bailey A.R.T. Gallery (☎ 788 8718; www.clementina.co.za; 20 Main Rd; ⊙ 10am-5pm Tue-Sun) For the full selection of Clementina van der Walt's distinctive tableware as well as one-off pieces.

Getting There & Around
The Simon's Town train line from Cape Town runs to Muizenberg, St James and Kalk Bay. If driving, the M4 leads directly to Muizenberg and connects with Main Rd which runs down the False Bay coast to Kalk Bay. The sights are all within walking distance of the train stations.

SIMON'S TOWN & BOULDERS
A naval town ever since colonial times, Simon's Town remains the main base for South Africa's navy. It's an attractive, Victorian town with a pretty harbour and an interesting Cape Muslim history. But the main reason most people head down this way is to visit the penguin colony at Boulders Beach.

For tourist information go to **Simon's Town Publicity Association** (☎ 786 2436; 111 St George's St, Simon's Town; ⊙ 9am-5.30pm Nov-Mar, 9am-5pm Mon-Fri, 9am-1pm Sat & Sun Apr-Oct).

Sights & Activities
BOULDERS BEACH
Some 3km south of Simon's Town is Boulders, an area with a number of large boulders and small sandy coves, within which you'll find **Boulders Beach** (☎ 701 8692; www.tmnp .co.za; adult/child R10/5; ⊙ 8am-5pm), part of Table Mountain National Park (p100) and famous for being home to a colony of 3000 African penguins. Delightful as they are, the penguins are also pretty stinky, which may put you off spending too long paddling with them.

There are two entrances to the penguins' protected area. The first, as you come along Queens Rd (the continuation of St George's St) from Simon's Town, is at the end of Seaforth Rd; the second is at Bellevue Rd, where you'll also find accommodation and eating options. You can observe the penguins from the boardwalk at Foxy Beach, but at Boulders Beach you can get in the water with them. The sea is calm and shallow in the coves, so Boulders is popular with families and can get extremely crowded, especially on holidays and at weekends.

HARBOUR CRUISES & KAYAKING
Among the several boat tour operators in Simon's Town is **Southern Right** (☎ 083-257 7760, 786 2136; Simon's Town Harbour Jetty; harbour cruise R25), which runs the popular *Spirit of Just Nuisance* cruise around the harbour. Speedboat trips to Cape Point and Seal Island are R250 and during the whale-watching season it also offers cruises to get up close to these magnificent animals.

It's also possible to kayak in the harbour and down the coast towards Cape Point (see p118 for more).

HERITAGE MUSEUM
This **museum** (☎ 786 2302; Almay House, King George Way, Simon's Town; adult/child R3/2; ⊙ 11am-4pm Tue-Fri, Sat & Sun by appointment only) is Simon's Town's most interesting museum. It includes displays on the Cape Muslim community of over 7000 people forcibly removed from here during the apartheid era. Nearby Alfred Lane leads to the handsome mosque and attached school built in 1926.

SIMON'S TOWN MUSEUM
This rambling **museum** (☎ 786 3046; Court Rd, Simon's Town; donation of R5 suggested; ⊙ 9am-4pm Mon-Fri, 10am-1pm Sat, 11am-3pm Sun) is about 600m south of the train station. Based in the old governor's residency (1777), its extensive exhibits trace the history of the town and port, and include a display on Just Nuisance, the Great Dane that was adopted as a navy mascot in WWII, and whose grave above the town makes for a healthy 1.5km walk.

SOUTH AFRICAN NAVAL MUSEUM
Definitely one for naval nuts, this **museum** (☎ 787 4635; St George's St, Simon's Town; admission free; ☎ 10am-4pm) nonetheless has plenty of interesting exhibits, including a mock submarine in which to play out adventure fantasies.

Sleeping & Eating
Boulders Beach Lodge (☎ 786 1758; www.boulders beach.co.za; 4 Boulders Pl, Boulders Beach; s/d/apt with breakfast R450/750/1000; P ✖) Close by the penguin colony, this smart guesthouse,

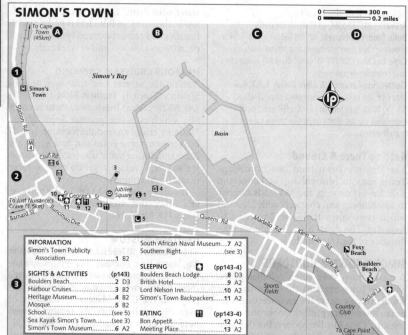

SIMON'S TOWN

with rooms decorated in wicker and wood, also has a range of good-sized apartments and a pleasant café with an outdoor deck.

British Hotel (☎ /fax 786 2214; www.british-hotel .co.za; 90 St George's St, Simon's Town; apt from R1000; 🖳) These stylish and quirkily decorated apartments with amazingly spacious bathrooms are set around a lovely courtyard. They're ideal for groups of friends or a family.

Lord Nelson Inn (☎ 786 1386; 58 St George's St, Simon's Town; s/d with breakfast R350/500) Above a small, old-fashioned pub, this is a pleasant, refurbished place, with plain but smart rooms. Some overlook the sea (which is largely obscured by a shed in the naval dockyards).

Simon's Town Backpackers (☎ 786 1964; www .capepax.co.za; 66 St George's St, Simon's Town; dm/d R70/200) Brightly painted rooms, a laid-back atmosphere and lots going on including bike hire, kayaking to Boulders beach and trips to Cape Point make this one very cool backpackers.

Bon Appetit (☎ 786 2412; 90 St George's St, Simon's Town; mains R80-90; 🕐 noon-2pm & 6.30-10pm Tue-Sun) Quaint and intimate French bistro serving classic dishes, such as twice-cooked cheese soufflé and *tarte tatin*. It has set menus for R140 or R160.

Meeting Place (☎ 786 1986; 98 St George's St, Simon's Town; mains R40; 🕐 9am-4pm Mon, 9am-9pm Tue-Sun) Relax on the balcony overlooking Simon's Town main street at this trendy deli-café, a foodie's delight.

Getting There & Around

See p143 for details on Muizenberg.

*Rikki*s (see p139 for details) meet all trains arriving at Simon's Town and go to Boulders and Cape Point.

CAPE OF GOOD HOPE NATURE RESERVE

You can easily spend a day enjoying the awesome scenery, fantastic walks and deserted beaches of **Cape Point** (Map pp94-5; ☎ 780 9010; www.capepoint.co.za; admission R35; 🕐 7am-6pm Sep-Apr, 7am-5pm May-Aug). If you come on one of the many tours that whip into the reserve, now part of Table Mountain National Park, pause at the tourist centre, walk to Cape Point and back, and then zip out again, you'll not even have seen the half of

DON'T FEED THE BABOONS!

There are signs all over Cape Point warning you not to feed the baboons. This isn't just some mean-spirited official stricture designed to keep baboons from developing a taste for potato crisps and chocolate. The baboons are highly aggressive and will quiet happily grab food from your hands or climb in the open doors and windows of your car to get at it. The damage inflicted might end up being more serious than baboon crap over your car seats, so keep an eye out and your food carefully hidden away.

it. Take your time to explore the reserve the way it should be: on foot. Pick up a map at the entrance gate if you intend to go walking, but bear in mind that there is minimal shade in the park and that the weather can change quickly.

It's not a difficult walk, but if you're feeling lazy a **funicular railway** (adult one way/return R20/29, child R10/15; ☽ 10am-5pm) runs up from beside the restaurant to the souvenir kiosk next to the old lighthouse (1860). The old lighthouse was too often obscured by mist and fog, so a new lighthouse was built at Dias Point in 1919, reached by a thrilling walkway along the rocks; if the winds are howling, as they often are, the old lighthouse is likely to be as far as you'll feel safe in going.

Numerous tour companies include Cape Point on their itineraries; both Day Trippers (p121) and Downhill Adventures (p116) are recommended because they offer the chance to cycle within the park. The only public transport to the Cape is with *rikkis*, which run from Simon's Town train station (p144). The best option is to hire a car for the day, so you can explore the rest of the peninsula.

CAPE FLATS

For the majority of Capetonians, home is in one of the poverty stricken townships sprawling across the shifting sands of the Cape Flats. Taking a tour – the only way of safely travelling here besides making friends with and being accompanied by a resident – is one of the most illuminating and life-affirming things you can do while in Cape Town. You'll learn a lot about

South African history and the cultures of Black South Africans.

The half-day itineraries of most township tours (p122) are similar. After starting in the Bo-Kaap for a brief discussion of Cape Town's colonial history, you'll move on to the District Six Museum (p100), then be driven to the Cape Flats to visit some or all of the following townships: Langa, Guguletu, Crossroads and Khayelitsha. Tour guides are generally flexible in where they go, and respond to the wishes of the group.

Places you'll visit will most likely include the brilliantly decorated **Guga S'Thebe Arts and Cultural Centre** (Map pp94-5; ☎ 695 3493; cnr Washington & Church Sts, Langa); the **Sivuyile Tourism Centre** (Map pp94-5; ☎ 637 8449) in Guguletu, which has an interesting photographic display on the townships, artists at work, an Internet café and a good gift shop; the Crossroads printing project of the **Philani Nutrition Centre** (Map pp94-5; ☎ 387 5124; www .philani.org.za); and Golden, a talented bloke who together with his family makes beautiful flowers from scrap tins in Khayelitsha.

If you can, visit Khayelitsha when the **Khayelitsha Craft Market** (Map pp94-5; ☎ 361 2904; St Michael's Church, Ncumo Rd, Harare, Khayelitsha; ☽ 9am-4pm Mon & Thu) is open. This is a great place to look for interesting souvenirs, and you can be sure that your money goes directly to the people who need it most. Sometimes a marimba band is playing and you can buy their CDs.

Sleeping

Of the several B&Bs springing up in the townships, we most recommend the following two.

Kopanong (Map pp94-5; ☎ /fax 361 2084; kopanong@ xsinet.co.za; Site C-329 Velani Cres, Khayelitsha; s/d with breakfast R210/360; ☐ ☐) All the home comforts are in place at the most upmarket of Khayelitsha's B&Bs, run by the dynamic Thope Lekau, who's also a registered guide and experienced development worker. There are two stylishly decorated rooms, one with private bathroom, the other with its own separate shower. A three-course dinner is R60/80 for vegetarian/meat.

Vicky's (Map pp94-5; ☎ 387 7104, 082-225 2986; www .journey.digitalspace.net/vicky.html; Site C 685A Kiyane St, Khayelitsha; s/d with breakfast & shared bathroom R170/340) The home Vicky Ntozini shares with her family is built of scrap but is charming nonetheless. There are two comfy rooms for guests and, since we last visited, an inside bathroom with toilet and shower courtesy of assistance by an international hotel chain. Apart from Vicky's bountiful hospitality, there's the added bonus of Cape Town's other Waterfront, a long-running and lively shebeen, right across the road.

Eating

If you want to try traditional Xhosa cuisine, arrange with a tour company (p122) or with a private guide to visit these places. Bookings are essential.

Eziko (Map pp94-5; ☎ 694 0434; cnr Washington St & Jungle Walk, Langa; mains R30-40; ☷ 9am-6pm Mon-Fri, 9am-10pm Sat) This is one the best places to eat in Langa; try the chef's special fried chicken or their traditional breakfast.

Lelapa (Map pp94-5; ☎ 694 2681; 49 Harlem Ave, Langa; buffet R75) Sheila serves up delicious buffets in her well-appointed home. She's well travelled and loves to chat with guests about life in the townships and elsewhere.

Gugule Afrika (Map pp94-5; ☎ 361 1975; 8 Lwandle Rd, Khayelitsha; mains R30) This catering training centre is a professional operation, with a full menu of very reasonably priced Western and African dishes.

Western Cape

WESTERN CAPE

The surf is pounding the rocks, throwing foam into the pink sky. The sun sets over the Indian Ocean making the water glow and the sand gleam. You're riding a horse by the sea, rugged coastline to the right, craggy cliffs to the left. Just another evening on the Garden Route.

Welcome to the Western Cape. A place so picture-perfect it's hard to describe without using clichés. The beauty here is mind-boggling, the diversity of the landscape unparalleled and the amount of adventures ready to be experienced almost overwhelming. Dive with sharks, jump out of an airplane, surf some of Southern Africa's best breaks, cruise with the whales, eat fresh crayfish in a whitewashed village, stand at the southernmost tip of Africa, sip the local brew and watch the children play an impromptu game of cricket in a township – their laughter creating music in the late afternoon stillness.

The Western Cape is jam-packed with First World amenities – classy hotels, top-notch restaurants, designer stores and modern shopping malls, and many Westerners may feel as if they never left home. But all that glitters is not gold, and amid the glossy tourism-brochure beauty it's easy to forget a major portion of the population still lives in abject poverty. At the edge of every town is a sprawling township of cardboard shacks and hungry children.

The Western Cape is also the country's most popular tourist destination, so you may feel a bit like a zebra in a herd travelling around here. But it's still a magical place, with ample opportunities to escape from the crowds. Try sipping world-class wines in a flowery garden; cruising the sun-drenched Karoo, where the sky and ground merge and spaces open up; or hiking through a green velvet mountain pass in the Cederberg.

HIGHLIGHTS

- Sipping wine in lush garden vineyards and gorging yourself on mouthwatering culinary masterpieces in the **Winelands** (p150)

- Surfing, skydiving, horse riding or just lounging on the beaches along the **Garden Route** (p188)

- Hiking past bizarre sandstone formations and San rock art in the rugged and desolate **Cederberg Wilderness Area** (p214)

- Enjoying scenery to soothe the soul along Western Cape's **southern coast** – a wonderful area to spot whales (p167)

- Marvelling in the silence, space and hospitality of the **Karoo** (p206) – check out the ostriches in **Oudtshoorn** (p186), relax in quaint **Prince Albert** (p206) and drive through the remarkable **Swartberg Pass** (p206)

★ Cederberg Wilderness Area
★ The Karoo
★ Winelands
★ Southern Coast
★ Garden Route

- POPULATION: 4,894,000   - AREA: 129,370 SQ KM

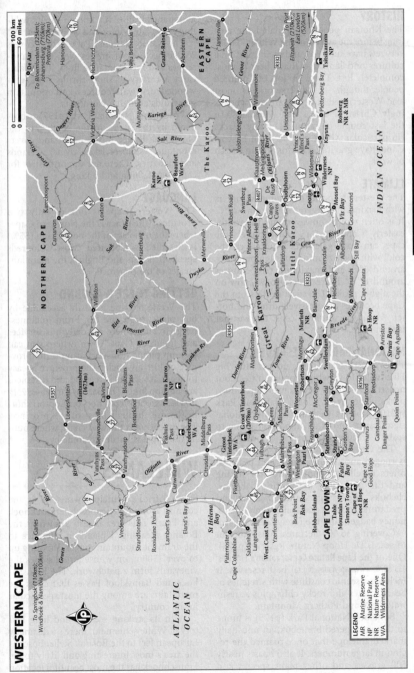

WESTERN CAPE

WESTERN CAPE

To Springbok (110km);
Windhoek & Namibia (1100km)

○ Garies

To Bloemfontein (325km);
Johannesburg (710km);
Pretoria (770km)

○ De Aar

100 km
60 miles

NORTHERN CAPE

EASTERN CAPE

To Port
Elizabeth (210km);
East London
(520km)

ATLANTIC OCEAN

INDIAN OCEAN

R357

Loeriesfontein

Nieuwoudtville

Calvinia

Hantamsberg
(1643m) ▲

Sutherland

Fraserburg

Loxton

Carnarvon

Williston

Vanrhynsdorp

Vanrhyns
Pass

Vredendal

Strandfontein

Rooidune Point

Lambert's Bay

Eland's Bay

St Helena
Bay

Paternoster

Cape Columbine

Saldanha

Langebaan

West Coast NP

Yzerfontein

Robben Island

CAPE TOWN

Table
Mountain NP

Simon's Town

Cape of
Good Hope NR

Cape of
Good Hope

False
Bay

Gordon's
Bay

Strand

Stellenbosch

Paarl

Wellington

Franschhoek

Bok Bay

Bok Point

Darling

Malmesbury

Tulbagh

Ceres

Worcester

Robertson

McGregor

Genadendal

Greyton

Caledon

Hermanus

Gansbaai

Danger Point

Quoin Point

Cape Agulhas

Struis Bay

Arniston

Bredasdorp

Stanford

Swellendam

Heidelberg

Riversdale

Albertinia

Still Bay

Whitesands

Cape Infanta

De Hoop
NR

Breede River

Barrydale

Montagu

Marloth
NR

Ladismith

Calitzdorp

Oudtshoorn

Cango
Caves

De
Rust

George

Mossel Bay

Vig Bay

Gourtismond

Wilderness

Wilderness
NP

Knysna

Plettenberg Bay

Robberg
NR & MR

Robberg
NR

Tsitsikamma
NP

Uniondale

Willowmore

Aberdeen

Graaff-Reinet

Jansenville

Nieu Bethesda

Hanover

Richmond

Murraysburg

Victoria West

Beaufort
West

Karoo
NP

Prince Albert

Prince Albert Road

Merweville

Matjiesfontein

Touws River

Swartberg
Pass

Prince
Alfred's
Pass

Seweweekspoort Pass
Seweweekspoort, Die Hell

The Karoo

Great Karoo

Little Karoo

Tankwa Karoo

Tankwa NP

Cederberg
WA

Pakhuis
Pass

Clanwilliam

Citrusdal

Piketberg

Groot
Winterhoek
WA

Groot
Winterhoek
(2078m) ▲

Mitchell's
Pass

Gydo
Pass

Bloukrans
Pass

Botterkloof
Pass

Middelburg
Pass

Groot
River

Onrus River

Groot River

Kariega

Salt River

Riet
River

Sak
River

Doring River

Renoster
River

Fish
River

Tankwa Ry

Olifants
River

Sout
River

Green
River

Dwyka

Gouritz
River

Gamka
River

Gamka
Pass

Sir Lowry's
Pass

Baviaanskloof
Pass

Du Toit's Pass

Bainskloof Pass

Michell's
Pass

Klaasfroom

Meiringspoort
Pass

Oudtshoorn

Kareebospoort

LEGEND
MR   Marine Reserve
NP   National Park
NR   Nature Reserve
WA   Wilderness Area

N1, N2, N7, N9, N10, N12
R27, R45, R46, R62, R63, R323, R332, R354, R357, R407

HISTORY

The Khoisan peoples populated the area long before the arrival of the Whites. Today very few have survived, and their traditional cultures and languages have been almost completely lost. There are lots of Coloured people, though, with diverse origins; most lead Westernised lifestyles, are overwhelmingly Christian and speak Afrikaans. In the last couple of centuries, many Blacks (in particular Xhosa peoples from Eastern Cape) have gravitated to this area in search of work.

CLIMATE

The Western Cape has dry, sunny summers with maximum temperatures around 28°C. It is often windy, however, and the south-easterly 'Cape Doctor', which buffets the cape, can reach gale force. Winters can be cold, with average minimum temperatures around 5°C, and maximum temperatures around 17°C. There is occasional snow on the higher peaks. The coast north from the Cape becomes progressively drier and hotter. Along the southern coast the weather is temperate.

NATIONAL PARKS & RESERVES

The Western Cape parks do not offer Big Five wildlife-viewing opportunities, but nevertheless there are some stupendous parks. The West Coast National Park (p210) protects wetlands of international significance and is an important home to seabird breeding colonies.

The Cederberg Wilderness Area (p214) is rugged and mountainous with peaks. It offers excellent opportunities for hiking and the possibility of spotting baboons, rheboks, klipspringers and grysboks; and predators such as caracals, Cape foxes, honey badgers and the rarely seen leopard.

Covering 36,000 hectares, plus 5km out to sea, is De Hoop Nature Reserve (p173). One of the **Cape Nature Conservation's** (☎ 028-435 5020; www.capenature.org.za) best reserves, it includes a scenic coastline with stretches of beach, dunes and rocky cliffs, plus a fresh-water lake and Potberg Mountain.

Bontebok National Park (p175) is home to the endangered bontebok, an unusually marked antelope that once roamed the region in large numbers. It also boasts nearly 500 grasses and other plant species and abundant birdlife. It's known for its wildflowers in late winter and early spring.

The Karoo National Park (p209) covers 33,000 hectares of impressive Karoo landscapes and representative flora. The plains carry a variety of short shrubs with well-wooded dry watercourses and mountain grasslands at higher elevations.

Wilderness National Park (p197) is bordered by the ocean in the south and the Outeniqua Range in the north and covers a unique system of lakes, rivers, wetlands and estuaries. There are opportunities for canoeing, fishing and hiking.

LANGUAGE

The Western Cape is one of only two provinces (the other is the Northern Cape) where the majority of the population (55%) is classified as Coloured. Most Coloureds speak Afrikaans and English, the main languages of the province.

GETTING THERE & AROUND

The Western Cape is easily accessible by bus, plane, train and car. From Johannesburg (Jo'burg) there are daily bus services and flights to Cape Town, where you can pick up public transport around the province or hire a vehicle. The province is easy to negotiate – roads are good and distances are not too long. The **Baz Bus** (☎ 021-439 2323; www.bazbus.com) offers a hop-on/hop-off shuttle service through most of the province. The exception is the west coast, where public transport is harder to come by.

WINELANDS

South Africa's principal wineland is the country around Stellenbosch, Franschhoek and Paarl. This area is also known as the Boland, meaning 'Upland', a reference to the dramatic mountain ranges, shooting up to over 1500m, on whose fertile slopes the vineyards form a patchwork. The Franschhoek and Bainskloof Passes that cross the mountains are among the most spectacular in the country.

With its striking scenery and long history of White settlement, there's a distinctly European feel to the Boland. Stellenbosch is the area's most interesting and lively town, Franschhoek has the most beautiful location and best dining options and Paarl is a busy commercial centre with plenty to see.

It is possible to see Stellenbosch and Paarl on day trips from Cape Town. Both are accessible by train, but Stellenbosch is the easiest to get around if you don't have a car. To do justice to the region and to visit the many wineries, you'll need to stay over and get yourself some wheels – bicycle wheels will do, if you're not too ambitious, but if you plan to pack in a lot of wineries, then a car is essential.

STELLENBOSCH & AROUND
☎ 021 / pop 184,000

Established on the banks of the Eerste River by Governor van der Stel in 1679, Stellenbosch is the second-oldest town (after Cape Town) in South Africa, and one of the best preserved. Full of architectural gems (Cape Dutch, Georgian and Victorian) and shaded by enormous oak trees, there are several interesting museums and decent sleeping, eating and nightlife options.

The Afrikaans-language University of Stellenbosch, established in 1918, continues to play an important role in Afrikaner politics and culture. There are over 17,000 students, which means that during term time, the town's nightlife can get wild – visit at the start of term in February during the Venster Versiering festival and you'll see what we mean!

Orientation

The train station is a short walk west of the centre. The train line effectively forms the western boundary of the town and the Eerste River the southern. Dorp St, which runs roughly parallel to the river, is the old town's main street and is lined with fine old buildings. The commercial centre lies between Dorp St and the university to the east of the Braak, the old town square.

Information
BOOKSHOPS

Ex Libris (Map p152; ☎ 886 6871; 18 Andringa St)
Exclusive Books (Map p152; ☎ 886 9277; 14 Andringa St)

INTERNET ACCESS

Fandangos Internet Café (Map p152; per hr R30) Mill St (☎ 887 4628); Drostdy Centre (☎ 887 7501; Bird St)
Java Café (Map p152; ☎ 887 6261; cnr Church & Andringa Sts; per hr R15) Stellenbosch's cheapest Internet access.

TOURIST INFORMATION

Stellenbosch Publicity Association (Map p152;
☎ 883 3584; www.stellenboschtourism.co.za; 36 Market St; ☼ 8am-6pm Mon-Fri, 9am-5pm Sat, 10am-4pm Sun) The staff here are extremely helpful. Pick up the excellent brochure *Discover Stellenbosch on Foot* (R2), with a walking-tour map and information on many of the historic buildings (also available in French and German). Also useful is the free brochure *Stellenbosch Wine Routes*, which gives information about opening times and tastings at many nearby wineries.

TRAVEL AGENCIES

Rennies Travel (Map p152; Bird St) A block from Dorp St, with a Thomas Cook foreign exchange office.

Sights & Activities

Stellenbosch has a number of museums, if you're tired of tasting wine. Taking a walk around town also is a pleasant way to pass an afternoon. **Guided walks** (per person R50), with a minimum of three people, leave from the Stellenbosch Publicity Association at 10am and 3pm.

VILLAGE MUSEUM

This **museum** (Map p152; ☎ 887 2902; 18 Ryneveld St; adult/child R15/10; ☼ 9.30am-5pm Mon-Sat, 2-5pm Sun) is a group of carefully restored and period-furnished houses dating from 1709 to 1850. The main entrance leads into the oldest of the buildings, the Schreuderhuis. The whole block, bounded by Ryneveld, Plein, Drostdy and Kerk Sts, is occupied by the museum and includes most of the buildings and some charming gardens. **Grosvenor House** is on the other side of Drostdy St.

TOY & MINIATURE MUSEUM

Behind the Publicity Association, in another historic building, is this delightfully surprising **museum** (Map p152; ☎ 887 7888; cnr Market & Herte Sts; adult/child R5/1; ☼ 9.30am-5pm Mon-Sat, 2-5pm Sun, closed Sun May-Aug). Many of the miniatures are amazingly detailed; the highlights are a model railway set and houses made entirely of icing sugar – get the guide to point out some of the best pieces.

THE BRAAK

At the north end of the **Braak** (Map p152; Town Sq), an open stretch of grass, you'll find the neo-Gothic **St Mary's on the Braak Church**, completed in 1852. To the west is the **VOC Kruithuis** (Powder House; admission free; ☼ 9.30am-1pm

STELLENBOSCH

0 ___ 300 m
0 ___ 0.2 miles

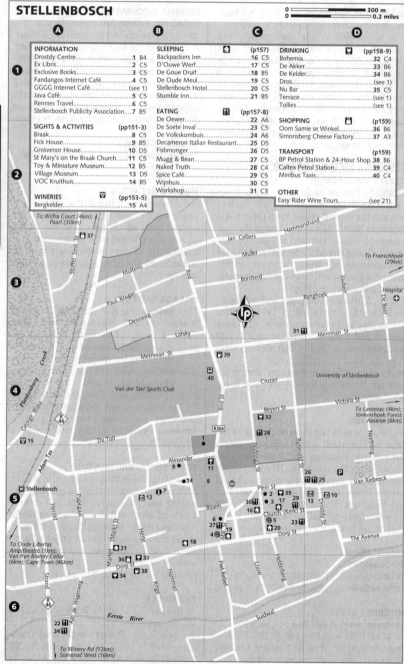

Mon-Fri), which was built in 1777 to store the town's weapons and gunpowder and now houses a small military museum. On the northwest corner is **Fick House**, also known as the Burgerhuis, a fine example of Cape Dutch style from the late 18th century. Most of this building is now occupied by Historical Homes of South Africa, established to preserve important architecture.

JONKERSHOEK FOREST RESERVE
This small **forest reserve** (Map p156; ☎ 866 1560; admission car/bicycle R110/5) is around 8km southeast of town along the WR4 set within a timber plantation. Here you'll find walking and biking trails.

Wineries
It's best to check directly with the wineries for the times of cellar tours. **Blaauwklippen** (Map p156; ☎ 880 0133; www.blaauwklippen.com; tastings R20; ☉ 9am-5pm), a rustic 300-year-old estate with several fine Cape Dutch buildings, is known for its red wines, particularly its Cabernet Sauvignon and Zinfandel. Cellar tours are by appointment and lunch is available (call for times, as they change according to the season). A good one for kids on weekends when it has horse and carriage rides around the estate (R10). Blaauwklippen is on the R44 towards Somerset West.

Bergkelder (Map p152; ☎ 809 8492; www.bergkelder .co.za; George Blake St; tastings R15; ☉ 8am-5pm Mon-Fri, 9am-3pm Sat) is an option if you don't have time to shuttle around the area's wineries, or want an introduction to what's on offer. The cellar tour (available in French and German as well as English) includes a slide show and tastings of up to 12 wines. You pour your own tastings, so take it easy or it might be your last stop for the day! The Bergkelder is a short walk from the train station.

Delaire (Map p156; ☎ 885 1756; www.delairewinery .co.za; tastings R10; ☉ 10am-5pm) is known as the 'vineyard in the sky' because of its high altitude location at the top of the Helshoogte Pass on the R310 towards Franschhoek. Naturally, the views are stunning and it's a friendly place with wheelchair access to the restaurant and picnics available from October to April (bookings essential). Try its Cabernet Sauvignon and Merlot.

Hartenberg Estate (Map p156; ☎ 882 2541; www .hartenbergestate.com; tastings free; ☉ 9am-5pm Mon-Fri, 9am-3pm Sat) was founded in 1692. Thanks to

a favourable microclimate, this estate produces many award-winning wines, notably its Cabernet Sauvignon, Merlot and Shiraz. Lunch is available from noon to 2pm (bookings essential). The estate is off Bottelary Rd, 10km northwest of Stellenbosch.

Lanzerac (Map p156; ☎ 886 5641; www.lanzerac wines.co.za; Jonkershoek Valley; tastings R16; ☉ 9am-4.30pm Mon-Thu, 9am-4pm Fri, 10am-2pm Sat, 11am-3pm Sun) produces a very good Merlot and quaffable Cabernet Sauvignon and Chardonnay. The tastings include a free glass and biscuits. Here you'll also find Stellenbosch's most luxurious hotel (see p157).

Morgenhof (Map p156; ☎ 889 5510; www.morgen hof.com; tastings R10; ☉ 9am-6pm Mon-Fri, 10am-5pm Sat & Sun Nov-Apr, 9am-4.30pm Mon-Fri, 10am-3pm Sat & Sun May-Oct) is an old estate on the slopes of Simonsberg that has fine architecture and a pretty rose garden. Light lunches are available and there's a coffee shop also serving breakfast from 9am to noon daily. Good wines include the Chenin Blanc and their Bordeaux-style blend. It's on the R44 towards Paarl.

Spier (Map p156; ☎ 809 1100; www.spier.co.za; tastings R12; ☉ 9am-5pm) has something for everyone. This mega-estate offers steam-train trips from Cape Town (call ☎ 419 5222 for information), horse riding, performing arts centres, beautifully restored Cape Dutch buildings and several restaurants, including the spectacular Moyo (see p158). The only aspect we're unsure about is the cheetah park, where listless animals pose for photos with the tourists. The wines produced here are nothing to shout about, but in the tasting you can try lots of other vineyards' wines. Check out the annual arts festival that runs from January to March – it's as good a reason as any for coming here. If you want to stay over there's a good Cape Malay–style hotel, the Village at Spier (see p157).

Van Ryn Brandy Cellar (Map p156; ☎ 881 3875; www.distell.co.za; Vlottenburg; tastings R15; ☉ 8am-5pm Mon-Fri, 9am-1.30pm Sat) is on the Western Cape Brandy Route (for more information see www.sabrandy.co.za). It generally runs three tours a day, including a tasting. In its boardroom you can view fine South African art. It's 8km southwest of Stellenbosch.

HELDERBERG
This area around Somerset West, 20km south of Stellenbosch, has some 20 wineries,

CAPE WINERIES Simon Richmond

It was Stellenbosch in the 1970s that first promoted a 'wine route', an idea that has since been enthusiastically taken up by 16 other parts of the country. Stellenbosch's wine route remains the largest, covering around 100 wineries; if you lump in the nearby areas of Franschhoek, Helderberg and Paarl, you're looking at over 200 wineries within a day's drive of Cape Town.

Several wineries are capitalising on the industry's popularity by adding on restaurants, accommodation and other attractions. Of these, we've selected some of the more notable ones, as well as vineyards that are renowned for their fine wines; you'll find them listed in the sections on Cape Town (see p114), Stellenbosch (see p153), Franschhoek (see p160), Paarl (see p165) and Robertson (see p180). For more information, the annual *John Platter's South African Wine Guide* is the place to look.

History

'Today, praise be the Lord, wine was pressed for the first time from Cape grapes.'

Jan Van Riebeeck, 2 February 1659

Although the founder of the Cape Colony, Jan Van Riebeeck, had planted vines and made wine himself, it was not until the arrival of Governor Simon Van Der Stel in 1679 that wine making began in earnest. Van Der Stel created Groot Constantia, the superb estate on the flanks of Table Mountain, and passed on his wine-making skills to the burghers settling around Stellenbosch.

Between 1688 and 1690, some 200 Huguenots arrived in the country. They were granted land in the region, particularly around Franschhoek, and although only a few had wine-making experience, they gave the infant industry fresh impetus.

For a long time, Cape wines other than those produced at Groot Constantia were not in great demand and most grapes ended up in brandy. But the industry received a boost in the early 19th century as war between Britain and France meant more South African wine was imported into the UK.

Apartheid-era sanctions and the power of the Kooperatieve Wijnbouwers Vereeniging (KWV), the cooperative formed in 1918 to control minimum prices, production areas and quota limits, didn't exactly encourage innovation, and hampered the industry. However, since 1992 KWV, now a private company, has lost much of its former influence.

Many new and progressive wine makers are leading South Africa's re-emergence onto the world market. New wine-producing areas are being established away from the hotter inland areas, in particular in the cooler coastal areas east of Cape Town around Mossel Bay, Walker Bay and Elgin Workers' Wines

Black empowerment in the wine industry is happening, but slowly. **Thabani** (☎ 021-882 8790; www.thabani.co.za; not open to the public) in Stellenbosch is South Africa's first wholly Black-owned wine company. They hit the big time in the US when Oprah served their lively Sauvignon Blanc at a party for poet Maya Angelou. Students of the wine maker Jabulani Ntshangase are now being snapped up by big vineyards, including KWV.

The **Fair Valley Workers Association** (Map p162; ☎ 863 2450; tastings & sales at Fairview, see p165) is a 17-hectare workers' farm next to Fairview. It's still developing its own vineyards but has already produced four seasons of Chenin Blanc (sold through the UK wine chain Oddbins) made with grapes bought in from Fairview, as well as a Sauvignon Blanc and a pinotage.

North of Paarl, at **Nelson's Creek** (see p165), the owner has donated part of the estate to his workers to produce their own wines. Under the label New Beginnings, these wines – a classic dry red, a rosé and a dry white – are being sold in the UK, the Netherlands and Japan.

Other worker empowerment wines to look out for include **Thandi** (☎ 844 0605; www.cluver.co.za; ◷ 9am-5pm Mon-Sat) from the Elgin area, available at Tesco in the UK, and **Tukulu** (☎ 809 8305; www.tukulu.co.za; not open to the public) from the Darling area. This highly successful operation has won awards for its pinotage and getting rave reviews for its Chenin Blanc.

All this has to be balanced against the facts of a Black and Coloured workforce of some 350,000 toiling in vineyards owned by 4500 Whites. The average monthly cash wage is R544, with women workers receiving even less. The infamous 'tot' system, whereby the wages of labourers are paid partly in wine, still happens and the consequences, socially and physiologically, have been disastrous.

Wines

The most common variety of white wine is Chenin Blanc, or *steen*. In the last decade or so, more fashionable varieties such as Chardonnay and Sauvignon Blanc have been planted on a wide scale. Other widely planted whites include Colombard, Sémillon, Crouchen Blanc (known as Cape riesling) and various sweet muscats. Table whites, especially Chardonnay, once tended to be heavily oaked and high in alcohol, but lighter, more fruity whites are now in the ascendancy. For good Sauvignon Blancs look to wineries located in the cooler wine-growing regions of Constantia, Elgin and Hermanus.

Older, more robust red varieties such as Shiraz, Cabernet Sauvignon and the Cape's own pinotage (a cross between Pinot Noir and Cinsault or Shiraz, which produces a very bold wine) are being challenged by lighter blends of Cabernet Sauvignon, Merlot, Shiraz and Cabernet Franc, making a style closer to Bordeaux styles. The reds attracting the highest prices are Cabernet Sauvignon and the Bordeaux-style blends. A buzz word of the moment is Cape Blend, which must contain at least 30% pinotage.

The Worcester region is the country's leading producer of fortified wines, including port, brandy and South Africa's own *hanepoot*. This dessert wine is made from the Mediterranean grape variety known as muscat of Alexandria to produce a strong, sweet and suitably high-alcohol tipple for the domestic market. In Worcester you'll also find the KWV Brandy Cellar, the largest in the world and the final stop on the Brandy Route, which runs from Van Ryn Brandy Cellar (see p151) at Vlottenburg, 8km southwest of Stellenbosch. For more information contact the **South African Brandy Foundation** (☎ 886 6381; www.sabrandy.co.za).

Top Five Wineries

The following are our favourite five wineries.

- **Boschendal** (p160) Fairytale location for this classic estate with fine wine, food and architecture.
- **Buitenverwachting** (p114) Enjoy a lovely picnic on an immaculate lawn, washed down with quaffable Chardonnay or Rhine riesling.
- **Cabrière Estate** (p160) Attend the Saturday morning cellar tour to witness the owner skilfully slice off the top of a sparkling bottle of wine with his sabre.
- **Fairview** (p165) Sample from a selection of some 23 wines, including the worker's empowerment wine Fair Valley, as well as many goats' and cows' milk cheeses.
- **Vergelegen** (p153) The Winelands' most elegant estate also produces some equally stylish wines, the flagship being its very fruity Vergelegen red.

including **Vergelegen** (Map p156; ☎ 847 1334; www.vergelegen.co.za; Lourensford Rd, Somerset West; admission R10; tastings R2-10; ⊙ 9.30am-4pm), arguably the most beautiful estate in the Cape. Simon van der Stel's son Willem first planted vines here in 1700. The buildings and elegant grounds have ravishing mountain views and a 'stately home' feel to them. On the dining front you can choose from the casual Rose Terrace overlooking the Rose Garden, the upmarket Lady Phillips Restaurant, or a picnic hamper (R180 for two people) – bookings are essential for the last two options.

Tours

Easy Rider Wine Tours (Map p152; ☎ 886 4651; www .jump.to/stumble; 12 Market St) is a long-established company offering good value for a full-day trip at R250 including lunch and all tastings. The wineries it visits sometimes changes but on the schedule at the time of research was Boschendal, Delaire, Fairview and Simonsig.

Anne Lee Steyn (☎ 083-631 5944; famsteyn@mweb .co.za) is a knowledgeable Stellenbosch-based guide who can arrange walking tours of the local wineries in the Simonsberg area. The walk is around 8km and costs R295 including a picnic lunch and tastings.

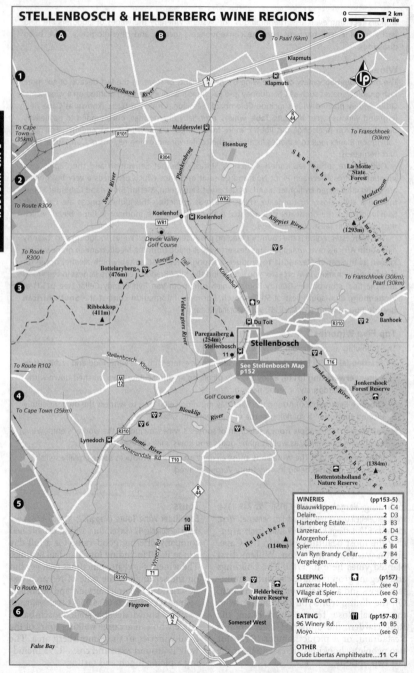

STELLENBOSCH & HELDERBERG WINE REGIONS

0 — 2 km
0 — 1 mile

To Paarl (6km)

Klapmuts

Klapmuts

To Cape Town (35km)

Mosselbank River

N1

Muldersvlei

R101

Elsenburg

R304

Plankenbrug

Skurweberg

La Motte State Forest

Meulspruit

Groot

Simonsberg

To Route R300

Swart River

WR2

Klippies River

Koelenhof

WR1

Koelenhof

Devon Valley Golf Course

(1293m)

To Route R300

Bottelaryberg (476m)

Vineyard Trail

Koelenhof

5

To Franschhoek (30km); Paarl (30km)

Ribbokkop (411m)

Veldwagens River

9

Du Toit

R310

2

Banhoek

To Route R102

Stellenbosch Kloof

Paregaaiberg (254m) Stellenbosch

11

Stellenbosch

See Stellenbosch Map p152

4

T16

Jonkershoek River

Jonkershoek Forest Reserve

M12

Golf Course

Stellenboschberge

To Cape Town (35km)

Blouklip

7

River

6

1

To Paarl

R310

Lynedoch

Bonte River

Annanandale Rd

T10

(1384m)

R44

Hottentotsholland Nature Reserve

10

Helderberg

(1140m)

To Route R102

R310

T1

Winery Rd

8

Helderberg Nature Reserve

Firgrove

N2

Somerset West

False Bay

WINERIES	(pp153-5)
Blaauwklippen	1 C4
Delaire	2 D3
Hartenberg Estate	3 B3
Lanzerac	4 D4
Morgenhof	5 C3
Spier	6 B4
Van Ryn Brandy Cellar	7 B4
Vergelegen	8 C6

SLEEPING	(p157)
Lanzerac Hotel	(see 4)
Village at Spier	(see 6)
Wilfra Court	9 C3

EATING	(pp157-8)
96 Winery Rd	10 B5
Moyo	(see 6)

OTHER	
Oude Libertas Amphitheatre	11 C4

Festivals & Events

The **Oude Libertas Amphitheatre** (Map p156; ☎ 809 7380; www.oudelibertas.co.za) and the Spier wine estate (see p153) both hold performing arts festivals between January and March.

The **Stellenbosch Festival** (www.stellenboschfesti val.co.za), which runs for two weeks at the end of September, celebrates music and the arts in various events around the town including a street carnival. The **Wine Festival** (www .wineroute.co.za) in early August offers visitors the chance to sample up to 400 different drops in one spot as well as attend talks and tutorials on wine.

The **Van der Stel Festival** at the end of September and early October combines with the Stellenbosch and Wine Festivals.

Sleeping

There's plenty of accommodation in Stellenbosch, particularly guesthouses; contact the Stellenbosch Publicity Association if you find all the recommendations listed here are booked up.

BUDGET

De Oude Meul (Map p152; ☎ 887 7085; www.deoude meul.snowball.co.za; 10A Mill St; s/d with breakfast R175/350; ⚁) Above an antiques shop in the centre of town, the accommodation here is very reasonable for the price (which is lower in winter). Some rooms have balconies.

Stumble Inn (Map p152; ☎ 887 4049; www.jump.to /stumble; 12 Market St; camp sites per person R40, dm R60, d with shared bathroom R160; ⚁ ⚁) With a lively and welcoming atmosphere, this place is split over two old houses, one with a small pool and the other with a pleasant garden. The owners are travellers themselves and are a good source of information. They also run Easy Rider Wine Tours (see p155) and rent bicycles for R50 per day.

Backpackers Inn (Map p152; ☎ 887 2020; bacpac1@ global.co.za; 1st fl, De Wett Centre; dm R60, d with shared bathroom R160; ⚁) Run by the folks from Stumble Inn, the rooms are spartan but brightly painted and it has a central location.

MID-RANGE

De Goue Druif (Map p156; ☎ 883 3555; 110 Dorp St; s/d with breakfast R600/650; ⚁ ⚁ ⚁) The name of this charming guesthouse in an old Cape Dutch building, run by a couple from Belgium, means 'the golden grape'. It has a small gym and sauna.

Stellenbosch Hotel (Map p152; ☎ 887 3644; www .stellenbosch.co.za/hotel; cnr Dorp & Andringa Sts; s/d with breakfast from R489/365; ⚁) This is a comfortable country-style hotel; some rooms have four-poster beds and others are self-catering. A section dating from 1743 houses the Jan Cats Brasserie, a good spot for a drink.

Wilfra Court (Map p156; ☎ /fax 889 6091; 16 Hine St, Cloetsville; s/d with breakfast R210/360) A homely place run by a friendly former mayor and his wife; there are only two rooms so book ahead. It's a fair way from the town centre so ask for directions.

TOP END

Lanzerac Hotel (Map p156; ☎ 887 1132; www.lanzerac .co.za; Jonkershoek Valley; s/d/ste with breakfast R1990/2700/3315; ⚁ ⚁ ⚁) This ultra-luxurious place consists of a 300-year-old manor house and winery. You don't even need plug adaptors since the spacious rooms are equipped with a range of sockets! Some suites have their own private pools.

D'Ouwe Werf (Map p152; ☎ 887 4608; www.ouwe werf.com; 30 Church St; s/d with breakfast R700/990; ⚁ ⚁) This is an appealing, old-style hotel (dating back to 1802) with a good restaurant. It's worth dropping by its shady courtyard for lunch. The more expensive luxury rooms are furnished with antiques and brass beds.

Village at Spier (Map p156; ☎ 809 1100; www .spier.co.za; Vlottenburg; d/ste with breakfast R1290/1950; ⚁ ⚁ ⚁) Forgo the usual Cape Dutch style in favour of a design copying the brightly painted houses found in Cape Town's Bo-Kaap. Rooms are large and well appointed.

Eating

There's no shortage of places to eat and drink, and several of the nearby vineyards have restaurants as well.

RESTAURANTS

De Volkskombuis (Map p152; ☎ 887 2121; Aan de Wagenweg; mains R75; ☾ lunch & dinner Mon-Sat, lunch Sun) An atmospheric place specialising in traditional Cape Malay cuisine – the terrace looks across fields to Stellenbosch Mountain. You can try sample plates of famous Cape Malay savoury and sweet dishes. Booking is advisable.

De Oewer (Map p152; ☎ 886 5431; Aan de Wagenweg; mains R70; ☾ lunch & dinner Mon-Sat, lunch Sun) Next to De Volkskombuis, De Oewer has an open-air section shaded by willow trees beside the river. It offers lighter meals with a more Mediterranean emphasis.

96 Winery Rd (Map p156; ☎ 842 2945; Zandberg Farm, Winery Rd; mains R70; ⊕ lunch & dinner Mon-Sat, lunch Sun) Off the R44 between Stellenbosch and Somerset West, this is one of the most respected restaurants in the area, known for its dry aged beef. It has a relaxed style and a belief in simply cooked, real food.

Moyo (Map p156; ☎ 809 1100; Spier Estate, Vlottenburg; buffet R150, per kg R98; ⊕ 11am-11pm) This place brings a fantasy vision of Africa to the midst of the Spier wine estate. It's a lot of fun, with face painting, roving musicians and dancers and alfresco dining in tents and up in the trees. The buffet is extensive and tasty, but you can pay per kilogram of food.

De Soete Inval (Map p152; ☎ 886 4842; 5 Ryneveld St; mains R50; ⊕ 9am-10pm) Known primarily for its choice of 40 different pancakes, this cheerful place also does a fine Indonesian *rystafel* (rice with many dishes) with six dishes for R75 or a half portion for R50.

Wijnhuis (Map p152; ☎ 887 7196; Andringa St; mains R50-100; ⊕ 10am-11pm) A stylish option with indoor and outdoor dining areas, an extensive menu and a wine list stretching to 350 different labels. Around 20 wines are available by the glass and it does tastings of six wines for R20.

Fishmonger (Map p152; ☎ 887 7835; cnr Ryneveld & Plein Sts; mains R50; ⊕ lunch & dinner) The choice for seafood. It's a snazzily designed place with a relaxed vibe. A platter goes for a reasonable R70.

Decameron Italian Restaurant (Map p152; ☎ 883 3331; 50 Plein St; mains R40-50; ⊕ noon-midnight Mon-Sat) Considered the town's best Italian restaurant, Decameron is good for either a quick pizza or a full meal. It has outdoor seating for those balmy evenings.

Workshop (Map p152; ☎ 887 9985; 34 Merriman St; mains R60; ⊕ 10.30-1am Mon-Sat) This place combines a spacious bistro/restaurant serving good-value fusion-cuisine dishes upstairs with a buzzy bar downstairs. It's popular with students from the nearby university.

CAFÉS & QUICK EATS

Mugg & Bean (Map p152; ☎ 883 2972; Mill St; mains from R30; ⊕ 7am-10pm) A reputable chain café, it's a good choice for breakfast with bagels, huge muffins and self-service bottomless cups of coffee.

Java Café (Map p152; ☎ 887 6261; cnr Church & Andringa Sts; snacks from R15; ⊕ 8.30am-11pm) A good range of drinks and snacks are available at this stylish café, with pavement tables. It also offers Stellenbosch's cheapest Internet access.

Spice Café (Map p152; ☎ 883 8480; 34 Church St; mains from R25; ⊕ 9am-5pm Mon-Fri, 9am-2pm Sat, 10am-2pm Sun) Situated in a brightly painted house with a courtyard shaded by a peppercorn tree, Spice Café offers a self-serve buffet and gourmet sandwiches.

Naked Truth (Map p152; ☎ 882 9672; 62 Andringa St; mains from R20; ⊕ 8.30am-9pm) A funky café decorated with some intriguing pieces of local art and photography, and with a quiet courtyard. The menu includes wraps, Thai curry and tempting homemade desserts.

Entertainment

Stellenbosch has a lively nightlife scene, geared towards the interests of the university students. It's safe to walk around the centre at night, so a pub-crawl could certainly be on the cards (if you're staying at the Stumble Inn one will probably be organised for you). All the places listed are open daily until very late.

Bohemia (Map p152; ☎ 882 8375; cnr Andringa & Beyers Sts) There is live music every Tuesday, Thursday and Sunday. Try the novelty hubble-bubble pipes (R25) with a range of different tobaccos.

De Kelder (Map p152; ☎ 883 3797; 63 Dorp St) A reasonably pleasant restaurant, bar and beer garden, it is popular with German backpackers.

De Akker (Map p152; ☎ 883 3512; 90 Dorp St) This is another classic student drinking-hole with pub meals from under R30. Upstairs is the Hidden Cellar, where bands occasionally play.

Nu Bar (Map p152; ☎ 886 8998; 51 Plein St) With more of a nightclub feel, it has a small dance floor beyond the long bar where the DJ pumps out hip-hop and house.

Dros (Map p152; ☎ 886 4856; Drostdy Centre, Bird St), the **Terrace** (Map p152; ☎ 887 194; Drostdy Centre, Bird St) and **Tollies** (Map p152; Drostdy Centre, Bird St), clustered together in the complex just off Bird St and north of the Braak, are among the liveliest bars; you can eat at all of them, but that's not what most patrons have in mind. If you're looking for a slightly more sophisticated option try **Fandangos Internet café** (☎ 887 7501; Drostdy Centre, Bird St), which is a cocktail bar and Internet café in the same complex.

Shopping
Simonsberg Cheese Factory (Map p152; ☎ 809 1017; 9 Stoffel Smit St; ☺ 9am-5pm Mon-Fri, 9am-12.30pm Sat) There are free tastings and the shop sells inexpensive cheese.

Oom Samie se Winkel (Map p152; Uncle Sammy's Shop; ☎ 887 0797; 84 Dorp St; ☺ 9am-5pm) Unashamedly touristy but still worth visiting for its curious range of goods – from high kitsch to genuine antiques and everything else in between.

Getting There & Away
BUS
Long-distance bus services charge high prices for this short sector to Cape Town and do not take bookings. You're better off using **Backpacker Bus** (☎ 082-809 9185; www.backpackerbus.co.za), which charges R130 one-way and will pick you up from where you are staying.

MINIBUS TAXI
A minibus taxi to Paarl is about R50 (45 minutes), but you'll probably have to change taxis en route at Pniel.

TRAIN
Metro trains run the 46km between Cape Town and Stellenbosch (1st class/economy R12/7.50, about one hour). Note there are no 2nd-class tickets. For inquiries, call **Stellenbosch station** (☎ 808 1111). To be safe, travel in the middle of the day.

Getting Around
With largely flat countryside (unless you try to cross Franschhoek Pass), this is good cycling territory. Bicycles can be hired from the Stumble Inn, the publicity association and Fandangos in the Drostdy Centre for R20 per hour or R90 for the day.

For local trips in a private taxi call **Daksi Cab** (☎ 082-854 1541).

FRANSCHHOEK
☎ 021 / pop 7000
The toughest decision you'll face in Franschhoek is where to eat. This booming village, nestling in one of the loveliest settings in the Cape, has so many fine restaurants and

wineries that you could find yourself lingering here longer than expected – not a bad thing, since Franschhoek is a good base from which to visit both Stellenbosch and Paarl as long as you have transport.

Wining and dining aside, there's an interesting museum, some decent walks in the surrounding mountains and plenty of galleries and boutiques to mop up any spare cash.

Orientation & Information
The town is clustered around Huguenot St. At the southern end it reaches a T-junction at Huguenot Memorial Park. Continue northeast along R45 for the spectacular Franschhoek Pass.

Internet access is available at the **Stationery Shop** (Map p160; Bordeaux St; R10 per ½hr; ☺ 9am-5pm).

Franschhoek Wine Valley Tourist Association (Map p160; ☎ 876 3603; www.franschhoek.org.za; Huguenot St; ☺ 9am-6pm Mon-Fri, 9am-5pm Sat, 10am-5pm Sun Sep-Apr) is to the left on the main street shortly after you enter the town. The staff can provide a map of the area's scenic walks and issue permits (R10) for walks in nearby forestry areas, as well as book accommodation. Call ahead for opening hours in other months.

Sights & Activities
HUGUENOT MEMORIAL MUSEUM
This engrossing **museum** (Map p160; ☎ 876 2532; Lambrecht St; adult/child R5/2; ☺ 9am-5pm Mon-Sat, 2-5pm Sun) celebrates South Africa's Huguenots (p30) and houses the genealogical records of their descendants. Some of the names of the original settlers, such as Malan, de Villiers, Malherbe and Roux, are among the most famous Afrikaner dynasties in the country. The museum also contains examples of some hefty Cape Dutch furniture. Behind the main complex is a pleasant café, in front is the **Huguenot Monument** (Map p160; adult/child R3/1; ☺ 9am-5pm) and across the road is the **annexe**, with displays on the Anglo-Boer War and natural history, plus a souvenir shop.

MONT ROCHELLE EQUESTRIAN CENTRE
For details about a horseback tour of the wine estates around town contact the **equestrian centre** (☎ 083-300 4368; fax 021-876 2363; per hr R80).

FRANSCHHOEK

To Chamonix (1km)

0 _____ 400 m
0 _____ 0.2 miles

SIGHTS & ACTIVITIES	(pp159-60)
Huguenot Fine Chocolates.........3 B2	
Huguenot Memorial Museum	
Annexe......................4 C3	
Huguenot Memorial Museum.....5 C3	
Huguenot Monument 6 C3	

WINERIES	(pp160-1)
Cabrière Estate......................7 B3	
Mont Rochelle.......................8 A3	

SLEEPING	(p161)
Auberge Bligny..........................9 B2	
Ballon Rouge.........................10 C2	
Cottage.................................11 B1	
La Cabrière Country House.......12 C3	
Le Quartier Français................13 A2	
Reeden Lodge........................14 A2	

To Haute Cabrière
Cellar (1.5km); La
Petit Ferme (1.5km);
Franschhoek Pass (2km)

Huguenot
Memorial Park

To La Couronne
(1.5km)

EATING	(pp161-3)
French Connection...................15 B2	
Topsi & Company....................16 B2	

HUGUENOT FINE CHOCOLATES

An empowerment programme helped give the two local Coloured guys who run this Belgian-style **chocolate shop** (Map p160; ☎ 876 4096; 62 Huguenot St) a leg up and now people are raving about their confections. Call them a day in advance to arrange a tour and chocolate-making demonstration including tasting of samples (R12).

Wineries

Many of Franschhoek's wineries are within walking distance of the town centre, but to reach Boschendal you'll need transport.

Boschendal (Map p162; ☎ 870 4210; www.boschendal.com; Pniel Rd; ⏱ 8.30am-4.30pm Nov-Apr, 8.30am-4.30pm Mon-Sat May-Oct), tucked beneath some awesome mountains, is the classic Winelands estate, with lovely architecture, food and wine. Note the Taphuis wine-tasting area (where tastings cost R12 or R20 for a formal tasting with a guide) is at the opposite end of the estate from the **Groote Drakenstein manor house** (admission R8) and restaurants. The blow-out buffet lunch (R180) in the main restaurant is mainly a group affair; far nicer,

especially in fine weather, is Le Café, where you can have a snack or something more substantial. Also very popular are 'Le Pique Nique' hampers (R87.50 per person, minimum two people), served under parasols on the lawn from mid-October to the end of April, for which you'll need to book (☎ 870 4274). Its reds, including Cabernet Sauvignon and Merlot, get top marks. Boschendal is on the R310 towards Stellenbosch.

Cabrière Estate (Map p160; ☎ 876 2630; www.cabriere.co.za; Berg St; tastings with/without cellar tour R25/20; ⏱ 9.30am-4.30pm Mon-Fri, 11am-2pm Sat; tours 11am & 3pm Mon-Fri, 11am Sat) offers tastings that include a couple of sparkling wines and one of the vineyard's excellent range of white, red and dessert wines and brandies. No wonder it's so popular. At the Saturday session, stand by for the proprietor's party trick of slicing open a bottle of bubbly with a sabre.

Chamonix (Map p162; ☎ 876 2498; www.chamonix.co.za; Uitkyk St; tastings R10; ⏱ 9.30am-4.30pm) has cellar tours at 11am and 3pm by appointment. The tasting room is in a converted blacksmith's; there's also a range of schnapps and mineral water to sample. The pretty **La Maison de Chamonix restaurant** (mains R70-90; ☺ noon-4pm Sat-Thu, noon-4pm & 6.30-9pm Fri) has a reasonably priced menu. There are also self-catering cottages amid the vineyards (see below).

Mont Rochelle (Map p160; ☎ 876 3000; montrochelle@wine.co.za; tastings R15; ☺ 10am-5pm Mon-Fri, 11am-5pm Sat year-round, 11am-3pm Sun Sep-Apr), another vineyard in a beautiful location, also offers great wines. It's one of the handful of vineyards owned by a Black businessman – Miko Rwayibare from the Congo. You can combine your wine tasting with a cheese tasting for an extra R10, and cellar tours (R10) are by appointment.

Sleeping

BUDGET
Cottage (Map p160; ☎ 876 2392; thecottage55@iafrica.com; 55 Huguenot St; s/d R250/320) There is just one cottage sleeping two, or four at a pinch, but it's a beauty. It's private, quiet, and is a few minutes' walk from the village centre.

Chamonix (Map p162; ☎ 876 2494; www.chamonix.co.za; Uitkyk St; cottages from R480) Pleasant cottages sleeping up to four are set in the middle of the vineyards (opposite). It's a 10-minute walk uphill north of Huguenot St.

Reeden Lodge (Map p160; ☎ 876 3174; www.reedenlodge.co.za; Fabriek St; cottages from R380; ☐ ☒) The lodge offers well-equipped self-catering cottages sleeping up to six people. They're located on a farm about 10 minutes' walk from town and it's good if you've got kids – there are sheep, a tree house and lots of space.

MID-RANGE
Ballon Rouge (Map p160; ☎ 876 2651; www.ballon-rouge.co.za; 7 Reservoir St East; s/d with breakfast R500/600; ☐ ☒) A small hotel with good-quality rooms opening on to the stoop. It also has a restaurant.

Auberge Bligny (Map p160; ☎ 876 3767; www.bligny.co.za; 28 Van Wyk St; s/d with breakfast R590/680; ☒) This is a guesthouse in a Victorian homestead with nine pleasant rooms and a shady garden.

TOP END
Le Quartier Français (Map p160; ☎ 876 2151; www.lequartier.co.za; 16 Huguenot St; d from R2350; ☒ ☐ ☒) This is one of the best places to stay in the Winelands. Set around a leafy court-yard and pool, guest rooms are very large with fireplaces, huge beds and stylish décor. There's also a fine restaurant here (see p161).

La Cabrière Country House (Map p160; ☎ 876 4780; www.lacabriere.co.za; Middagkrans Rd; d with breakfast R950; ☒ ☐ ☒) A modern boutique guesthouse that's a refreshing break from all that Cape Dutch architecture. There are only four sumptuously decorated rooms, very personal service and sweeping views to the mountains.

La Couronne (Map p162; ☎ 876 2770; www.lacouronnehotel.co.za; Robertsvlei Rd; d with breakfast from R1800; ☒ ☐ ☒) A boutique hotel-and-restaurant partly built into the hills, this place offers gilt-edged luxury and magnificent views across the valley.

Eating
Franschhoek is so small that it's easy to stroll around and see what appeals although if you want to eat at any of the following places advance booking is best. There are also good restaurants at the Boschendal (opposite) and Chamonix (opposite) wineries.

Le Quartier Français (Map p160; ☎ 876 2151; 16 Huguenot St; mains R75; ☺ lunch & dinner) As well as being a great place to stay (see p161), this place dazzles with the quality and creativity of its cooking; try dishes such as double-baked beetroot and rocket soufflé, lemon verbena roasted chicken, or the divine plum tartlet with currant syrup and verjuice. The hotel's bar does lighter meals for around R50.

La Petite Ferme (☎ 876 3016; Franschhoek Pass Rd; mains R80; ☺ noon-4pm) A must-visit for foodies who hanker for romantic views, boutique wines and smoked, de-boned salmon trout, its delicately flavoured signature dish. There's a helipad should you feel like choppering in from Cape Town and some luxurious rooms if you can't bear to leave.

Haute Cabrière Cellar (☎ 876 3688; Franschhoek Pass Rd; mains R80-90; ☺ noon-3pm daily, 7-9pm Wed-Mon) In a dramatic dining space in a cellar cut into the mountain side, each dish can be had either as a starter or main and all are paired with a Cabrière wine.

Topsi & Company (Map p160; ☎ 876 2952; 7 Reservoir St; mains R50-75; ☺ 12.30-3pm & 7.30-10pm Wed-Mon) Run by Topsi Venter, who should be accorded national-treasure status, it's

WESTERN CAPE

FRANSCHHOEK & PAARL WINE REGIONS

0 — 5 km
0 — 3 miles

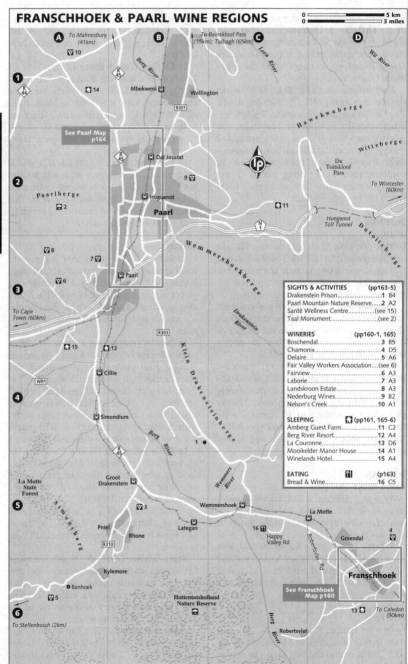

SIGHTS & ACTIVITIES   (pp163–5)
Drakenstein Prison........................1 B4
Paarl Mountain Nature Reserve.....2 A2
Santé Wellness Centre..............(see 15)
Taal Monument.........................(see 2)

WINERIES   (pp160–1, 165)
Boschendal..................................3 B5
Chamonix....................................4 D5
Delaire..5 A6
Fair Valley Workers Association....(see 6)
Fairview......................................6 A3
Laborie.......................................7 A3
Landskroon Estate........................8 A3
Nederburg Wines..........................9 B2
Nelson's Creek...........................10 A1

SLEEPING   (pp161, 165–6)
Amberg Guest Farm.....................11 C2
Berg River Resort.......................12 A4
La Couronne..............................13 D6
Mooikelder Manor House............14 A1
Winelands Hotel.........................15 A4

EATING   (p163)
Bread & Wine.............................16 C5

quirky and very relaxed, Topsi pops out from her open kitchen to serve the totally delicious food and chat with guests; you can BYO wine.

Bread & Wine (Map 162; ☎ 876 3692; Môreson Wine Farm, Happy Valley Rd, La Motte; mains R60; ☺ noon-6pm Tue-Sun) Hidden away down a dirt road as you approach town along R45, this place is worth searching out. It's known for its breads, pizzas, cured meats and tasty Mediterranean-style cuisine.

French Connection (Map p160; ☎ 876 4056; 48 Huguenot St; mains R50; ☺ lunch & dinner) A deservedly popular place with chequered red tablecloths that give it that ooh-la-la factor. The menu is bistro fare done to perfection.

Getting There & Away

The best way to reach Franschhoek is in your own vehicle. Shared taxis run from Paarl station (R7.50).

PAARL & AROUND

☎ 021 / pop 154,000

Less touristy and more spread out than Stellenbosch, Paarl is a large commercial centre, surrounded by mountains and vineyards, on the banks of the Berg River. There are vineyards and wineries within the sprawling town limits, including the huge Kooperatieve Wijnbouwers Vereeniging (KWV; see the boxed text p154).

Paarl is not really a town to tour on foot, but there is still quite a lot to see and do. There are some great walks in the Paarl Mountain Nature Reserve, some excellent Cape Dutch architecture and some significant monuments to Afrikaner culture.

Orientation & Information

Main St runs 11km along the entire length of the town, parallel to the Berg River and the train line. It's shaded by oaks and jacarandas and is lined with many historic buildings. The busy commercial centre is around Lady Grey St.

Paarl Tourism (Map p164; ☎ 872 3829; www.paarl online.com; 216 Main St; ☺ 9am-5pm Mon-Fri, 9am-1pm Sat, 10am-1pm Sun) has an excellent supply of information on the whole region and helpful staff.

Sights & Activities

Apart from the local wineries there are a few other worthwhile things to do in Paarl.

PAARL MUSEUM

This **museum** (Map p164; ☎ 872 2651; www.museums .org.za/paarlmuseum; 303 Main St; adult/child R5/ donation; ☺ 10am-5pm Mon-Fri) is housed in the Old Parsonage (Oude Pastorie) built in 1714. It has a fascinating collection of Cape Dutch antiques and relics of Huguenot and early Afrikaner culture. There's a bookcase modelled on King Solomon's temple, and display sections on the 'road to reconciliation', the old mosques of the local Muslim community and the Khoisan.

PAARL MOUNTAIN NATURE RESERVE

The three giant granite domes that dominate this popular reserve (Map p162) and loom over the western side of town apparently glisten like pearls if they are caught by the sun after a fall of rain – hence the name 'Paarl'. The reserve has mountain *fynbos* (literally 'fine bush', primarily proteas, heaths and ericas) and a particularly large number of proteas. There's a cultivated wildflower garden in the middle that's a nice spot for a picnic, and numerous walks with excellent views over the valley.

Access is from the 11km-long Jan Phillips Dr, which skirts the eastern edge of the reserve. The picnic ground is about 4km from Main St. A map showing walking trails is available from Paarl Tourism.

While up this way you could also visit the **Taal Monument** (adult/child R5/2; ☺ 8am-5pm). This is the giant needle-like edifice that commemorates the Afrikaans language. On a clear day there are stunning views from here as far as Cape Town.

DRAKENSTEIN PRISON

On 11 February 1990, Nelson Mandela ended his years in captivity here. With right arm raised and fist clenched in the Black power salute, he walked out the gates and greeted the world for the first time in 27 years, six months and seven days. The jail was then called the Victor Verster Prison, and it was here, not Robben Island, where Mandela spent his last two years of captivity in the relative comfort of the warders cottage, negotiating the end of apartheid. It's still a working prison so there are no tours. You can find it 9km south of Paarl along the R303 from exit 59 on the N1.

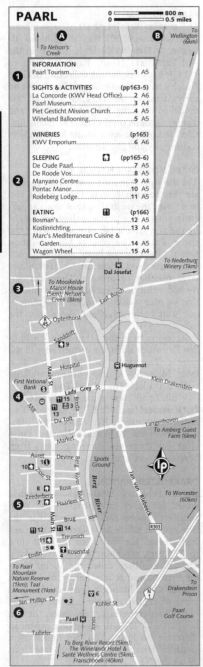

SANTÉ WELLNESS CENTRE

The chief selling point of this luxurious new **spa** (Map p162; ☎ 875 8200; www.santewell ness.co.za; Winelands Hotel, Klapmuts), around 7km southwest of Paarl, is its vinotherapy regime (R1645 with lunch), which includes a Shiraz body rub, Chardonnay cocoon wrap and Cabernet Sauvignon bath! There are lots of other treatments available as well as both indoor and outdoor pools.

WINELAND BALLOONING

You'll need to get up very early in the morning, but a hot-air balloon trip over the Winelands will be unforgettable. Contact **Wineland Ballooning** (Map p164; ☎ 863 3192; 64 Main St; per person R1550), which runs trips between November and April but only when the weather conditions are right.

WELLINGTON

This sedate and reasonably pretty town (Map p162) has a population of around 37,000 and is 10km north of Paarl. On the way here you'll likely pass through the large **Mbekweni** township, created in 1945 but with little infrastructure to match its half-century history.

The landowner whose property was used by the railway stipulated that all trains must stop in Wellington. This included King George VI's train in 1947 and today accounts for the brief halt by the *Blue Train* also.

The **Tourism Bureau** (☎ 873 4604; www.visitwe llington.com; 104 Main St) is next to the Andrew Murray Church. The friendly staff can provide a brochure and map of the wineries in the Wellington area, which are less touristy than Paarl's. A popular one is **Hildenbrand Wine & Olive Estate** (☎ /fax 873 4115; www.wine -estate-hildenbrand.co.za; tastings R5; s/d with breakfast R320/500; ☉ winery 10am-4pm; ▨), which also has a restaurant and good accommodation.

Bakkies B&B (☎ /fax 873 5161; www.bakkiesbb .co.za; Bainskloof Rd; s/d R150/260; ▨ ▢) offers good-value, well-equipped rooms in a lodge just above the Oasis café on the Bainskloof Rd. The rates include a permit to hike the Patatskloof Trail (below).

BAINSKLOOF PASS

This is one of the country's great mountain passes, with a superb caravan park halfway along. Thomas Bain developed the road

Pruning the grapevines in the countryside around Cape Town

JULIET COOMBE

Surfing at Kommetjie (p118) on the Cape Peninsula

PAUL KENNEDY

RICHARD I'ANSON

Wildflowers in the Cape of Good Hope Nature Reserve (p144), Cape Peninsula

Beach on the Cape Peninsula (p140)

CAROL POLICH

Cape gannets, Lambert's Bay (p213),
Western Cape

Historic winery in Franschhoek (p159),
Western Cape

Rain clouds over Karoo National Park (p209),
Western Cape

Farms and vineyards, Franschhoek (p159), Western Cape

through the pass between 1848 and 1852. Other than having its surface tarred, the road has not been altered since, and it is now a national monument. It's a magical drive, which would be even better to experience on bicycle.

The R301 runs from Wellington across Bainskloof to meet another road running south to Worcester and north to Ceres.

There are several nearby walks, including the five-hour **Bobbejaans River Walk** to a waterfall. This walk actually starts back at Eerste Tol and you need to buy a permit (R30), which is available from the Cape Nature Conservation desk at Cape Town Tourism (see p99).

The Patatskloof Trail is a long day-walk that begins and ends at the **Oasis Tea Room** (☎ 873 4231; 8.30am-6pm Thu-Sun), on the road leading up to the pass from Wellington. You can make it an overnight walk by arranging to stay in a cave on the trail.

Wineries

KWV Emporium (Map p164; ☎ 807 3007; www.kwv .co.za; Kohler St; tastings R20; 9am-4pm Mon-Sat) It's no longer the all-controlling body it used to be, but this remains one of the country's best-known wineries since its products are mostly sold overseas. Some KWV port and sherry is available inside South Africa, and its fortified wines, in particular, are among the world's best. The firm's impressive offices are at La Concorde on Paarl's Main St, but the cellar tours are at its complex near the railway line. Call for times of cellar tours (R20), which are worth taking if only to see the enormous Cathedral Cellar built in 1930.

Fairview (Map p162; ☎ 863 2450; www.fairview .co.za; tastings R10; 8.30am-5pm Mon-Fri, 8.30am-1pm Sat) A small and deservedly popular winery. Peacocks and goats in a tower (apparently goats love to climb) greet you on arrival. The tastings are great value since they cover some 23 wines *and* a wide range of goats' and cows' milk cheeses. You can sample and buy the pinotage and Chenin Blanc of the Fair Valley Workers Association (see the boxed text on p154) here too. Fairview is 5km southwest of Paarl off the R101.

Laborie (Map p162; ☎ 807 3390; www.kwv-inter national.com; Taillefert St; tastings R9; 9am-5pm daily Oct-Apr, 9am-5pm Mon-Sat May-Sep) KWV's attractive showcase vineyard, just off Main

St. It's known for its Shiraz and Alambic Brandy. The **restaurant** (☎ 807 3095; mains R45-70) is in an old Cape Dutch building and serves dishes such as Springbok shanks and kingklip.

Landskroon Estate (Map p162; ☎ 863 1039; tastings free; 8.30am-5pm Mon-Fri, 9am-1pm Sat) This estate represents five generations of the De Villiers family, who have been perfecting their wine-making skills on this pleasant estate. There's a nice terrace overlooking the vines on which you can quaff its Cabernet Sauvignons and celebrated port. The estate is off the R101, 6km south of Paarl.

Nederburg Wines (Map p162; ☎ 862 3104; www .nederburg.co.za; tastings R10; 8.30am-5pm Mon-Fri, 10am-2pm Sat) A big but professional and welcoming operation; the vast range of wines here are among the most widely available across the country. They offer an informative food and wine tasting (R17) that teaches you which types of flavour the wines will work best with. The picnic lunches cost R80 per person (December to March only, bookings essential) and are very popular. Nederburg is off the N1, 7km east of Paarl.

Nelson's Creek (Map p162; ☎ 869 8453; www.nel sonscreek.co.za; tastings free; 9am-5pm Mon-Fri, 9am-2pm Sat) is a forward-looking estate where the owner has donated land to workers to produce their own wines under the label New Beginnings. Wines to sample include the pinotage, Cabernet Sauvignon and Chardonnay. Cellar tours are by appointment and cost R20. It's around 15km north of the centre of Paarl on the R44.

For information about other wineries in the area, contact **Paarl Vintners** (☎ 872 3841).

Sleeping
BUDGET
Berg River Resort (Map p162; ☎ 863 1650; bergr@ mweb.co.za; camp sites R180, d chalets R425;) An attractive municipal camping ground beside the Berg River, 5km from Paarl on the N45 towards Franschhoek. Facilities include canoes, trampolines and a café.

Manyano Centre (Map p164; ☎ 872 2537; many anocentre@cci.org.za; Sanddrift St; dm with full board R110) An enormous accommodation complex with spartan three-bed dorms; you'll need to bring a sleeping bag. Call in advance, especially on weekends when it fills up with groups. Huguenot train station is closer than the main Paarl station.

De Roode Vos (Map p164; ☎/fax 872 5912; 152 Main St; s/d R150/240) This unspectacular guest-house offers clean lodgings and is about as cheap as you'll get in central Paarl.

MID-RANGE

Rodeberg Lodge (Map p164; ☎ 863 3202; www.rode berglodge.co.za; 74 Main Rd; s/d with breakfast R280/420; 🔊) Good rooms (some with air-con and TV) are sensibly located away from the busy main road. The hosts are friendly and breakfast is taken in the conservatory, opening onto a leafy garden.

Mooikelder Manor House (Map p162; ☎ 869 8787; www.capestay.co.za/mooikelder; Main Rd, Noorder Paarl; s/d with breakfast R275/500; 🖳 🔊) Around 5km north of the town centre in an elegant homestead once occupied by Cecil Rhodes, this is a lovely, quiet spot amid citrus orchards and with plenty of antique atmosphere in the rooms.

Amberg Guest Farm (Map p162; ☎/fax 862 0982; amberg@mweb.co.za; R101 along Du Toits Kloof Pass; s/d with breakfast R250/380; 🔊) Accommodation is in cottages (one of which is self-catering for R300) with spectacular views. The amiable hosts also run the Swiss-style Amberg Country Kitchen, serving Swiss specialities.

TOP END

Pontac Manor (Map p164; ☎ 872 0445; www.pon tac.com; 16 Zion St; s/d with breakfast R770/1050; 🔊 🔊) A small, stylish, Victorian-era hotel that commands a good view of the valley. The rooms are comfortable, there's one self-catering cottage and a restaurant, which is recommended.

De Oude Paarl (Map p164; ☎ 872 1002; www.de oudepaarl.com; 132 Main St; s/d with breakfast R650/930; 🔊 🖳 🔊) This is a new boutique-style hotel; the rooms have antique touches and there's a secluded courtyard at the back. Attached are shops selling a good selection of wine and delectable but pricey Belgian chocolates.

Winelands Hotel (Map p162; ☎ 875 8100; www .southernsun.com; Klapmuts; ste with breakfast R2300; 🔊 🖳 🔊) Paarl's luxury option; the newly planted vines are yet to fill out, which means the surrounding countryside is looking a bit barren and dusty. Inside the hotel rooms, it's king-sized beds, the latest in audio-visual equipment and decadent bathrooms all the way. The Santé Wellness Centre (p164) is attached.

Eating

Several of the local vineyards have restaurants or do picnic lunches and they are among the best places to eat.

Marc's Mediterranean Cuisine & Garden (Map p164; ☎ 863 3980; 129 Main Rd; mains R60-75; ⏰ noon-3pm Tue-Sun, 6pm-late Mon-Sat) The current favourite of restaurant reviewers, and with good reason. Patron Marc Friedrich has created a light and bright place with food to match and a Provence-style garden to dine in. Try the meze plate (R45) for lunch.

Wagon Wheel (Map p164; ☎ 872 5265; 57 Lady Grey St; mains R70; ⏰ noon-2pm Tue-Fri, 6pm-late Tue-Sat) More than your average steak joint, this cosy wood-panelled restaurant has won many awards and packs them in nightly. Next door they've added on Gabi's, a continental-style café-bar and nonsmoking section for the restaurant.

Kostinrichting (Map p164; ☎ 871 1353; 19 Pastorie Ave; mains R30; ⏰ lunch, closed Sun) Ideal if you're looking for a pleasant central café. It's in a Victorian building that once was a school, and has an attached crafts shop.

Bosman's (Map p164; ☎ 863 2727; Grande Roche, Plantasie St; mains R140; ⏰ lunch & dinner) If money is no object try this ritzy restaurant. It's undoubtedly classy, with chandeliers inside, flickering candles outside and a wine list that runs to over 50 pages! There are various set menus starting off at R175 for three courses.

Getting There & Away

BUS

All the major long-distance bus companies offer services going through Paarl, so it is easy to build it into your itinerary. The bus segment between Paarl and Cape Town is R90, so consider taking the cheaper train to Paarl and then linking up with the buses.

TRAIN

Metro trains run roughly every hour between Cape Town and Paarl (1st/economy class R14.5/8.50, 1¼ hours, Monday to Friday). Note there is no 2nd class. The services are less frequent on weekends. Take care to travel on trains during the busy part of the day, as robberies have been reported.

You can travel by train from Paarl to Stellenbosch: take a Cape Town–bound train and change at Muldersvlei.

Getting Around

If you don't have your own transport, your only option for getting around Paarl, apart from walking, is to call a taxi: try **Paarl Radio Taxis** (☎ 872 5671).

THE OVERBERG

The Overberg, which literally means 'Over the Mountains', is the region south and west of the Franschhoek Range, and south of the Wemmershoek and Riviersonderend Ranges, which form a natural barrier with the Breede River Valley.

Coming from Cape Town, the R44 from Strand, towards Hermanus around Cape Hangklip, is a thrilling coastal drive, in the same class as the Chapman's Peak Dr in Cape Town (p111). The first major stop is Hermanus, a popular seaside resort. In spring it's famous for the whales that frequent its shores (although it's so famous now that you might choose to do your whale-watching at a less crowded location along the coast).

If you're looking for somewhere quiet to hang out, both the miraculously undeveloped fishing village of Arniston and the De Hoop Nature Reserve will fill the bill. The best all-round base for the area is Swellendam, a historic and attractive town beneath the impressive Langeberg Mountains.

This region's wealth of *fynbos* is unmatched; most species flower somewhere in the period between autumn and spring. The climate basically follows the same pattern as Cape Town – a temperate Mediterranean climate with relatively mild winters and warm summers. Rain falls throughout the year but peaks in August, and it can be very windy any time.

KOGEL BAY
☎ 024

The best bit of the drive along the R44 from Cape Town is between Gordon's Bay and Kleinmond. The views are stunning. At times it feels as if the road is going to disappear into the sea. On one side is blue-green water, on the other rock strewn cliffs. The **Kogel Bay Pleasure Resort** (☎ 856 1286; fax 856 4741; R44; day visitors per person R6, per vehicle R12; camp sites R60) has camp sites and reasonable facilities on a fantastic beach (although it's

unsafe for swimming and sometimes windy). Bring all your own food. It's popular with South Africans during school holidays.

BETTY'S BAY
☎ 028

The small, scattered holiday village of Betty's Bay, just to the east of Cape Hangklip, is the next place worth a pause on the R44. Here you'll find the **Harold Porter National Botanical Gardens** (☎ 272 9311; adult/child R7/3; ☼ 8am-4.30pm Mon-Fri, 8am-5pm Sat & Sun), definitely worth visiting. There are paths exploring the area and, at the entrance, tearooms and a formal garden where you can picnic. Try the Leopard Kloof Trail, which leads through fern forests and up to a waterfall. It's 3km round-trip. Coming from Cape Town, look for the turn-off to the gardens after driving through Betty's Bay. Another worthwhile stop is at **Stony Point**, on the R44 coming from Cape Town before you reach Betty's Bay. Take a short stroll to the lookout point for a colony of **African penguins**. It's very picturesque with crashing waves and a sea of black-and-white birds.

KLEINMOND
☎ 028

Close to a wild and beautiful beach, Kleinmond, on the R44, is in a state of revival. The Harbour Rd area, quickly becoming quite chic, is a great place to spend an afternoon, eat some fresh seafood and browse through the art gallery and little shops. Stop by the **Abalone Hatchery** (☎ 271 5681; Harbour Rd; admission R8; ☼ 9am-4pm Mon-Fri), where they grow South Africa's six abalone species for export. It's a tiny place but worth a stroll. The area also has some reliable swells for surfers and some good walking.

Sleeping

Kleinmond Travellers Inn (☎ 082-263 6139; kleinmondtravelinn@hotmail.com; 31 Harbour Rd; camp sites per person R35, dm R50, d with shared bathroom R150) This sea-facing hotel is brightly painted and has fantastic sunset views. There's an outdoor bar with a fireplace, couches and a pool table.

Palmiet Caravan Park (☎ 271 4050; camp sites from R80) This caravan park is beside the beach on the western side of town, and you can hear the waves breaking from your tent. Follow the signs from the R44.

OVERBERG & ROUTE 62

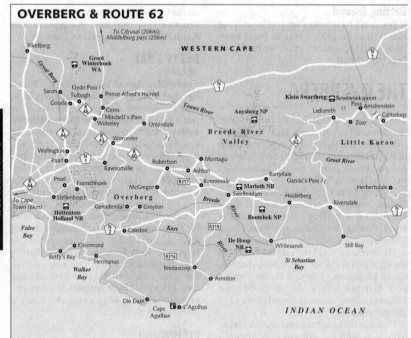

Eating

Café Caliente (☎ 082-263 6139; Harbour Rd; light meals R15-30) This café is owned by a former five-star restaurant chef and the cuisine, especially the pancakes, is delectable. The coffee is also stellar, as are the sweet snacks.

Alive Alive-O (☎ 271 3774; 35 Harbour Rd; mains R35-150) This outdoor beach-shack shellfish-bar claims to be the only restaurant in the country allowed to serve abalone. The shellfish, known for their aphrodisiac qualities, are fried in garlic butter and served in a wine cream sauce (R130 for 200g). Fresh prawns are also on the menu.

Café Atlantic & Café Europa (☎ 271 5107; 18 Harbour Rd; mains R30-500) Café Atlantic is a swanky cocktail bar, a rare find in such a tiny town, with big screen TVs, linen tablecloths and sunset views. the attached Café Europa has an interesting Greek-themed menu.

HERMANUS

☎ 028 / pop 24,700
Within day-tripping distance of Cape Town (122km), Hermanus was originally a fishing village and still retains vestiges of its heri-

tage. It's now best known as a place to view whales (see the boxed text on p171) and to dive with great white sharks.

There are some appealing beaches, most west of the town centre. Rocky hills, vaguely reminiscent of Scotland, surround the town, and there are good walks and a nature reserve protecting some of the prolific *fynbos*. The pleasant town centre, easily negotiated on foot and east of the new harbour, is well endowed with restaurants and shops.

Hermanus is packed during the school holidays in December and January.

Information
BOOKSHOPS
Book Cottage (☎ 313 0834; 10 Harbour Rd) Sells travel guides and other new books.
Hemmingway's Bookshop (☎ 312 2739; 4 Main Rd) Has an extensive collection of second-hand volumes.

INTERNET ACCESS
Hermanus Internet & Information Café (☎ 313 0277; Waterkant Bldg, Main Rd; per hr R40; ☺ 8am-8pm Mon-Fri, 9am-8pm Sat) Offers reliable and speedy Internet connections.

LEGEND

NP	National Park
NR	Nature Reserve
WA	Wilderness Area

TOURIST INFORMATION

Hermanus Tourism (☎ 312 2629; www.hermanus.co
.za; Old Station Bldg, Mitchell St; ☺ 9am-5pm Mon-Sat,
noon-5pm Sun) Has a large supply of information about
the area, including walks and drives in the surrounding
hills, and can book accommodation for you.

Sights & Activities

There is no shortage of outdoor activities
to be undertaken in Hermanus, and most
places to sleep can arrange anything from
sea kayaking to shark diving to local wine
tastings. Those looking for handicrafts can
check out the small daily market at Lemms
Corner, in the Market Sq off Main Rd; on
Saturday there's a craft market held there,
too.

SHARK-DIVING

Cage shark diving to view great whites is
heavily promoted in Hermanus, and there
are no fewer than eight operators based
here. The boats actually depart from Gansbaai, some 35km along the coast, but all
the companies transport you there. There's
no doubting the activity's popularity, but

it doesn't come without controversy. Operators use bait to attract the sharks to the
cage, which means that these killer fish are
being trained to associate humans with
food. It's not a pleasant scenario, especially
if you're a surfer, several of whom have
been attacked by sharks in the past.

With the majority of operators, an internationally recognised diving qualification is required in order to take part in
the dive, although some allow snorkellers into the cage. Most hotels and hostels can arrange shark-diving trips for
you. The most highly recommended operator is **Brian McFarlane** (☎ 312 2766; www
.hermanusinfo.co.za/greatwhite; trips R800), and he
is often booked solid. Another popular
choice is **Shark Lady Adventures** (☎ 313 3287;
www.sharklady.co.za; 61 Marine Dr; trips R850). The
shark lady herself, Kim Maclean, has been
running trips for 10 years. The trips include breakfast, lunch and diving gear.

WALKING

From town take the **Cliff Path Walking Trail**
that meanders along the sea to Grotto
Beach, a long narrow surf beach with excellent facilities. The walk takes about 1½
hours and along the way you'll pass Kraai-
water, a good whale-watching lookout, and
Laangbai and Voelklip beaches. The 1400-
hectare **Fernkloof Nature Reserve** (☎ 313 8100;
Fir Ave; admission free; ☺ 9am-5pm) is worth a visit
if you are interested in *fynbos*. They have
identified 1100 species so far. There is a
60km network of hiking trails for all fitness levels.

SEA KAYAKING

Walker Bay Adventures (☎ 314 0925; Prawn Flats;
kayaking R150) runs sea-kayaking tours that
give you the opportunity to see whales up
close and personal. The company also does
lagoon cruises and rents kayaks and boats.

OLD HARBOUR

The old harbour clings to the cliffs in front
of the town centre; here you'll find a small
and generally uninteresting **museum** (☎ 044-
312 1475; adult/child R2/1; ☺ 9am-1pm, 2-5pm Mon-Sat,
noon-4pm Sun) and a display of old fishing
boats. The museum's annexe, in the old
schoolhouse on the market square, displays some evocative old photographs of
the town and its fishermen.

WESTERN CAPE

WESTERN CAPE

HERMANUS

0 — 400 m
0 — 0.2 miles

To New Harbour (2km);
Cape Town (122km)

Mountain St
Dolphin St
Impala St
Flora St
Fourie St
Duiker St
Alberyn St

Main Rd

Hospital St
Fourie St
Albertyn St

De Coede St
Church St
Flower St
Myrtle St
Spence St
Patterson St
Magnolia St

Church St
Plein St
Westcliff St
Dirkeys St
Long St
Aberdeen St
Mitchell St
Colleger St
Lord Roberts St
High St

Hospital

Bochester St
Orothumno St
De Goede St
Westcliff St
Cliff St
Marine Dr
Park St
Main St
Lemms Cnt
Main Rd
Protea St
Sea St

Cliff Path Walking Trail

Ficks Pool

First National Bank

Boiling Pot
Castle Rock
Old Harbour

Walker Bay

Blow Hole

ATLANTIC OCEAN

To Grotto Beach (4km);
Fernkloof Nature
Reserve (5km);
Walker Bay
Adventures (6km);
De Kelders (55km);
Gansbaai (57km)

Sleeping

There's been an explosion of places to stay in Hermanus over the last few years, but in the holiday season the town can still be busting at the seams, so take care to book ahead. Hermanus Tourism will help you and there are agencies such as **Whale Route Accommodation** (☎ 314 1566; www.hermanus.co.za /accom/whaleroute) and the **Hermanus Accommodation Centre** (☎ 313 0004), which let houses and book other accommodation.

BUDGET

Budget travellers have a good selection of hostels in town.

Moby's Traveller's Lodge (☎ 313 2361; www.mo bys.co.za; 9 Mitchell St; dm R70, s/d with shared bathroom

R150/190; ☑) Travellers give this place rave reviews, and we agree. It's in a converted old hotel and you can party the night away at the big bar or chill out in the awesome rock pool with its own waterfall. Breakfast is included in the price and they also serve light snacks (R15).

Hermanus Backpackers (☎ 312 4293; moobag@ mweb.co.za; 26 Flower St; camp sites per person R40, dm R70, s/d with shared bathroom R100/200; ☑ ☑) This is a smashing place with clued-up staff, great décor and facilities, including a reed-roof bar. Free breakfast is served in the morning.

Zoete Inval Travellers Lodge (☎ 312 1242; www .zoeteinval.co.za; 23 Main Rd; dm R70, d with shared bath room R300) More a guesthouse than a back-

WATCHING THE WHALES

Between June and November, southern right whales *(Eubalaena australis)* come to Walker Bay to calve. There can be up to 70 whales in the bay at once. South Africa was a whaling nation until 1976 – this species was hunted to the verge of extinction but its numbers are now recovering. Humpback whales *(Megaptera novaeangliae)* are also sometimes seen.

Whales often come very close to shore and there are some excellent vantage points from the cliff paths that run from one end of Hermanus to the other. The best places are Castle Rock, Kraal Rock and Sievers Point. There's a telescope on the cliff top above the old harbour.

It's only recently that the people of Hermanus bothered to tell the outside world the whales were regular visitors. They took them for granted. Now, however, the tourism potential has been recognised and just about every business in town has adopted a whale logo. There's a **whale-spotters hotline** (☎ 0800 228 222) and a whale crier, who walks around town blowing on a kelp horn and carrying a blackboard that shows where whales have been recently sighted. A **Whale Festival** is held in late September or early October.

Despite all this hoopla, boat-viewing of whales is strictly regulated. No boat-viewing is allowed in the bay and jet skis are banned. There are only two boat-viewing operators licensed to operate in the seas outside the bay: **Southern Right Charters** (☎ 082-353 0550) and **Hawston Fishers** (☎ 082-396 8931). They charge around R250 for a one- to two-hour trip.

Although Hermanus is the best-known whale-watching site, whales can be seen all the way from False Bay (Cape Town) to Plettenberg Bay and beyond. The west coast also gets its share.

packer hostel, this is a quiet place with good amenities and nicely furnished rooms. Families are accommodated in four-person doubles.

MID-RANGE

Auberge Burgundy (☎ 313 1202; www.hermanus.co .za/accom/auberge; 16 Harbour Rd; s/d with breakfast R450/900; ☒) This is a wonderful place, built in the style of a Provençal villa, with fine facilities, wrought-iron balconies and unique art on the walls.

Windsor Hotel (☎ 312 3727; www.windsor-hotel .com; 49 Marine Dr; s/d with breakfast from R420/620) Situated on a cliff overlooking the ocean; naturally you'll want one of the more expensive sea-facing rooms that give you the opportunity to view whales without leaving your bed.

Kenjockity Guesthouse (☎ 312 1772; kenjock@ hermanus.co.za; 15 Church St; s/d R200/400) This guesthouse, the first in Hermanus, has a nice atmosphere and fair-sized rooms with wooden furniture and walls the same colour as the duvets.

Hermanus Esplanade (☎ 312 3610; clarkbro@ hermanus.co.za; 63 Marine Dr; flats from R250) Some of these cheery self-catering apartments with colourful furniture overlook the sea; the lowest rates on offer actually cover the whale-watching season from May to October.

TOP END

Marine Hermanus (☎ 313 1000; www.marine-her manus.co.za; Marine Dr; s/d with breakfast R1500/2500; ☒ ☐ ☒) Right on the sea with immaculate grounds and amenities, this place is as posh as a five-star hotel should be. The staff is very friendly and will work with what you're looking for – sea views or rooms with balconies. The hotel has two restaurants, both sea facing, open for dinner only, which serve nouveau South African cuisine. You can choose between two-courses (R155) and three-courses (R195).

Eating & Entertainment

There's no shortage of places to eat in Hermanus with new restaurants opening all the time.

Burgundy Restaurant (☎ 312 2800; Marine Dr; mains R60-95; ☽ lunch & dinner) Booking is essential at the Burgundy, one of the most acclaimed and popular restaurants in the province. It's in a pair of cottages, which are the oldest buildings in town (1875), with a garden and sea views. The menu is mostly seafood with a different vegetarian dish each day.

Marimba Café (☎ 312 2148; 108D Main Rd; mains R40-75; ☽ dinner) The lively atmosphere matches the eclectic menu at this recommended restaurant, where you can eat traditional African dishes from around the continent. The bar is perfect for a drink.

Fisherman's Cottage (☎ 312 3642; Lemms Cnr; mains R22-75; ⊗ lunch & dinner) Good cheap seafood is on offer at this restaurant in a white-washed cottage draped with fishing nets.

Rossi's Pizzeria & Italian Restaurant (☎ 312 2848; 10 High St; mains R22-40; ⊗ dinner) Delicious smells enchant your senses upon entrance into this low-key family restaurant that focuses on pizza and pasta.

Bientang's Cave (☎ 312 3454; Marine Dr; mains R55; ⊗ lunch & dinner) Nestled in the cliffs beside the water this really *is* a seaside cave, containing a good seafood restaurant with a children's menu.

Savannah Café (☎ 312 4259; Village Theatre, Marine Dr; mains from R20; ⊗ breakfast and lunch) Watch the whales frolic in the sea while eating the 'Whale of a Breakfast' – eggs, juice, coffee, bacon, chips, mushrooms and boerewors, among other items.

Zebra Crossing (☎ 312 3906; 121 Main Rd; mains R20-30; ⊗ lunch & dinner) This DJ bar with a funky zebra theme is *the* late-night party spot on weekends, and popular with backpackers. At other times there's an open fire and pool tables. Food is burgers and sandwiches.

Getting There & Away

All three hostels run a shuttle service (R20) to the Baz Bus drop-off point; otherwise there are no regular bus services to Hermanus from Cape Town.

CAPE AGULHAS

☎ 028

Welcome to the southernmost point of Africa. On a stormy day the low, shattered rocks and crashing seas can be atmospheric. Otherwise, Cape Agulhas isn't especially impressive and there's little reason to linger longer than it takes to snap a photo and peek at the nearby **lighthouse** (☎ 435 6222; adult/child R5/2; ⊗ 9am-4.15pm Mon-Sat, 9am-2pm Sun). Built in 1848, this is the second-oldest lighthouse in South Africa. If you're peckish, the **tearoom** (☎ 435 7506) here isn't bad, serving reasonably priced meals and snacks.

Rolling wheat and sheep country surround the region's largest town, **Bredasdorp**, through which you'll have to pass to reach the Cape by tarred road.

Cape Agulhas can be reached by car, or if you don't have wheels, several companies out of Swellendam offer day tours. For more information see p174.

ARNISTON

☎ 028

One of the Western Cape's gems, Arniston is a charming, undeveloped village in a dramatic, windswept setting. It is named after the vessel wrecked off its treacherous coast in 1815, which resulted in the loss of 344 lives. Colourful boats, warm blue-green waters and the backdrop of **Kassiesbaai**, the 200-year-old hamlet of whitewashed cottages that forms the core of Arniston, make for a pretty picture. South of Kassiesbaai is **Roman Beach** with white sand and gentle waves. It's a good place to bring the children as there are caves, coves and rock pools filled with sea urchins and colourful anemones at both ends. Be careful not to touch the sea urchins, though, as they can cause nasty cuts.

The village has no centralised area nor any real street signs, so finding your away around can sometimes be a challenge. Look for signs leading to the various eating and sleeping establishments.

Sleeping & Eating

Southwinds (☎ 445 9303; southwinds@kingsley.co.za; First Ave; d R500) This unique place blends rough whitewashed walls and wooden ceilings together and throws in interesting angles for good measure. The owner, John Midgely, is very friendly and extremely knowledgeable about the area. Ask about his 4WD eco-trip (R50, two hours) to see both the scant remains of the *Arniston* (practically covered by sand) and the cave. Apart from walking the dunes, the trip is a fine way to get a feel for this rugged coast washed by a beguilingly brilliant blue ocean.

Arniston Hotel (☎ 445 9000; www.arnistonhotel .co.za; s/d with breakfast R530/1060; ⚉) The Arniston is a luxury hotel facing the sea with a shipwreck theme – framed descriptions of events surrounding the boat wrecks and items salvaged from the boats themselves make up the décor. Sea- facing rooms have floor-to-ceiling windows. The classy ocean-view restaurant serves lunch (R30) and dinner (R45 to R90) and has an extensive wine list.

Die Herberg & South of Africa Backpackers' Resort (☎ 445 9240; www.southofafrica.co.za; s/d R279/390, with shared bathroom R130/210; ⚉) This backpackers is in a rather bizarre location, next to a neighbouring military test site signposted off the R316, 2km outside Arniston. It's a modern place with tons of amenities, including a gym, large pool, sauna and two full-sized billiard tables. There are two classes of rooms – cheaper backpacker doubles and more expensive en suite rooms, all with TV. The attached **Castaway Restaurant** (mains R20-50) has something for everyone, including the kids.

Die Waenhuis (☎ 445 9797; Dupreez St; mains from R30) This restaurant is full of character – the walls are covered in graffiti and candles grace the tables. It's also one of Arniston's only dining options; it serves a good range of dishes and is tucked behind the Arniston Centre general store.

DE HOOP NATURE RESERVE

Covering 36,000 hectares, plus 5km out to sea, is **De Hoop Nature Reserve** (☎ 028-542 1126; www.capenature.org.za; admission R20; camp sites R95, 4-person cottages from R285; ☉ 7am-6pm). This is one of the Cape Nature Conservation's best reserves, including a scenic coastline with stretches of beach, dunes and rocky cliffs, plus a freshwater lake and Potberg Mountain. Visitors come here to see both mountain and lowveld *fynbos* and a diverse cross section of coastal ecosystems. Fauna includes the Cape mountain zebra, the bontebok and a wealth of birdlife. The coast is an important breeding area for the southern right whale.

Although there are numerous day walks, an overnight mountain-bike trail and good snorkelling along the coast, the reserve's most interesting feature is the five-day **Whale Hiking Trail** (☎ 028-425 5020; per person R520). Covering 55km it offers excellent opportunities to see whales between June and December. Accommodation is in modern fully equipped self-catering cottages. The trail needs to be booked in advance, and only group bookings are accepted. You'll need a minimum of six and a maximum of 12 people. The fee includes shuttle service back to your car at the end of the trip. If you don't feel like carrying your own bags, your group can pay an extra R1200 (for six people) to have your belongings transported every morning to that night's overnight cottage.

Those just looking to spend the night in the reserve can choose from a variety of sleeping options, including basic cottages and a 10-person beach house. Accommodation prices include entrance fees into the reserve.

The reserve is about 260km from Cape Town, and the final 50km from either Bredasdorp or Swellendam is along gravel roads. The only access to the reserve is via Wydgeleë on the Bredasdorp to Malgas road. At Malgas a manually operated pont (river ferry) on the Breede River still operates (between dawn and dusk). The village of **Ouplaas**, 15km away, is the nearest place to buy fuel and supplies. If you don't have your own car you can reach the reserve by joining a tour (see p174).

SWELLENDAM
☎ 028 / pop 14,100

As well as being a historic and attractive town, dotted with old oaks and surrounded by rolling wheat country and mountains, Swellendam makes a great base for exploring the Overberg and the Little Karoo. It's a handy stop between Cape Town and the Garden Route, and even if you don't have wheels there's the chance to walk in indigenous forest quite close to town.

The town, dating back to 1776, is the third-oldest magisterial district in South Africa. It backs up against a spectacular ridge, part of the 1600m Langeberg Range, and is particularly impressive on a cloudy day when the mist rolls in over the mountains.

Information

The **Swellendam Tourism Bureau** (☎ 514 2770; Voortrek St; ☉ 9am-5pm Mon-Fri, 9am-12.30pm Sat) is in the old mission, or Oefeninghuis, on the main street. Note the twin clocks, one of which is permanently set at 12.15pm. This was the time for the daily service; the illiterate townspeople only had to match the working clock with the painted one to know when their presence was required.

The cheapest Internet connection is at **PC Connection Computers** (☎ 940 2751; 18 Voortrek St; per hr R30; ☉ 8.30am-5pm Mon-Fri, 9am-noon Sat).

Sights

The main sight in town is the excellent **Drostdy Museum** (☎ 514 1138; 18 Swellengrebel St; adult/child R10/1; ☉ 9am-4.45pm Mon-Fri, 10am-3.45pm Sat & Sun). The centrepiece is the beautiful *drostdy* itself, which dates from 1746. The museum ticket also covers entrance to the **Old Gaol**, where you'll find part of

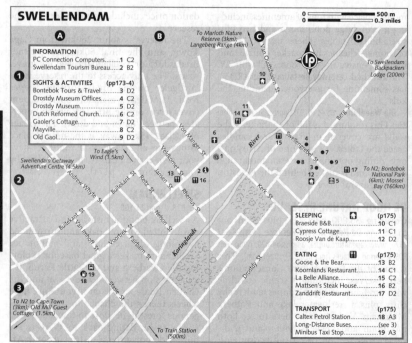

SWELLENDAM

0 — 500 m
0 — 0.3 miles

INFORMATION
PC Connection Computers..........1 C2
Swellendam Tourism Bureau......2 B2

SIGHTS & ACTIVITIES (pp173-4)
Bontebok Tours & Travel..............3 D2
Drostdy Museum Offices............4 C2
Drostdy Museum.........................5 D2
Dutch Reformed Church.............6 C2
Gaoler's Cottage.........................7 D2
Mayville......................................8 C2
Old Gaol.....................................9 D2

To Marloth Nature Reserve (3km);
Langeberg Range (4km)

To Swellendam Backpackers Lodge (200m)

To Eagle's Wind (1.5km)

Swellendam Getaway Adventure Centre (4.5km)

River

To N2; Bontebok National Park (6km); Mossel Bay (160km)

Korinlands

To N2 to Cape Town (3km); Old Mill Guest Cottages (1.5km)

To Train Station (500m)

SLEEPING (p175)
Braeside B&B...............................10 C1
Cypress Cottage...........................11 C1
Roosje Van de Kaap.....................12 D2

EATING (p175)
Goose & the Bear........................13 B2
Koornlands Restaurant................14 C1
La Belle Alliance.........................15 C2
Mattsen's Steak House................16 B2
Zanddrift Restaurant...................17 D2

TRANSPORT (p175)
Caltex Petrol Station...................18 A3
Long-Distance Buses...............(see 3)
Minibus Taxi Stop.......................19 A3

the original administrative buildings; the **Gaoler's Cottage** and a watermill; and **Mayville**, another residence dating back to 1853, with a formal Victorian garden.

Worthy of a picture is the **Dutch Reformed Church** (Voortrek St) in the centre of town. Swellendam residents swear it's the third-most-photographed site in the Southern Hemisphere. The church was built in 1911 in the eclectic style with baroque gables. The steeple is a replica of a famous Belgian steeple.

Activities

Swellendam has adventures for all ages, budgets and tastes. A good place to sort yourself out is at **Bontebok Tours & Travel** (☎ 514-3650; info@bontebok.co.za; 23 Swellengrebel St; ☽ 9am-6pm Mon-Sat, 10am-6pm Sun), which seems to arrange just about anything. Popular day trips include Cape Agulhas (R295), where you will have the option of quad biking for one hour (R180), De Hoop Nature Reserve (R295), day wine trails around Barrydale, Montagu, Ashton and Bonnievale (R295), and mountain-bike hire (R90 per day). The

company also arranges sunset cruises on a double-decker wooden raft on the lake near Buffeljachts Dam (R40).

For permits to walk in **Marloth Nature Reserve** in the Langeberg Range, 3km north of town, contact the **Nature Conservation Department** (☎ 514 1410; day permits R15) at the entrance to the reserve.

Two Feathers Horse Trails (☎ 082-494 8279; www .twofeathers.co.za; per hr R100) caters to inexperienced as well as experienced riders (but doesn't offer hard hats). Overnight rides into the Langeberg Range cost R1000. Two Feathers is located at the edge of the Marloth Nature Reserve. Advanced booking is essential.

Those interested in berry picking and liquor tasting should head to the **Swellendam Getaway Adventure Centre** (☎ 082-421 8555; off Andrew Whyte Rd; admission free; ☽ 8.30am-4.30pm Mon-Fri, 8.30am-1pm Sat). This working youngberry farm produces delicious liquors and homemade jams. We loved the honey liquor, but you can sample all 11 products. The farm is 4.5km outside Swellendam and accommodation is available (opposite).

Sleeping
The best places to stay are the many excellent B&Bs and guesthouses in and around Swellendam.

BUDGET
Swellendam Backpackers Lodge (☎ 514 2648; back pack@dorea.co.za; 5 Lichtenstein St; camp sites per person R40, dm R60, d with shared bathroom R170) Set on a huge plot of land with its own river this is an excellent hostel with enthusiastic management. There is a large fire circle with artsy chairs and an outdoor bar. Don't skip one of the homemade dinners (around R30), they are mouth watering and gigantic. The Baz Bus will drop you right outside.

Swellendam Getaway Adventure Centre (☎ 082-421 8555; off Andrew Whyte Rd; s/d with shared bathroom R125/250) On a working youngberry farm (see p174), this place has simple rustic rooms and a beautiful location right in the mountains. Guests are free to wander around the farm, pick berries and swim in the dam on the property. There's a self-catering kitchen.

MID-RANGE
Roosje Van de Kaap (☎ 514 3001; www.roosjevande kaap.com; 5 Drostdy St; s/d R275/400; ☒) Take a swim with a mountain view. This Cape country inn has nine cosy rooms and an excellent **restaurant** (mains R50-70) serving Cape Malay dishes and wood-fired-oven pizzas; it's open to the public, but booking is essential.

Cypress Cottage (☎ 514 3296; www.cypresscott age.info; 3 Voortrek St; s/d R250/500; ☒ ☒) There are five individually decorated rooms in this 200-year-old house with a gorgeous garden and a saltwater pool. Try an African-themed room complete with mosquito nets.

Braeside B&B (☎ 514 3325; www.braeside4u.home stead.com; 13 Van Oudtshoorn Rd; s/d with breakfast R350/500) This gracious Cape Edwardian home boasts fantastic views and really knowledgeable, friendly hosts.

Old Mill Guest Cottages (☎ 514 2790; www.old mill.co.za; 241 Voortrek St; d with breakfast from R400) This cute whitewashed cottage complex is behind the antiques/craft shop and has a pleasant café of the same name. Guests choose from a variety of tidy cottages.

Eating
Koornlands Restaurant (☎ 514 3567; 5 Voortrek St; mains R60; ☾ lunch & dinner) An eclectic menu of mostly game meat – everything from springbok loin to kudu – is served in an intimate candlelit setting at this locally recommended restaurant.

La Belle Alliance (☎ 514 2252; 1 Swellengrebel St; mains R20-50; ☾ breakfast & lunch) This appealing tearoom had the honour of serving Nelson Mandela in 1999. In an old Masonic lodge with shaded outdoor tables beside the Koringlands River, it's a good spot for lunch.

Mattsen's Steak House (☎ 514 2715; 44 Voortrek St; mains R30-60; ☾ lunch & dinner) The pizzas are delicious and if you're not starving, large enough for two, at this rather old-fashioned English-hunting-themed place with a very green interior.

Zanddrift Restaurant (☎ 514 1789; 132 Swellengrebel St; mains R45; ☾ breakfast & lunch) Breakfast (available all day) at the Zanddrift is a must, consisting of a huge platter of omelette, ham, cheese, pâté, fruit and so on. Other dishes depend on what's available that day. The building dates from 1757.

Goose & the Bear (☎ 514 3101; 35 Voortrek St; mains R25-50; ☾ lunch & dinner) Better known as a bar than a restaurant, this place is cosy and has occasional pool competitions. Standard pub meals are served.

Getting There & Away
All three major bus companies plus the Baz Bus pass through Swellendam on their runs between Cape Town and Port Elizabeth, stopping at Bontebok Tours and Travel (opposite), which is the Intercape, Greyhound, Translux and Baz Bus agent. Intercape fares include Cape Town (R85, 2½ hours, twice daily) and Mossel Bay (R90, two hours, daily).

Minibus taxis depart from corner of Voortrek and Stasie Sts, by the Caltex petrol station. Service includes Cape Town (R90, 2½ hours, daily) and Mossel Bay (R70, two hours, daily).

The weekly *Southern Cross* that runs between Cape Town and Oudtshoorn stops in Swellendam.

BONTEBOK NATIONAL PARK
Some 6km south of Swellendam is **Bontebok National Park** (☎ 028-514 2735; adult/child R60/30; camp sites R70, d cottages R180). This small chunk of land has been set aside to ensure the preservation of the endangered bontebok, an unusually marked antelope that once roamed the region in large numbers.

As a national park, Bontebok doesn't offer much competition to Kruger et al, but as a nice place to relax it's hard to beat. The park falls within the coastal *fynbos* area and is on the banks of the Breede River, where swimming is possible. It boasts nearly 500 grasses and other plant species; in the late winter and early spring, the veld (grassland) is covered with flowers. In addition to the bontebok, there is the rhebok, grysbok, duiker, red hartebeest and mountain zebra. Birdlife is abundant.

ROUTE 62

This area, promoted as the longest wine route in the world, encompasses both the Breede River Valley and the Little Karoo and stretches from the Winelands (p150) in the west to Uniondale, in the Little Karoo, in the east. Driving the route is an excellent hinterland alternative to the N2 for travel between Cape Town and the Garden Route.

Breathtaking mountain passes and intensively cultivated valleys, perfectly preserved 18th-century towns and vast stretches of semi-arid plains dotted with ostriches provide eye-candy, while delectable wine, country cafés, charming B&Bs and even a hot-springs resort enchant the palate and relax the body.

Europeans had settled most of the Breede River Valley by the beginning of the 18th century, but the area did not really take off until passes were pushed through the mountains in the 19th century. The headwaters of the Breede River (sometimes called the Breë), in the beautiful mountain-locked Ceres basin, escape via Mitchell's Pass and flow southeast for 310km before meeting the Indian Ocean at Whitesands. Many tributaries join the Breede, and by the time it reaches Robertson it has been transformed from a rushing mountain stream to a substantial river.

The Little (or Klein) Karoo is east of the Breede River Valley and bordered in the south by the Outeniqua and Langeberg Ranges and by the Swartberg Range in the north. It is more fertile and better watered than the harsher Great Karoo (p206 and p243) to the north.

The towns in this region are presented in the order they would be reached driving the route from Cape Town.

TULBAGH
☎ 023 / pop 31,000

Easy on the eyes and ringed by the dramatic Witsenberg Range, Tulbagh is one of the most complete examples of an 18th- and 19th-century Cape Dutch village in South Africa. Many buildings were substantially rebuilt after an earthquake in 1969, but it doesn't feel in the least bit fake due to painstaking restoration. A meander down Church St, lined with trees and flowering bushes, provides a unique brand of stress relief.

Although most of Tulbagh's surviving buildings date from the first half of the 19th century, the Tulbagh Valley was first settled in 1699. The village began to take shape after the construction of a church in 1743. It was to here, on the outer rim of the settled European areas, that early Boer families would bring their children out of the wilderness to be baptised.

Orientation & Information

Church St, the famous street in which every building has been declared a national monument, runs parallel to the town's main thoroughfare, Van der Stel St.

A visitor's first port of call should probably be the **tourist information centre** (☎ 230 1348; www.tulbagh.com; 14 Church St; 🕑 9am-5pm Mon-Fri, 9am-1pm Sat). Information and maps about the wine region can be found at **Tulbagh Wine Route** (☎ 230 1348; www.tulbaghwineroute.com; 4 Church St; 🕑 9am-5pm Mon-Fri, 9am-1pm Sat).

Sights & Activities

Wandering down Church St is a pleasant way to spend an afternoon. When you finish, take in a few wine tastings or visit the town's museum.

OUDE KERK VOLKSMUSEUM

The **Old Church Folk Museum** (☎ 230 1041; 1 Church St; adult/child R5/2; 🕑 9am-5pm Mon-Fri, 9am-4pm Sat, 11am-4pm Sun) is a mildly interesting museum made up of three buildings. Start at No 4, which has a photographic history of Church St, covering the earthquake and reconstruction; visit the beautiful Oude Kerk itself (1743); then go on to No 22, a reconstructed town dwelling from the 18th century.

Wineries

The Tulbagh valley produces a variety of wines and has a number of cellars to visit.

Wineries are well signposted. We particularly liked these three just outside town, and locals agreed.

Twee Jonge Gezellen (☎ 230-6820; tastings free; ✆ 9am-4pm Mon-Fri, 10am-2pm Sat), established in 1710, is the second-oldest family-owned wine estate in South Africa and the first to introduce night harvesting. Classic views and buildings along with friendly informed staff make a visit delectable. Follow the signs from the R46.

Drostdy Wines (☎ 230 1086; Van der Stel St; museum admission & tastings R8; ✆ 10am-12.30pm & 2-4.50pm Mon-Sat, 2.30-4.50pm Sun) was built in 1806 and is now a national monument. The wines produced here are sold worldwide. The place, which also houses a museum, was almost destroyed by the 1969 earthquake but has now been completely restored. The cellar offers candlelight tastings in the old slave quarters under the main building.

Rijk's Private Cellar (☎ 230 1623; www.rijks.co.za; Van der Stel St; tastings free; ✆ 9am-6pm Mon-Fri, 10am-4pm Sat) has won several awards for its Sauvignon Blanc, Shiraz and pinotage wines. It is in a lovely location 2km north of town.

Sleeping

There are numerous delicious sleeping and eating options in Tulbagh. Couples looking for a romantic destination won't be disappointed.

De Oude Herberg (☎ 230 0260; deoudeherbe@hotmail.com; 6 Church St; d from R440; mains R45; ☘) A guesthouse since 1885 (although not continuously), this is a very friendly place with antique furniture and a lovely patio. Each room is slightly different with classy touches like towels on the beds when you arrive. Its restaurant, which is open to nonguests, has an inventive menu focusing on food traditional to the region with excellent results; booking ahead for dinner is essential.

Tulbagh Country House (☎ 230 1171; 24 Church St; s/d with breakfast R250/440) Built in 1809, this pleasant place still retains the original wood ceilings and has a lived-in feel. The owner is a wealth of information about the surrounding region. There is a self-catering cottage for R150 per person.

Rijk's Country Hotel (☎ 230 1006; www.rijks.co.za; Van der Stel St; s/d R530/810; ☘) If you yearn to stay on a classy wine estate, this is the hotel for you. Located on the same property as the Rijk's Private Cellar, this place is

picturesque, romantic and overlooks a lake. There's a restaurant on the premises. The hotel is 2km north of the town centre.

Eating

Paddagang Restaurant (☎ 230 0242; 23 Church St; mains R50-60; ✆ breakfast, lunch & dinner) The town's most famous restaurant, in a beautiful old homestead with a vine-shaded courtyard, also serves snacks and light meals (R20 to R40). For dinner try one of their steaks followed by a mouthwatering desert. There's a good wine list, but little for vegetarians.

Reader's Restaurant (☎ 230 0087; 12 Church St; mains R20-50; ✆ lunch & dinner) This is a good choice. The menu changes daily, but you can expect food as varied as beef teriyaki and the Cape Malay dish, bobotie.

Forties (☎ 230 0567; 40 Church St; mains R40-60; ✆ dinner Wed-Sun) The hip industrial feel – think exposed walls and peeling plaster – at this lively pub comes in part from authentic earthquake damage. It's an excellent drinking choice and also serves pizza, pasta and steak.

Getting There & Around

One of the most interesting ways of visiting Tulbagh from Cape Town is to take one of the train trips organised by Mike and Rachel Barry at the **Duck Pond Holiday Chalets** (☎ 230 0665; day trip R500). You will ride the *Trans Karoo* as far as Wolseley, then be picked up and driven to Tulbagh, where you will be given a tour of the town, surrounding wineries and museums before being driven back to Cape Town.

Keep going along Van der Stel St past the Old Drostdy Museum and you'll come to a dead end at the head of the valley (overlooked by the rugged mountains of the Groot Winterhoek Wilderness Area). To get back to the R44 (running between Ceres and Piketberg, which is on the N7) go in the opposite direction down Van der Stel St. Halfway up the hill leading away from the town, turn right. There's a small, faded sign to Kaapstad (Cape Town) and Gouda.

CERES & AROUND
☎ 023 / pop 28,000

Sometimes referred to as the Switzerland of South Africa, the scenery surrounding Ceres is majestic. Located on the western side of a green and fertile bowl that is ringed by the rugged Skurweberg Range, the passes into the valley are particularly spectacular. But as attractive as the town is there's not a huge amount to linger here for. It might be best to make it a lunch stop in between spending the morning and afternoon exploring the exciting regional mountain passes.

Ceres is the most important deciduous fruit- and juice-producing district in South Africa, and seems remarkably prosperous in comparison with many regional towns. The surrounding countryside is densely populated and intensively farmed. The Ceres fruit juice that's been saving you from a diet of sugary drinks all over South Africa is packed here.

The valley has a very high rainfall, mostly between June and September, and four well-defined seasons. It can get very cold in winter, with temperatures dropping below zero (snow on the mountains) and hot in summer (36°C). It is most beautiful in spring and particularly in autumn, when the fruit trees change colour.

Orientation & Information

Coming off Mitchell's Pass you'll enter the town along the central Voortrekker St. The friendly **tourism bureau** (☎ 316 1051; www.ceres .org.za; cnr Owen & Voortrekker Sts; ☺ 8am-5pm Mon-Fri, 9am-noon Sat) is in the library. It has information on accommodation, tours and activities in the area.

Sights & Activities

Ceres was once a famous centre for making horse-drawn vehicles. Consequently, the **Togryers' Museum** (Transport Riders' Museum; ☎ 312 2045; 8 Oranje St; adult/child R3/1; ☺ 9am-1pm Mon-Fri, 9am-noon Sat) has an interesting collection of buggies, wagons and carriages. Oranje St is one street north of and parallel to Voortrekker St.

For some stupendous scenery don't miss a drive through the **Middelburg** and **Gydo Passes**. Coming from Citrusdal (p215) you almost immediately hit a very bumpy dirt road that takes you up into the Cederberg Wilderness Area (p214). Middelburg is an impressive pass but the really good views are on the Ceres side when you come out into a narrow valley completely walled by raw, rock hills with rich mineral colouring.

In stark contrast to the hills, the floor of the valley is irrigated, so it is usually emerald green, and there is a patchwork of orchards. The reds, ochres and purples of the rocky mountains, the blue of the sky, the blossom of the orchards, fresh green pastures, wildflowers, dams and wading birds combine to create a beautiful sight.

About 20km from Ceres you hit a sealed road. Coming south you feel as if you've lost altitude, so when you come out on the 1000m Gydo Pass overlooking the Ceres Valley, the world seems to drop away at your feet.

To experience a little history of the region take a drive over **Mitchell's Pass**. The Breede River, forcing its way between the mountains surrounding Ceres, provided the key to the development of the valley. Originally, the settlers dismantled their wagons and carried them over the mountain, but in 1765 a local farmer built a track along the river.

In 1846 the remarkable Thomas Bain began construction of a proper road. It was completed in 1848 and became the main route onto the South African plateau to the north, remaining so until the Hex River Pass was opened in 1875. Mitchell's Pass cut the travel time to Beaufort West from three weeks to one week. The pass has recently been rebuilt to highway standards, but you can still enjoy the views and appreciate what a remarkable engineer Bain was.

On the Ceres side of the pass is the **Toll House** (☎ 316 1571), where tolls were once collected; it's now a coffee shop and restaurant open daily, with braais every second Saturday.

Sleeping & Eating

The tourism bureau will help you find B&Bs and self-catering cottages if these places don't sound appealing.

Belmont Hotel (☎ 312 1150; belmont@intekom.co .za; Porter St; s/d from R290/490; 🏊) This large, old-fashioned hotel offers various types of accommodation in whitewashed cottages on large peaceful grounds. There are two dining options. **Pizza Nostra** (mains R30; ☺ closed Sun) is a casual family restaurant serving pizza, pasta and salads. **Oom Be Se Vat** (mains R70; ☺ closed Sun) is more upscale with a cosy atmosphere and log fires in the winter.

Die Herberg Guesthouse (☎ /fax 312 2325; 125 Voortrekker St; s/d R165/250) Rooms are simple and clean and come with TV at this comfortable, yet slightly old-fashioned place.

There is a **café** (meals 15-20; ✆ breakfast & lunch) serving light meals.

Getting There & Away
Kruger bus service (☎ 316 5901) runs basic daily buses to Cape Town; call for departure times and fares.

WORCESTER
☎ 023 / pop 95,000
A service centre for the rich farmland of the Breede River Valley, Worcester is a large and fairly nondescript place that needn't detain you longer than it takes to visit its farm museum and botanic gardens.

Most of the town lies to the south of the N1. There are some impressive old buildings near and around the edge of Church Sq (off High St). The **tourism bureau** (☎ 348 2795; 23 Baring St; ✆ 8am-4.30pm Mon-Fri, 8.30am-12.30pm Sat) is on the east side of Church Sq.

Sights & Activities
Worcester's things to see and do are its main attraction.

KLEINPLASIE FARM MUSEUM
This **farm museum** (☎ 342 2225; adult/child R12/5; ✆ 9am-4.30pm Mon-Sat, 10.30am-4.30pm Sun), is one of South Africa's best museums, and takes you from a Trekboer's hut to a complete functioning 18th-century farm complex. Located 1km from the town centre on the road to Robertson it's a 'live' museum, meaning there are people wandering around in period clothes and rolling tobacco, making soap, operating a smithy, milling wheat, spinning wool and so on. The place is fascinating and can easily absorb a couple of hours. A miniature train runs around the complex, leaving hourly.

At the museum shop you can sample and buy various flavours of the 60-proof *witblitz* (white lightning), a traditional Boer spirit distilled from fruit. To get the full taste, first inhale, then sip and roll the liquor around your mouth before swallowing and exhaling. Next door is the **Kleinplasse Winery**, where you can sample less potent libations.

KAROO NATIONAL BOTANIC GARDEN
This outstanding **garden** (☎ 347 0785; adult/child R9/5; ✆ 8am-4pm) takes in 140 hectares of semi-desert vegetation – with Karoo and *fynbos* elements – and 10 hectares of landscaped garden, where many of the plants have been labelled. If your interest has been piqued, this is an ideal opportunity to identify some of the extraordinary indigenous plants. The gardens are about 1km north of the N1 and 2.5km from the centre of town.

There is something to see at any time of the year; bulb plants flower in autumn, the aloes flower in winter and the annuals flower in spring. There's also a collection of weird stone plants and other succulents.

KVW CELLAR
Not as famous as its counterpart in Paarl (see p165), this cellar and **brandy distillery** (☎ 342 0255; cnr Church & Smith Sts; tours R13; ✆ 8am-4.30pm Mon-Fri) is the largest of its kind in the world under one roof. A must-see for brandy enthusiasts looking to sample the product; hour-long tours in English are held at 2pm.

Sleeping
Wykeham Lodge B&B (☎ 347 3467; wykehamlodge@telkomsa.net; 168 Church St; s/d with breakfast R275/400) This fine guesthouse is in a thatched-roof building dating from 1835. Rooms with wooden beams and floors face on to a quiet courtyard and there's also a large garden.

Kleinplasie Country Chalets (☎ 347 0091; Kleinplasie Farm Museum; d from R200) These four-person chalets attached to the Kleinplasie Farm Museum are simple yet comfortable enough for a night's stay.

Nekkies (☎ 343 2909; fax 343 2911; chalets from R250) These are smart wooden chalets with good facilities, overlooking the dam. Bikes are available for hire. Nekkies is 4.5km from Worcester at the Brandvlei Dam.

Burger Caravan Park (☎ 348 2765; fax 347 3671; De la Bat Rd; camp sites R45) This pretty ordinary place is close to the N1 and next to the town's swimming pool.

Eating
St Gerans (☎ 342 2800; 48 Church St; mains R40-60; ✆ lunch & dinner) This popular steak house in the town centre also does some seafood and chicken dishes, although there is little for vegetarians. There is a kid's menu and large wine list.

Kleinplasie Restaurant (☎ 347 5118; Kleinplasie Farm Museum; mains from R20; ✆ breakfast, lunch & dinner) Attached to the Kleinplasie Farm Museum (p179), this place offers traditional

Cape Malay/Afrikaner dishes such as bobotie and chicken pie; outdoor seating is available.

Getting There & Away

All **Translux** (☎ 021-449 3333; www.translux.co.za), **Greyhound** (☎ 021-505 6363; www.greyhound.co.za) and **Intercape** (☎ 0861 287 287; www.intercape.co.za) buses stop at the Shell Ultra City petrol station in town. Fares include Cape Town (R150, two hours, daily) and Jo'burg (R395, 17 hours, daily). The corner of Durban and Grey Sts is a good place to look for minibus taxis. Rates include Cape Town (R45, two hours, daily).

The daily *Trans Karoo* between Cape Town and Jo'burg stops in Worcester; the *Southern Cross* between Cape Town and Oudtshoorn stops at Worcester on Friday evening when heading east, early Monday morning when heading west. The extremely circuitous *Trans Oranje* to Durban also stops there. For bookings call ☎ 023-348 2203.

ROBERTSON

☎ 023 / pop 35,000

At the centre for one of the largest wine-growing areas in the country, and also famous for its horse studs, Robertson is clearly a prosperous town. With McGregor and Montagu both just a short drive away, however, there's not much reason to overnight here, although the surrounding vineyards should not be missed.

The helpful **Robertson Tourism Bureau** (☎ 626 4437; www.robertson.org.za; cnr Reitz & Voortrekker Sts; ⊙ 9am-1pm & 2-5pm Mon-Fri) can give you loads of information about the wine region, the R62 and hiking trails that take you into the mountains above Robertson.

Sights

SOEKERSHOF WALKABOUT

Tired of checking out wineries? Take a break and stretch your legs in these fabulous **gardens** (☎ 626-4134; Klaas Voogds West; adult/child R40/20; ⊙ 8am-4pm Wed-Sun), where you can wander through numerous mazes filled with indigenous plants and hedges as well as more than 1700 different species of succulents. Guided tours (adult/child R90/20) last about two hours, and there are also full-moon tours (R60). Soekershof is 8km past Robertson on the R60 heading towards Ashton. Turn left at the turn-off for Klaas

Voogds West. The entire operation shuts down for a month in July.

Wineries

The Robertson Wine Valley is worth a visit for its 27 wineries, its scenery and the general absence of tourist coaches. Ask the Robertson Tourism Bureau to provide you with a map of the wine region.

Van Louvern (☎ 615 1505; tastings free; ⊙ 8.30am-5pm Mon-Fri, 9am-1pm Sat) is by far our favourite wine tasting experience in the region. Tastings take place in the garden surrounded by trees planted for historical events – good and bad – like the day Mandela was released from prison or the day the Japanese bombed Pearl Harbour. Besides spectacular grounds this place has a different take on tastings. You'll pick what wines you want to try and be brought the entire bottle. You can choose as many bottles and pour as much as you like. The product is not bad either. Van Louvern is 15km from Robertson on the road to Bonnievale.

Tastings at **Graham Beck** (☎ 626 1214; www.grahambeckwines.co.za; tastings free; ⊙ 9am-5pm Mon-Fri, 10am-3pm Sat) are in a striking orange aircraft hangar-like building with huge plate-glass windows overlooking a long pool. The winery comes as a breath of fresh air after all those Cape Dutch estates – as do its eminently drinkable products. Its fizzy wines give French champagne a run for its money and the muscatel is heaven in a glass. The winery is off the R60 towards Worcester.

The **Robertson Winery** (☎ 626 3059; www.robertsonwine.co.za; Voortrekker St; tastings free; ⊙ 8am-5pm Mon-Thu, 8am-4.30pm Fri, 9am-1pm Sat) is more commercial and lacking in views, but is the region's oldest cellar. Unfortunately, it's located in a boring modern building smack in the middle of town. Still, it produces some decent products. The Sauvignon Blanc, Wide River Cabernet Sauvignon Reserve and semisweet wines are the ones to go for.

Sleeping & Eating

Amathunzi (☎ 626 1802; www.amathunzi.co.za; s/d with full board R1080/1440) This 3500-hectare game lodge with upmarket accommodation for 10 guests in thatched-roof cottages is well off the beaten track, and given that the price includes all meals, a game drive and a guided walk it's good value. Expect to see antelopes, zebras, wildebeests and, if you're very lucky, mountain leopards. The reserve is roughly 26km southwest of Robertson. Follow the signs from town.

Robertson Backpackers (☎ 626 1280; rbackpac kers@xsinet.co.za; 4 Dordrecht Ave; camp sites per person R30, dm R50, d with shared bathroom R140;) Dorms and doubles are spacious in this comfy house with friendly hosts. There's a big grassy backyard with a fire pit for chilling out at night, and wine tours of the region can be arranged.

Grand Hotel (☎ 626 3272; fax 626 1158; 68 Barry St; s/d R220/350;) The rooms, a couple with balconies, are of better quality than the foyer would suggest. The reasonably priced **Simone's Grill Room & Restaurant** (mains R40) serves a range of chicken, seafood and steak dishes.

Branewynsdraai (☎ 626 3202; 1 Kromhout St; mains R40; lunch & dinner) With a pleasant tea garden and more formal dining room, this restaurant specialises in local dishes and wines and has a children's menu. There is little for vegetarians. It's near the Shell petrol station on Voortrekker St.

Getting There & Away
Translux (☎ 021-449 3333; www.translux.co.za) buses stop at the train station. Fares include Oudtshoorn (R110, three hours, daily), Knysna (R135, five hours), Cape Town (R110, three hours, daily) and Port Elizabeth (R150, 6½ hours, daily).

Minibus taxis running between Cape Town (R40, three hours), Oudtshoorn (R110, three hours) and Montagu (R20, 30 minutes) stop at the Shell petrol station on the corner of Voortrekker and John Sts. Theoretically there is daily service, but when the buses actually show up is anyone's guess.

MCGREGOR
☎ 023
The tranquil village of McGregor feels like it belongs to another century – the mid-19th century to be precise, from when most of the buildings along its one major thoroughfare, Voortrekker St, date. Vineyards, orchards and vegetable gardens surround the town's thatched-roof cottages, many of which have been turned into B&Bs and self-catering units. There are some 30 wineries within half an hour's drive. Unsurprisingly, McGregor has become a place of retreat, and, with the magnificent Riviersonder-

end Mountains on its doorstep, a base for hiking. It is one end of the highly recommended Boesmanskloof Trail to Greyton (p182).

The **tourism bureau** (☎ 625 1954; Voortrekker St; 9am-5pm Mon-Fri, 10am-1pm Sat) is about halfway along Voortrekker St (there are no street numbers).

Activities
Both the Boesmanskloof Trail and the Vrolijkheid Nature Reserve offer excellent hiking opportunities in the area. Both are administered by the **Cape Nature Conservation** (☎ 028-435 5020; www.capenature.org.za; 7.30am-4pm), which has offices about 15km south of Robertson on the McGregor Rd.

Some argue the best reason for coming to McGregor is to hike the **Boesmanskloof Trail** to Greyton, roughly 14km through the spectacular *fynbos*-clad Riviersonderend Mountains. The trail actually starts at Die Galg, about 15km south of McGregor; you'll need your own transport to get here. To hike the entire trail costs R40/50 per person one-way/round trip, plus another R25 per day permit fee, and takes between four and six hours, making an overnight stay in Greyton the preferred option. Many people then hike back to Die Galg. It's slightly easier walking from McGregor to Greyton than in the opposite direction, and you'll notice that the start of the trail marks the end of a long-abandoned project to construct a pass across the range. It's best to book in advance, especially for weekends and during the holidays, since only 50 people per day are allowed on the trail.

If you don't fancy the full hike, it's quite possible to do a six-hour round-trip to the lovely **Oak Falls**, roughly 6km from Die Galg, where you can cool off with a swim in the tannin-stained waters. This costs R43 per person.

The **Vrolijkheid Nature Reserve** (admission per person R18), near the Cape Nature Conservation Offices on the McGregor Rd, offers day hikes in rugged and strikingly scenic landscapes. There are numerous succulents, dwarf trees and shrubs, as well as klipspringers, grysboks, grey rheboks and springboks and numerous species of birds. You can choose from a number of trails. Entrance is paid through an honesty box at the entrance to the reserve.

WESTERN CAPE

Sleeping & Eating

The tourism bureau has a full list of the accommodation around the village but doesn't take bookings. Eating options in McGregor are rather limited to where you sleep.

Temenos Country Retreat (☎ 625 1871; temenos@lando.co.za; cnr Bree St & Voortrekker Rd; s/d R210/280; 3-course dinner R75; ☒) These unique cottages set in spacious gardens are open to all (except children under 12), not just those on retreat. It's a peaceful place, with a decent lap pool, nooks for contemplation and a coffee shop. For those interested in a retreat the place offers massages, yoga, reiki and aromatherapy in the R50 to R200 range.

Old Mill Lodge (☎ 625 1841; www.mcgregor.org.za; Smit St; s/d R385/630; lunch R15-30, 3-course dinner R95) Environmentally friendly with wooden rafters and exposed thatched roofs, this place gives the discerning guest a unique stay. In a beautiful location surrounding an old mill there's a secluded pool and a private dam for bird-watching. The food is delicious, and homemade, and nonguests can book in for dinner or lunch. The Old Mill also can arrange reiki healings and crystal readings.

McGregor Country Cottages (☎ 625 1816; Voortrekker St; d R375) Located beside an apricot orchard at the north end of the village is this complex of seven whitewashed, thatched-roofed self-catering cottages, each with its own fireplace. Three of the cottages are wheelchair accessible. The entire place has a quaint farm-like feel with a cosy bar and sitting room and friendly hosts.

Whipstock Farm (☎ /fax 625 1733; whipstock@net active.co.za; s/d R250/500) Serenely located and tastefully decorated, this place offers accommodation in a variety of buildings, some historic. There is also fine food and friendly hosts who'll organise transfers to and from the Boesmanskloof Trail. Whipstock is 7km from McGregor on a dirt road towards the mountains.

Villagers Coffee Shop (☎ 625 1915; Voortrekker St; mains R15; ☼ lunch) This is a convivial country store that offers light meals and a refreshing range of homemade fruit juices. It also rents bicycles for R15 per hour, or R45 per day.

GREYTON
☎ 028

Although officially part of the Overberg region, we've included Greyton and the neighbouring village of Genadendal here because of their link to McGregor along the Boesmanskloof Trail.

Much more twee and polished than McGregor, even locals admit that the whitewashed, thatched-roof cottages of Greyton are a bit artificial. As pleasant as the village is, it needs to be seen in conjunction with the old Moravian Mission of Genadendal, with its well-preserved historic buildings that couldn't be more authentic.

Greyton comes into its own as a base for hiking in the Riviersonderend Mountains, which rise up in Gothic majesty immediately to the village's north. Apart from the Boesmanskloof Trail there are several shorter walks, as well as the two-day **Genadendal Trail** for the serious hiker. This is a 25.3km circular route that begins and ends at Genadendal's Moravian Church; for more details pick up the Cape Nature Conservation leaflet at the **tourist information office** (☎ 254 9414; ☼ 10am-noon & 2.30-4.30pm Mon-Sat) on the village's main road.

Genadendal Mission Station

Some 3km west of Greyton is Genadendal, the oldest mission station in South Africa, founded in 1738 and for a brief time the largest settlement in the colony after Cape Town. Entering the village from the R406, head down Main Rd until you arrive at the cluster of national monuments around Church Sq.

The Moravian Church is a handsome, simply decorated building. Opposite you'll find the **tourist information centre** (☎ 251 8291; ☼ 8.30am-5pm Mon-Fri, 10am-1pm Sat). There's a café here selling homemade bread, and souvenirs, including pottery.

The village's fascinating history is documented in the excellent **Mission Museum** (☎ 251 8582; adult/child R7/2; ☼ 9am-1pm & 2-5pm Mon-Thu, 9am-3.30pm Fri, 9am-1pm Sat), which is located in what was South Africa's first teacher training college. Elsewhere in this historic precinct is one of the oldest printing presses in the country, still in operation, and a water mill.

Sleeping & Eating

For its size, Greyton has a wide range of accommodation and places to stay.

High Hopes B&B (☎ /fax 254 9898; 89 Main Rd; d with breakfast from R450) One of the nicest places in town, High Hopes has tastefully furnished rooms, lovely gardens and a well-stocked library. Singles are negotiable and afternoon tea is thrown in for all guests. Convenient for hikers, it's the closest B&B to the start of the Boesmanskloof Trail.

Guinea Fowl (☎ 254 9550; www.longreyton.co.za; cnr DS Botha & Oak Sts; d with breakfast from R500; ☒) Comfortable and quiet, this guesthouse has a pool for summer, log fire for winter and good breakfasts year-round.

Posthaus Guesthouse (☎ 254 9995; fax 254 9920; Main Rd; d with breakfast from R400) Based around a pretty garden, the gimmick here is to name the rooms after Beatrix Potter characters (we told you Greyton was a twee place). Its English-style pub, The Ball & Bass, is a cosy place for a drink or meal.

Greyton Lodge (☎ 254 9876; greytonlodge@kingsley.co.za; 46 Main Rd; s/d with breakfast R450/600) A pair of stocks and rampant lion statues flank the entrance to this upmarket hotel in the old police station. There's a pool and a reasonably priced but unadventurous **bistro** (☒ 7-9pm).

The Oak & Vigne Café (☎ 254 9037; DS Botha St; mains from R30; ☒ breakfast & lunch) Evidence of the creeping 'yuppification' of Greyton is this trendy deli-art gallery-café, which is a fine place to grab a snack, chill out and watch the world go by.

Rosie's Restaurant (☎ 254 9640; 2 High St; mains from R40; ☒ dinner) The house specialities are wood-fired-oven pizzas (which are delicious and huge) and steaks.

Getting There & Away

If you're not hiking in from McGregor, the only way to Greyton is by your own transport. From Cape Town follow the N2 to just before Caledon and then take the R406. From Robertson take the R317 south to the N2 at Stormsvlei, then head west to Riviersonderend to connect with the R406.

MONTAGU

☎ 023 / pop 24,000

Founded in 1851, Montagu is the first town up the pass from the Breede River Valley – once you pop through the Kogmanskloof Pass near Robertson you are suddenly in a very different world. It's a good place to go if you want to escape the 21st century and get a brief taste of the Little Karoo.

Populated by artists and other escapees, country hospitality is spread thick here.

There are some 24 restored national monuments, but what is increasingly attracting more people is Montagu's splendid range of activities – swim in the hot springs, meander up Lover's Lane, take a hike, or eat a hearty meal in an old-world hotel. Montagu is the perfect retreat for couples looking for some space. Backpackers looking for a party might be happier elsewhere.

Orientation & Information

The town is small, so it's easy to get around on foot.

The **Tourism Bureau** (☎ 614 2471; www.montagu.org.za; 24 Bath St; ☒ 8.45am-6pm Mon-Fri, 9am-5pm Sat, 9am-noon & 3-5pm Sun) is particularly helpful and can provide information on accommodation (including a good range of B&Bs and self-catering cottages), hikes and other activities.

Internet access is available at **Printmore** (70 Bath St; per hr R20; ☒ 7.30am-5.30pm Mon-Fri, 8am-1pm Sat).

Sights & Activities

For a small country town, Montagu has enough to keep you entertained for a few days at least.

HOT SPRINGS & LOVER'S LANE TRAIL

Water from the **hot mineral springs** (☎ 614 1150; admission R22.50, parking R15; ☒ 8am-11pm) finds its way into the concrete pools at the Avalon Springs Hotel (p185), about 3km from town. Heated to 43°C, radioactive and renowned for their healing properties, the pools are a lively place on weekends, when many local families come for a soak.

A great way to get here is to hike along the gentle 2.2km Lover's Lane Trail, which starts at the car park at the end of Barry St. Pick up the *Hiking Trails* leaflet from the tourism bureau. The route leads past Montagu's top rock-climbing spots. For guidance on climbing and hiking in the area contact **Montagu Rock Adventures** (☎ 626 6083; humanvalues@xsinet.co.za).

TRACTOR-TRAILER RIDES

Niel Burger (☎ /fax 614 2471; adult/child R40/15; ☒ tours 10am & 2pm Wed & Sat), owner of the Protea Farm (p185), takes fun tractor-trailer rides to the top of the Langeberg Range, from where you can look way down into the Breede River Valley. Even locals enjoy

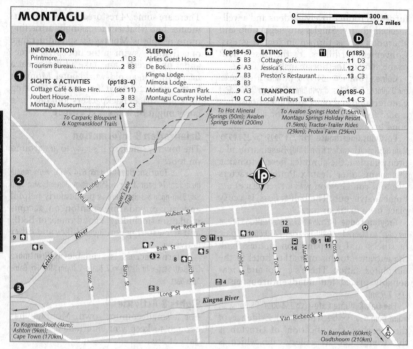

MONTAGU

| 0 | 300 m |
| 0 | 0.2 miles |

INFORMATION
Printmore.................................**1** D3
Tourism Bureau........................**2** B3

SIGHTS & ACTIVITIES (pp183-4)
Cottage Café & Bike Hire........(see 11)
Joubert House...........................**3** B3
Montagu Museum.....................**4** C3

SLEEPING (pp184-5)
Airlies Guest House..................**5** B3
De Bos.....................................**6** A3
Kingna Lodge...........................**7** B3
Mimosa Lodge.........................**8** B3
Montagu Caravan Park.............**9** A3
Montagu Country Hotel............**10** C2

EATING (p185)
Cottage Café............................**11** D3
Jessica's...................................**12** C2
Preston's Restaurant.................**13** C3

TRANSPORT (pp185-6)
Local Minibus Taxis..................**14** C3

To Carpark; Blowpunt & Kogmanskloof Trails

To Hot Mineral Springs (50m); Avalon Springs Hotel (200m)

To Avalon Springs Hotel (1.5km); Montagu Springs Holiday Resort (1.5km); Tractor-Trailer Rides (29km); Protea Farm (29km)

Tanner St
Mill St
Lovers Lane Trail
Joubert St
Piet Retief St
River
Kenie
Rose St
Barry St
Bath St
Church St
Long St
Kohler St
Du Toit St
Market St
Cross St
Van Riebeeck St
Kingna River

To Kogmanskloof (4km); Ashton (9km); Cape Town (170km)

To Barrydale (60km); Oudtshoorn (210km)

R62

---

the three-hour trip, so it must be something special. You can have a delicious lunch of *potjiekos* (traditional pot stew) with home-made bread for R40/10 per adult/child.

MONTAGU MUSEUM & JOUBERT HOUSE
Interesting displays and some good examples of antique furniture can be found at the **Montagu Museum** (☎ 614 1950; 41 Long St; adult/child R2/1; ☻ 9am-1pm & 2-5pm Mon-Fri, 10.30am-12.30pm Sat & Sun) in the old mission church.

   Joubert House (☎ 614 1774; 25 Long St; adult/child R2/1), a short walk away, is the oldest house in Montagu (built in 1853) and has been restored to its Victorian finery. It has the same opening hours as the museum.

HIKING
The **Bloupunt Trail** is 15.6km long and can be walked in six to eight hours; it traverses ravines and mountain streams, and climbs to 1000m. The flora includes proteas, ericas, aloes, gladioli and watsonias. The **Kogmanskloof Trail** is 12.1km and can be completed in four to six hours; it's not as steep as the Bloupunt Trail. Both trails start from the

car park at the end of Tanner St. To hike either trail costs R11 per person. The tourist bureau handles bookings for overnight cabins near the start of the trails. The **huts** (per person R50) are fairly basic (wood stoves, showers and toilet facilities), but they are cheap. There are also several **camp sites** (per person R30).

MOUNTAIN BIKING
Biking is a great way to see the surrounding countryside. To rent a mountain bike, call **Ron Brunings** (☎ /fax 614 1932; per day R55) or visit him at the **Cottage Café & Bike Hire** (78 Bath St). Ron also runs **Dusty Sprocket Trails** (brunings@lando.co.za), offering 10 guided mountain-bike trails in the area for all levels of skill; trails range from 12km to 43km.

Sleeping
Montagu has sleeping options both in and out of town. In town there are some lovely guesthouses, the model of country hospitality, that serve old-fashioned set-course dinners. Out of town you can choose from the hot-springs resort and a local farm stay.

BUDGET

De Bos (☎ /fax 614 2532; Bath St; camp sites per person R25, dm R40, s/d R120/150; ☒) This place has a barnyard-like feel – there are chickens running around. Dorms are in an old barn and there's a big self-catering kitchen. Bring your own bedding. On weekends there is a two-night minimum stay except for camping.

Montagu Caravan Park (☎ 082-920 7863; fax 614 3034; Bath St; camp sites per person R25, 4-person cabins/chalets R140/200) In a pleasant location with citrus trees and lots of shade and grass. The chalets come with bedding, cooking equipment and TVs. The park is at the far west end of Bath St.

MID-RANGE

Airlies Guest House (☎ 614 2943; www.beststay.co.za /airlies; Bath St; s/d with breakfast R250/500; ☒) The characterful Airlies is in a roomy thatched-roof white house with a swimming pool looking out on the mountains. The hosts are very obliging and the breakfast is excellent. Try for the room with the porch and the claw-foot bathtub.

Montagu Springs Holiday Resort (☎ 614 1050; www.montagusprings.co.za; Warmbronne Hot Springs; 4-person chalets from R280) These self-catering chalets are the cheaper option at the hotsprings resort. Those interested in waterfowl, pigeons and chickens should check out the 'feathered friends' sanctuary where more than 160 types of bird are on display. There are daily feedings.

Protea Farm (☎ 614 2471; 4-person cottages R300) Situated right at the top of the Langeberg Range, 29km from Montagu. There is a discount if you stay for longer than one night. Owner Niel Burger also runs tractor-trailer rides up the mountain (see p183).

TOP END

Kingna Lodge (☎ 614 1066; www.kingnalodge.co.za; 11 Bath St; s/d R360/570; ☒) Victoriana runs riot at this elegant guesthouse, where the five-course dinners (R170) draw rave reviews. Each room is uniquely decorated, but all come with marble bathrooms and fireplaces. Presidents Nelson Mandela and FW De Klerk both stayed here in 1995. Karoo hospitality exemplified.

Mimosa Lodge (☎ 614 2351; www.mimosa.co.za; Church St; s/d with breakfast R405/810; ☒) In a restored Edwardian landmark building with manicured gardens, an artful pool complete with a thatched-roof gazebo for shade and a small waterfall. The lodge does nightly five-course dinners for R135 that start with drinks in the garden. The dinners are open to nonguests, and are a highlight.

Avalon Springs Hotel (☎ 614 1150; www.avalonsprings.co.za; Warmbronne Hot Springs; s/d from R425/650) This luxury hotel and time-share complex draws good reviews, despite its rather kitsch décor and its mercenary policy of jacking up prices by 25% on weekends (when there's a two-night minimum stay) and at holiday times. As well as the outdoor hot-spring pools, massages, a gym and a 24-hour café are available.

Montagu Country Hotel (☎ 614 3125; www.montagucountryhotel.co.za; 27 Bath St; s/d R435/730; ☒) In a large pink building, this pleasant hotel with reasonably decorated rooms offers all the usual facilities, and has a pool, smart restaurant and bar. There is a lunch buffet serving local specialities for R45.

Eating

As well as meals in the Montagu Country Hotel, Mimosa Lodge and Kingna Lodge (for these last two you must book in advance), there are a few other options.

Jessica's (☎ 614 1805; 47 Bath St; mains R50-70; ☽ dinner) Named after the family dog, Jessica's serves up inventive bistro dishes such as butternut-squash gnocchi and ostrich stroganoff in a cosy atmosphere.

Preston's Restaurant (☎ 614 3013; 17 Bath St; breakfast R30, mains R40-70; ☽ breakfast, lunch & dinner) There's a variety of steak and seafood options as well as some veg options served in a lovely garden. Those looking for just a drink can head to the attached Thomas Bain Pub.

Cottage Café (78 Bath St; mains R10-30; ☽ breakfast & lunch) Light lunches are served in a grassy garden. The daily specials are usually tasty and good value. Those with a sweet tooth will enjoy the ice cream.

Getting There & Around

Translux (☎ 021-449 3333; www.translux.co.za) buses stop at Ashton, 9km from Montagu, on the run between Cape Town (R110, 2½ hours, daily) and Port Elizabeth (R150, six hours, daily).

JJ's Transport (☎ 614 3975; per person R30) runs a taxi service between town and the hot springs. The price includes a glass of wine. Call for bookings.

Local minibus taxis leave from the OK Supermarket on Bath St near the corner of Market St and run to Cape Town (R110, 3½ hours) and Oudtshoorn (R40, 2½ hours).

CALITZDORP

☎ 044 / pop 4500

This small town doesn't look very interesting from R62, which runs through the centre, but it's worth pausing briefly to explore the more attractive back streets. There's a small **museum** (cnr Van Riebeck & Geyser Sts; admission free; ☻ 9am-noon & 2-5pm Mon-Fri, 9am-noon Sat) and the sandstone **Dutch Reformed Church**, which is a national monument.

The **information centre** (☎ 213 3312; cnr Voortrek & Barry Sts; ☻ 9am-noon & 2-5pm Mon-Fri, 9am-noon Sat) can provide details on accommodation and the local wineries, which are famous for their ports and fortified wines.

Of the five wineries you can visit, **Die Krans** (☎ 213 3314; tastings free; ☻ 8am-5pm Mon-Fri, 9am-1pm Sat) is reckoned to be the best. Cellar tours are available if you book ahead. Follow the signs from R62. There's also a **port festival** held in July.

There are a few sleeping and eating options catering to visitors, including **Die Dorphuis** (☎ 213 3453; dorphuis@mweb.co.za; 4 Van Riebeck St; s/d with breakfast R150/300; ☒), which faces Calitzdorp's Dutch Reformed Church and offers a couple of rooms, one of which is self-catering. There's a **café-restaurant** (mains R20-40), serving snacks and traditional meals such as *eisbein* (a pork dish).

Ebenhart's Restaurant (☎ 213 3598; 13 Voortrek St; mains from R40; ☻ 9am-5pm) serves snacks and more substantial dishes in a shaded garden. It also sells hand-carved pipes made by South Africa's only pipe maker.

OUDTSHOORN

☎ 044 / pop 66,200

In Oudtshoorn it's all about the ostriches. The sedate tourist capital of the Little Karoo bills itself as the ostrich capital of the world and for good reason. The surrounding farmlands are thick with these birds, which have been bred hereabouts since the 1870s. At the turn of the 20th century such fortunes were made from the fashion for ostrich feathers that Oudtshoorn grew rich, and the so-called 'feather barons' built the grand houses that lend the town its distinct atmosphere today.

Although ostrich feathers have since fallen out of fashion, Oudtshoorn still turns a pretty penny from breeding the birds for meat and leather. The ostriches also pay their way with the tourists – so you can buy ostrich eggs, feathers and *biltong* (dried meat) all over town.

This sort of entertainment palls quickly, but Oudtshoorn is also a good base for exploring the different environments of the Little Karoo, the Garden Route (it's 55km to George along the N12) and the Great Karoo. The nearby Swartberg and Seweeekspoort Passes – two of South Africa's scenic highlights – are geological, floral and engineering masterpieces. Oudtshoorn has a strong Afrikaans feel, tree-lined streets, and shops and restaurants selling everything ostrich.

Orientation & Information

Since all the main attractions are beyond easy walking distance from town, your own transport, or a willingness to take a tour, or hitch, is virtually essential. The main commercial street is High (Hoog) St, to the east of Baron van Rheede St.

Next to the CP Nel Museum is the helpful **Oudtshoorn Tourism Bureau** (☎ 279 2532; www .oudtshoorn.com; Baron van Rheede St; ☻ 7am-4pm Mon-Fri). Ask here about the numerous B&Bs in town and about tours of the local sights. The **Tourism Information Centre** (☎ 272-6699; 35 Baron van Rheede St; ☻ 8am-5pm) also has area information and Internet access for R60 per hour.

Sights & Activities

Many of Oudtshoorn's sights are outside of the town limits. Some hostels and B&Bs offer discounts on attractions if you stay the night.

CP NEL MUSEUM & LE ROUX TOWNHOUSE

Extensive displays about ostriches, as well as Karoo history, make up this large and interesting **museum** (☎ 272 7306; 3 Baron van Rheede St; adult/child R10/3; ☻ 9am-5pm Mon-Sat). The museum, housed in a striking sandstone building completed in 1906 at the height of the ostrich fever, also features some impressive reconstructed Victorian shops and the interior of an 1896 synagogue transferred here when its original home was demolished.

Included in the ticket price is admission to the **Le Roux Townhouse** (☎ 272 3676; cnr Loop & High Sts; ☻ 9am-1pm & 2-5pm Mon-Fri). This place is decorated in authentic period furniture and is as good an example of a 'feather palace' as you're likely to see.

CANGO WILDLIFE RANCH & CHEETAHLAND

If you're all ostriched out, head to this **ranch** (☎ 272 5593; admission R40; ☺ 8am-5pm). It's got a bit of a zoo-like feel but has a good collection of wildlife and big cats (in rather small enclosures), including cheetahs, which you may pat for an extra R30 (funds go to the Cheetah Conservation Foundation). The ranch is 3km from town on the road out to Prince Albert. Other big cats here include lions, pumas and Bengal white tigers, and there are also crocodiles, alligators and other wild animals.

OSTRICH FARMS

What's a visit to Oudtshoorn without stopping by an ostrich show farm? There are four show farms in town, which offer guided tours of 45 minutes to one hour. There's little to choose between them; we found the staff at the **Oudtshoorn Ostrich Show Farm** (☎ 279 1861; Cango Caves Rd; adult/child R40/20; ☺ 8am-5pm) very informative. The **Highgate Ostrich Show Farm** (☎ 272 7115; www.highgate.co.za; adult/child R40/20; ☺ 8am-5pm) also gets good reviews. It's 10km from Oudtshoorn en route to Mossel Bay.

CANGO CAVES

Named after the Khoisan word for 'a wet place', the **Cango Caves** (☎ 272 7410; www.cangocaves.co.za; admission from R50; ☺ 9am-4pm) are heavily commercialised but impressive. There's a choice of tours on offer. The half-hour tour gives you just a glimpse – it's better to choose a longer tour. The longest tour is the most fun, but involves crawling through tight and damp places so is not recommended for the claustrophobic or unfit. The caves are 30km from Oudtshoorn.

MOUNTAIN-BIKE RIDES

If you're looking for a little exercise and a lot of thrill then hop on a mountain bike and ride from the top of Swartberg Pass down into Oudtshoorn. The **Oudtshoorn Adventure Centre** (☎ 272 3436; www.backpackersparadise.hostel.com; 148 Baron van Rheede St; tours from R140) at Backpackers Paradise hostel (see below) runs these trips, which depart daily at 8.30am. You'll be driven up and then cycle back to

town. Be warned, it's not all downhill and it's a long ride.

Sleeping

BUDGET

Backpackers' Paradise (☎ 272 3436; www.backpackersparadise.hostel.com; 148 Baron van Rheede St; camp sites per person R30, dm R60, s/d with shared bathroom from R130/150; ▣ ▣) In a large old house, this excellent hostel has a separate dorm-bed annexe, bar, ostrich braais and free ostrich-egg breakfasts (you'll be given an egg – cook it any way you please). They also offer discounts to area attractions and run an adventure centre that can set you up with a host of activities.

Oasis Shanti (☎ 279 1163; oasis@mailbox.co.za; 3 Church St; camp sites per person R35, dm R60, d with shared bathroom from R120; ▣) Friendly and well run, this hostel is in a large house with a good-sized yard and shady camping spots. The lounge has a roaring fireplace to take the chill out of cold nights and there are the requisite ostrich braais.

Kleinplaas Resort (☎ 272 5811; kleinpls@mweb.co.za; 171 Baron van Rheede St; camp sites R100, 4-person chalets R320; ▣) The fancier and pricier caravan park in town has a restaurant and a big pool.

NA Smit Caravan Park (☎ 272 2446; fax 279 1915; Park St; camp sites R85, rondavels R200; ▣) There's not much shade or grass, but facilities are decent. The kids will love the playground.

MID-RANGE

Oakdene Bed & Breakfast (☎ 272 3018; www.oakdene.co.za; 99 Baron van Rheede St; s/d R380/580; ▣ ▣) Elegant cottage furniture, ostrich eggs, linens with high thread counts and an earthy coloured paint job make each room special. The lush gardens and excellent pool just add to the charm, making a stay here worth the money.

Queen's Hotel (☎ 272 2101; www.queenshotel.co.za; cnr Baron van Rheede & Olivier Sts; s/d R540/600; ▣ ▣) This attractive old-style country hotel with spacious, understated rooms is refreshingly cool inside. It's an expansive place with ivy on the exterior walls and a faux marble entrance hall, yet it has an inviting appeal.

Shades of Africa (☎ 272 6430; shades@pixie.co.za; 238 Jan van Riebeeck Rd; s/d with breakfast R370/640; ▣) Colourful touches make this contemporary-styled guesthouse, with a small pool, a charming place to stay.

Adley House (☎ 272 4533; www.adleyhouse.co.za; 209 Jan van Riebeeck Rd; s/d with breakfast R295/600; ☒) Rooms in the 1905 'Feather Palace' have bags of charm, though the separate add-on ones less so. There's a couple of pools and smart outdoor braai and bar area.

La Pension (☎ 279 2445; www.lapension.co.za; 169 Church St; s/d with breakfast R350/480; ☒) A reliable choice with a decent range of rooms, La Pension includes some self-catering units with TV, plus a good-sized pool, sauna and a large garden.

Bisibee Guesthouse (☎ 272 4784; bisibee@hotmail.com; 171 Church St; s/d with breakfast R260/440) One of the first guesthouses in town, this is an immaculate but somewhat old-fashioned place.

Aan de Brug (☎ 272 2665; stemmet@mweb.co.za; 76 Church St; s/d with breakfast R180/300) Small and welcoming, this family-run place is close to the town centre.

Eating

As you'd expect, most places serve ostrich in one form or another.

Jemima's (☎ 272 0808; 94 Baron van Rheede St; mains from R50; ☽ lunch & dinner) Recognised as one of the country's finest restaurants, Jemima's delights both the palate and the eyes. It's the small touches that make this place so delightful – such as home-baked warm bread rolls served with an aubergine paste and the complimentary brownie with the bill.

De Fijne Keuken (☎ 272 6403; 114 Baron van Rheede St; mains R40-60; ☽ lunch & dinner) The funky atmosphere – bright-coloured walls plastered with old maps of the continent – is just another good mark for this highly recommended restaurant. The varied menu includes ostrich cooked every way imaginable, and a large selection of pastas.

The Godfather (☎ 272 5404; 61 Voortrekker St; R30-60; ☽ dinner) This convivial bar-restaurant serves all the usual Italian dishes and specialises in ostrich and venison. There's a good selection of board games to while away the evening, and live music on Saturday nights.

Secession Café-Bistro (☎ 272-3208; cnr Baron van Rheede & Olivier Sts; breakfast R30, mains R25; ☽ breakfast, lunch & dinner) Breakfast is served until 2.30pm and there are a huge number of choices. Otherwise dine on pasta, salads or sandwiches under umbrellas in the large flower garden.

Bernard's Taphuis (☎ 272 3208; Baron van Rheede St; mains R45-80; ☽ lunch & dinner) This place has a European flair, multiple selections for vegetarians and lots of ostrich dishes.

Rock Art Café (☎ 279 1927; 62 Baron van Rheede St; breakfast from R10, mains R30-55; ☽ lunch & dinner Mon-Sat, dinner Sun) A wide range of simple dishes is served at this often-busy bar, which has live music on Friday or Saturday.

Getting There & Around

Intercape (☎ 0861 287 287; www.intercape.co.za) has service to Jo'burg (R300, 14½ hours, daily). Otherwise you can take a **Translux bus** (☎ 021-449 3333; www.translux.co.za) to Mossel Bay (R60, one hour, daily) and from there you can get to multiple destinations (see p194).

The Baz Bus stops at George, from where you can arrange a transfer to Oudtshoorn with Backpackers' Paradise (R25).

Every Saturday the *Southern Cross* train leaves for Cape Town at 5pm.

Taxis aren't easy to find – try Union St near the Spar supermarket or check with the tourism bureau.

UNIONDALE

☎ 044

A small quiet town, Uniondale, 100km east of Oudtshoorn, is overlooked by an old fort and surrounded by a striking landscape of flat-topped kopje (little hills) and wheat fields. Uniondale is linked to Knysna on the Garden Route by the impressive Prince Alfred's Pass (p201), but there's no great reason to linger other than for a breather on the way to or from the coast.

If you arrive late and want to spend the night, try the **Cottages** (☎ 752 1554; Voortrekker St; d with breakfast R220), which has self-catering accommodation, and also serves meals and snacks in its pleasant garden.

GARDEN ROUTE

Want to scuba dive? Bungee jump? Sky dive? Hike in old growth forests? Quad bike through a wildlife reserve? Commune with monkeys? Chill out on the beach? It can all be accomplished on the always-popular Garden Route, which encompasses a verdant and highly attractive stretch of coastline from Mossel Bay in the west to just beyond Plettenberg Bay in the east.

Extensive lagoons that run behind a barrier of sand dunes and superb white beaches make up the Garden Route's outer fringes. Inland the Outeniqua and Tsitsikamma Ranges, which are between 1000m and 1700m high and crossed by some spectacular road passes, split the coast from the semidesert Karoo. It goes without saying – the scenery is stupendous, and constantly changing.

SURFING ALONG THE GARDEN ROUTE *David Malherbe & Nic Vorster*

As you travel up from Cape Town, the water gets a lot warmer. A spring suit or baggies in summer and autumn, and a good 3/2mm full suit in winter, is all you need. Local surfers are friendly and helpful if you show them the necessary respect. Tidal variations and changing wind directions are extremely important when it comes to the quality of the waves you'll find. There are a fantastic variety of waves. The following are some recommended breaks; there are many more for those who want to explore and make some local friends.

Still Point Bay

A right-point break, best at pushing tide; you can make waves from all the way outside to the inside. It's a long wave with sections and lots of cutting back into the juice. Does not hold a big swell, 4ft to 6ft is good, otherwise a strong rip. Southwesterly wind is perfect offshore.

Groot Jongensfontein

Right-breaking waves wrap into this small beautiful bay, 11km west of Still Bay. Playful fun waves, 3ft to 5ft. Needs a medium southwest swell with a rare northerly wind. Early mornings are a good time; better yet at low-to-medium tide.

Mossel Bay Peninsula

Offers no fewer than five excellent, consistent quality reef and point breaks, with many secretive waves to be found in the area. Check with locals about conditions and you could end up surfing waves many people, including South Africans, can only dream of! The main spots are Inner & Outer Pool, and Dingdang Reef, a left and right reef that works well on a big southwesterly or easterly direction swell. All these spots work on a west to southwest wind. Outers is a good right point, which has a very hollow, ledgy inside section that is usually better at lower tide and a 4ft to 5ft foot swell. Inners is a good right-hand point, with some nine sections. Watch out for rocks; it's better on a higher tide.

Herold's Bay

This is one of the rare spots that works on a northeasterly wind. It also picks up any swell that is around, so it is great for those small onshore days. There is usually a left wedge, coming off the left-hand corner.

Victoria Bay

Another beautiful small bay with a great right- hand break; early mornings or northwesterly winds are good, also OK on light southwesterly winds; holds 2ft to 8ft waves. Best at lowish-to-medium high tide. This is the home break of Springbok surfers Leonard Giles, David Pfaff and Sean Holmes.

Buffalo Bay

The point can get good, and works on a southwesterly wind. The 'Wild Side' picks up even more swell than Herold's Bay, if that happens to be flat, but it needs light wind conditions.

Plettenberg Bay

Offers some rare breaks, but is very fickle and inconsistent. Combine east or west swells with rare northwesterly or northerly winds and you'll surf some classic beach breaks.

GARDEN ROUTE

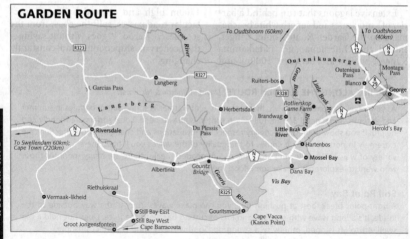

The Garden Route has some of the most significant tracts of indigenous forest in the country, including giant yellowwood trees and many wildflowers. The forests are still harvested commercially and there are also large eucalypt and pine plantations. The climate is mild and noticeably wetter than elsewhere; the highest chance of rainfall and grey days is from August to October.

The Garden Route caters to all kinds of travellers. Backpackers are taken care of with plenty of hostels, and mid-range and top-end folks will be pleased with the range of swanky hotels and charming guesthouses.

During the summer and South African school holidays prices soar and places quickly fill up, so it's best to book ahead. If you're looking for a base, the best bet is Knysna or Buffalo Bay, closely followed by Plettenberg Bay. The Garden Route is best done either in your own vehicle or on the Baz Bus's hop-on/hop-off bus service. Prices between Garden Route towns on the major coach companies are sky high – it costs almost as much to travel from Mossel Bay to Knysna as it does to go all the way to Cape Town. Remember, you don't have to be a backpacker to travel on the Baz Bus. The company will drop you off at one of the hostels, but most are centrally located.

Finally, although the Garden Route is unquestionably beautiful, it is also quite heavily (and sometimes tackily) developed, so if you leave South Africa without having seen the Garden Route it isn't a disaster, if you leave having seen only the Garden Route, it might be.

MOSSEL BAY

☎ 044 / pop 54,000

Once one of the jewels of the Garden Route, Mossel Bay (Mosselbaai) is now slightly marred by industrial sprawl, in particular the gas/petrol-conversion refinery on its outskirts. Despite this, the town centre has some attractive historic and sandstone buildings, quite a few good places to stay, plenty of activities, the only north-facing beach in the country and some top surf spots (see the boxed text on p189).

The first European to visit the bay was the Portuguese explorer Bartholomeu Dias in 1488. Vasco de Gama followed him in 1497. From then on many ships stopped to take on fresh water, and to barter for provisions with the Gouriqua Khoikhoi who lived in the region. A large milkwood tree beside the spring was used as a postal collection point – expeditions heading east would leave mail to be picked up by ships returning home. The spring and the tree still exist, and you can post letters (they receive a special post-mark) from a letterbox on the site.

Orientation & Information

The town lies on the northern slopes of Cape St Blaize. The museum complex, which overlooks the bay, is the best place to start your exploration. Marsh St, which runs through town, has a large concentration of restaur-

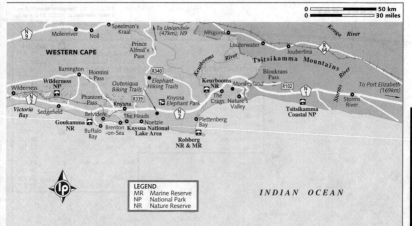

ants and pubs. The Point is the place to head for a late afternoon drink and to watch the surfers try their luck on the breaks. Santos Beach is the town's swimming beach.

The **Tourism Bureau** (☎ 691 2202; Market St; ☷ 8am-6pm Mon-Fri, 9am-1pm Sat & Sun) is very friendly and can help with accommodation bookings.

Sights
BARTHOLOMEU DIAS MARITIME MUSEUM
The highlight of the **museum complex** (☎ 691 1067; Market St; admission R5; ☷ Maritime & Shell Museums 9am-5pm Mon-Fri, 9am-4pm Sat & Sun; History Museum 9am-5pm Mon-Fri, 9am-1pm Sat) is the replica of the vessel that Dias used on his 1488 voyage of discovery. This caravel is incredibly small, and seeing it brings home the extraordinary skill and courage of the early explorers. The replica was built in Portugal and sailed to Mossel Bay in 1988 to commemorate the 500th anniversary of Dias' trip.

In addition to the maritime museum, the complex includes the **spring** where Dias watered the **postal tree**, the 1786 VOC **granary**, a **shell museum** (with some interesting aquarium tanks) and a local **history museum**.

BOTLIERSKOP GAME FARM
The **Botlierskop Game Farm** (☎ 696 6055; Little Brak River; admission from R300; ☷ 9am-noon & 3-6pm) offers the chance to view a vast range of wildlife, including lions, rhinos, buffaloes, giraffes and blue wildebeests, in excellent conditions. This is a place where animals

are bred for sale to other parks and although they are free to roam in 1500 hectares, the chances of spotting most breeds are high. The four lions – hand-reared, thus incapable of looking after themselves in the wild – are kept in a separate sanctuary. The most popular activity is the quad-bike rides (R550), which include a buffet serving South African dishes. There are also three-hour game drives (R360) including a buffet meal. The farm is around 20km east of Mossel Bay along the N2 (take the Little Brak River turn-off and follow the signs towards Sorgfontein). Booking ahead is recommended.

Activities
Mossel Bay is chock full of activities. There are regular boat trips on the **Romonza** (☎ 690 3101) and the **Seven Seas** (☎ 691 3371) to Seal Island from the harbour behind the train station. The trips last one hour and cost around R40. In late winter and spring it's not unusual to see whales on the trip. The *Romonza* also runs special whale-watching trips (R280, two hours) during the late winter/spring whale season.

Electrodive (☎ 690 7103; Santos Protea Hotel) is a family-run operation offering a number of diving and snorkelling options. In addition to PADI/NAUI courses (from R1800, four days), it does a four-hour introduction to diving (R390), charter dives (R110, two hours) and snorkelling trips (R150, two hours). The instructors are top-notch and very patient with beginners. While diving in Mossel Bay

MOSSEL BAY

INFORMATION	
Tourism Bureau	1 B3

SIGHTS & ACTIVITIES	(pp191-2)
Bartholomeu Dias Maritime Museum	2 B3
Boat Trips to Seal Island	3 C3
Electrodive	4 A2
Granary	5 B3
History Museum	6 B3
Postal Tree	7 B3
St Blaze Trail	8 D4
Shark Africa	9 C4
Shell Museum	10 B3
Spring	11 B3

SLEEPING	(pp192-3)
Bakke & Santos Caravan Parks	12 A1
Barnacles Backpackers	13 B3
Huis te Marquette	14 D3
Mossel Bay Backpackers	15 D3
Old Post Office Tree Manor	16 B3
Park House Lodge & Travel Centre	17 B3
Point Hotel	18 D4
Punt Caravan Park	19 D4
Santos Express	20 A2

EATING	(p193)
Jazzbury's	21 D3
Kingfisher	22 D4
Pavilion	23 A2
Post Tree Restaurant	24 B3
Tidals	25 D4
Trawlers	26 C3
Vingthai Restaurant	27 D3

offers the opportunity to see quite a lot of coral, fish and other sea creatures, remember these aren't tropical waters and you're not going to have the top-notch visibility.

Shark Africa (☎ 691 3796; sharkafrica@mweb.com; cnr Upper Cross & Kloof Sts; cost R900) organises cage dives and snorkelling to view great white sharks.

Face Adrenalin (☎ 697 7001; www.faceadrenalin .com; cost R170; ☾ 9am-5pm) offers bungee jumping off Gouritz Bridge 35km west of Mossel Bay. Ask about transfers at one of the hostels.

Skydivers can experience awesome views and possibly a beach landing when they jump with **Tandem Sky Dive** (☎ 082-824 8599; Mossel Bay Airfield; cost R1200).

Hikers should tackle the magnificent **St Blaze Trail**, running for 15km from the Point to Dana Bay (Danabaai) along the cliff tops. A round trip takes at least eight hours.

Sleeping

Mossel Bay has lots of accommodation options.

BUDGET

Barnacles Backpackers (☎ 690 4584; barnacles@mweb .co.za; 112 High St; dm R70, d with shared bathroom R190; ☐) Our favourite backpackers in town; each room is unique with funky furnishings and bright-coloured walls. The roof deck overlooks the ocean, the owners are friendly and very knowledgeable, and the doubles are an excellent-value option even if you don't usually stay in a backpackers.

Park House Lodge & Travel Centre (☎ 691 1937; www.park-house.co.za; 118 Montagu St; dm R70, d with shared bathroom from R180; ⊡) This place in a 130-year-old stone mansion is smartly decorated with nice linens, paintings on the wall and sturdy wood furniture. It also has beautiful pond-filled gardens.

Mossel Bay Backpackers (☎ 691 3182; www.gardenrouteadventures.com; 1 Marsh St; camp sites per person R45, dm R70, d with shared bathroom R190; ⊡ ⊠) Close by the beach at the Point and the bars on March St, this long-established place is reliable and well run. It offers a pool and bar; there are bicycles and boogie boards for rent.

Santos Express (☎ 691 1995; www.santosexpress.co.za; Santos Beach; d with breakfast & shared bathroom R179) The position of this converted train, right beside the beach, can't be beaten, even if the compartments are a bit cramped. You can choose between two and four sleeping cars. There's an attached **bar-restaurant** (mains R40-60) with a very large menu, overlooking the water.

There are three municipal **caravan parks** (☎ 691 2915; camp sites from R55, chalets from R160) in town. Bakke and Santos are next to each other on pretty Santos Beach. The Punt is on the Point and very close to the surf. Prices rise in the high season. All offer sea views.

MID-RANGE

Huis te Marquette (☎ 691 3182; marquette@pixie.co.za; 1 Marsh St; s/d from R300/520; ⊠) This classy, long-running guesthouse, near the Point, has its more-expensive rooms facing onto the pool. These come with spa baths. The place is attached to the Mossel Bay Backpackers and has a good bar.

Point Hotel (☎ 691 3512; www.pointhotel.co.za; Point Rd; s/d R500/650) This hotel is an eyesore but in a spectacular location, right above the wave-pounded rocks at the Point. All the spacious rooms have a balcony and ocean views.

TOP END

Old Post Office Tree Manor (☎ 691 3738; www.oldposttree.co.za; Market St; s/d R395/730; ⊠) More like a hotel than a guesthouse, the Old Post Office has nicely furnished characterful rooms. The hotel restaurant is the bright and eccentric **Gannet Restaurant** (lunch/dinner

R30/70) with a large seafood, meat and pizza menu. For a sea-facing sunset cocktail try the attached Blue Oyster Bar.

Eight Bells Mountain Inn (☎ 631 0000; www.eightbells.co.za; s/d R400/800; ⊠) This place is actually 35km north of Mossel Bay in a lovely mountain setting. Rooms are small but tastefully decorated with TVs and safes. There's a tea garden, **restaurant** (mains R30-60) and opportunities to hike and ride horses (R90 per hour) on the property.

Eating

Marsh St is a good place to check out at night – there are a number of pubs and restaurants lined up one after another.

Kingfisher (☎ 690 6390; Point Rd; mains R45-100; ☺ lunch & dinner) Locals say this is the best seafood restaurant in town. Besides good ocean views from the glassed-in balcony, you can choose between sushi, seafood platters, fish and salads.

Jazzbury's (☎ 691 1923; 11 Marsh St; mains R40-70; ☺ dinner) Come to Jazzbury's to try some traditional African dishes, such as mopani worms and Cape Malay food, as well as the more usual ostrich, beef and seafood creations.

Post Tree Restaurant (☎ 691 1177; cnr Riley & Powrie Sts; mains R50; ☺ lunch & dinner) The Post Tree gives friendly service, and serves a range of dishes, including interesting salads and pastas. Eat either indoors or in the candle-lit courtyard.

Vingthai Restaurant (☎ 690 8238; 12 Marsh St; mains R30-50; ☺ lunch & dinner) This place serves quite good Thai cuisine. Sit outside on the front porch and try the green curry and prawns (R52) for something different.

Pavilion (☎ 690 4567; Santos Beach; mains R40-60; ☺ lunch & dinner) In a 19th-century bathing pavilion (hence the name), this is a fine choice for a beachside meal. The menu offers just about everything.

Tidals (☎ 691 3777; Point Rd) This is a good spot for a sunset drink. It's right on the rocks at The Point, often has live music and draws a young crowd.

Trawlers (☎ 691 3073; 18 Marsh St; mains R17-50; ☺ lunch & dinner) Fishnet décor and maritime murals dominate this place. It serves inexpensive seafood-combo baskets, burgers and steaks. Looking for just a drink? Check out the long wooden bar. There's also a kids' menu.

Getting There & Away

Mossel Bay is off the highway, so long-distance buses don't come into town; they drop you at the Voorbaai Shell petrol station, 7km away. The hostels can usually collect you if you give notice. The Baz Bus will drop you in town.

Translux (☎ 021-449 3333; www.translux.co.za), **Greyhound** (☎ 021-505 6363; www.greyhound.co.za) and **Intercape** (☎ 0861 287 287; www.intercape .co.za) buses stop here on their Cape Town to Port Elizabeth services. Intercape fares from Mossel Bay include Knysna (R90, 1¾ hours, twice daily), Plettenberg Bay (R105, two hours, twice daily), Cape Town (R105, 7¾ hours, twice daily) and Port Elizabeth (R115, 5½ hours, twice daily).

GEORGE

☎ 044 / pop 116,300

George, the largest town on the Garden Route, was founded in 1811. It has some attractive old buildings, including the tiny St Mark's Cathedral and the more imposing Dutch Reformed Mother Church. But it's 8km from the coast and for most people, who come only to ride on the steam train service, there's no great reason to stay. Golf enthusiasts, however, may be drawn to stay and play the Fancourt Hotel, 10km outside town.

OUTENIQUA CHOO-TJOE

The **Outeniqua Choo-Tjoe** (☎ 044-801 8288 in George, ☎ 044-382 1361 in Knysna; adult/child one-way to Knysna R65/55), in operation since 1928, chugs at a leisurely pace along the coast and through the country from George to Knysna. It's a fantastic ride with some amazing scenery. Two trains run daily, departing from George at 9.30am and 2pm and leaving Knysna at 9.45am and 2.15pm. Reservations are recommended. You can also pick up the service in Wilderness.

The return trip from George is 7½ hours, so if you have to return to collect your car, consider taking the 9.30am train to Sedgefield (arriving 10.53am), then hopping across the platform onto the waiting train from Knysna (departing 10.58am) to return to George at 12.30pm. You'll still see some beautiful scenery on this section.

Orientation & Information

The N2 enters this sprawling town from the south on York St, which is a long, four-lane avenue, terminating at a T-junction with Courtenay St – head west for Oudtshoorn, east for Wilderness. The main commercial area is on the eastern side of York St around Hibernia and Market Sts.

The **tourism bureau** (☎ 801 9295; www.george tourism.co.za; 124 York St; ☉ 8am-4.30pm Mon-Fri, 9am-1pm Sat) has a lot of information and maps.

Sights

The starting point and terminus for journeys on the *Outeniqua Choo-Tjoe* steam train is the **Steam Train Museum** (☎ 801 8295; adult/child R5/2; ☉ 7.30am-6pm Mon-Sat), just off Courtenay St. It's worth visiting in its own right, especially if you're interested in trains. Some 11 locomotives and 15 carriages, as well as many detailed models, have found a retirement home here; some have been better cared for than others, but you can climb into most, including a carriage used by the British royal family in the 1940s.

Sleeping

French Lodge International (☎ 874 0345; www .frenchlodge.co.za; 29 York St; s/d R350/700; ✗ ☎) Cross a chic safari lodge with a little bit of France and you have this new hotel – the best deal in town. Rooms are in thatched-roof rondavels with satellite TV and a bathroom with a six-jet Jacuzzi. Décor is African safari motif – think giant wooden giraffes and hand-carved chairs. If that's not enough there's a **restaurant** (mains R50-100) featuring homemade French cuisine with a South African flair, an extensive wine list, including French champagne, and servers in old-fashioned suits.

Fancourt Hotel (☎ 804 0000; www.fancourt.com; Montagu St, Blanco; d from R1770; ✗ ☎) This is the area's most luxurious place, about 10km from the town centre, and has four 18-hole golf courses (two designed by Gary Player). In 2003 the Links Golf Course was the site of the President's cup, which pits the top 12 US golfers against the top 12 golfers from the rest of the world, excluding Europe. The hotel and country club has a range of top-notch accommodation options, a health spa and a few restaurants.

Protea Foresters Hotel (☎ 874 4488; foresters@ pixie.co.za; 123 York St; s/d R525/675; ✗) This functional, mid-range option is opposite the tourism bureau, and has frequent special deals.

George Tourist Resort (☎ 874 5205; fax 874 4255; York St; camp sites R75; ⊠) This large, flash caravan park on the edge of town has a restaurant, indoor heated pool, gym and minigolf course.

Eating

Reel n' Rustic (☎ -884 0707; Courtenay St; mains from R50; ⊗ lunch & dinner) Specialising in Creole and Cajun steaks and seafood, this is one of the best restaurants hereabouts, with another popular branch in nearby Wilderness. Booking at weekends is advised.

Copper Pot (☎ 870 7378; 12 Montagu St, Blanco; mains R60-100; ⊗ dinner) A George institution, this formal restaurant has an eclectic menu, ranging from curries to paella.

Butchers Block Pub & Grill House (☎ 874 3392; 127 York St; mains from R55; ⊗ lunch & dinner) As the name suggests, this is a meat-oriented place. There are all sizes and cuts of steaks. Mains come with onion rings, stir-fried veggies and a choice of potato. The atmospheric bar is a good place for a drink.

Getting There & Away

South African Airways (SAA; ☎ 0860 359 722; www .flysaa.com) and **Nationwide Airlines** (☎ 0861 737 737; www.nationwideair.co.za) fly to **George airport** (☎ 876 9310), which is about 15km south of town.

Most buses stop in St Mark's Sq, behind the Geronimo Spur steakhouse on the main street. **Translux** (☎ 021-449 3333; www.trans lux.co.za), **Greyhound** (☎ 021-505 6363; www.grey hound.co.za) and **Intercape** (☎ 0861 287 287; www .intercape.co.za) services stop here on their way from Cape Town to Port Elizabeth and on their runs between Jo'burg and the Garden Route. Intercape fares include Knysna (R85, one hour, twice daily), Mossel Bay (R80, 40 minutes, twice daily), Plettenberg Bay (R90, 1½ hours, twice daily), Port Elizabeth (R105, five hours, twice daily), Cape Town (R120, 6½ hours, twice daily), Bloemfontein (R260, 10 hours, daily) and Jo'burg (R355, 16 hours, daily).

The Baz Bus drops-off in town and you can call the hostels in Oudtshoorn for shuttle services there.

The weekly *Southern Cross* train between Cape Town and Oudtshoorn stops here.

AROUND GEORGE

There are a number of drives around George that make good day trips.

Montagu & Outeniqua Passes

One interesting drive from George is out on the Montagu Pass and back on the Outeniqua Pass (from Oudtshoorn). The Montagu Pass is a quiet dirt road that winds its way through the mountains; it was opened in 1847 and is now a national monument. Take a picnic, because there are some great picnic sites and beautiful *fynbos* to admire along the way. The views from the Outeniqua Pass are actually more spectacular than from the Montagu, but it's a main road, so it's a lot more difficult to stop when you want to.

Seven Passes Road

The Seven Passes Rd to Knysna used to be the main road link, and it is easy to imagine how difficult and dangerous it must have been for the pioneers and their ox-wagons. The road is still unsurfaced for quite a way and, thanks to the timber trucks, some parts are rough, so the trip will take two hours. It's a pleasant enough route but most of the countryside is now dominated by pine, gum trees and Port Jackson wattle, leaving only small patches of *fynbos* – if you want spectacular views, stick to the N2.

Herold's Bay
☎ 044

On a beautiful stretch of beach that provides consistent swells for surfers (see the boxed text on p189) is the sleepy village of Herold's Bay. With just one small shop and a couple of places to stay, it's generally quiet although it becomes very crowded on summer weekends. The town is 30km southwest of George. If you fancy staying the night try **Dutton's Cove** (☎ 851 0155; www .duttonscove.co.za; s/d R485/600; ⊠), which provides lovely upmarket accommodation in a peaceful setting. There are great views over the bay and a **restaurant** (mains from R50) with a large wine list.

Victoria Bay
☎ 044

Victoria Bay is tiny and picturesque, and sits at the foot of steep cliffs, around 20km south of George. It's a popular surf spot

WESTERN CAPE

(see the boxed text on p189). If you're set on staying the night, try either the **caravan park** (☎ /fax 889 0081; camp sites R70) or the self-catering **Sea Breeze Holiday Cottages** (☎ 889 0098; seabreeze@pixie.co.za; cottages from R150).

WILDERNESS
☎ 044

Dense old-growth forests, so thick with trees they seem to embrace you, give way to steep hills and pounding blue surf in Wilderness. This beautiful stretch of coastline, with rolling breakers, miles of white sand, sheltered lagoons and lush mountain hinterland, has made Wilderness very popular – but luckily the town does not come across as over-produced. The myriad of holiday homes blend into the verdant green hills, and as clichéd as it sounds, the tiny downtown can best be described as cute and charming. The only drawback is everything is quite widely scattered, making life very difficult if you don't have a vehicle.

The **Wilderness Tourism Bureau** (☎ 877 0045; Leila's Lane; ☼ 8am-6pm Mon-Fri, 9am-1pm & 3-5pm Sat high season) is just off the N2 as you pull into the village. It makes accommodation bookings and takes reservations for the *Outeniqua Choo-Tjoe* steam train (see the boxed text on p194).

Internet access is available at the **Internet Café** (☎ 877 0533; 5 Wilderness Centre; per hr R60; ☼ 8am-5pm).

Activities
Wilderness is jam-packed with activities. You can try **Eden Adventures** (☎ 877 0179; www.eden.co.za; Wilderness National Park) if you're looking to rent a canoe (R80 per half day) or mountain bike (R60 per half day), or try your hand at abseiling and kloofing (canyoning). The company also organises tours of the area. One popular trip (R185, four hours) combines canoeing with downhill cycling through the mountains.

Wilderness Adventures & Cossack Stunt Academy (☎ 850 1008; www.cossackstuntacademy.co.za; Seven Passes Rd) offers a three-hour horse ride to a waterfall where you can go swimming (R325), as well as sunrise and sunset rides in the mountains (R220). The academy is 19km from Wilderness. Take the N2 towards Knysna and exit at Hoekwil Rd and continue on until you hit Seven Passes Rd.

Sleeping & Eating
Palms Wilderness Guest House (☎ 877 1420; www.palms-wilderness.com; George Rd; s/d with breakfast R900/980; ☪) This is the fanciest place to stay, and blends into the surrounding landscape perfectly. Rooms are luxurious, it's a two-minute walk from the beach and there is a black-marble swimming pool. Its **restaurant** (mains R80) has a fusion menu and comes highly recommended.

Fairy Knowe Backpackers (☎ 877 1285; www.redcard.co.uk/fairyknowe; Dumbleton Rd; camp sites per person R50, dm R70, d with shared bathroom R200; 💻) Set in spacious, leafy grounds overlooking the Touws River, this 1874 farmhouse was the first in the area; it has yellowwood floors and some original fittings. The bar and café are in another pretty little building some distance away, so boozers won't keep you awake. It's a great place to relax, but numbers are limited so book ahead. The Baz Bus comes to the door and the steam train stops just along the lane. If you're driving, head into Wilderness town and follow the main road for 2km to the Fairy Knowe turn-off.

Beach House (☎ 877 0605; www.redcard.co.uk/fairyknowe; George Rd; dm R60, d with shared bathroom R180; 💻) Just 100m from Wilderness beach, this hostel has a spectacular location. The house and grounds are pretty nice too. Look for the turn-off before you pass Wilderness on the N2.

Pirate's Creek (☎ 877 1101; www.piratescreek.co.za; camp sites per adult/child R85/35, chalets from R450; ☪) This place is located on the N2 around 1km after the Wilderness turn-off. A good family option as there's lots of space and activities to keep the kids busy, including a nine-hole golf course, free canoes and a riverside restaurant. The wooden chalets are attractive, well equipped and right on the river. Prices rise sharply in high season.

Reel 'n Rustic's Wilderness Grille (☎ 877 0808; George Rd; mains R25-65; ☼ lunch & dinner) Sit outside among the trees and murals in the garden area. There is an interesting selection of steaks, from blackened sirloin to Cajun, as well as decent pizzas.

Penny Lane (☎ 877 0426; 1 George Rd; mains R40-85; ☼ breakfast, lunch & dinner) Popular with locals, Penny Lane specialises in seafood from all over the planet – everything from British fish and chips to fish with pesto or Cajun spices.

WILDERNESS NATIONAL PARK

This **national park** (☎ 877 1197; adult/child R60/30; ☒ 8am-5pm Jan-Nov, 8am-7pm Dec) encompasses the area from Wilderness and the Touws River in the west to Sedgefield and the Goukamma Nature Reserve in the east. The southern boundary is the ocean and the northern boundary is the Outeniqua Range. It covers a unique system of lakes, rivers, wetlands and estuaries that are vital for the survival of many species.

There are three types of lake in the park: drowned river valleys (eg Swartvlei); drowned low-lying areas among the dune system (eg Langvlei); and drowned basins that have been formed by wind action (eg Rondevlei). The rich birdlife includes the beautiful Knysna lourie and many species of kingfisher.

There are several nature trails taking in the lakes, the beach and the indigenous forest. The **Kingfisher Trail** is a day walk that traverses the region and includes a boardwalk across the intertidal zone of the Touws River. The lakes offer anglers, canoeists, windsurfers and sailors an ideal venue. Pedal boats and canoes can be hired at Ebb & Flow South camp, where there is also a small shop.

There are two similar **camps** (camp sites R140, d rondavels with shared bathroom R185, d forest cabins R320) in the park, Ebb & Flow North and Ebb & Flow South. The park is signposted from the N2. It's possible to walk there from Wilderness.

BUFFALO BAY

☎ 044

Picture a long surf beach with curvaceous white dunes and pounding waves. Picture a mostly deserted beach, as far as Garden Route beaches go, with only a tiny enclave of holiday homes on a point at one end, a beach shack backpackers about a kilometre down the road, and a nature reserve just a little past that. Picture all this and you have Buffalo Bay.

Here you'll find **Wild Side Backpackers** (☎ 383 0609; www.wildsidebackpacker.co.za; dm R70, d with shared bathroom R180, meals R30-50) run by the exuberant Elly and Garth. It's one of the best hostels in the country. You won't find a lot of luxury here – it's right on the beach and there's a constant battle to keep the sand out – but there's tons of atmos-

phere and attitude. The parties are legendary – partake in the famed 100 club (100 shots of beer in one hour) or just chill out in the lounge overlooking the ocean. There are nightly dinners, and some awesome surf spots in the area. If you're interested in a surf lesson it can be arranged, and the sunset horse rides along the beach are also very popular.

Buffalo Bay is 17km west of Knysna. From the N2 take the Buffalo Bay turnoff. You'll see Wild Side on the right-hand side of the road, or call for a pickup from Knysna.

During the day you can explore the **Goukamma Nature Reserve** (☎ 383 0042; admission R15; camp sites R50, 4-person rondavels R250; ☒ 9am-5pm). It's accessible from the Buffalo Bay road, and protects 14km of rocky coastline, sandstone cliffs, dunes covered with coastal *fynbos* and forest, and Groenvlei, a large freshwater lake. There are some small antelopes and much birdlife; 150 species, including the Knysna lourie, have been recorded.

Most of the reserve is accessible only by foot. There's an 8km circular trail and a 14km trail. A suspension bridge over the Goukamma River takes hikers to the start of the trail.

KNYSNA

☎ 044 / pop 38,100

Perched on the edge of a serene lagoon and surrounded by forests, Knysna (pronounced 'nie-snah') is one of the jewels of the Garden Route. It began as a timber port and shipbuilding centre, thanks to the lagoon and the rich indigenous forests of the area. Continuing the legacy of the timber industry are a number of excellent woodwork and furniture shops and a thriving artistic community.

With its sylvan setting, good places to stay, eat and drink, and wide range of activities, Knysna has plenty going for it. There's an **arts festival** in late September and early October, while in May the town goes gay with the **Pink Loerie Festival** (www.pinkloerie.com). In the holiday season, though, the sheer numbers of visitors threaten to overwhelm it and driving through the town can be hell.

Orientation & Information

Almost everything of importance is on Main St or at the bustling Waterfront area.

Knysna Tourism (Map p198; ☎ 382 5510; www
.knysna-info.co.za; 40 Main St; ⏰ 8.30am-5pm) is an
excellent information office, with very
knowledgeable staff. You can't miss the
place – there's an enormous elephant skeleton out front.

For Internet access try the **Adventure Café**
(Map p198; ☎ 382 4959; 1 Gray St; per hr R40; ⏰ 9am-
7pm). It's pretty fast.

Sights & Activities
KNYSNA LAGOON
Although regulated by the **South African
National (SAN) Parks Board** (Map p202; ☎ 012-428
9111; www.parks-sa.co.za; 643 Leyds St, Muckleneuk, Pretoria), Knysna Lagoon, covering 13 sq km,
is not a national park or wilderness area.

Much is still privately owned, and the lagoon is used by industry and for recreation. The town's famous oysters are bred
here – you can find out more about this
at the Knysna Oyster Company (p200) on
Thesen's Island.

The protected area starts just to the east of
Buffalo Bay and follows the coastline to the
mouth of the Noetzie River. The lagoon opens
up between two sandstone cliffs, known as
the Heads – once proclaimed by the British Royal Navy the most dangerous harbour
entrance in the world. There are good views
from a lookout on the eastern head, and a
nature trail on the western head.

The best way to appreciate the lagoon is
to take a cruise. The **MV John Benn** (Map p198;

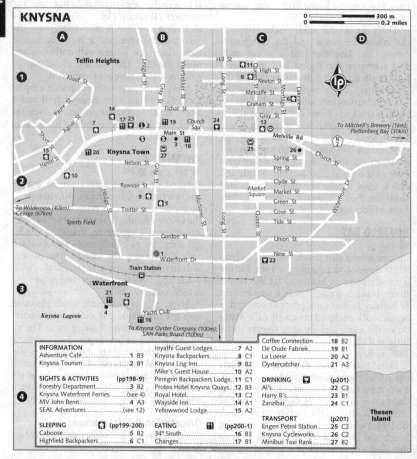

KNYSNA

0 _____ 300 m
0 _____ 0.2 miles

INFORMATION		
Adventure Café	1	B3
Knysna Tourism	2	B1

SIGHTS & ACTIVITIES	(pp198-9)	
Forestry Department	3	B2
Knysna Waterfront Ferries	(see 4)	
MV John Benn	4	A3
SEAL Adventures	(see 12)	

SLEEPING	(pp199-200)	
Caboose	5	B2
Highfield Backpackers	6	C1
Inyathi Guest Lodges	7	A2
Knysna Backpackers	8	C1
Knysna Log Inn	9	B2
Mike's Guest House	10	A2
Peregrin Backpackers Lodge	11	C1
Protea Hotel Knysna Quays	12	B3
Royal Hotel	13	C2
Wayside Inn	14	A1
Yellowwood Lodge	15	A2

EATING	(pp200-1)	
34° South	16	B3
Changes	17	B1
Coffee Connection	18	B2
De Oude Fabriek	19	B1
La Loerie	20	A2
Oystercatcher	21	A3

DRINKING	(p201)	
Al's	22	C3
Harry B's	23	B1
Zanzibar	24	C1

TRANSPORT	(p201)	
Engen Petrol Station	25	C2
Knysna Cycleworks	26	C2
Minibus Taxi Rank	27	B2

☎ 382 1697; www.featherbed.co.za; Waterfront; adult/child R220/50; ☯ departs 10am, 11.30am & 12.30pm) offers the recommended Featherbed cruise, a four-hour affair that includes lunch and takes you to the privately owned **Featherbed Nature Reserve** (Map p202), where you'll be driven around. The company also runs cheaper, shorter cruises.

Those searching for romance can take a 2½-hour sunset cruise that includes champagne and oysters. Contact **Knysna Waterfront Ferries** (Map p198; ☎ 382 5520; www.knysnaferries.co.za; Waterfront; tickets R250; ☯ departs 5pm).

MITCHELL'S BREWERY

A nice alternative to all that wine tasting is to drop by **Mitchell's Brewery** (Map p202; ☎ 382 4685; Arend St; tastings R10; ☯ tours 10.30am Mon-Fri). The beers, which include a draught lager, a bitter, a stout and an ale, can be found all over Western Cape.

TOWNSHIP TOURS & HOMESTAYS

Follow Gray St uphill and eventually you'll leave town and emerge on the wooded slopes of the hills behind. On top is the sprawling township of Concordia (Map p202), best visited on an excellent tour run by **Eco Afrika Tours** (☎ 082-925 0716) or **The Heads Adventure Centre** (Map p202; ☎ 384 0831; the Heads). Unlike many South African townships, Knysna's are not only quite safe, but have a different look. The humble homes are built mostly with timber from the nearby forests. The two-hour tours (R180) are led by local guides and take you through the usual township sites – schools, a visit to a tribal witch doctor and a shebeen – but then add a twist. You'll also get to visit the Grass Routes neighbourhood, the largest community of Rastafarians in the country. It's a unique and worthwhile experience.

If you want to stay overnight in either the Rastafarian community or in the township, contact Glendyrr at **Knysna Tourism** (Map p198; ☎ 382 5510; 40 Main St). The homestay costs R180 per night and includes breakfast. It just might be the highlight of your Garden Route experience.

KNYSNA FOREST TRAILS

There are excellent hikes in the Knysna forests, and you can book walking trails and collect maps and information at the **Forestry Department** (Map p198; ☎ 382 5466; Main St; ☯ 7.30am-1pm & 1.45-4pm Mon-Fri) office. Overnight hikes cost R15 per day including the use of trail huts.

The **Outeniqua Trail** is popular and takes a week to walk, although you can also do two- or three-day sections. The trail costs R30 per night to stay in a basic hut. You will need your own bedding. Mountainbike trails are being developed in the area and **Outeniqua Biking Trails** (Map pp190-91; ☎ 044-532 7644; exit N2 at Harkerville; per day R65) rents bikes and will give you a map to the surrounding trails. It also can arrange guided trips.

Other trails through the forests include the four **Elephant Trails** (Map pp190–91). These day walks cost R6. There are three elephants in the forest, but spotting one is so rare it's almost mythical.

OTHER ACTIVITIES

There are plenty of other activities on offer in the area; start by making inquiries at **The Heads Adventure Centre** (Map p202; ☎ 384 0831; the Heads). Among the possibilities are boat and short-entry scuba dives (R80 to R120) to some of South Africa's best spots. Snorkelling equipment can be rented for R70. Ask the guides to point out the good snorkelling trails. They may even go with you.

Quad biking trips in the Featherbed Nature Reserve are available with **SEAL Adventures** (Map p198; ☎ 381 0068; Shop 1, Protea Hotel Knysna Quays; 2½hr trip R280; ☯ departs 11am & 3.30pm). The company also runs an Awesome Foursome adventure trip – quad biking, abseiling, canoeing and cliff-jumping for R380.

There are also bike trails around the area; for more information on biking, and for bike rentals and maps, head to Knysna Cycleworks (p201).

Sleeping

Low-season competition between the several backpackers and many guesthouses in town keeps prices down, but in high season expect steep price hikes (except at the backpackers) and book ahead.

BUDGET

Highfield Backpackers (Map p198; ☎ 382 6266; highfields@hotmail.com; 2 Graham St; dm R70, d with shared bathroom from R180) Located in a spacious old house, Highfield feels like a B&B. Its focus is on doubles decorated with hard-wood floors, brass beds and nice linens.

Peregrin Backpackers Lodge (Map p198; ☎ 382 3747; peregrin@cyberpark.co.za; 16 High St; camp sites per person R50, dm R65, d with shared bathroom R170; 🖳) This place has lots of character. Rooms are clean and dorms not too cramped. All guests are given discount cards upon arrival for area bars and shops.

Caboose (Map p198; ☎ 382 5850; knysna@caboose .co.za; cnr Gray & Trotter Sts; s/d R130/180; 🖳) Perhaps the Caboose takes its train theme a little too seriously, as the rooms are about the same size as sleeping compartments: *tiny*. Still, the budget accommodation is good quality and there are plenty of spacious public areas.

Knysna Backpackers (Map p198; ☎ 382 2554; knybpack@netactive.co.za; 42 Queen St; dm R75, d with shared bathroom R180) You'll find mainly dorm beds at this large and spruce Victorian house on the hill a few blocks up from the main street. It tends to be quieter and more relaxing than other places. Rates include a light DIY breakfast.

Woodbourne Resort (Map p202; ☎ /fax 384 0316; woodb.kyn@pixie.co.za; George Rex Dr; camp sites per person R40, chalets from R220) Here you'll find spacious, shaded camping and simple chalets with TVs. It's a quiet place a little way out of town. Rates more than double during high season and holidays. Follow the signs to the Heads.

MID-RANGE

Inyathi Guest Lodges (Map p198; ☎ 382 7768; www .inyathi-sa.com; 52 Main St; s/d from R235/370) This is the most imaginatively designed guesthouse in Knysna, with a real African flair that avoids the kitsch. Accommodation is in uniquely decorated timber lodges – some with Victorian bathtubs, others with stained-glass windows. Excellent value for money and worth a stay.

Yellowwood Lodge (Map p198; ☎ 382 5906; www .yellowwoodlodge.co.za; 18 Handel St; s/d from R250/ 500; 🖳) A traditional and sumptuously decorated guesthouse, Yellowwood boasts a lovely garden setting and views of the lagoon.

Mike's Guest House (Map p198; ☎ 382 1728; dolp hins@mweb.co.za; 67 Main St; s/d with breakfast from R300/360; 🖳) Tidy, colourful rooms with TVs and some self-catering units make up this guesthouse on the main road.

Royal Hotel (Map p198; ☎ 382 1144; fax 382 2686; 24 Queen St; dm R85, s/d with breakfast R125/250) Although it might not be the smartest place in town, this great-value option has lots of

style, with its stripped pine floors and piano in the parlour.

Wayside Inn (Map p198; ☎ 382 6011; www.way sideinn.co.za; Pledge Sq; s/d R265/420) Intimate and well managed, the Wayside Inn has nicely decorated rooms and is in a handy location just off Main St by the cinema.

TOP END

Phantom Forest (☎ 386 0046; www.phantomforest .com; s/d R1600/2400; dinner R225; 🖳 🖳) This 137-hectare private ecoreserve, 6km west of Knysna along the Phantom Pass road, overlooks the lagoon and comprises 10 cleverly designed and elegantly decorated tree houses. Various activities, including conducted nature walks, are available. If nothing else, visit for the award-winning five-course Pan-African dinner served from 6.30pm to 8.30pm daily; booking is essential.

Protea Hotel Knysna Quays (Map p198; ☎ 382 5005; knysnaq@mweb.co.za; Waterfront Dr; s/d R780/1135; 🖳 🖳) Rooms are tastefully decorated at this stylish posh hotel, which is a better option than the other Protea on Main St. It has a very inviting pool and is just moments away from shopping and eating options at the Waterfront.

Knysna Log Inn (Map p198; ☎ 382 5835; log-inn@ mweb.co.za; 16 Gray St; s/d R350/700; 🖳 🖳) The Knysna Log Inn is said to be the largest log structure in the southern hemisphere. The rooms are comfortable enough, and there's a pool, but the whole place resembles a Disneyland exhibit a little too much.

Eating

34° South (Map p198; ☎ 382 7268; Waterfront; mains R35-80; 🕑 lunch & dinner) One of the best, this is a very tempting place with outdoor tables overlooking the water; go for a platter and choose from their vast range of salads and seafood pâtés. The sandwiches are also mouth watering.

Knysna Oyster Company (Map p202; ☎ 382 6941; www.mbendi.co.za/koyster; Thesen's Island; mains from R30; 🕑 lunch & dinner) This company grows its own oysters out in the lagoon; you can take a tour of the processing plant and have a tasting of a cultivated and wild oyster for R15 at its restaurant afterwards.

Changes (Map p198; ☎ 382 0456; Pledge Sq; mains R40-50; 🕑 dinner) This gay-friendly restaurant is popular all-round for its consistently good food and fun vibe. There's a different pasta, curry and crepe special every day. Sometimes there's live music.

Paquita's (Map p202; ☎ 384 0408; the Heads; mains from R20; ☺ breakfast, lunch & dinner) Seafood, steaks, pizza and pasta are available at this ideally located restaurant and bar next to the Heads. The views are stupendous – if this place was any closer to the water it would be in it – and it's a good spot for an afternoon drink. If you're lucky you may spot whales frolicking only metres away.

La Loerie (Map p198; ☎ 382 1616; 57 Main St; mains R60-80; ☺ dinner) Booking is essential at this deservedly popular but small place with copper pots hanging from the ceiling, linen napkins and a French flavour to its menu.

East Head Caffé (Map p202; ☎ 384 0933; the Heads; mains R30-40; ☺ breakfast, lunch & dinner) Our favourite breakfast spot. There's an outdoor deck overlooking the lagoon and ocean, and the smoked salmon, eggs and cream cheese breakfast (R36) is scrumptious.

Oystercatcher (Map p198; ☎ 382 9995; Knysna Quays; tapas R32; ☺ lunch & dinner) The Oystercatcher is a relaxed place serving four sizes of farmed oyster, and other seafood tapas dishes in a great waterside setting.

De Oude Fabriek (Map p198; ☎ 382 5723; cnr Main & Gray Sts; mains R45-80; ☺ lunch & dinner) This restaurant is a convivial spot to sample some interesting South African dishes – game meat, crocodile and Knysna oysters are all on the menu.

There are plenty of good snack and coffee places along Main St, including the excellent **Coffee Connection** (Map p198; ☺ breakfast & lunch), serving 36 types of coffee.

Entertainment

Starting off from Long St and heading west along Main St there are several bars worth a visit.

Zanzibar (Map p198; ☎ 382 0386; Main St) A relaxed vibe, a balcony area and a theatre where shows are held occasionally make this sophisticated joint one of Knysna's most popular night spots.

Harry B's (Map p198; ☎ 382 5065; 42 Main St; mains R70-90) Knysna's first residence (1863) now houses a very classy restaurant and bar.

Al's (Map p198; ☎ 382 6305; Queen St) This is a dance club and live-music venue – strictly a late-night affair. You'll know Al's is in business when you see the laser beam lighting up the sky.

Getting There & Away

BUS

The major bus companies, **Translux** (☎ 021-449 3333; www.translux.co.za), **Greyhound** (☎ 021-505 6363; www.greyhound.co.za) and **Intercape** (☎ 0861 287 287; www.intercape.co.za), all stop at the Engen petrol station; Baz Bus will take you where you want. For travel between nearby towns on the Garden Route, you're better off looking for a minibus taxi (see following) than travelling with the major bus lines, which are very expensive on short sectors.

Intercape fares include George (R85, one hour, twice daily), Mossel Bay (R90, 1¾ hours, twice daily), Port Elizabeth (R80, 3¾ hours, twice daily), Cape Town (R150, eight hours, twice daily) and Jo'burg (R385, 17 hours, daily).

MINIBUS TAXI

The main minibus taxi stop is behind Bloch's supermarket off Main St. Routes include Plettenberg Bay (R9, 30 minutes, daily) and Cape Town (R120, 7½ hours, daily).

TRAIN

The historic *Outeniqua Choo-Tjoe* steam train runs between Knysna and George daily except Saturday and public holidays. See the boxed text on p194 for details.

Getting Around

In Knysna there's a **Hertz Rent-a-Car** (☎ 876 9999). Even if you have a car, the summer traffic jams on the main street (much worse than anything you'll find in Cape Town) will make you look for alternative transport.

Knysna Cycleworks (☎ 382 5153; 3A Church St; per day R95) is one of several places selling and renting good bicycles.

AROUND KNYSNA
Prince Alfred's Pass

The Knysna-Avontour road climbs through the Outeniqua Range via the beautiful Prince Alfred's Pass, regarded by some as better than the Swartberg Pass. Be warned that the road is a bit rough and it's slow going.

Outside Knysna, the road passes pine and eucalypt plantations and indigenous forest (the home of Knysna's elephants). There are few really steep sections but the pass reaches a height of over 1000m, and there are great views to the north before the road winds into the Langkloof Valley.

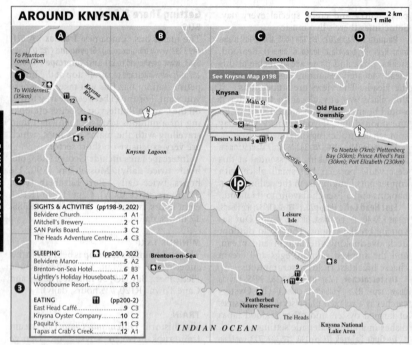

AROUND KNYSNA

0 — 2 km
0 — 1 mile

To Phantom Forest (2km)

To Wilderness (35km)

Knysna River

Concordia

See Knysna Map p198

Knysna
Main St

Old Place Township

Belvidere

Knysna Lagoon

Thesen's Island

To Noetzie (7km); Plettenberg Bay (30km); Prince Alfred's Pass (30km); Port Elizabeth (230km)

George Rex Dr

Leisure Isle

Brenton-on-Sea

Featherbed Nature Reserve

The Heads

INDIAN OCEAN

Knysna National Lake Area

SIGHTS & ACTIVITIES (pp198-9, 202)
Belvidere Church..........................1 A1
Mitchell's Brewery........................2 C1
SAN Parks Board...........................3 C2
The Heads Adventure Centre......4 C3

SLEEPING (pp200, 202)
Belvidere Manor...........................5 A2
Brenton-on-Sea Hotel..................6 B3
Lightley's Holiday Houseboats.....7 A1
Woodbourne Resort.....................8 D3

EATING (pp200-2)
East Head Caffé............................9 C3
Knysna Oyster Company.............10 C2
Paquita's....................................11 C3
Tapas at Crab's Creek.................12 A1

Belvidere & Brenton-on-Sea

There's a slightly creepy feel to immaculate Belvidere, around 10km west of Knysna on the road to Brenton-on-Sea. Still, it's worth a quick look for the beautiful Norman-style church built in the 1850s for a homesick Englishman, Thomas Duthie.

Belvidere Manor (Map p202; ☎ 387 1055; www.belvidere.co.za; Duthie Dr; d with breakfast R1040) is a collection of luxury guest cottages, some with lagoon views, in a garden setting. There is a **restaurant** (mains R80) serving regional dishes such as locally produced cheese, Karoo lamb and ostrich.

For a very different night's sleep check out **Lightley's Holiday Houseboats** (Map p202; ☎ 386 0007; www.houseboats.co.za; off the N2; 4-berth boats from R700), on the western side of the bridge over the Knysna River, which offers fully equipped houseboats. You can navigate up to 20km upriver from the Heads, but you have to pay extra for fuel. Rates vary radically depending on the boat and the season.

Tapas at Crab's Creek (Map p202; ☎ 386-0111; off the N2; mains R40; ☺ lunch & dinner) is a local

favourite watering hole, in a chilled out setting right on the lagoon. There are often afternoon drink specials. Try the chilli calamari appetizer (R30); it's fabulous.

Another 10km further, the *fynbos*-covered hills drop to Brenton-on-Sea, overlooking a magnificent 8km beach, stretching from the western head of Knysna Lagoon to Buffalo Bay. There's a small store where you can get some food; otherwise, bring your own or eat at the **Brenton-on-Sea Hotel** (Map p202; ☎ 381 0081; www.brentononsea.co.za; d R700), which has a fantastic location and a range of comfortable rooms and self-catering chalets overlooking the sea. The rates vary widely depending on the season.

Knysna to Plettenberg Bay

Not to be outdone by Captain Duthie at Belvidere, another romantic English family built holiday homes in a mock-castle-style at **Noetzie**, reached by a turn off along the N2, 10km east of Knysna. The homes are still privately owned, and are not as bad as you might imagine. Noetzie has a lovely surf beach (spacious but dangerous) and a sheltered lagoon running through a forested gorge. It's a steep trail between the car park and the beach.

Knysna Castles (☎ 375 0100; www.knysnacastles .com; d from R1300) is a four-bedroom home. If you're looking for a romantic getaway, renting one of these cosily decorated Noetzie castles right beside the beach might be just the ticket.

It's extremely unlikely that you will see the last remaining wild elephants that live in Knysna's forests, but you are sure to see them at **Knysna Elephant Park** (☎ 532 7732; www .knysna.co.za/elephant; admission R50; ⏰ 8.30am-5pm), 22km east of Knysna on the N2. Here small groups of visitors go on walking tours with the three elephants and a baby. It really is a delightful experience.

There are some good places to stay off the N2. The **Harkerville Forest Lodge & Backpackers** (☎ 532 7777; bacpac@mweb.co.za; camp sites per person R25, dm R65, d R250; 🏊) is where to head to if you're tired of the Garden Route's hustle. It's in an indigenous forest, and you have to drive down a dirt road to reach this cluster of wooden structures built around quite a few large trees. There's good hiking and horse riding in the area, and free pickups from Knysna or Plett.

Those in search of serious pampering can head to either Hunter's Country House or Tsala Treetop Lodge, both part of **Hunter Hotels** (☎ 532 7818; www.hunterhotels.com; d with breakfast from R1740; 🍴 🏊). The English-country-style Hunter's makes the perfect retreat. The 23 rooms are in garden cottages surrounding the main house. The Tsala Treetop Lodge is one of those places you go for serious luxury – inside the 10 suites, made of a combination of glass, wood and stone, you'll find silk curtains and African artwork. Outside you'll find your own private plunge pool. This place is the *crème de la crème* and you'll pay royally – doubles start at R4580. As expected both places feature exquisite dining options and a range of activities. The hotels are about 10km west of Plettenberg Bay just off the N2.

PLETTENBERG BAY

☎ 044 / pop 19,100

Plettenberg Bay, or 'Plett' as it's often known, is a resort town, with a rare combination of mountains, white sand and crystal-blue water. The town has a relaxed atmosphere with friendly locals, and if you want to be close to a beach it's a better place to stay than Knysna. There's not getting around it, Plett's a trendy and popular destination, so things tend to be upmarket. However, if you're on a budget there are hostels. The scenery to the east in particular is superb, with some of the best coast and indigenous forest in South Africa.

Orientation & Information

Plettenberg Bay is large and sprawling. The town centre is on a high promontory overlooking the Keurbooms River lagoon and Beacon Island.

The **Tourism Bureau** (☎ 533 4065; www.pletten bergbay.co.za; 1 Victoria Cottage, Kloof St; ⏰ 8.30am-5pm summer; 8.30am-5pm Mon-Fri, 9am-1pm Sat other times) has a great deal of useful information, ranging from accommodation to a craft trail and walks in the surrounding hills and reserves.

Internet access is available at the **Computer Shop & Internet Café** (☎ 533-6007; First National Bank Bldg, Main St; per hr R30; ⏰ 8.30am-6.30pm Mon-Fri, 9am-6pm Sat, 9am-4pm Sun).

Activities

Apart from lounging on the beaches or hiking on the Robberg Peninsula (p205) there's a lot to do in Plett; check with the Albergo for Backpackers (p204) as it can organise most things, often at a discount.

Boat trips to view dolphins and whales in season are available with **Ocean Blue Adventures** (☎ 533 5083; www.oceanadventures.co.za; Milkwood Centre, Hopewood St) and **Ocean Safaris** (☎ 533 4963; Milkwood Centre, Hopewood St). Trips cost about R270 for 2½ hours on 12-person boats.

Equitrailing (☎ 533 0599), located 11km east of Plett on the N2, offers horse riding through the forest for R100 per hour. **Dolphin Adventures** (☎ 083-590 3405) has sea kayaking (R200, 2½ hours) and catamaran sailing trips (R300, 2½ hours). It doesn't have an office in town, so just phone for a booking.

For skydiving try the recommended **Sky Dive Plettenberg Bay** (☎ 533 9048; Plettenberg Airport; tandem jump R1200), which offers outstanding views on the way down.

Those wanting to try surfing can take a lesson through the **International Surf School** (☎ 082-636 8431; R300 for 3½hr), which caters to all levels of surfers. It doesn't have an office, so just phone.

WESTERN CAPE

WESTERN CAPE

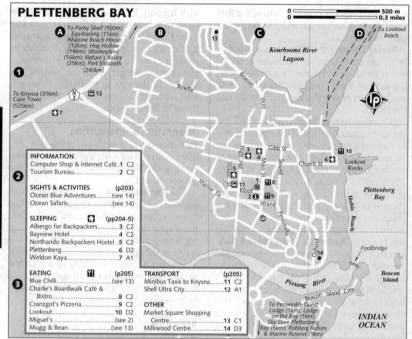

PLETTENBERG BAY

Sleeping

There is a great deal of holiday accommodation in town and nearby – in low season there are bargains. The tourism bureau has a full list and can tell you about the many camping options, all out of town. We've included both in and out of town options here.

BUDGET

If it's budget accommodation you're after, there are several good places to choose from.

Albergo for Backpackers (☎ 533 4434; www.alb ergo.co.za; 8 Church St; camp sites per person R50; dm R70, d with shared bathroom R200; ☐) Well run and friendly, Albergo encourages activities in town and in the area and can organise just about anything. Try for the upstairs dorm with huge windows and stellar ocean views from the balcony.

Abalone Beach House (☎ 535 9602; beachhouse@ global.co.za; 50 Ifafi Properties, Keurboomstrand; dm R70, d with shared bathroom R180; ☐) It's literally a hop to the beach from this great hostel run by friendly people. And what a beach! Surf and boogie boards can be hired (R10). To reach the beach house follow the Keurboomstrand signs from the N2 (about 6km east of Plett Bay), then turn into El Remo/Ifafi.

Northando Backpackers Hostel (☎ 533 0220; mwdeois@mweb.co.za; 3 Wilder St; dm R70, s/d with shared bathroom R200) Spotless and spacious, this YHA-affiliated hostel is a good choice if you're looking for peace and quiet. It has a homely feel.

MID-RANGE

Weldon Kaya (☎ 533 2437; fax 533 4364; s/d R300/460) Very funky accommodation can be found at this idealised version of a tribal village, with rooms in huts made of clay and straw. There are four wheelchair-friendly units, a pool and traditional music every Saturday night in the restaurant, which serves African dishes. It's off the N2 at the corner of Piesang Valley Rd.

Periwinkle Guest Lodge (☎ 533 1345; www.peri winkle.co.za; 75 Beachy Head Dr; d with breakfast from R1000) This bright, colourful beachfront guesthouse offers individually decorated rooms, all with great views – you might even be able to spot whales and dolphins.

Bayview Hotel (☎ 533 1961; fax 533 2059; cnr Main & Gibb Sts; s/d R245/490; 🔀) Right in the town centre, this is a small, serviceable and modern place with a range of rather plain rooms but a pleasant balcony.

TOP END

Plett Bay has some of the best luxury options in the region. You may never want to leave.

Plettenberg (☎ 533 2030; www.plettenberg.com; 40 Church St; s/d from R1250/2050; 🔀 🔁) The pool here alone is worth the stay – it's one that gives the illusion of ending in the sea. Built on a rocky headland with breathtaking vistas, this place is pure decadence with fantastic rooms, a spa and a 1st-class restaurant. Romantics can dine in the Wine Cellar surrounded by vintage bottles.

Lodge on the Bay (☎ 533 4724; www.thelodge.co .za; 77 Beachy Head Dr; d from R2800; 🔀 🔁) The highly sophisticated and ultra-modern Lodge has just six rooms and very personal service. There's a Japanese day spa on the premises. The place is worth splashing out on.

Hog Hollow (☎ 534 8879; www.hog-hollow.com; s/d with breakfast R1050/1500) Hog Hollow, 18km east of Plett along the N2, provides delightful accommodation in African art–decorated units, which are around an old farmhouse overlooking the forest. Each unit comes with a private wooden deck and hammock. It's possible to walk to Monkeyland (see p206) from here. A four-course dinner costs R150.

Eating

There are top-end restaurants at many of the top-end hotels. Otherwise you can choose from quite a few places in town.

Pansy Shell (☎ 533 6016; Old Nick Shopping Centre; mains R60; 🕑 dinner) This formal restaurant gets rave reviews for its steaks, seafood and overall ambience.

Miguel's (☎ 533 5056; cnr Marine Dr & Main St; breakfast/dinner R30/80; 🕑 breakfast, lunch & dinner) A modern place with an eclectic menu, it's bright and airy with floor-to-ceiling windows and patio seating. It's a good option any time of day.

Blue Chilli (☎ 533 5104; Market Sq Shopping Centre; mains from R30; 🕑 dinner) This is a lively Mexican restaurant and bar that comes highly recommended by locals.

Lookout (☎ 533 1379; Lookout Rocks; mains R40; 🕑 breakfast, lunch & dinner) With a deck overlooking the beach, this is a great place for a simple meal and perhaps views of dolphins surfing the waves.

Charlie's Boardwalk Café & Bistro (☎ 533 1420; 6 Yellowwoods Bldg, Main St; mains R15-50; 🕑 breakfast, lunch & dinner) A hang-out for local surfies as well as visitors, this pleasant café offers plenty of snacks and meals at reasonable prices.

Cranzgot's Pizzeria (☎ 533 1660; 9 Main St; mains R30-50; 🕑 breakfast, lunch & dinner) This perennial Plett favourite serves mouthwatering pizzas, pastas and char-grilled steaks. You might have to wait for a table in the evenings, but there is also a bar. You can take the kids here.

Mugg & Bean (☎ 533 1486; Market Sq Shopping Centre; mains R30-40; 🕑 breakfast, lunch & dinner) This ever-popular South African chain café does excellent breakfasts, bottomless coffees and sandwiches.

Getting There & Away

All the major buses stop at the Shell Ultra City on the N2; the Baz Bus will come into town. **Intercape** (☎ 0861 287 287; www.intercape .co.za) fares from Plett include: George (R90 1½ hours, three times daily), Port Elizabeth (R80, three hours, twice daily), Cape Town (R160, eight hours, twice daily), Jo'burg (R385, 18 hours, daily), Graaff-Reinet (R195, 5½ hours, daily) and Bloemfontein (R300, 12 hours, daily).

If you're heading to Knysna (R9, 30 minutes) you're better off taking a minibus taxi – services leave from the corner of Kloof and High Sts. Most other long-distance taxis stop at the Shell Ultra City on the highway.

AROUND PLETTENBERG BAY
Robberg Nature & Marine Reserve

This **reserve** (☎ 044-533 2125; admission R15; 🕑 7am-5pm Feb-Nov, 7am-8pm Dec-Jan), 9km southeast of Plettenberg Bay, protects a 4km-long peninsula with a rugged coastline of cliffs and rocks. There's a great circular walk approximately 11km long, with rich intertidal marine life and coastal-dune *fynbos*. The peninsula acts as a sort of marine speed bump to larger sea life, with mammals and fish spending time here before moving on. To get here head along Robberg Rd, off Piesang Valley Rd, until you see the signs.

Monkeyland

One of the best attractions in this area is **Monkeyland** (☎ 534 8906; www.monkeyland.co.za; adult/child R64/32; ☉ 8am-6pm), 16km east of Plett off the N2. Home to over 200 primates from 14 different species, this 12-hectare sanctuary helps rehabilitate wild monkeys that have been in zoos or private homes. The walking safari through a dense forest and across a 120m-long rope bridge is a brilliant way to find out about these creatures. There are plans to build the largest aviary in the southern hemisphere here, too. Oh, and did we mention the monkeys are really, really cute?

THE KAROO

There's something almost magical about the vast and arid Karoo. Maybe it's the wide-open spaces that make you feel so tiny, or maybe it's the towns, which make you feel you've been suspended in time. It's hard to pinpoint exactly, but there's something about this place way out in the middle of nowhere, where life moves slowly and the stars form a thick gravy soup in the night sky, that gets to you. The population is sparse, and off the main highways you can drive for hours without seeing another car.

The Karoo covers almost one-third of South Africa's total area. Translated out of Afrikaans it means 'great thirst land' and is big sheep country. Demarcated in the south and west by the coastal mountain ranges, and to the east and north by the mighty Orange River, it's often split into the Great Karoo and the Little Karoo, but it doesn't respect provincial boundaries and sprawls into the Eastern (p243) and Northern Capes (p491) as well. The section of the Karoo around the lovely town of Graaff-Reinet (p246) is possibly the most interesting. The Karoo National Park, outside of Beaufort West, is part of the Great Karoo.

PRINCE ALBERT & AROUND

☎ 023 / pop 1100

To many urban South Africans, Prince Albert – a charming village dating back to 1762 and dozing at the foot of the Swartberg Pass – represents an idyllic life in the Karoo. If you have your own transport, you can easily visit on a day trip from Oudtshoorn or even from the coast. Alternatively, stay in Prince Albert and make a day trip to Oudtshoorn via the spectacular Swartberg Pass and Meiringspoort, or – if the weather isn't too hot – consider going on a hike.

Despite being surrounded by very harsh country, the town is green and fertile (producing peaches, apricots, grapes and olives), thanks to the run-off from the mountain springs. A system of original water channels runs through town and most houses have a sluice gate, which they are entitled to open for a set period each week.

Sights & Activities

Prince Albert's best attractions are actually outside town. It's a good base for exploring the Karoo and hiking on the more than 100km of trails in the Swartberg Nature Reserve. Overnight walks have to be booked through **Cape Nature Conservation** (☎ 044-279

SWARTBERG PASS

Built by the brilliant engineer Thomas Bain, between 1881 and 1888, the Swartberg Pass is arguably the most spectacular in the country. It's 24km long and reaches nearly 1600m in height.

Proteas, watsonias and other *fynbos* are prolific. After the summit (Die Top) – where there are incredible views over the bleak Karoo and, on the other side, the greenery of the Little Karoo – the road meanders down into a fantastic geology of twisted sedimentary layers. The best picnic sites are on the northern side; the gorge narrows and in spring is full of pelargoniums. There are some quiet spots where you can sunbathe or swim.

Don't be put off by the warning signs at each end of the pass. It's a fairly easy drive as long as you take it very slowly. The road is narrow, there are very long drops and many of the corners are blind.

The hostels in Oudtshoorn will drive you and a bicycle to the top and you can ride back down. This is a huge buzz (although take along plenty of water), but the real beauty of the pass is deeper in, towards Prince Albert.

1739; Queen's Mall, Baron van Rheede St, Oudtshoorn). For guides, contact the Prince Albert of Saxe-Coburg Lodge (see below).

There's a good drive east to **Klaarstroom**, a tiny dorp (small town) along the foot of the mountains. The road runs along a valley, beneath the Groot Swartberg Range, which is cut by dramatic gullies, clefts and waterfalls. On the R329 between Prince Albert (40km) and Klaarstroom (10km), **Remhoogte Hiking Trail** can be walked in about five hours but there is a camping place on the trail.

Meiringspoort, south of Klaarstroom, on the N12 route between Beaufort West and Oudtshoorn, is an extraordinary place, following a river that cuts right through the Swartberg Range. It's not quite in the same class as Swartberg Pass, partly because it's a main road and partly because it's not as deep or as narrow.

On the road up to Prince Albert Rd station and at the station itself, keep an eye out for the work of local celebrity **Outa Lappies**, a septuagenarian artist and philosopher who makes 'something out of nothing'. His old homestead is on the R407, while his new cottage is opposite the station – it's the one with the tin toy windmills on the fence and a front yard full of junk creations.

Sleeping & Eating

Swartberg Hotel (☎ 541 1332; www.swartberg .co.za; 77 Church St; s/d with breakfast R345/500; 🖳 🕭) A charming small country inn; you can choose from thatched-roof huts or rooms in the main hotel. There are amazing gardens to relax in and the hotel organises area activities. The attached **coffee shop** (mains R18-35) looks out on the main road and is a popular spot for lunch or a homemade dessert. Also attached is the **Swartberg Arms** (mains R30), popular with locals for an evening pint. It has a large menu of pizzas and burgers as well as a kiddie menu.

Prince Albert of Saxe-Coburg Lodge (☎ 541 1267; www.saxecoburg.co.za; 60 Church St; s/d from R180/360; 🎇 🕭) The owners of this homely place are a great source of information and offer guided hikes in the area, including a three-day trip to Die Hell that's free as long as you stay at the lodge. Rooms come with satellite TVs and mosquito nets, and are lovely.

De Bergkant Lodge (☎ 541 1088; bergkant@iafrica .com; d with breakfast R1400; 🎇) Prince Albert's fanciest guesthouse has antique decorated rooms, with underfoot heating and air-conditioning as well as bathrooms with twin showers. An old fire truck is used for sundowner drives.

Onse Rus (☎ 541 1380; 47 Church St; s/d with breakfast R200/400) Onse Rus is a very appealing place with a thatched roof and friendly hosts. Lunches (R25) are also served on its grassy and shaded front garden.

Karoo Kombuis (☎ 541 1110; 18 Deurdrift St; mains R50; 🕑 dinner Mon-Sat) As good a reason to come to Prince Albert as any, this excellent restaurant serves traditional home-cooked dishes with panache. It offers either a three-course dinner (R80) or an à la carte menu. Bring your own drinks.

Sampie se Plaasstal (Church St; 🕑 9am-5pm) This is a simple but good farm-produce stall selling a range of snacks and refreshing home-made ginger beer.

Getting There & Away

Most people visit by driving over one of the area's passes from Oudtshoorn, or from the N1 between Cape Town and Jo'burg. However, if you've come for hiking there's no reason not to take a train, which is cheaper than the buses. There is no direct bus or train service to Prince Albert; the closest drop-off point is at the train station on Prince Albert Rd, 45km northwest of Prince Albert, which also serves as the long-distance-bus stop. Most places to stay will pick you up from the train station.

DIE HELL

In a narrow valley in the Swartberg Range is Die Hell, or Gamkaskloof. The first citizens of Die Hell were early Trekboers, who developed their own dialect. There was no road into Die Hell until the 1960s, and donkeys carried in the few goods the self-sufficient community needed from Prince Albert. Maybe it's a coincidence but within 30 years of the roads being built all the farmers had left. Now the area is part of a nature reserve where there is a camping ground.

The dirt road to Die Hell turns off the Swartberg Pass road about 20km from Prince Albert and extends for another 60km or so before hitting a dead end. Allow yourself the best part of a day to explore (or try hiking from Prince Albert), or you can camp here at Elandspad. There are also houses starting at R150 a double.

WESTERN CAPE

MATJIESFONTEIN

☎ 023

One of the most fascinating places in the Karoo, Matjiesfontein (pronounced 'mikeys-fontein') is a small railway siding around a grand hotel that has remained virtually unchanged for one hundred years. If you're passing this way, you should certainly pause to look around, or better still stay overnight.

The developer of the hotel and surrounding hamlet was one Jimmy Logan, a Scot whose rise through Cape society was so swift that by the age of 36 he not only was a member of parliament, but also ran every railway refreshment room between the Cape and Bulawayo (Zimbabwe). Matjiesfontein was his home base, and the hotel and other accommodation, together with the climate (the crisp air is likened to dry champagne), attracted wealthy people as a health resort.

As well as the attractive old buildings, including a church, courthouse and post office/general store, there's a fascinating **museum** (admission R3; �uclock 8am-5pm Tue, Thu, Sat & Sun, 8.30am-5.30pm Mon, Wed & Fri) in the train station that's a right old jumble sale, containing everything from trophy heads to a collection of commodes.

If you decide to stay, check out the **Lord Milner Hotel** (☎ 551 3011; www.matjiesfontein.com; s/d from R310/480; ☒), a classic period piece with bags of old-world charm. There is a range of comfortable rooms and an atmospheric reception area. Surprisingly, meals in the hotel's **dining room** (mains R40; �uclock 7-9pm), with waitresses in lace bobble caps, are reasonably priced and there is silver service to boot. At night have a drink in the Laird's Arms bar.

Matjiesfontein is just off the N1, 240km from Cape Town and 198km from Beaufort West. A night in the hotel would be worth a stopover on the *Trans Karoo* train trip between Jo'burg and Cape Town, though 24 hours here might be a bit long unless you have a good book. Alternatively, take the train from Cape Town (arriving at 2.46pm), stay the night and catch the 8.25am train back again the next day; it's a 5½-hour trip. The *Blue Train* also pauses here for an hour, with travellers being given a tour of town on the double-decker London bus that stands outside the station.

BEAUFORT WEST

☎ 023 / pop 35,400

Established in 1818, Beaufort West is not only the oldest town in the Karoo, but also the largest. In summer it becomes a sluice gate for the torrent of South Africans heading for the coast. Accommodation is booked out and prices rise. The town serves as a gateway for the nearby Karoo National Park (p249).

Tourist information (☎ 415 1488; cnr Donkin & Church Sts; �uclock 8am-4pm Mon-Fri) is on the main street in the old town hall opposite the church with the tall white spire. Next door is the **museum** (☎ 415 2308; Donkin St; adult/child R5/1; �uclock 8.30am-4.45pm Mon-Fri, 9am-noon Sat), which has displays on local-lad-made-good Dr Christiaan Barnard, who performed the world's first human heart transplant.

Sleeping

If you have tents and transport, go to the Karoo National Park. If not, there are plenty of options in town.

Matopo Inn (☎ 415 1055; fax 415 1080; 7 Bird St; s/d R275/320; breakfast/dinner R45/75; ☒) In the town's old *drostdy*, built in 1834, and set back from the northern end of Donkin St. The rooms have high ceilings, are spacious and decorated with antique furniture. The dinner is a four-course affair.

Ye Olde Thatch (☎ /fax 414 2209; 155 Donkin St; s/d R120/240, mains R40; ☒) There are only four rooms at this small guesthouse and restaurant at the southern end of town, but they're nicely decorated. The leopard-themed restaurant is cool and dark and serves Karoo specialities.

Springbok Lodge (☎ 415 2871; 17 Donkin St; s/d R120/240) In a rambling old Karoo farmhouse, rooms are set back from the road so you don't get street noises. Families can opt for the large self-catering cottages (R480), which sleep four.

Oasis Hotel (☎ /fax 414 3221; 66 Donkin St; d R250; ☒) The Oasis is a relic from the past, albeit in reasonable shape with friendly staff and large rooms.

Donkin House (☎ 414 4287; 14 Donkin St; s/d R160/280; ☒) Motel-style accommodation is on offer at this reasonable budget place at the northern end of the main road.

Formula 1 (☎ 415 2421; www.formula1hotels.com; 144 Donkin St; r R209; ☒) If all you need is a clean bed for the night this sterile chain hotel is good value.

Eating

Mac Young's (☎ 414 4068; 171 Donkin St; breakfast R30, mains R30-50; ☺ breakfast, lunch & dinner) In a strange location next to the Caltex petrol station the Scottish theme is played up to the hilt. The menu here is very large and includes pizza, pasta, seafood, burgers and something for the kids. There's also an Internet café (R15 per half-hour) inside.

Getting There & Away

Beaufort West is a junction for many bus services. **Translux** (☎ 021-449 3333; www.translux.co .za), **Greyhound** (☎ 021-505 6363; www.greyhound.co .za) and **Intercape** (☎ 0861-287 287; www.intercape .co.za) stop at the Total petrol station on Donkin St in the centre of town. Minibuses stop at the BP petrol station on Donkin St. Destinations include Jo'burg (R240, 12 hours, daily), Cape Town (R225, seven hours, daily) and Bloemfontein (R210, six hours, daily). From these cities you can then connect with buses to other parts of the country.

The *Trans Karoo* stops at the station on Church St on its daily journey between Cape Town and Jo'burg.

KAROO NATIONAL PARK

Just 5km to the north of Beaufort West, the **Karoo National Park** (☎ 012-343 1991; www.parks -sa.co.za; adult/child R60/30, camp sites R95, d cottages R380; ☺ 5am-10pm) was proclaimed in 1979, covers 33,000 hectares of impressive Karoo landscapes and representative flora and is run by the SAN Parks Board. The plains carry a variety of short shrubs, with well-wooded dry watercourses and mountain grasslands at higher elevations.

The park has 61 species of mammal, the most common of which are dassies (agile, rodent-like mammals, also called hyraxes) and bat-eared foxes. The antelope population is small but some species have been reintroduced and their numbers are growing. These include the springbok, kudu, gemsbok, reedbuck, red hartebeest and rhebok. The mountain zebra has also been reintroduced, as has the odd black rhino. There are a great many reptiles and birds.

Facilities include a shop and restaurant. There are two short nature trails and an 11km day walk. There are also vehicle routes and day or overnight 4WD guided trails.

Accommodation is either at pleasant camp sites or in Cape Dutch–style cottages. The cottages are fully equipped with kitchens, towels and bedding. Two of the cottages are handicapped accessible.

Public transport will take you to Beauford West (see p209), from where you will need to either hike in or catch a taxi from town; however the rest camp is 10km further into the park.

WEST COAST & SWARTLAND

Wild and jagged coastline and rugged and desolate mountains, a peaceful and quiet whitewashed fishing village and a country town serving up a big dish of South African cabaret all add to the West Coast and Swartland's charm. Although popular with Capetonians seeking a quick break, few overseas visitors head north of Cape Town and up through this region.

Those who do will find a long stretch of wild coastline to the west, home to anglers, resort towns and the West Coast National Park, a bird-lover's paradise. The coastal area is particularly spectacular in late winter and early spring when the dunes are carpeted with a stupendous array of wildflowers. The Cederberg Wilderness Area marks the region's eastern border. A hiker's playground, this remote area is a good place to get lost for a few days. In between the two, and roughly following the N7 north to south, is Swartland (Black Land), a rich agricultural area of rolling plains. It's believed the area's name derives from the dark foliage of the distinctive *renosterbus* scrub that covered the plains. Combined with the winter rainfall, the rich soil enables farmers to produce over 20% of South Africa's wheat, as well as high-quality wine. Here you'll find the country town of Darling, home of a South African entertainment icon Tannie Evita Bezuidenhout.

Most public transport through this area travels from Cape Town north along the N7, either going all the way to Springbok and Namibia or leaving the N7 and heading through Calvinia to Upington. Getting to the coastal towns west of the N7 isn't easy if you don't have a car.

DARLING

☎ 022

Once a quiet country town, Darling catapulted to fame by the presence of Tannie
Evita Bezuidenhout, the alter ego of actor
and satirist Pieter-Dirk Uys. Capetonians
make the 70km trek north by the dozens
on show nights to catch the uniquely South
African cabaret at **Evita se Perron** (☎ 492 2851;
www.evita.co.za; Evita's Platform; tickets R75; ☑ performances 2pm & 8pm Sat, 2pm Sun). The shows, featuring Pieter-Dirk Uys' characters, touch on
everything from South African politics to
history to ecology. Nothing is off limits – including the country's struggle with racism.
Although the shows include a fair smatter-
ing of Afrikaans, there's much for English-
speaking audiences to enjoy, and they are
often hilarious and thought-provoking.

The splendidly kitsch **theatre-restaurant**
(mains R20-40; ☑ lunch & dinner Tue-Sun), in a converted station building next to the railway,
is worth a visit in its own right. The theatre
is painted bright blues and reds, pink lights
are strung from the ceiling and the walls are
cluttered with old posters and paintings.
Food is traditional Afrikaans – chicken pie
and bobotie (curried mince with a topping
of savoury egg custard, usually served on
turmeric-flavoured rice).

While you're here take a walk around the
sculpture garden behind the theatre – pink-
tissue-paper ostriches and green mermaids
lounge in a sea of broken glass.

Darling is so close to Cape Town that
there's no pressing need to stay overnight, although if you choose to, there are some nice
guesthouses. The **Darling Guest House** (☎ 492
3062; 22 Pastorie St; s/d with breakfast R195/330) is an
elegant and imaginatively decorated place.

Arum Inn (☎ 492 3195; 5 Long St; s/d R180/270) has
lots of light and windows to make the big
rooms feel especially spacious. The place
welcomes children.

For an afternoon coffee or all day breakfast, don't miss **Through the Looking Glass**
(☎ 492 2858; 19 Main Rd; breakfast R30). This arty
café with an Internet connection (R40 per
hour) also serves sandwiches and homemade sweet treats.

To get to Darling, drive up the R27
from Cape Town and look for the signs.
It's worth inquiring about the occasional
Saturday excursions to Darling on the **Spier
Train** (☎ 021-419 5222). The 2½-hour trip includes a picnic lunch and admission to the
show at Evita se Perron.

WEST COAST NATIONAL PARK

Encompassing the clear, blue waters of the
Langebaan Lagoon and home to an enormous number of migratory wading birds
is the **West Coast National Park** (☎ 022-772 2144;
admission flower/nonflower season R60/15; ☑ 7am-7pm).
The park covers around 18,000 hectares
and is made up of a peculiar mix of semi-
independent zones, some of which are only
leased by the national park authorities.

The park protects wetlands of international significance and important seabird breeding colonies. Wading birds flock
here by the thousands in summer. The most
numerically dominant species is the curlew
sandpiper, which migrates north from the
sub-Antarctic in huge flocks. Flamingos,
Cape gannets, crowned cormorants, numerous gull species and African black oyster-
catchers are also here. The offshore islands
are home to colonies of jackass penguins.

The vegetation is predominantly made up
of stunted bushes, sedges and many flowering annuals and succulents. There are some
coastal *fynbos* in the east, and the park is
famous for its wildflower display, which is
usually between August and October. Several game species can be seen in the part
of the park known as the Postberg section,
which is open from August to September.
Game species include a variety of small antelopes, wildebeests, bonteboks and elands.

The park is only about 120km from Cape
Town, so it could easily be visited on a day
trip if you have transport. The roads in the
park are dirt and can be quite heavily corrugated. The park, which is clearly signposted,
begins 7km south of Langebaan. The return
trip from Langebaan to the northern end
of the Postberg section is more than 80km;
allow yourself plenty of time.

The only accommodation available in the
park is one houseboat, which costs R800
for four people. Book with the **SAN Parks
Board** (☎ 012-428 9111; www.parks-sa.co.za; 643 Leyds
St, Muckleneuk) in Pretoria.

LANGEBAAN

☎ 022

A rather unusual and beautiful location
overlooking the Langebaan Lagoon has
made this seaside resort a favourite holiday

destination with locals. If you're looking for untouched you might be happier elsewhere, but the town does support an excellent hotel, open-air seafood restaurants, phenomenal sunset views, superb sailing and windsurfing on the lagoon and a few good beaches, the best of which is **Langebaan beach**, in town, a favourite with swimmers. The town is also a good base for exploring the West Coast National Park.

The **Tourist Information Centre** (☎ 772 1515; www.langebaaninfo.com; end of Hoof St; ☽ 9am-5pm Mon-Fri, 9am-12.30pm Sat, 9am-noon Sun) has area information.

Sights & Activities
WEST COAST FOSSIL PARK
The first bear discovered south of the Sahara, lion-sized sabre-toothed cats, three-toed horses and short-necked giraffes are all on display at this **fossil park** (☎ 766-1606; www.museums.org.za/wcfp; admission R45; ☽ 10am-4pm Mon-Fri, 10am-1pm Sat & Sun) on R45 about 16km outside Langebaan. Tours depart daily at 11.30am and take you to the excavation sites. Children can sieve for their own fossils in a special display area.

HORSE RIDING
Two places offer opportunities to ride horses. At the **Oliphantskop Farm Inn** (☎ 772 2326; per hr R90) you can ride along the beach. The Inn is about 3km from Langebaan on the main road. Follow the signs. **Windstone Backpackers** (☎ 772 2326; R45; per hr R85) caters to beginning through advanced riders. You'll catch your own horse, groom it and then ride through the countryside. Windstone is off R45 about 16km from Langebaan.

Sleeping & Eating
Many of the sleeping options also double as restaurants.

Farmhouse (☎ 772 2062; www.thefarmhouselangebaan.co.za; 5 Egret St; s/d with breakfast R500/800; mains R50-80; ☒) This is by far Langebaan's best hotel, on a hill overlooking the bay with lovely sunset views. Rooms are large, with country décor and their own fireplaces. For such a classy place the restaurant is reasonably priced with a creative menu and a rustic, intimate dining room.

Oliphantskop Farm Inn (☎ /fax 772 2326; Main Rd; s/d R150/260; mains R50; ☒) An attractive place around 3km from town, across the road

from the Mykonos resort complex, Oliphantskop's restaurant has a good reputation with nice ambiance – cool and dark with rough white walls and a wooden ceiling. The menu is meat and seafood oriented and offers no vegetarian options.

Windstone Backpackers (☎ 766 1645; www.sawestcoast.com/windstone.html; camp sites per person R50, dm R70, d R180; ☒) Facilities here are quite good, and there's even an indoor swimming pool. The grounds are spacious with lots of trees and the accommodation rustic. Bring all the food and drinks you need for a stay, as this place is kind of in the middle of nowhere.

Club Mykonos (☎ 0800 226 770; theretha@clubmykonos.co.za; 4-person cabins R1550; ☒ ☒) There's a beautiful private beach here in a small alcove with lots of shells. The resort is good for families, as there is plenty here to entertain the kids. It's Greek-themed with pseudo-Mediterranean architecture. You'll either love it or hate it. There are no fewer than six outdoor swimming pools, a casino, restaurants and an arcade.

Die Strandloper (☎ 772 2490; mains R95; ☽ lunch Wed, Sat & Sun, dinner Wed-Sat) This is a rustic open-air seafood restaurant and bar on the beach, outside the town on the way to Mykonos Club, that has an all-you-can eat seafood menu. Call ahead to check it's open – sometimes it just closes.

Getting There & Away
Langebaan is an hour's drive north of Cape Town. You might be able to get here on the **West Coast Shuttle** (☎ 083-556 1777), which operates a minibus service (R60) from Cape Town to Mykonos Club. Otherwise no public transport runs to Langebaan.

SALDANHA
☎ 022
Dominated by an enormous iron-ore pier, navy yards and fish-processing factories, Saldanha is at the northern end of the same lagoon as Langebaan. Despite this, the town's bays are pleasant and, because they are sheltered, much warmer than the ocean. **Hoedjies Bay**, near the town centre, is the most popular for swimming.

The main road into town is Saldanha Rd, and Main (Hoof) Rd runs from the shopping centre up to the headland, along the back bay.

The helpful **information centre** (☎ 714 2088; www.capewestcoast.org; Van Riebeeck St; ☯ 8.30am-4.30pm Mon-Fri, 9am-noon Sat) is uphill from Saldanha Rd.

Boat trips (☎ 714 4235; www.sailboats.co.za; from R50, minimum 3 people) on the harbour and to offshore islands run from the Slipway restaurant in the docks right on the waterfront. There's a R2 charge to enter the harbour area.

Sleeping & Eating

Saldanha Bay Protea Hotel (☎ 714 1264; fax 714 4093; 51B Main Rd; s/d R350; mains R50-70; ☺ ☻) Overlooking the bay, this acceptable midrange chain hotel is much better value at the weekends when the rates drop. There's a lovely lounge looking out on the water. The attached Mussel Cracker Restaurant has the usual seafood, meat and pasta entrées in a classy dining room.

Strandloper Guesthouse (☎ 714 3099; www.strandloper.co.za; 52 Beach Rd; s/d with breakfast R295/395; ☻) Not much to look at from the outside but very pleasant inside; all the neat and tidy rooms have sea views.

Captain's Cabin (☎ 714 1716; 20 Main Rd; mains R30-50; ☯ breakfast, lunch & dinner) Laid-back with a tin-roofed bar and plenty of patio seating. It's a popular spot with lots of seafood as well as a decent selection of pastas and curries. There is often live music, and a big cocktail menu.

Slipway (☎ 714 4235; mains from R40; ☯ breakfast, lunch & dinner) In the docks, right on the waterfront, this is an atmospheric place for a lazy meal.

Getting There & Away

There's at least one minibus a day to Cape Town (about R25) from the corner of Main and Saldanha Rds. Local taxis (ask near the Spar supermarket) run north to Vredenburg (R5), where you can pick up taxis to Paternoster. It's difficult to make connections with taxis heading further up the coast because most run direct from Cape Town along the N7.

PATERNOSTER
☎ 022

Paternoster, a clutch of simple whitewashed homes with green roofs up against the blue sea, sparkles in the sun and is a feast for the eyes. This sleepy fishing village is a low-key kind of place where the local anglers live. Re-

cently it's been discovered by wealthy Capetonians looking for holiday houses. Property is now a hot commodity – there are 'sold' signs left and right and new guesthouses are opening every day. Paternoster is 15km from the missable inland town of Vredenburg.

The surrounding countryside is attractive, the rolling hills scattered with strange granite outcrops. The **Columbine Nature Reserve**, 3km past the town, protects 263 hectares of coastal *fynbos* around Cape Columbine. There's a small, basic **camping & caravan park** (Tietiesbaai; ☎ 752 1718; camp sites R20). Further north along the coast is the similar village of **St Helena Bay**, with a lovely sheltered stretch of water, but no real beach.

Sleeping & Eating

Paternoster is rather lacking in street signs; instead look out for the individual guesthouses signs. B&Bs are opening here on a daily basis, so it may be worth checking out a few places first. During the crayfish season (15 November to late December) you will see the tasty crustaceans for sale on the side of the road for between R25 and R40.

Ahoy! Guesthouse & Restaurant (☎ /fax 752 2725; s/d R220/440; mains R20-70) Some of the nicest rooms in Paternoster are found here – all immaculate with a white theme. There's a very blue kitchen for self-catering and a braai area for cooking your own crayfish; and it's all just a two-minute walk to the beach. The restaurant is seafood oriented. Try the big fish platter (R230), which includes crayfish and prawns and serves up to three people.

Paternoster Hotel (☎ /fax 752 2703; paternosterhotel@webnet.co.za; s/d R160/320) This rough-edged, quirky country hotel, virtually on the beachfront, is a popular venue for those interested in fishing. Its fish and crayfish braais are famous. We warn you, the bar is a feminist's nightmare.

Voorstrandt Restaurant (☎ 752 2038; Strandloperweg; mains R40-95; ☯ breakfast, lunch & dinner) You can hop from this designer red-and-green-painted beach shack right onto the sand. Specialising in seafood, this is also an excellent spot to watch the sunset over a beer.

ELAND'S BAY
☎ 022

Surfers and bird-spotters alike will love Eland's Bay. Mountains run down into the sea and the large lagoon is favoured by

---

GOOFY-FOOTER

Eland's Bay is a goofy-footer's (surfing with the right foot at the front of the board) paradise, with extremely fast left-point waves working at a range of swell sizes. The bay can hold a very big wave. The main left-point break is virtually in front of the hotel, towards the crayfish factory – it breaks along a rocky shelf in thick kelp, after southwesterly winds on a low and incoming tide. There's a right-beach break and more lefts on Baboon Point, along the gravel road past the crayfish factory.

---

all sorts of interesting waterbirds, including flamingos (although they are nomadic and don't hang around). The town itself, though, is ugly.

Accommodation boils down to the basic **municipal caravan park** (camp sites R52). The camp sites are right by the beach, so it's pretty exposed to the wind.

Sandveld Country Cottages (☎ 962 1609; cwykeham@mweb.co.za; R366; camp sites per person R40, cottages per person R80) is 35km from Eland's Bay. The self-catering cottages and camp sites on this farm are the best places to stay in the area.

If you're driving south, it's worth taking the dirt road that runs along the northern bank of the wide and reedy estuary. You can cross over at the hamlet of Rodelinghuys and head south through nice country to the village of Aurora or keep going to join the N7 at Piketberg.

Coming down the dirt road from Lambert's Bay, the turn-off to Eland's Bay takes you onto another dirt road but this has a toll of R15. If you don't want to pay this, head down the toll road a short way and there's a map showing the longer but free route.

LAMBERT'S BAY
☎ 027

A rookery of gannets and a classic seaside braai restaurant help diminish the rather unattractive nature of Lambert's Bay located on a bleak stretch of the West Coast and dominated by fish-processing factories. The **Crayfish Festival** on the first weekend of November is said to be quite lively.

The **information centre** (☎ 432 1000; Church St; 🕙 9am-1pm & 2-5pm Mon-Fri, 9am-1pm Sat) can tell you about area attractions.

Despite the overwhelming pong, birdlovers may be tempted to walk out onto a breakwater to the gannet rookery. Here thousands of aggressive birds mill around making a racket and snapping at each other. They lay eggs between September and November, and the chicks hatch 40 days later.

From July to January you might also spot some humpback whales off the coast, and dolphins are common throughout the year. For boat trips contact **Lambert's Bay Boat Charter** (☎ 432 1927).

Sleeping
Raston Gasthaus (☎ 432 2431; fax 432 2422; 24 Kiedeman St; s/d with breakfast R260/400; 🏊) This guesthouse is smart, if a bit over-the-top in its décor, which includes murals and a small pool.

Lambert Bay Hotel (☎ 432 1126; fax 432 1036; Voortrekker St; s/d with breakfast from R250/390; 🏊) Friendly and comfortable, this is the town's only hotel. It has a pool but is very close to the fish processing factory.

Lambert's Bay Caravan Park (☎ 432 2238; off Korporasie St; camp sites from R50) This place offers basic facilities north of town beside the beach.

Eating
Lambert Bay's two open-air restaurants, which you must book in advance (they'll only open if there are sufficient reservations), offer similar bust-a-gut buffets. To take full advantage set aside at least three hours to work your way through the fish, seafood stews, salads, home-made bread and jams.

Muisbosskerm (☎ 432 1017; meals R90, crayfish R115) This is the original open-air seafood restaurant, 5km south of town along the dirt road towards Eland's Bay, and it's right beside the sea. Bring your own drinks and be prepared to eat with your fingers or use a mussel shell as an impromptu spoon.

Bosduifklip (☎ 432 2735; meals R80) The cheaper, yet strangely slightly more formal of the open-air restaurants, it's 4km before Lambert's Bay just off the main road.

OLIFANTS RIVER VALLEY
The scenery changes dramatically at the Piekenaarskloof Pass; coming north on the N7 you suddenly overlook the intensively cultivated Olifants River Valley. The elephants that explorer Jan Danckaert came

upon in 1660, and which gave their name to the area, are long gone.

Today the river provides irrigation for hectares of grapevines and orange trees, which are beautifully maintained by a huge labour force. The comfortable bungalows of the White farmers are surrounded by green and leafy gardens, masking them from the shanties.

On the valley floor are some acclaimed wineries and coops, which specialise in white wine – you can get details of a wine route at tourist information centres. The eastern side is largely bounded by the spectacular Cederberg Range, which is protected by the extensive Cederberg Wilderness Area. Citrusdal and Clanwilliam, to the southwest and northwest of the wilderness area, are the two main towns in the region.

As an alternative to the N7, there's a spectacular partly tarred road (R303) between Citrusdal and Ceres, a great drive through the Cederberg Wilderness Area from Citrusdal to Clanwilliam, and another memorable route (R364) running between Clanwilliam and Calvinia (in Northern Cape to the northeast).

CEDERBERG WILDERNESS AREA

Bizarre-shaped weathered sandstone formations, San rock art, craggy and rugged mountains and green valleys all make the desolate **Cederberg** (adult/child R18/9) a must-see. The peaks and valleys extend roughly north–south for 100km, between Citrusdal and Vanrhynsdorp. A good proportion is protected by the 71,000-hectare Cederberg Wilderness Area, which is administered by **Cape Nature Conservation** (☎ 028-435 5020; www .capenature.org.za). The highest peaks are Sneeuberg (2027m) and Tafelberg (1969m). San paintings can be found on the rocks and in some of the area's caves.

The area is famous for its plant life, which is predominantly mountain *fynbos*. Spring is the best time to see the wildflowers, although there's plenty of interest at other times of the year. The vegetation varies with altitude but includes the Clanwilliam cedar (which gives the region its name) and the rare snowball protea. The Clanwilliam cedar survives only in relatively small numbers, growing between 1000m and 1500m, and the snowball protea (now limited to isolated pockets) grows only above the snow line.

There are small populations of baboons, rhEBOKS, klipspringers and grysboks; and predators such as caracals, Cape foxes, honey badgers and the rarely seen leopard.

Orientation & Information

The Cederberg is divided into three excellent hiking areas of around 24,000 hectares. Each area has a network of trails. However, this is a genuine wilderness area with a genuine wilderness ethos. You are *encouraged* to leave the trails, and little information is available on suggested routes. It's up to you to survive on your own. Similarly, you probably won't be given directions to the area's rock art. Work out for yourself where the Khoisan were likely to have lived.

There is a buffer zone of conserved land between the wilderness area and the farmland, and here more intrusive activities such as mountain biking are allowed.

There's no real season for walking; from May to the end of September expect rain and possibly snow. From December to April there's likely to be very little water.

A permit is required if you want to walk, and the number of visitors per hiking area is limited to 50 people. The maximum group size is 12 and, for safety, the minimum is two adults. Maps (R14) are available at the Algeria Camping Ground and the office of the **Chief Nature Conservator** (☎ 027-482 2812; Private Bag X6, Citrusdal 7340).

To be certain you'll get a permit, apply well in advance. Outside school holidays and weekends you may be able to get one on the spot, but you should definitely phone before arriving to make sure. Permits must be booked through the Chief Nature Conservation in Cape Town or online. Bookings open on 1 February for the March–June period, 1 June for July–October, and 1 October for November–February. The cost is R25 per person per day, plus the R18 park admission charge.

The entrance to the Algeria Camping Ground closes at 4.30pm (9pm on Friday). You won't be allowed in if you arrive late. You can only collect your permit (if you haven't already organised it in Cape Town or had it posted to you) during office hours, so if you're arriving on Friday evening you'll need to make arrangements.

There are no eating places in the area so you will need to bring your own food.

Sleeping

The camping fees do not include the park admission charge.

Algeria Camping Ground (☎ 027-482 2812; 6-person camp sites R95, d cottages R380) These are exceptional grounds in a beautiful, shaded site alongside the Rondegat River, which is the headwaters of the Olifants River. There are swimming holes and lovely spots to picnic. For those not interested in camping there are fully equipped stone cottages.

Kliphuis State Forest camping ground (☎ 027-482 2812; 6-person camp sites R65) Nestling in the forest, near the Pakhuis Pass on R364, about 15km northeast of Clanwilliam, this is another excellent camping ground. Surrounded by rock walls and cut by a fresh mountain stream, facilities are fairly spartan but there are toilets, showers and water.

You'll need to book either of these camp sites in the same way that you book hiking. There are number of basic huts and cottages for hikers in the wilderness area. These cost about R330/315 on weekends/weekdays for up to four people.

See both Citrusdal (p215) and Clanwilliam (p217) for places to stay outside the Cederberg Wilderness Area.

Getting There & Away

The Cederberg Range is about 200km from Cape Town, accessible from Citrusdal, Clanwilliam and the N7.

There are several roads into Algeria Camping Ground, and they all offer magnificent views. It takes about 45 minutes to get from Clanwilliam by car, much longer if you give in to normal human emotion and stop every now and again. Algeria is not signposted from Clanwilliam, but you just follow the road above the dam to the south. Algeria *is* signposted from the N7 and it's only 20 minutes from the main road; there's an amazing collection of plants, including proteas, along the side of the road.

There are some dusty but interesting back roads that run southeast through the hamlet of Cederberg and on to Ceres. There's a good but tough walk from the farm up to the Wolfsberg Crack, a well-known rock formation. Allow at least seven hours for the return trip.

Public transport into Algeria is nonexistent; walking from Citrusdal, the nearest town, will take about two days.

CITRUSDAL

☎ 022 / pop 4900

The small town of Citrusdal is a good base for exploring the Cederberg. August to September is wildflower season, and the displays can be spectacular. This is also one of the best times for hiking. Although the town itself is quaint, some of the most interesting and beautiful places to stay are in the surrounding mountains. Make sure to explore beyond the town limits – the scenery is stupendous.

The **tourism bureau** (☎ 921 3210; www.citrusdal .info; 39 Voortrekker St; ☽ 8am-5pm Mon-Fri, 8am-1pm Sat) can help you find accommodation in the area and provide information on mountain biking and hiking trails.

If the tourism bureau is closed, head over to **Craig Royston** (☎ 921 2963; Modderfontein Farm; ☽ 8am-5pm), in the large old farm building, 2km out of Citrusdal off the N7. It houses a café (meals are R25), a shop and a small museum – the old shop is where the farm workers still buy their supplies. It hasn't been renovated to within an inch of its life, and is a welcome relief after all those squeaky-clean tourist ventures. There are excellent light meals and you can sample (and buy) local wines. It's also a good place to come for information, and it holds monthly cabaret evenings in Afrikaans.

Sleeping

Elephant Leisure Resort (☎ 921 2204; d R450; 🖳 🖳) There is a private Jacuzzi on the porch of every chalet at this brand-new place in a serene location amid the trees and rocks. Accommodation is in either two- or four-person self-catering chalets with tiled floors, cheery walls and spotless bathrooms. There's a hot-springs swimming pool behind the main building. Elephant Leisure Resort is 9km outside Citrusdal; follow the signs.

Baths (☎ 921 3609; www.thebaths.co.za; camp sites per person R45, d from R270) In a glorious location thick with trees and right up against the craggy peaks is this health spa with two outdoor pools. It's a good place to relax for a couple of days. The pools have superb views and are family friendly. **Day visitors** (adult/child R20/10) are welcome. Prices jump on the weekends. At the time of research the Baths was building a restaurant which looked very promising – it was a modern

ROOIBOS TEA

Rooibos, literally 'red bush', is a red-coloured tea with a distinctive aroma. It's made from the leaves of the *Aspalathus linearis* plant, grown in the Cederberg region of Western Cape.

Malay slaves first discovered that the plant could be used to make a beverage, although it was not until the 20th century that a Russian immigrant Benjamin Ginsberg introduced it to the wider community, and it didn't become a cash crop until the 1930s. Despite this, some brands feature trek wagons and other icons of old Afrikanerdom.

The drink contains no caffeine and much less tannin than normal tea. This is probably its major health benefit, although it's claimed to have others, due to minute amounts of minerals such as iron, copper and magnesium. It's also a great thirst quencher, drunk straight or with lemon or milk.

Tours of one of the main packing plants, **Rooibos Ltd** (☎ 482 2155), just outside Clanwilliam, are available at 10am, 11.30am, 2pm and 3.30pm Monday to Friday.

affair with lots of glass and a fantastic patio. The place is about 18km from Citrusdal on the same road as the Elephant Leisure Resort. It is well signposted.

Staalwater (☎ 921 3337; cottage per person R100) The twisty dirt road climbs past grooves of citrus trees and flowering bushes before ending at the whitewashed farm buildings of Staalwater. The self-catering cottage sleeps eight. The property is large, and there are decent walks on the grounds. Staalwater is 12km from town on the way to the Baths.

Gekko Backpackers Lodge (☎ 921 3353; home .mweb.co.za/vi/vism; camp sites per person R30, dm R50, d with shared bathroom R140) A friendly low-key place on a large citrus farm, 17.5km from Citrusdal on the N7 towards Clanwilliam; activities here include tubing on the adjacent river or hiking through the mountains and caves on the enormous property – there are even San rock art trails on the grounds. Bring your own food, as there is no restaurant, just an honesty bar.

Tree Tops (☎ 921 3626; www.citrusdal.info/kardouw; d R200) In a poplar forest by the Olifants River, 12km further on from the Baths, the wooden chalets here are on stilts. It's a great place, but you'll need to bring everything with you and book well ahead.

Cederberg Lodge (☎ 921 2221; www.cedarberglodge .co.za; Voortrekker St; s/d R170/230; breakfast R40, mains R50; 🍴 🖥) Recently renovated, this hotel has large rooms with TVs. The attached restaurant focuses on meat and seafood.

Eating

Patrick's Restaurant (☎ 921 3062; 77 Voortrekker St; mains from R50; 🕑 noon-2.30pm Tue-Fri, 7-11pm Mon-Thu, 7pm-midnight Fri & Sat) This is the best,

and practically the only, place for dinner in town. It does good steaks and, for some reason, pizza with banana topping.

Uitspan Café (☎ 921 3273; 39 Voortrekker St; mains from R30; 🕑 breakfast & lunch) This bright café next to the tourism bureau does sandwiches, salads and cakes.

Getting There & Around

Intercape (☎ 0861 287 287; www.intercape.co.za) buses stop at the petrol station on the N7 highway outside town. Destinations include Cape Town (R125, three hours) and Springbok (R165, five hours).

There's an excellent scenic road (R303) over Middelburg Pass into the Koue (Cold) Bokkeveld and a beautiful valley on the other side, which is only topped by the Gydo Pass and the view over the Ceres Valley. The back road into the wilderness area is also excellent.

CLANWILLIAM

☎ 027 / pop 29,000

The adjacent dam and some adventurous dirt roads into the Cederberg make the compact town of Clanwilliam a popular weekend resort. Well-preserved examples of Cape Dutch architecture and trees line the main street. The dam is a favourite with water skiers.

The **information centre** (☎ 482 2024; 🕑 8.30am-5pm Mon-Sat, 8.30am-12.30pm Sat) is at the top end of the main street, across from the old *tronk* (jail in Afrikaans).

While up here, if you have the time, travel out to **Wuppertal** (inquiries ☎ 482 3410). This Moravian mission station, 74km southeast of Clanwilliam, dates back to 1830 and is reached along a gravel road. The original church and the workshops – where hand-made leather shoes (called *velskoene*) are still made – are worth seeing.

Sleeping & Eating

Clanwilliam Dam Municipal Caravan Park & Chalets (☎ 482 8000; camp sites R50, 6-person chalets R350) This caravan park overlooks the water-skiing action on the other side of the dam from the N7. Travellers arriving here after weeks in Namibia will be pleased to pitch their tents on lush, grassy sites. The chalets are very nice but you need to book ahead for school holidays and weekends.

Strassberger's Hotel Clanwilliam (☎ 482 1101; strassberger@lando.co.za; Main St; s/d R185/370; dinner R75; ☒) This comfortable and popular country pub has been well renovated. The rooms in the annexe (in a de-licensed pub nearby) are quite acceptable. There is a set-price dinner nightly.

Saint du Barrys (☎ /fax 482 1537; 13 Augsburg Dr; s/d with breakfast R300/500; ☒) This pleasant guesthouse is in a thatched-roof house with decent-sized rooms.

Bushman's Kloof (☎ 482 2627; www.bushmanskloof .co.za; s/d R2800/3800; ☒ ☒) This is an upmarket private reserve, 34km east of Clanwilliam along the Pakhuis Pass, known for its excellent San rock-art sites and extensive animal and birdlife. If you've got the cash, staff can also arrange fly-in safaris from Cape Town.

Reinhold's (☎ 482 2678; Main St; mains from R50; ☒ dinner Tue-Sat) This à la carte restaurant is run by the Strassberger's Hotel Clanwilliam and specialises in fish and grills. It's the most popular place in town for dinner. Book ahead as it often fills up.

Oliphantshuis (☎ 482 2301; Main St; mains from R40; ☒ dinner) A delightful garden with a cherub fountain makes this pub-restaurant in a big house a nice place for a drink on a hot night.

Getting There & Away

All the buses that go through Citrusdal also go through Clanwilliam. It's about 45 minutes between the two. Minibus taxis running between Springbok (R80, five hours) and Cape Town (R70, three hours) go through Clanwilliam, stopping at the post office.

Eastern Cape

Eastern Cape's long coastline extends from the forests of the Tsitsikamma National Park, eastwards past Cape St Francis and Jeffrey's Bay (famous for their surf), through Port Elizabeth and the Sunshine and Shipwreck Coasts to East London. Beyond East London, as far as Port Edward just over the border in KwaZulu-Natal, is the spectacular, subtropical Wild Coast. Inland, the genteel 'settler country' around Grahamstown gives way to the plains of the Karoo, dotted with intriguing towns such as Graaff-Reinet and artistic settlements like Nieu Bethesda.

This is a region of frontiers, with a long history of conflict. In the 19th century, land-hungry Boers and fierce Xhosa warriors fought eight wars along the Great Kei River, and British forces struggled to combat Boer guerrillas in the north. Later, leaders of the war on apartheid lived, and in some cases died, in the region. Famous Eastern Cape activists include President Thabo Mbeki, Nelson Mandela, Steve Biko, Robert Sobukwe, Chris Hani and Oliver Tambo.

Xhosa culture dominates the former apartheid homelands of Transkei and Ciskei, nominally independent republics that were used as a dumping ground for economically unviable populations. Today these regions celebrate their heritage with institutions such as the famous Nelson Mandela Museum in Umtata. For those who prefer natural history, a number of excellent wildlife parks, such as the Addo Elephant Park and the Shamwari Game Reserve, are making the Eastern Cape a viable (and malaria-free) safari alternative to eastern parks such as the Kruger.

EASTERN CAPE

HIGHLIGHTS

- Hiking or riding the spectacular **Wild Coast** with its crashing waves, shipwrecks, spectacular gorges and hidden waterfalls (p262)

- Puffing on a clay pipe or drinking millet beer in the Xhosa villages of the former **Transkei** (p262)

- Taking in the eerie, endless spaces and desolate valleys of the **Karoo** near Nieu Bethesda (p243)

- Admiring the 360-degree views or meditating in the forest glades of **Hogsback**, centre of New Age culture (p254)

- Spending tranquil hours by a waterhole with the elephants of **Addo Elephant National Park** (p235)

- Strolling down the well-kept streets of exquisite **Graaff-Reinet**, the most beautiful town in the province (p243)

- Searching for the elusive Cape clawless otter in the magnificent **Tsitsikamma National Park** (p222)

- Visiting the **Nelson Mandela Museum** in Umtata, a celebration of the life of Mandela and of the struggle for freedom (p271)

| POPULATION: 6,514,500 | AREA: 169,580 SQ KM |

EASTERN CAPE

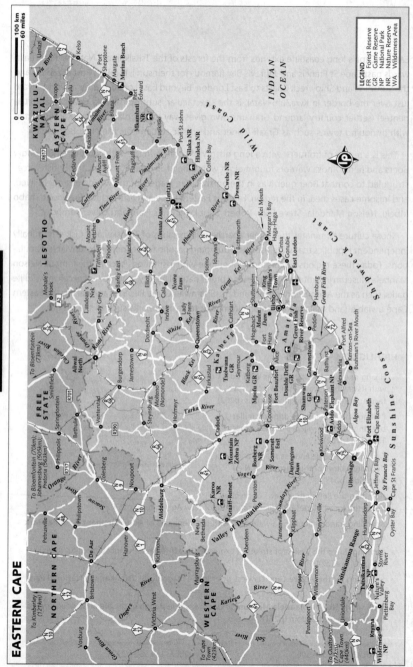

LEGEND
FR Forest Reserve
GR Game Reserve
NP National Park
NR Nature Reserve
WA Wilderness Area

CLIMATE

The rainfall and climate of Eastern Cape reflect the region's geographic variation, with a moderate climate on the coast, heavy rainfall (including snow in winter) in the mountains and low rainfall on the fringes of the Karoo. Average temperatures in East London and Port Elizabeth range from 26°C in summer to 21°C in the winter months of June–August, while further inland in the Karoo, temperature variations are far more extreme, with the thermometer plunging to around 6°C in winter, and rising as high as 40°C in summer.

NATIONAL PARKS & RESERVES

The Eastern Cape is scattered with national parks and private reserves, wildly varying in quality and facilities. Flora and fauna are just as varied – from the large pachyderms at Addo Elephant National Park (p235) and the rare Cape Mountain zebra at Mountain Zebra National Park (p245) near Cradock to the subtler attraction of rare plants in the remote Dwesa Nature Reserve (p266).

LANGUAGE

Start practising those tongue clicks – Xhosa is the predominant language in the Eastern Cape. Whites here speak either English or Afrikaans.

GETTING THERE & AROUND

Travelling around the western side of the Eastern Cape isn't too hard – numerous bus services ply the route between Cape Town, Port Elizabeth and East London (which also both have international airports), stopping at major towns on the way and continuing to Durban, Johannesburg (Jo'burg) and Pretoria.

Further off the beaten track, notably in the former Transkei and the Eastern Highlands, users of public transport will have to take to the minibus taxis to find their way into more obscure spots. Some places in the highlands and on the Wild Coast are only accessible on foot or horseback.

Even if you have your own car, travel isn't always simple – in many parts of the Wild Coast, for instance, there are no reliable maps and no signposts, but there are lots of stray cows, pigs and children wandering the roads.

WESTERN REGION

The western region includes the self-designated 'Sunshine Coast', which encompasses the coastline running from Nature's Valley to Port Alfred. Further inland is Grahamstown, at the heart of the region once settled by British immigrants. Also in this region are the recently extended Addo Elephant National Park and the upmarket Shamwari Game Reserve.

NATURE'S VALLEY

☎ 044

Nature's Valley is a small village nestled in yellowwood forest (*outeniqua* or 'they who bear honey'; thought to be derived from the name of a Khoisan group once resident in the forest) next to a magnificent beach in the west of Tsitsikamma National Park. This is where the Otter Trail ends and the Tsitsikamma Trail begins (see p222) but if you don't want to walk for that long, there are plenty of shorter hikes in the area.

Nature's Valley Trading Store & Information Centre (☎ /fax 531 6835; Beach Rd) is the hub of the village, incorporating a pub-restaurant and a small shop. Staff here can help with pamphlets on the surrounding area.

Sleeping & Eating

Nature's Valley Rest Camp (☎ 531 6700, bookings ☎ 012-428 9111; reservations@parks-sa.co.za; 1-2 person camp sites R100, forest huts d R230) This is the national park camping ground, east of town and a 2km walk from the beach. It's a lovely spot at the edge of a river with clean ablutions and shared kitchens and laundry. There's a 17% discount on forest huts from May to August and a 35% discount on camping from May to November.

Hikers Haven (☎ /fax 531 6805; patbond@mweb.co.za; 411 St Patrick's Ave; dm R70, d with breakfast R250) Just minutes from the beach, Hikers Haven is a large and very comfortable home with an attic dorm for backpackers and hikers. It's deservedly popular with Otter Trail groups, so bookings are essential. The guesthouse can arrange transport to the start of the Otter Trail.

Tourist Lodge (☎ 531 6681; 218 St Georges Ave; d R350) Self-catering apartments behind the owner's house, sleeping two or four people. Each has a kitchen, braai (barbecue), bathroom and garden area. There's a two-night minimum stay.

Tranquility Lodge (☎ 042-531 6663, 083-259 4609; www.tranquilitylodge.co.za; Beach Rd; s/d with breakfast R500/1000; 🖳) The only 'proper' hotel in Nature's Valley is just the place for some self-pampering after a hard hike. Rooms are very elegantly furnished with natural woods and unbleached cotton, and accommodation comes with some interesting trimmings including a personal mountain bike and kayak. There's a heated Jacuzzi, and fine food and wine on offer in the evenings.

Getting There & Away

There's no public transport to Nature's Valley, although the **Baz Bus** (☎ 021-439 2323; www.bazbus.com) will drop off or pick up here on request.

TSITSIKAMMA NATIONAL PARK

This **park** (adult/child R80/40; ⏲ 24hr at Storms River Mouth Rest Camp) protects 82km of coast between Plettenberg Bay and Humansdorp, including the area 5km out to sea.

The park lies at the foot of the Tsitsikamma Range and is cut by rivers that have carved deep ravines into the ancient forests. The flora varies from huge stinkwood and yellowwood trees to ferns, lilies, orchids and coastal fynbos, including proteas. It's a spectacular area to walk through.

The elusive Cape clawless otter, after which the Otter Trail is named, inhabits this park; there are also baboons, monkeys and small antelopes. Birdlife is plentiful.

Several short day walks give you a taste of the coastline if you don't have time to tackle the longer hikes such as the Otter Trail. The waterfall circuit (four hours) on the first part of the Otter Trail is recommended.

Orientation & Information

The main information centre for the national park is Storms River Mouth Rest Camp (opposite), 68km from Plettenberg Bay, 99km from Humansdorp and 8km from the N2. The park gate is 6km from the N2. It's 2km from the gate to the main camp, which has accommodation, a restaurant and a shop selling supplies, as well as an information/reception centre. You can also pay park entrance fees and get information at Nature's Valley Rest Camp (p221).

Otter, Dolphin & Tsitsikamma Trails

The 42km **Otter Trail** (per person R450) is one of the most acclaimed hikes in South Africa, hugging the coastline from Storms River Mouth to Nature's Valley. The walk, which lasts five days and four nights, involves fording a number of rivers and gives access to some superb stretches of coast. A good level of fitness is required for the walk, as it goes uphill and down quite steeply in many places.

Book the trail through the **South African National Parks office** (☎ 012-428 9111; www.parks-sa.co.za; 643 Leyds St, Muckleneuk) in Pretoria. The trail is usually booked up one year ahead. There are often cancellations, however, so it's always worth trying, especially if you are in a group of only two or three people (single hikers are not permitted).

Accommodation is in six-bed rest huts with mattresses but without bedding, cooking utensils or running water. Camping is not allowed.

The 64km **Tsitsikamma Trail** begins at Nature's Valley and ends at Storms River, running parallel to the Otter Trail but taking you inland through the forests. This hike also takes five days and four nights, although it's considered to be easier than the Otter Trail. You only need to pay accommodation costs for the hiking **huts** (per person per night R50).

Unlike the Otter Trail, there is little difficulty getting a booking, and midweek you may have the trail to yourself, except during school holidays. Accommodation is in huts. Book both the trail and accommodation through the **Forestry Department** (☎ 012-481 3615; Private Bag X313, Pretoria, 0001) in Pretoria or contact Nature's Valley Rest Camp (p221) for information.

The **Dolphin Trail** (per person R2250) is ideal for hikers who don't want to carry heavy equipment or sleep in huts. Accommodation on this three-night, four-day hike, which runs from Storms River Mouth to the banks of the Sandrif River, is in comfortable hotels, and luggage is carried on vehicles between overnight stops. The price includes all accommodation and meals, guides and a boat trip into the Storms River Gorge on the way back. To book, contact the **Tsitsikamma National Park office** (☎ 042-281 1607) or look at www.dolphintrail.co.za.

Sleeping & Eating

Storms River Mouth Rest Camp (bookings ☎ 012-428 9111; www.parks-sa.co.za; camp sites/forest huts/family cottages R140/230/730) This camp offers forest huts, chalets, cottages and 'oceanettes'; all except the forest huts are equipped with kitchens (including utensils), bedding and bathrooms. All accommodation except the forest huts is discounted by 10% between May and August. There's a 35% discount on camping from May to November.

Storms River Restaurant (☎ 042-281 1190; mains R70; ⏾ breakfast, lunch & dinner) at the reception complex has great views over the coast and reasonable prices. There's also a small shop and an outdoor terrace with a boardwalk over the rocks to the river mouth.

For information on Nature's Valley Rest Camp, see p221.

Getting There & Away

There is no public transport to either Nature's Valley or Storms River Mouth Rest Camps. Greyhound, Intercape and Translux buses run along the N2 (see p138 and p234 for contact details in Cape Town and Port Elizabeth), from where it's an 8km walk to Storms River Mouth. The **Baz Bus** (☎ 021-439 2323) stops at Nature's Valley (see p598 for more details).

STORMS RIVER

☎ 042

Watch out for confusion between Storms River village and Storms River Mouth in Tsitsikamma National Park. From the N2 the Storms River signpost points to the village that lies outside the national park. The turn-off is 4km east of the turn-off to the national park, which is signed as Storms River Mouth (or Stormsriviermund in Afrikaans).

Storms River is a tiny and scattered hamlet with tree-shaded lanes, a couple of places to stay and an outdoor centre. **Tsitsikamma Tourism Information Office** (☎ 280 3561; www.tsitsikamma.net) at the Petro Port petrol station on the N2 provides information.

East of the village on the N2 is the **Big Tree**, a huge, 36m-high yellowwood, and a forest with many fine examples of candlewood, stinkwood and assegai. The 4.2km **Ratel Trail** (admission R4) begins here, with signs describing the trees in this forest, one of the best preserved in South Africa.

Activities

The world's highest **bungee jump** (216m) is at the Bloukrans River Bridge, 21km west of Storms River directly under the N2. The jump costs R550, but if you're not sure if you can do it, you can walk out to the jumping-off point under the bridge for R80. There are also plans to introduce a 'Flying Fox' slide under the bridge. Book direct (☎ 281 1458; www.faceadrenalin.com) or through your hostel, or just turn up at the site between 9am and 5pm daily.

Most of the other activities on offer at Storms River are organised by **Storms River Adventures** (☎ 281 1836; www.stormsriver.com; Darnell St, Storms River), which offers heart-pumping activities such as black-water tubing (R295) down Storms River, abseiling (R120) and a tree canopy slide (R395), as well as mountain bike trails (R75) and a combined tubing, abseil and mountain bike day in Storms River Gorge (R495).

Sleeping & Eating

BUDGET

Storms River Rainbow Lodge (☎ 281 1530; rainbowl@lantic.net; 72 Darnell St; dm/d with shared bathroom R50/180; 🖳) This is a comfortable, quiet and homely backpackers, with lovely gardens at the back. There's one **self-catering cottage** (d R250) sleeping up to four or five people, and some rooms with private bathrooms inside the house. A healthy breakfast costs R25.

Tube 'n' Axe (☎ 281 1757; tube-n-axe@telkomsa.net; cnr Darnell & Saffron Sts; camp sites R50, dm/d with shared bathroom R70/200; 🖳) This is the more raucous of the two backpackers in Storms River Village – the dorms are small and near the bar, which pumps with adrenaline junkies reliving their experiences and sinking the hostel's own-brand beer. Quad biking and skydiving can be arranged.

MID-RANGE

Tsitsikamma Village Inn (☎ 281 1711; www.village-inn.co.za; d from R295; 🐾) This tranquil and genteel old-fashioned inn has rooms of different architectural styles, each with a four-poster bed and individual décor, set around a lawn. There's a restaurant and bar, which are popular with tour groups.

Ploughman's Rest (☎ 281 1726; www.ploughmansrest.co.za; 31 Formosa St; s/d with breakfast R205/370) This friendly B&B is just off the eastern side of the road before you enter Storms

River. Most rooms have an extra double bunk bed for kids, and self-catering studios are available.

Armagh Country Guest House (☎ 281 1557; www .thearmagh.com; d R350; 🖭) This homely guesthouse has a relaxing feel to it. The **Rafters restaurant** (meals R100; 🕑 lunch & dinner) serves hearty five-course dinners of home-cooked South African fare.

Bloukrans Backpackers Lodge (☎ 281 1450; www.tsitsikamma.org.za; dm/d with shared bathroom R65/140) This functional backpackers is right next to the bungee jump site and near the start of some shorter walking trails. You'll need a car – there are no facilities nearby.

TOP END

Tsitsikamma Lodge (☎ 250 3802; www.tsitsikamma .com; d low/high season R385/425, deluxe ste low/high season R405/445; 🖭) This lodge, 8km east of Storms River, is a group of log cabins set close together round a very tidy garden. The deluxe rooms have an open fireplace, spa bath and CD player. But it's too close to the road to have a wilderness feel, and all slightly tacky, particularly the coy 'striptease river trail'.

Getting There & Away

The **Baz Bus** (☎ 021-439 2323) stops at Storms River, but there's no other public transport to the village. Buses and minibus taxis running along the N2 could drop you off at Bloukrans River Bridge or Tsitsikamma Lodge, both right next to the road, from where it's a 2km walk.

HUMANSDORP

☎ 042

Humansdorp is an uninspiring town 87km southwest of Port Elizabeth. Its main interest for travellers lies in its position between the coastal resorts of Cape St Francis and St Francis Bay. This is where you'll get off the Greyhound bus en route for Jeffrey's Bay.

Information is available from the **Humansdorp Tourism Office** (☎ 295 1361; fax 291 0567; 24 Du Plessis St).

There are a number of B&Bs in Humansdorp; expect to pay around R120 per person. Contact the publicity association for details. The town's only hotel is the rundown **Palm Inn Hotel** (☎ /fax 295 1233; 16 Alexander St; d with breakfast R280).

Greyhound and Translux stop daily at the Total petrol station en route from Cape Town (R185, 10 hours) to Port Elizabeth. The **Baz Bus** (☎ 021-439 2323) will drop off or pick up at Wimpy on the main street on request.

CAPE ST FRANCIS

☎ 042

Cape St Francis, 22km south of Humansdorp, is a small and unpretentious town chiefly famous for the Seal Point and Bruce's Beauties surf breaks. If the surf's not up or you prefer land-based activities, you can walk up the **lighthouse** (admission R10), built in 1888 and the tallest masonry tower on the South African coast, or enjoy a late-afternoon drink at the so-called 'Sunset Rocks'. Whales can be seen offshore between July and November.

St Francis Bay is an ever-growing upmarket resort 10km north of Cape St Francis, partially constructed around a network of canals. Visiting off season, when many of the holiday homes are deserted, the town has a rather bleak and surreal air to it. It does, however, come to life in the high season, when it's jam-packed with sun-seeking yuppies zooming around the canals on speedboats or swimming off the beach.

There is some evidence to suggest that the scale of development around St Francis Bay is starting to impact on the supply of windblown sand to beaches in the area, an environmentally damaging phenomenon known as 'sand starvation'.

Sleeping & Eating

Seal Point Lodge & Backpackers (☎ 298 0284; www .seals.co.za; Da Gama Way; dm/d R70/200; 🖭) This well-located lodge is just 200m from the legendary Seal Point. Dorms are clean, and the spacious doubles in self-catering units are good value. Downstairs you'll find the lively **Full Stop Pub** (mains R15-25), which also does food. Boards and wetsuits can be hired, and hiking, fishing and kite surfing arranged.

Lyngenfjord House (☎ 298 0444, 082-557 4206; www.lyngenfjord.co.za; 7 Lyngenfjord Rd; s/d with breakfast R420/660; 🖭) A classy but friendly B&B, exquisitely furnished and surrounded by panoramic views. Dinner is available and includes local specialities such as blesbok and calamari. Some rooms have private balconies; try to get one facing the sea. Prices go up slightly in high season (December to April).

SURFING IN EASTERN CAPE *Chester Mackley & David Malherbe*

Eastern Cape's coast is one of the greatest and most consistent surfing regions in the world. Head the Kombi anywhere between Jeffrey's Bay and Port Edward for excellent, uncrowded surf, and meet some of the friendliest locals.

Jeffrey's Bay is world famous and those with the slightest interest in the motion of the waves will have heard of Supertubes. In July it hosts the Billabong Pro and in August the Pro Junior competition – partying, bands and a few hangovers are commonplace. Keep your eye on the low-pressure systems – anything below 970 millibars and you will be in heaven.

Heading north, **Port Elizabeth** is at its best with an unusual easterly swell or a big south swell and a southwesterly wind. With the right conditions, excellent waves can be found, particularly at the Fence, a hollow wedging left on the south side of the harbour wall.

Rock on to **Port Alfred** where there are excellent right-handers from the eastern pier of this sleepy fishing town.

Then on to **East London**, home of the legendary Nahoon Reef, a world-class right-hander known to be one of the most consistent waves in the country. This thick, juicy wave rises from deep water and thumps down on a boulder reef. If you find yourself stuck in the bowl, this wave will rattle your bones. Nahoon Beach and the Corner are the nursery for East London grommets and ideal for debutantes wanting to learn to surf. Buy the dudes at Buccaneers pub a beer and they'll let you in on Graveyards, Yellow Sands and Igoda.

Further north is **Wacky Point**, a great barrelling right-hander on a big swell. Then finally there's the **Wild Coast**, which boasts some of the most spectacular coastline you will ever see and point breaks reputed to be as good as Supertubes, some known and many others as yet unnamed and yet to be surfed.

EASTERN CAPE

Cape St Francis Resort (☎ 298 0054; www.cape stfrancis.co.za; Da Gama Way; camp sites/d R38/165, Christmas season R250/400; ☒) The various chalets and units at this well-run resort are big, clean and attractive, many with TV and outside kitchen. There's a restaurant, a small shop and a bar on site.

Getting There & Away
There's no public transport to Cape St Francis, but the Seal Point Backpackers (opposite) will pick up from the Baz Bus drop off at Humansdorp

JEFFREY'S BAY
☎ 042 / pop 11,800
Once a sleepy seaside town, 'J Bay' is now South Africa's foremost centre of surfing and surf culture. Boardies from all over the planet flock here to ride waves such as the famous Supertubes, once described as 'the most perfect wave in the world'. June to September are the best months for experienced surfers, but novices can learn year-round.

Development is raging at a furious pace, with shopping in the myriad clothing stores almost overtaking surfing as the main leisure activity, but so far the local board-waxing vibe has been retained. The biggest surf crowd comes to town every July for the Billabong Pro championship.

Information
There are several ATMs in Da Gama Rd, the main street.
Atlantic Internet Café (☎ 293 2399; Da Gama Rd; per min R0.50; ☒ 7.30am-5.30pm Mon-Fri, 8am-3pm Sat) Also puts digital photos onto CD and provides free tea and coffee.
Jeffrey's Bay Tourism (☎ 293 2923; fax 293 2924; Da Gama Rd; ☒ 8.30am-5pm Mon-Fri, 9am-noon Sat, 10am-2pm Sun) Friendly and helpful, and can make bookings for accommodation.

Sights & Activities
The **Shell Museum** (☎ 293 1111, ext 286; Drommedaris St; admission by donation; ☒ 9am-4pm Mon-Sat, 9am-1pm Sun), next to the information office, contains over 350 deep-water and rare shells. They look beautiful but rather sad in glass boxes out of the sea.

For nonsurfers, there is **windsurfing** and great **bird-watching** at Kabeljous Beach, **sandboarding** on nearby dunes, or **dolphin-** and **whale-watching** from many of the surrounding beaches. Sandboarding is just like snowboarding, with sand dunes replacing the

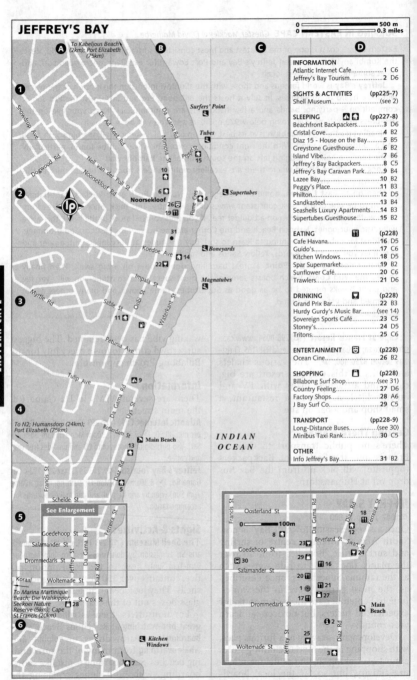

JEFFREY'S BAY

0 ————————— 500 m
0 ————————— 0.3 miles

INFORMATION
Atlantic Internet Cafe.................1 C6
Jeffrey's Bay Tourism.................2 D6

SIGHTS & ACTIVITIES   (pp225-7)
Shell Museum..........................(see 2)

SLEEPING   (pp227-8)
Beachfront Backpackers............3 D6
Cristal Cove............................4 B2
Diaz 15 - House on the Bay........5 B5
Greystone Guesthouse..............6 B2
Island Vibe.............................7 B6
Jeffrey's Bay Backpackers..........8 C5
Jeffrey's Bay Caravan Park.........9 B4
Lazee Bay..............................10 B2
Peggy's Place.........................11 B3
Philton...................................12 D5
Sandkasteel...........................13 B4
Seashells Luxury Apartments......14 B3
Supertubes Guesthouse............15 B2

EATING   (p228)
Cafe Havana..........................16 D5
Guido's..................................17 C6
Kitchen Windows.....................18 D5
Spar Supermarket....................19 B2
Sunflower Café........................20 C6
Trawlers................................21 D6

DRINKING   (p228)
Grand Prix Bar........................22 B3
Hurdy Gurdy's Music Bar..........(see 14)
Sovereign Sports Café...............23 C5
Stoney's.................................24 D5
Tritons...................................25 C6

ENTERTAINMENT   (p228)
Ocean Cine.............................26 B2

SHOPPING   (p228)
Billabong Surf Shop.................(see 31)
Country Feeling.......................27 D6
Factory Shops.........................28 A6
J Bay Surf Co..........................29 C5

TRANSPORT   (pp228-9)
Long-Distance Buses...............(see 30)
Minibus Taxi Rank...................30 C5

OTHER
Info Jeffrey's Bay....................31 B2

snow. At **Aloe Afrika Sandboarding** (☎ 082-576 4259; aloe@agnet.co.za; Marina Martinique; 2hr sessions R200), punters can try their luck on the slopes with instruction, while care is taken to minimise the impact on the environment.

Tours

Info Jeffrey's Bay (☎ 296 2563; www.infojeffreysbay .co.za; Da Gama Rd) is a private information office that can organise a range of tours and activities in the region, including horseriding, mountain biking, sandboarding, and township tours with local guides.

Sleeping

Like many places in this part of Eastern Cape, J Bay is rammed solid with holidaymakers between mid-December and mid-January, so you'll have to book way ahead for accommodation at this time. There's a good range of B&Bs and backpackers but no really upmarket hotels.

BUDGET

Island Vibe (☎ 293 1625; ivibe@lantic.net; 10 Dageraad St; camp sites/dm/d R40/60/200) The most popular backpackers in town, Island Vibe is a bit out of town but the attendant raft of surfies attests to its prime location. Activities on offer include **surf lessons** (incl board & wetsuit R170), drumming, horse-riding and kite surfing, plus of course plenty of drinking and partying. For those wanting a quieter time, the new, beautifully decorated beach house has double rooms only and a separate kitchen. Breakfast and dinner are on offer in the open-air restaurant.

Peggy's Place (☎ 082-506 4034; pegjbay@yahoo .com; 8A Oribi St; camp sites/dm/d R35/50/200) This is a rustic, friendly place in a comfortable old house on the outskirts of town, near the surf area and highly recommended by readers. A self-catering flat is available for R200/R300 in the low/high season.

Cristal Cove (☎ 293 2101; www.cristalcove.co.za; 49 Flame Cres; dm/d R60/180; 🖳) Offering clean, smart rooms within self-catering flats, Cristal Cove is a far cry from your run-of-the-mill backpackers. It's only 100m from the beach, very near Supertubes. Free pick-ups can be arranged from the buses at Humansdorp.

Jeffrey's Bay Backpackers (☎ 293 1379; back pac@netactive.co.za; 12 Jeffrey St; dm/s/d R50/80/120; 🖳) Quiet and functional but somewhat lacking in atmosphere, this backpackers is conveniently near the centre of town and has lots of local information. There are bicycles and surfboards for hire, surf lessons and a free shuttle to Supertubes when the surf's up.

Beachfront Backpackers (☎ 293 3363; 082-892 1689; 36 Diaz Rd; dm R50) Right on Main Beach, this place has pretty basic facilities but a great position and a friendly vibe. There's plenty of parking for the Kombi out front.

Jeffrey's Bay Caravan Park (☎ 200 2241; fax 293 1114; Da Gama Rd; camp sites low/high season R65/125) This park is a bit exposed but strategically located beside the sea midway between the town centre and the surf.

MID-RANGE

Jeffrey's Bay Tourism can put you in touch with a good selection of B&Bs and self-catering establishments.

Philton (☎ /fax 293 1287; 25 Diaz Rd; 2-/3-bedroom flats R250/460) Right on the beach, Philton doesn't look particularly good from the outside but don't be fooled. It has huge and excellent-value self-catering units with balconies and fantastic sea views. Prices go up by R50 in high season.

Lazee Bay (☎ /fax 296 2090; lazeebay@worldonline .co.za; 25 Mimosa St; d with breakfast R300; 🖳) This guesthouse has fabulously vibrant décor. The outside is painted bright blue and features ocean scenes, while the rooms, all different, have funky and comfortable furnishings, TV, minibar and great sea views. There's a pool deck, a braai area and a bar.

Supertubes Guesthouse (☎ 293 2957; www.super tubesguesthouse.co.za; 10/12 Pepper St; s/d with breakfast R350/500, s/d luxury rooms with breakfast R550/800; 🖳 🖳) Supertubes, as its name suggests, is right in J Bay's prime surfing spot and provides luxurious accommodation with very smart bedrooms, sharing a kitchen. Surf lessons can be arranged.

Diaz 15 – House on the Bay (☎ 293 1779; www .diaz15.co.za; 15 Diaz Rd; 2-bedroom flats low/high season R900/R1250; 🖳) This place has luxury apartments with tiled floors, leather sofas, and patio doors opening onto well-kept lawns. There's an infinity pool right on the ocean's doorstep.

Greystone Guesthouse (☎ 296 0616; greystone@ telkomsa.net; 11 Mimosa St; d with breakfast low/high season R360/500; 🖳 🖳) A friendly and fairly upmarket B&B with a range of rooms and studios. All are clean, new and modern, and many have a corner bath, fridge or kitchenette.

There's an outdoor Jacuzzi and a pool table too. Dinner can be arranged on request.

Sandkasteel (☎ 293 1505; www.sandkasteel.co.za; 3 Diaz Rd; 2-/3-bedroom flats R320/530) Good-value flats, each with a braai, close to the beach. There are units here for one person from R75.

Seashells Luxury Apartments (☎ 293 1104; www .seashell.co.za; 125 Da Gama Rd; 2-/3-bedroom flats R630/840; ☒) The spacious Seashells apartments are well located directly in front of Magnatubes.

Eating

Die Walskipper (☎ 082-800 9478; Marina Martinique; seafood platters R120; ☽ lunch & dinner Tue-Sat, lunch Sun) This alfresco restaurant is just metres from the lapping sea at the Marina Martinique beach. It specialises in seafood plus crocodile and ostrich steaks. At weekends, the long trestle tables are packed with locals enjoying giant platters of oysters, calamari, crab and langoustine.

Sunflower Café (☎ 293 1682; 20 Da Gama Rd; mains R40; ☽ breakfast, lunch & dinner, closed Wed & Sun evening) This bright, cheerful and friendly café does some healthy and vegetarian options.

Kitchen Windows (☎ 293 2430; Diaz Rd; mains R36-50; ☽ lunch & dinner Tue-Sun) One of the town's more upmarket eateries, with a great view of the sea and some splendid fresh fish to go with it. There's a good selection of salads for lunch. Enter on Diaz Rd.

Cafe Havana (☎ 293 3260; Malhoek Centre, Da Gama Rd; meals R20-30; ☽ breakfast & lunch daily, dinner in high season) Serving light meals such as pitta breads and salads, this café is the perfect spot for that early-morning caffeine fix.

Guido's (☎ 293 2288; 36 Da Gama Rd; pizzas R20-30; ☽ lunch & dinner) Guido's is part of a chain of neo-Italian restaurants that are very popular in the Eastern Cape. The interior features lots of plaster columns and fake Roman statues, and the menu consists mostly of passable pizzas and pasta dishes.

Tapas Lapa Seaside (☎ 292 0119; Marina Martinique; mains R50-85; ☽ dinner) Tapas Lapa is just across the car park from the seashore, so the sand on the floor has to be shovelled in! Meals feature decent seafood, and there's a bar next door.

Trawlers (☎ 293 1353; 19 Da Gama Rd; meals R15-25; ☽ breakfast, lunch & dinner) A greasy takeaway serving hamburgers, chips and calamari.

For self-caterers, there is a **Spar supermarket** (Da Gama Rd), which has a decent selection of food.

Entertainment

Tritons (☎ 293 3893; 12 Da Gama Rd) A traditional pub with a TV for sports, Triton's is a popular drinking spot. Dishes on the menu include big breakfasts and traditional South African *potjiekos* (meat and vegetables cooked in a cast-iron pot over an open fire).

Sovereign Sports Café (☎ 293 2311; Da Gama Rd) A cavernous and popular drinking spot with the requisite big screen TV. Hot dogs and burgers are available to sop up all that beer.

Stoney's (☎ 293 1801; Time Out Bldg, Ferreira St) Dishes up all the same ingredients as the other two – plus games machines and pool tables – but dispenses with food altogether.

Diagonally opposite each other are **Hurdy Gurdy's Music Bar** (Da Gama Rd) and the **Grand Prix Bar** (Da Gama Rd), which are a bit quieter than the others and see slightly older clientele.

Ocean Cine (☎ 296 2702; Wavecrest Centre, Da Gama Rd; admission R15) Near the Spar supermarket, screens current movies.

Shopping

The clothing industry has really taken off in J Bay, with much of the stuff on sale made and designed in the town itself. Make sure you check the various factory shops at the lower end of Da Gama Rd for the best bargains.

Clothing emporia in the town centre include **Country Feeling** (☎ 200 2611; Da Gama Rd), which also owns the Billabong franchises and the J Bay Surf Co; plus Quiksilver Boardriders Club, which has a nice coffee shop if it all gets too much; Roxy; Rip Curl; and a few local independent stores dotted around the high street.

J Bay Surf Co (☎ 293 1900; cnr Da Gama Rd & Goedehoop St) sells new surfboards for R2800 to R3000 and second-hand boards for R400 to R900. **Billabong Surf Shop** (☎ 296 1797; Da Gama Rd) hires boards for R15 per hour and wetsuits for R10 an hour, as well as stocking a big range of new and used boards.

Getting There & Away

The **Baz Bus** (☎ 021-439 2323) stops daily at hostels in both directions. A fare from Jeffrey's Bay to Cape Town costs R405 and takes 12 hours; Port Elizabeth to Jeffrey's Bay costs R70 and takes two hours. The **Sunshine Express** (☎ 293 2221) runs between Port Elizabeth and Jeffrey's Bay (R70, one hour). Buses leave from in front of the **Friendly Grocer** (Goedehoop St).

Minibus taxis also depart from the Friendly Grocer; it's R8 to Humansdorp (30 minutes) and R25 to Port Elizabeth (one hour).

PORT ELIZABETH

☎ 041 / pop 776,000

Port Elizabeth (commonly known as 'PE') is the Eastern Cape's biggest town and a major transport hub. The town is keen to market itself as a sunshine-filled holiday resort, and has branded itself the 'Nelson Mandela Bay', an area which incorporates the city centre, the nearby industrial area of Uitenhage and the huge, sprawling townships that surround them both.

While Port Elizabeth is a convenient place to stop for a rest, stock up on supplies or find onward transport, it's generally pretty charmless, and far from the best the Eastern Cape has to offer. If you do end up here for a few days, take a look at the interesting South End and Port Elizabeth museums (see right) or explore the vibrant shebeen scene of the surrounding townships.

Orientation & Information

The train station is just to the northwest of the city, which is circled by a ghastly freeway. The beachfront is to be found running between Humewood and Summerstrand, a couple of kilometres east of the centre. Shops and businesses are concentrated in the big malls: the Boardwalk at Summerstrand, and Greenacres, just west of the town centre on the R102.

INTERNET ACCESS

Boardwalk Internet Café (☎ 583 4725; the Boardwalk, Marine Dr, Summerstrand; per hr R40; ☼ 9.30am-8.30pm Mon-Sat, 10am-6pm Sun)

MONEY

AmEx (☎ 583 2025; the Boardwalk, Marine Dr, Summerstrand; ☼ 8am-10pm Mon-Fri, 10am-2pm Sat & Sun)
Rennies Foreign Exchange (☎ 368 5890; Walmer Park Shopping Centre; 9am-5pm Mon-Fri, 9am-noon Sat) About 3km from the town centre.

TOURIST INFORMATION

Nelson Mandela Bay Tourism (☎ 585 8884; www.nmbt.co.za; Donkin Reserve; ☼ 8am-4.30pm Mon-Fri, 9.30am-3.30pm Sat & Sun) Has an excellent supply of information and maps, including the Donkin Heritage Trail (R18), which details a two-hour walk around the

city's historic buildings. The information office is in the lighthouse building in Donkin Reserve. Its handy visitors' guide includes details of disabled-friendly sights and accommodation.

Dangers & Annoyances

The city centre can be dangerous at night – take a taxi if you're going out. The main beachfront, however, is considered one of the safest in the country.

Sights

SOUTH END MUSEUM

This small but fascinating **museum** (☎ 582 3325; admin@semuseum.co.za; cnr Walmer Blvd & Humewood Rd; admission free; ☼ 9am-4pm Mon-Fri, 10am-3pm Sat & Sun) records the multicultural and vibrant district of Port Elizabeth once known as South End. The apartheid bulldozers put an end to the neighbourhood during forced removals between 1965 and 1975 under the infamous Group Areas Act. The inhabitants, who included Blacks, Coloureds, Asians and Whites, were relocated to parts of the city designated by race.

BAYWORLD

One of the best and largest museum complexes in the country, **Bayworld** (☎ 584 0650; www.bayworld.co.za; Beach Rd; admission R32; ☼ 9am-12.45pm & 1.45-4.30pm) incorporates the Port Elizabeth Museum, an oceanarium and a snake park. Alongside the many stuffed and pickled marine mammals in the museum are some beautiful Xhosa beadwork incorporating modern materials, and a replica of the Algoasaurus dinosaur.

At the oceanarium, trained dolphins and seals perform at 11am and 3pm daily. It's an old-fashioned concept that may seem rather tacky and exploitative, but the shows still have the kids in raptures and at least carry a strong educational message about pollution and marine conservation.

NELSON MANDELA METROPOLITAN ART MUSEUM

Port Elizabeth's **art museum** (☎ 586 1030; www.artmuseum.co.za; 1 Park Dr, St George's Park; admission free; ☼ 9am-5pm Mon & Wed-Fri, 2-5pm Tue, Sat & Sun) is housed in two rather handsome buildings at the entrance to St George's Park. It has a permanent collection of paintings and sculpture by contemporary South African artists, some older British and Oriental

PORT ELIZABETH

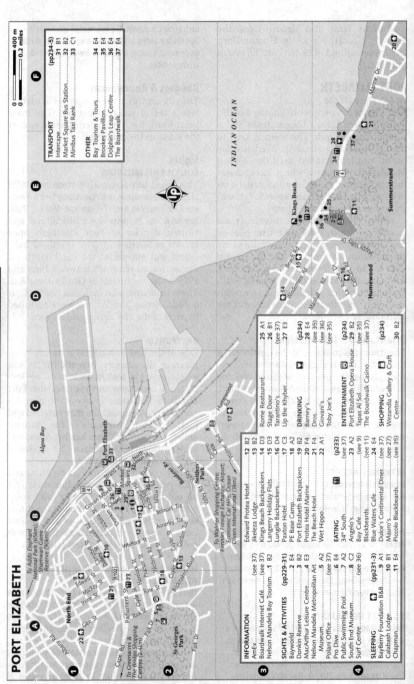

INFORMATION
AmEx.................................(see 37)
Boardwalk Internet Café.........(see 37)
Nelson Mandela Bay Tourism....1 B2

SIGHTS & ACTIVITIES (pp229-31)
Bayworld.............................2 E4
Donkin Reserve....................3 B2
MacArthur Leisure Centre........4 E3
Nelson Mandela Metropolitan Art
   Museum............................5 A2
Polani Office.......................6 E4
Pro Dive............................7 A2
Public Swimming Pool.............8 C2
South End Museum................(see 36)
Surf Centre........................(see 36)

SLEEPING (pp231-3)
BayBerry Foundation B&B..........9 A1
Calabash Lodge...................10 B1
Chapman..........................11 E4

Edward Protea Hotel.............12 B2
Jikeleza Lodge...................13 B2
Kings Beach Backpackers.........14 D3
Langerry Holiday Flats...........15 D3
Lungile Backpackers.............16 D4
Paxton Hotel.....................17 C3
PE Base Camp.....................18 A2
Port Elizabeth Backpackers......19 B2
Protea Hotel Marine.............20 F4
The Beach Hotel..................21 F4
Wet Hippo........................22 A1

EATING (p233)
34° South.......................(see 37)
Angelo's........................23 A2
Bay Cafe........................(see 9)
Blackbeards.....................(see 11)
Blue Waters Cafe.................24 E4
Dulce's Continental Diner.......(see 37)
Mauro's.........................(see 27)
Piccolo Blackbeards.............(see 35)

Rome Reataurant.................25 A1
Stage Door.......................26 B1
Tarantino's.....................(see 37)
Up the Khyber...................27 E3

DRINKING (p234)
Barney's.........................28 E4
Dros............................(see 35)
Giovani's.......................(see 36)
Toby Joe's......................(see 35)

ENTERTAINMENT (p234)
Port Elizabeth Opera House......29 B2
Tapas Al Sol....................(see 35)
The Boardwalk Casino............(see 37)

SHOPPING (p234)
Wezandla Gallery & Craft
   Centre.........................30 B2

TRANSPORT (pp234-5)
Intercape.......................31 B1
Market Square Bus Station.......32 B2
Minibus Taxi Rank...............33 C1

OTHER
Bay Tourism & Tours.............34 E4
Brookes Pavillion................35 E4
Dolphin's Leap Centre...........36 E4
The Boardwalk....................37 E4

0   400 m
0   0.2 miles

INDIAN OCEAN

Algoa Bay

works, plus regular rolling exhibitions and graduate shows.

DONKIN RESERVE

The Donkin Reserve is immediately behind the town centre and has good views over the bay. It's a handy point for getting your bearings. The **pyramid** on the reserve is a memorial to Elizabeth Donkin, the beloved wife of Sir Rufane Donkin, once the governor of Cape Province. A plaque on the pyramid pays tribute to: 'One of the most perfect human beings, who has given her name to the town below'.

Also on the reserve is the **Port Elizabeth Opera House**, the oldest in the country (see p233).

STEAM TRAIN

The **Apple Express** (bookings through Eas'capism ☎ 583 2030; the Boardwalk, Marine Dr, Summerstrand; adult/child R60/25; ☺ 10am Sat & Sun in high season) tourist steam train runs a day trip to Thornhill and back, with a two-hour stop for a braai. It crosses over the highest narrow-gauge bridge in the world.

Activities

The wide sandy beaches to the south of central Port Elizabeth make the town a major water sports venue. Kings Beach stretches from the harbour breakwater to Humewood Beach; both beaches are sheltered. Catamaran sailors and surfers make for Hobie Beach, which is 5km from the city centre.

If you prefer calmer waters, there's a rather beautiful **public swimming pool** (☎ 585 7751; St George's Park; adult/child R4/2.50; ☺ 7am-6pm Mon-Fri, 9am-6pm Sat, 10.30am-6pm Sun) in among the trees and lawns of St George's Park.

There's a bigger pool complex with a whale-viewing jetty at **MacArthur Leisure Centre** (☎ 586 3412; Kings Beach Promenade; adult/child R30/15; ☺ 8.30am-6pm Sep-Apr). The MacArthur complex includes a pool bar and two restaurants, with direct access to the beach.

Good **diving sites** around Port Elizabeth include some wrecks and the St Croix Islands, a marine reserve. Contact either **Ocean Divers International** (☎ 581 5121; www.odipe.co.za; 10 Albert Rd, Walmer) or **Pro Dive** (☎ 583 5316; www.prodive.co.za; Shark Rock Pier, Beach Rd, Summerstrand; per dive R275); both of these offer PADI and NAUI diving courses, starting at around R899.

The **Surf Centre** (☎ 083-656 8429; Marine Dr, Humewood; surfboards/body boards per day R100/180) sells and hires surfboards and body boards. Its surf school will teach you how to use them for R50 per hour.

Tours

Bay Tourism & Tours (☎ 584 0622; www.baytours.co.za; Beach Rd; ☺ 9am-5pm) runs local tours, including trips to Addo Elephant National Park (R490) and city/townships (R250).

There are several cross-cultural township tours, which give the opportunity to visit squatter camps, shebeens (drinking establishments, where you may get a traditional meal) and *abakhwetha* (initiation camps for boys). The guides are locals who are proud of the Port Elizabeth townships' part in the anti-apartheid struggle, and highlight places of historical and political interest along the way. The cost is from R200 to R250 per person for a half-day tour and includes a light lunch or dinner at a shebeen. Contact **Calabash Tours** (☎ 585 6162; calabash@iafrica.com), **Tanaqua Tours** (☎ 452 7692) or **Molo Tours** (☎ 082-970 4037).

Raggy Charters (☎ 073-152 2277) offers cruises led by a qualified marine biologist to St Croix, Jahleel and Benton Islands. You can see penguins, Cape fur seals, dolphins and whales on its half-day tour, which departs at 8am daily (R450).

For a sunset yacht cruise, including a fish barbeque, contact **Polani** (☎ 583 2141; info@polani.co.za; the Boardwalk, Marine Dr, Summerstrand). Boats go towards Cape Recife, and there's a good chance of seeing dolphins en route. The R120 price tag doesn't include drinks.

Sleeping

As you might imagine, Port Elizabeth is well provided with accommodation, mostly of a very good standard. The tourist office in Donkin Reserve can help with lists of B&Bs. Most of Port Elizabeth's fairly unexciting hotel choices are lined up along the beachfront.

BUDGET

Lungile Backpackers (☎ 582 2042; lungile@netactive.co.za; 12 La Roche Dr, Humewood; camp sites/dm/tw/d with shared bathroom R40/65/130/150; ☐ ☑) Port Elizabeth's most popular and busy backpackers is just a couple of minutes from the beachfront. The large entertaining area rocks most nights, and the dorms and tiny camping ground can get full when the Baz Bus arrives, so book ahead. There are also some handsome stone-flagged doubles with their own bathrooms (R175). The hostel does pick-ups from the airport and city centre bus stops.

Port Elizabeth Backpackers (☎ 586 0697; pebak pak@global.co.za; 7 Prospect Hill; dm/d with shared bathroom R70/160; 🖳) This friendly, laid-back hostel is in a 100-year-old building within walking distance of the city and places to eat and drink up on the headland. It's quieter and less ritzy than Lungile, but still very comfortable, with a braai area and a garden. Breakfast costs R20 – try its homemade bread! The hostel organises transport to the Owl House Backpackers in Nieu Bethesda (see p251).

Kings Beach Backpackers (☎ 585 8113; kingsb@ agnet.co.za; 41 Windermere Rd, Humewood; dm/d with shared bathroom R60/150; 🖳) Another quieter but friendly backpackers, with a big kitchen covered in the messages left by generations of travellers who've gone before. The staff can help organise tours in the area.

Wet Hippo (☎ 585 6350; www.wethippo.com; 14 Glen St, Richmond Hill; dm/d with shared bathroom R50/140; 🖳) Port Elizabeth's newest backpackers is pretty smart, with a sunny kitchen, a big pool and a pretty garden, all set in a leafy suburban street far from the hustle of the beachfront.

PE Base Camp (☎ 582 3285; helenegabriel@yahoo .com; 58 Western Rd; dm/s/d with shared bathroom R60/120/160; 🖳) Another new backpackers in an old house conveniently near the centre. There's a bar with pool table and a lounge with an open fireplace, plus an indoor braai.

Jikeleza Lodge (☎ 586 3721; winteam@hinet.co .za; 44 Cuyler St; camp sites/dm/s/d with shared bathroom R55/70/135/170; 🖳) Jikeleza Lodge is small and clean rather than especially charming, but there's a big garden and braai area, and it's a good place to organise township visits and other local tours.

MID-RANGE

Calabash Lodge (☎ 585 6162; 2 Dollery St, Central; s/d with breakfast R225/350) Calabash Lodge is by far the best-value and most charming B&B in town. It has clean, spacious rooms, each with different décor, from gingham to modern African prints. Photos of heroes of the liberation struggle line the walls, along with an

eclectic collection of hats! The lodge is very connected to Port Elizabeth's Black heritage – its Real City township tours (R200) focus on the history of the antiapartheid movement in the town (see p231).

BayBerry Fountain B&B (☎ 585 1558; info@bay berry.co.za; 7 Lutman St; s/d with breakfast R300/350) The upmarket BayBerry Fountain has very reasonable rates for elegant rooms with plenty of character. It's more of a guesthouse than a B&B, with an attractive **restaurant** (mains R30) and bar attached.

Edward Protea Hotel (☎ 586 2056; edward@pe hotels.co.za; Belmont Tce; s/d R400/530) The Edward Protea Hotel, in the heart of the city, is a gracious, old-style Edwardian hotel with comfortable rooms. It's a superior member of the Protea chain. A full English breakfast in the palm-filled courtyard restaurant costs R60.

Chapman (☎ 584 0678; www.chapman.co.za; 1 Lady Bea Cres, Brookes Hill, Summerstrand; s/d with breakfast R400/480; 🌊 🖳 ⚡) The family-run Chapman, overlooking the sea south of the city centre, is an upmarket choice with a waterfall horizon pool. Modern rooms have private balconies with sea views.

Paxton Hotel (☎ 585 9655; www.paxton.co.za; Carnarvon Pl, Humerail; s/d R475/600; 🌊 🖳 ⚡) This is a fairly characterless corporate hotel in a concrete tower halfway between the beach and the city centre. There are some wheelchair-adapted rooms available.

In addition to the places above, there are dozens of self-catering flats along the beachfront. If you're looking for a clean, no-frills apartment, head for **Langerry Holiday Flats** (☎ 585 2654; langerry@icon.co.za; 31 Beach Rd; 1-/2-bedroom flats R140/330). All flats have TV, telephone and kitchen, and the two-bedroom ones have a microwave. The same company also has other blocks in the area.

TOP END

Neither of Port Elizabeth's top-end hotels are much to write home about, but they both have good views of the sea.

The Beach Hotel (☎ 583 2161; reservations@pehot els.co.za; Marine Dr, Summerstrand; s/d with sea view R810/ 990, without sea view R670/810; 🌊 🖳 ⚡) The Beach Hotel is part of the Protea chain. The rooms have horrible mint green furnishings and paintwork but all the trimmings you'd expect, and it's well positioned opposite Hobie Beach and next to the Boardwalk. There are two restaurants, a bar and a coffee shop.

Protea Hotel Marine (☎ 583 2101; marine@pe hotels.co.za; Marine Dr, Summerstrand; s/d R970/1100; ✂ 🖫 🗷) The Protea Marine is one of the most expensive hotels in Port Elizabeth, so you'd think they could have increased the size of the swimming pool a bit – it's tiny, and right next to the road. Inside, things improve slightly, with a jazzy bar, a gym and comfortable, if characterless rooms with a bathroom and personal safe.

Eating

34° South (☎ 583 1085; the Boardwalk, Marine Dr, Summerstrand; dinner R45-100; ✆ lunch & dinner) Definitely one of Port Elizabeth's most attractive dining options, this restaurant-deli allows you to pick your own ingredients from the goodies served up at its counter, or opt for a more traditional seafood dish from the bistro-style menu. There's an extensive wine list, and a great selection of fine foods from all around the world on offer in the shop.

Angelo's (☎ 585 2929; Parliament St; mains R15-20; ✆ lunch & dinner) Angelo's is a small, casual restaurant with an imaginative menu and very good prices. It's popular, especially with the student crowd, so you might have to wait for a table, but it's well worth it.

Mauro's (☎ 582 2700; Beach Rd; mains R52-79; ✆ lunch & dinner Mon-Sat, lunch Sun) Mauro's is something of an anomaly among the bucket-and-spade kitsch of the beachfront – a Californian-style bistro with very good interior décor and trendy black-clad waiting staff. It's within the MacArthur Leisure Centre complex (see p231), and has some outside tables looking over beach.

Up the Khyber (☎ 582 2200; Beach Rd; mains R46-64; ✆ lunch & dinner) Next door to Mauro's, this is one of two fairly classy beachfront options within the MacArthur Leisure Centre. Indian food has recently taken a back seat to the usual steaks and burgers, but there are a couple of vegetarian and one vegan curry on the menu.

Blue Waters Café (☎ 583 4110; Marine Dr, Summerstrand; mains R30-90; ✆ lunch & dinner Mon-Sat, dinner Sun) A bright, lively café-restaurant with an imaginative menu – lots of seafood platters, salads and pasta, and a good black mushroom vegetarian dish. It's quite popular, so book ahead.

Stage Door (☎ 586 3553; Phoenix Hotel, 5 Chapel St; mains R25; ✆ lunch & dinner) The Stage Door has won awards for good-value pub grub, but the surroundings are a bit grungy and the area can be dodgy at night. It's popular with students and middle-aged rockers.

Rome Restaurant (☎ 586 2731; 63 Campbell St; mains R20-40; ✆ breakfast, lunch & dinner) Rome is a good pizza-and-pasta place with lunch specials from R10. The wine is reportedly often corked!

Blackbeard's (☎ 584 0678; Chapman Hotel, 1 Lady Bea Cres, Brookes Hill, Summerstrand; mains R70-90; ✆ breakfast & dinner) and its sister restaurant **Piccolo Blackbeard's** (Brookes Pavilion, Beach Rd, Humewood) specialise in seafood platters – you can pick the ingredients to create your own choice.

Most of Port Elizabeth's best cafés are in the Boardwalk Casino Complex in Summerstrand, at the far end of Beach Rd. The atmosphere is a bit artificial, but here you can at least sip a cappuccino in peace away from the plastic fast-food joints of the beachfront. Try Dulce's Continental Diner or Tarantino's for lunch.

Entertainment

Wednesday seems to be the biggest night in the pubs and clubs, although Friday and Saturday are popular as well.

Toby Joe's (☎ 584 0082; Brookes Pavilion, Beach Rd, Humewood; ✆ Tue-Sun) Port Elizabeth's current hotspot for the young and studenty crowd is this cavernous pub, filled to bursting every night with surfer types, glamorous girls and the requisite scowling bouncers. There are live DJs at weekends, karaoke on Thursday, and Sunday deck parties on the wooden terrace. A 'smart casual' dress policy means guys can expect to be turned away if they're wearing flip-flops.

Giovani's (☎ 586 3189; Dolphin's Leap Centre; ✆ nightly) A buzzy, trendy bar-diner with a fairly young crowd but a tad more sophistication than Toby Joe's. There's a big-screen TV, a long cocktail menu, loud music and American diner–style booths to cosy up in. It's busiest after 10pm on Friday.

Dros (☎ 585 1021; Brookes Pavilion, Beach Rd, Humewood) Part of the fast-growing South African chain, Dros is a favourite spot to quaff down a beer while watching the rugby. There's a pub grub menu and a good selection of wines too.

Tapas Al Sol (☎ 586 2159; Brookes Pavilion, Beach Rd, Humewood) No tapas here, but live bands play most nights and the Sunday afternoon deck party is legendary.

Barney's (☎ 503 4500; the Boardwalk, Marine Dr, Summerstrand) Barney's is an old-fashioned English-style pub 'n' grill. Test your drinking skills with the Beer Tower – a 3L cylinder cooled by ice.

Boardwalk Casino (☎ 507 7777; the Boardwalk, Marine Dr, Summerstrand; ⏰ 24hr) Try your luck on the slot machines or sample the dubious cabaret, but not before you've stashed your firearm in the special gun cloakroom near the entrance.

Port Elizabeth Opera House (☎ 586 3177; White's Rd) Port Elizabeth's opera house is the oldest in South Africa, with a beautiful 19th-century interior. It shows a lively programme of concerts, ballets, plays and jazz recitals – drop into the box office for the latest.

Cinema Starz (☎ 583 2000; the Boardwalk, Marine Pde; admission R20) Shows five screens of blockbusters.

Shopping

Wezandla Gallery & Craft Centre (☎ 585 1185; 27 Baakens St) This brightly coloured arts and crafts centre has a good selection of artefacts made by local groups and a small coffee shop. Staff can also help with tourist information.

Getting There & Away

AIR

SAA (☎ 507 1111) has daily flights between Jo'burg (R1000), Durban (R990), Cape Town (R1100) and Port Elizabeth. **SA Airlink** (☎ 0861 359 722) flies daily from Port Elizabeth to East London (around R750), Durban (R900) and Cape Town (R900). **Kulula.com** (☎ 0861 585 852) flies daily to Jo'burg. Fares start at around R500.

BUS

Greyhound (☎ 363 4555) buses depart from opposite Checkers at Greenacres Shopping Centre, around 3km from Humewood. Phone a private taxi or take a bus from the city centre – see opposite for details. Reservations can also be made at **Computicket** (☎ 083-915 8000; Greenacres Shopping Centre). **Translux** (☎ 392 1333; Ernst & Young bldg, Greenacres Shopping Centre, Ring Rd) also operates out of the Greenacres Shopping Centre. **Intercape** (☎ 586 0055) only accepts telephone bookings; the buses depart from the corner of Fleming and North Union Sts (behind the old post office).

To Cape Town

Translux has a daily bus to and from Cape Town (R190, 12 hours) via the Garden Route.

Intercape also has two daily Garden Route services linking Cape Town and Port Elizabeth (R215, 12 hours).

Greyhound stops in Port Elizabeth daily on the journey between Durban (R300, 15 hours) and Cape Town (R220, 12 hours).

The **Baz Bus** (☎ 021-439 2323) runs daily from Port Elizabeth to Cape Town (R840 one-way hop-on, hop-off).

To Johannesburg

Greyhound has nightly buses from Port Elizabeth to Jo'burg (R320, 15 hours) via East London. Translux has daily services from Port Elizabeth to Jo'burg (R350, 14½ hours) via Bloemfontein (R220, 10 hours) and Graaff-Reinet (R295, 11 hours). From February to September, Intercape has daily services from Port Elizabeth to Jo'burg (R310, 15 hours) via Graaff-Reinet (R180, four hours).

To Durban & East London

Translux runs to Durban daily (R280, 15 hours) via Grahamstown (R75, 2½ hours), East London (R125, five hours), Umtata (R170, nine hours) and Port Shepstone (R240, 13 hours). Greyhound runs to Durban daily (R300, 15 hours). Intercape runs between Port Elizabeth and East London daily (R99, five hours).

The **Baz Bus** (☎ 021-439 2323) runs Monday, Tuesday, Thursday, Friday and Sunday from Port Elizabeth to Durban, and returns on Monday, Wednesday Thursday, Saturday and Sunday; it's R720 for a one-way hop-on, hop-off ticket.

CAR

All the big car-rental operators have offices in Port Elizabeth or at the airport, including **Avis** (☎ 581 4291), **Budget** (☎ 581 4242) and **Imperial** (☎ 581 1268). Also try **Economic Car Hire** (☎ 581 5826; 104 Heugh Rd, Walmer).

MINIBUS TAXI

J-Bay Sunshine Express (☎ 042-293 2221) minibus taxis run between Jeffrey's Bay, Port Elizabeth and other coastal areas.

Most minibus taxis leave from the large townships surrounding Port Elizabeth and can be difficult to find. The **minibus taxi rank** (Strand St), a few blocks north of the bell tower, services the local area.

TRAIN

The **Shosholoza Meyl** (☎ 0860 008 888; www.spoornet .co.za) runs overnight to Jo'burg (1st/2nd class R365/R245, 18 hours) via Bloemfontein.

Getting Around

The **airport** (Allister Miller Rd, Walmer) is about 5km from the city centre. There's no public transport to the airport. A taxi costs around R55. Taxis and hire cars are available at the airport. For taxis, call **Hurter Cabs** (☎ 585 5500).

For information about bus services, contact **Algoa Bus Company** (☎ 404 1200), which runs scheduled central city services departing from the **Market Sq bus station** (Strand St).

ADDO ELEPHANT NATIONAL PARK

This **national park** (☎ 042-223 0556; quezettevd@ parks-sa.co.za; adult/child R80/40; ⏱ 7am-7pm) is 72km north of Port Elizabeth, near the Zuurberg Range in the Sundays River Valley. Addo's borders have recently been extended, and it now covers approximately 120,000 hectares.

The park protects the remnants of the huge elephant herds that once roamed Eastern Cape. When farmers started to develop the area at the beginning of the 20th century, they found themselves in conflict with the elephants. A man named Major Pretorius was commissioned to deal with the 'menace', and until he was stopped by a public outcry, he seemed likely to succeed. When Addo was proclaimed a national park in 1931, there were only 11 elephants left.

Today there are more than 300 elephants in the park, and you'd be unlucky not to see some. A day or two at Addo is a highlight of any visit to this part of the Eastern Cape, not only for the elephants but for the zebras, elands, kudus, warthogs and myriad birds you are likely to see as you drive around. There's even a chance of seeing lions and hyenas, which have recently been introduced to the park.

Information

The park's dirt roads can become impassable in the wet, so the park is closed if there has been heavy rain – if in doubt, call ahead. There is a well-stocked **shop** (⏱ 8am-7pm) at

the park headquarters, 7km from the village of Addo on the R335.

The elephants of Addo were once addicted to the oranges and grapefruits fed to them during droughts, and took to mobbing vehicles containing citrus fruit. For this reason, no citrus fruits of any kind are allowed in the park boundaries! Do *not* get out of your car except at designated climbout points, and if you're lucky enough to get close to the elephants, treat them with respect, however docile they may seem.

During the summer it's best to arrive at the park by mid-morning and to stake out one of the waterholes where the elephants tend to gather during the heat of the day. In the winter, early mornings are the best time to see animals. For optimum wildlife-spotting, pick up one of the **'hop-on rangers'** (R50) at the gate, who can give you advice on where to go and explain what you're looking at in interesting detail. The park's own **vehicle** (2hr drive per person R150) can also be used for elephant-spotting drives.

Horse trails (2hr ride per person R100) are available twice a day – they go through the Zuurberg section of the park, which doesn't contain the lions!

Sleeping & Eating

The park accommodation can get very booked up at busy periods, so always reserve in advance if possible.

Addo Rest Camp (bookings ☎ 012-343 1991; www .parks-sa.co.za; camp sites/safari tents/forest cabins with shared bathroom R95/220/300) Addo's main camping ground is at the main park headquarters. It's a great spot, with a picnic area and some of the accommodation overlooking a waterhole where elephants come to drink. Various accommodation options are available sleeping anything from two to six people, most of which are very well decorated and excellent value for money.

Addo also has a **bush camp** (1-4 people R440) and **bungalows** (1-4 people R120) in the northern section of the park, which have to be booked in their entirety. Inquire at the park headquarters for details.

Meals are also available at the park's **restaurant** (mains R25), which is presided over by the stuffed head of the legendary bull, Hapoor. If you've brought your own grub, the rest camp's shady picnic area has a fine view of the waterhole.

Several B&B places have sprung up around the tiny town of Addo, just a few kilometres from the park gate. **Chrislin** (☎ 042-233 0022; www.africanhuts-addo.co.za; d with breakfast R440; ☏) has friendly owners and very pretty African-style huts on a working citrus farm. A big braai dinner can be provided for R100 per person. Cheaper is **Homestead B&B** (☎ 042-233 0354; homestead@webmail.co.za; camp sites R25, backpackers s/d R100/180, B&B s/d 250/500; ☏), which has a few backpackers rooms and self-catering units, as well as camping, alongside the normal B&B accommodation. **Valley View** (☎ 042-233 0349; www.valleyview.co.za; r with breakfast R440; ☏) has big, spacious twin and double rooms, full of character, in a 100-year-old farmhouse.

Getting There & Away

The park is signposted from the N2. Alternatively you can travel via Uitenhage on the R75; there are attractive citrus farms along the banks of the Sundays River from Kirkwood to Uitenhage.

SHAMWARI GAME RESERVE

Undoubtedly the most high-powered of the Eastern Cape's many private wildlife reserves, **Shamwari** (☎ 042-203 1111; www.shamwari.com; r all inclusive R4920; ☒ ☐ ☏), 30km east of Addo Elephant National Park, is dedicated to restocking large tracts of reclaimed land with animals that were once common in the region before the advent of the farmers and big-game hunters. All of the Big Five (elephant, rhino, lion, leopard and buffalo) are present, and well-managed wildlife drives mean that you'll have a very good chance of seeing at least four of them during the course of a couple of days' stay. A two-night **camping trail** (per person R1200) is also available in the 3000 hectares of the reserve that have been set aside as an untouched Wilderness Area.

There are six different lodges within the reserve, ranging from Bayethe Lodge, a semi-tented camp nestling in the bush, to Bushman's River Lodge, a former settler home now restored with vibrant African interiors. Room rates vary from lodge to lodge, and many are discounted by as much as 50% during April, May and June. All rates are all inclusive – food, drinks and all activities.

Also on the reserve is the **Born Free Foundation** (☎ 042-203 1119; admission free; ⏱ 8.15-11.30am), an educational centre that provides a sanctuary for lions and leopards rescued from appalling conditions in zoos all over the world.

Shamwari's volunteer programme, **African Global Academy** (☎ 046-624 5449; www.africanglobalacademy.co.za), offers the chance to do hands-on conservation work at the various wildlife reserves in the Eastern Cape.

Shamwari can only be reached if you have your own car. If you're coming from Port Elizabeth, travel along the N2 towards Grahamstown for about 65km, take the Paterson turnoff (R342), continue for a further 7km, then turn right at the Shamwari sign.

GRAHAMSTOWN

☎ 046 / pop 64,300

Grahamstown is the capital of Settler Country. The town's genteel conservatism and English-style prettiness belie a bloody history (see p237). The town centre has some fine examples of Victorian and early Edwardian building styles, with beautiful powder blue and lemon yellow shop fronts. Two of the prettiest are **Grocott's Mail**, still a working newspaper office, and **Birch's Gentlemen's Outfitters**. The latter still has a marvellously old-fashioned 'slider', a pulley system that sends money and change across the ceiling to and from the central till. Staff will demonstrate if you ask them nicely.

Of course, the English weren't the only people to settle in Grahamstown. Visit the nearby townships for a glimpse into the culture of the Xhosa – once rulers of the region, they were defeated by British and Boer forces only after a fierce struggle.

Socially, the town is dominated by the students from Rhodes University, who are to be found packing out the pubs and bars during term time.

CITY OF SAINTS?

Grahamstown's nickname is 'City of Saints', an appellation that is generally thought to refer to the town's 40 churches. But another, more interesting theory comes from a message reportedly sent during one of the region's frontier wars. In reply to a requisition for carpentry tools, including a steel vice, the quartermaster wrote, 'We regret no vice in Grahamstown'. The reply from headquarters read: 'Then I believe, sir, you must all be saints'.

GRAHAMSTOWN

0 — 300 m
0 — 0.2 miles

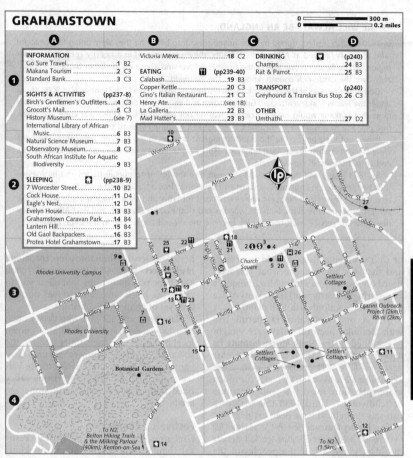

INFORMATION	
Go Sure Travel	1 B2
Makana Tourism	2 C3
Standard Bank	3 C3

SIGHTS & ACTIVITIES	(pp237-8)
Birch's Gentlemen's Outfitters	4 C3
Grocott's Mail	5 C3
History Museum	(see 7)
International Library of African Music	6 B3
Natural Science Museum	7 B3
Observatory Museum	8 C3
South African Institute for Aquatic Biodiversity	9 B3

SLEEPING	(pp238-9)
7 Worcester Street	10 B2
Cock House	11 D4
Eagle's Nest	12 D4
Evelyn House	13 B3
Grahamstown Caravan Park	14 B4
Lantern Hill	15 B4
Old Gaol Backpackers	16 B3
Protea Hotel Grahamstown	17 B3

EATING	(pp239-40)
Victoria Mews	18 C2
Calabash	19 B3
Copper Kettle	20 C3
Gino's Italian Restaurant	21 C3
Henry Ate	(see 18)
La Galleria	22 B3
Mad Hatter's	23 B3

DRINKING	(p240)
Champs	24 B3
Rat & Parrot	25 B3

TRANSPORT	(p240)
Greyhound & Translux Bus Stop	26 C3

OTHER	
Umthathi	27 D2

EASTERN CAPE

Information

Makana Tourism (☎ 622 3241; www.grahamstown .co.za; 63 High St; ⏰ 8.30am-5pm Mon-Fri, 9am-1pm Sat) is efficient and friendly. The office is in a small building next to the **Standard Bank** (Church Sq). It is an agent for Translux buses and also has **Internet access** (per hr R30).

Go Sure Travel (☎ 622 2235; marianl.gbstravel@ galileosa.co.za; Pepper Grove Mall, cnr African & Allen Sts) handles bookings for all local travel; it is also the agent for most car rental companies and cashes travellers cheques (no commission charged).

Sights

The most interesting of the various components of Grahamstown's **Albany Museum**

(☎ 622 4450; www.ru.ac.za/albany-museum) is the wonderfully eccentric **Observatory Museum** (Bathurst St; adult/child R8/5; ⏰ 9.30am-1pm & 2-5pm Mon-Fri, 10am-2pm Sat). It's an old house filled with eccentric Victorian memorabilia (look out for the commode disguised as a chest of drawers!). The highlight is the *camera obscura*, a complicated series of lenses, a bit like a periscope, which reflect a perfect panoramic image of the town onto a flat white disc hidden in a tower in the roof.

On the Rhodes University campus is the **International Library of African Music** (ILAM; ☎ 603 8557; http://ilam.ru.ac.za; Prince Alfred St, Rhodes University; ⏰ 8.30am-12.45pm & 2-5pm Mon-Fri, call ahead for appointments), a treasure trove of instruments and recordings. You can examine one of the 200

EASTERN CAPE

THERE WILL ALWAYS BE AN ENGLAND...

In 1820 English settlers, duped by their government into believing they were going to a peaceful land of plenty, arrived at Algoa Bay. In reality, they were arriving in a heavily contested border region, where Boers on one side of the Great Fish River and Xhosa on the other battled interminably over the cattle-rich country known as the Zuurveld.

Grahamstown was at the centre of the maelstrom. In 1819, in the Fifth Frontier War, 9000 Xhosa under the leader Makana attacked Grahamstown and very nearly defeated the garrison. The story goes that Makana would have succeeded had he not observed the Xhosa war code and given free passage to a woman who carried a hidden keg of gunpowder to the defenders.

It was not long before the thousand immigrant families found farming untenable. The odds were stacked against them: inexperience, hostile neighbours, labour shortages, floods, droughts and crop diseases all played a role.

By 1823 nearly half the settlers had retreated to the towns to pursue trades and businesses they had followed in England. Grahamstown developed into a trading and manufacturing centre, where axes, knives and blankets were exchanged for ivory and skins. Tradespeople among the settlers produced metal implements, wagons and clothes. Port Elizabeth and Port Alfred initially developed to service what had quickly become the second-largest city in the Cape Colony.

or so instruments, listen to field recordings and then try and emulate what you have heard on *nyanga* pipes from Mozambique, a *kora* (stringed instrument) from West Africa or a Ugandan *kalimba* (thumb piano).

The second coelacanth (a marine fish with limblike pectoral fins) ever caught is exhibited in the **South African Institute for Aquatic Biodiversity** (☎ 603 5800; www.jlbsmith.ru .ac.za; Prince Alfred St, Rhodes University; admission free; ☼ 8am-1pm & 2-5pm Mon-Fri), formerly the much more splendidly titled JLB Smith Institute of Ichthyology. Until 1938 this primitive fish was thought to have been extinct.

The **History Museum** (Somerset St; admission R5; ☼ 9am-1pm & 2-5pm Tue-Fri, 10am-1pm Sat) details the history and art of the peoples of the Eastern Cape, which includes the Xhosa and the 1820 settlers. The art exhibitions in its gallery change regularly.

Considerably less exciting, but worth half an hour on a rainy afternoon, is the **Natural Science Museum** (Somerset St; admission R5; ☼ 9am-1pm & 2-5pm Tue-Fri, 10am-1pm Sat), which depicts early human history and has some interesting artefacts, including a Xhosa hut.

Tours

There are plenty of opportunities to meet local Xhosa in the safe and friendly townships around Grahamstown. **Umthathi** (☎ 622 4450; www.umthathi.co.za; Station Bldg, High St), with an office in the old train station building, organises township visits including a traditional Xhosa meal (R50), and visits to a

herbal nursery in Rhini township. **Egazini Outreach Project** (☎ 083-428 9424; per group of 1-4 people R300) runs two-hour tours that allow you to relive the battle of Grahamstown through the eyes of young Xhosa historians.

Alan Weyer (☎ 622 7896; www.alanweyerstours .co.za; half-/full-day tours R300/650), a well-known local historian, conducts tours through the so-called 'Frontier Country' around Grahamstown. Some include a visit to the Valley of the Ancient Voices, a pristine valley filled with rock art, relics and stone age artefacts.

Festivals & Events

Grahamstown bills itself as 'Africa's Festival Capital', with events of various kinds happening several times a year. The biggest is the very successful **National Arts Festival** (☎ 603 1103; www.nafest.co.za) and its associated Fringe Festival. The Fringe alone has more than 200 events. The festival runs for nine days at the beginning of July, but accommodation at this time can be booked out a year in advance.

Growing in popularity is the **Makana Freedom Festival** (☎ 082-932 1304), held in late April, a festival of song and dance, with live bands playing in various venues in the townships around Grahamstown.

Sleeping

There are more than 40 B&Bs and 20 or so farmstays in the area; book with Makana Tourism for a full list.

BUDGET

Old Gaol Backpackers (☎ 636 1001; Somerset St; dm/d with shared bathroom R65/100) Built in 1824, the former jail – now a national monument – offers the chance to sleep in a genuine prison cell, complete with barred door and 19th-century graffiti. The rooms (or cells) are quite variable inside, so look at a few before deciding where you'll be interred. There's a cosy bar with wood-burning stove.

Umso Township Homestays (☎ 637 1632, 083-245 0496) Mrs Thabisa Xonxa arranges overnight homestays in good standard rooms in Grahamstown's townships. Ask Makana Tourism for more details.

Belton Hiking Trails & the Milking Parlour (☎ /fax 622 8395, 082-808 6139; farmhouse beds R75, cottage beds R150) At Belton Hiking Trails, 40km from Grahamstown on the R343 between Salem and Kenton-on-Sea, there is accommodation for 20 people in a converted farmhouse. The Milking Parlour next door is a fully equipped cottage for up to six guests. The main attractions are the walking trails (from 2.5km to 17km) in the Bushman's River Valley.

Grahamstown Caravan Park (☎ 603 6072; Grey St; camp sites/4-bed rondavels/5-bed chalets R45/120/250) The park is a wooded, hilly spot off the N2, although it's a bit of a walk from the town centre. Bedding is not supplied for the rondavels.

MID-RANGE

Lantern Hill (☎ 622 8782; www.imaginet.co.za/lantern hill; 2 Thompson St; R275/380) This friendly B&B has cosy and comfy wooden-floored rooms with TV and safe. Some rooms also have wheelchair ramps and bath rails. Owners Danny and Sterna Biermann speak German.

Cock House (☎ 636 1287; www.cockhouse.co.za; 10 Market St; s/d with breakfast R390/660) Named after William Cock, one of the 1820s settlers, the Cock House was once home to author Andre Brink. Today it's a National Monument and a hugely popular guesthouse, with chintzy, comfortable rooms in converted stables and a pretty garden. The rustic **restaurant** (3-course menu R105) is very highly regarded and often booked out.

Eagle's Nest (☎ 622 7189, 082-657 0359; www.grah amstown.co.za/eaglesnest; cnr Webber St & Shepperson Lane; s/d with breakfast R95/190; ☒) This good-value B&B has two studio flats sleeping two to four people, with a kitchenette and an outside terrace.

Victoria Mews (☎ 622 7208; www.hotelvictoria.co .za; 4-8 New St; s/d/f with breakfast R250/390/490; ☒) A good-value hotel in an old building next door to Gino's Italian Restaurant (see below). The rooms are simple but tasteful, with wooden floors, telephone and TV. Family rooms are also available here.

TOP END

7 Worcester Street (☎ 622 2843; www.worcesterstr eet.co.za; 7 Worcester St; s/d with breakfast R550/1100; ☒ ☒) This very luxurious guesthouse is filled with sumptuous period furniture and priceless artworks. The house was built in 1888 and once served as a student hostel – these days it provides accommodation to parents visiting their little darlings at Grahamstown's private boarding schools. Three-course dinner is available for R120.

Protea Hotel Grahamstown (☎ 622 2324; www .albanyhotels.co.za; 123 High St; s/d with breakfast R460/610; ☒) This hotel, in a characterless building in the centre of town, has modern but tasteful and fairly luxurious rooms with TV. There's a bar and a carvery restaurant.

Evelyn House (☎ 622 2324; www.albanyhotels.co .za; s/d with breakfast R520/730; ☒) An annex of the Protea Hotel Grahamstown and just across the road, this is quieter and more upmarket, with a small pool of its own.

Eating & Entertainment

Grahamstown's students drink hard and eat cheap, so there are a plethora of pubs and fast-food joints dotted around the town centre, plus some more upmarket options for when the folks come to visit.

La Galleria (☎ 622 3455; 13 New St; mains R40-50; ☽ dinner Tue-Sun) Bookings are essential at this smart, authentic Italian restaurant, which serves homemade pasta in a modern, arty setting.

Calabash (☎ 622 2366; 123 High St; mains R50-70; ☽ lunch & dinner) Calabash offers traditional South African food in a warm, ethnic-looking dining room. Xhosa hotpots are a speciality, and there are some veggie options such as spicy bean soup and stuffed squash. A lot of the menu, however, comprises the standard breaded calamari/T-bone steak fare.

Mad Hatter's (☎ 622 9411; 118 High St; mains R20-30; ☽ breakfast & lunch Mon-Sat, plus dinner Fri) Mad Hatter's is a bright and cheerful, studenty bistro serving all-day breakfasts, hearty stews and big sandwiches.

Henry Ate (☎ 622 7208; 4-8 New St; mains R39-95; ☾ dinner Mon-Sat) Next to the Victoria Mews hotel, this is a carnivore-friendly, Tudor-themed restaurant, whose menu features delights such as 'King Henry's Fire Spit', venison and 'wild boar' (actually pork knuckles).

Copper Kettle (☎ 622 4358; 7 Bathurst St; mains R30-40; ☾ lunch & dinner Mon-Sat) The old-fashioned Copper Kettle has a predictable menu of burgers, steaks and the like, but it's got a convivial bar, a cosy interior and friendly staff.

Gino's Italian Restaurant (☎ 622 7208; 8 New St, entrance via Hill St; R25-35; ☾ lunch & dinner) Grahamstown's most popular student restaurant is a very average pizza and pasta joint with an attached bar.

Rat & Parrot (☎ 622 5002; 59 New St; mains R20-30; ☾ lunch & dinner, closed Sun out of term time) The Rat is a pseudo-British drinking den and another popular student haunt, with loud music, a big-screen TV and a beer garden. The pub grub looks surprisingly decent, with healthy options such as chicken and mango salad and butternut ravioli.

Champs (Scott Ave) This place is a laddish sports bar with pool tables and live bands on Wednesday and Friday.

Getting There & Around

The **Bee Bus** (☎ 082-652 0798) runs to Port Elizabeth, Port Alfred and Kenton-on-Sea from Sunday to Friday, and **Mini Lux** (☎ 043-741 3107) runs to East London and Port Elizabeth from Sunday to Friday. Check with the tourist office for prices and times.

Intercape (☎ 622 2235) stops in Grahamstown on its daily run between Cape Town (R220, nine hours) and East London (R99, three hours).

Translux (☎ 622 3241) buses stop at the corner of Bathurst and High Sts on the daily run between Cape Town (R230, 15 hours), Port Elizabeth (R75, three hours) and Durban (R260, 12 hours), via East London and Umtata.

Greyhound (☎ 622 2235) buses also stop at the corner of Bathurst and High Sts on their way to Durban (R270, 13 hours) and Port Elizabeth (R70, two hours).

You'll find minibus taxis on Raglan St, but most leave from Rhini township. Destinations include Fort Beaufort (R19, two hours), King William's Town (R29, three hours), Port Elizabeth (R29, 2½ hours) and East London (R31, four hours).

BATHURST
☎ 046

On the road between Port Alfred and Grahamstown, this charming but scattered village with its narrow lanes and thick hedges is a famous Eastern Cape drinking spot, particularly during the annual December Ox Braai, a huge party that takes place around New Year's Eve every year. Open-air drinking and the barbecuing of vast quantities of meat are the main (printable) activities.

Near the turn-off to Bathurst (look for the Protea Hotel sign) is **Summerhill Farm** (☎ 625 0833; off the R67; tours adult/child R30/15; ☾ 9am-5pm Mon-Fri), which has the dubious honour of being home to the world's biggest pineapple – a rip-off of the Big Pineapple on the Sunshine Coast in Queensland, Australia. Standing 16.7m high, it is a mere 70cm taller than the original (and no, it's not real). There's also a reconstructed Xhosa village where you can buy handicrafts; meals are available from the Protea Hotel restaurant. Tours in a tractor include pineapple tasting and take place at 10am, noon and 3pm daily.

Watersmeeting Nature Reserve (☎ 425 0876; admission per vehicle R10, plus per person R5; ☾ 7am-5pm), just outside town, protects the start of the Kowie River, where fresh and tidal waters meet. There's bird-watching in the forests here, plus a nice view of the horseshoe bend in the river. The road down to the river is steep and shouldn't be attempted after rain.

The **Pig & Whistle Hotel** (☎ 625 0673; Kowie Rd; r R350; pub lunch R35; ☾ lunch & dinner) could be in England, which is not at all surprising considering it was built in 1831 and is in the centre of Settler Country. It's a popular stopping point on the Port Alfred–Grahamstown road for good-value pub lunches and Thai food on Friday and Saturday evening. The pub can also help out with information about canoe and hiking trails in the area. Try to get a room in the main house if you're staying – they have much more character than the newer ones in the garden.

PORT ALFRED
☎ 046 / pop 18,000

Port Alfred is a genteel seaside town that is being developed into an upmarket holiday resort. Outside the high season (from mid-December to mid-January) the town has a staid, quiet air to it, but in season it bustles with life and people come from other parts of the coast to soak up the holiday atmosphere. Needless to say, everything is much more expensive at this time. Out of season Port Alfred is busiest at weekends, when students from Grahamstown come to lounge on the beach and drink in the pubs.

Information

Palms Video (☎ 624 2182; Heritage Mall, Main St; per min R0.50; ☉ 9am-8pm) has Internet access.

Tourism Port Alfred (☎ 624 1235; www.portalfred tourism.co.za; Van der Riet St; ☉ 8am-4.30pm Mon-Fri, 8.30am-noon Sat), near the municipal offices on the western bank of the Kowie River, has brochures detailing accommodation, walks and canoe trails.

Activities

Three Sisters Horse Trails (☎ 675 1269; janwebb@ telkomsa.net; 1/1½hr trails R60/90, overnight trails for experienced riders incl accommodation R250) offers daily horse rides on the beach and through bushland.

For **surfers**, there are good right- and left-hand breaks at the river mouth; for golfers,

there's the beautiful **golf course**, one of the four 'Royals' in South Africa. There's also an 8km **walking trail** through the Kowie Nature Reserve – maps (R6.50) are available from the tourist office. For the fit, **Rufanes River Trails** (☎ 041-624 1469) has mountain bike trails.

The two-day **Kowie Canoe Trail** (☎ 041-624 2230; per person R80) is a fairly easy 18km canoe trip upriver from Port Alfred, with an overnight stay in a hut at Horseshoe Bend Nature Reserve. Mattresses, water and wood are provided, but you'll need your own food and bedding.

Keryn's Dive School & Maximum Exposure (☎ 624 4432; keryn@compushop.co.za; NAUI scuba-diving course R1485, Advanced Diver course R1100) offers diving courses and various other adventure activities. Diving is between May and August. Visibility is not outstanding (5m to 8m) but there are plenty of big fish, soft corals and raggy sharks. The same company rents out sandboards (R50 for two hours) and canoes with a map of the river route (R70 per half day). Waterskiing costs R320 per hour per boat (three people).

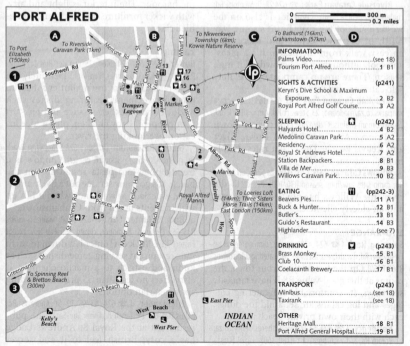

PORT ALFRED

0 — 300 m
0 — 0.2 miles

INFORMATION	
Palms Video	(see 18)
Tourism Port Alfred	1 B1

SIGHTS & ACTIVITIES	(p241)
Keryn's Dive School & Maximum Exposure	2 B2
Royal Port Alfred Golf Course	3 A2

SLEEPING	(p242)
Halyards Hotel	4 B2
Medolino Caravan Park	5 A2
Residency	6 A2
Royal St Andrews Hotel	7 A2
Station Backpackers	8 B1
Villa de Mer	9 B3
Willows Caravan Park	10 A2

EATING	(pp242-3)
Beavers Pies	11 A1
Buck & Hunter	12 B1
Butler's	13 B1
Guido's Restaurant	14 B3
Highlander	(see 7)

DRINKING	(p243)
Brass Monkey	15 B1
Club 10	16 B1
Coelacanth Brewery	17 B1

TRANSPORT	(p243)
Minibus	(see 18)
Taxirank	(see 18)

OTHER	
Heritage Mall	18 B1
Port Alfred General Hospital	19 B1

EASTERN CAPE

Sleeping

Tourism Port Alfred lists the town's numerous B&Bs.

BUDGET

Loeries Loft (☎ 675 1269; janwebb@telkomsa.net; r per person R50) Loeries Loft, 14km east of Port Alfred on the Three Sisters Horse Trails farm, is a very rustic tree house perched in the branches of a magnificent yellowwood tree beside the Riet River. This tranquil retreat is only for the adventurous; the loft is a 1½-hour walk (or horse ride) from the main farmhouse (a map is provided) and you must carry all your own supplies.

Station Backpackers (☎ 624 5869; www.thest ation.co.za; off Pascoe Cres; dm/d R60/150) This hostel, housed in the town's old train station, is going for the scruffy-funky look. However, it succeeds rather too well on the scruffy side, with dusty dorms, a grotty kitchen and lots of mosquitoes. The **Trainspotting** (☺ breakfast, lunch & dinner Mon-Sat) restaurant, with its bright and eccentric décor, is a popular dinner spot for local residents. Opening times are subject to demand.

Riverside Caravan Park (☎ 624 2230; Mentone Rd; chalets for 2 people R250) Riverside is also on the western side of the river but it's some way north of the town centre and more than an easy walk from the beach. It's a pleasant spot, although it gets crowded in high season. There are no camp sites here, only self-catering chalets.

Medolino Caravan Park (☎ 624 1651; www.cara vanparks.co.za/medolino; 23 Stewart Rd; camp sites R100, 2-/4-bedroom chalets R320/425) This park, in town off Princes Ave, is near both Kowie River and Kelly's Beach. The chalet rates double in high season.

Willows Caravan Park (☎ /fax 624 5201; off Albany Rd; camp sites low/high season R30/100) Next to the river, the Willows has powered camp sites and an elderly clientele.

MID-RANGE

Spinning Reel (☎ 624 4281; www.spinningreel.co.za; Freshwater Rd; d with breakfast R400, self-catering d/log cabins R160/R350) On the beach 4km from town, the rooms at this good-value B&B have fantastic sea views. Its comfortable self-catering cottages and log cabins are set amid the dunes, each with their own private beach access.

Residency (☎ 624 5382; www.theresidency.co.za; 11 Vroom Rd; s/d with breakfast R180/360) The Residency is a gracious B&B in a magnificently restored Victorian house dating from 1898. Its lovely rooms have freestanding enamel baths, wooden walls and sprigged cotton bedspreads. A big breakfast is served on the wide veranda every morning. Rates go up in high season.

Villa de Mer (☎ 624 2315; www.villademer.co.za; 22 West Beach Dr; s/d with breakfast from R245/390; ⊠ ⚫) A large ultramodern B&B right on the beachfront. Some of the smart rooms have their own fridge.

Royal St Andrews Lodge (☎ 624 1379; www.com pushop.co.za/standrew; St Andrews Rd; s/d with breakfast R290/500; ⊠ ⚫) This old-fashioned, mock-Scottish pub and inn opposite the golf course has some quaint Victorian-style rooms in the original building, plus more modern self-catering units in the garden. Its restaurant, the Highlander (below), rates a mention.

Halyards Hotel (☎ 624 2410; www.halyardshotel .com; Royal Alfred Marina, Albany Rd; s/d with breakfast R435/750; ⊠ ⚫) This comfy waterfront hotel with attractive Cape Cod–style architecture has large well-equipped rooms overlooking the harbour. The interior is light and airy, with wicker furniture and black- and white-tiled floors.

Eating

Butler's (☎ 041-624 3464; 25 Van der Riet St; mains R38-75; ☺ lunch & dinner Wed-Mon) Definitely the best restaurant in town, Butler's has an imaginative menu featuring dishes such as duck and blackberry sauce and *piri-piri* (hot peppers) baby chicken, plus a nice location overlooking the river.

Guido's Restaurant (☎ 041-624 5264; West Beach Dr; mains R20-45; ☺ lunch & dinner) Guido's is a trendy pizza-and-pasta restaurant on the beach. It's got slow service but a lively ambience, especially at weekends when it fills up with students down from Grahamstown.

Buck & Hunter (☎ 041-624 5960; Main St; mains R35-55; ☺ lunch & dinner, closed Sun Feb-Nov except Easter) The Buck & Hunter is a down to earth pub-restaurant serving game dishes such as kudu and ostrich to a macho clientele. It also offers no less than 35 pizzas, including six vegetarian options.

Highlander (☎ 624 1379; 19 St Andrews Rd; mains R25-65; ☺ lunch & dinner Tue-Sat) The pub-restaurant at the Royal St Andrews Lodge has a cosy, British feel to it and serves good-quality food, including an excellent Thai vegetable curry.

Beavers Pies (☎ 041-624 2760; Southwell Rd; pies R5; ⊗ 24hr) Beavers is a 24-hour takeaway serving cheap pies and other late-night post-beer delicacies.

Entertainment

Highlander (☎ 624 1379; 19 St Andrews Rd) Makes a charming local drinking hole, with sport on TV and a garrulous set of regulars.

Coelacanth Brewery (☎ 624 3373; www.oldfour legs.co.za; Wharf St) Port Alfred's own brewery – named after the famous 'fossil fish' first discovered off East London – was closed for renovations when we passed, but promises to be an interesting place to sample a pint of Old Fourlegs beer after you've seen it being brewed.

Club 10 (☎ 624 4953; admission R15; Wharf St; ⊗ Fri & Sat, nightly in Dec) Next door to the brewery, this disco pumps with tourists during the Christmas holiday season.

Brass Monkey (☎ 083-502 5539; cnr Wharf & Main Sts) This is another late-night venue, with a disco, bar and a pool table.

Getting There & Away

The **Baz Bus** (☎ 021-439 2323) stops at Port Alfred's Station Backpackers (opposite) on its run from Port Elizabeth (1½ hours) to Durban (12 hours) on Monday, Tuesday, Wednesday, Friday and Saturday.

The **minibus taxi rank** (Biscay Rd) is outside the Heritage Mall. There are daily services to Port Elizabeth (R45), Grahamstown (R20) and East London (R45). Local daily services include Bathurst (R7) and Kenton-on-Sea (R10).

KENTON-ON-SEA

☎ 046

Kenton-on-Sea, near Bushman's River Mouth (Boesmanriviermond), is an expensive resort on a beautiful bit of coast. It's not exactly wild and rugged, but good for a quiet holiday in unspoilt surroundings.

Kenton/Bushman's Publicity Association (☎ 648 2418; www.kenton.co.za) provides information on activities and accommodation. There is a 4km walking trail from the river mouth to Kwaaihoek, where Bartholomeu Dias erected a cross in 1488.

Bushman's Caravan Park (☎ 648 1227; www.cara vanparks.co.za/boesmans; camp sites low/high season R35/110) This caravan park is an attractive sheltered place where foreigners are warmly welcomed.

There is a daily minibus taxi service from Port Alfred to Kenton-on-Sea (R12).

THE KAROO

The Karoo is a vast semidesert stretching over miles of the great South African plateau inland from the Cape coast.

The Karoo's southeastern extension is in Eastern Cape and includes the exquisite town of Graaff-Reinet, the stunning scenery of Mountain Zebra National Park and the fascinating artistic community of Nieu Bethesda. It's one of the region's most intriguing areas, with an overwhelming sense of space and an arid beauty that stands in sharp contrast to the cheery holiday atmosphere of the western coastline.

Between December and February, temperatures in the Karoo towns can reach 45°C, and things barely cool down in March and April. June and July see the thermometer plummet to –5°C, with snow in the mountain passes and hard frosts. September to November are the best times to visit if you want to experience a moderate climate.

See p206 and p491 for more information about the western and northern sections of the Karoo.

MIDDELBURG

☎ 049

Middelburg is a nondescript town nestled in a plain with the spectacular Lootsberg Pass nearby. The **Middelburg-Karoo Publicity Association** (☎ /fax 842 2188; www.middelburgec.co .za; 8 Meintjies St; ⊗ 8am-4.30pm Mon-Fri) is a helpful source of information. The **Cultural History Museum** (☎ 842 1337; cnr Bennie & Du Plessis Sts; admission R2; ⊗ 8am-1pm & 2-4.30pm Mon-Fri) has memorabilia of the well-known playwright Athol Fugard, who once lived in the town.

Karoo Country Inn (☎ 842 1126; kci@yebo.co.za; cnr Meintjies & Loop Sts; s/d R259/335) The Karoo Country Inn, overlooking the pleasant town square, has the best value accommodation in town.

Intercape buses stop in Middelburg en route to Jo'burg/Pretoria (R250, 10 hours) via Graaff-Reinet (R100, 1½ hours). Translux buses also stop here.

EASTERN CAPE

CRADOCK

☎ 048 / pop 30,200

Cradock, on the banks of the Great Fish River, is 240km north of Port Elizabeth and was established as a military outpost in 1813. It is now a busy agricultural and commercial centre for the farming district along the river. The town centre is fairly scruffy, but there are some interesting old buildings, including a superb church built in 1867 and modelled on St Martin-in-the-Fields, London.

Information is available from the **Cradock Publicity Association** (☎ 881 2383; www.cradock.co .za; Stockenstroom St) in the town hall building. Internet access is available at **Ecelsis Computer Store** (☎ /fax 881 5103; lcoetzer@worldonline.co.za; Spar Shopping Centre, 12 Stockenstroom St; per min R0.85; ❤ 8.30am-8pm), opposite the information office. **Standard Bank** (Adderley St) and **ABSA Bank** (Adderley St) both have ATMs.

Sights

Olive Schreiner House (☎ 881 5251; 9 Cross St; admission by donation; ❤ 8.30am-12.45pm & 2-4.30pm Mon-Fri) is a good example of a typical Karoo house. Schreiner is best remembered for her provocative novel *Story of an African Farm*, which advocated views considered radical even by today's standards.

The **Great Fish River Museum** (☎ 881 4509; High St; admission by donation; ❤ 8am-4pm Mon-Fri) was originally the parsonage of the Dutch Reformed Church. The house was built in 1825 and the displays depict pioneer life in the 19th century.

Sleeping

Die Tuishuise Guesthouses (☎ 881 1322; www.tuish uise.co.za; 36 Market St; cottages with breakfast per person R250) In one of Cradock's old streets, 18 original cottages have been beautifully restored and are for rent. The enchanting cottages have various numbers of bedrooms, but all have a sitting room with fireplace, self-catering kitchen and garden. The smaller and more modest Garden Cottage (R340) with just one bedroom is also available. Breakfast is served at Victoria Manor (see below).

Audrey B&B (☎ 881 3853; 59 Sprigg St; s/d with breakfast R120/240) Cradock's most inexpensive B&B, Audrey's offers a warm welcome and big, clean rooms, some with TV.

Victoria Manor (☎ 881 1650; cnr Market & Voortrekker Sts; s/d R195/340) This very elegant old inn was built in 1840 and has atmospheric wood-panelled rooms. Breakfast costs R40. Cheaper rooms in the annexe (single/double R110/R200) are also available.

Heritage House B&B (☎ /fax 881 3210; 45 Bree St; s/d with breakfast R200/340; ☒) The homely Heritage House offers comfortable, rustic rooms and old-fashioned hospitality. Its garden is home to a springbok, several dogs and Adam the python!

Eating & Entertainment

Buffalo Dan (☎ 881 4321; Engen Garage, R61; mains R35; ❤ lunch & dinner Mon-Sat) The dubious title of Cradock's best restaurant belongs to this modest steakhouse on the way out of town towards Mountain Zebra National Park.

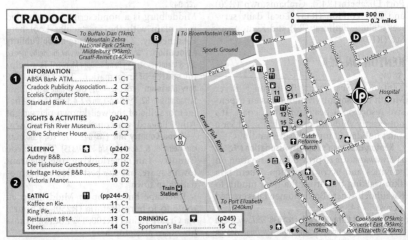

CRADOCK

0 ———— 300 m
0 ———— 0.2 miles

INFORMATION	
ABSA Bank ATM	1 C1
Cradock Publicity Association	2 C2
Ecelsis Computer Store	3 C2
Standard Bank	4 C1

SIGHTS & ACTIVITIES	(p244)
Great Fish River Museum	5 C2
Olive Schreiner House	6 C2

SLEEPING 🛏	(p244)
Audrey B&B	7 D2
Die Tuishuise Guesthouses	8 D2
Heritage House B&B	9 D2
Victoria Manor	10 D2

EATING 🍴	(pp244-5)
Kaffee en Kie	11 C1
King Pie	12 C1
Restaurant 1814	13 C1
Steers	14 C1

DRINKING 🍷	(p245)
Sportsman's Bar	15 C2

To Buffalo Dan (1km); Mountain Zebra National Park (25km); Middelburg (95km); Graaff-Reinet (140km)

To Bloemfontein (438km)

Sports Ground

Train Station

To Port Elizabeth (240km)

To Lemoenhoek (5km)

Cookhouse (75km); Somerset East (95km); Port Elizabeth (240km)

Dutch Reformed Church

Hospital

Kaffee en Kie (☎ 881 3779; Stockenstroom St; ☺ breakfast & lunch Mon-Sat) This café serves delicious breakfasts and is the only place in town that has half-decent coffee.

Restaurant 1814 (☎ 881 5390; 66 Stockenstroom St; mains R20-35; ☺ breakfast & lunch Mon-Sat) This place has a menu dedicated to burgers, pies and curries.

You can get your fast-food fix at **Steers** (Stockenstroom St) or **King Pie** (BP petrol station, Adderley St).

Sportsman's Bar (☎ 881 2431; cnr Stockenstroom & Durban Sts) is a great place to drink up the atmosphere with some of the more eccentric locals.

Getting There & Away

Translux runs daily to Cape Town (R225, 10 hours) via Graaff-Reinet (R100, two hours).

The **Shosholoza Meyl** (☎ 0860 008 888) *Algoa* train stops here en route between Port Elizabeth (six-/four-bed sleeper R70/105, 4½ hours) and Jo'burg (six-/four-bed sleeper R190/275, seven hours).

Most minibus taxis leave from the nearby township; ask at the petrol stations in town.

MOUNTAIN ZEBRA NATIONAL PARK

This **national park** (adult/child R60/30; ☺ 7am-7pm 1 Oct-30 Apr, 7am-6pm 1 May-30 Sept), 26km west of Cradock, is on the northern slopes of the Bankberg Range (2000m) and has superb views over the Karoo. The park protects one of the rarest animals in the world: the mountain zebra *(Equus zebra)*. The mountain zebra is distinguished from other zebra species by its small stature, reddish-brown nose and dewlap (a loose fold of skin hanging beneath the throat).

The park has superb mountain scenery, with the silence and space unique to the Karoo. Among the wide open spaces, thick patches of sweet thorn and wild olive are interspersed with rolling grasslands and succulents. The park also supports many antelope species. The largest predator is the caracal, and there are several species of small cats, genets, bat-eared foxes and black-backed jackals. Some 200 bird species have been recorded.

Information

The entrance gate is well signposted off the R61. It's quite feasible to get a taste of the park in a half-day excursion from Cradock.

You'll find a shop and restaurant in the main camp.

Activities

The park runs guided three night **trails** within the park on Monday and Thursday only – four people are needed for the trail to run, and no children under 12 are accepted. There's also a guided four-hour trail (R40). Various self-guided trails are also possible – ask at parks reception for details. A sunset guided **wildlife drive** costs R80 per adult. **Abseiling** (R170) can also be arranged at two sites within the park.

Sleeping & Eating

The park has a range of **accommodation** (bookings ☎ 048-881 2427; www.parks-sa.co.za/parks/mountain Zebra/default.html; camp sites/4-bed family cottages/6-bed guesthouses R70/335/600; ☒). The cottages at the park's rest camp are utilitarian but well-equipped, with their own bathrooms. The most interesting place to stay is at Doornhoek, a restored historic farmhouse, built in 1836 and hidden in a secluded valley. There is a 10% discount available from early June to mid-September, excluding school holidays.

The park headquarters has a restaurant called **Jabulani** (mains R40), with a decent selection of pasta, salad, steaks and burgers.

Getting There & Away

There's no public transport to the park so the only option is to bring your own car. One of the tour agencies in Graaff-Reinet (see p247) should be able to organise a day trip.

SOMERSET EAST

☎ 042 / pop 16,200

This attractive old town at the foot of the Bosberg Range (1600m) is sometimes referred to as the 'oasis of the Karoo', since the surrounding mountains mean that it receives a soaking 600mm of rainfall annually. After the dry country to the north and south, the rich forest on the mountain slopes is a surprise. There's no public transport to Somerset East, so you'll most likely only visit if you're passing in your own car.

The **Somerset East Tourist Office** (☎ 243 1333; Nojoli St; www.somerseteast.co.za; ☺ 7.45am-1pm & 1.45-4.30pm Mon-Fri) can help with local information.

The **museum** (☎ 243 1448; Beaufort St; ☉ 8am-1pm & 2-5pm Mon-Fri) is in a classic Georgian building at the top end of Beaufort St. There's a collection of Afrikaner memorabilia downstairs, and some interesting exhibitions about the liberation struggle upstairs.

Noah's Art (☎ 243 0620; www.noahs-art.co.za; 33 Nojoli St; s/d R150/300, with breakfast R180/360) is a cheerful pink-painted café-cum-curio shop–cum-B&B right in the middle of town, dedicated to promoting arts and crafts designed and made by locals.

BOSBERG NATURE RESERVE

This reserve covers 2000 hectares of thickly wooded ravines, dense grassland and Karoo shrubs. Most prominent of the larger animal species are mountain zebra and bushbuck. More than 83 bird species have been identified.

There are several hiking trails in the park, including the circular 15km-long **Bosberg Hiking Trail** (bookings ☎ 042-243 1333; per person R35), which has a 10-bed rest hut with toilet facilities. Hikers must register, and those planning to stay overnight must book in advance. The entrance to the reserve is 33km from Somerset East, along Auret Dr.

GRAAFF-REINET

☎ 049 / pop 35,400

Graaff-Reinet is often referred to as the 'jewel of the Karoo'. If you visit only one inland town in Eastern Cape, make it this one! It's the fourth-oldest European town in South Africa, and it has a superb architectural heritage with more than 220 buildings designated as national monuments. These range from Cape Dutch houses, with their distinctive gables, to classic flat-roofed Karoo cottages and ornate Victorian villas. Added to all this beauty is a charming small-town quirkiness, some excellent-value accommodation and a variety of eccentric local characters who add to the benignly surreal feel of the whole place.

The wild and beautiful Karoo Nature Reserve is within walking distance of Graaff-Reinet.

History

The interior of the Cape in the 18th century was a wild and dangerous place. When not fighting among themselves, the Boers did battle with the Khoisan in the Sneeu-berg and the Xhosa to the east around the Great Fish River. In an attempt to stem the chaos, the British sent a Landdrost (a sort of administrator/tax collector/magistrate) to Graaff-Reinet to establish a bit of law and order. The idea failed and the Landdrost was promptly thrown out by the town's citizens, who established an independent republic. The British regained a semblance of control soon afterwards, but were constantly harried by a joint force of Khoisan and Xhosa warriors and by the land-hungry Boers.

In the early 19th century, Boers seeking to escape the control of the Cape Town administration began their legendary Great Trek, and Graaff-Reinet became an important stepping stone for Voortrekkers heading north.

Orientation & Information

Graaff-Reinet is built in a cleft in the magnificent Sneeuberg Range on a bend of the Sundays River. The centre of town is very compact and easy to get around on foot.

Travel Café (p249) has a small **Internet café** (per min R0.75; ☉ 9am-4.30pm) attached to its restaurant. There's an **ABSA bank** (Church St) near the Dutch Reformed Church.

The helpful **Graaff-Reinet Publicity Association** (☎ 892 4248; www.graaffreinet.co.za; Church St; ☉ 8am-5pm Mon-Fri, 9am-noon Sat & Sun) has an abundance of maps and information about accommodation in the area.

Sights
MUSEUMS

You can buy a combined pass (R12) that gives access to the town's three museums. It's not valid on Sunday.

The **Hester Rupert Art Museum** (☎ 892 2121; Church St; adult/child R5/3; ☉ 9am-12.30pm & 2-5pm Mon-Fri, 9am-noon Sat & Sun) was originally a Dutch Reformed Mission church, consecrated in 1821. The beautiful interior space and permanent collection of paintings and sculptures are refreshingly contemporary after all the Victoriana at the town's other museums.

Pierneef Museum (☎ 892 6107; Middle St; admission free; ☉ 9am-12.30pm & 2-5pm Mon-Fri) is another very interesting contemporary art museum housing a set of panels by South African artist Jacob Hendrik Pierneef. Among the delicate, almost Japanese-looking paintings is one stunning rendition of the Valley of Desolation near Graaff-Reinet.

GRAAFF-REINET

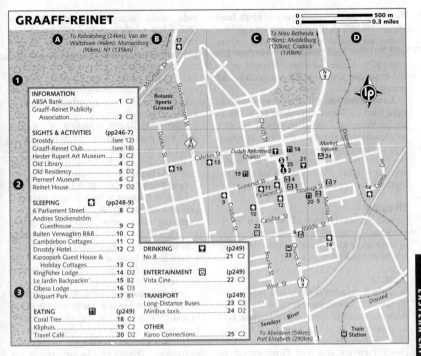

To Roboksberg (24km); Van der Waltshoek (46km); Murraysburg (90km); N1 (135km)

To Nieu Bethesda (55km); Middelburg (120km); Cradock (130km)

To Aberdeen (54km); Port Elizabeth (290km)

To Nieu Bethesda (55km); Middelburg (120km); Cradock (130km)

INFORMATION
ABSA Bank.....................................1 C2
Graaff-Reinet Publicity
   Association..............................2 C2

SIGHTS & ACTIVITIES (pp246-7)
Drostdy...................................(see 12)
Graaff-Reinet Club.................(see 18)
Hester Rupert Art Museum........3 C2
Old Library..................................4 C2
Old Residency............................5 D2
Pierneef Museum.......................6 C2
Reinet House..............................7 D2

SLEEPING (pp248-9)
6 Parliament Street....................8 C2
Andries Stockenström
   Guesthouse............................9 C2
Buiten Verwagten B&B.............10 C2
Cambdeboo Cottages...............11 C2
Drostdy Hotel...........................12 C2
Karoopark Guest House &
   Holiday Cottages...................13 C2
Kingfisher Lodge.......................14 D2
Le Jardin Backpackin'...............15 B2
Obesa Lodge.............................16 D3
Urquart Park.............................17 B1

EATING (p249)
Coral Tree................................18 C2
Kliphuis....................................19 C2
Travel Café...............................20 D2

DRINKING (p249)
No.8..21 C2

ENTERTAINMENT (p249)
Vista Cine.................................22 B2

TRANSPORT (p249)
Long-Distance Buses.................23 C3
Minibus taxis............................24 D2

OTHER
Karoo Connections....................25 C2

Botanic Sports Ground

Market Square

EASTERN CAPE

The **Old Library** (☎ 892 3801; cnr Church & Somerset Sts; adult/child R5/4; ☼ 8am-12.30pm & 2-5pm Mon-Fri, 9am-3pm Sat, 9am-4pm Sun) houses a collection of fossils from the Karoo (including some nasty-looking skulls of 'mammal-like, flesh-eating reptiles' from 230 million years ago) and an exhibition telling the life story of Robert Sobukwe, the pipe-smoking founder of the Pan African Congress. Much of his life was spent in jail or banned, so his children (one of whom rejoiced in the name Give Way Ye Imperialists) were brought up with the help of US tennis player Arthur Ashe.

Reinet House (☎ 892 3801; Murray St; adult/child R7/2; ☼ 8am-12.30pm & 2-5pm Mon-Fri, 9am-3pm Sat, 9am-4pm Sun), the Dutch Reformed parsonage built between 1806 and 1812, is a beautiful example of Cape Dutch architecture. The cobblestone rear courtyard has a grapevine planted in 1870 and now one of the largest in the world. The **Old Residency** (☎ 892 3801; Parsonage St; adult/child R5/2; ☼ 8am-noon & 2-5pm Mon-Fri, 9am-noon Sat) is another well-preserved 19th-century house with creaking wooden floors, now displaying a large collection of firearms.

DROSTDY

The residence of a Landdrost was known as a *drostdy* and included his office and courtroom as well as his family's living quarters. The Graaff-Reinet *drostdy* on Church St was built in 1806. Have a look at the old slave bell, which was restored and then, in an awful piece of irony, unveiled by former prime minister BJ Vorster, one of the arch criminals of apartheid. The *drostdy* is now a hotel (see p248)

GRAAFF-REINET CLUB

For something a little different, go along to the **Graaff-Reinet Club** (Church St). This one-time 'men's only' club, the second oldest in South Africa, has walls and halls adorned with numerous hunting trophies, including a giant pair of elephant feet that, unbelievably, someone saw fit to turn into wine coolers! Terrence and Nita Gush from Le Jardin Backpackin' (see p248) can get you an invitation.

Tours

Several readers have recommended the tours offered by Xolile Speelman, a lifelong township resident and owner of **Irhafu Tours** (☎ 082-844 2890). A three-hour township tour giving an insight into both Xhosa culture and history and modern township life costs R70. Xolile, who was brought up in the area, can also organise homestays and group meals.

Karoo Connections (☎ 892 3978; www.karootours .co.za; Church St) This company operates tours to the Valley of Desolation at sunset (R75; sundowners on request – the preferred drop is gin and tonic), Nieu Bethesda (R150) and the Karoo Nature Reserve (R75). It can also arrange wildlife drives, quad biking, microlighting, nature walks and city tours.

Sleeping

Graaff-Reinet is blessed with an overwhelming range of accommodation, most of it seriously good value compared to other towns in the Eastern Cape.

BUDGET

Le Jardin Backpackin' (☎ 892 5890, 082-644 4938; 103 Caledon St; s/d with shared bathroom R70/140; 🖭) A firm favourite with weary backpackers in need of a bit of pampering, Le Jardin provides homely rooms for excellent prices. Hosts Terrence and Nita Gush go out of their way to make their guests welcome and are both mines of information about the area's attractions.

MID-RANGE

Buiten Verwagten B&B (☎ 892 4504; www.buiten verwagten.co.za; 58 Bourke St; s/d with breakfast from R130/260; 🖳 🖭) The beautiful Buiten Verwagten, surrounded by a lovely garden, has charming rooms, some with self-catering facilities. Each is very different in décor and furnishings.

6 Parliament Street (☎ 892 6059; 7 Parliament St; s/d with breakfast R275/325) This very stylishly done up period cottage is ideal for a group of six people – the three bedrooms share two bathrooms. The wooden floors and antique furniture give the interior the same kind of feel as Reinet House or the Old Residency, but the old-fashioned look is offset by some contemporary touches such as satellite TV and sound system. Booking is through Travel Café on Parsonage St.

Obesa Lodge (☎ 082-588 5900; www.obesa.co.za; 64 Murray St; r R200, 2-bedroom cottages R300; 🖭) Something very different from Graaff-Reinet's

olde-worlde accommodation options – Obesa is a whole street of psychedelically coloured cottages with names like Moody Blues and Hey Mama. All have self-catering and braai facilities. Opposite the lodge is the owner's garden centre, which features an enormous collection of cacti from all over the world. Some reportedly have hallucinogenic qualities.

Kliphuis (☎ 892 2345; 46 Bourke St; r with breakfast R300) This popular restaurant (see opposite) also has two very charming cottage rooms in the garden. The bathrooms have Victorian claw baths but no showers.

Cambdeboo Cottages (☎ 892 3180; www.karoo park.co.za; 16 Parliament St; low/high season r R230/260, extra adult/child R65/45; 🖭) The modest but charming self-catering Cambdeboo Cottages are restored Karoo cottages, some featuring reed ceilings and yellowwood floors. There's a pool and a braai area. *Cambdeboo* is the Khoikhoi word for 'green valleys' and is used to describe the hills around Graaff-Reinet.

Karoopark Guest House & Holiday Cottages (☎ 892 2557; www.karoopark.co.za; 81 Caledon St; s/d with breakfast R140/310; 🖭) The friendly Karoopark has adequate self-contained cottages as well as comfortable but *very* chintzy rooms in its guesthouse. There's an a la carte restaurant for dinner, and breakfast is R40.

Urquart Park (☎ /fax 892 2136; Stockenstroom St; camp sites/rondavels/bungalows/chalets R50/100/120/300) To the north of town near the Van Ryneveld Dam, Urquart has pretty views towards the Karoo Nature Reserve. The good-quality chalets have their own kitchens.

TOP END

Andries Stockenström Guesthouse (☎ 892 4575; 100 Cradock St; r with half board from R630; 🖭 🖭) 'Possibly the best meal we ate in South Africa' was the verdict of one diner at this very upmarket B&B, famed in particular for its sumptuous four-course dinners. The Karoo-style haute cuisine is available to guests only, so you'll have to book in if you want to sample the award-winning menu.

Drostdy Hotel (☎ 892 2161; www.drostdy.co.za; 30 Church St; s/d R407/638; 🖭) The main part of this beautiful old hotel is in Graaff-Reinet's restored *drostdy*. The courtyard café is particularly enchanting, surrounded by fruit trees and the scent of flowers from the stunning gardens. The reception and the hotel restaurant are in the *drostdy*, while guests stay in restored mid-19th-century cottages, originally built for freed slaves along Stretch's Crt.

Kingfisher Lodge (☎ 892 2657; 33 Cypress Grove; s/d from R230/280; ⊠) The upmarket Kingfisher Lodge has lovely gardens and its own wine cellar. Breakfast is available for R30.

Eating

Coral Tree (☎ 892 5947; 3 Church St; mains R35-50; ✆ lunch & dinner Mon-Sat) This excellent café-restaurant specialises in local dishes such as Karoo schnitzel and springbok and ostrich carpaccio. There are a couple of good veggie options too. When fresh fish arrives from the coast, the place is booked solid. There's also a small shop here selling local arts and crafts, handmade pickles and delicacies such as kudu salami.

Kliphuis (☎ 892 2345; 46 Bourke St; mains R30-50; ✆ breakfast, lunch & dinner) Kliphuis is one of Graaff-Reinet's most popular eating spots, with Sunday lunch of Karoo lamb or venison a speciality. The rest of the menu is refreshingly grease-free, with dishes such as moussaka and quiche.

Travel Café (☎ 892 6059; 3 Parsonage St; light meals R10-20; ✆ breakfast & lunch) This café-restaurant serves delicious cakes, lunches and sandwiches, plus big cooked breakfasts. There's also an Internet café and a small curio shop.

Entertainment

No. 8 (☎ 892 4464; Somerset St) Graaff-Reinet's best drinking option as well as being a very decent restaurant, with dishes like Karoo lamb chops (R55) and springbok pies (R40) on the menu. The convivial bar leads out onto a wide veranda for summer evenings. There's a good selection of wines too.

Vista Cine (☎ 891 0260; 17 Bourke St; admission R10; ✆ 2.30pm & 8pm Fri & Sat, 8pm Mon) This is surely one of the most enchanting cinemas in the world – a lemon-yellow former church, perfectly preserved on the outside but with a tiny little fleapit auditorium fitted inside. Hand-written announcements on the projector screen call for 'no remarks to be passed during the film'.

Getting There & Away

BUS

Long-distance buses stop at Kudu Motors on Church St. The Publicity Association office acts as the Translux agent. Translux stops here on the run from Cape Town (R225, 8½ hours) to Queenstown (R125, three hours) via Cradock (R100, 1½ hours).

Intercape passes through Graaff-Reinet daily on its run between Jo'burg (R265, 11 hours) and Port Elizabeth (R205, three hours).

MINIBUS TAXIS

Minibus taxis leave from Market Sq. Major destinations are Port Elizabeth, Cape Town and Jo'burg.

AROUND GRAAFF-REINET
Farm Trails

Several farmers of the Cambdeboo region have developed walks and activities on their beautiful properties.

Rheboksberg (☎ 049-891 8004; s/d with breakfast R110/220) The friendly Rheboksberg farm, 24km northwest of Graaff-Reinet, is highly recommended. Dinner is available for an extra R40.

Van Der Waltshoek (☎ 049-845 9007; s/d with breakfast R130/160) Some 46km northwest of Graaff-Reinet, Van der Waltshoek is a historical farm with great walking all around. Dinner is R50.

KAROO NATURE RESERVE

This reserve, which virtually surrounds Graaff-Reinet, protects 16,000 hectares of mountainous veld typical of the Karoo. There are plenty of animals, but the real draw is the spectacular rock formations and great views overlooking the town and the plains. The reserve is subdivided into three main sections: the wildlife-viewing area to the north of the dam, the western section with the Valley of Desolation and the eastern section with the overnight hiking trail.

In the **wildlife-viewing area** (admission free; ✆ 7am-dusk) there are buffaloes, elands, kudus, hartebeests, wildebeests, springboks, the rare Cape Mountain Zebra and a host of smaller mammals. Bird species include black eagles, blue cranes and kori bustards. Visitors must stay in their vehicles.

The **Valley of Desolation** (admission free; ✆ 24hr) is the nature reserve's most popular sight. It's a hauntingly beautiful valley with an outstanding view – the rugged, piled dolorite columns of the valley are set against the backdrop of the endless Karoo plains. The town is also visible, nestled in a bend of the Sundays

EASTERN CAPE

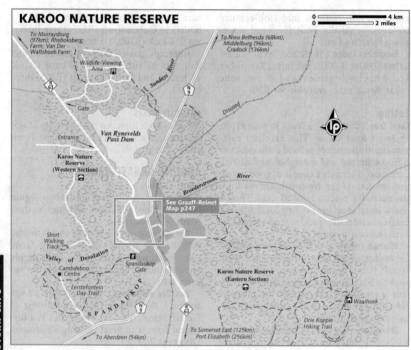

KAROO NATURE RESERVE

0 — 4 km
0 — 2 miles

To Murraysburg (97km); Rheboksberg; Farm; Van Der Waltshoek Farm

Wildlife-Viewing Area

Sundays River

R63

Gate

N9

To Nieu Bethesda (68km); Middelburg (96km); Cradock (136km)

Disused

Entrance

Van Rynevelds Pass Dam

Karoo Nature Reserve (Western Section)

Broederstroom

River

See Graaff-Reinet Map p247

Short Walking Track

Valley of Desolation
Cambdeboo Centre

Spandaukop Gate

Eerstefontein Day Trail

S P A N D A U K O P

N9

R63

Karoo Nature Reserve (Eastern Section)

Waaihoek

Drie Koppie Hiking Trail

To Aberdeen (54km)

To Somerset East (125km); Port Elizabeth (256km)

River. The valley can be reached by car on a steep but sealed road, and there's a 1.5km circuit walk. It's the sort of place that makes you wish you were an eagle. The best times to come are at sunrise or sunset.

The **Eerstefontein Day Trail** is also in the western section and has three trail options: 5km, 11km and 14km long. The information office supplies a map. Free permits are available from a self-help permit box at the Spandaukop gate. A longer, overnight trail in the eastern section, the **Drie Koppie Trail**, costs R15 per person and can be booked with the **Nature Reserve office** (☎ 049-892 3453) or by contacting **Karoo Connections** (p248) in Graaff-Reinet.

You'll need to have your own car to get around the reserve, or contact Karoo Connections in Graaff-Reinet for a tour. Accommodation is only available in Graaff-Reinet.

NIEU BETHESDA
☎ 049

The tiny, isolated village of Nieu Bethesda, once one of the most obscure places in South Africa, has achieved worldwide

fame as the home of the extraordinary **Owl House** (☎ 841 1603; adult/child & student R12/6; 8am-6pm). It was the home, studio and life's work of Helen Martins (1898–1976). Lying ill in bed one night, 'Miss Helen' resolved to bring light and colour into her drab, grey life by transforming her physical environment. Over the next 30 years she worked with a passion verging on obsession, first adorning the inside of the house with crushed glass and brightly coloured paint, then filling the yard outside with giant cement owls, camels, acrobats and mermaids, all created from everyday materials such as cement, broken bottles and wire. At the age of 78, worn down by arthritis and blindness, she committed suicide, leaving behind instructions that her house was to be preserved as a testament to her vision.

The idea of a lone woman creating such weird things in this tiny village in the middle of the Karoo is mind-boggling. It certainly serves to shake the standard view of apartheid-era South Africa as a drab and conformist society.

These days Nieu Bethesda has become a minor artistic colony, with dirt roads, a brewery, some good accommodation and a couple of pretty cafés. It's a great place to kick back for a few days and contemplate life amid the vast open spaces on all sides.

Nieu Bethesda is 55km from Graaff-Reinet. The drive here is very scenic with the Sneeuberg Range dominating the region as you approach; there are several turn-offs from the N9 between Graaff-Reinet and Middelburg. The biggest peak in the region, **Compassberg** (2502m), can be climbed in 2½ hours – the start of the hike is 35km out of town, at Compassberg farm. Ask in the village for directions. Petrol is not available in Nieu Bethesda.

Sleeping

The **Accommodation Booking Agency** (☎ 841 1623; Main Rd) arranges accommodation in guesthouses in and around Nieu Bethesda.

Owl House Backpackers (☎ 841 1642; owlhouse@ global.co.za; Martin St; camp sites/dm/d R35/65/160) A tranquil, ecofriendly place with very funky interior spaces and a fantastic, painted tower room in the garden (R200). The friendly owners can organise trips to Graaff-Reinet, visits to Khoisan painting sites, and donkey cart rides. It also hires bikes (R50/R30 per half/full day). Meals can be arranged.

Outsiders B&B (☎ 841 1642; owlhouse@global .co.za; Martin St; d with breakfast R300) This stylish B&B has cool, spacious rooms decorated with artistic touches such as lamps made from reclaimed metal. There's also a **restaurant** (mains R35; ☯ breakfast, lunch & dinner) and craft shop here.

Ganora Guest Farm (☎ 841 1302; www.ganora .co.za; cottages per person R150) If you'd rather be out of town under the soaring skies of the Karoo, this working sheep farm 7km out of the village is an excellent option, with well-decorated self-catering cottages of various sizes. Meals can be arranged (dinner R50, breakfast R35). Day tours are also available (book ahead). A visit to the fossil museum or rock-art sites costs R30 per person; a fossil walk is R40.

Stokkiesdraai Guesthouse (☎/fax 841 1658; Murray St; s/d R100/170) Old horse stables have been ingeniously converted into modest but comfortable self-catering cottages. The guesthouse also serves continental breakfasts (R15) and dinners (R45).

Eating

Egbert's Place (☎ 841 1716; Main Rd; ☯ breakfast, lunch & dinner Wed-Sun) This is a combined bring-your-own restaurant and bookshop. There's a great range of new and second-hand books, plus tasty, wholesome meals such as pork chops and lemon meringue pie. The food menu has no prices, so customers simply put whatever payment they think fit into an old red kettle! It's worth booking ahead for supper at busier times.

Village Inn Coffee Shop (☎ 841 1635; mains R10-30; ☯ breakfast & lunch Tue-Sun) This small coffee shop just down from the Owl House serves light lunches, sandwiches and cakes. There's also a small second-hand bookshop here. Dinner is available if you order in advance.

Two Goats Deli & Brewery (☎ 841 1602; Pienaar St; ☯ lunch Wed-Sun) Across a bridge from the main part of the village, is this excellent place to buy goat's milk cheeses, have a cold meat lunch or simply quaff lots of homemade Two Goats beer! Dinner is available in high season.

Getting There & Away

There is no public transport to Nieu Bethesda, but if you're in a group, lifts can be arranged from Nieu Bethesda – ask at Le Jardin Backpackin' (p248) for help.

AMATOLA

The stretch of coast and hinterland known as Amatola (from Xhosa for 'Calves') extends from the Great Fish River to the Great Kei River on the so-called Shipwreck Coast, and inland as far as Queenstown. It includes the surf-side city of East London, the enchanting mountain village of Hogsback, and the little-visited and wild government wildlife reserves of Mpofu, Double Drift and Tsolwana. Much of this area was the former Xhosa homeland of Ciskei.

SHIPWRECK COAST

The coast between the Great Fish River and East London is also known as the Shipwreck Coast, as it is the graveyard for many ships. The 64km **Shipwreck Hiking Trail** (per person per night R20) leads from the Great Fish River to the Ncera River, but it is possible to do any section as there are several easy entry and exit points. This is one of the few walking

EASTERN CAPE

areas in South Africa where hikers can set their own pace and camp more or less where they choose. They are rewarded with wild, unspoilt sections of surf beach, rich coastal vegetation and beautiful estuaries. The trail must be booked through the **Department of Water Affairs & Forestry** (☎ 043-642 2571, 043-604 5433; amatolHK@dwaf.co.za; 9 Chamberlain St) in King William's Town.

Hamburg

☎ 040

The small village of Hamburg, on the wide river flats at the mouth of the Keiskamma River, is near some of the best coast in South Africa. The river flats are home to many birds, especially migrating waders in summer. They also offer good fishing.

Oyster Lodge (☎ 678 1020; oyster@magicmaqil .co.za; 279 Main Rd; camp sites/dm/d R35/60/160; 🖳 🐂) From the outside the excellent Oyster Lodge is not much to look at, but don't be put off – inside it's spacious, clean and welcoming. There's a garden and braai area and a large deck out the back overlooking the river. **Meals** (dinner R25) are available, and kayaks and bikes can be hired.

Pelican Place (☎ 073-485 7048; Main Rd; www.the pelicanplace.co.za; 1-/2-/3-bedroom cottages low season R200/250/350, high season R300/350/450) This new, upmarket place has self-catering units of various sizes and a restaurant on site.

There's a daily minibus taxi to/from East London, which is about 100km to the east. The **Baz Bus** (☎ 021-439 2323) picks up and drops off here.

EASTERN CAPE GAME RESERVES

☎ 040

There are three main wildlife reserves administered by the **Eastern Cape Tourism Board** (☎ 635 2115; reservation@ectourism.co.za; www.ecto urism.co.za; PO Box 186, Bisho). All the reserves organise wildlife viewing, and many have multi-day walking trails available – contact the reserves directly for details. You'll need to be self-sufficient with food and water to visit the reserves.

Tsolwana Game Reserve (☎ 845 1112; adult/child R6/3, plus per car R20; ☽ 8am-6pm) is 57km south-west of Queenstown. The park is managed in conjunction with the local Tsolwana people, who benefit directly from the jobs and revenue produced. It protects some rugged Karoo landscape south of the spec-

tacular **Tafelberg** (1965m) and adjoining the Swart Kei River. The reserve's rolling plains are interspersed with valleys, cliffs, waterfalls, caves and gullies. There is a diverse range of animals including large herds of antelopes, rhinos, giraffes and mountain zebras. Wildlife viewing is possible in the **park's vehicle** (up to 4 people R160).

Double Drift Game Reserve (☎ 653 8010; ect bdd@icon.co.za; adult/child R6/3, plus per car R20; ☽ 8am-5pm), between Fort Beaufort and Alice, has been combined with the Sam Knott Nature Reserve and the Andries Vosloo Kudu Reserve to form the **Great Fish River Reserve**. There is much large wildlife to be seen in this area of thick bushveld, which is sandwiched between the Great Fish and Keiskamma Rivers.

To the north of Fort Beaufort is **Mpofu Game Reserve** (☎ 864 9450; adult/child R6/3, plus per car R20; ☽ 8am-5pm), where you are likely to see *mpofu* (eland), a large antelope. The grassland and valley bushveld make the region ideal for wildlife viewing. The three-day **Katberg Trail** starts here (see p255).

Sleeping

Tsolwana Game Reserve has three comfortable **lodges** (up to 4 people R485-650, plus per additional person R120-165) in old farmhouses. There are also two trail huts here, Phumlani and Fundani.

Double Drift Game Reserve also has three comfortable lodges: **Double Drift** (4-person r R580), **Mbabala** (4-person r R580) and **Nottingham Lodge** (4-person r R580).

Mpofu Game Reserve has two lodges: **Ntloni** (4-person r R580) and **Mpofu** (4-person r R580).

Getting There & Away

You'll need your own vehicle to visit all these reserves. Some are remote and hard to find – phone the lodges for directions and leave plenty of time to get there.

KING WILLIAM'S TOWN

☎ 043

Established by the London Missionary Society in 1826, King William's Town (known as 'King' or 'KWT') was a colonial capital and an important military base in the interminable struggle with the Xhosa. The main reason for a visit is the excellent Amathole Museum, or before beginning the Amatola Trail (see p254).

Hiking trails must be booked through the **Department of Water Affairs & Forestry** (☎ 642 2571, 604 5433; amatolHK@dwaf.co.za; 9 Chamberlain St).

Sights

The **Amathole Museum** (☎ 642 4506; 3 Albert Rd; admission R5; ☺ 9am-4.30pm Mon-Fri, 10am-1pm Sat) is one of the finest in the region, with an excellent **Xhosa Gallery** featuring in-depth explanations of Xhosa culture, mysticism and history. There are some wonderful examples of beadwork, plus wire cars made by local artists.

Pride of place in the natural history section is given to the stuffed corpse of Huberta, a hippo that became famous between 1928 and 1931 when she wandered down the coast from St Lucia in Natal – more than 1000km away – to the vicinity of King William's Town. The King of England declared she was to be left in peace, but she was shot by local farmers, causing a national outcry.

Sleeping & Eating

There are a limited number of sleeping options in KWT, but many are overpriced, so it's probably better to stay in East London and visit for the day. The town **library** (☎ 642 3391; Ayliff St; ☺ 9am-5.30pm Mon-Fri, 9am-1pm Sat) can provide a list of guesthouses and B&Bs.

STEVE BIKO

Steve Biko (1946–77) is buried in the Ginsberg cemetery just outside King William's Town. His insistence that people must begin by changing their own attitudes and feelings of inferiority – a process he called Black Consciousness – created a movement that is credited with playing a huge part in the downfall of apartheid.

This former medical student from the University of Natal refused to be silenced by the persecution of the apartheid government, and was eventually put under house arrest and banned from speaking in public. In 1977 he was detained in Port Elizabeth for 26 days under the Terrorism Act. He died in police custody after a series of brutal assaults.

To reach Biko's grave, follow Cathcart St south of the town and turn left down a dirt track that is signposted to the cemetery.

Dreamers Guest House (☎ 642 3012; www.dreamersguesthouse.com; 29 Gordon St; s/d with breakfast R290/390; ☒) This is a fairly upmarket guesthouse in a smart Victorian house. The spacious but fussy wooden-floored rooms have TV. **Meals** (dinner R65) are available and trips to local Xhosa villages can be arranged.

Grosvenor Lodge (☎ 642 1440; fax 604 7205; 48 Taylor St; s/d with breakfast R340/435) Centrally located, this small hotel has expensive but adequate rooms and a cosy bar-restaurant, the **King's Head** (mains R26; ☺ lunch & dinner). Its annexe, **Grosvenor Guest Lodge** (☎ 642 1440; fax 604 7205; 10 Bryson St; s/d with breakfast R280/360) is in a restored farmhouse in a quiet area of town.

Getting There & Away

Buses arrive at and depart from the **Engen One petrol station** (Cathcart St). Intercape buses stop in KWT on their daily run between Cape Town (R240, eight hours) and East London (R80, one hour). Translux buses run to Cape Town (R340, 18 hours).

Greyhound also stops in town on its daily run between Jo'burg/Pretoria (R310, 12 hours) and East London (R85, one hour) via Bloemfontein (R205, six hours).

Minibus taxis run from KWT to Bisho.

BISHO

☎ 040 / pop 138,000

Bisho, once capital of Ciskei, is now the administrative capital of Eastern Cape. The centre of Bisho was built to house Ciskei's bureaucrats and politicians, so there is a compact bunch of suitably grandiose and ugly public buildings, which are now in the service of the new provincial bureaucracy.

Regular minibuses run from the King William's Town train station to Bisho.

AMATOLA & KATBERG MOUNTAINS

The area north and west of King William's Town is partly degraded grazing land and partly rugged mountains with remnant indigenous forest. There are some good walks. When the mists are down on the Amatola Mountains, the forests take on an eerie silence.

The easiest way into this area is via King William's Town or Queenstown. **City to City** (☎ 011-773 2762) daily buses stop in Katberg, Seymour and Alice on the Jo'burg–King William's Town run. There are occasional minibus taxis too.

Amatola Trail

The 105km, six-day **Amatola Trail** (per person R150) begins at the Maden Dam, 23km north of King William's Town, and ends at the Tyumie River near Hogsback. Accommodation is in huts.

The Amatola Trail ranks as one of South Africa's top mountain walks, but it is pretty tough and should only be attempted if you are reasonably experienced and fit. Walkers are rewarded with great views, although about a third of the walk goes through dense forest and numerous streams with waterfalls and swimming holes. Shorter sections of the hike are available outside school holidays. Guides can also be arranged.

The trail must be booked with the **Department of Water Affairs & Forestry** (☎ 043-642 2571, 043-604 5433; amatolHK@dwaf.co.za; 9 Chamberlain St) in King William's Town.

Alice & Around

☎ 040 / pop 9800

Alice is a busy little town near the **University of Fort Hare**. The university was established in 1916 and has played an important role in the development of Southern Africa. Former students include Steve Biko, Nelson Mandela and Robert Mugabe. Parts of the original Fort Hare are also preserved in the grounds.

Within the campus, the excellent **De Beers Centenary Art Gallery** (☎ 602 2277; admission free; 7.30am-4.30pm Mon-Fri) has some very important work by contemporary South African artists, plus archive material on Steve Biko, Black Consciousness and the ANC.

Frequent minibus taxis run from King William's Town to the main gates of the university and to Alice; they cost R10. From Alice to Fort Beaufort is R5. A minibus taxi to Hogsback will cost about R20, but you'll probably have to change taxis en route.

Fort Beaufort

☎ 046 / pop 26,400

In 1846 a Xhosa man called Tsili stole an axe from a shop in Fort Beaufort. In a masterly display of overreaction, a British force invaded the Xhosa province of Queen Adelaide, beginning the Seventh Frontier War, known as the War of the Axe (1846–47). Today, Fort Beaufort has left such drama long behind and is a quiet, attractive and unassuming little town.

The **Historical Museum** (☎ 645 1555; fbmuseum@procomp.co.za; 44 Durban St; adult/child R2/0.50; 8.30am-5pm Mon-Fri, 8.30am-12.45pm Sat) is in the old officers' mess, bursting with memorabilia from firearms to fossils. The local publicity association is based here.

Savoy Hotel (☎ 645 1146; 53 Durban St; s/d R175/250;) This fairly decent little hotel opposite the museum has uninspiring but clean rooms with TV. There's a pretty garden and an a la carte **restaurant** (mains R35-50). Look out for newspaper clippings in the lobby relating to a UFO sighting in the town in 1972!

Town Lodge (☎ /fax 645 1598; townlodge@procomp.co.za; 114 Campbell St; s/d R160/240) This friendly little guesthouse has simple, cool rooms with TV and fan, plus a **restaurant** (mains R40).

The only public transport to Fort Beaufort is by minibus taxis, which leave several times a day from Alice (R5, 30 minutes)

Hogsback

☎ 045

Hogsback is a magical resort 1300m up the beautiful Amatola Mountains, about 100km northwest of Bisho. The small village has nothing more than a sprinkling of holiday homes and old-style mountain guesthouses, with mind-boggling views of mountains and forested valleys in all directions. Locals make much of the fact that JRR Tolkien was inspired to write *The Hobbit* in Hogsback, but in reality he left the place when he was five years old. Still, it's certainly easy to imagine a scene from one of his books happening here.

The steepest slopes around Hogsback are still covered in beautiful rainforest: yellowwood, assegai and tree fuchsia are all present. There are also, sadly, extensive pine plantations on land that was once indigenous forest. The peaks of the hills are high and bare, with 'bristles' reminiscent of a hog's back – hence the town's name.

On one side of the village is the mystical **ecoshrine** (adult/child R10/free; 10am-5.30pm Wed, Sat & Sun), a cement sculpture and garden that celebrates the forces of nature.

There are some great walks, bike rides and drives in the area. Some of the best roads are unsealed, so check locally before trying anything ambitious, and definitely think twice if it's been snowing (some snow falls in 10 months out of 12!). Be prepared for rain at any time, and in winter for temperatures that can drop to –1°C.

The hogs made of mud that you'll see being sold along the road (R10 to R15) are not fired; when they get wet they make a hell of a mess.

INFORMATION

The **information office** (11am-noon Mon-Fri) is on the main road; during peak season it's open longer hours.

There's an ATM in the Hogsback Inn, just off the main road.

SLEEPING & EATING

Hogsback has several very charming guesthouses and B&Bs, plus a couple of rather faded hotels.

Away with the Fairies (962 1031; hogsback1@iafrica.com; Hydrangea Lane; camp sites/dm/d with shared bathroom R40/65/160;) An interesting backpackers, the interiors are painted with fantastical designs featuring nubile fairies, and there's a log fire in the lounge that crackles cosily on cold evenings. The views from the lush garden and the double rooms are heartstopping. Most popular spot for those 'deep and meaningful' conversations is the tree house, perched in the forest among parrots and monkeys. The Hog & Hobbit bar is the spot to sink a few beers in the evenings. There are hearty **meals** (dinner R35), **mountain bikes** (per day R50) for hire, lots of rock climbing, and **horse trails** (per person R85) on offer.

Edge (962 1159; theedge@execunet.co.za; Bluff End; self-catering cottages from R220;) This is a collection of 10 stunningly decorated self-catering cottages strung out along the mountain's edge. The cottages all have one big bedroom (there's one twin and one family unit) with a log fire and TV, plus separate bathroom and kitchen. The more expensive (up to R650) have astonishing views too. The vibe here is peace, quiet and relaxation rather than raucous partying. It's an unbeatable place for a healthy rest – or a romantic weekend.

Also on site is a healthy and wholesome restaurant, **Tea Thyme** (mains R15-40; breakfast & lunch), and a mystical labyrinth, reminiscent of the patterns formed by crop circles (for more information on this, see www .besc.co.za/hogsback.htm).

To find the Edge, follow the signs from the main road (look for the pink triangle).

Granny Mouse House (962 1259; ingi@iafrica.com; 1 Nutswood Dr; s/d with breakfast R185/370;) This is a charming little B&B with rooms in an old wattle and daub house, plus a self-catering cottage in the garden. It's well known for its delicious organic dinners (R80). The very friendly owner speaks French and German.

High on the Hogs (962 1032; highhogs@telkomsa .net; Hydrangea Lane; 2-bedroom cottages R300;) The big two-bedroom cottage in the garden has a log fire and a full kitchen, and can sleep six in total. Its cheery pub, the Three Hogs Inn, serves big pre-hiking breakfasts (R25) and pub grub–style lunches.

Somerset Garden (962 1307; cnr Main Rd & Plaatje's Kraal; lunch R30, 4-course dinner R75; lunch & dinner) This restaurant is inside a private house and specialises in Afrikaner cooking, with dishes such as chicken livers in balsamic vinegar. Vegetarians and vegans are welcome – book ahead to discuss your requirements as there is no set menu. There's no alcohol licence either, so bring your own wine.

GETTING THERE & AWAY

The easiest way to get to Hogsback without a car is by shuttle bus from the Sugarshack Backpackers (p257) in East London, Buccaneer's Backpackers (p264) in Cintsa, or Old Gaol Backpackers (p239) in Grahamstown to Away with the Fairies on Monday, Tuesday, Thursday, Friday and Sunday (R45 one way). Beware of trying to come to Hogsback for a single night – you'll regret it!

Katberg & Around

040

Katberg, 110km northwest of Bisho, is a small town at the foot of a wooded range. The surrounding area is still much as it was when it was Ciskei: overworked and underfunded.

The road over the pass from Hogsback is unsealed, and although it is in a reasonable condition, check locally before tackling it after a lot of rain or snow.

The 50km, three-day **Katberg Trail** (bookings /fax 043-642 2571; per person per night R30) begins in Mpofu Game Reserve and ends at the Katberg Forest Station, just below the Katberg Pass. Accommodation in timber cabins is provided. It's a hike of medium difficulty and you cover a reasonable distance.

Katberg Hotel (653 1010; phkatberg@mweb .co.za; s/d with breakfast & dinner R305/610, weekend R275/550;) About 8km from Katberg, this upmarket hotel provides horse riding and tennis, plus lots of excellent walks in the surrounding area.

There's no official public transport into Katberg, but you may be able to find a lift or a minibus taxi going there from King William's Town or Alice (about R10).

EAST LONDON

☎ 043 / pop 423,500

East London is the country's largest river port, with a good surf beach and a spectacular bay that curves round to huge sand hills. Its Khoisan name means 'Place of the Buffalos', and the whole area has been named 'Buffalo City' by the tourism authorities.

If it is the quintessential beach/surfer lifestyle you are after, East London is definitely the right place to gravitate to – it's perfect for making contacts before heading to Jeffrey's Bay. Otherwise, the town's charms are somewhat limited, so most people don't spend much time here before heading up the spectacular Wild Coast to the north or south down the Sunshine Coast. There are, however, some good canoe and kayak trails in the surrounding nature reserves, and some beautiful beaches to the east of town.

Orientation

The main street in the centre is Oxford St, with the city centre extending from about Argyle St south to Fleet St. Fleet St runs east, and eventually, after a few corners and name changes, meets the Esplanade, where all the beachfront hotels and restaurants are situated. To the west, around Buffalo St, is a run-down and slightly edgy area dominated by the minibus taxi ranks.

Orient Beach, which is east of the river mouth, is popular with families and has a tidal pool. Eastern Beach is the long main beach fronting the Esplanade, but Nahoon Reef on the northern headland is better for surfing.

The massive and sprawling township of Mdantsane, 15km from town, is the second-largest township in South Africa after Soweto.

Information

MONEY

There are ATMs for all the major banks on Oxford St. For safety, only use ATMs during the day; better still, use one of the ATMs in the **Vincent Park shopping centre** (Devereux Ave) instead.

POST & COMMUNICATIONS

The main post office is halfway up Oxford St; there's a row of Telkom telephone boxes nearby. For Internet access, try **Cyber Lounge** (☎ 083-375 9040; 58 Beach Rd, Nahoon; per 21min R20; 🕒 8.30am-7.30pm Mon-Thu, 8.30am-6.30pm Fri, 10am-6pm Sat, 3-6pm Sun) or Guido's restaurant (pp260–1), though this place has a fairly slow connection.

TOURIST INFORMATION

There are two tourist offices in East London, both in **King's Tourist Centre** (cnr Longfellow & Aquarium Rds) on the beachfront. Staff at both offices are friendly but fairly clueless – the best they can do is hand out endless brochures and a few fairly useful maps.

Buffalo City Tourism (☎ 722 6015; www.visitbuffalocity.co.za; 🕒 8am-4.30pm Mon-Fri, 9am-2pm Sat, 9am-1pm Sun) Deals with matters relating to the city itself.

Eastern Cape Tourism Board (☎ 701 9600; www.ectourism.co.za; 🕒 8am-4.30pm Mon-Fri) Covers the wider area.

TRAVEL AGENCIES

Wild Coast Holiday Reservations (☎ 743 6181; www.wildcoastholidays.co.za; King's Tourist Centre, cnr Longfellow & Aquarium Rds) books accommodation and hiking trails in the Transkei.

Dangers & Annoyances

The eastern end of Eastern Beach and the area around Nahoon River mouth are not considered safe to walk on. Take care on the Esplanade and get a taxi home from anywhere in East London after dark. Watch out for pickpockets if you end up in the area around Buffalo St and the minibus taxi ranks.

Sights & Activities

The **East London Museum** (☎ 743 0686; Dawson Rd; admission R5; 🕒 9.30am-5pm Mon-Fri, 2-5pm Sat, 11am-4pm Sun) shot to fame in 1938 when the young curator, Marjorie Latimer, discovered a strange-looking fish on a vessel in East London harbour. It turned out to be a coelancanth, a type of fish thought to have become extinct over 50 million years ago. To find it still in existence was the marine equivalent of stumbling upon a living dinosaur. The fish was named *Latimeria chalumnae* in honour of its finder, and over five thousand people came to the museum on the first day it was exhibited. Coelacanths have since been discovered all over the world, but the stuffed original is still on display at the museum. Other exhibits at the museum include trace-fossil human footprints and a living beehive.

The **Ann Bryant Art Gallery** (☎ 722 4044; St Marks Rd; admission free; ♥ 9.30am-5pm Mon-Fri, 9.30am-noon Sat), south of the museum, is in an old mansion featuring an eclectic collection of paintings and sculptures, mostly by South African artists. There's also a small coffee shop here.

Gately House (☎ 722 2141; 1 Park Gates Rd; adult/child R1/free; ♥ 10am-1pm & 2-5pm Tue-Thu, 10am-1pm Fri, 3-5pm Sat & Sun) was the residence of the first mayor of East London, John Gately, and still contains all his original furniture. It's near the entrance to Queen's Park, but it's easiest to access the house by walking up from the zoo.

If you have children, the small **East London zoo** (☎ 722 1171; adult/child R9.90/6.60; ♥ 9am-5pm Mon-Sun) at Queen's Park, and a small **aquarium** (☎ 705 2637; Esplanade; adult/child R13.20/8.30; ♥ 9am-5pm Mon-Sun) on the beachfront. Otherwise try the **Water World Fun Park** (☎ 748 4265; admission R20; ♥ 9am-5pm Sep-Easter) in West Bank (near the racetrack), where kids can ride endlessly on the supertube and speed slides.

If there are a group of you, you can take a sunset cruise on the **Miscky yacht** (☎ 735 2232, 083-953 8899; cruises per person R50). It leaves at 6pm from Latimer's Landing, just south of Settler's Way; bookings are essential.

The best **surfing** is at Nahoon Reef at the southern end of Nahoon Beach. If you'd like to do some lengths or pump some iron while you're in town, head for the **Virgin Active Gym** (☎ 743 3777; Esplanade; ♥ 5.30am-9pm Mon-Fri, 7am-7pm Sat & Sun). Day membership costs R75.

Tours

Various half-day tours of the city and the surrounding area can be organised; contact the tourist office or one of the following companies:

Amatola Tours (☎ 748 3037; info@amatour.co.za; 20 Currie St, Quigney) Offers tours to places of interest around the city, including the townships.

Imonti Tours (☎ 745 3884; 26 Venice Rd, Morningside) Organises tours to the townships of Mdantsane and Zwelitsha, and to Bisho and King William's Town. There are also full-day tours to Qunu in the Transkei, where Nelson Mandela spent his childhood.

Off Road Adventures (☎ 082-783 1288; 4wd@mweb .co.za) Provides cultural, 4WD and canoeing trails in the countryside surrounding East London. Canoe trips centre on the Fish or Breda Rivers and are suitable for beginners as well as experienced paddlers. Multi-day trips to Dwesa Nature Reserve or even Lesotho can also be arranged.

Sleeping

As you might imagine, East London has a plethora of accommodation in all price ranges. Unless you're a surfer you might be better off opting for one of the uptown hotels and B&Bs rather than the pretty scruffy beachfront. There are no really top-end hotels in East London.

BUDGET

Niki Nana Backpackers (☎ 722 8509; www.nikinana .co.za; 4 Hillview Rd; camp sites/dm/d with shared bathroom R35/65/150; ⊠) This backpackers, easily recognisable by its striking zebra-striped facade, is small but perfectly formed, with comfy inside spaces plus a private garden with a large swimming pool and braai area. Meals can be arranged on request.

Sugarshack Backpackers (☎ 722 8240; www.sug arshack.co.za; Eastern Esplanade, Eastern Beach; camp sites/dm/d with shared bathroom R35/55/140; ⊠) With the beach just metres away, the surf's always up at this lively backpackers. Activities on offer include waterskiing (R160), paintballing (R75) and cliff jumping (R25). Surfboard hire (R50) and two-hour lessons (R75) are always available. After a day's hanging 10, you can have a drink at the Shack's bar or next door at Buccaneers pub, which rocks until dawn. This is a place to cut loose, not to sleep – which is just as well as the smallish dorms are pretty close to the party area. If you just can't tear yourself away, the hostel also offers a visa extension service (R475).

East London Backpackers (☎ 781 1122, 084-782 7780; www.elbackpackers.co.za; 11 Quanza St; dm/s/d with shared bathroom R60/100/140, d R160; ⊠) This well-maintained place is much quieter than Sugar Shack, but somewhat lacking in atmosphere. The dorms are spacious and clean and there is a braai area and a plunge pool. There are also good-quality doubles with their own bathroom.

Mike's Guest House (☎ 743 3647; mikes@his.co.za; 22 Clifford St; s/d with shared bathroom R100/160, s/d R170/220) Up a rather dubious looking road

EAST LONDON

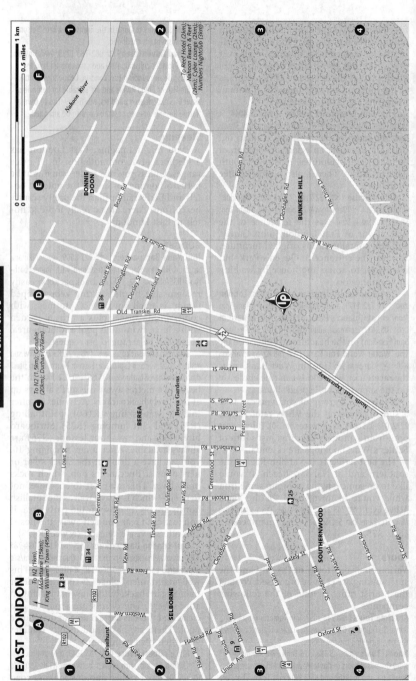

To N2 (1km); Mdantsane (15km); King William's Town (45km)

To N2 (1.5km); Gonubie (20km); Durban (675km)

To Reef Hotel (2km); Nahoon Beach Hotel (2km); Cyber Lounge (2km); Numbers Nightclub (3km)

Nahoon River

BONNIE DOON

BUNKERS HILL

BEREA

SELBORNE

SOUTHERNWOOD

North East Expressway

OLd Transkei Rd

Epsom Rd

Gleneagles Rd

The Drive Rd

John Baillie Rd

Beach Rd

Schultz Rd

Smartt Rd
Kennington Rd
Dersley St
Beresford Rd

Lowe St

Devereux Ave

Oakhill Rd

Kew Rd

Frere Rd

Tindale Rd

Darlington Rd

Jarvis Rd

Ashley Rd

Cleydon Rd

Lincoln Rd

Chamberlain Rd

Greenwood St

Pearce Street

Tecoma St

Castle St

Suffolk Rd

Berea Gardens

Latimer St

Western Ave

Beatty Rd

Haig Rd

Halstead Rd

Smuts Rd

Union Ave

Dawson Rd

Light Road

Gately St

St Mark's Rd

St Andrew's Rd

St George's Rd

Oxford St

Chiselhurst

R102

36

38

34

41

14

24

25

9

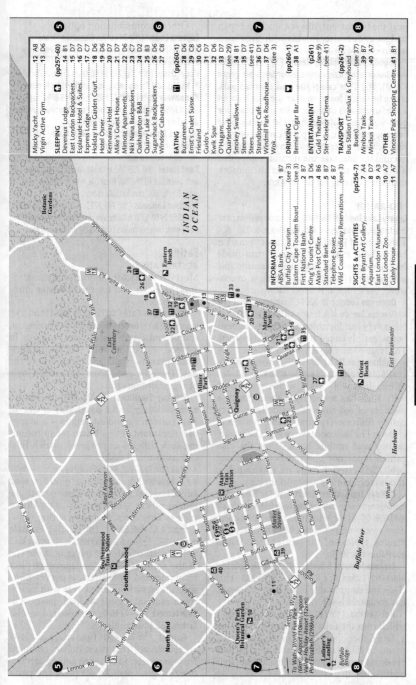

Miscky Yacht...........................12 A8
Virgin Active Gym....................13 D6

SLEEPING (pp257–60)
Devereux Lodge.........................14 B1
East London Backpackers...........15 D7
Esplanade Hotel & Suites............16 D7
Express Lodge...........................17 C7
Holiday Inn Garden Court...........18 D6
Hotel Osner..............................19 D6
Kennaway Hotel.........................20 D7
Mike's Guest House....................21 D7
Mimosa Apartments...................22 D6
Niki Nana Backpackers...............23 D7
Oakhampton B&B.......................24 D2
Quarry Lake Inn........................25 B3
Sugarshack Backpackers.............26 D6
Windsor Cabanas.......................27 C8

EATING (pp260–1)
Buccaneers...............................28 D6
Ernst's Chalet Suisse..................29 C8
Friesland..................................30 C6
Guido's....................................31 D7
Kwik Spar................................32 D6
O'Hagans.................................33 D7
Quarterdeck............................(see 29)
Smokey Swallows......................34 B1
Steers......................................35 D7
Strandloper Cafe....................(see 41)
Windmill Park Roadhouse...........37 D6
Wok.....................................(see 3)

DRINKING (pp260–1)
Bernie's Cigar Bar......................38 A1

ENTERTAINMENT (p261)
Guild Theatre..........................(see 9)
Ster-Kinekor Cinema...............(see 41)

TRANSPORT (pp261–2)
Bus Station (Translux & Greyhound
  Buses).................................(see 37)
Minibus Taxis............................39 B7
Minibus Taxis............................40 A7

OTHER
Vincent Park Shopping Centre....41 B1

INFORMATION
ABSA Bank....................................1 B7
Buffalo City Tourism...................(see 3)
Eastern Cape Tourism Board........2 B7
First National Bank.......................3 D6
King's Tourist Centre....................4 B6
Main Post Office..........................5 B7
Standard Bank.............................6 B7
Wild Coast Holiday Reservations...(see 3)

SIGHTS & ACTIVITIES (pp256–7)
Ann Bryant Art Gallery..................7 A4
Aquarium....................................8 D7
East London Museum....................9 A3
East London Zoo........................10 A7
Gately House.............................11 A7

INDIAN OCEAN

Botanic Gardens

Eastern Beach

Marine Park

Orient Beach

East Breakwater

Harbour

Wharf

Buffalo River

Latimer's Landing

Buffalo Bridge

To Water World Fun Park
(6km); Areena Riverside
Resort & Lagoon Valley
Holiday Resort (12km);
Port Elizabeth (298km)

near the beachfront, this is a spick and span budget guesthouse. Rooms with their own bathroom are also available.

Lagoon Valley Holiday Resort (☎ 736 9785/9753; www.lagoonvalley.co.za; camp sites/rondavels per person R54/131; 🐾) This camp site and caravan park is in a beautiful location near the beach about 18km southwest of town. It's a great place for bird-watching – more than 150 species have been spotted here. The place can get busy in high season, when prices also go up slightly. To find the site, take the turn-off signposted 'Cove Rock' about 3.5km after the airport, then keep driving for about 4km.

MID-RANGE

Quarry Lake Inn (☎ 707 5400; www.quarrylakeinn.co.za; Quartzite Dr, Selbourne; s/d with breakfast R506/720; 🐾) This is one of East London's most upmarket hotels, built next to a tranquil man-made lake. The rooms are elegant and comfortable with modern facilities, including a microwave, bar fridge and small sitting area.

Devereux Lodge (☎ 726 9459; coastdev@iafrica.com; 7A Devereux Ave; s/d with breakfast R364/433; 🖳) Another very comfortable and upmarket guesthouse, mainly aimed at visiting businessmen. The huge rooms have TV and fridge.

Oakhampton B&B (☎ 726 9963; www.oakhampton .co.za; 8 Okehampton Rd; s/d with breakfast R220/330; 🐾) Minimalists will swoon – this impossibly frilly B&B has a Victorian theme, with a plethora of red roses, china dolls and lacy doilies filling every conceivable nook and cranny. The bedrooms have brass bedstead, canopy and antique linen, while the lush garden holds not one but two swimming pools. Self-catering units are also available, and honeymooners get satin sheets.

Holiday Inn Garden Court (☎ 722 7260; gceast london@southernsun.com; cnr John Bailie Rd & Moore St; s/d R599/699; 🐾 🖳 🐾) Rooms at this safe choice have sweeping sea views but are otherwise blandly typical of the genre. Breakfast is available for R68.

Esplanade Hotel & Suites (☎ 722 2518; esphotel@ iafrica.com; Clifford St; s R220-260, d R260-290) This clean and comfortable hotel, near the beach, has rooms with sea views.

Kat Leisure (☎ 743 3433; osaccom@iafrica.com), which runs the following places to stay, has a virtual monopoly of the hotels and apartments in East London. Places that include breakfast provide a pre-packed airline-style continental affair.

Other accommodation options:

Express Lodge (☎ 743 0182; Fitzpatrick St; s/d R145/215) Rooms here include a kitchenette with fridge and microwave.

Hotel Osner (☎ /fax 743 3433; Court Cres; s/d/family R310/360/600) Breezy rooms that are ideal for families.

Kennaway Hotel (☎ 722 5531; fax 743 0792; Esplanade; d R450) Over-the-top colonial-style rooms, heavy on the velour furnishings but quite luxurious.

Mimosa Apartments (☎ 743 3433; Marine Tce; s/d with breakfast R220/280) Good-value units with kitchenette, often booked out.

Reef Hotel (☎ 735 1620; 18 Harewood Dr, Nahoon; s/d with breakfast R230/280) Near the river in Nahoon, this place has bright, comfortable rooms.

Windsor Cabanas (☎ 743 2225; Marine Tce; s/d with breakfast R480/575) A fairly upmarket Mediterranean-style place with cheaper rooms (R255/325) in the courtyard.

Eating
RESTAURANTS

Most of the beachfront hotels have restaurants. You can also try the following mid-range places:

Strandloper Café (☎ 735 4570; 95 Old Transkei Rd; mains R58-88; 🕑 dinner Mon-Sat) This very elegant, simple and classy restaurant specialises in seafood, with dishes such as chilli and coriander prawns, paella and Cajun fish of the day. There's a good wine list and a couple of veggie options too.

Smokey Swallows (☎ 727 1349; Devereux Ave; mains R60-100; 🕑 lunch & dinner) This is one of East London's trendiest venues – a lounge bar–restaurant with a bistro menu including such delights as peppered ostrich fillet and hand-rolled sushi.

Wok (☎ 722 2902; King's Tourist Centre, cnr Longfellow & Aquarium Rds; mains R30-50; 🕑 lunch & dinner Tue-Sat, lunch Sun) This smart diner next to the tourist offices serves Asian fusion dishes such as Thai curry, sushi and spring rolls.

Ernst's Chalet Suisse (☎ 743 2102; Esplanade; mains R35-85; 🕑 lunch & dinner Mon-Fri, dinner Sat, lunch Sun) In a rather unlovely building at the end of the seafront, this is an upmarket place recommended by readers. It serves Swiss specialities such as diced veal with mushroom sauce alongside seafood dishes. The **Quarterdeck** (☎ 722 1840), next door, does old-fashioned pub meals.

Guido's (☎ 743 4441; Esplanade; mains R20-40; 🕑 lunch & dinner) This chain Italian, complete with faux-Grecian columns and a water feature, is a good standby for pizza and pasta.

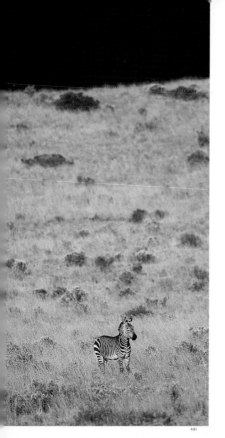

Mountain Zebra National Park (p245),
Eastern Cape

Xhosa boy from the Transkei region
(p262), Wild Coast, Eastern Cape

Diving near Port Elizabeth (p231),
Eastern Cape

Sandboarding on the dunes at Jeffrey's Bay (p225), Eastern Cape

Zulu woman, KwaZulu-Natal

Rickshaw puller (p287), Durban, KwaZulu-Natal

Entrance to Victoria St Market (p296), Durban, KwaZulu-Natal

Farmland in the Drakensberg range (p323), KwaZulu-Natal

O'Hagans (☎ 822 2982; Aquarium Complex, Esplanade; mains R30-50; ⏰ lunch & dinner) This popular pub 'n' grill is good for a sunset drink on the sea-facing deck. The fake Irish menu includes things like 'Tipperary Roast Chicken' and 'Shamrock Burger' but it's all pretty tasty and good value, if a bit unoriginal. No shorts may be worn after 7pm.

Buccaneers (☎ 743 5171; Eastern Esplanade; mains R15-40; ⏰ lunch & dinner) Next to Sugarshack Backpackers, this down-to-earth pub serves steaks, toasted sandwiches and pizzas to soak up the alcohol.

CAFES & QUICK EATS

Fast-food options include **Friesland** (cnr Goldschmidt & Tennyson Sts) and **Steers** with its four branches on Oxford St in the centre of town; in the Vincent Park Shopping Centre, the Papagallo Building on the Esplanade; and on the waterfront in Nahoon.

Windmill Park Roadhouse (☎ 722 2908; Moore St; mains R15-20; ⏰ breakfast, lunch & dinner) This fast-food joint at the bus station brings your burger or toastie directly to your car.

SELF-CATERING

If you're self-catering, the most convenient shop is **Kwik Spar** (Marine Tce) in front of Mimosa Apartments.

Entertainment

BARS & NIGHTCLUBS

Buccaneers (☎ 743 5171; Esplanade) What this surfy, hard-drinking pub lacks in sophistication, it makes up for in popularity – as well as food (see above), there's happy hour from 8pm to 9.30pm on Wednesday, and live bands Wednesday, Thursday and Friday.

Numbers Nightclub (☎ 748 4425; the Hub, Beacon Bay) This long-established nightclub recently moved out to Beacon Bay from the centre of town, but it's still the best-loved disco in the city.

Bernie's Cigar Bar (☎ 726 3792; 10 Balfour Rd; ⏰ Mon-Sat) This attractive, relaxed bar has live music Wednesday to Saturday.

O'Hagans (☎ 743 8713; Aquarium Complex, Esplanade) This traditional pub is good on Friday night. The terrace perfect for a beer or meal (see above) on a sunny afternoon.

Smokey Swallows (☎ 727 1349; Devereux Ave) The first Sunday of the month there's live jazz and the third Sunday has live blues at this sophisticated bar-restaurant (see p260).

CINEMAS & THEATRES

Ster-Kinekor Cinema (☎ 726 8122; Vincent Park Shopping Centre, Devereux Ave; admission R15) Shows the latest movies.

Guild Theatre (☎ 743 0704; Dawson Rd) This is East London's main theatre. Everything from ballet performances to beauty contests takes place here.

Getting There & Away

AIR

The airport is 10km from the centre. **South African Airways** (SAA; ☎ 706 0203) has an office at the airport and flies from East London daily to Port Elizabeth (around R700), Durban (around R1100) and Cape Town (around R1650).

BUS

Translux, Greyhound and SA Connection stop at the **Windmill Park Roadhouse** (Moore St). Intercape buses stop at the **main train station** (Station St) and at the airport.

Translux (☎ 700 1999) has daily buses to Umtata (R115, four hours), Port Elizabeth (R155, four hours), Durban (R185, 10 hours), Cape Town (R320, 15 hours) and Jo'burg/Pretoria (R320, 14 hours).

Greyhound (☎ 743 9284) has a daily bus between Durban (R200, 10 hours) and Cape Town (R360, 16 hours) via Port Elizabeth (R125, five hours).

Intercape (☎ 743 9284) has daily buses from East London to Cape Town (R289, 7½ hours) and Port Elizabeth (R99, five hours).

SA Connection (☎ 086-110 2426) has buses weekly to Jo'burg (R315) and a twice-weekly connection to Cape Town (R330).

The **Baz Bus** (☎ 021-439 2323) runs from Port Elizabeth to Durban via East London Monday, Tuesday, Wednesday Friday and Saturday. It runs in the other direction Monday, Tuesday, Thursday, Friday and Sunday. It picks up from hostels.

MINIBUS TAXI

On the corner of Buffalo and Argyle Sts are long-distance minibus taxis to destinations north of East London. Nearby on the corner of Caxton and Gillwell Sts are minibus taxis for King William's Town, Bisho and the local area. The following are sample fares: King William's Town (R13, one hour), Butterworth (R32, three hours), Umtata (R63, five hours), Port Elizabeth

(R70, six hours), Jo'burg (R170, 15 hours) and Cape Town (R190, 18 hours).

TRAIN
The overnight **Shosholoza Meyl** (☎ 0860 008 888) *Amatola* from East London to Jo'burg (1st/2nd class R335/235, 18 hours) departs daily via Bloemfontein.

Getting Around
Most city buses stop at the city hall on Oxford St. For information on times and routes, contact **Buffalo City Municipal Buses** (☎ 705 2666).

For private taxis, contact **Border Taxis** (☎ 722 3946).

GONUBIE
☎ 043
So close to East London that it's almost a suburb, Gonubie has a small nature reserve and a stretch of rather rocky beach.

The impressive **White House** (☎ 740 0344; www.thewhitehousebandb.co.za; 10 Whitthaus St; s/d with breakfast R295/395; ☒) has glass windows for panoramic views of cliffs and sea – you can watch whales and dolphins passing by while you're having breakfast! There's a helipad too, should you need one.

The **Blue Waters Lodge** (☎ 740 2019; bwlodge@ iafrica.com; 7th St; s/d low season R120/190, high season R207/334; ☒) is a friendly family-run place with fairly basic facilities.

Gonubie Caravan Park (☎ 705 9748; fax 740 5937; camp sites/2-bedroom chalets low season R35/236, high season R104/478) is the best budget option in Gonubie, with log cabin–style chalets right on the beach.

To get to Gonubie, return to the N2 from East London, then follow the signposts leading down to the village. There's no public transport.

WILD COAST

Just north of East London is the start of the famous Wild Coast, a beautiful area of dramatic beaches and indigenous forest running east of the N2 all the way to Port Edward in Natal. This area is also often still referred to as the Transkei, after the apartheid homeland that once covered this part of the country.

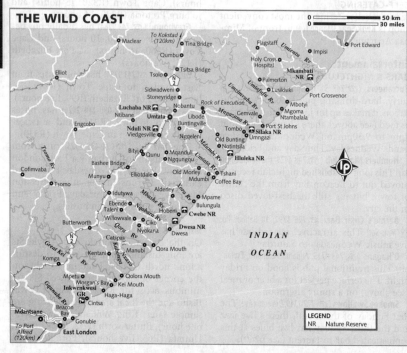

THE WILD COAST

The Wild Coast got its name from the many ships that were wrecked by the unforgiving storms and rocky shores of this part of the coast. In later years, a few captains needing a quick insurance claim chose to run their ships aground and trust that the region's reputation would save too many awkward questions!

This is one of the most unspoilt, rural and wild areas of South Africa. The spectacular coastline with its surf-pounded beaches, waterfalls and river estuaries is perfectly complemented by the green, rolling hills and steep-sided gorges to be found inland. This is the best place to get to know the Xhosa people who still live traditionally in villages of round, brightly painted huts dotted across the hillsides.

If you plan to hike or drive around inland Transkei, always ask permission before camping. Don't drive after dark, and remember that most of the roads here don't appear on maps, and signposts are few and far between. It's also important to watch out for animals and people in the middle of the roads. Unsealed roads can be impassable after rain.

Summers on the coast are hot and humid. Inland, many areas have winter frosts. Most rain falls in March and spring (September–November).

TOURS

Even if guided tours aren't your usual style, the following outfits can help immeasurably in understanding the rich and complex culture of the Xhosa and AmaMpondo peoples who inhabit the Wild Coast. If time is a consideration, it's also handy to let someone else sort out the fairly complex logistics of travelling around an area with few mapped roads, English speakers or tourist facilities.

African Heartland Journeys (☎ 043-734 3012, 082-327 3944; www.africanheartland.co.za) This very well-regarded tour company runs small-group adventure tours into the area across the Great Kei River from their base at Buccaneer's Backpackers in Cintsa. The accommodation varies from rural village homestays to comfortable hotels, and tours encompass travel by Land Rover, canoe, horse, mountain bike or even light aircraft. Inspirational guides lead groups to waterfalls, forests, beaches and villages, all with the emphasis on getting to know 'the colourful and courageous Xhosa nation'. Single and multi-day journeys are possible from a

EASTERN CAPE

THE XHOSA

Travelling along the southwestern Wild Coast is an excellent way to get to know Xhosa culture. You may hear the term 'red people', which refers to the red clay and red clothes worn by many adults. Clothing, colours and beaded jewellery all indicate a Xhosa's subgroup. The Tembu and Bomvana, for example, favour red and orange ochres in the dyeing of their clothing, while the Pondo and Mpondomise use light blue. The isiDanga – a long turquoise necklace that identifies the wearer to their ancestors – is also still seen today.

Belief in witches (male and female) among the Xhosa is strong, and witch burning is not unknown. Most witchcraft is considered evil, with possession by depraved spirits a major fear. A main source of evil are tokoloshe, mythical man-like creatures who live in water but are also kept by witches. One reason that many Xhosa keep their beds raised high off the ground is to avoid being caught in their sleep by the tiny tokoloshe.

The iGqirha (spiritual healer) is empowered to deal with both the forces of nature and the trouble caused by witches, and so holds an important place in traditional society. The iXhwele (herbalist) performs some magic but is more concerned with health. Both of these healers are often referred to as sangomas.

Many Xhosa have the top of their left-hand little finger removed during childhood to prevent misfortune. Puberty and marriage rituals also play a central role. Boys must not be seen by women during the three-month initiation period following circumcision; during this time the boys disguise themselves with white clay, or in intricate costumes made of dried palm leaves. In the female puberty ritual, a girl is confined in a darkened hut while her friends tour the area singing for gifts. Unmarried girls wear short skirts, which are worn longer as marriage approaches. Married women wear long skirts and cover their breasts. They often put white clay on their faces, wear large, turban-like cloth hats and may smoke long-stemmed pipes.

variety of different starting points. Tents and camping equipment are provided.

Wild Coast Trails (☎ 039-305 6455; www.wildcoast .org.za; amadiba@euwildcoast.za.org) The Wild Coast Trails project runs horse-riding, hiking and canoeing routes of different lengths up and down the most beautiful and isolated parts of the coast between Coffee Bay and Port Edward in Natal. Guides and hosts are drawn from local AmaMpondo and Amadiba communities, supported by local hotels and private companies. Accommodation is in comfortable tented camps, guesthouses or local homes, and the trails go through nature reserves, along beaches and into rural villages. Along the way guests visit shipwrecks, spectacular rock formations, waterfalls and nature reserves as well as shebeens, sangomas (traditional healers) and traditional celebrations. Day rides are also available at various locations on the Wild Coast.

EAST LONDON TO KEI MOUTH

The East Coast Resorts turn-off from the N2 will get you to most of the resorts closest to East London, the most attractive of which is Cintsa. The excellent Strandloper Trails (see opposite) are the best introduction to this part of the coastline.

Cintsa

☎ 043 / pop

Next to a beautiful sweep of unspoilt white beach, 38km from East London, Cintsa comprises two small, pretty villages, Cintsa East and Cintsa West. It's definitely the best place on this part of the coast to hang out for a few days (or weeks). Also in the area is the private, upmarket **Inkenkwesi Game Reserve** (☎ 734 3234; www.inkwenkwezi.com; day visits

per person R195; ⏰ 8am-4pm), which contains four of the Big Five (only elephants are missing). Any of the accommodation listed can help organise activities.

SLEEPING & EATING

Cintsa offers several good accommodation options and an excellent restaurant.

Buccaneer's Backpackers (☎ /fax 743 3012, 734 3749; cintsabp@iafrica.com; Cintsa West; camp sites/dm/d with shared bathroom R45/70/160; ▢ ▢) One of the most celebrated hostels in South Africa, Buccaneer's is a big place, with dozens of activities on offer and a great party vibe. Despite this, it still retains its character and personal touch, with the Price family working flat out to make sure their guests feel welcome. There's also enough space to make sure that those who want peace and quiet can find it here.

As well as comfortable dorms and rooms, there are also **safari tents** (R140) and **cottages** (R240) with their own bathrooms and private sundecks. Among the many activities on offer at 'Bucks' are free canoes and surfboards, a surf school, horse riding, booze cruises and school visits (the nearby Belugha school is supported partially by donations from guests). There is also a volleyball court, bar, poolside café, climbing wall, and a daily free activity with free wine. On Saturday evening there's a candlelit Xhosa dinner party featuring traditional dishes. **Meals** (breakfast R15-40, mains R45-60) are available and on Sunday, the Prices prepare a free breakfast for guests, served in their dining room.

Buccaneer's is also the base of the excellent **African Heartland Tours** (see p263), which offers single and multi-day trips into the Transkei.

THE XHOSA CATTLE KILLING

In 1856 a young Xhosa girl named Nongqawuse went down to the banks of the Gxarha stream, just east of the Great Kei River, to help keep birds away from her uncle's fields. When she returned, she announced that she had met with the spirits of dead ancestors, who told her that the Xhosa must slaughter all their vast herds of cattle and cease to cultivate their fields. When this was done, all the ancestors would return from the dead, bringing with them herds of fat, glossy cattle, and drive the White men into the sea.

To the Xhosa, their cattle dying en masse from European diseases and their chiefs reeling in the wake of a succession of frontier wars with the land-hungry Boers, it was a vision of hope. In the aftermath of the prophecy, over 100,000 Xhosa slaughtered their own cattle and slowly starved to death. The British governor of the province, Sir George Grey, rounded up the survivors to be used as slave labour and gave their abandoned lands to White settlers.

To get to Buccaneer's, follow the Cintsa West turn-off for about 200m until you reach the entrance; the main buildings are a further 2km along the dirt road.

Moonshine Bay (☎ 7343590; cintsa-moonshine@isat .co.za; Main Rd, Cintsa West; camp sites/dm/d with shared bathroom R35/60/150; ☒) Much smaller and quieter than Buccaneer's, Moonshine has a big bar and upstairs terrace, tennis and squash courts and comfortable African-theme rooms. It also offers horse riding and free snorkel gear. Breakfast is free on Saturday. To get there, follow the directions for Buccaneer's but continue on past the Buccaneer's entrance until the end of the sealed road.

Gables (☎ 738 5353; www.gables.co.za; Kabeljou Cres, Cintsa East; s/d with breakfast R420/620; ☒) This B&B is one of Cintsa's grandest options, with fantastic views and a lovely round swimming pool.

Dolphin View (☎ 738 5432; dabeat@mweb.co.za; 18 Dolphin Dr, Cintsa East; s/d with breakfast R160/320) Far more modest but very charming, this little B&B has just a couple of rooms, all very good value, with TV, microwave, radio and CD player.

Michaela's of Cintsa (☎ 738 5139; Steenbras Dr, Cintsa East; mains R49-69; ☒ lunch & dinner Wed-Mon) Michaela's offers fusion-style food with South African ingredients. Book early for Sunday lunches. Wooden stairs lead diners up through a mini-rainforest to the restaurant; for the less fit there is always the air-conditioned funicular!

GETTING THERE & AWAY
To reach Cintsa from East London, take Exit 26 (East Coast Resorts) off the N2. Double back under the freeway and follow the road for 1km to the Cintsa East turn-off. The Cintsa West turn-off is another 16km further on.

Morgan's Bay & Kei Mouth
☎ 043
Along the coast from Cintsa, and reached by turning off the N2 onto the R349, is the village of Morgan's Bay, a good place for some peace and quiet and for beachcombing and surfing. Prices skyrocket and places get booked solid between mid-December and mid-January.

Just after Morgan's Bay and slightly more developed, Kei Mouth is the last resort before the beginning of the rural former homeland of Transkei, which is reached by taking the 'pont' **vehicle ferry** (per car R40; ☒ 7am-6pm) across the Great Kei River.

Yellowwood Park (☎ 841 1598; camp sites R45 plus R10 per person; hut shelters s/d R35/90), located about 1km from Morgan's Bay, is a very tranquil and ecofriendly camp site, frequented by birds and monkeys. Local Xhosa guides give guided river trails. Lifts can be arranged from East London or Mooiplaas on the N2.

Hotels in the area include the **Kei Mouth Beach Hotel** (☎ 841 1017; www.keimouthbeachhotel .co.za; Kei Mouth; r low/high season R275/370; ☒), a fairly staid hotel with good views; and **Mitford Lodge** (☎ 841 1510; www.morgansbay.co.za; Morgan's Bay; dm/d/t R65/200/350), a clean budget hotel with rustic décor and restaurant. Alternatively, the **Morgan Bay Hotel** (☎ 841 1062; www .morganbay.co.za; r with breakfast & dinner low/high season R245/275) is a light and airy family hotel with a Mediterranean feel and a bar serving pub grub. There's also a **camping ground** (camp sites low/high season R75/215) next door.

Strandloper Trails
The 60km, five-day **Strandloper Hiking Trail** (R220) and the one-night **Strandloper Canoe Trail** (bookings ☎ 043-841 1046; http://strandlopertrail .tripod.com) runs between Morgan's Bay and Gonubie, just outside East London. It's a fairly easy trail, but good fitness is required. The Strandlopers ('Beach Walkers') were a Khoisan tribe who lived on the coast but disappeared as a distinct group after White settlement. You'll need a copy of the tide tables published in the Daily Dispatch newspaper in East London, as there are several estuaries to cross.

There are four overnight huts and the cost of staying in these is included in the booking fee. Camping on the beach is prohibited, but most of the coastal hotels have camp sites.

GREAT KEI RIVER TO COFFEE BAY
There are a number of hotels and resorts along the stretch of coast from the Great Kei River to Coffee Bay. Most can be booked through **Wild Coast Holiday Reservations** (☎ 043-743 6181; www.wildcoastholidays.co.za; King's tourist Centre, cnr Longfellow & Aquarium Rds) in East London. Most places cater to fishermen and South African families; prices rise sharply around Christmas and Easter. There's no public

EASTERN CAPE

transport on this part of the coast, so you'll need your own vehicle.

The following is just a selection of the options available, listed from south to north.

Trennery's Hotel (☎ 043-498 0004; www.wheretostay .co.za/trennerys; s/d with full board R350/420; ☒) About 16km north of the 'pont' ferry, Trennery's has attractive thatched bungalows, a bit run-down on the inside but still comfortable. There's a basic restaurant, a lovely beach, gardens and a pool.

Wavecrest Resort Hotel (☎ /fax 047-498 0022; www .wavecrest.co.za; s/d with full board R330/660; ☒) The wooden deck at this smart hotel has amazing views over sand dunes at the mouth of the Nxaxo River. It's reached from Butterworth via Kentani; turn left at Kentani.

Kob Inn (☎ /fax 047-499 0011; http://kobinn.hypermart .net; s/d with full board R325/650) This family hotel can be reached by car from Idutywa via Willowvale. There are some good hiking trails in the area.

Haven (☎ 047-576 8904/8906; fax 047-576 8905; s/d with full board R265/530) The Haven is a good base for exploring Cwebe Nature Reserve, close to the mouth of the Mbashe River. Coming from the south, you can reach it via Elliotdale; turn off at the village of Qunu, 31km south of Umtata. It is about 70km from Qunu to the hotel and the road is unsealed from Elliotdale. If you're coming from the north, turn off at Viedgesville, 20km south of Umtata.

Bulungula Backpackers (☎ 047-557 8900; www.bul ungula.com; camp site per person/dm/d with shared bath-room R30/55/130; ☐) This new and very community-conscious hostel promises to be something very special, if only for its position overlooking one of the most spectacular beaches on the Wild Coast. It's 4km north of the Xora river mouth and around two hours drive from Coffee Bay. Getting there is a mission (part of the journey involves a hovercraft transfer), but if you're interested in Xhosa culture, ecotourism or simply a cracking good party, put this on your 'must-do' list. It's essential to contact Bulungula in advance to get directions and let them know you're coming.

Dwesa & Cwebe Nature Reserves

These adjoining reserves take in about 6000 hectares of coastal land. Both have tracts of forest as well as good beaches and hiking trails. The reserves are separated by the Mbashe River. The only way to get to either reserve is with your own vehicle.

Dwesa Nature Reserve (bookings ☎ 047-499 0073; day visitors R10; ⏱ 6am-6pm) is one of the most remote and beautiful reserves in South Africa, bounded by the Mbashe River in the north and the Nqabara River in the south. You may see the herd of eland come down to the beach near the Kobole estuary in the late afternoon. Other species present include buffalo and white rhino. If you want to hike, you must take a **ranger** (per day R40) with you.

To get to Dwesa, go to Willowvale and ask directions there – the road has many junctions, very few of which are signposted.

In **Cwebe Nature Reserve** (bookings ☎ 040-635 2115; day visitors R10; ⏱ 6am-6pm), you can walk to the Mbanyana Falls or to the lagoon, where if you are lucky, you may see Cape clawless otters in the late afternoon. On the southern edge of the reserve near the Mbashe is a small cluster of white mangroves where crabs and mudskippers are found near the stems.

To get to Cwebe, take the Elliotdale (Xhora) turn-off from the N2 (about 40km southwest of Umtata), then follow signs to the Haven hotel.

There is **self-catering accommodation** (2-bedroom bungalows R150) at Dwesa, and **camping** (camp sites R10) at both Cwebe and Dwesa.

COFFEE BAY
☎ 047

No one is sure how tiny Coffee Bay got its name, but there is a theory that a ship wrecked here in 1863 deposited its cargo of coffee beans on the beach. These days, this once remote hamlet is a backpacker's mecca, with two busy hostels and a couple of more upmarket hotels jostling for space in the village centre. In between, a few hopeful locals hover, trying to sell *dagga* (marijuana), curios and day trips.

Coffee Bay itself is a fairly scruffy place, but the surrounding scenery is dramatic, with a beautiful kilometre-long beach set in front of towering cliffs. The two backpacker hostels, Bomvu Paradise and the Coffee Shack, run all sorts of day trips, including **horse riding** (2hr treks about R150), **guided hikes** (from R50), **cultural visits** (from R60) and **surfing trips** (R60).

Sleeping & Eating

Competition is fierce for backpacker bucks in Coffee Bay.

Bomvu Paradise (☎ 575 2073; www.bomvuback packers.com; camp sites/dm/d with shared bathroom R40/ 70/150) Bomvu is an imaginatively designed backpackers with horses grazing among the tents on the lawn and tame exotic birds fluttering around the garden. There's a drum-making and drumming school (not ideal if you're trying to sleep, but great fun otherwise), a yoga school, a surf shop and a pretty restaurant serving wholesome organic breakfasts and lunches. The dorms and rooms are rustic, comfortable and funky and the staff very efficient and friendly. The hostel hosts regular music and dance festivals in a natural amphitheatre nearby.

Coffee Shack (☎ 043-575 2048; www.coffeeshack .co.za; camp sites/dm/d with shared bathroom R40/70/180; 🖳) Just across the road from Bomvu, the Coffee Shack has a definite party vibe, with regular live local music in the evenings. This is an excellent place to learn to surf – owner David Malherbe was a surfing champion. Try to get a room across the river from the main hostel – the ablutions are better and it's more peaceful. Three-course dinners are available for R35, with free *potjekos* on Sunday night. If you're coming from elsewhere in the Transkei, the hostel offers a shuttle service – the first pick-up is free.

Ocean View Hotel (☎ 575 2005; www.oceanview .co.za; s/d with half board R405/600, without sea views R351/520; 🅿 🖳 🏊) Ocean View has good-quality bungalow-style rooms, with a deck overlooking the ocean. There is a **restaurant** (set dinner R80) and seafood snacks are served in the bar in the evenings. Prices go up in high season.

You can buy mussels, crayfish and other seafood from locals and there's a well-stocked grocery store.

Getting There & Away

If you're driving to Coffee Bay, take the sealed road that leaves the N2 at Viedgesville. When you reach Coffee Bay, continue past the derelict Lagoon Hotel, cross the river and you will come to the backpackers' enclave. A minibus taxi from Umtata to Coffee Bay costs R22 and takes one hour. The backpacker hostels meet the **Baz Bus** (☎ 021-439 2323) at the Shell Ultra City, 4km south of Umtata.

AROUND COFFEE BAY

The walking around Coffee Bay is spectacular – one of the best walks is to the **Hole in the Wall**, a rock formation featuring an impressive natural hole that has been carved through the cliffs by the pounding of the ocean. The signposted turn-off to the Hole in the Wall is about 30km before

Coffee Bay. There is also a direct unsealed road from Coffee Bay (about 8km).

Mdumbi Backpackers (☎ 047-575 0437, 083-749 1615; fax 047-568 6775; camp sites/dm/d with shared bathroom R20/50/120) This is a great place really to get away from it all – a rural backpackers in the grounds of a mission set in rolling hills next to a secluded beach. There are lots of water-based activities (the surf can be phenomenal here) and lots of opportunities to meet the local Xhosa people in a genuine setting. Think space, silence, great views and lots of early nights. To get here, turn off the Coffee Bay road to Mdumbi and follow the signs. The **Back 2 Back shuttle bus** (☎ 082-400 3335; back2back@absamail.co.za) drops off here from its base in Port St Johns (see p270).

Hole in the Wall Hotel (☎ 047-575 0009; http:// home.intekom.com/holeinthewall; s/d with half board R265/ 530; 🖳 🏊) About 8km south of Coffee Bay, this fenced-in hotel has plain rooms and good-value, well-decorated self-catering cottages (R300 for a two-bedroom unit). The landmark after which the hotel is named is a 2km walk away. Prices go up sharply in the high season, when the hotel gets very busy with holidaying families.

Hole in the Wall Backpackers (☎ 083-317 8786; holeitwh@iafrica.com; camp sites/dm/d with shared bathroom R40/60/140) Within the Hole in the Wall hotel complex is this no-nonsense backpackers that's had great reviews from readers. Facilities include use of the hotel's swimming pool and volleyball court, plus **horse riding** (per hr R50). Meals are available at the hotel (breakfast R30, dinner R60).

COFFEE BAY TO PORT ST JOHNS

The route between Coffee Bay and Port St Johns takes in the Hluleka and Silaka Nature Reserves, as well as Mpande village, home of the well-known Kraal Backpackers (p268). It's a great route to walk, but there have been reports of ambushes and muggings along the way, so it may be best to take a local guide. See p263 for details.

Hluleka Nature Reserve

Midway between Coffee Bay and Port St Johns is **Hluleka Nature Reserve** (admission R5; ⏱ 8am-5pm), which combines a rocky seashore with lagoons and an evergreen forest. Burchell's zebras, blesboks and blue wildebeest have all been introduced.

To get to the reserve, take the road from Umtata to Port St Johns and turn right at Libode, about 30km from Umtata. The reserve is about 90km further on.

Silaka Nature Reserve

This small coastal reserve (admission R5; ☙ 6am-6pm), 6.5km south of Port St Johns, runs from Second Beach to Sugarloaf Rock. By the shoreline are many interesting tidal rock pools. Near the estuary, where the Gxwaleni flows into the sea, aloes grow down almost to the water. Clawless otters are often seen on the beach and white-breasted cormorants clamber up onto Bird Island. It's a magical place.

Sleeping & Eating

Kraal Backpackers (☎ 082-871 4964; www.thekraal -backpackers.co.za; camp sites/dm with shared bathroom R45/65) This is a down-to-earth, ecofriendly backpackers that gets rave reviews from travellers. There is no electricity, no TV and no telephone – just peace, a friendly vibe and spectacular scenery on all sides. Nearby villagers look upon it as an extension of their community and come to sell fish and vegetables; visitors are welcome to go with them to their shebeens or visit the local sangoma. Hiking, horse riding, surfing and kayaking are all on offer. **Meals** (dinner R35-60) are available.

The turn-off to the Kraal is 70km from Umtata and 20km from Port St Johns at Tombo Stores. From here it's signposted all the way. It is a 30- to 40-minute drive on a rough road from the turn-off to Mpande, where the Kraal is situated. To get here by public transport, get to the Shell Ultra City in Umtata, then take a minibus taxi (R30) from there – just say you want to go to the Kraal. It's best to ring ahead before turning up. The **Back 2 Back shuttle bus** (☎ 082-400 3335; back2back@absamail.co.za) from Port St Johns (p270) also stops here.

Umngazi River Bungalows (☎ 047-564 1115; www.umngazi.co.za; s/d with full board R588/840; ☒) This very popular and relaxed resort is at the mouth of the Umngazi River, about 21km south of Port St Johns. As well as the bustling, family-orientated main hotel, there are more secluded honeymoon cottages and a bush camp. Lots of activities are on offer, including canoeing through mangroves, fishing, mountain biking and hik-

ing. Rates go up in high season. There's no public transport to Umngazi. To get there in your own car from Port St Johns, take the Umtata road for 10km to the Umngazi turn-off. Turn left, and travel 11km to the hotel.

Accommodation in Hluleka is in self-catering wooden **chalets** (R230) for up to six people. In Silaka, you can stay in thatched **bungalows** (R200). To book either, call the **Eastern Cape Tourism Board** (☎ 040-635 2115) in Bisho. Bring all your own provisions.

PORT ST JOHNS

☎ 047 / pop 1900

The deliciously laid-back Port St Johns is a magnet for hippy types both young and old. This idyllic little town on the coast at the mouth of the Umzimvubu River has tropical vegetation, dramatic cliffs, great beaches, no traffic jams and absolutely no stress. Many travellers, lulled by the clinking of wind chimes and the sound of the waves, succumb to the famous 'Pondo Fever' and stay for months.

A favourite sunset spot is **Mt Thesiger**, a hill with one of the most spectacular views on the Wild Coast. It's on the banks of the Umzimvubu River, just west of the town centre.

The **tourist office** (☎ 564 1206; www.portstjohns .org.za/tourism.htm) is located on the main road into Port St Johns. The Island Backpackers Lodge (opposite) has **Internet access** (per min R1) available.

Sleeping & Eating

The emphasis in Port St Johns is on backpackers' accommodation, but there are a few more upmarket options too. Most of the eating options are within the hostels and hotels themselves – or you could always do what the locals do – buy cheap mussels, crayfish and fish and cook your own meal.

Amapondo Backpackers (☎ 564 1344, 083-315 3103; www.amapondo.co.za; Second Beach Rd; camp sites/dm/d with shared bathroom R35/65/160) Four kilometres from the town centre, this is a beautiful hostel with a great view of Port St Johns' idyllic Second Beach. There's a very peaceful, gentle atmosphere, compounded by the holistic massage treatments on offer. The double rooms are sensational, with beds raised on platforms and elegantly draped mosquito nets. Activities at Amapondo include **horse riding** (per day R150), boat trips, dive charters, canoeing and surfing – plus plenty of lying around in hammocks. **Meals** (breakfast R10-32, dinner R25-50) are available and the relaxed bar gets lively with locals and travellers at night.

Gwyneth's Barn & Ekuphumleni (☎ /fax 564 1506; www.mrinfo.co.za; off Pussfoot Lane, First Beach; d with shared bathroom R220, 2-bedroom cottage R350-440) Ekuphumleni (meaning 'Place to Rest') is an adorable group of wooden self-catering rooms set among indigenous bushland. A raised walkway connects the cottages to a shared braai area, kitchenette and a dreamy outdoor shower. Each room is beautifully decorated, with scented candles and fluffy towels – the only drawback is that they're a bit close together. Accommodation is also available in the main house, Gwyneth's Barn, and in a two-bedroom cottage on the adjoining property. Meals can be provided on request. To get there follow the signs from Main St.

Island Backpackers Lodge (☎ 564 1958; www .theislandbackpackers.co.za; 341 Berea Rd; dm/d/tr with shared bathroom R65/175/185; 🖳) During the day this hostel is an island in a sea of calm, but at night it comes alive as a popular **restaurant** (dishes R35-50) and night spot. There's an all-day deli selling Middle Eastern delights like hummus and falafels, prepared from organic ingredients. A full 'Israeli breakfast' is R30. At night the well-decorated dining room serves an eclectic menu of international dishes, with an excellent choice for veggies.

Jungle Monkey (☎ 564 1517; junglemonkeybp@ yahoo.co.uk; 340 Berea Rd; camp sites/dm/d with shared bathroom R40/65/160) Right next door to the Island, Jungle Monkey has hippy-chic paintings on the walls, a garden full of hammocks and a bar with a pool table in the garage. It offers hiking, **horse riding** (per day R140) and special rates for long stays. There's a big camping area and a typically Port St Johns arty-crafty feel.

Cremorne Hotel (☎ 564 1113; www.cremorne.co.za; camp sites R50, cabins without bedding per person R90, s/d with breakfast R252/504; 🖳) Clean, comfortable rooms and rustic fishermans' cabins are on offer at this friendly, rather family hotel, in a spectacular location over the ferry from town on the banks of the Umzimvubu River. There's a cosy pub and a restaurant. Four-bedroom self-catering cottages are also available (R480).

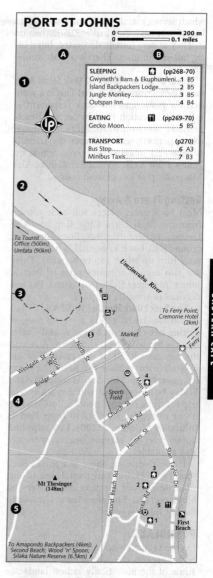

PORT ST JOHNS

SLEEPING	🏠	(pp268-70)
Gwyneth's Barn & Ekuphumleni..........1		B5
Island Backpackers Lodge..........2		B5
Jungle Monkey..........3		B5
Outspan Inn..........4		B4

EATING	🍴	(pp269-70)
Gecko Moon..........5		B5

TRANSPORT		(p270)
Bus Stop..........6		A3
Minibus Taxis..........7		B3

Outspan Inn (☎ 564 1240; www.outspaninn.co.za; Main St; s/d with breakfast R250/430; 🖳) This hotel has slightly dingy rooms with brass bedsteads, but a lovely garden with excellent birdlife. The restaurant has been recommended by readers.

Gecko Moon (☎ 564 8354; Stan Taylor Dr; mains R35-45) This snazzy and popular restaurant which serves mainly pizza and pasta dishes has a few **rooms** (s/d with breakfast R225/390) behind it. They're very funkily decorated, but a little hot in summer. There's a craft studio here too.

Wood 'n' Spoon (☎ 083-532 8869; Second Beach; mains R35-55; ☾ dinner only Thu-Tue) This is a wonderfully rustic and laid-back restaurant in a fantastic location right by Second Beach, around 6.5km from town. The funky 'salvage' décor perfectly complements the friendly service and imaginative menu, which includes a few Swiss specialities such as Alpe Macaroni, plus lots of fresh seafood.

Getting There & Away
Most backpacker places will pick you up from the Shell Ultra City, 4km south of Umtata (where the Baz Bus stops) for around R40, but it's essential to book ahead (and turn up when you've booked). There are also regular minibus taxis to Port St Johns from here (R30, two hours). For bus services to Umtata, see p272.

The **Back 2 Back Shuttle** (☎ 082-400 3335; back 2back@absamail.co.za) offers a useful way of getting between Port St Johns and Coffee Bay via the back-road shortcuts. A ride in the bus costs R120, or you can 'follow on' in your own vehicle for R50. The service operates on Monday, Wednesday and Friday both ways, but will make a special trip for three or more people. You can hop on or off at the Kraal (R40 from Port St Johns) or Mdumbi (R100). Day trips and horse rides to various beauty spots are also available.

If you're driving, there is a good sealed road to Lusikisiki and then 17km of dirt road; watch out for maniacal drivers on blind corners. The road from Umtata to Port St Johns is sealed.

PONDOLAND
On the 110km stretch of coast between Port St Johns and the Umtamvuna River lies some of the biologically richest landscape in the whole region. This area is the site of the proposed new Pondoland National Park. More controversial are plans to divert the course of the N2 highway through the area and start mining operations on the coastal sand dunes.

North of the Kokstad corridor is an isolated tract of Eastern Cape created by apart-

heid area land policies, with Umzimkulu as its main centre.

The 8000-hectare **Mkambati Nature Reserve** (admission R5; ☾ 6am-6pm) encompasses expanses of grassland, dotted with forest and flanked by the Msikaba and Mtentu River Gorges. The reserve's great scenery is a haven for a spectacular variety of birds, including trumpeter hornbill and African fish eagle. Animal species include eland and red hartebeest.

There are canoe and walking trails, or you can hire the park's own open vehicle and guide for a wildlife drive. A shop sells basic food. **Self-catering units** (☎ 040-635 2115; 10-bed lodges R 515, cottages per person R53) are available. You get there from Flagstaff, which is 65km south of the N2. Take the turn-off to Holy Cross Hospital, just north of Flagstaff. There are also buses running from Port St Johns to Msikaba, on the southern edge of the reserve.

The only hotel in this area is the glitzy and over-the-top **Wild Coast Sun Casino & Country Club** (☎ 039-305 9111; r R1350-1560; ☒) It's reached from the Kokstad region via Bizana on the R61. If coming from Durban, turn off the N2 at Port Shepstone and follow the R61 (there are numerous signs along the way).

If this isn't really your style, you could opt for a tented camp or a village homestay on one of the trips operated by **Wild Coast Trails** (see p264).

UMTATA
☎ 047 / pop 79,000
Umtata, the main town in the former Transkei, was founded in 1871, when Europeans settled on the Umtata River at the request of the Thembu tribe to act as a buffer against Pondo raiders. It's a scruffy, lively place with a fearsome but probably exaggerated reputation for crime. Commonsense precautions apply – don't carry your valuables in obvious places, and stay out of the city centre after dark.

The area around Umtata is now famed as the childhood home of Nelson Mandela. The first president of free South Africa was born in the village of **Mveso** on the Mbashe River, but he spent most of his childhood at **Qunu**, 31km south of Umtata. A museum that incorporates both these areas has been built to commemorate the man who be-

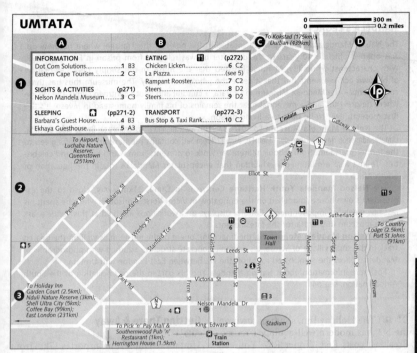

UMTATA

INFORMATION	
Dot Com Solutions...................1 B3	
Eastern Cape Tourism..............2 C3	

SIGHTS & ACTIVITIES	(p271)
Nelson Mandela Museum........3 C3	

SLEEPING	(pp271-2)
Barbara's Guest House.............4 B3	
Ekhaya Guesthouse.................5 A3	

EATING	(p272)
Chicken Licken........................6 C2	
La Piazza................................(see 5)	
Rampant Rooster....................7 C2	
Steers....................................8 D2	
Steers....................................9 D2	

TRANSPORT	(pp272-3)
Bus Stop & Taxi Rank............10 C2	

came the symbol of freedom and reconciliation for the new South Africa (see p272).

Orientation & Information

Most banks and businesses are in the centre of Umtata around Sutherland St. There is a branch of **Eastern Cape Tourism** (☎ 531 5290; ectbwc@icon.co.za; 64 Owen St; ⏰ 8am-4.30pm Mon-Fri), plus an **information caravan** (⏰ 8am-4.30pm Mon-Fri, 9.30am-3pm Sat & Sun) at the Shell Ultra City petrol station, 4km from town.

Internet access is available at **Dot Com Solutions** (☎ 532 2572; 45 Nelson Mandela Dr; per hr R30; ⏰ 7.30am-6pm Mon-Fri, 9am-2pm Sat).

Sights

The highlight of any trip to Umtata is the **Nelson Mandela Museum** (see the boxed text on p272), which charts the inspirational life of South Africa's former president.

Nduli Nature Reserve is in a valley 3km south of Umtata, while **Luchaba Nature Reserve** is on the Umtata Dam, next to the water-sports area. Both have zebra, wildebeest and antelope species, as well as many wetland birds.

Sleeping

There's a complete dearth of decent budget accommodation in Umtata, so if you find yourself needing to stay the night here, be prepared to fork out.

Herrington House (☎ /fax 532 5692; 46 Vukutu St; s/d with half board R331/547) This is a good option 1.5km from the centre – a smart B&B with a big restaurant and bar, and satellite TV in every room. Ring ahead and they'll pick you up from the bus at Ultra City.

Ekhaya Guesthouse (☎ 072-432 7244; fax 532 4007; 36 Delville Rd; s/d with breakfast R379/500) This is a smart new place on the edge of the golf course. There's a pretty garden with a braai area and modern rooms with TV.

Country Lodge (☎ /fax 532 5730, 501 2812; clodge@wildcoast.co.za; Port St Johns Rd; s/d R250/370) Situated just 2.5km out of town on the Port St Johns road, this lodge is a great relief after Umtata's urban hustle, with chickens and guinea fowl pecking peacefully around in the shady garden. Breakfast (R35) and dinner (R55) are available.

Holiday Inn Garden Court (☎ 537 0181; tembisan@southernsun.com; Myezo Park, off N2; s/d R589/699;

MANDELA'S LEGACY

The Nelson Mandela Museum project, located in the heart of the Transkei where he grew up, was opened officially 10 years to the day after he was released from prison in February 1990. With characteristic humility, Mandela insisted that the museum not simply be a celebration of his own achievements but that it serve the whole community. The museum thus has three components – the Mandela Museum in Umtata, a cultural and youth centre in Qunu, the village where he grew up, and a memorial near the remains of his family homestead in Mveso. It's the first museum ever to be built to a living person.

The **Nelson Mandela Museum** (☎ 047-532 5110; www.mandelamuseum.org.za; Bunga Bldg, Owen St, Umtata; admission free; 🕓 9am-4pm Mon-Fri, 9am-12.30pm Sat) contains the honours and gifts given to the former president, from schoolchildrens' artwork to presents from world leaders and celebrities. There's also a multimedia exhibition that encapsulates Mandela's role in the liberation of South Africa.

The **Nelson Mandela Youth Heritage Centre** is in Qunu, 31km away, close to the ex-president's own house (modelled on the bungalow in Victor Vorster prison in which he spent his last few weeks of imprisonment). Cultural displays and workshops are held at this venue – ask at the museum in Umtata for the latest events.

The **Nelson Mandela Monument**, the final component of the museum, is well off the beaten track in the small village of Mveso. It's a simple concrete structure adorned with photographs of Mandela. Follow the signposted route off the N2 between East London and Umtata.

For more information about Nelson Mandela and his part in the reconciliation of the South African nation, see p41.

🚫 🍴) The Holiday Inn, south of town on the N2, has modern well-equipped rooms. Breakfast costs R68, dinner R87. You can book in advance to be picked up from Shell Ultra City.

Barbara's Guest House (☎ 531 1751; fax 531 1754; 55 Nelson Mandela Dr; s/d with half board R325/465) Umtata's least expensive option is a faded and fairly depressing looking place, but it's conveniently easy to find and the meals are surprisingly good.

Eating

La Piazza (☎ 531 0795; 36 Delville Rd; mains R22-32; 🕓 lunch & dinner Mon-Sat) This no-nonsense restaurant in the Umtata Country Club serves a decent range of pizza, pasta and chops. It does room service for the Ekhaya Guesthouse.

Southernwood Pub 'n' Restaurant (Anton's; ☎ 083-305 321; Pick 'n' Pay Complex, Southernwood; mains R20-40; 🕓 lunch & dinner Mon-Sat) Another reasonable option is this straightforward pizza and seafood joint just outside the town centre.

For chicken fanciers, **Chicken Licken** (Sutherland St) and **Rampant Rooster** (Sutherland St) are found at the western end of Sutherland St. There are two branches of Steers on Sutherland St.

Getting There & Away

AIR
Umtata's Mantanzima airport is 17km from the city. **SA Airlink** (☎ 536 0024) has daily services to Jo'burg (R1000).

BUS
Translux has a daily service from Cape Town (R350, 17 hours) to Umtata.

Greyhound (☎ 531 0603) stops in Umtata on its daily run between Durban (R200, six hours) and Cape Town (R400, 20 hours). Local bus company DMJ Transport is reputedly much faster and cheaper than either of the above (Umtata–Cape Town R220, 13 hours) – inquire at Shell Ultra City.

The **Baz Bus** (☎ 021-439 2323) passes through Umtata on its Port Elizabeth–Durban run Monday, Tuesday, Wednesday, Friday and Saturday; it runs in the other direction Monday, Tuesday, Thursday, Friday and Sunday.

Translux, Greyhound and the Baz Bus stop at the Shell Ultra City, which is the pick-up point for backpacker shuttles heading to the coast.

MINIBUS TAXI
These depart from both Shell Ultra City and the main bus stop and taxi rank near Bridge St. Destinations include Port St Johns or the

Kraal backpackers (R30), Coffee Bay (R25) and East London (R70).

NORTH-EASTERN HIGHLANDS

Ravishingly beautiful and refreshingly free of tourist hype, the North-Eastern Highlands are bounded on three sides by the Transkei and have a short border (but no border crossing) with Lesotho. Summer in this part of the Drakensberg brings excellent hiking and fishing, while winter brings snowfalls and the opportunity to ski (although most of the pistes are artificial). Watch out for harsh weather conditions in the high passes at all times of the year. In the more remote parts, you'll need your own vehicle.

QUEENSTOWN

☎ 045 / pop 55,800

This fairly uninteresting town was established in 1847 and laid out in the shape of a hexagon for defence purposes. This pattern enabled defenders to shoot down the streets from a central point.

The **Chris Hani Area Regional Tourism Office** (☎ /fax 839 2265; sarto@eci.co.za; Shop 14, the Mall) is in the Pick 'n' Pay complex.

Sleeping & Eating

Alisa Cottage (☎ /fax 839 2761; 37 Haig Ave; s/d with breakfast R140/220; 🛋) The best place to stay in town is the extremely good-value Alisa Cottage. Each room is a flat, with a sitting area, small kitchen and TV.

Hexagon Guest House (☎ 838 4036; 7 Longview Cres & 38 Buxton St; s/d with breakfast R220/310) Both parts of this guesthouse are in quiet streets and offer decent rooms.

Black Swan (☎ 839 7475; cnr Grey St & Ebden Sts; mains R20-50; 🍴 lunch & dinner Mon-Sat) This restaurant has a nicely decorated interior and a good menu featuring fish, pasta and a few vegetarian dishes.

Getting There & Away

Queenstown is the hub for all transport in and out of the Highlands.

EASTERN CAPE

NORTH-EASTERN HIGHLANDS

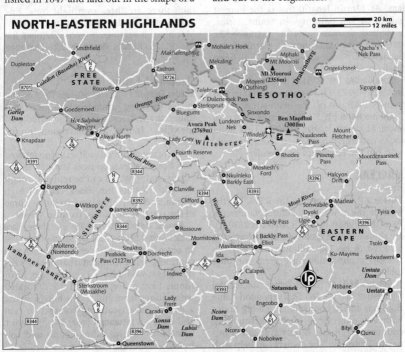

Greyhound passes through Queenstown on the Jo'burg/Pretoria to Port Elizabeth run (Port Elizabeth R150, 5½ hours; Jo'burg R260, 9½ hours). All buses stop at the Shell Ultra City petrol station on Cathcart St. Greyhound buses also run from Queenstown to Aliwal North (R110, two hours). Translux runs daily to Cape Town (R230, 13 hours).

City to City (☎ 011-773 2762) buses have daily services to Jo'burg/Pretoria (R100). Another daily City to City bus runs from Jo'burg to Idutywa via Queenstown (R90).

From the **minibus taxi rank** (cnr Victoria & Komani Sts) you can travel to Cathcart (R15), Stutterheim (R20), King William's Town (R40) and East London (R80).

ELLIOT

☎ 045 / pop 11,900

Nestled in a particularly scenic region southeast of Barkly East, Elliot is the centre of a very interesting area.

On Denorbin farm, near Barkly Pass between Barkly East and Elliot, are some well-preserved examples of **San rock paintings**. At 32m in length, this is the longest gallery of San paintings in South Africa. It depicts shamans entering a trance-like state while dancing. The rock paintings can be viewed by prior arrangement. Call **Gavin Small** (☎ 971 9052).

Rose Garden (☎ 931 1158; 10 Dampier St; s/d with breakfast R140/280) This is a comfortable and homely B&B just off the main street.

Merino Hotel (☎ 931 2987; greg@imaginet.co.za; Maclear Rd; s/d with breakfast R140/220) This hotel looks extremely forbidding from the outside, but the managers are friendly.

MACLEAR

☎ 045

This is a trading town on the R396. Northwest of the town, just before Naudesnek Pass (the highest in South Africa at 2620m), are some exposed **fossilised dinosaur footprints** believed to be 200 million years old. The streams around town are great for **trout fishing**.

Declan's B&B (☎ 932 1071; declan@xsinet.co.za; s/d with breakfast R180/300; 🖳) This very good-value B&B has smart, cool rooms in a big house with stunning views of the surrounding countryside. Dinner is only available Monday to Thursday. The owners can help with

tourist information. The **Royal Hotel** (☎ 932 1176, fax 932 1003; Van Reibeeck St; mains R25) can provide dinner at other times.

RHODES & TIFFINDELL

☎ 045

Locals jokingly refer to **Rhodes** as 'the centre of the universe'. It's definitely the best place in the Highlands – a jewel of a little village almost entirely comprised of quaint old buildings, grassy meadows and rusting farm machinery.

There's an ATM (small amounts only) at Walkerbouts Inn.

Tiffindell (2800m), about 23km up a mountain pass (4WD only) from Rhodes, is a purpose-built winter sports resort. Its snow-making facilities mean that a season of 95 days is possible here. With only 1.5km of piste on a good day, however, the resort is more popular with those who prefer to spend their time in South Africa's highest pub.

The **Ben Macdhui Hiking Trail** (☎ 974 9305) is not too steep for the Drakensberg range, but parts of the route run over rough terrain; there are three overnight huts. Enquire at the Rhodes Hotel for more details. Mountain bikers arrive every October for the 82km **Rhodes Mountain Bike Challenge** (☎ 974 9290).

Sleeping & Eating

Rhodes Campsite (☎ 974 9290; camp sites R35) The village camping ground is in a great spot under shady trees right in the middle of the village. Inquire at Walkerbouts Inn for the key.

There are numerous self-catering **cottages** (www.highlandsinfo.co.za; per person from R105) in the village centre, which can be rented through the Walkerbouts Inn. Book early in high season, and wrap up warm in winter – some of the cottages only have paraffin stoves.

Rhodes Hotel (☎ 974 9305; www.rhodesvillage .co.za; s/d with half board R300/600, self-catering cottages per person from R105) Rhodes' only hotel is a charming establishment that looks very much as it would have a century ago. Most rooms have a fireplace and are decorated with antique furnishings. The hotel also has a couple of self-catering cottages to rent and there's a **restaurant** (mains R40; 🕑 breakfast, lunch & dinner). Horse riding, tennis and volleyball are on offer here too.

Walkerbouts Inn (☎ 974 9290; www.walkerbouts
.co.za; s/d with half board R370/540) Walkerbouts is
a cosy B&B with a very convivial bar. Try
the home-brewed Highland beer, or their
infamous 'Fall About Stout'. Genial host
Dave Walker is a mine of information on
everything and anything in the area. **Meals**
(pizzas R25, 3-course dinner R65) are available in the
evenings; nonresidents will need to book.

Tiffindell Ski Resort (☎ 011-787 9090, 974 9005/
4/8; www.snow.co.za; 4-bed chalets in summer R285, 3-night
winter ski packages per person from R1500) The resort's
winter package price includes ski-lift charges,
equipment hire, emergency medical facilities
and meals in the restaurant. Summer activities include mountain biking, horse riding,
grass skiing and rock climbing.

Getting There & Away
The road to Rhodes from Barkly East is
fine for 2WD cars, but don't attempt the
route from Maclear unless you have a 4WD,
and ring ahead to check weather conditions. The road to Tiffindell always requires
4WD, but the resort lays on a free shuttle –
call for details.

BARKLY EAST
☎ 045 / pop 7500
On the R58, this town with its scenic and
mountainous location bills itself as the 'Switzerland of South Africa'. In reality, however, it
has little magic in comparison with Rhodes,
just 60km away. The **Magic Moments** (☎ 082-
499 2388; 5 Molteno St; ◷ 9am-4.30pm Mon-Sat) craft
shop can help with tourist information and
occasionally has Internet access.

The **trout fishing** near Barkly East is
reputedly some of the best in the country.
Keen anglers should contact the **Wild Trout
Association** (☎ 974 9290; www.wildtrout.co.za).

Barkly East Caravan Park (☎ 971 0123/0299; Victoria Park; camp sites per tent R30) This has clean
ablution facilities and pleasant sites. Inquire
at FK's Sports Bar in town for details.

Old Mill Inn (☎ 971 0277; fax 971 0972; cnr White &
De Smidt Sts; s/d R160/320) This olde-worlde inn
has charming, good-value Victorian-style
rooms, a bar and a **restaurant** (mains R30-80). It
can also help with tourist info.

LADY GREY
☎ 051
Lady Grey is a sleepy little town surrounded
by spectacular views, with the Witteberge

mountain range's Joubert's Pass, one of the
highest in the country, as an impressive
backdrop. Tourist information is available
from the **At Home Coffee Shop** (☎ 603 0176;
Martin St).

Baggers & Packers (☎ 603 0346; 53 Heut St; johan
dp@telkomsa.net; camp sites/dm/d with shared bathroom
R35/50/120) is a hikers' guesthouse in a former
mission church is charmingly crumbling
and a bit eccentric, with higgledy-piggledy
rooms in various outhouses in the garden.

The very pretty and well-kept **Comfrey
Cottage** (☎ 603 0407; www.comfreycottage.co.za; 51-
59 Stephenson St; s/d R180/360, with half board R300/600)
is actually a set of cottages situated around
a park-like garden right at the foot of the
mountains.

The private nature reserve **Lammergeier
Adventure Trails** (☎ 603 1114; www.adventuretrails
.co.za; cottages per person R135, with full board R350),
halfway between Lady Grey and Barkly
East, features spectacular scenery and a
range of ways to enjoy it, from quad biking
to tubing on rivers. There are several multi-
day circular hiking trails to choose from.

City to City (☎ 011-773 2762) buses leave
Jo'burg travelling to Lady Grey (R80) on
Monday, Wednesday and Friday at 8am;
there is also a Friday service at 7pm.

ALIWAL NORTH
☎ 051 / pop 23,300
Obscure Aliwal North, on the border between the Free State and Eastern Cape, was
South Africa's third-biggest tourist destination in the early 20th century. The reason?
A thermal spa whose waters are supposed
to have health-giving properties. These days
the **spa complex** (admission R15; ◷ 6am-10pm) has
dwindled to a few grubby swimming pools,
but the countryside around the town is still
ravishing. Contact the **Eastern Cape Tourism
Board** (☎ 633 3567; ectban@intekom.co.za; 97 Somerset
St) for information.

At the southern end of town is a **Boer Concentration Camp Memorial** dedicated to the 700-
plus Afrikaners who died in the British-run
camp.

Sleeping & Eating
There are plenty of places to stay near the
spa, but the best options are outside the
town centre.

Conville (☎ 633 2203; www.conville-farm.com; s/d
with breakfast R170/300) This flamboyant 1906

farmhouse was designed by famed architect Herbert Baker, and sits in stunning gardens overlooking a lake. Inside, it's rather grand, with brass beds and antique furniture.

Toll Inn (☎ 634 1541; tolherberg@xsinet.co.za; Lady Grey St; s/d with breakfast R275/440, self-catering units s/d R230/350) A shame it's so near the road but this former government toll station still makes a charming B&B, with smart rooms with TV and kitchenette in converted stables. Self-catering units are also available.

Riverside Pub 'n' Grill (☎ 633 3282; 1 Aliwal St; mains R40-50; ⏰ lunch & dinner) Located on the banks of the Orange River, the terrace at this restaurant is a good place for evening drinks.

Welgemoed Chalets (☎ 633 2692; cnr Duncan & Dirkie Uys Sts; 4-/6-person chalets R180/210) This

place is the best of the options near the spa, with self-catering chalets and a communal braai area.

Pink Lady Steakhouse (☎ 684 2189; 14 Dan Pienaar Ave; mains R45-55; ⏰ lunch & dinner Mon-Fri, dinner Sat) A popular spot with local diners.

Getting There & Away

A daily **City to City** (☎ 011-773 2762) bus stops here on the Jo'burg–Idutywa (via Queenstown) run.

Translux, Greyhound and Intercape services stop at Nobby's Restaurant (on the N6), near the junction with the R58. City to City buses stop at the Balmoral Hotel.

The **minibus taxi rank** (Grey St) is near the corner of Somerset St.

KwaZulu-Natal

KwaZulu-Natal

An eclectic mix of cultures and landscapes come together in one of South Africa's great melting pots, KwaZulu-Natal. Tumbling tribal settlements exist alongside the glassy canyons of Durban's giant shopping malls, while downtown streets, packed to bursting with all the electric atmosphere of workaday African life, are in stark contrast to the empty sweeps of beach, mountainside and savanna that rank among the continent's great, protected wildernesses. Throw in the wildlife, the historic intrigue of the battlefields of the Anglo-Zulu and Anglo-Boer War, and the sand, sea and surf of the coast's glossy resort towns, and you've got a seductive mix of local idiosyncrasies and classic continental highlights. Little wonder then that this is one of the world's favourite South African destinations.

Heading east from the awesome peaks and unforgettable vistas of the stunning Drakensberg mountain range, KwaZulu-Natal has its metropolitan heart in the colossal port of Durban and its nearby historic capital, Pietermaritzburg. The beaches along this stretch of coast are peppered with resorts and draw the bulk of visiting sun-worshippers. Head north and you enter Zululand and Maputaland, home to some of the country's finest national parks, most evocative traditional settlements and wildest countryside. Northwest of Durban, around the towns of Ladysmith and Dundee, you will find KwaZulu-Natal's historic heartland, where the history of the province was thrashed out on the battlefields of the Anglo-Zulu and Anglo-Boer Wars. In KwaZulu-Natal, there really is something for everyone.

HIGHLIGHTS

- Vanishing down the beaten track to the pristine beaches of **Kosi Mouth** (p320)

- Hiking the peaks of the Drakensberg's magnificent Amphitheatre in **Royal Natal National Park** (p326)

- Driving through the clouds over the **Sani Pass** to Lesotho (p333)

- Living the summer big-time amongst the bars and beaches of **Durban** (p295)

- Reliving the timeless clashes of the Anglo-Zulu War at **Isandlwana** (p347) and **Rorke's Drift** (p347)

- Diving or snorkelling in the stunning waters of **Sodwana Bay** (p318)

- Hiking through the Big Five stomping ground of **Hluhluwe-Imfolozi Park** (p313) or sitting near a pan at dawn at **Mkhuze Game Reserve** (p320)

- Hanging out with the hippos at sunset at the **Greater St Lucia Wetland Park** (p315)

- Wandering through the museums and galleries of the heritage city, **Pietermaritzburg** (p337)

POPULATION: 10,070,000 | AREA: 92,100 SQ KM

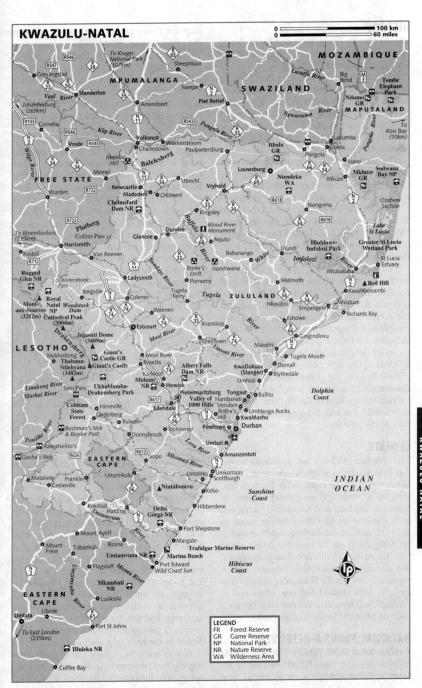

KWAZULU-NATAL

0 — 100 km
0 — 60 miles

MOZAMBIQUE

MPUMALANGA

SWAZILAND

MAPUTALAND

FREE STATE

LESOTHO

ZULULAND

Dolphin Coast

INDIAN OCEAN

Sunshine Coast

EASTERN CAPE

Hibiscus Coast

LEGEND
FR   Forest Reserve
GR   Game Reserve
NP   National Park
NR   Nature Reserve
WA   Wilderness Area

KWAZULU-NATAL

HISTORY

Battled over by Boers, Brits and Zulus, Natal was named by Portuguese explorer Vasco da Gama, who sighted the coastline on Christmas Day 1497, and named it for the natal day of Jesus. It took the British Empire more than 300 years to set its sights on the region, proclaiming it a colony in 1843. Briefly linked to the Cape Colony in 1845, Natal again became a separate colony in 1856, when its European population numbered less than 5000.

The introduction of Indian indentured labour in the 1860s – sections of the province still retain a subcontinental feel – and the subsequent development of commercial agriculture (mainly sugar) boosted development, and the colony thrived from 1895, when train lines linked Durban's port (dredged to accommodate big ships) with the booming Witwatersrand.

The recorded history of the province up until the Union of South Africa is full of conflict: the *mfecane* (the 'forced migration' of South African tribes); the Boer-Zulu and the Anglo-Zulu Wars, which saw the Zulu kingdom subjugated; and the two wars between the British and the Boers. See p32 for more details about the origin and development of the *mfecane*.

Just before the 1994 elections, Natal Province was renamed KwaZulu-Natal, in belated recognition of the fact that the Zulu heartland of KwaZulu comprises a large part of the province.

CLIMATE

The weather (and the water, thanks to the Agulhas current) stays warm year-round along much of the coast, with Durban lapping up a heady 230 sunny days a year. In summer, the heat and humidity, combined with the crowds that flood to the coast to enjoy it, can be exhausting, with temperatures regularly in the mid-30s. Most of the interior enjoys similarly balmy conditions, but sudden and explosive thunderstorms, especially in the Drakensberg mountains and the hills around Eshowe, often roll in during the afternoon. Winter even brings a dusting of snow to the higher peaks.

NATIONAL PARKS & RESERVES

KwaZulu-Natal (KZN) Wildlife (☎ 033-845 1000; www.kznwildlife.com; Queen Elizabeth Park, Duncan McKenzie Dr, Pietermaritzburg) is an essential first stop for those planning to spend time in the province's excellent parks and reserves. Accommodation within the parks ranges from humble camp sites to luxurious lodges; the free *Fees & Charges* booklet lists accommodation options and prices, as well as entrance charges, for all KZN Wildlife reserves. Maps to the parks are also available here.

Camp sites are booked directly with individual parks, but all other accommodation *must* be booked in advance through either the Pietermaritzburg office, or the **KZN Wildlife booking office** (☎ 031-304 4934) on the first floor of Tourist Junction (p285) in Durban. You can book in person, by phone, or via email.

While many of the parks are a must-see for animal lovers and the outdoorsy, their campgrounds are also an excellent choice for those touring South Africa on a budget.

If you only have time to visit one or two reserves, highlights include the Royal Natal National Park (p326) for Drakensberg vistas, Hluhluwe-Imfolozi (p313) for wildlife and Kosi Bay (p320) and the Greater St Lucia Wetland Park (p315) for classic coastal scenery.

LANGUAGE

Eleven official languages are spoken in KwaZulu-Natal, but English, Zulu, Xhosa and Afrikaans are most widely used. Also see the Language chapter, p615.

GETTING THERE & AROUND

Durban, with flights, buses and trains to destinations across the country, is KwaZulu-Natal's undisputed transport hub, and at least nationally, the city is well connected. Getting around the province itself, however, is a different story. While long-distance coaches run to Port Shepstone, Margate and Kokstad in the south, Richard's Bay, Empangeni and Vryheid in the north and a string of towns including Estcourt, Ladysmith and Newcastle in the west, many of the more remote locations are a headache to get to on public transport. Minibus taxis provide a useful back-up, but distances are large and relying on them as your sole means of getting about will mean many long hours in the back of a cramped van.

If you want to explore the region's true highlights (Drakensberg, the parks and reserves, and the battlefields), you are better off hiring a car. Durban has dozens of operators, and cars with generous mileage allowances can be had for as little as R175 a day. Most roads are good, but a few locations – the Sani Pass (which you can easily take a tour to from Underberg), Tembe Elephant Park and occasionally Kosi Bay (which you can hitch to from KwaNgwanase) – require a 4WD, if you want to remain completely independent.

The Baz Bus links most of the province's hostels.

See p596 and individual Getting There & Away sections for more details.

DURBAN

☎ 031 / pop 2,531,000

Summer-season Durban is a city with an eye on the surf and its mind on the party. Stretching along a swathe of butter-yellow sand, South Africa's third-largest city (known as eThekweni in Zulu) has long been one of the country's great escapes, offering a lively, if slightly tacky, pre-packaged seaside experience on the very doorstep of KwaZulu-Natal's teeming metropolitan hub. Traditionally the silly-season stomping ground of White tourists from Johannesburg (Jo'burg) and Pretoria, 21st-century Durban now caters to a more cosmopolitan market, with visitors of all creeds and colours living it up along the city's seafront esplanade.

Not surprisingly, the mix of Bermuda shorts, peroxide surfie hairdos, hotels and snack bars that is Durban's high-rise beachfront remains the city's trademark: a multimile stretch of sun, sea, sand and a little bit of sin. Investment, most notably in the form of the new uShaka Marine World development, is now pouring in and gloss is slowly but surely returning to sections of the beach that had previously deteriorated into no-go zones. Like the Jo'burgers heading home at the end of summer, parts of Durban's seafront still look a little bleary-eyed. Derelict buildings and peeling paint strip the sheen from the streets backing the shore and when the sun goes in, Durban tends to lose its shimmer.

But then there's plenty more to Durban than the four S's. The affluent and altogether more sedate suburbs of Berea, Morningside and Greyville are chock-a-block with bars, eateries and chattering, upper-echelon Durbanites, while the city centre, peppered with some grandiose colonial buildings, throbs to a distinctly African beat. Home to the largest concentration of people of Indian descent in the country, Durban also boasts a distinctive Asian twang, with the marketplaces and streets of the Indian area teeming with the sights, sounds and scents of the subcontinent.

HISTORY

It took some time for Durban to be established. Natal Bay, on which Durban is centred, provided refuge for seafarers at least as early as 1685, and it's thought that Vasco da Gama anchored here in 1497. Though the Dutch bought a large area of land around the bay from a local chief in 1690, their ships didn't make it across the sand bar at the entrance to the bay until 1705, by which time the chief had died, and his son refused to acknowledge the deal.

With a good port established at Delagoa Bay (now Maputo in Mozambique), Natal Bay attracted little attention from Europeans until 1824, when Henry Fynn and Francis Farewell set up a base here to trade for ivory with the Zulu. Shaka, a powerful Zulu chief (see p32 for more information), granted land around the bay to the trading company and it was accepted in the name of King George IV.

The settlement was slow to prosper, partly because of the chaos Shaka was causing in the area. By 1835 there was a small town with a mission station, and that year it took the name D'Urban, after the Cape Colony governor.

In 1837 the Voortrekkers crossed the Drakensberg and founded Pietermaritzburg, 80km northwest of Durban. The next year, after Durban was evacuated during a raid by the Zulu, the Boers claimed control. It was re-occupied by a British force later that year, but the Boers stuck by their claim. The British sent troops to Durban to secure the settlement, but were defeated by the Boers at the Battle of Congella in 1842.

The Boers retained control for a month until a British frigate arrived (fetched by teenager Dick King, who rode the 1000km of wild country between Durban and Grahamstown in Eastern Cape in 10 days) and dislodged them. The next year, Natal was annexed by the British, and Durban began its growth as an important colonial port

KWAZULU-NATAL

DURBAN

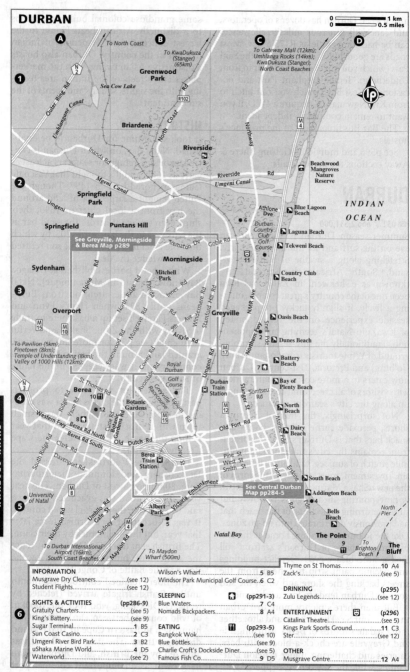

0 ————————— 1 km
0 ————————— 0.5 miles

To North Coast

A

B

To KwaDukuza
(Stanger)
(65km)

C

To Gateway Mall (12km);
Umhlanga Rocks (14km);
KwaDukuza (Stanger);
North Coast Beaches

D

1

Outer Ring Rd

N2

Sea Cow Lake

Greenwood Park

R102

North Coast Rd

Umhlangane Canal

Briardene

Inanda Rd

M4

Northway

2

Mgeni Canal

Riverside

3

Riverside Rd

Umgeni Canal

**Beachwood
Mangroves
Nature
Reserve**

INDIAN
OCEAN

Umgeni Rd

**Springfield
Park**

Springfield

Puntans Hill

Athlone Dve

6

**Blue Lagoon
Beach**

**Durban
Country
Club
Golf
Course**

Laguna Beach

Tekweni Beach

See Greyville, Morningside
& Berea Map p289

Trematon Dr

Goble Rd

Morningside

11

**Country Club
Beach**

3

Sydenham

Alpine Rd

North Ridge Rd

Florida Rd

Mitchell
Park

Innes Rd

Windermere Rd

Stanford Hill Rd

Greyville

NMR Ave

Snell Pde

Oasis Beach

Overport

M15

M10

Essenwood Rd

Musgrave Rd

9th Ave

Argyle Rd

M17

Northern Fwy

M2

Dunes Beach

To Pavilion (5km);
Pinetown (8km);
Temple of Understanding (8km);
Valley of 1000 Hills (12km);

Cowey Rd

Avondale Rd

**Royal
Durban
Golf Course**

Umgeni Rd

7

**Battery
Beach**

**Bay of
Plenty Beach**

4

N3

St Thomas Rd

Ridge Rd

Vause Rd

10

12

Berea Rd

Berea Rd North

Berea Rd South

Botanic Gardens Rd

Currie Rd

8

Berea

**Botanic
Gardens**

**Greyville
Racecourse**

Greyville
Epsom
Rd

**Durban
Train
Station**

Stanger St

Somtseu Rd

M12

**North
Beach**

**Dairy
Beach**

Western Fwy

Clark Rd

South Ridge Rd

Nicholson Rd

Davenport Rd

M8

Old Dutch Rd

Old Fort Rd

M15

Marine Pde

5

University
of Natal

Umbilo Rd

Gale St

Sydney Rd

M4

Maydon Rd

**Berea
Train
Station**

Grey St

Pine St

West St

Smith St

Point Rd

Erskine

South Beach

Addington Beach

4

**Bells
Beach**

North
Pier

To Durban International
Airport (16km);
South Coast Beaches

**Albert
Park**

1

5

Victoria Embankment

To Maydon
Wharf (500m)

Nata Bay

See Central Durban
Map pp284–5

9

The Point

To
Brighton
Beach

**The
Bluff**

---

city. In 1860 the first indentured Indian labourers arrived to work the cane fields. Despite the unjust system – slave labour by another name – many free Indian settlers arrived, including, in 1893, Mohandas Gandhi (see the boxed text on p36).

ORIENTATION

Marine Pde, which fronts the beach, is Durban's focal point. Many mid-range places to stay and eat are on the parade and in the streets behind it, as are many of the entertainment venues. Once almost derelict, the Point, which runs along the spit south of Marine Pde, is slowly being revived with the building of the huge uShaka Marine World theme park, but sections of Point Rd and adjoining streets should still be avoided.

West St starts as a mall, but further west it becomes one of central Durban's main streets. The city hall and the centre of town are about 1km west of the beach, straddling West and Smith Sts.

On the western side of the city centre, around Grey and Victoria Sts, is the Indian area. There's a bustle and vibrancy present here that is missing from most commercial districts in South Africa.

Near the Indian area, especially around Berea train station, thousands of Zulu have set up camp in an extraordinarily jumbled 'township' right on the city centre's doorstep. Most of these people are near destitute and live in appalling conditions, so conspicuously wealthy tourists are obvious targets.

The suburb of Berea (pronounced b-*ree*-a) is further inland, on a ridge overlooking the city centre. The ridge marks the beginning of the wealthy suburbs, including Greyville and Morningside, rich with pubs, clubs, eateries and hostels, and the lively Florida and Windermere Rd. Wild elephants roamed the Berea Ridge well into the 1850s; these days, it's the best place to take a breather from the bustling centre.

The Umgeni River marks the northern boundary of the city, although the suburbs have sprawled over the river all the way up the coast to Umhlanga Rocks, a big resort and retirement town. Inland from Umhlanga Rocks is Phoenix, an Indian residential area named after Gandhi's commune.

On the city's western fringe is Pinetown, a vast collection of dormitory suburbs. A fair proportion of Durban's mainly Black population lives in townships surrounding the city. These include Richmond Farm, KwaMashu, Lindelani, Ntuzuma and the Greater Inanda area.

INFORMATION
Bookshops
Adam's & Co (Map pp284–5; ☎ 304 8571; 341 West St) Good bookshop with a second outlet at the Musgrave Centre in Berea.
Steve & Toni's (Map pp284–5; ☎ 301 2801; 7 Mark Lane; ☷ 7.30am-4.30pm Mon-Fri, 8am-4pm Sat) Bookshop with an exchange service. They also buy books on a Wednesday (phone ahead).

Emergency
Ambulance (☎ 10177)
General Emergency (☎ 361 0000)
Main Police Station (Map pp284–5; ☎ 10111; Stanger Rd) North of the city centre.
Police Office (Map pp284–5; ☎ 368 3399; Marine Pde) Near Funworld on the beach.

Internet Access
Most of the hostels offer Internet access. Charges start at about R25 per hour. Other options:
Internet Café (Map pp284–5; ☎ 305 6998; 1st fl, the Workshop, Aliwal St; per 30 min R20; ☷ 8.30am-7pm Mon-Fri, 8.30am-6pm Sat & Sun) In the city centre.
Internet Café (Map p289; ☎ 207 2156; 1st fl, Overport City Shopping Centre, 430 Ridge Rd; per 30min R20; ☷ 8.30am-5.30pm Mon-Fri, 9am-2pm Sat) Near Hippo Hide.

Laundry
McKleens (Map pp284–5; ☎ 337 5722; Palmer St; ☷ 8am-5pm)
Musgrave Dry Cleaners (Map p282; ☎ 201 1936; 2nd fl, Musgrave Centre, Musgrave Rd; ☷ 8am-5pm Mon-Fri, 9am-2pm Sat)

Medical Services
Addington Hospital (Map pp284–5; ☎ 327 2000; Prince St) For emergencies.
Medical Centre (Map pp284–5; ☎ 031-304 9767; cnr Smith & Broad Sts; ☷ 9am-8pm) Charges R100 for general medical and dental consultations.
Travel Doctor (Map pp284–5; ☎ 360 1122; International Convention Centre, 45 Ordnance Rd; ☷ 8am-4pm Mon-Fri, 8am-noon Sat) For travel-related advice.

Money
There are banks with ATMs and change facilities across the city.

KWAZULU-NATAL

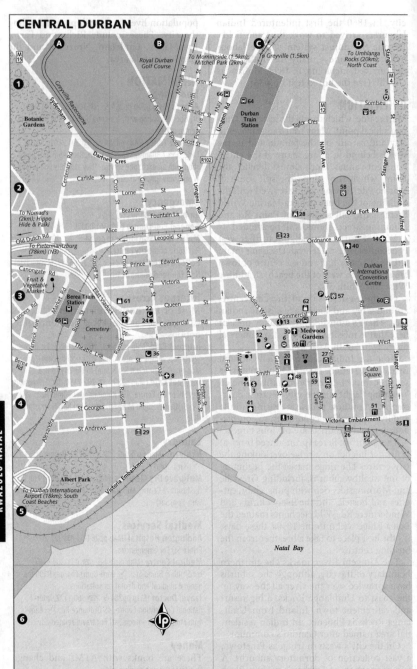

CENTRAL DURBAN

KWAZULU-NATAL

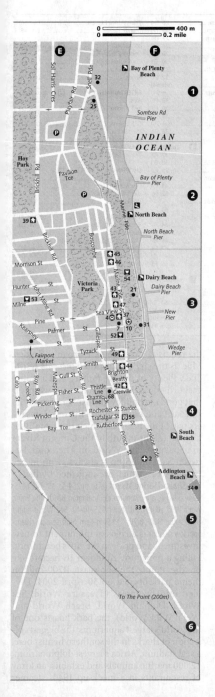

American Express (Map pp284–5; ☎ 301 5541; 11th fl, Nedbank Bldg, Durban Club Lane; ☉ 8.30am-4.30pm Mon-Fri, 9-11am Sat) Accessed from the lane leading from Smith Street to the Durban Manor Hotel.

Rennies Travel (Map pp284–5; ☎ 305 5722; ground fl, 333 Smith St; ☉ 8.30am-4.30pm Mon-Fri, 8.30-11.30am Sat) An agent for Thomas Cook with several branches around town.

Post

Branch post office (Map pp284–5; Sea View St; ☉ 8am-4.30pm Mon-Fri, 8am-noon Sat) By the beach near Funworld.

Main post office (Map pp284–5; cnr West & Gardiner Sts; ☉ 8am-4.30pm Mon-Fri, 8am-noon Sat) Has a poste restante service.

Tourist Information

The main tourist information centre is in the old train station (built in 1894) and is known as **Tourist Junction** (Map pp284–5; 160 Pine St, cnr Soldiers Way; ☉ 8am-5pm Mon-Fri, 9am-2pm Sat). In here, you will find **Durban Africa** (☎ 304 4934; www.durbanexperience.co.za; 1st fl, Tourist Junction), which covers Durban; and the **KwaZulu-Natal Tourism Authority Information Office** (☎ 366 7516/7; www.zulu.org.za; ground fl, Tourist Junction), which deals with the province as a whole.

There are also various booking agencies in the complex, including **KZN Wildlife** (☎ 304 4934; www.kznwildlife.com; 1st fl, Tourist Junction), where you can reserve accommodation in KZN Wildlife parks and reserves; and **South African Parks Reservations** (☎ 304 4934; www.parks-sa.co.za; 1st fl, Tourist Junction), which takes accommodation bookings for national parks across the country.

Pick up a free copy of the bi-monthly *What's On in Durban* pamphlet at Tourist Junction. The monthly *Durban for All Seasons* is available from most hotels. There is also information in the *KwaZulu-Natal Experience* magazine.

There are also several other **Durban Africa tourist offices** (www.durbanexperience.co.za) Airport (☎ 451 6950; arrivals hall; ☉ 7am-9pm); Marine Pde (Map pp284–5; ☎ 332 2595; next to Joe Kool's; ☉ 8am-5pm Mon-Fri, 8am-4pm Sat & Sun).

Travel Agencies

Student Flights (Map p282; ☎ 202 5995; fax 202 1108; Shop 324, Musgrave Centre, Musgrave Rd; ☉ 8.30am-5pm Mon-Fri, 9am-noon Sat) Specialises in discounted student and backpacker flights.

DANGERS & ANNOYANCES

Crime is a stark reality in Durban, especially during summer, when thieves tend to follow tourists to the beach. While the beach promenade itself is relatively well patrolled, pickpockets remain a problem and particular care should be taken in nearby streets, especially around Point Rd and the area surrounding the Wheel Shopping Centre. Extra care should also be taken around Berea train station and the informal settlements nearby.

Many areas are potentially dangerous at night and central Durban is transformed into a ghost town as people head to beachfront and suburban nightspots. If you have a car, make sure you park it in a locked garage after dark.

Wherever you are, if you are confronted by armed muggers, hand over your valuables immediately!

SIGHTS
Beachfront

Come here for the sunshine and you will probably leave thinking that Durban is little more than the sum of its beaches – which wouldn't be unreasonable. With more than 6km of warm-water beaches (protected by

the requisite shark nets), Durban's 'Golden Mile' is the city's undisputed *pièce de résistance*. Plenty of seaside fanfare and a smorgasbord of bars and restaurants whip up that good ole holiday atmosphere, while the sun, surf and sand provide the rest. Lifesavers patrol the beaches, which run from Blue Lagoon (at the mouth of the Umgeni River) to uShaka Marine World on The Point, between 8am and 5pm – always swim in patrolled areas, which are indicated by flags.

uShaka Marine World (Map pp284-5; ☎ 368 6675; www.ushakamarineworld.co.za; Addington Beach, the Point; Wet'n'Wild adult/child/senior R55/40/40, Sea World adult/child/senior R80/50/70; ⏰ 9am-6pm high season, 10am-5pm low season) is a colossal monument to new investment and pride in the city's beachfront. Filling a previously rundown 16-hectare site on the Point, the showcase R700-million theme park opened on 30 April 2004. Divided into five areas (Treasure World, Sea World, Dolphin World, Beach World and Wet'n'Wild World), the park boasts one of the world's largest aquariums, the biggest collection of sharks in the southern hemisphere, a seal stadium, Africa's largest dolphinarium, 12,000 marine animals and exhibits, an array of restaurants in a mock-up 1940s steamer wreck, a shopping centre, enough freshwater rides to make you seasick and a spread of beaches featuring activities from jet-skiing and volleyball to surfing and sailing.

North of uShaka, the **Promenade** is the pedestrianise tourist superhighway running up the beach from Smith St. On the other side of the road, particularly along Marine Pde, you will find the canyon of high-rise hotels, bars, restaurants and nightclubs typical of seaside cities from Florida to Queensland.

About a dozen rickshaws ply their trade along the beachfront, many sporting exotic Zulu regalia. In 1904 there were about 2000 registered rickshaw pullers, and it was an important means of transport. A five-minute ride costs about R20 plus a few rand for the mandatory photo.

After uShaka, the beachfront's other paying attractions are a bit of a letdown. A few, however, make for a good afternoon out.

The oh-so-glitzy **Sun Coast Casino** (Map p282; ☎ 328 3000; www.suncoastcasino.co.za; Snell Pde) features restaurants, slot machines and cinema screens, but also houses **Waterworld** (☎ 337 6336; adult/child R30/23; ☑ 8.30am-5pm), a watery labyrinth of flumes, pools, shoots and pipes ideal for scorching summer days.

On the Umgeni River, **Umgeni River Bird Park** (Map p282; ☎ 579 4600; Riverside Rd; adult/child R25/18; ☑ 9am-4.30pm) makes for a relaxing escape from the throng. At the mouth of the Umgeni you will see many species of water birds coming and going as they please.

Back towards Marine Pde, **Mini Town** (Map p282; ☎ 337 7892; 114 Snell Pde; adult/child R12/6; ☑ 9.30am-4.30pm) is a typically tacky model city with replicas of Durban's best-known buildings. The nearby **Snake Park** (Map pp284-5; ☎ 073-156 9606; Snell Pde; adult/child R15/8; ☑ 9am-4.30pm) has plenty of serpents and about five venom-milking demonstrations daily.

Right back in the thick of things, **Funworld** (Map pp284-5; Marine Pde; admission R10; ☑ 11am-5pm Tue-Wed, 11am-10pm Thu-Sat) is a busy little amusement park with pools and rides for the kids.

Victoria Embankment

Maydon Wharf, which runs along the southwestern side of the harbour, contains the **Sugar Terminal** (Map pp284-5; ☎ 365 8153; 51 Maydon Rd; adult/concession R10/5; tours 8.30am, 10am, 11.30am & 2pm Mon-Thu, 8.30am, 10am & 11am Fri), which offers an insight into the sugar trade that made Durban big.

A little further north, **Wilson's Wharf** (Map p282; www.wilsonswharf.co.za) is a typically hip waterside development, with a clutch of decent eateries (p293), boat-charter outfits (p295), shops and a theatre (p295).

Dick King Statue (Map pp284-5; Victoria Embankment), near Gardiner St, commemorates the historic ride of this teenager in 1842 to fetch a British frigate, after the Boers took control of Durban.

Sarie Marais (Map pp284-5; ☎ 305 4022; Victoria Embankment; adult/child R40/20; ☑ 9am-5pm) runs pleasure cruises from the nearby Gardiner St Jetty. It also has a **booking office** (Map pp284-5; ☎ 305 4022) near Funworld on the beachfront.

The **Natal Maritime Museum** (Map pp284-5; ☎ 311 2230; Maritime Dr; adult/child R3/1.50; ☑ 8am-3.45pm Mon-Sat, from 11am Sun) is on a service road running parallel to Victoria Embankment – enter on the corner of Fenton St and Victoria Embankment. It has two tugboats and the minesweeper SAS *Durban*. You can clamber all over the boats.

Further along Maritime Dr is the **BAT Centre** (p295), a Bohemian arts centre with shops, an artist's studio, live music, and a bar-restaurant all cut through with a lively trans-Africa theme.

The **Vasco da Gama Clock** (Map pp284–5), a florid Victorian monument on the Embankment, just east of Stanger St, was presented by the Portuguese government in 1897, the 400th anniversary of Vasco da Gama's sighting of Natal.

Durban's **harbour** is the busiest in Africa (and the ninth busiest in the world) and much of the activity centres on the Shipping Terminal near Stanger St, where there are public viewing areas. You can also see the activity on the water from the ferry that runs across the harbour mouth from North Pier on the Point to South Pier on the Bluff.

Down at the southern end of the beachfront, the Point is an old area on a spit of land between the harbour and the ocean. At the very end of the Point you can watch ships coming through the narrow heads into the harbour. The dense indigenous forest on the Bluff, across the narrow channel, is in stark contrast to the sprawling city. Point Rd, leading down to the Point, runs through a very run-down area and is definitely unsafe at night.

KWAZULU-NATAL

City Centre
Map pp284–5

Dominating the city centre is the opulent, but slightly spooky, 1910 **city hall** (☎ 311 1111; Smith St), an incongruous cocktail of modern Renaissance architecture and palm trees next to a minibus taxi rank. In front of the hall is Francis Farewell Sq, where Fynn and Farewell made their camp in 1824.

Inside city hall is the **Natural Science Museum** (☎ 311 2256; Smith St; admission free; ☯ 8.30am-4pm Mon-Sat, 11am-4pm Sun). Check out the cockroach display, the reconstructed dodo and the life-sized dinosaur model. There are sometimes free films here – some dull, some very good.

Upstairs is the **Art Gallery** (☎ 311 2265; admission free; ☯ 8.30am-4pm Mon-Sat, 11am-4pm Sun), which houses a good collection of contemporary South African works, especially Zulu arts and crafts. In particular, look out for the collection of baskets from Hlabisa, finely woven from a variety of grasses and incorporating striking natural colours.

The **municipal library** (☎ 311 2217; ☯ 8.30am-5pm Mon-Fri, 8.30am-1pm Sat) is in this complex.

The **Old Courthouse Museum** (☎ 311 2229; 77 Aliwal St; admission free; ☯ 8.30am-4pm Mon-Sat, 11am-4pm Sun) is in the beautiful 1863 courthouse behind the city hall. It offers an interesting insight into the highs and lows of colonial living.

On the eastern side of the main post office on West St is **Church Sq**, with its old vicarage and the 1909 **St Paul's Church** at the rear on Pine St. Near Church Sq is **Medwood Gardens**, the most relaxing place to take five from the bustle of central Durban.

The excellent **KwaMuhle Museum** (☎ 311 2223; 130 Ordnance Rd; admission free; ☯ 8.30am-4pm Mon-Sat, 11am-4pm Sun) is in the former Bantu Administration building. The museum has a display (with good oral history tapes) on the 'Durban System' by which Whites subjugated Blacks, and temporary exhibitions relating to Zulu culture and contemporary issues.

Old Fort, north of the centre on Old Fort Rd, is where the British were besieged by the Boers in 1842. Here, you can access **Warriors Gate** (☎ 307 3337; Old Fort Rd; admission free; ☯ 11am-3pm Tue-Fri, 10am-noon Sat, 11am-3pm Sun), which is the general headquarters of MOTH (Memorable Order of Tin Hats), a former servicepersons' club. There's a small collection of militaria here.

In the southwest of town, the **Old House Museum** (☎ 311 2261; 31 St Andrews St; ☯ 8.30am-4pm Mon-Sat, 11am-4pm Sun) is the restored home of Natal's first prime minister.

Indian Area
Map pp284–5

The big **Juma Mosque** (☎ 306 0026; cnr Queen & Grey Sts; ☯ 9am-4pm Mon-Fri, 9am-11am Sat) is the largest in the southern hemisphere; call ahead for a guided tour. Madrassa Arcade runs between the mosque and the Catholic Emmanuel Cathedral.

Alayam Hindu Temple (Somtseu Rd; ☯ 7am-6pm) is the oldest and biggest in South Africa. It's away from the main Indian area, on Somtseu Rd, which runs between Stanger St and NMR Ave.

See p296 for information on the popular Victoria St Market.

Greyville, Morningside & Berea

The **Campbell Collections** (Map p289; ☎ 207 3432; 220 Marriott Rd; admission R15; ☯ by appointment only), on the corner of Marriott and Essenwood Rds, are well worth seeing. Muckleneuk, a superb house designed by Sir Herbert Baker, holds the documents and artefacts collected by Dr Killie Campbell and her father Sir Marshall Campbell (KwaMashu township is named after him), which are extremely important records of early Natal and Zulu culture.

Killie Campbell began collecting works by Black artists 60 years before the Durban Gallery did, and she was the first patron of Barbara Tyrrell. Tyrrell trained as a fashion illustrator in Europe in the 1930s, but on returning home to South Africa, she decided that recording the traditional costumes of the indigenous peoples was more important than illustrating catalogues of the latest Paris couture. Her paintings convey the clothing and decoration, and the grace of the people wearing them. You can buy cards of her work or a portfolio of limited-edition prints at the Campbell Collections shop.

The house itself is worth seeing; it contains some wonderful old Cape Dutch furniture.

Mitchell Park, at the top of Florida Rd, has a small **zoo** (Map p289; ☎ 312 2318; 10 Ferndale Rd; adult/child R3/2; ☯ 8am-4pm), with a few animals, and the Blue Zoo (p294), an outdoor restaurant.

The 20-hectare **Botanic Gardens** (Map pp284-5; ☎ 201 1303; Sydenham Rd; admission free; ☯ 9.30am-12.30pm & 2-4.45pm, Orchid House 7.30am-5.45pm), west of Greyville Racecourse, has one of the rarest cycads, *Encephalartos woodii*, as well as

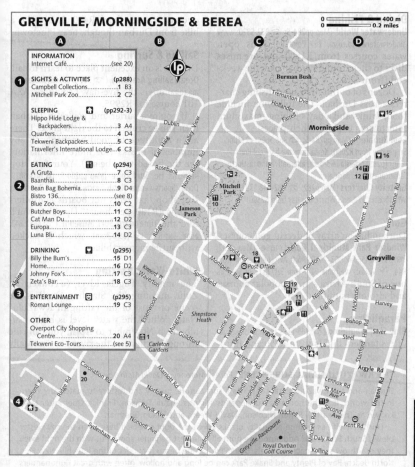

GREYVILLE, MORNINGSIDE & BEREA

0 ————————— 400 m
0 ————————— 0.2 miles

---

many species of bromeliad. There is also a picturesque tea garden.

Temple of Understanding

This **temple** (☎ 403 3328; Bhaktieedanta Sami Rd; ☼ 9am-4pm), 8km west of Durban, is the biggest Hare Krishna temple in the southern hemisphere. It's an unusual building, and now houses a vegetarian restaurant. Follow the N3 towards Pietermaritzburg and then branch off to the N2 south. Take the Chatsworth turn-off and turn right towards the centre of Chatsworth.

ACTIVITIES

It is an irony of modern times that most of the more accessible 'outdoor' activities

take place in the giant Gateway Mall (p304), 16km north of central Durban, near Umhlanga Rocks.

Canoeing

Each January the popular Dusi Marathon starts 80km inland at Pietermaritzburg and ends at the mouth of the Umgeni River.

Trips of nearby rivers can be organised through **180° Adventures** (☎ 566 4955; www.180 .co.za).

Cycling

Durban Mountain Bike Club (☎ 312 9076) runs informal Saturday afternoon rides. You simply give them a call and find out where they are meeting.

Diving & Fishing

Underwater World (Map pp284-5; ☎ 332 5820; www .underwaterworld.co.za; 251 Point Rd) runs open water courses from R1500 and organises dives to sites around Durban over the weekend (from R120).

Dozens of outfits offer sport-fishing charters across Durban. The following include food, drinks and a day's fishing (maximum four to six people) in their prices.

Cool Runnings (Map pp284-5; ☎ 368 5604; 49 Milne St; per day from R2000) Kevin from the bar Cool Runnings (p295) offers a laid-back, alternative and distinctly Jamaican-style experience.

Gratuity Charters (Map p282; ☎ 082-448 1781; Wharfsiders, Wilson's Wharf; per day from R2500)

Golf

Durban has an array of decent golf courses. **Windsor Park Municipal Golf Course** (Map p282; ☎ 312 2245; fax 303 2479; NMR Ave; per person from R44; ☺ visitors welcome 9am-1pm Sat, 8-11am Sun) is one of South Africa's most popular courses and also offers tuition.

Paragliding

Blue Sky Paragliding (☎ 765 1318; www.blusky.co.za) offers tandem flights from R250 and intro-

ductory courses from R450. It is quite a hike from Durban though, near Pinetown.

Sailing & Surfing

Durban is an excellent place to learn to sail. **Ocean Sailing Academy** (☎ 301 5726; www.oceansail ing.co.za) offers the five-day, beginner's ASA 101 course for R2995.

If you're a surfer and you're in Durban then you've cruised to the right place. There are a multitude of good beaches with any number of breaks (for more information, see the boxed text, below). Your first stop should be **Surf Zone** (Map pp284-5; ☎ 368 5818; Ocean Sports Centre, North Beach; ☺ 8am-4.30pm), a surf shop that rents out boards and offers lessons (R180 per hour). Upstairs, you'll find the **Time-warp Surf Museum** (☎ 368 5842; admission R10; ☺ 10am-4pm), which is packed with surfie memorabilia.

White-Water Rafting

The mighty Tugela River (uThukela in Zulu, meaning 'the Startling One') is the scene of most of the rafting in KwaZulu-Natal. When the water level is high, usually from November to April, you can ride through sections of the river known locally

---

THE KWAZULU-NATAL SURF SCENE   *Patrick Moroney & David Malherbe*

Durban and the KwaZulu-Natal coast has a surf culture, quality and history to match anywhere in the world. It is the home of true legends such as Shaun Tomson, Frankie Oberholzer (also known as The Search), Simon Nicolson, David Weare and Shaun Gossman.

Durban itself has a range of quality breaks, given the right swell, all best when the sou'wester blows. South Beach and Addington are normally the best beginner spots, but with the right swell they can throw some gaping barrels. Dairy Pier has the best left-hander of the lot while New Pier, North Beach, Bay of Plenty and Snake Park can be long and hollow, often with great right-handers breaking off the piers. If town starts getting a little too crowded, then head for the northern town beaches, Battery and Tekweni, which can produce quality waves with fewer people in the water. Joe Kool's (p293), right on North Beach, is the most popular postsurfing *jol* (party).

The Bluff, just south of Durban, has some good spots, with the infamous Cave Rock being its showpiece. Often compared with Hawaii's Backdoor, the Rock is for experienced surfers only.

The KwaZulu-Natal coast really comes into its own on the north and south coasts, which offer a selection of world-class point breaks and the chance to get away from the city crowds. The coast is best in winter, from April to August, before 10am or 11am, when you're basically guaranteed a northwest land breeze. When solid groundswells roll in from the south, you are assured solid waves. On the north coast the best-known spots are Westbrook (arguably the hollowest wave around), Ballito Bay and Zinkwazi Beach. The south coast offers Greenpoint, Scottburgh, Happy Wanderers, St Michaels and The Spot (all right-handers). Each produces incredibly rideable 1m to 2.5m-plus grinders over rock and sand bottom, with the occasional ride that is a couple of hundred metres. Plenty of barrels are around, but check with locals to be safe. Lucien Beach, near Margate, is the place to check when the northeasterly is blowing. Further south are more right-hand points along the Transkei Wild Coast (p225), with plenty of quality waves between.

as Horrible Horace, the Rollercoaster, Four-Man Hole and the Tugela Ravine. When the water is bad on the Tugela, you may have more luck on the Unkomaas. **180° Adventures** (☎ 566 4955; www.180.co.za) offers rafting on both rivers for R450 per day.

TOURS

Perhaps the best way to experience Durban is in the company of someone who knows what they are looking at. **Durban Africa** (☎ 304 4934; www.durbanexperience.co.za; 1st fl, Tourist Junction) runs walking tours of the city (adult/child R40/20) at 9.30am Monday to Friday for three hours. Township tours can also be arranged through Durban Africa. **Umkhumbane Tours** (☎ 309 7058) is one such provider, offering a full-day tour of Durban and the neighbouring Inanda township for R350 per person.

The **Ricksha Bus** (☎ 083-289 0509; fax 205 5713; adult/child R40/20) collects passengers from Tourist Junction at 1.30pm on Tuesday, Thursday and Sunday for a 2½-hour city tour in an open-top bus. Pay as you hop on.

Most hostels arrange backpacker-oriented tours and activities in the Durban area and around KwaZulu-Natal. By far the largest range is offered by **Tekweni Eco-Tours** (Map p289; ☎ 303 1199; tekwenitours@mweb.co.za; 169 Ninth Ave), based at Tekweni Backpackers (p293) in Durban.

FESTIVALS & EVENTS

JANUARY/FEBRUARY

Kavadi Festival This major Hindu festival is held twice a year (January to February and April to May). It honours the god Muruga, who heals and dispels misfortune, and, as a sign of devotion, much self-inflicted pain accompanies the ceremony.

APRIL/MAY

Draupadi festival An 18-day festival, in honour of the goddess Draupadi, culminates in fire walking.

JULY/AUGUST

Mariamman For 10 days during July and August the Mariamman, or Porridge Festival, is celebrated.

NOVEMBER

Diwali The three-day Diwali is also known as the Festival of Lights.

DECEMBER

Ratha Yatra The colourful five-day Hare Krishna festival Ratha Yatra, is also known as the Festival of Chariots.

SLEEPING

A worthwhile first call is Durban Africa's accommodation website www.bookabedahead.co.za, which allows you to browse and book online. Alternatively, pop into **Durban Africa** (☎ 304 4934; www.durbanexperience.co.za; 1st fl, Tourist Junction), which can help you out, whatever your budget.

Durban doesn't have the range of hostels you'll find in Cape Town or Jo'burg, but there are some good ones here, and more are opening all the time. Most are some way west and northwest of the city centre in the wealthier suburbs. Many will, however, collect you from the airport or train station, and they usually arrange trips to the beach and other places of interest. Many top-end places line the beachfront, but some of the nicest places are scattered across the city centre and suburbs.

Beachfront

MID-RANGE

Holiday Inn Garden Court – South Beach (Map pp284-5; ☎ 337 2231; www.southernsun.com; 73 Marine Pde; r R429; P ❄ ❖) With simple, modern styling, this unpretentious place has sparkling floors and decent rooms. As far as beachfront mid-rangers go, it takes some beating.

Durban Spa (Map pp284-5; ☎ 332 9366; www.durbanspa.co.za; 57 Marine Pde; r R400; P ❄ ❖) A bit like a giant swimming-pool complex – it is, after all, a spa – this immaculate place has large, self-catering units with TVs, microwaves, dishwashers and all. And then, of course, you can always head downstairs and use the sauna.

Parade Hotel (Map pp284-5; ☎ 337 4565; www.paradehotel.co.za; 191 Marine Pde; s/d with breakfast R230/320; P ❄) The Parade Hotel is a bit old, with a slightly dowdy array of 1970s salesroom furniture, but it's a comfortable place and at these prices definitely worth a look.

Palace Hotel (Map pp284-5; ☎ 332 8351; fax 332 8307; 221 Marine Pde; r R475; P ❄) It's hardly palatial, with a little too much cyan in the colour scheme, but the self-catering apartments are fine, if you want to spend your days on the beach.

Tropicana (Map pp284-5; ☎ 368 1511; tropican@iafrica.com; 85 Marine Pde; s/d R429/658; P ❄) The bright and breezy Tropicana is another beachfront tower, with spacious rooms, boasting air-con and TV.

KWAZULU-NATAL

TOP FIVE DURBAN SLEEPING

■ Quarters (opposite)

■ Royal Hotel (right)

■ Durban Hilton International (right)

■ Protea Hotel Edward International (below)

■ Hippo Hide Lodge & Backpackers (right)

Blue Waters (Map p282; ☎ 332 4272; fax 337 5817; 175 Snell Pde; s/d with breakfast R300/440; P ⊠) Blue Waters is a classic hotel on the northern end of the beachfront, away from the crowded Promenade.

TOP END

Protea Hotel Edward Durban (Map pp284-5; ☎ 337 3681; www.proteahotels.com/edwarddurban; 149 Marine Pde; s/d R800/950; P ⊠ 🖳 ♨) King of the seafront hotels, this is classic and comfortable, with tip-top rooms, fresh polish smells and stylish décor making up for the requisite piped music.

Balmoral (Map pp284-5; ☎ 368 5940; www.raya -hotels.co.za; 125 Marine Pde; s/d with breakfast R630/785; P ⊠) Making the odd concession to colonial-era splendour, this beachfront place has lashings of understated style and plenty of plush rooms.

Holiday Inn Garden Court – Marine Parade (Map pp284-5; ☎ 337 3341; 167 Marine Pde; s/d R634/728; P ⊠ 🖳) The best of Holiday Inn's four beachfront offerings, this comes from the steel-and-glass school of architecture, with fresh, modern décor, uncluttered rooms and acres of polished floors.

Victoria Embankment

MID-RANGE

Durban Manor (Map pp284-5; ☎ 366 0700; fax 366 0701; 93-96 Victoria Embankment; s/d with breakfast R380/490; P ⊠) Housed in the opulent Durban Club, one of the city's finest colonial-era landmarks and a solid jumble of Victorian and Edwardian architectural elements, the owners of this hotel seem rather smug about transforming this formerly snooty institution into a mid-range hotel. 'Once exclusive, now inclusive' (or so the publicity pamphlet reads), Durban Manor has lost much of the Club's former glory, but renovations are planned and prices are reasonable.

City Centre   Map pp284–5

BUDGET

Banana Backpackers (☎ 368 4062; aroutes@iafrica .com; 61 Pine St; dm/tw/d with shared bathroom R60/ 140/170; 🖳) Beach-bum backpackers will love the location, but staying here is a bit of a roller-coaster ride. The owner makes a big effort and the facilities are good, but it can get noisy enough to drive you bananas.

MID-RANGE

City Lodge (☎ 332 1447; www.citylodge.co.za; cnr Brickhill & Old Fort Rds; s/d R320/460; P ⊠) This secure place offers motel styling and slick service. It doesn't ooze charm, but it does have everything you would want for the price, including a quiet spot near the beach.

TOP END

Royal Hotel (☎ 333 6000; www.theroyal.co.za; 267 Smith St; s/d with breakfast R1310/1670; P ⊠ 🖳) Overlooking the city hall, the Royal is one book you shouldn't judge by its cover. A nondescript tiled tower block on the outside, this five-star institution is actually one of the city's swankiest offerings. Specials go as low as R550 per room.

Durban Hilton International (☎ 336 8100; www .hilton.com; 12 Walnut St; r with breakfast R1670; P ⊠ 🖳 ♨) Glitzy and chic, this slick, modern behemoth is arguably Durban's most exclusive hotel, with crowds of business travellers and local movers-and-shakers filling the downstairs bar. Some excellent deals take rooms down to as little as R800.

Greyville, Morningside & Berea

BUDGET

Hippo Hide Lodge & Backpackers (Map p289; ☎ 207 4366; www.hippohide.co.za; 2 Jesmond Rd; dm/s/d with shared bathroom R70/100/170; P 🖳 ♨) Small enough to maintain that family feel, but big enough to keep the new faces coming, this groovy little place pulls in the punters with its friendly, informal style and consistently high standards. It's out on a limb in terms of location, but huddled up around the miniature bar, wallowing in the rock pool or kicking back in the TV room, you won't much care.

Nomads Backpackers (Map p289; ☎ 202 9709; nomads.durban.co.za; 70 Essenwood Rd, Berea; dm R60 d with/without bathroom R200/160; P 🖳 ♨) Another graduate from the school of suburban backpacking, this pleasant place is only a

Beadwork for sale, Johannesburg, Gauteng

Oranges for sale, Gauteng

Small street mall, Johannesburg, Gauteng

Wooden masks at Bruma Lake Market World (p394), Johannesburg, Gauteng

Wall mural of Nelson Mandela, Soweto (p399), Gauteng

RICHARD I'ANSON

Brightly painted house in Soweto (p399), Gauteng

JANE SWEENEY

RICHARD I'ANSON

Woman at an outdoor market, Soweto (p399), Gauteng

Statue of Paul Kruger, the 'Old Lion', Church Sq (p409), Pretoria, Gauteng

RICHARD I

skip and jump away from the cinemas and cappuccino bars of the Musgrave Centre. And if you can't be bothered with that, you can always sip a few sundowners in the Bambooza bar before slipping into the swimming pool.

Tekweni Backpackers (Map p289; ☎ 303 1433; www .tekwenibackpackers.co.za; 169 Ninth Ave, Morningside; dm/ s/d with shared bathroom R80/130/200; **P** 🖳) It's not the glossiest spot on the backpacker circuit, but with top notch information and tour bookings through Tekweni Eco-Tours, it's no surprise that the beds fill up quicker than you can say 'another tequila slammer please'. On the doorstep of vibrant Florida Rd, and with a reputation as a bit of a party hostel itself, this is the place for those wanting to plan big trips in raucous, sociable surrounds.

Traveller's International Lodge (Map p289; ☎ 303 1064; 743 Currie Rd, Morningside; dm/s/d with shared bathroom R75/150/180; **P** 🖳) This pleasant, if a little scruffy, family-run place is for those after more hush than rush. Friendly faces and relaxing, quiet(ish) surrounds make for a relaxing hostel stay.

MID-RANGE

Quarters (Map p289; ☎ 303 5246; quarters@icon.co.za; 101 Florida Rd; r R565; **P** 😽) Right in the throbbing heart of Durban's most fashionable eating and drinking quarter, this attractive boutique hotel balances colonial glamour with small-scale home comforts. The cosy rooms have tasteful soft furnishings and balconies, and the restaurant is one of the best in the area.

EATING

Finding a decent bite to eat in Durban is rarely difficult, although variety is a little harder to come by. Without doubt, your best bet for a good feed is to head to the suburbs. Many of the following eateries double as bars once the plates have been cleared.

TOP FIVE DURBAN EATING

- Famous Fish Co (right)
- Trans-Africa Express (right)
- Bean Bag Bohemia (p294)
- Ulundi (p294)
- Zack's (right)

Beachfront
Map pp284–5

While the beachfront is chock-a-block with cheap and cheerful diners, you'll be hard-pressed to find much more than the usual spread of burgers, pizza and candy floss.

Joe Kool's (☎ 332 9697; Lower Marine Pde, North Beach; mains R20-45; 😽 breakfast, lunch & dinner) Joe Kool's is a popular nightspot with a restaurant promoted as the 'world's worst restaurant' – a statement that is not too far from the truth come midnight on a Saturday – but it does serve a great Sunday morning fry-up.

Saagris (☎ 332 7922; 167 Marine Pde; mains R35-65; 😽 lunch & dinner; 😽) This decent Indian restaurant, in the Holiday Inn Garden Court – Marine Parade, specialises in delicious seafood curries as well as dishes from the tandoori oven, though atmosphere is not its strong suit.

Victoria Embankment

The new Wilson's Wharf development on Victoria Embankment has a good choice of seaside eats and there is a clutch of decent seafood places around King's Battery at the end of the Point.

Zack's (Map p289; ☎ 305 1677; Wilson's Wharf, Victoria Embankment; mains R30-80; 😽 lunch & dinner; 😽) Offering café-style dining, this stylish eatery serves quality bistro fare washed down with a good blast of fresh sea air. Try the Mozambican Calamari and Mussel Pasta (R55).

Charlie Croft's Dockside Diner (Map p289; ☎ 307 2935; Wilson's Wharf, Victoria Embankment; mains R30-70; 😽 lunch & dinner; 😽) A foodie pub in the chain mould, this whips up some great steak and seafood specialties in a lively, bar-style atmosphere.

Trans-Africa Express (Map pp284-5; ☎ 332 0804; 1st fl, Bat Centre, Victoria Embankment; mains R25-60; 😽 lunch & dinner) Upstairs at the Bat Centre, with terrace views over the docks, this restaurant serves hearty, healthy fare with a zesty African twist.

Famous Fish Co (Map p289; ☎ 368 1060; King's Battery, the Point; mains R40-100; 😽 lunch & dinner; 😽) Something of a Durban institution, with as dreamy a sea view as the city gets (you'll have to ignore the cargo ships), this reliable fish restaurant has fed such luminaries as Danny Glover, Jimmy Carter and the Springboks.

Blue Bottles (Map p289; ☎ 332 2787; King's Battery, the Point; mains R30-80; 😽 lunch & dinner; 😽) Mountains of fresh fish, occasional live music, plenty of big windows for big views and a lively Caribbean twist conspire to make the trek down here worthwhile.

City Centre
Map pp284–5

Takeaway places around the city have good Indian snacks including *bunny chow*, a half or quarter loaf of bread hollowed out and filled with beans, traditionally, or curry stew. There are countless places like this around **Victoria St Market** (p296). There's also usually someone with a braai (barbecue) cooking sausages near the main post office – follow your nose for a cheap lunch.

For a decent selection of fast food chains, check out the back entrance of the **Workshop** (p296).

Roma Revolving Restaurant (☎ 332 3337; 32nd fl, John Ross House, Victoria Embankment; mains R35-70; ⏰ lunch & dinner; ❄ ✕) One of only 37 revolving restaurants worldwide, this reasonably priced Italian eatery offers stunning views over Durban. The fact that John Ross House has a touch of the Leaning Tower of Pisa about it doesn't fill you with confidence though.

Garden Bistro (☎ 304 1461; Medwood Gardens, 232A West St; mains R15-30; ⏰ lunch & dinner) Inexpensive, outdoors and a great place to read your snail mail, this little café offers a welcome oasis from the crowds of West St.

The **Royal Hotel** (p292) has a number of restaurants: **Ulundi** (mains R50-90) is the place to sample a Bombay fish curry or a lamb dish; the Royal Carvery has a set menu (starting with sherry) for both lunch and dinner; the **Royal Grill** (mains R70-150), a little more adventurous and more expensive, is where you can dine à la carte.

Greyville, Morningside & Berea

Durban's more affluent suburbs are filled with eateries – some adventurous, some not so – which come and go on a culinary whim. Most whip up the same staple spread of pasta, steak and pizza, usually pepped up with a selection of Indian and African specialties. Prices are generally fair and standards reliable. The adjoining arteries of Florida and Windermere Rds are the best places to start.

Bean Bag Bohemia (Map p289; ☎ 309 6019; 18 Windermere Rd; mains R25-50; ⏰ breakfast, lunch & dinner) A temple to kitsch (check out the Greek-god doorway and the turquoise staff shirts), this bar-cum-eatery serves a wholesome range of Mediterranean fare, from hummus-topped burgers to a range of hearty pastas. The beer flows until late.

Butcher Boys (Map p289; 312 8248; 170 Florida Rd; mains R30-70; ⏰ lunch & dinner; ❄) If you haven't already sworn never to go near a braai again, the meat aficionados here whip up a mean steak. Fill up on the sunny terrace or soak up the ambience in the stylish interior.

Baanthai (Map p289; ☎ 303 4270; 138 Florida Rd; mains R30-60; ⏰ lunch & dinner; ❄) Wafts of (culinary) Bangkok drift from the door of this reasonably authentic Thai restaurant, which offers a reliable, if slightly predictable, selection of the old favourites.

Bistro 136 (Map p289; ☎ 303 3440; 136 Florida Rd; mains R40-100; ⏰ lunch & dinner; ❄) In the same building as Baanthai, this classy little bistro serves up an old-school style of cooking, with oysters, duck and game playing a starring role on the menu. The large windows open out for that Parisian streetside effect.

A Gruta (Map p289; ☎ 312 8675; 200C Florida Rd; mains R30-75; ⏰ lunch & dinner; ❄) If you aren't heading on to Mozambique (or Portugal for that matter), this is a great place to sample the flavours of Iberia. It fills up at night, making for a fab, if slightly cheesy, Mediterranean-style ambience.

Europa (Map p289; ☎ 312 1099; 167 Florida Rd; mains R25-60; ⏰ lunch & dinner) This little slice of contemporary Italia offers tasty pizza and frothy cappuccino.

Blue Zoo (Map p289; ☎ 303 3568; Mitchell Park; mains R20-40; ⏰ breakfast, lunch & dinner) In the heart of sleepy Mitchell Park, this is a mellow spot to caffeinate over bleary breakfasts or long lunches.

Cat Man Du (Map p289; ☎ 312 7893; 411 Windermere Rd; mains R30-80; ⏰ lunch & dinner) More Hispanic than Nepalese, this groovy diner serves excellent Mediterranean tucker (and Cuban cigars) in warm, atmospheric surrounds.

Luna Blu (Map p289; ☎ 312 4665; 427 Windermere Rd; mains R25-40; ⏰ lunch & dinner) Small restaurant, big aromas. Offering a range of gourmet toppings (Thai chicken, gorgonzola, roast lamb) this is the ideal place to order that special takeaway pizza (free delivery).

Thyme on St Thomas (Map p282; Tinsley House, 225 Musgrave Rd; snacks R15-30; ⏰ breakfast & lunch; ❄) This fashionable café, with décor straight from an interior-design magazine, is the perfect place to chat philosophy over coffee.

Bangkok Wok (Map p282; ☎ 201 8557; 225 Musgrave Rd; mains R25-60; ☺ lunch & dinner; ☒) This upmarket Thai place boasts svelte modern-meets-traditional décor and fresh, zesty cooking.

DRINKING

As ever, while there are plenty of basic drinking and dancing dens along the beachfront and through the city centre (watch what you wander into), most of the best options are found in the suburbs.

Zeta's Bar (Map p289; ☎ 303 7049; 258 Florida Rd; ☺ Tue-Sat) Voluptuous red-plush seats and curvy soft lines provide the backdrop for this lounge lizard's favourite. Sip your cocktail and watch the beautiful people – or just have a cold beer on the terrace. It's closed on Sunday and Monday.

Home (Map p289; ☎ 303 3694; cnr Windermere & Innes Rds) Oh-so-stylish bar promising 'better living through social intercourse'. Yep, it's pretentious, but it also provides a great opportunity to don your glad rags and smooch with interior-designer types.

Johnny Fox's (Map p289; ☎ 303 5404; 295 Florida Rd) This no-nonsense Irish bar, set in a plush colonial villa, serves up a passable pint of Guinness and a fair dose of *craic*. It's worth coming along just to hang out on the terrace like a sugar baron.

Billy the Bum's (Map p289; ☎ 303 1988; 504 Windermere Rd, Morningside) Attracting a crowd of Durban's upwardly mobile, this suburban cocktail bar is reliably raucous.

Zulu Legends (Map p282; ☎ 201 0733; Musgrave Centre) A hot spot in the Musgrave Centre, this is a chic cocktail bar with a fun atmosphere and delicious food.

Cool Runnings (Map pp284-5; ☎ 368 5604; 49 Milne St) The original Cool Runnings is rougher around the edges than the franchises elsewhere in South Africa; it retains a truly Rasta Bohemian feel and it stays open until 6am. Come late (it fills up after 11pm) and catch a cab (this is not an area to walk around).

Joe Kool's (Map pp284-5; ☎ 332 9697; Lower Marine Pde, North Beach) The inevitable finish line for any day on the beach, this venerable nightspot cooks up a cocktail of cold beer, big screen TV, dance music and feisty crowds. Sunday night is party night.

Rivets (Map pp284-5; ☎ 336 8100; Durban Hilton, 12 Walnut St) As glossy as you'd expect a bar in the guts of the Hilton to be, Rivets boasts weekend DJs, chi-chi décor, a contingent of the beautiful set and pricey cocktails.

Cockney Pride Pub (Map pp284-5; ☎ 337 5511; cnr Marine Pde & West St) This little slice of East London features all the authentic features of a true English boozer: pub tucker, caricatures of the regulars on the walls, billows of smoke and stained carpets.

ENTERTAINMENT

Durban is a lively city with a vibrant cultural scene. Many events, from the Natal Sharks games to Shakespeare performances, can be booked through **Computicket** (Map pp284-5; ☎ 083-915 8000; 1st fl, the Workshop, Commercial Rd; ☺ 8.30am-4.30pm Mon-Fri, 8.30am-noon Sat).

The **Durban Exhibition Centre** (DEC; Map pp284-5; ☎ 301 7763; Aliwal St) hosts occasional shows and events.

Cinemas

There are cinemas in all of the major malls:
CSE Cinema (Map pp284-5; ☎ 304 0329; the Workshop)
Imax (☎ 566 4415; Gateway, Umhlanga Ridge) Big screen action in the Gateway Mall (p296).
Ster (Map p282; ☎ 0860 300 222; www.sterkinekor.com; Musgrave Centre, Musgrave Rd)
Ster (☎ 566 3222; www.sterkinekor.com; Gateway, Umhlanga Ridge) In the Gateway Mall (p296).

Gay & Lesbian Venues

Axis (Map pp284-5; ☎ 332 2603; cnr Gillespie & Rutherford Sts) This is a popular gay nightclub catering to both men and women. It plays a good range of dance, house and garage music.

Roman Lounge (Map p289; ☎ 303 9023; 202 Florida Rd, Morningside) Right in the heart of the bar district, this is a good place to hook up and caters to both men and women.

Live Music

KwaZulu-Natal Philharmonic Orchestra (☎ 369 9438; www.kznpo.co.za) The orchestra has an interesting spring concert programme with weekly performances in the city hall. It plays in the Botanic Gardens some Sundays.

The jazz scene in Durban deserves special mention. There is a real blend of styles using American jazz rhythms as a base. Imagine the effect a sprinkling of Indian classical, indigenous South African and township jazz influences has on the sound.

BAT Centre (Map pp284-5; ☎ 332 0451; www.batcentre.co.za; 45 Marine Pl, Victoria Embankment) One of Durban's more interesting haunts, this ever-popular venue features everything from DJs on Friday and Saturday nights to a drum circle on Tuesday evenings. It also plays host to regular performances by the best jazz musicians in the country.

Rivets (Map pp284-5; ☎ 336 8100; Durban Hilton, 12 Walnut St) From 8pm on Thursday nights, this bar (p295) turns into a smooth jazz club with a range of performances from up-and-comers and genre veterans.

Rainbow Restaurant & Jazz Club (☎ 702 9161; 23 Stanfield Lane, Pinetown) It's way out in Pinetown, 8km west of the centre, but in the 1980s this was the first restaurant in Natal to cater to Blacks in a so-called 'White area'. Developing a reputation as a centre of the jazz scene, it now features weekly concerts and headline acts on the first Sunday of the month.

The local press has been bemoaning the shrinking contemporary live music scene in Durban and gigs are few and far between. Ask around in bars for the latest.

Nightclubs

Tilt (Map pp284-5; ☎ 306 9356; 11 Walnut Rd) One of Durban's classier clubs, this place shares DJs with the Hilton's Rivets bar. Friday is often the big one, with thumping dance music working up the tribal rhythm.

Sport

Several different types of football are played in KwaZulu-Natal, but the most popular is soccer. Professional teams such as AmaZulu and Manning Rangers play in town, and international teams also visit.

King's Park Sports Ground (Map p282; ☎ 312 5022; Jackson Dr) With 60,000 seats, King's Park is home to the **Natal Sharks** (www.sharksrugby .co.za) rugby team.

Kingsmead Cricket Ground (Map pp284-5; ☎ 335 4200; 2 Kingsmead Close) Cricket fever is cured here, where the international knockabouts are hosted.

Theatre

Natal Playhouse (Map pp284-5; ☎ 369 9444; www .playhousecompany.com; Smith St) Opposite the city hall, Durban's central theatre has dance, drama and music most nights.

Other venues:

Barnyard Theatre (☎ 566 3945; www.barnyardtheatre.co .za; Gateway, Umhlanga Ridge) In the Gateway Mall (p296).

Catalina Theatre (Map p289; ☎ 305 6889; Wilson's Wharf, Victoria Embankment)

SHOPPING

Victoria St Market (Map pp284-5; ☎ 306 4021, Victoria St; 6am-6pm Mon-Sat, 6am-4pm Sun) At the western end of Victoria St, this is the hub of the Indian community and offers a typically rip-roaring, subcontinental shopping experience, with more than 160 stalls selling wares from across Asia. It's the main tourist attraction in the area, but watch your wallet. Grey St, between Victoria and West Sts, is the main shopping area. Prices are low and you can bargain. Most Muslim shops close between noon and 2pm on Friday.

African Art Centre (Map pp284-5; ☎ 301 2717; www.afriart.org.za; 160 Pine St; 8.30am-5pm Mon-Fri, 9am-1pm Sat) In the building that houses the Tourist Junction, this is not a curio shop, but a nonprofit gallery with work by rural craftspeople and artists. It also sells some 'authentic' pieces, which are usually old and were made for traditional use. Local dealers and galleries often snap these up.

Workshop (Map pp284-5; ☎ 304 9894; 99 Aliwal St; 8.30am-5pm Mon-Fri, 9am-5pm Sat, 10am-5pm Sun) A shopping centre in a former railway building (a train shed, hence the huge doors), which became redundant when the new station opened.

While the shops in the city centre and the shopping centres in the nearby suburbs (especially the Musgrave Centre in Berea) will cater to most of your needs, if you want to see where the wealthy minority hides from the poor majority, in a glitzy local version of the American Dream, drop into the enormous **Pavilion** (☎ 265 0558; Westville; 9am-6pm Mon-Fri, 9am-5pm Sat, 10am-5pm Sun). It's on the city's outskirts but is a quick drive from the centre on the N3 towards Pietermaritzburg. The region's even larger behemoth is the **Gateway Mall** (Map p303; ☎ 566 2332; www.gatewayworld.co.za; 1 Palm Blvd, Umhlanga Ridge; 9am-7pm Mon-Thu, 9am-9pm Fri-Sat, 9am-6pm Sun), 16km north of central Durban. A **shuttle bus** (☎ 083-545 9006; fare R5) links the Workshop and Gateway every two hours from 7.30am until 7.30pm.

On Sunday a **flea market** (Map pp284-5; Aliwal St) is held in the South Plaza of the Durban Exhibition Centre.

GETTING THERE & AWAY
Air

Durban International Airport (☎ 451 6666) is off the N2, 16km south of the city. **Student Flights** (p285) is a good first stop for flights.

KWAZULU-NATAL

Several airlines link Durban with South Africa's other main centres. Prices quoted are for the cheapest available one-way fares.

Comair (☎ 011-921 0222; www.comair.co.za) links Durban and Jo'burg daily (R431).

Kulula (☎ 0861 585 852; www.kulula.com), South Africa's no-frills airline, links Durban with Jo'burg (R250) and Cape Town (R500) at least once daily.

Nationwide Airlines (☎ 408 9300; www.nationwideair.co.za) flies at least once daily to Jo'burg (R463), Cape Town (R502) and Port Elizabeth (R365).

South African Airlink (SAAirlink; ☎ 011-978 1111; www.saairlink.co.za) flies daily to Port Elizabeth (R900), Bloemfontein (R1000) and Nelspruit (R1300).

South African Airways (SAA; ☎ 250 1111/3; www.flysaa.com) flies to Jo'burg (R310), Port Elizabeth (R990), East London (R1100), Cape Town (R805), George (R1150) and Nelspruit (R1300) at least once daily.

Bus

The **Baz Bus** (Map pp284-5; ☎ 304 9099; www.bazbus.com; 1st fl, Tourist Junction; ☺ 8.30am-4.30pm Mon-Fri, 8.30am-noon Sat) has an office next to Durban Africa. One-way hop-on/-off prices start at R1520 for Cape Town and R1800 for Jo'burg via Drakensberg.

Most long-distance buses leave from the rear of Durban train station (Map pp284-5). If you're going to the station by car, enter from NMR Ave, not Umgeni Rd. The following long-distance bus companies have their offices here.

Eldo Coaches (☎ 307 3363) has three buses daily to Jo'burg (R165, eight hours).

Greyhound (☎ 309 7830; www.greyhound.co.za) has daily buses to Richard's Bay (R120, three hours), Jo'burg (R185, eight hours), Cape Town (R465, 22 hours), Port Elizabeth (R300, 15 hours) and Port Shepstone (R85, 1½ hours). They also run daily to Pietermaritzburg (R80, one hour), Estcourt (R95, two hours), Ladysmith (R140, four hours) and Newcastle (R160, 5½ hours), as well as to Vryheid (R160, six hours) and Paulpietersburg (R165, 6½ hours).

You can also book at the Greyhound office for the **Margate Mini Coach** (☎ 039-312 1406), which links Durban and Margate twice daily (R70, 2½ hours).

Intercape (☎ 0861 287 287; www.intercape.co.za) has daily buses to Jo'burg (R125, eight hours), Cape Town (R460, 22 hours), Gaborone (via Jo'burg) (R245, 15 hours) and Maputo (R200, 15 hours), via Jo'burg.

Luxliner (☎ 305 9090; www.luxliner.co.za) links Durban with Ladysmith (R160, 3½ hours) and Newcastle (R180, five hours) en route between Margate (R90, 2½ hours) and Jo'burg International Airport (R185, eight hours). It runs on Tuesday, Thursday and Sunday.

Translux (☎ 308 8111; www.translux.co.za) has daily buses to Jo'burg (R150, eight hours) and Cape Town (R465, 22 hours). City to City buses go to destinations across the country.

Car

Comet Car Rental (☎ 765 4009; www.cometcar.co.za) offers some of the best rates in town, including 300km free per day and full insurance. Its offices are a long way from town, in Hillcrest, but they deliver and pick up from addresses throughout Durban.

Most major car-rental companies also have offices at the airport:
Avis (☎ 0860 021 111)
Budget (☎ 0860 016 622)
Imperial (☎ 0860 131 000)

Hitching

Although we don't recommend it, if you do choose to hitch, and are heading south, hitch from the M4 interchange near Albert Park. The N2 north starts at the top end of Stanger St.

Minibus Taxi

Some long-distance minibus taxis leave from stops in the streets opposite the Umgeni Rd entrance to the train station. To Jo'burg it costs R110, and to the Swaziland border it costs about R100. Other taxis, running mainly to the south coast and the Transkei region of Eastern Cape, leave from around the Berea train station.

Train

Durban train station (☎ 0860 008 888; Umgeni Rd) is huge. Main services include the *Trans Natal*, which leaves Durban daily (except Tuesday & Saturday) for Jo'burg (1st/2nd class R250/165, 12½ hours), and the *Trans Oranje*, which makes the run to Cape Town (R645/435, 38 hours) every Wednesday.

There are also commuter trains running down the coast as far south as Kelso and north to KwaDukuza (Stanger). You can catch southbound commuter trains at Berea train station as well as at Durban station. Note that even hardy travellers report feeling unsafe on these trains.

GETTING AROUND
To/From the Airport
An **airport shuttle** (☎ 465 1660) runs to the airport from near the corner of Aliwal and Smith Sts for R25. Some hostels can get discounts and pick-ups for backpackers on the return trip. By taxi, the same trip should cost about R120.

Bus
The main bus terminal and information centre is on Commercial Rd across from the Workshop.

The **Mynah** (☎ 307 3503) service of small, frequent buses covers most of the central and beachfront areas. The disadvantage is that the service stops early in the evening on most routes. Trips cost around R4 and you get a slight discount if you prebuy 10 tickets. Routes are as follows: North Beach, South Beach, Musgrave Rd Circle, Mitchell Park Circle, the Ridge/Vause, Botanic Gardens, Kensington/Mathias Rd.

Additional services are provided by the large **Durban Transport** (☎ 309 5942) buses, which depart from the station across from the Workshop.

Taxi
A taxi between the beach and the train station costs about R25. **Bunny Cabs** (☎ 332 2914) operates 24 hours a day.

Tekweni Eco-Tours (p289; ☎ 303 1199; tekwenitours@mweb.co.za; 169 Ninth Ave) will pick you up and drop you off pretty much anywhere in town for only R25.

WEST OF DURBAN

PINETOWN
☎ 031
Pinetown, a centre of light industry, is the third-biggest population centre in KwaZulu-Natal and the second-largest industrial area. There are areas of this city that possess a certain charm, including Paradise Valley and Marianhill Nature Reserves and the Japanese Gardens in Sarnia, but it is most worth visiting for its famous **Rainbow Restaurant & Jazz Club** (p296).

VALLEY OF 1000 HILLS
☎ 031
A pleasant, hassle-free getaway from the steamy streets of downtown Durban, the Valley of 1000 Hills runs from the city's western outskirts to Nagle Dam, east of Pietermaritzburg. The rolling hills, sleepy villages and traditional Zulu communities are the main reason visitors drive through here, usually on the R103, which begins in Hillcrest, off the M13 freeway. You can also get to Hillcrest from the N3 between Durban and Pietermaritzburg. If you want to see more of the valley, you'll have to head north from this road, which just skirts the southern edge.

Information
Thousand Hills Tourism (☎ 777 1874; www.1000hills.kzn.org.za; Old Main Rd, Botha's Hill; ☉ 8am-4pm Mon-Fri, 10.30am-1.30pm Sat & Sun) offers the useful *1000 Hills Experience* brochure, listing six routes through the region and stacks of places to stay and eat.

Sights & Activities
About halfway between Durban and Pietermaritzburg, off the N3, the **Shongweni Resource Reserve** (Map p300; ☎ 769 1238; fax 769 1125; admission R10; ☉ 8am-5pm) protects a river valley and grassland, and has quite a few mammals and birds. Horse riding and canoeing are available, but you must book ahead. No accommodation is available.

There's a reptile park and a traditional Zulu village complete with touristy cultural displays at the **PheZulu Safari Park** (☎ 777 1000; www.phezulusafaripark.co.za; Old Main Rd, Botha's Hill; adult/child R50/25; ☉ shows 10am, 11.30am, 2pm & 3.30pm).

The **Umgeni Steam Railway** (☎ 082-353 6003; adult/child R60/40) operates out of the old Kloof station (now home of the Stoker's Arms Tavern). The 1000 Hills Choo-Choo service departs on the last Sunday of every month at 8.45am and 12.30pm and huffs and puffs its way through the area for about an hour.

Tekweni Eco-Tours (p291) in Durban runs tours (R350) to the Zulu village of isiThumba, where you meet traditional healers. For an extra R150, you can stay over in a local house.

Sleeping

Chantecler (☎ 765 2613; chantecler@mweb.co.za; 76 Clement Stott Rd, Botha's Hill; s/d with breakfast R420/610; ✗) Bafflingly named after Chaucer's rooster, this thatched place oozes high-country class, with pleasant gardens, water features aplenty and old-meets-new styling.

Rob Roy (☎ 777 1305; robroyhotel@mweb.co.za; Rob Roy Cres, Botha's Hill; s/d with breakfast R320/460; ✗) With great views from the tea garden and an animal farmyard to keep the kids occupied while you admire them, this nice mid-ranger has all the usual hotel comforts.

Valley Trust (☎ 716 6800; www.thevalleytrust.org.za; off Old Main Rd, Nyuswa; s/d with shared bathroom R60/120) Home of the Simunye Handicraft Project, which promotes traditional handicrafts to raise funds for local development projects, this place offers cheap, clean beds in basic rooms and allows you to camp for free.

Eating

Many Durbanites visit the hills for the food. The Chantecler and Rob Roy have restaurants and several train stations in the area, such as Botha's Hill and Kloof, have been renovated as English-style pubs and tea gardens.

New Swan & Rail (☎ 765 8091; Inanda Rd, Hillcrest; mains R25-55) Occupying the old Hillcrest railway station, which is now a National Heritage Site, this pleasant pub oozes rural English charm and offers scrumptious pub grub. It is closed on Monday.

Pot & Kettle (☎ 777 1312; 168 Old Main Rd, Botha's Hill; mains R25-45) A casual restaurant with a delightful outdoor terrace overlooking the valley.

SOUTH OF DURBAN

There are some good beaches on the south coast, the strip between Durban and Port Edward, just across the Umtamvuna River from the Transkei region of Eastern Cape. There are also shoulder-to-shoulder resorts for much of the 150km, and in summer there isn't a lot of room to move.

The south coast begins at Amanzimtoti, a huge resort and residential area about 10km from Durban International Airport. Further south the major centres are Umkomaas, Scottburgh, Park Rynie and Hibberdene. This area is called the Sunshine Coast. A large built-up area begins just after Hibberdene, centring on Port Shepstone and Margate, about 10km south. This region, the Hibiscus Coast, continues almost unbroken to Marina Beach near the Trafalgar Marine Reserve. Port Edward is the last centre before Transkei and the Umtamvuna River.

SUNSHINE COAST

The Sunshine Coast stretches about 60km from Amanzimtoti to Hibberdene. All the beaches are easily accessible from the N2 but the area suffers from its proximity to Durban – Amanzimtoti is almost in the shadow of the southern industrial areas.

Amanzimtoti & Kingsburgh
☎ 031

Called 'Toti' for short, Amanzimtoti (Sweet Waters) is a high-rise jungle of apartment blocks. Warner Beach is at the southern end of Amanzimtoti, and while it's still a built-up area, the atmosphere is more relaxed. From here Amanzimtoti merges into Kingsburgh, which has a number of beaches, to the south. Neither resort offers anything you can't get in Durban.

The **Amanzimtoti Information Office** (☎ 903 7498; fax 903 7493; 95-97 Beach Rd; ☾ 8am-12.30pm & 1-4pm Mon-Sat) isn't far from the Inyoni Rocks.

SLEEPING

There are plenty of B&Bs, flats and holiday homes – visit the Amanzimtoti Information Office for details. There are also many caravan parks in the area, although they fill up in January and prices are high.

Angle Rock Backpackers (☎ 916 7007; www.anglerock.co.za; 5 Ellcock Rd, Warner Beach; camp sites R45, dm R80, d with shared bathroom R180-190) Angle Rock Backpackers is right by the beach and offers surfing lessons. The facilities are good. Management does free pick-ups from Durban. Take Exit 133 (Kingsburgh) off the N2.

Protea Hotel Karridene (☎ 916 7228; sales2@karridene.co.za; Old Coast Rd, Illovo Beach; s/d R935/1000; ✗ ✦) Luxury comes in the Protea package here, but you don't get a whole lot for your rand. More reasonable 'specials' pull the price down to the R600 mark.

Umkomaas to Mtwalume
☎ 039

The main towns on this strip are Umkomaas, Scottburgh, Park Rynie, Kelso and Pennington. You can get tourist information from

KWAZULU-NATAL

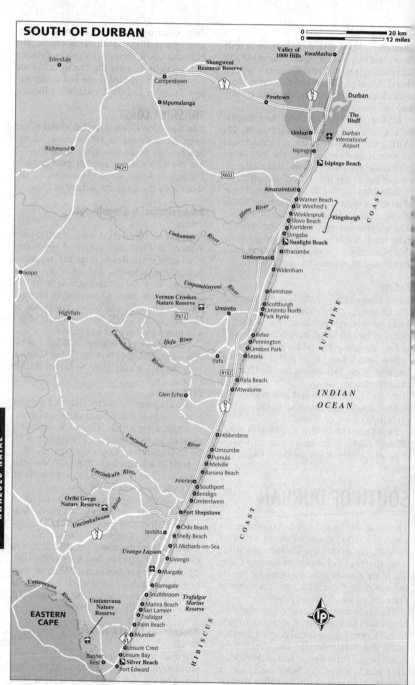

SOUTH OF DURBAN

0 _____ 20 km
0 _____ 12 miles

Edendale

Shongweni
Resource Reserve

Valley of
1000 Hills   KwaMashu

Camperdown

N3

Pinetown

N2

Durban

Mpumalanga

The
Bluff

Umlazi

Durban
International
Airport

Isipingo

Richmond

R624

R603

Isipingo Beach

Amanzimtoti

Warner Beach
St Winifred's
Winklespruit   Kingsburgh
Illovo Beach
Karridene
Umgaba
Sunlight Beach
Ilfracombe

Illovo River

Umkomaas River

Umkomaas

Widenham

Ixopo

Umpambinyoni River

Renishaw

Vernon Crookes
Nature Reserve   Umzinto

R612

Scottburgh
Umzinto North
Park Rynie

Highflats

Ifafa River

Kelso
Pennington
Umdoni Park
Sezela

SUNSHINE COAST

Umtwalume River

Ifafa

R102

Ifafa Beach

Glen Echo

Mtwalume

INDIAN
OCEAN

Umzumbe River

Hibberdene

Umzumbe
Pumula
Melville
Banana Beach

Umzimkulu River

Anerley
Southport
Bendigo
Umtentweni
Port Shepstone

Oribi Gorge
Nature Reserve

Umzimkulwana River

N2

Izotsha

Oslo Beach
Shelly Beach
St Michaels-on-Sea

COAST

Uvongo Lagoon

Uvongo

Margate

Umtamvuna River

Ramsgate
Southbroom
Marina Beach
San Lameer
Trafalgar
Palm Beach

Trafalgar
Marine
Reserve

EASTERN
CAPE

Umtamvuna
Nature
Reserve

R61

Munster
Leisure Crest
Leisure Bay
Silver Beach
Port Edward

Banner
Rest

HIBISCUS COAST

KWAZULU-NATAL

he Blue Marlin hotel (below) in Scottburgh. There are plenty of little eateries on offer to satisfy tummy grumbles.

The highlight of this strip has got to be the **Aliwal Shoal**, a fantastic dive site, with soft corals and plenty of ragged-mouth sharks, off Unkomaas. There's also a wreck dive. **Aliwal Dive Charters** (☎ 973 2542; www.aliwal shoalscubadiving.co.za), on the main road past the village; and **Aliwal Shoal Adventures** (☎ 973 1077; aliwalshoaladventures@worldonline.co.za; 24 Harvey St), in the village itself, offer dive courses, and individual dives (from R140).

SLEEPING
There are plenty of B&Bs and in low season you might get away with R110 per person.

Aliwal Shoal Adventures (☎ 973 1077; aliwalsho aladventures@worldonline.co.za; 24 Harvey St, Unkomaas; dm/d R70/180) A backpackers-cum-dive shop, ASA is a good spot for cheap sleeps and energetic post-dive banter.

Aliwal Dive Charters (☎ 973 2542; www.aliwal shoalscubadiving.co.za; r with/without bathroom R180/110) This Unkomaas diving outfit has some cheap, but slightly bleak, rooms for weary bubble blowers. Positioned right on the beach, they come with complimentary sea noises.

La La Manzi (☎ 973 0161; lala@sco.eastcoast.co.za; Unkomaas; s/d with breakfast R180/260) La La Manzi, meaning 'Sleeping Waters', also draws the divers and the atmosphere is lively. They also have cheaper rooms with shared bathroom (singles/doubles R100/200).

Blue Marlin (☎ 031-978 3361; www.bluemarlin .co.za; 180 Scott St, Scottburgh; s/d with breakfast R220/440; 🏊) Lifted straight out of the English Riviera, the Blue Marlin is fresh, airy and unpretentious.

Vernon Crookes Nature Reserve
Inland from Park Rynie, off the R612 past Umzinto, this **reserve** (☎ 033-845 1000; www.kzn wildlife.com; admission R10; 🕐 6am-6pm) has abundant mammal and bird species and some indigenous forest. If you walk through the reserve, beware of ticks.

Accommodation is offered by **KZN Wildlife** (☎ 033-845 1000; 2-bed huts per person R90).

HIBISCUS COAST
This section of the south coast stretches from Hibberdene to Port Edward. The tizzy resort of Margate, which throbs to the beat of Gauteng's youth during the holidays, is the main tourist centre, but the Oribi Gorge Nature Reserve and the area around the Umtamvuna Nature Reserve, near sleepy Port Edward, are the biggest draw cards for those looking for a little more rest and a little less play.

You can get information about the Hibiscus Coast from **Hibiscus Coast Tourism** (☎ 039-312 2322; www.hibiscuscoast.kzn.org.za; Panorama Pde, Main Beach, Margate; 🕐 8.30am-4pm Mon-Fri, 9am-noon Sat). Its useful *Southern Explorer* brochure is a must-have for any wannabe visitor.

Port Shepstone & Around
☎ 039 / pop 29,000
The industrial town of Port Shepstone is of little interest to tourists, but motorcycle enthusiasts can hire Yamaha Ténérés from **Motozulu** (☎ 695 0348; www.motozu.lu.ms; 9 Eden Valley Rd) to explore the local area. The bikes cost from R500 per day to hire, or you can take longer, guided safaris through Lesotho and the Transkei.

During the summer, the steam-powered **Banana Express** (☎ 682 4821; acrailmc@venturenet .co.za) runs daily (except Monday) from the station next to the King Prawn pub on the beachfront. Seven different tour options, including the Oribi Gorge (R300), are on offer – guides meet you from the train at the appropriate stop and fees include lunch and park entrance fees. All tours depart at 10.30am.

SLEEPING
There are plenty of hotels in Port Shepstone, but two backpackers on the strip of coast north of Port Shepstone are well worth a stopover.

Mantis & Moon Backpacker Lodge (☎ 684 6256; travelsa@saol.com; 7/178 Station Rd, Umzumbe; dm/d R70/200, camp sites R45; 🏊) In the village of Umzumbe, this mellow spot, in a thick knot of tropical bush, seems to move in slow motion, with heaps of atmosphere and a distinctly Caribbean vibe.

Spot Backpackers (☎ 695 1318; spotbackpackers@ netactive.co.za; Ambleside Rd, Umtentweni; dm/d with shared bathroom R65/160, camp sites R45) Closer to Port Shepstone, this is another well-regarded place. From its spot right on the beach you can fill your days with swimming, surfing and scuba diving or just relax and soak up the sun.

KWAZULU-NATAL

GETTING THERE & AWAY

Greyhound (☎ 031-309 7830; www.greyhound.co.za) has daily buses between Port Shepstone and Durban (R85, 1½ hours). If you are staying at one of the backpackers, ask the driver to drop you in Umzumbe or Umtentweni.

Oribi Gorge Nature Reserve

This **nature reserve** (☎ 039-315 0112; www.kznwildlife.com; admission R10, 2-bed huts R102, camp sites R30; ☽ 6am-6pm) is inland from Port Shepstone, off the N2. The spectacular gorge, on the Umzimkulwana River, is one of the highlights of the south coast. Apart from the scenery, there are many animals and birds, and a mountain-bike trail.

Oribi Gorge Hotel (☎ 039-687 0253; oribigorge@worldonline.co.za; s/d with breakfast R395/590) is a large place overlooking the gorge and charges an entrance fee (R10) to its attached viewpoint. It's 11km off the N2 along the Oribi Flats Rd. The hotel is also home to **Wild 5 Adventures** (☎ 082-566 7424), which offers a 130m Gorge Swing off Lehr's Falls (R280), abseiling (R170) and white-water rafting (R295).

Margate & Around

☎ 039 / pop 34,000

The south coast's tourist mecca is loud and lively, with a string of bars and clubs pumping up the volume, and a knot of hotels putting up the visitors. Somewhat similar to its English namesake, this is not a 'glamour' resort, but it is a decent place to let your hair down, if you're into the bump-and-grind brand of beach life. Go smell that tanning lotion!

Nearby Ramsgate is a quieter version of Margate, with a nice little beach.

Ocean Safaris (☎ 695 2714; www.oceansafaris.co.za; Shelly Beach; adult/child R160/110) runs whale-watching tours between the end of May and October from the Ski Boat Club on Shelly Beach, north of Margate.

SLEEPING & EATING

Sometimes it seems there are more hotels than people in Margate, but beds can still come at a premium during the high season.

Margate Backpackers (☎ 312 2176; ulrika@venturenet.co.za; 14 Collis Rd, Margate; dm/d with shared bathroom R60/150, camp sites R40) The homely Margate Backpackers is relatively quiet for a hostel,

where a pool table, satellite TV and upbeat staff provide the entertainment.

Wailana Beach Lodge (☎ 314 4606; wailana@iafica.com; 436 Ashmead Dr, Margate; s/d with breakfast R390/330; ☒ ☒) This svelte guesthouse, 200m from the sea in nearby Ramsgate, has five 'designer' bedrooms with contemporary, individual styling and private sun decks, leafy gardens and a bar.

Sunlawns Hotel (☎ /fax 312 1078; Uplands Rd, Margate; s/d with breakfast R200/400; ☒ ☒) This long-established hotel has delightful old-English charm. There is a 'Ladies Lounge' and pub as well as a good-sized pool.

Margate Hotel (☎ 312 1410; info@margatehotel.co.za; Marine Dr, Margate; s/d with breakfast R400/500; ☒) This place is a little plain, but it is in a top location (if you want to be in the heart of things) on the main drag.

Keg & Galleon (☎ 312 2575; Marine Dr, Margate; mains R20-55; ☽ breakfast, lunch & dinner) This busy boozer is typical of Margate's eating and drinking options. Icy beer and decent pub grub draw the tourists, who flock here to be amply fed and watered.

GETTING THERE & AWAY

SA Airlink (☎ 031-250 1111) flies daily between Margate and Jo'burg (R826).

The **Margate Mini Coach** (☎ 031-312 1406) links Durban and Margate twice daily (once on a Saturday). It costs R70 single, or R90 for a same-day return. On Thursday, it also travels south to the Wild Coast Sun Casino, just over the border in Eastern Cape (R55). Book through Hibiscus Coast Tourism (p301).

Luxliner (☎ 317 4628; www.luxliner.co.za) has an office in Hibiscus Coast Tourism in Margate, and runs coaches on Tuesday, Thursday and Sunday between Margate and Jo'burg (R225, 10 hours).

Port Edward & Around

☎ 039

The little village of Port Edward itself is rather unspectacular, but the surrounding area makes a pleasant escape from the concrete jungle.

The **tourist information office** (☎ 311 1211; ☽ 8.30am-4pm Mon-Fri) is on the main road to the beach and can help with accommodation.

On a gorge on the Umtamvuna River, which forms part of the border with Eastern Cape, the beautiful **Umtamvuna Nature Reserve** (☎ 311 2383; www.kznwildlife.com; admission

R10; 7am-5pm) is densely forested, with wild-flowers in spring. There are quite a number of mammals and birds, including peregrine falcons. This reserve has a twin across the Umtamvuna Gorge in Eastern Cape.

Beware of bilharzia in the river. To get to the reserve, head to Banner Rest, a small town southwest of Port Edward, and drive north towards Izingolweni for a few kilometres.

The **Umtamvuna Mountain Bike Trail** (☎ 311 1130; clearwater@venturenet.co.za; per trail R15; per 2hr R55) operates out of Clearwater Chalets and rents out bikes for use on a network of trails above the gorge.

There are a couple of small restaurants and a supermarket in Port Edward, but it's best to bring some of your own food if you are staying at the hostels.

SLEEPING

There is no accommodation in the reserve itself, though there are options just outside.

Vuna Valley Backpackers (☎ 083-992 6999; vuna valley@hotmail.com; dm/d with shared bathroom R60/150) A minute's walk from the entrance to Umtamvuna Nature Reserve, this rustic place has castle styling (you'll have to wait and see), nice gardens, a Bohemian atmosphere and a collection of (friendly) motley dogs.

Clearwater Chalets (☎ 311 1130; clearwater@ven turenet.co.za; s/d with shared bathroom R60/120) This seriously spartan backpackers has plenty of rural appeal and stunning views over the gorge. To get there from Port Edward, cross the R61 and head towards Harding, then pass Old Pont Rd and turn left at Coastals.

NORTH OF DURBAN

The stretch of coast from Umhlanga Rocks north to the Tugela River is less developed than the coast south of Durban, and the beaches are better. For those after a quieter time, the north coast's profusion of time-share apartments and retirement villages means this stretch of coast is rather more sedate than many of the beaches south of Durban.

Before swimming at the beaches on the north coast, you might want to check the status of the shark netting. Some towns have removed the netting because it was killing

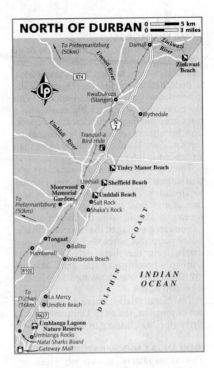

NORTH OF DURBAN

too many sharks – sharks 'drown' if they can't keep water flowing through their gills.

Other than some commuter services between Durban and Umhlanga Rocks there is very little public transport along the coast. There are, however, commuter trains and plenty of buses and minibus taxis between Durban and KwaDukuza and other inland towns. They can get very crowded, so are a possible haven for petty thieves.

UMHLANGA ROCKS

☎ 031

The buckle of Durban's chi-chi commuter belt, Umhlanga is an affluent mix of upmarket beach resort and moneyed suburbia. Umhlanga means 'Place of Reeds' (the 'h' is pronounced something like a 'sh').

On the mall, near the intersection of Lagoon Dr and Lighthouse St (the continuation of the road in from the main Durban road), **Infonet Cafe** (☎ 561 1397; per 30min/1hr R15/25; 8am-10pm) is an Internet café that doubles as an information office.

ABSA (Granada Centre) has an ATM and change facilities.

KWAZULU-NATAL

Sights & Activities

NATAL SHARKS BOARD

A research institute, the **Natal Sharks Board** (☎ 566 0400; 1A Herrwood Dr; audiovisual & dissection adult/child R15/10; ⊗ 8am-4pm Mon-Fri, noon-6pm Sun) is dedicated to studying sharks, specifically in relation to their danger to humans. With the great white shark – a big shark with a fearsome, but largely undeserved reputation for attacks on humans – frequenting the KwaZulu-Natal coast, this is more than an academic interest.

There are audiovisual presentations and shark dissections at 9am and 2pm Tuesday to Thursday. The presentation and dissection is also held at 2pm on Sunday. The squeamish should avoid the dissection.

You can go along in the boat with Sharks Board personnel, when they collect trapped sharks from the shark nets that protect Durban's beachfront. The daily **boat trip** (☎ 082-403 9206; Durban Harbour; trip R150; ⊗ 6.30am) takes two hours.

The Natal Sharks Board is about 2km out of town, up the steep Umhlanga Rocks Drive (the M12 leading to the N3).

UMHLANGA LAGOON NATURE RESERVE

This **nature reserve** (admission free; ⊗ 6am-6pm) is on a river mouth just north of town. Despite its small size (26 hectares) there are many bird species. The trails lead through dune forest, across the lagoon and onto the beach.

GATEWAY MALL

There are plenty of activities on offer at this mall (p296). You can surf a giant artificial wave at the **Wavehouse** (☎ 570 9200; www.wavehouse.co.za; per hr R30; ⊗ 9am-9pm); scale the **Rock** (☎ 566 5016; climbs from R25; ⊗ 9am-9pm), a 23m climbing wall; thrash the half-pipes in the **Skate Park** (☎ 570 9200; per day R20; ⊗ 9am-9pm); or go off-road driving at the **4WD Track** (☎ 566 3140; per driver R20; ⊗ 9am-5.30pm). And if that's not enough, **180° Adventures** (☎ 566 4955; www.180.co.za; Shop G216, Getaway Zone, Gateway Mall) can organise just about anything you can't do in the mall, from diving and hiking to sea-kayaking and white-water rafting.

Sleeping

Umhlanga is crowded with holiday apartments, most of which are close to the beach.

They fill up in high season, when you'd be lucky to rent one for less than a week but outside peak times it's possible to take one for two days. A two-bedroom serviced apartment in low/high season starts at about R300/500 per night; contact **Umhlanga Accommodation** (☎ 561 2012; www.umhlangaaccommodation.co.za; Protea Mall, Chartwell Dr; ⊗ 8.30am-4.30pm Mon-Fri, 8.30-11.30am Sat) for help.

Hotel prices vary enormously depending on the season. The following are average prices – expect a 10% fluctuation either way in low/high season.

Oyster Box (☎ 561 2233; www.oysterbox.co.za; 2 Lighthouse Rd; s/d with breakfast R400/640; ⊗ ⊗) In the shadow of Umhlanga's lighthouse, this spot exudes colonial-era grace, with an old-school atmosphere that offers an antidote to Umhlanga's trademark concrete towers.

Beverley Hills Sun Intercontinental (☎ 561 2221; www.southernsun.com; Lighthouse Rd; s/d R1800/2500; ⊗ ⊗ ⊗) They didn't pull the stops out on the exterior, but this top-notch classic is deliciously stylish on the inside. It's the perfect place for a platinum-card splurge.

Pendlebury's B&B (☎ 561 4853; www.wheretostay.co.za/pendleburys.htm; s/d with breakfast R400/670; ⊗ ⊗) A regular at the national AA hotel and guesthouse awards, this posh retreat has more trimmings than you can shake your guidebook at, including a bar, a Jacuzzi, a pool and 'jet showers' in the superslick rooms (d R790).

Also recommended:

Umhlanga Guest House (☎ 561 1100; umhlangabb@telkomsa.net; 7 Campbell Dr; s/d with breakfast R250/500; ⊗ ⊗) For relaxing atmosphere and soft furnishings.

Umhlanga Protea Hotel (☎ 561 4413; umprotea@iafrica.com; cnr Lighthouse Rd & Chartwell Dr; s/d with breakfast R700/900; ⊗) For the predictable Protea package.

Eating

Sugar Club (☎ 561 2211; Lighthouse Rd; mains R60-365; ⊗ lunch & dinner; ⊗) This swish eatery, at the Beverly Hills Sun Intercontinental, scores rave reviews in the local press and consistently lives up to expectations with its innovative cooking and sophisticated styling. This is the place to dress up.

George & Dragon (☎ 561 5850; Granada Centre; mains R20-50; ⊗ breakfast, lunch & dinner) In the main mall area, next to Infonet Cafe, this lively boozer has basic, tasty eats and beer aplenty.

Getting There & Away

A commuter bus (R15, 40 minutes) runs regularly from near Infonet Cafe in Umhlanga to Durban.

Umhlanga Taxis (☎ 561 1846) makes the run to Durban airport for R180.

DOLPHIN COAST

☎ 032

The Dolphin Coast starts near Ballito and stretches north to the Tugela River. It includes the areas of Tongaat, Ballito, Shaka's Rock, Salt Rock, Umhlali, Blythdale, KwaDukuza and Zwinkazi Beach. The coast gets its name from the pods of bottlenose dolphins that frolic offshore.

Dolphin Coast Publicity (☎ 946 1997; www.dolphincoast.co.za; Ballito Dr; ◷ 8.30am-4.30pm Mon-Fri, 8.30am-noon Sat) is near the BP petrol station, just where you leave the N2 to enter Ballito. It books B&Bs and lists other accommodation.

Tongaat

A big, sedate sugar town with some fine old buildings, Tongaat is on the train line running north from Durban. With a large Indian population, Tongaat is home to a handful of temples including the small but fascinating **Shri Jagganath Puri Temple**.

Ballito to Sheffield Beach

Ballito, Shaka's Rock, Umhlali, Salt Rock and Sheffield Beach form a continuous, settled strip, although the density of settlement is nothing like that on the south coast. They are connected by the old coast road, so you don't have to jump back and forth on the N2 to travel between them.

SLEEPING

Much of the accommodation is in apartments, and in high season most are let by the week. A good rental agency in Ballito is **Realty 1** (☎ 946 2141; fax 946 1789; cnr Sandra & Compensation Beach Rds).

Ballito Manor (☎ 946 3290; www.ballitomanor.com; 102B Compensation Beach Rd; s/d R1580/2100; ❄ 💻 🏊) This seriously sumptuous boutique hotel has staff with flight-attendant smiles, stately interiors, a luxurious day spa for tip-top pampering and beautiful tropical gardens.

Dolphin Holiday Resort (☎ 946 2187; fax 946 3490; Dolphin Cres, Ballito; r R350, camp sites R160) This resort has camping in lush surrounds and some pleasant cottages.

KwaDukuza (Stanger)

☎ 032 / pop 36,700

In July 1825, Shaka established KwaDukuza as his capital. Also known as Stanger, this is a rough-and-ready town, far removed from the neat, suburban settlements of the coast. There's not a whole lot to soak up here, but it is a main service centre for the region and it's worth a flying stop, if you are following the Zulu trail.

Throughout KwaDukuza there are fading reminders of the town's regal heritage. In the centre of town, near the old police station, is the site of **Shaka's royal residence**. In front of the municipal offices in Roodt St is an **old mkuhla tree** (Natal mahogany), reputedly the site of Shaka's councils. A large fig tree stood in the Nyakambi kraal at the opposite end of KwaDukuza, marking the spot where, in September 1828, Shaka was murdered by his half-brothers Dingaan and Umhlanga.

On Couper St are the **Shaka Memorial Gardens**, where you can see the memorial stone erected in 1932 over Shaka's burial chamber, which was originally a grain pit.

The **Dukuza Interpretive Centre** (☎ 552 7210; 5 King Shaka St; admission by donation; ◷ 8am-4pm Mon-Fri, 9am-4pm Sat & Sun) can organise **tours** (around R30) of the Shaka sites. **Dukuza Museum** (☎ 437 5075; King Shaka St; admission by donation; ◷ 8am-4.30pm Mon-Fri), opposite, has related historical exhibits.

There are no hotels in KwaDukuza.

Minibus taxis link KwaDukuza with Durban (R15, one hour) and towns along the coast.

Blythedale

☎ 032

Blythedale is a quiet seaside village with a sandy (shark-net) beach and crashing surf.

Mini Villas (☎ 551 1277; minivillas@mweb.co.za; Umvoti Dr; r R229) offers excellent-value two-bed, self-catering villas.

La Mouette Caravan Park (☎ 551 2547; www.caravanparks.co.za/lamouette; 1 Umvoti Dr; camp sites R45), which is right on the beach, has braai facilities and is a decent spot for committed campers. Prices skyrocket in the summer months.

There are a few simple eateries in town.

Occasional minibus taxis run between Blythedale and KwaDukuza (R5, 15 minutes), 7km away.

ZULULAND & MAPUTALAND

Evoking images of wild landscapes and tribal rhythms, this beautiful swathe of KwaZulu-Natal offers a different face of South Africa, where deserted beaches, mist-clad hills and traditional settlements steal the limelight from the ordered stretch of suburban developments running up the coast from Durban to meet it. Dominated by the Zulu tribal group, the region offers a fascinating insight into one of the country's most enigmatic, and best-known cultures. However, while the name Zulu (which means Heaven), aptly describes the rolling expanses that dominate the landscape here, it doesn't tell the whole story. Intense poverty and all the social problems that come with it are still commonplace here, and much of the population still struggles with a hand-to-mouth existence. Head off the main roads and this becomes glaringly obvious.

Extending in a rough triangle from the mouth of the Tugela River to the Mozambique border, and across to Vryheid in the west, Zululand is most visited for the spectacular Hluhluwe-Imfolozi Park and its many traditional Zulu villages. But there is plenty more besides. In fact, the portion known as Maputaland, which fills the area

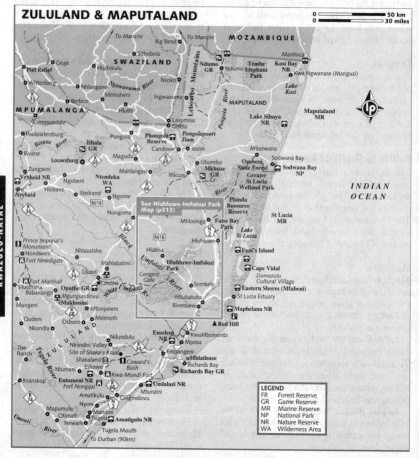

ZULULAND & MAPUTALAND

east of the N2 and north of the Mtubatuba–St Lucia road is one of the wildest and most fascinating regions of South Africa and an absolute must for nature lovers. Taking its name from the Maputo River, which splits into the Usutu and Pongola Rivers on the Mozambique border, this large stretch of coastline includes some of the country's true highlights, including the wonderfully diverse and perennially photogenic Greater St Lucia Wetland Park and the coffee-table book vistas of Kosi Bay. Sparsely populated and uncompromisingly untamed, these regions, away from the scattered resort towns, offer a glimpse of the wild heart of Africa.

The climate becomes steadily hotter as you go north and, thanks to the warm Indian Ocean, summers are steamy and almost tropical. The humid coastal air causes frequent dense mists on the inland hills, reducing visibility to a few metres. If driving, be careful of pedestrians and animals suddenly appearing around a corner.

There is a good network of minibus taxis and local-bus companies covering this area. However, timetables and routes are vague, so be prepared for delays and hassles.

The Baz Bus (p594) also goes up the coast, on the run between Durban and Jo'burg via Swaziland.

TUGELA MOUTH
☎ 032

The sprawl of resort-town suburbia comes to an end with Blythedale, giving way to an altogether wilder landscape at the mouth of the mighty Tugela River. With one of the most unspoilt sweeps of sand in the region (beware, there are a lot of sharks here – seek local advice if you want to swim), the small town of Tugela Mouth, which sits on the north bank of the Tugela estuary and on the very boundary of Zululand, is a soporific, undeveloped alternative to the gloss and glitz of the tried-and-tested holiday centres. Fantastic fishing (including the unusual lobotes), and a remote, otherworldly atmosphere only bolster the appeal.

Amatigulu Nature Reserve (☎ 453 0155; www .kznwildlife.com; adult/child R10/5; ☙ 6am-6pm) is 10km north of Tugela, off the N2, and features giraffes, zebras and antelopes across its 2100 hectares. There are also four walking trails through the park. **Camp sites** (per per-

---

son R21) are available. You'll need your own transport to get to the reserve.

Emolweni (☎ 458 4133; w2wog@lantic.net; s/d R50/100; 🛉) is a rustic, no-frills place with heaps of Bohemian, beachfront charisma. It faces straight onto the sand dunes and offers blissfully empty days of swimming, sunbathing and sundowner sipping. There are only a few cottages on offer, but the place is owned by the couple behind the Cool Runnings bar chain and an *Endless Summer* atmosphere prevails. If you're a fishing junkie, Wayne's your man.

Getting here without a car is a headache, but you can hop off the minibus taxis running between Durban and Richard's Bay at the Tugela Mouth off-ramp (R15, about one hour north of Durban). If you call ahead, Emolweni will pick you up from here.

GINGINDLOVU
☎ 035

Crowds and dust are Gingindlovu's trademarks, but there are two very good accommodation options in the area, making it a good pit stop on the route north. The town was once one of King Cetshwayo's strongholds and two battles of the Anglo-Zulu War of 1879 were fought in the vicinity.

Mine Own Country House (☎ 337 1262; fax 337 1025; s/d with breakfast R500/700), in an opulent villa, is surrounded by sugar plantations and has lashings of colonial-era nostalgia. It's 4km north of Gingindlovu, off the R102.

If you are bleary-eyed and bloated after an overdose of Durban high life, **Inyezane** (☎ 082-704 4766; inyezane@ethniczulu.com; camp site R40, dm/d with shared bathroom R60/180; 🛉 🖳 🛉) has the antidote. Wrapped up in the hush of rural Zululand, with on-site herbal baths, mud baths and aromatherapy sessions, this is the place for a good old rustic detox. There's also an art studio. Inyezane is on an old plantation near Gingindlovu, off the D134, and on the Baz Bus route – by far the easiest way of getting here without a car.

MTUNZINI
☎ 035

A little oasis of tearooms and neatly tended lawns surrounded by the wild, rolling hills of Zululand, Mtunzini screams 'Europe' in the heart of Africa. But there is more to this pretty village than coffee mornings and herbaceous borders. Sitting above a lush sweep of rare Raffia palms, themselves home to even rarer palmnut vultures, Mtunzini makes an excellent base for exploring this beautiful slice of Zululand.

The town had a colourful beginning. John Dunn, the first European to settle in the area, was granted land by King Cetshwayo. He became something of a chief himself, took 49 wives and sired 117 children. He held court here under a tree, hence the town's name (*mtunzi* is Zulu for 'shade'). After the British defeated Cetshwayo and divided the kingdom, Dunn was one of the chiefs granted power. It wasn't until recently that the descendants of Dunn and the descendants of Cetshwayo were formally reconciled.

Information

There is a **tourist information office** (☎ 340 2897; Station Rd; ☻ 9am-6pm Mon-Thu, 9am-9pm Fri & Sat) in the Fat Cat Coffee Shop.

ABSA (Hely Hutchinson Rd) has an ATM at the top of town.

Sights & Activities

Near the mouth of the Mlalazi River, there is lush tropical forest where you'll find the **Raffia Palm Monument** (admission free; ☻ 24hr). The palms (*Raphia Australis*) were first planted here in 1916 from seeds sent to the local magistrate by the Director of Prisons in Pretoria. The idea was to use the palm's fibres to make brooms for the prison service, but it was soon established that they were too short and the commercial enterprise came to an end. The palms flourished, however, and by 1942 had been declared a National Monument. There is a wooden boardwalk through the grove – the palms are home to the **palmnut vulture** (*Gypohierax angolensis*), South Africa's rarest breeding bird-of-prey.

The entrance to **Umlalazi Nature Reserve** (☎ 340 1836; www.kznwildlife.com; admission R10; ☻ 5am-10pm) is 1.5km east of town, on the coast. Here, you will find the Indaba Tree, where John Dunn held his court gatherings; the remains of John Dunn's Pool, which he

built so his wives could swim safely; and plenty of the crocs he was afraid he would lose his loved ones to.

Sleeping & Eating

KZN Wildlife (☎ 340 1836; www.kznwildlife.com; camp sites R50, 5-bed log cabins per person R162) offers accommodation in the Umlalazi Nature Reserve. All accommodation, except camp sites, must be booked through KZN Wildlife in Pietermaritzburg or Durban.

Trade Winds Country Inn (☎ 340 2533; trade winds@microweb.co.za; Hely Hutchinson Rd; s/d with breakfast R249/385) Fresh and clean with motel 'styling', this is a reliable, if slightly bland, option. You can get a good feed at the attached **Tides Inn** (mains R30-70; ☻ breakfast, lunch & dinner) restaurant.

Mtunzini Chalets (☎ 340 1953; fax 340 1955; 4-/5-bed chalets R495/550; ☒) These spacious chalets are in a densely forested nature reserve by the sea. This is a very attractive place with good facilities including a pool, a bar and private beach access. During school holidays it fills up, but at other times it's a tranquil escape.

Clay Oven (☎ 340 1262; 32 Hely Hutchinson Rd; mains R25-60; ☻ lunch & dinner) This stylish diner whips up excellent steaks, pizza and pasta, and serves them on the breezy wooden terrace or in the refined interior. And yes, it does have a clay oven.

UMHLATHUZE (RICHARD'S BAY & EMPANGENI)
☎ 035 / pop 115,000

The new name for a sprawling conurbation incorporating the port of **Richard's Bay** and the nearby town of **Empangeni**, uMhlathuze is a web of roads connecting very little. Both centres are perfectly pleasant, but as a tourist you are unlikely to do much more in them than change buses or stop for a bite to eat.

The most convenient tourist office is the central Empangeni branch of the **uMhlathuze Tourism Association** (☎ 792 1283; emptour@ microweb; cnr Pearce Singel & Turnbull Sts; ☻ 8am-4pm Mon-Fri, 9am-noon Sat), which doubles as the Greyhound agent.

The main office of **uMhlathuze Tourism Association** (☎ 753 3909; rbtour@uthungulu.co.za; ☻ 8am-4pm Mon-Fri, 10am-2pm Sat) is in **Reptile City** (☎ 753 5901; admission R15; ☻ 8am-4pm Mon-Fri, 10am-2pm Sat), a ho-hum reptile park 6.4km out of central Richard's Bay, en route to Meerensee.

Also at Reptile City, **Bird Life South Africa** (☎ 753 5644; www.birdlife.org.za; ☺ 7.30am-4pm Mon-Fri, 7.30am-noon Sat & Sun) organises guides and tours for keen birders (there are more than 600 species in the region). Call ahead to discuss your requirements and prices.

Empangeni Arts & Crafts Centre (☎ 772 7622; artcraft@freemail.absa.co.za; Turnbull St; ☺ 9am-4pm Mon-Fri, 9am-2pm Sat), by the tourist association office, is worth a browse.

Sleeping

Woodpecker Inn (☎ 786 1230; fax 786 1243; Pelican Pde, Richard's Bay; s/d R245/320; ⊠ ⊠) Offering thatched, country comforts in a garden setting, this swanky place has a bar, swish rooms with en suite and a 12-bed, self-catering lodge (R1296).

Also recommended:

Harbour Lights (☎ 796 6239; www.harbourlights.co.za; camp sites R55, s/d R155/310, huts per person R55) A decent range of affordable accommodation for tight budgets. It's off the N3, between Richard's Bay and Empangeni.

Protea Hotel (☎ 772 3322; www.proteahotels.com; 64 Turnbull St, Empangeni; s/d R565/681; ⊠ ⊠) For reliable, mid-range comforts in the centre of Empangeni.

Getting There & Away

Greyhound buses stop at the Empangeni branch of the uMhlathuze Tourism Association (opposite), where you can also get tickets and information; and by McDonalds, next to the Bay Hospital in Richard's Bay. Buses run daily to Durban (R145, 2½ hours) and Jo'burg (R205, eight hours). Most of the surrounding towns can be reached from here by minibus taxi.

ESHOWE

☎ 035 / pop 14,700

Zululand is at its most idiosyncratic in the rolling green hills that run in chains west of the ocean. Eshowe – a name said to echo the sound made by wind in the trees – stands among them. The centre has a rural, rough-and-tumble atmosphere, but the suburbs are leafy and quiet. It is well placed for exploring the wider region and there are some decent attractions and accommodation options on offer.

Eshowe was Cetshwayo's stronghold before he moved to Ondini, and like Ondini it was destroyed during the Anglo-Zulu War.

ZULU FESTIVALS

Throughout the year there are a few major festivals that celebrate the rich culture of the Zulu people. These peaceful and joyous occasions involve colourful displays of traditional singing and dancing and are not to be missed. For further details about these events contact Graham Chennels at the **George Hotel & Zululand Backpackers** (☎ 035-474 4919) in Eshowe.

King Shaka Day Festival

On the last Saturday in September, thousands of Zulus converge on KwaDukuza (formerly Stanger) for the King Shaka Day Festival. The annual event, attended by the current Zulu king, pays homage to the Zulu hero.

Reed Dance

Every year thousands of young bare-breasted Zulu 'maidens' gather before their king, honouring the ancient tradition of the Reed Dance. In days long gone, the king would select a new bride from the mass of beautiful young maidens presented before him. The dance takes place on the Saturday before the King Shaka Day Festival at King Nyonkeni's Palace, which lies between Nongoma and Ulundi.

Shembe Festival

During the month of October, more than 30,000 Zulus gather at Judea, 15km east of Eshowe, for the annual Shembe Festival. This eye-opening festival celebrates the Shembe, the Church of the Holy Nazareth Baptists – an unofficial religion that somehow manages to combine Zulu traditions with Christianity. Presiding over the festivities is the church's saviour, Prophet Mbusi Vimbeni Shembe. Throughout the festival the emphasis is on celebration, with much dancing and singing and the blowing of the horns of Jericho.

The British occupied the site and built Fort Nongqai in 1883, establishing Eshowe as the administrative centre of their newly captured territory.

Information

For information on the area, visit **uMlalazi Municipality Publicity & Tourism Office** (☎ 474 1141; www.umlalazi.org.za; cnr Hutchinson & Osborne Rds; ☷ 7.30am-4pm Mon-Thu, 7.30am-3pm Fri). You can check email down the road at **Eshowe Computers** (☎ 474 5441; Osborne Rd; per hr R25; ☷ 8am-4.30pm Mon-Fri) and change money at **ABSA** (Miku Bldg, Osborne Rd), which also has an ATM.

Sights & Activities

The **Fort Nongqayi Museum Village** (☎ 474 1141; fax 474 4976; Nongqayi Rd; adult/child R20/4; ☷ 7.30am-4pm Mon-Fri, from 9am Sat & Sun) is based around the three-turreted, mud-and-brick Fort Nongqayi (there were not enough bricks to erect the fourth tower). The entrance fee includes access to the Zululand Historical Museum, with artefacts and Victoriana; the excellent Vukani Zulu Basketing Collection; the Zululand Missionary Museum, which offers an insight into the first missionaries in the region; and the Museum Crafter's Market, where local crafts are sold.

From the museum you can also walk to **Mpushini Falls** (40 minutes return) – though don't swim in or drink the water as there is a risk of bilharzia here.

When war approached, King Shaka used to hide his wives in the eerie swathe of forest that now makes up the 200-hectare **Dlinza Forest Reserve** (☎ 474 4029; www.zbr.co.za/board walk; admission free; ☷ 6am-6pm). There is prolific birdlife – look out for crowned eagles (*Stephanoaetus coronatus*) – and there are some walking trails, some of which are believed to have been made by British soldiers stationed here after the Anglo-Zulu War. The 100m-long **Dlinza Forest Aerial Boardwalk** (adult/child R25/5) offers some great views as it passes through the canopy.

Entumeni Nature Reserve (☎ 474 5084; admission free; ☷ 6am-6pm) is larger than Dlinza, and preserves indigenous mist-belt forest. It's 16km west of town, off the road to Ntumeni.

Sleeping & Eating

George Hotel & Zululand Backpackers (☎ 474 4919; www.eshowe.com; 38 Main St; s/d with breakfast R225/295; ☐ ☐) Housed in an attractive,

whitewashed building that oozes colonial-era pretensions, the George packs out on a Friday night for Eshowe's party of the week. Despite looking a little hungover itself these days, this Zululand institution, which includes a microbrewery, a tour company that offers 101 activities, and a **backpacker hostel** (camp sites R45, dm/s/d with shared bathroom R75/120/180), has plenty of life in it yet.

Amble Inn (☎ 474 1300; ambleinn@corpdial.co.za; 116 Main St; s/d with breakfast R215/295) Filling the guts of an old British Army brothel, this place blends B&B comforts with a certain ramshackle, backpacker charm. Ask nicely and the owner, from Middlesbrough, might give you a ride in his Rolls-Royce.

Adam's Outpost (☎ 474 1787; mains R25-60; ☷ lunch & dinner) With a garden café out front and a surprisingly cosy, corrugated iron restaurant, complete with real fireplaces and candles, for smarter eats behind, this little gem tops Eshowe's culinary roll call.

Getting There & Away

Minibus taxis leave from the Kwik Spar car park on the main street to Empangeni (R20, one hour) and Melmoth (R12, 45 minutes) – the best place to catch taxis deeper into Zululand.

Washesha Buses (☎ 477 4504) runs services in the area including a scenic but rough run on dirt roads through forest areas to Nkandla (R30, two hours). There's no accommodation at Nkandla, but you can get a taxi from there to Melmoth, where there's a hotel. A bus from Eshowe to Empangeni costs around R17. For more information ask at the office, behind KFC on the main street.

NKWALINI VALLEY

Shaka's kraal (fortified village), KwaBulawayo, once loomed over this beautiful valley but today the valley is regimented into citrus orchards and cane fields rather than impi (Zulu warriors). From Eshowe head north for 6km on the R66, and turn right onto the R230 (a dirt road that will eventually get you to the R34).

Across the road from the KwaBulawayo marker is **Coward's Bush**, now just another marker, where warriors who returned from battle without their spears, or who had received wounds in the back, were executed.

Further west, a few kilometres before the R230 meets the R66, the **Mandwe Cross** was erected in the 1930s, against the wishes of the Zulu. There are excellent views from the hill.

Shakaland

Created as a set for the telemovie *Shaka Zulu*, the Protea-managed **Shakaland** (☎ 035-460 0912; www.shakaland.com; Nandi Experience R185; ☽ display 11am) whips up an incongruous, but entertaining, blend of perma-grin Disneyesque service and informative authenticity. The Nandi Experience (Nandi was Shaka's mother) is a display of Zulu culture and customs (including lunch). You can also stay overnight at the four-star **hotel** (s/d with Nandi Experience & full board R1025/865).

Shakaland is at Norman Hurst Farm, Nkwalini, a few kilometres off the R66 and 14km north of Eshowe.

MELMOTH

☎ 035 / pop 3800

Named after the first resident commissioner of Zululand, Melmoth is a small town dozing in the hills, on the point of going to seed.

Melmoth Inn (☎ 450 2074; Victoria St; s/d R250/320), in the centre of town, is a reasonable option. There is a noisy bar out the back though.

From here, you can catch minibus taxis to Eshowe (R12, 45 minutes) and Ulundi (R12, 45 minutes).

ULUNDI

☎ 035 / pop 15,200

Once the hub of the powerful Zulu empire, Ulundi has lost much of its regal bearing, with brightly coloured box houses replacing the traditional huts of old. Now the joint capital of KwaZulu-Natal (with Pietermaritzburg), 21st-century Ulundi is a functional, bureaucratic centre, which sprawls across the surrounding hills. For Zulu fanatics, however, there are still plenty of historic sites to explore in the immediate area.

Information

Zululand Tourism (☎ 870 0812; www.zululand.org.za; Princess Magogo St; ☽ 7.30am-5pm Mon-Fri) has an office in the centrally located municipal building and offers information on the whole of Zululand. **Ulundi Tourism** (☎ 083-766 5942; Princess Magogo St; ☽ 7.30am-5pm Mon-Fri) can also be found here.

There are plenty of banks, with ATMs, in town.

Sights

ONDINI

Established as Cetshwayo's capital in 1873, **Ondini** (High Place; ☎ 870 2050; admission R10; ☽ 8am-4pm Mon-Fri, 9am-4pm Sat & Sun) was razed by British troops after the Battle of Ulundi (July 1879), the final engagement of the 1879 Anglo-Zulu War.

It took the British nearly six months to defeat the Zulu army, but the Battle of Ulundi went the same way as most of the campaign, with 10 to 15 times more Zulus killed than British. Part of the reason for the British victory at Ulundi was that they adopted the Boer laager tactic, with troops forming a hollow square to protect the cavalry, which attacked only after the Zulu army had exhausted itself trying to penetrate the walls.

The royal kraal section of the Ondini site has been rebuilt and you can see where archaeological digs have uncovered the floors of identifiable buildings. The floors, of mud and cow dung, were preserved by the heat of the fires, which destroyed the huts above. The huge area is enclosed in a defensive perimeter of gnarled branches.

Also at Ondini is the **KwaZulu Cultural-Historical Museum** (included in admission fee; ☽ 8am-4pm Mon-Fri, 9am-4pm Sat & Sun) with good exhibits on Zulu history and culture and an excellent audiovisual show. It also has one of the country's best collections of beadwork on display. You can buy souvenirs, including some interesting books.

To get to Ondini, take the 'Cultural Museum' turn-off from the highway just south of Ulundi centre and keep going for about 5km on a dirt road. Minibus taxis occasionally pass Ondini. This road continues on to Hluhluwe-Imfolozi Park and should be tarred by 2006.

En route to Ondini, you will also pass the **Ulundi Battlefield** (admission free; ☽ 24hr), where there is a small memorial.

CITY CENTRE

The former **KwaZulu Legislative Assembly** is just north of the train line, and has some unique tapestries charting a course through Zulu history. The building isn't always open to visitors, but you can organise **tours** (around R25) through Ulundi Tourism.

Opposite the Legislative Assembly is the site of King Mpande's *iKhanda* (palace), **kwaNodwengu**. Mpande won control from Dingaan after the disaster at Blood River (see p348). He seized power with assistance from the Boers but Zululand declined during his reign. The king's grave is there, but there's little else to see.

AROUND ULUNDI

Opathe Game Reserve (☎ 870 5000; www.kzn wildlife.com; adult/child/vehicle R15/10/15; ☼ 7am-6pm), 10km from Ulundi on the R66 towards Melmoth, is only open to 4WD vehicles, but has a good spread of wildlife, including rhinos.

A place of great significance to the Zulu is **eMakhosini** (Valley of the Kings). The great *makhosi* (chiefs) Nkhosinkulu, Senzangakhona (father of Shaka, Dingaan and Mpande) and Dinizulu are buried here. A number of big developments are planned for this region – check with Ulundi Tourism.

Sleeping

Holiday Inn Garden Court (☎ 870 1012; fax 870 1220; Princess Magogo St; s/d R609/789; ☒ 🖳 🕸) Catering to passing dignitaries and bureaucrats, this offers the predictably safe comforts of a chain hotel.

Ondini (☎ 870 2050; s/d with breakfast R195/350) Accommodation is also available in rondavels inside the Ondini complex. Unless you've made other arrangements, you must be there by 6pm.

Getting There & Away

The minibus-taxi park is opposite the Holiday Inn, with services to destinations including Vryheid (R30, 2¼ hours) and Eshowe (R24, 1½ hours).

MGUNGUNDLOVU

This was Dingaan's capital from 1829 to 1839, and it was here that Pieter Retief and the other Voortrekkers were killed by their host in 1838, the event that precipitated the Boer-Zulu War. (There are several variations of the spelling of Mgungundlovu, including Ungungundhlovu.) There's a small **museum** (admission R5; ☼ 8am-5pm) and a monument to the Voortrekkers nearby. In 1990 excavations revealed the site of Dingaan's *ndlunkulu* (great hut).

The site is 5km off the R34, running between Melmoth and Vryheid. Turn off to the left (west) about 5km northeast of the intersection with the R66 to Ulundi.

BABANANGO
☎ 035

En route to the Battlefields, Babanango is best known for Stan's Pub at the Babanango Hotel, a favourite drinking hole of Michael Caine during the filming of *Zulu*.

Stan is no longer with us, but the new owners of the **Babanango Hotel** (☎ 835 0029; 16 Justice St; s/d R220/390) have brought this 'cult' hotel back from the brink, with a fresh facelift and plenty of spirit. If you're on your way to Rorke's Drift (p347), the next leg of the Michael Caine pilgrimage, you might as well get watered in the bar here first.

KWAMBONAMBI
☎ 035

KwaMbonambi (often called Kwambo) is a tiny town off the N2, between Empangeni and Mtubatuba. There's no real reason to stop, but the excellent Cuckoos Nest hostel makes an ideal base for backpackers exploring St Lucia, Hluhluwe-Imfolozi and surrounding attractions.

Some believe that KwaMbonambi means 'Place of the Gathering of Kings', while others believe it means 'Place of the Blacksmith', as Shaka's spears were made here.

Cuckoos Nest (☎ 580 1001; cuckoos@mweb.co.za; 28 Albizia St; dm/d/t with shared bathroom R55/140/180; 🕸), off the beaten track and slightly eccentric, is a vibrant hostel with a good buzz, a lush, tropical setting and a vaguely 'eco' feel about it. You can stay in a **tree house** (d R140), expand the left side of your brain in the 'craft corner' or join the sing-along around the braai. Staff also arrange tours to the surrounding parks and reserves.

The Baz Bus stops in Kwambonambi on its Durban-to-Swaziland route.

MTUBATUBA & AROUND
☎ 035

The name Mtubatuba comes from a local chief, Mthubuthubu, meaning 'He who was Pummelled Out', referring to his difficult birth. After a stroll through the chaotic centre you may feel much the same.

The main reason to visit is that buses and minibus taxis run through here on the way south to Durban, north to Pongola (via Hluhluwe and Mkuze) and west into

Zululand. Coming from those destinations, Mtubatuba is the stop for St Lucia (St Lucia Estuary is 25km east; take the R8 by minibus taxi).

On the southern side of Mtubatuba is Riverview, a poor but neat town with a sugar mill.

Wendy's B&B Country Lodge (☎ 550 0407; www .wendybnb.co.za; 3 Riverview Rd, Riverview; r with breakfast R470; ⚉) drips with soft furnishings and offers a hint of homey *Out of Africa* charm. This cosy, four-star B&B provides a warm welcome, an in-house restaurant and pub, and some more opulent, honeymoon-style rooms (R600).

HLUHLUWE-IMFOLOZI PARK

☎ 035

One of South Africa's finest and most evocative parks, **Hluhluwe-Imfolozi Park** (☎ 550 8476; www.kznwildlife.com; adult/child R70/35; ⚉ 5am-7pm Nov-Feb, 6am-6pm Mar-Oct) is best visited in winter as the animals can range widely without congregating at water sources, although the lush vegetation sometimes makes viewing difficult. However, summer visits can also be very rewarding, especially at Imfolozi where there is more-open savanna country.

The two reserves of Hluhluwe and Imfolozi were first proclaimed in 1895, but for all intents and purposes (you only pay once) now comprise a single park covering 96,000 hectares.

The park has lions, elephants, rhinos (black and white), leopards, giraffes and wild dogs. The land is quite hilly except on the river flats: the White Imfolozi River flows through Imfolozi, and the Black Imfolozi forms the northern border of the park; the Hluhluwe River bisects Hluhluwe, and the dam on it attracts wildlife.

A highlight of the park is the **Centenary Centre** (⚉ 8am-4pm), a wildlife-holding centre with an attached museum and information centre in the eastern section of Umfolozi. The centre, which incorporates rhino enclosures and antelope pens (open 9am to 3pm), was established to allow visitors to view animals in transit to their new homes.

The wildlife drives here are very popular. The Hilltop Camp (p314) offers morning and night drives, while the Mpila Camp (p314) offers night drives only. The drives are open to resort residents only and cost R150 per person.

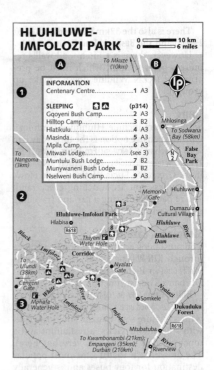

HLUHLUWE-IMFOLOZI PARK

0 — 10 km
0 — 6 miles

To Mkuze
('10km)

INFORMATION
Centenary Centre...................1 A3

SLEEPING (p314)
Gqoyeni Bush Camp.................2 A3
Hilltop Camp.........................3 B2
Hlatikulu............................4 A3
Masinda.............................5 A3
Mpila Camp..........................6 A3
Mtwazi Lodge.....................(see 3)
Muntulu Bush Lodge.................7 B2
Munywaneni Bush Lodge..........8 B2
Nselweni Bush Camp...............9 A3

To Nangoma (3km)
To Ulundi (38km)
Mhlosinga
To Sodwana Bay (58km)
False Bay Park
Memorial Gate
Hluhluwe
Dumazulu Cultural Village
Hluhluwe-Imfolozi Park
Hlabisa
R618
Thiyeni Water Hole
Hluhluwe River
Hluhluwe Dam
Black
Imfolozi
Corridor
Cengeni Gate
Mphafa Water Hole
Imfolozi River
Nyalazi Gate
Somkele
Nyalazi
Dukuduku Forest
Mtubatuba
R618
To Kwambonambi (21km); Empangeni (35km); Durban (210km)
Riverview

Bear in mind that while they are low risk, the reserves are in a malarial area and there are lots of mosquitoes – come prepared.

Wilderness Trails

One of Imfolozi's main attractions is its trail system, in a special 24,000-hectare wilderness area. On the **Traditional Trail** (R2340; 3 days & 4 nights) hikers are accompanied by an armed ranger and donkeys to carry supplies. Hikers spend three days walking in the reserve covering an average of 12km to 15km each day. The first and last nights are spent at a base camp, with two nights out in the wilderness area. Bookings are accepted up to six months in advance and it's advisable to book early, with alternative dates if possible. All meals and equipment are included in the cost, and full payment is required in advance.

A variation on this is the **Primitive Trail** (R2580; 4 days & 4 nights), on which you carry the equipment and food (provided) and sleep under the stars. Some consider the Primitive Trail to be more fun as you get to participate more (for example, hikers must sit up in 1½-hour watches during the night).

KWAZULU-NATAL

There is also the 32km **Weekend Trail** (R1320; 2 nights) and the **Bushveld Trail** (R1410; 2 nights).

However, there is a hitch – all walks require a party of four, which must be prearranged (KZN Wildlife doesn't make up groups).

Tours

Several tours include Hluhluwe-Umfolozi. One inexpensive option is the three-day trip with Durban's **Tekweni Eco-Tours** (☎ 031-303 1199; www.tekweniecotours.co.za), which also takes in the Greater St Lucia Wetland Park. However, unless you are watching every rand, you're better off hiring a car and travelling at your own pace through the park.

Sleeping & Eating

You must book accommodation in advance through **KZN Wildlife** (☎ 033-845 1000; www.kzn wildlife.com) in Pietermaritzburg (p337) or at Durban's Tourist Junction (p337).

Hilltop Camp (☎ 562 0848; rest huts/chalets per person R209/424, 2-bed units with full board per person R424) is the signature resort on the Hluhluwe side, with stupendous views, a restaurant and a much-needed bar (it gets very hot here). The drawback is that it's the most popular destination for tour buses and is generally quite busy. If you want peace and quiet, try one of the accommodation centres in Imfolozi, which are smaller.

If you're after a bush lodge, try **Muntulu Bush Lodge** (8-bed bush lodges per person R468, minimum R2808), perched high above the Hluhluwe River; or **Munyawaneni Bush Lodge** (8-bed bush lodges per person R468, minimum R2808), which is secluded and self-contained. There's also a fully hosted and catered nine-bed lodge at **Mtwazi Lodge** (per person, including wildlife drives & walks R1800).

The main accommodation centre on the Imfolozi side is **Mpila Camp** (4-bed rest huts per person R194, 2-bed safari camps per person R220) in the centre of the reserve. **Masinda** (9-bed lodge per person incl game drives & walks 1800R), near the Centenary Centre, is fully hosted and catered. There is also accommodation available at **Nselweni Bush Camp** (8-bed bush camps per person R290), **Gqoyeni Bush Camp** (8-bed bush camps per person R468) and **Hlatikulu** (8-bed bush camps per person R468).

Be warned: all accommodation options are billed per person but are subject to a minimum charge. Additionally, if you are self-catering, remember to bring your own food!

Getting There & Away

The main entrance, Memorial Gate, is about 15km west of the N2, about 50km north of Mtubatuba. Alternatively, just after Mtubatuba, turn left off the N2 onto the R618 to Nongoma, entering the reserve through the Nyalazi Gate.

Imfolozi also has a gate on the western side, Cengeni Gate, accessible by rough roads (though they should be tarred by 2006) from Ulundi (do not take this route after dark as there are some big potholes as well as some low-level banditry). Petrol is available at Mpila Camp in Imfolozi and at Hilltop Camp in Hluhluwe, where you can also get diesel.

HLUHLUWE

☎ 035 / pop 3200

Hluhluwe village (roughly pronounced 'shloo-shloo-wee') is located to the northeast of Hluhluwe-Imfolozi Park. Here, next to the Engen petrol station on the main road through town, you will find the **Hluhluwe Tourism Association** (☎ 562 0353; www.hluh luwe.net; Bush Rd; ☼ 8am-5pm Mon-Fri, 9am-4pm Sat & Sun), which can offer useful advice on accommodation and transport in the area.

You can also indulge in some local retail therapy at **Ilala Weavers** (☎ 562 0630; www .ilala.co.za; ☼ 8am-5pm Mon-Fri, 9am-4pm Sat & Sat), which has an excellent selection of Zulu handicrafts and aims to make local women more self-sufficient. Some 2000 Zulus now contribute to the works on offer.

Sleeping

Isinkwe Backpackers Lodge (☎ 562 2258; www .isinkwe.co.za; dm/d with shared bathroom R65/140; ☒) Right by Dumazulu Cultural Village (opposite), this is about as close as you can get to a bona fide bush-lodge backpackers. Set in a sweep of virgin bush, it offers Zulu dancing, a nature trail, tours to the surrounding parks and a cocktail bar for that essential sundowner.

Zululand Tree Lodge (☎ 562 1020; s/d with full board R1580/2100; ☒) Seven kilometres outside Hluhluwe, near the wildlife park, this romantic spot offers dreamy, thatched tree houses and some self-catering, four-bed safari lodges (R530).

Hluhluwe Hotel (☎ 562 0251; www.hluhluwe hotel.co.za; 104 Bush Rd; s/d with breakfast R500/860; 🍽 🐾) The thatched roof here adds a certain charm, but this passable place remains 80% motel. It is right in the centre of the village though.

AROUND HLUHLUWE
Dumazulu Cultural Village

South of Hluhluwe, **Dumazulu Cultural Village** (☎ 035-562 2260; dumazulu@goodersons.co.za; admission R88; shows at 8.15am, 11am & 3.15pm), east of the N2, is one of the better 'Zulu experience' villages (including the requisite snake and crocodile park). Lunch and dinner are available.

Dumazulu Lodge (☎ 031-337 4222; intsales@good ersons.co.za; r with breakfast R660), next to the village, offers some upmarket bush comforts.

GREATER ST LUCIA WETLAND PARK
☎ 035

Up there on the podium with the world's great ecotourist destinations, Greater St Lucia Wetland Park is a phenomenal stretch of natural beauty, with a fabulously diverse mix of environments and wildlife. Now a Unesco World Heritage Site, the park stretches for 80 glorious kilometres, from Sodwana Bay, in the north of Maputaland, to Mapelane, at the southern end of Lake St Lucia. With the Indian Ocean on one side, and Lake St Lucia on the other, the park protects no fewer than five distinct ecosystems, offering everything from offshore reefs and beaches, to sedge swamps, bushveld and fossil corals.

Lake St Lucia itself is in fact a large and meandering estuary (Africa's largest) with a narrow sea entrance, and its depth and salinity alter depending on seasonal and ecological factors. It is mainly shallow and the warm water is crowded with fish, which in turn attract huge numbers of water birds. There are lots of pelicans and flamingos in the area, and fish eagles breed around here, while frogs make a din during the summer mating season. However, the Lake St Lucia area is best known as a crocodile and hippo reserve.

Needless to say, Lake St Lucia and its nearby ocean beaches pull big crowds during the holiday season and St Lucia Estuary, the main resort, is abuzz with safari-suited tourists, neon signs and trundling Land Rovers during the busiest weeks. That said, hippos still amble down the town's quieter

> **WARNING**
>
> This is a malarial area, and there are lots of mosquitoes. Ticks and leeches can be a problem. Also be aware of crocs and hippos: both can be deadly. Be careful at night, as this is when hippos roam. In more remote areas hippos might be encountered on shore during the day – maintain your distance and retreat quietly. Sharks sometimes venture up near the St Lucia Estuary.

streets and away from the main centre, the park becomes blissfully peaceful.

The Greater St Lucia Wetland Park is a baffling jigsaw of different reserves, each with their own gate fees and accommodation options. Your best bet is to spend a night in St Lucia Estuary, where you can organise boat trips on the lake, visit the KZN Wildlife office (p316) and get your bearings.

All the parks and reserves are administered by KZN Wildlife, but there is private accommodation in the town of St Lucia Estuary.

Remember that all KZN Wildlife accommodation other than camping must be booked in Pietermaritzburg or at Durban's Tourist Junction.

Hiking Trails

The main trails are all in the Eastern Shores (Mfabeni) area. They are the guided and fully catered **St Lucia Wilderness Trail** (per person R1550; 4 days) and the self-catering 40km **Mziki** (per person per night R66; 3 days) and 65km **Emoyeni** (per person per night R52; 5 days) trails, both accompanied by a field ranger. For more information, see p317.

There are also day walks, detailed in KZN Wildlife literature available at the office at St Lucia Estuary.

Tours

Countless tours are on offer and as many tour operators provide them. Most of the hostels run their own tours and guesthouses will fix you up using a number of trusted providers. The following are in St Lucia Estuary.

St Lucia Tours & Charters (☎ 590 1259; www .zululink.co.za; cnr MacKenzie & Katonkel Rds; ⏰ 6.30am-6pm) doubles as the tourist office and is a worthwhile first stop. As well as offering twice-daily boat tours on the lake (R45), it also runs tours to Hluhluwe (R375, minimum four) and Cape Vidal (R325, minimum four), as well as more specialist hippo tours (R90, minimum six) and whale-watching trips (R400, 1 June to 30 November only).

Shaka Barker Tours (☎ 590 1162; info@shakabarker .co.za; Hornbill St), at the Hornbill House B&B (below), also offers six-hour turtle tours (R150), which include dinner on the beach.

St Lucia Estuary

Most visitors to St Lucia gravitate towards its main resort town at some point. As a result, this pleasant little village, situated just where Lake St Lucia tips into the sea, has become a hotbed of activity during the peak months and the best place for a comfortable bed, a cold beer and a good feed the rest of the time. The main drag, MacKenzie St, is packed with restaurants, lively hostels and bars, but the quieter avenues behind offer a touch more hush and a good selection of mid-market B&Bs.

INFORMATION

St Lucia Tours & Charters (☎ 590 1259; www.zululink .co.za; cnr MacKenzie St & Katonkel Rd; ☉ 6.30am-6pm) offers plenty of information and tour bookings. There is another office on the corner of MacKenzie and the R618.

KZN Wildlife (☎ 590 1340; fax 590 1343; Pelican Rd; ☉ 8am-12.30pm & 2-4.30pm) offers information on the reserves and takes bookings for the camp sites.

There is an **Internet café** (☎ 590 1056; 310 MacKenzie St; per hr R30; ☉ 7am-10pm) at BiB's International Backpackers (right).

First National Bank (MacKenzie St) and **Standard Bank** (MacKenzie St) both have ATMs.

SIGHTS

About 1km north of St Lucia, on the road to Cape Vidal, is the **Crocodile Centre** (☎ 590 1386; croc-centre@kznnca.org.za; adult/child R25/20; ☉ 8.30am-4.30pm Mon-Fri, 8.30am-5pm Sat, 9am-4pm Sun), where a fine array of crocs can be seen in their not-so-natural habitat.

SLEEPING

There is rarely a shortage of places to stay, but it is worth booking ahead during the summer months. St Lucia Tours & Charters (above) can help with bookings.

In St Lucia Estuary itself, you can camp at sites run by **KZN Wildlife** (☎ 590 1340; www .kznwildlife.com; Pelican Rd; Sugarloaf camp sites per person R65, Eden Park R55).

Santa Lucia Guest House (☎ 590 1151; www.san talucia.co.za; 30 Pelican St; s/d with breakfast R300/530; ✴ ☒) This highly acclaimed B&B adds some luxury to the usual standard fare. Some of the décor is a little old-fashioned and the owners can be overwhelmingly friendly, but the rooms have hotel trimmings and the service is excellent.

Hornbill House (☎ 590 1071; www.forafrica.co .za/hornbill; 43 Hornbill St; s/d with breakfast R245/390; ✴ ☒) All the homey B&B comforts come for less at this cheery place, a few streets back from the main drag. The owners, who run a tour company, know their stuff and there's a nice garden for loafing in.

BiB's International Backpackers (☎ 590 1056; www.bibs.co.za; 310 MacKenzie St; camp sites R40, dm/d with shared bathroom R60/150, d with bathroom R180; ☒ ☐) If it happens anywhere, it happens here. Occupying a sprawling, and slightly rickety, barn conversion, BiB's offers all the backpacker staples, from a busy bar and excellent tours, to a huge kitchen for cooking, meeting and greeting. The rooms are a touch tarnished, but the atmosphere is top-notch.

St Lucia Heritage International Backpackers (☎ 590 1968; 70 MacKenzie St; dm/s/d with shared bathroom R60/80/160, d with air-con R240; ☒ ☐) A little smarter and a little sturdier than BiB's, this spot caters to the better-heeled backpacker, offering some nice, new air-con rooms as well as the usual rough-and-ready sleeps.

EATING

The Quarterdeck (☎ 590 1116; MacKenzie St; mains R25-75; ☉ breakfast, lunch & dinner) With a slightly tacky maritime theme, this lively place serves up mountainous portions and plenty of atmosphere. Steaks and seafood top the billing, but come nightfall, the outside terrace takes on a bustling, bar-style buzz. There's a late-night drinking den below.

St Pizza (☎ 590 1048; MacKenzie St; mains R30-60; ☉ lunch & dinner) Pizza with a South African spin (they'll even put biltong on top) is on the menu here. There's a big, shady terrace for long summer dinners.

Alfredo's Italian Restaurant (☎ 590 1150; MacKenzie St; mains R30-50; ☉ lunch & dinner) St Lucia's little Italy whips up pizza, pasta and salads just like Mamma used to make.

GETTING THERE & AWAY

Fast Fotos (☎ 082-445 0057; cnr MacKenzie St & R618; ☽ 8am-4pm Mon-Fri, 8am-2pm Sat, 10am-2pm Sun) operates a shuttle to Durban (provided all seats are filled; seven seats R850, three hours), Sodwana Bay (R160, two hours) and Richard's Bay (R50, 45 minutes), where you can pick up the Greyhound service (Fast Fotos can sell you a ticket).

Backpackers tend to travel on the Baz Bus route.

Maphelana Nature Reserve

South across the estuary from St Lucia Estuary, **Maphelana Nature Reserve** (☎ 590 1407; www.kznwildlife.com; adult/child R20/10; ☽ 6am-8pm) is a popular fishing spot.

There is accommodation offered by **KZN Wildlife** (☎ 033-845 1000; www.kznwildlife.com; camp sites per person R56, 5-bed cabins per person R186). Minimum charges apply.

Although Maphelana is across the estuary from St Lucia Estuary, travel between St Lucia Estuary and Maphelana is circuitous unless you have a boat. Maphelana is reached by 40km of sandy and sometimes tricky road from KwaMbonambi, off the N2 south of Mtubatuba. Follow the KwaMbonambi Lighthouse sign.

Eastern Shores (Mfabeni) Reserve

Two kilometres north of St Lucia Estuary, on the eastern side of the lake, is the boom gate for the **Eastern Shores (Mfabeni) Reserve** (☎ 590 9002; www.kznwildlife.com; adult/child/vehicle R20/15/35; ☽ 6am-6pm), which has the sea on its eastern flank. This section of the park has an excellent selection of wildlife, including rhinos, buffaloes, hippos, crocodiles, elephants and leopards, and a variety of eco-systems from rocky shore and swamp to open grassland. Fourteen kilometres north of the boom gate are the **Mission Rocks**, where you will find the **ranger station** (☎ 590 9002) for the walking trails (see below). At low tide, the Mission Rocks are covered in rock pools containing a fabulous array of sea life.

You can drive through the reserve on a day trip, but by far the best way to see this section of the park is to take one of the trails offered by KZN Wildlife.

HIKING TRAILS

The **Mziki Trail** (☎ 590 9002; per person per night R66) is a guided, three-day trail of about 40km.

In fact, the route is made up of three, distinct one-day trails, which span out from the Mount Tabor Base Camp, where accommodation is in a basic, eight-bed hut. The trails take in a wide range of habitats, running along the lakeshore, through indigenous forest and sand dunes and then down 8km of uninhabited coastline. Reservations should be made on the listed phone number and you should check in at the Mission Rocks ranger station between 2pm and 4pm on the first day. You must bring your own food.

The **Emoyeni Trail** (☎ 590 9002; per person from R104) is a guided, five-day excursion. The trail is 65km long and you stay each of the four nights in a different camp. The trail offers an in-depth insight into the ecosystems and history of the area – there used to be a WWII British radar observation post on Mt Tabor. Reservations should be made on the listed phone number and you should check in at the Mission Rocks ranger station before noon on the first day. You must bring your own food, cooking equipment, sleeping bag and tent.

The **St Lucia Wilderness Trail** (☎ 590 9002; per person R1550) is a fully catered, guided trail. The first and last nights are spent in Bhangazi tented base camp, overlooking Lake Bhangazi, while the intermediary two nights are spent in the wilderness area. As well as guided day walks, canoeing and snorkelling are also on offer. Reservations should be made on the listed phone number and you will be met at the Bhangazi Complex boom gate (below), 40km north of St Lucia Estuary on the first day. Trails begin on Saturday and only operate between April and October.

Cape Vidal

This **coastal camp** (☎ 590 9024; www.kznwildlife .com; adult/child/vehicle R20/15/35; ☽ 6am-6pm) takes in the land between the lake and the ocean, north of Cape Vidal itself. Some of the forested sand dunes are 150m high and the beaches are excellent for snorkelling and swimming.

There is KZN Wildlife accommodation at the **Bhangazi Complex** (☎ 033-845 1000; www.kzn wildlife.com; camp sites R66, 5–8-bed log cabins per person R202, 8-bed bush lodge R319), near Lake Bhangazi. Minimum charges apply. This is the starting point for the St Lucia Wilderness Trail (above).

KWAZULU-NATAL

From St Lucia head north, past the Crocodile Centre and through the entrance gates. Cape Vidal is approximately 35km further on.

Fani's Island

On the western shore of the lake, **Fani's Island** (☎ 550 9035; www.kznwildlife.com; adult/child R20/10, camp sites per person R48, 2-bed rest huts per person R138; ☻ 6am-8pm) offers one of the most secluded camps, and excellent fishing and bird-watching. The 5km Umkhiwane trail is a must for ornithologists. There are **camp sites** and **rest huts**. Follow signs to Charter's Creek from the N2 north of Mtubatuba.

False Bay Park

One of the geologically oldest parts of the St Lucia Wetland area, **False Bay Park** (☎ 562 0061; www.kznwildlife.com; adult/child R20/10; ☻ 6am-8pm) is well known for its fossils and runs along the western shore of Lake St Lucia. As well as the lake's hippos and crocs, the park has several antelope species and other animals, including zebras and warthogs. It is only 3km across, but comprises sand forest, thornveld and savanna. There are three hiking trails through the park averaging around 8km each; contact Dugandlovu Rustic Camp (right) for details.

MARINE TURTLES

Five species of turtle live off the South African coast but only two actually nest on the coast: the leatherback turtle *(Dermochelys coriacea)* and the loggerhead turtle *(Caretta caretta)*. The nesting areas of the leatherback extend from the St Lucia mouth north into Mozambique, but the loggerhead only nests in the Maputaland Marine Reserve.

Both species nest at night in summer. The female moves above the high-tide mark, finds a suitable site and lays her eggs. The loggerheads' breeding area is more varied as they clamber over rocks in the intertidal zone; leatherbacks will only nest on sandy beaches.

About 70 days later, the hatchlings scramble out of the nest at night and make a dash for the sea. Only one or two of each thousand hatchlings will survive until maturity. The females return 12 to 15 years later to the very same beach to nest.

In the northern part of False Bay is the **Mpophomeni Trail**, which is divided into two routes that are both suitable for families; the longer 10km section takes about four to five hours, and the shorter 7km section takes three hours.

Dugandlovu Rustic Camp (☎ 562 0061; camp sites per person R52, 4-bed rustic huts per person R120) is on the Dugandlovu Trail, about 9km from the entrance gate; you can drive to the camping site.

The main road into the park runs from Hluhluwe village, off the N2. Hluhluwe village is also the nearest place to buy fuel and other supplies.

SODWANA BAY
☎ 035

Never far from the top of the scribbled list marked 'Places I Must See In South Africa', Sodwana Bay, at the very northern tip of the Greater St Lucia Wetland Park, isn't a whole lot more than sand, sea and silence. And yet that's its appeal. Isolated and peaceful (outside the holidays), this little slice of paradise offers stunning coastal scenery, the world's most southerly coral reefs, walking trails and some serious fishing. There is a small village (Sodwana Bay) here, but the two nearby parks provide most of the highlights.

Sodwana Bay National Park (☎ 571 0051; www.kznwildlife.com; adult/child R20/15; ☻ 6am-6pm) is on the coast, east of Mkuze. There are some animals, and the dunes, swamps and offshore coral reefs are well worth visiting, but the area can become very congested during holidays. Over Christmas there are turtle-viewing tours (R150 per person).

For a more peaceful look at a similar ecosystem, head south to the adjoining **Ozabeni State Forest** (☎ 571 0268; www.kznwildlife.com; adult/child/vehicle R15/10/15; ☻ 6am-6pm), which runs all the way down to Lake St Lucia. Bird-watchers are in for a treat here, as over 330 species have been recorded. North of the lake is a prohibited area.

As well as diving (see the boxed text on opposite), **Ocean Links** (☎ 571 5000, 083-654 7204; ☻ 8.30am-4.30pm Mon-Fri, 8.30am-noon Sat), in a psychedelic store on the main street of the village, organises dolphin-watching, whale-watching and turtle tours (from R150 per person). Nearby, **Off Road Fun** (☎ 082-785 7704) offers quad-bike tours (R150).

SNORKELLING & DIVING

The coastline near Sodwana Bay, which includes the southernmost coral reefs in Africa, is a diver's paradise. Schools of fish glide through the beautiful coral, turtles swim by, and moray eels peer inquisitively from rock crevices. Predominantly soft coral over hard, the reef has one of the world's highest recorded numbers of tropical-fish species. All of these wonders can be seen using scuba or snorkelling equipment, and excellent visibility and warm winter waters allow for diving year-round.

Popular snorkelling spots are Cape Vidal, Two-Mile Reef off Sodwana Bay, Mabibi and the Kosi Mouth with its famous 'aquarium', so named because of the diversity of fish. Scuba divers should head for Tenedos Shoal, between the Mlalazi River and Port Durnford, and Five-Mile, Seven-Mile and Nine-Mile Reefs. Courses are held at Two-Mile Reef.

Sodwana Bay Lodge (☎ 035-571 0095; www.sodwanadivelodge.co.za) specialises in Professional Association of Diving Instructors (PADI) diving packages (two nights accommodation, meals and three dives costs R1284 per person). There are also individual dives (R150) on offer. **Coral Divers** (☎ 035-571 0290; coraldivers@mweb.co.za) also offers PADI courses (PADI Open Water costs R1650). Both offer equipment hire.

You can access the Internet at **Vis Agie Charters** (☎ 571 0104; per hr R30), at the bottom of the main street. The nearest ATM is in Mbazwana, 14km west.

Sleeping & Eating

KZN Wildlife (☎ 033-845 1000; www.kznwildlife.com; Ozabeni camp sites per person R28, Sodwana Bay National Park camp sites/5-bed cabins per person R40/198) offers camping at Ozabeni; and both camping and cabins at Sodwana Bay National Park. Minimum charges apply.

Sodwana Bay Lodge (☎ 571 0095; www.sodwana divelodge.co.za; s/d with half board R562/998) This slick place caters to high-life divers. It rents out quad bikes (R150 per hour) and offers horse-riding trips (R180 for two hours). It's on the main road through the village.

Coral Divers (☎ 571 0290; coraldivers@mweb.co.za; Sodwana Bay National Park; s/d with shared bathroom from R90/180; 🐾 🖳) This five-star Professional Association of Diving Instructors (PADI) resort has a fabulous setting, satellite TV, a pool, a bar and lashings of personality. However, as the site is within Sodwana Bay National Park, you pay an extra charge for entry. For R100, staff will pick you up from Hluhluwe.

For dive prices at these two places, see the boxed text above.

Getting There & Away

There are two road routes from the N2. The northern route leaves the highway about 8km north of Mkuze and runs up into the Lebombo Mountains to the small town of Jozini. After Jozini it's a dirt road running through flat country. The southern route is sealed the whole way and leaves the N2 north of the turn-off for Hluhluwe village. Both routes converge at the village of Mbazwana, from where it's about 20km to the park.

Minibus taxis run from the N2 up to Jozini. From there to Sodwana Bay you shouldn't have trouble finding transport (taxis) as it's a fairly densely populated region. There are far fewer taxis on the southern route but there is a fair amount of tourist traffic, so hitching should be easy.

Fast Fotos (p317), in St Lucia Estuary, runs a shuttle between Sodwana Bay and St Lucia Estuary.

MKUZE

☎ 035

Mkuze, a small town on the N2 and the Mkuze River, is west of a pass over the Lebombo range. The road through the pass is one route to Sodwana Bay. **Ghost Mountain**, south of the town, was an important burial place for the Ndwandwe tribe and has a reputation for eerie occurrences, usually confined to strange lights and noises. Occasionally human bones, which date from a big battle between rival Zulu factions in 1884, are found near Ghost Mountain.

Ghost Mountain Inn (☎ 573 1025; ghostinn@iafrica .com; s/d with breakfast R440/740; 🌐 🖳) boasts a recent facelift, which has brought a touch of the modern to this pleasant, old-school place. Blooming gardens, tennis courts and drives to the Mkhuze Game Reserve all add to the appeal.

MKHUZE GAME RESERVE

Established in 1912, this **reserve** (☎ 035-573 9001; www.kznwildlife.com; adult/child/vehicle R30/15/35; ☺ 6am-6pm), covering some 36,000 hectares, lacks lions and elephants but just about every other sought-after animal is represented, as well as more than 400 species of birds, including the rare Pel's fishing owl (Scotopelia peli).

Better still, the reserve has hides at water-holes, which offer some of the best wildlife viewing in the country. Morning is the best time.

Wildlife drives (R90) are available. Fuel is sold at the main gate.

KZN Wildlife (☎ 033-845 1000; www.kznwildlife .com; Nhlonhlela camp sites per person R55, Mantuma 2- & 4-bed safari camps & chalets per person R230) offers camping at Nhlonhlela, and safari camps and chalets at Mantuma. Minimum charges apply.

From the north you can get to the game reserve from Mkuze town; from the south, turn off the N2 around 35km north of Hluhluwe village.

PHINDA RESOURCE RESERVE

This 17,000-hectare reserve, to the north-west of Lake St Lucia, is very much an 'ecotourism' showpiece. It was set up by the Conservation Corporation, a private-reserve chain.

There are nine different ecosystems in the park. They include hilly terrain, sand forest, riverine woodland, natural pans and savanna grasslands. This diversity attracts a great variety of birdlife (more than 360 species) and promotes a diverse range of plant life. There are about 10,000 animals, many re-introduced, including nyala and the rare suni antelope (Neotragus moscha-tus). Lion and cheetah kills can occasion-ally be spotted and leopards are now seen during wildlife drives. In addition to these, there are also accompanied walks, canoeing and river-boat cruises on offer.

The only problem with Phinda is that all the 'eco' features don't come cheap: low-season doubles with full board and activities start at R4120. Bookings can be made through **Conservation Corporation Africa** (☎ 011-809 4300; fax 011-809 4400).

To get there, take the Southern Maputa-land turn-off from the N2 and follow the signs.

LAKE SIBAYA NATURE RESERVE

Protecting the largest freshwater lake in South Africa, **Lake Sibaya Nature Reserve** (www .kznwildlife.com; adult/child/vehicle R20/10/35; ☺ 6am-6pm) covers between 60 and 70 sq km, de-pending on the water level. It lies very close to the coast, and between the eastern shore and the sea is a range of sand dunes up to 165m high. There are hippos, some crocs and a large range of birdlife (more than 280 species have been recorded). The lake is popular for fishing; you can hire boats (complete with skipper) for fishing trips.

There is no accommodation in the re-serve. The main route to the reserve is via the village of Mbazwana, south of the lake, either from Mkuze or from Mhlosinga, off the N2 north of Hluhluwe village.

KOSI BAY NATURE RESERVE

The jewel of the KwaZulu coast, **Kosi Bay Na-ture Reserve** (☎ 035-592 0234; www.kznwildlife.com; adult/child/vehicle R20/15/15; ☺ 6am-6pm) features a string of four lakes, Nhlange, Mpungwini, Sifungwe and Amanzimnyama, that tip down the hillside into an estuary lined with some of the most beautiful (and quietest) beaches in South Africa. Fig, mangrove and raffia-palm forests provide the greenery, while a coral reef offers excellent snorkel-ling just offshore.

There are antelope species in the drier country and hippos, Zambezi sharks and some crocs in the lake system. More than 250 bird species have been identified there, including the rare palmnut vulture. The research station at the reserve studies the local population of leatherback turtles; dur-ing the nesting season (December to Janu-ary) there are turtle-viewing tours. Canoes are also available for hire.

The 44km **Kosi Bay Trail** (4 days per person R285) is a self-catered, guided hike around the Kosi estuarine system, stopping each night in remote camps, which focus on different aspects of the reserve. This trail includes a walk to the estuary at Kosi Mouth.

There are camp sites and basic cabins in the reserve, but very little else. **KwaNgwanase** (also called Manguzi) is the nearest serv-ice centre, some 10km west of the reserve, and you will find shops and an ATM here. The access roads to Kosi Bay – particularly the track to the Kosi Mouth section – can get very bad, and you may need a 4WD.

The Total petrol station, on the main road through KwaNgwanase, is a good place to ask about the state of the roads and the best spot to try and hitch into the reserve with a passing 4WD.

SLEEPING & EATING

KZN Wildlife (☎ 033-845 1000; www.kznwildlife.com; camp sites per person R65, 2- & 4-bed cabins per person R223) offers camping and cabin accommodation – minimum charges apply.

I Gwala Gwala Lodge (☎ 035-592 9250, 084-588 0564; s/d R150/300, camp sites R75) Around 1km from the parks board office on the Kosi Bay Camp access road, this excellent place offers transfers to all beaches, picks up from Mkuze and organises snorkelling, dolphin swims, boat trips and diving. Accommodation is in chalets.

Utshwayelo Campsite (☎ 035-592 9626, 073-134 3318; camp sites per person R55) This quiet, community-run camp site offers camping right by the parks board office on the Kosi Bay Mouth access road. You can walk to one of the country's best beaches in 20 minutes.

Lapa Lapa Lodge (☎ 035-592 9055; lapa-lapa@den .co.za; Main Rd, KwaNgwanase; camp sites R50, s/d R150/ 300) Just outside KwaNgwanase, on the main road towards Kosi Bay, this place offers reasonable rooms, camping and the Rocky Reef Bar. All mock rock and fish tanks, this relatively lively bar has pool tables and cold beer. It also offers **meals** (mains R25 to R50).

GETTING THERE & AWAY

To get to Kosi Bay, take the Jozini turn-off from the N2 and head towards Ndumo Game Reserve but turn hard right (east) just before Ndumo village. There is also a sealed road between Mbazwana and Phelandaba, cutting hours off the route from Sodwana Bay. There are two main access roads into the reserve north of KwaNgwanase. The first (7km north) leads to Kosi Bay Camp and the second (19km north) leads to Kosi Bay Mouth. Both may require a 4WD.

City to City (☎ 031-308 8111; www.translux.co.za) links KwaNgwanase (Manguzi) with Durban (R100, 5½ hours).

TEMBE ELEPHANT PARK

Heading back to the N2 from Kosi Bay, South Africa's last free-ranging elephants are protected in the sandveld (dry, sandy belt) forests of **Tembe Elephant Park** (☎ 035-592 0545; www.tembe.co.za; adult/child/vehicle R30/15/35; ☺ 6am-6pm) on the Mozambique border. There are now about 160 elephants in the area, many of them the last remnants of elephant herds from the Maputo Elephant Reserve, saved from Mozambique's civil war. There are also white rhinos and leopards.

Although this is a KZN Wildlife park, the accommodation is privately run.

Tembe Lodge (☎ 035-592 05455; www.tembe.co.za; r with full board from R800) offers accommodation in secluded safari tents built on wooden platforms. In the centre of the camp there is a large dining area, a shaded pool and braai facilities. The prices include meals and activities.

There's a sealed road all the way to Tembe, but only 4WD vehicles are allowed to drive through the park.

NDUMO GAME RESERVE

A little further west, this **reserve** (☎ 035-591 0004; www.kznwildlife.com; adult/child/vehicle R30/15/35; ☺ 6am-6pm) is beside the Mozambique border and close to the Swaziland border, about 100km north of Mkuze. On some 10,000 hectares, there are black and white rhinos, hippos, crocodiles and antelope species but it is the birdlife on the Pongola and Usutu Rivers, and their flood plains and pans, which attracts visitors. It's known as a 'mini Okavango'.

Guided walks (R35) for wildlife viewing and bird-watching, and vehicle tours (R90) are available. This is the southernmost limit of the range of many bird species and the reserve is a favourite of bird-watchers, with more than 400 species recorded.

Fuel and limited supplies are usually available 2km outside the park gate.

Camping and rest huts are offered by **KZN Wildlife Accommodation** (☎ 033-845 1000; www .kznwildlife.com; camp sites per person R48, 2-bed rest huts per person R176) – minimum charges apply.

PONGOLA
☎ 034

Back on the N2, Pongola is a small town in a sugar-growing district near the Mpumalanga and Swaziland borders. There's an ATM, and petrol is available 24 hours.

Southeast of Pongola (you'll see it from the N2, which is the western border) is the **Phongola Reserve** (☎ 435 1012; www.kznwildlife.com; adult/child/vehicle R16/11/20; ☺ 6am-6pm), a lovely

KWAZULU-NATAL

area backed by the Lebombo range and encompassing a large lake, on which you can go boating.

Sleeping

KZN Wildlife (☎ 033-845 1000; www.kznwildlife.com; camp sites per person R46) has camping in Phongola Reserve.

Pongola Country Lodge (☎ 413 1352; fax 413 1353; 14 Jan Mielie St; s/d R250/290) Modern, comfortable and central, this is a good bet for an overnight stay in Pongola.

Riverview Backpackers (☎ 413 1713; fax 413 2100; dm/d with shared bathroom R70/180, camp sites R35) Riverview Backpackers, on an old sugar farm south of Pongola, is a rustic place with a lush garden. To get there follow the N2 south, then turn right before the biltong stall and follow this for about 1km, turn left, then right, then follow the signs.

ITHALA GAME RESERVE

KZN Wildlife's **Ithala Game Reserve** (☎ 034-983 2540; www.kznwildlife.com; adult/child/vehicle R30/15/30; ☻ 6am-6pm) has all the trappings of a private game reserve but much lower prices. It also doesn't get the crowds that flock into Hluhluwe-Imfolozi, as it's slightly off the main routes.

Most of the 30,000 hectares are taken up by the steep valleys of six rivers (tributaries of the Pongola), with some open grassland on the heights, rugged outcrops and about 25% bushveld.

Animals, mostly reintroduced, include black and white rhinos, elephants, tsessebes (the only herd in KwaZulu-Natal), nyalas, hyenas, buffaloes, baboons, leopards and cheetahs. There are more than 75 mammal species in the park, plus crocodiles and 100 or so other species of amphibians and reptiles, and 20 species of indigenous fish. The diverse habitats support more than 320 species of bird, including the endangered southern bald ibis (*Geronticus calvus*).

There are also **wildlife drives** (per person R46) and **guided walks** (per person R35).

Sleeping

Ntshondwe (☎ 033-845 1000; www.kznwildlife.com; self-catering 2-bed chalets per person R320, 2-bed units per person R290; ☙) is the main centre, with superb views of the reserve below. Facilities include a restaurant, shop and swimming pool. There's a full-board option for the units, on request.

There's also camping available at **Mhlangeni** (☎ 033-845 1000; www.kznwildlife.com; camp sites per person R36).

Minimum charges apply.

Getting There & Away

Ithala is reached from Louwsburg, about 55km northeast of Vryheid on the R69, and about the same distance southwest of Pongola via the R66 and the R69. Louwsburg is much smaller than many maps indicate.

NTENDEKA WILDERNESS AREA

This **wilderness area** (☎ 035-867 1883; admission R30; ☻ 6am-6pm) is a truly beautiful grassland and indigenous coastal and inland tropical forest, with some dramatic dolerite and sandstone cliffs (Ntendeka means 'Place of Precipitous Heights'). More than 180 species of trees, 60 species of ferns and 190 species of birds have been recorded. The rare Ngoye red squirrel is found in the forest and unusual birds such as the blue swallow (*Hirundo atrocaerulea*) and cuckoo hawk (*Aviceda cuculoides*) can also be spotted. The wilderness area is bordered by **Ngome State Forest**, a good example of inland tropical forest.

This is an important region in Zulu history as Cetshwayo was once holed up here; his rock-shelter refuge is in the northeastern corner of the park. Another famous figure to hide out here was Mzilikazi, one of Shaka's disloyal generals. Mzilikazi was eventually chased north, where his descendants established the Ndebele tribe in the Pretoria area and the Matabele in present-day Zimbabwe.

There are walking trails but it is not possible to drive through the wilderness area. There's a **camp site** (per person R45) with ablution facilities on the northeastern edge of the park; this is the only place in the wilderness where you can camp.

Getting There & Away

The nearest big town is Nongoma (which is an important trading town but has no facilities for visitors), along 50km of unsealed road. Nongoma is about 60km northeast of Ulundi. Alternatively, get to Ntendeka by travelling east from Vryheid on the R618 for about 70km, or south from Pongola on the R66, then northwest on the R618.

VRYHEID

☎ 034 / pop 63,600

Vryheid (Liberty) is the largest town in northern Zululand. Today Vryheid is an agricultural and coal-mining centre but in 1884 it was the capital of the Nieuwe Republiek, which was absorbed into the Zuid-Afrikaansche Republiek (ZAR; South African Republic) four years later. After the Anglo-Boer War, the area was transferred to Natal. There are Anglo-Boer War sites and several people offer guided tours of the battlefields.

Vryheid Information Office (☎ 982 2133; inform ation@vhd.dorea.co.za; cnr Market & High Sts) can provide information on the surrounding area, and on tours of the battlefields.

There are two worthwhile museums in town. The **Nieuwe Republiek Museum** (☎ 982 2133; Landdrost St; admission free; � 7.30am-4pm Mon-Fri, by appointment Sat & Sun), in the Old Raadsaal building, is devoted to the short-lived Nieuwe Republiek. South of the main street, Kerk St, is the **Lucas Meijer Museum** (☎ 982 2133; cnr Landdrost & Mark Sts; � 7.30am-4pm Mon-Fri, by appointment Sat & Sun). This small local history museum is in the old Lucas Meijer House (Meijer was the only president of the Nieuwe Republiek).

Sleeping

Villa Prince Imperial (☎ 983 2610; princeimperial@ intekom.co.za; 201 Deputasie St; s/d with breakfast R300/500; ☒) Offering a splash of frontier-town luxury, the Villa Prince, at the base of Lancaster Hill, is Vryheid's most upmarket hotel. Its stylish rooms all have TV, tea-and-coffee facilities and even a hair dryer.

Oxford Lodge (☎ 980 9280; fax 981 5673; cnr Kerk & Deputasie Sts; s/d with breakfast R240/320) In a large old house, the Oxford Lodge offers a homier, old-school alternative.

Vryheid Lodge (☎ 981 5201; fax 981 5467; 200 Kerk St; s/d R150/210) In town, the Vryheid Lodge is a more frugal option.

Getting There & Away

Greyhound (Durban ☎ 031-334 9700; www.greyhound .co.za) runs daily coaches between Durban and Vryheid (R160, six hours).

The well-organised minibus-taxi park is near the train station. Vryheid is the centre for minibus taxis in this part of KwaZulu-Natal. Services from Vryheid include: Ulundi (R20, 1½ hours), Dundee (R20, 1¼

hours), Pongola (R25, two hours), Eshowe (R30, 2½ hours), Durban (R50, four hours), via Melmoth, and Jo'burg (R75, five hours).

PAULPIETERSBURG

☎ 034 / pop 8500

This town is a centre for timber and agricultural production, and gets its name from Paul Kruger and Pieter Joubert. Paulpietersburg has many descendants of the original German settlers from the Hermannsburg Missionary Society established in 1848. The main German towns the settlers came from are Gluckstadt, Braunschweig and Luneberg.

The **Paulpietersburg Publicity Association** (☎ 995 1650; fax 995 1255; 10 Hoog St; � 8.30am-4.30pm Mon-Fri) has information on the town and the surrounding area.

Natal Spa (☎ 995 0307; www.natalspa.co.za; r with breakfast R350), on the banks of the Bivaan River, outside of town, boasts 162 bird species, and hot and cold mineral pools for soaking away the wildlife drive aches and pains.

Greyhound (Durban ☎ 031-334 9700; www.grey hound.co.za) runs daily coaches between Durban and Paulpietersburg (R160, 6½ hours).

DRAKENSBERG

A wall between states and the roof of the nation, the tabletop peaks of the Drakensberg range, which form the boundary between South Africa and the mountain kingdom of Lesotho, offer some of the country's most awe-inspiring landscapes, and provided the backdrop for the film *Zulu* and the inspiration for a million picture postcards. This vast 243,000-hectare sweep of basalt summits and buttresses was formally granted World Heritage status in November 2000, when it was renamed the **Ukhahl-amba-Drakensberg Park**. Today, some of the vistas, particularly the unforgettable curve of the Amphitheatre in the Royal Natal National Park, are so recognisably South African that they have become tourist-brochure clichés. But that doesn't make them any less magnificent. If any landscape lives up to its airbrushed, publicity-shot alter ego, it is the jagged, green sweep of the Drakensberg.

Drakensberg means 'Dragon Mountains'; the Zulu named it Quathlamba, meaning 'Battlement of Spears'. The Zulu word is a

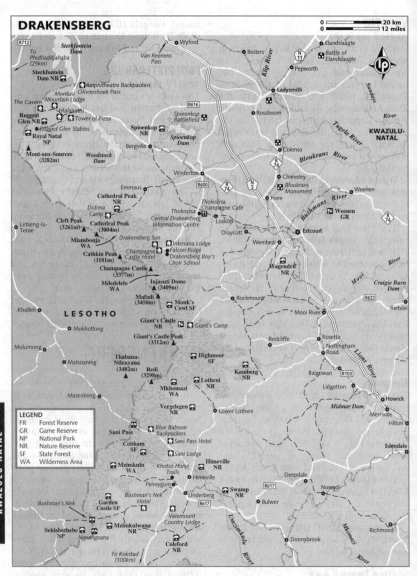

DRAKENSBERG

| 0 | | 20 km |
| 0 | | 12 miles |

LEGEND

FR	Forest Reserve
GR	Game Reserve
NP	National Park
NR	Nature Reserve
SF	State Forest
WA	Wilderness Area

more accurate description of the sheer escarpment but the Afrikaans name captures something of the Drakensberg's otherworldly atmosphere. People have lived here for thousands of years – this is evident by the many San rock-art sites – yet many of its peaks were first climbed little more than 50 years ago (for details, see the boxed text on p325).

The San, already under pressure from the tribes that had moved into the Drakensberg foothills, were finally destroyed with the coming of White settlers. Some moved to Lesotho, where they were absorbed into the Basotho population, but many were killed or simply starved when their hunting grounds were occupied by others. Khoisan

TAMING THE DRAGONS

The mountains of South Africa don't stand as a single, solid range like the European Alps. They are a series of ranges, each imbued with its own particular character. The most majestic of the ranges is the Drakensberg, stretching from Eastern Cape to Northern Province. The peaks of the Drakensberg in KwaZulu-Natal were the last of the 'dragons' to be tamed by mountaineers, as most activity had concentrated on peaks near Cape Town – the Mountain Club was formed there in 1891.

In 1888, Reverend A Stocker, a member of the Alpine Club, was the first to climb Champagne Castle (3377m) and Sterkhorn Peak. He also attempted, but failed to summit, Cathkin Peak (3181m); this was not climbed until 1912, when it was scaled by a group that included a Black guide called Melatu. Cathedral Peak (3004m) was conquered by two climbers, R Kingdon and D Bassett-Smith, in 1917.

The next intensive period of climbing was in the 1940s. Dick Barry attempted the Monk's Cowl (3234m) in 1938, but was killed doing so. In 1942 a group led by Hans Wongtschowski scaled its basalt faces. Two years later, Hans and his wife Elsa clawed up the seemingly impregnable Bell (2991m).

The region's greatest challenge was the Devil's Tooth (3022m), which, after several attempts, was conquered in 1950. In 1954, shortly after it was surveyed, Thabana-Ntlenyana (Little Black Mountain) was climbed as a relatively simple excursion. Thabana-Ntlenyana is in Lesotho and, at 3482m, is Southern Africa's highest peak.

---

cattle raids annoyed the White settlers to the extent that the settlers forced several Black tribes to relocate into the Drakensberg foothills to act as a buffer between the Whites and the Khoisan. These early 'Bantu locations' meant that there was little development in the area, which later allowed the creation of a chain of parks and reserves.

ORIENTATION

The Ukhahlamba-Drakensberg Park, which is actually several spectacular parks in and around the Drakensberg range, is usually divided into three sections, although the distinctions aren't strict. The Northern Berg runs from the Golden Gate Highlands National Park in Free State (see p363) to the Royal Natal National Park. Harrismith and Bergville are sizable towns in this area.

The Central Berg's main feature is Giant's Castle Game Reserve, the largest reserve in the area. North of Giant's Castle is Cathedral Peak and two wilderness areas. Estcourt and Winterton are towns adjacent to the central Drakensberg.

The Southern Berg runs down to the Transkei area of Eastern Cape. There's a huge wilderness area here and the Sani Pass route into southern Lesotho. Pietermaritzburg to the east and Kokstad to the south are the main access points to the southern Drakensberg and up in the hills are some pleasant little towns, notably Underberg and Himeville.

David Bristow's books *Guide to the Drakensberg* and *Best Walks of the Drakensberg* are useful references for those planning to explore the region. KZN Wildlife sells six 1:50,000 topographic maps, which detail hiking trails, camp sites etc, for around R30 each. They're available from KZN Wildlife's headquarters in Pietermaritzburg, the various park offices and some shops in the area.

INFORMATION

KZN Wildlife (☎ 033-845 1000; www.kznwildlife.com), in Pietermaritzburg (p337) can provide information on the various parks and accommodation options. In general, you must book all KZN Wildlife accommodation (except camping) in advance through either the Pietermaritzburg or Durban Tourist Junction (p325) branches. There are also several local information offices:

Central Drakensberg Information Centre (☎ 036-488 1207; www.cdic.co.za; Thokozisa; ☉ 9am-6pm) Based in the Thokozisa complex, 13km outside Winterton on the R600, this private enterprise is extremely helpful. It also has Internet access.

Okhahlamba Drakensberg Tourism (☎ 036-448 1557; www.drakensberg.org.za; Tatham Rd, Bergville; ☉ 9am-4.30pm Mon-Fri, 9am-1pm Sat) Based in Bergville and covers the northern and central Drakensberg.

Southern Drakensberg Sani Saunter (☎ 033-701 1471; www.sanisaunter.com; Clocktower Centre, Old Main Rd, Underberg; ☉ 9am-4.30pm Mon-Fri, 9am-1pm Sat) Covers the southern region from Underberg.

CLIMATE

The frosts come in winter, but the rain falls in summer. While the summer weather forecasts, posted in each of the KZN Wildlife park offices, often make bleak reading for those hoping for blue skies and sunshine, you can often bet on clear, dry mornings, with the thunderheads only rolling in during the afternoon. Whenever you visit, always carry wet-weather gear, and be prepared for icy conditions and snowfalls, if you are crossing the high peaks in winter.

HIKING

The Ukhahlamba-Drakensberg Park has some superb walks and hikes, ranging from gentle day walks to strenuous hikes of two or more days. The trails in the Mkhomazi and Mzimkulu Wilderness Areas, and the Mzimkulwana Nature Reserve, in the southern Drakensberg, offer some of the most remote and rugged hiking in South Africa. For the less experienced there's also the five-day Giant's Cup Trail, running from near Sani Pass Hotel down to Bushman's Nek (p334).

Summer hiking can be made frustrating, and sometimes even dangerous, by flooding rivers; in winter, frosts and snow are the main hazards. April and May are the best months for hiking.

Make sure you get the relevant maps (see Orientation, p283), which show trails and have essential information for hikers.

Permits are needed on most of the hikes; get them from KZN Wildlife offices at the various trailheads. Trail accommodation is often in huts (which means you don't need a tent). In northern Drakensberg accommodation must be booked well in advance, but in southern Drakensberg this isn't such a problem.

SLEEPING

The perfect way to see the Ukhahlamba-Drakensberg Park is to stay at one of KZN Wildlife's excellent reserves. The biggest and most popular are Royal Natal and Giant's Castle, but accommodation and camp sites can also be found in the state forests and other reserves.

Usually more expensive than the parks board's accommodation are the private resorts, which dot the foothills near Royal Natal and Giant's Castle.

GETTING THERE & AROUND

There is little public transport in the northern and central Drakensberg, although there is a lot of tourist traffic. With so many resorts all needing staff there are some minibus taxis. The main jumping-off points are on or near the N3; for more information, see Estcourt (p343), Mooi River (p340), Winterton (p329) and Bergville (p328). The Baz Bus drops off and picks up at a couple of hostels in the area. Through hostels in Durban you can arrange a lift to the hostels near Sani Pass and Himeville.

Sani Pass is the best-known Drakensberg route into Lesotho. There are other passes over the escarpment but most don't connect with anything in Lesotho larger than a walking track (if that).

Many back roads in the Drakensberg area are unsealed and after rain some are impassable – stick to the main routes.

NORTHERN BERG

An ideal stopover on the journey between Durban and Jo'burg, the Northern Berg is crowned with the beautiful Royal Natal National Park and some wonderfully empty spaces.

Royal Natal National Park

☎ 036

Spanning out from some of the range's loftiest summits, the 8000-hectare **Royal Natal Park** (☎ 438 6310; www.kznwildlife.com; adult/child R25/15; ⏰ 5am-6pm) has a presence that far outstrips its relatively meagre size, with many of the surrounding peaks rising as high into the air as the park stretches across. With some of the Drakensberg's most dramatic and accessible scenery, the park is crowned by the sublime Amphitheatre, an 8km wall of cliff and canyon, which is spectacular from below and even more so from up on high. Here the Tugela Falls drop 850m in five stages (the top one often freezes in winter). Looming up behind is Mont-aux-Sources (3282m), so called because the Tugela, Elands and Western Khubedu Rivers rise here; the latter eventually becomes the Orange River and flows all the way to the Atlantic.

Other notable peaks in the area are Devil's Tooth, the Eastern Buttress and the Sentinel. Rugged Glen Nature Reserve adjoins the park on the northeastern side.

The park's **visitors centre** (☺ 8am-12.30pm & 2-4.30pm) is about 1km in from the main gate. There's also a shop selling basic provisions, where you can pick up a copy of KZN Wildlife's excellent booklet *Royal Natal Walks & Climbs* (R10), which includes descriptions of walks and a sketch map. Fuel is available in the park.

WILDLIFE
With plentiful water, a range of more than 1500m in altitude and distinct areas such as plateaus, cliffs and valleys, it isn't surprising that the park's flora is extremely varied. Broadly speaking, much of the park is covered in grassland, with protea savanna at lower altitudes. This grassland depends on fire for reproduction and to discourage other vegetation. In areas that escape the park's periodic fires, scrub takes over. At lower levels, but confined to valleys, are small yellowwood forests. At higher altitudes grass yields to heath and scrub.

Royal Natal is not as rich in wildlife as Giant's Castle and other sections of the Drakensberg but there is still quite a lot to be seen. Of the six species of antelope, the most common is the mountain reedbuck. Hyraxes are everywhere, as are hares. Royal Natal also has a large population of baboons, the feeding of which has become a growing problem. If you see baboons, please avoid giving them food – as the signs in the visitors centre make quite clear: 'You Feed 'Em, We Shoot 'Em!'.

If you have your own tackle, there is also good trout fishing here. Permits are available from the visitors centre for R60.

ROCK ART
There are several San rock-art sites, although Royal Natal's are fewer and not as well preserved as those at Giant's Castle; the latter has many more rock shelters and caves, and has suffered less from vandalism. The notable sites are Sigubudu Shelter, north of the road just past the main gate, and Cannibal Caves, on Surprise Ridge, outside the park's northern boundary.

HIKING TRAILS
Except for the **Amphitheatre-to-Cathedral** (62km, four to five days) and the **Mont-aux-Sources** (20km, 10 hours) hikes, all of the 30-odd walks in Royal Natal are day walks. Only 50 day visitors and 50 overnighters are

allowed on Mont-aux-Sources (3282m) each day. The hike to the summit starts from the Mahai camp site and takes you up to Basotho Gate and the Sentinel car park, from where you take the chain ladder up to the summit. However, if you are short of time you can drive to the Sentinel car park on the road from Phuthaditjhaba in QwaQwa (p364), shortening the hike by five hours.

If you plan to camp on the mountain, you should book with the **Free State Agriculture Department** (☎ 058-713 5071) in Phuthaditjhaba. Otherwise there's a basic hut on the escarpment near Tugela Falls. Unlike other KZN Wildlife accommodation, you don't need to book (except for registering before walking here) and there's no fee for the hut, but an overnight hiking permit costs R30.

Independent local guides can be booked through the visitors centre, or through **Elijah** (☎ 083-575 0762), or **Reginald** (☎ 083-340 2067). Per person prices (minimum group sizes apply) include: Tiger Falls, Lookout Rock and Gudu Bush (R15, two hours), Tugela Gorge (R20, six hours) and the Amphitheatre Summit (R35, nine hours).

HORSE RIDING
Just outside the park gates, **Rugged Glen Stables** (☎ 036-438 6422) organises a wide range of horse-riding activities, including two-day trails (R495 per person).

CLIMBING
Some of the peaks and faces were first climbed by mountaineers just over 50 years ago, and the park has become a mecca for climbers. You must apply for a permit from the KZN Wildlife office before you attempt a climb; unless you are experienced, it may not be granted. Take your passport, if you plan to venture into Lesotho.

SLEEPING & EATING
Tendele (☎ 033-845 1000; chalets per person R276) The park's main camp has a variety of accommodation, including some reasonable two-bed chalets – minimum charges apply. It must be booked in advance through KZN Wildlife in Pietermaritzburg (p337) or Durban (p285). You can also camp at **Mahai** (☎ 438 6303; fax 438 6231; camp sites per person R58) inside the park, or in the nearby **Rugged Glen Nature Reserve** (☎ 438 6303; fax 438 6231; camp sites per person R52).

KWAZULU-NATAL

The following places are all outside the park.

Amphitheatre Backpackers (☎ 438 6106; amphi backpackers@worldonline.co.za; camp sites R35, dm/d with shared bathroom R75/160; 🖳) Off the R74, in the heart of the Pocolane Nature Reserve at Oliviershoek Pass (1780m), this relatively spartan place boasts the type of views that can make grown men weep. An in-house Sotho guide conducts tours into the darker corners of Lesotho, and there's also a bar where you can restore aching limbs afterwards.

Hlalanathi (☎ 438 6308; hlalanathi@xsinet.co.za; camp sites per person R50, 2-/4-bed chalets R300/630; 🐾) With a location lifted straight from an African chocolate box, and a clutch of tourism accolades to boot, this pretty resort offers camping or some excellent on a finger of land overlooking the Tugela River.

Tower of Pizza (☎ 036-438 6480; s/d with breakfast R250/340; 🖳) Yep, there really is a tower, and they really do serve (very good) pizza in it. They also offer comfortable rooms and an Internet café. The Tower is right next to Hlalanathi.

The Cavern (☎ 438 6270; www.cavernberg.co.za; s/d with full board R600/800) North of Royal Natal, this award-winning resort offers family-friendly service in lush forest surrounds. There's even babysitting available.

Montusi Mountain Lodge (☎ 438 6243; www.mon tusi.za.net; s/d with half board R850/1300; 🐾 🖳 🐾) With oodles of bush-lodge exclusivity, this opulent place blends a thatch-and-fireplace homeliness with plenty of five-star comforts, including 4WD trails, trout fishing and some very swish chalets. It's en route to The Cavern.

GETTING THERE & AWAY
The road into Royal Natal runs off the R74, about 30km northwest of Bergville and about 5km from Oliviershoek Pass.

Bergville
☎ 036
Small and a little rough around the edges, Bergville is nevertheless a useful jumping-off point for the northern Drakensberg.

The **Okhahlamba Drakensberg Tourism** (☎ 448 1557; www.drakensberg.org.za; Tatham Rd; ⏲ 9am-4.30pm Mon-Fri, 9am-1pm Sat) has an office here. You will also find an **ABSA** (Tatham Rd) bank and ATM.

SLEEPING & EATING
Sanford Park Lodge (☎ 448 1001; sanfordparklodge@ mweb.co.za; s/d with half board R390/660) One of Bergville's swankiest options, the Sanford offers cosy rooms in thatched rondavels or in a creaking, 150-year-old farmhouse. It's a few kilometres out of Bergville, off the road to Ladysmith (the R616).

Drakensberg Inn (☎ 448 2946; brizet@futurenet .co.za; 3 Tatham Rd; s/d with breakfast R200/360) A terrace restaurant, real fires and a comfortable communal lounge all help to spice up this slightly plain, small town inn.

Bergville B&B (☎ 448 1003; bergvillebb@starmail .co.za; 11 Berea Rd; s/d with breakfast R160/320; 🐾) Just behind the main street, this pleasant, thatched place has a decent little bar with a pool table, neatly trimmed gardens and reasonable rooms.

GETTING THERE & AWAY
None of the long-distance bus lines run very close to Bergville. You'll have to get to Ladysmith and take a minibus taxi from there (R14, 45 minutes). A daily Greyhound bus stops at Estcourt and Ladysmith.

The minibus taxi park is behind the tourist office. Taxis run into the Royal Natal National Park area for about R10 but few run all the way to the park entrance.

CENTRAL BERG
Crowned with some of the Drakensberg's most formidable peaks – Giant's Castle Peak (3312m), the Monk's Cowl (3234m) and Champagne Castle (3377m) are found here – the Central Berg is a big hit with climbers. But with dramatic scenery aplenty, this beautiful region is just as popular with those who prefer to admire their mountains from a safe distance.

The area between Cathedral Peak and Giant's Castle comprises two wilderness areas, Mlambonja and Mdedelelo (together some 35,000 hectares). Both are administered by KZN Wildlife. Grey rheboks, klipspringers and mountain reedbucks occur naturally in the area.

Just off Dragon Peaks road is **Drakensberg Boys' Choir School** (☎ 036-468 1012; www.dbchoir.co .za). There are public performances at 3.30pm on Wednesdays during term time. Also not to be missed are the falcon-flying demonstrations and informative talks at **Falcon Ridge** (☎ 082-774 6398; adult/child R20/10; ⏲ talks 10.30am).

Thokozisa (☎ 036-488 1273; thokozisa@futurest co.za), 13km out of Winterton on the R600, is a new arts and crafts village, housing the extremely helpful **Central Drakensberg Information Centre** (☎ 036-488 1207; www.cdic.co.za; ☷ 9am-6pm), which has Internet access, a clutch of crafts shops and a couple of good restaurants.

Cathedral Peak Nature Reserve
☎ 036

In the shadow of the ramparts of Cathedral Peak, **Cathedral Peak Nature Reserve** (☎ 488 3000; www.kznwildlife.com; adult/child R15/10; ☷ 6am-6pm) backs up against a colossal escarpment of peaks between Royal Natal National Park and Giant's Castle, west of Winterton. With the Bell (2930m), the Horns (3005m) and Cleft Peak (3281m) on the horizon, this is a beautifully photogenic park. Cathedral Peak is a long day's climb (10km, seven hours return) but other than being physically fit, no special ability or equipment is required (ask at the park office for trail details).

The **Didima San Art Centre** (☎ 488 1332; adult/child R40/20; ☷ 8am-4pm), 1km into the park, offers an excellent, multimedia insight into San rock art.

The **park office** (☎ 488 8000; www.kznwildlife.com), in Didima Camp (below), sells permits for the scenic drive (4WD only) up Mike's Pass (R35) and arranges guides.

SLEEPING & EATING
Didima Camp (☎ 033-845 1000; www.kznwildlife.com; camp sites per person R42, chalets per person R320; ☒ ☖) One of KZN Wildlife's swankiest offerings, this upmarket, thatched lodge boasts huge views, a restaurant, tennis courts, lashings of elegant style and a range of excellent two- and four-bed self-catering chalets (full-board options are also available on request). Book through KZN Wildlife in Pietermaritzburg (p337) or Durban (p285). Minimum charges do apply.

There is also camping near the main gate.

Winterton
☎ 036

Quaint and sedate, this peaceful little town is the gateway to the central Drakensberg and makes a pleasant, if unspectacular, stopover. **Winterton Museum** (☎ 488 1885; Kerk St; admission by donation; ☷ 9am-3pm Mon-Fri, 9am-noon Sat) offers a wee insight into San rock

art and Drakensberg geology, and doubles as an information office, if you can find anyone in it.

SLEEPING & EATING
Bridge Lodge (☎ 488 1554; thebridge@futurenet.co.za; Main Rd; s/d R160/260) Doubling as the town's favoured nightspot (Friday's the big one), this has a pleasant thatched restaurant and reasonably priced, but slightly dowdy, rooms. Renovations are on the cards.

Lilac Lodge (☎ 488 1025; www.wheretostay.co.za /lilaclodge; Springfield Rd; s/d with breakfast R160/320) Combining B&B comforts with a slither of Bohemian hippy chic, this colourful little place sits in a pleasant garden with a covered bar-terrace.

Thokozisa Champagne Café (☎ 488 1827; Thokozisa; mains R20-60; ☷ lunch & dinner) In the Thokozisa crafts village (p328), this lively little place serves a delicious range of burgers, wraps, pastas and salads in bright and breezy surrounds.

GETTING THERE & AWAY
From here, there are minibus taxis to Cathedral Peak (R10, 40 minutes), Bergville (R8, 30 minutes) and Estcourt (R10, 45 minutes).

Monk's Cowl State Forest
☎ 036

Monk's Cowl (☎ 468 1103; www.kznwildlife.com; adult/child R15/10; ☷ 6am-6pm), another stunning slice of the Drakensberg range, offers superb hiking and rock climbing. Within Monk's Cowl State Forest are the two peaks Monk's Cowl and Champagne Castle.

The **park office** (☎ 468 1103; camp sites per person R52) is 3km beyond Champagne Castle Hotel, which is at the end of the R600 running southwest from Winterton. The office takes bookings for camping and **overnight hiking** (per person R30).

SLEEPING & EATING
As well as camping in the state forest, there are also some other accommodation options in the area.

Inkosana Lodge (☎ 468 1202; www.inkosana.co.za; dm/d with shared bathroom R75/200; ☖) Inkosana is a bit of an institution among backpackers, with a surprisingly fresh, cheery ambience and easy access to some of the country's most beautiful scenery (it offers a free shuttle to many of the trailheads). It's on the R600, en route to Champagne Castle.

Champagne Castle Hotel (☎ 468 1063; www .champagnecastle.co.za; s/d with full board R560/920; ☒) The ever-reliable Champagne Castle is one of the best-known resorts, conveniently located in the mountains at the end of the road to Champagne Castle Peak, off the R600. Staff will collect you (for a small fee) from Estcourt (a Greyhound stop).

Drakensberg Sun (☎ 468 1000; constance@south ernsun.com; f with breakfast R949; ☒) This chain-style place, located just before Champagne Castle Hotel en route to Champagne Castle Peak, quotes for family rooms, meaning that up to two children can stay in the room for free. Standards are predictably high.

Giant's Castle Nature Reserve

Rising up to Injasuti Dome (3409m), South Africa's highest peak, **Giant's Castle Nature Reserve** (☎ 036-353 3718; www.kznwildlife.com; adult/child R20/10; ☒ 6am-6pm) is one of the Drakensberg's loftiest parks – even its lowest point sits at 1300m above sea level. Established in 1903, mainly to protect the eland, it is a rugged, remote and popular destination, with huge forest reserves to the north and south and Lesotho's barren plateau over the escarpment to the west.

Limited supplies (including fuel) are available at Giant's Camp (opposite) and there's a basic shop selling limited provisions.

WILDLIFE

The reserve is mainly grassland, wooded gorges and high basalt cliffs with small forests in the valleys. There's also some protea savanna and, during spring, swathes of wildflowers.

The reserve is home to several species of antelope, with relatively large numbers of elands, mountain reedbucks, grey rheboks and oribis. The rarest antelope is the klipspringer, which is sometimes spotted on the higher slopes. The rarest species is a small short-tailed rodent called the ice rat, which lives in the boulders near the mountain summits. Altogether there are thought to be about 60 mammal species.

The rare lammergeier, or bearded vulture (*Gypaetus barbatus*), which is found only in the Drakensberg, nests in the reserve. Reserve staff put out meat on weekend mornings between May and September to encourage the birds to feed here. The **Lammergeier Hide** (☎ 036-353 3718; fax 353 3775; per person R150) has been built nearby, and is the best place to see the vultures. The hide is extremely popular and you may need to book (preferably by fax) months in advance.

ROCK ART

Giant's Castle Game Reserve is rich in San rock art, with at least 50 sites. It is thought that the last San lived here at the beginning of the 20th century.

The two main sites of paintings are Main Cave and Battle Cave. **Main Cave** (admission R20; ☒ 9am-3pm) is 2km south of Giant's Camp (a 30-minute walk) and must be visited as part of a tour that departs from Giant's Camp every hour, on the hour, during the cave's opening times.

Battle Cave (admission R20; ☒ 24hr) is near Injisuthi and must be visited on a self-guided tour. It's an 8km walk each way; there's a good chance of seeing wildlife en route. The cave's name reflects the paintings here, which record a clash between San groups.

HIKING

Trails begin at Giant's Camp and lead to Meander Hut (5.5km, two hours), on a cliff above the Meander Valley; Giant's Hut (10.5km, four hours), under Giant's Castle itself; and Bannerman's Hut (11km, 4½ hours), close to the escarpment near Bannerman's Pass.

Hikers can stay at **mountain huts** (R30) for which you'll need sleeping bags and cooking utensils. The fee for the huts is a one-off 'hiking fee'. If you're planning to walk between huts rather than return to Giant's Camp, you have to arrange to collect keys. Unless you've booked the entire, you must share it with other hikers.

There are other trails. The booklet *Giant's Castle Day Walks* (R5), available at Giant's Camp gives details and has a basic map of the trails. Before setting out on a long walk you must fill in the rescue register.

Don't confuse trails here with the Giant's Cup Trail (p334), further south in the Drakensberg.

SLEEPING

There are several accommodation centres inside the reserve, as well as trail huts and caves for hikers. Note that hikers are not allowed to light fires, so you'll need to bring a stove. There's a small supermarket near Giant's Camp.

Giant's Camp (☎ 033-845 1000; www.kznwildlife .com; mountain hut/chalets per person R62/206) The main camp has two- and four-bed chalets and a four-bed mountain hut. Book through KZN Wildlife in Pietermaritzburg (p337) or Durban (p285).

Injasuti Hutted Camp (☎ 036-431 7849; camp sites per person R48) This secluded and pleasant spot on the northern side of the reserve has camping sites.

Note that minimum charges do apply.

There are several places outside the reserve, on and around the R600, which runs southwest from Winterton towards Cathkin Peak and Champagne Castle. The following places also dish up decent meals.

Mount Lebanon Park (☎ 033-263 2214; lebanon park@freemail.absa.co.za; dm/d with shared bathroom R90/180) This relaxed farm is on a 500-hectare property on the edge of Giant's Castle Reserve, off Giant's Castle Rd. Phone for directions or a pick-up from Mooi River. The Baz Bus, Greyhound and trains stop at Mooi River.

Drakensberg International Backpackers (☎ 033-263 7241; wildchild@telkomsa.net; 21 Highmoor Rd; dm/d with shared bathroom R65/165, camp sites R40; 🖳) This mellow backpackers offers easy access to the higher peaks. Staff meet the Baz Bus in Mooi River and run a daily shuttle from Durban and Pietermaritzburg (phone ahead).

GETTING THERE & AWAY
Giant's Camp

The roads from both Mooi River and Estcourt are now sealed – do not take the unsealed back roads as they can become unpassable and robberies have been reported.

Infrequent minibus taxis run from Estcourt to villages near the main entrance (KwaDlamini, Mahlutshini and KwaMankonjane) but these are still several kilometres from Giant's Camp.

Minibus taxis also pass near here running between Estcourt and the large village of Malutshini on the Bushman's River, where you turn off for Giant's Camp.

Injasuti

The Injasuti camp is accessible from the township of Loskop, northwest of Estcourt. Turn south 4km west of Loskop or 6km east of the R600; the road is signposted.

SOUTHERN BERG

Best accessed from the pleasant towns of Himeville and Underberg, the Southern Berg boasts one of the region's highlights: the journey up to Lesotho over the Sani Pass. As well as some great walks, including the fabulous Giant's Cup Trail, the region also offers a smorgasbord of state forests and wilderness areas.

Southern Drakensberg Wilderness Areas

Four state forests, Highmoor, Mkhomazi, Cobham and Garden Castle, all run south from Giant's Castle to beyond Bushman's Nek, to meet Lesotho's Sehlabathebe National Park at the top of the escarpment. The big Mkhomazi Wilderness Area and the Mzimkulu Wilderness Area are in the state forests.

The wilderness areas are near the escarpment and to the east are Kamberg, Lotheni, Vergelegen and Mzimkulwana Nature Reserves. A spur of Mzimkulwana follows the Mkhomazana River (and the road) down from the Sani Pass, separating the two wilderness areas.

These areas are administered by KZN Wildlife. Overnight-hiking permits cost R30.

COBHAM STATE FOREST

The Mzimkulu Wilderness Area and the Mzimkulwana Nature Reserve are in **Cobham State Forest** (☎ 033-702 0831; www.kznwildlife .com; adult/child R15/10; ☾ 6am-6pm). The park office is about 15km from Himeville on the D7; it's a good place to get information on the many hiking trails in the area, some with trail huts (R60 per person). Basic camp sites (R34 per person) are available.

GARDEN CASTLE STATE FOREST

The park office of **Garden Castle** (☎ 033-701 1823; www.kznwildlife.com; adult/child R15/10, camp sites per person R34, huts per person R60; ☾ 6am-6pm) is 30km west of Underberg – carry along the road past Khotso Horse Trails and Pennygum (p332).

You can hike to the top of the nearby escarpment and back in about eight hours, if you're physically fit.

There are trail huts on some of the walks and a limited number of camp sites are available.

KWAZULU-NATAL

HIGHMOOR STATE FOREST

Part of the Mkhomazi Wilderness Area falls within the boundaries of **Highmoor** (☎ 033-263 7240; www.kznwildlife.com; adult/child per person R40; ◷ 6am-6pm). The park office is off the road from Rosetta to Giant's Castle and Kamberg. Turn off to the south just past the sign to Kamberg, 31km from Rosetta.

Camp sites are available.

KAMBERG NATURE RESERVE

Southeast of Giant's Castle and a little away from the main escarpment area, **Kamberg Nature Reserve** (☎ 033-267 7251; www.kznwildlife.com; adult/child R15/10, 2-bed huts R297; ◷ 6am-6pm) has a number of antelope species and guided rock-art walks on a Sunday.

The cheapest accommodation is in two-bed rest huts.

You can get there from Rosetta, off the N3 south of Mooi River, travelling via either Nottingham Road or Redcliffe.

LOTHENI NATURE RESERVE

Lotheni (☎ 033-702 0540; www.kznwildlife.com; adult/child R15/10; ◷ 6am-6pm) has a Settlers' Museum and some very good days walks.

KZN Wildlife (☎ 033-845 1000; camp sites R48, 3-bed chalets per person R164) offers camping and chalets.

The access road runs from the hamlet of Lower Lotheni, about 30km northeast of Himeville or 65km southwest of Nottingham Road (off Mooi River). The roads aren't great and heavy rain can close them. They are, however, some of the most scenic in South Africa, with the Drakensberg as a backdrop and many picturesque Zulu villages in the area.

MKHOMAZI STATE FOREST

Forming the southern part of the Mkhomazi Wilderness Area, **Mkhomazi State Forest** (☎ 033-263 6444; www.kznwildlife.com; adult/child R15/10; ◷ 6am-6pm) includes the 1200-hectare **Vergelegen Nature Reserve** (☎ 033-702 0712; www.kznwildlife.com; adult/child R15/10; ◷ 6am-6pm). There are no established camp sites in the area, but you can camp on hikes (R30). The turn-off to the state forest is 44km from Nottingham Road, off the Lower Lotheni to Sani Pass road, at the Mzinga River. From there the state forest is another 2km.

Underberg

☎ 033 / pop 1500

Clustered in the foothills of the southern Drakensberg, this small farming town fills up in summer, when Durbanites head to the peaks for a breath of the fresh stuff. Himeville, just down the road, is a quieter, more-pleasant place to stay.

INFORMATION

The **Southern Drakensberg Sani Saunter Information Office** (☎ 701 1471; www.sanisaunter.com; Clocktower Centre, Old Main Rd; ◷ 9am-4.30pm Mon-Fri, 9am-1pm Sat & Sun) publishes an excellent Sani Saunter map and booklet (free) listing dozens of hotels, hostels, restaurants and tour guides.

In the same shopping complex, you will also find **White Cottage Books** (☎ 701 2059; ◷ 9am-5pm Mon-Fri, 9am-2pm Sat & Sun), which sells a wide range of local maps; and **Sani Pass Tours** (☎ 701 1064; www.sanipasstours.com; day tours per person R240; ◷ 9am-5pm Mon-Fri, 9am-2pm Sat & Sun), which offers day tours up the Sani Pass, as well as packages tailored to more specialist interests. It also takes bookings for the Sani Top Chalet (p531).

You can access the Internet at **NUD Entertainment** (☎ 701 1317; Old Main Rd; ◷ 10am-6pm), further down the road, next to Spar. A **First National Bank** (Old Main Rd) and ATM is nearby.

SIGHTS & ACTIVITIES

Khotso Horse Trails (☎ 701 1502; www.khotsotrails.co.za) offers rides and treks in the area. It's about 7km northwest of Underberg. Nearby, **Pennygum** (☎ 701 1023) rents out rafts for (relatively) gentle, river drifting (R90 per person).

The **Splashy Fen Festival**, held in April, is a long-running music festival featuring gentle alternative styles. It's held 20km from Underberg, on the road to Drakensberg Gardens.

SLEEPING & EATING

Underberg Inn (☎ 701 1412; Old Main Rd; dm/s/d with breakfast R70/190/320) Old-world-meets-spit-and-sawdust, Underberg's eponymous inn has seen better days, but the bar's good for a tipple and the rooms are fine after a nightcap.

Valemount Country Lodge (☎ 701 1686; www.valemountafrica.com; s/d with breakfast R385/680) This cosy, thatched farmhouse B&B oozes graceful charm, with roaring fires in winter and

48 hectares of grounds to explore when things heat up again. It's 8km from Underberg on the Kokstad road.

Polo (☎ 033-701 1675; R617; mains R40-70; ☺ lunch & dinner; ☷) Decorated with polo memorabilia and with a terrace for knocking down the post-tournament bubbly, this excellent little bistro whips up a fabulous selection of grills and an ever-changing array of specials. It's 500m out of town, on the road to Bulwer (R617).

GETTING THERE & AWAY

Sani Pass Carriers (☎ 701 1017; sanipasscarriers@wandata.com) runs minibuses to Underberg from Kokstad (R80, two hours), Pietermaritzburg (R85, two hours) and Durban (R130, three hours). Return fares are slightly cheaper than buying two one-way tickets. Call ahead to book.

Minibus taxis run to Himeville (R3, 10 minutes) and Pietermaritzburg (R25, 1½ hours) and you might find one running to the Sani Pass Hotel (p531).

Himeville
☎ 033

A skip and a jump from Underberg, Himeville is a prettier, more-sedate jumping-off point for the southern Drakensberg.

The **Himeville Museum** (☎ 702 1184; admission by donation; ☺ 9am-12.30pm) is a highlight. Housed in the last laager built in South Africa (c 1896), which was also the first building in Himeville, the museum now contains an incredible array of bric-a-brac, from the Union Jack flown at the siege of Ladysmith to a map of El Alamein signed by Montgomery. The curator will give you a guided tour.

KZN Wildlife's **Himeville Nature Reserve** (☎ 702 1036; www.kznwildlife.com; admission R10; ☺ 6am-6pm), on the northeastern side of town, is popular for trout fishing (permits R50) and there are a few antelopes around.

SLEEPING & EATING

KZN Wildlife Accommodation (☎ 033-845 1000; www.kznwildlife.com; camp sites R44) The camp site is in the Himeville Nature Reserve, not far from town.

Himeville Arms (☎ 702 1305; www.himevillehotel.co.za; Main Rd; d with/without bathroom R420/150) Seemingly beamed here from the midst of quaint Middle England, this homey inn has a cosy bar, comfy rooms and lashings of rustic, village-green atmosphere.

Rosewood Cottage (☎ 702 1290; Main Rd; s/d with breakfast R190/350) All blooming roses and chocolate-box décor, this idyllic thatched cottage has great views of the Sani Pass, a delightful garden and a brace of attractive rooms. It's about 300m further down the main road from the Himeville Arms.

See p334 for information on a couple of hostels near Himeville, on the road to Sani Pass.

GETTING THERE & AWAY

About the only regular transport from Himeville are minibus taxis to Underberg (R3, 10 minutes).

See Sani Pass (below) for details on transport into Lesotho.

The road from Himeville to Nottingham Road is well worth driving. The distance between the two towns is 92km, with 60km on a dirt road that winds through some spectacular country. The section between Himeville and Lower Lotheni is well gravelled. The section between Lower Lotheni and the sealed road that runs to Nottingham Road has at least one hill that could give 2WD vehicles problems after heavy rain.

Sani Pass
☎ 033

The drive up the Sani Pass is a trip to the roof of South Africa: a winding, bone-breaking ride through the clouds to the kingdom of Lesotho. At 2865m, this is the highest pass in the country and the vistas are magical, offering stunning views out across the Umkhomazana River to the north and looming cliffs, almost directly above, to the south. There are hikes in almost every direction and inexpensive horse rides are available. Amazingly, this is also the only road link between Lesotho and KwaZulu-Natal.

At the top of the pass, just beyond the Lesotho border crossing, is the **Sani Top Chalet** (p531). Various operators run 4WD trips up to the chalet (see opposite).

Daily minibus taxis bring people from Mokhotlong (Lesotho, R50 between Mokhotlong and Underberg) to South Africa for shopping; if there's a spare seat going back, this would be the cheapest option, and you would get to a town, not just the isolated lodge at the top of the pass. Ask around in

Himeville or at Blue Baboon Backpackers (below). You need a passport to cross into Lesotho. The border is open daily from 8am to 4pm on the South African side (until 5pm on the Lesotho side).

SLEEPING

The following places are all at the bottom of the pass.

Sani Lodge (☎ 702 0330; www.sani-lodge.co.za; dm/d with shared bathroom R60/15, camp sites R40; ☐) Owned by the author of *A Backpacker's Guide to Lesotho*, Sani Lodge tops the pops in the local-knowledge stakes, offering a range of fabulous tours and more insider tips than you'll be able to digest at this altitude. And if you've already had enough of Lesotho, there's always the bar with panoramic views and cheap drinks. It's about 10km from Himeville on the Sani Pass road.

Blue Baboon Backpackers (☎ 702 0340; dm/d with shared bathroom R45/150; ☐) Boasting 100 acres of back garden (every one of them beautiful) and claiming to house the last pub before Lesotho (we couldn't find another), the Blue Baboon offers a menagerie of free-roaming animals, plenty of activities and tip-top tucker. It's 5km further along the Sani Pass road from the Sani Pass Hotel.

Sani Pass Hotel (☎ 702 1320; www.sanipasshotel .co.za; r with half board R750) This decent three-star hotel, complete with guards and razor-wire fence, is on the Sani Pass road, 14km from Himeville.

Giant's Cup Trail

If you are planning to stretch your legs anywhere in South Africa, this is the place to do it. Without doubt, the Giant's Cup Trail (68km, five days), running from Sani Pass to Bushman's Nek, is one of the nation's great walks. Any reasonably fit person can walk it, so it's very popular. Early booking (up to nine months ahead, through KZN Wildlife in Pietermaritzburg) is advisable. Although the walking is relatively easy, the usual precautions for the Drakensberg apply – expect severe cold snaps at any time of the year.

The stages are: day one, 14km; day two, 9km; day three, 12km; day four, 13km; and day five, 12km. Highlights include the **Bathplug Cave** with San rock paintings, beautiful

Crane Tarn and breathtaking mountain scenery on day four.

Camping is not permitted on this trail, so accommodation is in limited shared huts (R60 per person) – thus the need to book ahead. No firewood is available so you'll need a stove and fuel. Sani Lodge (opposite) is almost at the head of the trail; arrange for the lodge to pick you up from Himeville or Underberg.

Bushman's Nek

☎ 033

This is a South Africa–Lesotho border post. From here there are hiking trails up into the escarpment, including to Lesotho's Sehlabathebe National Park. You can walk in or hire a horse for about R50. How often do you get to enter a country on horseback? You can't drive in.

Accommodation options include the **Bushman's Nek Hotel** (☎ 701 1460; r with half board R300), about 20km east of the border post, and the **Silverstreams Caravan Park** (☎ 701 1249; www.silverstreams.co.za; camp sites per person R70), which has camping right next to the border.

EAST GRIQUALAND

Historically, the Voortrekkers had been moving into the Griqua territory between the Vaal and Orange Rivers, around Philippolis, since the 1820s. The Griqua chief, Adam Kok III, realising that there would soon be no land left, encouraged his people to sell off their remaining titles and move elsewhere.

In 1861, Kok's entire community of 2000, along with about 20,000 cattle, began their epic, two-year journey over the rugged mountains of Lesotho to Nomansland, a region on the far side of the Drakensberg. When they reached the southern slopes of Mt Currie, they set up camp. Later, in 1869, they moved to the present site of Kokstad. Nomansland was called East Griqualand after it was annexed by the Cape in 1874. Kok died the following year when he was thrown from his cart.

Kokstad

☎ 039 / pop 25,100

Kokstad is named in honour of Adam Kok III. It lies 1280m above sea level in the Umzimhlava River valley, between Mt

Currie and the Ngele Mountains. Today it's a bustling little place with some solid buildings and excellent transport connections.

The **Kokstad Municipality** (☎ 727 3133; fax 727 3676; 75 Hope St; ☺ 8.30am-4.30pm Mon-Fri, 8.30am-noon Sat) has information on the area.

The pleasant **East Griqualand Museum** (Main St; adult/child R5/2; ☺ 9am-4pm Mon-Fri, 9am-noon Sat) has some interesting information on the history of the Griquas, as well as the usual small-town relics.

SLEEPING

Mount Currie Inn (☎ 727 2178; fax 727 2196; s/d R353/461) This hotel, on the outskirts of town on the main road leading to the N2, is without doubt the best place to stay in Kokstad. There's a petrol station and a Wimpy fast-food outlet at the front, which doesn't bode well, but it's actually a very nice hotel with a pleasant bar and the good Tipsy Trout restaurant.

The municipal **caravan park** (☎ 727 3133; camp sites per person R25), next to the sports ground near the town centre, is a last resort.

GETTING THERE & AWAY

Sure Travel (☎ 727 3124; Hope St; ☺ 8am-4.30pm Mon-Fri, 8-11am Sat) is the agent for Translux buses, which stop at Wimpy, a little way out of town on the Durban–Umtata road, and run daily to destinations including Durban (R130, four hours) and Port Elizabeth (R270, 11 hours).

The minibus-taxi park is between Hope and Main Sts, and regular taxis or buses go to Pietermaritzburg (R45, 4½ hours) and Durban (R45, 4½ hours).

Around Kokstad

A few kilometres north of Kokstad, off the R626 to Franklin, is KZN Wildlife's **Mount Currie Nature Reserve** (☎ 039-727 3844; www.kznwildlife.com; admission Mon-Fri R6, Sat & Sun R9; ☺ 6am-6pm). There are walking trails and several antelope species in this grassy, 1800-hectare reserve. A memorial marks the site of Adam Kok's first laager. You can camp (R34 per person) or stay in a two-bed squaredavel (R100 per person) – book direct.

There is an isolated chunk of Eastern Cape, northeast of Kokstad, called Umzimkulu (also the name of the main town, see p170). The R56 through this area makes for an interesting drive.

THE MIDLANDS

The Midlands run northwest from Durban to Estcourt, skirting Zululand to the northeast. This is mainly farming country with little to interest visitors. The main town is Pietermaritzburg – KwaZulu-Natal's joint capital along with Ulundi.

West of Pietermaritzburg is picturesque, hilly country, with horse studs and plenty of European trees. This area was settled mainly by English farmers and looks a little like England's West Country, with craft centres, galleries and tearooms taking centre stage.

The excellent *Midlands Meander* brochure (www.midlandsmeander.co.za), available from one of the larger tourist offices, has maps and exhaustive listings for the area.

PIETERMARITZBURG

☎ 033 / pop 457,000

Billed as the heritage city, Pietermaritzburg takes a step away from the metropolitan South Africa of busy streets and suburban shopping malls. Its grand historic buildings hark back to an age of pith helmets and midday martinis, while its large Indian community brings echoes of the subcontinent. Pietermaritzburg has its own, unique brand of workaday chaos, but after the bump-and-grind of downtown Durban, KwaZulu-Natal's joint capital (the other is Ulundi) is an altogether leafier and more sedate place.

History

After defeating the Zulu at the decisive Battle of Blood River (p348), the Voortrekkers began to establish their republic of Natal. Pietermaritzburg (usually known as PMB) was named in honour of leader Pieter Mauritz Retief, and was founded in 1838 as the capital (later the 'u' was dropped and, in 1938, it was decreed that Voortrekker leader Gert Maritz be remembered in the title). In 1841 the Boers built their Church of the Vow here to honour the Blood River promise. The British annexed Natal in 1843 but they retained Pietermaritzburg – well positioned and less humid than Durban, and already a neat little town – as the capital.

Orientation

The central grid of Pietermaritzburg contains most places of interest to travellers

PIETERMARITZBURG

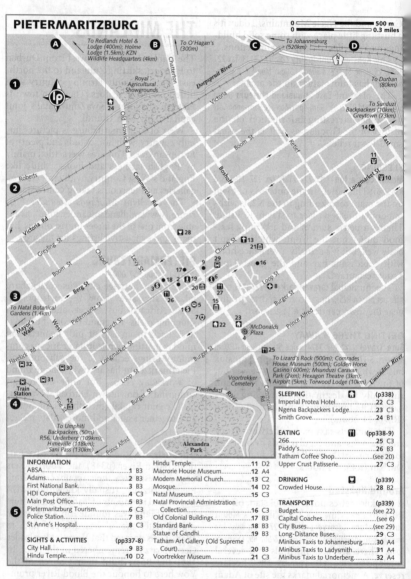

0 — 500 m
0 — 0.3 miles

and is easy to get around. However, as is becoming common in South Africa, White-run businesses are continuing to flee the city centre. Southeast of the centre is the University of Natal.

The northern end of the city, beyond Retief St, is a largely Indian commercial district. It shuts down at night and is the

most-unsafe part of the city centre. North of here is the Indian residential area of Northdale (with suburbs such as Bombay Heights and Mysore Ridge). To the southwest of the city is Edendale, the Black dormitory suburb. To the northwest, on the Old Howick Rd, beyond Queen Elizabeth Park, is the village of Hilton, a leafy and slightly twee residential area. Hilton is only about 10km from Pietermaritzburg but it's a long way up. If it's rainy in Pietermaritzburg, then Hilton will probably be in the clouds.

Information

BOOKSHOPS
Adams (☎ 394 6830; 230 Church St; ☺ 8.30am-4.30pm Mon-Fri) Has a wide selection of books and maps.

EMERGENCY
Police Station (☎ 342 2211; Loop St)

INTERNET ACCESS
HDI Computers (☎ 345 1133; sales@hdi.co.za; Mc-Donald's Plaza, cnr Commercial Rd & Burger St; per hr R32; ☺ 8am-5pm Mon-Fri, 8am-12.30pm Sat)

MEDICAL SERVICES
St Anne's Hospital (☎ 897 5000; Loop St)

MONEY
There are several banks across town:
ABSA (Longmarket St) Next to the post office, ABSA has an ATM and change facilities.
First National Bank (Church St)

POST
Main post office (Longmarket St)

TOURIST INFORMATION
KZN Wildlife Headquarters (☎ 845 1000; www.kzn wildlife.com; Queen Elizabeth Park, Duncan McKenzie Dr; ☺ 8am-5pm Mon-Fri, 8am-noon Sat) provides information and accommodation bookings for all KZN Wildlife parks and reserves. To get to the office, head out to the Old Howick Rd (Commercial Rd) and after some kilometres you'll come to a roundabout – don't go straight ahead (to Hilton) but take the road veering to the right. This road has a very small sign directing you to 'QE Park', which is 2km further on. Some minibus taxis running to Hilton pass this roundabout.
Pietermaritzburg Tourism (☎ 345 1348; admin@ pmbtourism.org.za; 117 Commercial Rd; ☺ 8am-5pm Mon-Fri, 8am-1pm Sat) is a useful first stop for information on the city.

Sights & Activities

In keeping with Pietermaritzburg's self-styled role as the 'heritage city', one of its finest sights is the **Tatham Art Gallery** (☎ 342 1804; fax 394 9831; Commercial Rd; admission free; ☺ 10am-6pm Tue-Sun), which was started in 1903 by Mrs Ada Tatham. Housed in the beautiful Old Supreme Court, it contains a fine collection of French and English 19th- and early 20th-century works. Every 15 minutes, little figurines appear out of the building's Ormulu clock to chime the bells. The nearby, colonial-era **City Hall** (cnr Church St & Commercial Rd) is the largest all-redbrick building in the southern hemisphere.

The artworks in the **Natal Provincial Administration Collection** (☎ 345 3201; 330 Longmarket St; ☺ by appointment only), which include some of the finest examples of indigenous art, are also worth an hour or so.

At the **Macrorie House Museum** (☎ 394 2161; 11 Loop St; adult/child R5/2; ☺ 11am-4pm Mon, 9am-1pm Tue-Fri) are displays of items related to early British settlement. For another view, visit the **Voortrekker Museum** (☎ 394 6834; cnr Longmarket & Boshoff Sts; adult/child R5/2; ☺ 9am-4pm Mon-Fri, 9am-1pm Sat), near the city hall. The museum is in the Church of the Vow, built in 1841 to fulfil the Voortrekkers' part of the Blood River bargain. Afrikaner icons on display include Retief's prayer book and water bottle, and a replica of a trek wagon. The words of the Vow are in the **Modern Memorial Church** next door.

The **Natal Museum** (☎ 345 1404; 237 Loop St; adult/child R4/1; ☺ 9am-4pm Mon-Fri, 2-5pm Sat), covered in giant (model) creepy-crawlies, has a range of displays, including African ethnography.

The **Comrades House Museum** (☎ 897 8650; Connaught Rd; admission free; ☺ 8.30am-1pm Mon-Fri) is packed with memorabilia from the Comrades Marathon (p338). Connaught Rd is off Durban Rd, an extension of Commercial Rd.

Natal Botanical Gardens (☎ 344 3585; Swartskop St; adult/child R7/3; ☺ 8am-6pm), 2km west of the train station on the continuation of Berg St, has exotic species and a garden of indigenous mist-belt flora.

Back in the centre, there are two **Hindu temples** at the northern end of Longmarket St. The main **mosque** is nearby, on East St. A **statue of Gandhi**, who was famously ejected from a first-class carriage at Pietermaritzburg station, also stands defiant opposite the old colonial buildings on Church St.

Architect Phillip Dudgeon modelled the **Standard Bank** (Church St Mall), on the Bank of Ireland in Belfast. Rather less highbrow is **Peggy the Pegasus**, which stands 14m tall and qualifies for the spurious accolade of being

KWAZULU-NATAL

the largest horse statue in the world. It is at the entrance to the **Golden Horse Casino** (☎ 395 8136; 45 New England Rd).

Tours

Pietermaritzburg Tourism (p337) organises city walking (R80 per person) and driving (R150 per person) tours.

Festivals & Events

The **Comrades Marathon** (☎ 897 8650; www.comrades.com), staged in late May or early June, is the most famous athletics event in South Africa. Conceived in 1921 to honour comrades who fought in WWI, the event sees runners from around the world complete the 89km slog between Pietermaritzburg and Durban.

Sleeping

BUDGET

Umphiti Backpackers (☎ 394 3490; umphiti@mweb .co.za; 317 Bulwer St; dm/tw with shared bathroom R70/160, d R200) A Bohemian backpacker vibe, mixed up with some Victorian architectural grandeur, conspire to make this place the city's best bet for the budget traveller. Specialising in adventure sports, it's also a great place to get active.

Ngena Backpackers Lodge (☎ 345 6237; ngena@ sai.co.za; 293 Burger St; dm/d R70/200) It's central, semi-fortified (for the paranoid) and clean, but this convenient place lacks atmosphere and they won't take South African travellers.

Sunduzi Backpackers (☎ 390 1023, 083-435 2805; Bishopstowe) Once in the centre, this decent cheapie has recently moved to a new location, out in the sticks, in Bishopstowe. It isn't all that convenient for Pietermaritzburg, but standards are good and staff will pick you up (probably the only way you'll find it).

Msunduzi Caravan Park (☎ 386 5342; fax 346 2662; 50 Cleland Rd; camp sites per person R50) This camping spot is nearly 5km from the train station. Head southeast on Commercial Rd, which becomes Durban Rd after you cross the creek. Go left onto Blackburn Rd across the freeway, then take the first road to the right.

MID-RANGE & TOP END

There are many B&Bs in the area; Pietermaritzburg Tourism can help with bookings.

Redlands Hotel & Lodge (☎ 394 3333; www .guestnet.co.za; cnr Howick Rd & George McFarlane Lane; s/d R495/615; ☒ ☒) Swish and stately, this elegant place offers grand, colonial-style surrounds and personal service. The spacious grounds add to the escape-from-it-all ambience. It's north of the centre on Old Howick Rd, past the Royal Agricultural Showgrounds.

Torwood Lodge (☎ 033-390 1072; www.torwood .co.za; tw R350; ☒) With a quaint rural setting and lungfuls of fresh air, this excellent out-of-town option is great for those seeking city days and rustic nights. It's 10km out of town (see the website for directions), but there are pick-ups from the centre.

Holme Lodge (☎ 347 3808; www.pietermaritzburg.co .za/holmelodge; 18 Clifton Rd; s/d with breakfast R240/360; ☒) With just a couple of rooms, this cosy B&B, about 3km north of the centre, retains a welcoming, family feel. There's a pool to lounge around on those balmy summer afternoons and a braai to fire up afterwards.

Smith Grove (☎ 345 3963, 082-691 4161; 37 Old Howick Rd; s/d R175/310) This basic B&B offers no-fuss home comforts and nicely decorated, individually styled rooms.

Imperial Protea Hotel (☎ 342 6551; imperial@ iafrica.com; 224 Loop St; s/d with breakfast R705/790; ☒) With more history than most, this was the spot the French Prince Imperial rode out from prior to coming to a sticky end during the 1879 Anglo-Zulu War. A few of the old fixtures and fittings survive and the rooms are good value if you catch a special (as low as R549).

Eating

266 (☎ 345 5084; 266 Prince Alfred; mains R30-90; ☺ lunch & dinner; ☒) Arguably Pietermaritzburg's best eatery, this atmospheric place slides neatly into the 'heritage city' theme, with a breezy terrace for pink gins out front and a formal restaurant area serving excellent seafood, pasta and grills inside. The zebra-print tablecloths really have to go though.

Tatham Coffee Shop (☎ 342 8327; Commercial Rd; lunch R10-35; ☺ breakfast & lunch) Upstairs at the Tatham Gallery, this arty little café whips up a range of fresh, healthy fare. At lunchtime, it fills up with the local business set, who clamour for a table on the balcony. It is open during gallery hours.

O'Hagan's (☎ 342 9658; Chatterton Rd; mains R20-60; ☺ lunch & dinner; ☒) Soak up the *craic* at this recently assembled, Irish kit pub. There's a typically Celtic bar buzz and a decent menu featuring all the usual Emerald Isle favourites.

KWAZULU-NATAL

Upper Crust Patisserie (☎ 342 7625; 272 Longmarket St; sandwiches R10-25; ☾ breakfast & lunch) This upmarket snack shop serves gourmet sandwiches out of a lovely old colonial building.

Other recommendations:

Lizard's Rock (☎ 345 7745; Durban Rd; mains R25-50; ☾ lunch & dinner; ☷) A funky restaurant southeast of the centre.

Paddy's (☎ 345 4835; 22 Timber St; mains R10-30; ☾ breakfast, lunch & dinner) Greasy spoon meets Tudor tearoom serving some very cheap eats.

Entertainment

Crowded House (☎ 345 5977; 99 Commercial Rd; ☾ 8pm-4am Tue-Sat) Late night boozers head here, where 'Pigs Night' means you can down as many drinks as you can stomach in two hours for only R25.

There are several theatres including the **Hexagon** (☎ 260 5537; Golf Rd), which is part of Natal University. It's about 3km south of the centre, off Durban Rd. For all entertainment bookings, call **Computicket** (☎ 083-915 8000).

Getting There & Away

AIR

SAAirlink (☎ 031-250 1111), with an office at the airport, flies to Jo'burg daily (R658).

BUS

Capital Coaches (☎ 342 3026; capitalcoach@sai.co.za; 117 Commercial Rd; ☾ 8.30am-4.15pm Mon-Fri, 8am-12.30pm Sat), in the same building as Pietermaritzburg Tourism, is the local agent for all the major coach companies including Greyhound, Translux, City to City, Intercape, Luxliner and Eldo. Prices are similar across the board, although City to City fares tend to be about a third lower than those quoted here. Destinations offered by the listed companies from Pietermaritzburg include: Jo'burg (R195, seven hours); Pretoria (R195, eight hours); Cape Town (R470, 22 hours); Port Elizabeth (R310, 15 hours); Durban (R40, one hour) and Lusaka (R630, 31 hours).

Cheetah Coaches (☎ 342 0266) runs daily between Durban, Pietermaritzburg and Durban International Airport. The fare to Durban is R40.

Sani Pass Carriers (☎ 701 1017; sanipasscarriers@ wandata.com) runs buses up into southern Drakensberg. See p333 for more details.

CAR

Most of the major car rental companies have agents here. **Budget** (☎ 342 8433; ☾ 8am-5pm Mon-Fri, 8am-noon Sat) is based in the Imperial Protea Hotel (opposite).

HITCHING

Lonely Planet does not recommend hitching. However, if you are hitching on the N3, get off at Exit 81 (Church St) for the city centre, Exit 76 (northbound) or Exit 74 (southbound) for the municipal caravan park.

MINIBUS TAXI

Minibus taxis generally congregate near the train station. Destinations from Pietermaritzburg include: Durban (R20, one hour), Estcourt (R25, 1¾ hours), Ladysmith (R30, 2½ hours), Underberg (R30, 2½ hours), Newcastle (R40, four hours) and Jo'burg (R90, eight hours). Other taxis depart from Market Sq (behind Pietermaritzburg Tourism).

TRAIN

Pietermaritzburg is serviced by the *Trans Natal*, which runs daily (except Tuesday and Saturday) to Jo'burg (1st/2nd class R185/125, 10 hours) and Durban (R45/30, two hours); and the *Trans Oranje*, which heads to Cape Town (1st/2nd class R530/360, 36 hours) on Wednesday, returning on a Monday. There is a **train information line** (☎ 0860 008 888).

Getting Around

The main rank for city-area buses is on the road running behind Pietermaritzburg Tourism.

For a taxi, phone **Yellow Cabs/Metro Taxis** (☎ 397 1910).

AROUND PIETERMARITZBURG
Howick & Around
☎ 033

In the town of Howick, about 25km northwest of Pietermaritzburg on the N3, are the popular **Howick Falls**, which you can abseil down – call **Over The Top Adventures** (☎ 082-736 3651). Just before the falls there is the small **Howick Museum** (admission free; ☾ 9am-noon & 2-3.30pm Tue-Fri, 10am-3pm Sat), an unabashedly parochial celebration of the town.

Umgeni Valley Nature Reserve (☎ 330 3931; www.wildlifesociety.org.za/umgeni.htm; 1 Karkloof Rd; admission R10; ☾ 8am-4.30pm) is nearby, with

---

END OF FREEDOM

One of the most significant events in South Africa's apartheid history occurred in the KwaZulu-Natal Midlands.

In August 1962 it was just outside Howick that Nelson Mandela's days of freedom ended and his lengthy incarceration began.

Mandela, disguised as a chauffer, had been driving to Johannesburg along the Old Howick Rd with Umkhonto we Sizwe (Spear of the Nation, MK) member Cecil Williams, when their car was stopped by police.

The actual spot of his arrest on the R103 is now marked by a memorial, which Mandela unveiled himself in 1996.

---

giraffes, zebras antelopes and six walking trails. Around 260 bird species have been recorded here.

Midmar Nature Reserve (☎ 330 2067; www .kznwildlife.com; admission R10; ☒ 6am-6pm) is 7km from Howick off the Greytown Rd. Although there are some animals in the reserve, it is mainly a recreation area, and has water sports on the dam.

In Karkloof, 14km north of Howick, **Karkloof Canopy Tours** (☎ 033-330 3415; www.kark loofcanopytour.co.za; groups up to six R395; ☒ 8am-3pm) conduct three-hour tours through the canopy of Karkloof forest. Do not attempt this if you have vertigo; book ahead.

SLEEPING
Midmar Nature Reserve (☎ 845 1000; www.kznwild life.com; Munro Bay; camp sites R46, chalet R162) You can camp or take a two-bed chalet at Munro Bay in the reserve.

Windermere Guest House (☎ 330 8284; winder meregh@yebo.co.za; 11 Windermere Pl; s/d with breakfast R225/450; ☒) Not far from the waterfall, this olde-worlde place has log fires for winter and a pool for summer. The rooms are beautifully furnished and the pace is sedate.

Albert Falls Resources Reserve
This **reserve** (☎ 033-569 1202; fax 033-569 1371; admission R10; ☒ 6am-6pm) is 25km from Pietermaritzburg, off the road north to Greytown. **Camp sites** (per person R40) are available. Note that there have been outbreaks of bilharzia associated with the dam.

Ecabazini Zulu Cultural Homestead (☎ 342 1928; r with half board per person R150) Ecabazini has

accommodation in traditional huts. There are traditional meals and cultural displays, but you'll need your own linen and towel. Visits are by prior arrangement only. Book through a backpacker agency such as Tekweni Eco-Tours (p291) in Durban.

MOOI RIVER
☎ 033 / pop 10,000

Mooi River is a nondescript town but the early Voortrekkers probably had high hopes for it, as *mooi* means 'beautiful'. The Zulu were more matter of fact, calling it Mpofana, 'Place of the Eland'. The surrounding countryside, especially to the west, is worth exploring. It's horse-stud country on rolling hills dotted with old European trees.

Mooi River is closer to Giant's Castle than Estcourt and, while there are fewer minibus taxis, the town is right on the N3 so hitching to and from here may be easier.

Gleneagles Guest House (☎ 263 2883; www.glen eagles.co.za; Claughton Tce; s/d with breakfast R220/400) Just off the Giant's Castle Rd, this restored manor offers traditionally styled rooms and bags of home comforts.

Riverbank Caravan Park (☎ /fax 263 2144; Greytown Rd; camp sites R35, r R170) This reasonable caravan park also has two-bed chalets.

There are some excellent country guesthouses in the surrounding area – for details, see Nottingham Road & Around (below).

Getting There & Away
Greyhound buses running between Durban (R50, 1½ hours) and Jo'burg/Pretoria (R185, 7½ hours) stop at the Wimpy, at the big truck stop on the Rosetta road near the N3, 1km from the centre.

The *Trans Oranje* and *Trans Natal* trains stop here. Book tickets at the goods office, across the tracks from the old station.

Minibus taxis aren't frequent and run mainly to nearby villages.

NOTTINGHAM ROAD & AROUND
☎ 033

The quaint little town of Nottingham Road was so-named to honour the Nottinghamshire Regiment of the British Army, which was garrisoned here. After the Cape Winelands, this is probably the most gentrified rural area in the country; there are some excellent guesthouses, and most have extensive gardens.

Quaint with a capital 'Q' is **Thatchings** (☎ 266 6275; www.thatchings.co.za; Curry's Post Rd; s/d with breakfast R250/500). This thatched place boasts 135 acres of fairy-tale garden, three stocked trout ponds and trimmings galore – right down to the goose-down duvets.

Granny Mouse Country House (☎ 234 4071; www.grannymouse.co.za; Old Main Rd; s/d with breakfast R400/800), near the village of Balgowan, south of Mooi River, is one of the better-known accommodation options. It's off the R103, a scenic road running parallel to the N3 between Howick and Mooi River. It also offers mid-week specials.

Hartford House (☎ 263 2713; www.hartford.co.za; s/d with breakfast from R440/880; 🖃 🖳), which was the home of a former Natal prime minister,

is one of the country's top luxury lodges, with rooms starting at the listed prices and going up as high as your credit rating will take you.

BATTLEFIELDS

Big game, big mountains and big waves may top the agenda for many visitors to the province, but the history of KwaZulu-Natal is intrinsically linked to its battlefields and it was the stage on which many of the country's bloodiest chapters were played out. KwaZulu-Natal is where the British Empire was crushed by a Zulu army at Isandlwana, where they subsequently staged the heroic

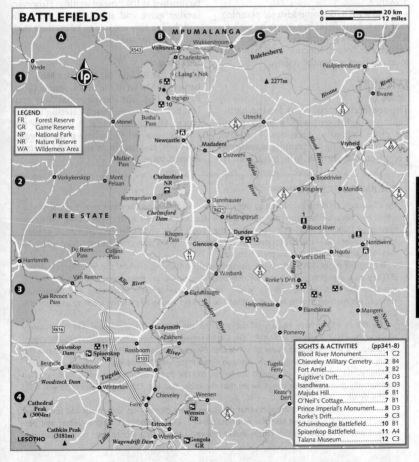

defence of Rorke's Drift, where the Boers and the Brits slogged it out at Ladysmith and Spioenkop, and where less than 600 Voortrekkers avenged the murder of their leader Piet Retief by defeating a force of 12,000 Zulus at Blood River.

Roughly following the N11 and R33 roads and occupying an area that stretches north from Estcourt to the Free State and Mpumalanga borders, the Battlefields can be a headache to get to without a car. Without a guide, you may also be left feeling like you are traipsing through a string of empty fields. Take a tour, however, or do some swatting up before you go and the so-called Battlefields Route can be one of the most rewarding experiences in the province.

If you want to do some advance planning, visit www.battlefields.kzn.org.za or pick up KZN Tourism's *Battlefields Route* brochure – available at Tourist Junction (p283) or from tourist offices across the region.

ESTCOURT
☎ 036

The southern access point for the battlefields region, Estcourt is still a fair slog from the more interesting locations. That said, this sedate farming community is well connected on the Durban to Jo'burg/Pretoria bus route and there are some decent wildlife reserves on the doorstep.

Bushman's River Tourism Association (☎ 352 6253; brta@futurest.co.za; Old Civic Bldg, Upper Harding St; ☺ 8am-4pm Mon-Fri) can help with accommodation. **Makarios Reservations** (☎ 352 5187; makariosres@absamail.co.za; ☺ 8am-4pm Mon-Fri), in the same building, can also book battlefield tours and transport.

Fort Durnford (☎ 352 3000; admission by donation; ☺ 9am-12.30pm & 1.30-4pm), which is now a museum, was built in 1874 to protect Estcourt from Zulu attack. There are interesting displays and a reconstructed Zulu village in the grounds.

Gongola Game Reserve (☎ 083-309 2166), a few kilometres southeast of Estcourt, had yet to be finished at the time of writing. However, smaller game had already been moved in and the Big Five are said to be on their way. Call ahead for the latest.

Sleeping

Sewula (☎ 352 2485, 082-824 0329; r R600) Slap bang in the heart of the new Gongola Game Reserve, this four-star place has four opulent cottages around a self-catering kitchen block. The bonus is that if you book one cottage, you get the whole place to yourself – oh, and that lions should be roaming around soon.

THE BATTLE OF SPIOENKOP

On 23 January 1900 the British, led by General Buller, made a second attempt to relieve Ladysmith, which had been under siege by the Boers since late October 1899. At Trichardt's Drift, 500 Boers prevented 15,000 of his men from crossing the Tugela River, and Buller decided that he needed to take Spioenkop – the flat-topped hill would make a good gun emplacement from which to clear the annoying Boers from their trenches.

During the night, 1700 British troops climbed the hill and chased off the few Boers guarding it. They dug a trench and waited for morning. Meanwhile the Boer commander, Louis Botha, heard of the raid. He ordered his field guns to be trained onto Spioenkop and positioned some of his men on nearby hills. A further 400 soldiers began to climb Spioenkop as the misty dawn broke.

The British might have beaten off the 400, but the mist finally lifted, and was immediately replaced by a hail of bullets and shells. The British retreated to their trench and by mid-afternoon, continuous shellfire caused many to surrender. By now, reinforcements were on hand and the Boers could not overrun the trench. A bloody stalemate was developing.

After sunset, the British evacuated the hill; so did the Boers. Both retreats were accomplished so smoothly that neither side was aware that the other had left. That night Spioenkop was held by the dead.

It was not until the next morning that the Boers again climbed up Spioenkop and found that it was theirs. The Boers had killed or wounded 1340 British – Gandhi's stretcher-bearer unit performed with distinction at this battle. Buller relieved Ladysmith a month later on 28 February.

Ashtonville Terraces (☎ 352 7770; dlsa@telkomsa .net; 76 Albert St; s/d with breakfast R220/320; 🅿 🖵) Owned by a local newspaper magnate – most handy if you need information – this homey place is in a lovely colonial villa, ringed by tropical gardens and boasting plenty of slick extras such as Victorian baths and massive breakfasts.

Darkest Africa (☎ 354 1806; darkestafrica@lantic .net; camp sites R40, dm R60) Out near Weenen Nature Reserve (below), this no-frills place is indeed a trip back into the days of Livingstone et al. There's no electricity and beds are in basic huts, but the atmosphere is truly wild. Call ahead for directions and pick-up.

Getting There & Away

BUS

Greyhound (☎ 031-309 7830; www.greyhound.co.za) buses stop outside the Bushman's River Tourism Association office (opposite) – you also book tickets here. They run daily to Durban (R95, two hours) and Jo'burg (R170, 7½ hours).

MINIBUS TAXI

The main minibus taxi rank is at the bottom of Phillips St, in the town centre, downhill from the post office. Fares from Estcourt include: Winterton (R10, 40 minutes), Ladysmith (R18, one hour), Pietermaritzburg (R25, 1¾ hours), Durban (R35, 2½ hours) and Jo'burg (R80, eight hours).

AROUND ESTCOURT

Around 25km northeast of Estcourt is the 5000-hectare **Weenen Game Reserve** (☎ 036-354 7013; www.kznwildlife.com; adult/child/vehicle R10/10/15; 🕑 6am-6pm), which has black and white rhinos, buffaloes, giraffes and several antelope species, including the rare roan. There are three good walking trails: Impofu (2km), Beacon View (3km) and Reclamation (2km). The reserve also has camp sites (R38 per person) and five-bed cottages (R102 per person) – minimum charges apply.

Almost at the point where the R103 meets the R74, 16km north of Estcourt, is the site where the young Winston Churchill was captured by the Boers in 1899 when they derailed the armoured train he was travelling in; there is a **plaque** just off the road.

COLENSO

☎ 036

Colenso, a crumbling, frontier-style town, was once the British base during the Relief of Ladysmith. As well as Spioenkop, there are several other Anglo-Boer War battlefields near here, most examples of the triumph of Boer guerrilla tactics over British imperial discipline.

There is a museum and some memorial sites relating to the Battle of Colenso (December 1899) – another disaster for the hapless General Buller at the hands of Louis Botha. The **tourist office** (☎ 422 2112; Main Rd; 🕑 8.30am-12.30pm & 1.30-4.30pm), in the Revenue Office, hands out the keys to the **museum** (admission free), which is in the toll house adjacent to the bridge.

Lord Roberts' only son, Freddy, was among those slaughtered here (with about 1100 other British); he is buried in the **Chieveley Military Cemetery**, south of the town.

Sleeping

Umsuluzi Riverside Lodge (☎ 352 9801; umsuluzi@ miwen.co.za; camp sites R155, cottages per person R290, with full board R490) This private game reserve, 8km southeast of Colenso, features stunning surrounds, horse-riding and mountain-biking. The slick, safari-style accommodation includes a tented bus camp, self-catering cottages, and cottages with full board.

SPIOENKOP NATURE RESERVE

The 6000-hectare **Spioenkop Nature Reserve** (☎ 036-488 1578; www.kznwildlife.com; admission R10; 🕑 6am-6pm) is based on the Spioenkop Dam on the Tugela River. The reserve is handy for most of the area's battlefield sites and not too far from the Drakensberg for day trips into the range. There are two reserves in the resort; animals include white rhinos, giraffes, zebras and various antelope species. There's a swimming pool and horse riding, and tours of the Spioenkop battlefield are available.

iPika (bush camps per person R138, camp sites per person R48) inside the reserve, offers camping and four-bed tented bush camps. Book all accommodation directly through the reserve.

The reserve is north of Bergville but the entrance is on the eastern side, off the R600, which runs between the N3 and Winterton. If you are coming from the south on the N3,

KWAZULU-NATAL

take the turn-off to the R74 to get to Winterton. You will need a car to get here.

LADYSMITH
☎ 036

Ladysmith was named after the wife of Cape governor Sir Harry Smith, but it could well have had a much more colourful name. She wasn't just plain Lady Smith, she was Lady Juana Maria de los Dolores Smith.

The town achieved fame during the 1899–1902 Anglo-Boer War, when it was besieged by Boer forces for 118 days. Apart from the historical aspect – several buildings in the city centre were here during the siege – Ladysmith is a pleasant place to walk around.

Information

ABSA (cnr Queen & Murchison Sts) Has two branches on the same crossroads, one with a currency exchange and one with an ATM.

Police Station (☎ 638 3309; King St) By the NG Kerk.

PostNet (☎ 631 3042; Oval Shopping Centre, Queen St; per hr R30; 🕑 8am-5pm Mon-Fri, 8am-1pm Sat) Offers Internet access.

Tourist Information Office (☎ 637 2992; www .ladysmith.co.za; 🕑 9am-4pm Mon-Fri, 9am-1pm Sat) In the Siege Museum. Ask about guided tours of the Battlefields here.

Sights & Activities

The very good **Siege Museum** (☎ 637 2231; adult/ child R2/1; 🕑 9am-4pm Mon-Fri, 9am-1pm Sat), next to the town hall in the Market House (built in

1884), was used to store rations during the siege. You can pick up a walking-tour map of Ladysmith here.

There's also the small **Cultural Museum** (☎ 637 2231; 25 Keate St; adult/child R2/1; 🕑 9am-4pm Mon-Fri), with displays including a room dedicated to Ladysmith Black Mambazo.

Outside the town hall are two guns, **Castor** and **Pollux**, used by the British in defence of Ladysmith. Nearby is a replica of **Long Tom**, a Boer gun capable of heaving a shell 10km. Long Tom was put out of action by a British raiding party during the siege, but not before it had caused a great deal of damage.

On the corner of King St and Settlers Dr is the police station, which includes the wall with loopholes from the original **Zulu Fort**, built as a refuge from Zulu attack.

Sleeping

The municipal **caravan park** (☎ 637 6804; fax 637 3151; camp site per person R25) is on the northern side of town; follow Poort Rd over the hill, where it becomes the Harrismith road. It is only manned between 7.30am and 4.15pm.

Peaches & Cream (☎ 631 0954; fax 631 1233; 4 Berea Rd; s/d with breakfast R230/350; 🖳) With décor from a colonial-era home improvement programme, immaculately tended lawns, high ceilings and trimmings aplenty, Peaches & Cream combines plush hotel styling with some welcome B&B charm.

LADYSMITH map

Buller's Rest Lodge (☎ 637 6154; www.bullers restlodge.co.za; 61 Cove Cres; s/d with breakfast R250/325) Scrumptious home cooking, the snug 'Boer War' pub and fabulous views from the sundeck earn this place a clutch of gold stars.

Royal Hotel (☎ 637 2176; royal@intekom.co.za; 140 Murchison St; s/d with breakfast R280/450) The 'leaders in friendliness and service' (their words, not ours) have obscured some of this hotel's lovely old features with some 1980s renovations. Still, there's a good pub and it's right in the heart of things.

Boer & Brit (☎ 631 2184; fax 637 3957; 47-49 Convent Rd; s/d with breakfast R150/220; 🐾) With a little slice of jungle for a garden, a braai area and a lively feel (don't worry, Boer War politics are not on the menu), this pleasant little place will also give you a tent to camp in if you're trying to save the pennies. It's north of the centre, off Berea Rd.

Natalasia Hotel (☎ 637 6821; 342 Kandahar Ave; s/d R100/150) The modern Natalasia Hotel has cheap passable rooms.

Eating

There are several eateries in the Oval Shopping Centre behind the Siege Museum.

About Thyme (☎ 635 5827; 5 Berea Rd; mains R30-60; 🕑 lunch & dinner) This snug bistro, filled with Victorian-era bric-a-brac, serves up an excellent range of seafood, as well as the usual grills.

Tipsy Trouper (☎ 637 2176; 140 Murchison St; mains R20-50; 🕑 lunch & dinner) 'Your Country Needs You…To Serve in the International Booze Battalion'. Well, that's what their merchandising says anyway. They serve English pub grub, decent beer and if you drink 32 different brews in 40 days, they'll etch your name on a brass plaque. It's in the Royal Hotel.

Mario's (☎ 637 2176; 140 Murchison St; mains R20-50; 🕑 lunch & dinner) Also in the Royal, Mario's is an Italian restaurant with lunch specials such as tagliatelle.

Getting There & Away

BUS

Sure Destinations Travel (☎ 631 0831; San Marco Centre, cnr Francis & Harrismith Rds; 🕑 8.30am-4.30pm Mon-Fri) is the local Greyhound agent. The daily buses, which leave from a stop next to the Caltex garage on Murchison Rd, connect Ladysmith with Durban (R140, four hours), Jo'burg (R165, six hours), Pretoria

(R165, seven hours) and Cape Town (R370, 19 hours).

MINIBUS TAXI

The main taxi rank is east of the town centre near the corner of Queen and Lyell Sts. Taxis bound for Harrismith and Jo'burg are nearby on Alexandra St. Some destinations are Newcastle (R20, 1½ hours), Durban (R40, 3½ hours) and Jo'burg (R80, seven hours).

TRAIN

The *Trans Oranje* (Durban to Cape Town) and the daily *Trans Natal* (Durban to Jo'burg/ Pretoria) both stop here, but at inconvenient times. For more details see p605.

NEWCASTLE & AROUND

☎ 034 / Newcastle pop 309,000

Now twinned with its UK namesake, Newcastle lacks the big-city feel of its English counterpart. As a coal-mining and steel-producing centre, however, it does share the same no-nonsense atmosphere.

The **tourist information office** (☎ 315 3318; www.tourismnewcastle.co.za; Scott St; 🕑 9am-4pm Mon-Fri, 9.30-10.30am Sat) is in the colonial-era town hall.

There's an Anglo-Boer War museum in **Fort Amiel** (☎ 328 7621; admission R5; 🕑 9am-1pm Tue-Thu, 11am-4pm Fri, 9am-1pm Sat), which was established in 1876 when the British anticipated conflict with the Zulu.

The turn-off to **Chelmsford Nature Reserve** (☎ 351 1753; www.kznwildlife.com; admission R10; 🕑 6am-6pm) is on the R23, 25km south of Newcastle. As well as water sports on the dam, there's a wildlife reserve with white rhinos.

Sleeping & Eating

KZN Wildlife (☎ 033-845 1000; www.kznwildlife.com; camp sites per person R40, 5-bed chalets per person R110) offers camping and chalets in Chelmsford Nature Reserve.

Cannon Lodge (☎ 315 2307; fax 315 2308; 96 Allen St; s/d with breakfast R210/290) In a red-brick, colonial-style building, this B&B combines clean, motel-style rooms with a vibrant, English-style pub serving lunches and dinners.

Newcastle Inn (☎ 312 8151; fax 312 4142; cnr Hunter & Victoria Rds; s/d R242/332; 🐾 🐾) Predictable and reliable, this is a decent, business-style offering.

Getting There & Away

Sure Travel (☎ 312 6006; Allen St; ☼ 8.30am-4.30pm Mon-Fri, 9am-noon Sat), on the road to Volksrust, is the local Greyhound agent. Buses run daily to Jo'burg (R185, five hours) and Durban (R160, 5½ hours) from the Shell petrol station on Allen St.

The daily *Trans Natal* train runs to Jo'burg and Durban.

Car-rental companies with agents in Newcastle include **Imperial** (☎ 312 2806; Volksrust St), which is based at the Mortimer Toyota garage – continue down Allen St.

MAJUBA HILL

The first Anglo-Boer War ended abruptly, 40km north of Newcastle, with the British defeat at Majuba Hill in early 1881. The **site** (adult/child R10/5; ☼ 8am-4pm Mon-Fri, 9am-4pm Sat & Sun) has been restored and a map is available. The Laing's Nek and Schuinshoogte battlefields are also signposted.

Peace negotiations took place at **O'Neill's Cottage** in the foothills near Majuba. The cottage, used as a hospital during the battle, has been restored and has a photographic display.

UTRECHT

☎ 034 / pop 3500

Today a quiet little town in prime cattle country, Utrecht was once the capital of one of the original Voortrekker republics, this one measuring just 30km by 65km. The town was the British headquarters during the Anglo-Zulu War, and a number of fine 19th-century buildings remain. The **Utrecht Information Bureau** (☎ 331 3613; www.utrecht.co.za; Voor St; ☼ 7.30am-4pm Mon-Fri) is in the centre and there's a **museum** (admission R5; ☼ 9am-noon Mon-Fri) in the old parsonage.

Mangosuthu Crafts Village (☎ 331 3613; upuba@ worldonline.co.za; 1 Voor St; r with shared bathroom R90) has irresistibly cheap accommodation.

DUNDEE

☎ 034 / pop 29,000

Coal mines pepper the surrounds, but Dundee is another planned swathe of middle-class, South African suburbia. There's not much to do, but it's a decent base for exploring the region's history.

Tourism Dundee (☎ 212 2121; fax 218 2837; Victoria St; ☼ 9am-4.30pm), by the gardens in the centre, can put you in touch with battlefield guides, who charge between R300 and R500 for a one-day tour of sites including Rorke's Drift and Isandlwana.

On the Vryheid road, 1.5km out of town, is **Talana Museum** (☎ 212 2654; www.talana.co.za; adult/child R10/1; ☼ 8am-4.30pm Mon-Fri, 10am-4.30pm Sat & Sun), dedicated to 'small men who had to take root or die, not to the captains and kings who departed'. It's a large place with several old buildings and displays on coal mining and local history, including both the Anglo-Zulu and the Anglo-Boer Wars.

East of Dundee, 52km away via the R33 and R66, is the regional centre of **Nqutu**, an important trading centre for the surrounding Zulu community. There is a small **information centre** (☎ 271 0915; ☼ 9am-4pm Mon-Fri).

A further 30km north of Nqutu, near Nondweni, is the memorial to the Prince Imperial Louis Napoleon, the last of the Bonaparte dynasty, who was killed here on 1 June 1879.

Sleeping

Royal Country Inn (☎ 212 2147; royal@dundee.kzn .co.za; Victoria St; backpacker s/d R160/360, s/d with breakfast R265/420) With oodles of late 19th-century charm, an English-style pub fit for a spot of post–Rorke's Drift R 'n' R and cosy rooms named after the battle's Victoria Cross recipients, this is a great little place to stay during a tour of the battlefields.

Penny Farthing Country House (☎ 642 1925; www .pennyf.co.za; s/d with half board R485/800; ⚹) In the midst of a 7500-acre beef and game farm, this homey place offers snug accommodation, big spaces and a warm, sociable atmosphere. You can also crash in the cheaper stables (singles/doubles with shared bathroom R200/400). It's 30km south of Dundee on the R33 towards Greytown and well placed for visits to Rorke's Drift and Isandlwana.

Kwa Rie (☎ 212 2333; Tandy Rd; camp sites R55, s/d R120/190; ⚹) Featuring quirky architecture borrowed from *The Flintstones*, this pleasant little place has camping sites and comfortable chalets. It's 1.5km southwest of the centre – head down Victoria St.

Getting There & Away

There is very little transport connecting Dundee. You can arrange a pick-up with **PMB Heritage Tours** (☎ 212 4040), which makes the run to Ladysmith (R300, maximum four people).

ISANDLWANA & RORKE'S DRIFT

☎ 034

If you have seen *Zulu*, the film that made Michael Caine a star, you will have doubtless heard of Rorke's Drift, a victory of the misty-eyed variety, where, on 22/23 January 1879, 139 British soldiers successfully defended a small mission station from 4000 Zulu warriors. A propaganda-minded Queen Victoria lavished 11 Victoria Crosses on the survivors and the battle was assured its dramatic place in British military history.

For the full picture, however, you must travel 15km across the plain to Isandlwana, the precursor of Rorke's Drift, where only hours earlier the Zulus dealt the Empire one of its great battlefield disasters by annihilating the main body of the British force in devastating style. Tellingly, *Zulu Dawn*, the film made about Isandlwana, never became the cult classic *Zulu* is now. Victories sell better than defeats.

Ideally, the two battlefields should be visited together. Start at the **Isandlwana Visitors centre** (☎ 271 8165; adult/child R10/5; 8am-4pm Mon-Fri, 9am-4pm Sat & Sun), where there is a small museum. Here, you can pay your entrance fee and pick up a copy of the *Isandlwana Battlefield Self-Guided Trails* booklet (R3), which provides the background of the battle as well as details of walks through the site. The battlefield itself is extremely evocative. Spread out from the base of Isandlwana hill, white cairns and memorials mark the spot where each British soldier fell – the hillside is peppered with them.

If you have seen *Zulu*, which was filmed in the Drakensberg, the scenery around Rorke's Drift may come as a bit of a disappointment. The landscape is still beautifully rugged, however, and the **Rorke's Drift Museum** (☎ 642 1687; adult/child R10/5; 8am-4pm Mon-Fri, 9am-4pm Sat & Sun), located on the site of the original mission station, is excellent. The Zulu know this site as Shiyane, their name for the hill at the back of the village. The *Rorke's Drift-Shiyane Self-Guided Trail* brochure (R3) is helpful for understanding the close nature of the fighting in this battle.

Next to the museum, you will also find the **Evangelical Lutheran Church Art & Craft Centre** (☎ 642 1627; admission by donation; 8.30am-4.30pm Mon-Fri, 9am-2pm Sat & Sun). As one of the few places to offer artistic training to Black artists during apartheid, the centre boasts a proud history, with such names as Gordon Mbatha, Cyprian Shilakoe and Daniel Rakgoathe among its alumni. Funds are now at a premium, but you can still witness the artists at work. For an authoritative guide to the centre in its heyday, pick up a copy of *Rorke's Drift – Empowering Prints* by Philippa Hobbs and Elizabeth Rankin.

About 10km from Rorke's Drift is **Fugitive's Drift**. Two British soldiers were killed here while attempting to rescue the Queen's Colours.

Sleeping

Rorke's Drift Lodge (☎ 642 1805; www.rorkesdriftlodge.co.za; Rorke's Drift; s/d with half board R285/570;) On a large farm, with wonderful views over the Battlefields, this excellent

---

THE BATTLE OF ISANDLWANA

It hardly bears thinking about. When a soldier from one of the five British armies sent to invade Zululand peered over a ridge on 22 January 1879, he was confronted not with an empty stretch of savanna, but with 25,000 Zulu warriors, crouching in the grass less than a kilometre away. They had intended to delay their attack until the following day, the day after the full moon, but once discovered moved into battle formation – two enclosing horns on the flanks and the main force in the centre – and fell on the British, catching them off guard and unprepared. By the end of the day, the British column had been annihilated and the Anglo-Zulu War, for the invaders at least, had got off to a very bad start.

Meanwhile, the small British contingent that had remained at Rorke's Drift (where the army had crossed into Zululand) to guard supplies, heard of the disaster and fortified their camp. They were attacked by about 4000 Zulus but the defenders, numbering fewer than 100 fit soldiers, held on through the night until a relief column arrived. Victoria Crosses were lavished on the defenders – 11 in all – and another couple went to the two officers who died defending the Queen's Colours at Fugitive's Drift, about 10km south of Rorke's Drift.

place offers plenty of old-fashioned hospitality and bush-lodge peace and quiet. It is 5km up a rough track from the Rorke's Drift Museum – turn left out of the museum and you will see the sign on the right. Call ahead for pick-ups from Ladysmith and Dundee.

Fugitive's Drift Lodge (☎ 642 1843; www.fugitives-drift-lodge.com; Fugitive's Drift; s/d with half board R1850/2700; ✖ 🖳 🐾) Run by Battlefields authority David Rattray (tours from R495), this opulent private game reserve is dripping in colonial-style class and military memorabilia. Expect to pay 50% more during the summer season, but there are also rooms in a slightly less glamorous guesthouse (singles/doubles with half board R1395/1800). It is by Fugitive's Drift, about 10km from Rorke's Drift.

Getting There & Away
The battle sites are southeast of Dundee. Isandlwana is about 70km from Dundee, off the R66; Rorke's Drift is 42km from Dundee, accessible from the R66 or R33 (the R33 turn-off is 13km south of Dundee). The roads to both battlefields can be dusty and rough. A dirt road connects Isandlwana and Rorke's Drift.

BLOOD RIVER MONUMENT
On 16 December 1838 a small force of Voortrekkers avenged the massacre of Piet Retief's diplomatic party by crushing an army of 12,000 Zulus. More than 3000 Zulus died – the river ran red with their blood – while the Voortrekkers barely sustained a single casualty. The battle became a seminal event in Afrikaner history. The victory came to be seen as the fulfilment of God's side of the bargain and seemed to prove that the Boers had a divine mandate to conquer and 'civilise' Southern Africa, and that they were in fact a chosen people.

However, Afrikaner nationalism and the significance attached to Blood River simultaneously grew in strength and it has been argued (by Leach in *The Afrikaners – Their Last Great Trek* and others) that the importance of Blood River was deliberately heightened and manipulated for political ends. The standard interpretation of the victory meshed with the former apartheid regime's world view: hordes of untrustworthy Black savages were beaten by Boers who were on an Old Testament–style mission from God.

The battle site is marked by a full-scale bronze recreation of the 64-wagon laager. The cairn of stones was built by the Boers after the battle to mark the centre of their laager. The monument and the nearby **Blood River Museum** (☎ 034-632 1695; adult/child R12/5; ☽ 8am-5pm) are 20km southeast of the R33; the turn-off is 27km from Dundee and 45km from Vryheid.

Interestingly, the **Ncome Museum** (☎ 034-271 8121; admission by donation; ☽ 8am-4.30pm) is on the other side of the river, offering a 're-interpretation' from the Zulu perspective.

Free State

CONTENTS

Free State

In the landlocked Free State, tiny *dorps* (towns) are interspersed with huge fields of sun-flowers, and farmers in floppy hats and overalls drive estate cars full of sheep over bumpy roads. Groups of Tswana ladies sit comfortably in the shade of sandstone shop fronts, but in the Dutch Reformed Churches and blue-rinsed ladies' baking circles, dreams of an Afrikaner Arcadia still linger. Outside the towns, brightly painted Sotho houses dot the waving veld, and some of the best San rock art in the country adorns the walls of hidden caves.

The Free State landscape consists largely of the grasslands of the Southern African plateau. To the east are the highlands with their weirdly eroded sandstone hills, which glow bright gold every sunset. There are important gold mines in and around Welkom and diamonds are also mined in Free State. The western half of the province is rolling grazing country, while the hillier east is a major grain-growing region.

Nelson Mandela once said that when he visited the Free State, he felt that nothing could shut him in and that his thoughts could roam as far as the horizons. While the Free State is never going to feature highly on any traveller's itinerary, it's a place that grows on you slowly as you absorb the pace of life and get to know the eccentric characters that inhabit the middle-of-nowhere places scattered throughout it. It's an ideal place for a farm- or homestay, a camping trip or a multinight hiking trail. If you're craving a bit of nightlife and culture, head for Bloemfontein, the region's studenty and lively capital.

HIGHLIGHTS

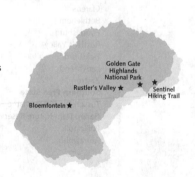

- The surprisingly funky and alternative night-life scene in **Bloemfontein** (p356), with its emphasis on down-to-earth live rock music

- The **Sentinel Hiking Trail** (p364), which leads up over the dizzying heights of the Drak-ensberg plateau and all the way down into KwaZulu-Natal

- Bloemfontein's strikingly beautiful and tranquil **Oliewenhuis Art Museum** (p354)

- The hippie mecca of **Rustler's Valley** (p366), with its brightly painted cottages, New Age therapies and stunning views

- The eerie sandstone formations of the famous **Golden Gate Highlands National Park** (p363), home to the rare bearded vulture, black eagle and jackal buzzard

| POPULATION: 2,749,300 | AREA: 129,480 SQ KM |

FREE STAE

FREE STATE

LEGEND
GR   Game Reserve
NP   National Park
NR   Nature Reserve

100 km
60 miles

HISTORY

Free State's borders reflect the prominent role it has played in the power struggles of South Africa's history. To the east, across the Caledon River, is Lesotho, where forbidding mountains combined with the strategic warfare of the Sotho king Moshoeshoe the Great halted the tide of Boer expansion. To the southeast, however, Free State spills across the river as the mountains dwindle into flat grassland – this area proved harder for Moshoeshoe to defend.

The Voortrekkers established their first settlement near modern-day Thaba 'Nchu, and various embryonic republics then came and went, in addition to a period of British sovereignty after the 1899–1902 Anglo-Boer War.

The 'Orange Free State' was created in 1854, with Bloemfontein as the capital. The 'Orange' part of the province's title was dropped in 1994, following South Africa's first democratic elections.

CLIMATE

The eastern highveld region, which includes the Free State, experiences a dry, sunny climate from June to August, with showers, thunderstorms and hail between October and April. Snow falls thickly each winter around the foothills of the Maluti Mountains, near the Golden Gate Highlands National Park in the eastern highlands.

LANGUAGE

Sesotho is the most dominant tongue in the Free State, followed by Afrikaans, Xhosa, Setswana, Zulu and English (just 2% of the Free State's inhabitants speak English as a first language).

GETTING THERE & AROUND

Bloemfontein is well served by public transport, with trains and buses stopping here on their way to and from Johannesburg (Jo'burg) and Pretoria and southern parts of the country. Likewise, it's easy to get to and from Lesotho – taxis and buses leave Thaba 'Nchu and Bloemfontein daily for the border.

Elsewhere in the province, you'll need to take your own vehicle, or rely on the sporadic minibus taxis.

BLOEMFONTEIN

☎ 051 / pop 349,000

Bloemfontein (or 'Bloem' as it is usually called) is the provincial capital of Free State and South Africa's judicial capital. In Afrikaans it means 'Fountain of Flowers'; its Tswana name, Manguang, more intriguingly, means 'Place of Cheetahs'. In 1854 when it became the capital of the new Orange Free State, it was a struggling frontier village in constant danger of being wiped out by the soldiers of Sotho king Moshoeshoe. By the end of Johannes Brand's 25-year term as president, however, Bloem had grown into a wealthy city with imposing buildings and rail links to the coast.

These days, Bloem is one of the more pleasant cities in South Africa, with attractive leafy suburbs, some imposing architecture (particularly in the area around President Brand Street), a hip, student-led nightlife and a relaxed atmosphere on the streets.

There are quite a few destitute whites wandering the streets of Bloem, begging and trying to 'keep an eye on cars' for a few rand.

ORIENTATION

There are endless sprawling suburbs in Bloemfontein but the central area is laid out on a grid and is easy to navigate. Hoffman Sq is the centre of the downtown area. Botshabelo, on the Thaba 'Nchu road, is one of the largest townships in the country.

INFORMATION

Internet Access

Connix Internet (☎ 448 5648; Loch Logan Waterfront; per hr R30) A flash place in the Waterfront shopping centre, with fast connections and prices to match.

Money

There are banks with ATMs in the town centre and handy ATMs at the Tourist Centre and at the Waterfront; there's an Amex office in the Mimosa Mall and a branch of ABSA (with bureau de change) in the Pick 'n' Pay Centre opposite the western side of the Mimosa Mall.

Post

Main post office (Groenendal St) Near Hoffman Sq.

FREE STATE

BLOEMFONTEIN

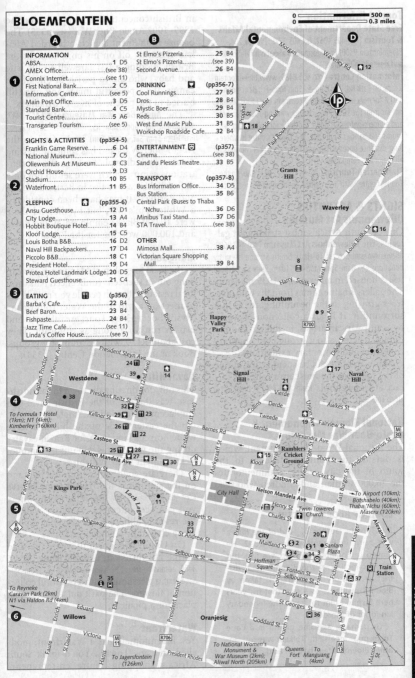

INFORMATION
ABSA..............................1 D5
AMEX Office....................(see 38)
Connix Internet................(see 11)
First National Bank............2 C5
Information Centre............(see 5)
Main Post Office...............3 D5
Standard Bank..................4 C5
Tourist Centre..................5 A6
Transgariep Tourism..........(see 5)

SIGHTS & ACTIVITIES (pp354-5)
Franklin Game Reserve.........6 D4
National Museum................7 C5
Oliewenhuis Art Museum.......8 C3
Orchid House....................9 D3
Stadium...........................10 B5
Waterfront........................11 B5

SLEEPING (pp355-6)
Ansu Guesthouse................12 D1
City Lodge........................13 A4
Hobbit Boutique Hotel.........14 B4
Kloof Lodge......................15 C5
Louis Botha B&B................16 D2
Naval Hill Backpackers........17 C1
Piccolo B&B......................18 C1
President Hotel..................19 D4
Protea Hotel Landmark Lodge.20 D5
Steward Guesthouse............21 C4

EATING (p356)
Barba's Cafe.....................22 B4
Beef Baron.......................23 B4
Fishpaste.........................24 B4
Jazz Time Café..................(see 11)
Linda's Coffee House..........(see 5)

St Elmo's Pizzeria...............25 B4
St Elmo's Pizzeria...............(see 39)
Second Avenue...................26 B4

DRINKING (pp356-7)
Cool Runnings....................27 B5
Dros................................28 B4
Mystic Boer.......................29 B4
Reds................................30 B5
West End Music Pub............31 B5
Workshop Roadside Cafe......32 B4

ENTERTAINMENT (p357)
Cinema.............................(see 38)
Sand du Plessis Theatre.........33 B5

TRANSPORT (pp357-8)
Bus Information Office..........34 D5
Bus Station........................35 B6
Central Park (Buses to Thaba
'Nchu.............................36 D6
Minibus Taxi Stand..............37 D6
STA Travel.........................(see 38)

OTHER
Mimosa Mall......................38 A4
Victorian Square Shopping
Mall...............................39 B4

FREE STATE

Tourist Information

Free State Department of Environmental Affairs & Tourism (☎ 405 4062; fax 403 3778; PO Box 264, Bloemfontein 9300) For information about national parks and reserves in the area.

Information Centre (☎ 405 8489; www.bloemfontein .co.za; 60 Park Rd; ☺ 8am-4.15pm Mon-Fri; 8am-noon Sat) A friendly and very helpful centre in the Tourist Centre, not far from the stadium. Pick up a walking-tour map here and a *Bloemfontein Art Route* brochure for galleries, museums and handicraft outlets. The Tourist Centre is where long-distance buses arrive, and there are ticket counters for all major bus companies.

Transgariep Tourism (☎ 447 1362) Next door to the Tourist Centre, with information about most of Free State.

SIGHTS & ACTIVITIES
Oliewenhuis Art Museum

One of South Africa's most striking art galleries, the **Oliewenhuis Art Museum** (☎ 447 9609; oliewen@nasmus.co.za; 16 Harry Smith St; admission by donation; ☺ 8am-5pm Mon-Fri, 10am-5pm Sat, 1-5pm Sun) is housed in an exquisite 1935 mansion. The gallery's name comes from the wild olive trees growing in the beautiful gardens that surround it. It holds a collection of works by South African artists, including Thomas Baines. There's also a strong contemporary collection and temporary exhibitions.

Many an hour can be spent lazing at one of the tables in the museum's café, the Terrace at Oliewenhuis (mains R20-35; ☺ breakfast & lunch Tue-Sun).

National Women's Monument & Anglo-Boer War Museum

The National Women's Monument, which is outside the military museum to the south of the city centre, commemorates the 26,000 women and children who died in British concentration camps during the 1899–1902 Anglo-Boer War (see p355). The bronze monument depicts a bearded Afrikaner, setting off on his pony to fight the British, bidding a last farewell to his wife and baby, who are to perish in one of the camps. It's a powerful image and one still buried in the psyche of many Afrikaners.

The **Anglo-Boer War Museum** (☎ 447 3447; Monument Rd; admission R5; ☺ 8am-4.30pm Mon-Fri, 10am-5pm Sat, 2-5pm Sun) is devoted to the Anglo-Boer Wars and has some interesting displays including photos from the concentrations camps, which were set up not only in South Africa, but also in Bermuda, India and Portugal. It may have been considered a White-man's war, but by the end there were 10,000 Blacks employed by the Boers and 100,000 working for the British.

Manguang

In the local township of Manguang you can hang out in shebeens (unlicenced bars) and local restaurants with people you're unlikely to meet on a trip to the Waterfront or the Mystic Boer (p356). Tours are informal and usually run for as long as you want. They cost about R180, with discounts for groups. Book at the Information Centre (p354).

Naval Hill

This hill, dominating the town to the north-east, was the site of the British naval-gun emplacements during the Anglo-Boer War. On the eastern side of the hill is a large white horse, a landmark for British cavalry during the war; it was laid out by a home-sick regiment from Wiltshire.

There are good views from the hill, and on the summit is the **Franklin Game Reserve** (☎ 405 8124; admission free; ☺ 8am-5pm), where you can see antelopes. You can walk in the reserve, although one traveller reports being chased by a wildebeest!

On Union Ave, north of where the road up the hill turns off, is **Orchid House** (☎ 405 8488; admission free; ☺ 10am-6pm Mon-Fri, 10am-5pm Sat & Sun), a glasshouse with a beautiful collection of flowers. The park outside is a great place for a picnic.

Waterfront

Yes, Bloemfontein has a Waterfront, modelled on Cape Town's. You'd think South Africa's shopping centre entrepreneurs

---

LORD OF BLOEMFONTEIN

JRR Tolkein, author of *Lord of the Rings*, was born in Bloemfontein in 1892. He moved to England when he was five, but his recollection of the Bloemfontein district as 'hot, dry and barren' is taken by Bloem's residents as a sign that his years here inspired him to create the legendary kingdom of Mordor.

Or perhaps, as some graffiti in a Cape Town pub once said, 'Tolkein was just another Bloemfontein boy on acid'…

CONCENTRATION CAMPS

The British had the dubious honour of inventing the concentration camp, during the 1899–1902 Anglo-Boer War. Guerrilla bands of Afrikaners, helped by farmers, were reportedly harassing the British troops. In response the British took on a 'scorched earth' policy in the countryside, burning the farms of suspected combatants and shipping their wives and children off to concentration camps. As a consequence, by the end of the war 26,000 Afrikaner women and children had died of disease and malnutrition, which accounted for more than 70% of the total Afrikaner losses in the war. There were also concentration camps created for blacks and of the 80,000 interned, an estimated 14,000 people died.

could come up with something a bit more original. Although it's a bit tacky, Bloem's Waterfront is a lot more pleasant than the huge shopping malls that are popping up on the outskirts of so many South African cities. It's outside, set on a small body of water, and the atmosphere is relaxed – it's a great place for kids. For travellers there are plenty of services, including ATMs, an Internet café, cheap eats and a cinema.

National Museum

A great re-creation of a 19th-century street, complete with sound effects, is the most interesting display at this **museum** (☎ 447 9609; 36 Aliwal St; admission R5; ☒ 8am-5pm Mon-Fri, 10am-5pm Sat, noon-5.30pm Sun). There is also a shop and a café here.

Bloemfontein has dozens of smaller museums, mostly centred on the old governmental buildings around President Brand St. Ask at the Information Centre for details.

SLEEPING

The Information Centre has a full list of accommodation and makes bookings. Note that rooms can be scarce on cricket- and rugby-match weekends.

Budget

Naval Hill Backpackers (☎ 430 7266, 082-579 6509; www.navalhillbackpackers.co.za; Delville St; camp sites per person/dm/d with shared bathroom R45/70/160; P ☐)

Pretty much the only 'traditional' backpackers in the Free State, this is an old water-pumping station (1902) that has been converted into an über-cool hostel with funky industrial décor. Unfortunately, the staff at the time of research gave the distinct impression that the guests were intruding on their own private party, leading to a very cliquey atmosphere. Facilities are good, however, and if the personnel change, this will be an excellent budget option. Activities and transport to Lesotho can be arranged here.

Louis Botha B&B (☎ 436 4533; mwctrade@absamail .co.za; 18 Louis Botha St; dm/d with shared bathroom R70/140; P ☐) In a private home, in the leafy suburb of Waverley, the Louis Botha describes itself as less of a backpackers and more of a B&B. It's not a place for party animals, but its wooden-floored rooms are clean and comfortable, and there's a garden at the back. Breakfast is available for R25.

Reyneke Caravan Park (☎ 523 3888; fax 523 3887; Petrusburg Rd; camp sites R70, s/d chalets R180/220) Two kilometres out of town, this well-organised park has a swimming pool, a trampoline and a basketball court. This is a good place for kids.

Mid-Range

Ansu Guesthouse (☎ 436 4654; ansu@symok.co.za; 80 Waverley Rd; s/d R165/220; P ☒) The Ansu is a good suburban choice; the very smart rooms all have TV, and there's a tennis court in the leafy garden. Breakfast (R45) and dinner (R65) can be arranged with advance notice.

Steward Guesthouse (☎ /fax 448 4828; 85 Aliwal St; s/d with breakfast R250/350; P) This new guesthouse has beautiful big rooms in an old mansion, each with Victorian baths and old-fashioned washbasins. Try to get a room at the back, as the ones nearer the road can be a bit noisy. Meals can be arranged on request.

Piccolo B&B (☎ 436 1483; kay@imaginet.co.za; 4 Prophet St; r with breakfast R300; P) This is a homely suburban B&B. The comfortable rooms all have TV, and some can sleep four people. A self-catering flat is also available.

Kloof Lodge (☎ 447 7603; kloof@global.co.za; 7 Kellner St; s/d with breakfast R295/400; P ☒) This is a comfortable and central option, with clean rooms with fan, TV and phone. There's a bar and a restaurant here too. Book ahead as it's often full.

Formula 1 Hotel (☎ 444 3523, fax 444 3825; cnr Nelson Mandela Dr & Kriega St; r R299; P ⊠) This cut-price hotel west of Kings Park is a bit claustrophobic but cheap and spotless. Rooms sleep up to three people (in a double bed and a bunk).

Top End

Hobbit Boutique Hotel (☎ /fax 447 0663; www.hobbit .co.za; 19 President Steyn Ave, Westdene; s/d with breakfast R495/660; P ⊠ 💻 🐾) This very charming little hotel, made from two 1921 houses, is the winner of numerous awards for service and décor. The cottage-style bedrooms have sprigged counterpanes and painted bathtubs, plus a couple of teddy bears apiece.

President Hotel (☎ 430 1111; preshot@iafrica.com; 1 Union Ave; s/d with breakfast R440/510; P ⊠ 💻 🐾) It's considerably less charming than the Hobbit Boutique Hotel, but nonetheless the President offers clean rooms with TV and telephone.

Protea Hotel Landmark Lodge (☎ 430 8000; bloemf@iafrica.com; Sanlam Plaza, East Burger St; s/d R470/516; P 💻) This smart corporate hotel has all the facilities you'd expect from a Protea, but it's not in a very salubrious part of town.

City Lodge (☎ 444 2974; clbloem.resv@citylodge.co .za; cnr Nelson Mandela & General Dan Pienaar Aves; s/d R450/540; P ⊠ 💻) The comfortable City Lodge is part of a very successful chain of business-traveller refuges. Rooms are spotlessly clean and have TV and phone.

EATING

Many of the hotels and guesthouses do their own meals in the evenings, but there are a few good restaurants in Bloem plus all the usual fast-food joints in the Waterfront and Mimosa Mall shopping centres.

Fishpaste (☎ 430 2662; 31 President Steyn Ave; mains R30-50; ✋ lunch & dinner Mon-Fri, dinner Sat) Fishpaste is a rare thing – a Free State restaurant with a trendy, funky interior and an interesting modern fusion menu. Choose from blackened Canadian salmon with green bean salad, Vietnamese prawn rolls or rolled pork fillet. The fashionably black-clad staff are super-friendly, the bar is buzzy and the prices are extremely reasonable. In a class of its own.

Barba's Café (☎ 430 2542; 16 2nd Ave; Mon-Sat; mains R38, meze for two R140; ✋ breakfast, lunch & dinner) Barba's is recommended by locals

and rightly so: it's one of Bloem's hidden secrets. The Greek specialities, including chicken souvlaki (R38), are delicious. It also has a large cocktail list and live music on Wednesdays.

Jazz Time Café (☎ 430 5727; Waterfront; mains R20-50; ✋ lunch & dinner) This hip eatery has an interesting menu featuring zippy *zivas* – Yemeni-style layered dough wrapped around a variety of fillings (such as Cajun chicken, feta and avocado), folded and toasted. There are cocktails and jazz recitals in the evenings – unusual in the rock-orientated Bloemfontein music scene.

Beef Baron (☎ 447 4290; 22 2nd Ave, Westdene; mains R50; ✋ dinner Mon-Sat, lunch Sun) This cosy steakhouse has carnivore delights such as rump *rossini*.

Second Avenue (☎ 448 3088; mains R20-40; ✋ lunch & dinner) The eager waiting staff at this tacky, studenty diner-cum-bar sometimes take to the streets and wave examples of the salads and burgers on offer under the noses of unsuspecting passers-by. If you're in a drinking mood, have a go at the 'tower of beer'.

St Elmo's Pizzeria (☎ 447 9999; cnr Zastron & Kellner Sts; mains R25-45; ✋ lunch & dinner) St Elmo's does good wood-fired pizza, and baguettes coated in melted cheese. There is also a branch at Victorian Sq Shopping Centre.

Linda's Coffee House (☎ 430 6436; Park Rd; mains R17-32; ✋ breakfast, lunch & dinner) Near the information desk at the Tourist Centre, Linda's is open 24 hours and does good breakfasts (and coffee) for those early bus arrivals.

ENTERTAINMENT

As a university town, Bloemfontein has a good range of places to drink, party and, increasingly, listen to live music. The music on offer is universally alternative rock, so if this isn't your scene, you may be disappointed. The corners of 2nd Ave and Kellner St, and Zastron St and Nelson Mandela Ave bustle with revellers in the evening and compete for the nightlife scene with the Waterfront.

Mystic Boer (☎ 430 2206; 84 Kellner St) Bloem's most popular pub and live music venue provides an eccentric twist to Afrikaner culture, with psychedelic pictures of long-bearded Boers on the walls. One 'big' band plays per month, plus there are regular gigs by unsigned rock and (sometimes) hip-hop outfits. The bar specialises in tequila, while pizza and burgers provide the fuel.

Cool Runnings (☎ 430 7364; admission R5-10; 163 Nelson Mandela Ave) This is part of a nationwide chain of Caribbean-themed bar-restaurants, with DJs and live bands at weekends and karaoke on Sundays. Forget about reggae – the music on offer is the ubiquitous rock and blues.

Workshop Roadside Cafe (☎ 447 2761; cnr 2nd Ave & President Reitz St) This is a large, raucous pub with loud music, a big-screen TV and a reputation as a bit of a bikers' hangout. When we visited, however, the clientele comprised mainly of portly blokes with moustaches boogying on down to tunes by Shania Twain. Sophisticated it ain't, but it's a good place to sink a few beers.

Reds (132 Nelson Mandela Ave; ☯ Wed, Fri & Sat) This dark and deafening club, filled with spinning lights and spotty youths, plays slightly more up-tempo music than many other places in Bloem.

West End Music Pub (☎ 430 5485; 142A Nelson Mandela Ave; ☯ closed Sun) This large sticky-floored venue has a slightly rough atmosphere and a pool table.

Dros (☎ 448 7840; 149 Zastron St) A conservative hang-out with mainly Afrikaner patrons. Stick to the drinks; the food is ordinary.

Sand du Plessis Theatre (☎ 552 4071; cnr Markgraaff & St Andrews Sts) The local paper lists music, ballet, drama and opera performances held at this striking modern building in the town centre.

There are cinemas in the Mimosa Mall and at the Waterfront.

GETTING THERE & AWAY
Air
Bloemfontein airport is 10km from the city centre and there is no transport to/from the airport, except by private taxi.

SA Airlink (☎ 433 3225) and Nationwide Airlines connect Bloemfontein with Cape Town (one way R1200), Durban (around R1000), George, Kimberley, Port Elizabeth, Upington and Jo'burg (R980).

STA Travel (☎ 444 6062; laudep@statravel.co.za), in the Mimosa Mall, can organise flights.

Bus
Long-distance buses leave from the Tourist Centre. **Translux** (☎ 408 4888; www.translux.co.za) runs daily buses to Durban (R220, nine

hours), Jo'burg/Pretoria (R185, five hours), Port Elizabeth (R220, nine hours), East London (R195, seven hours), Knysna (R290, 12 hours) and Cape Town (R350, 10 hours).

Greyhound (☎ 447 1558; www.greyhound.co.za) runs daily buses to Durban (R230, 9½ hours), Pretoria (R200, seven hours), Cape Town (R360, 12 hours) and Port Elizabeth (R230, 10 hours). **Intercape** (☎ 0861 287 287; www.intercape.co.za) runs to Jo'burg (R190, five hours) and Cape Town (R345, 13 hours) daily.

A bus called Interstate runs from the Information Centre in Bloem to Thaba 'Nchu every hour (R10). There's also a shuttle bus to Bloem run by the hotels in Thaba 'Nchu daily except Tuesday and Thursday. The ticket price of R50 includes vouchers for drinks, food and a game on the casino tables. Book both at the Tourist Office.

Big Sky Buses run from the Central Park shopping centre on St Georges St to Maseru in Lesotho (R45, three hours) at 6.30am Monday to Friday.

Minibus Taxi
Most minibus taxis leave from opposite the train station for Maseru (Lesotho; around R45), Kimberley (R50) and Jo'burg (R80).

Train
The **Shosholoza Meyl** (☎ 0860 008 888; www.spoornet.co.za) *Trans Oranje* runs weekly via Bloemfontein between Cape Town (1st/2nd/economy class R390/265/155) and Durban (R270/185/110). The *Algoa* runs five times weekly via Bloemfontein between Jo'burg (1st/2nd/economy R145/100/55, about seven hours) and Port Elizabeth (R235/160/95). The *Amatola* runs five times weekly via Bloemfontein on the run between Jo'burg (1st/2nd/economy R145/100/55) and East London (R210/145/85). The *Diamond Express* runs three times weekly between Bloemfontein and Jo'burg (1st/2nd/economy R145/100/90).

GETTING AROUND
Bloem's public-bus system, Interstate, provides infrequent services that finish early in the evening. The best place for schedules and information is the **Interstate office** (☎ 448 4951) in the Central Park shopping centre. There is also an information office in Hoffman Sq.

FREE

If you're after a private taxi, try **President Taxis** (☎ 522 3399).

AROUND BLOEMFONTEIN
Thaba 'Nchu
☎ 051 / pop 38,300

Thaba 'Nchu (ta-*baan*-chu, meaning 'Black Mountain') is a small Tswana town to the east of Bloemfontein. The surrounding area was once a small piece of the scattered Bophuthatswana homeland, and this too was known as Thaba 'Nchu. As with most homelands, a Sun casino was built here.

There's an information office on the main street, at the other end of town from the supermarkets. Unless you're a compulsive gambler, it's hard to see any reason to stop here.

The **Naledi Sun** (☎ 875 1060; fax 875 2329; 3 Bridge St; R350; ❷ ❷) has the usual Sun comforts.

Thaba 'Nchu Sun (☎ 871 4200; fax 873 2161; N8; r with breakfast R818; ❷ ❷) is about 10km from Thaba 'Nchu and is more expensive, but for high rollers the casino is here.

For details of buses between Thaba 'Nchu and Bloemfontein, see p357. From Thaba 'Nchu, regular minibuses run to the Lesotho border (R35, around two hours). You can walk across the border and get minibuses on the other side into the centre of Maseru.

There's a free shuttle that operates between town and the Naledi and Thaba 'Nchu Sun hotels.

Maria Moroka National Park
Just outside Thaba 'Nchu in the hills is this small **national park** (☎ 873 2427), which protects zebras, elands and red hartebeests among other species. There are a couple of hiking trails plus some self-catering **chalets** (per person R90). You can also do guided wildlife drives with the rangers. You'll need your own vehicle to get there.

NORTHERN FREE STATE

Gold was discovered in Free State in April 1938 and a rush started immediately. Now the Free State goldfields produce more than a third of the country's output.

The Canna Circle region, comprising Reitz, Heilbron and Frankfort, takes its name from the annual cultivation of masses of colourful canna plants. These are in bloom from the end of December to April, and each of the towns within the Circle cultivates plants of a different colour. If you are travelling between Jo'burg and Free State's Eastern Highlands, it is easy to deviate to several of these pleasant towns. If a farm holiday is your bag, you have come to the right place.

The extraction of gold is centred on three industrial – and far less pleasant – towns: Welkom, Virginia and Odendaalsrus. Much of the region is given over to intensive farming, mainly maize. Kroonstad is the largest town between Jo'burg and Bloemfontein.

WINBURG
☎ 051 / pop 11,100

It's difficult to imagine that this sleepy little town, founded in 1842, was the first capital of a Boer republic in present-day Free State. It was in the dining room of Ford's Hotel (now a large shop on the town square) that the leaders of five Voortrekker groups finally agreed to form a government under the leadership of Piet Retief.

Tourist information is available at the **library** (☎ 881 0003; ❷ Mon-Fri), in the town square.

The **church** on the Winburg town square was used as a hospital and school during the 1899–1902 Anglo-Boer War. There are some old photos of the town here.

The **Voortrekker Monument**, about 3km from town, comprises five columns symbolising the five trek parties led by Louis Trichardt, Hendrik Potgieter, Gert Maritz, Piet Retief and Pieter Uys, all of whom created the republic. You'll probably have noticed that just about every town in the Free State has variations of these as street names!

The only decent option in town, **Winburg Guesthouse** (☎ 881 0233; fax 881 0234; 1 Church St; s/d R170/270) has small, tidy rooms with TV and telephone. The attached restaurant and bar are probably your best eating and drinking options.

Getting There & Away
City to City buses between Welkom and Thaba 'Nchu, Maseru and Ficksburg stop here. Other buses running along the N1 stop out on the highway, from where you can walk into town, hail down a minibus taxi or catch a private taxi.

There are a few minibus taxis running to the Goldfields area and some heading towards Bloemfontein. Ask at the petrol station on the northern edge of town.

AROUND WINBURG

Off the N1, about 20km north of Winburg and 70km south of Kroonstad, is the **Willem Pretorius Game Reserve** (☎ 057-651 4003; admission R20; ☺ 7am-6.30pm). Split in two by the Sand River and Allemanskraal Dam, the reserve encompasses two different ecosystems: grassy plains with large herds of eland, blesbok, springbok, black wildebeest and zebras; and, further north, the bushy mountain region with baboons, mountain reedbuck and duiker. White rhino and buffalo are equally at home on either side of the reserve.

There are 10 self-catering chalets on the reserve, as well as a restaurant and small shop. There is also a bush camp that sleeps 16. Fishing is popular here (you need to get a Free State angling licence from the resort) and there are hiking trails.

A range of accommodation is available at **Aldam Resort** (☎ 057-652 2200; fax 652 0014; camp sites from R50; 2-bed chalets R370, 4-bed units R485), much of which has magnificent views over Allemanskraal Dam. Rates increase on weekends and in high season.

WELKOM

☎ 057 / pop 246,000
This modern town is at the centre of the Goldfields area. It's something of a showpiece, as it was completely planned – there are no traffic lights, which is touted as proof of a masterpiece of town planning. However, this just means that it's sprawling, soulless and hell to get around, if you don't have your own transport.

Orientation

Stateway is Free State's main street. Not far from Stateway is Mooi St, with most of the central shopping area in its horseshoe curve. The First National Bank is on Elizabeth St, the Standard Bank is on Tulbagh St, and the main post office is on Bok St.

Information

The **information centre** (☎ 352 9244; ☺ 8am-4.30pm Mon-Fri) is in the clock tower at the civic centre on Stateway. The staff are friendly but they don't have much information.

Sights & Activities

Tours of the **mines** in Welkom, and those in the nearby town of Virginia can be arranged but you'll need to contact the Welkom information centre in advance.

The area's huge mine-evaporation pans are home to a wide variety of **birdlife**, including the greater and lesser flamingo and the grey-headed gull. More than 200 species of bird have been seen around the city, including 90% of all waterfowl species found in South Africa.

Try Flamingo Pan, off the R30 just west of the town, or Witpan at Oppenheimer Park, about 4km southeast of the town centre on the continuation of Stateway. Two other bird-watching spots are Theronia and Flamingo Lakes.

Sleeping & Eating

Stanville Inn (☎ 353 2452; 180 Tempest Rd; s/d R150/180; ☒) The Stanville has spick-and-span budget rooms with TV and telephone. It's opposite Dagbreek Primary School.

Welkom Inn (☎ 357 3361; w-inn@global.co.za; cnr Stateway & Tempest Rd; s/d R298/338; ☒ ☒) This place is three-star rated and is a few blocks

---

THE BATTLES FOR THE FREE STATE

Bloody battles between various enemies have raged across much of the land that is now the Free State. In 1836 Voortrekker Afrikaners, led by Hendrik Potgieter, fought a desperate battle against the Ndebele warriors of the legendary king Mzilikazi at Vegkop, south of Heilbron. When confronted by the Ndebele, who followed the Zulu fighting method of encircling their enemies, fifty of the Voortrekkers formed their wagons into a circle and held off their attackers.

In May 1900, battles raged between English and Boer forces near the Sand River, which flows though the northern Free State. During a battle at Biddulphsberg, between Winburg and Bethlehem, the veld caught fire and many British soldiers perished in the flames. But in July of the same year the war was over, a major Boer force, led by General Prinsloo, capitulated at Surrender Hill near Fouriesburg.

east of the centre. Neat rooms have TV and telephone. There's a restaurant and a bar here.

Saddles Steak Ranch (☎ 353 4248; Stateway; mains R40-50) Opposite the Sanlam Plaza, Saddles has decent steaks. If you're thirsty, try O'Hagan's Bar in the Welkom Inn.

Getting There & Away

Being a mining town, Welkom is a major depot for City to City buses, with a few services to Jo'burg/Pretoria, and more to the QwaQwa region, Lesotho and the Transkei.

Several Intercape services stop daily in town on their way to destinations including Cape Town (R370, 15 hours) Bloemfontein (R110, two hours) and Jo'burg (R175, four hours). Greyhound buses stop at the Orange Hotel on Stateway, on the way to Cape Town (R360, 14 hours).

The minibus taxis in the supermarket car park in town are mainly for the local area but you may find long-distance taxis here for Jo'burg (R55) or Cape Town (R130) in the early morning.

KROONSTAD

☎ 056 / pop 90,800

Kroonstad, on the N1, is a typical large rural Free State town. It dates back to 1855, and the Voortrekker Sarel Celliers was one of the first settlers here. Kroonstad may have been named after the Voortrekker's horse, Kroon!

There's Internet access at **Compuwise** (☎ 213 4368; cnr Orange & President Sts; per hr R20; ☼ 7.30am-5pm Mon-Fri, 7.30am-1pm Sat) in the centre of town.

Sights & Activities

The **old market building** opposite the pretty magistrate's building, on the corner of Mark and Murray Sts, is a national monument. Upstairs in the library there's the small **Sarel Celliers Museum** (☎ 216 9249; ☼ 10am-4pm Mon-Fri).

You can see the **Celliers statue** in the grounds of the impressive NG Moederkerk (Mother Church) on Cross St. Celliers is standing on a gun carriage making the Blood River vow.

Kroon Park (admission R20) offers swimming and other water activities (p360).

The national tournament of Jukskei (an Afrikaner game in which clubs are tossed at a peg) is held annually in Kroonstad.

The 4000-hectare **Koppies Dam Nature Reserve** (☎ 72 ext 2522; ☼ 7am-9pm) northeast of Kroonstad, is on the Rhenoster River. It is home to various wildlife species and water birds, but fishing is the main pursuit, with yellowfish, barbell, mudfish and carp taken in abundance. Windsurfing, sailing, and water-skiing are also very popular here. There are camping sites with ablution facilities in the reserve.

Sleeping & Eating

Arcadia Guesthouse (☎ 212 8280; arcadia@gcs.co.za; s/d with breakfast R280/350) This guesthouse is in the midst of a large garden scattered with faux-Greek statues. The very smart, classically themed rooms make it the best place to stay in Kroonstad. It's extremely well signposted from most arteries into town. Dinner can be arranged (R60).

Kroon Park (☎ 213 1942; fax 213 1941; camp sites R45, 2-/4-person chalets R200/250; ☼) This is more like a resort than a municipal park, with a couple of swimming pools, river tubing and boat rides. There are some beautiful camping spots on the river's edge. It's well signposted in town. Prices are higher at Christmas and Easter, and at these times you'll need to book ahead. There's a R100 deposit for accommodation, and a weekend supplement of R50.

Shalom Guesthouse (☎ 217 5717; fax 212 6228; Louw St; s/d R170/230; ☼ ☼) This is a basic but respectable guesthouse near the centre of town with recently refurbished rooms, some with TV.

Angelo's Trattoria (☎ 213 2833; 38 Reitz St; pizza R30-40; ☼ lunch & dinner) Pizza with biltong, fettucine with steak, burgers and crumbed mushrooms on the menu – it's all Italian here, but it does have a nice cosy interior. Opposite the mosque.

Trinity Coffee Shop (☎ 082-518 0585; breakfast R15-20; ☼ breakfast & lunch Mon-Sat) This pretty little coffee shop is opposite the Shalom Guesthouse. It does breakfasts, salads and toasted sandwiches.

Getting There & Away

BUS

The City to City bus service between Welkom and Jo'burg stops at the train station.

There are three daily Translux services (between Jo'burg/Pretoria and either East London, Port Elizabeth or Paarl), which stop out on the highway at the Shell Ultra

City, as does Greyhound's Jo'burg/Pretoria to Port Elizabeth service.

MINIBUS TAXI
The minibus taxi rank is opposite the train station. Most minibus taxis go to relatively nearby towns only, although there are occasional services to Jo'burg – get there early in the morning.

TRAIN
The *Trans Oranje* train stops here on its weekly run between Durban (1st/2nd/economy class R210/145/85, 14 hours) and Cape Town (R445/305/180, 24 hours). See p605 for more details of this service.

PARYS & VREDEFORT DOME
☎ 056 / pop 45,400
Parys, right on the border with the North-West Province, is handy for visiting Vredefort Dome, an area of hills created by the impact of a gigantic meteorite 2000 million years ago. The same cataclysmic impact created the Witwatersrand gold-bearing reefs. Vredefort is the oldest and largest meteorite impact site on earth, measuring around 200km in diameter.

Today the area consists of valleys, ravines and cliffs, covered in lush flora and home to a variety of different plants, animals and birds. Activities on offer range from abseiling to white-water rafting.

The **Parys Info Centre** (☎ 817 2986; www.parys info.co.za; 62b Bree St; ☯ 8am-5pm Mon-Fri, 8am-1pm Sat) does bookings for the many adventure trails and camping sites in the Dome area.

Sleeping & Eating
Waterfront Guesthouse (☎ 083-452 6504; devills@ global.co.za; 22 Grewar Ave; s/d with breakfast R150/300) A very friendly and good-value place down by the Vaal river.

Suikerbos (☎ 018-294 3857; www.suikerbos.co.za; camp sites R60, dm/cottage per person R35/60, chalet R250-350) Bookings are essential for this farm/reserve in which herds of impala graze peacefully between the buildings.

Mirro's (☎ 817 7191; 62 Bree St; mains R20-50; ☯ lunch & dinner Tue-Sun) This little restaurant does half-decent pizza, steaks and burgers.

Getting There & Away
Minibus taxis link Parys with Potchefstroom in the North-West Province. From there you can find onward transport to Jo'burg or Pretoria.

EASTERN HIGHLANDS

This is the most beautiful part of Free State, stretching from Zastron in the south to Harrismith in the north, and following the Lesotho border. Roughly, it is the area that fringes the R26 and the R49 east of Bethlehem to Harrismith. In addition to being a tremendously scenic area, it is also archaeologically and historically important. The drives alone, past sandstone monoliths that tower above rolling fields, are reason enough to visit.

HARRISMITH
☎ 058 / pop 35,200
Harrismith is a quiet rural centre, well situated for exploring the northern Drakensberg, the QwaQwa area and Golden Gate Highlands National Park. It probably has the best facilities for travellers in the area.

The **Harrismith Marketing Bureau** (☎ 622 3525; fax 623 0923; Pretoria St; ☯ 9am-5pm Mon-Fri) in the town hall can help with local information.

There's Internet access at the **Koppie Shop** (Stuart St; per min R0.60; ☯ 9am-5pm Mon-Fri).

Sights & Activities
The extensive **botanic gardens** (☎ 623 1078; admission R5; ☯ 7am-7pm Sep-May, 7.30am-7pm Jun-Aug), about 5km south of town at the foot of the Platberg, have many plant species from the Drakensberg. Walking on the slopes of the Platberg you may see a few antelope species – there was once a nature reserve here.

The information centre arranges **tours** (R25) of Intabazwe, a township on a hill outside town, and can also arrange **half-board accommodation** (r with dinner & breakfast around R150) there. It's inspiring to see a small, conservative town promoting this sort of thing, and the peaceful township is small enough for visitors to get a good feel for township life. Unusually for Free State, both Zulu and Sotho people live here.

Sleeping & Eating
Harrismith International Backpackers (☎ 058-623 0007; jmantz@oldmutualpfa.com; 44 Piet Retief St; camp sites per person/dm/d with shared bathroom R30/55/140).

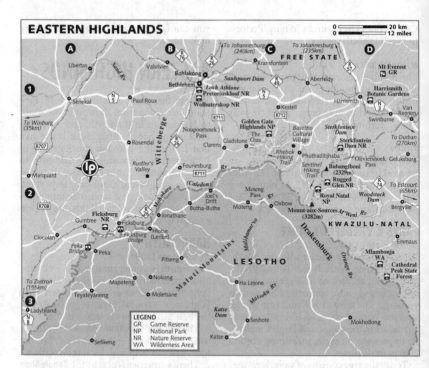

EASTERN HIGHLANDS

LEGEND
GR Game Reserve
NP National Park
NR Nature Reserve
WA Wilderness Area

There's a garden and braai (barbecue) facilities in this comfy B&B-cum-backpackers. The staff can do pick-ups from major bus stops in the area.

Harrismith Inn (☎ 622 1011; harrismithinn@dorea .co.za; McKechnie St; s/d R268/363; ✗ 🖳 🕿) This is a modern hotel, next to Spur and similar to a Holiday Inn. The good-value rooms have TV and telephone. The hotel has its own restaurant and bar.

Harrismith Country Lodge (☎ 622 2151; fax 622 2152; 100 McKechnie St; s/d R169/219) The name of this ugly concrete motel situated behind the BP station is presumably ironic; however it should do at a pinch, if you only need somewhere to stop for the night. It's opposite the Harrismith Inn at the N5 junction.

Pringles Country Inn (☎ 623 0255; louise@pringles -wimpy.co.za; Bergview 1-stop, Warden St; s/d R240/360; ✗) This is another, newer motel, no more rural than the Harrismith Country Lodge, but at least it has a decent restaurant and smart rooms, some with fridges.

Pringles (☎ 623 0255; Bergview 1-stop, Warden St; mains R20-50; ✆ lunch & dinner Mon-Sat, lunch Sun)

The best dining option in town serves old-fashioned stodge such as bangers and mash, and lamb hotpot.

Spur (☎ 623 1319; McKechnie St; mains R20-45; ✆ breakfast, lunch & dinner) Next to the Harrismith Inn, Spur has a great playroom for kids. It also does some tasty Mexican dishes.

Getting There & Away

BUS

Translux runs daily services to Durban (R150, four hours), Bloemfontein (R145, five hours), Jo'burg (R150, four hours) and Cape Town (R370, 17 hours), which stop at the Harrismith Country Lodge on Mc-Kechnie St.

The Baz Bus also stops here (at the Shell garage on the N3) on its Jo'burg-to-Durban run, if you book ahead.

MINIBUS TAXI

Minibus taxis run to Phuthaditjhaba (R10; see p364), from where you'll have a much larger choice of routes and more frequent minibus taxis.

TRAIN

The *Trans Oranje* train stops here daily between Durban (1st/2nd/economy class R135/95/55, eight hours) and Cape Town (R525/355/210, over 24 hours). See p605 for details.

AROUND HARRISMITH

The small **Sterkfontein Dam Nature Reserve** (☎ 058-622 3520; admission per vehicle R25; ☯ 7.30am-10pm) is in the Drakensberg foothills, 23km south of Harrismith on the Oliviershoek Pass road into KwaZulu-Natal. This is a very beautiful area, and looking out over this expansive dam with rugged peaks as a backdrop is like gazing across an inland sea. At one of the many viewpoints there's a vulture 'restaurant', but there's no set day or time for feeding. Sunset cruises on the dam's lake are available.

Camp sites (R40) are available, and there are **4-bed chalets** (R200).

GOLDEN GATE HIGHLANDS NATIONAL PARK

Golden Gate (☎ 058-255 0012; fax 255 0022; admission R60), which is being extended to incorporate the former QwaQwa Highlands National Park, preserves the unique and spectacular scenery of the foothills of the Maluti Mountains. The western approach to the park is guarded by the immense, sandstone Brandwag rocks, typical of the scenery within the park, which turn a glowing golden colour in the late afternoon and give the park its name.

There are also quite a few animals, including grey rheboks, blesboks, elands, oribis, Burchell's zebras, jackals, baboons and numerous bird species, including the rare bearded and Cape vulture as well as the endangered bald ibis. Hiking is the main reason to come here, but there are also plenty of shorter walking trails and scenic, twisting roads to drive on.

Winters in the park can be very cold, with frost and snow; summers are mild but rain falls at this time and cold snaps are possible: if you're out hiking, take warm clothing. Buy entry permits at the park reception.

Rhebok Hiking Trail

This well-maintained, circular, 33km **trail** (two days per person R60) is a great way to see the park. The trail takes its name from the grey rhebok, a species of antelope that prefers exposed mountain plateaus, and you will probably see them when hiking. The trail starts at the Glen Reenen Rest Camp, next to the park reception, and on the second day the track climbs up to a viewpoint on the side of Generaalskop (2732m), the highest point in the park, from where Mont-aux-Sources and the Malutis can be seen. The return trail to Glen Reenen passes Langtoon Dam.

There are some steep sections so hikers need to be reasonably fit. The trail is limited to 18 people and must be booked through the **South African National (SAN) Parks Board** (☎ 012-428 9111; www.parks-sa.co.za).

There are also shorter hiking trails in the foothills, ranging from 45 minutes to half a day. Ask at the park reception for details.

Horse Riding

If you prefer four legs to two, horse trails are a great way to see the park. **Gladstone Stables** (☎ 058-255 0951), near the park reception, organises rides to beautiful spots like Cathedral Cave (per hour R30).

Basotho Cultural Village

Within the park, under the lee of Vulture Mountain, you'll find the small **Basotho Cultural Village** (☎ 058-721 0300; basotho@dorea.co.za; tours R15; ☯ 8am-4.30pm Mon-Fri, 8am-5pm Sat & Sun). It's essentially an open-air museum, peopled by actors depicting various aspects of traditional Basotho life. There's a curio shop and an outdoor **restaurant** (☯ lunch & dinner) serving a few Sotho dishes. Try the home-made ginger beer. A guided **hiking trail** (per person R20, two hours) explores medicinal and other plants, and a rock-art site.

You can stay in two-person self-catering **rondavels** (R380). Bring your own food.

This is a friendly place, with a lot of good information on traditional culture, but it's essentially artificial and idealised. To see how most Sotho live, take a township tour in nearby Harrismith (p361), or cross the border into Lesotho (p516).

Sleeping

Glen Reenen Rest Camp (☎ 011-428 9111; 2-person camp sites R95, 2-person chalets R380) The park's main rest camp has well-maintained chalets and camping spots, but it gets very busy with South African families in high season. There's a shop here selling basic supplies.

Two other rest camps are planned within the newly-extended Golden Gate area, one at the Basotho Cultural Village.

Protea Hotel Golden Gate (☎ 058-255 1000; www.proteahotels.com/goldengate; self-catering chalets d R470, s/d with breakfast R468/580, buffet dinner R80; 🖳) The park's only 'proper' hotel is a pretty good member of the Protea hotel chain, with wonderful views from the terrace and a snug coffee shop. Ask for a room at the front when booking.

Getting There & Away

The R712 is a sealed road that runs into the park from Clarens, south of Bethlehem. Minibus taxis run between Bethlehem and Harrismith, via Clarens and Phuthaditjhaba, and go right through the park. Alternatively, with your own vehicle you can approach from Harrismith on the R74 and then the R712.

PHUTHADITJHABA & AROUND

☎ 058 / pop 43,800

Phuthaditjhaba, about 50km southwest of Harrismith, was the capital of the apartheid homeland of QwaQwa (master the 'click' pronunciation and you'll win friends). QwaQwa (meaning 'Whiter than White'), was named after the sandstone hill that dominates the area. It was created in the early 1980s as a homeland for southern Sotho people. The dumping of 200,000 people on a tiny patch of agriculturally unviable land, remote from employment centres, was one of the more obscene acts of apartheid. Today, the highlands around Phuthaditjhaba (which means 'meeting place of all nations') are great hiking country.

The **QwaQwa information centre** (☎ 713 0012; fax 713 4342; ⏱ 8am-4.30pm Mon-Fri, 8am-9pm Sat & Sun), on the road through town, has hiking information.

Sentinel Hiking Trail

The most famous of the hiking trails in the area is the 10km **Sentinel Hiking Trail**, which commences in Free State and ends in KwaZulu-Natal. The trail starts at the Sentinel car park, on the way up to Witsieshoek Mountain Resort Hotel at an altitude of 2540m, and runs for 4km to the top of the Drakensberg plateau, where the average height is 3000m. It's about a two-hour ascent for those of medium fitness. At one point you have to use a chain ladder that runs up over a set of sheer rocks. Those who find the ladder frightening can take the route up The Gully, which emerges at Beacon Buttress (although some hikers argue this route is even more hair-raising!). The reward for the steep ascent is majestic mountain scenery and the opportunity to climb Mont-aux-Sources (3282m; p326).

Sleeping & Eating

Witsieshoek Mountain Resort Hotel (☎ 713 6361; fax 713 5274; s/d with breakfast R195/390, dinner R55) About 15km south of Phuthaditjhaba, this is reputedly South Africa's highest-altitude hotel and is a good source for local hiking information. The accommodation, however, is pretty basic.

There are several rudimentary cafés and hotels in Phuthaditjhaba – ask the information centre for recommendations.

Getting There & Away

Minibus taxis from Phuthaditjhaba to Harrismith (R10) and Bethlehem (R35), usually via Clarens, run daily.

If you're driving into Phuthaditjhaba from the north, you'll eventually get through the urban sprawl to the tourist information centre (look for a cluster of tall thatched roofs on the left). If you're heading for the Witsieshoek Mountain Resort Hotel or the Sentinel Hiking Trail, turn left at the traffic lights at the information centre and keep going.

CLARENS

☎ 058

This pretty little town, on the junction of the R712 and the R711 (a back road between Bethlehem and Fouriesburg), is surrounded by large limestone rocks, such as Titanic Rock, with the magnificent Maluti Mountains forming a backdrop.

Artists have set up studios in and around Clarens and there are galleries and craft shops lining the edges of the central village square. Unfortunately many of them are pretty tacky, and the village centre has a distinctly tourist-orientated feel. Worth a detour is the excellent **Bibliophile** (☎ 256 1692; 313 Church St), a quaint bookshop with a huge range of titles as well as jazz CDs and local cheeses. Other 'essentials for a civilised life' on offer are olive oil, imported pasta and Italian coffee.

The **Highlands Tourist & Information Centre** (☎ 256 1542; clarens@bhm.dorea.co.za; ☾ 8am-5pm Mon-Thu, 8am-6pm Fri, 8am-4pm Sat & Sun) had unenthusiastic staff when we visited and little in the way of literature.

Activities
There are lots of opportunities for **fly-fishing** in dams and rivers around here. Rainbow and brown trout are usually on offer and it costs around R70 per day including a rod. Casting is the trickiest part! Ask at the **Something Else** (☎ 256 1389; Market St, Clarens) curio shop for permits.

Mountain Odyssey Tourism (☎ 256 1173; odyssey@isat.co.za) organises open-vehicle safaris into Golden Gate National Park as well as quad-biking trails.

Sleeping & Eating
Village Square Guesthouse (☎ 256 1064; villagehouse@isat.co.za; Main St; s/d with breakfast R290/450) If you want to be right in among the action around the village green, opt for one of the big, smartly decorated rooms here. All have TV and electric blankets for those chilly highland nights.

Patcham Place (☎ 256 1017; patcham@netactive.co.za; 262 Church St; s/d with breakfast R260/390) This B&B is another good central option: its comfortable rooms with fridge and balcony, inside the owner's house.

Clarens Inn (☎ 256 1119; schwim@netactive.co.za; 93 Van Reenan St; camp sites R40, s from R80) Clarens Inn is a good budget option against the mountain at the bottom of Van Reenen St (after the Le Roux turn-off). Accommodation is in a variety of dorms and cottages, with some having open fires and en suite bathrooms.

Bokpoort Holiday Farm & Game Ranch (☎ 256 1181; www.bokpoort.co.za; s/d with breakfast R190/380) This farmstay is backpacker-friendly and in a great spot between Clarens and Golden Gate. Horse riding on western saddles is available and there are mountain-bike trails (but you must have your own bike). To get here, travel 5km from Clarens on the Golden Gate road, then turn off at the big Bokpoort Holiday Farm sign and drive another 3km along the dirt road.

Clementines Restaurant (☎ 256 1616; 315 Church St; mains R45-60; ☾ lunch & dinner Tue-Sun) This is a wonderfully cosy restaurant serving fantastic food that's a bit pricey but well worth it.

Try the butternut soup or the local speciality, pan-fried trout (R58).

Street Café (☎ 256 1064; Hoof St; mains R20-40; ☾ lunch & dinner) This is a good place for a pizza, or a drink in the pub next door.

Getting There & Away
Minibus taxis run between Bethlehem and Harrismith, travelling via Clarens and Phuthaditjhaba.

BETHLEHEM
☎ 058 / pop 59,800
Bethlehem was established by Voortrekkers on the farm Pretoriuskloof in 1864. Not content with the biblical name they chose for their town, the devout newcomers also gave the name Jordaan to the river that flows through it. Bethlehem is now a large town and the main commercial centre of eastern Free State.

The **tourist information office** (☎ 303 5732; info@bethlehem.org.za; ☾ 7.30am-1pm & 2-4pm Mon-Fri) is in the civic centre on Muller St, near the corner of Roux St.

The obligatory shopping centre, the Metropolitan, has a coffee shop, a pharmacy and a cinema.

Sights & Activities
As usual for this area, there are some impressive sandstone buildings, including the **old magistrate's office**, on the corner of Louw and Van der Merwe Sts, and the **NG Moederkerk** in the town centre. Also right in town is the tiny **Pretoriuskloof Nature Reserve** (adult/child R5/2; ☾ 8am-5pm Apr-Sep, 7.30am-6pm Oct-Mar) on the banks of the Jordaan near the corner of Kerk and Kort Sts. Just outside of town is the **Wolhuterskop Game & Nature Reserve** (☎ 303 5732), which has several species of antelope. There are horse trails and a one-night hiking route here. Book through the tourist information office in town.

Sleeping & Eating
There are some good B&Bs in the area. The tourist information office has a full list.

Fisant & Bokmakierie Guesthouse (☎ 303 7144; fisant@isat.co.za; 8-10 Thoi Oosthuyse St; s/d with breakfast R260/340; ☒) This well-established, acclaimed guesthouse is the best in town. The owners are very friendly and each room is tastefully furnished, with some quirky single rooms in the garden. **Dinner** (R60) can be arranged on weekday evenings. There are also some larger self-catering units available at their other property, Hoephoep, near the hospital. If there's no room at the inn, the staff can help find alternative options.

La Croché (☎ 303 9229; www.lacroche.co.za; cnr Kerk & Theron Sts; s/d R260/370) Some of the rooms at this upmarket guesthouse have Jacuzzis – ask when booking. It's next door to O'Hagans, which is handy for breakfast or evening drinks.

Park Hotel (☎/fax 303 5191; 23 Muller St; s R120-220, d R160-270, breakfast R30) On the corner of High St, the Park Hotel is an old-fashioned hotel built in 1928. The quaint polished-wood bar is a good place to watch a rugby match with the Afrikaner locals. The budget rooms across the street are basic, but clean. The **restaurant** (3-course meal R65) in Park Hotel is the best-value place to eat in Bethlehem. Their standard pub fare is reasonably priced.

O'Hagan's (☎ 303 0919; 8 Theron St; mains R25-50; ☺ breakfast, lunch & dinner) O'Hagan's serves above-average pub fare, and is definitely the best of the chain restaurants in town.

Nix Pub (Kerk St) Across from the church, this is a cosy place for a drink and it has decent pub meals too.

Debonairs Pizza, KFC and Nando's are all within a few hundred metres of each other around Muller St, near the Metropolitan shopping centre.

Getting There & Away
BUS
Translux runs daily to Durban (R160, five hours) and Cape Town (R360, 16 hours), as does Greyhound at similar fares. Translux buses stop at Top Grill on Church St and Greyhound stops at Wimpy, on the corner of Muller and Hospital Sts.

MINIBUS TAXI
The minibus-taxi ranks are around the corner of Cambridge and Gholf Sts, north of the town centre on the way to the train station. There are minibus taxis to Harrismith via Clarens.

TRAIN
The *Trans Oranje* train stops here on its weekly run between Durban (1st/2nd/economy class R170/115/65, 10 hours) and Cape Town (R492/335/200).

FOURIESBURG
☎ 058

Fouriesburg is 12km north of the Caledonspoort border post for Lesotho. The town is surrounded by mountains: the Witteberge to the west; and the Maluti Mountains to the east. Two nearby peaks, Snijmanshoek and Visierskerf, are the highest in Free State.

Fouriesburg was a stronghold in the Anglo-Boer War and was pronounced the capital of Free State after the British occupied Bethlehem.

There are a number of fine old **sandstone buildings** in the town including President Steyn's house.

About 11km outside Fouriesburg, and just 800m from the Lesotho border, **Camelroc Guest Farm** (☎ 223 0368; www.camelroc.co.za; camp sites per person R30, s/d with breakfast R195/390) has fine views over the Maluti Mountains. There are self-catering cottages and several hiking and 4WD trails also on offer.

RUSTLER'S VALLEY
☎ 051

This remote valley in the heart of the conservative Free State is the vanguard of the 'dare to be different' movement in the new South Africa. The valley, centred on the famous Rustler's Valley Retreat, attracts a diverse crowd: yuppies from Jo'burg, remnant hippies from all parts of the continent and 'ideas' people from all over the globe.

If you grow tired of contemplating your navel, you can swim or fish in the many dams, walk up onto sandstone escarpments, climb imposing Nyakalesoba (Witchdoctor's Eye) or ride a horse into the labyrinthine dongas all around.

Rustler's Valley Retreat (☎/fax 933 3939; www .rustlers.co.za; camp sites per person/dm/d R35/60/250; ❂) is the original hippy hangout, and is a lot more polished and better organised than you might expect. It's proof that just because you're in tune with nature doesn't mean you can't have a hot shower or a gourmet meal (try their venison goujons or herb tagliatelle, but make sure you book ahead for dinner).

The individually painted cottages with private bathrooms are superb, as is the glass-fronted restaurant with panoramic views over the valley. The once-legendary music festival no longer happens here, but it's been replaced with a calendar of smaller events, most notably the One World festival at Easter. There are also a variety of workshops on offer, from drumming to permaculture or creativity. Give the staff a call if you need a lift from Ficksburg (R20). Children are very welcome.

Franshoek Guest Farm (☎ 933 2828, 072-128 7356; www.franshoek.co.za; s/d with breakfast R230/460; 🖳 🕿) is a working farm with comfortable sandstone cottages in its garden, a terrific round swimming pool and great views of the valley. Try to get the honeymoon suite with its open fire. A polo package, with full board, thoroughbred ponies and instruction from a pro, costs R1500 per day.

Getting There & Away
Rustler's Valley Retreat does pick-ups (R20) from Ficksburg. If you have your own vehicle, the main turn-off is about 25km south of Fouriesburg on the R26 to Ficksburg. Follow the signposts down a dirt road that crosses a train line. From the turn-off it is about 12km to Rustler's.

FICKSBURG
☎ 051
Ficksburg is a pretty place with some fine **sandstone buildings** including the town hall, the NG Kerk and the post office.

The mild summers and cold winters of this area are good for growing stone fruits, and Ficksburg is the centre of the Free State's cherry industry. There's a Cherry Festival in November but September and October are the best times to see the trees in bloom. The **Cherry Trail** is a tourist route around the district; there are several orchards to visit, various art and craft shops and guest farms. Get a map from the **tourist office** (☎ 933 2130; 🕑 9am-4.30pm Mon-Fri) in the Caltex office on the main road, or visit www.cherryfestival.co.za.

Sleeping & Eating
Bella Rosa Guesthouse (☎ 933 2623; bellarosa@tel komsa.net; 21 Bloem St; s/d with breakfast R250/390; 🖳) This excellent guesthouse does a roaring trade. Dinner can be arranged, and there's a bar here too.

Thom Park (☎ 083-592 1267; Voortrekker St; camp sites R40) The green and shady municipal caravan park is right in the middle of town, opposite Bella Rosa Guesthouse.

Hotel Hoogland (☎ 933 2214; fax 933 2750; 37 Voortrekker St; s/d with breakfast R180/300, budget s/d

R120/200) This standard hotel has a big gift shop and tourist information centre downstairs. The budget rooms are more or less exactly the same as the more expensive standard rooms – both have private bathrooms. The restaurant has a patronising 'ladies' menu featuring dainty delights such as chicken croquettes (R25).

Bottling Co Pub & Restaurant (☎ 933 2404; 57 Piet Retief St; mains R38-48; 🕑 lunch & dinner Mon-Sat) This place has an imaginative menu with a couple of veggie options and is a top little spot for an evening beer.

Lemon Cottage coffee shop (Kestell St; 🕑 lunch Mon-Sat) Try this ladylike coffee shop for lunch – its club sandwiches could feed three people.

Getting There & Away
Coming from Jo'burg, you can get to Ficksburg by taking a minibus taxi to Bethlehem. At Bethlehem change to a minibus taxi for Ficksburg (R20, one hour).

LADYBRAND
☎ 051 / pop 17,300
Ladybrand, also on the R26, is around 16km from Maseru, Lesotho's capital.

There are some handsome **sandstone buildings** including the town hall and the old magistrate's court. **Catharina Brand Museum** (☎ 924 5131; malotiinfo@xsinet.co.za; 17 Church St; 🕑 8am-5pm Mon-Fri) has archaeological displays including rock paintings and instruments, and tools dating back to the Stone Age. You will find the tourist office here too.

Ashes taken from an ancient hearth in the **Rose Cottage Cave**, not far from Ladybrand, prove that the area was inhabited by humans 55,000 years ago. There are also over 300 San rock-art sites in caves in the area around the town.

About 12km from Ladybrand is one of the quaintest churches you are ever likely to see. **Modderpoort Cave Church**, built in 1869, is nestled under a huge boulder in scenic surroundings. Apply for permission to visit at the tourist office.

Sleeping & Eating
Fort Amity (☎ 924 3131; fax 924 1633; 18 van Riebeeck St; s/d with breakfast R300/450, luxury s/d R350/600; 🖳 🕿) This isn't a fort but an imposing grey-brick house, which these days is home to a very smart B&B. The luxury rooms have

their own balcony and fridge and the large, manicured garden holds a tennis court.

Cranberry Cottage (☎ 924 2290; crancott@xsinet .co.za; 37 Beeton St; s/d R297/470; 🖳 🐾) This is perhaps the most interesting B&B in town. It offers luxury accommodation, as well as good-value rooms in the disused train station 800m away. The three-course fusion-style dinner (R95) is recommended. There's also a small gift shop here.

Casa Romana B&B (☎ 924 1627; casaromana@xsi net.co.za; 34 Piet Retief St; s/d with breakfast R285/480; 🖳) The rooms in this smart pink-painted B&B have TV, minibar and safe. The establishment also runs the **Impero Romana restaurant** (11 Church St; mains R20-60; 🕙 lunch & dinner Mon-Sat), with sophisticated food and good service.

Country Lodge (☎ 924 3209; fax 924 2611; 19 Joubert St; s/d with breakfast R210/290) Ladybrand's only hotel is a small friendly place with TV in every room. Some rooms also have fans.

Leliehoek Holiday Resort (☎ 924 0260; Leliehoek Ave; camp sites per person R30, 2-/3-person chalets R240/280) Located 2km south of the town hall, Leliehoek is a peaceful spot.

Getting There & Away
Minibus taxis can be found near the church on Piet Retief St. Most run to nearby areas, including Ficksburg (R20, one hour). For a wider choice of destinations, take a minibus taxi to Maseru Bridge (R5), at the Lesotho border, and find a long-distance taxi in the big minibus-taxi rank there.

ZASTRON
☎ 051 / 12,500
Zastron, on the R726, is a quiet little town in the foothills of the Aasvoëlberg and Maluti Mountains. It's the centre of a rural community and, with Lesotho forming an arc around this section of Free State, Zastron has long-established trading links with the mountain kingdom.

There are some **San paintings** in the area; the best are in the Seekoei and Hoffman Caves. The **Eye of Zastron**, a mildly interesting rock formation with a 9m hole, is best seen from the road to Aliwal North. There are also various walks and climbs that you can do.

The three-star **Maluti Hotel** (☎ /fax 673 2112; 22 Hoofe St; s/d with breakfast R165/300) has the Horse & Hound pub on site.

The nearest town in Lesotho is Mohale's Hoek, 55km away on a dirt road.

SOUTHERN FREE STATE

Southern Free State typifies much of the province: it's dusty, harsh and dry. It's pretty much an area that you'll just transit through, although some of the small old towns such as Philippolis are worth a look.

TUSSEN DIE RIVIERE GAME FARM
☎ 051
This 23,000-hectare **reserve** (☎ /fax 754 0026; 763 1114; admission per vehicle R20; 🕙 dawn-dusk Sep-Apr) has more animals than any other reserve in Free State. There are mostly small mammals and various species of antelope but also white rhinos and hippos. The country is varied, with plains and ridges and a long frontage on the Orange River. For keen hikers, there are the 7km Middelpunt, the 12km Klipstapel and the 16km Orange River hiking trails; water must be carried on all of them.

There are **camp sites** (with/without power R50/ 30), and inexpensive two-person **chalets** (with shared bathroom R150). There is a communal sitting- and dining-room complex with a bar, kitchen and a large braai area, but no food is available here. The entrance gate is on the road between Bethulie and Smithfield (R701), about 15km from Bethulie, or 65km east of the N1. There's no public transport, so you'll need your own vehicle.

GARIEP DAM NATURE RESERVE
☎ 051
West of Tussen Die Riviere, on the Orange River, this 13,000-hectare **reserve** (☎ 754 0026; admission per vehicle R20) surrounds one of the largest dams in South Africa (it used to be called the Hendrik Verwoerd Dam). Be warned, the dam is described in brochures as 'a mecca for motorboats'. During February each year the world's longest inland rubber-duck race takes place on the Gariep Dam. The event, which runs over a distance of 500km, is completed in one day.

There are three **chalets** (R250) in the reserve, or there are **camp sites** (R45).

There's quite a lot of accommodation in the town of Gariep Dam, near the dam wall at the western end. The town was built to house the workers constructing the dam. There are several B&Bs charging from R120 per person.

Aventura Midwaters Resort (☎ /fax 754 0045; fax 754 0135; camp sites/2-person chalets R100/550) is well laid-out. The opportunity for water sports here makes it expensive – rates go up in high season.

Gariep Dam Hotel (☎ 754 0060; s/d R235/380) is pricey but comfortable; breakfast is extra.

PHILIPPOLIS
☎ 051

On the R717, Philippolis is a beautiful little place; it's the oldest town in Free State, founded in 1823 as a mission station. The Griquas, who settled here in 1826, sold the town and then trekked overland, through Lesotho, to settle in Griqualand East (p334). Seventy-five buildings within the town have been declared national monuments, including the NG Kerk, the library and many places built in Karoo style. For more information about the town, contact the **Philippolis Information Office** (☎ 084-581 0149; www.philippolis.org.za).

If you've ever fancied spending a night in jail, the **Old Jail** (☎ 082-550 4421; s/d R100/200) is your big chance. The town's former jail has been converted into basic but comfortable self-catering accommodation. The prison also has a honeymoon suite!

FAURESMITH
☎ 051

Fauresmith is famous for the train line that runs along the main street. North of town on the Petrusburg road is the 4500-hectare **Kalkfontein Dam Nature Reserve** (☎ 722 1441; admission per vehicle R20), a great place to see the local fishermen harvesting yellowfish. Camping and angling are the main activities on offer. There are no shops and visitors must bring their own provisions and equipment. There are **camp sites** (R30) with braai areas and toilets.

Gauteng

CONTENTS

On the surface, Gauteng (southern Sotho for 'Place of Gold' and pronounced 'how-teng') is the small province with the deep pocket, a province that grew rich on the back of the gold rush and kept plenty aside for a rainy day. Incorporating the cities of Johannesburg (Jo'burg) and Pretoria, it is now the country's metropolitan powerhouse, accounting for 34% of South Africa's gross domestic product (GDP) and, perhaps more extraordinarily, 10% of the GDP of all Africa. Fly through Gauteng's opulent suburbs then, and you will encounter an Africa of corporate headquarters, six-lane freeways, neon-capped shopping malls and German-built saloons, all cut through with the cosmopolitan high-life demanded by those with bulging wallets.

There is a flipside to this gold sovereign however, and while a minority gloats in the Gauteng big time, plenty more exist beneath the veneer, among some of the country's starkest urban poverty. Positive change is sweeping through parts of Soweto, with a growing tourist industry and booming entrepreneurship bolstering the township's once derelict economy, but other sections remain hopelessly destitute, with tens of thousands still living in shacks without electricity and running water. The province's perennial crime problem is perhaps the inevitable consequence of the stark polarities of Gauteng living.

But there is much more to this fascinating province than money, or the blatant lack of it. From Pretoria, the fast-changing one-time capital of the apartheid system, to the vibrant streets of Soweto, where the daily struggle against segregation was lived out, Gauteng is choc-a-bloc with the history of South Africa. City sprawl has long since ingested many of the province's open spaces, but if you want to explore the urban jungle, with all its idiosyncrasies and intrigue, there is no better place to do it.

HIGHLIGHTS

- Soaking up the new Johannesburg (Jo'burg) in **Newtown's cultural precinct** (p381)

- Watching Jo'Burg's **Old Melville** drift by from a roadside café (p389)

- Getting up-close-and-personal with a baby King Cheetah at the **De Wildt Cheetah & Research Centre** (p419)

- Rocking around the clock on Pretoria's party strip, **Burnett St** (p415)

- Exploring the historic heartlands of the world's best-known township, **Soweto**, and live it up with locals in a shebeen (p401)

- Catching the Jo'burg derby as Kaizer Chiefs and Orlando Pirates clash on the **football** pitch (p393)

- POPULATION: 9,839,000

- AREA: 17,010 SQ KM

GAUTENG

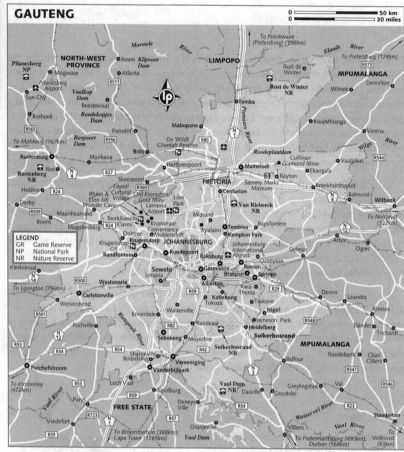

HISTORY

Gauteng has many strands to its tangled history and the longest reaches as far back as humankind itself. Dubbed the Cradle of Humankind, the northwestern corner of Gauteng is thought to have played a key role in human evolution, with sites across the region yielding up as many as 850 sets of hominid remains. In 1947, Dr Robert Broom made one of the most famous discoveries in Sterkfontein Caves (p403), when he uncovered the 2.5-million-year-old fossilised skull of the affectionately named Mrs Ples.

Despite the massive disruption caused by the Zulu wars, when many local Blacks left the region, the area now called Gauteng remained a relatively quiet, chiefly rural place right through until the end of the 19th century. A number of different tribes lived in the region and there is evidence of mining activities dating as far back as the Iron Age, but it was only in 1886, when gold was discovered, that the area was catapulted into the modern age.

Boers, escaping British rule in the Cape Colony, had been here since the mid-19th century, founding the independent Zuid-Afrikaansche Republiek (ZAR) and establishing its capital in the then frontier village of Pretoria. But as the British turned their attentions to the colossal profits being made in the gold mines, it was only a matter of time before the events that led to the 1899–1902 Anglo-Boer War were set in motion.

The British won and the fledgling city of Jo'burg exploded into life, but little had changed for the thousands of Black miners. It was a theme that would persist throughout the coming century. With apartheid later being managed out of Pretoria, and the townships surrounding Jo'burg, not least of them Soweto, becoming the hub of both the system's worst abuses and its most energetic opponents, Gauteng, which was then known as Transvaal, was centre stage in South Africa's all-too-familiar 20th-century drama.

The 21st century has started in a new light. Transvaal has been renamed Gauteng, a Black president now rules out of Pretoria and the country's new Constitutional Court has been built on the site of Jo'burg's most infamous apartheid-era jail, the Old Fort. However it remains to be seen whether the new century will finally bring Gauteng's poor their slice of the pie.

See p374 and p405 for more information.

CLIMATE

Largely on the highveld, the big cities of Gauteng benefit from the cooling effects of altitude. Both Jo'burg and Pretoria can become baking hot in summer, but a fresh breeze can often be relied on to take the sting out of a Jo'burg January. At this time of year, cloudless days and plenty of sunshine are common.

Winters can get chilly, and frosts and freezing temperatures are not unknown. It has even been known for Jo'burg to get a dusting of snow. Early summer (September–October) and autumn (March–April) offer the best weather for a visit.

NATIONAL PARKS & RESERVES

Concrete streets, rather than open spaces, predominate in largely metropolitan Gauteng, but there are still a few decent day-trip escapes to be had. Suikerbosrand Nature Reserve, Krugersdorp Game Reserve and especially the Rhino & Lion Nature Reserve, near Jo'burg (see p403), offer a reasonable spread of wildlife and a sense of the great outdoors, while the De Wildt Cheetah Research Centre (p419), near Pretoria, remains one of Gauteng's great attractions.

LANGUAGE

English is widely spoken in Gauteng, although Afrikaans is often the language of choice among Whites in Pretoria. Sesotho, Sepedi, Setswana and Zulu are the main languages spoken among Blacks, although many will communicate using the hybrid melange of South African languages that developed in the townships.

DANGERS & ANNOYANCES

Crime is a daily reality in Gauteng, and Jo'burg in particular, but the risks should always be kept in perspective. The worst crime is often limited to individual suburbs and so there is absolutely no need to feel trapped in your hotel room. Local advice is gold dust when it comes to having a good, safe time in the big cities: ask for it, listen to it and then go out there and enjoy yourself.

See p378 and p409 for more information.

GETTING THERE & AROUND

As South Africa's major national and international transport hubs, there aren't many places you can't get to from Jo'burg and Pretoria. **Johannesburg International Airport** (JIA; ☎ 011-921 6911; www.johannesburg-jnb.com), easily accessible from Pretoria and Jo'burg, has flights to regional centres across the country, with airlines covering many of the smaller towns as well. Durban, Cape Town and Port Elizabeth are also connected to Jo'burg via a network of no-frills budget airlines – by far the best way of getting between the big cities.

South Africa's long-distance bus companies, **Translux** (☎ 011-774 3333; www.translux.co.za), **Greyhound** (☎ 012-323 1154; www.greyhound.co.za) and **Intercape Mainliner** (☎ 0861 287 287, 021-380 4400; www.intercape.co.za), also link Jo'burg and Pretoria with just about anywhere you would want to go. Both cities are often served by the same services, with buses heading north starting at Jo'burg's Park Station, before passing through Pretoria, and services heading south commencing in Pretoria, before stopping in Jo'burg. Prices are reasonable, with fares to destinations as far as Cape Town rarely exceeding R400. If you are backpacking, the **Baz Bus** (☎ 021-439 2323; www.bazbus.com) links up with most of Gauteng's hostels.

Trains, although slower, are also an option and several named services pass through both Jo'burg and Pretoria en route to destinations including Musina, near the Zimbabwe border, Cape Town, Bloemfontein, Durban and Kimberley. If you have hired a car, you can even put your vehicle on the *Trans Karoo* and ship it all the way to the Cape.

Hiring a car is easy in both cities and prices are competitive. If you are staying in Gauteng, there are few sights you can't reach as part of a tour, or via public bus, but Jo'burg remains a city of car owners and having one will make getting around easier – beware of carjackers though. Despite its size, it isn't too much of a headache getting out of Jo'burg and onto the main, interstate highways.

If you are strapped for cash, minibus taxis also depart Jo'burg for destinations across the country and prices tend to be considerably lower than those charged by the main bus companies.

See individual Getting There & Away sections for more details. See the Transport chapter (p587) for details of connections between Gauteng's major cities and neighbouring countries.

JOHANNESBURG

☎ 011 / pop 4.9 million

With as many faces as the Rainbow Nation itself, the great big beating heart of South Africa has long played a Jekyll-and-Hyde role in the global consciousness. Often the stage on which the epic of this extraordinary nation has been played out, the colossus of Jo'burg, with all its thrills and foibles, is today a fascinating, multitudinous city, where all the ups and downs of 21st-century South Africa can be witnessed in three, multicolour dimensions.

In the past, the city's darker personality proved the most enduring. The Jo'burg of the newsflash was a city where fear and loathing reigned supreme, a city where spiralling gun crime and poverty had manifested itself in a society where one half of the population stagnated, while the other looked on impassively through coils of razor wire.

As ever, there is an iota of truth to the stereotypes. Jo'burg does bear the scars of South Africa's turbulent 20th century, and many will be slow to heal. Stark inequalities persist: wealthy northern suburbs like Sandton and Melville bristle with glossy shopping precincts, chic restaurants and electric fences; while the worst slums of the townships are a world apart, and poignant reminders that only the tip of the Jo'burg iceberg sits in the First World, while so much of it remains hidden, in the Third.

But armed with a new self-confidence, ironically most pronounced in the infamous township of Soweto, Africa's giant hub is fast introducing itself to a healthy new diet of urban renewal and social regeneration. Blacks are increasingly moving into the wealthy, formerly snow-white, suburbs; tourists and investors are flooding into Soweto; and developments in the central Newtown district are providing the city with a communal hub where Jo'burg's many faces can come together as one. From the recently erected Mandela Bridge, which symbolically connects previously divided sections of the city, to the new Constitutional Court, built on the site of one of the country's most infamous, apartheid-era prisons, Jo'burg's 21st-century monuments herald a new era of optimism.

Perhaps more than in any other big city (and at more than 2500 sq km, Jo'burg is *big*), it pays to keep your wits about you. Advances in the battle against crime have yet to win the war, and local advice is often the surest way of avoiding a costly run-in with its more sinister elements. Aware of its shortcomings and determined to make a difference, Jo'burg is an extraordinarily friendly and informal city, and not one to hide away in – get out there and live the big time.

HISTORY

At the beginning of 1886 the undistinguished stretch of the Transvaal highveld that was to become Jo'burg consisted of four sleepy farms: Braamfontein, Doornfontein, Turffontein and Langlaagte. In March of that year, however, an Australian prospector, George Harrison, found traces of gold on Langlaagte. Harrison didn't realise that he had stumbled on the only surface outcrop of the richest gold-bearing reef ever discovered. He sold his claim for £10.

Within a matter of months, thousands of diggers descended on this site. Because the gold was deep – in reef form, not the more easily accessible alluvial form – mining was quickly concentrated in the hands of men who had the capital to finance large underground mines. Mining magnates, who had made their money at the Kimberley diamond field, bought up the small claims and soon came to be known as the Randlords.

By 1889 Jo'burg was the largest town in Southern Africa – a rowdy city of bars and brothels. The multicultural fortune-seekers – Blacks and Whites – were regarded with deep distrust by the Boers, the Transvaal government and especially by the president, Paul Kruger. Kruger introduced electoral laws that effectively restricted voting rights to the Boers, and laws aimed at controlling the movement of Blacks were passed.

The tensions between the Randlords and uitlanders (outsiders) on one side, and the Transvaal government on the other, were crucial factors in the events that led to the 1899–1902 Anglo-Boer War. Jo'burg, which already had a population in excess of 100,000, became a ghost town during the war. It recovered quickly when the British took control and massive new mines were developed to the east and west.

Although gold-mining remained the backbone of the city's economy, manufacturing industries soon began to spring up, gaining fresh impetus during WWII. Under increasing pressure in the countryside, thousands of Blacks moved to the city in search of jobs. Racial segregation had become entrenched during the interwar years, and from the 1930s onwards, vast squatter camps had sprung up around Jo'burg.

Under Black leadership these camps became well-organised cities, despite their gross overcrowding and negligible services. But in the late 1940s, many were destroyed by the authorities, and the people were moved to new suburbs known as the South-Western Townships, now shortened to Soweto.

The official development of apartheid during the 1960s did nothing to slow the expansion of the city or the arrival of Black squatters. Large-scale violence finally broke out in 1976, when the Soweto Students' Representative Council organised protests against the use of Afrikaans (regarded as the language of the oppressor) in Black schools. Police opened fire on a student march and over the next 12 months more than 1000 would die fighting the apartheid system.

The regulations of apartheid were finally abandoned in February 1990 and since the 1994 elections the city has, in theory, been free of discriminatory laws. The Black townships have been integrated into the municipal government system: the city centre is vibrant with Black hawkers and street stalls; and inner suburbs have become multiracial.

Unfortunately, serious problems remain. Crime is rampant and middle-class Whites are retreating to the north where new shopping malls and satellite business centres are mushrooming.

Gold-mining is no longer undertaken in the city area, and the old, pale-yellow mine dumps that created such a surreal landscape on the edge of the city are being reprocessed. Modern recovery methods allow the mining companies to extract as much gold from these waste tailings today as was found in the raw ore 100 years ago. The classic view of Jo'burg – a mine dump in the foreground and skyscrapers in the background – will be retained, however, as some dumps are being preserved as historical monuments.

ORIENTATION

Despite its size, it's not difficult to find your way around Jo'burg, although cars reign supreme here and getting around without one can be time-consuming. JIA is 25km northeast of the city centre, and accessible by freeway. Regular buses connect the airport with Park Station on the northern edge of the city centre (see p395 for more information on JIA and Park Station).

PHOTOGRAPHING JOHANNESBURG

Carrying a camera around Johannesburg (Jo'burg) is as good as wearing a sign saying 'Mug Me'. Even in the relative safety of the northern suburbs you will never see Jo'burgers carrying cameras; to do so is to make yourself an unnecessarily attractive target.

The introduction of double-decker tourist buses (see p398) has been a blessing for all photographers. These buses, especially the open-topped City Slicker bus, provide the perfect platform from which to shoot photos. They're fairly slow moving, take interesting routes, are high enough to see over the walls of the wealthy suburbs and make you remote enough that most people don't even see the camera. But most importantly, they're safe enough for you to wave your camera around as much as you like.

GAUTENG

JOHANNESBURG

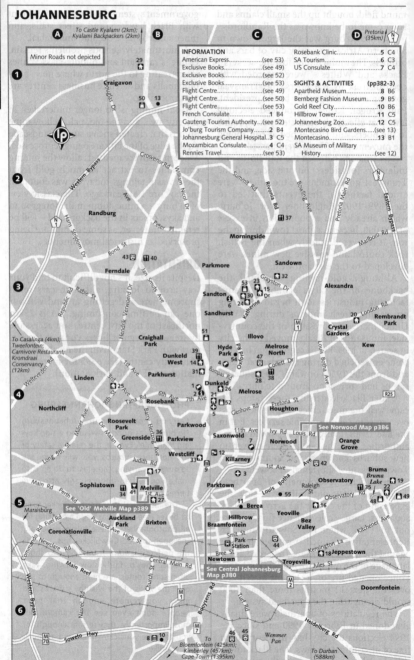

Ⓐ To Castle Kyalami (2km); Kyalami Backpackers (2km) Ⓑ   Ⓒ   Ⓓ Pretoria (35km)

Minor Roads not depicted

INFORMATION
American Express...................(see 53)
Exclusive Books....................(see 49)
Exclusive Books....................(see 52)
Exclusive Books....................(see 53)
Flight Centre........................(see 49)
Flight Centre........................(see 50)
Flight Centre........................(see 53)
French Consulate.........................1 B4
Gauteng Tourism Authority....(see 52)
Jo'burg Tourism Company........2 B4
Johannesburg General Hospital..3 C5
Mozambican Consulate..............4 C4
Rennies Travel.......................(see 53)

Rosebank Clinic........................5 C4
SA Tourism...............................6 C3
US Consulate............................7 C4

SIGHTS & ACTIVITIES (pp382–3)
Apartheid Museum....................8 B6
Bernberg Fashion Museum.........9 B5
Gold Reef City........................10 B6
Hillbrow Tower........................11 C5
Johannesburg Zoo...................12 C5
Montecasino Bird Gardens.....(see 13)
Montecasino..........................13 B1
SA Museum of Military
History.............................(see 12)

See Norwood Map p386

See 'Old' Melville Map p389

See Central Johannesburg
Map p380

0 ——————— 4 km
0 ——————— 2 miles

E   **F**

Modderfontein

To AECI
Dynamite Factory
Museum (2km)

To Caesars
Casino (9.5km);
Duneden Hotel
(4km); Airport
Backpackers
(11km);
Johannesburg
International
Airport & Holiday
Inn Garden Court
& City Lodge
(18km); Emerald
Guest House
(20km)

Sydonia St

Stanhope St

M2
Eastern Bypass

The city centre, which is laid out on a straightforward grid, is dominated by office blocks, in particular the 50-storey Carlton Centre on Commissioner St. There's no reason to stay in the city centre; after the shops close, the centre becomes a virtual ghost town. However, redevelopment of the Newtown cultural precinct, at the southwestern edge of the city, is at the core of an effort to clean up central Jo'burg. North of the city centre, a steep ridge runs west–east from Braamfontein across to the dangerous suburb of Hillbrow. To the northeast of the centre is the equally dangerous Yeoville.

The northern suburbs are predominantly White middle- and upper-class areas, within an arc formed by the N1 and N3 freeways. These suburbs of big houses, big trees and big fences are where most travellers stay. Sterile shopping malls form the centre of most social life, although there are a few pockets of resistance. The inner-suburban restaurant enclaves of Melville and Norwood make a refreshing change.

The Black townships ring the city and are a stark contrast to the northern suburbs. Conditions within them range from stereotypically suburban to appalling. The main township is Soweto (p399) but there are also big townships at Tokoza (south of Alberton), Kwa-Thema and Tsakane (southeast and south of Brakpan, respectively), Daveyton (east of Benoni), Tembisa (to the northeast) and Alexandra (inside the N3 freeway to the northeast of the city centre).

Maps

For maps try the **Map Office** (Map pp376–7; ☎ 339 4941; Ground fl, Standard House, 40 De Korte St, Braamfontein; ⏰ 8am-4pm Mon-Fri) This place sells government maps of all South African provinces for R35 a sheet.

INFORMATION
Bookshops

Book Dealers of Melville (Map p389; ☎ 726 4054; 12 7th St, Melville; ⏰ 10am-9pm) Has a good antiquarian selection and buys second-hand books (2.30-5.30pm Tue & Thu).

Exclusive Books Eastgate Mall (☎ 622 4870; upper fl; ⏰ 9am-10pm); Rosebank Mall (☎ 447 3028; level 3, the Zone; ⏰ 9am-9pm); Sandton City Mall (☎ 883 1010; lower level; ⏰ 9am-9pm Mon-Sat, 9am-7pm Sun) This chain is the best in town, with the widest range of local press, travel guides and international newspapers.

Emergency

AIDS line (☎ 0800 012 322)
Ambulance (☎ 10111)
Fire (☎ 10111)
Lifeline (☎ 728 1347)
Police (Map p380; ☎ 10111; Headquarters, Main Rd)
Rape Crisis Line (☎ 806 1888)
St John's Ambulance (☎ 10777)

Internet Access

Most hostels and hotels have Internet facilities, charging anything from R20 to R60 per hour. Alternatively, most Jo'burg malls and suburbs have an Internet café – Post-Net has stores across town. **Out of Print Books** (Map p389; ☎ 482 6026; 78 4th Ave, Melville; per min R1; ⊗ 10am-9pm), in the centre of Melville, is open later than most.

Medical Services

Medical services are of a high standard but they are expensive, so make sure you're insured. Hospitals include:
Johannesburg General Hospital (Map pp376-7; ☎ 488 4911; M1/Jubilee Rd, Parktown) A public hospital.
Rosebank Clinic (Map pp376-7; ☎ 328 0500; 14 Sturdee Ave, Rosebank; ⊗ 7am-10pm) A private hospital in the northern suburbs, with casualty, GP and specialist services.

Money

There are banks with ATMs and change facilities across town. American Express and Rennies Travel (an agent for Thomas Cook) have branches in major malls including:
American Express Jo'burg International Airport (☎ 390 1233; JIA; ⊗ 5am-9pm); Sandton (Map pp376-7; ☎ 883 9009; Shop B36c, level 5, Sandton City Mall; ⊗ 9am-6pm Mon-Sat, 10am-5pm Sun)
Rennies Travel Jo'burg International Airport (JIA; ☎ 390-1040; ⊗ 5.30am-9pm); Sandton (Map pp376-7; ☎ 884 4035; Sandton City Mall; ⊗ 9am-6pm Mon-Fri, 9am-3pm Sat, 10am-1pm Sun)

Post

Main post office (Map p380; ☎ 0800 110 226; Jeppe St; ⊗ 8.30am-4.30pm Mon-Fri, 8.30am-noon Sat). There is a poste restante service; do be careful about having anything too valuable sent here.

Tourist Information

Different offices provide information depending on whether you are interested in Jo'burg, Gauteng, or South Africa as a whole. The following organisations have a monopoly on most of the best information.

Gauteng Tourism Authority (Map pp376-7; ☎ 327 2000; www.gauteng.net; upper level, Rosebank Mall, Rosebank; ⊗ 8am-5pm Mon-Fri) For information on the whole of Gauteng.
Jo'burg Tourism Company (Map pp376-7; ☎ 214 0700; deon@joburgtourism.com; ground fl, Grosvenor Cnr, 195 Jan Smuts Ave, Parktown North; ⊗ 8am-5pm Mon-Fri) Covers the city of Jo'burg.
SA Tourism (Map pp376-7; ☎ 895 3000; fax 895 3001; 90 Protea Rd, Sandton; ⊗ 8am-5pm Mon-Fri) Can be contacted for general South Africa information.

Travel Agencies

There are dozens of agencies in Jo'burg, and many hotels and hostels also arrange bookings. For flight bargains, check the *Star* newspaper's travel lift-out on Saturday.
Flight Centre (Central Bookings ☎ 0860 400 747); Eastgate (Map pp376-7; ☎ 616 7008; Shop L3, Eastgate Mall; ⊗ 9am-5.30pm Mon-Fri, 9am-3pm Sat); Fourways (Map pp376-7; ☎ 467 0050; Shop G43, Fourways Mall; ⊗ 9am-5.30pm Mon-Fri, 9am-2.30pm Sat); Sandton (Map pp376-7; ☎ 784 1571; Shop L80, Sandton Mall; ⊗ 9am-5.30pm Mon-Fri, 9am-3pm Sat) Specialises in discounted flights and has branches in most major malls.

DANGERS & ANNOYANCES

Crime is a big problem in Jo'burg, but it is important to put things in perspective: remember that most travellers come and go without incident and that much of the crime afflicts suburbs you would have little reason to stray into. The secret to success is simple: seek local advice, listen to it and remain aware of what's going on around you.

A couple of important things to remember are that you are really very unlikely to become the victim of a violent crime – even criminals understand that assault and murder attract far more attention from the authorities than robbery alone – and that you are most vulnerable when using an ATM (see the boxed text on p574).

For everything else see the boxed text on opposite, and when you think of all those stories you've seen or read, remember that the media doesn't usually report good news, and then get out there and enjoy yourself.

SIGHTS & ACTIVITIES
City Centre & Newtown
CITY CENTRE   Map p380

The city centre choked and largely died in the mid-1990s, with many White businesses fleeing to the northern suburbs, leaving

---

SURVIVING JOHANNESBURG'S DANGERS & ANNOYANCES

Few tourists run into serious trouble in Johannesburg (Jo'burg) and despite the odd horror story, you really don't want to spend your time here hiding away in a hotel room – there's just too much fun to be had. That said, the city's crime statistics do make uncomfortable reading and so it is well worth taking a little extra care when you are out and about.

If your hostel/hotel transport does not arrive at the airport, bus station or train station when expected, catch a legitimate taxi to your intended destination (even pay up to R250). This small investment may save the contents of your backpack and money belt. Don't become one of the many independent travellers who lose the lot in their first moments in the city, ie those trying to walk or catch a bus to their accommodation to save money. Never walk out of Park Station with luggage unless you're getting straight into a car.

Store your valuables in the hostel/hotel safe and when you head off to explore the city, try not to dress too conspicuously, take only what money you think you will need and keep maps and swinging cameras to an absolute minimum – you want to blend in, not stand out. The odds of being robbed are relatively low, but making yourself more of a target is never a good idea.

The northern suburbs and the cultural precinct in Newtown are generally safe to walk around, but be very careful about venturing into sections of the inner city without getting local advice first. The central business district teems with people during the day, but becomes empty, and dangerous, after sundown. The inner city suburbs of Hillbrow – with the exception of Constitution Hill – and Yeoville are now de facto no-go zones at any time of day and you shouldn't even think about wandering through them without an extremely savvy local guide.

Have a healthy respect for your circumstances but don't be overly paranoid – most of the people you meet are genuine and not trying to rip you off.

If you are mugged, which is unlikely, and a knife or gun appears, give them all they want. A smile often goes a long way to ameliorate the situation.

If you are driving make sure the car doors are locked; when you're at stop lights leave a car's length between you and the vehicle in front so you can drive away if necessary – running a red light is not illegal if you're in reasonable fear of assault. When you park your car, immobilise it or attach a gear-stick lock or a steering-wheel lock – or do all three.

The Jo'burg–Pretoria Metro train is targeted by muggers these days, so don't go to Pretoria this way.

---

the district to vanish under a mountain of none-too-promising crime statistics. The area retains its edgy atmosphere today, but regeneration projects in Newtown to the south and university-oriented Braamfontein to the north, are gradually helping to boost confidence in the heart of the city.

There are plenty of colonial-era buildings that are worth a look: the presently closed **Rissik St Post Office** (Rissik St) and **City Hall** (cnr Rissik & Market Sts), now a sometime concert venue, are among the finest. Sights aside, the thousands of hawkers and the smells of corn and beef being cooked at street-side stalls give the centre an African atmosphere that you won't find in the northern suburbs and that alone makes it worth a well-planned visit. See the boxed texts on above and p375.

On the Noord St side of the Joubert Park is the **Johannesburg Art Gallery** (☎ 725 3130; Joubert Park; admission free; ☟ 10am-5pm Tue-Sun). This place has a reputable collection of European and South African landscape and figurative paintings, and several exhibitions featuring more adventurous contemporary work and long-overdue retrospectives of Black artists.

To get an overview of the hub of Jo'burg, take the lift to the **Top of Africa** (☎ 308 1331; 50th fl, Carlton Centre, 152 Commissioner St; adult/child R7.50/5; ☟ 9am-7pm). From the quiet remoteness of the observation deck, the sprawling city seems positively serene. The entrance is via a special lift one floor below street level and you can admire the views over lunch at the **Marung restaurant** (☎ 331 1438).

BRAAMFONTEIN Map p380

The suburb of Braamfontein focuses around the **University of Witwatersrand** (☎ 717 1000; Jan Smuts Ave, Braamfontein), more commonly known as Wits (pronounced 'Vits') University, and there are plans to transform this currently

CENTRAL JOHANNESBURG

0 _____ 500 m
0 _____ 0.3 miles

INFORMATION

Botswanan Consulate	1 B4
Main Post Office	2 C5
Map Office	3 A4
SA Police Headquarters	4 A6
Swaziland Consulate	5 A4
Zimbabwe Consulate	6 B6

SIGHTS & ACTIVITIES (pp378–83)

Bus Factory	7 A6
City Hall	8 C6
Constitution Hill	9 C3
Drum Cafe	(see 7)
Getrude Posel Gallery	10 A4
Johannesburg Art Gallery	11 D4
Mary Fitzgerald Sq.	12 A5
Museum Africa	13 A5
Nelson Mandela Bridge	14 B5
Planetarium	(see 10)
Rissik St Post Office (closed)	15 C6
SAB World of Beer	16 A6
St Mary's Anglican Cathedral	17 C5
Sci-Bono Discovery Centre	18 A6
Soweto Art Gallery	19 B6
Standard Bank Foundation Collection of African Tribal Art	(see 10)
Top of Africa	20 D6
Turbine Hall	21 A5
University of Witwatersrand	22 A3
Women's Gaol	(see 9)
Workers' Museum	23 A6

SLEEPING (p385)

Devonshire Hotel	24 B4
Formule 1 Hotel Park Station	25 C4
Protea Hotel Parktonian	26 B4

EATING (pp388–9)

Gramadoela's	(see 35)
Guildhall Bar & Restaurant	27 B6
Kapitan's	28 B6
Moyo's	(see 35)

DRINKING (p391)

Horror Cafe	29 A6

ENTERTAINMENT (pp392–4)

Carfax	30 B5
Civic Theatre	31 B3
Kaizer Chiefs Store	32 C6
Kippie's Jazz International	33 A5
Laboratory	34 A5
Market Theatre	35 A5
Mega Music Warehouse	36 A6
Shaft	37 A4
Windybrow Centre for the Arts	38 D4
Wits Theatre Complex	(see 10)

SHOPPING (p394)

Beautiful Things	(see 7)
Kohinoor	39 B6
Market Square Market	40 A5

TRANSPORT (pp395–8)

Long-Distance Buses Booking Offices	41 C4
Metrobus Terminal	42 C6
Taxis to Bulawayo, Zimbabwe	43 C4
Taxis to Durban	44 C5
Taxis to Lesotho, Bloemfontein, Kroonstad & Ficksburg	45 D4
Taxis to Maputo (Mozambique)	46 C4
Taxis to Pretoria	47 C5
Taxis to Rosebank & Sandton	48 C5
Taxis to Soweto	49 D5
Taxis to Upington, Kimberley & Cape Town	50 C4

OTHER

Department of Home Affairs	51 B5

quiet area into a lively student ghetto. Wits University is the largest English-language university in the country, with over 20,000 students. It's an attractive campus and you can visit the worthwhile **Gertrude Posel Gallery** (☎ 717 1365; gallery@atlas.wits.ac.za; ground fl, Senate House; admission free; ⌚ 10am-4pm Tue-Fri); the **Standard Bank Foundation Collection of African Tribal Art**, which includes masks, Ndebele fertility dolls and beadwork; **Jan Smuts House** to see Smuts' study; the **Planetarium** (☎ 717 1390; Yale Rd; shows adult/concession R25/10; ⌚ 8.30am-4pm), which you can look around for free, or attend shows on Friday (8pm), Saturday (3pm) and Sunday (4pm). You can get a cheap café meal at the **Student Union Building**.

NEWTOWN   Map p380
Known as Brickfields at the turn of the 20th century, Newtown was once the centre of a thriving brick-making industry, booming on the back of the area's rich clay deposits. In April 1904, the fire brigade unceremoniously torched most of the buildings to combat an outbreak of bubonic plague and it was subsequently renamed Newtown. Today, Newtown is at the centre of efforts to rejuvenate the downtown area and on 20 July 2003, the showcase Nelson Mandela Bridge, which links it with Braamfontein, was opened, breathing fresh life into streets that had long been left to the dogs.

Surrounded by museums and cafés, Newtown's cultural precinct, which occupies the newly brushed-up **Mary Fitzgerald Sq** (named after South Africa's first female trade unionist), is a good place to start a tour of central Jo'burg. As well as being the staging ground for a number of annual events (check Jo'burg City's website www .joburg.org.za for details), it's also simply a good place to watch the city drift past. The square is decorated with an array of heads carved by Newtown artists from old railway sleepers.

At the heart of the cultural precinct, **Museum Africa** (☎ 833 5624; museumafrica@joburg .org.za; 121 Bree St; adult/child R7/2; ⌚ 9am-5pm Tue-Sun) is now housed in the impressive old Bree St fruit market, next to the Market Theatre complex. The superb exhibition on the Treason Trials (1956–61), which featured most of the important figures in the 'new' South Africa, is a must-see for anyone looking for a better understanding of the country's more recent history. The Transformations exhibition details the evolution of Jo'burg and includes a simulated descent into one of the gold mines. The Sophiatown display is outstanding. There's also a large collection of rock art, a geological museum, a display on Gandhi's time in Jo'burg and the Bensusan Museum of Photography, which charts the history of photography and has regular exhibitions by famous South African snappers.

The nearby **Market Theatre** complex (p394), with its shows, bars and restaurants, is an excellent place to while away a few hours between museum visits.

Looming over Newtown is the **Nelson Mandela Bridge** (www.mandelabridge.co.za). Officially opened by Nelson Mandela on 20 July 2003 (two days after his 85th birthday), the 295m, cable-stayed bridge is the longest of its kind in Southern Africa, can support 3,000 cars per hour and cost a hefty R120 million to erect (oh, the things they tell you in the PR brochures). It isn't the most impressive structure in Jo'burg, but it is an enduring symbol of efforts to resurrect long-forgotten sections of the city and an ongoing source of pride.

The **SAB World of Beer** (☎ 836 4900; 15 President St; admission R10; ⌚ 10am-6pm Tue-Sat) delves into that other great, if slightly less cultural, South African pursuit: beer drinking. It unlocks the secrets of the country's brewing industries (malting, mashing and wort boiling), from the time when the crudely brewed sorghum beer first passed the lips of early Africans. In the Ales Pavilion, the European tradition of brewing ales and lagers is described; sorghum brewing is covered in the Ukhamba exhibition and there is a recreation of a 1965 Soweto shebeen (unlicenced bar) – all heavenly for appreciators of the amber fluid. The guided tour takes about 90 minutes and runs every half hour.

The small, but significant, **Soweto Art Gallery** (☎ 492 1109; Suite 34, 2nd fl, Victory House, cnr Commissioner & Harrison Sts; admission free; ⌚ 8am-6pm Mon-Fri, 8am-1pm Sat) is directed by well-known Sowetan artist Peter Sibeko and is one of the few places contemporary Black artists from the townships can exhibit their paintings and sculptures. All works are for sale and offer a worthwhile insight into life in the townships.

Much of the area around Mary Fitzgerald Sq was once taken up by a giant power station – builders keep running into the foundations of the colossal cooling towers. The huge **Turbine Hall** (cnr Jeppe & Bezuidenhout Sts) next to the SAB World of Beer, is one of the city's more impressive buildings – a kind of Battersea Power Station for Jo'burg. Although derelict, the fantastic interior was used to launch the New Mini and there are several, tentative plans in the pipeline to transform the space into something more user-friendly. If you hear of an event being hosted here, shift hell or high water to get hold of a ticket.

In the Electric Workshop building, you'll find the brand new **Sci-Bono Discovery Centre** (☎ 082-575 6688; www.sci-bono.co.za; Bezuidenhout St). It had yet to open at time of writing, but the space will include a science museum and an interactive learning experience, promising to become an excellent way to fill a couple of hours. If you have children in tow, there will be plenty to keep them occupied.

In the restored Electricity Department's compound you'll find the **Workers' Museum** (☎ 832 2447; 52 Jeppe St; admission free; ⊗ 9am-5pm Mon-Sat). It was built in 1910 for 300-plus municipal workers and has been declared a national monument, but it is not as inspiring as it could be. There is a Workers' Library, a resource centre and a display of the living conditions of migrant workers.

South of the cultural precinct, you will find the newly refurbished **Bus Factory** (2 President St), which includes Beautiful Things (p394), a new initiative exhibiting and selling crafts from across South Africa, and the **Drum Cafe** (☎ 834 4464; www.drumcafe.com; ⊗ 9am-4pm), which has a free drum museum and stages regular drumming events.

HILLBROW & CONSTITUTION HILL

Crowned by the looming, 269m **Hillbrow Tower** (Map pp376-7; Goldreich St), Hillbrow was once among the liveliest and most interesting suburbs in the city, becoming one of the first districts in Jo'burg to witness the cracks opening in the shell of apartheid when it was designated the nation's first 'Grey Area' – a zone where Blacks and Whites could live side by side. These days, however, it also has a reputation for very real lawlessness and a trip into its guts, without an extremely savvy guide (see p383), is not recommended.

At a time when high-profile developments are being erected in washed-out areas throughout the city, however, it is no accident that the ever-egalitarian Rainbow Nation chose to build its new Constitutional Court on the very edge of Hillbrow. With any luck the court, the surrounding Constitutional Hill development and the investment they will attract, will start to change this suburb's sinking fortunes.

The **Constitution Hill** (Map p380; ☎ 688 7856; Kotze St; adult/child R20/10; ⊗ 9am-5pm Wed-Mon) development had yet to be completed at the time of writing, but promises to become one of the city's chief tourist attractions. Built within the ramparts of the **Old Fort**, which dates from 1892 and was once the city's most notorious prison, the development focuses on South Africa's new **Constitutional Court**. Ruling on constitutional and human-rights matters, the court itself is a very real symbol of the changing South Africa: a *lekgotla* (place of gathering) rising from the ashes of one of the city's most poignant apartheid-system monuments. The modern structure incorporates sections of the old prison walls, and large windows, which allow visitors to watch proceedings, symbolise the sense of transparency that is at the heart of the new South Africa's constitution.

As well as gaining access to the court, visitors will also be able to take tours of the Old Fort's various sections, including the **Awaiting Trial Block**, which held the 156 treason triallists – led by Nelson Mandela – of 1956; the notorious **Number Four** section, which held Black, male prisoners; and the **Women's Gaol**, where female offenders (their offence was often simply failing to produce an identity card) were incarcerated. The final development, which will include a hotel and restaurants, should be fully completed by 2006, but some areas, such as the court and large sections of the Old Fort, including the Women's Gaol, are already open to the public – call ahead for the latest.

Northern Suburbs   Map pp376-7

Montecasino (☎ 510 7777; www.montecasino.co.za; William Nicol Dr, Fourways) consistently draws more visitors than any other attraction in Jo'burg. Based around a large casino, the development features an entire 'Tuscan village under one roof', with a menagerie of restaurants, shops, bars, the **Pieter Toerien Theatre** (p394) and the pleasant **Montecasino Bird Gardens** (☎ 511 1864; adult/child R10/5; ⊙ 9am-5pm), where you can get a blast of country air in the heart of the city. The designers of the 'Tuscan village' left authenticity at the door, but it makes a rather unique change from the sparkling floors and muzak of many of the city's shopping malls.

Perhaps it's South Africa's fascination with guns, or maybe it's the country's bloody history, but every year the **South African National Museum of Military History** (☎ 646 5513; www.militarymuseum.co.za; 22 Erlswold Way, Saxonwold; adult/child R10/5; ⊙ 9am-4.30pm) is one of Jo'burg's most popular museums. If gunpowder is your thing you'll find this museum is actually quite well done. You can see artefacts and implements of destruction from the 1899–1902 Anglo-Boer War through to the Namibian wars. The museum is at the eastern end of the grounds of the Jo'burg Zoo.

The **Johannesburg Zoo** (☎ 646 2000; www.jhbzoo.org.za; Jan Smuts Ave, Westcliff; adult/child R24/16; ⊙ 8.30am-5.30pm) has a reasonable array of the fierce and the furry. It seems rather bizarre going to a zoo in Africa but you can combine a visit to Jo'burg Zoo with the South African National Museum of Military History. The zoo is about 4km north of the city centre; it has a particularly interesting wild-dog enclosure. There are also **night tours** (R60) three times a week (no children); book through the zoo.

Also worth checking out is the **Bernberg Fashion Museum** (☎ 646 0716; cnr Duncombe Rd & Jan Smuts Ave, Forest Town; admission free; ⊙ 9am-5pm Tue-Sat), which has a variety of fashions from yesteryear on display, and the **AECI Dynamite Factory Museum** (☎ 309 4700; 2 Main St, Modderfontein; ⊙ 10am-2pm Mon & Fri, 2-4.30pm Wed), which is housed in an original 1895 homestead and charts the development of South Africa's explosives industry (a crucial factor in Jo'burg's development as a mining centre).

Southern Suburbs   Map pp376–7

In stark contrast to the nearby Gold Reef City theme park, the **Apartheid Museum** (☎ 309 4700; www.apartheidmuseum.org; cnr Gold Reef Rd & Northern Parkway; adult/child R25/12; ⊙ 10am-5pm Tue-Sun) takes a long, hard look at South Africa's era of segregation. With plenty of attention to detail and overall effect – visitors are handed a card stating their race when they arrive and are required to enter the exhibit through their allotted gate – this remains one of South Africa's most evocative museums. Charting the course of several South Africans through the apartheid era, the museum uses film, text, audio and live accounts to provide a colourful insight into the architecture, implementation and eventual unravelling of the apartheid system. If you are on your way to Soweto, where the excellent Hector Pieterson Museum pads out the story, this is an absolute must. It is 8km south of the city centre, just off the M1 freeway.

Nearby, **Gold Reef City** (☎ 248 6800; www.goldreefcity.co.za; Gold Reef Rd; admission R70, children under 120cm free; ⊙ 9.30am-5pm Tue-Sun) also has one foot in the past, but this time provides a light-hearted and reasonably rip-roaring take on gold-rush Jo'burg. Ninety per cent Disneyland clone, this theme park only offers a token nod to historical authenticity, but provides ample means for filling a spare afternoon, especially if you have kids in tow.

It features scary rides, a Victorian fun fair and various reconstructions, including a bank, brewery, pub and newspaper office. Visitors can go 220m down a shaft to see a gold mine from the inside (an extra R45), watch a gold pour and see an entertaining programme of tribal or 'gumboot' dancing.

There are numerous places to eat and drink, the Gold Reef City Arts & Crafts Centre and an expensive craft/souvenir shop. There are often special programmes on the weekend, sometimes with live music performed in an open-sided amphitheatre, and fireworks. Check the entertainment section in the *Star*.

If you want to stay over, the excellent Protea Gold Reef City Hotel is here (p388).

Beside the theme park is the **casino** (☎ 248 5000; ⊙ 24hr). Unfortunately, it's a bit tricky to reach by public transport and a taxi would be expensive, but it's included in most Jo'burg day tours. The attached Gold Reef City Casino Hotel (p388) has rooms.

TOURS

All Jo'burg budget hostels should have information on cheap packages to Kruger National Park and on the best (and cheapest) travel links to Cape Town, Durban, Swaziland, Lesotho, Namibia, Botswana, Zimbabwe and Mozambique. Almost all

GAY & LESBIAN JOHANNESBURG

Johannesburg (Jo'burg) has a thriving gay scene and, since the liberalisation of the constitution in 1994, has become a centre for gays and lesbians from across Africa. Gays are well organised and increasingly accepted – a far cry from the puritanical attitudes of the past.

The annual **Gay Pride March** (☎ 082-547 2486; www.sapride.org), held on the last weekend of September, is the focal point, but by no means the only organised activity. In fact, one of the highlights is taking a **Queer Johannesburg Tour** (p383), which will give you the lay of the land.

A number of gay-oriented websites provide the best source of information on the city's gay scene, including events listings and details of where to go and what to see: www.q.co.za, www .mask.org.za and www.heavensgate.co.za are all packed with useful background material. See p393 for some gay and lesbian club listings.

Also contact the **Lesbian & Gay Equality Project** (Map pp376-77; ☎ 487 3810; 36 Grafton Rd, Yeoville). For other sources of information see p577.

can book Soweto tours as well. If you phone ahead, the following tour companies will arrange a pick-you or tell you how to get to the rendezvous (see also p402).

Imbizo Tours (☎ 838 2667) Specialises in tours to Jo'burg's gritty townships, including half-day tours to Alexandra (per person R280), perhaps the city's grimmest township, and Soweto (per person R280). Also evening Soweto shebeen tours (per person R600), where you get to eat and drink it up with the locals.

Take-A-Tour (☎ 624 1676; www.takeatour.info) Tours of Soweto (per person R280), as well as trips through Jo'burg's city centre and heritage sites (per person R280).

Queer Johannesburg Tours (bookings ☎ 717 1963; anthonym@library.wits.ac.za) Run on the first Sunday of the month by the **Gay & Lesbian Archives of South Africa** (☎ 717 4239; www.gala.wits.ac.za), at Wits University. Gay or straight, the tours offer a fascinating insight into gay Jo'burg, taking you deep into the heart of Hillbrow and Soweto, and providing plenty of background on the role homosexuality played in the gold mines and the struggle against apartheid. Tours start at 9am, last four hours, and cost R300 per person.

Walks Tours (☎ 444 1639; www.walktours.co.za; per person from R100) Offers regular weekend walking tours around parts of Jo'burg as diverse as the city centre, Sandton, Troyeville, Parktown and Alexandra township. The walks go for between three and six hours and are led by well-informed guides. The only downside is that unless you can get enough people together for a private tour, you might have to wait weeks for the walk you want.

Parktown and Westcliff Heritage Trust (☎ 482 3349; per person from R150) Leads several tours through the more salubrious sections of town.

FESTIVALS & EVENTS

The big **Arts Alive Festival** (☎ 549 2315; www.art salive.co.za) is held in September. Since South Africa's liberation, the arts have been going

through an exciting time, with an explosion of optimism and mainstream acceptance of long-suppressed talents. A strong element in the festival is the workshops that reveal the continent's rich cultures, denigrated for so long by the Eurocentrism of the apartheid years. The festival is a particularly good time to hear excellent music, on and off the official program. Most events are staged in Newtown.

Other festivals include the **Joy of Jazz Festival** (☎ 832 1641; www.joyofjazz.co.za) staged in venues across Newtown in late August; the annual **Gay Pride March** (☎ 082-547 2486; www .sapride.org), held on the last Saturday of September; the **Rand Easter Show** at the National Exhibition Centre in April; and **Chinese New Year** at Wemmer Pan, south of the centre.

SLEEPING

Hotels and hostels are scattered across Jo'burg with the only pattern being a steady drift north. The range of quality is broad, from the bare basics of some hostels to the opulence and perma-smile service of the many five-star hotels. Some Jo'burg hostels will allow you to pitch a tent, but it's wise to check before you arrive. (If backyards are not to your liking, the best caravan parks that permit camping are in the far south of the province, see p404.)

The agency **Portfolio** (☎ 880 3414; www.port foliocollection.com) lists a number of top B&Bs, mainly in the northern suburbs; they're upmarket and reasonably expensive, with singles from R200 to R400, and doubles from R300 to R500.

If you're looking to party, a bed near Melville or Norwood would be handy if you can find one. Otherwise the Rosebank and, increasingly, Fourways areas have decent after-hours entertainment. Places in the northern suburbs tend to be quite spread out, with few obvious accommodation ghettoes. In fact, many suburbs are served by a single hotel in each range, meaning that visiting a number of places before you settle on your favourite is the privilege of those with a car.

There are a few options in the city centre and prices can be very reasonable, but standards tend to be lower and the streets considerably less secure.

Yeoville was for years a backpacker favourite but is not any more. All of the hostels have either closed or relocated to safer areas.

When you arrive in Jo'burg most hostels will pick you up from the airport or Park Station for free. If a car doesn't show up, call the hostel or get a taxi. Nearly all of the hostels are on the route of the Baz Bus (see p395). Internet and satellite TV facilities are standard and most hotels will organise tours to Soweto, Kruger National Park and elsewhere.

City Centre & Newtown   Map p380
In terms of accommodation, central Jo'burg can't touch the smarter suburbs. That said, if you are keen on hanging around Newtown and the Market Theatre complex, these places will save you a few bob in taxi fares.

BUDGET
Most of the budget hotels in the city centre, Berea and Hillbrow are run down and depressing. You can't really go out at night on foot and you can get a backpackers double somewhere safer for the same price as a double room here, so there's not much argument for staying.

TOP FIVE JOHANNESBURG SLEEPING

- Saxon Hotel (p387)
- Grace (p387)
- Ten Bompas (p387)
- Die Agterplaas (right)
- Backpackers Ritz (p386)

Formule 1 Hotel Park Station (☎ 720 2111; fax 720 2112; Park Station; r with shared bathroom R169) This place offers basic rooms for a basic price. It is near the northeast corner of the huge Park Station complex and might appeal if you arrive late. It's a short walk from the main bus and train arrivals hall, and you can sleep up to three people in the room for the same price.

MID-RANGE
Some of the better hotels in this area are good value, as the escalating crime rate has chased away custom.

Devonshire Hotel (☎ 339 5611; www.orion-hotels .com; cnr Melle & Jorissen Sts; s/d with breakfast R360/420; **P**) On the doorstep of Wits University (p378) and the Civic Theatre (p394), this Braamfontein mid-ranger has all the mod cons and clean rooms.

TOP END
Protea Hotel Parktonian (☎ 403 5741; www.protea hotels.com; 120 De Korte St, Braamfontein; s/d with break-fast R630/770; **P** 🛇) The Parktonian is the best hotel in the central Jo'burg area and draws visiting business types.

Melville
BUDGET
Pension Idube (Map pp376-7; ☎ 482 4055; idube@ mail.com; 11 Walton Ave, Auckland Park; d with/without bathroom R190/260; **P** 🛈) The pension is very close to trendy Melville and only 5km from the city centre – a big plus in itself. It is secure, has off-road parking, serves inexpensive meals and has a patio that is the launch pad for some excellent braais.

MID-RANGE
Die Agterplaas (Map pp376-7; ☎ 726 8452; agter plaas@icon.co.za; 66 Sixth Ave, Melville; s/d with break-fast R385/395; 🛇) Oozing 'old' Melville grace, this colonial-era villa has lashings of comfy class, with Oregon pine flooring, a sun terrace and plenty of old school bric-a-brac for décor.

Norwood
BUDGET
Ascot Hotel (Map p386; ☎ 483 1101; cnr Grant Ave & Algernon Rd; s/d with breakfast R180/210) Norwood's central hotel has reasonably priced rooms and there's a decent English-style pub below for late-night knees-ups.

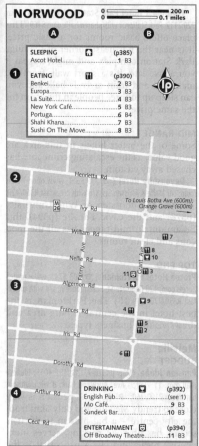

Northern Suburbs   Map pp376–7

BUDGET

Backpackers Ritz (☎ 325 7125; www.backpackers-ritz
.co.za; 1A North Rd, Dunkeld West; dm/s/d with shared bathroom R75/130/190; P 🔌 💻) A safe hop-and-
a-skip from Hyde Park Mall, and plenty of
bars and restaurants, this popular place is
just off Jan Smuts Ave. Of all the hostels in
huge old mansions, this is undoubtedly the
most impressive. The historic building offers
stunning views across the city and some of
the best dorm-room views you could hope
to see. It has a pool, a crypt-like bar and a
strong emphasis on security. Well worth it.

Rockey's of Fourways (☎ 465 4219; www.backin
africa.com; 22 Campbell Rd, Fourways; camp sites/dm/s/d
with shared bathroom R45/65/155/180; P 🔌 💻) A

die throw from the Montecasino complex
and Fourways mall, this friendly place has
spacious gardens, obliging hosts and the
usual backpacker comforts. It gets consistently good reports from travellers.

Gemini Backpackers (☎ 882 6845; www.gemini
backpackers.com; 1 Van Gelder Rd, Crystal Gardens; camp
sites/dm/s/d with shared bathroom R45/60/110/150;
P 🔌 💻) Offering a decent dose of backpacker plush, this place is bursting with
facilities, including a travel desk, volleyball
and tennis courts, a gym and a video library
for film buffs. It's a bit out of the way, but
staff will pick you up from the airport and
there's a daily shuttle to the shops.

Kyalami Backpackers (☎ 318 3258; www.kyala
mibackpackers.co.za; 15 Village Rd, Blue Hills, Kyalami;
camp sites/dm/s/d with shared bathroom R30/65/100/150;
P 🔌 💻) This quiet place offers novelties
aplenty including an on-site diving school,
roaming ostriches and a pet pig named
Winnie. The pool's heated for taking away
those Jo'burg winter chills.

MID-RANGE

Castle Kyalami (☎ 799 7676; www.planethotels.co.za;
66 Pine Rd, Kyalami; s/d with breakfast R650/950; P
🔌 🔌) One of Jo'burg's true oddities, this
mock castle was built by a Greek millionaire
set on constructing a super-status seat for
his extended family. The Arthurian styling
borders on the irrecoverably naff, but the
rooms are plush and the setting outstanding. There's also an excellent spa for serious pampering, with a variety of treatments
available to suit all budgets.

Don Suites Apartments at Rosebank (☎ 880
1666; fax 880 3366; 10 Tyrwhitt Ave; s/d with breakfast
R530/655; P 🔌) This is the only Black-owned
hotel chain in the land and it offers excellent rooms. This place is no exception.

Holiday Inn Garden Court (www.southernsun.com;
s/d R590/725 with breakfast; P 🔌) JIA (☎ 392 1062;
2 Hulley Rd) Sandton (☎ 884 5660; cnr Katherine St & Rivonia Rd) The reliable, if a little frumpy, Holiday Inn chain has a number of hotels across
town. Most offer cheaper weekend rates.

Protea Hotel Wanderers (☎ 770 5500; www
.proteahotels.com; cnr Rudd Rd & Corlett Dr; s/d with
breakfast R865/990; P 🔌 🔌) The perfect spot
for cricket aficionados, this Protea offering
straddles the mid- and top-end divide.

Linden Hotel (☎ /fax 782 4905; cnr 7th St & 4th
Ave, Linden; s/d with breakfast R300/360; P 🔌) This
is an attractive, comfortable, personalised

hotel. Unfortunately, it's a long way north-west of the city. It has a restaurant and a 'ladies' bar'.

City Lodge (www.citylodge.co.za; s/d from R495/620; P ⊠ ♨) JIA (☎ 392 1750; Sandvale Rd, Edenvale); Sandton (☎ 444 5300; Katherine Dr) Offers good-value accommodation. Worthwhile discounts are available to those who book over the Internet.

Town Lodge Sandton (☎ 784 8850; www.citylodge .co.za; cnr Grayston Dr & Webber Rd; s/d from R390/460; P ⊠ ♨) Part of the City Lodge group, it offers a little less for a little less than the City Lodges.

TOP END

Saxon Hotel (☎ 292 6000; www.thesaxon.com; 36 Saxon Rd, Sandhurst, Sandton; r with breakfast R4150; P ⊠ ♨ ☐) For the person with everything, this is one of those places you simply have to bed down in before you die. Scooping the 2003 World's Best Boutique Hotel accolade at the World Travel Awards, this gorgeous place offers no-holds-barred luxury. Needless to say, when it came to getting some peace and quiet while putting the finishing touches to his autobiography, this was the spot Nelson Mandela chose to pen his memoirs.

Westcliff (☎ 646 2400; www.westcliff.co.za; 67 Jan Smuts Ave, Westcliff; r with breakfast R2275; P ⊠ ♨ ☐) With a majestic setting above the zoo, this opulent place has no-expense-spared décor and a reputation for effortless exclusivity. This is the place to max out your credit card on a well-deserved splurge.

Palazzo Inter-Continental Montecasino (☎ 510 3000; www.southernsun.com; Montecasino Blvd, Fourways; r with breakfast R1300; P ⊠ ♨ ☐) Boasting graceful Tuscan styling, this glossy number mixes Mediterranean charm with superslick service and all the usual five-star trimmings. The adjacent Montecasino development provides plenty to do, if you are twiddling your thumbs after dark.

Intercontinental Sandton Sun & Towers (☎ 780 5000; www.southernsun.com; cnr Fifth & Alice Sts; s R2145-2365, d R2365-2570; P ⊠ ♨ ☐) Just across the road from the Sandton City and Sandton Sq malls (p394), this place is the pride of the Southern Sun Group. The Sandton Sun caters for the wealthy, while the Towers pampers the megarich.

Grace (☎ 280 7300; www.grace.co.za; 54 Bath Ave, Rosebank; s/d with breakfast R2400/2700; P ⊠) Offering a distinctly personal big-city experi-ence, this stylish boutique hotel caters to a galaxy of stars, honeymooners and well-heeled business travellers. Compared to many five-star hotels, this place is still small enough to make you feel at home.

Ten Bompas (☎ 325 2442; www.tenbompas.com; 10 Bompas Rd, Dunkeld West; r with breakfast R2400; P ⊠ ♨) With only ten individually styled suites, this upper-echelon place offers five-star exclusivity and a free minibar – come with a thirst.

Park Hyatt (☎ 280 1234; www.johannesburg.hyatt .com; 191 Oxford Rd, Rosebank; s/d R1160/1460; P ⊠ ♨ ☐) With a great spot in the heart of the northern suburbs, this reliable place offers plenty of five-star, chain-hotel luxury. It is the staple of the city's visiting business travellers

Eastern Suburbs   Map pp376–7
BUDGET
Diamond Digger's Lodge (☎ 624 1676; www.oneand only.co.za; 36 Doris St, Kensington; dm/d with shared bathroom; P ♨ ☐) With an in-house travel agency, this is a reasonably convenient base for exploring the city centre and Soweto. There's a Jacuzzi for a spot of late night nuz-zling with your new clinch, a big-screen home cinema and a pub for post-tour frolics.

Airport Backpackers (☎ 394 0485; air backp@m web.co.za; 3 Mohawk St, Rhodesfield, Kempton Park; camp sites/dm/s/d with shared bathroom R50/80/150/180; P ♨) Just 2km from the airport (free pick-ups and drop-offs), this is a top place for coming off the jet lag and settling into your holiday, with a pleasant *lapa* bar (a low-walled building with a thatched roof) and a decent pool. Down the road from Caesar's Casino, it is also a good bet for those who would rather save their pennies for the roulette wheel.

Eastgate Backpackers (☎ 616 2741; egatebp@net active.co.za; 41 Hans Pirow Rd, Bruma; dm/s/d with shared bathroom R60/140/160; P ♨ ☐) Only walking distance from Bruma Lake Market World (p394), this clean two-storey mansion has a vibey, laid-back atmosphere.

MID-RANGE
Cottages Guest House (☎ 487 2829; fax 487 2404; 30 Gill St, Observatory; s/d R345/400 with breakfast; P ⊠ ♨) A self-styled 'English country es-tate', this delightful place offers plenty of quiet, rural calm in the heart of the big city. The cottages are thatched and there are

self-catering options and weekend specials (double including breakfast R345).

Holiday Inn Garden Court (☎ 622 0570; www .southernsun.com; Ernest Oppenheimer Dr; s/d R590/725 with breakfast; **P** **⊠**) Part of the Holiday Inn Garden Court chain (p386).

Holiday Inn Express Eastgate (☎ 622 0060; www.southernsun.com; 8 South Blvd, Bruma; s/d with breakfast R402/433; **P** **⊠**) Almost next door to the more upmarket Holiday Inn Garden Court, this is a cheaper incarnation of the same basic product.

Emerald Guest House (☎ 394 1198; fax 975 1822; 19 Halifax St, Rhodesfield, Kempton Park; s/d R250/350; **P** **⊠** **⊠** **⊒**) Within easy striking distance of the airport, this has plenty of home comforts and decent rooms. It looks a little dated, but the facilities are good and it makes a convenient stopover, if you have an early flight. Airport transfers are offered.

Duneden Hotel (☎ /fax 453 2002; 46 Van Riebeeck Ave, Edenvale; s/d R310/420; **P** **⊠** **⊠**) Another option close to the airport, this passable mid-ranger has a bar, tennis courts and a gym. Again, it's worth considering if you are flying in or out in the wee, small hours.

Southern Suburbs   Map pp376–7
MID-RANGE

Protea Hotel Gold Reef City (☎ 248 5700; www.pro teahotels.com; Gold Reef Rd; s/d with breakfast R595/840; **P** **⊠**) Slap-bang in the heart of the Gold Reef City theme park, with old Jo'burg styling, this excellent place has charming rooms and bags of upmarket Wild West character. Eight kilometres south of the city centre, and actually inside the theme-park gates, it is also probably the most secure hotel in all Jo'burg.

TOP END

Gold Reef City Casino Hotel (☎ 248 5152; www.three cities.co.za; cnr Northern Parkway & Data Cres, Ormonde; s/d R780/1050; **P** **⊠**) You are likely to spend as much again in the casino, but the opulent rooms are quite good value at this place, 8km south of the city centre by Gold Reef City.

EATING

Jo'burg is stacked with places to eat, satisfying every whim, craving, occasion and budget. Unfortunately for visitors, especially those without cars, most of the best places are scattered around the northern

suburbs and they can be difficult to find. The big hotels have restaurants and in shopping centres you'll find franchised steakhouses such as Spur Ranch and Italian places such as Panarotti's.

For self-caterers, head to the glitzy supermarkets in the bowels of every shopping mall for the widest range of produce.

City Centre & Newtown   Map p380
There are a clutch of excellent restaurants around the cultural precinct in Newtown and a few quirky, historic places further north in the city centre itself. There's no shortage of takeaways but they are not inspiring, eg roasted mealies. For a cheap meal of mealie pap (maize stew) and braaied (barbecued) meat, try the stalls on and nearby Diagonal St – just follow your nose.

Gramadoela's (☎ 838 6960; Bree St, Newtown; mains R40-90; ⏰ lunch & dinner; **⊠**) Full of curios and character, this Newtown classic in the Market Theatre complex whips up a mean mix of African and Asian cuisine, blending recipes that range from the Cape to Cairo and adding a distinctly Malay twist. Diners include such luminaries as Hillary Clinton, Denzel Washington and Nelson Mandela, and the gay-friendly flag flies over the door.

Moyo's (☎ 838 1715; www.moyo.co.za; Bree St; mains R30-80; ⏰ lunch & dinner; **⊠**) In the Market Theatre complex, this stylish eatery mingles a touch of cigar-puffing exclusivity, with plenty of candlelit African charm. Fresh, herb-packed cooking forms the backbone of the innovative menu and there's a top-notch wine list for vinophiles.

Guildhall Bar & Restaurant (☎ 833 1770; 88 Market St; mains R25-50; ⏰ lunch & dinner) Established way back in 1888, this was one of the city's first bars and if the nicotine-stained, wood-panelled walls could talk, they could doubtless spin a yarn or two. You can while away

---

TOP FIVE JOHANNESBURG EATING

- Yum (p391)
- Gramadoela's (p388)
- Kapitan's (p389)
- Moyo's (p388)
- Café Mezza Luna (p389)

the day in the dark English-style pub below, or sit out on the upstairs balcony and watch the City of Gold pass you by over a pie and chips.

Kapitan's (☎ 834 8048; 11A Kort St; mains R25-60; ⏰ lunch & dinner) Don't be put off by the grubby stairwell, Kapitan's (just behind Diagonal St) is a Jo'burg institution. The authentic Indian food has been attracting luminaries for years – Nelson Mandela and Oliver Tambo used to eat here in the 1950s, when they had a law office nearby.

Melville

Northwest of Braamfontein, Melville has become the trendiest eating strip in Jo'burg. Restaurants and cafés have sprung up in the area around 7th St, known as 'Old Melville', and around the busier Main Rd about 1km away, known as 'New Melville'.

The best food is in Old Melville, where a Bohemian, youthful atmosphere prevails. Most of the cafés have outdoor seating and in the warmer months 7th St takes on a Parisian ambience, with patrons sipping drinks and watching the world go by from pavement tables.

CAFÉS & QUICK EATS

Spiro's Cafe (Map p389; ☎ 482 1162; cnr 7th St & 2nd Ave; mains R20-50; ⏰ breakfast, lunch & dinner) With terrace seating outside and huge, comfy sofas inside, this place heaves at breakfast time. Come nightfall, it serves up some tasty restaurant tucker before slowly transforming into a bar.

Wild Olive (Map p389; ☎ 726 8306; 7th St; sandwiches R20; ⏰ lunch) This little place serves up some big, bourgeois sarnies and a selection of delicious deli treats. It closes at 4.30pm.

RESTAURANTS

Café Mezza Luna (Map p389; ☎ 482 2477; www.hellosa.co.za; 9A 7th St; mains R35-90; ⏰ lunch & dinner; ⏰) With plenty of elegant, Mediterranean-style character and a terrace setting, this charming place serves up everything from calamari and kingfish to stacks of wonderful South African meat.

Soi (Map p389; ☎ 726 5775; cnr 7th St & 3rd Ave; mains R45-90; ⏰ lunch & dinner; ⏰) Flash, oh-so-trendy Asian décor gives this place a hip, stylish edge. The Thai and Vietnamese food is fresh and zesty, and there's a bar full of beautiful people attached.

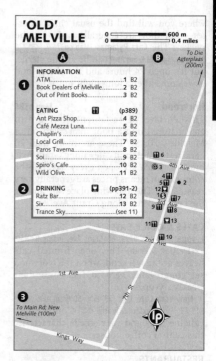

'OLD' MELVILLE

0	600 m
0	0.4 miles

INFORMATION
ATM.....................................1 B2
Book Dealers of Melville..........2 B2
Out of Print Books..................3 B2

EATING (p389)
Ant Pizza Shop......................4 B2
Café Mezza Luna....................5 B2
Chaplin's..............................6 B2
Local Grill.............................7 B2
Paros Taverna........................8 B2
Soi......................................9 B2
Spiro's Cafe.........................10 B2
Wild Olive...........................11 B2

DRINKING (pp391-2)
Ratz Bar..............................12 B2
Six......................................13 B2
Trance Sky........................(see 11)

Chaplin's (Map p389; ☎ 482 4657; 85 4th Ave; mains R50-90; ⏰ lunch & dinner; ⏰) This twee little bistro whips up some legendary food, and in an area where new places come and go in a flash, remains one of the true veterans. European meat and fish dishes predominate.

Local Grill (Map p389; ☎ 727 2890; cnr 7th St & 3rd Ave; mains R50-150; ⏰ lunch & dinner; ⏰) The only place for a hardcore meat feast, this upmarket steakhouse serves sublime aged cuts in modern surrounds. They also claim to cater to vegetarians.

Paros Taverna (Map p389; ☎ 482 4781; cnr 7th St & 3rd Ave; mains R40-75; ⏰ lunch & dinner; ⏰) With fresh, white-and-blue taverna décor and tasty Greek eats, this little piece of the Mediterranean gets lively at the weekends. On Saturday morning, they're still sweeping up the smashed plates from the night before.

Ant Pizza Shop (Map p389; ☎ 726 2614; 11 7th St; mains R30-45; ⏰ lunch & dinner) This hole-in-the wall Italian eatery has a distinctly Bohemian edge and whips up tasty pizzas in snug surrounds.

Eateries in New Melville are generally not as good as those around 7th St – this is

GAUTENG

where you will find the usual chain eateries – but they are generally easier on the pocket. The **Catz Pyjamas** (Map pp376-7; ☎ 726 8596; cnr Main Rd & 3rd Ave) can be a little sterile, but it's open 24 hours and the cheap food is welcome after a long night out.

Norwood   Map p386

This enclave of restaurants has grown and matured into a poor man's version of Melville's 7th St. There are more than 20 bars, restaurants and cafés along Grant Ave, most of which are open every day. All the competition means prices are generally very reasonable. The following places are among the best, and run along Grant Ave.

CAFÉS & QUICK EATS

Europa (☎ 483 0799; 66 Grant Ave; mains R20-50; 🕐 breakfast & lunch) This open-fronted café heaves at the weekend, when the Norwood set congregates here to tuck into their weekly fry-up.

   New York Café (☎ 728 4606; 50 Grant Ave; snacks R15-25; 🕐 breakfast & lunch; 🔀) Comfy sofas, caffeine fixes and cake smells characterise this central coffee house.

RESTAURANTS

La Suite (☎ 728 9262; cnr Grant & Francis St; mains R40-80; 🕐 lunch & dinner; 🔀) This is one of Norwood's plusher eateries, with wicker chairs on the pavement and coffee-and-cream décor inside. There's a wide range of local and European dishes on the menu, or you can dig into the lunchtime buffet.

   Benkei (☎ 483 3296; 48 Grant Ave; mains R25-50; 🕐 lunch & dinner; 🔀) This jazzy Japanese place attracts Norwood's young trendies with its fashionable styling and authentic cooking. If you have had enough meat, the sushi offers welcome reprieve from the braai.

   Sushi on the Move (☎ 483 0293; 76 Grant Ave; mains R25-45; 🕐 lunch & dinner) This on-the-hop Japanese place has a rotating sushi counter and does deliveries.

   Shahi Khana (☎ 728 8157; 80 Grant Ave; mains R30-60; 🕐 lunch & dinner; 🔀) Offering reliable Indian fare, this is the place to get your eyes watering and your tastebuds tingling.

   Portuga (☎ 728 0415; 37 Grant Ave; mains R25-45 🕐 lunch & dinner) This place brings all the flavours of Mozambique to its seafood menu. The setting is quite basic, but the food's good value.

Northern Suburbs   Map pp376–7

The many eating options in these mainly White suburbs are centred on the huge shopping malls that form the core of northern suburbs society. The expensive cafés and restaurants are uniformly slick and are often chain operations. Many are devoid of individuality and, in Sandton, completely lacking in atmosphere once the shops have closed.

   But for all their formulaic qualities there is some good food to be found. For a dose of fun with your food, head to Rosebank or stroll through Melrose Arch, where there are a number of excellent options.

   Not far from Melville, the suburb of Greenside also boasts a clutch of decent eateries. The area is rather more middle-aged – this is not a party zone – but a few of the restaurants draw punters from across the city. The restaurants are in a little cluster on Gleneagles Rd and Greenway, just off Barry Hertzog Ave.

Moyo's (☎ 684 1477; www.moyo.co.za; 5 Melrose Sq, Melrose Arch; mains R30-80; 🕐 lunch & dinner; 🔀) Oozing chi-chi African charm, this busy place offers a wide range of contemporary African eats. There's a stylish cigar bar and a huge wine cellar where they hold tastings.

   Cranks (☎ 880 3442, Shop 52, Rosebank Mall; mains R35-55; 🕐 lunch & dinner; 🔀) Still going after almost 20 years, Cranks was one of the first Thai-Vietnamese places in Jo'burg. Among the tried-and-tested favourites is fish fillet with lemongrass (R45).

   Paros Taverna (☎ 788 4976; Hutton Court, Jan Smuts Ave, Hyde Park; mains R30-75; 🕐 lunch & dinner; 🔀) The Paros is another of the irrepressible Greek places that punctuate Jo'burg, emphasising their existence most nights with a cacophony of smashing crockery and the not-so-Greek twirlings of a belly dancer. The food here is pretty good, reasonably priced and comes in huge portions.

   Codfather (☎ 803 2077; cnr 1st Ave & Rivonia Rd, Morningside; mains R40-80; 🕐 lunch & dinner; 🔀) Near Sandton, the Codfather is one of the best-value seafood restaurants in Jo'burg. There is a huge selection of fresh fish (flown from the coast daily) that you can have cooked however you like.

   Swiss Inn (☎ 789 3314; 170 Hendrik Verwoerd Dr, Randburg; mains R40-140; 🕐 lunch & dinner; 🔀) Looking very Swiss, right down to the clinically clean bathrooms, this place is worth the long drive. Locals rave about the ambience and the international menu.

Yum (☎ 486 1645; www.yum.co.za; 26 Gleneagles Rd; mains R40-200; ☯ lunch & dinner; ✗) One of the city's most celebrated dining rooms – they have even published their own cook book – Yum specialises in innovative fusion cooking, with an emphasis on top-notch ingredients and lashings of culinary flair. It closes for most of the month of January.

Ove Flo (☎ 486 4576; 116 Greenway; mains R40-90; ☯ lunch & dinner; ✗) This Parisian-style bistro is a good spot for romantic dining, with an atmospheric, womb-red interior, plenty of gold-edged mirrors for checking your hair in, and a menu offering everything from pizza to roast lamb.

Karma (☎ 646 8555; cnr Barry Hertzog Ave & Gleneagles Rd; mains R40-70; ☯ lunch & dinner; ✗) Bringing traditional Indian cooking into the 21st century, this stylish place puts a contemporary spin on the old favourites and offers a smorgasbord of tasty vegetarian dishes for those sick of the South African meat feast.

Tantra (☎ 646 3502; cnr Barry Hertzog Ave & Gleneagles Rd; mains R30-70; ☯ lunch & dinner; ✗) A self-styled 'Easy Thai Diner', Tantra runs with the cheeky erotic theme, offering courses from 'Foreplay' to 'A Little on the Side'. The food is accordingly fresh, zesty and tasty.

Circle (☎ 646 3744; 141 Greenway; mains R40-80; ☯ lunch & dinner; ✗) With everything from South African tuna and Scottish venison to Indonesian nasi goreng and the plain old sandwich, this informal, popular place is a restaurant for all seasons, with something on the menu to suit every fancy and appetite.

Eastern Suburbs

Near Bruma Lake is Derrick Ave, Cyrildene, off Observatory Rd, where a new Chinatown (Map pp376–7) with a number of cheap restaurants, has sprung up. Represented are Taiwanese, Korean, Sichuan, Shanghai and Hong Kong styles served in those lifeless places with Formica-top tables and plastic chairs; most close at about 9.30pm.

Sun Fat (Map pp376-7; ☎ 615 1392, 14 Derrick Ave; mains R25-50; ☯ lunch & dinner) Sure, it doesn't sound appetising, but the honey roast pork in syrup (R30) is a treat.

Carnivore (☎ 957 2099; Misty Hills Country Hotel, Muldersdrift Rd, Muldersdrift; mains R50-150; ☯ lunch & dinner; ✗) This is the place to go, if you are inclined to eat some of the animals you

have seen in South Africa's parks. There is a selection of salads and desserts, *potjiekos* (a variety of meat and vegetables stewed in an iron pot), soups, and all-the-meat-you-can-eat carved from Maasai tribal sword skewers at your table.

DRINKING

Jo'burg is renowned as the party capital of Africa and we are inclined to agree. There is a constantly changing mix of bars, pubs and clubs, ranging from the outrageous to the downright conservative; whatever you prefer, you'll find somewhere to feel comfortable. Jo'burg's one-time drinking haunts of Hillbrow and Yeoville are now too edgy to wander around, with much of the nightlife moving into the northern suburbs, particularly around Melville, Norwood and Rosebank – just ask around. The area around the cultural precinct in Newtown also has a few decent places for a tipple.

For other venues, see p392.

City Centre & Newtown   Map p380

Horror Cafe (☎ 838 6735; 5 Becker St, Newtown) The neon green décor is appropriately horrible, but big crowds, and its proximity to the SAB World of Beer (p381), ensure that this venue is never short of action. On Thursdays, thumping reggae provides the soundtrack for much of the area, while on Friday the scene goes 'underground rave'. Saturday is gay and lesbian night.

Guildhall Bar & Restaurant (☎ 833 1770; 88 Market St) Jo'burg's oldest pub is a great place to soak up some history while stoking the fires with a pint or two of lager. There's an upstairs terrace for city-centre people-watching and food available (see p388).

Melville

Cool Runnings (Map pp376-7; ☎ 482 4786; 27A 4th Ave) Reggae is going through something of a renaissance in Jo'burg at the moment and so it is no surprise that this franchise of Jamaican-style bars is hitting the big time. A relaxed atmosphere, thumping bass-lines and late, lively nights are a sure thing.

Ratz Bar (Map p389; ☎ 726 2019; 9B 7th St) This cosy place, with rats daubed on the walls rather than running across the floors, plays big sounds from Wednesday to Saturday, and has a two-for-one happy hour on cocktails from 5pm to 7pm.

Trance Sky (Map p389; ☎ 615 4397; 7th St) The pun itself deserves a few brownie points, but the whirly décor and trance-style tunes set the pace at this lively, late night joint.

Six (Map p389; ☎ 482 8306; 7th St) They haven't pulled out many stops decorating this place – the generous might call it 'industrial chic' – but it stays open later than most during the week, there are some decent cocktails on show, and punters come for the vibrant, unpretentious atmosphere.

Punter & Trouserleg (Map p380; ☎ 726 1030; 1st fl, Melville Tce, cnr 5th Ave & Main Rd) This spot is guaranteed to appeal to youthful backpackers. It is generally full of sexy young things partaking in the regular beer-and-shooter specials and boogieing to commercial music.

Norwood   Map p386

Sundeck Bar (☎ 728 2279; 72 Grant Ave) Popular with pathological people-watchers, the upstairs terrace bar at this place is the perfect spot to sip a cocktail and watch Norwood drift by.

Mo Café (☎ 728 8256; Grant Ave) This camp, retro-style affair offers beautiful people, stacks of irony and lashings of orange décor. Fashionable facial hair is a must.

English Pub (☎ 483 1101; cnr Algernon St & Grant Ave) Offering plenty of rough-and-tumble action and an English pub–style ambience, this is a good spot at the weekends for determined drinking and lively banter.

ENTERTAINMENT

The best entertainment guide is in Friday's *Mail & Guardian*. 'Tonight' in the *Star* is also good. For entertainment bookings by credit card, contact **Computicket** (☎ 340 8000; www.computicket.com), which can arrange seats for almost every theatre, cinema and sports venue. For parties and get-togethers, check out www.jhblive.co.za and www.brag.co.za.

Cinemas

Huge cinema centres can be found across Jo'burg, with almost every shopping centre boasting one. **Ster Kinekor** (central bookings ☎ 0860 300 222; www.sterkinekor.com) has the widest distribution of multiplexes, with screens in the Fourways, Westgate, Eastgate, Sandton and Rosebank malls.

If it's a large screen that you're seeking, the grandest addition to Jo'burg's entertainment scene is the **Imax Theatre** (Map p380; ☎ 325 6182; Hyde Park Mall, Jan Smuts Ave, Hyde Park).

Live Music & Nightclubs

Jo'burg is home to a thriving live music scene, and on any given night you can see rock, pop, kwaito, jungle, jazz and hip-hop acts, and all manner of house and techno (see p59 for more on kwaito and other local sounds). On weekends, the Jo'burgers really come out to play and regularly hold enormous raves. There's little pattern to the spread of venues, but you'd be safe to assume that in most cases the further north you go the tamer they become.

If you want to get a sense of what central Jo'burg has to offer, the area around the Newtown cultural precinct (Map p380), with its bars, eateries, theatres and music venues, is the best place to kick off an evening.

CLASSICAL

Johannesburg Philharmonic Orchestra (☎ 789 2733; www.jpo.co.za) The city's budding orchestra stages a regular circuit of concerts, utilising venues from Wits University to City Hall. Call or check their website for the latest programme.

CONTEMPORARY

The suburban venues tend to cater to a whiter crowd, but things are changing as more Blacks move into the suburbs. Being where they are, prices also tend to be a little higher – and watch what you wear, dress codes apply.

Carfax (Map p380; ☎ 834 9187; 39 Pim St, Newtown) This industrial space is one of the hottest club tickets in town, with weekend DJs and a house-oriented music scene. It's big, loud and a whole lotta fun.

Kippie's Jazz International (Map p380; ☎ 833 3316; www.kippies.co.za; Bree St, Newtown) Kippie's is a small but very popular jazz venue, named after the great Kippie 'Morolong' Moeketsi. It's a 'must do' when in Jo'burg as it's one of the best places to see South African jazz talent, which happens to be exceptional. Gigs and events kick off on Friday and Saturday nights at around 9.30pm; a cover charge of R40 usually applies.

Mega Music Warehouse (Map p380; ☎ 834 2761; cnr Gough & Jeppe Sts, Newtown) This medium-sized venue hosts a decent spread of gigs from Western rock to African kwaito. It doesn't open its door every weekend, so check the local press for the latest events.

Kilimanjaro (Map pp376–7; ☎ 214 4300; 17 High St, Melrose Arch, Melrose) Extremely swoosh (there's a 'smart-casual' policy and the bouncers mean it) and packed with the beautiful set, this glossy suburban number plays everything from African tribal rhythms, to hardcore techno. Cocktails (from R25) are the drink of choice and there is an R80 cover charge at the weekend.

206 Live (Map pp376–7; ☎ 728 5333; 206 Louis Botha Ave, Orange Grove) Garage, ragga, drum 'n' bass and rock tracks keep the feet tapping here. Next door, 208 keeps the flag flying over the local hip-hop crowd.

Blues Room (Map pp376–7; ☎ 784 5527/8; www .bluesroom.co.za; Lower level, Village Walk Shopping Centre, cnr Rivonia Rd & Maude St, Sandown) This blues and jazz venue makes the occasional foray into rock and is notoriously gay-friendly. The atmosphere is easy-going and welcoming.

GAY & LESBIAN VENUES

Gay and lesbian venues open and close with disconcerting regularity in Jo'burg, so it is worth checking before you head out. Hillbrow used to be Jo'burg's gay capital, but increasing crime has driven many of the venues out. A few places still remain in Braamfontein, the best bet for mingling with a mainly Black crowd, while Melville is fast becoming the city's new (largely White) gay Mecca.

Club Bitch (Map pp376–7; ☎ 084-405 9164; www .bitchonline.co.za; Metro Centre, cnr Hendrik Verwoerd Dr & Jan Smuts Ave; admission R20) The city gay scene's big Saturday night bash kicks off at this giant new opening. Holding two thousand partygoers in its six bars and dance floors, this is the behemoth, with wild crowds, thumping tunes and lashings of action. Things get rolling at about 11pm, when the cover charge also goes up to R40.

Oh! Bar (Map pp376–7; info@brandoh.com; cnr 4th & Main Rd, Melville) After a huge Saturday, this is the place to keep things rolling (at a slightly gentler pace) on Sunday. Catering to a more upmarket, trendier and altogether more discerning crowd, this slick bar-club hosts the scene's big Remedy Sunday event. Dance music keeps pulses racing from 8pm until 2am. It costs R20 if you enter after 9pm.

Shaft (Map p380; 14 Juta St, Braamfontein; ⊙ from 4pm Mon-Thu, from noon Fri-Sun) The Braamfontein

gay scene has taken a knock in recent years, but this is a decent place to check out the scene in quieter surrounds. It is also the place to come to, if you want to mingle with a Black crowd.

Sport

South Africans love their sport. Their inability to prove themselves the world's best (due to international sanctions) arguably contributed to the dismantling of apartheid.

CRICKET

The most important cricket venue is **Wanderers Cricket Ground** (Map pp376–7; ☎ 788 1008; Corlett Dr, Illovo). Just off the M1 freeway to Pretoria, this is one of the most beautiful cricket grounds in the world, and one of the few where you can watch an international match and braai yourself a steak at the same time.

FOOTBALL

The **Rand Stadium** (Map pp376–7), near Turffontein; **FNB Stadium** (Map p399), further east on Baragwanath Rd near Soweto; and, increasingly, **Ellis Park** (above) are the major venues for football, which is the sport Black South Africans follow most passionately. The most popular teams are also the greatest rivals: Soweto teams the Orlando Pirates (known as the 'Bucs') and the 'mighty, all conquering' Kaizer Chiefs. The annual league derby between the two teams is a highlight, uniting communities from across the city. Dates change every year depending on the league schedules.

RUGBY

Jo'burg boasts some excellent venues, the pick of which is **Ellis Park** (Map pp376–7; ☎ 402 8644; www.sarugby.net; Doornfontein), just to the east of the city centre. Ellis Park is the headquarters of rugby union and was the scene of one of the new nation's proudest moments – victory in the 1995 World Cup. Rugby supporters are fanatical, and Ellis Park can hold 70,000 – a Saturday afternoon at the rugby can be an almost religious experience. During the winter months, the stadium hosts some of the massively attended Super 12 matches.

Following in the footsteps of the marketing savvy clubs of the European leagues, the Kaizer Chiefs have even opened up their own **merchandising store** (Map pp376–7; ☎ 838 6477; Ghandi Sq; ⊙ 8.30am–4.30pm Mon-Fri).

GAUTENG

OTHER SPORTS

Kyalami (Map p372; ☎ 466 2800), off the M1 between Jo'burg and Pretoria, is the venue for motor sports.

There are several horse-racing tracks but the best known is **Turffontein Race Course** (Map pp376-7; ☎ 681 1500), 3km south of the city. There are race meetings most weeks.

Theatres

Market Theatre (Map p380; ☎ 832 1641; www.markettheatre.co.za; Bree St) The Market Theatre is the most important venue for live theatre. There are three live theatre venues – the Main, Laager and Barney Simon Theatres – as well as galleries, a café and the excellent Kippie's Jazz International (p392). There is always some interesting theatre, ranging from sharply critical contemporary plays to musicals and stand-up comedy – check the programme in the *Mail & Guardian* entertainment section.

Laboratory (Map p380; ☎ 836 0516) An offshoot of the Market Theatre and acts as a showcase for community talent. There are free local theatre shows every Saturday at 1pm.

Civic Theatre (Map p380; ☎ 877 6800; www.showbusiness.co.za; Loveday St, Braamfontein) Located near Wits University, this theatre offers a variety of productions in its Main and Tesson Theatres.

Pieter Toerien Theatre (Map pp376-7; ☎ 511 1818; Montecasino, William Nicol Dr, Fourways) In the Montecasino development, this is a family-oriented place, offering plenty of cabaret-style entertainment.

Off Broadway Theatre (Map p386; ☎ 403 1563; 59 Grant Ave, Norwood) Specialises in cabaret, but offers some artier shows too.

Wits Theatre Complex (Map p380; ☎ 717 1381; Jorissen St, Braamfontein) Stages the university's productions.

Windybrow Centre for the Arts (Map p380; ☎ 720 7009; cnr Nugget & Pietersen Sts, Hillbrow) A good testing ground for emerging Black playwrights.

SHOPPING
Arts & Crafts

Rosebank Rooftop Market (Map pp376-7; ☎ 788 5530) One of the most convenient places to shop for traditional carvings, beadwork, jewellery and fertility dolls. Held every Sunday in Rosebank Mall.

Beautiful Things (Map p380; ☎ 492 3696; Bus Factory, 2 President St, Newtown; ☺ 10am-4pm) A community-run initiative selling arts and crafts from across the country.

Bruma Lake Market World (Map pp376-7; ☎ 622 9648; Observatory Rd) By Bruma Lake, this place sells a wide range of crafts and lots of kitsch.

Faraday Market (cnr Eloff St & N2) This new market is an interesting place to wander around, with plenty of *muti* (traditional medicine) stalls.

Market Sq Market (Map p380; Bree St) Held on Saturday mornings in the car park opposite the Market Theatre. There's a lively, cheerful atmosphere (with buskers), and although most of the stalls sell flea-market rubbish, there are also some reasonable crafts amid the dross.

Malls

Jo'burg prides itself on its shops, and the city's malls are up there with the best. Jammed with Western consumer goods of every description, it sometimes seems like they are as much a wealthy White habitat as a place to go shopping.

Eastgate Mall (Map pp376-7; ☎ 616 2209) Off the N12 just east of Bruma Lake. Boasts of being Africa's largest mall.

Fourways Mall (Map pp376-7; ☎ 465 6095; William Nicol Dr)

Hyde Park Mall (Map pp376-7; William Nicol Dr)

Rosebank Mall (Map pp376-7; ☎ 788 5530; Craddock Ave) If you're after serious retail therapy, head to this interlocking series of malls, with central parking on the corner of Cradock Ave and Baker St.

Sandton City Mall (Map pp376-7; ☎ 883 2011; Rivonia Rd) Very plush.

Sandton Sq Mall (Map pp376-7; ☎ 784 2750; Rivonia Rd) Adjoining and similar to Sandton City Mall.

A short walk from Newtown, you'll find **Oriental Plaza** (☎ 838 6752; Bree St, Fordsburg; ☺ 9am-5pm Mon-Fri, 8.30am-3pm Sat). It has over 350 Indian-owned shops. If you have a rough idea of prices and don't mind bargaining, you will make some good purchases. At the least, you'll find cheap, delicious samosas.

Music

You can get most titles in the big malls.

Kohinoor (Map p380; ☎ 834 1361; 54 Market St) is one of the best sources of ethnic/African music, and sells everything from kwaito to jazz.

GETTING THERE & AWAY

Air

South Africa's major international and domestic airport is **JIA** (☎ 921 6911; www .johannesburg-jnb.com). For more information, including international flight connections, see p587.

Distances in South Africa are large, so if you're in a hurry, some domestic flights are definitely worth considering. For regular flights to national and regional destinations try **South African Airways** (SAA; ☎ 0860 359 722, 978 1111; www.flysaa.com), **South African Airlink** (SAAirlink; ☎ 978 1111; www.saairlink.co.za) and **South African Express** (☎ 978 5577; www.saex press.co.za). All flights can be booked through SAA, which also has offices in the domestic and international terminals of JIA.

Services include the following (prices are the cheapest, one-way, advance purchase fares).

Destination	One-way fare (R)
Cape Town	630 (3-day advance)
Durban	310 (3-day advance)
East London	700 (7-day advance)
Kimberley	730 (14-day advance)
Manzini (Swaziland)	600 (7-day advance)
Maseru (Lesotho)	570 (7-day advance)
Nelspruit	720 (7-day advance)
Polokwane (Pietersburg)	720 (7-day advance)
Upington	1185 (7-day advance)

Smaller budget airlines, including Comair, Kululua and Nationwide, also link Jo'burg with major destinations and often offer the cheapest fares. For contact details and details of other airline offices in Jo'burg, see p587.

Bus

Park Station (Map p380) was the result of a huge and much-needed redevelopment of the 22 city blocks bound by Wolmarans, Rissik, De Villiers, Hoek, Noord and Wanderers Sts. A Metro concourse was built for Metro trains from platform Nos 1 to 10, and a road-transport interchange has now been built over the web of train tracks between the Metro concourse and Wanderers St to deal with about 150 long-distance taxis and 1200 minibus taxis.

A number of international bus services leave Jo'burg for Mozambique (p594), Lesotho (p593), Botswana (p593), Namibia (p594), Swaziland (p594) and Zimbabwe (p595).

The main long-distance bus lines (national and international) depart from and arrive at the Park Station transit centre, in the northwest corner of the site, where you will also find their respective booking offices. There is also a **Jo'burg information desk** (☎ 337 6650).

BAZ BUS

Backpackers can now be connected from Jo'burg to the most popular parts of the region (Swaziland, Durban, Garden Route and Cape Town) by **Baz Bus** (☎ 021-439 2323; www.bazbus.com), which picks up at hostels in Jo'burg and Pretoria, saving you the hassle of going into the city to arrange transport. All hostels have current timetables and prices. For more, see p598.

OTHER BUS COMPANIES

The most comprehensive range of services to/from Jo'burg is provided by the government-owned lines, **Translux** (☎ 774 3333; www .translux.co.za) and **City to City** (☎ 773 2762). For more information on these, plus the other major bus lines – **Greyhound** (☎ 012-323 1154; www.greyhound.co.za) and **Intercape** (☎ 0861 287 287; www.intercape.co.za) – see p598.

With the exception of City to City buses, which commence in Jo'burg, all services that are not heading north commence in Pretoria at the Pretoria station.

TO CAPE TOWN

Translux has at least one bus running daily to Cape Town (R380, 19 hours) via Bloemfontein (R180, six hours). There are also daily services to Cape Town (R380, 18 hours) via Kimberley (R185, seven hours).

Greyhound has daily buses to Cape Town (R400, 18½ hours) via Bloemfontein (R175, six hours) and Kimberley (R190, seven hours).

Intercape also runs to Cape Town (R400, 19 hours) via Upington (R260, 10 hours). From Upington, you can also get an Intercape bus to Windhoek, Namibia (R250, 12 hours), but there isn't a direct connection.

TO DURBAN & KWAZULU-NATAL

Greyhound has four daily buses to Durban (R185, eight hours), including slower services that run through Newcastle (R185, five hours), Ladysmith (R165, six hours) and Estcourt (R170, 7½ hours), and then onto Richard's Bay (R205, eight hours). Translux has at least one bus a day to Durban (R150, eight hours), as does Intercape (R125, eight hours).

Eldo Coaches (☎ 773 4552), also based at Park Station, has three buses daily to Durban (R165, eight hours).

TO MPUMALANGA & KRUGER NATIONAL PARK
The nearest large town to Kruger National Park is Nelspruit. Greyhound runs there daily (R165, five hours). Note that this service starts in Jo'burg and picks up in Pretoria an hour later. Translux runs to Maputo, Mozambique daily (R200, eight hours) via Nelspruit (R130, 4½ hours); this service also starts in Jo'burg and picks up in Pretoria an hour later.

City to City has some slow, cheap services from Jo'burg to Nelspruit (R80, seven hours) and Hazyview (R75, eight hours). Hazyview is closer to Kruger than Nelspruit, and has backpacker hostels that can arrange trips into the park (p431).

Translux also has daily buses running to Phalaborwa (R165, 7½ hours), which is another access point for the Kruger National Park.

TO THE NORTH
Several services run north up the N1. Translux has a daily bus to Bulawayo, Zimbabwe, via Beitbridge. The journey times and fares are: Polokwane (Pietersburg; R130, five hours), Makhado (Louis Trichardt; R175, 5½ hours), Musina (R200, 7½ hours), Beitbridge (R210, eight hours) and Bulawayo (R230, 15 hours). They also have services that head east through Limpopo, stopping in Tzaneen (R135, 6½ hours) and Phalaborwa (R150, 7½ hours).

Greyhound has daily services (except Sat) to Harare, Zimbabwe (R350, 17 hours), and Bulawayo (R220, 15 hours) that stop in Polokwane (Pietersburg; R130, five hours).

Intercape also heads north to Gaborone, Botswana (R135, seven hours).

There are daily City to City services to Sibasa, in Limpopo's Venda region (R85, 8½ hours). These services, which wind north through townships and ex-homelands, also stop in major towns on the N1.

North Link Tours (☎ 015-291 1867) runs buses between Jo'burg and Polokwane (Pietersburg; R100, 4½ hours) via Pretoria, and the smaller towns en route. From Polokwane, there are connections to Tzaneen and Phalaborwa.

TO THE SOUTH
Translux operates a daily service to East London (R320, 14 hours) via Bloemfontein. There's also a daily service to Bloemfontein (R180, six hours). Translux also has five services a week (not on Sunday and Tuesday) from Jo'burg to Port Elizabeth (R350, 14½ hours) via Bloemfontein (R220, 10 hours) and Graaff-Reinet (R295, 14½ hours), and a Tuesday and Sunday service via Cradock (R300, 14½ hours).

Intercape has daily services to Port Elizabeth via Cradock (R310, 15 hours) and on to Plettenberg Bay (R385, 18 hours).

Greyhound has daily buses that travel overnight from Jo'burg to Port Elizabeth (R320, 15 hours) and East London (R310, 13 hours).

Translux runs to Knysna (R385) via Kimberley three times weekly or Bloemfontein four times weekly, then Oudtshoorn, Mossel Bay and George (all R355 from Jo'burg); the trip takes 17 hours. Intercape also operates to Knysna for the same price.

City to City runs to Umtata (R115), the closest large town to Port St Johns and Coffee Bay, daily at 7pm. There are daily City to City services to Lusikisiki via Pietermaritzburg (R110) and to Idutywa via Queenstown (R115); call for times as they can vary substantially. Translux and Greyhound both run to Umtata (R220, 12½ hours); Translux runs on Sunday, Tuesday, Thursday and Friday and Greyhound runs daily except Saturday.

Car
All the major rental operators have counters at JIA and at various locations around the city. It is well worth calculating the length of your planned journey before you settle for a deal though. With many of the main operators offering a limited number of free kilometres, and distances in South Africa piling on the miles, you may end up with a nasty bill when it comes to returning the car. For listings of major rental agencies, see p600.

A range of local firms also rent cars, usually at lower prices. If you're looking for a long-term rental, it's worth ringing around for the best deal.

Comet Car Rental (☎ 453 0188; www.cometcar.co.za) Offers excellent rates including 350km free per day and full insurance (something of a novelty here). Free pick-up and drop-off throughout Jo'burg. If you book through a hostel, you will also get preferential backpacker rates.

Swan's Rent-a-Car (☎ 975 0799; www.swans.co.za) A smaller company, offering older, but well-maintained cars at some of the lowest rates available. Can also pick up and drop off throughout Jo'burg.

Hitching

We say don't hitch – especially here – but people do. Heading north, a popular place to begin hitching is on the M1, a couple of kilometres northwest of Yeoville. The N12 running east towards Kruger begins just east of Eastgate Mall. Heading south on the N1 (to Cape Town) you could try hitching on one of the freeway on-ramps.

The hostels always have notice boards with details of free or shared-cost lifts. Don't expect hostels to take any responsibility – it is up to you to check out the lift-giver and to decide whether or not you wish to travel with that person.

Minibus Taxi

A new road-transport interchange has been built in Park Station, over the train tracks between the Metro Concourse and Wanderers St, to deal with the majority of minibus taxis. It is intended that this will streamline the old set-up, which saw taxis leaving from terminals all around Joubert Park. The new system will slowly kick in, meaning that taxi ranks will be chopping and changing over the next year or so. The best bet for now is to head to the Park Station concourse first, where taxi marshals can point you in the right direction. Because of the risk of mugging, it isn't a good idea to go searching for a taxi while carrying your luggage. Go down and collect information, then return in a taxi, luggage and all.

At the time of writing, as well as the services leaving from Park Station, you could also find minibus taxis going in the direction of Kimberley, Cape Town and Upington on Wanderers St near Leyds St; Bulawayo taxis at the northern end of King George St; Pretoria taxis on Noord St; Lesotho, Bloemfontein (and other Free State destinations) on Noord St, east of Joubert Park; and Durban taxis near the corner of Wanderers and Noord Sts. Fares tend to fluctuate in line with petrol prices, but rates for trips from Jo'burg include:

Destination	Fare (R)
Bulawayo (Zimbabwe)	200
Cape Town	250
Durban	110
Gaborone (Botswana)	85
Harrismith	65
Kimberley	120
Komatipoort	125
Manzini (Swaziland)	90
Maputo (Mozambique)	150
Nelspruit	110
Polokwane (Pietersburg)	75
Pretoria	20
Thohoyandou (Venda)	90
Tzaneen	90

As well as these taxis, which only leave when they're full, there are a few door-to-door services you can book through hostels.

Train

For information on train services to/from Jo'burg and elsewhere in the country, see p605. Tickets can be booked at the Spoornet kiosk on the main concourse at Jo'burg's Park Station.

GETTING AROUND
To/From the Airport

JIA is located about 25km east of central Johannesburg in Kempton Park. There are plenty of touts at the airport, so ensure you only settle for a reputable taxi or shuttle company.

The **Magic Bus** (☎ 608 1662) is the main shuttle-bus service between JIA and the northern suburbs. It leaves half-hourly for expensive hotels in Sandton (R80) and hourly for similar establishments in Rosebank (R80) and Randburg (R90). Door-to-door services cost more. **Airport Link** (☎ 884 3957) is another reputable, airport shuttle.

Between 5am and 10pm, buses run every half hour between JIA and Park Station (R60, 45 minutes); call **Metropolitan Bus Services** (Metrobus; Map p380 ☎ 403 4300; www .mbus.co.za) for details. The area immediately around Park Station is confusing and known for muggings, so heading straight here is not to be advised if you are carrying your bags.

Taxis are expensive at between R200 and R300, depending on where you're going. Meters will generally be used, otherwise agree on a price before you get into the cab.

Most hostels will collect you from the airport, and some still 'tout' there.

Bus

Metropolitan Bus Services (Metrobus; Map pp376–7; ☎ 403 4300; www.mbus.co.za) runs services covering 108 routes in the Greater Jo'burg area. The main bus terminal is at Gandhi Sq, two blocks west of the Carlton Centre, and fares work on a zone system ranging from zone one (R3) to zone eight (R10). Tickets, however, have largely been replaced with a tag system. Travellers buy tags from the bus terminal and the cost of the journey is automatically deducted each time you travel, as with a prepaid phonecard. Normal, adult tags are green in colour and come in denominations of 52 trips monthly, 44 trips monthly, 14 trips weekly, 12 trips weekly and 10 trips weekly. The monthly tags must be used within 35 days, while the other tags have an expiry date of 10 days. At the time of writing, you could still pay for journeys with cash, but this may change – check before you try to use a bus.

The following routes are useful (and there is a useful, interactive route-finder map at www.mbus.co.za):

Route No	Destinations
5	Parktown, Houghton, Rosebank & Illovo
22	Yeoville & Bruma Lake
75	Braamfontein, Auckland Park & Melville
80	Rosebank & Dunkeld via Jan Smuts Ave

HOP-ON, HOP-OFF BUS

The hop-on, hop-off, open-topped **City Slicker** (☎ 403 4300; www.mbus.co.za) buses, which are run by Metropolitan Bus Services, began operating in late 2000 and offer one of the best ways to see Jo'burg (see the boxed text on p375).

The double-deckers pick up from five of Sandton's best hotels, heading to Rosebank and the zoo before winding through the mansions of Parktown, Melville's 7th St and the Oriental Plaza on its way to the city centre.

City stops include the Newtown cultural precinct and the Carlton Centre. The three-hour route ends in Soweto, via Gold Reef City. The return trip takes the same route. It operates between 9am and 9pm, with one-day (R70), two-day (R120) and three-day (R150) passes available. Buy them on the bus or through **Computicket** (☎ 340 8000). Bus stops are marked around town; call ahead for more details.

Minibus Taxi

Fares differ depending on routes, but R4 will get you around the inner suburbs and the city centre and R6 will get you almost anywhere. It's easy enough to catch a minibus taxi into the city and, if you're waiting at a bus stop, the chances are a taxi will show up before the bus does. If you do take a minibus taxi into central Jo'burg, be sure to get off before it reaches the end of the route – avoid the taxi ranks as they are a mugging zone. Getting a minibus taxi home from the city is a more difficult proposition. Even locals often give up and take the bus.

There's a complex system of hand/finger signals to tell a passing taxi where you want to go (drivers will stop if they are going the same way). Just raising your index finger in the air will stop most taxis – but it means 'town'. A down-turned index finger means 'Sandton'. The last three fingers held up is 'Dobsonville, Soweto'.

Taxi

Taxis are an expensive but necessary evil in this city. They all operate meters, which unfortunately seem to vary markedly in their assessment, if they work at all. Consequently, it's wise to ask a local the likely price and agree on a fare at the outset. From Park Station to Rosebank should cost between R50 and R70, and significantly more to Sandton. Three reputable firms are **International taxi** (☎ 390 1502), **Maxi Taxi Cabs** (☎ 648 1212) and **Rose's Radio Taxis** (☎ 403 9625).

Train

For inquiries about **Metro** (☎ 773 5878) train services call, or visit the helpful information office in the Park Station concourse. There has been a very serious problem with violent crime on the Metro system, mostly on those lines connecting with Black townships. The Jo'burg–Pretoria Metro line should also be avoided.

SOWETO

☎ 011 / pop 1.5 million

The idea was simple. Move anyone who wasn't White as far away from the 'chosen race' as possible, but still close enough for them to be used as cheap labour. Thus was born the South-Western Townships, or Soweto, traditionally the biggest, most political, violent and dynamic, and best known of South Africa's townships.

But while the history of Soweto is intrinsically linked to the wider struggle against apartheid, the township has since embarked on a journey of self-discovery that is as much about the future as the past. Tourists now flood into the area, attracted by some of the most poignant landmarks in South Africa's historical narrative (the Mandela Museum, the Hector Pieterson Museum, the Regina Mundi Church), but after an initial exodus, local Blacks are also returning to the township, intent on forging a new identity for their community.

And so the face of this sprawling community – anything from 1.5 million (the official census figure) to 3.5 million (local estimates) people live in Soweto – is changing. Large sections of the township are still characterised by tin shacks and desperate poverty, while others, such as the Diepkloof Extension and Orlando West, are indicative of the growth of a new, moneyed class. After growing up with the Western media's stereotypical image of Soweto as a crime-ridden

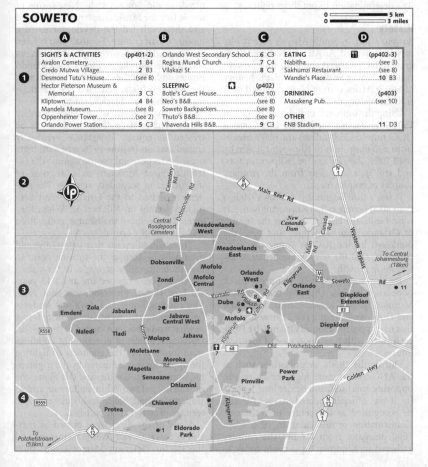

SOWETO

0 ———— 5 km
0 ———— 3 miles

SIGHTS & ACTIVITIES	(pp401-2)
Avalon Cemetery	1 B4
Credo Mutwa Village	2 B3
Desmond Tutu's House	(see 8)
Hector Pieterson Museum & Memorial	3 C3
Kliptown	4 B4
Mandela Museum	(see 8)
Oppenheimer Tower	(see 2)
Orlando Power Station	5 C3

Orlando West Secondary School	6 C3
Regina Mundi Church	7 C4
Vilakazi St	8 C3
SLEEPING 🏠	(p402)
Botle's Guest House	(see 10)
Neo's B&B	(see 8)
Soweto Backpackers	(see 8)
Thuto's B&B	(see 8)
Vhavenda Hills B&B	9 C3

EATING 🍴	(pp402-3)
Nabitha	(see 3)
Sakhumzi Restaurant	(see 8)
Wandie's Place	10 B3
DRINKING	(p403)
Masakeng Pub	(see 10)
OTHER	
FNB Stadium	11 D3

wasteland, the sprinkler-fed lawns of these middle-class suburbs may well seem rather incongruous.

Which is not to say that modern Soweto is a bed of roses – far from it. Vilakazi St may be the only street in the world to boast two Nobel peace laureates (Nelson Mandela and Desmond Tutu), both heroes in the Black community's struggle for freedom, but now the apartheid system has been dismantled, new heroes will have to emerge in the battle against poverty, HIV/AIDS and crime. A resolution will be a long time coming, but Soweto remains a fascinating, living example of all that is good and bad in South Africa, suffering from the nation's devastating social problems, but also riding high on a community's determination to put them right.

History

Soweto's role in South Africa's recent history is unrivalled. As African National Congress (ANC) stalwart and long-time Soweto resident Walter Sisulu once said, the history of South Africa cannot be understood outside the history of Soweto.

Using the outbreak of bubonic plague in 1904 as an excuse, the Jo'burg City Council (JCC) moved 1358 Indians and 600 Africans from a Jo'burg slum to Klipspruit, 18km by road from the city centre (Klipspruit was, and still is, a long way from the primary sources of employment).

It was a slow beginning, and by 1919 less than 4000 people called Klipspruit home. It wasn't until the late 1930s, after the suburb of Orlando had been built and cynically marketed by the JCC as 'Somewhat of a paradise', that the population began its astonishing growth.

By the end of WWII, Jo'burg's Black population had risen by more than 400,000. Moroka, Jabavu, Meadowlands, Diepkloof and Dube were among the 21 new suburbs that had appeared around Orlando by 1958, each filled with row upon row of identical houses.

During the 1950s, organisations such as the ANC took a more high-profile role in opposing apartheid and before long Soweto (as it was officially named in 1961) would be recognised as the centre of resistance. Confirmation of this came in 1955 when 3000 delegates from around the country gathered in Kliptown Sq (known today as

Freedom Sq) at the Congress of the People. The result was the Freedom Charter, which is the central pillar of ANC philosophy and integral to the new constitution.

The demands of the charter were not unreasonable, but the response was less than sympathetic and resistance was forced underground in 1960 after the Sharpeville Massacre (p38). Sowetans spent the next 15 years in a state of definite uncertainty – definite they wanted change but uncertain as to how and when it would come.

While the struggle continued at a slower pace over these years, it was not the only change taking place in Soweto. The demographics of the townships were changing, and as second-generation Sowetans matured, so did Soweto style. New forms of music (see the Music chapter, p54) emerged and the youth led the developments of a unique urban culture. Football also offered an escape, and massive support for teams such as the Moroka Swallows, the Orlando Pirates and, after they split from the Pirates, the Kaizer Chiefs, reflected the development of an urban Black identity.

The development of this new identity only served to strengthen the desire to be treated as equals. Resistance eventually spilled over on 16 June 1976, when students organised a peaceful protest against the introduction of Afrikaans as a language of instruction in secondary schools. The students marched to the Orlando West Secondary School on Vilakazi St. When they arrived and refused to disburse, police fired tear gas into the crowd.

The chain of events that followed would eventually be seen as the turning point in the whole liberation struggle. In the resulting chaos police opened fire and a 13-year-old boy, Hector Pieterson, was shot dead. The ensuing hours and days saw students fight running battles with the security forces in what would become known as the Soweto Uprising. Dozens of government buildings were torched, but the euphoria of fighting the oppressor was tempered by the frightening human cost. On the first day alone, the official toll put two White policemen and 23 students as dead, but in reality closer to 200 teenage protesters had perished.

Many of the dead were buried as martyrs in Soweto's vast Avalon Cemetery, and the Hector Pieterson Memorial was built to commemorate all those who died in the struggle.

Within days, world opinion had turned irreversibly against the apartheid regime and Soweto became the most potent symbol of resistance to a racist South Africa.

Scenes of burning cars, burning people and mass funerals flowed out of Soweto throughout the 1980s, as the death throes of apartheid swept over the country. Mandela was released in 1990 and returned to live in his tiny home in Vilakazi St, just 200m from Archbishop Desmond Tutu. Tutu still lives here, while Mandela's old home has been converted into a museum.

However, Mandela's release was no panacea. Encouraged by the government, supporters of rival political parties murdered each other by the hundreds in the run up to the 1994 free elections. In the early 1990s, Soweto was one of the most dangerous places on earth.

More recently life has been stable, and since 1994 Sowetans have had ownership rights over their properties. The relative calm has been further compounded by a number of redevelopment projects, including the transformation of Hector Pieterson Sq into a memorial and major visitor attraction, growing tourist traffic and the return of many middle-class Blacks. In 2000, Soweto was finally brought back into the fold when it was officially incorporated into the city of Jo'burg.

For a fabulous insight into Soweto's history, pick up a copy of Peter Magubane's photographic record *Soweto*.

Visiting Soweto

It may seem grotesque to treat Soweto as just another attraction but a tourist trail through the township is now well established and most Sowetans are excited about the interest the world is showing in their community. Without doubt, the easiest and safest way to visit is on a tour, but moves are being made to improve the signposting (a perennial problem), and the infrastructure is now such that a self-guided tour is not out of the question – heed local advice carefully, if you choose to do this, and stick to the area surrounding Vilakazi St and Hector Pieterson Sq. If you want some extra flexibility, and would prefer to avoid the aloofness of an organised tour, perhaps

the best option is to take a tour as far as Vilakazi St (the greatest danger is getting hopelessly lost on the way into Soweto) and then rely on your guesthouse owner to get you safely between the various attractions. However you choose to see Soweto, the following attractions appear on most tour itineraries, or can be visited on their own.

The first stop on most tours is the **Mandela Museum** (☎ 083-530 1521; 8115 Ngakane St; adult/child R20/10; ◷ 9.30am-5pm), just off Vilakazi St. This was the house Nelson Mandela shared with his first wife, Evelyn, and it is filled with fascinating photographs and clutter. Among the exhibits is a letter from the State of Michigan asking George Bush Senior to apologise for the role the CIA played in Mandela's 1962 arrest. Needless to say, they never did. Just down Vilakazi St, by the Sakhumzi Restaurant (p402), is **Desmond Tutu's house**.

North of Vilakazi St is Soweto's showcase **Hector Pieterson Sq**. Named after the 13-year-old who was shot dead in the run-up to the Soweto uprising (see p400), the square now features the poignant **Hector Pieterson Memorial** and the excellent **Hector Pieterson Museum** (☎ 011-536 0611; cnr Khumalo & Pela St; adult/child R10/5; ◷ 10am-5pm), which offers an insight into Sowetan life and the history of the independence struggle. From the square, a line of shrubs leads up Moema St to the site where he was shot outside the school.

South of here, down Klipspruit Valley Rd, is the **Regina Mundi Church** (Mkhize St; admission by donation), which, as a community meeting place, was central to the struggle against apartheid. The police often retaliated and you can still see bullet holes in the ceiling to the right of the main altar. The right-hand, 'community' altar rail is also chipped from where it was smashed by the butt of a police rifle. In recognition of the church's role in the struggle, several hearings of the Truth & Reconciliation Committee were heard here.

Other sights include the **Credo Mutwa Village** (Bolani Rd; admission free), which was largely destroyed after the artist who built it made controversial comments about the 1976 uprising; and the **Oppenheimer Tower** (Bolani Rd; admission free), erected in gratitude to the Chairman of the Anglo-American Corporation, Sir Ernest Oppenheimer, who in 1956 organised a loan from the Chamber of Mines to build 14,000 homes, improving living standards for thousands of Sowetans. You can also visit **Avalon cemetery**, where you will find the graves of Hector Pieterson (Plot EC462) and Joe Slovo (Plot B35311), leader of the South African Communist Party.

Kliptown, to the southwest of Orlando West, was established back in 1904 and is the oldest settlement in Johannesburg to accommodate all races. It was also the site of the adoption of the Freedom Charter on 26 June 1955. It is very run-down today, but plans for a redeveloped hub on the Walter Susulu Sq of Dedication, including a Soweto Tourist Information Centre and a Kliptown Museum, are in the offing. The full development should be open by June 2005. Check www.jda.org.za for progress reports.

Tours

Dozens of companies offer tours of Soweto (see p383 for more details). **KDR Sports & Adventure Travel** (☎ 326 1700; www.soweto.co.za) is a well-connected outfit and can also book accommodation in Soweto. It runs excellent Soweto day tours for R430 per person, or R510 per person including Jo'burg. The website is also a good source of information on the township.

Sleeping

Once almost unthinkable, staying over in Soweto is now both perfectly possible and one of the most rewarding ways of getting a sense of the place. At last count there were more than 30 functional B&Bs in the township, most in the immediate vicinity of Vilakazi St. While going through a tour company remains by far the best and safest way of organising a foray into the guesthouses, you can book directly through the guesthouses themselves. Most owners will then be more than happy to show you around. The **Soweto Accommodation Association** (☎ 936 8123; nrwaxa@hotmail.com) is a community-run enterprise organised out of Thuto's B&B (p402) and can help find you a room or advise on safety issues.

Most of the following places offer comfortable rooms with private bathrooms in a small, middle-class home. In general, accommodation in Soweto does not come cheap, but remember that tourism has become a major source of income for this area.

Soweto Backpackers (☎ 326 1700; www.soweto backpackers.co.za; 10823 A Powe St; dm/s/d with shared bathroom R70/85/170) A couple of years back, few

would have expected Soweto to have its own backpackers. And yet here it is. Standards are basic, but the beds are cheap and the owner is a great source of information on the township.

Neo's B&B (☎ 536 0413, 082-629 2284; 8041 Bocela St; s/d R190/380 with breakfast) In a vintage Sowetan home, this tiny place offers cosy comforts on the very doorstep of the township's major attractions. There is a thatched deck outside for evening eating.

Thuto's B&B (☎ 936 8123, 072-376 9205; 8123 Ngakane St; s/d with breakfast R350/500) Right opposite the Mandela Museum, this is Soweto's second-oldest B&B. It isn't the best, but the owner, Anastacia, promises to show her guests how the Black middle classes really live.

Vhavenda Hills B&B (☎ 936 0411, 082-213 1630; 11749 Mampuru; s/d R250/500; ⊠ ▣) Just off Klipspruit Valley Rd and a short hop from Vilakazi St, this slick, whitewashed place is one of the township's smartest options, with huge rooms, Internet access and an in-house tour company (Vhupo Cruiserline Tours) that organises walking tours of Soweto and driving trips across South Africa.

Botle's Guest House (☎ 982 1872, 082-838 1886; 648 Monyane St; d with/without bathroom R250/350; ⊠) A good example of Soweto's growing prosperity, the owner of this place demolished her breeze-block bungalow to build a guesthouse. With typically Sowetan, mock-Versace décor, it offers a cash bar, a small restaurant space for breakfast and a TV in every room. It is near Wandie's Place (p402).

Eating & Entertainment

When you're visiting Soweto, you'll find that you're never more than a short stagger from a drinking establishment, the quality of which varies greatly. In the squatter camps the favourite tonic is the African beer made from maize meal. It comes in 1L plastic bottles for R5, and is definitely an acquired taste. For most Sowetans a trip to the pub involves sitting in a neighbour's front room and being served lager from a cooler.

But Soweto is changing. With a growing number of tourists and wealthier locals looking for a slicker place to eat and drink, several decent bars and restaurants have sprung up around the township. Some even have a reputation that has spread into the northern suburbs of Jo'burg itself.

Wandie's Place (☎ 982 2796; www.wandiesplace .co.za; 618 Dube; buffet R45) Soweto's original and most-famous nightspot remains in pole position in the eating and drinking stakes. Fast expanding, it now has several different spaces, each packed to bursting by 9pm. Cape wineries have even been known to come here to host tastings. The buffet is fabulous.

Sakhumzi Restaurant (☎ 939 4427; www.sakhum zi.co.za; 6980 Vilakazi St; mains R20-40) Opening in the very heart of the Vilakazi St area, this excellent little eatery draws a steady stream of tourists and locals alike. The food is tasty, there are sometimes jazz bands playing in the evening, and tours of the area can be arranged.

Nabitha (☎ 082-785 7190; 6877 Vilakazi St; mains R25-55) Nabitha means 'to taste – expensively' in Zulu and this brand-new opening aptly represents the township's changing face. Stylish and open-fronted, it serves a delicious combination of contemporary and traditional African fare and a decent selection of drinks.

Masakeng Pub (☎ 982 8034; 649 Kinini St; mains R20-40) Home of the Soweto Beer Festival (in October), this lively place has an outside braai area, an Internet café, a big-screen telly and ice-cold beer.

Getting There & Away

At present, by far the best way to get to Soweto is on a tour. However, if you do want to explore the township at your own pace, which is perfectly possible, organise transport through a tour operator, book

into a B&B and ask the guesthouse owner (preferably in advance) to show you the lie of the land.

AROUND JOHANNESBURG

WESTERN GAUTENG

The **Kromdraai Palaeontological Reserve**, also referred to as the Cradle of Humankind, is a Unesco World Heritage Site, with at least a dozen sites offering up a fabulous array of palaeontological material.

In fact, the **Sterkfontein Caves** (☎ 956 6342; Sterkfontein Caves Rd; adult/child R20/10; ☺ 9am-4.30pm Tue-Sun), on Johannesburg's doorstep, are one of the most significant archaeological and palaeontological sites in the world – up there with Olduvai Gorge in Tanzania. The discovery in 1998 of 'Mr Ples', an almost complete 3.5 million-year-old hominid skeleton, has renewed interest in this veritable time capsule. See the boxed text below for more information.

Be warned, the caves' limestone interior has been mined out so they are not attractive caves. The pokey **Broom Museum** (admission free) contains fossils from some of the more significant finds. Tours of the caves are conducted every half-hour.

Not far away is the **Old Kromdraai Gold Mine** (☎ 957 0211; Ibis Ridge Farm, Kromdraai Rd; adult/child R25/10; ☺ 9am-5pm Sat & Sun, Tue-Fri by appointment). This was the first gold mine on the

---

STERKFONTEIN CAVES

The Sterkfontein Caves were formed by the solution of dolomite beneath the water table, a process that began about 2.5 billion years ago. But it is that which was washed in much later (3.5 million years ago) that has spurred latter-day interest: deposits rich with bones.

In August 1936, Dr Robert Broom visited the caves after learning that extinct baboon fossils had been found in the dumps left from crude lime quarrying. A week after arriving in the area he had found the first adult skull of an 'ape-man', believed to be 2.6 to three million years old – he named it *Australopithecus transvaalensis*. In 1947, the cranium of 'Mrs Ples' was blasted out of the debris and almost 10 years later, in 1956, Dr CK Brain discovered much younger stone tools. In 1995, the significance of the articulating foot bones of 'Little Foot' was revealed – their relationship to an ankle bone indicated that this 'ape-man', our ancestor, walked upright. In all, Sterkfontein has so far given up more than 600 hominid fossils, making it the most bountiful site for evidence of *A. transvaalensis*.

Sterkfontein is significant as it indicates that erect walking creatures (hominids) roamed and hunted across this landscape more than three million years ago, side by side with several other now-extinct species (eg giant leaf-eating monkeys, hunting hyena and sabre-toothed cats).

Witwatersrand. Guided tours leave the converted shed every hour.

In the Swartkop Mountains is the **Rhino & Lion Nature Reserve** (☎ 957 0109; Kromdraai Rd; adult/child R50/20; ☺ 8am-5pm). This place goes from strength to strength and is a good option for those who cannot afford the time to go to Kruger National Park. You can see cheetahs, wild dogs (painted wolves), buffaloes, lions and rhinos close up and there is a vulture hide for keen birdwatchers. There is a comfortable **chalet** (four people R400) in a camp within the reserve, and **wildlife drives** (R100) are offered.

West of the Rhino & Lion Nature Reserve, and just off Kromdraai Rd, is **Wonder Cave** (☎ 957 0034; Kromdraai Rd; adult/child R50/25; ☺ 8am-4pm Mon-Fri, 8am-5pm Sat & Sun). With some beautiful formations, Wonder Cave is a good fillip for those that came to Sterkfontein expecting a pristine interior. Wonder Cave is nothing more than a commercial tourist cave, however. Visit Sterkfontein for the prehistory before you come here. Tours run hourly.

Krugersdorp Game Reserve (☎ 665 1735; adult/ child R15/5; ☺ 8am-5pm), a small grassland reserve 7km west of Krugersdorp on the R24 in the direction of Magaliesberg, has four of the Big Five (no elephant). Within the reserve, **Ngonyama Lion Lodge** (☎ 665 4342; Rustenberg Rd; d R350) has a range of accommodation and is a good bet for those wishing to stay out of town.

Near Lanseria airport is a **Lion Park** (☎ 460 1814; Old Pretoria Rd/R55; admission R75; ☺ 8.30am-5pm Mon-Fri, 8.30am-6pm Sat & Sun). This place, on the R55, is notable for its 'tree-climbing lions', terrible takeaways and *lekker jol festing* (good partying) Afrikaners. If you do go, avoid going on a Sunday at all costs when the crowds descend in legions.

SOUTHERN GAUTENG

This area, with its cities of Vereeniging, Sebokeng and Vanderbijlpark, is dissected by the Vaal River and is very rich in history. The natural barrier of the Vaal River – the *gij!garib* (tawny) to the San, *lekoa* (erratic) to the Sotho, and *vaal* (dirty) to the Afrikaners – has been an important dividing line in Southern African history, separating the 'Transvaal' from the south.

The Treaty of Vereeniging was negotiated near the Vaal, effectively ending the 1899–

1902 Anglo-Boer War, and in more recent times southern Gauteng has been an important place in the struggle for freedom.

It was at Sharpeville and Evaton, on 21 March 1960, that Black civilians protested against the pass laws by publicly burning their passbooks. The police opened fire on the protestors at Sharpeville, killing 69 and wounding about 180; most were shot in the back. Now, 21 March is commemorated in South Africa as Human Rights Day.

In 1984 in Sebokeng, the security forces violently reacted to a Black boycott of rent and service tariffs, tearing apart townships looking for activists. About 95 people were killed. These slaughters galvanised the Black population into a more unified force, and ultimately hastened the fall of apartheid.

Named after the sugar bush *Protea caffra*, the **Suikerbosrand Nature Reserve** (☎ 904 3930; Klip River Rd; adult/child R20/10, plus vehicle R15; ☺ 6.30am-5.30pm Oct-Apr, 7am-5.30pm Mar-Sep) is nestled between the N3 and R59 freeways, and can be reached by either. There are 66km of walking trails, several drives and the historic **Diepkloof Farm Museum** (☎ 904 3933; admission free), originally built in 1850 by Voortrekker Gabriel Marais, and renovated in the 1970s after being burnt during the Boer War. Its opening hours are the same as for the reserve.

Camping is available 25km from Meyerton at **Aventura Kareekloof** (☎ 016-365 5334; fax 016-365 5628; camp sites R85), which has plenty of space, or the adjoining **Aventura Heidelbergkloof** (☎ 016-341 2413; fax 341 6758; R23 near Heidelberg; camp sites R85). Look for signs from Meyerton or call for directions before setting off.

PRETORIA

☎ 012 / pop 1.47 million

In May 2001, forty years to the day after South Africa was declared a republic, a colossal bust of Johannes Gerhardus (JG) Strijdom, an architect of apartheid, toppled from its plinth in Pretoria's JG Strijdom Sq and cracked in two. In a city that has become a living monument to the changing South Africa, it was a poignant moment.

With deep roots in the country's Afrikaner-dominated past, and as the city where the mechanisms of apartheid were both engineered and administered, Pretoria (known as 'Tshwane' by the Sotho population, and 'ePitoli' in township-speak) has been forced to don a new face for the 20th century. As South Africa's administrative capital, this former hub of White supremacy, built on the twin Boer dreams of independence from the British and dominance of the Blacks, is now home to a growing number of Black civil servants, importing the multiculturalism that had previously been resisted by the rule of law. Against many other parts of the country, stately Pretoria is proof positive that affluence is no longer an entirely White privilege.

Only 50km apart (and the gap is closing fast as suburbs on both sides of the divide expand), the cities of Pretoria and Jo'burg remain very different. Pretoria remains uncompromisingly 'Boer' and the bump-and-grind of downtown Jo'burg here gives way to a slower-paced, more reserved way of life. Jacarandas again bring colour to the streets in October and November, but Pretoria also retains a faint whiff of the old school, with fewer skyscrapers and a flush of latter-day buildings.

Majority rule has brought scores of embassies back to the leafy suburbs of Arcadia and Hatfield, but not everything has changed – the military and educational institutions associated with the capital remain. The universities are huge and tens of thousands of students drive Pretoria's vibrant nightlife.

There are several sites that must be seen. The looming Voortrekker Monument and the neofascist lines of JG Strijdom Sq are very different but are united in their hardline Afrikaner origins. The Union Buildings are architecturally classic, while the charm of Church Sq is best appreciated from the benches of Cafe Riche (p413). Burgers Park, an English garden, is a midcity oasis and a relaxing spot for lunch. After dark, the music and cuisine centres of Hatfield and Brooklyn are buzzing; meanwhile jazz is played in the township shebeens.

This is a far more relaxed place than Jo'burg, but there has been a sharp rise in crime in recent years, with the city centre and Sunnyside copping most of the flak. Most of the city is safe by day, but things change fast so take all the usual precautions and a large dose of local advice.

HISTORY

The area around the Apies River was well watered and fertile, so it supported a large population of cattle farmers for hundreds of years. These were Nguni-speaking peoples (from the same origin as the Zulus and Swazis), who came to be known as the Ndebele by the Sotho people of the Transvaal, and as the Matabele by the Europeans.

However, the disruption caused by the Zulu wars resulted in massive dislocation. Much of the Black population was slaughtered and most of the remaining people fled north into present-day Zimbabwe. In 1841, the first Boers trekked into a temporary vacuum. With no-one around, they calmly laid claim to the land that would become their capital, thus beginning the long-held myth that White people arrived in the area first.

By the time the British granted independence to the ZAR in the early 1850s, there were estimated to be 15,000 Whites and 100,000 Blacks living between the Vaal and Limpopo Rivers. The Whites were widely scattered, and in 1853 two farms on the Apies River were bought as the site for the republic's capital. The ZAR was a shaky institution. There were ongoing wars with the Black tribes, and violent disputes among the Boers themselves. Pretoria, which was named after Andries Pretorius, the hero of Blood River (p33), was the scene of fighting during the Boer civil war (1863–69).

Pretoria was nothing more than a tiny frontier village with a grandiose title, but the servants of the British Empire were watching it with growing misgivings. They acted in 1877, annexing the republic. The Boers went to war – Pretoria came under siege at the beginning of 1881 – and won back their independence.

The discovery of gold on the Witwatersrand in the late 1880s revolutionised the situation and within 20 years the Boers would again be at war with the British. Pretoria was abandoned by President Paul Kruger and the Boer forces in June 1900, but the war ground on until 31 May 1902, when the Treaty of Vereeniging was signed at Melrose House.

With the British making efforts towards reconciliation, self-government was again granted to the Transvaal in 1906, and through an unwieldy compromise Pretoria was made the administrative capital. The

PRETORIA

INFORMATION

ABSA ATM	**1** G4
Australian Embassy	**2** F4
Backpacker Student Travel	(see 46)
Botswanan High Commission	**3** H2
Canadian High Commission	**4** G4
Department of Home Affairs	**5** B4
First National Bank	**6** B4
First National Bank	**7** G4
French Embassy	**8** F3
German Embassy	**9** H4
Irish Embassy	**10** H3
Kodak Express	(see 45)
Laundromat	(see 76)
Lethotho Embassy	**11** B4
Main Post Office	**12** A4
Mozambiquan High Commission	**13** D3
Namibian Embassy	**14** E3
Nedbank	(see 45)
Netherlands Embassy	**15** F4
New Zealand Embassy	**16** G4
Odyssey Internet Cafe	(see 76)

Police Station	**17** B6
Police Station	**18** D5
Protea Book House	**19** G4
STA Travel	**20** G4
Swazi Embassy	**21** E3
Tourist Information Centre	**22** A4
UK High Commission	**23** H3
US Embassy	**24** F4
Zimbabwean High Commission	**25** E3

SIGHTS & ACTIVITIES (pp409–11)

African Window	**26** A5
Church Square	**27** B4
City Hall	**28** A5
Dutch Reformed Church (Paul Kruger's Church)	**29** A4
JG Stijdom Square	**30** B4
Melrose House	**31** B5
Pass Office	(see 32)
Paul Kruger House Museum	**32** A4
Pretoria Art Museum	**33** E4
Pretoria National Zoological	

Gardens	**34** B3
SA Police Museum	**35** A4
Transvaal Museum	**36** B5
Union Buildings	**37** E3

SLEEPING (pp412–13)

B'Guest House	**38** E4
Burgerspark Hotel	**39** B5
Hotel 224	**40** D4
Kia Ora	**41** B5
La Maison	**42** G3
Malvern House	**43** D4
Manhattan Hotel	**44** B5
Manor Protea House	**45** G4
North South Backpackers	**46** H4
Orange Court Lodge	**47** D3
Parkview Hotel	**48** D4
Pretoria Backpackers	**49** F5
Sheraton Pretoria	**50** E4
That's It	**51** F4
Victoria Hotel	**52** B5

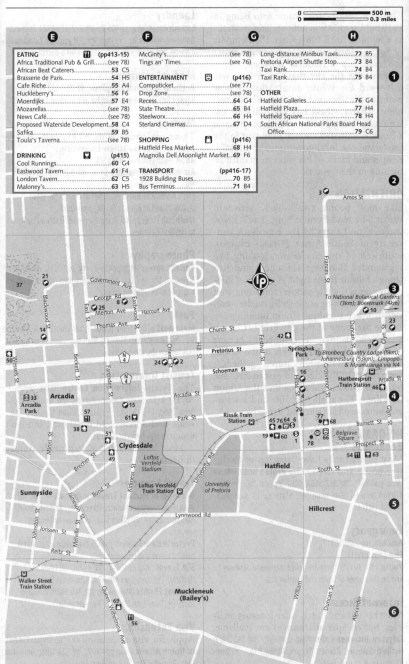

Union of South Africa came into being in 1910 but Pretoria was not to regain its status as a republic until 1961, when the Republic of South Africa came into existence under the leadership of Hendrik Verwoerd.

Ironically, the city that for so long was a byword for White domination is now home to the liberated country's Black president. Thabo Mbeki has his office in the Union Buildings, while a Black mayor and a Black-dominated council hold seat in the less grandiose local government buildings. Kruger and many of his successors must be turning in their graves.

ORIENTATION

Like most people you'll likely arrive in Pretoria by road from Jo'burg. You'll know you're almost there by the enormous University of South Africa (Unisa) campus, southwest of the city centre, looking like a grounded Battlestar Galactica, stretched along a hillside to the right. A couple of kilometres on is the city proper, spreading west to east below a long kopje (hill), on the south side of which stand the Union Buildings.

The backbone of the city grid is Church St, which, at 26km, is claimed to be one of the longest straight streets in the world. Church St runs through Church Sq, the historic centre of the city, and east to Arcadia, home to hotels, embassies and the Union Buildings. The main nightlife and restaurant zones are Hatfield and Brooklyn.

INFORMATION
Bookshops

Most of the malls have branches of Exclusive Books and CNA. The **Protea Book House** (Map pp406-7; ☎ 362 5683; 1067 Burnett St; ☽ 9am-4.30pm Mon-Fri, 9am-noon Sat) also sells second-hand titles.

Emergency
Ambulance (☎ 10111)
Fire (☎ 10111)
Police (☎ 10111) There are police stations on Railway St and on the corner of Leyds and Esselen Sts.

Internet Access

Most hostels and hotels offer Internet facilities, but cheaper alternatives are available. **Odyssey Internet Cafe** (Map pp406-7; ☎ 362 2467; Hatfield Galleries, Burnett St; per 30min R15; ☽ 9am-11pm) is a good bet.

Laundry
Laundromat (Map pp406-7; ☎ 072-329 8222; Hatfield Galleries, Burnett St; ☽ 7am-9pm) If you aren't staying in a hostel, this place will clean your kit for a decent price.

Medical services
Pretoria Academic Hospital (☎ 011-354 1000; Dr Savage Rd) The place to head for in a medical emergency.

Money

There are banks with ATMs and change facilities across town including:
ABSA (Map pp406-7; Hilda St)
American Express (Map p414; ☎ 346 2599; Brooklyn Mall; ☽ 9am-5pm)
First National Bank Branches at Church Sq (Map pp406-7) and at Burnett St (Map pp406-7).
Nedbank (Map pp406-7; cnr Burnett & Festival Sts) Next to Hatfield Galleries.

Photography
Kodak Express (Map pp406-7; ☎ 362 0678; cnr Burnett & Festival Sts; ☽ 8am-6pm Mon-Fri, 8am-1pm Sat) Offers a one-hour developing service.

Post
Main post office (Map pp406-7; cnr Church St & Church Sq; ☽ 8am-4.30pm Mon-Fri, 8am-noon Sat) In an historic building on the main square.

Tourist Information

The **Tourist Information Centre** (Map pp406-7; ☎ 337 4337; www.tshwane.gov.za; Old Nederlandsche Bank Bldg, Church Sq; ☽ 8am-3.45pm Mon-Fri) has some useful maps and brochures, but isn't much help beyond that.

Most hostels and hotels provide similar information.

Travel Agencies
Backpacker Student Travel (Map pp406-7; ☎ 362 0989; info@northsouthbackpackers.com) At North South Backpackers (p412); offers tour- and travel-planning services.
Pretoria Backpackers (p412) This backpackers has a helpful travel and tour agency.
STA Travel (Map pp406-7; ☎ 342 5292; Hilda St, Hatfield; ☽ 9am-5pm Mon-Fri, 9am-noon Sat)
Student Flights (Map p414; ☎ 460 9889; Brooklyn Mall; ☽ 9am-5pm Mon-Fri, 9am-noon Sat)

Visa Extensions

Apply for visa extensions at the **Department of Home Affairs** (Map pp406-7; ☎ 324 1860; Sentrakor Bldg; Pretorius St; ☽ 8am-3pm Mon-Fri).

DANGERS & ANNOYANCES

Rated South Africa's 'happiest city' in a recent poll, with the best quality of life in the country, Pretoria is certainly safer and more relaxed than Jo'burg. That said, crime rates have been rising steadily in recent years. The city centre and Sunnyside have been worst hit, with restaurants and other businesses moving to the safer Hatfield and Brooklyn areas. The square roughly formed by Vermeulen, Du Toit, Boom and Schubert Sts has a bad reputation.

It's important to remember that almost two million people live in Pretoria and live relatively regular lives, so don't be scared into never leaving your lodgings. At the same time, things change quickly in South Africa, and Pretoria is no exception – always seek local advice before venturing into the unknown, and take all the usual precautions; see p573 for more information.

SIGHTS & ACTIVITIES
Voortrekker Monument & Museum

The intimidating **Voortrekker Monument & Museum** (Map p418; ☎ 323 0682; Eeufees Rd; adult/child R22/8, plus vehicle R10; ☉ 8am-6pm) is hallowed turf for many Afrikaners. Built between 1938 and 1949 to commemorate the achievements of the Voortrekkers, who trekked north over the coastal mountains of the Cape into the heart of the African veld, the structure remains a looming symbol of the Boers' pioneering and independent spirit. In particular, it commemorates the Battle of Blood River on 16 December 1838, during which 470 Boers, under the command of Andries Pretorius, defeated approximately 12,000 Zulus. Supposedly, three 'trekkers were wounded and 3000 Zulus were killed.

The 'trekkers went on to found independent republics that in many ways form the genesis of modern South Africa. In terms of drama, determination, courage, vision and tragedy, their story surpasses the history of European colonists (or invaders if you like) anywhere else in the world. Some Afrikaners go one step further, saying that the trek parallels the biblical Exodus, and that the Battle of Blood River was a miracle that can only be explained by divine intervention, proof that the 'trekkers were a chosen people.

The monument was built at the time of a great resurgence of Afrikaner nationalism. The scars of their defeat in the 1889–1902 Anglo-Boer War were still fresh and the monument provided an emotional focal point for the Afrikaners' ongoing struggle. The building's inauguration in 1949 was attended by 250,000 people. It remains a powerful symbol of the 'White tribe of Africa' and their historical relationship to South Africa.

The edifice is surrounded by a stone wall carved with 64 wagons in a traditional defensive laager (circle). The building itself is a huge stone cube inspired by the ruins of Great Zimbabwe. Inside, a bas-relief tells the story of the trek and of the Battle of Blood River. On 16 December a shaft of light falls on the words *Ons vir jou, Suid Africa* ('We for thee, South Africa'). A staircase and elevator lead to the roof and a great panoramic view of Pretoria and the Transvaal highveld.

In the basement there is an excellent small museum that reconstructs the lives of the 'trekkers, and a magnificent tapestry that almost eclipses the bas-relief above in its combination of naive artistry and tubthumping chauvinism.

The monument is 3km south of the city and is clearly signposted from the N1 freeway. It is possible to catch the Voortrekkerhoogte or Valhalla bus from Kruger St near the corner of Church Sq. Ask the driver to let you off at the entrance road to the monument, from where it is a 10-minute walk uphill.

Church Square   Map pp406–7

At the heart of Pretoria, Church Sq is surrounded by imposing public buildings. These include the **Ou Raadsaal (Old Government) building** on the southern side; the **Old Capitol Theatre** in the northwestern corner; the **First National Bank** in the northeastern; the **Palace of Justice**, where the Rivonia Trial that sentenced Nelson Mandela to life imprisonment was held, on the northern side; the **Old Nederlandsche Bank building**, which adjoins the Cafe Riche and houses the Tourist Information Centre (p408); and the **main post office** at the western side. Look for the clock, surrounded by **nude figures** by Anton van Wouw, above the Church Sq entrance to the post office.

In the centre, the **'Old Lion'**, Paul Kruger, looks disapprovingly at office workers lounging on the grass. The bronze figures of Kruger and the sentries, also by Van Wouw, were cast in Italy at the turn of the century, but lay in storage until 1954. In the early days, Boers from the surrounding country-side would gather in the square every three months for communion.

Paul Kruger House Museum
Map pp406–7

A short walk west from Church Sq, the residence of Paul Kruger, has been turned into the **Paul Kruger House Museum** (☎ 326 9172; 60 Church St; adult/child R10/5; ☀ 8am-4.30pm Mon-Fri). It's interesting, but, partly due to its setting right on a busy street, it's difficult to get a feeling for the man (unlike at Smuts' House Museum, Doornkloof; p417), despite the fact that he was undoubtedly an extraordinary human being.

There are clues. The house is unpretentious, although there would have been few grander homes when it was built in 1883. Among all sorts of bric-a-brac there's the knife that Kruger used to amputate his thumb after a shooting accident. The **Dutch Reformed Church**, where he worshipped and preached, is across the road.

Immediately left of the house is the neo-Georgian 1932 **Pass Office**. Hated by Blacks for its function of racial classification, the building was nevertheless known to them as GaMothle, 'Beautiful Place', because the friezes and tableaux decorating it represented Black African peoples. Sadly it's now falling into disrepair and is not open to the public, but there are interesting explanations of its history outside.

Melrose House

Opposite Burgers Park is **Melrose House** (Map pp406–7; ☎ 322 2805; 275 Jacob Maré St; adult/child R5/3; ☀ 10am-5pm Tue-Sun). This neobaroque mansion was built in 1886 for George Heys, and it's a somewhat fanciful cross between English Victorian and Cape Dutch styles.

During the 1899–1902 Anglo-Boer War (sometimes known as the Second War of Independence), Lords Roberts and Kitchener (both British commanders) lived here. On 31 May 1902 the Treaty of Vereeniging, which marked the end of the war, was signed in the dining room. The house is a national monument.

Transvaal Museum

Opposite City Hall, this **museum** (Map pp406–7; ☎ 322 7632; Paul Kruger St; adult/child R8/5; ☀ 9am-5pm Mon-Sat, 11am-5pm Sun) has static displays of animals and birds in glass exhibition cases. After the wildlife parks elsewhere in the country, perusing a collection of stuffed animals is a bit of letdown, but at least you don't have to worry about rampant buffalo. The most dramatic exhibit is the enormous skeleton of a whale outside the building.

South Africa Police Museum

The newly renovated **police museum** (Map pp406–7; cnr Pretorius & Volkstem Sts; adult/child R8/5; ☀ 9am-5pm Mon-Sat, 11am-5pm Sun) is one of the city's better museums, with scores of exhibits covering the turbulent history of the nation's police force. Many of the items date back to the apartheid era, when South Africa was a de facto police state.

African Window

Concentrating on the archaeological and anthropological records of Southern Africa, **African Window** (Map pp406–7; ☎ 324 6082; 102 Visagie St; adult/child R8/5; ☀ 8am-4pm) focuses on the tribes of Gauteng, incorporating some San engravings, a traditional restaurant and regular dance and art exhibitions.

Pretoria Art Museum

Off Schoeman St, a kilometre or so east of the city centre, this **art museum** (Map pp406–7; ☎ 344 1807; Arcadia Park; adult/child R5/3; ☀ 10am-5pm Tue & Thu-Sat, 10am-8pm Wed, noon-5pm Sun) has displays of South African art from many periods of the country's history. It's a good place to get a feel for the contrasting influences that make up modern South Africa.

Pretoria National Zoological Gardens

About 1km north of the city centre are the **zoological gardens** (Map pp406–7; ☎ 328 3265, cnr Paul Kruger & Boom Sts; adult/child R32/19; ☀ 8am-6pm). The national zoo is an impressive and pleasant enough spot to while away an afternoon. There is an aquarium here, as well as a decent cafeteria and some areas of lawn. The highlight is probably the cable car that runs up to the top of a kopje that overlooks the city.

There are regular guided evening trips (R25 per person).

Heroes' Acre Cemetery

Around 1.5km west of Church Sq you'll find this **cemetery** (Map p418; Church St; ☀ 8am-6pm), the burial place of a number of historical figures including Andries Pretorius,

Paul Kruger and Hendrik Verwoerd. Henry H 'Breaker' Morant, the Australian Boer War antihero executed by the British for war crimes, is also buried here – look for the low sign pointing to the grave stone from one of the north-south avenues. If you miss this, you'll never find it.

To get here by bus, take the West Park No 2 or Danville service from Church Sq.

JG Strijdom Square

A striking example of neofascist architecture, the square (Map pp406-7) was until recently dominated by a huge bust of JG Strijdom, the prime minister from 1954 to 1958 and an architect of apartheid, and a group of charging horses (apparently an archetypal heroic and martial image). But in an incredibly ironic twist of fate, in May 2001 Strijdom's head crashed down from its mount and cracked in two – 40 years to the day after South Africa was declared a republic. Exactly what will become of the square remains to be seen, although you can be fairly sure the new government won't be resurrecting Strijdom.

Union Buildings

These buildings (Map pp406-7) are the headquarters of government, South Africa's equivalent of the Kremlin. The impressive red sandstone structures – with a self-conscious imperial grandeur – are surrounded by expansive gardens and are home to the presidential offices.

The architect was Sir Herbert Baker (see the boxed text below), who was responsible for many of the best public buildings constructed immediately after the Union of South Africa was formed.

The buildings are quite a long walk from the city centre; alternatively catch just about any bus heading east on Church St, and walk up through the gardens.

TOURS

Backpacker Student Travel (☎ 362 0989; info@north southbackpackers.com), at North South Backpackers (see p412) runs a range of tours to destinations including a local diamond mine (per person R250), Pretoria city (R200), Soweto (R350) and the Apartheid Museum (R330) in Johannesburg.

Pretoria Backpackers (p412) also offers a wide range of packages.

FESTIVALS & EVENTS

The immensely popular **Pretoria Show** is held during the third week of August at the showgrounds. **Oppikoppi Music Festival** (www.oppikoppi .co.za) is a Woodstock-type bash, where local

---

SIR HERBERT BAKER

The day after a mob of angry rail commuters vented their frustration by burning down Pretoria station in February 2001, the gutted shell of the building seemed destined for demolition. It's a measure of the respect that South Africans have for its architect, Sir Herbert Baker, that by the following day money had been found to rebuild the station, and talk of demolition was a distant memory.

Born in Kent in 1862, Baker arrived in South Africa 29 years later to visit his brother and his cousin, the latter an admiral with the Royal Navy based in Cape Town. His timing was perfect and through the well-connected admiral he soon formed a friendship with the colony's richest and most powerful man, Cecil John Rhodes.

This carefully cultivated relationship would be a turning point in Baker's life. Rhodes commissioned Baker to redesign his home, and the young architect took the radical step of using the vernacular Cape gable on a double-storey building. The result was the timeless magnificence that is Groote Schuur in Cape Town – Rhodes was delighted.

Baker was prolific and designed an eclectic mix of homes and public buildings for the colony and its wealthiest citizens, many of whom made their fortune on the Witwatersrand goldfields. His credits include a raft of mansions in Johannesburg's Parktown district, the South African Institute for Medical Research in Braamfontein, St George's Cathedral in Cape Town, the Sunnyside and Arcadia cathedrals in Pretoria and the work for which he is best remembered, the classical lines of the imposing Union Buildings (p411).

Baker left for India in 1913, eventually returning to England where he worked on South Africa House in London's Trafalgar Sq. He died in 1946 and is buried in Westminster Cathedral.

and international rock bands congregate in a celebration of peace, love and music. It is staged once or twice a year – visit their website for the latest programme details.

SLEEPING

Pretoria has plenty of hostels and hotels of every description. Hatfield, with its bars and restaurants, has developed into something of a backpackers ghetto and some of the best, cheap places to stay are in this area. The well-to-do streets of Hatfield, Brooklyn and New Muckleneuk are also the best places to start looking for mid-range B&B options.

With plenty of cash passing through Pretoria, the city also has its fair share of upmarket business and boutique hotels. Again, these tend to be east of the centre, out towards the wealthier suburbs.

Staying in the centre is a good idea if you want to explore Pretoria's heartlands, and while wandering the streets of downtown Pretoria is not to be recommended after dark, it makes a lot more sense than staying in the centre of Jo'burg. This central area also has its fair share of cheapies.

Budget

North South Backpackers (Map pp406-7; ☎ 362 0989; info@northsouthbackpackers.com; 355 Glyn St, Hatfield; camp sites/dm/s/d with shared bath R35/50/150/180; ⓟ ☀ 💻) Within stumbling distance of the highlife of Burnett St, this excellent hostel has a tirelessly convivial buzz and trimmings (including a savvy travel agency) aplenty. There's a pleasant garden for summer lounging and a cosy sitting room with a real fire for winter warming. The budget dorms, in a separate house, are guaranteed to be the cheapest in town.

Pretoria Backpackers (Map pp406-7; ☎ 343 9754; ptaback@netactive.co.za; 425 Farenden St; dm/s/d with shared bathroom R60/150/180; ⓟ ☀ 💻) Another option within striking distance of the Hatfield good-time, this comfortable place also has roaring fires in the winter and small dorms for that personal feel. They also have a useful in-house travel and tour agency.

Bronberg Country Lodge (☎ 811 0497; www.bron bergbackpackers.co.za; Plot 207, Lynwood Rd, Tiegerpoort; camp sites/dm/d R45/60/180; ⓟ) On the eastern reaches of Pretoria, this rustic place offers a breath of fresh, country air on the boundary of the city. After a busy day's sightseeing, this is the perfect spot to escape back into the bush, or reinvigorate weary feet with a soak in the Jacuzzi.

Kia Ora (Map pp406-7; ☎ 322 4803; kia-ora@vak aneo.co.za; 257 Jacob Maré St; dm/s/d with shared bathroom R60/140/180) Right next to Melrose House, this decent spot is the best bet, if you want to spend some time exploring the city centre and its many museums.

Malvern House (Map pp406-7; ☎ 341 7212; www .malvernhouse.co.za; 575 Schoeman St, Arcadia; s with/without bathroom R125/95, d with/without bathroom R180/140; ⓟ ☒) This large guesthouse is within walking distance of the city. It's spotlessly clean and comfortable and breakfast is included. There are competitive rates for longer stays.

Parkview Hotel (Map pp406-7; ☎ 325 6787; kol met@mweb.co.za; 179 Zeederberg St, Arcadia; s/d R100/150; ⓟ) Opposite the Union Buildings' gardens, this hotel is Spartan but friendly and clean. Rooms are small but each has a shower. Toilets are shared.

Fountains Valley Caravan Park (Map p418; ☎ 440 2121; fax 341 3960; camp sites R55; ⓟ 💧) Just off the M18, south of Pretoria, this is a good facility, with plenty of sites, a pool, a restaurant and tennis courts.

Mid-Range

If you are looking for homey, B&B-style accommodation, it is well worth contacting the **Bed & Breakfast Association of Pretoria** (☎ 083-212 1989; www.accommodationinpretoria.co.za).

Crane's Nest Guesthouse (Map p414; ☎ 460 7223; cranesnest@absamail.co.za; 212 Boshoff St; s/d R350/560; ⓟ ☒) This salubriously suburban B&B sits in the chi-chi section of New Muckleneuk, right next to the bird sanctuary – a big bonus in itself. It is a flick overpriced, but the rooms, overlooking a pleasant garden, are very comfortable.

B'Guest House (Map pp406-7; ☎ 344 0524; louis strydom@mweb.co.za; 751 Park St; s/d R300/395; ⓟ ☒) With a groovy painted gate, this place is a little old-fashioned, but offers a flick of old-world grace and a lush courtyard garden. The breakfast buffet costs R35 and the owner will give you plenty of chat while serving it.

Hotel 224 (Map pp406-7; ☎ 440 5281; www .hotel224.com; cnr Schoeman & Leyds Sts, Arcadia; s/d R220/250; ⓟ ☒) This high-rise hotel sells itself as Pretoria's premier budget location. The amenities just about slip it into the mid-range category however, and while things are now looking a little worn, it remains pretty good value for money.

That's It (Map pp406-7; ☎ 344 3404; www.thatsit .co.za; 5 Brecher St, Clydesdale; s/d with breakfast R210/320; P ✗ ✗) Located near the corner of Farenden St, this is a guesthouse in a leafy suburb, not far from Loftus Versfeld. It's a pleasant house with good-sized rooms, a garden and a pool.

Manhattan Hotel (Map pp406-7; ☎ 322 7635; fax 320 0721; 247 Scheiding St; r with breakfast R300; P ✗) More upmarket, but rather less charming, this is one of the few Black-run hotels in town. It's clean, comfortable and handy for Pretoria Station.

Orange Court Lodge (Map pp406-7; ☎ 326 6346; orange@lantic.co.za; 540 Vermeulen St; 1-/2-/3-bedroom apt R400/800/1200; P ✗) On the corner of Hamilton St, this oasis among concrete blocks is an excellent option. It offers serviced apartments, with phone, TV, kitchen and linen in a historic building.

Top End
Sheraton Pretoria (Map pp406-7; ☎ 429 9999; www .sheraton.com; cnr Church & Wessels St; r R565; P ✗ ✗ ☐) Pretoria's glitziest offering, this classy place saw Britain's Queen Liz shun the official guest residence in favour of one (or a whole floor) of their sparkling rooms. It offers all the reliable, spic-and-span Sheraton trimmings and top-notch service.

Victoria Hotel (Map pp406-7; ☎ 323 6054; fax 324 2426; 200 Scheiding St; s/d with breakfast R375/475; P ✗) Built in 1894, this gracious, historic place has ten Victorian-style rooms with all the creature comforts. It is a great place to stay if you want a whiff of old Pretoria and offers a more idiosyncratic brand of top-end experience.

La Maison (Map pp406-7; ☎ 430 4341; www.la maison.co.za; 235 Hilda St, Hatfield; s/d with breakfast R500/650; P ✗ ✗) Housed in 'Hatfield Castle', a slightly ostentatious 1922 property in leafy Hatfield, La Maison oozes boutique-hotel exclusivity, with only six individually decorated rooms, a pool and a very pleasant rooftop terrace. With an ongoing reputation for fine food, this is also a great spot for a slap-up, culinary splurge.

Manor Protea Hotel (Map pp406-7; ☎ 362 7077; mphotel@satis.co.za; cnr Burnett & Festival Sts, Hatfield; s/d R475/520; P ✗) Up an escalator from Burnett St, this hotel beats the Sheraton on location, but for the price fails to compete

on any other level. It's plain, but perennially reliable.

Burgerspark Hotel (Map pp406-7; ☎ 322 7500; hotel@burgerspark.co.za; cnr Van der Walt & Minaar Sts; s/d R380/450; P ✗) Opposite the well-manicured Burgers Park, this place is big, efficient and central.

EATING
Food in Pretoria is generally of a high standard and prices, especially when compared with those in Jo'burg, are very reasonable. There are a few places in the city centre but most people head to Hatfield, Brooklyn and New Muckleneuk. Most eateries seem to be concentrated along a few streets, so if there's nothing that appeals to you here, just choose a street and cruise.

City Centre   Map pp406-7
Cafe Riche (☎ 328 3173; 2 Church St; mains R25-50; ☽ lunch & dinner) One of Pretoria's more historic eateries, Cafe Riche enjoys a choice spot right in the heart of the city's Church Sq. The passing action, which you can view over a beer from the terrace outside, is the chief selling point, but the food isn't bad either.

Safika (☎ 320 0274; 357 Visagie St; mains R25-50; ☽ lunch & dinner) Looking more like a cafeteria than a restaurant, Safika serves cheap and tasty food from across Africa. The fish curry is delicious.

Hatfield   Map pp406-7
Hatfield is one of the main beneficiaries of the growing security problem in the centre of Pretoria. Burnett St is thriving. It's full of restaurants, cafés and bars and is safe at any hour. If you're out for a drink and a feed, bustling Hatfield Sq on Burnett St is the place to start.

Brasserie de Paris (☎ 342 5057; 525 Duncan St; mains R45-100; ☽ lunch & dinner; ✗) With chic, Art Nouveau trimmings and a Parisian ambience, this snug French bistro is one of Hatfield's best. Duck, game and beef dishes pad out the excellent menu and the food is enough to make you lie back and think of the Moulin Rouge.

News Cafe (☎ 362 7190; Hatfield Sq, Burnett St; mains R25-50; ☽ lunch & dinner; ✗) Cocktails draw the punters to this lively haunt, but they usually end up eating. Fried, gut-busting drinking food tops the billing, but it's a good place to start your night out with a quick bite to eat.

Mozarellas (☎ 362 6464; Hatfield Sq, Burnett St; mains R30-70; ☽ lunch & dinner; ☒) This Italian-style place is a firm favourite with locals and makes a decent stab at all the old favourites. Come nightfall, the outside tables in the square pack out, and a cheery Mediterranean atmosphere prevails. The wine can get pricey though.

Toula's Taverna (☎ 362 7166; Hatfield Sq, Burnett St; mains R30-70; ☽ lunch & dinner; ☒) With a touch of tacky, resort-like Mediterranean style (including the requisite giant pepper grinders), this busy spot has plenty of Greek eats and a decent cocktail menu.

Africa Traditional Pub & Grill (☎ 362 1604; Hatfield Sq, Burnett St; mains R20-40; ☽ breakfast, lunch & dinner) This tiny place doubles as a cosy bar, but it does decent breakfasts from 7am, and snacks all day. If you blink, you'll miss it.

Brooklyn & New Muckleneuk

As the dining and nightlife has moved eastwards, the area around Middle and Fehrsen Sts has become home to a host of good restaurants. The food is generally better and more expensive than in Hatfield. Apart from the following places, you will find all of the staple, cheap-and-cheerful takeaways in the adjoining shopping malls.

Cynthia's Indigo Moon (Map p414; ☎ 346 8926; 283 Dey St; mains R50-150; ☽ lunch & dinner; ☒) Accolades and glowing press reviews galore decorate the entrance hall, while the restaurant itself is surrounded by the colossal wine cellar. A lot of cows died to make this menu possible, but the steak is fabulous, the seafood sublime and the atmosphere cosy and stylish.

Crawdaddy's (Map p414; ☎ 460 0589; Shop 3, Brooklyn Piazza, cnr Middle & Dey Sts; mains R35-60; ☽ lunch & dinner; ☒) With a flick of the Louisiana swamp about it, this Deep South surf-and-turf place has a jumping, bar-style atmosphere and solid steak and seafood tucker.

Villamoura (Map p414; ☎ 346 1650; 273 Middle St; mains R60-160; ☽ lunch & dinner; ☒) This flash Mozambique-Portuguese place serves excellent seafood and a good range of Mediterranean-style specialties. And if you have an eye for detail, the tablecloths are starched, the butter comes in decorative balls and the bread is fresh. What more could you want?

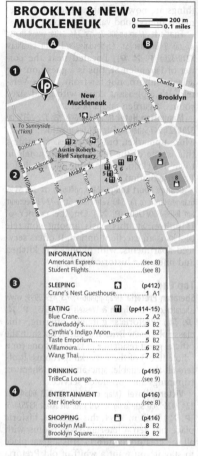

BROOKLYN & NEW MUCKLENEUK

0 _____ 200 m
0 _____ 0.1 miles

INFORMATION	
American Express	(see 8)
Student Flights	(see 8)
SLEEPING 🏠	(p412)
Crane's Nest Guesthouse	1 A1
EATING 🍴	(pp414-15)
Blue Crane	2 A2
Crawdaddy's	3 B2
Cynthia's Indigo Moon	4 B2
Taste Emporium	5 B2
Villamoura	6 B2
Wang Thai	7 B2
DRINKING	(p415)
TriBeCa Lounge	(see 9)
ENTERTAINMENT	(p416)
Ster Kinekor	(see 8)
SHOPPING 🛍	(p416)
Brooklyn Mall	8 B2
Brooklyn Square	9 B2

Blue Crane (Map p414; ☎ 460 7615; Melk St; mains R40-80; ☽ lunch & dinner; ☒) The Blue Crane is part of the Austin Roberts Bird Sanctuary – the Roberts of the famous bird books. The restaurant overlooks a lake that is the breeding site for the endangered blue crane, South Africa's national bird. It does Afrikaner *potjiekos* (a variety of meat and vegetables stewed in an iron pot) and the pub is great at sundown. The entrance to the restaurant is off Melk St, which is a right turn off Middle St as you head west.

Taste Emporium (Map p414; ☎ 460 7181; 279 Dey St; mains R40-110; ☽ lunch & dinner; ☒) With a menu divided into sections, including 'From the Garden', 'From the Sea' and 'From the Farm', this place believes eating is about good ingredients, cooked simply. Piles of fresh wood and an open front add a rustic twist to the simple, neutral décor.

Wang Thai (Map p414; ☎ 346 6230; 281 Middle St; mains R40-100; 😋 lunch & dinner; 😢) Offering 'Royal Thai Cuisine', this upmarket eatery is decorated with an array of upper-echelon bric-a-brac, seemingly purchased from an expensive Bangkok souvenir shop. Standards are high, the food is good and it is a reported favourite of the Thai ambassador.

Huckleberry's (Map pp406-7; ☎ 346 4588; Magnolia Dell, Queen Wilhelmina Dr; mains R25-60; 😋 lunch & dinner; 😢) Right by the stream in the shade of the willow trees, this bright yellow café and pizzeria is excellent for well-priced, lazy summer lunches.

Sunnyside & Arcadia

A shadow has fallen across Esselen St, Sunnyside, and it's not the eating experience it once was. There's a depressing field of take-away chains scattered among the pawn and porn shops, with the odd café and restaurant thrown in. However, there are a couple of places still worth visiting around the olde-worlde Oeverzicht Art Village (Map pp406–7), in Sunnyside, as well as a few upmarket options in the suburban streets of Arcadia. A waterside development, planned for a site just off Esselen St, may yet help to turn things around.

Africa Beat Caterers (Map pp406-7; ☎ 341 3926; 115 Gerhard Moerdyk St; mains R15-30; 😋 lunch & dinner) This area is packed with cutesy, historic villas and this little place is in one of them. There's a sun terrace out front and they serve up a regular mix of cheap, tasty food and live music.

Moerdijks (Map pp406-7; ☎ 344 4856; cnr Park & Beckett St; mains R35-100; 😋 lunch & dinner; 😢) This upmarket place has pride of place in a graceful Dutch villa, with old-school styling, pleasant gardens and the type of food empires were built on.

DRINKING

There are several bars and nightspots in trendy Hatfield, catering for all types. Yet again, Hatfield Sq is a good place to start, but remember that 'guns, fireworks and motorbikes are strictly prohibited'. Unusually for South Africa, Burnett St offers a high density of bars, eateries and clubs; all cut through with lashings of backpacker bravado and student shenanigans. You can wander between venues easily and safely, saving the endless taxi journeys that usually punctuate a night in a big South African city. The easiest pub crawl in the country.

Cool Runnings (Map pp406-7; ☎ 362 0100; 1075 Burnett St) Reggae rules the roost at this perennially popular drinking haunt, but anyone's welcome at the party. Days start slow and lazy, while nights get hot, steamy and really quite drunken after 10pm.

McGinty's (Map pp406-7; ☎ 362 7176; Hatfield Sq, Burnett St) This Irish kit pub has walls covered in Emerald Isle paraphernalia and lashings of have-a-nice-day, commercial *craic*.

Herr Gunther's (Map pp406-7; ☎ 362 6975; Hatfield Sq, Burnett St) A Germanic answer to the Irish bar, this raucous place serves 2L jugs of beer and sausages to soak them up.

Maloney's (Map pp406-7; ☎ 362 2883; Duncan Walk, Duncan St) As if to prove the old corporate adage that you can never have enough Irish pubs, here's another. And it's worth another night's drinking all to itself.

Tings an' Times (Map pp406-7; ☎ 362 5537; Hatfield Galleries, 1066 Burnett St) This laid-back place calls itself a pita bar, but is much more about drinking than eating. It offers great ambience for late-night philosophising or just chilling.

TriBeCa Lounge (Map pp406-7; ☎ 460 3068; Brooklyn Sq, Veale St) Coffees and cocktails create the mood at this trendy café-bar. At weekends, it fills up with the beautiful set, who stop in for a quick looser, after a hard afternoon at the mall.

Eastwood Tavern (Map pp406-7; ☎ 344 0243; cnr Eastwood & Park Sts) This Arcadia institution is packed before, during and after any rugby encounter. You're not likely to meet any Blacks here though. In the summer, a fine mist is sprayed over the beer garden to keep the boozers standing.

London Tavern (Map pp406-7; ☎ 341 1116; cnr Jeppe & Kotze Sts) Most of the 'action' in Sunnyside now involves disrobing, but this remains a lively, reasonable boozer, if you fancy getting a sense of the place over a beer.

Oppikoppi Bar (Map p414; ☎ 082-499 7668) On Magasyn Hill (opposite the Voortrekker Monument), this is one of the best-located pubs in Pretoria. The views over the city are great, particularly at sunset, and they offer DIY braais.

ENTERTAINMENT
Cinemas

There are several large cinema complexes in Pretoria. The *Pretoria News* lists screenings daily.

Menlyn Park Drive-In (Map p418; ☎ 348 8766; Menlyn Park Shopping Centre) On the roof of the Menlyn Park Shopping Centre, this is the spot to catch a movie from the comfort of your car.

Imax Theatre (Map p418; ☎ 368 1168; Menlyn Park Shopping Centre) Big-screen oohs-and-aahs.

Ster Kinekor (Map p414; ☎ 0860 300 222; Brooklyn Mall, Fehrson St, Brooklyn) All the usual Hollywood blockbusters, along with appropriately large tubs of popcorn.

Sterland Cinemas (Map pp406-7; ☎ 0860 300 222; cnr Pretorius & Jeppe Sts, Arcadia) Shows Hollywood blockbusters.

Live Music & Nightclubs

Despite being home to a large student population, Pretoria's live-music scene can be a bit of a damp squib. Check out the *Pretoria News* for the latest listings. If there's nothing that tickles your fancy, there are plenty of nightclubs to boogie the night away in.

Recess (Map pp406-7; ☎ 362 6630; 1076 Burnett St) Anything but a recess, Hatfield's biggest-ever club has five bars, pool tables, dance floors, laser shows, outside seating and Miami Beach styling. On the downside, you'll probably leave deaf.

Steelworx (Map pp406-7; ☎ 362 6623; 1st fl, cnr Burnett & Grosvenor Sts) With a distinctly industrial theme, this is the last late-night stop on the Hatfield circuit.

Drop Zone (Map pp406-7; ☎ 362 6528; Hatfield Sq) Despite the name, this is reputedly the pick-up joint for Pretoria's student population. It is essentially a disco, but the odd band does make an appearance.

The surrounding townships, especially Mamelodi and Atteridgeville have plenty of shebeens; these are best visited with a Black friend or as part of a tour. It's estimated that Gauteng has over 36,000 shebeens.

Theatres

Most shows can be booked through **Computicket** (☎ 083-915 8000; www.computicket.com; Hatfield Plaza, Burnett St; ☷ 8.30am-4.30pm Mon-Sat).

State Theatre (Map pp406-7; ☎ 392 4000; www.statetheatre.co.za; cnr Prinsloo & Church Sts) Designed by Hans and Roelf Botha, who dreamt up JG Strijdom Sq (p409), this huge theatre complex hosts a range of high-culture productions (including opera, music, ballet and theatre) in its five theatres: the Arena, Studio, Opera, Drama and Momentum. You can take guided tours of the building (R20).

Barnyard Theatre (Map p418; ☎ 368 1555; top fl, Menlyn Park Shopping Centre) Out of town in Menlyn Park Shopping Centre, also stages shows.

SHOPPING

Apart from the big **Brooklyn Mall** (Map p414), **Brooklyn Sq** (Map p414) and **Menlyn Park** (Map p418) shopping centres, where you will find all the usual air-conditioned chain stores, Pretoria is best known for its markets.

Boeremark (Map p418; ☎ 082-416 3900; Meiring Naude Rd; ☷ 6-9am Sat) East of the centre, and opposite the CSIR complex, this market is run by the Transvaal Agricultural Union and is the place to find fresh produce and old-style Boers, with traditional food and music.

Hatfield Flea Market (Map pp406-7; ☎ 362 5941; Hatfield Plaza car park, Burnett St, Hatfield; ☷ 9.30am-5.30pm Sun) Peddling the usual flea-market paraphernalia, as well as some African stuff you can't import from China.

Magnolia Dell Moonlight Market (Map pp406-7; ☎ 308 8820; Magnolia Dell, Queen Wilhelmina Ave, New Muckleneuk; ☷ 5.30-9.30pm Fri) Staged on the last Friday evening of the month. It is an excellent event and is the place to pick up local crafts.

GETTING THERE & AWAY
Air

See p373 and p395 for information on arriving at JIA.

Bus

Most national and international bus services commence in Pretoria before picking up in Jo'burg, unless the general direction is north. Most long-distance buses leave from the **1928 Building** (Map pp406-7; Scheiding St) in the Pretoria train-station forecourt. You will also find their booking and information offices here.

Most **Translux** (☎ 011-774 3333; www.translux.co.za), **City to City** (☎ 011-773 2762), **Intercape** (☎ 0861 287 287; www.intercape.co.za) and **Greyhound** (☎ 323 1154; www.greyhound.co.za) services running from Jo'burg to Durban, the south coast and Cape Town originate in Pretoria. Services running north up the N1 also stop here – see p395 for full details of these services.

Translux, Greyhound and Intercape fares from Pretoria are identical to those from Jo'burg regardless of the one-hour difference in time. If you only want to go between the two cities, it will cost about R30.

Baz Bus (Cape Town ☎ 021-439 2323; www.bazbus .com) will pick up and drop off at Pretoria hostels.

North Link Tours (☎ 323 0379) also runs from the 1928 Building, north to Polokwane (Pietersburg; R80, 3½ hours), Tzaneen (R140, five hours) and Phalaborwa (R180, 6½ hours).

Car

The larger local and international companies are represented in Pretoria; see p600 for details. For the best value, try **Swans Rent a Car** (☎ 082-658 0078; www.swans.co.za) or **Comet Car Rental** (☎ 011-453 0188; www.cometcar.co.za). If you book ahead of time, these companies deliver.

Minibus Taxis

Minibus taxis go from the main terminal by the train station and travel to a host of destinations including Jo'burg (R20).

Train

The historic Pretoria train station was rebuilt at a cost of R35 million after it was burned down by angry commuters in February 2001, and things are now back to normal. Despite commuter frustrations, most long-distance trains run on time, which is just as well as they seem to take forever.

Main Line (☎ 0860 008 888, www.spoornet.co.za) trains running through Pretoria are the *Trans Karoo* (daily from Pretoria to Kimberley and Cape Town) and the *Komati* (daily from Jo'burg to Komatipoort via Nelspruit). The *Bosvelder* runs north via Polokwane (Pietersburg) to Musina, near the Zimbabwe border. Fares from Pretoria for 1st/2nd class are R15/10 less or more than from Jo'burg, depending on your direction of travel. The luxury *Blue Train*, which links Pretoria, Jo'burg and Cape Town originates here (see p605 for details of the 'name train' services).

Pretoria train station is about a 20-minute walk from the city centre. Buses run along Paul Kruger St to Church Sq, the main local bus terminal.

METRO

Warnings first: there have been many robberies at gunpoint on the Metro, and we don't recommend travelling between Pretoria and Jo'burg by Metro.

A 1st-class train ticket to Jo'burg on the Metro system is R15. The journey takes over an hour. From Monday to Friday, trains run every half hour early in the morning, then hourly until 10pm. On weekends, trains run about every 1½ hours.

GETTING AROUND
To/From the Airport

If you call ahead, most hostels, and many hotels, will pick you up for free.

Pretoria Airport Shuttle (Map pp406-7; ☎ 320 3303) leaves from the Protea Hotel (corner of Visagie and Van der Walt Sts in central Pretoria) on the hour between 6am and 10pm. It costs R80 (the same if they pick up from a hostel) or R95 to/from Hatfield.

Get You There (☎ 346 3175) operates shuttle buses between JIA and Pretoria. The company does not have a set timetable but runs day and night about every hour, charging R95 to/from hostels and hotels.

Bus & Minibus Taxi

There's an extensive network of local buses. A booklet of timetables and route maps is available from the inquiry office in the main **bus terminus** (Map pp406-7; ☎ 308 0839; Church Sq) or from pharmacies. Fares range from R5 to R7, depending on the distance. Some services, including the No 3 bus to Sunnyside, run until about 10.30pm – unusually late for South Africa. Other handy buses include Nos 5 and 8, which run between Church Sq and Brooklyn via Burnett St in Hatfield.

Minibus taxis run just about everywhere and the standard fare is about R4. You won't see many White faces on these buses, but that doesn't mean they're unsafe. Seek local advice before you ride.

Taxi

There are taxi ranks on the corner of Church and Van der Walt Sts, and on the corner of Pretorius and Paul Kruger Sts. Or you could call **Rixi Taxis** (☎ 0800 325 807).

AROUND PRETORIA

Gauteng is perhaps better known for its cities than its countryside, but there are more than a few gems out in the sticks, if you have had

GAUTENG

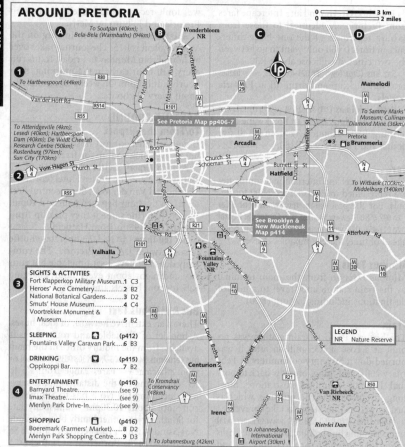

AROUND PRETORIA

0 ——— 3 km
0 ——— 2 miles

SIGHTS & ACTIVITIES
Fort Klapperkop Military Museum..1 C3
Heroes' Acre Cemetery..................2 B2
National Botanical Gardens..........3 D2
Smuts' House Museum...................4 C4
Voortrekker Monument &
Museum..................................5 B2

SLEEPING 🏠 (p412)
Fountains Valley Caravan Park....6 B3

DRINKING 🍷 (p415)
Oppikoppi Bar...............................7 B2

ENTERTAINMENT (p416)
Barnyard Theatre.......................(see 9)
Imax Theatre.............................(see 9)
Menlyn Park Drive-In...............(see 9)

SHOPPING 🛍 (p416)
Boeremark (Farmers' Market).....8 D2
Menlyn Park Shopping Centre.....9 D3

LEGEND
NR   Nature Reserve

enough urban living. The De Wildt Cheetah
Research Centre is a particular treat.

SMUTS' HOUSE MUSEUM

General JC Smuts was a brilliant scholar,
Boer general, politician and international
statesman. An architect of the Union of South
Africa, he was the country's prime minister
from 1919 to 1924, and 1939 to 1948.

Smuts' home was once known as Doornkloof and has been turned into an excellent
museum (Map p418; ☎ 012-667 1176; smutshouse@
worldonline.co.za); Nelmapius Rd, Irene; adult/child R10/5,
garden free; ☺ 9.30am-4.30pm Mon-Fri, 9.30am-5pm Sat
& Sun). It is worth visiting if you have private
transport and are travelling to/from Pretoria.
The wood-and-iron building was a British of-

ficers' mess at Middelburg but Smuts bought
it and re-erected it on his 1600-hectare property at Irene, 16km south of Pretoria. Surrounded by a wide veranda and shaded by
trees, it has a family atmosphere, and gives a
vivid insight into Smuts' amazing life.

Unfortunately, there is no access by
public transport. The house is signposted
from both the N14 freeway (R28) and the
R21. The most direct route from Pretoria is
along Louis Botha Ave to Irene.

FORT KLAPPERKOP MILITARY MUSEUM

This **fort** (Map p418; ☎ 082-807 5278; Johann Rissik Dr; adult/child R10/5; ☺ 10am-3.30pm) is one of
the best preserved in South Africa. Located

6km south of the city, a shot was never fired from here in anger, but it now illustrates South Africa's military history from 1852 to the end of the 1899–1902 Anglo-Boer War. There are panoramic views across the city and the region.

NATIONAL BOTANICAL GARDENS

Around 9km east of the city centre, these **gardens** (Map p418; ☎ 012-804 3200; Cussonia Ave, Brummeria; adult/child R10/5; � 6am-6pm) cover 77 hectares and are planted with indigenous flora from around the country. The 20,000-odd plant species are labelled and grouped according to their region of origin, so a visit is a must for keen botanists.

By car, head east along Church St (R104) for about 8km, then turn right into Cussonia Rd; the gardens are on the left-hand side. Take the Meyerspark or Murrayfield bus from Church Sq.

SAMMY MARKS' MUSEUM

This **museum** (Map p372; ☎ 012-803 6158; R104, Old Bronkhorstspruit Rd; adult/child R20/10; � 9am-4pm Tue-Fri, 10am-4pm Sat & Sun) is housed in one of South Africa's most splendid Victorian mansions, dating from 1884. Sammy Marks was an English magnate who had his fingers in a lot of pies: industrial, mining and agricultural. It is a good example of the sort of house you can build for yourself if you strike it rich (and an example of the expensive goodies with which you can fill it).

CULLINAN DIAMOND MINE

After visiting Sammy Marks' Museum, go north to historic Cullinan, a pretty 100-year-old village full of quaint Herbert Baker architecture. It is best explored on a sluggish, Sunday afternoon stroll. The village is home to Cullinan Diamond Mine (Map p372) one of the biggest and most productive diamond-bearing kimberlite pipes in the world. It has produced three of the largest diamonds ever found. The largest, the 3106-carat Cullinan, as it was called, was 11cm by 6cm in rough form and was presented to King Edward VII. You can don a tin hat and organise a tour of the mine through **Premier Diamond Tours** (☎ 012-734 0081, 083-261 3550; tours from R30).

To get here, take the N4 east and the Hans Strijdom off-ramp, then turn left and follow the signs.

DE WILDT CHEETAH RESEARCH CENTRE

Just past Hartbeespoort, about 50km northwest of Pretoria, is the **De Wildt Cheetah Research Centre** (Map p372; ☎ 012-504 1921; www .dewildt.org.za; Farm 22, R513 Pretoria North Rd; admission R100; tours by appointment), famous for its breeding success of rare and endangered animals. If you only make it to one reserve in South Africa, go to this one.

Work began at De Wildt in the 1960s, when the cheetah was regarded as highly endangered. Seven offspring were successfully bred in captivity – more than at any reserve in the world at the time. To a large degree it's thanks to the work done here that the cheetah is now off the endangered species list.

The king cheetah, with its distinctive black pelt pattern, was successfully bred at De Wildt in 1981; it was previously thought to be extinct. These magnificent animals are very rare and you probably won't see one outside of the reserve, at least not this close up.

As well as cheetahs, visitors can see other animals such as wild dogs, brown hyenas, servals, caracals, honey badgers, meerkats, a few different antelope species, and vultures.

Tours provide a fascinating insight into some of Africa's most endangered predators. In an open truck you'll see cheetahs of different age groups being fed, and learn about their precarious existence in the wild. Bookings are essential and you should call at least a week in advance.

To get to De Wildt from Pretoria (via Hartbeespoort), take the R5131 northwest for 34km – the centre is on the left, about half a kilometre off the main road.

LESEDI CULTURAL VILLAGE

For a day out of town and a dose of culture, check out the **Lesedi Cultural Village** (Map p372; ☎ 012-205 1394; lesedi@pixie.co.za; � tours 11.30am & 4.30pm), which is very touristy but gets a lot of good reports from readers.

Lesedi means 'Place of Light' and there's plenty of dancing, singing and traditional African meals; Xhosa, Ndebele, Pedi, Zulu and Sotho cultures are all represented. The full 'African Experience' costs R250, or you can opt for lunch or dinner only (R100).

Lesedi is southwest of Pretoria and north of Lanseria airport. It's a good idea to book, if you're going for the full meal and show. Accommodation is also available and is booked directly through the village.

Mpumalanga

It's in unassuming Mpumalanga (Place of the Rising Sun; pronounced M-poo-ma lan-ga) where the plateaus of the highveld begin their spectacular tumble onto the lowveld plains at the dramatic Drakensberg Escarpment. Here is the main gateway to Kruger National Park, some of Africa's best private game reserves (see the Kruger National Park chapter, p440), and the impressive Blyde River Canyon. Other attractions include rafting and hiking, abundant scenic drives and vistas, world-class rock climbing, kloofing opportunities, ballooning, and historic towns. Many visitors regard Mpumalanga as little more than a doormat for Kruger park, but the province is well worth visiting in its own right, and is an ideal stop if you're travelling between Johannesburg (Jo'burg) and Kruger, or northern KwaZulu-Natal.

When planning your itinerary, you can ignore much of Mpumalanga's industrialised west. The interesting parts start around tiny Dullstroom, which is trying to build a name for itself as a trout-fishing mecca and getaway for nature-hungry Gauteng residents. Nearby is Waterval Boven, with some of South Africa's best rock climbing. Northeast is the heart of Mpumalanga, with the quaint gold rush town of Pilgrim's Rest; the beautiful Long Tom Pass; Graskop, with its vistas over the lowveld and good mountain biking; and the attractive tourist town of Sabie. From here, head down into the lowveld, where the centre of action is Nelspruit. From Nelspruit, Kruger park's Numbi and Malelane gates are both an easy drive away, as is the Mozambique border at Komatipoort. Alternatively, head south to the charming old gold-mining town of Barberton and on into Swaziland. In Mpumalanga's far south is Piet Retief, a convenient transit junction if you're en route to Swaziland or KwaZulu-Natal.

Towns in this chapter are organised roughly counter clockwise west to east, and north to south.

HIGHLIGHTS

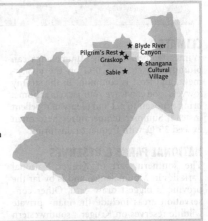

- Hiking, cycling or rafting around **Sabie**, taking in the cool mountain air and beautiful views (p425)

- Dining on pancakes in **Graskop** (p429) or **Pilgrim's Rest** (p428)

- Exploring the **Blyde River Canyon** on foot (p429)

- Getting a taste of Shangaan life at **Shangana Cultural Village** near Hazyview (p431)

Pilgrim's Rest ★ ★ Blyde River Canyon
Graskop ★ ★ Shangana Cultural Village
Sabie ★

■ POPULATION: 2.8 MILLION   ■ AREA: 79,490 SQ KM

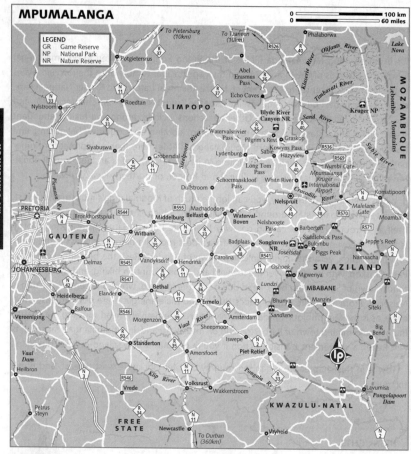

CLIMATE

Winter temperatures in Mpumalanga can plummet to close to 0°C on the escarpment, and frost is common. In the steamy lowveld, you can leave your jackets at home; bring a mosquito net and plenty of repellent instead. Summer temperatures here often exceed 35°C, with frequent rainstorms.

NATIONAL PARKS & RESERVES

The southern part of Kruger National Park lies in Mpumalanga, and is by far the province's biggest draw card. Other conservation areas include the many private wildlife reserves on Kruger's southwestern edge (p451), and the Blyde River Canyon Nature Reserve (p429).

LANGUAGE

Swati, Zulu and Ndebele are the main languages spoken in Mpumalanga, but it's easy to get by with English. In and around Nelspruit, you'll also hear alot of Afrikaans.

GETTING THERE & AROUND

There are good domestic and regional air connections via Mpumalanga Kruger International Airport (MKIA), about 28km northeast of Nelspruit off the R40.

Mpumalanga is crossed by an extensive network of good tarmac roads. While there are frequent bus and minibus connections to/from Nelspruit, public transport is scarce away from major routes, and hire car is definitely the best way of exploring.

MPUMALANGA...

■ is South Africa's second smallest province;

■ is the country's second largest citrus-growing area;

■ encompasses all or part of the former homelands of KaNgwane, KwaNdebele, Gazankulu, Lebowa and Bophu-thatswana;

■ has South Africa's second-lowest adult literacy rate (75.5%);

■ is the fifth most densely populated province (38 people per sq km), with about 7% of the total population, of whom about 89% are African and 9% white.

A passenger train line cuts through the middle of the province, connecting Jo'burg with Komatipoort and Maputo (Mozambique), via Nelspruit.

For details of air, road and train connections to/from Jo'burg, see p435. For details of connections between Nelspruit and Kruger National Park, see p450. For information on crossing between Nelspruit and Swaziland and Mozambique, see p594 and p594, respectively.

DRAKENSBERG ESCARPMENT

The Drakensberg escarpment (the section here is known as the Klein Drakensberg or the Transvaal Drakensberg) marks the point where the highveld plunges down over 1000m, before spilling out onto the eastern lowveld. It's one of South Africa's most scenic areas, marked by dramatic cliffs, stunning views and an abundance of adventure activities, including kloofing, rock climbing and white-water rafting. It's also prime holiday territory, which means that accommodation is pricier than in some other parts of the country, and invariably fills up during high season. While it's possible to get around via minibus taxi, the going is slow; car hire is the best option for really exploring the area.

DULLSTROOM

☎ 013 / pop 2000

This chic, attractive town is in the heart of trout country. It's surrounded by rolling hills studded with rocky outcrops, stands of pine and small lakes, and exudes the ambience of a genteel English country estate. If you're an angling aficionado, it's a reasonable place to stop en route between Jo'burg (260km west) and points further east.

Along the main road (Hugenote St) at the southern end of town you'll find a **tourist information centre** (☎ 254 0200; info@dullstroom .co.za; 🕑 8.30am-5pm Mon-Fri, 9am-noon Sat) and a collection of bait and tackle shops. There's an ATM at First National Bank at the main junction.

For budget lodging, try either the **Caravan Park** (camp sites R50, caravans R60), signposted on the northern edge of town past Dullstroom Inn, or the small **Charilo B&B** (☎ 013-254 0250; charilo@worldonline.co.za; Machteld St; s/d with breakfast R250/380), near the caravan park turnoff.

Dullstroom Inn (☎ 254 0071; dullstroominn@dulls troom.net; Teding van Berkhout St; s/d with breakfast R287/500) is an unassuming place with cosy rooms and the **Old English Pub restaurant** (mains from R40; 🕑 lunch & dinner). is on the north-western edge of town.

Critchley Hackle (☎ 254 0999; www.critchleyhackle .co.za; Teding van Berkhout St; s/d with breakfast from R740/1150) is an elegant mansion with its own trout pond, and beautiful grounds planted with rose bushes. It's at the northeastern edge of town, signposted from the main road. Children under 12 aren't permitted.

Scones and tea are Dullstroom's culinary specialities. Places to sample these include **Rose Pancakes** (☎ 254 0218; Hugenote St; light meals from R25; 🕑 lunch & dinner), which also offers cappuccino and light meals, and **Cranberry Cafe** (Hugenote St; light meals from R25; 🕑 8am-5.30pm), both at the main junction. For something more substantial, try **Die Tonteldoos Bistro** (☎ 254 0115; Hugenote St; meals from R30; 🕑 7am-5pm Mon-Wed, 7am-7pm Thu-Sun), an award-winning place in the town centre with a large menu and excellent food. **Tuscany Restaurant & Pizza** (Hugenote St; mains from R35; 🕑 lunch & dinner) and **Casa Portuguesa** (Hugenote St; mains R35-55; 🕑 lunch & dinner), both at the southern edge of town, are less expensive.

Minibus taxis pass Dullstroom en route to/from Belfast, stopping along the main

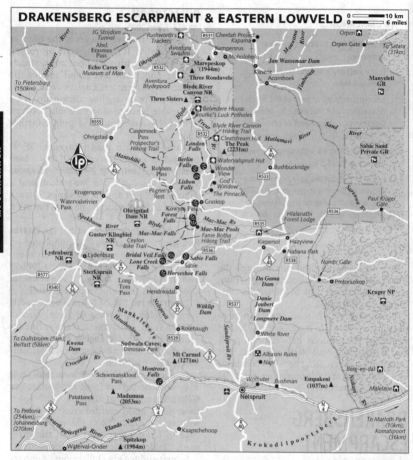

DRAKENSBERG ESCARPMENT & EASTERN LOWVELD

road, but the main way to get here and around is with your own vehicle.

WATERVAL BOVEN
☎ 013

This tiny town is in scenic countryside just off the N4, and is known mainly as a base for some superb rock climbing. There's also the chance to abseil at the Elands River Waterfall (from which the town takes its name) or, for the more sedate, to ride a **steam train** (☎ 011-825 4304; return adult/child R50/30; 2hr; ☉ Sun) to the hamlet of **Waterval Onder**, about 4km further east along the N4.

Elandskrans Mountain Resort (☎ 257 0175; next .resource@next.co.za; camp sites R65, 4-/6-person chalets R380/510; ☒) This place is set near the edge of

the escarpment, with camping, self-catering chalets (bring your own towels), hot- and cold-water pools and a trampoline. It's just out of town along the extension of Fifth Ave towards Slaaihoek.

Aloes (☎ 013-257 7037; www.mpumalanga-venues .co.za/thealoesbp.htm; dm R60, d with shared bathroom R180) is a laid-back backpackers set on its own in a woodsy setting in Waterval Onder. You can arrange hiking, abseiling and more here, and buy any aloe product you could want. Meals are available on request, and the **Baz Bus** (☎ 021-439 2323; www.bazbus.com) stops here en route between Jo'burg and Nelspruit.

Minibus taxis to Nelspruit cost R25 (two hours).

LYDENBURG

☎ 013 / pop 19,000

Lydenburg (Town of Suffering) was established by Voortrekkers in 1849 and was once the capital of the Republic of Lydenburg. It's also where the famous **Lydenburg Heads** were found. These seven terracotta masks date to the 6th century AD, when they may have been used in initiation rituals, and are among the earliest African sculpture forms known in Southern Africa.

Today Lydenburg is a quiet service centre for the farming district and one of Mpumalanga's more modest touristic offerings, unless you're interested in history. East of town along the R37 is the beautiful **Long Tom Pass** (2150m), one of Mpumalanga's more scenic drives.

There are ATMs at First National Bank and ABSA, opposite each other on Voortrekker St near Kantoor St. **4U Computers** (Kantoor St), one block north of Voortrekker St, has Internet access.

About 2km east of town along the R37 is the **Gustav Klingbiel Nature Reserve** (admission R10; ☑ 8am-4pm Mon-Fri, 8am-5pm Sat & Sun), with lots of birds, a small population of antelopes and short hiking trails, plus Iron Age sites and Anglo-Boer War trenches. Also at the reserve is the very worthwhile **Lydenburg Museum** (☎ 235 2121; Long Tom Pass Rd; ☑ 8am-1pm & 2-4pm Mon-Fri, 8am-5pm Sat & Sun), with a fascinating collection of animal and human terracotta masks, and replicas of the Lydenburg Heads. (The originals are in the South African Museum in Cape Town, p105.)

Sleeping & Eating

Uitspan Caravan Park (☎ 235 2914; uitspanlyd@lantic.net; Viljoen St; camp sites from R70, s/d rondavels R155/215, s/d chalets R175/275; ☑) This well-maintained place is on the road to Jo'burg. The chalets come with bathroom and kitchenette, while the rondavels have bedding and fridge only.

Manor Guest House (☎ 235 2099; cnr Viljoen & Potgier Sts; s/d with breakfast R230/400; ☑) An indulgent, four-star B&B with a nice garden.

Lemon Tree Cafe & Take Away (☎ 235 3383; 31 Voortrekker St), diagonally opposite the post office, and the cosy **Vroutjies Coffee Shop** (☎ 235 3016; 13 Voortrekker St; ☑ 8.30am-4.30pm Mon-Fri, 8am-2pm Sat) have light meals. There's a **Superspar** (cnr Voortrekker & Kantoor Sts) for self-caterers.

Getting There & Away

The minibus taxi stop is in the town centre off Voortrekker St, with daily vehicles to Sabie (R20, one hour) and Belfast (R30, 1½ hours). City to City services also stop here (R90) on their Jo'burg–Phalaborwa run.

SABIE

☎ 013 / elevation 1100m

From Lydenburg, the R37 winds over the spectacular Long Tom pass before dropping down through valleys blanketed with pine forests to the picturesque tourist hub and logging centre of Sabie. Its attractions include a cool climate, trout fishing, extensive pine and eucalyptus plantations in the surrounding area, almost unlimited possibilities for outdoor activities, and easy access to Kruger National Park.

Next to each other in the town centre are a helpful **tourist information office** (☎ 764 1125; www.panoramainfo.co.za; Market Sq; ☑ 8am-5pm Mon-Fri, 8am-1pm Sat), an **Internet café** (☑ 8am-6pm Mon-Sat), and a First National Bank with ATM.

Sights & Activities

The area around Sabie is dotted with beautiful **waterfalls** (admission to each R5). These include **Sabie Falls**, just north of town on the R532 to Graskop; the 70m **Bridal Veil Falls**, northwest of Sabie off Old Lydenburg Rd; the 68m **Lone Creek Falls**, also off Old Lydenburg Rd, and with wheelchair access on the right-hand path; and the nearby **Horseshoe Falls**, about 5km southwest of Lone Creek Falls. The popular **Mac-Mac Falls**, about 12km north of Sabie off the R532 to Graskop, take their name from the many Scottish names on the local mining register. About 3km southeast of the falls are the **Mac-Mac Pools**, where you can swim.

Komatiland Forestry Museum (☎ 764 1058; cnr Ford St & Tenth Lane; adult/child R5/3; ☑ 8.30am-4.30pm Mon-Fri, 8.30am-noon Sat) has displays on local forests and the timber industry. It has wheelchair access. Also here is the **Komatiland Forests Ecotourism office** (☎ 764 1392, 012-481 3615; ecoklf@mweb.co.za), which has information and make bookings for hiking trails around Sabie, and elsewhere in Mpumalanga.

For horse riding contact the tourist information office, **Fern Tree Park Riding School** (☎ 764 2215; ftp@cybertrade.co.za) or **Golden Monkey** (☎ 737 8191; www.big5country.com); rates average R60 per hour. Golden Monkey can also

MPUMALANGA

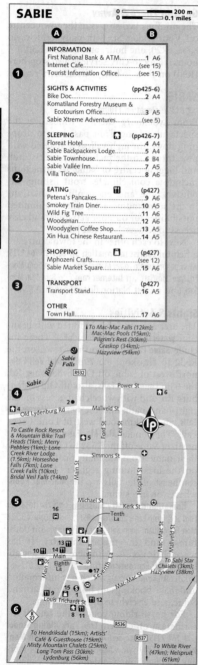

SABIE

0 —————— 200 m
0 —————— 0.1 miles

INFORMATION
First National Bank & ATM.............1 A6
Internet Cafe.............................(see 15)
Tourist Information Office..........(see 15)

SIGHTS & ACTIVITIES (pp425-6)
Bike Doc...................................2 A4
Komatiland Forestry Museum &
    Ecotourism Office..................3 A5
Sabie Xtreme Adventures.............(see 5)

SLEEPING (pp426-7)
Floreat Hotel.............................4 A4
Sabie Backpackers Lodge..............5 A4
Sabie Townhouse........................6 B4
Sabie Vallée Inn.........................7 A5
Villa Ticino...............................8 A6

EATING (p427)
Petena's Pancakes.......................9 A6
Smokey Train Diner....................10 A5
Wild Fig Tree...........................11 A6
Woodsman...............................12 A6
Woodyglen Coffee Shop................13 A5
Xin Hua Chinese Restaurant..........14 A5

SHOPPING (p427)
Mphozeni Crafts........................(see 12)
Sabie Market Square....................15 A5

TRANSPORT (p427)
Transport Stand.........................16 A5

OTHER
Town Hall................................17 A6

To Mac-Mac Falls (12km);
Mac-Mac Pools (15km);
Pilgrim's Rest (30km);
Graskop (34km);
Hazyview (54km)

Sabie Falls

Sabie River

R532

Power St

6

Old Lydenburg Rd

2

Maliveld St

To Castle Rock Resort
& Mountain Bike Trail
Heads (1km); Merry
Pebbles (1km); Lone
Creek River Lodge
(1.5km); Horseshoe
Falls (7km); Lone
Creek Falls (10km);
Bridal Veil Falls (14km)

5

Ford St
Lea St

Main St

Simmons St

Hospital St

Michael St

Kerk St

16

Tenth La

3
7

13 14
10

Main
Eighth
La

15

17

Sixth La
Seventh La

Mac-Mac St
Maliveld St

To Sabi Star
Chalets (3km);
Hazyview (38km)

9

Louis Trichardt St

12

8 11

R536

Mac-Mac St

To Hendriksdal (15km); Artists'
Café & Guesthouse (15km);
Misty Mountain Chalets (25km);
Long Tom Pass (30km);
Lydenburg (56km)

R537

To White River
(47km); Nelspruit
(61km)

arrange hot-air balloon flights (per person about R1550) in the area around Sabie.

There are several excellent mountain-bike trails, ranging from 13km to 45km and starting at Castle Rock Resort, near Merry Pebbles (below). Permits, which you'll need to ride on the trails, cost R20 and can be arranged at **Bike Doc** (☎ 013-764 1034, 082-878 5527; bikedoc@lantic.net; cnr Main St & Old Lydenburg Rd), which also has bike rental (per hour/day including helmet R30/180) and can help with repairs.

Hardy Ventures (☎ 751 1693; www.hardyventure .com) and Sabie Xtreme Adventures (contact through Sabie Backpackers Lodge, below) can help organise abseiling, white-water rafting on the Blyde and Sabie Rivers, kloofing and bungee jumping.

Sleeping

Sabie Backpackers Lodge (☎ 764 2118; Main St; camp sites per person R35, dm R60, d with shared bathroom R130) This popular establishment is the only backpackers in town and the base for Sabie Xtreme Adventures (above). It's in a small house, with cooking facilities.

Merry Pebbles (☎ 764 2266; www.merrypebbles .co.za; camp sites per person R85; 4-/8-person chalets R550/1100) Just north of town off Old Lydenburg Rd, Merry Pebbles is a large camping park in shaded, spacious grounds on the banks of the Sabie River. It's ideal for families. Rates increase exorbitantly over Easter weekend.

Sabie Vallée Inn (☎ 764 2182; sabievi@netactive .co.za; Tenth Lane; d with breakfast R560, d cabins with breakfast R640) A straightforward, centrally located place with no-frills rooms in the main building, some log cabins behind and a restaurant.

Sabie Townhouse (☎ 764 2292; www.sabietown house.co.za; Power St; s/d R350/630; 🛋) This up-scale B&B is a good choice for a treat, with arched windows, plush rooms with private entrances, and a quiet location.

Villa Ticino (☎ 764 2598; www.villaticino.co.za; cnr Louis Trichardt & Second Lane; s/d with breakfast R350/470) Villa Ticino is a comfortable Swiss-run B&B in the town centre with an old-world atmosphere and good breakfasts.

Lone Creek River Lodge (☎ 764 2611; www .lonecreek.co.za; Old Lydenburg Rd; s/d R1065/1630, s/d cabins from R460/660) Sabie's most upscale ac-commodation, with plush rooms in the main building backing on to the Sabie River, and comfortable two-storey self-catering cabins across the road. It's about 1.5km southwest of town. The **restaurant** (buffet R95; ☺ lunch & dinner) has a delicious Sunday lunch buffet; reservations are required.

Floreat Hotel (☎ 764 2160; www.floreat.co.za; Old Lydenburg Rd; s/d with breakfast R440/495) An unassuming place with comfortable brick cottages set around a large lawn, and a **restaurant** (meals around R45; ☺ lunch & dinner). The Sabie River – here quite small – runs along the edge of the property.

Artists' Café & Guest House (☎ 764 2309; arts cafe@mweb.co.za; s/d with breakfast R285/530) This charming place is in Hendriksdal, about 15km south of Sabie along the R37. Accommodation is in old train station buildings that have been converted into rooms, and there's a very good Italian **restaurant** (meals R50; ☺ lunch & dinner).

Misty Mountain Chalets (☎ 764 3377; www.misty mountain.co.za; s/d with breakfast R360/600, per additional person R200) This rustic but comfortable place is along the R37 at the Long Tom Pass, about 25km from Sabie. It's an ideal base for mountain biking (bring your own bike), birdwatching or relaxing. Accommodation is in fully equipped two-, four- or six-person self-catering cottages with fireplaces, and there's a **restaurant** (meals R40-65; ☺ lunch & dinner).

Eating

Sabie has an excellent assortment of restaurants, only a small sampling of which are listed here.

Petena's Pancakes (☎ 764 1541; Main Rd; pancakes about R20; ☺ 9am-5.30pm Tue-Sat, 10am-5.30pm Sun) Dine on your choice of sweet or savoury pancakes in a cosy setting.

Woodsman (☎ 764 2204; www.thewoodsman.co.za; cnr R536 & Mac-Mac St; mains R40-60; ☺ breakfast, lunch & dinner) A tasty Greek menu, pleasant outdoor eating area and central location are the draws here. They also have nice **rooms** (s/d with breakfast R250/450), including some with a small terrace.

Wild Fig Tree (☎ 764 3098, 013-764 2239; mark uren@soft.co.za; 6 Third Lane; meals R35-65; ☺ breakfast, lunch & dinner) This place features local specialities such as biltong pâté, ostrich fillet and homemade apple pie, all filling and delicious. They also have Internet access and a **guesthouse** (s/d with breakfast R200/370).

Smokey Train Diner (☎ 764 3445; Main Rd; mains about R40; ☺ lunch & dinner) An Afrikaner diner,

with some seating at booths in a refurbished train car, and more on a large patio. The menu features *potjiekos* (stew cooked in a three-legged pot) and other Afrikaner dishes, plus a range of burgers and other standards.

Xin Hua Chinese Restaurant (☎ 764 2222; Main Rd; mains R20; ☺ lunch & dinner) Good Chinese food and fast service.

Woodyglen Coffee Shop (☎ 764 2209; Main Rd; breakfast from R25, lunch about R35; ☺ 7.30am-5pm Mon-Fri, 8am-1pm Sat & Sun) This pleasant eatery in the town centre features muffins, wholegrains and light meals.

There's a **Spar** (Main Rd) north of Market Sq.

Shopping

There are several craft shops in the town centre, including Mphozeni Crafts, next door to Woodsman restaurant. Market Sq in the town centre has a small collection of shops, and an Internet café.

Getting There & Away

There are daily buses from Jo'burg to Nelspruit, from where you can get minibus taxis to Sabie (R15, one hour between Nelspruit and Sabie). Minibus taxis also run frequently to/from Hazyview (R15, one hour). The transport stand is behind Spar supermarket on Main Rd, with an office that dispenses timetable information. The tourist information office (p425) can help arrange charter vehicles for lifts in the area.

PILGRIM'S REST
☎ 013

Gold was discovered at tiny Pilgrim's Rest in 1873, and for 10 years the area buzzed with diggers working small-scale alluvial claims. When the big operators arrived in the 1880s, Pilgrim's Rest became a company town, and when the gold finally fizzled out in 1972 the town was sold to the government as a ready-made historical village (it's now a national monument). It's a bit overdone, but an agreeable enough stop if you like quaint historical places and don't mind the tourist throngs, which are particularly heavy on weekends. Visitor activity centres around Uptown. Downtown – about 1.2km down the road – is quieter, with a few restaurants and craft outlets.

There's an **information centre** (☎ 768 1060; Main St, Uptown; ☺ 9am-12.45pm & 1.15-4.30pm) at the museums building, and an ATM just down the road. Just up from Royal Hotel is a stand selling colourful batiks.

Sights & Activities

The town's three main **museums** (☎ 768 1060; total admission R10) feature a printing shop, a restored home and a general store. More interesting is historic **Alanglade** (☎ 768 1060; admission R20, guided tours R20; ☼ 11am & 2pm Mon-Sat), a former mine-manager's residence at the northern edge of town furnished with period objects from the 1920s. Just east of town along the Graskop road is the open-air **Diggings Museum** (guided tours R5) where you can see how gold was panned. You need to visit on a tour, arranged through the information centre.

Sleeping

Pilgrims Rest Caravan Park (☎ 768 1427; pilgrims camp@mweb.co.za; camp sites per person R40, 2-person tented accommodation R140, d with shared bathroom R145; ⏾) The cheapest place in town, with fixed tents, basic rooms and large grounds. It's just past Downtown on the Blyde River.

Royal Hotel (☎ 768 1100; www.royal-hotel.co.za; s/d with breakfast R310/590; ⏾) This is the historic centrepiece of Uptown and a fine example of wooden Victorian architecture. The rooms are elegantly furnished in period style and include brass four-poster beds. Church Bar, adjoining, is a good spot for a drink.

Beretta's (☎ 768 1066; www.berettas.co.za; s/d with breakfast R190/240, cottages per person about R250) Beretta's is one of the less expensive places, with simple, comfortable rooms in a small house set between Uptown and Downtown, and meals at their restaurant down the road. They also have two self-catering cottages.

In addition to the hotels in town, there are several places along the scenic stretch of R533 leading up towards Robber's Pass (1770m). **Inn on Robber's Pass** (☎ 768 1491; innonrp@global.co.za; s/d with half board from R335/590) has cosy, rustic cottages with fireplaces, a restaurant and a self-catering guesthouse. It's about 15km from Pilgrim's Rest; no children under 14. **Crystal Springs Mountain Lodge** (☎ 768 5050; info@crystalsprings.co.za; s/d with breakfast R425/600; ⏾) is a large resort-style place 9km from Pilgrim's Rest and a good choice for families. Accommodation is in self-catering chalets taking two to eight people, and there are several pools, trampolines, mini-golf and more.

Eating

Scott's Cafe (☎ 768 1061; Uptown; meals from R25) A busy eatery with a large menu selection and a craft shop.

Pilgrim's Pantry (☎ 768 1042; pancakes about R29; ☼ 8am-6pm) This cosy coffee shop and pancake house has pleasant seating on the porch.

Chaitow's Restaurant (☎ 768 1389; meals R22-40; ☼ 8am-5pm) Chaitow's is a small, trendy place opposite Royal Hotel featuring pastas, seafood and gourmet fare.

Getting There & Away

Sporadic minibus taxis run between Pilgrim's Rest and Graskop (R7, 30 minutes), but most traffic along this road is in private vehicles.

GRASKOP

☎ 013 / elevation 1450m

Graskop sits at the top of Kowyns Pass, on the edge of the Drakensberg escarpment. The town itself is plain, lacking the woodsy ambience of Sabie, however nearby are some spectacular views of the lowveld almost 1000m below. A walking trail that includes places described in the popular South African classic *Jock of the Bushveld* starts at the Graskop Municipal Holiday Resort (below), where you can get a map. The surrounding area is also good for mountain biking.

The best places for information are the **tourist information office** (☎ 767 1833; wild@iafrica .com; Pilgrim St; ☼ 8am-5pm Mon-Sat), inside Spar supermarket and Green Castle Backpackers (below). There's an ATM at **First National Bank** (Kerk St), just north of Louis Trichardt St, and an **Internet café** (Louis Trichardt St) next to Graskop Hotel.

Sleeping

Graskop Municipal Holiday Resort (☎ 767 1126; Louis Trichardt St; caravan & camp sites R60, 2-/3-/5-person chalets R190/260/440; ⏾) This place is worth considering if you're just looking for a base, rather than ambience.

Green Castle Backpackers (☎ 767 1761; gras kop@global.co.za; 69 Eeufees St; camp sites per person R35, dm R65, d with shared bathroom R160) This backpackers is in an unmistakeable castle-like building west of the centre across the train line. The owner is enthusiastic about the surroundings and arranges good trips, including kloofing, cave-crawling and hiking.

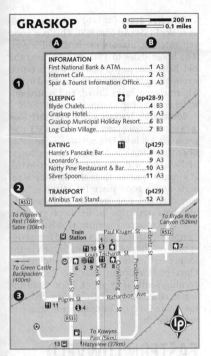

Log Cabin Village (☎ 767 1974; www.logcabin.co.za; Louis Trichardt St; s/d chalets R230/300; 🖳) A fenced-in compound in a central location close to the pancake eateries, with pleasant self-contained chalets with TVs and fireplaces.

Blyde Chalets (☎ 767 1316; info@graskop.info; Louis Trichardt St; 2-/3-person chalets from R270/300; 🖳) Blyde Chalets is an appealing, modern place with various levels of self-catering chalets, all spotless and comfortable. It's opposite Log Cabin Village.

Graskop Hotel (☎ 767 1244; info@graskophotel.co.za; cnr Main & Louis Trichardt Sts; s/d with breakfast R265/470) This is a surprisingly charming hotel, with efficient staff and spacious rooms. Avoid those facing the street as timber trucks roll by in the night.

Eating & Drinking

Graskop is a gourmet's delight, with pancakes the highlight.

Harrie's Pancake Bar (☎ 767 1273; Louis Trichardt St; pancakes R12-30; 🕑 8am-5.30pm) A classic pancake eatery with a cosy atmosphere, fast service and a wide range of sweet and savoury pancakes.

Silver Spoon (☎ 767 1039; Louis Trichardt St; pancakes from R15; 🕑 7am-6pm) Just across the road from Harrie's and a good alternative, with an even larger menu.

For relief from pancakes, or in the evenings, try **Notty Pine Restaurant & Bar** (☎ 767 1030; Pilgrim St; meals R35-50; 🕑 lunch & dinner Sat-Thu, dinner Fri), known for its excellent trout dishes, or **Leonardo's** (☎ 767 1078; Louis Trichardt St; meals R40-60; 🕑 lunch & dinner Mon-Sat) with good Italian food.

Getting There & Away

The minibus taxi stand is at the southern end of Main St, with daily morning departures to Pilgrim's Rest (R7, 30 minutes), Sabie (R10, 40 minutes) and Hazyview (R12, one hour).

BLYDE RIVER CANYON

The Blyde River's spectacular canyon is nearly 30km long and one of South Africa's most impressive natural features. Much of it is rimmed by the 26,000-hectare **Blyde River Canyon Nature Reserve** (admission per person R20), which snakes north from Graskop, following the escarpment and meeting the Blyde River as it carves its way down to the lowveld. Most visitors drive along the edge of the canyon, with stops at the many wonderful viewpoints, but if you have the time, it's well worth exploring on foot.

Heading north from Graskop, look first for the **Pinnacle**, an impressive rock formation jutting out from the escarpment. (Lock up your vehicle here as there have been thefts.) Just to the north along the 534 (a loop off the R532) are **Wonder View** and **God's Window** – two viewpoints with amazing vistas and batteries of souvenir sellers. At God's Window watch for the short trail leading to a point with good views over the lowveld, 1000m below. The Blyde River canyon starts north of here, near **Bourke's Luck Potholes**. These bizarre cylindrical holes were carved into the rock by whirlpools near the confluence of the Blyde and Treuer rivers. There's a **visitor's centre** (☎ 013-769 6019) where you can pay the reserve entry fee and get information on the canyon's geology, flora and fauna.

Continuing north past Bourke's Luck Potholes and into the heart of the nature reserve, you'll reach a viewpoint overlooking the **Three Rondavels** – huge cylinders of rock with hut-like pointed 'roofs' rising out of the far wall of the canyon. There are a number of short walks in the surrounding area to points where you can look down to the Blydepoort Dam at the reserve's far north. West of here, outside the reserve and off the R36, are **Echo Caves** where Stone Age relics have been found. The caves get their name from dripstone formations that echo when tapped. Nearby, and reached via the same turnoff from the R36, is the rather mediocre open-air **Museum of Man** (adult/child R10/5; ☺ 8am-5pm), an archaeological site with rock paintings and other finds.

Hiking

The main route is the popular and very scenic **Blyde River Canyon Hiking Trail** (R60; 2½ days), which begins at Paradise Camp and finishes at Bourke's Luck Potholes. The first night is spent at Watervalspruit Hut, and the second at Clearstream Hut. Bookings should be made through the **Mpumalanga Parks Board** (☎ 013-759 5432; mpbinfo@cis.co.za). As it's a one-way route, you'll need to sort out onward transport from the end of the trail.

The short but reasonably strenuous **Belevedere Day Walk** (R5; 5hr) takes you in a circular route to the Belvedere hydroelectric power station at Bourke's Luck Potholes. The station was built in 1911 and was once the largest of its kind in the southern hemisphere. Bookings should be made at Potholes.

Sleeping

It's easy to explore the canyon by car as a day jaunt from Graskop, Sabie or Pilgrim's Rest. If you're continuing further north, a good alternative is to stay in or around the nature reserve, or in Hoedspruit (p474). Ask about low-season and midweek discounts.

Aventura Resort Blydepoort (☎ 013-769 8005; www.aventura.co.za; camp sites R110 plus per person R22; 2-/4-person self-catering chalets R505/685; ⊉) This popular resort is located just off the R532, and is convenient for discovering the surrounding area. It offers a full range of resort amenities, including a golf course nearby, horse and hiking trails and easy access to Graskop.

Aventura Resort Swadini (☎ 015-795 5141; www.aventura.co.za; camp sites R110 plus per person R22, 6-person self-catering chalet R850; ☒ ⊉) Accommodation here is made more appealing by the good location and impressive views. In addition to hiking, the resort can organise white-water rafting, abseiling and more. It's at the northern end of the reserve along the Blyde River, and about 5km from Blydepoort Dam.

Belvedere House (☎ 013-759 5432; mpbinfo@cis.co.za; Mon-Fri R540, Sat & Sun R650) This is a good self-catering place with beautiful views. The house dates to 1915 and sits near the old Belvedere power station with a porch overlooking the canyon. It's operated by the Mpumalanga Parks Board, and rented out in its entirety (up to nine persons).

Rushworth's Trackers (☎ 015-795 5033; www.trackers.truepath.com; camp sites per person R35, r per person with half board R290, self-catering r per person R160) This is in a good setting just northwest of Swadini, with views over the lowveld. It's much quieter than the Aventura resorts and a good place for relaxing. Staff can also help you organise bird-watching and botanical trips on the large grounds. The easiest access is from Hoedspruit (in Limpopo province, and accessed from Nelspruit via the R40, or from Sabie via the longer but more scenic R532 and R527). Once in Hoedspruit, take the R527 west, turning south after about 20km onto the small Driehoek road (just after crossing the Blyde River). Continue for 6.5km, and watch for the signs.

EASTERN LOWVELD

It's in Mpumalanga's hot, dry eastern lowveld where you'll get a taste for bygone days, when vast bush-covered expanses were the playing fields for the ancestors of the animals that now roam Kruger park. While the area lacks the drama and scenic splendour of the Drakensberg Escarpment, it has numerous attractions. These include its location at Kruger park's doorstep, good infrastructure, easy access and a laid-back, untouristed pace away from major towns. The lowveld's rich history spans the millennia, from the earliest formation of the earth's crust (some of the world's oldest rocks are near Barberton), to the 19th-century heyday of the Voortrekkers and gold miners, to today's rapidly melting racial pot.

HAZYVIEW
☎ 013

Hazyview is a small village dominated by several large shopping centres. It's a convenient gateway to Kruger National Park via the Phabeni (12km), Numbi (15km) or Paul Kruger (47km) Gates.

Information

The helpful **Hazyview Tourism Association** (☎ 737 7414; Pick 'n' Pay Centre; ☼ 9am-6pm Mon-Fri, 8.30am-1pm Sat) is next to Simunye Shopping Centre. In the same complex is Haznet Internet Café, an ATM, and a Checkers supermarket.

About 5km north of town along the R535 is **Shangana Cultural Village** (☎ 737 7000; www .shangana.co.za; ☼ 9am-5pm), which is well worth a stop to get a feel for Shangaan culture. At various times of day it features a market, farming activity, house building, displays of uniforms and weaponry of the *masocho* (warriors), the relation of customs and history by a *sangoma* (witch doctor or herbalist), cooking, singing, dancing and the imbibing of *byala* (traditional beer). Day tours cost R55, midday visits with traditional meal from R115, and the evening program with a good dinner costs R170. Also here is Marula Crafts Market.

Sleeping & Eating

Thika Tika Guest Farm (☎ 737 8108; thika@lowveld .com; camp sites per person R40, dm/d R60/160) Thika Tika is in a beautiful setting about 4km west of Hazyview along the R536 to Sabie. It's well worth the extra drive, with great backpacker accommodation, two-storey chalets on a small river, a braai (barbecue) area and self-catering facilities, and a huge lawn. There are no catered meals.

Big 5 Backpackers (☎ 082-645 8248; hazyeye@soft .co.za; dm/d R75/200; ☒) This popular backpackers is in a wooded setting with a 'contemplation area', cooking facilities and safaris to Kruger. It's 3km up from the junction of the R40 and the R538; watch for the large, purple sign.

Kruger Park Backpackers (☎ 737 7224; info@kr ugerparkbackpackers.com; camp sites per person R35, dm R65, d huts with shared bathroom R150; ☒) Another spacious place, with trips to Kruger and accommodation in dorms or Zulu huts. It's about 2km south of the four-way stop, and about 500m along the road to Kruger's Numbi Gate.

Gecko Bushpackers & Campsite (☎ 737 8140; www.gecko-bushpackers.co.za; dm R65, d with/without bathroom R190/170; ☒) This backpackers is about 2.5km from Hazyview just off the R536 to Sabie. It has bright dorm rooms, some doubles, shaded camping, a self-catering area and pool table. Meals can also be arranged.

Rissington Inn (☎ 737 7700; www.rissington.co.za; d R540-900; ☒ ☒) An upscale retreat, with comfortable rooms in thatched, white cottages, and views over Kruger in the distance.

Thulamela (☎ 737 7171; www.thulamela.co.za; s/d cottages R455/760) Another upscale, comfortable place. It's set in the bush about 13km from Kruger, with majestic views and free-roaming wildlife in the area. Children under 16 aren't permitted. To get here, take the Umbhaba turn-off from the R40.

Hotel Numbi (☎ 737 7301; www.hotelnumbi.co.za; s/d with breakfast R395/590; ☒) Hotel Numbi has a colonial-era ambience, spacious grounds, the good **Pioneer Grill** (mains from R40) with views over the lawn and a less expensive pub menu inside. It's just south of the four-way stop.

Hippo Hollow (☎ 737 7752; www.hippohollow.co .za; s/d chalet R500/750; ☒) This is a large, sprawling resort-style complex on the Sabie River about 2.5km from Hazyview. Accommodation is in two- and four-bed chalets with braai area and small kitchenette, or in hotel rooms overlooking the river. There's also a restaurant.

For meals try **Hysterical Hornbill** (☎ 737 7404; mains R35-60; ☼ lunch & dinner), a pub and restaurant serving seafood, plus pub fare and some vegetarian dishes. There are also several fast-food places at Simunye Centre, including **Nando's** (☎ 737 6768) for chicken, and the **Italian Stallion** (☎ 737 6416) for pizzas. For something more intimate, head to **Tree Tops Restaurant** (☎ 737 8294; meals R60-80; ☼ dinner Mon-Sat), which features a mix of continental and local cuisine. It's 10km from Hazyview along the R36 to Sabie.

Getting There & Away

City to City's daily Jo'burg–Acornhoek bus stops at Hazyview (R75 from Jo'burg). The backpackers places do pick-ups from Nelspruit from about R15 (and some will do pick-ups at no charge if you book a Kruger safari with them).

Minibus taxis go daily to Nelspruit (R15, one hour) and Sabie (R15, one hour).

WHITE RIVER

☎ 013 / pop 13,000 / elevation 950m

White River (Witrivier) is a green, pleasant little town dating back to the days of the Anglo-Boer Wars. It's a bit higher and less humid than nearby Nelspruit, and worth a short stop. The town is the self-styled 'nut capital of South Africa', and just south of White River off the R40, you can visit some plantations.

The **tourist office** (☎ 750 1073; info@lowveld.info; ☺ 8am-5pm Mon-Fri, 8am-1pm Sat) is at the Casterbridge Centre about 2km north of town off the R40. There's an ATM at **First National Bank** (Tom Lawrence St) and an **Internet café** (cnr Tom Lawrence & Peter Graham Sts) nearby.

Hardy Ventures (☎ 751 1693; www.hardyventure .com) organises various adrenalin activities in the area, including rafting trips on the Sabie, Olifants and Blyde Rivers and hiking.

Sleeping

Lalela (☎ 751 2812; hawk@yebo.co.za; camp sites per person R35, dm R60, d with shared bathroom R150; 🖳 🍴) Lalela is a backpackers set on a farm, with accommodation in simple tepees or in the farmhouse, and windsurfing boards and a sailboat available for relaxation. It has self-catering facilities or meals if you want them. It's about 1.5km off Plaston Rd and signposted. Pick-ups from Nelspruit are available, and lifts to Swaziland can be organised.

Karula Hotel (☎ 751 2277; www.karulahotel.co.za; Old Plaston Rd; s/d with breakfast from R225/320; 🏊 🍴) This colonial-style hotel is the best midrange choice. Rooms are pleasant, especially those in the 'luxury' wing, and the grounds – rimmed by jacaranda and bougainvillea – are relaxing. It's on a quiet, winding section of the R538.

White River Lodge (☎ 751 1100; www.whiteriver lodge.co.za; cnr Kruger Park Rd & Alie van Bergen St; s/d with breakfast R242/418; 🏊 🍴) A modern place lacking in atmosphere, but with a convenient location along the main road, and the standard amenities.

Outside town are several comfortable places, which are good if you want to spend a few days relaxing in the countryside. **Igwala Gwala Country Lodge** (☎ 750 1723; www .igwalagwala.co.za; d with breakfast from R395; 🍴) is about 3km south of White River off the R40 and signposted, with nice gardens and accommodation in plush attached suites (no children allowed). **Greenway Woods Resort** (☎ 751 1094; www.greenway.co.za; 6-person chalets R850; 🏊 🍴) is a large resort about 6km from White River near the golf course. The self-catering chalets have fireplaces, and there's a restaurant. **Numbela** (☎ 751 3356; www.numbela .co.za; d with breakfast R700) is a small, charming

getaway with two beautiful self-contained cottages; no children under 12 allowed. It's about 20km north of White River along the R40. **Hulala Lakeside Lodge** (☎ 764 1893; www .hulala.co.za; s/d with half board from R710/1100; 🍴), a large resort with a waterside setting, canoeing and row-boating, and rooms with fireplaces is north of White River, signposted along the R40.

Eating

Bag-dad Cafe (☎ 751 1777; meals from R30, set menu R85; ☺ from 10am) This is a delightful bar and restaurant attached to a craft shop. It's about 2km from the town centre along the R40 to Hazyview, and opposite the tourist information office.

Other places for a meal include **Jürgen's German Restaurant** (☎ 751 2895; 30 Alie van Bergen St; mains from R40; ☺ lunch & dinner Sun-Fri, dinner Sat), bookings essential; and the **Meating Place Restaurant & Steak House** (☎ 750 1076; Tom Lawrence St; mains from R35; ☺ lunch & dinner), with a **pizzeria** (pizzas from R25) adjoining.

Getting There & Around

Minibus taxis go throughout the day to/from Nelspruit (R5, 20 minutes) and Hazyview (R12, one hour).

NELSPRUIT

☎ 013 / pop 236,000

Nelspruit, Mpumalanga's largest town and provincial capital, sprawls along the Crocodile River Valley in the steamy, subtropical lowveld. It has plenty of ATMs, supermarkets, restaurants and pubs, and makes a good stocking-up point before setting off into the wilds of Kruger National Park, or heading into Swaziland.

Orientation

At the centre of things, or at least trying to be, is the Promenade Centre, with a modest selection of shops and restaurants. Opposite are the ticket offices for Translux and other long-distance buses. Just southwest, between Louis Trichardt St (the N4) and Bester St, is the main business district. Spreading out southeast from here are quiet residential streets with numerous B&Bs. About 5km north of town off the White River road is the large Riverside Mall, which has taken much of Promenade Centre's business, and is the best place to shop.

MPUMALANGA

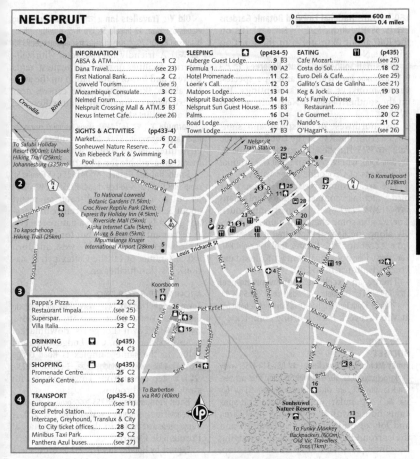

NELSPRUIT

0   600 m
0   0.4 miles

Information

The helpful **Lowveld Tourism** (☎ 755 1988/9; nelspruit@soft.co.za; cnr General Dan Pienaar & Louis Trichardt Sts; ☒ 8am-5pm Mon-Fri, 8am-1pm Sat), at Nelspruit Crossing Mall, sells City Bug and Greyhound tickets, takes bookings for all national parks, including Kruger, and can help arrange accommodation and tours.

Nelmed Forum (☎ 755 1541; www.nwlmwd.world online.co.za; cnr Nel & Rothery Sts) offers 24-hour emergency medical care.

There are numerous ATMs, including at **ABSA** (Brown St), and at **Nelspruit Crossing Mall** (cnr General Dan Pienaar & Louis Trichardt Sts). **First National Bank** (Bester St) does foreign exchange.

For Internet access, try **Nexus Internet Cafe** (Sonpark Centre; per hr R28; ☒ 8am-7pm Mon-Fri, 9am-

8pm Sat, 11am-5pm Sun), opposite Town Lodge, or **Alpha Internet** (1st fl, Riverside Mall; per hr R26; ☒ 9am-9pm Sun-Thu, 9am-11pm Fri & Sat).

The long-standing **Dana Travel** (☎ 753 3571; dananlp@galileosa.co.za; cnr Louis Trichardt & Paul Kruger Sts) can help with air tickets and other travel arrangements.

The **Mozambique consulate** (☎ 753 2089; 64 Bester St; ☒ 8am-4pm Mon-Fri) does same-day visa processing (between 8am and 11am only).

Sights & Activities

Nelspruit's lively produce **market** (cnr Brown & Currie Sts) is worth a look. If you're after something quieter, take a stroll among manicured stands of flowers, gnarled baobabs and patches of indigenous forest in the

150-hectare **National Lowveld Botanic Gardens** (☎ 752 5531; adult/child R5/2; ✆ 8am-6pm). It's on the R40 about 2km north of the junction with the N4.

The small **Sonheuwel Nature Reserve** (☎ 759 9111; admission free) features antelope species, vervet monkeys and rock paintings. It's on the southern edge of Nelspruit, off Van Wijk St.

Just northwest of Nelspruit and signposted from the R40 is the **Croc River Reptile Park** (☎ 752 5511; reptile@pixie.co.za; adult/child R30/15; ✆ 8am-5pm), where you can meet the original inhabitants of Crocodile River Valley.

The area around Nelspruit is good for bird-watching; contact **Lawson's Bird Safaris** (☎ 741 2458; www.lawsons.co.za) to organise tours. There's also some challenging hiking, notably along the **Kaapschehoop trail** (per night R47; 2, 3 or 4 days) and the **Uitsoek trail** (per night R47; 1 or 2 days). For bookings, contact Komatiland Forests Ecotourism (p425).

There's an excellent 50m **swimming pool** (☎ 759 9411; Drysdale St; adult/child R5.50/4.40; ✆ 10am-5.30pm Tue-Sat, 1-5.30pm Sun & public holidays) at Van Riebeeck Park sporting complex.

Sleeping
BUDGET

Funky Monkey Backpackers (☎ 083-310 4755; www .funkymonkeys.co.za; 102 Van Wijk St; camp sites per person R35, dm R60, s/d with shared bathroom R110/160; 🖳 🖭) A popular, well-run place in a spacious house, with a pool table, braai area and lots of information on Nelspruit and the surrounding area, plus help arranging Mozambique itineraries. It's a Baz Bus stop, and pick-ups from the bus terminal can be arranged.

Nelspruit Backpackers (☎ 741 2237; nelback@ hotmail.com; 9 Andries Pretorius St; camp sites per person R45, dm R70, d with shared bathroom R120; 🖭) This laid-back, basic backpackers (and Baz Bus stop) is equipped with a kitchenette, bar and pool table, and borders Sonheuwel Nature Reserve. It's run by Mbombela safaris, and can organise itineraries in the area. Look for the house painted like a South African flag.

Nelspruit Sun Guest House (☎ 741 2253; gho eks@iafrica.com; 7 De Villiers St; dm R65, d with/without bathroom R195/150; 🖭) This place has a range of comfortable, clean accommodation slightly classier than the backpackers, and without the party environment. The Baz Bus stops here.

Old Vic Travellers Inn (☎ 744 0993; www.krug erandom.co.za; 12 Impala St; dm R75, d with/without bathroom R250/170, 4-person self-catering cottages R380; 🖳 🖭) A friendly backpackers, with self-catering facilities or meals on request, tents for rent and lots of information on the area. It's about 3km south of the centre, near an extension of Sonheuwel Nature Reserve, and a Baz Bus stop.

Formula 1 (☎ 741 4490; www.formula1.co.za; cnr N4 & Kaapschehoop St; r R199; 🖭) Box-like but efficient three-person rooms, with continental breakfast available for an extra R18.

Safubi Holiday Resort (☎ 741 3253; 45 Graniet St; camp sites R120; 2-/4-/6-bed chalets R295/395/495; 🖭) Safubi is a well-kept self-catering resort about 2.5km from the town centre in pleasant grounds backing on to a nature reserve. A restaurant is planned, but for now bring your own food. Take the N4 west, and turn left at Graniet St (at the Caltex petrol station); it's 1km further on.

MID-RANGE & TOP END

Town Lodge (☎ 741 1444; www.citylodge.co.za; cnr General Dan Pienaar & Koorsboom Sts; s/d R330/390; 🖭 🖳 🖭) Town Lodge is downmarket from its sister chain, City Lodge, but good value. In the same complex is **Road Lodge** (☎ 741 1805; www.citylodge.co.za; 3-person r R230; 🖭), a step down from Town Lodge, with straightforward rooms.

Hotel Promenade (☎ 753 3000; promenade@prom enadehotel.co.za; s/d with breakfast R420/510; 🖭) A very pleasant hotel in the old town hall at Promenade Centre.

Express by Holiday Inn (☎ 757 0000; contactus@ southernsun.com; cnr White River Rd & Government Blvd; d with breakfast R429; 🖭 🖭) This branch of the Holiday Inn chain has all the standard amenities, and is a decent option if you have a car. It's in a sterile setting off the White River road, about 5km north of Nelspruit in the Emnotweni complex next to Riverside Mall.

Auberge Guest Lodge (☎ 741 2866; auberge@ global.co.za; 3 de Villiers St; s/d with breakfast R225/325) A quiet, well-maintained guesthouse with comfortable rooms in the main house, and a small yard. It's just down from Town Lodge.

Matopos Lodge (☎ 753 3549; matopo@mweb.co .za; 14 Sheppard Ave; s/d with breakfast R245/350; 🖭) Rooms at this comfortable place have ceiling fans, and some have balconies. It's in a quiet setting about 15 minutes on foot from the centre near Van Riebeeck Park.

Palms (☎ 755 4374; 25 Van Wijk St; s/d with breakfast R270/400; 🖳) An attractive B&B with leafy surroundings and weekend discounts.

Loerie's Call (☎ 752 4844; info@loeriescall.co.za; 2 du Preez St; s/d with breakfast from R380/500; 🖳) One of Nelspruit's classiest guesthouses. The rooms are set apart from the main house, each with their own entrance.

Eating & Drinking

Villa Italia (☎ 752 5780; cnr Louis Trichardt & Paul Kruger Sts; mains R35-60; 🕑 lunch & dinner) This popular place has been around for years. It serves a wide range of good pastas, pizzas and other Italian fare.

Costa do Sol (☎ 752 6382; cnr Louis Trichardt & Paul Kruger Sts; meals R40-50; 🕑 lunch & dinner Mon-Sat) A quaint little Portuguese place opposite Villa Italia featuring seafood, good soups and classic Portuguese cuisine.

Ku's Family Chinese Restaurant (☎ 741 3989; cnr General Dan Pienaar & Piet Retief Sts; mains from R23; 🕑 lunch & dinner Tue-Sun) Ku's is in Sonpark Centre, opposite Town Lodge. It offers straightforward Chinese food in a no-frills dining room; there's better seating out on the porch.

Keg & Jock (☎ 755 4969; Ferriera St; mains from R30; 🕑 lunch & dinner) Some of the best pub meals in town are available here, with a particularly interesting selection of salads. Outside are nice, shady tables amidst the ferns, ideal for enjoying a drink.

O'Hagan's (☎ 741 3580; cnr General Dan Pienaar & Piet Retief Sts; mains from R35) O'Hagan's is more homogenised than Keg & Jock, but it's a decent spot for a drink and pub food. It's in Sonpark Centre, opposite Town Lodge.

Le Gourmet (☎ 755 1941; cnr Branders & Voortrekker Sts; mains R50-75; 🕑 lunch & dinner Tue-Fri, dinner Sat & Sun) This intimate place features French cuisine and game dishes, and makes an ideal candlelight splurge.

Old Vic (☎ 755 3350; Nel St) A good spot for beers, a game of pool or meeting locals and other travellers. It's near Nelmed Forum.

Cafe Mozart (☎ 752 2637; Promenade Centre; light meals R25-35) is a long-standing place that has good sandwiches, salads and desserts, plus good speciality coffees. Also in Promenade Centre are the **Euro Deli & Cafe** (☎ 755 3425; light meals R25-35), with sandwiches and continental dishes, and the no-frills **Restaurant Impala**

(meals R25-30; 🕑 lunch & dinner Mon-Sat) with Indian sit-down and take-away meals, all halal.

For fast food, head to Brown St, where you'll find Nando's and the similar Gallito's Casa de Galinha. Opposite is **Pappa's Pizza** (☎ 755 1660), which draws a good crowd with its tasty pizzas and open porch seating. Riverside Mall is also a good bet, with branches of most chain fast-foods and several coffee houses, including **Mugg & Bean** (☎ 757 1036; snacks from R20), which also serves sandwiches and muffins.

For self-caterers, there's a huge **Superspar** (cnr General Dan Pienaar & Louis Trichardt Sts) at Nelspruit Crossings Mall.

Shopping

The biggest shopping centres are the glitzy Riverside Mall (about 5km north of town off the R40, with a wide range of stores), and Nelspruit Crossing (with various shops and ATM facilities, see p433). Promenade Centre has a reasonable array of eateries and shops, while Sonpark Centre has an Internet café and a few restaurants.

Getting There & Around

AIR

MKIA (p587) is the closest commercial airport. There are daily flights with **South African Airways** (SAA; ☎ 0860 359 722; www.flysaa.com) and **SAAirlink** (☎ 011-978 1111; www.saairlink.co.za) to Jo'burg (R1000; one hour), Cape Town (R2000; 2¼ hours) and Durban (R1300; 1½ hours). **Nationwide Airlines** (☎ 0861 737 737; www.nationwideair.co.za) flights also connect Nelspruit several times weekly with Jo'burg and Cape Town.

BUS

Baz Bus connects Nelspruit with Jo'burg/ Pretoria and Manzini (Swaziland), and stops at all the backpackers in town.

Intercape (☎ 0861 287 287; www.intercape.co .za), **Greyhound** (☎ 012-323 1154; www.greyhound .co.za) and **Translux** (☎ 011-774 3333; www.trans lux.co.za) all go daily between Jo'burg (and Pretoria) and Maputo (Mozambique) via Nelspruit. Their ticket offices are together on Louis Trichardt St, just up from Henshall St, and opposite Promenade Mall. Panthera Azul (p594) also stops in Nelspruit – at the **Excel petrol station** (cnr Bell & Louis Trichardt Sts) – on its run between Jo'burg and Maputo.

CAR RENTAL

Avis (☎ 741 1087), **Budget** (☎ 741 3871), **Europcar** (☎ 741 3062) and **Imperial** (☎ 741 2834) have offices at the airport. Europcar also has a desk at Hotel Promenade.

MINIBUS TAXI

The local bus and minibus taxi park is on the corner of Bester and Henshall Sts. Minibus taxi destinations and fares include White River (R5, 20 minutes), Barberton (R12, 40 minutes), Sabie (R15, one hour), Hazyview (R15, one hour), Graskop (R25, 1½ hours), Komatipoort (R45, two hours) and Jo'burg (R110, five hours).

City Bug (☎ 741 4114; www.citybug.co.za) operates a convenient shuttle service in town for R20 per person door-to-door. They also have a chauffeur service to/from Kruger Mpumalanga International Airport, a weekly shuttle to Durban (R380 per person one-way) and a three-times-daily shuttle between Nelspruit and Johannesburg International Airport (R180 per person).

TRAIN

The *Komati* (see p594) runs daily between Jo'burg and Komatipoort via Nelspruit.

MALELANE

☎ 013

Malelane is a small, bustling town between the N4 and the banks of the Crocodile River, on the southwestern border of Kruger National Park. It's a reasonable base before heading into the park, with Score and Spar supermarkets, petrol stations, and a Nedbank that does foreign exchange. Vast sugarcane plantations cover the surrounding area.

You can arrange tours of nearby Matsulu township (about 30km west of Malelane, bordering the southwestern corner of Kruger park) with **Zozi's** (☎ 778 8849, 082-668 1577; tours per person R275). The tours take about three hours and include visits to a sangoma (traditional witch doctor) and the local school.

River Cottage (☎ 790 0825; s/d with breakfast R250/400, 6-person cottage R1000) is a well-tended place sitting on the Crocodile River just west of town. The smaller cottages are set back on a clipped lawn, while the six-person one is close to the river; all are self-catering, with their own braai areas.

Lino's Lodge & Deck Restaurant (☎ 790 0793; s/d with breakfast R250/400; ☯ restaurant breakfast & lunch Tue-Sun, dinner Tue-Sat) offers good dining, especially seafood, on a nice open deck. There's also accommodation in pleasant white and green cottages on the banks of the river. It's just west of River Cottage, and reached via a long, frangipani-lined driveway.

River House Lodge (☎ 790 1333; riverhouse@m web.co.za; 22 Visarend St; d with half board R1480) is an elegant five-star thatched estate with B&B style accommodation. All rooms have their own small terraces, and there are attractive gardens bordering the river. It's west of River Cottage and signposted from the main road.

KOMATIPOORT

☎ 013 / pop 4700

This border town is at the foot of the Lebombo Mountains, near the confluence of the Komati and Crocodile Rivers and only 10km away from Kruger park's Crocodile Bridge Gate. It's a convenient stop if you're travelling to/from Mozambique or Swaziland.

Duve (☎ 790 7559; 79 Rissik St), a craft shop, provides tourist information. **ABSA** (Rissik St), near the town entrance, has an ATM and foreign exchange. Also here are Spar and Score supermarkets and petrol stations.

Sleeping & Eating

Komati River Chalets (☎ 790 7623; s/d with breakfast R245/400, 5-/7-person self-catering chalets R650/950; ⛱) This good-value place has plain stucco-and-thatch chalets set around large clipped grounds, a popular pub and tiger fishing in season. It's signposted from the N4, and just over the railroad tracks, with a second access route signposted from town.

Hippo's Restaurant & Lodge (☎ 793 8155; hippos restaurant@telkomsa.net; 80 Rissik St; ☯ breakfast, lunch & dinner) Hippo's, next to Duve, has a large menu selection featuring filling portions of meat and fish. Adjoining is **Pioneers Guest Lodge** (s/d R195/240; ⛱ ☏).

Trees Too (☎ 793 8262; s/d with breakfast R270/400; ☏) A small, very nice private home with B&B accommodation around a small garden. It's on a leafy side street about 500m in from Rissik St and signposted.

Restaurante Tambarina (☎ 790 7057; Rissik St; mains R40-55; ☯ lunch & dinner) Tambarina is a good place to sample prawns and Portuguese fare before heading over the border into Mozambique. It's opposite the Duve tourist information shop.

Getting There & Away

Minibus taxis leave from just off Rissik St near the Score supermarket, and regularly do the run between Komatipoort and Maputo (R60, 1½ to two hours). If you're driving, there are two tolls along the N4 on the Mozambique side.

BARBERTON

☎ 013 / pop 29,500

Alluring Barberton dates to the gold rush days of the late 19th century, when it was a boom town and home to South Africa's first stock exchange. However, most miners soon moved on to the newly discovered Rand fields near Jo'burg, and Barberton's prominence declined. All working gold mines in the region are now over 100 years old.

Although Barberton is usually completely overlooked by tourists, it makes a good stop if you want to see a 'typical' South African town, while enjoying the amenities. It's also within easy reach of Nelspruit (45km north) and Kruger, and a good base for excursions. The big township just outside Barberton is Emjindini.

The helpful **Tourist Information Centre** (☎ 712 2121 ask for tourist info; www.barberton.info; Market Sq, Crown St; ☯ 8am-1pm & 2-4.30pm Mon-Fri, 8.30am-noon Sat) in the town centre can assist with accommodation, tours of historic sites, and day hikes in the area. There are ATMs at **First National Bank** (Crown St) and in **Shoprite** (Crown St).

Sights & Activities

Barberton boasts several restored houses dating to the late 19th and early 20th centuries. All are open for touring and give a glimpse into the town's early history. They include **Belhaven House** (Lee St; adult/child R8/4; ☯ Mon-Fri); **Stopforth House** (Bowness St; admission included in Belhaven ticket; ☯ Mon-Fri) and **Fernlea House** (Lee St; admission included in Belhaven ticket; ☯ 8.30am-4pm Mon-Fri).

Barberton Museum (☎ 712 4281; Pilgrim St; admission free; ☯ 9am-4pm) is also worth a look. Next door is **Umjindi Gallery** (☯ 8am-5pm Mon-Fri, 9am-1pm Sat), with various crafts and a jewellery workshop where you can watch the artists at work.

Located just off the eastern end of Judge St is an iron and wood **blockhouse** from the

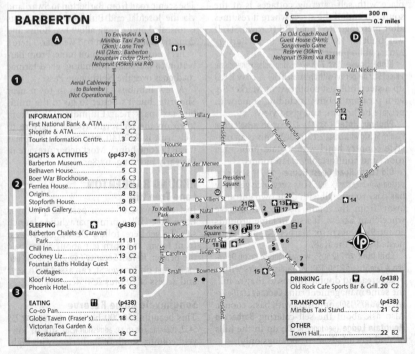

BARBERTON

0 ——— 300 m
0 ——— 0.2 miles

To Emjindini & Minibus Taxi Park (2km); Lone Tree Hill (2km); Barberton Mountain Lodge (2km); Nelspruit (45km) via R40

To Old Coach Road Guest House (9km); Songimvelo Game Reserve (30km); Nelspruit (53km) via R38

Aerial Cableway to Bulembu (Not Operational)

Van Niekerk

INFORMATION	
First National Bank & ATM	1 C2
Shoprite & ATM	2 C2
Tourist Information Centre	3 C2

SIGHTS & ACTIVITIES	(pp437-8)
Barberton Museum	4 C2
Belhaven House	5 C3
Boer War Blockhouse	6 C3
Fernlea House	7 C3
Origins	8 B2
Stopforth House	9 B3
Umjindi Gallery	10 C2

SLEEPING ⭑	(p438)
Barberton Chalets & Caravan Park	11 B1
Chill Inn	12 D1
Cockney Liz	13 C2
Fountain Baths Holiday Guest Cottages	14 D2
Kloof House	15 C3
Phoenix Hotel	16 C3

EATING 🍴	(p438)
Co-co Pan	17 C2
Globe Tavern (Fraser's)	18 C3
Victorian Tea Garden & Restaurant	19 C2

DRINKING 🍸	(p438)
Old Rock Cafe Sports Bar & Grill	20 C2

TRANSPORT	(p438)
Minibus Taxi Stand	21 C2

OTHER	
Town Hall	22 B2

MPUMALANGA

Anglo-Boer War, part of the chain built by the British when the war entered its guerrilla phase. On the southwestern edge of town is a currently nonfunctional 20.3km **aerial cableway**. When operating, it is purported to be the longest industrial cableway in the world, bringing asbestos down from a mine in Swaziland. Coal is carried in the other direction to provide counterweight.

Origins (☎ 712 5055; www.origins.co.za; 20 Sheba Rd) runs various tours, including a good Eureka City Ghost Town tour of the old Barberton gold mines. They also do pickups from Nelspruit for R50 plus R10 per additional person.

Sleeping

Barberton Chalets & Caravan Park (☎ 712 3323; walmec@soft.co.za; General St; camp sites per person R50, caravan sites R60, 2-person chalets R220) This caravan park is conveniently close to the town centre, with lots of shade and grassy areas, camping and self-catering chalets.

Fountain Baths Holiday Guest Cottages (☎ 712 2707; fountainbaths@hotmail.com; 48 Pilgrim St; cottages per person with breakfast R120) This good-value place with self-catering cottages is at the southern end of the street where it resumes after merging into Sheba Rd (Crown St). It was built in 1885 and used to be Barberton's public pool.

Kloof House (☎ 712 4268; kloofhuis@xsinet.co.za; 1 Kloof St; r per person with breakfast R150) A cosy B&B up a steep hill just southeast of Market Sq, with pleasant rooms, including some with private bathroom, and good views.

Phoenix Hotel (☎ 712 4211; phoenix@soft.co.za; Pilgrim St; s/d with breakfast R180/300) This is an old-style country hotel with a staid pub, a tea room and comfortable, clean rooms.

Old Coach Road Guest House (☎ 719 9755; r per person with breakfast R200) This very nice getaway has cosy rooms, all with their own entrance away from the main house. Some have wheelchair access. It's set in large grounds about 9km north of Barberton, and signposted from the R38.

Chill Inn (☎ 712 5055; www.origins.co.za; cnr De Villiers & Tate Sts; s/d R150/300) A backpackers with a braai area and double rooms. If they're full, the same management runs **Cockney Liz** (De Villiers St; s/d R75/150), opposite, with basic rooms. Also ask about the self-catering **Barberton Mountain Lodge** (per lodge R800), up in the hills behind town (advance bookings only).

Eating & Entertainment

Co-co Pan (☎ 712 2653; Crown St; mains R25-35; 9am-6pm Mon-Sat) This casual eatery opposite the museum is a good budget choice, with burgers, salads and other basics. Entry is through a small general shop.

Victorian Tea Garden & Restaurant (☎ 712 4985; light meals from R25; 9am-5pm Mon-Fri, 9am-2pm Sat) The gazebo here is a great spot to relax and watch the passing parade. It's between Pilgrim and Crown Sts, and next to the tourist information office. The menu features sandwiches and fast food.

Globe Tavern (Fraser's; ☎ 712 3952; 18 Pilgrim St; mains R45-60; lunch & dinner Tue-Sat) Fraser's is in the historic old Globe Tavern, with an agreeable ambience and excellent meals featuring impeccably prepared fish, chicken and meat dishes.

Old Rock Cafe Sports Bar & Grill (De Villiers St; dinner Mon-Sat) The best place to go for a drink, and to find out what's happening in town. They also have meals and sometimes a bonfire in the yard. It's next to Cockney Liz.

Getting There & Away

The scenic road from Barberton to Swaziland via the Josefdal and Bulembu border posts is unsealed and rough; allow two hours and don't try it in a 2WD in bad weather. There's a check post at the Bulembu mine. From Barberton to Badplaas, a winding, good tarmac road goes over the Nelshoogte Pass.

A few minibus taxis stop in town near Shoprite, but it's better to go to the minibus taxi park near Emjindini (3km from town on the Nelspruit road). The fare to Nelspruit is R12 (40 minutes), to Badplaas it is R17 (one hour). Most departures are in the early morning, by 8am.

AROUND BARBERTON
Lone Tree Hill

Just southwest of town past the prison is Lone Tree Hill, a prime paragliding launch site. To get here, follow De Villiers St west from town, and turn left about 500m past the prison. **Hi Tech Security** (☎ 712 3256; McPherson St), just off Kruger St, can assist with keys and access (R20 plus R50 deposit).

Songimvelo Game Reserve

This beautiful 56,000-hectare **reserve** (☎ 759 5432; mpbinfo@cis.co.za; admission R50) sits in lowveld country south of Barberton, with high-altitude grassland areas on its eastern edge along the mountainous Swaziland border. There are no lions, but there are numerous other introduced species, including elephants, zebras, giraffes and various antelopes, and both walking and horse riding are popular. (Note that walking is limited to certain areas, and walkers must be accompanied by a guide.) Songimvelo is also home to some of earth's oldest rocks – perhaps dating to 4000 million years ago – and to some interesting archaeological sites. You can stay overnight at **Kromdraai Camp** (cabins per person R40), with simple self-catering, 4-person wooden cabins.

BADPLAAS
☎ 017

If relaxing in **thermal springs** (person/vehicle per day R45/25) appeals, Badplaas is worth a short stop. Rising up on the horizon are the dramatic Hlumuhlumu Mountains.

Aventura Badplaas (☎ 844 1022; www.aventura .co.za; camp sites R110, r R565, 2-/4-bed self-catering chalets R583/R805; ✖) is the best place to stay if you want a resort atmosphere, complete with beauty treatments and a choice of chalets or double rooms. There's also a caravan park, and admission to the hot springs is included in the room rates.

Badplaas Valley Inn (☎ 844 1040; s/d with breakfast R200/300) is smaller, simpler and quieter than the Aventura next door. In addition to nice rooms, it offers a bar, restaurant and TV room.

Minibus taxis run between Badplaas and Machadodorp, via the N4 (R15, one hour), and Barberton (R17, one hour).

PIET RETIEF
☎ 017 / pop 32,000

This solid, medium-sized town is the largest in southern Mpumalanga, and a convenient stopping point en route to Swaziland or KwaZulu-Natal. About 80km southwest of Piet Retief near Wakkerstroom is a vast area of grasslands, known for its excellent birdwatching. It's slated to become the centre of the yet-to-be-declared Ekangala Grassland Biosphere Reserve. The area south of Piet Retief is also known for its many Anglo-Boer War battlefields.

There's a small **tourist information office** (☎ 826 5477; 10A Piet Retief St; ✆ 8am-1pm & 2-5pm Mon-Fri, 8am-1pm Sat) between Church and Mark Sts, with a new one set to open soon near the sports grounds at the northeastern edge of town. There are ATMs at First National Bank and ABSA, both on Church St in the town centre, and Internet access at the Green Door Cafe (below).

Sleeping & Eating

Lala's Lodge (☎ 826 1838, 083-302 2466; camp sites per person R35, dm R70, r per person with breakfast R200) Lala's, with dorms and doubles and a communal lounge, may be worth checking if you're on a tight budget. It's about 1.5km north of town, signposted off the N2 towards Ermelo.

Green Door Guest House (☎ 826 3208; www.the greendoor.co.za; 1 Market St; s/d with breakfast R203/275) A popular place with lots of rooms, some with interesting African decoration. The same management runs the **Green Door Restaurant** (☎ 826 3208; Church St; mains from R27; ✆ 11am-10pm Mon-Fri, dinner Sat), with tasty, filling meals. Adjoining is a cosy bar known for its wide selection of beers, and for its collections of ties, caps and more. In the same complex is Green Door Cafe, with wholegrain snacks, good coffee and an Internet connection.

LA Guest House (☎ 826 2837, 082-292 2163; 3 Market St; s/d R190/280) This comfortable B&B has immaculate, spacious rooms, two with small cooking areas, and a yard. It's in a quiet location just a few blocks from the town centre.

Bossie's Inn (☎ 826 3285; bossiesinn@megaweb .co.za; cnr Market & North End Sts; s/d R200/300) Another pleasant and well-located B&B.

Near Wakkerstroom, try **Wetlands Lodge** (☎ 730 0101; d with half board R550), just off the R543, with a fireplace and a well-stocked library; or the much larger **Weaver's Nest Country Village** (☎ 730 0115; www.weavers.co.za; s/d with half board R525/810, 4-person cottages R700), also signposted off the R543, with rooms and self-catering cottages.

Getting There & Away

Greyhound stops in town at Waterside Lodge on the southern end of Church St on its daily Pretoria–Durban run. The fare from Piet Retief to Pretoria is R130; to Durban it's R170. City to City also comes here from Johannesburg.

The minibus taxi stand is at the back of SuperMac (Kerk and Brand Sts). From here to the Swaziland border post at Mahamba costs R10 (30 minutes).

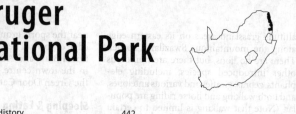

Kruger National Park

CONTENTS

With its vast savannas, abundant wildlife and long conservation history, Kruger National Park is one of the best safari destinations in the world. It's reputed to have the greatest variety of animals of any park on the continent, with lions, leopards, elephants, Cape buffaloes and black rhinos (the Big Five), plus cheetahs, giraffes, hippos, antelopes and many species of smaller animals all wandering around a stunning lowveld setting. Topping it all off is an excellent infrastructure that makes everything readily accessible. It's likely to be one of the highlights of your travels in Southern Africa.

Thanks to Kruger's infrastructure, which includes an extensive network of sealed roads and comfortable camps, the park does not offer a true wilderness experience (although some would argue that the walking trails and northern Kruger approach this ideal). Yet, this shouldn't deter you: the sounds and scents of the bush are never more than a few metres away, and often much easier (and less expensive) to enjoy than elsewhere on the continent. And, as long as you avoid weekends and school holidays, or stick to areas north of Phalaborwa Gate and along gravel roads, it's easy to travel for an hour or more without seeing another vehicle. You'll hardly notice that you're in the most visited wildlife park in Africa. An additional plus: since many of the animals are used to the presence of cars, it's often possible to observe them from within close range.

Southern Kruger is the most popular section of the park, with the highest animal concentrations and the easiest access. Central Kruger, with its grasslands and thornveld, is renowned for its lions. Further north, mopani takes over as the dominant vegetation. This is a favoured food of elephants, and you'll see these giant creatures in abundance here. Kruger is at its best in the far north, around Punda Maria and Pafuri. Here, although animal concentrations are somewhat lower, the bush setting and wilderness atmosphere are all-enveloping.

KRUGER NATIONAL PARK

HIGHLIGHTS

- Exploring Kruger's hidden corners on one of its excellent **wilderness trails** (p445)
- Staying in a remote **bushveld camp** and falling asleep to the sounds of hippos grunting in a nearby river (p449)
- Taking a **night drive** and spotting the shining yellow eyes of one of the big cats gleaming from the roadside (p444)
- Sitting at a **water hole** at dawn, watching creation come alive (p444)
- Pampering yourself with a few nights at one of the luxurious **private game reserves** bordering the park (p451)

- TELEPHONE CODE: 013   - AREA: 20,000 SQ KM

KRUGER NATIONAL PARK

```
0 ─────── 40 km
0 ─────── 20 miles
```

LEGEND

CA	Conservation Area
FR	Forest Reserve
GR	Game Reserve
NP	National Park
NR	Nature Reserve
WA	Wilderness Area

HISTORY

The San were the first people to see Kruger's animals, and they have left their mark in rock paintings at numerous sites throughout the park. Prior to the San, various hominid species wandered the lowveld as much as 500,000 years ago. From around 500AD, Nguni peoples had settled in.

The area that is now Kruger first came under protection in 1898, when Paul Kruger (president of the Transvaal Republic and an avid hunter) established the Sabie Game Reserve, between the Sabie and Crocodile Rivers, as a controlled hunting area. In 1902, following the second Anglo-Boer War, James Stevenson Hamilton became the reserve's first warden. Stevenson Hamilton was also the first to see the tourism potential of wildlife, and to bring a true conservation vision to the area. In 1926, Sabie Game Reserve was joined with neighbouring Shingwedzi Game Reserve and various private farms to become Kruger National Park, and in 1927 the park was opened to the public.

Since then, Kruger has become a major research and conservation centre and one of Africa's premier wildlife-watching destinations. In the early '90s, most of the fences came down between Kruger and the private game reserves lining the park's western edge. In 2002, Kruger – together with Zimbabwe's Gonarezhou National Park, and

Limpopo National Park in Mozambique – became part of the giant **Great Limpopo Transfrontier Park** (www.greatlimpopopark.com). The park is still in its earliest stages and not yet operational as a transborder entity, but once infrastructure is in place, Kruger's wildlife will ultimately have a 35,000 sq km area in which to roam.

ORIENTATION

Kruger is a long, narrow wedge bordered by Mozambique to the east, Limpopo province to the west and Mpumalanga to the west and south. It averages about 65km across, and is about 350km long. Rimming the park to the west, and sharing the same unfenced terrain, is a chain of private game reserves.

Terrain ranging from flat to gently undulating covers the majority of the park, with the Lebombo Mountains rising up to the east along the Mozambique border. Major rivers flowing across Kruger from west to east include the Limpopo, Luvuvhu, Shingwedzi, Letaba, Olifants, Timbavati and Sabie.

There are nine entry gates (*heks* in Afrikaans). On the park's southern edge are Malelane and Crocodile Bridge Gates, both readily accessible from the N4 from Johannesburg (Jo'burg). The Numbi, Phabeni and Paul Kruger Gates are easily accessed from Hazyview (turn off the N4 before Nelspruit); Paul Kruger Gate is the closest to Skukuza (p447), Kruger's main rest camp. Orpen, to the west, is convenient if you're coming from the Blyde River area. Phalaborwa is near Polokwane; Punda Maria is reached via Makhado (Louis Trichardt); and Pafuri, in the far north, is accessed from Thohoyandou in the Venda region.

The park is laced with a network of sealed roads (about 700km in total), one of which runs along its entire spine. These, together with more lightly travelled gravel side roads, form a road network of about 1900km.

INFORMATION
Bookings

Accommodation can be booked through **South African National (SAN) Parks central reservations office** (☎ 012-428 9111; www.parks-sa.co .za; 643 Leyds St, Muckleneuk, Pretoria). It's also possible to book directly through **Lowveld Tourism** (p433), **Cape Town Tourism** (p99), and at the **Tourist Junction** (p285) in Durban. All of these local tourism offices have Kruger

---

KRUGER'S POPULATION

Kruger National Park's population is made up of:

- 147 mammal species
- 507 bird species
- 114 reptile species
- 49 fish species
- 34 types of amphibians
- one million human visitors per year

---

maps and publications, and they are also sold in the park in the larger rest camps.

Phone bookings are possible with credit card. Written applications for rest camps and wilderness trails can be made up to 13 months in advance. Except in the high season (school holidays, Christmas and Easter) and weekends, bookings are advisable but not essential.

Entry

Day or overnight entry to the park costs R120/60 for adults/children, with significant discounts available for South African citizens and residents, and for South African Development Community (SADC) nationals. The SAN Parks Wild Card (p63) also applies to Kruger.

Bicycles, motorcycles and open vehicles are not permitted to enter the park. During school holidays you can stay in the park for a maximum of 10 days, and at any one rest camp for five days (10 days if you're camping). Throughout the year, park authorities restrict the total number of visitors within the park, so in the high season it pays to arrive early if you don't have a booking.

Entry gate opening times vary slightly with the season, and are currently as follows.

Month	Gates/camps open (am)	Gates/camps close (pm)
Jan	4.30/5.00	6.30
Feb	5.30	6.30
Mar	5.30	6.00
Apr	6.00	6.00
May–Aug	6.30	5.30
Sep	6.00	6.00
Oct	6.00/5.30	6.00
Nov & Dec	5.30/4.30	6.30

It's an offence to arrive late at a camp and you can be fined for doing so (the camps are fenced). With speed limits of 50km/h on sealed roads and 40km/h on dirt roads (monitored by rangers with radars), it can take a while to travel from camp to camp, especially if you encounter a traffic jam near an interesting animal.

PLANT & ANIMAL DISTRIBUTION

Kruger encompasses a variety of landscapes and ecosystems, with each ecosystem favoured by particular species. Most mammals are distributed throughout the park, but some show a distinct preference for particular regions. The excellent *Find It* booklet, available from the park shops located at some of the bigger camps and at the National Parks office in Pretoria, points out the most likely places to see all the major animals.

Impalas, buffaloes, Burchell's zebras, blue wildebeests, kudus, waterbucks, baboons, vervet monkeys, cheetahs, leopards and other smaller predators are all widespread. Birdlife is prolific along the rivers and north of the Luvuvhu River.

Rainfall is highest (700mm a year) in the southwestern corner between the Olifants and Crocodile Rivers. The area is thickly wooded and has a variety of trees including acacias, bushwillows, sycamore figs and flowering species such as the red-and-orange coral tree. This terrain is particularly favoured by white rhinos and buffaloes, but is less favoured by antelope and, therefore, by predators.

The eastern section of the park, to the south of the Olifants River on the plains around Satara rest camp and south to the Crocodile River, experiences reasonable rainfall (600mm) and has fertile soils. There are expanses of good grazing, with buffalo grass and red grass interspersed with acacia thorn trees (especially knobthorn), leadwood and marula trees. In this region there are large populations of impalas, zebras, wildebeests, giraffes and black rhinos. Joining them are predators, particularly lions, who prey on impalas, zebras and blue wildebeests.

North of the Olifants River the rainfall drops below 500mm and the dominant tree is mopani. This grows widely in the west, among red bushwillow, but has a tougher time on the basalt plains of the northeast, where it tends to be more stunted. The mopani is a favoured food of elephants, which are most common north of Olifants River, and is also eaten by tsessebes, elands, roans and sables.

Perhaps the most interesting area is in the far north around Punda Maria and Pafuri, which has a higher rainfall (close to 700mm at Punda Maria) than the mopani country. This enables it to support a wider variety of plants (baobabs are particularly noticeable), and greater wildlife concentrations. There is woodland, bushveld, grass plains and, between the Luvuvhu and Limpopo Rivers, a tropical riverine forest.

All of Kruger's rivers have riverine forest along their banks, often with enormous fig trees, which supports populations of bushbuck and nyala.

ACTIVITIES

Kruger is exceptionally well organised, with a plethora of activities to enhance your wildlife-watching. When planning an itinerary, keep in mind that the closer you can get to the bush, and the more time you can devote to becoming acquainted with its sounds, smells and rhythms, the more rewarding your experience will be. Although it's possible to get a sense for Kruger in a day, the park merits at least four to five days, and ideally at least a week. If the bush really gets into your blood, there's enough here to keep you coming back for a lifetime.

Interspersed with whatever activities you do, allow plenty of time for simply sitting still – preferably by a water hole, river or lake. The silence will soon become filled with nature's symphony, and you'll be able to watch Kruger come to life before you. Even without seeing a single animal, it's an incomparable experience to stand on a rise with Kruger stretching out before you, and savour the indescribable, primeval majesty of having such vast tracts set aside solely to protect earth's natural splendour.

Wildlife Drives

Dawn (three hours), midmorning (two hours), sunset (three hours) and night (two hours) wildlife drives are available at most rest camps, and offer good chances to maximise your safari experience, especially as you'll have a ranger to point out interesting features. The drives are scheduled to take advantage of the natural rhythms of the wildlife, as many animals, including lions, leopards and rhinos, are at their most active from first light to around 10am, and then again later in the day. The drives are done in 10- or 20-seat vehicles, and cost between R85 and R140 per person, depending on the time and vehicle size.

Bush Walks

Better than the drives are guided morning and afternoon bush walks (per person morning/afternoon R210/165), which are possible at all the larger camps, including Satara, Skukuza, Lower Sabie and Pretoriuskop. These are highly popular, and are an excellent way to experience Kruger at close range. All walks are accompanied by armed rangers. The morning walk – when you'll have a better chance of seeing wildlife on the move – is particularly recommended.

Wilderness Trails

Kruger's wilderness walking trails are one of the park's highlights, and a major attraction of the Southern African safari experience. They are done in small groups (maximum eight people), guided by highly knowledgeable armed guides and offer a superb opportunity to get a much more intimate sense of the bush than would ever be possible in a vehicle. The walks are not particularly strenuous, covering about 20km per day at a modest pace, and are appropriate for anyone who is reasonably fit. The itinerary of each walk is determined by the interests of the group, the time of year and the disposition of the wildlife.

Most wilderness trail walks last two days and three nights, with departures on Wednesday and Sunday afternoon. They cost R2050 per person, including accommodation in rustic, pleasant huts, plus food and equipment. Bring your own beer and wine if you'd like a drink. The walks are extremely popular, and should be booked well in advance.

Brief descriptions of Kruger's seven wilderness trails follow.

Bushman Trail Near the Berg-en-dal rest camp in the southwestern corner of the park. This trail features treks to San rock paintings, plus the chance to see white rhinos, lions and large herds of antelope.

Metsimetsi Trail Midway between Lower Sabie and Satara rest camps on the eastern border of the park. The terrain consists of undulating savanna, ravines and the rocky gorge of the N'waswitsontso River. Because the river flows year-round, the surrounding area is noted for its abundant wildlife, including elephants and black rhinos.

Napi Trail Runs through mixed bushveld, midway between Skukuza and Pretoriuskop rest camps. This area is home to white and black rhinos, lions, leopards, cheetahs, wild dogs, buffaloes and elephants, and the trail is known for the opportunities it offers for seeing the Big Five, plus its excellent birding.

Nyalaland Trail In the far north of the park near the Luvuvhu River, a region of strikingly diverse ecosystems. The trail is most memorable for its beauty and its wilderness ambience, rather than for opportunities to witness the Big Five. Birdlife is prolific and the area is a paradise for ornithologists.

Olifants Trail Based in the eastern part of the park on the Olifants River. With its superb riverine setting, this trail offers the chance to get close to elephants, hippos, crocodiles and more, and is also known for its birding. Species you may see include fish eagles and the rare Pels fishing owl.

Sweni Trail A highly rewarding trail near Satara rest camp. Many lions are attracted to the herds of wildebeests, zebras and buffaloes here – all against a highly evocative backdrop of vast grassy plains.

Wolhuter Trail Based in southern Kruger near the Bushman Trail, in an area inhabited by lions and white rhinos. The name commemorates legendary father and son rangers Harry and Henry Wolhuter. You can find out more about Harry's exploits, including the time when he wrestled a lion, at the Stevenson-Hamilton Museum in Skukuza rest camp.

Bird-Watching

There is excellent bird-watching throughout Kruger, with the far north (from Punda Maria Gate up past Pafuri Gate) arguably one of the best birding areas on the continent. There are a handful of hides scattered throughout the park; see the birding pages on the website for **SAN Parks** (www.parks-sa.co.za) for a listing of their locations. Several of the bushveld camps (p449) also have their own hides, and some of the larger camps run bird-watching excursions on request. There is also an annual 24-hour **Birding Big Day** in January. For information on this, and other birding activities in the park, contact **SAN Parks Honorary Rangers** (☎ 012-426 5026).

Mountain Biking

There are currently three mountain-bike trails (per person R300) in Kruger, ranging from 12km to 24km. Full-day trails can also be arranged for R600. All are based out of **Olifants** (☎ 735 6606) in central Kruger,

WILDLIFE-WATCHING

It's a game of chance, but thanks to the variety and sheer numbers of animals in Kruger, you have a better probability of spotting wildlife here than anywhere else in the region. Viewing is best in the cooler, drier winter season, when trees lose their leaves and plant growth is sparser, improving visibility. Also at this time animals tend to be concentrated around the dwindling water sources, and there are fewer mosquitoes. However, the landscape is more attractive in summer, with fresh green growth and a plethora of newborns.

Whatever time of year you visit, patience and perseverance are vital prerequisites for rewarding wildlife-watching. Drive slowly, stop frequently, and disengage the motor. It's amazing how often you first notice an animal, and only after stopping the car realise that there are many others in the vicinity. Even elephants can be well camouflaged when not in motion. Sitting still and staking out a water hole is always rewarding. Rest camps provide maps that have a 'coloured pin system' showing where animals have been spotted in the area that day and on the previous day – a good place to start.

Thanks to Kruger's excellent road system, you can get off the main roads quite easily, and won't need a 4WD for most secondary gravel roads. (If it has been raining heavily, check with rangers at your rest camp for routes that should be avoided.) Sunglasses and binoculars are essential.

Though different animals display varying behaviour at different times of the day (and tend to be more active in the morning and again in the late afternoon and evening), they don't follow rules, so there is always something to be seen. The more you know about the animals (especially their distribution and behaviour) the better your chance of finding them, so it's worth buying one of the detailed books available at the rest camp shops. Some tips:

- Watch for big cats enjoying the breezes from rocky knolls; leopards will often rest high off the ground in tree branches.
- Circling vultures and parked cars are two obvious signs of something interesting, as are excited motorists attempting to flag you down.
- Warthogs, baboons, zebras, giraffes and many antelope species will happily graze together, so if you see one species, there will often be more close by.
- The presence of feeding herbivores does not preclude the possibility of a predator in the vicinity. Look carefully, as predators are expert stalkers and may not be obvious. Many animals do, however, seem to know whether a predator is actually hunting; if it isn't they will be quite relaxed in its presence.
- Antelopes will be nervous and alert if they are aware of a predator on the hunt, but may not immediately flee. They know they can nearly always outrun a predator if they have a sufficient head start, so they maintain a 'flight distance' between themselves and the threat. If the hunter encroaches, the antelope will move, but will try to keep the hunter in sight. If the hunter charges, the antelope will flee, though may not go far.
- Avoid driving too close to the animals, so as not to disturb their natural behaviour. If you do approach, be slow and steady, without sudden movements.
- Avoid frequent stopping and starting of the car engine – if you stop, it's best to stay put for a while. However bear in mind that engine vibrations may create a problem with camera shake. There are a few designated spots in Kruger where you are permitted to get out of your car.

and should be booked at least several days in advance directly through the camp, or through central reservations (p443).

4WD Trails

The longest and most established of Kruger's 4WD trails is the **Lebombo Motorised Eco Trail**, a rough, rugged 500km 4WD route along the eastern boundary of the park, departing from Crocodile Bridge and ending at Pafuri. The trail lasts five days and costs R4750 per vehicle (maximum of four people per vehicle). You'll need to provide your own vehicle, food and drink (it's completely self-catering). Only five vehicles are permitted at a time on the trail (plus the vehicle of the ranger who accompanies you). Book well in advance through central reservations (p443).

There are also four shorter trails, all averaging about four hours, and costing R460 per vehicle plus a R100 refundable deposit. They (and the points where you can reserve them) are: **Northern Plains Adventure Trail** (Shingwedzi camp); **Nonokani Adventure Trail** (Phalaborwa Gate); **Mananga Adventure Trail** (Satara camp); **Madlabantu Adventure Trail** (Pretoriuskop camp). All are closed after rains, and can only be booked on the morning of the day that you want to drive, with a maximum of six vehicles per trail per day. There are no facilities (including ablutions) along any of the trails, so bring whatever you'll need, plus ideally a global position system (GPS).

Golf

There's a nine-hole golf course at Skukuza (R75); bring your own clubs.

SLEEPING & EATING

Kruger boasts various types of accommodation, all of high standard. Bookings can be made through central reservations, or at one of the local tourist offices that take Kruger bookings (see p443 for all contacts).

Most visitors stay in one of the park's 12 rest camps. These offer camping, plus a range of huts, bungalows and cottages and several other styles of accommodation, as well as shops, restaurants and other facilities. Several of the rest camps have satellite camps, which are set some distance away, and are much more rustic, without any facilities.

There are also five bushveld camps – smaller, more remote clusters of self-catering cottages without shops or restaurants; and two bush lodges, which are set in the middle of the wilderness, and must be booked in their entirety by a single group. Finally, there are several private concessions within Kruger offering five-star comforts.

Another possibility is to stay outside the park. For budget travellers, the best places for this are Hazyview (p431) and Nelspruit (p434). At the opposite end of the spectrum, there's very luxurious accommodation in many of the private reserves bordering Kruger to the west (p451).

Rest Camps

The larger rest camps are like small towns in the middle of the bush, though remarkably unobtrusive, considering the facilities they offer and the volume of visitors they host. All rest camps are fenced, attractively laid out, and immaculately maintained, and all have electricity. Most also have shops and reasonable restaurants with reasonable prices (mains about R40 to R55), plus shared cooking facilities (sinks, hotplates and braais), public telephones, and fuel supplies (petrol and diesel). There are swimming pools at Berg-en-dal, Pretoriuskop (a converted natural rock pool), Lower Sabie, Skukuza, Mopani and Shingwedzi, banks at Skukuza and Letaba, and an ATM at Skukuza. Wildlife drives and bush walks can be arranged at all of the rest camps.

Accommodation in the rest camps varies but usually comprises huts, bungalows and cottages. All are supplied with bedding and towels, and most have air-con or fans. If a kitchen is not part of the accommodation (ie, if there is a communal kitchen only), visitors must bring their own cooking and eating utensils.

Huts (two people around R140 to R200) are rustic, and the cheapest option, with shared ablutions and communal cooking facilities. They sleep between two and six people, depending on the camp, and some have fridges.

Bungalows (two people around R420 to R460) are almost always en suite, and range from simple units with communal cooking facilities to more luxurious versions with kitchenettes.

Cottages (up to four people about R790) are the next step up in both comfort and price. They usually have a living room area, as well as kitchen and bathroom, and come in several sizes, including multibedroom 'family cottages'.

Some camps also offer the option of staying in safari tents (two people about R220), all of which are furnished, take from two to four people, and have a refrigerator and fan. Most have shared kitchen and ablutions facilities. Several camps – notably Lower Sabie rest camp and Tamboti satellite camp (near Orpen) – also have safari tents with private bathroom and cooking facilities (from R360 to R475 for two people).

For those with tents or caravans, camping (camp sites for one to two people R95, per extra person R30, maximum of six extra people) is available at many rest camps (the exceptions are noted); booking is not generally necessary. Many tent sites are not equipped with power points.

Facilities for disabled persons are available at Berg-en-dal, Crocodile Bridge, Pretoriuskop, Lower Sabie, Skukuza, Satara, Olifants, Letaba, Mopani, Shingwedzi and Tamboti. The website for **SAN Parks** (www .parks-sa.co.za) has an excellent overview of conditions at each camp for disabled travellers, and is well worth browsing when planning your travels.

Note that bookings for all rest camps should be made through central reservations, or at one of the local tourist offices that take Kruger bookings (see p443); the numbers listed in this section are for specific rest camp information and emergencies only.

Berg-en-dal (☎ 735 6106) A medium-sized camp near Malelane Gate, and one of the most modern, with bungalows and family cottages sleeping up to six people. It's laid out in attractive natural bush landscape on the banks of the Matjulu River, about 5km from a water hole popular with rhinos. There's a visitors centre and nature trails. About 9km away on the southern border of Kruger, is the small and – except for its size – not particularly appealing **Malelane satellite camp**. Other than camping and a few bungalows, there are no facilities. If you want to stay here, you'll need to register at Malelane Gate.

Crocodile Bridge (☎ 735 6012) This small camp is near the Crocodile River just in from Crocodile Bridge Gate, and is a good choice if you've arrived in Kruger too late to drive further into the park. There are crocodile and hippo pools a few kilometres away, and zebras, impalas, buffaloes and wildebeests in the surrounding acacia. Accommodation is in bungalows or a safari tent. There is no restaurant, and diesel fuel is not available.

Pretoriuskop (☎ 735 5128) This is Kruger's oldest camp, and one of its largest. It's located near Numbi Gate, in higher country than other places in the park, and is thus a bit cooler in summer. Accommodation is in huts, bungalows, and several large cottages sleeping between six and nine people. The surrounding country is attractive, with granite outcrops, and is frequented by white rhinos. The camp has an old-style charm and includes a natural rock swimming pool that is popular with kids.

Lower Sabie (☎ 735 6056) This medium-sized camp, about one hour (35km) from Crocodile Bridge Gate, has a beautiful setting in a prime wildlife-viewing region. It overlooks a dam on the Sabie River that attracts many animals, and elephants, buffaloes, cheetahs and rhinos are often seen in the surrounding country. For sleeping, there's a good selection of huts, safari tents, bungalows and cottages. Campsites here have individual water taps.

Skukuza (☎ 735 4152) On the Sabie River, Skukuza is the main camp in Kruger, with facilities similar to those in a small town. There's a bank with an ATM, an Automobile Association (AA) workshop garage, a doctor, a library, the police, a post office, a small museum and a helpful information centre. There's also an extensive range of accommodation, including luxury bungalows and various cottages. Apart from its size, the main drawbacks are the slightly sanitised feel and the campsites, which are distinctly average.

Orpen (☎ 735 6355) Near Orpen Gate, this is a small, attractive camp with a nearby water hole that attracts wildlife. There's no restaurant; cooking facilities are shared and no utensils are provided. Some accommodation doesn't have electricity, so bring a torch. There are two satellite camps near Orpen. **Maroela**, 4km northeast, has basic camp sites with power points. The appealing **Tamboti**, 4km east, has nice safari tents, complete with wildlife wandering around outside. Some of the tents have private bathrooms and kitchens, and two have wheelchair access ramps. For both Maroela and Tamboti, you'll need to check in at Orpen.

Satara (☎ 735 6306) East of Orpen Gate, Satara is situated in an area of flat and fertile plains that attracts large numbers of grazing animals. While its setting isn't that appealing (mainly because of the lack of any raised viewpoints), it has the highest lion population in the entire park. There are several water holes; you can see one of them from the terrace of the pleasant self-serve restaurant. Satara is also Kruger's second-largest camp, with a full range of facilities. About 45km north of Satara near the Olifants River is **Balule satellite camp**, with camping and several rustic three-person huts. It's wonderfully quiet and atmospheric, and at night you'll almost certainly hear hippos grunting in the river. There's no electricity (kerosene lanterns are available at the camp, but bring a torch). There's a large freezer and a stove, but otherwise, you'll need to bring everything in with you, including cooking utensils. Although Balule is much closer to Olifants camp (11km further north), check-in must be done through Satara.

Olifants (☎ 735 6606) This camp has a fantastic position on the bluff high above the Olifants River and offers spectacular views. From the camp you can see elephants, hippos and many other animals as they come down to the river 100m below. Much of the camp is terraced and some of the huts are perched on the edge of the cliffs. There are no camp sites at Olifants, but it's possible to camp at nearby Balule satellite camp (p448).

Letaba (☎ 735 6636) About 20km to the north, Letaba has excellent views over a wide bend of the Letaba River. It's an attractive camp with lots of shade, trees and grassy camp sites. There are plenty of animals, especially in winter, and a restaurant overlooking the river. The Elephant Hall museum here focuses on the elephant and includes mounted tusks of the big bulls (Mafunyane, Dzombo, Shingwedzi and Shawu) that have died in the park. There are sections on poaching, the illegal ivory trade, geomorphology and biology, plus descriptions of elephant habits.

Mopani (☎ 735 6536) This good, modern rest camp is on the edge of the Pioneer Dam, 45km north of Letaba. The buildings are all of natural materials and thatch, and the overall impression is highly aesthetic. There are no camp sites, but about 3km away is **Shipandani** – a 'sleepover' hide with mattresses, bed linens, a modest collection of cooking utensils and toilet facilities. It can take up to six people.

Shingwedzi (☎ 735 6806) The large Shingwedzi is an old-style place in the northern section of the park, with many huts and cottages arranged in circles and shaded by tall mopani trees and palms. A restaurant overlooks the Shingwedzi River and there's a swimming pool. There are excellent drives in the vicinity.

Punda Maria (☎ 735 6873) The northernmost rest camp, Punda Maria is in sandveld (dry, sandy belt) country by Dimbo Mountain. It's a long-established place with an agreeable wilderness ambience. The area's ecology is fascinating and supports a wide range of animals, including lions and elephants.

Bushveld Camps

Bushveld camps are an excellent option if you want more of a wilderness experience than is possible at the rest camps, and are equipped for self-catering. Most are reasonably close to a rest camp where supplies can be bought. All have solar power, so electrical appliances other than lights, fans and fridges cannot be used. Bookings (made through central reservations or at one of the local tourist offices that take Kruger bookings, see p443) are essential. At most of the bushveld camps, it's possible to arrange night drives and bush walks. Accommodation is in cottages, all with private bathroom, most of which sleep up to six people. Prices range from R675 to R795 for four people, plus R170 per additional person.

Bateleur If you make it to northern Kruger, it's well worth staying a few nights here. It's the smallest and nicest of the bushveld camps – rustic but comfortable, with a good setting, a wilderness ambience and a small pan on the edge of the camp, plus two dams nearby which offer some excellent bird-watching. It's in northern Kruger, about 35km southwest of Shingwedzi.

Biyamiti On the southern border of Kruger, between Malelane and Crocodile Bridge Gates, in an easily accessed area known for its lions and other representatives of the Big Five. It's about twice as large as Bateleur, accommodating up to 70 people in thatched cottages with a pleasant, semipampered feel.

Talamati This lies about 30km southeast of Orpen Gate on the N'waswitsontso River in an exceptionally wildlife-rich area. It has two- and four-person cottages with basic kitchen facilities, plus a more luxurious four-person cottage, and several hides overlooking the nearby water hole.

Shimuwini This camp is on the Letaba River, 50km northeast of Phalaborwa Gate in a riverine setting that's ideal for bird-watching. It has a bird hide overlooking the dam, and accommodation in two- to six-person cottages.

Sirheni In a lightly wooded area about 40km northwest of Shingwedzi in Kruger's far north, Sirheni, like Shimuwini, is on a dam. It's an excellent spot for birding, with the added appeal of more of a wilderness atmosphere. It also offers a good population of antelopes, and the chance to see lion, leopard and cheetah.

Bush Lodges

Kruger's two bush lodges are set off on their own and must be reserved in their entirety. The idea is to have as remote a bush experience as possible, in the privacy of your own group. There are no facilities other than equipped kitchens, braai areas and bedding; you'll need to bring all supplies in with you. For both lodges, you need to make reservations before arrival, either through central reservations (p443), or at any Kruger gate or rest camp. Neither lodge has electricity, other than solar power for lights and fans.

Roodewal (up to 4 people R1350, per additional person R280) About 28km northeast of Orpen Gate, Roodewal takes up to 19 people in a cottage and several bungalows.

Boulders (up to 4 people R1500, per additional person R280) About 23km southwest of Mopani rest camp, Boulders takes up to 12 people in six rooms.

Private Concessions

Kruger's private concessions are all located in wildlife-rich areas of the park and offer the chance to go on safari while enjoying all the amenities. Accommodation (in luxury tents or lodges) should be booked directly with the relevant concession operator. (There are also links from the SAN Parks website.) Prices start around R4500 per person. They include the following:

Jock Safari Lodge (☎ 735 5200; www.jocksafarilodge .com) In southern Kruger, about halfway between Bergen-dal and Skukuza rest camps.

Singita Lebombo Lodge (see p452)

Rhino Post Camp (☎ 011-467 1886; www.zulunet.co .za) Near Skukuza rest camp on the Mutlumuvi River.

Lukimbi Safari Lodge (☎ 011-888 3713; www .lukimbi.com) Near the southern border of the park, and just southwest of Biyamiti bushveld camp.

GETTING THERE & AROUND
Air

SAAirlink (☎ 011-978 1111; www.saairlink.co.za) has daily flights linking both Jo'burg and Cape Town with Mpumalanga Kruger International Airport (MKIA) near Nelspruit (for Numbi, Malelane and Crocodile Bridge Gates), and with Kruger Park Gateway Airport in Phalaborwa (2km from Phalaborwa Gate). Sample fares and flight times: Jo'burg to Phalaborwa (R1100 one-way, one hour); Jo'burg to MKIA (R1000, one hour); Cape Town to MKIA (R2000, 2¼ hours). SAAirlink also has daily flights connecting Cape Town with Hoedspruit (for Orpen Gate) via Sun City (R2200, 3¼ hours).

South African Airways (SAA; ☎ 0860 359 722, 011-978 1111; www.flysaa.com) flies six times weekly between Durban and MKIA (R1300, 1½ hours), while **South African Express** (☎ 011-978 5577; www.saexpress.co.za) flies daily between Jo'burg and Hoedspruit Eastgate Airport (R1200, 1½ hours), with connections to Cape Town. **Nationwide Airlines** (☎ 0861 737 737, 011-327 3000; www.nationwideair.co.za) is another airline to check, with several flights weekly connecting both Cape Town and Jo'burg with MKIA.

Bus & Minibus Taxi

For most visitors, Nelspruit is the most convenient large town near Kruger, and is well served by bus and minibus taxi to and from Jo'burg (see p436). Numbi Gate is about 50km away, and Malelane Gate about 65km away. Phalaborwa, in the north on the edge of Kruger, is being increasingly promoted as a gateway for northern Kruger. It is served by regular bus services to/from Jo'burg and elsewhere in South Africa (see p474). Hoedspruit is another possible hub, with reasonable bus connections to elsewhere in South Africa (see p474). It's also the most convenient gateway for many of the private reserves bordering Kruger, and an easy 70km drive from the park's Orpen Gate. From the Venda region in Limpopo province, minibus taxis run close to the Punda Maria Gate.

Car

Skukuza rest camp is 500km from Jo'burg (six hours); Punda Maria is about 620km from Jo'burg (eight hours). **Avis** (☎ 735 5651; www.avis.co.za) has a branch at Skukuza, and there is car rental from the Nelspruit, Hoedspruit and Phalaborwa airports.

Most visitors drive themselves around the park, and this is the best way to experience Kruger. If you're running low on funds, hiring a car between three or four people for a few days is relatively cheap (see p600).

Organised Tours

At the budget level, the best places to contact are the backpacker lodges in Hazyview (p431) and Nelspruit (p434), all of which can organise tours into Kruger from about R450 per day, plus entry fees and meals. Another good budget option is **African Routes** (☎ 031-563 5080; www.africanroutes.co.za; see p605), which also includes Swaziland and the Drakensberg in its Kruger itineraries.

If you're on a tight schedule, and want to connect directly from Jo'burg or Cape Town, **SA Airlink Tours** (www.airlinktours.com) runs various flight-accommodation packages between Jo'burg and central Kruger.

Other operators include **Wildlife Safaris** (www.wildlifesaf.co.za), which has four-day panorama tours taking in the Blyde River and Kruger for R4214 per person, including half board; **Bundu Safari Company** (☎ 011-675 0767; www.bundusafaris.co.za; see p605), which offers four-day Kruger tours for about R2500 per person; and many of the other tour operators listed in the Transport chapter (p605), most of which organise Kruger itineraries.

Train

The *Komati* (p605) runs from Jo'burg via Nelspruit to Komatipoort (1st/2nd/economy class R185/130/70), which is about 12km from Kruger's Crocodile Bridge Gate.

PRIVATE GAME RESERVES

Spreading over a vast lowveld area just west of Kruger is a string of private reserves that offer comparable wildlife-watching to what you'll experience in the park. The main reserves – Sabie Sand, Manyeleti and Timbavati – directly border Kruger (with no fences), and the same Big Five populations that roam the park are also at home here.

Most lodges and camps in the private reserves are pricey – from around R2000 to over R6000 per person sharing, all-inclusive. However, together with the handful of new private concessions operating within the park's boundaries (see p405), the private reserves offer among Africa's best opportunities for safari connoisseurs, and are the place to go for those who want to experience the bush in the lap of luxury.

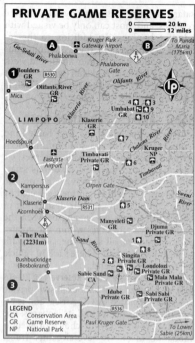

PRIVATE GAME RESERVES

LEGEND	
CA	Conservation Area
GR	Game Reserve
NP	National Park

SLEEPING	🏠 (pp452-3)
Chitwa Chitwa Private Game Lodges	1 B3
Exeter Private Game Lodges	2 B3
Gomo Gomo	3 B1
Inkwazi Bush Camp	4 B1
Khoka Moya	5 B2
Ngala	6 B2
Ngala	7 B2
Nkorho Bush Lodge	8 B3
Tanda Tula	9 B1
Umlani Bush Camp	10 B1

If your budget permits, it's also worth considering the private reserves as a complement to spending a few nights in the park. The rangers can be a wealth of knowledge, and because of the personalised safari attention, can train you in the art of wildlife-watching before you head to Kruger for a self-guided trip. The major reserves and a few of their camps are described following. There are many more lodges and dozens of operators handling tours in this area. Before booking, it's well worth browsing some of the websites, and talking to a travel agent or tour operator (including some of those listed on p605) to help you find a good deal. Note that even if you arrive with your own vehicle, self-drive safaris aren't permitted in any of the private reserves, and most can only be visited with advance booking. In addition to the reserves described here, there are numerous other smaller ones further north and west, including Klaserie, Makalali (which doesn't share any borders with Kruger) and Balule (also no borders with Kruger).

SABIE SAND CONSERVATION AREA

Within the borders of the large Sabie Sand Conservation Area are some of Southern Africa's best-known private reserves, as well as some of the most luxurious safari lodges and best wildlife-viewing on the continent. The area is routinely selected by safari connoisseurs as their destination of choice. As there's no fencing between the various private reserves within the greater Sabie Sand area, all share the same wealth of birds and animals. There's a R50 vehicle fee to enter Sabie Sand.

Londolozi Private Game Reserve (☎ 011-809 4300; www.londolozi.com) This exclusive private reserve is operated by CC Africa, and is renowned for its luxury and its leopards. For sleeping, you have your choice of accommodation in one of several camps (most notable is the intimate Tree Camp), or in an equally comfortable lodge – all with excellent settings along the Sand River. Londolozi describes itself as 'unashamedly exclusive', and is the place to go if you want a five-star-plus experience in the bush, combined with excellent wildlife-watching.

Singita Private Game Reserve (☎ 021-683 3424; www.singita.co.za) Singita has been distinguished by the top-end travel industry as one of the best resorts in Africa, and one of the world's top travel destinations. Its Lebombo Lodge draws most of the attention, with a superb riverine location, an excess of amenities and impeccable service. It's operated as a private concession within Kruger's boundaries, on the park's western edge, southeast of Satara rest camp.

Chitwa Chitwa Private Game Lodges (☎ 011-883-1354; www.chitwa.co.za) Chitwa Chitwa suffers a bit in the shadows of Londolozi and Singita, but offers good value, especially at its beautiful, waterside Game Lodge.

Nkorho Bush Lodge (☎ 735 5367; www.nkorho .com) In the northern part of Sabie Sand, this is one of the more moderately priced lodges, with comfortable thatched chalets

set around grassy grounds, and a low-key ambience.

Djuma Game Reserve (☎ 735 5118; www.djuma .co.za) Djuma is notable for its straightforward, good-value accommodation. The most intriguing option here is Vuyatela Lodge, where local culture has been incorporated into every aspect of the building. It's an ideal choice if you're interested in learning about local people as well as the local wildlife.

Mala Mala Game Reserve (☎ 011-268 2388; www .malamala.com) Mala Mala competes with Londolozi and Singita for distinction as one of the region's most luxurious reserves, though it's not quite as polished as its two neighbours. Excellent wildlife-viewing compensates, and staff make every effort to ensure you spot the Big Five.

Other places to check out include the following:

Exeter Private Game Lodges (☎ 741 3180, www .exeter-lodges.com) An upscale entity managing several lodges in western and southern Sabie Sand, notably the exclusive Leadwood and Dulini lodges.

Idube Private Game Reserve (☎ 011-888 3713, www.idube.com) Nice and comfortable, without the finesse of some of the other places, but with a more manageable price tag.

Sabi Sabi Private Game Reserve (☎ 011-483 3939; www.sabisabi.com) Known especially for its lions and for its subterranean and ultraluxurious Earth Lodge.

MANYELETI GAME RESERVE

During the apartheid era, Manyeleti was the only game reserve that Blacks were permitted to use. Today, it's the least crowded of the private game reserves, with only a few camps. It's possible to see all the Big Five here, although with somewhat more effort than in Sabie Sands, its neighbour to the south. As compensation, accommodation here is significantly less expensive than in Sabie Sands.

Khoka Moya (Capture the Spirit; ☎ 015-793 1729; all-inclusive s/d R1500/2000) A small place, taking a maximum of 16 people. It's also one of the cheaper places in the private reserves, with accommodation in rustic cabins raised a bit off the ground on stilts.

TIMBAVATI PRIVATE GAME RESERVE

Timbavati was originally known for its white lion population, although it's the yellow versions you'll see today. It's less crowded

Ndebele artist outside homestead

JANE SWEENEY

Main street of Pilgrim's Rest (p427),
Mpumalanga

RICHARD I'ANSON

RICHARD I'ANSON

Firecracker wildflowers in the Blyde
River Canyon Nature Reserve (p429),
Mpumalanga

Blyde River Canyon (p429), Mpumalanga

JANE SWEENEY

CAROL POLICH

Yawning baboon, Kruger National
Park (p440)

Young impala ram, Kruger National Park
(p440)

LUKE HUNTER

Ground hornbill, Kruger National Park (p440)

MITCH REARDON

Olifants River, Kruger National Park (p440)

RICHARD

than Sabie Sand, and its accommodation – while lacking the sumptuous settings of the lodges in Sabie Sand – tends to be more reasonably priced, without foregoing too many amenities. There's a R90 per person conservation fee and R65 vehicle entry fee to pay when entering the reserve.

Tanda Tula (☎ 021-794 6500; www.tandatula.co.za; all-inclusive s/d from R4200/7800) Timbavati's most luxurious option, with cosy safari tents, and a water hole practically at your doorstep. Children under 12 aren't permitted.

Ngala (☎ 011-809 4300; www.ccafrica.com; all-inclusive tent per person sharing R4800, lodge per person sharing R2600-6800) A subdued but luxurious place in a superb location on the border of Kruger, and managed by CC Africa. Accommodation is in your choice of a safari tent or lodge (prices for the lodge vary depending on the season), and comes with all the amenities.

Inkwazi Bush Camp (☎ 015-793 1836; www.inkwazi.co.za; s/d with full board and activities R1170/1740, self-catering with activities R875/1150) A good 'budget' choice, with accommodation in straightforward chalets or tents. It's located on the Nhalaralumi River in northern Timbavati.

Umlani Bushcamp (☎ 012-346 4028; www.umlani.co.za; s/d R1950/3400) A good place if you want to immerse yourself in the bush, with no electricity, and accommodation in simple but comfortable reed bungalows.

Gomo Gomo (☎ 752 3954; www.gomogomo.co.za; s/d R1490/2280) Another of the more moderately priced places, with rustic chalets and tents.

Limpopo

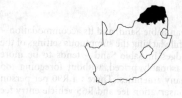

CONTENTS

Somewhat eclipsed by the Kruger National Park, which runs along its eastern border, Limpopo (formerly known as Northern Province) tends not to feature on the standard tourist itinerary, with many travellers only watching it slide past as they head north on the bus to Zimbabwe. But the empty spaces of this remote province, made all the more special by being off the well-trodden tourist circuit, have their own unique appeal, with plenty to satisfy the wannabe pioneer.

Following the N1 highway north, first impressions of Limpopo are of a low, flat sweep, studded with baobab trees and characterised by mile-upon-mile of dusty savannah. The highway, which runs arrow-straight the whole way to Zimbabwe, neatly bisects the province en route and its main towns, Polokwane (Pietersburg) and Makhado (Louis Trichardt), pleasant clusters of neat suburbia that offer welcome reprieve from days on the road.

But there is plenty more to the picture. At Makhado, the road is itself bisected by the lush Soutpansberg range, which suddenly rises out of the plain in a broad, green wave. Here, stunning views and wilderness walks offer a totally different Limpopo experience.

East of the N1, the landscape changes once again, giving way to the tropical fruit farms of the Letaba Valley, the cycad forests that surround the realm of the mystical Rain Queen and the intriguing traditional homeland of the Venda people. The western section of the province boasts the beautiful Waterberg range and a clutch of wildlife parks.

Tourist offices divide Limpopo into four distinct geographical areas: Capricorn in the south, Bushveld in the west, Valley of the Olifants in the east, and Soutpansberg in the north. You can pick up useful brochures on each from tourist offices across the province.

LIMPOPO

HIGHLIGHTS

- Soaking up the prehistory in the **Vhembe Dongola National Park** (p466)
- Hiking through the lush green peaks of the **Soutpansberg range** (p465)
- Saddling up the horses for a ride through the hills of **Haenertsburg** (p469)
- Munching through the mangoes in the fruit-growing centre of **Tzaneen** (p470)
- Skirting around the sacred sites of the mysterious **Venda Region** (p466)
- Getting drenched with the Rain Queen in **GaModjadji** (p472)

■ POPULATION: 5,482,000   ■ AREA: 123,910 SQ KM

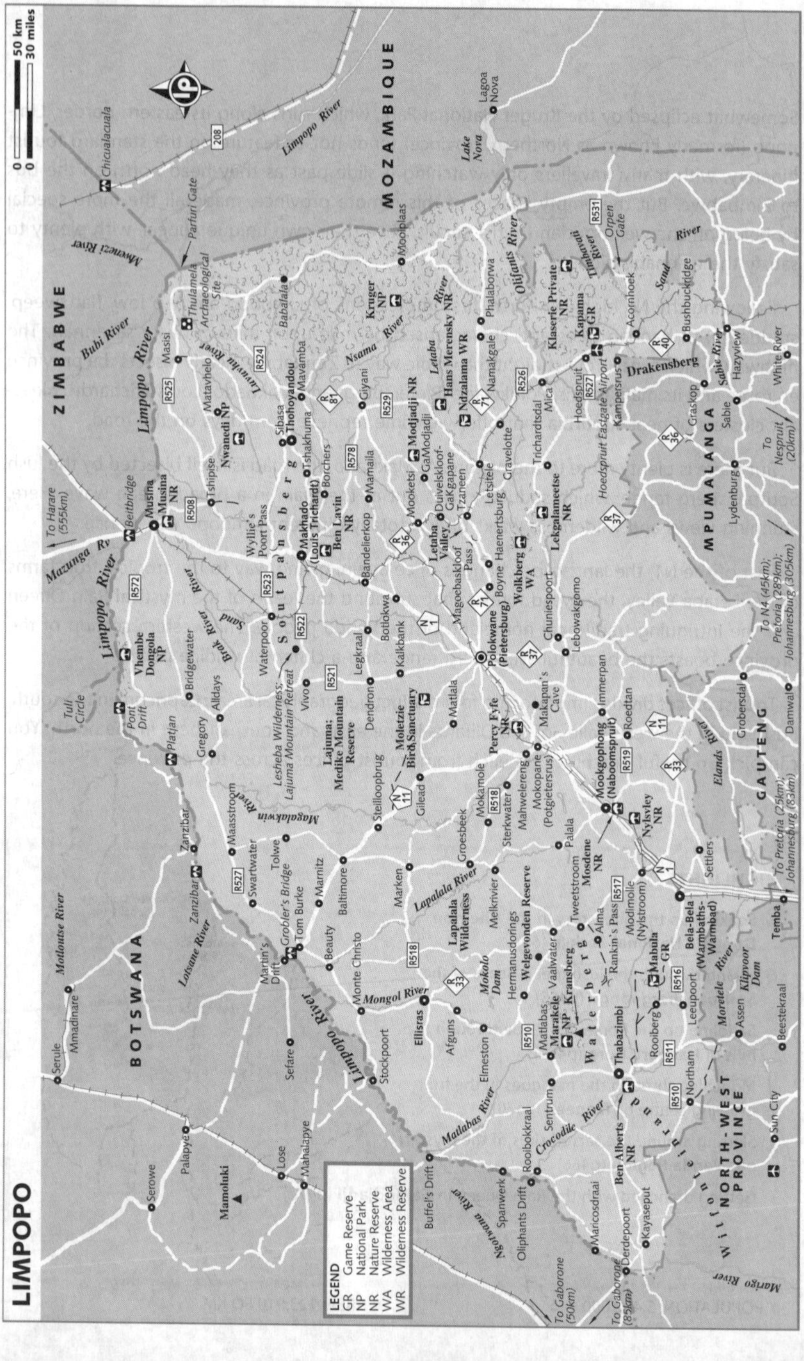

LIMPOPO
LEGEND
GR Game Reserve
NP National Park
NR Nature Reserve
WA Wilderness Area
WR Wilderness Reserve
0 50 km
0 30 miles
ZIMBABWE
MOZAMBIQUE
BOTSWANA
MPUMALANGA
GAUTENG
NORTH-WEST PROVINCE
Limpopo River
Mwenezi River
Bubi River
Chicualacuala
208
Parfuri Gate
Thulamela Archaeological Site
Kruger NP
Lake Nova
Lagoa Nova
Mooiplaas
Babalala
Masisi
Matavhelo
Luvuvhu River
R524
Mavamba
Sibasa
Thohoyandou
Tshakhuma
Nwanedi NP
Tshipise
Musina
Musina NR
Beitbridge
To Harare (555km)
Mazunga Rv
R508
R572
R525
Vhembe Dongola NP
Pont Drift
Tuli Circle
Platjan
Gregory
Alldays
Bridgewater
Brak River
Sand River
Waterpoor
R523
Wyllie's Poort Pass
Soutpansberg
Makhado (Louis Trichardt)
Ben Lavin NR
Borchers
R578
Mamaila
Giyani
R81
R529
Nsama River
Modjadji NR
GaModjadji
Mooketsi
Duivelskloof-GaKgapane
Tzaneen
Letaba Valley
Magoebaskloof Pass
Haenertsburg
Letsitele
Gravelotte
Hans Merensky NR
Ndzalama WR
Letaba River
R71
Namakgale
Phalaborwa
Olifants River
Mica
R526
Trichardtsdal
Klaserie Private NR
Kapama GR
Timbavati River
Orpen Gate
R531
Hoedspruit
R527
Hoedspruit Eastgate Airport
Kampersrus
Acornhoek
Sand River
Bushbuckridge
R40
Drakensberg
Graskop
R36
Sabie
Sabie River
Hazyview
White River
Lydenburg
To Nelspruit (20km)
To N4 (45km); Pretoria (289km); Johannesburg (305km)
R37
Lekgalameetse NR
Wolkberg WA
Boyne
Chuniespoort
Lebowakgomo
Polokwane (Pietersburg)
N1
R36
Bandelierkop
Bandelierkop
Botlokwa
Kalkbank
Legkraal
Dendron
Vivo
R521
R522
Lesheba Wilderness; Lajuma Mountain Retreat
Lajuma: Medike Mountain Reserve
Moletzie Bird Sanctuary
Matlala
Percy Fyfe NR
Makapan's Cave
Immerpan
Roedtan
N11
Mookgophong (Naboomspruit)
R519
R33
Elands River
Grobersdal
Damwal
Mokopane (Potgietersrus)
Mahwelereng
Sterkwater
R518
Mokamole
Gilead
Steilloopbrug
N11
Magalakwin River
Maasstroom
Zanzibar
Swartwater
R527
Tolwe
Marnitz
Baltimore
Marken
Groesbeek
Lapalala River
Lapalala Wilderness
Melkrivier
Palala
Mosdene NR
Nylsvley NR
Modimolle (Nylstroom)
Settlers
Bela-Bela (Warmbaths-Warmbad)
To Pretoria (25km); Johannesburg (83km)
Temba
Tweetstroom
Alma
Rankin's Pass
Waterberg
Welgevonden Reserve
Hermanusdorings
Vaalwater
Mokolo Dam
Mahula GR
R516
Leeupoort
Moretele River
Klipvoor Dam
Assen
Beestekraal
Grobler's Bridge
Tom Burke
Martin's Drift
Lotsane River
Motloutse River
Mmadinare
Serule
Beauty
Monte Christo
R518
R33
Mongol River
Ellisras
Afguns
Elmeston
Stockpoort
Sefare
Marakele NP
Kransberg
Matlabas
R510
Thabazimbi
Rooiberg
R511
Northam
R510
Sentrum
Crocodile River
Matlabas River
Rooibokkraal
Ben Alberts NR
Witfonteinrand
Sun City
Buffel's Drift
Ngotwane River
Spanwerk
Oliphants Drift
Maricosdraai
Derdepoort
Kayaseput
Marigo River
To Gaborone (50km)
To Gaborone (85km)
Mamoluki
Serowe
Palapye
Lose
Mahalapye

LIMPOPO

HISTORY

After the battlefields of KwaZulu-Natal and the antiapartheid struggle of Soweto, it is easy to overlook Limpopo's history. But the province has a rich past that spans millions of years. Makapan's Caves, near Mokopane, offered up an archaeological record stretching back to protohuman times – including human tools from more than 500,000 years ago – while Mapungubwe, in the Vhembe Dongola National Park, was at the heart of one of Africa's most technologically advanced African civilisations, once holding sway over an area of 30,000 sq km and enjoying its heyday in the 8th and 9th centuries.

The Voortrekkers made this region home in the mid-19th century, establishing their base in Pietersburg (now Polokwane) in 1886. Conflict with the local Ndebele people – one clash, in 1854, took place at Makapan's Caves – marked a period of resistance against the settlers, but Northern Province, as it later became known, settled into quiet for much of the 20th century. In recognition of its distinctly African origins, many of the region's towns have been renamed in recent years and the name of the province was itself changed to Limpopo at the turn of the 21st century.

CLIMATE

In general, Limpopo is hot and dry and gets steadily hotter as you head north. The high peaks of the Soutpansberg range provide cooler, damper conditions and the rolling hills of the Letaba Valley and Venda regions also get more than their fair share of mist and drizzle.

NATIONAL PARKS & RESERVES

The **Limpopo Tourism and Parks Board** (☎ 015-290 7300; www.limpopotourism.org.za; cnr Kerk & Grobler Sts; ☺ 8am-4.30pm Mon-Fri), in Polokwane, provides information on most of the region's parks and reserves. Highlights include the Vhembe Dongola National Park, on the Zimbabwe border. Limpopo is also home to numerous private wildlife reserves. The best of these are contiguous with Kruger National Park, and are covered in that chapter (see p451).

LANGUAGE

English and Afrikaans are widely spoken, but Afrikaans remains the language of choice in most areas.

WARNING

Take precautions against malaria and bilharzia while in Limpopo. For more information, see p609.

GETTING THERE & AROUND

Limpopo is bisected by the excellent N1 highway (a toll road as far as Polokwane), which runs from Johannesburg (Jo'burg) and Pretoria to the Zimbabwe border at Beitbridge. Many of the province's large towns are on this artery and most are connected to Jo'burg and Pretoria via the **Translux** (www.translux.co.za) and **Greyhound** (www.greyhound.co.za) buses which run this way en route to Bulawayo and Harare. The *Bosvelder* train runs an almost identical route, but more slowly. Long-distance buses also link the regional capital, Polokwane, with destinations along the R71, including Tzaneen and Phalaborwa, on the edge of the Kruger National Park. Other destinations can be hard to access without a car, but minibus taxis do link most parts of the province.

Hiring a car is the best way to see Limpopo (most roads are good), but if you want to save some miles, you can also fly from Jo'burg to Polokwane, Phalaborwa or Hoedspruit, near Kruger's Orpen Gate, and hire a car there.

See p596 and individual Getting There & Away sections for more details.

CAPRICORN

The Capricorn region includes little more than Polokwane (Pietersburg), the provincial capital. The tropic of Capricorn crosses the N1 halfway between Polokwane and Makhado (Louis Trichardt).

POLOKWANE (PIETERSBURG)

☎ 015 / pop 140,000

A rather agreeably sedate cluster of suburban streets surrounding a bustling, commercial centre, Polokwane was founded in 1886 by Voortrekkers seeking to escape the usual cocktail of tropical disease and 'hostile natives'. Much of this conflict now seems to have dissipated and if you are wandering through the backstreets of South Africa's safest provincial capital these days, the biggest risk seems to be getting soaked by an overzealous garden sprinkler.

Information

MEDICAL SERVICES & EMERGENCY

Pietersburg Hospital (☎ 015-287 5000; cnr Hospital & Dorp Sts) For medical attention.

Police Station (☎ 015-290 6000; cnr Schoeman & Bodenstein Sts)

MONEY

There are plenty of banks throughout the town. **ABSA** (Landdros Mare St) has an ATM and change facilities.

TOURIST INFORMATION

Limpopo Tourism & Parks Board (☎ 015-290 7300; www.limpopotourism.org.za; cnr Kerk & Grobler Sts; ☉ 8am-4.30pm Mon-Fri) Covers the whole province and offers the useful *Limpopo Explorer* map and *Limpopo Tourist Factfiler* guide.

Polokwane Municipality Local Development Office (☎ 015-290 2010; www.polokwane.org.za; Civic Sq, Landdros Mare St; ☉ 8am-4pm Mon-Fri) Has limited town information.

TRAVEL AGENCIES

Triple K Travel Services (☎ 015-291 5748; info@triple ktravel.co.za; Shop 7, Library Gardens; ☉ 8am-4.30pm Mon-Fri, 8am-noon Sat) Offers bus and flight bookings.

Sights & Activities

Polokwane Game Reserve (☎ 015-290 2331; adult/child/vehicle R9/6/12; ☉ 7am-6.30pm) is one of the largest municipal wildlife reserves in the country, with 21 wildlife species including zebras, giraffes and white rhinos, and a 20km hiking trail. It is south of the town centre in Union Park.

The **Bakone Malapa Northern Sotho Open-Air Museum** (☎ 295 2432; adult/child R3/1.50; ☉ 8am-12.30pm & 1.30-3.30pm), 9km southeast of Polo-

kwane on the R37 to Chuniespoort, is devoted to northern Sotho culture and includes an authentic 'living' village. There are archaeological remains and paintings dating back to AD 1000 and there's evidence of Ndebele iron and copper smelting.

The **Hugh Exton Photographic Museum** (☎ 290 2180; Civic Sq; admission free; ☉ 9am-3.30pm Mon-Fri) documents the first 50 years of the city's history through 23,000 glass slides. Nearby is the beautiful Victorian-era **Irish House** (cnr Thabo Mbeki & Market Sts).

Sleeping

As is the case in much of Limpopo, accommodation options are concentrated mainly in the mid-range bracket. Those wanting some luxury will be better off at an upmarket guesthouse, while budget travellers will struggle.

Vivaldi Guest House (☎ 295 6162; vivaldi1@mweb .co.za; 2 Voortrekker St; s/d with breakfast R275/340; ✷) Surrounded by a garden filled with rare cycads and with a soundtrack provided by a brace of talking parrots, this tip-top hideaway offers friendly welcomes and oodles of home comforts.

Travellers Lodge (☎ 291 5511; incatrav@worldon line.co.za; 43 Bok St; s/d R225/250; ✷) Despite the name, this smart, self-catering place doesn't cater to the backpacker market. If you want to whip up your own meals, however, this peaceful place is an excellent choice.

Cycad Guest House (☎ 291 2181; mariadp@mweb .co.za; cnr Schoeman & Suid Sts; s/d with breakfast R330/420; ✷) Best filed in the drawer marked 'motel-style', this glossy, modern place falls on the practical side of the functional/cosy divide, earning its gold stars for cleanliness and slick service.

Plumtree Lodge (☎ 295 6153; plumtree@pixie.co .za; 138 Marshall St; s/d with breakfast R330/435; ✷ ▣) The crowds vote with their feet at this busy little place, where rooms are in twee bungalows and all the couch potato creature comforts come as standard.

Polokwane Game Reserve (☎ 290 2331) The reserve has camping (R45 per tent) and two-bed chalets (R114).

Other recommendations:

Holiday Inn Garden Court (☎ 291 2030; higcpolokw ane@southernsun.com; Thabo Mbeki St; s/d with breakfast R410/566; ✷ ▣) For the smartest, business-style beds in town.

Northern Star (☎ /fax 295 8980; 46 Landdros Mare St; s/d R150/200) For cheap, central sleeps.

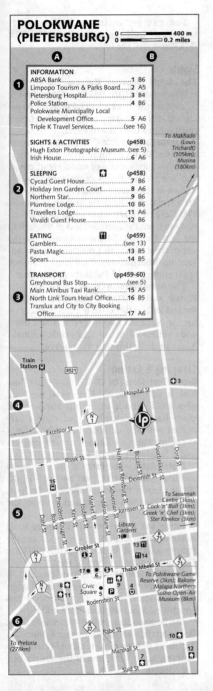

Eating & Entertainment

You can find all the usual takeaways in Library Gardens, but the Savannah Centre on Grobler St offers the widest selection of steak-based eats.

Cock 'n' Bull (☎ 296 0961; Savannah Centre; mains R30-70; ☻ lunch & dinner; ✖) This pub-style offering serves up steaks the size of a springbok's thighs in yee-haa surrounds. There's big-screen sport and ice-cold beer to wash away the indigestion, and outdoor seating for those who prefer their meat *al fresco*.

Greek 'n' Chef (☎ 296 0662; Savannah Centre; mains R25-65; ☻ lunch & dinner; ✖) It's not all that Greek, but there's some fine rump on offer and a good selection of seafood and pastas. Haloumi and calamari bring a flick of Mediterranean flavour.

Spears (☎ 295 8146; Checkers Centre; Hans Van Rensburg St; mains R25-65; ☻ lunch & dinner; ✖) This lively place brings a little more Middle American razzle-dazzle to the veld, with cow-print seating, meat feasts and karaoke on a Saturday.

Pasta Magic (☎ 291 1770; 1st fl, Palm Centre, Grobler St; mains R20-50; ☻ breakfast, lunch & dinner; ✖) Italian eats and good old fish and chips (you may see either being eaten for breakfast) are whipped up in this central eatery.

Gamblers (☎ 291 1890; 1st fl, Palm Centre, Grobler St) This saloon-style drinking den keeps the beer flowing until the last person's standing. At weekends, there's plenty of action involving booze, singing and banter.

Ster Kinekor (☎ 0860 300 222; Savannah Centre) Catch all the latest Hollywood flicks at this cinema.

Getting There & Away

AIR

SAAirlink (☎ 288 0166; www.saairlink.co.za), with offices at the airport, flies daily to/from Jo'burg (R1145 one-way).

BUS

Translux (☎ 295 5548; www.translux.co.za; cnr Joubert & Thabo Mbeki Sts) runs services to Pretoria (R120, 3½ hours), Jo'burg (R130, 4½ hours), Harare (R400, 12 hours) and Lusaka (R400, 24 hours). It also runs the cheaper **City to City** buses, which serve a number of smaller towns.

Greyhound (☎ 011-276 8500; www.greyhound.co.za) links Polokwane with Jo'burg (R140, 4½ hours) and Harare (R265, 12 hours). There isn't an office in town, but you can book through Triple K Travel Services (p458). Buses stop on Civic Sq.

North Link Tours (☎ 291 1867; 13 Library Gardens, Hans Van Rensburg St) runs daily (10am) buses between Polokwane and Jo'burg. They stop at Mokopane (R25, 40 minutes), Mookgophong (R35, 1¼ hours), Pretoria (R80, 3½ hours) and Jo'burg (R100, 4½ hours). Buses depart from outside Library Gardens.

MINIBUS TAXI

The main minibus taxi rank is on the corner of President Kruger and Devenish Sts. Destinations and fares from Polokwane include Thohoyandou (R25, 2½ hours), Makhado (R16, 1¼ hours) and Jo'burg (R75, five hours).

TRAIN

The *Bosvelder* (☎ 086-000 8888) passes through Polokwane daily (except Saturday) en-route between Jo'burg and Musina. Fares include: Jo'burg (1st/2nd class R110/75, eight hours), Makhado (1st/2nd class R70/40, four hours) and Musina (1st/2nd class R100/70, 7¼ hours).

BUSHVELD

The Bushveld region occupies the southwestern section of the province and is flat, dry and the most typical of South African savannah. It includes a string of towns along the N1, including Mokopane (Potgietersrus), Mookgophong (Naboomspruit) and Modimolle (Nylstroom), as well as the holiday resort of Bela-Bela (Warmbaths). West of the N1, the bushveld turns into the rolling mountains and scenic valleys of the Waterberg Range.

MOKOPANE (POTGIETERSRUS) & AROUND

☎ 015 / pop 100,000

This conservative town (they all seem to be up this way), 227km north of Pretoria, was settled early by Voortrekkers, not without resistance from the people already living there.

The **Bosveld Publicity Association** (☎ 491 8458; www.mogalakwena.org.za; 97 Thabo Mbeki Dr; ☺ 7.30am-4.30pm Mon-Fri, 9am-noon Sat) is on the R101 and has plenty of local information.

You can get online at **PostNet** (☎ 491 1317; Shoprite Centre, Thabo Mbeki Dr; per 15min R10; ☺ 8.30am-4.30pm Mon-Fri).

Sights

The **Arend Dieperink Museum** (☎ 491 8458; adult/student/child R3/1/1; ☺ 7.30am-4.30pm Mon-Fri), located at the back of the Publicity Association, tells the story of the local people's resistance to the Voortrekkers.

Makapan's Caves (☎ 491 8458; sabek@mub.co.za; adult/student R25/15), 23km northeast of town, is a palaeontological site of world significance, and has yielded bones of an early human, known as *Australopithecus africanus*, radiocarbon-dated to be three million years old. The Cave of Hearths records human development from the Early Stone Age through to the Iron Age. In 1854, the caves were also the site of chief Makapan's resistance to the advancing Voortrekkers. You must pre-book visits at the Bosveld Publicity Association.

The **Game Breeding Centre** (☎ 491 4314; Thabo Mbeki Dr; adult/child R12/6; ☺ 8am-3pm Mon-Fri, 8am-4pm Sat & Sun), on the R101, is a breeding centre for the National Zoo in Pretoria and has a wide variety of native and exotic animals. You can drive through the reserve.

Sleeping & Eating

Koos Se Tonteldoos (☎ 491 4317, 082-979 0833; Thabo Mbeki Dr; s/d R180/250; ☒) Housed at the back of a small antique store, this atmospheric place has individually styled rooms furnished with the choicest bric-a-brac from the shop. There's a kitchen for self-caterers and a braai in the yard out the back.

Protea Hotel – The Park (☎ 491 3101; ppark@mweb.co.za; Thabo Mbeki Dr; r with breakfast R455; ☒ ☒) It's hardly the embodiment of glamour, but this business-style option is about the plushest choice in town.

Lonely Oak Lodge (☎ 491 4563; Hooge St; s/d including breakfast R225/325) It's a touch on the frumpy side, but the rooms in this place are OK, in a functional kind of way.

Oaks Pub & Grill (☎ 491 4355; Hooge St; mains R25-55; ☺ lunch & dinner) Adjoining Lonely Oak Lodge, this dark diner offers lively, bar-style eats (read: steaks and seafood) until midnight.

San Domingo Spur (☎ 491 4500; Shoprite Centre, Thabo Mbeki Dr; mains R20-60; ☺ lunch & dinner; ☒) Yep, it's a perennially predictable chain restaurant, but it's still one of the town's better options.

Getting There & Away

Translux and **City to City** (☎ 491 8457; www.trans lux.co.za; Thabo Mbeki Dr), next to the Wimpy res- taurant, have buses to Polokwane (R45, one hour) and Jo'burg (R85, three hours).

Northern Link (☎ 491 4124; Thabo Mbeki Dr) buses run to Polokwane (R25, one hour) and Jo'burg (R85, three hours). You can buy tickets from Oasis Lodge Hotel on the main road through town – they stop here too.

Polokwane to Mokopane costs about R20 in a minibus taxi.

MOOKGOPHONG (NABOOMSPRUIT) & AROUND

☎ 014

Still plain old 'Naboom' to its Afrikaans residents, this innocuous little town sits at the hub of a rich agricultural area. Conser- vative, small-town attitudes prevail, but the local, home-distilled brandy (mampoer) in- jects a little life come the weekend.

You can get some **tourist information** (☎ 743 1111; Louis Trichardt St; ☼ 9am-4pm Mon-Fri) from the municipality offices by the old locomotive.

The 3000-hectare **Nylsvley Nature Reserve** (☎ 743 1074; adult/child/vehicle R15/7.50/7; ☼ 6am- 6pm), 20km south of Naboom, is one of the country's best places to see birds and has a basic **camp site** (☎ 743 1074; camping R40 per tent). For the reserve, head 13km south on the N1 and turn east on to the road to Boekenhout.

Sleeping

Die Frei Gastehuis (☎ 743 2981; guesthouse@mjvn.co .za; 80 Vierde St; s/d with breakfast R175/350) In an old school villa complete with corrugated iron roof, this guest house has a tropical garden and a big terrace for cocktail sipping. Head up Louis Trichardt St, turn right at the post office, keep going and it's on the left.

Inyathi Game Lodge (☎ 743 2762; www.inyathig amelodge.co.za; tented camps/cottages R120/140 per person; ☟) Giraffes, kudus and zebras stroll through the grounds of this well-equipped lodge. There are four-bed cottages and tented camps (without bedding). Oh, and a pub too.

Getting There & Away

Translux (☎ 015-491 8457; www.translux.co.za) and **North Link Tours** (☎ 015-291 1867) buses stop in town; the fare to Polokwane is R75/35 (1¼ hours) respectively.

Minibus taxis run to Mokopane (R15, 30 minutes).

MODIMOLLE (NYLSTROOM)

☎ 014 / pop 20,000

Modimolle, a small town in cattle coun- try, was named Nylstroom by Voortrekkers who thought they'd found the source of the Nile. After all, the river here seemed to fit the biblical description of the Nile: it was a river, it was in Africa and it had papyrus reeds growing along the banks.

The **Tourism Association** (☎ 717 5211; cnr Kerk & Field Sts; ☼ 9am-5pm Mon-Fri, 9am-noon Sat) pro- vides information at a stand in the library.

Avuxeni Stokkiesdraai Motel & Caravan Park (☎ 717 4005; fax 717 5997; camping R80, r R385) This place, 3km north of Modimolle on the R101 to Mookgophong, has everything for the weary Voortrekker wishing to rest, water the horses, oil the wagon wheels and play putt-putt. You can camp, or stay in the at- tached motel (breakfast is included).

Shangri-La Country Lodge (☎ 718 1600; r R605) This lodge, 10km from the Kranskop toll- gate, has thatched rondavels in a magnificent bush setting – it's perfect for escaping the hustle and bustle of the cities for a few days. It's off the R33 on the Eersbewoond road.

BELA-BELA (WARMBATHS)

☎ 014 / pop 37,200

As close as Limpopo gets to a resort town, Bela-Bela (Warmbaths) has grown on the back of the hot springs discovered by the Tswana in the early 19th century. Around 22,000 litres of the warm stuff bubble out of the earth every hour and there's no shortage of folk from the big cities to soak it up.

Bela-Bela Community Tourism Association (☎ 736 3694; www.belabelatourism.co.za; the Water- front, Old Pretoria Rd; ☼ 8am-5pm Mon-Fri, 9am-2pm Sat) is in the Waterfront development, on the main road into town.

The **hydro spa** (☎ 736 2200; www.aventura.co.za; Voortrekker St; adult/child R40/30; ☼ 7am-4pm & 5- 10pm), at the Aventura Resort, is said to be the second biggest of its kind in the world and certainly sits at the centre of the Bela- Bela universe. Discounted rates are available from 5pm to 10pm (adult/child R25/15).

Sleeping & Eating

Aventura Spa Warmbaths (☎ 736 2200; www.avent ura.co.za; Voortrekker St; camp sites per person R30 plus per tent R65, s/d with breakfast R680/750, 2-bed chalet R560; ☒ ☟) Swimming pool smells pervade every nook and cranny, but the town's headline resort offers comfortable rooms, camping and self-catering, two-bed chalets. Watersports are also on offer.

Elephant Springs Hotel (☎ 736 2101; www.avuxeni.com; 31 Sutter Rd; s/d with breakfast R455/670; 🄿 🄿) A quick stroll from the spa, this is a typical resort-style hotel, with plenty of colour, but not a whole lot of atmosphere.

De Draai Gastehuis (☎ 736 4379, 082-820 0673; s/d with breakfast R165/330) This comfy place offers a refreshing alternative to the resort hotels. It's 10km north of town – if you are coming from the south, turn right at the first set of traffic lights after the bridge (opposite the cinema) and keep going.

There are numerous places to eat at the Waterfront.

O'Hagans (☎ 736 5068; the Waterfront, Old Pretoria Rd; mains R30-60; 🕑 lunch & dinner; 🄿) Bring on the green paint and the Dublin car boot sale bric-a-brac. This Irish theme-pub offers tasty food and decent beer.

Baobab (☎ 736 5136; ABSA Bosveld Kompleks; cnr Marx & Potgeiter Sts; mains R30-70; 🕑 lunch & dinner; 🄿) Between the Waterfront and the spa, this bright and breezy pizzeria cooks up generous pizzas in cheerful surrounds.

Getting There & Away

Translux (☎ 015-295 5548; www.translux.co.za) buses run through Bela-Bela en route between Jo'burg (R90, two hours) and Polokwane (R90, 2½ hours).

Minibus taxis run from behind the cinema on the corner of Marx and Potgeiter Sts to towns in the area including Modimolle (R10, 20 minutes).

THE WATERBERG

The 150km-long Waterberg range, which makes up part of the Bushveld region, stretches from Thabazimbi in the south to the Lapalala River in the northeast. It is a wild and inspirational place, with *sourveld* (a type of grassland) and bushveld etched by rivers. The rolling terrain is ideal for exploring on horseback, and several operators are based here (for some listings, see p569).

Thabazimbi

☎ 014 / pop 10,300
Thabazimbi (Mountain of Iron) is 129km north of Rustenburg on the R510. Nearby is the imposing Kransberg (2100m), the highest peak of the Waterberg.

Ben Alberts Nature Reserve (☎ 777 1670; admission R15; 🕑 6am-6pm), about 7km south of town, has an abundance of wildlife and good wildlife-viewing vantage points. Accommodation in the reserve is in chalets (R170 for two people).

Hotel Kransberg (☎ 777 1588, fax 772 1589; s/d with breakfast R255/330) is a comfortable hotel with the Rhino Restaurant and Buffalo Pub attached. There are also 'economy' rooms (singles/doubles R190/280).

Marakele National Park

This rather isolated **national park** (☎ 014-777 1745; adult/child R60/30; 🕑 7.30am-6pm) is in the heart of the Waterberg, in spectacular mountain country. Elephants, rhinos and many other large wildlife species, apart from lions, are now resident, with many having been relocated from Kruger National Park. The birdlife is prolific and includes the largest colony of the endangered Cape vulture (*Gyps coprotheres*) in the world (800 breeding pairs).

It can be reached from Thabazimbi by tarred road – in the park itself the roads deteriorate markedly. A 4WD is needed to access some of the best trails.

The **booking office** (🕑 from 8am) is on the Thabazimbi–Alma road, 3km from where this road intersects with the Matlabas–Rooiberg road; entry is on the left and is signposted (this last 3km is on a limestone road).

There is four-bed tented accommodation in the **safari camp** (d R500, extras per person R90). These furnished tents, on the banks of the Matlabas River, have a bathroom, and kitchen with refrigerator and stove. There are communal barbecue facilities.

The more rustic **bush camp** (huts R500) has A-frame huts which sleep four, but you must bring your own towels and linen.

Lapalala Wilderness

This 25,600-hectare **wilderness area** (☎ 014-755 4395; 🕑 7am-6pm) is an area of high ecological value, with a number of animals, including black rhinos, white rhinos, zebras, blue wildebeests and several species of antelopes, as well as hippos and crocodiles. More than 270 species of birds have been recorded. Unfortunately, unless you stay here, you can only come as a day visitor to watch the rhino feeding (adult/child R20/10), held Monday to Saturday at 4pm.

Ask the rangers to point out the unusual termite mounds built under layers in the sandstone. It appears that ants have managed to lift the sandstone slabs and build beneath them, earning them the name 'Arnold Schwarzenegger ants'.

Small self-catering bush camps are scattered through the wilderness; accommodation ranges from R135 to R220 per person. There are cooking facilities but you must bring your own supplies. The minimum stay is two nights and there are mid-week specials; book in advance as Lapalala is popular.

The **Rhino Cultural Museum** (☎ 014-755 4428; adult/child R5/2; ☒ 9am-5pm Tue-Sun), by the Melkrivier school, offers a detailed insight into all things rhinoceros.

The Lapalala Wilderness is north of Modimolle, in the heart of the Waterberg. From Modimolle take the R33 to Vaalwater and from there head in the direction of Melkrivier. Take the turn-off to Melkrivier school 40km from Vaalwater, and continue for 25km to Lapalala.

Sleeping

Zeederburg Cottage & Backpackers (☎ 014-755 3538; www.zeederbergs.co.za; camping R30, dm/d R60/150; ☒ ☒) The only backpackers in this area, friendly Zeederburg is located just off the R33, about 2km past Vaalwater (coming from Modimolle) – it's behind the Spar supermarket. It is conveniently situated halfway between Lapalala and Marakele.

SOUTPANSBERG

The Soutpansberg region incorporates the most northern part of South Africa, scraping southern Zimbabwe. The rainforest of the Soutpansberg is strikingly lush compared with the hot, dry lowveld to the north. The N1 towns of Makhado (Louis Trichardt) and Musina are here, as is the ancient Venda region to the east.

MAKHADO (LOUIS TRICHARDT)

☎ 015 / pop 86,000

After the harsh country to their north and south, the lush peaks of the Soutpansberg range provide a much-needed breath of fresh air. What better setting for a town than right at their base? Makhado itself is of limited appeal, but its location makes it an excellent jumping-off point for exploring the nearby mountains, or delving into the Venda region to the east.

Information

The **Soutpansberg Tourist Office** (☎ 516 0040; www.tourismsoutpansberg.co.za; Songozwi St; ☒ 8am-4.30pm Mon-Fri, 8am-noon Sat) is useful. You'll see it as you pass through town on the N1.

The **ABSA** (cnr Songozwi & Krogh Sts) and **First National** (cnr Songozwi & Krogh Sts) banks both have ATMs and change facilities.

PCS Computers (☎ 516 4122; 84 Krogh St; R15 per 30min; ☒ 8am-5pm Mon-Fri, 9am-2pm Sat) offers Internet access.

The **police station** (☎ 519 4300; Krogh St) is at the northern end of Krogh St. **Du Toit Pharmacy** (☎ 516 4072; 13A Songozwi St; ☒ 8.30am-4.30pm Mon-Fri) is near the caravan park.

Activities

The spectacular mountains are the major draw card here, boasting extraordinary diversity of flora and fauna, including 615 of South Africa's 900 bird species. The following operators run tours:

Face Africa (☎ 516 2076; facaf@mweb.co.za; R1200 per day, maximum four)

4 Frontiers (☎ 516 2282; info@fourfrontiers.co.za; R1400 per day, maximum four)

Schoemansdal Environmental Education Centre (☎ 516 4881; sdaleec@lantic.net)

Sleeping

There are several options in Makhado itself, but the best way to soak up the Soutpansberg is to stay in the hills above town – ask tourist information for a map.

Ultimate Guest House (☎ 517 7005; ultimategh@lantic.net; s/d with breakfast R230/330; ☒) With buckets of quirky character and colourful, individually styled rooms, this beautifully remote place prides itself on its convivial atmosphere and infectious bonhomie. It's 10km from the centre – turn left 100m after Mountain View and head 1km along the dirt track (it's on your right).

Tuinhuis (☎ 517 7222, 082-781 7249; s/d with breakfast R225/450; ☒) Further along the same track, this offers more rustic charm, with sweeping views, glossy rooms and fabulously friendly hosts (they even wash your car).

Mountain View Hotel (☎ 517 7031; www.mountainviewhotel.co.za; s/d with breakfast R275/385) This resort-style place, on the road to Musina,

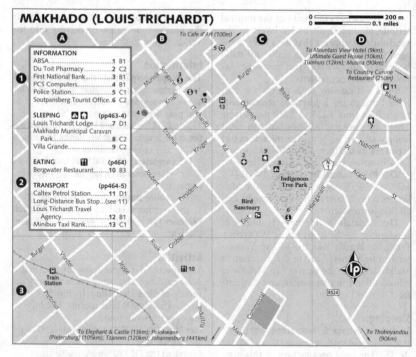

MAKHADO (LOUIS TRICHARDT)

INFORMATION
ABSA..............................1 B1
Du Toit Pharmacy..............2 C2
First National Bank............3 B1
PCS Computers..................4 B1
Police Station..................5 C1
Soutpansberg Tourist Office..6 C2

SLEEPING (pp463-4)
Louis Trichardt Lodge.........7 D1
Makhado Municipal Caravan
Park...............................8 C2
Villa Grande.....................9 C2

EATING (p464)
Bergwater Restaurant.........10 B3

TRANSPORT (pp464-5)
Caltex Petrol Station.........11 D1
Long-Distance Bus Stop...(see 11)
Louis Trichardt Travel
Agency...........................12 B1
Minibus Taxi Rank.............13 C1

---

has clipped gardens, charming staff and the (often empty) Merry Monk pub. The rooms, however, are a little dowdy.

Louis Trichardt Lodge (☎ 516 2222; fax 516 2232; Hlanganani St) This welcoming place on the main road through town is a bit basic, but it has large self-catering rooms that work out very cheap for big groups – you pay R170 for the first person and R60 for everyone thereafter (maximum six).

Other recommendations:

Makhado Municipal Caravan Park (☎ 516 0212; www.caravanparks.co.za/makhado; Grobler St; camp site per person R40) For central camping.

Villa Grande (☎ /fax 516 1161; 104 Grobler St; s/d R200/275) For attractive, smarter sleeps.

Eating

Cafe d'Art (☎ 516 5760; 129 Krogh St; mains R20-50; breakfast, lunch & dinner) Kicking back in the garden listening to the chirruping crickets, or sitting inside among the African paintings and pottery, this is a top spot for lazy breakfasts, lunches and light dinners.

Country Cuisine Restaurant (☎ 516 4452; Koraalbloom St; mains R40-80; lunch & dinner) With big,

social tables for impromptu get-togethers, this simple, African-style place is awash with zebra print and carved wood. Meat feasts come as standard, but they also do buffets. It's behind the Multimark store.

Bergwater Restaurant (☎ 516 0262; 5 Rissik St; mains R30-60; lunch & dinner;) The pub/ restaurant of the Bergwater Hotel has OK food, a pool table and sport on TV – the signs remind you to leave your firearms at home.

Elephant & Castle (☎ 516 5540; mains R20-35; lunch & dinner;) If you're heading south, save your appetite for this cosy inn, 13km out of town on the N1.

Getting There & Away

The **Louis Trichardt Travel Agency** (☎ 516 5042; 8am-1pm & 2-4pm Mon-Fri, 9-11am Sat), down an alley off Burger St, is the local agent for Greyhound and Translux/City to City buses. Most buses linking Makhado with Jo'burg (R175, 5½ hours) and Harare (R375, 11 hours) stop by the Caltex petrol station on the corner of the N1 and Baobab St.

The train station is at the southwestern end of Kruger St. The *Bosvelder* (☎ 086-000 8888) stops here and links Makhado with Jo'burg (1st/2nd class R150/105, 11 hours) and Musina (1st/2nd class R70/40, 3½ hours).

The minibus taxi rank is in the Shoprite supermarket car park off Burger St, a block northeast of Trichardt St. Destinations and fares from Louis Trichardt include Thohoyandou (R20, 1½ hours), Polokwane (R16, 1¼ hours), Beitbridge on the Zimbabwe border (R25, 1½ hours) and Musina (R25, 1¼ hours).

AROUND MAKHADO
Soutpansberg Hiking Trails

The two-day 20.5km **Hanglip Trail** includes a climb up a 1719m peak; it begins at Hanglip forest station. Take precautions against malaria, bilharzia and ticks. Overnight accommodation is in huts and there's a trail fee of R40 per person per day, which includes a good walking map. Contact the **Soutpansberg Tourist Office** (p463) for more information and details of how to make reservations.

SLEEPING

Lesheba Wilderness (☎ 015-593 0076; www.leshe ba.co.za; rondavel/full-board r per person R250/850) Perched in the clouds, this excellent hideaway is based on a Venda-style village, recreated with the help of acclaimed Venda artist, Noria Mabasa. Surrounded by wildlife, including rare brown hyenas and leopards, and with greenery supplied by 340 tree species, the resort offers self-catering accommodation in rondavels, or a full-board option in bedrooms with cosy fireplaces and groovy outdoor showers. It's 36km west of Makhado on the R522.

Lajuma Mountain Retreat (☎ 015-593 0352; www .lajuma.com; bungalow/lodge per person R120/150) The retreat is 7km off the R522 between Makhado and Vivo on the flanks of Letjuma (Soutpansberg's highest peak). This beautiful region is a hiker's paradise and there are archaeological sites, rare animals and a host of outdoor activities. Self-catering accommodation is at a number of sites, from basic bungalows to a more opulent lodge. Meals are available if you twist their arm ahead of arrival. Call ahead to check road conditions.

Ben Lavin Nature Reserve

Well worth a visit, this **reserve** (☎ 015-516 4534; www.satis.co.za/benlavin; adult/child R30/10; ☉ 6am-6pm) covers 2500 hectares. There are

several walking and mountain bike trails. The reserve contains 240 bird species, as well as giraffes, zebras and jackals.

Camping (camp sites per person R40) is available, or there are **huts** (d R215, per additional person R68) and **lodges** (d R265, per additional person R80).

Take the N1 south from Makhado for about 3.5km, then take the Fort Edward turn-off to the left. After a short distance, you'll see the entrance gate on your left.

MUSINA
☎ 015 / pop 20,000

The closest town to the Zimbabwe border, Musina is a hot, dusty settlement, with a frontier feel to it. The town grew around the copper mines, which began operating in 1905 and are still functioning today. Away from the mines the town centre is a sleepy place, but there are moves to promote Musina as a regional centre in its own right, along with nearby tourist attractions such as the excellent Vhembe Dongola National Park.

Information

ABSA (National Rd) Has change facilities and an ATM. It is on the N1 as it passes through the centre of town.
Computer Shop Internet Caf' (☎ 534 1206; National Rd; R15 per 30min; ☉ 8.30am-4.30pm Mon-Fri) North of the ABSA, this place offers sluggish web surfing.
Limpopo Travel (☎ 534 2220; limpopotrav@lantic.net; National Rd; ☉ 8.30am-4.30pm Mon-Fri) Can help with all travel bookings.
Musina Tourism (☎ 534 3500; musinatourism@ hotmail.com; National Rd; ☉ 8.30am-4pm Mon-Fri) In a thatched hut on the way into town on the N1 from Polokwane.

Sights

Giant **baobab** (*Adansonia digitata*) trees characterise the region and it is on the road south of here that you will see some of the grandest – the largest in the country, near Sagole, is 3000 years old! Legend has it that the gods inverted the trees, which used to roam unhindered, so that their roots faced skywards.

Musina Nature Reserve (☎ 534 3235; adult/car R5/7; ☉ 8.30am-4pm Mon-Fri), 5km south of the town off the N1, was established to protect the baobabs. There are animals such as nyalas and kudus. You can camp in **permanent tents** (per person R40), all with reed-enclosed *lapa* areas, or stay in one of the **chalets** (s R120).

LIMPOPO

Sleeping & Eating

Guesthouse Musina B&B (☎ 534 3517, 082-780 0579; Irwin St; s/d with breakfast R350/450; 🐾) The name's hardly punchy, but the rooms, clustered around a butter-yellow villa and full of soft furnishings, are tasteful and spotless.

Ilala Country Lodge (☎ 534 3220; Venetia Mine Rd; s/d R250/300; 🏊) This pleasant lodge has some very nice self-catering units, surrounded by plenty of bush-style hush and big, open spaces. It is 8km from Musina, signposted from the Beitbridge road.

Limpopo River Lodge (☎ 534 0204; National Rd; s/d R115/180, with shared bathroom R100/150; 🐾) Inspiration didn't play a role in the planning of this place, and the décor is rather flaky, but the rooms are fine and mercifully cheap for Limpopo.

Impala Lelie Hotel (☎ 534 0127; National Rd; mains R35-70; 🕐 lunch & dinner; 🐾) Right next to Baobab Caravan Park, this hotel has a dark, raucous sports bar and an upmarket (for Musina) restaurant.

Getting There & Away

The Zimbabwean border at Beitbridge, 14km north of Musina, is open 24 hours. If you are coming from Zimbabwe, there is a large taxi rank on the South African side of the border, 1km from the crossing itself. For detailed information on crossing the border into Zimbabwe, see p591.

BUS

Translux (☎ 295 5548; www.translux.co.za) buses on the Jo'burg–Harare route stop at the Limpopo River Lodge (see previous). Jo'burg costs R190 (7½ hours); Harare costs R300 (10 hours).

MINIBUS TAXI

If you're coming from Zimbabwe and want to take a minibus taxi further south than Musina, catch one at the border as there are many more there than in Musina. Destinations and fares from Musina include Makhado (R25, 1½ hours), Polokwane (R35, 2½ hours) and Jo'burg (R95, 7½ hours). Taxis between the border and Musina cost R10 (20 minutes).

TRAIN

The daily (except Saturday) *Bosvelder* (☎ 086-000 8888) terminates at Musina. It travels (very slowly) to Jo'burg (1st/2nd class R185/125, 14 hours) via Makhado and Polokwane.

VHEMBE DONGOLA NATIONAL PARK

Declared a World Heritage Site in 2003, the **Vhembe Dongola National Park** (☎ 015-534 0102; bernardv@limpopo.co.za; adult/child R30/15; 🕐 6am-6pm) was opened up to the public in mid-2004. Covering 28,000 hectares and incorporating many of South Africa's most significant Iron and Stone Age sites, the park promises to become Limpopo's premier attraction (it is still early days and more animals have yet to be moved in). Expected to boast populations of all of the Big Five, potential for wildlife-spotting will be almost unparalleled – especially if plans to incorporate the park into an 800,000-hectare Trans-Frontier Conservation Area that will stretch into Botswana and Zimbabwe come to fruition.

But the park is as much about history as wildlife. Centred on **Mapungubwe Hill**, the finest Iron Age Site in the country is a rip-roaring field day for archaeology buffs. The hill offers an excellent insight into Africa's 8th-century Zimbabwe civilisation and many of the artefacts will soon be returned to the site for viewing in a museum. Short walks (R30) and fully-catered, three-day trails (R1800) to the major sites are already available.

You can **camp** (R70), or stay in opulent, two-bed **chalets** (R400; 🐾 🏊) with pools and air-con.

The park is at the confluence of the Shashe and Limpopo rivers, north of the Musina to Pontdrift road.

As developments were still being made at the time of writing, call ahead to check the current status of facilities.

VENDA REGION

Perhaps the most enigmatic section of the Soutpansberg region, this is the traditional homeland of the Venda people, who moved to the area from modern-day Zimbabwe at the start of the 18th century. Long neglected under the apartheid regime, the Venda region is a world away from the South Africa of uptown Jo'burg; here even a short diversion from the freeway takes you through an Africa of mist-clad hilltops, dusty streets and mud huts. A land where myth and legend continue to play a major role in everyday life, Venda is peppered

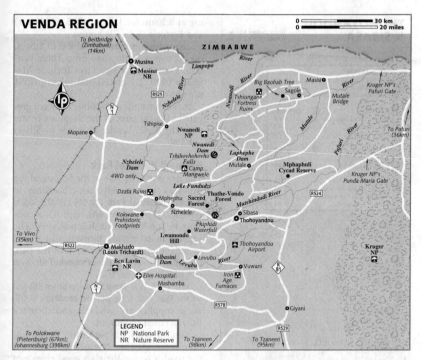

VENDA REGION

0 ____ 30 km
0 ____ 20 miles

(Map labels, reading across the region:)

To Beitbridge (Zimbabwe) (14km)

ZIMBABWE

Musina
Musina NR

Limpopo River

R525

Nzhelele River

Nwanedi River

Big Baobab Tree   Masisi

Tshiungane Fortress Ruins   Sagole

Mutale Bridge   Kruger NP's Pafuri Gate

Mopane

Tshipise

Nwanedi NP

Nwanedi Dam
Tshihovhohovho Falls

Luphephe Dam
Mutale

Mphaphuli Cycad Reserve

Kruger NP's Punda Maria Gate

To Pafuri (36km)

Mutale River

Pafuri River

Nzhelele Dam
4WD only

Camp Mangwele

Dzata Ruins
Mphephu   Sacred Forest   Thathe-Vondo Forest

Lake Fundzi

Mutshindudi River

R524

Nzhelele

Kokwane Prehistoric Footprints

Phiphidi Waterfall

Sibasa
Thohoyandou

To Vivo (35km)

R522

Lwamondo Hill

Thohoyandou Airport

Kruger NP

Makhado (Louis Trichardt)

Ben Lavin NR

Albasini Dam   Levubu   Levubu River

Vuwani

R81

Elim Hospital
Mashamba

Iron Age Furnaces

To Polokwane (Pietersburg) (67km);
Johannesburg (398km)

R578

Giyani

R529

LEGEND
NP National Park
NR Nature Reserve

To Tzaneen (98km)   To Tzaneen (95km)

---

with lakes and forests that are of great religious significance and the region continues to support a thriving artistic heritage.

Thohoyandou & Sibasa

☎ 015 / pop 50,000

Created as the capital of the apartheid-era Venda Homeland, the city of Thohoyandou blends some impressively functional town-planning with a healthy dose of African chaos, matching a looming shopping centre and adjacent casino resort with all the push-and-shove of the backstreet marketplace. The adjacent town of Sibasa is a few kilometres north. Most public transport leaves from Sibasa.

Thohoyandou is an easy 65km drive to Kruger's Punda Maria Gate, and a good entry/exit point if you plan to explore the park's far north.

Standard Bank (Mphephu St), on the main road through Thohoyandou, has an ATM. There is a second branch opposite the minibus taxi rank in Sibasa.

Thohoyandou Arts & Culture Centre (☎ 082-401 9756; Punda Maria Rd, Thohoyandou; ☻ 6am-6pm)

is a useful first stop. In addition to selling crafts (some good, some not so good) from around the region, manager Mashudu Dima also organises tours. Full-/half-day tours (R250/150, minimum three people) include transport, village visits and a trip to Lake Fundudzi. Those interested in the arts, should ask to meet Noria Mabasa, one of the region's best-known female artists, who sculpts traditional figures in clay and wood (wood was traditionally a 'men only' medium).

SLEEPING & EATING

Vevisa Lodge (☎ 962 5252; vevisa@iafrica.com; 758 Mphephu St; s/d with breakfast R250/295) This new place opts for mock-traditional decor, with fake mud walls and thatched roofs, and has clean rooms.

Tusk Venda (☎ 962 4600; www.tusk-resorts.co.za; Mphephu St; s/d with breakfast R435/630; 🖳 🖺) A little slice of Vegas in the heart of Venda, this casino resort looks rather incongruous among the local hustle and bustle. It offers plenty of trimmings and plenty of ways to fritter away a penny or two.

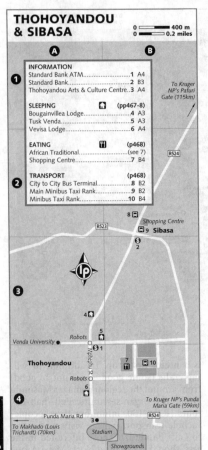

THOHOYANDOU & SIBASA

0 ————— 400 m
0 ————— 0.2 miles

INFORMATION
Standard Bank ATM..........................1 A4
Standard Bank....................................2 B3
Thohoyandou Arts & Culture Centre..3 A4

SLEEPING (pp467-8)
Bougainvillea Lodge..........................4 A3
Tusk Venda.......................................5 A3
Vevisa Lodge....................................6 A4

EATING (p468)
African Traditional..........................(see 7)
Shopping Centre...............................7 B4

TRANSPORT (p468)
City to City Bus Terminal..................8 B2
Main Minibus Taxi Rank....................9 B2
Minibus Taxi Rank..........................10 B4

To Kruger NP's Pafuri Gate (115km)

R524

8
Shopping Centre
9 Sibasa
R523
2

3

4

5
Venda University ● Robots
1
Thohoyandou
Robots
7
10

6

To Kruger NP's Punda Maria Gate (59km)

Punda Maria Rd
3 ●
R524
To Makhado (Louis Trichardt) (70km)
Stadium
Showgrounds

Bougainvillea Lodge (☎ 962 4064; mweb1325@mweb.co.za; Mphephu St; s/d with breakfast R250/325) As promised by the name, there is plenty of blooming bougainvillea here – and plenty of smiles too.

All the usual fast-food establishments are represented in the shopping centre. **African Traditional** (buffet R12; ⏱ lunch & dinner), in the heart of the centre, offers something a little different, including a good selection of local favourites: chicken heart, chicken gizzard and lamb stew.

GETTING THERE & AWAY

City to City (☎ 295 5548; www.translux.co.za) buses run from a terminal just up the R524 from the centre of Sibasa. They leave every morn-

ing at 8.30am for Jo'burg (R85, 8½ hours) and Pretoria (R85, 7½ hours).

The main minibus taxi rank is in Sibasa, on the corner of the road from Thohoyandou. Destinations and fares include Makhado (R20, 1½ hours) and Jo'burg (R90, nine hours).

In Thohoyandou, minibus taxis congregate in the car park of the shopping centre near the Tusk Venda. The fare to Sibasa is R2.50.

Nwanedi National Park

The dry northern side of the Soutpansberg provides an extremely scenic backdrop to **Nwanedi National Park** (☎ 015-539 0723; adult/vehicle R5/7; ⏱ 6am-6pm), although it's a contrast to the Venda's lush landscapes. The vegetation is mainly mopani and mixed woodland and the major walk in the park is to the very scenic **Tshihovhohovho Falls**. You can hire canoes for R45.

The park has **camp sites** (per person R20, plus per tent R50), and four-person **rondavels** (R300). Basic supplies are available and there's a fully licensed restaurant.

You can reach the park from Thohoyandou, entering at the Nwanedi gate; though the road is scenic there's a good chance of getting lost, and there are several kilometres of bad dirt road. It's simpler to come via Tshipise and enter from the west. Tshipise is the nearest place to buy fuel.

Nwanedi also makes a good combination with northern Kruger. A possible itinerary is to head from Thohoyandou to Kruger's Punda Maria Gate, exit Kruger via the park's northernmost Pafuri Gate, then continue on to Nwanedi and Tshipise.

Lake Fundudzi & Around

This lake is a sacred site, as its water is believed to have come from the great sea that covered the earth before land was created. The python god, who holds an important place in the rites of the Venda's matriarchal culture and once required human sacrifice, lives here. The lake is 35km northwest of Thohoyandou, but you can't visit it without permission from the lake's priestess, which is unlikely to be granted. The easiest way to catch a glimpse of the lake is to take a tour from Thohoyandou or Makhado.

Near the lake is **Thathe-Vondo Forest** (admission R5; ⏱ 8am-4pm Mon-Fri, 8am-5pm Sat & Sun),

LIMPOPO

with a (usually) drivable dirt track leading to a section of Holy Forest (13km) and a pleasant viewpoint (17km), with vistas over Lake Fundudzi.

SLEEPING

Camp Mangwele (☎ 072-631 6670; camp site R40 per person) North of Lake Fundudzi, this camping ground is situated within the rugged country of the Soutpansberg, and is accessible only by a 4WD with high ground clearance. There are hot showers, braai facilities and firewood; many activities, including scrambling, rock climbing and mountain biking, are within range of the camp. There is also an on-site **tour guide** (☎ 082-768 8801).

To get to Camp Mangwele, head first to Makhado (not the former Louis Trichardt, but the smaller town to the north). Some 2km northeast of Makhado, turn north towards Musekwa. Follow this road for 21.7km, then turn right (east) and follow the road towards Tshixwadza. After 9km there is a signboard indicating Mangwele Pothole (slightly worrying in itself); follow this road south for 1km until you reach the camp.

VALLEY OF THE OLIFANTS

The eastern reaches of Limpopo present yet another face of this diverse province. The region is culturally very rich, being the traditional home of the Tsonga-Shangaan and Lobedu peoples. It is also popular for a north–south traverse through Kruger National Park or a visit to one of the many private wildlife reserves in the Hoedspruit area (see p474). The main town of Tzaneen, and the pretty village of Haenertsburg, in the Letaba Valley, make pleasant bases for trips into the scenic Modjadji and Magoebaskloof areas.

LETABA VALLEY

The Letaba Valley is east of Polokwane, between two chunks of the former Lebowa Homeland. The valley is subtropical and lush, with tea plantations and crops of tropical fruits below, and forested hills above.

At Haenertsburg the road splits in two, with the R71 reaching Tzaneen via the steep Magoebaskloof Pass, while the R528 runs along the more gentle George's Valley.

Haenertsburg
☎ 015

Tucked into green peaks reminiscent of the Scottish Highlands, sedate little Haenertsburg offers an oasis of rural hush for those wanting to escape from it all. Established during the 1887 gold rush, the village appears to have kept a little aside for a rainy day, retaining an affluent, suburban atmosphere.

INFORMATION

Magoebaskloof Tourist Association (☎ 276 5047; www.magoebaskloof.com; Rissik St; ⌚ 8am-5pm Mon-Fri, 9am-noon Sat & Sun) has plenty of information and offers **Internet access** (per 30min R15).

There is an **ABSA** (Rissik St) ATM in the Tank Trap store next door.

ACTIVITIES

Hiking trails near Haenertsburg include the 11km **Louis Chang-uion Trail**, which has spectacular views; and the **Bifrost Mountain Trails**, which pass waterfalls and ascend to the summit of Iron Crown (2126m).

Haenertsburg is also well endowed with operators offering outdoorsy activities.

Filly's Way (☎ 082-294 8349; michelle@slm.co.za), 2km west of town on the R71, offers one-hour (R110), one-day (R380) and two-day (R1850) horse trails.

Magoebaskloof Mountain Bike Trails (☎ 083-564 9445; mmbt@webmail.co.za) can point you in the direction of five colour-coded bike trails, or take you on a guided ride. You'll need your own bike though.

The **Growth Centre** (☎ 276 2712, 072-277 4809), 6km east of town on the R71 towards Tzaneen, offers holistic health remedies, reflexology and meditation. It is signposted on the road as Stanford Lake Lodge.

SLEEPING & EATING

Chalets (☎ 276 4264; thechalets@942.co.za; R71; s/d R150/300) These fairytale twee, Swiss-style chalets, 1km from town on the R71, are great value for keen self-caterers.

Bali Will Will (☎ 276 2212; glmccomb@absamail .co.za; camp sites per person R40, s/d with breakfast R185/370) The rooms in this quiet, farm-style place are a little worn, but the setting is sublime. It's located 2km out of town (follow the signs from the R71), but staff will pick you up from the village if you phone ahead.

LIMPOPO

Magoebaskloof Hotel (☎ 276 4776; www.magoe baskloof.co.za; R71; s/d with breakfast R250/500; ❄ ⚲) This business-standard place boasts monkeys, top views, plenty of trimmings and a Dutch-style pub for post-activity rehydration. It is 10km out of town, on the R71 towards Tzaneen.

Iron Crown Tavern (☎ 276 4755; mains R15-40; ☽ lunch & dinner; ❄) In keeping with the village atmosphere, this lively tavern offers decent pub grub and a good dose of drinking den character.

GETTING THERE & AWAY
Beyer's Bus Service (☎ 307 5959, 082-434 3449) stops at Picasso's restaurant on the R71 on Wednesday, Friday and Sunday en route between Pretoria and Tzaneen. Fares from Haenertsburg include Tzaneen (R30, 30 minutes), Polokwane (R40, 40 minutes) and Pretoria (R150, 5½ hours).

Magoebaskloof Pass
The Magoebaskloof is the escarpment on the edge of the highveld, and the road here drops quickly down to Tzaneen and the lowveld, passing through plantations and large tracts of thick indigenous forest.

The high summer rainfall means there are a number of waterfalls in the area including **Debengeni Falls** in the De Hoek State Forest. To get here, turn west off the R71 at Bruphy Sawmills.

Two recommended walking trails are the two-day, 21km **Debengeni Falls Trail** and the three-day, 40km **Dokolewa Waterfall Trail**. Overnight stays for the Dokolewa Waterfall Trail are in huts near waterfalls and streams.

Speak to the Magoebaskloof Tourist Association (p469) in Haenertsburg about bookings.

TZANEEN & AROUND
☎ 015 / pop 80,000
At the hub of a rich fruit-growing area, Tzaneen, the largest town near the Letaba Valley and the second-largest in Limpopo, is perhaps best known for its avocados and mangoes – be sure to try some. Surrounded by lush, subtropical hills, this is a pleasant spot with plenty of quiet corners. At the heart of this region, it also makes a convenient base for exploring the Valley of the Olifants.

Information
ABSA (Danie Joubert St) Has an ATM and change facilities.
First National (Danie Joubert St) ATM and change facilities.
Limpopo Parks & Tourism Board (☎ 307 7244; www .tzaneen.com; R71; ☽ 8am-5pm Mon-Fri, 8am-1pm Sat & Sun) On the R71 towards Phalaborwa, has plenty of useful information on the region.
Post Office (Lannie Lane) Behind Danie Joubert St.
Speedphone (☎ 307 5933; Ground fl, Tzaneng Mall, Danie Joubert St; R15 per 30min; ☽ 8.30am-4.30pm Mon-Fri) Offers Internet access.
Tzaneen Hospital (☎ 307 4475; Hospital St) Southeast of the centre.

Sights
Tzaneen Museum (☎ 307 8056; Agatha St; donation welcome; ☽ 9am-4pm Mon-Fri, 9am-noon Sat) has an interesting collection of Tsonga cultural artefacts including a Rain Queen ceremonial drum, and looks back at 2000 years of tribal pottery and art.

Sleeping
Satvik Backpackers Village (☎ 307 3920; satvik@pi xie.co.za; George's Valley Rd; camp site R35, dm/d R70/160) Less technicolour tacky than many backpackers, Satvik offers a more rustic blend of budget accommodation, with a farm setting and beds in old workers' cottages.

Fairview River Lodge (☎ 307 2679; www.tzaneen .co.za/fairview; s/d R325/400; ❄) One of the town's swankiest options, this thatched, four-star place has some very comfortable self-catering chalets and a leafy tropical garden. If you ask, there are also some basic rooms for R200.

Arborpark Lodge (☎ 307 1831; arborpark@mweb.co .za; cnr Soetdoring & Geelhout Sts; dm/s/d with breakfast R85/265/360; ❄) Appealing to both the better-heeled backpacker and the committed mid-ranger, this motel-style offering has a laundromat, a pub and a good restaurant. It's quite a way from the centre, but staff will collect you if you call ahead.

Silver Palms Lodge (☎ 307 3092; cnr Monument & Voortrekker Sts; s/d economy R205/250, standard R240/265; ❄ ⚲) This glossy little place has nice rooms and a 1980s-style bar around a pleasant pool area.

Eating
The dining scene is painfully ordinary.
Villa Italia (☎ 307 2795; Danie Joubert St; mains R30-60; ☽ lunch & dinner; ❄) Villa Italia whips up a decent spread of Mediterranean fare and could be your best bet for a sit-down meal.

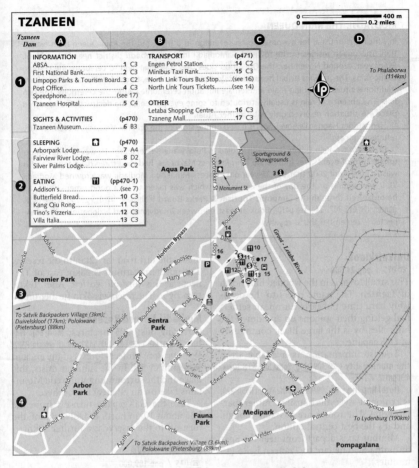

TZANEEN

INFORMATION	
ABSA	1 C3
First National Bank	2 C3
Limpopo Parks & Tourism Board	3 C2
Post Office	4 C3
Speedphone	(see 17)
Tzaneen Hospital	5 C4

SIGHTS & ACTIVITIES	(p470)
Tzaneen Museum	6 B3

SLEEPING	(p470)
Arborpark Lodge	7 A4
Fairview River Lodge	8 D2
Silver Palms Lodge	9 C2

EATING	(pp470-1)
Addison's	(see 7)
Butterfield Bread	10 C3
Kang Qiu Rong	11 C3
Tino's Pizzeria	12 C3
Villa Italia	13 C3

TRANSPORT	(p471)
Engen Petrol Station	14 C2
Minibus Taxi Rank	15 C3
North Link Tours Bus Stop	(see 16)
North Link Tours Tickets	(see 14)

OTHER	
Letaba Shopping Centre	16 C3
Tzaneng Mall	17 C3

Butterfield Bread (Danie Joubert St; breakfast & lunch) This reliable bakery chain is a good spot for fresh bread and tasty treats.

Kang Qiu Rong (☎ 072-307 5451; 30 Morgan St; mains R30-50; lunch & dinner) Glamorous? No. But Chinese is a novelty here and this spartan place whips up a few decent Asian dishes.

Tino's Pizzeria (☎ 307 1893; Agatha St; mains R25-45; lunch & dinner;) This place has been around for a while now and the pizzas are still reliably good.

Addison's (☎ 307 6261; cnr Soetdoring & Geelhout Sts; mains R25-60; lunch & dinner;) In Arborpark Lodge, this is a lively little eatery, with a decent pub in which to wash your food down afterwards.

Getting There & Away

North Link Tours buses stop at the rear of the Letaba Boulevard shopping centre. They run from Phalaborwa (R70, 1½ hours) to Jo'burg (R140, six hours) via Tzaneen, four days a week. You can book tickets at the **Engen petrol station** (☎ 307 2930; Danie Joubert St).

Translux buses run to Pretoria (R130, 4½ hours), Jo'burg (R130, 5½ hours) and Phalaborwa (R95, one hour). Book tickets at the Limpopo Parks & Tourism Board (p458).

Most minibus taxis depart from a rank behind the Tzaneng Mall. Destinations and fares from Tzaneen include Duivelskloof (R6, 15 minutes) and Haenertsburg (R10, 30 minutes).

LIMPOPO

MODJADJI, THE RAIN QUEEN

In Africa it is unusual for a woman to be sovereign of a tribe, but the Rain Queen is an exception. The queen resides in the town of GaModjadji in the Bolebodu district near Duivelskloof. Every year, around November, the Queen presides over a festival held to celebrate the coming of the rains. The *indunas* (tribal headmen) select people to dance, to call for rain, and to perform traditional rituals, including male and female initiation ceremonies. After the ceremony, the rain falls. The absence of rain is usually attributed to some event such as the destruction of a sacred place – a situation resolved only with further ritual.

Henry Rider Haggard's novel, *She*, is based on the story of the original Modjadji, a 16th-century refugee princess.

In June 2001, Rain Queen, Modjadji V, died in Polokwane (Pietersburg). However, in an unfortunate turn of events, her immediate heir, Princess Makheala, had died three days earlier and it wasn't until April 2003 that the 25-year-old Princess Mmakobo Modjadji was crowned Modjadji VI. It was raining on the day of the ceremony, which was taken to be a good omen. Visits can be organised through the **Limpopo Tourism & Parks Board** (Polokwane ☎ 015-290 7300; see p458; Tzaneen ☎ 015-307 7244; see p470). Book at least one week in advance and a donation will be expected – remember this is royalty.

Duivelskloof

☎ 015 / pop 24,500

This small town is in the wooded hills north of Tzaneen. The name refers to the devilishly hard time the early European settlers had getting their wagons up and down the hills. Nearby is the large Black community of GaKgapane.

Tourist information is available from the **municipality** (☎ 309 9246; Botha St; ✆ 8.30am-4.30pm Mon-Fri).

Hotel Imp Inn (☎ 309 9253; Botha St; s/d R150/220) is a colonial-style villa housing a rather spartan hotel. The rooms are passable though, and it's the best central option.

Minibus taxis depart from near the Spar on Botha St. The fare to Tzaneen is R6 (15 minutes).

Ndzalama Wildlife Reserve

Based on Ndzalama, a spectacular, phallic rock formation, this **reserve** (☎ 015-307 3065; ndzalama@pixie.co.za), near Letsitele, is a hidden gem, built around stunning rocky hillocks. The emphasis is not so much on the Big Five (although everything but buffalo is represented), but rather on the subtle nuances of the bush. No day visitors are allowed into the reserve (you have to stay).

Self-catering **accommodation** (2-bed chalet from R400) is available. You must book in advance.

To get to the reserve from Tzaneen or Phalaborwa, take the R71. The southern turn-off is 9km north of Gravelotte; turn right and follow the dirt road for 12km to the reserve. The northern turn-off is 28km east of Tzaneen; at this turn-off, go left. After 16km, turn right. The reserve is 4km further on.

Modjadji Nature Reserve

Covering just 305 hectares, **Modjadji Nature Reserve** (☎ 082-393 5551; adult/vehicle R5/7; ✆ 7.30am-4pm) protects forests of the ancient Modjadji cycad. In the summer mists, this place and the surrounding Vulovedu Mountains take on an ethereal atmosphere.

Take the GaKgapane turn-off from the R36 about 10km north of Duivelskloof; the turn-off to the reserve is a further 18km.

PHALABORWA

☎ 015 / pop 109,000

Phalaborwa is a neatly tended stretch of well-watered suburbia – the 'Beware Hippos' signs seem rather out of place – with a group of guest houses and hotels thriving on the back of the town's proximity to the Kruger National Park. Phalaborwa means 'Better than the South', and was so called because Nguni tribes returned here after a foray to the south. Boozers, however, will be more interested to hear that the town is home to South Africa's famed Amarula cream liqueur.

Phalaborwa makes an ideal starting point if you're intending to explore central and northern Kruger. It's being increasingly promoted as a base for exploring the park, and has a good and rapidly expanding range of accommodation and other facilities for doing this. For people with limited time in South Africa, it is possible to visit Kruger by flying from Jo'burg to Phalaborwa, hiring a car for touring the park and then returning the car at Phalaborwa airport before returning by air to Jo'burg (see p474).

Information

The Phalaborwa gate into Kruger National Park is 3km from town.

Bollanoto Tourism Centre (☎ 781 7267; www .phalaborwa.co.za; cnr Hendrick van Eck & Pres Steyn Sts; ☺ 8am-4.30pm Mon-Fri, 9am-noon Sat) has lots of information and is the best place to book tours of Kruger and the surrounding area. The tours include morning walks (R350 per person including breakfast, four hours) and microlight flights (R200 per 30 minutes).

Net-o-Mania (☎ 781 7812; Shop 2, Phalaborwa Mall, Nelson Mandela St; R8.50 per 15min; ☺ 8.20am-4.30pm Mon-Fri) offers Internet access.

Sights & Activities

You can tour the nearby **copper mine** (fax 780 2813; maggie.mapurazi@palabora.co.za; admission free), said to boast the largest man-made hole in Africa, at 9am on Friday, but you must fax or email in advance.

The Bollanoto Tourism Centre (see p473) can book **day tours** (per person R180) to the local township, Namakgale.

The **Hans Merensky Estate** (☎ 781 3931; www .hansmerensky.com; Club Rd; 9/18-hole round R250/350), just south of Phalaborwa, has an 18-hole championship golf course with a difference: here you have to hold your shot while wildlife, elephants included, crosses the fairways. Be careful – the wildlife is 'wild'.

Sleeping

There are scores of places to stay in Phalaborwa; many of the best are just out of town in the bush.

BUDGET
Elephant Walk (☎ 781 5860; elephant.walk@nix.co.za; 30 Anna Scheepers Ave; camp sites R50, dm/s/d with shared bathroom R60/100/150, d R280) Close enough to Kruger to hear the lions roar, this is a great spot to plan your foray into the park. The owners will pick you up from the centre of town and offer an excellent range of reasonably priced tours and activities. The ensuite doubles are glossier.

Daan & Zena's (☎ 781 6049; www.daanzena.co.za; 15 Birkenhead St; s/d R180/330, with shared bathroom R150/260; 🅿 🖭) Bridging the gap between backpackers and B&B, this place is brought to life by lashings of colourful paint and a friendly atmosphere. It's a tad crumbly and prices are a bit high, but it's a good spot if you're looking for a comfy bed and a youthful vibe.

MID-RANGE & TOP END
Bed In The Bush (☎ 781 1139; bushbed@lantic.net; s/d R450/600; 🅿) Leopards, elephants and more than 60 bird species call this quiet farm home. The four-star grading promises plenty of home comforts, but the setting is bona fide wild. It's 6km north of town, en route to Masorini Lodge, but pick-ups are available if you call ahead.

Sefapane Lodge (☎ 781 7041; www.sefapane.co.za; cnr Koper & Essenhout Sts; s/d with breakfast R400/700; 🅿 🖭) Sefapane has plenty of safari-park styling, a sunken bar, one of the town's best eateries and a whiff of genuine exclusivity. Accommodation is in rondavels.

Masorini Lodge (☎ 781 3579; www.masorini.co.za; s/d R295/450) Out in the sticks, this atmospheric place has self-catering accommodation in thatched A-frames, complete with patio, kitchenette and braai. As you enter town from Tzaneen, turn left (north) on Spekboom St and keep going for 8km.

Phuza Moya (☎ 793 1971; www.phuzamoya.co.za; s/d with full-board & wildlife drives R1875/2500; 🅿 🖭) About as glamorous as the bush gets, this seriously stylish place only takes 24 guests at a time – and they are soon swallowed up by the surrounding 2800 hectares of private wildlife reserve. Elegant and serene, accommodation is in thatched lodges, or some spectacularly chi-chi safari tents. It is about an hour out of town on the S30 between Mica and the R36. Head south from Phalaborwa on the Lydenburg road.

Eating

The Phalaborwa Mall, on Nelson Mandela St, has the usual food chains. For posh eats, the restaurant at Sefapane Lodge is excellent.

Juba's Grill House (☎ 781 7834; Shop 1, Phalaborwa Mall; mains R40-90; ☺ lunch & dinner; 🅿) The fact that it is in a mall slightly detracts from the atmosphere, but the sizzling griddle turns out some fine slabs of meat and there are plenty of salad and seafood options for those who have had their fill of the red stuff.

LIMPOPO

Buffalo Pub & Grill (☎ 781 0829; 1 Lekkerbreek St; mains R30-70; ⏱ lunch & dinner; 🖳) There's more meat on offer at this popular place, but there's a nice terrace for al fresco dining and plenty of African trimmings.

Getting There & Away

AIR
SAAirlink (☎ 781 5823; www.saairlink.co.za), with an office at the airport, flies daily to Jo'burg (R1100).

BUS
Sure Turn Key Travel (☎ 781 7761; Shop 42, Phalaborwa Mall, Nelson Mandela St; ⏱ 8.30am-4.30pm Mon-Fri, 9am-noon Sat) is the local agent for Translux and City to City buses. Translux services travel via Polokwane and connect Phalaborwa with Tzaneen (R95, one hour), Polokwane (R95, 2½ hours), Makhado (R170, four hours), Pretoria (R165, six hours) and Jo'burg (R165, seven hours). City to City buses travel to Jo'burg (R135, 9½ hours) via Middleburg, and are cheaper but slower. Prices for both companies include a booking fee of R20.

North Link Tours buses run to Tzaneen (R70, 1½ hours) and Polokwane (R80, 2½ hours), where there are connections to Jo'burg and towns en-route. You can buy tickets from Bollanoto Tourism Centre (p473).

CAR
Hiring a car is often the cheapest way of seeing the Kruger Park. **Avis** (☎ 781 3169; ⏱ 8am-6pm Mon-Fri, 10.30am-1pm Sat, 4-6pm Sun), **Imperial** (☎ 781 0376; ⏱ as Avis) and **Budget** (☎ 781 5404; ⏱ as Avis) all have offices at the airport.

MINIBUS TAXI
There aren't many minibus taxis in this area, and most run from the township of Namakgale (R4, 20 minutes). From here, you can catch connections to Tzaneen (R35, 1½ hours).

HOEDSPRUIT & AROUND
☎ 015
There's not a whole lot in Hoedspruit but 200 neat houses and a large Air Force base – which is scaling down. It is, however, within striking distance of Kruger's Orpen gate (67km), and makes a convenient launching point for exploring the central and northern sections of the park. It's also one of

the main access towns for Timbavati and several of the other private wildlife reserves bordering western Kruger (see p451), with good air connections to/from Jo'burg.

Information
The **Tourist Information Centre** (☎ 082-800 1300; Kamogelo Centre, Main Rd; ⏱ 8am-5pm) is on the R527, next to the Wimpy fast-food outlet. There is an **ABSA** (Main Rd) ATM nearby.

McFarlane Safaris (☎ 793 3000; www.mcfarlane safaris.co.za; ⏱ 8am-5pm Mon-Fri, 8am-noon Sat), by the Total petrol station on the R40, runs upmarket safaris in and around Kruger. **Off-Beat Safaris** (☎ 793 2422) runs horse safaris (R150 for two hours) from a nearby farm. It also offers **accommodation** (s/d R220/440).

Loerie Guesthouse (☎ 793 3990; fax 793 2779; 85 Jakkals St; s/d R165/270) specialises in warm welcomes and home cooking (breakfast R35, dinner R60). It is signposted off Main Rd.

Getting There & Away
SA Express (☎ 793 3681) flies daily out of Hoedspruit Eastgate airport (7km) to Jo'burg (R1200 one-way) and five times a week (not Tuesday and Saturday) to Cape Town (R2200 one-way).

You can hire a car with **Avis** (☎ 793 2014), at the airport.

There is a minibus taxi rank near the train station, with services to Phalaborwa (R25, 1½ hours).

Nyani Cultural Village
Home of the descendants of former local chief Kapama, **Nyani Cultural Village** (☎ 083-512 4865; Guernsey Rd; admission R50; ⏱ 10am-5pm Mon-Fri) offers an interesting insight into how traditional Shangaan families live. The village recreates all aspects of tribal culture, and chief Axon Khosa is happy to explain traditional medicines and aspects of Tsonga life. Admission includes a one-hour tour and **lunch** (R35) is available. There's also evening tours (including dinner and dancing) for R100. If you want to eat, book ahead.

The village is on the road heading towards Thornybush Game Reserve, 4km from Route 40, near Klaserie Dam.

Safari Backpackers & Bushcamp (☎ 793 3816; Route 531; dm/d with shared bathroom R60/160; 🖳) is a bush camp offering a true wildlife-park experience at a backpacker's price. It is just past Nyani Cultural Village.

North-West Province

The North-West Province takes in much of the area once covered by the fragmented apartheid homeland of Bophuthatswana (often shortened to 'Bop'), dumping ground for thousands of 'relocated' Tswana people. The nominally independent homeland became famous for the excesses of the White South African men, who visited its casinos and pleasure resorts for interracial encounters with prostitutes, which would have been illegal in South Africa itself. Today, however, the most famous of the apartheid-era resorts, Sun City, has been reclaimed as a holiday destination by Black and Asian families from the surrounding area.

The North-West Province was the site of a complex and sophisticated iron-age civilisation centred on the 'lost city' of Kaditshwene, about 30km north of modern-day Zeerust. The people who lived here had an economy so developed they traded copper and iron jewellery with China. By 1820, when European missionaries first visited the city, it was bigger than Cape Town. In the end the peace-loving inhabitants of Kaditshwene were no match for the aggression of the Sotho, displaced by Zulu incursions into the Free State. The city was sacked by a horde of 40,000 people and fell into ruins.

Diamonds were discovered in the province in the 1870s, resulting in an enormous rush to the fields around Lichtenburg. Mining is still important here and there are extensive platinum mines near Rustenburg.

Today, the best-known places in the province are still the famously kitsch Sun City and Lost City casino resort complexes, along with the excellent Madikwe and Pilanesberg National Parks.

HIGHLIGHTS

- Riding the wave pool or braving a fake earthquake in **Sun City**, once a glittering icon of apartheid, now a playground for every kind of South African (p478)

- Exploring rocky valleys and extinct volcanoes and getting up close to rhino, leopard and elephant at **Pilanesberg National Park** (p480)

- Staying under canvas in a bush camp or driving in search of lion, giraffe or the endangered wild dog in **Madikwe Game Reserve** (p482)

- Mellowing out and listening to live music while absorbing the eccentric vibes of the **Revel Inn** near Rustenburg (p478)

- POPULATION: 3,669,349
- AREA: 116,320 SQ KM

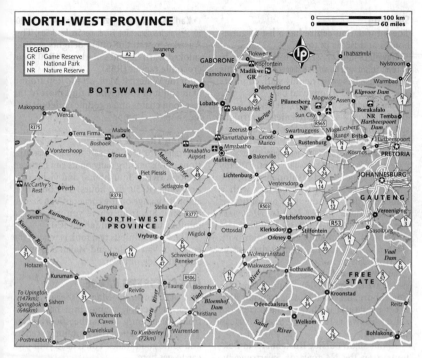

NORTH-WEST PROVINCE

LEGEND
GR Game Reserve
NP National Park
NR Nature Reserve

CLIMATE

Summer temperatures range between 22°C and 34°C and winter brings with it dry, sunny days and chilly nights. The average winter (May–July) temperature is 15.5°C but can range from an average of 2°C to 20°C in a single day. The summer months (August–March) bring brief, refreshing afternoon thunderstorms.

LANGUAGE

Setswana is the principal language spoken in the North-West Province; most Whites speak Afrikaans, with a minority having English as their first language.

GETTING THERE & AROUND

The principal towns in the province, Mafikeng and Rustenburg, are well connected by bus with Johannesburg (Jo'burg) and Pretoria. Potchefstroom is also a transport hub. Buses also run regularly to Gaborone in Botswana via Zeerust. The main border crossing is Ramatlabama, north of Mafikeng.

Elsewhere in the province, especially the sparsely populated west, public transport is sporadic and you'll most likely need your own vehicle to get around. Car hire is available through **Avis** (www.avis.co.za) Pilanesberg Airport (☎ 014-552 1501); Mafikeng (☎ 018-385 1114); Potchefstroom (☎ 018-290 8535) and **Imperial Car Hire** (www.imperialcarrental.co.za) Pilanesberg Airport (☎ 014-552 1767); Mafikeng (☎ 018-381 7447).

RUSTENBURG

☎ 014 / pop 123,000

Rustenburg is a large and prosperous mining town, founded in 1841, which lies at the western edge of the Magaliesberg Range about 115km northwest of Jo'burg; Thlabane is the huge Black township nearby. There's no particular reason to come to Rustenburg, but it makes a handy base for visiting Sun City or Pilanesburg National Park.

On the way into town, you'll find the well-stocked **tourist information centre** (☎ 597 0904; ☒ 7.30am-5pm Mon-Fri, 8am-1pm Sat) between Plein and Van Staden Sts. There is also an art gallery here and an arts and crafts shop. There's Internet access at **Copy Express** (per hr R30; ☎ 592 1970; Biblio Plaza).

Sleeping

The information centre has a list of guesthouses and B&Bs in town.

Traveller's Inn (☎ 592 7658; travinn@mweb.co.za; 99 Leyds St; s/d with breakfast & dinner R260/520) This guesthouse has very friendly staff, comfortable rooms and a convivial bar.

Tom's Lodge (☎ 592 0435; 51 Heystek St; s/d R150/220) Tom's is a convenient overnight stop, reminiscent of a block of flats. Rooms are compact and tidy.

Joan's B&B (☎ 533 3086; joan@joansbnb.co.za; 61 Wildevy Ave, Protea Park; s/d with breakfast R130/220) Joan's is a good old-fashioned B&B; the owners serve a hearty breakfast with a smile. Just don't get them on to politics…

Cashane Hotel (☎ 592 8541; fax 592 3016; 66 Steen St; s/d with breakfast R245/350; 🕃) This is a convenient, cheap and central option with clean rooms. Ask for a room at the back as the front can be noisy.

Bushwillows B&B (☎ 537 2333; wjmcgill@lantic .net; s/d with breakfast R140/280) Some 12km from Rustenburg, off the R24, this tranquil B&B is set in natural bush, and the owner (an artist) knows a lot about South African wildlife.

About 50km outside Rustenberg, at Bokfontein on the N4 towards Swartruggens, lies one of the province's best-kept secrets. The **Revel Inn** (☎ 072-225 7182; www.revelin.co.za; camping/dm/d with shared bathroom R30/40/120, bungalows R240; dinner R35; 🕃) lies deep in the rural heartland of Afrikanerdom, nestled in a green valley next to a small stream. Once through the gate, however, any preconceptions are quickly dispelled by a riot of psychedelic paintings and a crowd of eccentric regulars who like to party – hard.

At sporadic intervals Revel Inn hosts mini music festivals with live drumming, DJs or such esoteric events as the Magic Carpet Carnival and the Spring Love Party. When there's no party on, you could well have the place to yourself, so simply recline in a hammock, chill out in a tree house, or float in the perfectly circular pool and contemplate the sky, man…

Eating

Royal Dutchman (☎ 537 3626; 58 Nelson Mandela; mains R60-80; 🕃 lunch & dinner Mon-Fri, dinner Sat) This dark and cosy restaurant has dining booths and a decent menu including lots of seafood. Try the rollmop herrings (R31).

Karl's Bauernstube (☎ 537 2128; R24; mains R20-50; 🕃 lunch & dinner Tue-Fri, dinner Sat, lunch Sun) This Austrian restaurant offers delights such as smoked warthog and sauerkraut (R40), and crocodile ragout (R35).

In the Waterfall Mall, off the R30 around 3km south of town, you'll find most of the fast-food chains and a couple of decent coffee shops.

Getting There & Away

Intercape (☎ 0861 287 287; www.intercape.co.za) stops in Rustenburg daily on its run between Pretoria (R105, four hours) and Gaborone, Botswana (R150, five hours) The bus stops at the BP garage on the corner of Van Staden and Smit Sts, from where you can catch a minibus taxi into town (about R5).

The main minibus taxi rank is west of the corner of Van Staden and Malan Sts, on the Sun City side of town.

MAGALIESBERG RANGE

The 120km-long Magaliesberg Range, north of the N4, swings in a half moon from Rustenburg to Hartbeespoort Dam. The region has attractive mountain scenery and some good walks. You'll need your own car to get here.

At the western end of the range is **Kgaswane Mountain Reserve** (☎ 014-533 2050; admission R20; 🕃 8am-4pm). The area is dominated by rocky ridges and wooded ravines, and lies to the south of Rustenburg. You may see hyenas, black-backed jackals and small antelopes.

The **Hunter's Rest Hotel** (☎ 014-537 2140; www.huntersrest.co.za; s/d with dinner & breakfast R530/900; 🕃) is an attractive resort, with a big swimming pool and a golf course, in the Magaliesberg Range, 14km south of Rustenburg; follow the signs.

SUN CITY

☎ 014

The legendary creation of entrepreneur Sol Kerzner, **Sun City** (admission R60) is a large entertainment and hotel complex with hundreds of casino tables and acres of slot machines. It's dominated by the fairly spectacular Lost City, an extraordinary piece of kitsch that claims to symbolise African heritage. In fact it has less to do with African heritage than Disneyland Paris has to do with French heritage, but it's still mildly entertaining, and some of the hotels are fabulous. Don't expect Vegas, however: unless you are determined to put in several hours on the slot machines in the entertainment centre, or at the casino tables in one of the hotels, the complex can essentially be explored in a couple of hours.

Sun City started as an apartheid-era haven for wealthy Whites, but these days one of its best features is the mix of Black, White and especially Asian people who flock here at weekends. Losers at the tables can also console themselves with the thought that they are helping to pay over 3500 salaries.

Orientation & Information

The car park for day visitors is at the entrance, about 2km from the entertainment centre. An elevated 'sky' train shuttles from the car park to the Cascades hotel and the entertainment centre.

The **welcome centre** (☎ 557 1544; ⏱ 9am-8pm Sun-Thu, 8-1am Fri & Sat) at the entrance to the entertainment centre has maps and just about any information you could possibly need.

Admission to Sun City gives you R30 in 'Sunbucks' to be spent at the various restaurants and shops in the resort (unfortunately you can't gamble with them). One or two of the attractions have separate entry charges, notably the Valley of the Waves, which costs another R55.

Sights & Activities

The best part of Sun City is undeniably the **Lost City**, which is entered over a bridge flanked by life-sized fake elephants, and basically consists of **Valley of the Waves**, a pool with a large-scale wave-making machine. Every hour or so a voice booms out some nonsense about lost civilisations and earthquakes from a hidden mike, and the bridge shakes while dry ice pours out of either side.

In the heart of the Lost City is the **Palace of the Lost City**, a hotel that could inspire hallucinations, but access is prohibited to all but the lucky – and wealthy – guests.

Kids can enjoy 'tubing' the Lazy River, riding the water slides or joining in the fun at the Kamp Kwena activity centre during summer.

Eighteen holes at the superb **Gary Player Country Club** or the **Lost City Golf Course** costs R400 (R350 for hotel guests).

Near the main entrance is **Kwena Gardens Crocodile Sanctuary** (R40), which is home to the world's biggest captive crocs. Feeding time is 4.30pm. **Waterworld**, on the shores of a large artificial lake, has facilities for parasailing (R275), jet-skiing (R135) and water-skiing (R140).

Gametrackers Outdoors Adventures (www.gametrac.co.za) runs wildlife drives and activities into the neighbouring Pilanesberg National Park (p480). Book at their desk in the information centre, but if you're going to stay in Pilanesberg too, bear in mind that the prices are cheaper if you book within the park.

Sleeping

If the Sun City hotels are too expensive (and you have your own transport), consider staying at Pilanesberg National Park (p480) and making the complex a day trip only. The town of Rustenburg (see p477) is also close enough to use as a base.

All the following hotels can be booked through **Sun City** (☎ 557 1000; fax 557 1902; www.suncity.co.za) or **Sun International central reservations** (☎ 011-780 7800; www.suninternational.com).

Palace of the Lost City (tw/f R3590/4490; ▨ ▣) The Palace's ludicrously over-the-top décor – check the enormous marble elephants dancing a jig around the fountains in the main restaurant – is so bad, it's almost good. The rooms, though luxurious, are a bit unimaginative compared with the public spaces.

Sun City Cabanas (tw/f R1240/1575; ▨ ▣) This is the cheapest alternative; it's laid-back and aimed at family groups.

Sun City Hotel (tw/f R1865/2050; ▨ ▣ The most lively of the hotels, with gambling facilities on the premises, as well as a number of restaurants, a nightclub and an entertainment centre.

The Cascades (tw/f R2090/2295; ▨ ▣) The Cascades has been displaced by the Palace of the Lost City as the most luxurious hotel in the complex, but the rooms are still easily described as palatial.

Eating

All the hotels have a selection of restaurants. Palm Terrace in Sun City Cabanas is the cheapest. There are plenty of fast-food joints in the entertainment centre. Your 30 Sunbucks will just about get you a burger and a soft drink.

Getting There & Away

AIR

Tiny Pilanesberg Airport once gloried in the name 'Pilanesberg International Airport', when it was the home of Bop Air, the airline of the former 'independent' homeland of Bophuthatswana. It's about 9km east of the Sun City complex. **SAAirlink** (☎ 011-978 1111; www.saairlink.co.za) operates flights six times a week from Jo'burg (R500) and three times a week from Cape Town (R1000). From the airport, you'll need to hire a car or arrange for your hotel to pick you up.

CAR

If you are on a tight budget, get a group together, hire a car and tour both Sun City and Pilanesberg National Park in the same day. For car hire information, see p477.

Surprisingly, the Sun City complex is poorly signposted, so navigators will really need to concentrate to not miss it. From Jo'burg it's a two-hour drive. The most straightforward route is via Rustenburg and Boshoek on the R565; a clever navigator could make it shorter via the R556. Both roads run north from the N4.

PILANESBERG NATIONAL PARK

This **national park** (☎ 014-555 5356; adult/child R20/10, per vehicle R15) lies just north of Sun City, so it is easy to combine a visit to both. Don't be fooled, by its proximity to Sun City, into thinking this is some kind of tacky superannuated zoo – it protects over 500 sq km of an unusual complex of extinct volcanoes, and is the fourth-largest national park in South Africa. The scenery is impressive, with towering rocky outcrops in the centre of the park, particularly in the area around Mankwe Lake, which is the centre of an extinct 1200-million-year-old volcano.

Since 1979, when Operation Genesis brought dozens of translocated animal species to the park, Pilanesberg has been home to extensive populations of many of Africa's most impressive animals. There are white and black rhinos, elephants, giraffes, hippos, buffalos, a wide variety of antelopes (including sables, elands, kudus and gemsboks), zebras, leopards, lions, jackals, hyenas and cheetahs. Since early 2000, African wild dogs can be seen here too. The region also has a diverse population of birds – over 300 species have been recorded.

There is an excellent 100km network of gravel roads, hides and picnic spots, and some good-value accommodation. Since it is no more than 25km from one end of the park to the other, it is easy to cover the range of different environments in the park and to see a wide variety of animals. To do any real justice to it, however, you need a full day. On no account miss the viewpoints over the crater from Lenong Lookout.

You'll need your own car to visit the park; see p477 for information on car hire.

Orientation & Information

There are four gates into Pilanesberg. Enter from the direction of Sun City using either Bakubung Gate to the west (via R556) or Manyane Gate to the northeast (via the R556 and R510 if you're coming from Pretoria and Jo'burg).

A useful information booklet and map (R10) is available at the main park gates, where overnight visitors must enter and report to the **reception office** (☎ 014-555 5355; ☻ 24hr).

Gates into the park proper (beyond the reception area and camp sites) are open as outlined in the table below.

Months	Gates open (am)	Gates close (pm)
Nov-Feb	5.30	7.00
Mar-Apr	6.00	6.30
May-Aug	6.30	6.00
Sep-Oct	6.00	6.30

There is an **information centre** (☎ 014-555 7931; www.parksnorthwest.co.za/pilanesberg) with an interpretative display and shop in an old magistrates court in the centre of the park; the shop sells curios, refreshments and a range of basic food items.

Activities

Gametrackers Outdoor Adventures (www.game trac.co.za) runs a dizzying variety of activities within the park. Book at its offices at Manyane or Bakgatla Complexes (p481), or at the Sun City welcome centre (p479). A scheduled daily 2½-hour wildlife drive costs R200; try tracking rhino on foot with a guide (R260). If you get lucky at the Sun City casino, splash out on a balloon flight (per person including champagne and breakfast R2300).

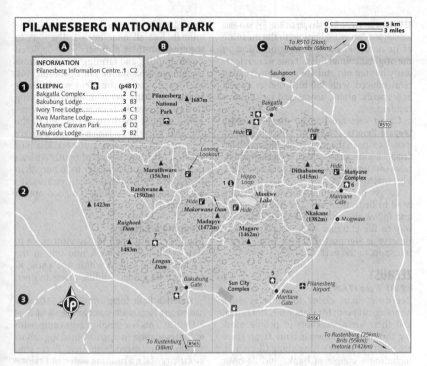

PILANESBERG NATIONAL PARK

0 — 5 km
0 — 3 miles

INFORMATION
Pilanesberg Information Centre..1 C2

SLEEPING (p481)
Bakgatla Complex.....................2 C1
Bakubung Lodge......................3 B3
Ivory Tree Lodge.....................4 C1
Kwa Maritane Lodge................5 C3
Manyane Caravan Park.............6 D2
Tshukudu Lodge.....................7 B2

To R510 (2km);
Thabazimbi (68km)

Saulspoort

Pilanesberg
National
Park
1687m

Bakgatla
Gate

R510

Hide

Hide

Lenong
Lookout

Maruthware
(1563m)

Hippo
Loop

Dithabaneng
(1415m)

Hide

Manyane
Complex

Ratshwane
(1502m)

Mankwe
Lake

Manyane
Gate

1423m

Hide
Makorwane Dam

Hide

Nkakane
(1382m)

Mogwase

Ruighoek
Dam

Madapye
(1472m)

Magare
(1462m)

1483m

Lengau
Dam

Bakubung
Gate

Sun City
Complex

Pilanesberg
Airport

Kwa
Maritane
Gate

R556

To Rustenburg
(38km) R565

To Rustenburg (35km);
Brits (55km);
Pretoria (142km)

Mankwe Safaris (☎ 014-555 7056; www.mankwe safaris.co.za) also runs a variety of activities; enquire at its office next to the Manyane Gate reception office. Wildlife drives with a bush braai (barbecue) cost R320, walking trails are R200 and the company can also organise museum trips and cultural tourism activities.

Sleeping & Eating

Manyane Complex & Caravan Park (☎ 014-555 5351; www.goldenleopard.co.za; camp & caravan sites R120, 2-person safari tent with breakfast R350, 2-person chalet with breakfast R340;) Near Manyane Gate, this complex is thoughtfully designed and laid out, with high-quality facilities. There's a small pool, a bar, a shop with a reasonable range of food items and a decent restaurant.

Bakgatla Complex (☎ 014-555 5351; www.golden leopard.co.za; camp sites R120-150, safari tent with breakfast R330, 4-/6-person chalet with breakfast per person R320/280;) There is a big range of accommodation options available here. This is a smaller camp to the northwest of Manyane gate.

Ivory Tree Lodge (☎ 011-706 8781; www.africanan thology.co.za; s/d with full board & activities R2680/3500;

) The rates quoted at this newly opened luxury lodge will no doubt go up sharply once it's better established.

Kwa Maritane Lodge (☎ 011-806 6806; www .legacyhotels.co.za; s/d with breakfast & dinner R1330/1880;), **Bakubung Lodge** (☎ 011-806 6806; www.legacyhotels.co.za; s/d with breakfast & dinner R1330/1880;) and **Tshukudu Lodge** (☎ 011-806 6806; www.legacyhotels.co.za; s/d with full board & activities R3360/4790;), all run by Legacy hotels, are the park's main luxury options. Bakubong and Kwa Maritane are essentially similar, with around 80 rooms, large dining rooms and tennis courts. The accommodation here is of a very good standard and the hotels have still managed to retain a bit of taste and character, though neither exactly represents a wild bush experience. Tshukudu is more exclusive, with just six luxury cottages, each with a sunken bath that has a view over the surrounding hills.

BORAKALALO NATIONAL PARK

Located in the northeastern corner of the province on the Moratele River and the Klipvoor Dam, this **national park** (☎ 012-729

NORTH-WEST PROVINCE

3337; entry per person R15, plus per car R10; 5am-8pm summer, 6am-7pm winter) lives up to the meaning of its name: Place of Relaxation. Most of the original animal inhabitants were relentlessly hunted out and are now slowly being reintroduced, with 350 bird species as well as leopards, otters, zebras and jackals now resident.

Camp sites are booked through **Golden Leopard Resorts** (014-555 6135; goldres@iafrica .com). Camps in the reserve are **Pitjane Fishing Camp** (camp sites per person R55); at **Phuduphudu** (4-person safari tents R390) and **Moretele** (camp sites R55, 4-bed safari tents R250).

To get here from Pretoria and Jo'burg head to Brits, then take the R511 to Assen and follow the signs to Klipvoor Dam; the way to the entrance of Borakalalo Nature Reserve is signposted. There is no public transport to the park.

ZEERUST
018 / pop 17,600

Zeerust's main claim to fame is as a jumping-off point for Gaborone, Botswana, and there are always lots of people moving through. The town is quite large; there are plenty of shops strung along Church St, including a couple of banks and 24-hour petrol stations. There are a couple of basic hotels on the main street.

The **tourist information office** (642 1081; Church St; 7.30am-4pm Mon-Fri) in the municipal building has information on the local Mampoer Route, which refers to a fiery distilled liquor brewed in the region.

Intercape (0861 287 287; www.intercape.co.za) passes through Zeerust on its daily run between Pretoria (R125, two hours) and Gaborone (R70, three hours). The bus stops at the Chicken Licken in Church St.

The minibus taxi rank is on Church St on the Mafikeng side of town.

MADIKWE GAME RESERVE
One of the largest reserves in South Africa, **Madikwe** (083-629 8282) comprises 760 sq km of bushveld, savanna grassland and riverine forest on the edge of the Kalahari Desert. The reserve was created in 1991, not only to protect endangered wildlife, but as a job-creation scheme and a way of providing a more sustainable environment for local people. A massive translocation operation, called Operation Phoenix, brought more than 10,000 animals into the area. The animals had all once been indigenous to the area, but their numbers were depleted due to hunting and farming pressures from the human inhabitants. The operation took over seven years to complete, with animals (including entire herds of elephant) being flown or driven in from various other reserves around Southern Africa. All of the Big Five, plus the endangered wild dog, are now present, together with over 350 bird species. Madikwe is one of South Africa's best-kept secrets: it's nearer to Jo'burg than the Kruger Park but has far less visitors. It's also malaria-free, making it a good option for children.

Sleeping & Eating
Madikwe is not open to day visitors, so to visit you'll have to book into one of the 24 lodges and camps within the park, all of which do guided wildlife drives in open vehicles.

Mosethla Bush Camp (011-444 9345; www .thebushcamp.com; s/d with shared bathroom & full board R1459/2190) This is a simple, rustic camp, with accommodation in open-fronted log cabins within an unfenced bush area. There's no electricity and no running water, but canvas bucket showers and hot water boilers ensure it's still very comfortable. Rates include bush walks, wildlife drives and all meals.

Jaci's Lodges (083-700 2071; www.madikwe.com; s/d with full board & activities R5700/7590, children R1260;) For sheer luxury, panache and design flair, Jaci's two lodges – Safari Lodge and Tree Lodge – can compete with anywhere else in Africa. The quality of guiding is also excellent, ensuring guests have the best chance of seeing great wildlife during their stay. Unusually for such an upmarket place, Jaci's welcomes children and has babysitters and various kids' activities for when parents need a break.

Getting There & Away
It takes about four hours to drive from Gauteng to the reserve gates via the N4 and the R510 from Rustenburg, or R505 from Zeerust. Buses on their way from Gaborone can be prevailed upon to stop in the reserve, while at the other end of the scale there is also a regular scheduled flight from Jo'burg airport. Ask about either of these options when booking your accommodation.

MAFIKENG

☎ 018 / pop 50,900

Mafikeng and Mmabatho were originally twin towns about 3km apart, but are now combined and Mmabatho is part of Mafikeng. Mmabatho was built as the capital of the 'independent' homeland of Bophuthatswana, and became famous for the monumental and absurd buildings erected by corrupt Bophu thatswana president, Lucas Mangope.

Today Mafikeng is a friendly and relaxed town with a large middle-class Black population. The main reason to visit is the excellent Mafikeng Museum, one of the best in the country.

History

Mafeking (as the Europeans called it) was established as the administrative capital of the British Protectorate of Bechuanaland (present-day Botswana). The small frontier town, led by British colonel Lord Baden-Powell, was besieged by Boer forces from October 1899 to May 1900. The siege was in many ways a civilised affair, with the besieging Boers coming into town on Sundays to attend church. However, it was seized upon by the heroics-hungry Victorian press as a symbol of British courage and steadfastness. During the siege Baden-Powell created a cadet corps for the town's boys, which was the forerunner to his Boy Scout movement.

In reality, the British officers dined on oyster patties and roast suckling pig in their mess while the Baralong and Mfengu people, who sustained equal casualties in the service of the colonialists, lived on dogs and locusts. The Baralong military hero Mathakong Ko-

dumela, who saw his troops massacred by the Boers several times while raiding for cattle to feed the town, was dismissed by Baden-Powell as 'uncooperative' when he asked for arms to defend them.

Orientation

It's easy to get around Mafikeng on foot. Most shops and banks are around the central local bus station. It's 5km from the centre of Mafikeng to the Megacity shopping mall in Mmabatho; catch one of the many local buses. Megacity is a useful starting point if you are heading further north or west; you'll find banks, a post office and a Pick 'n' Pay supermarket here.

Information

MONEY

First National Bank (Robinson St), between Main and Shippard Sts, **ABSA** (cnr Warren & Main Sts) and **Standard Bank** (cnr Main & Robinson Sts) all have ATMs and can change travellers cheques or cash at a pinch.

POST & COMMUNICATIONS

The main post office is next to Megacity. There is another post office on Carrington St between Main and Martin Sts. There's an **Internet café** (☎ 384 9071; per hr R20; ☼ 8.30am-5.30pm Mon-Thu; 8.30am-4.30pm Fri, 9am-2pm Sat) in the Megacity shopping mall.

TOURIST INFORMATION

Check out the grandiose **Mafikeng Tourism Info & Development Centre** (☎ 381 3155; www.tour ismnorthwest.co.za; cnr Licthenburg Rd & Nelson Mandela Dr; ☼ 8am-6pm Mon-Fri, 8am-noon Sat) at the

---

NO HOME, NO LANDS

During the 1970s the Batloung inhabitants of Botshabelo, near Mafikeng, were forcibly removed from their well-established villages, farms and towns and 'resettled' in areas of arid, unfertile bush as part of the homelands policy. White farmers were given the plots left behind at 40% of their market value, while the original landowners received no compensation. In many cases, the dispossessed Batloung had watched their homes and possessions being bulldozed before they were removed.

After the reversal of the homelands policy in the 1990s, the displaced community began taking action to get their land back. In 1991, a group of White extremists led by Eugene Terreblanche attacked the families who had returned to Botshabelo. The final steps in the return of the Batloung to their rightful lands were only completed in 2001. In a final act of defiance, one departing farmer even poisoned the fruit trees in his orchard before he left.

Visit the excellent Mafikeng Museum (see p484) to learn more about the machinations of the apartheid government in this part of South Africa.

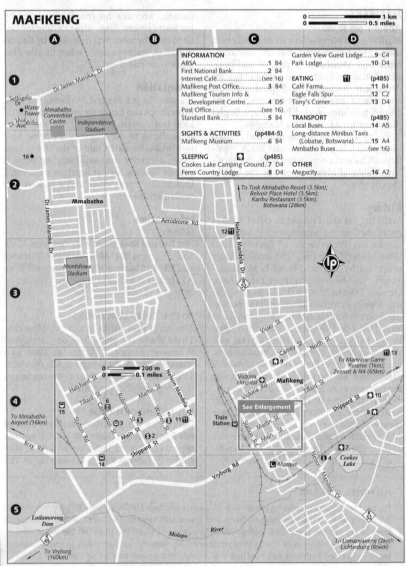

MAFIKENG

0 — 1 km
0 — 0.5 miles

INFORMATION
ABSA...1 B4
First National Bank....................2 B4
Internet Café.......................(see 16)
Mafikeng Post Office..................3 B4
Mafikeng Tourism Info &
   Development Centre..............4 D5
Post Office...........................(see 16)
Standard Bank............................5 B4

SIGHTS & ACTIVITIES   (pp484-5)
Mafikeng Museum.........................6 B4

SLEEPING 🏠   (p485)
Cookes Lake Camping Ground.7 D4
Ferns Country Lodge...................8 D4

Garden View Guest Lodge.......9 C4
Park Lodge.................................10 D4

EATING 🍴   (p485)
Café Farma.................................11 B4
Eagle Falls Spur.........................12 C2
Tony's Corner...........................13 D4

TRANSPORT   (p485)
Local Buses................................14 A5
Long-distance Minibus Taxis
   (Lobatse, Botswana)...........15 A4
Mmbatho Buses..................(see 16)

OTHER
Megacity.................................16 A2

To Tusk Mmabatho Resort (3.5km);
Belvoir Place Hotel (3.5km);
Karibu Restaurant (3.5km);
Botswana (28km)

Setlogelo Dr
Water Tower
Mmabatho Convention Centre
Independence Stadium
Dr James Maroka Dr
Dr Mok Ave
Gobo
16

Mmabatho

Aerodrome Rd

Montshiwa Stadium

Nelson Mandela Dr

Visser St

Carney St
North St
9

To Manyane Game Reserve (1km);
Zeerust & N4 (65km)
13

Victoria Hospital
Victoria Rd
Mafikeng

Tillard St

Shippard St
10
8

0 — 200 m
0 — 0.1 miles

Hatchard St
Tillard St
Robinson St
Martin St
Warren St
Carrington St
Station Rd
6
15
5
3
11
2
Main St
Shippard St
14

See Enlargement

Train Station
Station Rd
Martin St
Main St

Vryburg Rd
Mosque
4
7
Cookes Lake

To Mmabatho Airport (16km)
Bray Rd

Lotlamoreng Dam

To Vryburg (160km)

Molopo   River

To Lomanyaneng (2km);
Lichtenburg (65km)

Cookes Lake Camping Ground. It even has some badly stuffed animal heads on the walls!

Sights

The excellent **Mafikeng Museum** (☎ 381 6102; cnr Carrington & Martin Sts; admission by donation; ⏰ 8am-4pm Mon-Fri, 10am-1pm Sat) has reams of

interesting and quirky information about the history of Mafikeng from prehistoric times onwards. Among the many displays in the museum is an exhibit charting the rise of the Boy Scout movement, and an entire room dedicated to the famous siege, with original photographs and letters, and good information about the forgotten role

Cape Flat Lizard, Augrabies Falls National Park (p507), Northern Cape

LUKE HUNTER

CAROL POLICH

Quiver tree, Namaqualand (p508), Northern Cape

Gemsbok or South African Oryx, Kgalagadi Transfrontier Park (p503), Northern Cape

CAROL POLICH

CAROL POLICH

Wildebeest, Kgalagadi Transfrontier Park (p503), Northern Cape

LUKE HUNTER

Auob riverbed, Kgalagadi Transfrontier Park (p503), Northern Cape

LUKE H

Ravine through the Augrabies Falls National Park (p507), Northern Cape

African daisies in the Goegap Nature Reserve (p511), Northern Cape

ROB DRUM

played by the town's Black population. There's also some information about the 'lost city' of Kaditshwene, and a small coffee shop.

Sleeping

There are a few B&Bs in town, starting at around R150 per person. Ask at the tourist office for a complete list.

Garden View Guest Lodge (☎ 381 3110; cnr North & Havenga Sts; s with/without bathroom R240/150, d with/without bathroom R320/220; ☒) This is the best that Mafikeng has to offer at a reasonable price. The spick-and-span rooms have TV, fridge and kitchenette, and there's a very convivial restaurant-bar.

Ferns Country Lodge (☎ 381 5971; ferns@world online.co.za; 12 Cook St; s/d R399/513; ☒ ☐ ☒) Ferns is stylish and elegant with ultramodern furnishings and a beautiful garden. It's well signposted off Shippard St.

Park Lodge (☎ 381 6753; fax 381 1683; 70 Shippard St; s/d with breakfast R180/230) The small but uncluttered rooms here all have TV. Dinner is available for R39.

Belvoir Place Hotel (☎ 386 2222; fax 386 2100; ihtm@iafrica.co.za; Nelson Mandela Dr; s/d with breakfast R340/550; ☒ ☒) If you can take the horrid 1980s décor, this is a fairly luxurious place that forms part of a hotel training school. Each of the enormous rooms has TV, safe, fridge and telephone. The hotel is 3.5km from the town centre.

Tusk Mmabatho Resort (☎ 389 1111; mmabat ho@tusk-resorts.co.za; Nelson Mandela Dr; s/d R580/840; ☒ ☐ ☒) Mafikeng's luxury option, this opulent resort and casino, 3.5km from the town centre, is a legacy of the old Bophuthatswana homeland.

Cookes Lake Camping Ground (☎ 381 5611; camp sites R15 plus per person R15) Inside the Manyane Game Reserve, Cookes has recently been upgraded and now offers decent facilities.

Eating

Café Farma (☎ 381 4906; 17 Nelson Mandela Dr; lunches R20; ☒ breakfast & lunch Mon-Sat) In Era's Pharmacy, this is *the* place for breakfast, light meals and heavy cakes.

Karibu Restaurant (☎ 386 2222; Nelson Mandela Dr; mains R45-80; ☒ lunch & dinner) It's not cheap, but this grand restaurant in the Belvoir Place Hotel does good meals (try the veggie curry). It also has delightfully old-fashioned service: the plates come covered with silver

domes, which the tuxedoed waiters remove with a flourish.

Tony's Corner (☎ 381 0700; 12 Gemsbok St; seafood R49-55; ☒ lunch & dinner Mon-Sat) This upmarket pub-restaurant has an interesting menu including duck, stir-fry and plenty of seafood dishes.

Eagle Falls Spur (☎ 381 0347; cnr Nelson Mandela Dr & Aerodrome Rd; meals R20-45) This steak restaurant has specials such as steak and calamari (surf 'n' turf) and kids burgers with free drinks.

Getting There & Around

Many people come through Mafikeng on their way to/from Botswana. Ramatlabama, 24km to the north, is the busiest border post and lies on the main route to/from Gaborone (Botswana).

SAAirlink (☎ 011-978 1111; www.saairlink.co.za) has flights four days a week to Jo'burg (R900) with connections to other cities. The airport is 16km northwest of Mafikeng. The Tusk Mmabatho Resort can arrange airport pick-ups for guests. For car-hire information, see p477.

Mmbatho Buses (☎ 381 2680; Megacity) run daily from Megacity to Jo'burg (R95, six hours).

Long-distance minibus taxis leave from the forecourt of the Mafikeng train station, headed for the Botswana border (R5, running all day); Zeerust (R12); Lobatse (Botswana; R17); Vryburg (R30, very few taxis); Gaborone (R35); and Rustenburg (R30). As usual, most leave early in the morning.

Numerous city buses ply the route between Mafikeng (from the corner of Main St and Station Rd) and Megacity for a few rand.

POTCHEFSTROOM

☎ 018 / pop 122,100

Potchefstroom, known locally as 'Potch', is off the N12 about 115km southwest of Jo'burg. It was the first European town to be established in the former Transvaal, and remains staunchly conservative. It's a large town, verging on a city, which looks rather unappealing from the main road. There are, however, some pleasant leafy suburbs around the university.

Maps of Potch and the Vredefort Dome in neighbouring Free State (p361) are available at the **Tourist Information Office** (☎ 293 1611; cnr Potgieter & Church Sts).

Sleeping & Eating

Willows Garden Hotel (☎ 297 6285; willowsgch@mweb .co.za; cnr N12 & Mooiriver St; s/d with breakfast R365/475; ❄ 🖳 🕱) This smart, modern business-style hotel has all the mod cons you'd expect. Dros restaurant next door provides room service.

Lake Holiday Resort (☎ 299 5473; fax 299 5475; camp sites R75, 2-person rondavels with shared bathroom R115, family 'longdavel' R265; 🕱) The whole of Potch can be found here on a sunny weekend. The resort's facilities include fairground attractions, boats, a café and plenty of braais.

Paljas Backpackers B&B (☎ 018-267 1815; Esselen St; dm/s/d with shared bathroom R80/100/200) This is a clean, inexpensive place aimed at groups of visiting students. There's a self-catering kitchen and a homely lounge. It does pickups from the bus stop (R10).

Getting There & Away

Intercape (☎ 0861 287 287; www.intercape.co.za) buses stop in Potch on their daily run between Pretoria (R85, 3½ hours) and Upington in the Northern Cape (R225, eight hours). **Greyhound** (☎ 012-323 1154; www.greyhound.co.za) buses run from Potch to Cape Town (R400, 16 hours) and Jo'burg (R100, two hours). **Translux** (☎ 011-774 3333; www.translux.co.za) also runs to Johannesburg (R90, two hours).

The *Trans Karoo* train also stops here on the way between Pretoria (1st/2nd class R80/60, five hours) and Cape Town (R450/305, 24 hours). See p605 for more details of this service.

Northern Cape

Perspectives are skewed in South Africa's largest, yet least-populated, province, the Northern Cape. The sky consumes you and the larger-than-life solitary landscapes make you comprehend your minuteness in the scope of the entire universe. A place of haunting beauty, the Northern Cape has roads that seem to stretch on forever into the great unknown. It's easy to lose yourself in the vastness, to find yourself mesmerised by the red sands of the Kalahari or by lions stalking prey across South Africa's most wild and remote national parks.

It's a province full of surprises. A long, hard drive across the Karoo can lead to a town in the middle of nowhere, where life moves as slowly as it always has and nothing ever seems to change. Soak it up with a late-afternoon beer at a café with the locals or a wander past the old colonial buildings of a one-street town.

When the sun sinks low in Namaqualand, famous for its extraordinary spring flowers, it's one of those big orange-balled sunsets that remind you of the Africa of tourist brochures. The land then dissolves into the black velvet sky for your own personal planetarium show, where the stars give the illusion of being more plentiful than anywhere else in the world. And just when you think you're in the middle of a never-ending desert, you'll be hit with another surprise: the landscape will turn green, you'll pass grapes ripening on the vines and you'll hit the banks of the mighty Orange River, the lifeline that runs through the country.

HIGHLIGHTS

- Watch **Namaqualand** blossom into an astounding display of wildflowers in the spring (p509)

- Spot a black-maned lion letting out a ferocious roar in **Kgalagadi Transfrontier Park** – a remote and pristine area teeming with wildlife (p503)

- Raft the mighty **Orange River** and then take in the splendour of **Augrabies Falls National Park** (p507)

- Hike the barren trails in **Richtersveld National Park**, a stunning mountainous desert (p513)

- Revel in the red and white sands, bleached grasses and psychedelic sunsets of the **Kalahari**, a vast and mythical land (p498)

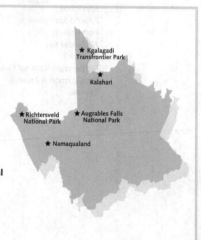

★ Kgalagadi Transfrontier Park

★ Kalahari

★ Richtersveld National Park

★ Augrables Falls National Park

★ Namaqualand

- POPULATION: 814,000

- AREA: 361,830 SQ KM

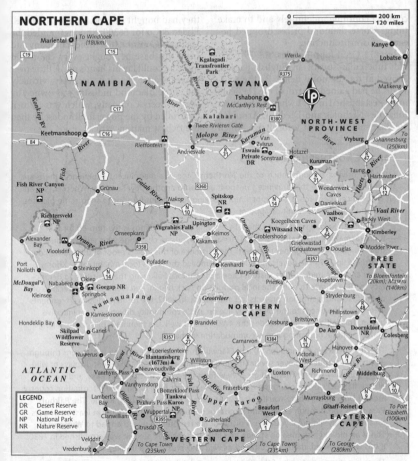

NORTHERN CAPE

HISTORY

The modern history of the Northern Cape has been shaped by the richness the seemingly barren earth has yielded. On a fateful day in 1866 a young man by the name of Erasmus Jacobs saw a pretty white pebble shimmering on the arid ground near Kimberley and picked it up. In his hand he held a 21.25 caret yellow diamond called Eureka, and life in the province was never quite the same.

In 1871 diamonds were discovered at a small hill that came to be known as Colesberg Koppie (later Kimberley), and the excavation of the mine known as the Big Hole commenced. By 1872 there were an estimated 50,000 miners in the vicinity. It was thought the diamonds lay at a depth of

15m to 18m, which allowed virtually anyone with a shovel to get at them. A number of problems faced the diggers, not the least of which was how to allow each miner access to their claims (which measured about 7m by 9m). These small claims were even further subdivided, and eventually there were 1600 claims and over 30,000 men toiling in an area measuring roughly 200m by 300m.

The miners soon found the diamonds continued as they dug further and further down. And as they did so the difficulties of managing the mine, rapidly resembling an insane anthill, increased. An elaborate web of ropes and pulleys, which were used to haul out the gravel, soon crisscrossed the ever-growing crater. This kind of chaos couldn't continue indefinitely and to make things worse diamond prices dropped because of overproduction.

In 1871 Cecil John Rhodes, the 19-year-old, tubercular son of an English parson, arrived at the diamond fields. By the mid-1870s he had gained control of the De Beers mine – established in 1871 when the brothers Johannes Nicholas and Diederik Arnoldus De Beer sold their farm Vooruitzigt, which they had bought in 1860 for £50, to Dunell Ebden & Co for £6300. Rhodes founded the De Beers Consolidated Mines company and from this base he bought every claim and mine he could lay his hands on. A little over 20 years after the first discovery, virtually the entire diamond industry was owned by the De Beers Company, which was in turn controlled by the powerful Rhodes, by then the richest man in Africa.

TOP FIVE NORTHERN CAPE DRIVES

Although driving through much of the Northern Cape is a magnificent experience, there are some drives that take this province's unspoilt appeal to another level entirely. Whether you are an experienced back-roads driver, or simply looking for a beautiful spot to snap some pictures, we're sure these roads won't disappoint.

▪ Just outside Kakamas (p506) on the N14 heading towards Keimos is the turn-off for the **Riemvasmaak 4WD Trails** (☎ 054-431-0945). Here you can challenge your skills on three trails ranging from beginner to expert. The existence of this area is proof of the triumph over apartheid. In 1973 the government forcibly removed the area's local inhabitants – Xhosa, Nama and Coloured – to the Eastern Cape and Namibia. Following the transition to democracy in 1994 efforts to bring the local population back began, and Riemvasmaak became one of the first land restitution projects in South Africa. In 2002, the formerly displaced residents were given the deeds to the plots they live on and a community driven tourism initiative began. This initiative now includes the 4WD trails as well as a mountain bike route, hiking paths, a natural hot spring and accommodation in chalets.

▪ The R364 between Calvinia (p514) and Clanwilliam in the Western Cape (p216) runs through empty countryside and over several magnificent passes. There are excellent displays of wildflowers in early spring. There's a great view from the top of **Botterkloof Pass**, and a couple of nice flat rocks overlooking the gorge that are perfect for a picnic. You hit irrigation country around Doringbos, where you'll find dramatic views of the Cederberg Range. The **Pakhuis Pass** takes you through an amazing jumble of multicoloured rocks. Allow at least two hours for the journey – more if you have a picnic or are tempted to take the road to **Wuppertal**. This is an old Rhenish mission station and little has changed since it was established in 1830. It has whitewashed, thatched cottages, as well as cypresses and donkeys.

▪ There is a stunning stretch of the R27 between Calvinia and Vanrhynsdorp in the Western Cape with magnificent views over the Knersvlakte Plain from **Vanrhyns Pass**. In spring there can be a breathtaking contrast between the green and fertile wheat fields, the flowers at the top of the pass and the desert far below.

▪ The local dirt roads around **Hondeklip Bay** on the Northern Cape's coastline are spectacular. After climbing through rocky hills you drop onto the desert-like coastal plain, which is dotted with enormous diamond mines. The flora is fascinating – make sure you take time to walk around, even if it's just off the side of the road. A 2WD is OK for this area.

▪ The **Namakwa 4WD Route** traverses some of South Africa's most remote and rugged territory east and south of Richtersveld National Park (p512). The route has been divided into two parts: Pella Mission Station to Vioolsdrif and Vioolsdrif to Alexander Bay. To drive either route you must first obtain a permit from the **Tourism Information Office** (☎ 027-712 2011) in Springbok (p509). Permits cost R150 per vehicle per route and include a detailed map and information on designated camp sites along the way. The first route, designed for novice drivers, traverses 328km and takes between two and four days to drive. The second route, designed for more experienced drivers, is 284km long and is usually completed in six hours.

CLIMATE

The Northern Cape is a land of extremes. The province is semidesert and summer temperatures in the Kalahari and the Karoo often soar above 40°C during the day and drop below freezing at night.

Rainfall in the region is scant, with annual precipitation between 50mm and 400mm, most of which falls in the western areas of the province. This rain leads to magnificent spring (July–November) wildflowers in Namaqualand. The Orange River runs through the Northern Cape and the river valleys are so fertile the area is called the Green Kalahari.

NATIONAL PARKS & RESERVES

The Northern Cape has the country's most remote national parks, and some of its most spectacular. In the far north of the province, bordering Botswana and Namibia, is the outstanding Kgalagadi Transfrontier Park (p503), one of Africa's new parks joining conservation areas across international borders (see p63) and the result of a merger between the Kalahari-Gemsbok National Park in South Africa and the Mabuasehube-Gemsbok National Park in Botswana.

The wildest of all of South Africa's national parks is the Richtersveld National Park (p512), in a very remote location on the Namibian border in the northwest corner of the province. The area is a spectacular wilderness offering excellent hiking opportunities and the chance to spot wildlife, mostly small mammals. The park is only accessible by 4WD, and due to the amount of time it takes to reach it, day visitors are discouraged. It's best to visit the park on an organised tour.

Another major park in the region is Augrabies Falls National Park (p507) where the Orange River plunges over a series of waterfalls. It is easily accessible in a 2WD vehicle.

The province is also home to quite a few nature reserves including the Witsand Nature Reserve (p502), 200km east of Upington, where you can feast your eyes on a giant white sand dune; and Spitskop Nature Reserve (p502), which has a number of unusual species such as the black springbok and the black zebra.

LANGUAGE

The Northern Cape is one of only two provinces in South Africa (the other is Western Cape) where Coloureds, and not Blacks, make up the majority of the population. Afrikaans is the most widely spoken language with about 66% of the province speaking it. The indigenous population is varied and includes the San, who can still be seen around the Kalahari (small numbers of San continue to lead semitraditional lifestyles in isolated parts of neighbouring Botswana), the Tswana and some Khoikhoi groups. Setswana (19%) and isiXhosa (6%) are the other main languages. English is spoken everywhere.

GETTING THERE & AROUND

The Northern Cape is easily accessible by car, bus, train and plane. With the exception of the Kgalagadi Transfrontier and Richtersveld National Parks, where private vehicle hire is a necessity, with a little patience most places can be reached by bus. There is daily bus service between the transportation hubs of Kimberly and Colesberg from both Cape Town and Johannesburg (Jo'burg). Buses to and from Cape Town, Jo'burg and Windhoek, Namibia, also pass through Upington and Springbok at least three times a week. **South African Airlink** (SAAirlink; ☎ 054-838 3337; www.saairlink.co.za) has flights from Jo'burg and Cape Town to Kimberly and Upington. **National Airlines** (☎ 021-934 0350; www.flynal.com) has flights to Springbok and Alexander Bay, a good jumping off point for the Richtersveld, from both Cape Town and Jo'burg.

Public transport within the province is generally straight forward, and you won't be kept waiting anywhere for too long. If you're on a tight budget, but still want to experience the Kgalagadi on your own, it's possible to pick up a rental car in Upington for a couple of days, although prices are generally higher than if you rent in one of the country's major cities.

KIMBERLEY & UPPER KAROO

Kimberley, capital of the Northern Cape, is the main centre of the *diamantveld* (diamond fields). The north–south N12, an alternative route between Jo'burg and Cape Town, passes through Kimberley and crosses the east–west N10 at Britstown in the Upper Karoo.

Kimberley is a captivating place and the surrounding area is rich in Anglo-Boer War history. The Upper Karoo, part of the Great Karoo (p206 and p243), is sprinkled with small towns, scrub brush and little else; it's probably the least enticing portion of the expansive Karoo. However, nearly everyone driving the N1 between Cape Town and Jo'burg stops for the night in Colesberg, as it's about halfway between the two cities.

KIMBERLEY

☎ 053 / pop 166,000

Step inside one of Kimberley's atmospheric old pubs with dark smoky interiors, scarred wooden tables and last century's Castle Lager posters, and you get the feeling you've been transported back to the rough-and-ready gold mining days. Spend a night in one of the old world hotels, the slightly shabby air only adding to its charm, and you might wake up thinking it's the late 1800s.

This is the city where De Beers Consolidated Mines began; where Cecil John Rhodes (p494) and Ernest Oppenheimer (mining magnate and mayor of Kimberley) made their fortunes. It's been more than a century now, and yet Kimberley is still synonymous with diamonds, and mining continues.

And after a long slog across the Karoo the relatively bright lights of Kimberley are a welcome sight. The Big Hole is amazing, there are some excellent galleries in town, Galeshewe township is inextricably linked with the history of the struggle against apartheid, and the silence of the Karoo will be forgotten amid the din of Kimberley's busy pubs.

Orientation

The town centre is a tangle of streets, a legacy of the not-so-distant days when Kimberley was a rowdy shantytown, sprawling across flat and open veld. If you're trying to find the train station, look for the red-and-white communications tower. The tourist tram, which departs from the town hall, is a good means of getting your bearings.

The satellite township of Galeshewe is northwest of the city centre.

Information

Small World Net Café (☎ 831 3484; 42 Sidney St; per hr R30; ☽ 9am-5pm Mon-Fri) is where to go to surf the net.

The **Diamantveld Visitors Centre** (☎ 832 7298; tourism@kbymun.org.za; Bultfontein Rd; ☽ 8am-5pm Mon-Fri, 8am-noon Sat) has brochures and good maps of Kimberley and Northern Cape and can arrange tours of the area.

Sights & Activities

Kimberly has enough historical sights to keep you entertained for a day or two.

KIMBERLEY MINE MUSEUM

Step back in time and browse for ladies shoes, bottled water or petticoats at this excellent open-air **museum** (☎ 833 1557; West Circular Rd; adult/child R25/15; ☽ 8am-6pm) set up as a reconstruction of Kimberley in the 1880s. Complete with streets, miners cottages, shops, auction rooms and a tavern, there are 48 original or facsimile buildings in total. De Beers Hall has a collection of diamonds and there are demonstration models of diamond-recovery technology. There's also a dramatic view over the Big Hole.

Children will love the diamond dig where they'll be given a large bucket of rocks to sift through; if you find a diamond you win a prize. The museum is on the western side of the Big Hole.

THE BIG HOLE

The largest hole in the world dug entirely by manual labour, the Big Hole is 800m deep. Water now fills it to within 150m of the surface, which still leaves an impressive void, but don't forget that there is over four times as much hole below the water's surface.

The Kimberley Mine, which took over after open-cast mining could no longer continue, went to a depth of around 1100m. It closed in 1914. Altogether, 14.5 million carats of diamonds are believed to have been removed. In other words, 28 million tonnes of earth and rock were removed for just three tonnes of diamonds. For the best view of the Big Hole, you need to enter via the museum (and pay the museum's admission fee).

ANGLO-BOER WAR BATTLEFIELDS

Kimberley holds a significant place in the history of the 1899–1902 war between the British and the Boers. After swift early victories the Boers got bogged down in lengthy sieges at Kimberley, as well as Ladysmith in

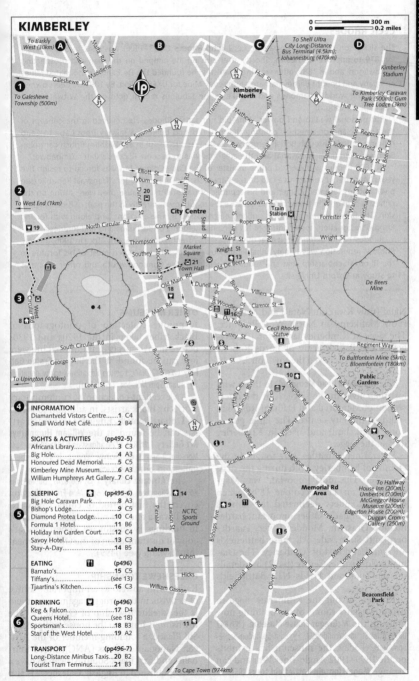

KIMBERLEY

0 — 300 m
0 — 0.2 miles

To Barkly West (30km) **A**
To Galeshewe Township (500m)
Galeshewe Rd
Pniel Rd
Malfa St
Madeliefie Ave

B

C
To Shell Ultra City Long-Distance Bus Terminal (4.5km); Johannesburg (470km)

D
Kimberley Stadium
To Kimberley Caravan Park (500m); Gum Tree Lodge (3km)

1

Cecil Sussman St
Transvaal Rd
Quinn Rd
Hull St
Willis St
Mathews St
Diagonal St
Kimberley North

Gladstone Ave
Regent St
Oxford St
Judge St
Piccadilly St
Gray St
Short St
Taylor St
Searle St
Warren St
Merriman St
De Beers Tce
Innes St

2
To West End (1km)
19

Elliott St
Tyburn St
Duncan St
20
Transvaal Rd
Cemetery St
City Centre
Goodwin St
Roper St
Stead St
Ward St
Quinn St
Forrester St
Wright St
Train Station
North Circular Rd
Compound St
Thompson St
Southey St
Stockdale St
Market Square
Knight St
Town Hall 21
Old De Beers Rd

6
3
8
West Circular Rd
Old Main Rd
18
Dunell St
New Main Rd
Jones St
Bean St
Woodley St
3
Chapel St
Du Toitspan Rd
Villiers St
Clarence St
Cecil Rhodes Statue
De Beers Mine
Regiment Way
4

South Circular Rd
George St
To Upington (400km)
Long St
Bultfontein Rd
Sydney St
Currey St
York St
Lennox St
Chapel St
Tiffany Cres
Jan Smuts Blvd
12
10
7
Hospital Rd
Park Rd
Todd La
Du Toitspan Rd
Spencer La
Harley St
Etienne Rd
Cornwall St
Public Gardens
To Bultfontein Mine (5km); Bloemfontein (180km)

@ 2
Angel St
Eureka St
1
Jubilee St
Cullinan Cres
Lyndhurst St
Synagogue St
Henderson St
Memorial Rd
17
Cornwall St
To Halfway House Inn (200m); Umbertos (200m); McGregor House Museum (200m); Edgerton House (200m); Duggan Cronin Gallery (250m)

4
INFORMATION
Diamantveld Vistors Centre.......1 C4
Small World Net Café..............2 B4

SIGHTS & ACTIVITIES (pp492-5)
Africana Library...................3 C3
Big Hole..........................4 A3
Honoured Dead Memorial...........5 C5
Kimberley Mine Museum............6 A3
William Humphreys Art Gallery....7 C4

SLEEPING (pp495-6)
Big Hole Caravan Park.............8 A3
Bishop's Lodge....................9 C5
Diamond Protea Lodge.............10 C4
Formula 1 Hotel..................11 B6
Holiday Inn Garden Court........12 C4
Savoy Hotel......................13 C3
Stay-A-Day.......................14 B5

EATING (p496)
Barnato's........................15 C5
Tiffany's......................(see 13)
Tjaartina's Kitchen..............16 C3

DRINKING (p496)
Keg & Falcon.....................17 D4
Queens Hotel...................(see 18)
Sportsman's......................18 B3
Star of the West Hotel...........19 A2

TRANSPORT (pp496-7)
Long-Distance Minibus Taxis.....20 B2
Tourist Tram Terminus...........21 B3

Scanlan St
Dalham Rd
Memorial Rd Area
Memorial Rd
Oliver Rd
Vortrekker St
Miner St
Loop La
Carrington Rd
Beaconsfield Park
14
NCTC Sports Ground
Pienaar
Lawson St
Bishops Ave
9
16
15
5
Labram
Cohen
Hicks
William Gasson
11
Poole St
To Cape Town (974km)

5

6

CECIL RHODES

The sickly son of an English parson, Cecil John Rhodes (1853–1906) was sent to South Africa in 1870 to improve his health. Shortly after arriving, he jumped on the diamond prospecting bandwagon, and in 1887, after working feverishly, he founded the De Beers Consolidated Mines company and bought Barney Barnato's Kimberley Mine for UK£5 million. By 1891 De Beers owned 90% of the world's diamonds and a stake in the fabulous reef of gold on the Witwatersrand (near Johannesburg).

But personal wealth and power alone did not satisfy Rhodes. He believed in the concept of the empire, and dreamed of 'painting the map red' and building a railway from Cape to Cairo running entirely through British territory. Rhodes was successful in establishing British control in Bechuanaland (later Botswana) and the area that was to become Rhodesia (later Zimbabwe).

In 1890 Rhodes was elected prime minister of the Cape Colony, but was forced to resign five years later after encouraging a raid on the Witwatersrand, in Paul Kruger's Transvaal Republic (see p34). Rhodes resented Kruger and his republic of pastoralists because they were sitting on the richest reef of gold in the world and because the republic was directly in the path of British expansion. The British government was publicly embarrassed by these actions, and along with forcing Rhodes' resignation, took control of his personal fiefdoms of Bechuanaland and Rhodesia.

Rhodes' health deteriorated after these disasters. After his death in South Africa in 1906, though, Rhodes' reputation was largely rehabilitated by his will, which devoted most of his fortune to the Rhodes Scholarship that still sends winners from the Commonwealth and other countries to study at Oxford University.

Natal (now KwaZulu-Natal) and Mafeking (now Mafikeng) in North-West Province. The siege of Kimberley lasted for 124 days before the British army of Lords Roberts and Kitchener relieved the town on 15 February 1900.

The **Honoured Dead Memorial**, to those who lost their lives in the siege, is at the intersection of Memorial and Dalham Rds, 6km south of the city centre. The large gun is Long Cecil, built and used in Kimberley during the siege.

Several major battles were fought in the vicinity of Kimberley, both during the siege and after. The most important was Magersfontein on 11 December 1899, when entrenched Boers decimated the famous Highland Brigade. Other important battles include Graspan, Modder River, Paardeberg and Sunnyside. All these battlefields are south and east of Kimberley. The Diamantveld Visitors Centre (p492) has details on the Diamond Fields N12 Battlefields Route.

Rhodes sat out the Kimberley siege in two downstairs rooms of the building now housing the **McGregor House Museum** (☎ 842 0099; Atlas St; adult/child R8/4; ◷ 9am-5pm Mon-Sat, 2-5pm Sun). Today, the museum has exhibits on the 1899–1902 Anglo-Boer War and can arrange **Magersfontein battlefield tours** (R5).

OTHER MUSEUMS

A unique collection of photographs of Black tribes taken in the 1920s and 1930s before many aspects of traditional life were lost can be found at the **Duggan Cronin Gallery** (☎ 842 0099; Egerton Rd; admission by donation; ◷ 10am-5pm Mon-Sat, 2-5pm Sun).

An excellent collection of contemporary works by Black artists, in addition to pieces by Dutch, Flemish, English and French artists can be found at the **William Humphreys Art Gallery** (☎ 831 1724; admission R2; ◷ 10am-5pm Mon-Sat, 2-5pm Sun). Some argue it's the best gallery in South Africa.

The **Africana Library** (☎ 180 6247; Du Toitspan Rd; admission free; ◷ 10am-5pm Mon-Fri) collection covers the first period of contact between the Tswana and the missionaries. Included in holdings is missionary Robert Moffat's copy of his translation of the Old Testament into Tswana (see p499).

GALESHEWE TOWNSHIP

Rating with Soweto as an important source of activists in the struggle against apartheid is the satellite township of Galeshewe. The township is home to the house and grave of Sol Plaatje, a founding member of the African National Congress (ANC), noted journalist and first Black South African to have a novel published in English. Galeshewe is also the home of Robert Sobukwe, founder and first president of the then–Pan African Congress (PAC). Galeshewe was where the Self Help Scheme was implemented by Helen Joseph, former secretary of the Federation of South African Women and an organiser of the 1956 mass demonstration in Pretoria against the extension of regulations governing the carrying of passes (see p37).

A tour of Galeshewe may well be one of the highlights of your stay in South Africa. Unlike Soweto, tours of this township are not common. You can tailor an itinerary to suit your interests; some of the notable things to see are places associated with Robert Sobukwe and Sol Plaatje. However, it is the opportunity to see how the majority of South Africans live, and how the ANC's commitment to provide housing for people living in abject poverty is progressing, that makes a tour so absorbing. Much new housing has been provided, but the reality is that there is too many people and too little money.

The spirit of the people in Galeshewe is undeniable and you'll be met with a smile and a handshake from adults, and laughter and waves from kids.

Tours

The Diamantveld Visitors Centre (p492) has a list of registered tour guides in Kimberley.

De Beers Tours (☎ 842 1321; tours R15; ⏰ 9am & 11am Mon-Fri) Groups visit the diamond treatment and recovery plants at Bultfontein Mine 5km east of the centre on the city's outskirts. Tours depart from the visitors centre at the Bultfontein Mine gate.

Underground Tours (☎ 842 1321; tours R80; ⏰ 9.30am Mon, 8am Tue-Fri) Also run by De Beers, this is the more adventuresome of the mine tours. Descend deep under the earth and get a feel for the life of a miner. You can't wear contact lenses because of the pressure at the depths you'll descend to, and you have to be over 16 to go on one of these 3½-hour tours. The tours depart from the visitors centre at the mine gate.

Fikile (Michael) Bili (☎ 083-692 6058; tours R150) Michael is a guide operating tours into Galeshewe. He is very familiar with the history of the area, and the horrors of apartheid are brought to life with his vivid descriptions. He is also passionate about improving conditions in the township. These daily tours are highly recommended and run for about three hours. Call for departure times and to arrange pick-up.

Sleeping

Kimberley has options for all budgets.

BUDGET

Stay-A-Day (☎ 832 7239; 72 Lawson St; dm R50, s/d with shared bathroom R95/160) Rooms are tiny, but tidy. If the place is empty ask to stay in a double for the price of a dorm. Formerly an orphanage, the proceeds go towards the existing children's home near the property.

Gum Tree Lodge (☎ 832 8577; fax 831 5409; cnr Hull St & Bloemfontein Rd; dm R50, s/d with shared bathroom R90/160; 🏊) Big and spread out, this former jail is a good place to bring the family – there is a playground and lots of grass. Accommodation is in fairly basic flats with a stove and fridge. It's about 3km east of the town centre.

Big Hole Caravan Park (☎ 830 6322; West Circular Rd; camp sites R25 plus per person R15; 🏊) Trees, grassy areas on which to pitch your tent and a central location make this an appealing camping option. The swimming pool is a good cool-off spot on a hot day.

Kimberley Caravan Park (☎ 082-442 5097; Hull St; camp sites R45) Shady and friendly, this is another camping option 500m east of town.

MID-RANGE

If none of these options sound appealing head to the Diamantveld Visitors Centre, which has details on more B&Bs.

Savoy Hotel (☎ 832 6211; 15 Old De Beers Rd; s/d R290/330) This gracious and old-fashioned hotel is excellent value, and a stay here is almost like stepping back in time.

Bishop's Lodge (☎ 831 7876; www.bishopslodge .co.za; 9 Bishops Ave; d R245, 2-person flats R355; 🏊 🏊) Modern and spotless inside. Inviting pool and braai area outside. The self-contained flats come with sitting rooms, TV and full kitchenettes.

Halfway House Inn (☎ 831 6324; 229 Du Toitspan Rd; s/d R160/190) If you're hoping to literally 'stumble into bed' this is a good option – the place is attached to a lively pub. Those seeking quiet, look elsewhere. Rooms are large and come with TV.

Formula 1 Hotel (☎ 831 2552; www.formula1hotels .co.za; cnr Memorial & Welgevonden Aves; r R200; 🏊) For clean, quality rooms head to this South African chain. It's a little way out of town, but good value for money.

TOP END

Edgerton House (☎ 831 1150; 5 Edgerton Rd; d R990; 🏊 🏊) Exquisite furniture, African hospitality and a tea garden make this charming guesthouse the best luxury option in Kimberley. It has the honour of having had Nelson Mandela stay on more than one occasion.

Holiday Inn Garden Court (☎ 833 1751; fax 832 1814; 120 Du Toitspan Rd; s/d R480/570; ✗ 🖳) This large hotel delivers high standards at a reasonable price and often has weekend specials. Children stay free.

Diamond Protea Lodge (☎ 831 1281; dplkim@glo bal.co.za; 124 Du Toitspan Rd; s/d R400/450; ✗) Another option for high standard, yet chain hotel–styled rooms – although this Protea's rooms are larger than usual. There are often specials.

Eating

Umbertos (☎ 832 5741; 229 Du Toitspan Rd; mains R30-60; 🕑 lunch & dinner; ✗) Big hearty portions of Italian food are served along with loads of ambiance. For dining choose either the rooftop patio with its pretty sunset views or the more intimate downstairs area – with a red and white theme. Occasionally Umberto himself gets up and gives an impromptu opera solo.

Star of the West Hotel (☎ 832 6463; North Circular Rd; mains R35; 🕑 breakfast, lunch & dinner) This place is old and atmospheric: to walk through the thick wooden door is to step back into Kimberley's rough-and-ready mining days. Tables are scarred and old posters and newspaper clippings grace the walls (this was a men-only pub until the late 1980s!). Food is pub grub, the clientele mostly local. Despite its past, women won't feel uncomfortable eating or drinking (see p496) here.

Tiffany's (☎ 832 6211; Old De Beers Rd; mains R25-50; 🕑 breakfast, lunch & dinner) This is a lovely, if very pink, old-style restaurant in the Savoy hotel with good service and a varied menu – including a few vegetarian options. The old leather-and-wood bar adjoining Tiffany's is good for a quiet drink before dinner.

Barnato's (☎ 833 4110; 6 Dalham Rd; mains R60-90; 🕑 lunch & dinner Mon-Fri, dinner Sat, lunch Sun) One of the poshest and most popular places in town for top-end food.

Tjaartina's Kitchen (☎ 831 5856; 75A Du Toitspan Rd; mains R7; 🕑 breakfast & lunch) Try this eatery for cheap African food, including traditional dishes such as *bunny chow*, a curry served in a bread basket. It also does cheap burgers.

Entertainment

Kimberley is one of the few towns in the country with a range of decent pubs, some of which have been around from the time diamonds were the town's lifeblood. In fact at one time the number of bars in the city apparently twice outnumbered its churches.

Star of the West Hotel (☎ 832 6463; North Circular Rd) There are often live bands in the big beer garden. Pool tables and a cocktail bar upstairs add to the ambience.

Halfway House Inn (☎ 831 6324; 229 Du Toitspan Rd) Once a ride-in bar (a concept invented by Rhodes, who was afraid to dismount from his horse and reveal his true height), the Half has pool tables downstairs and live music on Friday and Saturday nights in the pleasant rooftop beer garden.

Queens Hotel & Sportsman's (☎ 831 3704; 12 Stockdale St) In the centre of town this large pub in the hotel gets rowdy on weekends and has gambling. Sportman's is the attached disco.

Keg & Falcon (☎ 833 2075; 187 Du Toitspan Rd; mains R35-60) Tired of partying with the very young? Head here. You have to be over 23 to get in and the dress code is smart casual. It also serves food.

Getting There & Away

AIR

SA Express (☎ 011-978-5315; www.saexpress.co.za) has regular direct services from Jo'burg (R1000, 1½ hours). **SAAirlink** (☎ 054-838 3337; www.saairlink.co.za) has a direct service to Cape Town (R1585, two hours).

BUS

Translux (☎ 011-774-3333; www.translux.co.za) stops in Kimberley on its run between Jo'burg/ Pretoria (R185, seven hours, daily) and Cape Town (R290, 10 hours, daily).

Greyhound (☎ 012-323 1154; www.greyhound.co .za) has the cheapest service between Jo'burg and Kimberley (R190, seven hours, daily). **Intercape** (☎ 0861 287 287; www.intercape.co.za) also has a service to Kimberley.

Book tickets for all three companies through **Tickets for Africa** (☎ 832 6043; Diamantveld Visitors Centre). Buses stop at the Shell Ultra City long-distance bus terminal on the N12.

MINIBUS TAXI

The main minibus taxi area is around the Indian shopping centre on Duncan St in the city centre (where there's a produce market and takeaways). Destinations from Kimberley include Bloemfontein (R50, 2½ hours),

Kuruman (R75, two hours), Jo'burg (R120, seven hours), Upington (R75, four hours) and Cape Town (R135, 10 hours).

TRAIN

For information on trains call **Spoornet** (☎ 838 2111; www.spoornet.co.za). The *Trans Karoo* runs daily between Cape Town (R150, 18 hours, daily) and Jo'burg/Pretoria (R80, nine hours, daily) via Kimberley; the *Diamond Express* runs overnight between Jo'burg/Pretoria and Bloemfontein via Kimberley (R80, nine hours, three times weekly); and the *Trans Oranje* between Cape Town and Durban (R120, 18 hours, weekly) takes a slow and circuitous route via Kimberley.

Getting Around

The Kimberley airport is about 7km south of the city centre. A taxi costs about R150.

Kimberley has one surviving antique tram (one-way/return R7/14) that departs from the terminus near the town hall every hour on the hour (9am to 4pm daily) and runs to the mine museum.

A minibus taxi around town costs about R1.30. For a private taxi from the pubs, try **AA Taxi** (☎ 861 4015) or **Rikki's Taxi** (☎ 083-342 2533).

VAALBOS NATIONAL PARK

This is the only **national park** (☎ 561 0088; adult/child R60/30) in South Africa where three distinct ecosystems are present: Karoo, *grassveld* (grasslands) and Kalahari. Proclaimed in 1986 and divided in two by a belt of private land, the park is 61km northwest of Kimberley on the R31. If you want to stay the night you can **camp** (camp sites R75) or stay in one of the **self-catering cottages** (up to 4 people R350). Note: you must bring all your supplies with you, as the park does not have restaurant or shopping facilities.

DE AAR

☎ 053 / pop 26,000

De Aar is a major service centre for the Karoo, but its claim to fame is as a railway junction – it's one of the busiest in South Africa. De Aar is too big to be called a one-horse town – maybe it's a two-horse town. The author Olive Schreiner (who wrote *Women and Labour*) lived here from 1907 to 1913. There is little to see or do here except appreciate small-town life.

The **De Aar Hotel** (☎ 631 2181; Friedlander St; s/d R160/240; 🟌) is a large well-maintained place with a pleasant feel. It's not luxurious, but the bathrooms are spotless and the rooms have TV. There is an attached restaurant and bar.

The **Upstairs Restaurant** (☎ 631 1000; cnr Hoof & Voortrekker Sts; mains R25-50; 🕑 breakfast, lunch & dinner) has a rather extensive menu of seafood, pasta, pizza and various meats. Eat on the upstairs patio and catch all the town's action on the main drag below.

Trains that pass through here are the *Trans Karoo* and the *Blue Train* (Jo'burg/Pretoria–Cape Town), and the *Trans Oranje* (Durban–Bloemfontein–Kimberley–Cape Town); see p605.

BRITSTOWN

☎ 053

At the centre of a prosperous sheep-grazing area in the Upper Karoo is orderly, pleasant and tiny Britstown, at the crossroads of the N10 and the N12. If you find yourself here at dusk and want to stay the night try the long-established **Transkaroo Country Lodge** (☎ 672 0027; fax 672 0363; s/d R180/350; 🟌 🟋). It has a provincial French feel with a cosy lounge, friendly staff and quaintly furnished, immaculate rooms. The attached restaurant and bar does a dinner buffet for R75 and light lunches. It also runs activities such as bird-watching trips, and excursions to San rock-art sites.

Minibuses pass through Britstown; ask at the Transkaroo Country Lodge.

COLESBERG

☎ 051 / pop 12,000

Colesberg makes a good halfway stopping point on the N1 between Cape Town and Jo'burg. Drive through it enough times and it starts to grow on you. A classic Karoo town, Colesberg is an attractive place. Founded in 1829, many old buildings have survived including a beautiful **Dutch Reformed church** (1866). There are also shops with verandas fronting onto the main street, and charming old houses and cottages on the side streets.

Colesberg's friendly **information centre** (☎ 753 0678; belinda@mjvn.co.za; Murray St; 🕑 8am-4.30pm Mon-Fri) is in the town museum. If you're yearning to surf the Web try the **Colesberg Apteek** (☎ 753 0618; 18 Church St; per hr R60; 🕑 9am-5pm Mon-Sat).

Sleeping

Most of the town's accommodation options are found along Church St, which is sometimes spelled the Afrikaans way – Kerk St.

Light House (☎ 753 0043; 40A Church St; d R220) The best option in town, the Light House is located in a large rambling home with stately, well-appointed and airy rooms.

Colesberg Lodge (☎ 753 0734; fax 753 0667; Church St; d R270-360; 🌡 🐾) Rooms come in three classes – budget, regular and luxury – at this quality hotel. The budget rooms only have fans, while the luxury rooms have air-con and TV. There's also a bar and restaurant attached.

Colesberg Backpackers (☎ 753 0582; 39 Church St; dm R50, d with shared bathroom R120) A homely place right on the main drag, this backpackers doesn't have tons of atmosphere but it's quiet and makes for a good-value overnight stop. Often empty, you'll probably have the dorm to yourself.

Sunset Chalets (☎ 082-493 8814; 14 Torenberg St; s/d R80/160) Conveniently situated on the right when you first come into town from the south on the N1, Sunset has red-brick thatched cottages, and a playground for the kids.

Eating

Bordeaux Coffee Shop & Restaurant (☎ 753 1582; 7A Church St; breakfast R15-30, light meals R15; mains R30-50; 🕑 breakfast, lunch & dinner) Cosy atmosphere inside, and a suburban garden outside make this Colesberg's best eating option. There is a decent wine list and the calamari appetiser (R18) is appealing. Vegetarians might be happier elsewhere.

JC's Pizzeria (☎ 753 1170; 29 Church St; mains R28-52; 🕑 lunch & dinner) The menu features pizzas, pastas and steaks, although it does pizzas best. Sit outside under the vines or inside among the twinkling candles. The best option for vegetarians in Colesberg.

Getting There & Around

Translux (☎ 011-774-3333; www.translux.co.za) and **Intercape** (☎ 0861 287 287; www.intercape.co.za) both pass through Colesberg on their Jo'burg (R225, 7½ hours, daily) to Cape Town (R305, 9½ hours, daily) run and stop at the Shell Ultra to the north of town on the N1. Intercape also has services to Bloemfontein (R110, 2½ hours, daily).

AROUND COLESBERG

North of Colesberg, and just off the R369, you'll find **Doornkloof Nature Reserve** (☎ 051-753 1315; janniedoornkr@hotmail.com; adult/child R5/3; 🕑 8am-6pm). Both here and on the shores of Vanderkloof Dam it's possible to see mountain reedbucks, duikers, kudus and steenboks (and if you're very lucky: aardvarks, aardwolfs and bat-eared foxes).

There is an overnight **hut** (up to 4 people R88), but you'll need your own bedding, food and cooking utensils. There are also very basic **camp sites** (per night R35).

THE KALAHARI

With stunning sunsets, endless sun-seared, shifting red and white sands, fertile green fields and ripening red grapes on thick brown vines, the Kalahari region is one of South Africa's gems. A timeless magical place, it will enchant and mystify long after you depart. Solitary stretches of space spin on into infinity and shapes are distorted under a blanket of shimmering heat. You may feel you are the last person alive on a deserted planet. Laurens Van der Post brought the world of the Kalahari alive in many of his books including the *Lost World of the Kalahari* and *A Far Off Place.*

The desert is not limited to South Africa, but actually covers much of Botswana and its fingers extend into Angola and Namibia as well. In South Africa it's divided into two distinct areas – the arid, semidesert and desert regions on its periphery and the 'green' Kalahari, the irrigated, fertile region along the banks of the Orange River. Most visitors to the country miss the Kalahari. Don't. Even the extra driving it takes to reach the Kgalagadi Transfrontier Park is well worth it.

KURUMAN

☎ 053 / pop 9,000

At the edge of rough and wild country, this evocative frontier town is an oasis in the desert – thanks to a permanent water supply in the shape of an amazing natural spring. Kuruman's name derives from a San word, but the Batlhaping, a Batswana tribe, also settled in the area c1800.

West of Kuruman there's a long, empty stretch of road to Upington, and a landscape of low, sandy ranges.

The main road is called simply that, and most businesses are concentrated around the intersection of this and Voortrekker/Tsening Sts. Adjacent to the Eye of Kuruman is a useful **tourist office** (☎ 712 1095; Main Rd; ☉ 8am-4.30pm Mon-Fri, 8am-12.30pm Sat).

Sights & Activities
Kuruman is worth an out-of-the-way stop if birds of prey fascinate you. The **Raptor Rehabilitation Centre** (☎ 712 0620; Tsening Rd; admission free; ☉ 8am-4.30pm Mon-Fri) provides a map of the best routes to follow in search of these creatures. The Kalahari is home to 40 of South Africa's 67 raptor and vulture species, although they now have to share the skies with a recent influx of human soarers. Kuruman has become world renowned as a **paragliding** centre, with several height and distance records achieved here.

The **Eye of Kuruman** (Main Rd; adult/child R1/0.50) is the natural spring that produces 18 to 20 million litres of water per day, every day. It has never faltered. The surrounding area has been developed into a pleasant-enough picnic spot, and is a good place to break your journey – note the masked weaverbirds and their nests over the pond.

Sleeping
Riverfield Guesthouse (☎ 712 0003; 12 Seodin Rd; s/d with breakfast R210/330; ☒) Run by the ebullient Alfie, the bar here is a great meeting place, the rooms good value (especially the cosy rondavel) and the breakfasts mighty.

Kuruman Caravan Park (☎ 712 1479; Voortrekker St; camp sites R50, chalets R200) Not a bad place to shack up for the night – the chalets are well equipped and comfortable. Camp sites are mostly shady, and it's all a short walk from the town centre.

Eldorado Motel (☎ 712 2191; Main Rd; s/d R250/390; ☒ ☒) Those looking for standard modern motel features should head here. Prices drop on weekends.

Eating
Over-de-Voor (☎ 712 3224; Hoof St; mains from R25; ☉ lunch & dinner) Over-de-Voor, which serves 'Kalahari cuisine', is the town's best eating place. Vegetarians beware – it serves meat plus meat.

Tavern Bar (☎ 712 1148; Main Rd; ☉ breakfast, lunch & dinner) This fiercely conservative Afrikaner bastion is in the Grand Hotel. The

ennui here can be cut with a knife – though it does have a *boerewors* (spicy sausage) collection as a centrepiece!

De Oude Drostdy (☎ 712 0620; Main Rd; snacks from R10; ☉ breakfast & lunch) Next to the Eye, this is a good choice for coffee and a snack.

Getting There & Around
Intercape (☎ 0861 287 287; www.intercape.co.za) stops daily in Kuruman on its way between Jo'burg (R175, seven hours) and Upington (R120, three hours).

The taxi rank is next to the Shop Rite supermarket on Voortrekker St.

MOFFAT MISSION
☎ 053
The first White settlement in the area, the London Missionary Society established the **Moffat mission** (☎ 732 1352; adult/child R5/2; ☉ 8am-5pm Mon-Sat, 3-5pm Sun) in 1816 to work with the local Batlhaping people. The mission site was chosen due to this part of the valley's cultivability.

It was named after Robert and Mary Moffat, two Scots who worked at the mission from 1817 to 1870. They converted the Batlhaping to Christianity, started a school and translated the Bible into Tswana. The mission became a famous staging point for explorers and missionaries heading further into Africa. The Moffats' daughter, Mary, married David Livingstone in the mission church, which is a stone and thatch building with 800 seats.

The mission is a quiet and atmospheric spot shaded by large trees that provide a perfect escape from the desert heat. It is along the R31 to Hotazel, about 4km from the N14.

HOTAZEL TO VAN ZYLSRUS
☎ 053
The most interesting thing about Hotazel is its name. Say it quickly: 'hot as hell'. Van Zylsrus is a dusty little frontier town, one of the most isolated in South Africa. There's a stop sign, a petrol station, post office and pub – all the necessities of life!

The reason either is mentioned is that about halfway between the two, near Sonstraal, lies the superb **Tswalu Private Desert Reserve** (☎ 781 9211; fax 781 9316; s/d with full board R6600/8800; ☒ ☒). South Africa's largest private wildlife reserve, it is something special, offering the chance to spot rare animals such as the black rhino, sable and roan in a stunningly beautiful landscape. The staff are very experienced, and it's possible to tailor a safari to your own interests. As you'd expect for the price, accommodation and rations are top notch, imaginative and blend incongruously into the surrounding landscape. The pool is particularly alluring.

UPINGTON
☎ 054 / pop 53,000

Orderly and prosperous, Upington is the principal commercial town in the far north, and in the midst of an intensively cultivated area, thanks to limitless sunlight and irrigation water. After a long trip across the Kalahari the sight of wheat and cotton and grapes and fruit growing in an oasis of green will be startling. Wide boulevards slightly cluttered with supermarkets and chain stores line the centre of town, but step onto one of the side streets and you'll enter a different world. Here lazy river views and endless rows of trees create a calm and quiet atmosphere perfect for an afternoon stroll (if the heat is not too stifling). Upington is a good place to stock up on supplies for a visit to Kgalagadi Transfrontier Park (p503).

Information
The First National Bank is on the northwestern corner of Schröder and Hill Sts; the Standard Bank is on the corner of Hill and Scott Sts.

The helpful **tourist office** (☎ 332 6046; green kal@mweb.co.za; ☉ 8am-5pm Mon-Fri, 9am-noon Sat) is in the Kalahari Oranje Museum.

There is Internet access at **Café de Net** (☎ 331 2252; Pick 'n Pay Centre; per hr R30; ☉ 9am-5pm Mon-Fri); look for it behind the Dros pub. You can also get on-line at the Kalahari Junction Backpackers (p501).

Tours
Kalahari Safaris (☎ 332 5653; www.kalahari-safaris .ch) Readers highly recommend this company, run by Kalahari Junction Backpackers (p501), which does camping and deluxe safaris to Kgalagadi, Augrabies Falls and Witsand Nature Reserve. The three-day Kalahari

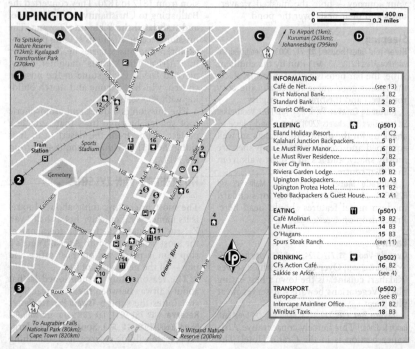

UPINGTON

0 —————— 400 m
0 —————— 0.2 miles

To Spitskop
Nature Reserve
(12km); Kgalagadi
Transfrontier Park
(270km)

To Airport (1km);
Kuruman (263km);
Johannesburg (795km)

Train Station

Sports Stadium

Cemetery

Orange River

To Augrabies Falls
National Park (80km);
Cape Town (820km)

To Witsand Nature
Reserve (200km)

safari in Kgalagadi starts at R2990 and includes all fees, equipment and meals. A one-day safari to Augrabies Falls costs R650.

Kalahari Adventure Centre (☎ 331 1286; www .kalahari.co.za; 12 Mark St) This company runs five-day Kgalagadi camping safaris for R3950, including entrance fees and meals. Tours depart from Upington Backpackers (p501) on Mondays.

Sleeping

Spitskop Nature Reserve (p502) is a good alternative accommodation option, and is close to town.

BUDGET

Kalahari Junction Backpackers (☎ 332 5653; www .kalahari-safaris.ch; 3 Oranje St; dm from R50; 🖵 🖭) Under renovation when we stopped by, this place has potential for being a good stopover spot. It's run by the people who operate Kalahari Safaris (p500).

Upington Backpackers (☎ 331 1286; www.kala hari.co.za; 12 Mark St; dm R75, d with shared bathroom R150) The new kid on the block, this place was just opening when we were researching. It's run by the Kalahari Adventure Centre (p507), which runs rafting and canoe trips down the Orange River, so it's a good place to stay at if you're looking for adventure sport info.

Yebo Backpackers & Guest House (☎ 331 2496; danie.eng@lantic.net; 21 Morant St; camp sites per person R35, dm R50, d with shared bathroom from R170; 🖭) Dorms are large and the beds are not bunked. Yebo is a sprawling place with large grassy gardens. The pool is perfect for cooling down on a hot summer day.

Eiland Holiday Resort (☎ /fax 334 0286; camp sites R50, r from R120) A good range of huts and bungalows, all varying in price, make this another option and the best for camping. The resort is a fair walk from town, on the eastern bank of the Orange River.

MID-RANGE & TOP END

Budler St has some gorgeous guesthouses with grassed areas overlooking the river.

Le Must River Residence (☎ 332 3971; www .lemustupington.com; 14 Budler St; s/d from R390/580; 🖭 🖭) The classiest of the Le Must franchises, this guesthouse is by far the most exclusive place to stay in Upington and well worth the price. Service and facilities are impeccable. Rooms are luxuriously decor-

ated with antique furniture and African themes and come with satellite TV; the grounds are a work of art.

Le Must River Manor (☎ 332 3971; www.lemust upington.com; 12 Murray Ave; s/d from R295/395; 🖭 🖭) For those on a tighter budget the quality at the River Manor is only slightly less luxurious than the River Residence, and well worth a stay.

Riviera Garden Lodge (☎ 332 6554; 16 Budler St; d with breakfast R390; 🖭) This excellent lodge has two cosy rooms with flowery bedspreads, and a fantastic garden area with trees and fountains extending down to the river.

River City Inn (☎ 331 1971; cnr Park & Scott Sts; s/d R225/285; 🖭) A step up from the backpackers, but still affordable to those on a budget, this is a good splurge option if you need a night with TV and air-con. We get many readers' letters praising this inn. Beware, if you have a vehicle there is no off-street parking.

Upington Protea Hotel (☎ 337 8400; fax 337 8499; 24 Schröder St; s/d R400/475; 🖭 🖭) This is one of two Protea hotels in town. Rooms are comfortable, but sterile. It has a lovely swimming pool.

Eating

Le Must (☎ 332 3971; 11 Schröder St; mains from R60; 🕑 lunch & dinner) The best eating option in town. The food is excellent and of far better quality than you usually find in a country town. The Cape Malayan pot-fried lamb flavoured with tamarind strongly reasserts the restaurant's name.

O'Hagans (☎ 331 2005; 20 Schröder St; mains R35-60; 🕑 breakfast, lunch & dinner) O'Hagans has the best food of the 'chain' pubs. The menu here is very good, and the portions are generous, especially the seafood. And you can't beat the location – sit outside on the patio overlooking the river. There are often drink specials.

Café Molinari (☎ 331 2928; Pick 'n Pay Centre; breakfast R18-36, mains R24-35; 🖭) We loved the variety of breakfast options here. Lunch focuses on sandwiches, pastas and salads. There's a big stack of magazines to thumb through while waiting for your food.

Spurs Steak Ranch (☎ 331 1240; 24 Schröder St; mains from R30; 🕑 breakfast, lunch & dinner) Under the Upington Protea Hotel, Spurs has the usual grills to keep carnivores happy, as well as salads for herbivores.

Entertainment

Sakkie se Arkie (☎ 082-564 5447; admission R35) A sundowner cruise on the Orange River is the perfect way to start your evening. Admission covers the cruise; drinks are extra. The company picks up from many of the riverfront guesthouses.

CFs Action Café (☎ 332 1414; 65 Market St) A dance floor and pool tables draw a young rowdy crowd.

O'Hagans (☎ 331 2005; 20 Schröder St) The outdoor patio is pleasant on a warm night for a tipple as well as for food (see p501). O'Hagans generally entertains an Afrikaner horde. There is a good range of beers and a few decent wines.

Getting There & Away

AIR

If you're short on time and want to see the Kgalagadi it may be worth flying into Upington and then renting a car. **SAAirlink** (☎ 838 3337; www.saairlink.co.za) flies to/from Jo'burg (R1665, daily) and to/from Cape Town (R1665, Sunday to Friday). Upington hotels usually provide a free taxi from the airport.

BUS

Two Intercape services run through Upington and provide good links to the rest of the country. For tickets go to the **Intercape Mainliner office** (☎ 332 6091; Lutz St). Buses run to Jo'burg and Pretoria (R260, 10 hours, daily), Windhoek, Namibia (R250, 12 hours, four times weekly), Cape Town (R220, 10½ hours, four times weekly) and Calvinia (R145, five hours, four times weekly).

CAR RENTAL

Car hire is generally more expensive here than in Jo'burg or Cape Town. There's an agent for **Avis** (☎ 332 4746) at Upington airport. There is a **Europcar** (☎ 082-426 8489) agent inside the River City Inn. They rent 4WDs for about R900 per day, and compact cars for R340. If you know when you're going to be in Upington try checking out www.travelocity.com a few weeks in advance, as there are often deals on car hire through major rental companies.

MINIBUS TAXI

You'll find taxis nearby the Checkers supermarket near the corner of Mark and Bas-son Sts. Not all long-distance taxis leave from here but it's a good place to start asking. Fares from Upington include Jo'burg (R170, 10 hours), Cape Town (R180, 10 hours) and Windhoek (R170, 10 hours).

VIP Taxis (☎ 027-851 8780 in Port Nolloth) operates a weekday taxi service from Port Nolloth to Upington, via Springbok. It costs R80 to travel from Upington to Springbok. Call to arrange pick-up.

AROUND UPINGTON

It is the unusual species that make the small **Spitskop Nature Reserve** (☎ 054-332 1336; teuns@intekom.co.za; adult/child R12/6; camp sites per adult/child R25/12, huts/chalets per person R60/80) about 13km north of Upington so interesting. Most intriguing are the black springbok (there are six), whose colour results from genetic mutations that are seldom seen. The all 'black' zebra you see dominating a group of female zebra is a runt of a pony who decided to take over the herd – just look at the intensity on his face when he rounds up one of the females who breaks away. The camels are remnants of those that the German cameleers left in the region after skirmishes during WWI.

The reserve also has gemsboks, springboks, wildebeests, bonteboks, zebra and elands among other smaller animals.

There are short hiking trails and a novice 4WD trail. You can view wildlife through a telescope from the top of the prominent Spitskop.

Accommodation includes sandy, shady camp sites, a four-bed chalet and, most fascinating of all, a rustic, isolated 'veld hut' in the middle of the reserve (bring your own bedding). There is no electricity in the hut, which sleeps five.

WITSAND NATURE RESERVE

The beauty of this **nature reserve** (☎ 053-313 1062; www.witsandkalahari.co.za; adult/child R15/7.50; ⏱ 8am-6pm) has a soundtrack. As if a park based on a 9km-wide by 2km-long by 100m-high white sand dune standing out in stark contrast to the typical red Kalahari sands surrounding it weren't enough – when the wind blows the sand sings. Known as 'roaring sands' the effect is created by the movement of air across the dunes and creates a bass, organ-like sound; walking on the sands produces a muted groan.

The reserve is approximately 200km east of Upington (or 200km southwest of Kuruman). You can walk anywhere in the park, but 4WDs are restricted to the roads. A bird hide and mountain bike (per day R50) and dune board (per day R70) hire provide added entertainment.

There's a delightful bush camp with two swimming pools and 10 thatch-roofed, open-plan, tastefully decorated **self-catering lodges** (per adult/child R190/95; ✷). The lodges have three bedrooms and can sleep up to six people. On weekends there is a minimum charge of R570 per lodge. The reserve does not have a restaurant or bar, but for R725 per person a chef will prepare you dinner and breakfast in your lodge. The fee also includes your accommodation, park entrance fee and a guided walk. Advance booking is essential. **Camping** (camp sites per person R80) is also an option.

KGALAGADI TRANSFRONTIER PARK

A giant black-maned lion napping under the shade of a camel thorn tree in a landscape of varying shades of red and orange terrain is an awesome sight. Add herds of gentle looking gemsbok picking their way through the sparse vegetation, those massive orange and pink sunsets Africa is famous for, and a chance to view wildlife without the crowds of South Africa's more popular parks and you're set for an unforgettable experience. The **Kgalagadi Transfrontier Park** (☎ 054-561 0021; www.parks-sa.co.za; adult/child R120/60) was proclaimed in April 1999 and is the result of a merger between the former Kalahari-Gemsbok National Park in South Africa and the Mabuasehube-Gemsbok National Park in Botswana.

The accessible section of the park lies in the triangular segment of South African territory between Namibia and Botswana. This region covers 9591 sq km. The protected area continues on the Botswana side of the border (there are no fences) for a further 28,400 sq km. South Africa's side of the park was proclaimed in 1931 and Botswana's in 1938. Kgalagadi is one of the largest protected wilderness areas in Africa, allowing the unhindered migration of antelopes, which are forced to travel great distances in times of drought to reach water and food.

Although the countryside is described as semidesert (with around 200mm of rain a year) it is richer than it appears and sup-

KGALAGADI TRANSFRONTIER PARK

0 ——— 40 km
0 ——— 20 miles

ports large populations of birds, reptiles, rodents, small mammals and antelopes. These in turn support a large population of predators. Most of the animals are remarkably tolerant of cars. This allows you to get extraordinarily close to animals that are otherwise wild – it's as if you are invisible.

The landscape is hauntingly beautiful. The Nossob and Auob Rivers (usually dry) run through the park and meet each other a few kilometres north of the entrance, at Twee Rivieren rest camp. Much of the wildlife is concentrated in these river beds, so they are easy to spot. The only significant human interference in the park's ecology are the windmills and water holes.

In the south of the park, the Nossob river bed is between 100m and 500m wide, with grey camel thorn trees growing between the limestone banks. In the north the river bed opens up to more than a kilometre wide, and becomes sandy. The bed of the Auob is narrower and deeper. Between the two rivers, the Kalahari dunes are characteristically red due to iron oxide. In other areas the sand varies from pink and yellowish to grey.

Orientation & Information

Visitors are restricted to four gravel/sand roads – one running up the bed of the Nossob River, one running up the bed of the Auob River (there are also some small loop roads), and two linking these. Make sure to take one of the roads linking the rivers for unobstructed views of the empty expanses of the Kalahari. Visitors must remain in their cars, except at a small number of designated picnic spots.

The best time to visit is in June and July when the days are coolest (below freezing at night) and the animals have been drawn to the bores along the dry river beds. August is windy and, for some reason, a favourite time for tour buses. September to October is the wet season and if it does rain, many of the animals scatter out across the plain to take advantage of the fresh pastures. November is quiet, and daily temperatures start to rise. Despite the fact that temperatures frequently reach 45°C in December and January, the chalets in the park are fully booked during the school holidays.

All the rest camps have shops where basic groceries, soft drinks and alcohol can be purchased (fresh vegetables are hard to come by); these are open from 7am until 30 minutes after the gates close. Petrol and diesel are available at each camp. There are public phones, a pub, a swimming pool and an information centre detailing the history of the park and giving details of the flora and fauna (there are also slide shows four nights a week) at Twee Rivieren rest camp.

The gate opening hours change based on month, but generally follow the rising and setting sun. Gates open between 5.30am and 7.30am and shut between 6pm and 7pm.

The speed limit is 50km/h. The minimum travelling time from the entrance gate at Twee Rivieren to Nossob rest camp is 3½ hours and to Mata Mata rest camp it's 2½ hours. Allow plenty of time to get to the camps as no driving is permitted after dark.

If you want to venture into the Botswana side of the park, this is only possible via a 4WD trail. You need to make arrangements with the **Botswana Department of Wildlife & National Parks** (☎ 09-267 580774) in Gaborone. Staff at park headquarters in Twee Rivieren organise sundowner night drives for R85 per person, giving you the chance to spot some of the park's nocturnal species.

Flora

Only hardy plants survive the periodic droughts that afflict the Kalahari. Many have adapted so that they germinate and produce seed within four weeks of a shower of rain.

The river beds have the widest variety of flora. The Nossob River is dominated by camel thorn trees (Acacia erioloba) in the north and grey camel thorn trees (A. haematoxylon) in the south. Sociable weaverbirds favour the camel thorns for their huge nests, and all sorts of creatures feed off the foliage and seeds.

Various grasses and woody shrubs survive on the dunes. There are occasional shepherd's trees (Boscia albitrunca), which have white bark and a dense thicket of short low branches where many animals take refuge in the heat of the day. The driedoring shrub (Rhigozum trichotomum), with fine leaves and forked branches, is the most common shrub in the park.

Many of the animals depend on plants as their source of moisture. In particular, the tsamma (Citrillus lanatus), a creeper with melon-like fruit, is an important source of water. There are several prickly cucumbers that are important for the survival of animals, especially the gemsbok.

Fauna

Finding fauna requires luck, patience and a little intelligence. There is no guarantee that you will see one of the big predators but you are more likely to here than in many other places. Most of the region's wildlife, with the exception of elephants, rhinos and zebras, are found in the park.

There are 19 species of predator here, including the dark-maned Kalahari lion, cheetah, leopard, wild dog, spotted hyena, black-backed jackal, bat-eared fox, Cape fox, honey badger and meerkat. The most numerous antelope is the springbok but there are also large numbers of gemsbok, eland, red hartebeest and blue wildebeest.

Spend an hour or so in the morning and the afternoon by a water hole. Watch for signs of agitation among herds of antelope – they don't automatically flee at the sight of a predator but wait until the predator commits itself to a charge before they run. Be sure to keep an eye on the top of the ridges overlooking the river beds, especially near herds of grazers, as these are good places to spot predators surveying their next meal. The lions like to walk along the side of the road because the soft dust is kind to their paws. Look for recent prints, as the lion may have moved off the road at the sound of your vehicle. Binoculars are essential (see the boxed text on p446 for more tips).

BIRDS

Some 215 species of bird have been recorded here. Sighting birds of prey is a real treat and they are incredibly numerous; the Mata Mata road is especially good. Some of the most impressive species are the bateleur eagle, martial eagle, red-necked falcon, pygmy falcon, pale chanting goshawk and tawny eagle.

Two common birds are the secretary bird, seen strutting self-importantly over the clay pans, and the kori bustard, the largest flying bird in Southern Africa.

A distinctive sight is the huge thatched nests of the sociable weaverbird. The birds live in many-chambered nests that can last for more than a century and are inhabited by as many as 200 birds at a time. They weave twigs and straw together in the crowns of acacias, on quiver trees and atop telephone poles.

Sleeping & Eating

There is accommodation both inside and outside the park. The park's only restaurant is at Twee Rivieren rest camp. Since park fees are now based on a daily rate if you arrive late in the afternoon you may want to spend the night outside the park to avoid paying that day's fees and head in early the next morning.

INSIDE THE PARK

There are three rest camps and three luxury wilderness camps. Camp sites are usually available but booking is advised for huts and

chalets from June to September, and during holiday periods. Book with the **South African National (SAN) Parks Board** (☎ 012-428 9111; www .parks-sa.co.za; 643 Leyds St, Muckleneuk, Pretoria).

All rest camps have **camp sites** (per 2 people R80, per extra person R30) without electricity and with shared ablutions facilities.

All camps also have a range of huts, bungalows and cottages equipped with bedding, towels, cooking and eating utensils, kitchens and bathrooms.

Twee Rivieren (4-bed cottages per 2 people R395, 6-bed family chalets per 4 people R560, both per extra adult/ child R90/45; ⊠ 🖫) This is the closet camp to the park's entrance, and the one with the most facilities. It's also the only rest camp with a swimming pool, restaurant and air-con.

Mata Mata (park-home d with shared bathroom R240, chalet d R335, 6-person chalets per 4 people R560, per extra adult/child R90/45) This camp is 2½ hours drive from Twee Rivieren rest camp on the park's western boundary with Namibia. Surrounded by thorny Kalahari dune bushveld it's a good place to spot giraffe. There are a limited number of park homes and chalets so booking is advised.

Nossob (2-person chalets R335, 4-person guesthouse R660) Situated within the dry riverbed of the Nossob, this camp is a good place to spot predators; it even has a predator information centre. The camp is a 3½ hour drive from Twee Rivieren rest camp.

Three new luxury wilderness camps have recently opened in the park. We've heard mixed reviews, although they do give you the opportunity to really get off the beaten path. The camps are not fenced, which means animals can wander in at will; a ranger is on duty at all times. Make sure you stock up on petrol and drinking water before visiting these camps, as neither is available on site. All three camps have been designed to accommodate disabled people.

Bitterpan Camp (2-person cabins R500) Bitterpan can only be reached with a 4WD vehicle. A stilted camp overlooking a water hole, accommodation is in reed and canvas cabins with roofs of corrugated iron sheet covered in reeds, making the entire place blend into the landscape. The camp is located on a one-way 4WD route starting from Nossob and will allow you to access a very remote portion of the park. It takes about 2½ hours to drive from Nossob to Bitterpan, so either start early in the day or spend the night at Nossob first. Leaving Bitterpan it takes about three hours to drive back to Twee Rivieren. There is a 6m lookout tower for wildlife-viewing, as well as a one-way 15km drive to look for animals.

Grootkolk Camp (2-person cabins R560) Nestled amid red sand dunes, and only 20km from Union's End where South Africa, Botswana and Namibia meet, this camp is a six-hour drive from Twee Rivieren rest camp. The camp has desert cabins made from sand bags and canvas – definitely a different sleeping experience. At night the silence and the stars will overwhelm you.

Kalahari Tent Camp (2-person desert tents R600, 3-person family tents R695, honeymoon tents R700; 🏊) This is the most accessible of the wilderness camps, and the most luxurious. Only 3km from Mata Mata rest camp, accommodation is in 15 desert tents created out of wood, sand and canvas and decorated with rustic furnishings. The swimming pool is lovely.

Lion's Den Restaurant (breakfast/dinner from R30/60; ⏱ 7.30-9am & 6.30-9pm) This pleasant place overlooking the camp in Twee Rivieren offers surprisingly reasonable value. The menu is mostly meat- and seafood-oriented, with only one vegetarian option. There's also a snack bar selling burgers and other takeaways. If you're coming for dinner, let the staff know by 6pm.

OUTSIDE THE PARK

Kalahari Trails Nature Reserve (☎ 054902 ask for 91634; www.kalahari-trails.co.za; camp sites R60, s/d from R100/200) Run by a former professor of animal behaviour and desert ecology, this 3500 hectare reserve is located 35km from the Twee Rivieren gate on the R360 towards Andrievale. The reserve has all the wildlife located inside the park, with the exception of the big cats, and allows visitors to experience the Kalahari they will not see from a car. Morning and evening dune walks (R35 per person) teach you about the smallest of dune creatures and the geology of the area; wildlife drives (R45, three hours) teach you basic tracking skills. Responsible tourism is emphasised heavily here – the host hopes visitors leave with a deeper respect for the Kalahari and all that lives in it.

Accommodation is basically self-catering, although breakfast (R35) and dinner (R50) can be organised if you call ahead. There are a variety of sleeping options from tented bush chalets 2km into the reserve to a guesthouse sleeping four. For a different look at the magnificent world of the Kalahari we highly recommend stopping by the reserve.

Molopo Lodge (☎ 054-511 0008; www.molopo.co.za; d with breakfast R342; 🍴 🏊) This lodge is located where the tarmac ends, about 60km before the Twee Rivieren gate on the R360. It is an attractive place built in the traditional African safari lodge style, and offers surprisingly good value for money. Accommodation is in thatched roof huts, and the lounge area is covered in animal skins. There's a large porch for relaxing and a great swimming pool. It makes a good stop either before or after a park visit. Children aged 12 and under stay half price. There is also a restaurant.

Rooiduin (☎ 082-589-6659; camp sites per person R25) Rooiduin is about 32km from the Twee Rivieren gate on the road into the park, and is a unique camping option. Camp sites are under wooden structures to keep the blowing sand away. Rooiduin rents sandboards for R25 per day, including a short lesson. It also offers horse riding on the dunes for R50 per half hour.

Getting There & Away

It's a solid six-hour drive from Kuruman to Twee Rivieren (385km). The drive from Upington to Twee Rivieren gate is 250km, made up of about 190km on bitumen and 60km on dirt roads (the bitumen is gradually being extended).

Be very careful driving on the dirt roads as we've had several letters from travellers who wrecked their cars on this trip. If you stop, don't pull too far off the road or you might become bogged in the sand. Beware of patches of deep sand and loose gravel, which makes corners treacherous. Petrol is not available between Upington and Twee Rivieren, so start out with a full tank.

It's important to carry water, as you may have to wait a while for help if you break down.

KEIMOS & KAKAMAS
☎ 054

For those that think the Kalahari is all desert, dust and heat, the lush towns of Keimos and Kakamas will come as a pleasant surprise. The N14 southwest of Upington follows the course of the Orange River and

ORANGE RIVER WINE ROUTE

Although not as well known as its Western Cape counterparts, the wine region along the banks of the Orange River is starting to take off. Tastings here are much less of a pretentious affair, and meandering between the vineyards run by the Orange River Wine Cellars Cooperative is a pleasant way to spend an afternoon. The towns of Keimos and Kakamas make good bases from which to explore this region.

Winemaking in the region dates back to the early 1900s when vineyards were planted in the fertile river valley for raisin production. However, it was discovered that the sultana grape was much more suitable for wine than raisin production, and in 1965 the Orange River Wine Cellars was born. The first grapes were harvested in Upington in 1968, and since then the co-op has grown to be the largest in South Africa with about 750 members and five cellars concentrated along the N10 and N14. The cellars produce about 30 different products, including grape juice concentrates.

Just outside Keimos and Kakamas, the **Keimos cellar** (☎ 054-461 1006; admission free; ☻ 8am-5pm Mon-Fri, 8.30am-noon Sat) and **Kakamas cellar** (☎ 054-431 0830; admission free; ☻ 8am-5pm Mon-Fri, 8.30am-noon Sat) are worth a visit. Look for the Keimos/Kakamas Wine Trail signs. Both cellars offer tastings, and during harvest time (mid-January to mid-March) tours of the vineyards and a chance to chat with the winemaker.

passes through oases of vineyards (still irrigated with the aid of wooden water wheels) and the quaint and quiet little towns of Keimos and Kakamas. Keimos is particularly lush with palm tree–lined streets and plenty of green grass. The turn-off to Augrabies Falls National Park is at Kakamas.

For sleeping try **Die Werf** (☎ 461 1634; Keimos; s/d R215/308; light meals R10, mains R30-60; ☻ ☻) with its large expanse of green lawns. There's also an inviting swimming pool, self-contained chalets, a restaurant and a bar. Die Werf is on the N14, if you're coming from Upington it will be on your right side just before town.

The **Kalahari Gateway Hotel** (☎ 431 0838; www .kalaharigateway.co.za; Main Rd, Kakamas; s/d R275/385; ☻ ☻) has newly renovated massive rooms with coffee tables, couches and TVs. The zebra-themed **restaurant** (mains from R50, pizzas R30) and bar inside the hotel serves an assortment of steak and seafood dishes, as well as pasta, burgers and pizzas. There is a large wine list focusing on regional wines. KG's Sportsbar is attached to the hotel and has the same menu, but drinks here are about a third of the price. The Kalahari Gateway also provides information on the area and can arrange 4WD hire.

AUGRABIES FALLS NATIONAL PARK

For much more than just an impressive waterfall visit this **national park** (☎ 054-452 9200; adult/child R60/30; ☻ dawn-dusk). Certainly

the falls can be spectacular (particularly if they are carrying a lot of water) but the most interesting facet of the park is the fascinating desert/riverine ecosystems on either side of the river.

The name of the falls derives from the Namaqua word for 'Place of Great Noise'. The Orange River meanders across the plain from the east but following an uplift in the land around 500 million years ago it began to wear a deep ravine into the underlying granite. The ravine is 18km long and has several impressive cataracts. The main falls drop 56m, while the Bridal Veil Falls on the northern side drop 75m.

The park has a harsh climate, with an average rainfall of only 107mm and daytime summer temperatures that often reach 40°C. The flora includes kokerboom aloes, the Namaqua fig, several varieties of thorn trees, and succulents. The park has 47 species of mammal (most of which are small) including klipspringer and other antelope species, rock dassie and ground squirrel.

Activities

The three-hour **Dassie Trail** is well worth doing, particularly if your time is short. It involves clambering over rocks through some magical landscape – if you haven't seen any of the cute little rock dassies yet, this is your big chance.

The popular three-day, 40km **Klipspringer Hiking Trail** (per person R125) runs along the southern bank of the Orange River. Two nights are spent in huts built from local stone (these can sleep 12 people). Camping is not allowed. Hikers must supply their own sleeping bags and food. Advance booking is advised. The trail is closed from mid-October to the end of March because of the heat. The **Gariep 3-in-1 Route** includes canoeing, walking and mountain biking; book and check out prices at the visitors centre when you enter the park.

The **Kalahari Adventure Centre** (☎ 054-451 0177; www.kalahari.co.za) runs canoeing and rafting on the Orange River. Try its very popular 'Augrabies Rush'. You will raft an exciting grade 2 to 3, 8km section of the river in inflatable kayaks. The take-out point is only 300m above the falls; it costs R275 per person and is loads of fun. It also runs a five-day/four-night canoe trail for R1695. The trip covers 60km, includes all meals, and is well worth the cost. Its office is 10km outside the park on the road from Kakamas. Follow the signs.

Sleeping & Eating

Accommodation in the park can be booked through the **SAN Parks Board** (☎ 012-428 9111; www.parks-sa.co.za; 643 Leyds St, Muckleneuk, Pretoria), or you can take your chance and just show up, there's often space. Options include **camp sites** (per 2 people R100, per extra person R35) and a variety of **self-contained chalets** (from R350). Many of the chalets have outstanding views and are within earshot of the falls.

There's a cafeteria where you can buy sandwiches and cold drinks, and a **restaurant** (mains around R60; ☾ lunch & dinner) with meals such as fillet steak or chicken. Cold water is free from the dispenser – you'll probably drink it dry if you are here in summer.

The friendly **Augrabies Falls Backpackers** (☎ 054-451-0177; www.kalahari.co.za; camp sites per person R30, s/d with shared bathroom R75/150) has a great reed bar for watching the distant thunderclouds build, a chilled out atmosphere and clean, comfortable rooms with animal-print-patterned bedding. Run by the Kalahari Adventure Centre (p508), the staff are very friendly and knowledgeable. Make sure to take part in one of their dinners (R35) – they are positively scrumptious. The backpackers are about 10km before Augrabies Falls National Park on the road from Kakamas. Follow the signs.

Getting There & Away

Private transport is recommended. The park is 38km northwest of Kakamas and 120km from Upington. The Kalahari Adventure Centre will pick up from Upington (and other towns in the area). The shuttle fare is R150 per person (minimum of four).

NAMAKWA

This rugged region in the northwestern Northern Cape combines the unspoilt expanses of Namaqualand and the Hantam Karoo and covers a vast area stretching from the Namibian border in the north to the west coast's bleak beaches, then south towards Vanrhynsdorp in the Western Cape before merging with the area known as Bushmanland in the east.

The region has a noticeable 'frontier atmosphere' due largely to its bleak and beautiful landscape, and the presence of diamond miners. This is a land of immense sky and stark country. At night the sky is bright with stars, too many to try to count, and it's easy to drive for ages without seeing another car.

The cold Antarctic Benguela current runs up the west coast, lowering temperatures and severely limiting rainfall, creating a barren desert-like environment. However, this apparently inhospitable place produces one of the world's natural wonders. After decent winter rains there is an extraordinary explosion of spring flowers that cover the boulder-strewn mountains and plains with a multicoloured carpet.

The area is sparsely populated, mainly by Afrikaans-speaking sheep farmers, and in the northwest by the Namaqua, a Khoikhoi tribe. The Namaqua were famous for their metal-working skills, particularly in the copper that occurs in the region. Not surprisingly, this attracted the attention of Dutch explorers, who came into contact with the tribe in 1661. Because of the region's isolation, however, the Namaqualand copper rush did not properly begin until the 1850s. The first commercial mine (now a national monument) was established just outside Springbok in 1852, and there are still a number of working mines including one at Nababeep.

Namakwa is also an important source for alluvial diamonds. In 1925 a young soldier

WILDFLOWERS OF NAMAQUALAND

For the majority of the year Namaqualand appears a barren wasteland where seemingly nothing but the hardiest shrubs can survive. But with the winter rains comes the revelation of a secret: the dry lands are transformed into a kaleidoscope of colour as daisies, perennial herbs, aloes, lilies and a host of other species blanket the ground creating a sight that will enchant and mesmerise the eye, the artists pallet and the photographers lens. At this time visitors are drawn from all over the world to this often-forgotten corner of the country. All in all about 4000 species of plant grow in the region.

The optimum time to visit varies from year to year, but you have the best chance of catching the flowers at their peak between mid-August and mid-September (sometimes the season can begin early in August and extend to mid-October). The best flower areas vary from year to year, so it is essential to get local advice on where to go. Bear in mind most varieties of wildflower are protected by law, and you can incur heavy fines if you pick them.

The flowers depend on rainfall, which is variable, and the blooms can shrivel quickly in hot winds. Many of the flowers are light sensitive and only open during bright sunshine. Overcast conditions, which generally only last a day or two, will significantly reduce the display, and even on sunny days the flowers only open properly from around 10am to 4pm. They also face the sun (basically northwards), so it is best to travel with the sun behind you.

There are generally good flowers east of the N7 between Garies and Springbok. Other reliable flower-viewing routes are between Springbok and Port Nolloth, and through Kamiesberg, which is southeast of Kamieskroon in the direction of Garies. The Goegap Nature Reserve, east of Springbok, and the hills around Nababeep are also good.

Jack Carstens found a glittering stone near Port Nolloth. Prospectors converged on the area, and it soon became clear that an enormously rich source of diamonds had been discovered. All the major west-coast alluvial fields are now classified as prohibited areas and are closed to the general public. Diamonds are only bought and sold by licensed traders.

You may meet locals who offer to sell you cheap diamonds – not only is this highly illegal, you may end up with a fake. For more information, see the boxed text on p512.

SPRINGBOK

☎ 027 / pop 10,400

In a valley surrounded by harsh rocky hills that explode with colour in the flower season lies the town of Springbok. Outside the flower season there's little to see or do here, although there is something alluring about the town's remoteness. The air always feels fresh, the desolate landscape is endearing and step outside at night and it will be thoroughly still and quiet.

The first European-run copper mine, the Blue Mine, was established on the town's outskirts in 1852. From a rough-and-tumble frontier town, Springbok has been transformed into a busy service centre

for the copper and diamond mines in the region.

In the 1920s, Springbok had a large population of Jews who traded in the region. Most have moved away and their synagogue (built in 1929) has been converted into a small but good **museum** (☎ 712 2011; admission free; ⏱ 9am-4pm Mon-Fri).

Orientation & Information

The town is quite spread-out but most places are within walking distance of the small kopje in the elbow of the main street's right-angled bend. The kopje is covered with the strange local flora.

The **Tourism Information Office** (☎ 718 2985; Voortrekker St; ⏱ 7.30am-4.15pm Mon-Fri, 9am-noon Sat & Sun) has loads of info about flowers, attractions and drives in the area.

To surf the web stop by the **Something Online Internet Café** (☎ 712 2561; 59 Voortrekker St; per hr R60; ⏱ 8am-5pm Mon-Fri).

Sleeping

During flower season accommodation in Springbok can fill up. The tourist office can tell you about private, overflow accommodation. There is a big difference between low-season prices (given here) and flower-season prices.

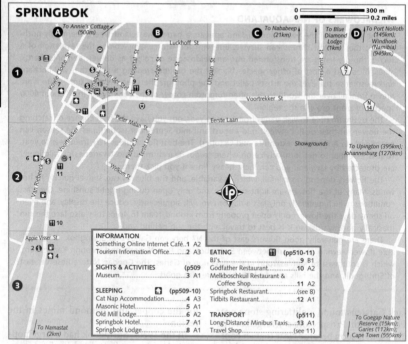

SPRINGBOK

Cat Nap Accommodation (☎ 718 1905; www.adven tureaddicts.com/aa/richtersveld.htm; Voortrekker St; dm/d R70/R250, tr per person R80; 🛇) This place caters to all budgets. Backpackers can choose from dorms in a barn, or the one backpacker triple. Rooms are lovely and come with TVs and animal-print duvets. The photography on the walls is amazing, making this one of the town's best options. Tours to the Richtersveld National Park can be arranged here.

Annie's Cottage (☎ 712 1451; annie@springbokinfo .com; 4 King St; s/d from R185/370; 🛋) The 10 rooms are uniquely decorated, each one different and each one beautiful. The pool and garden area is quaint with fountains, trees, flowers and benches. Rooms are variety of prices depending on amenities. An excellent choice.

Blue Diamond Lodge (☎ 718 2624; 19 Union St; s/d with breakfast R270/400; 🛋) Travellers give this place good reviews. North of the centre it's attractive with neat units set around a swimming pool, a resident macaw and a trail up the mountain behind the lodge with good views.

Springbok Hotel (☎ 712 1161; fax 712 1932; 87 Van Riebeeck St; s/d R150/250; 🛇) Good value for

money, rooms are simple and clean with TVs and telephones. They all look the same. There is an attached **restaurant** (mains R35-70) with a variety of options, including a kids' menu.

Springbok Lodge (☎ 712 1321; fax 712 2718; 37 Voortrekker St; s/d from R120/220) This place is actually a collection of old houses scattered around town that have been steadily upgraded over the years; rooms range in size from the small Matchbox to the sizable Die Gewelhuis and Die Ark.

Old Mill Lodge (☎ 718 1705; 69 Van Riebeeck St; s/d R280/370) Pleasantly situated up against the rocks on a quiet side street. The grounds are more impressive than the rooms – well maintained with fountains and plenty of green grass.

Masonic Hotel (☎ 712 1505; fax 712 1730; 2 Van Riebeeck St; s/d R186/303) This fine Art Deco edifice has been upgraded and there is a great balcony.

Eating

BJ's (☎ 718 2270; cnr Van der Stel & Hospital Sts; mains R35-50; 🛇) Very reasonably priced steak cooked the way you like it is served in this basement restaurant with a wine-cellar feel. White archways, wooden beams and leopard-skin print make up the décor. Classical music adds to the ambiance, and the food does not disappoint. Vegetarians will be happier elsewhere.

Melkboschkuil Restaurant & Coffee Shop (☎ 718 1789; 75 Voortrekker St; mains R40-70) This place likes to experiment with various types of booze in their dishes, some with better results than others, although they are all generally tasty. The chef can cook a springbok in more ways than you ever imagined.

Springbok Restaurant (☎ 712 1321; 37 Voortrekker St; breakfast R18-25, mains R25-50; ☷) Pictures and animal heads clutter the walls and seating is at plastic dinner tables. There is a good breakfast selection. Lunch and dinner include steaks, chicken and schnitzel as well as pizza and burgers.

Titbits Restaurant (☎ 718 1455; cnr Namakwa & Voortrekker Sts; mains R25-50) Plenty of pasta options are served in a very pink interior. There's also a balcony and a kids' menu.

Godfather Restaurant (☎ 02251-81877; Voortrekker St; mains R25-50) This simple, small place has a large menu – everything from meat to pasta to sandwiches, very peppy music and a fun bar in the back.

Getting There & Away

AIR
National Airlines (Springbok ☎ 712 2061, Cape Town 021-934 0350; www.flynal.com) has flights from Cape Town (R950, Monday to Friday).

BUS
Intercape (☎ 0861 287 287; www.intercape.co.za) has buses to Cape Town (R210, 7½ hours, twice weekly) that leave from opposite the Springbok Lodge near the kopje. Buses leave for Windhoek, Namibia (R330, 12 hours, four times weekly) at 6.45pm from the same spot. Book at the small **travel shop** (☎ 072-171 3081, ask for Madelein) behind the Melkboschkuil Restaurant.

CAR RENTAL
Springbok is a popular jumping off point for the Richtersveld National Park and exploring Namibia. For 4WD hire, stop by **Cat Nap Accommodation** (☎ 718 1905; Voortrekker St); they rent vehicles for R700 per day, or R850 per day including camping equipment. These prices include unlimited kilo-

metres and insurance. Other rental options can be found by asking at the Springbok Lodge, the tourism information office or at the small travel shop behind the Melkboschkuil Restaurant.

MINIBUS TAXI
Van Wyk's Busdiens (☎ 021-559 1601) run a daily door-to-door taxi to Cape Town (R160, five hours) and Kamieskroon (R45, one hour). You'll find ordinary minibus taxis at the taxi rank opposite the First National Bank near the kopje. Destinations include Cape Town (R160, five hours, daily) and Port Nolloth (R40, 2½ hours, five times weekly).

VIP Taxis (☎ 851 8780) operates a taxi from Springbok to Upington (R80, four hours, Monday to Friday) that departs from the Masonic Hotel.

AROUND SPRINGBOK
Nababeep
☎ 027
Nababeep is the site of a large copper mine, and the surrounding hills have spectacular blooms in flower season. For those interested in mining, a visit to the **Nababeep Mine Museum** (☎ 713 8121; admission free; ☷ 9am-5pm) is worthwhile.

Nababeep Hotel (☎ 713 8151; s/d R101/186) is a simple country hotel on the town's main street that also serves meals. Breakfasts are about R40 and dinners from R65. Prices go up considerably here in flower season.

Nababeep is 16km northwest of Springbok on the N7. Public transportation options are sporadic. Ask at the minibus stop in Springbok if there are any minibuses heading in this direction.

Goegap Nature Reserve
Don't miss this semidesert **nature reserve** (☎ 712 1880; admission R10; ☷ 7.45am-4.15pm), famous for its extraordinary display of spring flowers and a nursery of 200 amazing Karoo and Namaqualand succulents at the **Hester Malan Wildflower Garden**.

There are a couple of driving routes around the reserve, but you'll see more on one of the circular walks (4km, 5.5km and 7km). There are two incredible **mountain-biking routes** (14km and 20km), which are particularly memorable during flower season; bring your own bikes. There's a biking permit fee of R7 per person.

PORT NOLLOTH

☎ 027 / pop 5000

Port Nolloth is a sandy and exposed little place with a certain fascination. Originally developed as the shipping point for the region's copper, it is now dependent on the small fishing boats that catch diamonds and crayfish. The boats are fitted with pumps, and divers vacuum up the diamond-bearing gravel found on the ocean floor. The town has attracted a multicultural group of fortune-seekers and they give it a frontier vitality.

Bedrock (☎ 851 8865; www.bedrocklodge.co.za; d from R200) is a friendly and comfortable place located in one of the old wooden cottages lining the seafront. With big rooms and sea views, it's a social must as it's owned by local personality Grazia de Beer, better known as Mama. Turn right onto the beachfront road as you come into town and the Bedrock is the second building along. Mama also owns a couple of nearby houses, so a range of accommodation options is available.

The **Crow's Nest** (meals R20-40) is attached to the Bedrock, and serves seafood, meat, pasta dishes and pizza.

Captain Pete's Tavern (mains R25-40) is across from the Scotia Inn Hotel and owned by a diamond diver who struck it rich. It's not a bad place to pop in for a drink.

There is little public transport, and hitching from the N7 turn-off at Steinkopf would be slow. **VIP Taxis** (☎ 851 8780) operate a taxi to Springbok (R40, 2½ hours, five times a week).

ALEXANDER BAY

☎ 027

The archetypal remote seaside community of Alexander Bay is a government-controlled diamond mine on the southern bank of the mouth of the Orange River (Namibia is on the north side). The road from Port Nolloth is open to the public but the Namibian border is closed. Restrictions on access are slowly lifting, though, and the town is looking at its tourism potential. Activities include **mine tours** (☎ 831 1330; ☼ 8am Thu), which should be booked one day in advance. Bird-watchers come here looking for Barlow's lark, which is found nowhere else in the world.

Brandkaros (☎ 831 1856; fax 831 1390; camp sites per person R50, d R150; ☻) is a citrus farm by the river about 30km northeast of Alexan-

---

---

der Bay. It has a great swimming pool. The farm is en route to Richtersveld National Park and is a good base from which to tour this area. Accommodation is in self-catering rondavels. Bring your own food.

VIOOLSDRIF

☎ 027

This town is at the border post with Namibia on the N7, 677km north of Cape Town. The short drive from Steinkopf, with its views of the Orange River carving its way through desolate mountains, is spectacular. The border is open from 7am to 7pm.

Peace of Paradise (☎ 761 8968; www.peaceofparadise.co.za; camp sites R150, s/d R200/300) is 22km west of Vioolsdrif on the banks of the Orange River. It's very pleasant with hot showers, clean toilets and electricity for campers, as well as canoes for hire. There are San engravings 100m from the camp, and you can cool off with a swim in the river.

RICHTERSVELD NATIONAL PARK

Located in a mountainous desert – a spectacular wilderness of jagged rocky peaks, grotesque rock formations, deep ravines, and gorges – is this enormous (185,000 hectares) **national park** (☎ 027-831 1506; PO Box 406, Alexander Bay 8290; adult/child R80/40; ☼ 7am-6pm). It is located in the northern loop of the Orange River, northwest of Vioolsdrif and the N7. The park is the property of the local Nama people who continue to lead a semitraditional, seminomadic pastoral existence; hopefully they will benefit from increased job opportunities from tourism and the rent paid by the park authorities.

The hiking possibilities, in this surreal almost lunar-like landscape, are excellent though demanding. Despite its apparent barrenness, the region has a prolific variety of succulents – 30% of South Africa's known succulent species grow here.

At present, most of the park is virtually inaccessible without a properly equipped expedition and local guides. The southern section is accessible by high clearance 2WD vehicles (such as a bakkie) but it would be worth checking this before going in.

Fill up your tank at Alexander Bay before entering the park; fuel emergencies are only dealt with at Sendelingsdrift.

Hiking Trails

Three hiking trails have been established in the park. The **Ventersvalle Trail** (42km, four days) encompasses the mountainous southwest wilderness; the **Lelieshoek-Oemsberg Trail** (23km, three days) takes in a huge amphitheatre and waterfall; and the **Kodaspiek Trail** (15km, two days) allows the average walker to view stunning mountain desert scenery. Accommodation is in *matjieshuis* (traditional woven Nama 'mat' huts) and there are field toilets. The trails are only open from April to September and you must take a guide with you. For information about prices contact the **SAN Parks Board** (☎ 012-343 9770; www .parks-sa.co.za; 643 Leyds St, Muckleneuk, Pretoria).

Tours

An organised tour could be the easiest way to visit this remote park. The **Richtersveld Challenge** (☎ 027-718 1905; www.adventureaddicts .com/aa/richtersveld.htm) is run by Springbok photographer Rey van Rensburg, and operates between April and October. Rey is enthusiastic, experienced and very know ledgeable about the area. A five-day vehicle tour costs R650 per person per day including camping equipment and meals

(minimum of 8 people). Try to book a few months in advance.

Marius Opperman (☎ 027-851 8041, 083-314 3351) operates the 'Richtersveld Experience' out of Port Nolloth. Tours are about R540 per person per day (minimum of four people). You'll need your own bedding and you should book in advance.

Sleeping & Eating

Options include **camp sites** (per 2 people R100) and the **Arieb Guest Cottage** (per 4 people R650, per extra person R180) that can accommodate up to 10 people. Accommodation must be booked through the SAN Parks Board. There is only one cottage available.

Also within Richtersveld is **Eksteenfontein** (☎ 027-851 8775; r per person R60; meals R25), a community guesthouse hosted by Nama people. Traditional meals are also prepared.

KAMIESKROON & AROUND
☎ 027

Craggy mountains and boulder-strewn hills surround this little town. The feel is desolate and remote, and many of the roads in town are still not paved. The name Kamieskroon means 'Jumble' or 'Huddles Together' in Nama. It's a great spot to get away from it all and to explore the area, especially in flower season.

The **town clerk** (☎ 672 1627; Voortrekker St; ☼ 9am-5pm Mon-Fri) serves as the tourist information office.

About 18km southwest of Kamieskroon is the **Skilpad Wildflower Reserve** (☎ 672-1948; admission R60; ☼ 8am-4pm), which was established by the World Wide Fund for Nature (WWF) to increase awareness of the floral heritage and biodiversity of Namaqualand. The shrubland and old wheat fields burst into flower (Namaqualand daisies) in spring, often surpassing all other areas in the region. At the time of research the Namaqua National Park was in the process of being designated, and eventually may incorporate this wildflower reserve.

Kamieskroon Bed & Breakfast (☎ 672 1652; Charlotta St; s/d with breakfast R140/280) is a relaxing little oasis, which makes a good base and has all the creature comforts.

Kamieskroon Hotel & Caravan Park (☎ 672 1614; kamieshotel@kingsley.co.za; camp sites per person R45, s/d R150/250; ☒) is just off the N7; follow the signs. It's very comfortable and deservedly popular, especially from July to September (when bookings are essential and prices rise). It serves a set price dinner every night for R80 and breakfast for R35. During flower season it runs photographic workshops.

Kamieskroon is 80km south of Springbok on the N7. **Van Wyk's Busdiens** (☎ 021-559 1601) runs a bus service to Springbok (R45, one hour, daily). From here, if you're looking for a little scenic adventure, head west to Hondeklip Bay. While the town itself is just a smaller, less interesting version of Port Nolloth, the local dirt roads are spectacular.

CALVINIA
☎ 027 / pop 8100

Calvinia, an attractive town surrounded by 'Wild West' country, is the main centre of the Hantam Karoo. As the church clock quietly tolls the hours it's easy to imagine that decades, if not centuries, have slipped away. The nearby township is very friendly, with several convivial eateries and shebeens (unlicenced bars).

The **tourist information office** (☎ 341 1712; 44 Church St; ☺ 8am-1pm & 2-5pm Mon-Fri, 8am-noon Sat), which adjoins the museum is very well organised. Staff can provide a walking-tour map of town and will help you arrange accommodation; bookings are advisable in flower season.

Sights
For a small country town, the **Calvinia Museum** (☎ 341 1712; 44 Church St; admission R2; ☺ 8am-5pm Mon-Fri, 8am-noon Sat) is of a surprisingly high standard and definitely worth visiting. The main building was a synagogue – it's incongruous but not unusual to find disused Jewish buildings in tiny, remote South African towns. The museum concentrates on the White settlement of the region, including sheep and farming activities, and there are some wonderful oddities such as a four-legged ostrich chick (a fake used by a travelling con artist), and a room devoted to the lives of a local set of quadruplets.

Sleeping & Eating
The restored historic buildings, which now operate as guesthouses, are good places to stay.

Die Tuishuis, Die Dorphuis & Die Hantamhuis (☎ 341 1606; www.calvinia.co.za; Hoop St; s/d from R195/320; mains R90) These are a complex of antique guesthouses and a café that are some of the oldest buildings in town. Die Tuishuis and Die Dorphuis are your lodging options: both are furnished with antiques and offer a variety of elegant rooms. Candles and romantic music set the atmosphere for traditional three-course dinners served in Die Hantamhuis; meals include old favourites such as mutton on a stick.

Pionierslot (☎ 341 1263; 35 Water St; s/d with breakfast R170/300) One of the nicest B&Bs in town. The owners here are hospitable without being overwhelming.

Hantam Hotel (☎ 341 1512; fax 341 2462; Kerk St; s/d with breakfast R140/240; ☒) This place is plain, but comfortable and as clean as a whistle. The hotel's steakhouse, the **Busibee** (breakfast R30; mains R50; ☺ breakfast, lunch & dinner) has braaied lamb as a perennial feature.

Cobusegat (☎ 341 2326; caves per person R60, stone houses per person R80) Definitely a unique experience, this place is actually 116km south of Calvinia on the R355. Accommodation is in self-catering caves – OK really they are more like over-hanging rocks enclosed three-quarters of the way around and complete with electricity, fridges and a stove. Each cave can accommodate up to eight people. The place also has two thatched-roof stone houses. The area boasts glacier scrapings from the last ice age.

Die Blou Nartjie Restaurant (☎ 341 1484; Pionierslot; mains R30-70; ☺ lunch & dinner Mon-Sat) The range of dishes at this excellent restaurant is limited but very good quality for such a small town. We love an open kitchen! Traditional bobotie (curried mincemeat topped with beaten egg, and served with turmeric rice and chutney) is delicious.

Getting There & Away
Intercape (☎ 0861 287 287; www.intercape.co.za) has buses to Cape Town (R170, six hours, four times weekly) and to Upington (R145, five hours, four times weekly). Book at the **travel agency** (☎ 344 1373) incongruously situated in the *slaghuis* (butchers). Buses stop at the *trokkie* (truck) stop on the western side of town.

Lesotho

DI JONES

Lesotho

LESOTHO

Preparing food as a good-luck offering for travelling, Lesotho

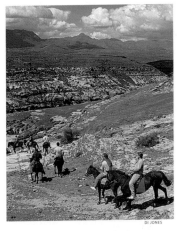

Pony trekking (p534), Malealea, Lesotho

Overlooking the gorge near Quthing (p535), Lesotho

Above the Makhaleng River valley,
Malealea (p533), Lesotho

Basotho boy, Malealea, Lesotho

Fields in bloom, Malealea (p533), Lesotho

Lesotho (le-*soo*-too) – Southern Africa's 'kingdom in the sky' – is a stunningly beautiful, mountainous country about the size of Belgium, nestled island-like in the middle of South Africa. It came into being during the tumultuous years of the early 19th century, when both the *difaqane* (forced migration) and Boer incursions into the hinterlands were at their height. Under the leadership of the legendary king Moshoeshoe the Great, the Basotho people sought sanctuary and strategic advantage amid the forbidding terrain of the Drakensberg and Maluti ranges. The nation they forged has managed to resist more recent pressures as well, and continues to be an intriguing anomaly in a sea of modernity.

The only way to reach Lesotho is via South Africa, and it is a fascinating detour from travels in its larger neighbour. Among the country's attractions are: superb mountain scenery; the opportunity to meet and stay with people living traditional lifestyles; endless hiking trails; and the chance to explore remote areas on Basotho ponies. Throughout, you'll find Lesotho refreshingly free of the after-effects of apartheid, with proud, friendly people and a laid-back pace.

While infrastructure is not what it is in most areas of South Africa, it's quite possible to enjoy the amenities. The country boasts a handful of comfortable hotels and lodges, and with an ordinary rental car you can reach most areas. If you're of a more adventurous bent, public transport is good (albeit slow) in much of the country, or you can just head off on foot.

Attractions of the 'lowland' areas (all of which are still above 1000m) include craft shopping around Teyateyaneng, and following in the footsteps of dinosaurs around Quthing and Hlotse. Yet, it's in the highlands in the northeast and centre that Lesotho is at its most beautiful. Here, towering peaks climb over 3000m, riven by verdant valleys and tumbling streams, and hiking or pony trekking from village to village are the best ways of exploring.

HIGHLIGHTS

- Pony trekking around **Malealea** and **Semonkong** (pp533–4)
- Making it up the **Sani Pass** via mountain bike or 4WD, and enjoying the vistas from the top (p531)
- Revelling in the splendid isolation of **Sehlabathebe National Park** (p537), **Ts'ehlanyane National Park** (p529) or **Bokong Nature Reserve** (p533)
- Hiking in the **northern highlands** (p529)
- Craft shopping in **Teyateyaneng** (p527), **Hlotse** (p528) or **Maseru** (p525)

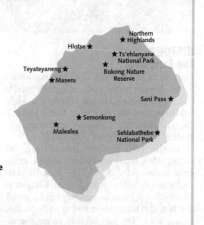

- POPULATION: 2.2 MILLION
- AREA: 30,344 SQ KM

LESOTHO

0	50 km
0	30 miles

LEGEND
NP   National Park
NR   National Reserve
GR   Game Reserve
FR   Forest Reserve
WA   Wilderness Area

HISTORY
The Early Days

Lesotho is the homeland of the Basotho – Sotho-Tswana peoples who originally lived in small chiefdoms scattered around the highveld in present-day Free State. Cattle and cultivation were their economic mainstays, and trading was at the heart of daily life.

As the 19th century moved into full swing, this comparatively tranquil existence came under threat. The Voortrekkers and various White entrepreneurs began to encroach on Basotho grazing lands, which the Basotho themselves had already pushed to capacity. On top of this came the *difaqane* (see p32), which was just beginning to unleash its wave of destruction.

Yet, unlike neighbouring groups, many of whom were dispersed or decimated, the Basotho managed to come out of this period more united. This was largely due to the leadership of the brilliant Moshoeshoe the Great, a village chief who managed to rally his people and forge a powerful kingdom. To do this, Moshoeshoe first led his own villagers to the mountain stronghold of Butha-Buthe where he established a base from which he was able to resist the early incursions of the *difaqane*. In 1824, to enhance his position, Moshoeshoe began a policy of assisting refugees of the *difaqane* in return for their help with his own defence. He moved his headquarters to the more easily defended hilltop perch of

Thaba-Bosiu, from where he repulsed wave after wave of invaders.

By 1840 Moshoeshoe's rule was firmly entrenched. His people numbered about 40,000, and his power base was protected by groups who had settled on outlying lands and were partially under his authority. Ultimately, Moshoeshoe was able to bring these various peoples together as part of the loosely federated Basotho state, which, by the time of his death in 1870, had a population exceeding 150,000.

While all this was going on, Moshoeshoe had also begun to welcome Christian missionaries into his territory. The first to arrive, in 1833, were from the Paris Evangelical Missionary Society. Moshoeshoe made one of them his adviser, and the sophisticated diplomacy that had marked his dealings with local chiefs now extended to his dealings with the Europeans. The missions, often situated in remote parts of the kingdom, served as tangible symbols of his authority. In return for some Christianisation of Basotho customs, the missionaries were disposed to defend the rights of 'their' Basotho against a rising new threat: Boer and British expansion.

Defending the Territory

The Basotho spent much of the early and mid-19th century fending off Boer forays into their areas. In 1843 – in response to continuing Boer incursions – Moshoeshoe allied himself with the British Cape Colony government. While the resulting treaties defined his borders, they did little to stop squabbles with the Boers, who had established themselves in the fertile lowveld west of the Mohokare (Caledon) River. In 1858 tensions peaked with the outbreak of the Orange Free State-Basotho War. This was followed in 1865 by a second war between the Boers and the Basotho. After gaining an early victory, Moshoeshoe began to suffer setbacks, and was ultimately forced to sign away much of his western lowlands.

In 1868 Moshoeshoe again called on the British, this time bypassing the Cape Colony administration and heading straight to the imperial government in London. It had become obvious that no treaty between the Boers and the Basotho would hold for long, and the British viewed continual war between the Orange Free State and Baso-

tholand as bad for their own interests. To resolve the situation, the British annexed Basotholand.

The decade after Moshoeshoe's death (in 1870) was marked by ongoing squabbles over succession, and increasing colonial infringements on Basotho autonomy. After briefly changing hands between the British imperial government and the Cape Colony, Basotholand again came under direct British control in 1884. One unexpected benefit of this was that, when the Union of South Africa was created in 1910, Basotholand was a British protectorate and was not included in the Union. If the Cape Colony had retained control, Lesotho would have become part of South Africa, and later a Homeland under the apartheid regime.

Independence at Last

During the early 20th century, migrant labour to South Africa increased, and the Basotho gained greater autonomy under the British administration. The main local governing entity during this period was the Basotholand National Council, an advisory body to the colonial government. In the mid-1950s the council requested internal self-government, with elections to determine its members. Meanwhile, political parties had begun to form, led by the Basotholand Congress Party (BCP, similar to South Africa's African National Congress) and the Basotholand National Party (BNP), a conservative group headed by Chief Leabua Jonathan.

Lesotho's first elections in 1960 were won by the BCP, which made full independence from Britain the first item on its agenda. Agreement was reached, with independence to come into effect in 1966. At the next elections, in 1965, the BCP lost to the BNP. Chief Jonathan became the first prime minister of the newly independent Kingdom of Lesotho, with King Moshoeshoe II as nominal head of state.

Chief Jonathan's rule was unpopular, and in the 1970 election, the BCP regained power. Chief Jonathan responded by suspending the constitution, arresting and then expelling the king, and banning opposition parties. Lesotho effectively became a one-party state.

Chief Jonathan was deposed in a military coup in 1986, and Moshoeshoe II

LESOTHO

was restored as head of state. Yet the calm didn't last. Following ongoing power disputes between the king and the coup leader, Moshoeshoe II was deposed in favour of his son, Prince Mohato Bereng Seeisa (Letsie III). Elections in 1993 returned the BCP to government. In 1995 Letsie III abdicated in favour of his father, who again managed to bring some semblance of order to Lesotho. Less than a year after being reinstated, Moshoeshoe II was killed when his 4WD plunged over a cliff in the Maluti Mountains. Letsie III was again made king.

The BCP was split between those who wanted the then–Prime Minister, Ntsu Mokhehle, to remain as leader and those who opposed him. In response, Mokhehle formed the breakaway Lesotho Congress for Democracy (LCD) and continued to govern, with the BCP now in the opposition. Mokhehle died in 1998, and Pakalitha Mosisili took over the leadership of the LCD. Later that year, the LCD won a landslide victory in elections that were declared reasonably fair by international observers, but were widely protested within Lesotho. Tensions between the public service and the government became acute, and the military was also split. In September 1998 the government called on its Southern African Development Community (SADC) treaty partners – Botswana, South Africa and Zimbabwe – to help it restore order in the country. Rebel elements of the Lesotho army resisted, resulting in heavy fighting and widespread looting in Maseru. Elec-

tions – initially scheduled for 2000 – were finally held in May 2002. The LCD won, and Prime Minister Pakalitha Mosisili began his second five-year term.

Current Events

Lesotho today looks uncertainly towards the future. Although its literacy rate is comparatively high (about 82%), its democracy is only moderately stable at best, it ranks among the poorest countries in the region and it has few natural resources other than water. From the latter half of the 19th century, Lesotho's main export was labour, with approximately 60% of males working in South Africa, primarily in the mining industry. Over the past decade, these numbers have dropped by almost half with the closing of several South African mines. Unemployment is now estimated at about 40% to 45%, with the domestic economy unable to take up the slack.

Overshadowing all of this is the spectre of AIDS. The infection rate is estimated at about 31% country wide – one of the highest in the region and the world – and at an astronomical 40% in Maseru, with no signs of decreasing. Although the government has taken limited steps to address the situation, scarce resources and a continued high level of social stigma attached to the disease hinder efforts to combat it.

CLIMATE

Clear, cold winters, with frosts and snow in the highlands, await you in Lesotho, so pack warm clothing. In the summer (late November to March), dramatic thunderstorms are common, as are all-enveloping clouds of thick mist. Temperatures at this time can rise to over 30°C in the valleys, though it's usually much cooler than this in the mountains, even dropping below freezing. Nearly all of Lesotho's rain falls between October and April. Throughout the year, the weather is notoriously changeable.

Visits are possible at any time, with spring and autumn optimal. For more information about when to go, see p13.

NATIONAL PARKS & RESERVES

Sehlabathebe is Lesotho's most famous national park, and until recently was its only one. While you won't encounter the Big Five here, its high-altitude grasslands, lakes,

---

STATELY MATTERS IN THE MOUNTAIN KINGDOM

Lesotho's hereditary monarchy is nowhere near as strong a force in day-to-day life as is the monarchy in nearby Swaziland. While the Basotho king (currently Letsie III) is head of state, he does not exercise executive power. Under traditional law, the king can be deposed by a majority vote of the College of Chiefs.

The real power lies with the cabinet, headed by the prime minister, and with parliament. Parliament is bicameral, consisting of a 120-member elected national assembly and a non-elected senate, comprised of 22 chiefs and 11 nominated members.

bogs and otherworldly rock formations offer a wonderful wilderness experience and are ideal for hiking or just getting away from it all. Sehlabathebe is under the jurisdiction of the Parks Office of the Ministry of Forestry & Land Reclamation. For contact details and more information, see p537.

The country's other main conservation areas – Ts'ehlanyane National Park (p529), Bokong Nature Reserve (p533) and the Liphofung Cultural Site Reserve (p530) – are all under the jurisdiction of the **Lesotho Highlands Development Authority Nature Reserves** (LHDA; ☎ 2246 0723, 2291 3206; www.lesotho parks.com), which handles all accommodation bookings. All have simple accommodation, established trails and helpful staff, and are relatively easily accessed and well worth visiting. Accommodation in the three LHDA reserves (prices are given in the individual listings) is discounted by 50% from May through July.

LANGUAGE
The official languages are South Sotho (Sesotho) and English. For some useful words and phrases in South Sotho, see the Language chapter (p615). For more on Sotho language and culture, see www.sesotho.web.za.

DANGERS & ANNOYANCES
High unemployment rates and a weak economy have resulted in an increase in armed robberies, break-ins and carjackings. Most assaults have occurred in Maseru, with foreign aid workers and diplomats being targeted – caution is advised. Outside urban centres, crime is negligible.

If you're hiking without a guide, you might be hassled for money or 'gifts' by shepherds in remote areas, and there's a very slight risk of robbery.

Several lives are lost each year from lightning strikes; keep off high ground during an electrical storm and avoid camping in the open. Waterproof clothing is essential for hiking and pony trekking.

GETTING THERE & AROUND
It's possible to fly to Lesotho from South Africa, but most travellers enter by bus or private vehicle. For details, see the Transport chapter (p587). Once in Lesotho, there are good bus and minibus taxi net-

LESOTHO SAMPLER
Lesotho is an adventure traveller's destination *par excellence*. Hire a car, or brush up on your pony- or public transport–riding skills, and set off into the country's more remote corners. Some possible routes:

- Enter Lesotho at Tele Bridge by Quthing, and make your way east via Mt Moorosi, Mphaki and Qacha's Nek to Sehlabathebe National Park.

- Take in some of Southern Africa's most impressive scenery on a circuit from Butha-Buthe to Oxbow and Mokhotlong (with a possible detour to Sani Top), then back via Thaba-Tseka and the Katse Dam.

- Travel in a loop from Maseru via Morija to Malealea, continue on pony to Semonkong and then make your way back to Maseru via Roma.

works that cover the country. See p598 for bus information and p604 for minibus taxi information.

For charter flights within Lesotho, the best contact is **Mission Aviation** (☎ 2232 5699), based at Moshoeshoe International Airport near Maseru.

MASERU
pop 150,000 / elevation 1600m
Maseru sprawls across Lesotho's lower-lying western edge, rimmed by the Berea and Qeme Plateaus. For much of its history, the city has been a quiet backwater, and if you're coming from Johannesburg (Jo'burg), you might think that it still is. However, over the past three decades, Maseru has rapidly expanded, and boasts a modest array of amenities. Among its attractions: a temperate climate, well-stocked shops, a decent selection of restaurants and hotels, and peppy people. Although many travellers bypass the capital completely, it makes an agreeable stop for a day or two, and is a good place to sort out logistics and stock up on supplies before heading into the highlands.

Despite a major city rebuilding program, you'll still see scars of the 1998 invasion by troops from SADC member states (see p520).

Orientation

Maseru's main street is Kingsway, which was paved in 1947 for a visit by the British royals and long remained the capital's only tarmac road. It runs from the Maseru Bridge border crossing southeast through the centre of town to the Circle – a major traffic roundabout best identified by the spires of the large Catholic cathedral on its eastern edge. At the Circle, Kingsway splits into Lesotho's two major traffic arteries: Main North Rd (for Teyateyaneng and other points north) and Main South Rd (for Mohale's Hoek and points south). A new bypass road rims the city to the south. About midway along on Kingsway is the distinctive conical Basotho Hat building, a good landmark.

MAPS

The **Department of Land, Surveys & Physical Planning** (☎ 2232 6367, 2232 2818; Lerotholi Rd; ☽ 8am-3pm Mon-Fri) sells a good 1:10,000 map of Maseru (M50, 2002). Look for the brown building marked 'LSPP'. The Tourist Information Office (p522) also sells a Maseru map (M5).

Information

BOOKSHOPS

Basotho Hat (☎ 2232 2523; Kingsway; ☽ 8am-4.30pm Mon-Sat) This craft shop (p525) has books on Lesotho.
CNA (LNDC Centre, Kingsway) The best bookshop in the area.
Maseru Book Centre (Kingsway) Near Nedbank.

CULTURAL CENTRES

Alliance Française (☎ 2232 5722; Kingsway; ☽ 8.30am-6.30pm Mon-Thu, 8.30am-5pm Fri, 9-11am Sat) Offers French-language lessons, and can organise Sotho tutors for groups.

EMERGENCY

Ambulance (☎ 114)
Fire Department (☎ 115)
Police (☎ 112)

INTERNET ACCESS

Leo (Orpen Rd; per min M0.80; ☽ 8am-5pm Mon-Fri, 9am-1pm Sat) The best and cheapest place for Internet access; behind the Basotho Hat building.
Lesotho Sun (☽ 8am-7pm Mon-Sat, 9am-1pm Sun) This hotel (p524) also has an Internet café.

MEDICAL SERVICES

For anything serious, you'll need to go to South Africa. In an emergency, also try contacting your embassy (p576), as most keep lists of recommended practitioners.
Maseru Private Hospital (☎ 2231 3260) In Ha Thetsane, about 7km south of Maseru.
Queen Elizabeth II Hospital (☎ 2231 2501; Kingsway) Near Lesotho Sun.

MONEY

The top-end hotels will do forex transactions (at poor rates). Otherwise try the following:
International Business Centre (Ground fl, Lesotho Bank Tower, Kingsway; ☽ 8.30am-3.30pm Mon-Fri, 8.30-11am Sat)
Nedbank (Kingsway) Does forex transactions Monday to Friday.
Standard Bank (Kingsway) Has an ATM.

POST

Post office (cnr Kingsway & Palace Rd) Has unreliable poste restante.

TELEPHONE

International phone calls are expensive; if possible, wait until you are in South Africa.
Public call centre (Kingsway) Opposite the Tourist Information Office.
Public phone shop (LNDC Centre, Kingsway)

TOURIST INFORMATION & TRAVEL AGENCIES

City Centre Maseru Travel (☎ 2231 4536; maseru travel@galileosa.co.za; Kingsway) Next to Nedbank, does regional and international flight bookings. It can also arrange tickets for Intercape and other long-distance buses, as well as private long-distance taxis within Lesotho.
Tourist Information Office (☎ 2231 2427, 2231 3760; ☽ 8am-4.30pm Mon-Fri, 8.30am-1pm Sat) Managed by the Lesotho Tourist Board. A helpful office with lots of brochures, information on public transport and free but dated Maseru city maps.

Dangers & Annoyances

Maseru is reasonably safe, but walking around at night, especially off the main street, is not recommended. Bag-snatching and pickpocketing are the main risks during the day.

Sights & Activities

Although Maseru has few sights, just walking around the town and getting a feel for Lesotho life can be enjoyable. If you're feeling more adventurous, there are several good **walks** on the mountain ridges

MASERU

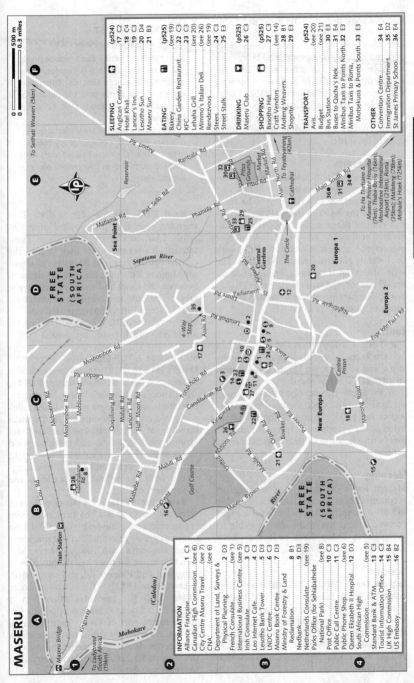

0 ____ 500 m
0 ____ 0.3 miles

INFORMATION
Alliance Française...............................1 C3
Canadian High Commission..........(see 6)
City Centre Maseru Travel..............(see 7)
CNA..(see 6)
Department of Land, Surveys &
Physical Planning..........................2 D3
French Consulate...........................(see 1)
International Business Centre.........(see 5)
Irish Consulate.................................3 C3
Leo Internet Cafe..............................4 C3
Lesotho Bank Tower.........................5 D3
LNDC Centre.....................................6 C3
Maseru Book Centre..........................7 D3
Ministry of Forestry & Land
Reclamation....................................8 B1
Nedbank...9 D3
Netherlands Consulate..................(see 19)
Parks Office (for Sehlabathebe
National Park)...............................(see 8)
Post Office.......................................10 C3
Public Call Centre...........................11 C3
Public Phone Shop.........................(see 6)
Queen Elizabeth II Hospital............12 D3
South African High
Commission..................................(see 5)
Standard Bank & ATM.....................13 C3
Tourist Information Office................14 C3
UK High Commission......................15 B4
US Embassy......................................16 B2

SLEEPING (pp524)
Anglican Centre.............................17 C2
Hotel Khali.....................................18 C4
Lancer's Inn....................................19 C3
Lesotho Sun...................................20 D4
Maseru Sun.....................................21 B3

EATING (pp525)
Bakery..(see 19)
China Garden Restaurant..............22 C3
KFC..23 C3
Lehaha Grill...............................(see 20)
Mimmo's Italian Deli...................(see 26)
Rendezvous................................(see 19)
Steers..24 C3
Street Stalls....................................25 E3

DRINKING (pp525)
Maseru Club...................................26 C3

SHOPPING (pp525)
Basotho Hat...................................27 C3
Craft Vendors.............................(see 14)
Moteng Weavers............................28 B1
Shoprite..29 E3

TRANSPORT (pp524)
Avis..(see 21)
Budget..30 D3
Bus Station....................................31 E4
Minibus Taxis to Points North.......32 E3
Minibus Taxis to Points South.......33 E3
Motsekuoa & Points South............33 E3

OTHER
Convention Centre.........................34 E4
Immigration Department................35 D2
St James Primary School................36 E4

that overlook the city. The most accessible begins at the gate of the Lesotho Sun hotel and takes you up to a plateau with views over the city. Go in a group, and leave your valuables behind. For other walks, look for a copy of *Hill Walks In & Around Maseru*, available at the **Basotho Hat** (☎ 2232 2523; Kingsway; ☺ 8am-4.30pm Mon-Sat) craft shop.

Another possibility is heading into the urban villages surrounding Maseru for a taste of local life.

Quirky Maseru

Finding yourself with nothing to do in Maseru? Set yourself down on a bench and watch the parade of hats go by. The most obvious is the Basotho hat, with its distinctive conical shape and curious top adornment. The Basotho know it as *mokorotlo* or *molianyeoe*, and often wear it together with the brightly patterned Basotho blanket. The style of the hat is supposedly modelled on the shape of Qiloane Hill, near Thaba-Bosiu. The hats are sold as souvenirs at craft shops throughout Lesotho.

Tours

The Tourist Information Office (p522) in Maseru keeps an updated list of tour operators, and all the main lodges listed in this chapter can arrange tours.

A few South African operators run tours up Sani Pass and over the border into Lesotho; see p333. Several of the operators listed in the Transport chapter also include forays into Lesotho in their itineraries; see p605.

Sleeping

Maseru has a decidedly modest range of accommodation, though you should be able to find something that will suit for a night or two. Alternatively, it's also possible to overnight in Thaba-Bosiu or Roma – both easy drives from the capital.

BUDGET

Anglican Centre (☎ 2232 2046; dm/tw with shared bathroom M50/100) Maseru's only real budget option has austere but clean rooms, and meals available with advance notice. It's about 500m north of Kingsway on the bend where Assisi Rd becomes Lancer's Rd. If you get lost, ask for St James Church, which is next door.

> ### A GOOD BREAKFAST & A HOT SHOWER
>
> Most hotels in Lesotho don't include breakfast in their prices. In this chapter, we've noted those places that do. Otherwise, expect to pay about M40 per person for standard fare and about M80 for a full breakfast buffet.
>
> Also on the topic of amenities: a shower is a rare luxury in Lesotho. Many places – even some of the nicer hotels – only have baths, though almost everywhere has piping hot water.

Hotel Khali (☎ 5816 0329; d M285) This friendly, rambling place offers undistinguished but comfortable rooms and a restaurant. It's set off on its own behind the central prison, south of Kingsway and just off Manong Rd. A shuttle runs on demand between the hotel and town. Alternatively, take a Thetsane minibus from Pioneer Rd near Lancer's Inn to the signposted turn-off for the suburb of New Europa. The hotel is about 800m further and signposted.

MID-RANGE & TOP END

Lancer's Inn (☎ 2231 2114; lancers-inn@ilesotho.com; cnr Kingsway & Pioneer Rd; s/d with breakfast M395/495; 🖭) Lancer's is Maseru's best-value accommodation, with pleasant rooms and a colonial-era ambience. Rooms are in the main building or in self-catering rondavels set around small grounds, and there's a good restaurant. The hotel caters primarily to business travellers, and also offers long-term rentals. It's behind Alliance Française in the town centre.

Maseru Sun (☎ 2231 2434; maseru@sunint.co.za; 12 Orpen Rd; r M820; 🖭 🏊) The attractions here are comfortable, modern rooms looking out onto grassy grounds, and slot machines to eat any extra cash you may have. Maseru Sun is just southwest of the junction of Kingsway and Pioneer Rd, and signposted.

Lesotho Sun (☎ 2231 3111; lesoresv@sunint.co.za; r M840; 🖭 🖳 🏊) Lesotho's other Sun is perched on a quiet hillside overlooking the southeastern part of town. Apart from its setting, it boasts a casino, two restaurants and rooms similar in standard to those at the Maseru Sun, and is similarly overpriced for what you get.

Eating

Happily, Maseru offers more variety for dining out than for accommodation, with several good restaurants.

Rendezvous (☎ 2231 2114; Lancer's Inn, Kingsway; mains M50-70; ☺ lunch & dinner) A rustic feel, large menu and reliable meals are on offer at Rendezvous, one of Maseru's nicer dining spots.

China Garden Restaurant (☎ 5896 1605, 5891 9513; Orpen Rd; mains M40-50; ☺ lunch & dinner) Tasty food and reasonable prices compensate for the rather drab dining area, and make this a good spot for an informal meal. It also does takeaway. The restaurant is set back, just off Kingsway near the Basotho Hat.

Mimmo's Italian Deli (☎ 2232 4979; Maseru Club, United Nations Rd; mains from M30; ☺ lunch & dinner) Mimmo's, a favourite with the local expat community, serves good pasta and pizza in agreeable surroundings.

Lehaha Grill (☎ 2231 3111; Lesotho Sun; meals from M50; ☺ dinner) This upscale place features a three-course menu and à la carte selections. If nothing suits, Chinese food is usually served during the evening in the Sun's second **restaurant** (☺ lunch & dinner) next door. Also watch for the new restaurant planned to open soon in the Basotho Hat building.

On the eastern end of Kingsway near Shoprite are **street stalls** (meals about M5; ☺ lunch) selling grilled meat, curry and rice. For Western fast food, KFC and Steers are both on Kingsway. Shoprite is the best option for self-caterers.

Next to Lancer's Inn is a good **bakery** (☺ 7am-8.30pm), with pies, cakes and other delicacies.

Drinking & Entertainment

Popular meeting spots include **Lancer's Inn** (p524), **Maseru Club** (☎ 2232 6008; United Nations Rd) and the bar/slot-machine lounges at the two Sun hotels.

Shopping

Basotho Hat (☎ 2232 2523; Kingsway; ☺ 8am-4.30pm Mon-Sat) This government-run craft shop is the best place to start, although prices are generally higher than elsewhere in the country. If you plan on walking or pony trekking, the horsehair fly whisks sold here make good investments.

The **craft vendors** (Kingsway) in front of the Tourist Information Office have a supply of woven Basotho hats and other souvenirs.

For tapestries, try **Moteng Weavers** (☎ 2231 1773; Raboshabane Rd), near the train station, and **Seithati Weavers** (☎ 2231 3975), about 7km from town along the airport road. For self-catering the best selection is at Shoprite, just off the circle.

Getting There & Away

For reaching Maseru from South Africa, see the Transport chapter (p596).

There are three main transport stands: near the Circle next to Shoprite for minibus taxis to Roma, Motsekuoa (for Malealea) and other points south; just off Main North Rd near Pitso Grounds (take the turn-off by the KFC sign) for minibus taxis to points north; and, about a block away from here, reached via the same turn-off, for large buses to points south and north. Buses to Qacha's Nek have their own (unmarked) stop along Main South Rd, just past St James Primary School, near the Convention Centre.

For car rental agencies, **Avis** (☎ 2232 0087) is based at Lesotho Sun, and **Budget** (☎ 2231 6344) is at Maseru Sun. Both agencies have kiosks at the airport.

Getting Around

TO/FROM THE AIRPORT

Moshoeshoe International Airport is 21km from town, off Main South Rd. Minibus taxis (from the transport stand next to Shoprite) cost M10. Alternatively, you can arrange transport with the Hotel Khali shuttle (p524), or from about M50 with one of the private taxi companies listed following.

MINIBUS TAXI

The standard minibus taxi fare around town is M2. The main taxi companies are **Moonlite** (☎ 2231 2695) and **Planet Shuttle** (☎ 2231 7777). Both can also be chartered for long-distance transport elsewhere in the country.

AROUND MASERU

If Maseru doesn't hold you, the surrounding area offers several attractions, all of which make easy day or overnight excursions from the capital. They're covered here clockwise, from north to south.

Thaba-Bosiu

About 25km east of Maseru is the famed and flat-topped Thaba-Bosiu (Mountain at Night), where King Moshoeshoe the Great established his mountain stronghold in 1824 (see p518). It's regarded as the birthplace of the Basotho nation, and – although quite an unassuming spot – is Lesotho's most important historical site.

The origins of its name are unclear. Some people say it may have been bestowed because the site was first occupied at night, while a more plausible legend suggests that Thaba-Bosiu, a hill in daylight, grows into a mountain at night-time.

At the mountain's base is a **visitors information centre** (admission M5; ☸ 8am-4.30pm) which has maps and an information pamphlet available. An official guide will accompany you on the short walk to the top of the mountain, for which you should pay a tip.

From the summit, there are good views over the surrounding area, including to **Qiloane Hill**, which allegedly provided the inspiration for the Basotho hat. Also at the summit are the remains of fortifications, Moshoeshoe's grave and parts of his original settlement.

Mmelesi Lodge (☎ 5250 0006, 2700 0601; s/d M180/230) is a friendly, well-organised place about 2km before the visitors information centre, and is the only accommodation available. Not many tourists stay here, but it does a brisk local business, with reasonable rooms and a good restaurant.

GETTING THERE & AWAY
Minibuses to Thaba-Bosiu (M5, 30 minutes) depart from Maseru at the transport stand next to Shoprite. If you're driving, take Main South Rd to the Roma turn-off; after about 6km take the signposted road left. Thaba-Bosiu is 10km further along.

Ha Baroana
Ha Baroana is one of Lesotho's more important rock-art sites. It's worth a visit if you have extra time, although neglect and vandalism have taken their toll.

To get here, take the Roma turn-off on the Main South Rd and follow this about 8km to the Thaba-Tseka junction. Follow the northern fork (to Thaba-Tseka) about 12km to Nazareth village. Just before Nazareth, there's a signposted gravel track to the paintings. Follow this 3km to Ha Khotso village, turn right at a football field and continue 2.5km to a hilltop overlooking a gorge. A footpath zigzags down the hillside

to the rock shelter with the paintings. Minibus taxis will take you as far as Nazareth.

Roma
Nestled amid sandstone cliffs about 35km southeast of Maseru, Roma was established in the 1860s as a mission town. Today it's Lesotho's centre of learning, with the country's only university, as well as several seminaries and secondary schools. The southern entry/exit to Roma takes you through a striking gorge landscape, and is best travelled during the morning or late afternoon when the lower sun lights the cliffs to full advantage.

The pleasant **Trading Post Guest House** (☎ 2234 0202/67, 082-773 2180; tradingpost@leo.co.ls; camp sites per person M35, rondavels per person M150, s/d with shared bathroom M100/200) is part of a trading post that has been here since 1903, together with the Thorn family, who own the guesthouse. There's no restaurant, but you can use the kitchen; breakfast is available (M30). The Trading Post runs pony trekking, and can help you sort out hiking, 4WD trails and other activities. About 1.5km away are some *minwane* (dinosaur footprints). The guesthouse is at the western end of town, signposted off the main (Semonkong) road from Maseru.

About 35km southeast along the same road is Ramabanta village, where the same owners run **Trading Post Adventures Guest House** (camp sites per person M35, s/d with shared bathroom M100/200) with self-catering facilities, and the chance to link up Roma, Ramabanta and other places in the area on overnight hikes. Bookings are taken for Trading Post Adventures Guest House through the Trading Post Guest House.

The humble **Speakeasy Restaurant** (meals M8), on the main road, serves basic fare.

Minibus taxis run throughout the day to/from Maseru (M6, 30 minutes). They depart Maseru from the stand next to Shoprite.

Morija
Morija is a tiny town with a long past, and the site of the first European mission in Lesotho. It's easy to get to, and well worth visiting if you're interested in Lesotho's history and culture. Before coming, hunt up a copy of Tim Couzens' *Murder at Morija*, which attempts to get behind the 1920 poisoning of one of the country's early missionaries.

SIGHTS & ACTIVITIES

Morija Museum & Archives (☎ 2236 0308; www
.morijafest.com; admission M6; ☼ 8am-5pm Mon-Sat,
noon-5pm Sun) is an impressive place including archives from the early mission, interesting information on Lesotho's collection
of dinosaur footprints and more. Staff are
knowledgeable, and the exhibits are very
well presented.

Morija Arts & Cultural Festival (www.morijafest
.com) is a popular event held annually in early
October. It highlights the diversity of Basotho
culture through dance, music and theatre,
and includes horse racing and *moraba-raba*
(the African equivalent of chess) competitions. The festival began in 1999 as a means
of reuniting the people of Lesotho after the
turmoil created by the 1998 invasion.

Other places of interest include the good
Maeder House Crafts Centre (☎ 2236 0487; ☼ 9am-
5pm Mon-Sat, noon-5pm Sun), near the museum,
and Lesotho's first **printing press**, on the same
grounds. **Pony trekking** can be organised
through the museum, as can overnight **walks**
(per person with half board & bedding M200, plus M150
per guide per day) on the nearby Makhoarane
Plateau.

SLEEPING & EATING

Ha Matela (Morija Guest House; ☎ 2231 6555, or through
Morija Museum; r per person M120) This pleasant and
comfortable stone-and-thatch cottage on the
edge of Morija has good views and peaceful surroundings. It accommodates up to 14
guests. Meals can be arranged, and there's a
kitchen. Take the road up from the museum
about 1.5km, turning right at the signpost.

Mophato Oa Morija (☎ 2236 0219; camp sites
per person M25, dm M60) Located near the museum, Mophato Oa Morija is an ecumenical
conference centre that is sometimes willing to accommodate travellers. Meals can
be arranged. Take the first right after the
museum and wind your way back about
700m – ask locals to point out the way.

GETTING THERE & AWAY

Minibus taxis run throughout the day between Maseru and Morija (M6, 45 minutes,
40km).

NORTHERN LESOTHO

Northern Lesotho – the area from Maseru
up to Butha-Buthe – is relatively densely
populated, and dotted with a series of bustling lowland towns. Most are of little interest to visitors, except for Teyateyaneng and
Hlotse (Leribe), both of which offer some
good craft shopping. The area is also convenient as an entry or exit point to/from
South Africa and as the main gateway to the
spectacular northeastern highlands. If you're
driving, it's worth allowing at least half a day
to drive through this part of the country en
route to points north and east. If you're travelling on public transport, Teyateyaneng and
Hlotse are the best overnight stops.

Teyateyaneng

Teyateyaneng (Place of Quick Sands; usually known simply as 'TY') has been developed as the craft centre of Lesotho, and
is well worth a stop to buy tapestries or
watch them being made.

Some of the best come from **Helang Basali
Crafts** (☎ 2250 0382; ☼ 8am-5pm Mon-Sat, 10am-5pm
Sun) at St Agnes Mission, about 2km before
Teyateyaneng and signposted to the east of
the Maseru road. Other good places (both
open similar hours) include Sesotho Design, near Blue Mountain Inn, and Hatooa
Mose Mosali, just west of the main road at
the town entrance. At Helang Basali and
Sesotho Design you can watch the weavers
at work.

Blue Mountain Inn (☎ 2250 0362; s/d M190/220)
is the main place to stay, with simple, good
rooms in a shaded compound, and a restaurant. It's about 1km off the main road
and signposted.

Ka Pitseng (☎ 2250 1368; s/d with shared bathroom
M150/180) is a small house, with simple rooms
and meals on request. It's signposted just off
the main road at the southern end of town.

Minibus taxis run throughout the day
between Teyateyaneng and Maseru (M8,
45 minutes, 35km). Chartering a taxi from
Maseru costs about M100 one way.

Maputsoe

This border town, 86km north of Maseru, is
across the Mohokare (Caledon) River from
the Free State town of Ficksburg, and of no
appeal other than as a transit point.

The **Sekekete Hotel** (☎ 2243 0621; s/d about
M145/170) is rough and run-down; it's much
better to stay across the border (p367).

Maputsoe is a major transport junction,
and for northbound transport from Maseru, you'll usually need to change vehicles

LESOTHO

here. Minibus taxis to both Maseru (M14, one hour) and Hlotse (M7, 30 minutes) run throughout the day.

Hlotse (Leribe)

Hlotse (also known as Leribe) is a large town and a regional market hub. It served as an administrative centre under the British, as witnessed by a few old buildings slowly decaying in the leafy streets. The main sight is the crumbling **Major Bell's Tower** near the market. It was built in 1879, and spent most of its career as a storehouse for government records.

The good **Leribe Craft Centre** (☎ 2240 0323; ⏲ 8am-4.30pm), just off the main road at the northern end of town, sells a range of high-quality woollen goods at reasonable prices.

There are several sets of **dinosaur footprints** near Hlotse. The first is a few kilometres south of town at Tsikoane village. Just south of Hlotse, take the small dirt road to the right towards some rocky outcrops. Follow it up to the church and ask someone to direct you to the *minwane*. From here, it's about a 1km slog up the mountainside to a series of caves. The prints are clearly visible on the rock ceiling.

About 7km north of Hlotse are the Subeng River dinosaur footprints. At the signpost indicating the river, walk down about 250m to a concrete causeway. The rather worn footprints of at least three species of dinosaur are about 15m downstream on the right bank.

If you're heading into the highlands, Hlotse is the last good place to stock up.

SLEEPING & EATING

Farmers' Training Centre (☎ 2240 0226; dm M25) This place is geared more towards farmers than intrepid backpackers, but it's possible to bunk here for the night. It's about 3km north of town off the road to Butha-Buthe. Take the first major left (west) turn-off after the mosque, and follow the dirt road around until you see the tractor and the Lesotho Agricultural College sign.

Leribe Hotel (☎ 2240 0559; Main St; s/d M175/240; meals from M25) An old-style hotel, and one of the nicer places in this part of Lesotho. There's good, clean accommodation in the main building or in private rondavels, and an invitingly green and leafy tea garden and meals. The hotel is about 100m uphill

from the central junction, on the main road through town.

GETTING THERE & AWAY

Minibus taxis run throughout the day between Hlotse and Maseru (M20, 1½ hours), usually with a change of vehicles at Maputsoe. There are also several vehicles daily between Hlotse and Katse (M30, 2½ hours), and between Hlotse and Butha-Buthe (M7, 40 minutes), many originating further south.

Butha-Buthe

Butha-Buthe (Place of Lying Down) was named by King Moshoeshoe the Great, because it was here that his people first retreated during the chaos of the *difaqane*. The town itself is small and scrappy, but redeemed by its attractive setting alongside the Hlotse River, with the beautiful Maluti Mountains as a backdrop.

The **Ha Thabo Ramakatane Hostel** (☎ 2246 1290; dm M35) – the name means 'Mr Ramakatane's Hostel' – is about 3.5km from Butha-Buthe in the village of Ha Sechele. There's no electricity, everything's very basic, and you'll need to bring all food and supplies from town, but it's a good dip into local life. You cook using gas and fetch your own water just as the villagers do. Turn off the main road at the sign for St Paul's High School in central Butha-Buthe, go left after the school, then take the next right. If you get lost, ask for the hostel.

Crocodile Inn (☎ 2246 0223; Reserve Rd; s/d from M171/200) The accommodation here is simple but clean, and it's a better place to stay than you might guess by looking at the outside. There are some average rooms in the main building, and newer, nicer rondavels out the back. The restaurant is Butha-Buthe's main dining establishment. The hotel is about 500m off the main road, and signposted at the southern end of town near the hospital.

GETTING THERE & AWAY

There are several minibus taxis daily between Maseru and Butha-Buthe via Maputsoe, where you'll usually need to change vehicles. From Maputsoe to Butha-Buthe costs M10 and takes about 20 minutes. There's also a daily bus to Mokhotlong, departing by about 8am. Butha-Buthe is the last reliable place to get petrol.

CULTURE BASOTHO-STYLE

Traditional Basotho culture is flourishing, and colourful celebrations marking milestones, such as birth, puberty, marriage and death, are a central part of village life. While hiking you may see the *lekolulo*, a flute-like instrument played by herd boys; the *thomo*, a stringed instrument played by women; and the *setolo-tolo*, a stringed instrument played with the mouth by men. Cattle hold an important position in daily life, both as sacrificial animals and as important symbols of wealth. Crop cultivation and weather are also central, and form the heart of many traditions.

The Basotho believe in a Supreme Being and place a great deal of emphasis on *balimo* (ancestors), who act as intermediaries between people and the capricious forces of nature and the spirit world. Evil is a constant danger, caused by *boloi* (witchcraft; witches can be either male or female) and *thkolosi* (small, maliciously playful beings, similar to the Xhosa's *tokoloshe*). If you're being bothered by these forces, head to the nearest *ngaka* – a learned man, part sorcerer and part doctor – who can combat them. Basotho are traditionally buried in a sitting position, facing the rising sun and ready to leap up when called.

Some snippets of Basotho traditional wisdom:

- toasting fresh rather than stale bread is bad because it causes rheumatism;
- when straining beer, take an occasional drink or your hands will swell;
- a spider in a hut should not be hurt – it's the strength of the family;
- a howling dog must be silenced immediately or it will bring evil.

Ts'ehlanyane National Park

This LHDA-administered **park** (admission per person M15, per vehicle M5) protects a beautiful 5600-hectare patch of rugged wilderness, including one of Lesotho's only stands of indigenous forest. It's7 about as away from it all as you can get, and if you're equipped for hiking, it's a superb stop.

For accommodation, there's a **conference centre** (r per person M60) at the park entrance with doubles and triples; various **camp sites** (per person from M20); a **tented camping area** (per person M50, minimum 2 people) with safari-style tents; and, a **'bush camp'** (rondavels M200 plus per person M40) with stone rondavels. Bookings can be made through LHDA (p520). Bring your own food and cooking equipment.

In addition to day walks, there's a challenging 39km hiking trail from Ts'ehlanyane southwest to Bokong Nature Reserve (p533) through some of Lesotho's most dramatic terrain. **Pony trekking** (per half/full day M50/75) can be arranged through LHDA with advance notice.

If you're driving, take the signposted turn-off from the main road about 8km south of Butha-Buthe, from where it's 31km further on a gravel access road (easily negotiable in 2WD). Occasional taxis run from Butha-Buthe towards Khabo, on the access road, from where you'll need to walk or hitch.

NORTHEASTERN & CENTRAL HIGHLANDS

Northeast of Butha-Buthe, the road begins to climb into some of the most spectacular scenery you'll see in Southern Africa. South Africa does a good job of marketing its portion of the Drakensberg escarpment, but for raw beauty, it can't compare with that in Lesotho, where the combination of snow (in winter), low population density and stunning highland panoramas is hard to beat. All the areas covered in this section are excellent for hiking, but you'll need to be fully equipped with a four-season sleeping bag, waterproof gear, topographical maps and a compass. Trout fishing is reputed to be top-notch.

'Muela

About halfway between Butha-Buthe and Oxbow is a signposted turn-off for 'Muela Lodge. The 'lodge' is about 7km from the main road, although there's nothing here yet, except a small stone house perched on a rise amid some great scenery. However, more is planned, including a craft centre and possibly accommodation. The nearby hydroelectric power station is part of the Lesotho Highlands Water Project (p532). Check with LHDA (p520) for an update on facilities at 'Muela. When things get going, the area would make a good base for hikes.

LESOTHO

Liphofung Cultural Site Reserve

Just beyond 'Muela is the signposted turn-off for this small LHDA-administered reserve (p520). The main attraction is a cave with some San paintings and Stone-Age artefacts. King Moshoeshoe the Great is also rumoured to have stopped here on his travels around Lesotho.

There is a **visitors centre** (adult/child M15/5; 8am-4.30pm Mon-Fri, 9am-4.30pm Sat & Sun), with a small shop selling local crafts. Accommodation is in two simple stone four-person **rondavels** (per person M50) with kitchen facilities (a minimum of two people can stay); or **camping** (per person M20). Hot showers are available; you'll need to bring your own food. There are various day hikes, and you can arrange **pony trekking** (half/full day M50/75) with advance notice.

Liphofung is an easy 1.5km walk down from the main road along a tarmac access ramp. Via public transport, take a taxi heading from Butha-Buthe towards Moteng, and get off at the Liphofung turn-off (M6, 25 minutes). If you stay overnight at Liphofung, the bus to Mokhotlong passes the turn-off at about 10.30am.

Oxbow

Oxbow, reached after crossing the dramatic Moteng Pass (2820m), consists of a few huts and a couple of lodges nestled amid some wonderful mountain scenery, and is an ideal place to get away from the bustle while still enjoying the amenities. The area regularly receives snow in winter, and boasts a 1.5km ski slope. It's also popular with South African trout anglers and bird-watchers. Except for a small supply of basics at the shop at New Oxbow Lodge, there's nowhere to stock up.

The appealing **New Oxbow Lodge** (☎ 051-933 2247 in South Africa; www.oxbow.co.za; camp sites per person M35, s/d with breakfast M310/545), on the banks of the Malibamat'so River, has an alpine feel, comfortable chalet-style accommodation, a cosy bar and a good restaurant. The owner is very knowledgeable about Lesotho, and the lodge rents skis. Half-board arrangements are available, as are triples and quads.

A few kilometres further north is a **private chalet** (www.clubmaluti.co.za; dm M65), run jointly by the Maluti and Witwatersrand University ski clubs. It's sometimes possible to sleep here, although weekends during winter are crowded.

About 10km past Oxbow off the road to Mokhotlong is the site of the planned **Afri-Ski ski resort** (www.afriski.co.za). Completion is still well in the future.

The bus between Maseru and Mokhotlong (p531) will drop you at Oxbow (M40, 4½ hours); if you're heading to Mokhotlong, it passes Oxbow at about noon. Several minibus taxis run daily between Butha-Buthe and Oxbow (M25, 1½ hours). The route follows a series of hairpin turns up the pass, and can be treacherous in snow and ice.

Mokhotlong

From Oxbow, a mostly good tarmac road winds its way over a series of 3200m-plus passes and through some superb high-altitude scenery before dropping down to Mokhotlong (Place of the Bald Ibis). The route was the original **Roof of Africa Rally** (www.roofofafrica.org.ls) course.

Mokhotlong is the main town in eastern Lesotho, but it is still very much an outpost, and has something of a Wild West feel to it. There's not much to do other than watch life go by, with the locals on their horses, sporting Basotho hats and blankets. However, the Senqu (Orange) River – Lesotho's main waterway – has its source near Mokhotlong, and the town makes a good base for walks. There are a number of reasonably well-stocked shops; petrol (expensive at M5 per litre) and diesel are sometimes available.

SLEEPING & EATING

Farmer Training Centre (dm M25) This is the cheapest place in town, with cold-water washing facilities and a kitchen. It's at the far end of town, past the library.

Senqu Hotel (☎ 2292 0330; s/d M180/200, with shared bathroom M90/120) The main place in Mokhotlong, with adequate but undistinguished rooms, and a restaurant. It's at the western end of town along the main road.

Mokhotlong Hotel (☎ 2292 0212; s/d M156/198) In the unlikely event that the Senqu is full, Mokhotlong Hotel – at the opposite end of town – is worth a try. Rooms are basic, and better in the 'new block', where they have a TV and bathroom.

Molumong Guesthouse & Backpackers (☎ 033-345 7045 in South Africa; molumong@worldonline.co.za; camp sites per person M40, dm/d M70/160) Most travellers head out of town to Molumong (pronounced 'modimong'), signposted about 15km southwest of Mokhotlong off the road to Thaba-Tseka. Look for the red-roofed building with 'Molumong' on its roof. The guesthouse was once a colonial trading post, and offers a peaceful self-catering experience. Rooms are simple and bright, with no electricity, TV or telephones; just the stars. Bring whatever food you'll need from Mokhotlong.

Thia-Lala Butchery & Cafe A good shop in the town centre next to the library, with takeaway sandwiches and a range of basics, including chilled juices.

GETTING THERE & AWAY

There are a few minibus taxis daily to/from Butha-Buthe (M40, six hours). A bus goes daily to/from Maseru, departing in each direction by about 8am (M50, eight hours), except on Sunday (Mokhotlong to Maseru only) and Saturday (Maseru to Mokhotlong only). There's also a daily minibus taxi from Mokhotlong to Sani Top, which continues on to Underberg (South Africa) via the Sani Pass. It departs from Mokhotlong daily at 6am (M50, five hours to Underberg). Minibus taxis to Linakaneng (on the Thaba-Tseka road) will drop you by Molumong Guesthouse. For transport from Molumong to Sani Pass, head back to the Sani Pass junction, 4km from Mokhotlong centre.

Sani Top

Sani Top sits atop the steep Sani Pass, the only dependable road into Lesotho through the Drakensberg range in KwaZulu-Natal. It offers wonderful views on clear days and unlimited hiking possibilities. Among the options are:

Thabana-Ntlenyana (3482m) This is a popular, but long and arduous, hike. Thabana-Ntlenyana is Africa's highest peak south of Mt Kilimanjaro. The mountain's height was only calculated in 1951 and not confirmed by satellite technology until 30 years later. There's a path, but a guide would be handy. It's also possible to do the ascent on horseback.

Hodgson's Peaks (3257m) A much easier walk 6km south, from where you can see into Sehlabathebe National Park and KwaZulu-Natal.

Sehlabathebe National Park A rugged three-day hike from Sani Top Chalet south along the remote escarpment edge to Sehlabathebe National Park; only try this one if you're well prepared, experienced and in a group of at least three people.

Other hikes in this area are outlined in the excellent booklet *A Backpackers' Guide to Lesotho* by Russell Suchet – available at Maseru craft shops (p525), the Morija Museum (p527) and through Sani Lodge (p334).

SLEEPING & EATING

Sani Top Chalet (☎ 033-702 1158 in South Africa; www.sanitopchalet.co.za; camp sites per person M35, dm M70, r with half board per person M275) On the edge of the escarpment at a lofty 2874m, this popular place boasts the highest bar in Africa. Also on offer are simple, cosy rooms with shared bathroom, a backpackers dorm, cooking facilities and meals. In winter the snow is sometimes deep enough for skiing (there are a few pieces of antique equipment); pony trekking can be arranged with advance notice.

There are also several good hostels on the KwaZulu-Natal side of the pass; see p334.

GETTING THERE & AWAY

A minibus taxi runs daily from Mokhotlong via Sani Top down to Underberg (South Africa) and back (M50, five hours).

If you're driving, you'll need a 4WD to go up the pass; 2WD with clearance can make it down, though with difficulty. The South African border crossing is open 8am to 4pm daily; the Lesotho side stays open until 5pm to let the last vehicles through. Hitching is best on weekends.

Hostels on the KwaZulu-Natal side arrange transport up the pass, and various agencies in Himeville and Underberg (the nearest South African towns) arrange tours.

Thaba-Tseka

Thaba-Tseka is a remote town on the western edge of the Central Range, over the sometimes-tricky Mokhoabong Pass. It was established in 1980 as a centre for the mountain district. Today, it's a scrappy place with little to interest you, other than serving as a convenient transport junction for travel north to Katse or west to Maseru.

The **Farmer Training Centre** (☎ 2290 0201; dm M25) has similar standards as Farmer Training Centres elsewhere. It's on the street behind the post office.

Mountain Star Hotel (☎ 2290 0415; s/d M120/150) is Thaba-Tseka's main hotel, with a new wing along the main road in the centre of town and the original building about 1.5km

---

LESOTHO HIGHLANDS WATER PROJECT

The Lesotho Highlands Water Project (LHWP) is an ambitious scheme developed jointly by Lesotho and South Africa to harness Lesotho's abundant water resources. The project, being implemented in stages, will result in five major dams, many smaller ones and approximately 200km of tunnels, and will provide water and electricity for a large tract of Southern Africa.

Immediate effects of this development include vastly improved roads and telecommunications in the interior of the country – bringing innumerable benefits, including new jobs, for the residents of many remote villages.

However, there are major detrimental effects as well. These include flooding of significant portions of Lesotho's already scarce arable land and potential silting problems. Another unknown is the impact on Namibia, a downstream user with its own water shortage problems. Billboards in each village warning of AIDS hint at other risks caused by easier contact with the outside world now that the road network has been improved. For more background on the water project see www.lhwp.org.ls.

---

further along the same road. Rooms are adequate and meals are available.

Three buses run daily between Maseru and Thaba-Tseka (M27, seven hours), departing from Maseru between about 9am and 11am. There's no public transport south from Thaba-Tseka to Sehonghong and Qacha's Nek, though it's sometimes possible to negotiate a lift with a truck driver. From Thaba-Tseka to Mokhotlong, get a minibus taxi to Linakaneng (M20, two hours), and from there another to Mokhotlong (M10, two hours). Several minibus taxis travel daily along the unsealed but good road from Thaba-Tseka to Katse, and on to Hlotse (M50, five hours).

Basotho Pony Trekking Centre

About 85km west of Thaba-Tseka, and also easily accessed from Maseru, is the **Basotho Pony Trekking Centre** (☎ 2231 7284), on the top of God Help Me Pass. It's much more no frills and DIY than the other pony trekking places, but this is the place to come if you want to ride away from the crowds.

Treks range from two hours (per person about M35) to seven days (per person M405, minimum four people), with discounts for groups.

Accommodation on overnight treks is in villages en route (per person M20, with your own tent M10). You'll need to bring all your own food and a stove; the centre provides a pack mule for your gear. There's nowhere to stay at the centre, so if you plan to depart in the morning, you'll need to camp (there's a grubby, but hot, shower). The closest hotel is **Mabotlenyane Lodge**

(☎ 2234 7766, 5886 4352; s/d M180/320), about 20km west along the road to Maseru, with basic rooms, a bar and meals.

Buses between Thaba-Tseka and Maseru will drop you at the centre (M10, 1½ hours between the pony centre and Maseru).

Katse

Tiny Katse's main claim to fame is as the base for the Lesotho Highlands Water Project and the site of Africa's highest dam (185m). There's a well-organised **information office** (☎ 2291 0276), with a video about the dam, tours of the dam daily at 9am and 1.30pm, and a viewpoint over the dam wall.

The dam's lake is serene, ringed by steep, green hillsides, and if you have the budget to stay in the lodge, it makes a relaxing pause on travels through the highlands. Fishing is allowed from the sides; permits are on sale at the information office (M10).

Katse Lodge (☎ 2291 0202; s/d with breakfast M253/456) is the only place to stay, with modern rooms, a restaurant overlooking the lake and a bar; advance bookings are recommended. To get here, follow signs for Katse village, and turn off into the staff housing compound.

GETTING THERE & AWAY

The 122km road between Hlotse and Katse is excellent, although steep and winding, and slick in the rain. Allow at least two hours for driving, longer if going by public transport.

Minibus taxis go daily from Hlotse to Katse (M40, 3½ hours), with some continuing on to Thaba-Tseka (M50), sometimes with a change at Pitseng. In Katse, public transport stops near the Katse village junction. Hitching is usually easy.

If you're driving, Katse Lodge is at the far end of Katse village, past the barrier gate. The information office is about 2km east of here along the main road.

Hikers may be interested in the small boat that ferries locals across the dam to Ha Sepinare village (M5). The launch point is reached by following the path leading down to the water from next to Lesotho Bank at the entrance to Katse village.

Bokong Nature Reserve

Bokong has perhaps the most dramatic setting of the three LHDA reserves, with stunning vistas over the Lepaqoa Valley from the **visitors centre** (adult/child M5/3; ⏰ 8am-5pm), various short walks and a good, rugged two- to three-day hike to Ts'ehlanyane National Park (p529). Not far from the visitors centre is an impressive waterfall, near where you can **camp** (per person M20) or overnight in a very basic four-person **hut** (per person M40) – bring your own food, sleeping bag, mattress and stove. **Guides** (per person M20) are available, and **pony trekking** (per half/full day M50/75) can be arranged. The reserve sits at just over 3000m and gets cold at night, so come prepared. Bookings can be made through LHDA (p521).

Bokong lies roughly midway between Katse and Hlotse at the top of Mafika-Lisiu Pass (3090m). Minibus taxis from Hlotse will drop you at the visitors centre (M15, 1½ hours); when leaving, you may need to wait a while before one passes by with space.

Semonkong

Semonkong (Place of Smoke) is a one-horse town in a serene setting in the Thaba Putsoa range. It makes a great base for pony trekking and hiking, including to **Maletsunyane Falls** (192m), a 1½ hour walk away. The falls are at their most impressive in summer, and are best appreciated from the bottom of the gorge, where there are **camp sites** (per person M20). Also worth seeing are **Ketane Falls** (122m), a rewarding day's ride (30km) from Semonkong.

The peaceful and recommended **Semonkong Lodge** (☎ /fax 051-933 3106 in South Africa; www.placeofsmoke.co.ls; camp sites per person M35, dm/s/d M80/220/360), near the Maletsunyane River, is the place to stay. It has camping,

good dorm-style rondavels set away from the lodge and comfortable rooms, plus a good restaurant and a bar. The owners can help you organise hiking, pony trekking and more. It's on the edge of town, and signposted from the town centre.

GETTING THERE & AWAY

Semonkong is about 120km southeast of Maseru, past Roma. The final 70km are gravel, though in reasonable condition (negotiable with 2WD). Allow three to four hours from Maseru. Buses between Maseru and Semonkong (M20) leave from either place in the morning, arriving in late afternoon. The road dead-ends at Semonkong; an excellent alternative to retracing your steps is to hike south to Christ the King mission on the Quthing–Qacha's Nek road (see p536).

SOUTHERN LESOTHO

Southern Lesotho – from Mafeteng and Malealea southwards, across to Sehlabathebe National Park in the southeast – is less developed than the northwest between Maseru and Butha-Buthe. There are no tarmac roads east of Qacha's Nek, and public transport connections take more time than in the north. None of this should deter you, however. The region is highly rewarding, with scenery rivalling that in the highlands to the north, numerous opportunities for immersing yourself in local history and culture, and an enticing off-the-beaten-track feel.

Malealea

Tiny Malealea village is many travellers' introduction to Lesotho life, and makes an excellent place to start exploring the country. Activities centre around Malealea Lodge (p534), which is appropriately advertised as 'Lesotho in a nutshell'. You can go on a well-organised pony trek from here or wander freely through the hills and villages.

The surrounding valleys have been occupied for centuries, as shown by the many **San rock paintings**.

PONY TREKKING

It's possible to arrange **pony treks** (per person per day/overnight M150/200) to any destination that you fancy. Popular routes include: Ribaneng Waterfall (two days, one night); Ribaneng and Ketane waterfalls (four days, three nights); and, Semonkong (five to six days).

PONY TREKKING & HIKING

Pony trekking is one of Lesotho's top drawcards. It's done on sure-footed Basotho ponies, the result of crossbreeding between short Javanese horses and European full mounts. King Moshoeshoe the Great is recorded as having ridden a Basotho pony in 1830. Since that time, these animals have become an integral part of life in the highlands, and the preferred mode of transport for many villagers.

Advance booking is recommended, and no prior riding experience is necessary. Whatever your experience level, expect to be sore after a day in the saddle. For overnight treks, you'll need to bring food (stock up in Maseru), a sleeping bag and warm, waterproof clothing. Places to organise treks include:

- Basotho Pony Trekking Centre (p532)
- Malealea Lodge (below)
- Semonkong Lodge (p533)
- LHDA conservation areas: Ts'ehlanyane National Park (p529); Bokong Nature Reserve (p533); and the Liphofung Cultural Site Reserve (p530).

Hiking rivals pony trekking as the best way to explore Lesotho. Plan a day in Maseru to buy topographical maps and stock up on food and supplies. Any specialist hiking supplies, including a compass, should be brought from South Africa. Once on the trail, respect the cairns that mark graves. However, a mound of stones near a trail, especially between two hills, should be added to by passing travellers, who ensure their good luck by spitting on a stone and throwing it onto the pile.

Several lodges have worked out trail networks in their areas, including Malealea and Semonkong. The owner of Fuleng Guest House (p536) is also helpful with hikes. For more hiking possibilities, see the Sani Top section (p531).

Bring food, a sleeping bag, rainwear, sunscreen, warm clothing, a torch (flashlight) and water purification tablets. It's possible to stay in Basotho village huts along the way for M30 per person per night.

HIKING

Malealea Lodge (right) has route maps for hikes and can arrange pack ponies for your gear. Nearby destinations include: **Botso'ela Waterfall** (two hours return); **Pitseng Gorge** (six hours return, bring swimwear); **Pitseng Plateau** (one hour return); and along the Makhaleng River. The scenery throughout is stunning, and all walks include visits to surrounding villages. Overnight and longer jaunts are also possible.

OTHER ACTIVITIES

Flat-water **rafting** can be arranged, water levels permitting, on the Makhaleng River. It's best around December and January, and not possible from May through August. **Abseiling** is also possible, as are **4WD trips** across rugged terrain in an open 4WD. The lodge can also point you to some good, scenic

drives, including one along the road forming part of the Roof of Africa Rally (www .roofofafrica.org.ls).

SLEEPING & EATING

Malealea Lodge (☎ 051-447 3200, 082-552 4215 both in South Africa; www.malealea.co.ls; camp sites per person M40, backpacker huts per person with shared bathroom M70, r per person M135-180) Malealea Lodge began life in 1905 as a trading post, established by teacher, diamond miner and soldier Mervyn Smith. Since then, it's grown considerably and is now the hub of local life. The lodge, which is run by the very helpful Mick and Di Jones, is impressively integrated into the surrounding community. In 2003 it was the overall winner in the prestigious Imvelo responsible tourism awards for Southern Africa, and a significant portion of tourist revenue goes directly to supporting projects in the area.

Accommodation options range from a camp sites and two-person backpacker huts (huts with linen available for M90) in a good, wooded setting away from the lodge, to simple, cosy rooms and rondavels. Book in advance if possible. There's no phone at the lodge (just a radio), so allow a few days for your booking to go through. The lodge also has a bar, good meals (breakfast/lunch/dinner M35/40/60), self-catering facilities and a fully stocked shop nearby. Almost every night it's possible to hear one of the local children's choirs practising on the grounds.

GETTING THERE & AWAY

Two Sprinter minibus taxis connect Maseru and Malealea, departing Maseru at noon and 5pm, and Malealea at 6.30am and 2.30pm (M14, two hours, 83km). Otherwise, catch a minibus taxi from the transport stand next to Shoprite in Maseru and take it to the junction town of Motsekuoa (M10, two hours), from where there are frequent connections to Malealea (M7, 30 minutes).

If you're driving, head south from Maseru on Main South Rd for 52km to Motsekuoa. Here, look for the Malealea Lodge sign and the collection of minibus taxis. Turn left (east) onto a tarmac road and follow it for 24km. When you reach the signposted turn-off to Malealea, it's 7km further along an unsealed road to the lodge. Shortly before reaching the lodge is **Gates of Paradise Pass**, with stunning views of your destination and a plaque announcing, 'Wayfarer – Pause and look upon a gateway of Paradise'.

It's also possible to approach Malealea from the south, via Mpharane and Masemouse, but the road is rough and most drivers travel via Motsekuoa.

Mafeteng

Mafeteng (Place of Lefeta's People) is an important bus and minibus taxi interchange, a border junction (it's just 22km to Wepener in Free State) and a possible stocking-up point before heading further south. It's named after an early magistrate Emile Rolland, who was known as Lefeta (One who Passes By) to the local Basotho. In the town centre is a small **statue** commemorating soldiers of the Cape Mounted Rifles who fell in the Gun War of 1880.

Mafeteng Hotel (☎ 2270 0236; s/d from M200/250) is an agreeable place, signposted from the main road at the southern end of town, and the best choice. It has standard rooms, nice garden cottages, a restaurant and a popular disco.

Golden Hotel (☎ 2270 0566; s/d M175/240) lies at the northern edge of town along the main road, with adequate rooms and meals.

Frequent minibus taxis connect Mafeteng with Maseru (M14, 1½ hours) and Mohale's Hoek (M9, one hour). For Quthing, change at Mohale's Hoek.

Mohale's Hoek

Mohale's Hoek takes its name from the younger brother of King Moshoeshoe the Great, Mohale, who in 1884 gave this land to the British for administrative purposes. The town centre is agreeable enough, and a better spot to overnight than Mafeteng.

Monateng Lodge (☎ 2278 5337; s/d M170/200) is the cheapest choice, with simple rooms and a restaurant. It's along the main road at the northern end of town.

Hotel Mount Maluti (☎ 2278 5224; m.m.h@leo.co.ls; s/d with breakfast M234/342) is a pleasant hotel boasting large gardens, comfortable rooms and a good restaurant. It's about 500m off the main road and signposted.

Minibus taxis depart each morning for Quthing (M10, 45 minutes) and throughout the day to Mafeteng (M9, one hour). There are also several minibus taxis daily to Maseru (M22, 2½ hours, 125km) and a bus (M20).

Quthing

Quthing – the southernmost major town in Lesotho – is also known as Moyeni (Place of the Wind). It was established in 1877, abandoned during the Gun War of 1880 and then rebuilt at the present site.

Activity centres around Lower Quthing (Lower Moyeni), spread out along the main road. Up on the hill overlooking the Senqu (Orange) River gorge is Upper Quthing (Upper Moyeni), the former colonial administrative centre, with a post office, hospital, police station, hotel and some good views. Minibus taxis between Lower and Upper Quthing charge M2.

SIGHTS & ACTIVITIES

Masitise Cave House Museum (admission free, but donation appreciated) is an intriguing place about 5km west of Quthing. It's part of an old mission that was built directly into a San rock shelter in 1866 by Reverend David-Frédéric Ellenberger, a Swiss who was among the first missionaries to Lesotho.

The cave house has been converted into a small museum, with interesting displays on local culture and history. There's a cast of a dinosaur footprint in the ceiling and San paintings nearby. To get here, take the signposted turn-off for Masitise Primary School and follow the road about 1.5km back past the small church. The caretaker's house (for the key to the cave house) is just behind, and the museum about five minutes further on foot. Accommodation is planned for the future.

Quthing's other claim to fame is a proliferation of **dinosaur footprints** in the surrounding area. The most easily accessible are just off the main road to Mt Moorosi; watch for the small, pink building to your left. It's just a short walk down to the footprints, which are believed to be 180 million years old.

Between Quthing and Masitise, and visible from the main road, is **Villa Maria Mission**, with a striking, twin-spired sandstone church. About 10km southeast of town near Qomoqomong is a collection of **San paintings**. Several minibus taxis ply this route daily; once in Qomoqomong, ask at the General Dealer's store to arrange a guide for the 20-minute walk to the paintings.

The road from Quthing to Qacha's Nek is one of Lesotho's most beautiful drives, taking you along the winding Senqu (Orange) River gorge and through some impressive canyon scenery before climbing up onto the escarpment. If you're equipped, the whole area is ideal for hiking. En route is the village of **Mt Moorosi**; the pretty **Mphaki** village, a possible base for hiking; and **Christ the King Mission**, with wide views over the Senqu River valley. From the mission, it's a good two- to three-day hike north to Semonkong (p533).

SLEEPING & EATING

Merino Stud Farm (r per person M45, with shared bathroom M25) The cheapest rooms in town. The Stud Farm is located about 2.5km from Upper Quthing and is signposted from the end of the tarmac road. Meals can be arranged.

Fuleng Guest House (☎ 2275 0260; r per person from M50) A friendly place with rooms and thatched rondavels. The owner is enthusiastic about establishing tourism in Quthing, and can arrange guides for hikes

and excursions. If you want a good local experience, it's well worth stopping here for a few nights. The rooms and rondavels have bathrooms, and are very reasonably priced for what you get; meals can be arranged. It's in Lower Quthing and signposted from the main road just before the bend.

Mountain Side Hotel (☎ 2275 0257; s/d M200/274) The better of Quthing's two hotels, this place has faded but spacious rooms and a decent restaurant. Ask for a room in the main building; those at the back are very cramped. It's about 100m down the dirt lane leading off the main road, where the hill from Lower Quthing begins to climb to Upper Quthing.

Orange River Hotel (s/d M260/300) This once-grand hotel, perched on the edge of the escarpment in Upper Quthing, now stands virtually derelict. Its less-than-average rooms have wide views across the gorge to the hills behind. If you decide to stay here, you'll likely be the only one. Meals can be arranged.

For an inexpensive meal, head to the well-stocked, no-name shop selling grilled chicken, omelettes and other fast food in Lower Quthing, just before Fuleng Guest House.

In Mphaki, there's a **Farmers' Training Centre** (dm M25) with a kitchen, and a few small shops nearby.

GETTING THERE & AWAY

A bus departs from Quthing daily for Qacha's Nek at about 9am (M30, five hours), and several minibus taxis go to Maseru (M35, 3½ hours). The transport stand is in Lower Quthing in front of the Ellerine's store. The Quthing–Qacha's Nek road is tarmac the entire way, except for about 30km starting shortly east of Mphaki.

Qacha's Nek

Originally a mission station, Qacha's Nek was founded in 1888 near the pass (1980m) of the same name. It's a pleasant place with an attractive church and a variety of other colonial-era sandstone buildings. Nearby are stands of California redwood trees, some over 25m high.

The **Farmer Training Centre** (☎ 2295 0231; dm M25) has similar standards to other Farmer Training Centres. It's just off the main road at the western end of town; turn at the 'For-

RAIN-MAKING CEREMONY

It's not likely you'll be wishing for rain while visiting Sehlabathebe, but just in case, here's a description of the ceremony for rainmaking, as detailed in the pamphlet *Customs & Superstitions in Basotholand* by Justinus Sechefo.

A first attempt at bringing rain is made by the men of the village, who climb to the top of a nearby mountain and kill every animal they can find. The entrails of the animals are thrown into streams and the men return home, drenched from the heavy rain. If the rain isn't falling, the village calls in a *moroka-pula* (rainmaker).

If the men fail, it's the turn of the village's young women. Theirs is the ceremony of last resort. They go to a neighbouring village and the quickest of them enters a hut and steals the *lesokoana*, which can be any wooden cooking utensil. She flees from the village with the *lesokoana*, raising the alarm herself if she hasn't already been spotted. When the village women run out to reclaim the *lesokoana*, the young women toss it back and forth, sometimes losing it and sometimes regaining it. This game attracts spectators from both villages and ends when one group makes it back to their village with the *lesokoana*.

The winners enter the village, their heads and waists bedecked with green leaves, singing joyously. Even if the ceremony still fails to bring rain, at least everyone stops worrying about the drought for a while.

LESOTHO

estry Division Nursery & Office' sign just east of the Lesotho Bank.

Anna's B&B (☎ 2295 0374; s M75-125, d M135-250) is on the main road, diagonally opposite the Farmer Training Centre. It has clean, pleasant rooms in the new wing, and some less appealing ones with a shared bathroom in the old wing.

Hotel Nthatuoa (☎ 2295 0260; s/d M150/200) is a nice place, and has simple but agreeable rooms and a restaurant. Rooms with a TV are available for an extra M45. It's signposted along the main road at the northern edge of town.

GETTING THERE & AWAY

There's a daily bus between Maseru and Qacha's Nek departing from Maseru between 5am and 6am (M50, nine hours), and a daily bus from Qacha's Nek to Sehlabathebe National Park departing from Qacha's Nek about noon (M25, five hours). The Quthing bus leaves Qacha's Nek at 9am (M30, five hours).

Sehlabathebe National Park

Lesotho's first national park, proclaimed in 1970, is remote, rugged and beautiful, and getting there is always an adventure. The major attractions are the park's sense of separation from the rest of the world, as well as its highly rewarding wilderness hiking and its trout fishing. It's also home to a few rare birds, the odd rhebok or baboon and

the Maloti minnow (thought to be extinct but rediscovered on the Tsoelikana River). Hiking and horse riding are the main ways to explore.

You'll need to bring all your food, and be well prepared for the elements. This is a summer-rainfall area, and thick mist, potentially hazardous to hikers, is common. Winters are clear but cold at night, with occasional light snowfalls.

SLEEPING & EATING

Sehlabathebe Park Lodge (camp sites per person M20, r per person M30) This rustic but pleasant self-catering lodge offers good value, and is the only place to stay in the park. (Camping is permitted throughout the park, though there are no facilities besides plenty of water.) Bring all your own food, plus extra petrol or diesel, as there's none available at the park. Accommodation should be booked in advance through the Ministry of Forestry & Land Reclamation's **Parks Office** (☎ 2232 3600; just off Raboshabane Rd, Maseru). The lodge takes up to 12 people, and has bedding and a fully equipped kitchen.

If you're travelling by public transport, the buses reach Sehlabathebe in the evening, which means you'll need to overnight in Mavuka village near the park gate and continue to the park the next day. The **Range Management Education Centre** (dm M35), 1.5km down the Sehonghong road, has dorm beds and meals.

GETTING THERE & AWAY

There's an airstrip at Paolosi, about 3km south of Mavuka, for charter flights.

A daily bus connects Qacha's Nek and Sehlabathebe, departing from Qacha's Nek at noon and Sehlabathebe at 5.30am (M30, 4½ hours). The bus terminates in Mavuka village, near the park gate. From here, it's about 12km further on foot to the lodge. You can also arrange with the Parks Office (p537) in Maseru for horses to come and meet you at the gate and ride in to the lodge (M40 per horse, one-way).

If you're driving, the main route into the park is via Quthing and Qacha's Nek. The road from Qacha's Nek is unpaved but in reasonable condition, and negotiable at most times of year in 2WD. You can arrange to leave your vehicle at the police station in Paolosi village while you're in the park. It's also possible at some times of the year to reach Sehlabathebe from the north from Thaba-Tseka, via Taung, Sehonghong and Matabeng. This route is rough even with 4WD; check on conditions locally before setting off. Note that 4WD tracks sometimes become impassable after heavy rains, and it's possible that once at the park you could be stuck waiting for a swollen river to go down before you can leave.

Probably the simplest way into the park is to hike the 10km up the escarpment from Bushman's Nek in KwaZulu-Natal. From Bushman's Nek to the Nkonkoana Gate border crossing takes about six hours. You can also take a horse up or down for M50. This can be arranged with the park lodge, or at the Parks Office (p537) in Maseru.

Swaziland

ARIADNE VAN ZANDBERGEN

Swaziland

Swaziland comes as a breath of fresh air after travelling through South Africa. With its laid-back ambience, friendly people and relative lack of racial animosities, it's a complete change of pace from its larger neighbour. Most visitors take away memories of smiling adults and waving children, particularly if they spend any time in the countryside – which is anywhere outside the main towns of Mbabane and Manzini.

During apartheid, Swaziland was known primarily for its casinos and nightclubs – forbidden pleasures in apartheid-era South Africa. Since the dismantling of apartheid this reputation has faded fast. Today the country's attractions include rewarding, affordable and delightfully low-key wildlife-watching, stunning mountain panoramas and a lively traditional culture. Swaziland also boasts superb walking and an excellent selection of high-quality handicrafts. Overseeing all this is one of Africa's last reigning monarchs. The monarchy has its critics, but combined with the Swazis' distinguished history of resistance to the Boers, the British and the Zulus, it has fostered a strong sense of national pride, and local culture is flourishing.

Travelling in Swaziland is easy. There's accommodation to suit every taste, ranging from a decent network of hostels to family-friendly hotels and upscale retreats, and plenty to keep you busy. It's feasible to drive around the entire country in a few days, but it's well worth lingering at least a week, especially if you plan to do any hiking. It's also worth timing your visit to coincide with one of the national festivals, notably the Incwala ceremony or the Umhlanga (Reed) dance (p550), to get a taste of the cultural vitality for which Swaziland is so renowned.

SWAZILAND

HIGHLIGHTS

- Watching wildlife – including rare black rhinos in the wild – at the excellent **Mkhaya Game Reserve** (p560)
- Hiking in **Malolotja Nature Reserve**, one of Southern Africa's most enchanting wilderness areas (p557)
- Witnessing Swazi culture in full force at the Umhlanga (Reed) dance or Incwala ceremony at **Lobamba** (p552)
- Taking advantage of some of Southern Africa's best craft shopping in the **Ezulwini Valley** (p552) and the **Malkerns Valley** (p554)
- Shooting white-water rapids on the **Usutu River** (p560)
- Cycling or walking around **Mlilwane Wildlife Sanctuary**, and relaxing in its comfortable bargain lodges (p552)
- Exploring the **Ezulwini Valley**, Swaziland's royal heartland (p549)

★ Malolotja Nature Reserve

Mlilwane Wildlife Sanctuary ★ ★ Ezulwini Valley
★ Lobamba

Malkerns Valley
★ Mkhaya Game Reserve
Usutu River ★

| POPULATION: 990,000 | AREA: 17,364 SQ KM |

SWAZILAND

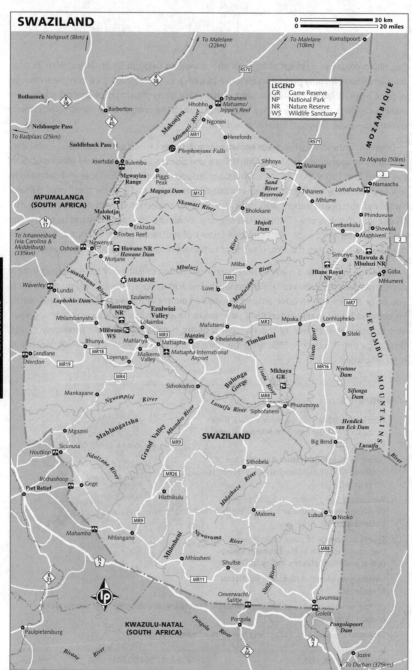

SWAZILAND

To Nelspruit (8km)
To Malelane (22km)
To Malelane (10km)
Komatipoort

R570

LEGEND
GR Game Reserve
NP National Park
NR Nature Reserve
WS Wildlife Sanctuary

Bothasnek

R38

Barberton

R40

Nelshoogte Pass
To Badplaas (25km)

Saddleback Pass

Hhohho
Tshaneni Matsamo/ Jeppe's Reef
Ngonini

Makonjwa

Mlumati River

MR1

Herefords

R571

MOZAMBIQUE

Phophonyane Falls

Sihhoya
Mananga

To Maputo (50km)

Josefsdal Bulembu
Piggs Peak

Mgwayiza Range

Maguga Dam

M13

Sand River Reservoir
Tshaneni
Mhlume

Lomahasha
Namaacha

Nkomati River

Bholekane

R2

MPUMALANGA (SOUTH AFRICA)

Malolotja NR

Enkhaba
Forbes Reef

Mnjoli Dam

River

Phinduvuke
Tambankulu
Shewula
Maphiveni

To Johannesburg (via Carolina & Middelburg) (335km)

N17

Oshoek Ngwenya
Motjane

Hawane NR
Hawane Dam

Mbuluzi

MR5

Mliba

River

Mbuluzane River

Simunye
Hlane Royal NP

Mlawula & Mbuluzi NR
Goba
Mhlumeni

Waverley
Lundzi

Luphohlo Dam

MBABANE

Ezulwini

Mantenga NR
Lobamba

Ezulwini Valley

Luve

Mpisi

MR7

MBABANE

LEBOMBO MOUNTAINS

Mhlambanyatsi

Mlilwane WS
Mahlanya
Bhunya

Matsapha

MR3

Manzini Hhelehhele
Mafutseni

Timbutini

MR3

Mpaka

Lonhlupheko

Siteki

Sandlane
Nerston

MR18

MR19

Loyengo
Malkerns Valley

Matsapha International Airport

Balunga Gorge

Usutu River

Mkhaya GR

MR16

Nyetane Dam

Sifunga Dam

Mankayane

Ngwempisi
River

Sidvokodvo

Lusutfu River

MR8
Siphofaneni

Phuzumoya

Hendick van Eck Dam

Mgazini

Mahlangatsha

Grand Valley

Mbondvo River

MR9

SWAZILAND

Big Bend

Lusutfu

Sicunusa
Houtkop

Ndotzane River

MR26

Sithobela

River

Bothashoop
Gege

Piet Retief

MR9

Hlathikulu

Mlalahuze River

Maloma

Lubuli
Nsoko

Mahamba
Nhlangano

Mhlosheni

Ngwavuma River

Sithobela

MR8

MR11

N2

Mhlosheni
Sihultse

Sitila River

R33

Onverwacht/ Salitje

Lavumisa

KWAZULU-NATAL (SOUTH AFRICA)

Pongola River

Pongola

Golela

Pongolapoort Dam

Paulpietersburg

Bivane River

R66

N2

Jozini
To Durban (375km)

0 ____ 30 km
0 ____ 20 miles

HISTORY
The Beginnings of a Nation

The area that is now Swaziland has been inhabited for millennia, and human-like remains possibly dating back as far as 100,000 years have been discovered around the Lebombo Mountains in eastern Swaziland. However, today's Swazis trace their ancestors to much more recent arrivals. By around AD500, various Nguni groups had made their way to the region as part of the great Bantu migrations (p28). One of these groups settled in the area around present-day Maputo (Mozambique), eventually founding the Dlamini dynasty. In the mid-18th century, in response to increasing pressure from other clans in the area, the Dlamini king, Ngwane III, led his people southwest to the Pongola River, in present-day southern Swaziland and northern KwaZulu-Natal. This became the first Swazi heartland, and today, Swazis consider Ngwane III to have been their first king.

It was Ngwane's successor, Sobhuza I, who established a base in the Ezulwini Valley, which still remains the centre of Swazi royalty and ritual. Following Sobhuza I on the throne was the renowned King Mswazi (or Mswati), after whom the Swazi take their name. Despite considerable pressure from the neighbouring Zulu, Mswazi succeeded in unifying the whole kingdom. He also extended Swazi territory northwards as far as Hhohho in what is now northwestern Swaziland, largely in response to continued Zulu incursions on Swazi lands to the south. By the time he died in 1868, the foundations of the young Swazi nation were secure.

From the mid-19th century, Swaziland began to attract increasing numbers of European farmers in search of land for their cattle, as well as hunters, traders and missionaries. Mswazi's successor, Mbandzeni, inherited a kingdom rife with European carpetbaggers, and proved much weaker at reining them in than Mswazi. Under Mbandzeni, increasing amounts of the kingdom's land were alienated through leases granted to Europeans, with bribes for the king featuring heavily in some of the deals.

Over the next decades, the Swazis saw their territory whittled away as the British and Boers jostled for power in the area. In 1902, following the second Anglo-Boer War (p34), the Boers withdrew and the British took control of Swaziland as a protectorate.

Struggle for Independence

Swazi history in the early 20th century centred around the ongoing struggle for independence. Under the leadership of King Sobhuza II (guided by the capable hands of his mother acting as regent while Sobhuza was a child), the Swazis succeeded in obtaining much of their original territory back. This was done in part by direct purchase and in part by British government decree. By the time of independence in 1968, about two-thirds of the kingdom was again under Swazi control. This was a major development, as Swazi kings are considered to hold the kingdom in trust for their subjects, and land ownership is thus more than just a political and economic issue. Having a large proportion of the country owned by foreigners threatened the credibility of the monarchy and the viability of Swazi culture. It was also during this time that many Swazis began seeking work as migrant labourers in the Witwatersrand mines, in part to raise money to buy back their lands.

In 1960 King Sobhuza II proposed the creation of a Legislative Council, to be composed of Europeans elected along European lines, and a National Council formed in accordance with Swazi culture. One of the Swazi political parties formed at this time was the Mbokodvo (Grindstone) National Movement, which pledged to maintain traditional Swazi culture while eschewing racial discrimination. When the British finally agreed to elections in 1964, Mbokodvo won a majority. At the next elections, in 1967, it won all the seats. Independence was finally achieved – the culmination of a long and remarkably non-violent path – on 6 September 1968, 66 years after the start of the British protectorate.

The first Swazi constitution was largely a British creation, and in 1973 the king suspended it on the grounds that it did not accord with Swazi culture. Four years later parliament reconvened under a new constitution vesting all power in the king.

Sobhuza II died in 1982 as the world's longest-reigning monarch. Most significant among his accomplishments was his success in ensuring the continued existence of his country and culture, under threat since his father's reign. He is still referred to as 'the late king'. In 1986 the young Mswati III ascended the throne, where he continues today to represent and maintain the traditional Swazi way of life, and to assert his pre-eminence, for better and often worse, as absolute monarch.

Current Events

Swaziland is run by King Mswati III and a small core of advisers (Council of Ministers). Most Swazis seem happy with (or perhaps apathetic to) their political system, and focus instead on ensuring that their culture survives in the face of modernisation. However, there is an undercurrent of political dissent, and the movement for democratic change has slowly gained momentum over the past decade. In 1996 the king appointed a constitutional review commission, and in 2003 a new constitution was finally unveiled – though it was promptly dismissed by reform-minded Swazis as doing little more than preserving the status quo.

Opposition parties are officially banned, but several exist. The main ones are People's United Democratic Movement (Pudemo) and Swaziland Youth Congress (Swayoco), both of which enjoy only limited support. In addition, the trade union movement has long been agitating for change, though there is a royal ban on its meetings. Yet, despite these political tensions and increasing popular dissatisfaction with recent abuses of royal privilege, it's likely that the king and his advisers will continue to hold the upper hand in Swazi politics for the foreseeable future. Even reformers call only for modification of the monarchy (demanding a constitutional instead of an absolute monarchy), rather than its complete abandonment.

Putting these constitutional wranglings into sharp perspective is the scourge of AIDS: Swaziland has the third-highest HIV prevalence rate in the world (34.4% for adults between 15 and 49 years of age), and life expectancy has fallen as a result from 58 years to 33 years, with the downward spiral continuing. There are currently more than 12,000 AIDS orphans in the country, with this number predicted to increase to constitute over 12% of the population by 2010.

CLIMATE

Most of Swaziland enjoys a climate similar to that of South Africa's eastern lowveld, with rainy, steamy summers and agreeably cooler winters. Between December and February, temperatures occasionally exceed 40°C and torrential thunderstorms are common. May to August are the coolest months. In the higher-lying areas of the west, winters bring cool, crisp nights and sometimes even frost.

NATIONAL PARKS & RESERVES

Swaziland has five main reserves, reflecting the tiny country's impressively diverse topography. Easiest to get to is Mlilwane Wildlife Sanctuary (p552) in the Ezulwini Valley, which is privately run by **Royal Swazi Big Game Parks** (☎ 528 3944; www.biggameparks.org), based at Mlilwane. Also under the same jurisdiction, and both well worth visiting, are the excellent Mkhaya Game Reserve (p560), with black rhinos and many other animals, and Hlane Royal National Park (p558).

In the northwestern highlands is the beautiful Malolotja Nature Reserve (p557), known for its hiking trails. It, together with Mlawula Nature Reserve (p559) in the eastern lowveld and tiny Mantenga Nature Reserve (p549) in the Ezulwini Valley, is run by the **National Trust Commission** (☎ 416 1151, 416 1178; www.sntc.org.sz; p549), with its head office at the National Museum in Lobamba (Ezulwini Valley) and a bookings representative at the Ezulwini Tourist Office (p549).

LANGUAGE

The official languages are Swati and English, and English is the official written language. For information on Swati, see the Language chapter (p615).

DANGERS & ANNOYANCES

Street crime in Mbabane and Manzini is rising, so take common-sense precautions, especially at night.

Schistosomiasis (bilharzia) and malaria are both present in Swaziland; see p611 and p610 for information on avoiding these diseases.

GETTING THERE & AROUND

There are flights into Swaziland from Johannesburg (Jo'burg) and Durban in South Africa and from Maputo in Mozambique; see p589.

Swazi Express Airways (☎ 518 6840; www.swazi express.com), together with its sister company, Steffen Air Charters, operates charter flights within the kingdom and the region.

Most travellers enter Swaziland overland. For details of border posts, see p592. For bus connections, see p594 and for information on driving around Swaziland, including car hire, see p599.

Once in Swaziland, there is a good network of minibuses covering the country. There are private taxis in Mbabane, the Ezulwini Valley and Manzini. See the Getting Around sections of these areas for details.

MBABANE

pop 60,000

Mbabane (pronounced mm-bah-ban) is Swaziland's capital and second-largest city. There isn't much to see or do here – the adjacent Ezulwini Valley has most of the attractions – but it's a relaxing town in a lovely setting in the Dlangeni Hills, and a good place to get things done. Mbabane is growing fast and has recently seen a surge in commercial development, making it a sharp contrast to the surrounding rural areas.

During the colonial era, the British originally had their base in Manzini, but moved it in 1902 to Mbabane to take advantage of the cooler climate in the hills.

Orientation

Street names in Mbabane seem to be perpetually in the process of being changed. To complicate things, often only one or two signposts are changed, so a street will be signposted in one section with the new name and elsewhere with the old.

The main street is Gwamile St (formerly Allister Miller St), which runs roughly north–south through the town centre. Just off its southern end is Swazi Plaza, a large shopping mall with the tourist information office, bank and an ATM, an Internet centre and a good range of shops. Just across the street is Mbabane's other main shopping centre, the Mall.

The city's central commercial area is easily negotiated on foot. Away from here, the streets become green and residential as they wind over the hills, and a car is handy if you'll be staying in any outlying B&Bs.

MAPS

The tourist information office (p546) has a free map with Mbabane and Manzini on one side, and the whole country on the reverse.

Information

BOOKSHOPS

Webster's (120 Dzeliwe St) The best-stocked bookshop in Mbabane.

EMERGENCY
Fire ☎ 404 3333
Police ☎ 404 2221, 999

INTERNET ACCESS
There are Internet centres at Swazi Post, located upstairs at Swazi Plaza, and in the Mall, next to Spar. Rates average E25 per half hour.

MEDICAL SERVICES
Mbabane Clinic (☎ 404 2423; St Michael's Rd) For emergencies try this clinic in the southwest corner of town just off the bypass road.
Mbabane Pharmacy (☎ 404 2817; Gwamile St) In the town centre and well stocked.

MONEY
The only ATMs that accept international cards are at the Standard Bank in Swazi Plaza, and at the Royal Swazi Sun Hotel outside Mbabane in the nearby Ezulwini Valley.
First National Bank (Msunduza St) Changes cash and travellers cheques, and has an ATM that accepts most credit cards.
Nedbank (Swazi Plaza) Changes cash and travellers cheques.
Standard Bank (Swazi Plaza) Use the machine marked 'international transactions'. Standard Bank also changes cash and travellers cheques (bring your purchase agreement for travellers cheques).

POST
Post office (Msunduza St) There's poste restante here, though it's not particularly reliable. You can also make international (though not reverse-charge) calls here.

TOURIST INFORMATION
Tourist information office (☎ 404 9693; www.welc ometoswaziland.com; ☼ 8am-5pm Mon-Fri, 9am-noon Sat) At the edge of Swazi Plaza. In addition to maps and brochures, you can pick up copies of various free publications with the latest on hotels, restaurants and entertainment. These include *What's Happening in Swaziland* and the smaller *What's on in Swaziland*.

TRAVEL AGENCIES
Harvey World Travel (☎ 404 1538; www.harvey world.co.za; Swazi Plaza) Can assist with flight bookings and other travel arrangements.
Royal Swazi National Airways Office (Swazi Plaza) Helpful with booking regional flights.

Sights & Activities
Walking around the town centre, shopping and taking care of errands is the main activity in Mbabane for most travellers. It's worth detouring through the **Swazi Market**, with good but pricey crafts, fresh produce and more.

About 8km northeast of Mbabane is **Sibebe Rock**, a massive granite dome hulking over the surrounding countryside. Much of the rock is completely sheer and dangerous if you should fall, but it's a good adrenalin charge if you're reasonably fit and relish looking down steep rock faces. Swazi Trails (p549) offers three-hour nontechnical climbs up the rock for E325 per person.

Tours
Many of the tour operators listed in the Transport chapter (p605) include short detours into Swaziland in their itineraries. Once in Swaziland, the main operator is the very keyed-in Swazi Trails (p549), based in the Mantenga Craft Centre in Ezulwini Valley, which can organise rafting, hikes and tours to wherever you'd like to go.

For a taste of rural Swazi life, a good contact is Myxo of Myxo's Place (p555). As part of his **Liphupho Lami Camp Holidays** (www .earthfoot.org/sz.htm), he organises day and overnight tours to his home village, 65km south of Manzini. For E340 per person, you can learn mat weaving, visit the local school and otherwise immerse yourself in local village life. Advance booking is essential.

Sleeping
Mbabane has a decent selection of accommodation, and is a better place to overnight than nearby Manzini, which has limited appeal.

BUDGET
Thokoza Church Centre (☎ 404 6681; Polinjane Rd; d E40, with shared bathroom E35) The rooms are basic and unappealing, but this is one of the cheapest places in town, and often full. Inexpensive meals can be arranged. To get here from Gwamile St on foot, turn onto Mhlonhlo (Walker) St, cross the bridge at the bottom of the hill, turn left at the police station and head up Polinjane Rd for about 10 minutes. Take a taxi at night (E7 from Swazi Plaza).

Flying Rhino (☎ 611 7897; swronny@yahoo.de; 18 Mabandla (Mission) St; camp sites per person E35, dm E50, d with shared bathroom E150) Laid-back, chilled out and within walking distance of the town centre. Flying Rhino is a no-frills backpackers in a private house, with all the basics, including meals if you want them. Staff are

MBABANE

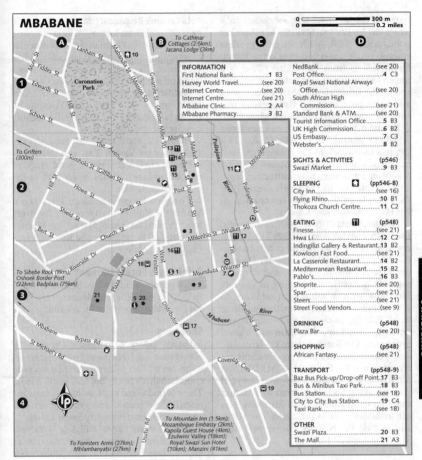

SWAZILAND

very helpful with information on things to do in Swaziland, and can assist with organising visas and onward travel in Mozambique. It's about 10 minutes on foot from the town centre, off Gwamile St.

Grifters (☎ 404 5342, 617 0218; info@grifterslodge .com; End St; camp sites per person E35, dm E50, d with shared bathroom E150) Another laid-back place, in a house within walking distance of the town centre. Meals are available, and staff can help you sort out onward travel. Grifters is off Somhlolo Rd (Gilfillan St).

MID-RANGE & TOP END
Cathmar Cottages (☎ 404 3387; www.swazilodgings .com/cathmar; 167 Lukhalo St; camp sites per person E40, s/d from E220/275) Various self-catering units

clustered together up on a hill in a quiet residential area about 3.5km north of the town centre. All have TV and mini-fridge, and range from OK to quite nice. Meals and group discounts are also available.

City Inn (☎ 404 2406; cityinn@realnet.co.sz; Gwamile St; s/d with breakfast E275/350) This is the most central hotel, and somewhat of a Mbabane institution, though it's a bit frayed around the edges these days. Ask for a room in the renovated west wing.

Kapola Guest House (☎ 404 0906; www.kapola _eden.co.sz; MR3; s/d with breakfast E230/420) Kapola is good value, with pleasant rooms, a common area and a relaxing porch. It's about 5km from Mbabane just off the MR3; watch for the wall painted with flags.

Jacana Lodge (☎ 405 0277; www.jacanalodge.co
.sz; s/d with breakfast from E230/330; 🐾) Another
good-value B&B, with bright, spotless
rooms, and a quiet location on a hilltop
about 3.5km from the centre. There's a
queen room with its own balcony and bathroom (the other rooms share bathrooms),
and a tiny pool. Staff can also organise reasonably priced tours of Swaziland.

Mountain Inn (☎ 404 2781; www.mountaininn
.sz; s/d with breakfast from E525/670; ❄ 🐾) This
inn is a throwback to the colonial era, and
Mbabane's most luxurious option. It offers
a genteel ambience, pool, attractive lawn,
comfortable rooms, and panoramas over
the valley from the inviting **restaurant** (mains
from E45; 🕑 breakfast, lunch & dinner).

Foresters Arms (☎ 467 4177; www.foresters
arms.co.za; s/d with half board E638/1208) The Foresters Arms is 27km southwest of Mbabane in
the hills around Mhlambanyatsi (Watering Place of the Buffaloes), and it makes
a good alternative to sleeping in the city
for those with a vehicle. In addition to
cosy rooms, it boasts attractive gardens,
trout fishing, horse riding, water sports
on the nearby Luphohlo Dam and a good
restaurant. On Sunday there's a large and
very popular lunch buffet (reservations are
recommended). Follow the MR19 from
Mbabane; it's tarmac the whole way. If
you're leaving Swaziland from here, rather
than retracing your steps to Mbabane, you
can continue southwest along the MR19
and exit via the Nerston border post near
Sandlane.

Eating

Pablo's (☎ 404 2406; Gwamile St; burgers from E12,
breakfast from E20; 🕑 breakfast, lunch & dinner) This
place is next to the City Inn, and lacking in
atmosphere, though it's one of the better
budget options. On offer are burgers, pizza,
steak dishes and breakfasts.

Indingilizi Gallery & Restaurant (☎ 404 6213;
indingi@realnet.co.sz; 112 Dzeliwe St; snacks from E15; light
meals from E35; 🕑 8am-5pm Mon-Fri, 8.30am-2pm Sat)
This relaxed outdoor café offers quiches,
salads and similar fare, plus decadent desserts and good craft shopping at the adjoining gallery.

Hwa Li (☎ 404 5986; Dhlan'ubeka House, Mhlonhlo
St; mains from E30; 🕑 lunch & dinner Mon-Sat) A good
spot for spring rolls, chow mein and spicy
soups.

La Casserole Restaurant (☎ 404 6426; Gwamile St;
mains E40-65; 🕑 lunch & dinner) A long-standing
place, featuring German and continental
cuisine and a pizza oven. It also offers a few
vegetarian dishes, plus a good wine selection and a pleasant outside patio.

Mediterranean Restaurant (☎ 404 3212, Gwamile St; mains E40-70; 🕑 lunch & dinner) Despite its
name, tasty curries and other Indian delicacies are the specialities here.

Finesse (☎ 404 5936; the Mall; mains from E30;
🕑 lunch & dinner Mon-Sat) This restaurant has
a French chef, and serves a good range of
seafood and meat dishes, many with an Indian Ocean flavour.

There's a Shoprite at Swazi Plaza and a
Spar at the Mall. For fast food, try the street
food vendors at Swazi Market on Warner
(Msunduza) St; or Steers and Kowloon Fast
Food in the Mall.

Drinking & Entertainment

Most people head to the Ezulwini Valley
(p552) for nightlife. In Mbabane, try **Plaza
Bar** (Swazi Plaza), a popular local haunt.

Shopping

Indingilizi Gallery & Restaurant (☎ 404 6213;
indingi@realnet.co.sz; 112 Dzeliwe St; 🕑 8am-5pm Mon-Fri,
8.30am-2pm Sat) This gallery has an idiosyncratic
collection that's pricey but well worth a look.
There is traditional craft, including some interesting old pieces, and excellent art and
craftwork by contemporary Swazi artists.

African Fantasy (☎ 404 0205; Shop 11, the Mall)
African Fantasy offers a great selection of
locally made T-shirts and cards; it also has a
branch at Mantenga Craft Centre (p552).

Getting There & Around

The main bus and minibus taxi park is just
behind Swazi Plaza. The best place to catch
a minibus taxi to Jo'burg is Manzini. See
p587 for more information on connections
to/from South Africa and Mozambique.
City to City has its own bus station at the
southern end of town off the main road.

There are several minibus taxis daily to
Piggs Peak (E7, one hour); Ngwenya and
the Oshoek border post (E6, 40 minutes);
and Malkerns Valley (E6, 45 minutes). All
vehicles heading towards Manzini (E5, 35
minutes) and points east pass through the
Ezulwini Valley, although most take the
bypass road.

Printed textile, Mantenga Craft Centre (p552), Ezulwini Valley, Swaziland

RICHARD I'ANSON

White rhino, Hlane Royal National Park (p558), Swaziland

ARIADNE VAN ZANDBERGEN

ARIADNE VAN ZANDBERGEN

Boy drinking porridge from a clay bowl, Swazi Cultural Village (p550), Swaziland

Sunset over the private Mkhaya Game Reserve (p560), Swaziland

RICHARD I'ANSON

Young dancer at a ceremony, Mbabane (p545), Swaziland

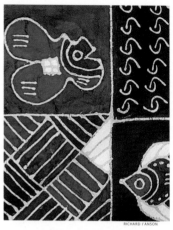

Printed textile, Mantenga Craft Centre (p552), Ezulwini Valley, Swaziland

Woman sitting outside beehive hut, Swaziland

Flowering aloe, Mlilwane Wildlife Sanctuary (p552), Swaziland

Nonshared taxis congregate just outside the transport park behind Swazi Plaza. At night, you can also usually find one near the City Inn. Alternatively try calling **SD Tel Taxi** (☎ 404 0966). Nonshared taxis to the Ezulwini Valley cost at least E40, more to the far end of the valley (from E60), and still more if hired at night. To Matsapha Airport, expect to pay from E80.

The Baz Bus pick-up/drop-off point is at the Shell station at the entrance to town.

EZULWINI VALLEY

The Ezulwini Valley – Swaziland's royal heartland and tourism centre – begins just outside Mbabane and extends down past Lobamba, 18km away. For most of Swazi history, it's been home to the Swazi royal family. It's possible to whiz through on the MR3 bypass road, but if you want to see anything, you'll need to take the old MR103. Don't let the tacky-hotel-strip atmosphere along some sections deter you: just in from the road is some beautiful woodland scenery, with brilliant orange flame trees, flowering jacarandas and views over the surrounding mountains. There's a good selection of places to stay here and some of the best craft shopping in Southern Africa.

Information

The **Ezulwini Tourist Office** (☎ 442 4206) is based at the Mantenga Craft Centre. Staff are helpful and supply a decent range of information about accommodation, activities and things to see in the valley and around Swaziland. They also take bookings for Malolotja, Mlawula and Mantenga Nature Reserves.

Swazi Trails (☎ 416 2180; www.swazitrails.co.sz) organises activities and tours all over the kingdom and also has an office at the craft centre.

For accommodation in Mlilwane Wildlife Sanctuary, Mkhaya Game Reserve and Hlane Royal National Park, contact **Royal Swazi Big Game Parks** (☎ 528 3117; www.biggameparks.org), accessed through the Mlilwane Wildlife Sanctuary.

The National Trust Commission (see p545), headquarters of the Mlawula, Malolotja and Mantenga Nature Reserves, is based at the National Museum in Lobamba.

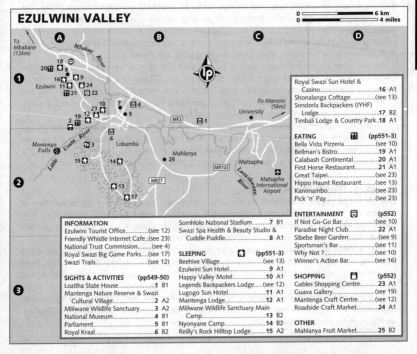

EZULWINI VALLEY

0 — 6 km
0 — 4 miles

To Mbabane (12km)
Mbabane River
Ezulwini
To Manzini (5km)
University
MR3
Mantenga Falls
Usutu River
Little Usutu River
Lobamba
Mahlanya
Matsapha
MR103
Lwusushwana River
Matsapha International Airport
MR27

Royal Swazi Sun Hotel & Casino................................16 A1
Shonalanga Cottage.............(see 13)
Sondzela Backpackers (IYHF) Lodge.................................17 B2
Timbali Lodge & Country Park..18 A1

EATING (pp551–3)
Bella Vista Pizzeria................(see 10)
Bellman's Bistro....................19 A1
Calabash Continental............20 A1
First Horse Restaurant..........21 A1
Great Taipei.........................(see 23)
Hippo Haunt Restaurant.......(see 13)
Kanimambo.........................(see 23)
Pick 'n' Pay.........................(see 23)

ENTERTAINMENT (p552)
If Not Go-Go Bar...................(see 10)
Paradise Night Club...............22 A1
Sibebe Beer Garden...............(see 9)
Sportsman's Bar....................(see 11)
Why Not ?............................(see 10)
Winner's Action Bar...............(see 16)

SHOPPING (p552)
Gables Shopping Centre.........23 A1
Guava Gallery.......................(see 19)
Mantenga Craft Centre..........(see 12)
Roadside Craft Market...........24 A1

OTHER
Mahlanya Fruit Market..........25 B2

INFORMATION
Ezulwini Tourist Office.............(see 12)
Friendly Whistle Internet Cafe..(see 23)
National Trust Commission.......(see 4)
Royal Swazi Big Game Parks....(see 17)
Swazi Trails.............................(see 12)

SIGHTS & ACTIVITIES (pp549–50)
Lozitha State House.....................1 B1
Mantenga Nature Reserve & Swazi Cultural Village......................2 A2
Mlilwane Wildlife Sanctuary........3 A2
National Museum........................4 B1
Parliament.................................5 B1
Royal Kraal................................6 B2

Somhlolo National Stadium..........7 B1
Swazi Spa Health & Beauty Studio & Cuddle Puddle........................8 A1

SLEEPING (pp551–3)
Beehive Village.......................(see 13)
Ezulwini Sun Hotel......................9 A1
Happy Valley Motel....................10 A1
Legends Backpackers Lodge.....(see 12)
Lugogo Sun Hotel.....................11 A1
Mantenga Lodge.......................12 A1
Mlilwane Wildlife Sanctuary Main Camp...................................13 B2
Nyonyane Camp......................14 B2
Reilly's Rock Hilltop Lodge........15 A2

To get online, try **Friendly Whistle Internet Cafe** (per half hr E20) in the Gables Shopping Centre, opposite the Happy Valley Motel.

The closest ATM is at the Royal Swazi Sun Hotel & Casino.

Lobamba

Lobamba is the heart of Swaziland's Royal Valley – a position it has held since the early days of the Swazi monarchy. The royal Embo State Palace was built by the British – in grand proportions, as it had to house the entire royal clan (Sobhuza II had 600 children). It isn't open to visitors, and photos aren't allowed. Swazi kings now live in **Lozitha State House**, about 10km from Lobamba.

To see the monarchy in action, head to the **Royal Kraal** during the Incwala ceremony or the Umhlanga (Reed) dance (below). It's next to Lozitha State House. Just north of here towards the main road is **Somhlolo**

National Stadium, which hosts sports events (mainly soccer) and important state occasions, such as coronations.

The nearby **National Museum** (adult/child E10/5; 8am-4pm Mon-Fri, 10am-4pm Sat & Sun) has some interesting displays of Swazi culture, as well as a traditional beehive village and cattle byre.

Next to the museum is the **parliament**, which is sometimes open to visitors; if you want to visit, wear neat clothes and use the side entrance. Across the road from the museum is a **memorial** to King Sobhuza II, the most revered of Swazi kings.

About 3km from Mantenga Lodge is **Mantenga Nature Reserve** (adult/child E20/10; 6am-6pm), which also includes the **Swazi Cultural Village** (guided tour adult/child E20/10) and is under the auspices of the National Trust Commission. The cultural village has authentic beehive huts and cultural displays, and it's

---

SWAZI CEREMONIES

Incwala

Incwala (also known as Ncwala) is the most sacred ceremony of the Swazi people. It is a 'first fruits' ceremony, where the king gives permission for his people to eat the first crops of the new year. Preparation for the Incwala begins some weeks in advance, according to the cycle of the moon. *Bemanti* (learned men) journey to the Lebombo Mountains to gather plants; other *bemanti* collect water from Swaziland's rivers and some travel across the mountains to the Indian Ocean to skim foam from the waves. Meanwhile, the king goes into retreat.

On the night of the full moon, young men all over the kingdom harvest branches of the *lusekwane*, a small tree, and begin a long trek to the Royal Kraal at Lobamba. They arrive at dawn, and use their branches to build a kraal. If a branch has wilted, it is seen as a sign that the young man bearing it has had illicit sex. Songs prohibited during the rest of the year are sung, and the *bemanti* arrive with their plants, water and foam.

On the third day of the ceremony a bull is sacrificed. On the fourth day, to the pleadings of all the regiments of Swaziland, the king comes out of his retreat and dances before his people. He eats a pumpkin, the sign that Swazis can eat the new year's crops. Two days later there's a ritual burning of all the items used in the ceremony, after which the rains are expected to fall.

Umhlanga (Reed) Dance

Though not as sacred as the Incwala, the Umhlanga (Reed) dance serves a similar function in drawing the nation together and reminding the people of their relationship to the king. It is something like a week-long debutante ball for marriageable young Swazi women, who journey from all over the kingdom to help repair the queen mother's home at Lobamba.

After arriving at Lobamba, they spend a day resting, then set off in search of reeds, some not returning until the fourth night. On the sixth day the reed dance is performed as they carry their reeds to the queen mother. The dance is repeated the next day. Those carrying torches (flashlights) have searched for reeds by night; those with red feathers in their hair are princesses.

As the Swazi queen mother must not be of the royal clan, the reed dance is also a showcase of potential wives for the king. As with the Incwala, there are signs that identify the unchaste – an incentive to avoid pre-marital sex.

possible to take guided tours and watch the **sibhaca dance** (adult/child E10/3; ☺ 11.15am & 3.15pm). Nearby, and part of the reserve, are **Mantenga Falls**, which you can visit on guided walks.

For some relaxation after running around to all these places, head to the Royal Valley's own **hot mineral springs** (☎ 416 1164; adult/child E5/2; ☺ 6am-11pm), also known as the Cuddle Puddle. These mineral waters are warm and live up to their name. In the same complex is the **Swazi Spa Health & Beauty Studio** (☎ 416 1164; ☺ 10am-6pm), with aromatherapy steam tube, oxygen multistep and Jacuzzi.

SLEEPING
There's no accommodation in Lobamba village itself, but there are plenty of options in the immediate vicinity.

Budget
For more budget options in the Lobamba area, see Sleeping & Eating under Mlilwane Wildlife Sanctuary (p552).

Legends Backpackers Lodge (☎ 416 1870; leg ends@mailfly.com; camp sites per person E40, dm E60, d with shared bathroom E160; ▯) This good backpackers is opposite the Mantenga Craft Centre. It has the usual features – dorms, doubles and lots of travel information, plus Internet connection and easy access to the Swazi Trails office (just across the road).

Mid-Range
There are several good mid-range accommodation options available.

Mantenga Lodge (☎ 416 1049; reservations@mant engalodge.com; s/d with breakfast from E350/460; ☒) A relaxed place with comfortable, unassuming rooms in a wooded setting about 1.5km off the main road. There's also a good restaurant, with a dining patio overlooking the hills and stands of flame trees. Take the signposted turn-off for the Mantenga Craft Centre; the hotel is 500m further along this road.

Happy Valley Motel (☎ 416 1061; happyvalley@ africaonline.co.sz; r E370; ☒) Not much ambience from the outside, but inside, rooms are agreeable and well equipped. As an added bonus, your room price includes free entry to the Why Not? disco and the If Not Go-Go Bar (p552) – all in keeping with the hotel's description of itself as a 'mecca of entertainment'. Mid-week discounts are available, and children under 12 years old

stay for free. It's along the MR103, opposite the turn-off for Mantenga Lodge.

Timbali Lodge & Country Park (☎ 416 1156; timbali@africaonline.co.sz; s/d with breakfast E400/550, 4-person cottages E600; ☒) This moderately upscale place, at the western end of the valley, at the western end of the valley, has modern, self-catering cottages set in pleasant, grassy grounds.

Mantenga Nature Reserve (☎ 416 1151, 416 1178; mnr@africaonline.co.sz; beehive huts per person Mon-Fri E40, Sat & Sun E60, tented chalets per person with breakfast E250) Mantenga Nature Reserve has some comfortably rustic en suite safari-style tents with small porches. You can also stay in traditional beehive huts at the Cultural Village, and there's a restaurant featuring Swazi delicacies.

Top End
Top-end lodging is dominated by the Sun chain, which has three properties here, all clustered together along the MR3 about 6km northwest of Lobamba and about 3km from Mbabane. Rates are always changing, so inquire in advance. All offer weekend specials at some times of the year for about half price and all have restaurants.

Royal Swazi Sun Hotel & Casino (☎ 416 5000; www.swazisun.sz; s/d E1070/1150; ☒ ▯ ☒) The most luxurious of the three Sun hotels, with a golf course, casino, tennis courts, Internet café, ATM and Kamp Kwena for children.

Lugogo Sun Hotel (☎ 416 4000; www.swazisun.sz; s/d E720/780; ☒ ☒) The largest of the Swazi Suns, on the same grounds as the Royal Swazi Sun, and slightly more low-key.

Ezulwini Sun Hotel (☎ 416 3000; www.swazisun .sz; s/d E720/780; ☒ ☒) Across the road from the other two Sun hotels, this complex has the usual international hotel features, such as pools and tennis courts.

EATING
Calabash Continental (☎ 416 1187; mains E40-70; ☺ lunch & dinner) German and Swiss cuisine are the highlights at this popular and long-standing place. It's at the upper end of Ezulwini Valley, and also easily accessible from Mbabane.

First Horse Restaurant (☎ 416 2272, 416 1137; mains from E35; ☺ lunch & dinner) This is another old-timer, featuring large servings of seafood, steaks and desserts in a dark, pub-style atmosphere.

Bella Vista Pizzeria (☎ 416 1061; pizza from E30; ☺ dinner) Bella Vista is at Happy Valley Motel along the MR103, and does a brisk local business.

Bellman's Bistro (light meals from E30; ☺ 9am-5pm Tue-Sat, 10am-5pm Sun) A chic eatery at Guava Gallery, just before Swazi Cultural Village, with salads, soups and lunch fare.

Opposite Bella Vista is the Gables Shopping Centre, with a Pick 'n' Pay and several good restaurants. **Kanimambo** (☎ 416 3549; mains E35-60) features Portuguese and Mozambican cuisine, and **Great Taipei** (☎ 416 2300; mains from E35; ☺ lunch & dinner) is the place to go for chop suey and other Chinese dishes.

ENTERTAINMENT

Why Not? (☎ 416 1061; Happy Valley Hotel; admission E25 Mon-Fri, E30 Sat & Sun) Swaziland's best-known nightspot, with a continually changing program of bands, plus some less salubrious entertainment as well. Also here is the dimly lit and somewhat tawdry If Not Go-Go Bar (entry to Why Not? includes If Not).

There are also several nightspots at the Sun hotels, including **Sibebe Beer Garden** (☎ 416 1201; Ezulwini Sun Hotel), with live music and meals; **Sportsman's Bar** (☎ 416 1550; Lugogo Sun Hotel), with a pub night on Wednesday; and **Winner's Action Bar** (Royal Swazi Sun Hotel), with live music on Friday.

Paradise Night Club (MR103), just east of the Ezulwini Sun Hotel, is an African theme bar, with meals in the evening and bands some nights.

Also check out what's playing at House on Fire, in Malkerns Valley (p554).

SHOPPING

The Ezulwini Valley, together with the nearby Malkerns Valley, offers some of the best craft shopping in the region, with a wide selection, high quality and reasonable prices. Places to check out include **Mantenga Craft Centre** (☎ 416 1136), on the access road leading to Mantenga Lodge, with numerous shops featuring everything from weaving and tapestries to candles, woodcarvings and T-shirts, and **Guava Gallery** (☎ 416 1343; ☺ 9am-5pm Tue-Sat, 10am-5pm Sun), a chic boutique with various local crafts. There's also a well-stocked roadside craft market along the M103 just south of the Ezulwini Sun Hotel.

GETTING THERE & AWAY

Nonshared taxis from Mbabane cost E40 to E60, depending on how far down the valley you go. For a pick-up from the Ezulwini Valley, you'll have to call a Mbabane-based taxi service.

During the day you could get on a Manzini-bound minibus, but make sure the driver knows that you want to alight in the valley, as many aren't keen on stopping.

If you're driving from either Mbabane or Manzini, take the Ezulwini Valley/Lobamba exit off the bypass road. This puts you on the MR103, from where everything is well signposted.

Mlilwane Wildlife Sanctuary

This tranquil **private reserve** (☎ 528 3943; www.biggameparks.co.sz; admission E25; ☺ 6am-5pm) near Lobamba was Swaziland's first protected area, created by conservationist Ted Reilly on his family farm in the 1950s. Reilly later opened Mkhaya Game Reserve and supervised the establishment of Hlane Royal National Park. Read about conservation efforts at the reserve (and throughout the kingdom) in *The Mlilwane Story*, available from the sanctuary. Mlilwane means 'Little Fire', named after the many fires started by lightning strikes in the region.

While the reserve doesn't have the drama or vastness of some of the South African parks, it's very accessible and well worth a visit. Its terrain is dominated by the precipitous Nyonyane (Little Bird) peak, with several fine walks in the area. Animals to be seen include zebras, giraffes, warthogs, many antelope species, crocodiles, hippos and a variety of birds. In summer, you may spot black eagles near Nyonyane.

Activities on offer in the reserve include **walking** (per person per hr with guide E25), two-hour **vehicle safaris** (per person E120), **cycling** (per person per hr E55) and horse riding.

Mlilwane gets very busy during South African school holidays. The entrance is 2km southeast of the Happy Valley Motel on the old Mbabane–Manzini road, and signposted from the turn-off. At the entrance gate you can get a sanctuary map. Night access is via an alternate gate.

SLEEPING & EATING

All accommodation in the sanctuary can be booked in advance at **Royal Swazi Big Game**

Parks (☎ 528 3117; www.biggameparks.org), located behind Sondzela Backpackers (IYHF) Lodge. It can be reached either through the wildlife sanctuary, or via Malkerns, though there's no real reason to go there as you can make bookings via telephone or email. Bookings need to be paid in advance, either via post or credit card.

Mlilwane Wildlife Sanctuary Main Camp (camp sites per person E40, dm E80, s/d 2-person huts E240/340) This camp is set in a scenic location about 3.5km from the entry gate, complete with simple thatched huts – including traditional **beehive huts** (s/d E240/340, with shared bathroom E150/240) – and the occasional warthog snuffling around. There's a small shop, the **Hippo Haunt restaurant** (mains from E30), and an area for braais.

Shonalanga Cottage (s/d E290/380, per additional person E110) This spacious self-catering cottage is near the main camp, and a good choice for families.

Nyonyane Camp (s/d E250/350) On the eastern border of the sanctuary, about 5km from the entry gate, and a perfect spot to be if you want to get away from everyone. Accommodation is in well-equipped self-catering cabins, and there's a braai area.

Sondzela Backpackers (IYHF) Lodge (camp sites E40, dm E50, s/d with shared bathroom E100/160, s/d rondavels E115/190) Sondzela is in the southern part of the reserve, around 1.5km beyond the camp, and about 2km from Malandela's Homestead and Gone Rural in Malkerns Valley. It calls itself 'Africa's Rolls Royce of Backpacker Hostels', and when you get here, you'll see why. It's spacious, with large gardens, telephones, a central living area including the Hog & Wart Bar, and a hilltop perch that gives it one of the best backpackers' settings in Southern Africa. The pickup point is at Malandela's Homestead in Malkerns Valley, where the Baz Bus stops; this is about 2km west of the Mahlanya fruit market on the old Manzini–Mbabane road. If you're driving, you'll need to use the main Mlilwane Wildlife Sanctuary entrance, pay the entry fee and drive through the park to reach Sondzela.

Reilly's Rock Hilltop Lodge (s/d from E650/1100) The most luxurious accommodation in the reserve and in Swaziland. 'The Rock' has a colourful history: it was the first dwelling in Swaziland to have electric lighting, and the original structure was built in exchange for

an UK£80 ox wagon. There are wide views over the reserve from the veranda, and an aloe garden surrounding.

MALKERNS VALLEY
About 7km south of Lobamba on the MR103 is the turn-off to the fertile Malkerns Valley, known for its arts and crafts outlets, and together with the Ezulwini Valley, offering some of Southern Africa's best craft shopping.

There's Internet access and tourist information at **Sigubhu Internet Cafe** (☎ 528 3423; per 30min E20) at Malandela's.

Sleeping & Eating
For budget accommodation, also check out Sondzela Backpackers (IYHF) Lodge (left), which is readily accessible from Malkerns Valley.

Eco-Vision (☎ 528 3561; ecovision@zanet.co.za; dm E75, d with shared bathroom E180; 💻) A small place with basic rooms that focuses on letting visitors sample Swazi culture. Staff can help organise excursions in the area or onwards into Mozambique. It's on the main road near Swazi Candles.

Malandela's Homestead (☎ 528 3115; entrées from E15, mains E30-60; ✽ lunch & dinner Mon-Sat, lunch Sun) One of the best restaurants in the region, with good old-fashioned meals and serving an array of meat and seafood dishes. Watch for the popular prawn nights. The same management also offers very nice rooms, plus gardens and pool, at **Malandela's B&B** (☎ 605 2598, 528 3448; r per person with breakfast E150; ✍), just behind Malandela's Homestead. Malandela's is along the MR27, about 1km from the junction with the MR103.

Nyanza Cottages (Nyanza Horse Trails; ☎ 528 3090; nyanza@africaonline.co.sz; dm E65, caravan s/d E160/220, d E190, cottages per adult about E220) A working farm with stables, and a great place to stay. The comfortable cottages sleep four, have a galley-style kitchen, are secluded and over-look pasture land. The kids can help out on the farm and there's as much horse rid-ing as you'd like (per hour/day E80/370). There's also a small backpackers' dorm and a well-equipped caravan that takes up to six people. Bring your own towels for the backpackers, caravan and camping. Nyanza is located just off the main road, signposted next to Baobab Batik.

Willows Lodge (☎ 602 1284; www.swaziwillows .com; s/d E250/370, with breakfast E280/410) This place is set off the MR27 in Malkerns Valley, near Malandela's Homestead. It has five pleasant self-catering cottages (each sleeping three people) set around the grounds of a sugar cane farm, and a small bar.

Entertainment

House on Fire (☎ 528 2001; houseonfire@africaonline .co.sz) A happening performance venue based at Malandela's Homestead that hosts Af-rican theatre, music and films, as well as other forms of entertainment. Give it a call to see what's on.

Shopping

There's some excellent shopping in the Malkerns Valley.

Gone Rural (☎ 528 3439, 528 3078) The place to go for baskets, mats and traditional clay pots made by a large, successful women's cooperative. Upstairs you can watch the Lutindzi grass being dyed before the weav-ing. It's based at Malandela's Homestead. Also here are Baobab Too, offering colour-ful African batiks; and Southern Country, selling handmade leather goods.

Swazi Candles (☎ 528 3219; swazicandles@realnet .co.sz) This signposted shop is 7km south of the MR103/Malkerns turn-off and sells candles in every shape and colour you can imagine, with some in the shape of African animals (elephants, rhinos, hippos etc).

Baobab Batik (☎ 528 3177) Next to Nyanza Cottages, 1km on from Swazi Candles, it's a small place that's worth a poke around, particularly if you're in the market for a wall hanging.

Getting There & Away

The Baz Bus stops at Malandela's Home-stead, just outside Gone Rural. This is the pick-up point for Sondzela Backpackers Lodge in Mlilwane Wildlife Sanctuary. You can also get minibus taxis between here and the Ezulwini Valley for about E3. As the craft shops and places to stay are spread out, you'll really need a car to get around.

MANZINI
pop 80,000

Manzini started out as the combined ad-ministrative centre for the squabbling Brit-ish and Boers between 1890 and 1902. So adversarial was their relationship that dur-ing the Anglo-Boer War a renegade Boer *kommando* (militia unit) burned the town down. Today things are much calmer, and Manzini plods more or less placidly along as Swaziland's industrial centre. It's con-siderably larger than Mbabane, though not large at all compared to its South African counterparts. Manzini is also Swaziland's main transport hub, so you're likely to pass through here if you're getting around on public transport. Otherwise, it's of minimal appeal – it's much better to base yourself in Mbabane or the Ezulwini Valley. Take care at night, and watch for pickpockets. Especially on weekends, Manzini fills up with Mozam-bicans who come over to take advantage of the cheaper shopping, so you're likely to hear some Portuguese or Shangaan.

Manzini's main drawcard is its colourful **market** (cnr Mhlakuvane & Mancishane Sts; ✽ closed Sun). The best day to visit is Thursday, when the normal produce displays are comple-mented by a great selection of handicrafts. If you get there at dawn, you can watch the vendors from rural areas bringing in their handicrafts to sell to the retailers. The mar-ket also has a wide selection of textiles.

Orientation

Central Manzini is set out in a grid pattern, with most of the activity on or around Ngwane St and Nkoseluhlaza St, the main east–west thoroughfares. The large Bhunu Mall, with a good range of shops, is on Ngwane St between Sandlane and Louw Sts. Behind, on Nkoseluhlaza St, is a Shoprite.

Information

Standard Bank (cnr Ngwane & Masalesikhundleni Sts) does foreign exchange (on Monday to Friday only). There's an Internet café in Bhunu Mall (on the 1st floor, opposite Milady's), and another at **Swazi Post** (cnr Nkoseluhlaza & Martin Sts).

Sleeping

Swaziland Backpackers (☎ 518 7225; swazilandbackpackers@realnet.co.sz; camp sites per person E35, dm E60, d with shared bathroom E160; 🖳 🐾) A well-run, clean place with a bar and email facilities, laundry service, kitchen (it also serves breakfast and dinner), and a small pool. It's about 8km west of town along the M103 towards Ezulwini Valley, opposite the Chinese Agricultural Centre compound. It's a Baz Bus stop.

Myxo's Place (☎ 505 8363, 604 4102; wozanawe@realnet.co.sz, camp sites per person E35, dm E60, d with shared bathroom E150) Chilled out, popular and Swaziland's only Swazi-owned and run backpackers, it offers all types of activities, including drumming lessons, plus cultural tours to Myxo's (the owner's) village, giving visitors the opportunity to gain insight into rural Swazi life (see p546). You can also stay in a beehive hut. Advance bookings are essential, both for Myxo's Place and the village tours. It's 6km from Manzini off the road to Big Bend. The signposted turn-off is at the Big Surprise Bottle Store, where any minibus taxi from Manzini to Hhelehhele will drop you. From there, it's about 1km further on foot and signposted. The closest Baz Bus pick-up/drop-off point is at the Big Surprise Bottle Store. Private taxis from Manzini charge about E30.

Matsapha Inn (☎ 518 6893; MR103; s/d E210/280) This utilitarian place is not far from the airport. It has clean, spartan rooms and a restaurant.

MANZINI

0 ———————— 400 m
0 ———————— 0.2 miles

Park Hotel (☎ 505 7423; 9 Mancishane St; s/d E195/250; ☒) The Park Hotel is nothing special, but it's the nicest place in central Manzini. Rooms are decent, all with small balconies, air-con, TV and telephones. It's at the eastern end of town, a block up from the police station.

Gibela Getaway (☎ 505 3024; www.visitswazi.com /gibela/; self-catering s/d E86/171, s/d with breakfast E217/ 285; 3-person cottages E285) This good B&B is about 10km northeast of Manzini off the main road, but nicer than the places in town and worth the drive. It has two rooms in the main house that share a bathroom, and several self-catering cottages and rooms, all in a scenic farm setting.

Eating

Fontana di Trevi Pizzeria (☎ 505 3608; the Hub, cnr Villiers & Mhlakuvane Sts; pizza from E30, breakfast from E20; ☽ breakfast, lunch & dinner) This place does a little bit of everything at reasonable prices, and is one of the better spots in town to get a decent coffee. In addition to pizza, it serves pasta, salads and burgers.

Mozambique Hotel & Restaurant (☎ 505 2489; Mahleka St; mains E30-55; ☽ lunch & dinner) A good place to get a taste of life across the border, with delicious prawns and seafood, various Portuguese dishes, and a good selection of Portuguese and South African wines.

Gil Vincente Restaurant (☎ 505 3874; Ilanga Centre, Martin St; mains E40-60; ☽ breakfast, lunch & dinner Tue-Sun) Another good spot for Portuguese and Mozambican dishes.

On Louw St in town are a few basic food outlets that are open during the day; the most notable is OK Restaurant. Bhunu Mall houses various fast-food places, including Nando's. There's also KFC, Debonaire's Pizza and Kowloon Fast Foods on Ngwane St.

Shopping

Bhunu Mall (Ngwane St) is the main shopping centre, with fast food, an array of stores and a Shoprite (entrance on Nkoseluhlaza St) to the back.

Getting There & Away

The main bus and minibus taxi park is at the northern end of Louw St, where you can also find some non-shared taxis. A minibus taxi trip up the Ezulwini Valley to Mbabane costs E5 (35 minutes). A nonshared taxi to Matsapha International Airport costs

around E45. Minibus taxis to Mozambique leave from the car park next to KFC.

For transport to/from South Africa, see the Transport chapter (p596).

NORTHERN SWAZILAND

It's in Swaziland's beautiful north that you'll find the country's best scenery, with mountains, woodlands, streams, plunging ravines and waterfalls. Away from the MR1, which runs from near Oshoek border post northeast to Jeppe's Reef border, all roads are unpaved, though easily negotiable with 2WD during most of the year. Especially in the summer months, heavy mists roll in that can limit visibility to almost zero.

Ngwenya

Tiny Ngwenya (The Crocodile), 5km east of the border with Mpumalanga, is the first town you'll reach if you're arriving in Swaziland via Oshoek. If you can't wait until you reach the Ezulwini Valley to do your shopping, there are several craft outlets here, including **Ngwenya Glass Factory** (☎ 442 4142; ☽ 7am-4pm), which uses recycled glass to create beautiful African animal and bird figures, and **Endlotane Studios/Phumulanga Swaziland Tapestries** (☎ 442 4196; ☽ 8am-5pm), which features beautiful tapestries and lets you watch the weavers at work. Both are within 1km of each other and signposted from the main road.

Also here is the **Ngwenya iron ore mine** (admission E5 ☽ 8am-4pm Sat, Sun & holidays), dating from around 40,000 BC and one of the world's oldest known mines. The mine is part of Malolotja Nature Reserve (p557). There's an entrance signposted near the Ngwenya Glass Factory, although you can't continue on into the rest of Malolotja from here. You can also reach the mine from the main entrance to Malolotja Nature Reserve. To visit the mine, including visits made by vehicle, you'll need to be accompanied by a ranger, which should be booked a day in advance.

Nearby, on the opposite side of the MR1, is **Hawane Dam** and the small **Hawane Nature Reserve** (no facilities).

SLEEPING & EATING

Hawane Village (☎ 442 4744; www.hawane.co.sz; beehive huts per person E136) A good choice if you want to go horse riding, or have a base for visiting Malolotja Nature Reserve and the surrounding area. Accommodation is in four-person beehive huts in a small enclosure, and there's the Taste of Africa Restaurant, with Kenyan, Mozambican and other dishes. It's about 8km up the Piggs Peak road from the junction of the MR1 and MR3, and 1.5km off the main road.

Malolotja Nature Reserve
This beautiful highveld/middleveld **reserve** (☎ 416 1151, 442 4241; www.sntc.org.sz; adult/child E20/10; ☻ 6am-6pm) is a true wilderness area, rugged and in the most part unspoiled. It's also an excellent walking destination, with a 200km network of hiking trails, and an ornithologist's paradise, with over 280 species of birds, including several rare species. Wildflowers and rare plants are added attractions, with several – including the Woolly, Barberton and Kaapschehoop cycads – found only in this part of Africa.

Various antelope species make Malolotja their home, as do herds of zebras, some wildebeest and even some elephants. The terrain ranges from mountainous to high-altitude grassland to forest to lower-lying bushveld. The reserve is laced by streams and cut by three rivers, including the Komati River, which flows east through a gorge in a series of falls and rapids until it meets the lowveld.

Hiking trails range from short walks to a week-long jaunt that extends from Ngwenya in the south to the Mgwayiza Range in the north. For all longer walks, you'll need to bring whatever food you'll need, as well as a camp stove, as fires are not permitted outside the base camp. You'll also need to arrange a free permit and map with the reserve office at the entrance gate. Wildlife drives can also be arranged.

In addition to Ngwenya Mine (see p556), it's also possible to visit **Forbes Reef gold mine** in Forbes Reef Forest towards the centre of the reserve.

Accommodation consists of **camping** (per person at main camp/on trails E40/20), either at the well-equipped main site, with ablutions and braai area, or along the overnight trails (no facilities). There are also pleasant, fully equipped self-catering **log cabins** (per person E150), each of which sleeps a maximum of six persons. Book through the Ezulwini Tourist Office (p549) or directly with the National Trust Commission (p545).

The entrance gate for Malolotja is about 35km northwest of Mbabane, along the Piggs Peak road (MR1); minibus taxis will drop you here.

Piggs Peak & Around
The small town of Piggs Peak was named after a prospector who found gold here in 1884. There was a rush, but only one deep mine ever made much money, and it has been closed for 40 years.

Piggs Peak is in a highly scenic, hilly section of the country, with one of the highlights **Phophonyane Falls** about 8km north of town. It's also the centre of Swaziland's logging industry, which is based on the huge pine plantations in the area. There are a couple of petrol stations, a bank or two (though no foreign-exchange facilities) and a gritty 'frontier' atmosphere.

In addition to the scenery, the Piggs Peak area is known for its handicrafts. A good place to check these out is at the Peak Craft Centre just north of Orion Pigg's Peak Hotel & Casino, where you'll find **Ethnic Bound** (☎ 437 3099; lungi@africaonline.co.sz), which specialises in African fabrics, and **Likhweti Kraft** (☎ 437 3127), a branch of **Tintsaba Crafts** (☎ 437 1260; www.tintsaba.com), which sells sisal baskets, jewellery and many other Swazi crafts. There are also numerous craft vendors along the road up from Mbabane.

SLEEPING & EATING
Highlands Inn (☎ 437 1144; s/d with breakfast E160/300) This inn, 1km south of the town centre on the main road, is the only place to stay in town itself and only worth considering if you're on a tight budget. Tintsaba Crafts, and **Woodcutter's Restaurant** (mains from E15; ☻ breakfast, lunch & dinner) are both attached to the restaurant.

Orion Piggs Peak Hotel & Casino (☎ 437 1104; gmpiggspeak@orion-hotels.co.za; d with half board E1380) About 10km northeast of Piggs Peak, this place is on the road to the Jeppe's Reef border post, with upscale rooms (all with views), a casino and a full range of amenities. Midweek specials are often available.

Phophonyane Lodge (☎ 437 1319; www.phopho nyane.co.sz; tents E420-600, s/d cottages from E600/840) This serene place lies northeast of Piggs Peak on a river in its own nature reserve of lush indigenous forest. It's one of the nicest places to stay in Swaziland. It has walking

SWAZILAND

trails around the river and waterfall, and you can swim in the rock pools. Accommodation is in comfortable cottages or East African–style luxury safari tents. Excellent meals are available at the **Dining Hut** (mains from E40; ☺ breakfast, lunch & dinner), which also features an interesting collection of masks from Mali. The cottages also have facilities for self-catering.

Entry to the reserve and therefore the lodge is an additional E20/10 per adult/child. Day visitors are charged E30/20 per adult/child to enter the surrounding reserve. The lodge is about 14km from Piggs Peak: head northeast (towards the casino), and the signposted turn-off (minibus taxis will drop you here) is about 1.5km before the casino. Continue down this road until you cross a bridge over a waterfall; the turn-off to the lodge is about 500m further, on the right. You can arrange with the lodge to be picked up from Piggs Peak; a taxi costs about E35.

GETTING THERE & AWAY

If you're heading east towards Hlane Royal National Park, the roads are mainly dirt and they're in reasonably rough condition, although a 2WD can handle them if you take it slowly.

The stretch of dirt road running west from Piggs Peak to Barberton (Mpumalanga) through Bulembu is rough. The descent can take up to two hours, and shouldn't be attempted in wet conditions.

The minibus taxi stand is next to the market at the top end of the main street, with several vehicles daily to Mbabane (E7, one hour).

EASTERN SWAZILAND

The Eastern Swaziland lowveld nestles in the shadow of the Lebombo Mountains, within an easy drive of the Mozambique border. The area is known for its sugarcane plantations, as well as for rewarding wildlife-watching at Hlane Royal National Park, Mlawula Nature Reserve and Mkhaya Game Reserve.

Simunye

Simunye is a manicured sugar-company town with little of interest for travellers, except as a possible stocking-up point for visiting the nearby Hlane park, or Mlawula and Mbuluzi nature reserves.

Tambankulu Country Club B&B (☎ 373 7111; tam@realnet.co.sz; s/d E222/318; 🅿 🅡) is a comfortable place, with modern attached cottages in nice gardens, a restaurant, swimming pool, gymnasium, tennis court, golf course and whatever other amenities you could want. It's under the same management as Mbuluzi Nature Reserve (opposite), and can arrange visits there. The club is north of Simunye and about 8km west of the junction at Maphiveni, off the Tshaneni road.

Simunye Country Club (☎ 383 8600; tlitschka@simunye.co.sz; s E267, s/d cottages E336/463; 🅿 🅡) has small single rooms, modern self-catering cottages and a good restaurant. It's intended for sugar workers, but temporary visitor memberships are available, which allow you to use the facilities (swimming pool, golf course, tennis and squash courts).

Shewula Mountain Camp (☎ 605 1160, 603 1931; shewula@realnet.co.sz; r per person E75) This community-owned camp is in the Lebombo Mountains about 15km northeast of Simunye as the crow flies (about 35km by road). It gives a chance to go on guided 'cultural walks' to nearby villages, or nature and bird-watching walks (guided walks per person E10). It's a good way to experience rural life away from the crowds, and to enjoy some wonderful views. For accommodation, there's camping or basic rondavels, with shared ablutions and self-catering facilities. Local meals can also be arranged (breakfast/lunch/dinner E25/40/40, must be booked in advance) or you can self-cater. The camp does pick-ups from Simunye or you can organise a visit through Swazi Trails (p549). If you're arriving via public transport, get a minibus taxi from Simunye to Phinduvuke (E8, one hour) and ask to be dropped at Shewula.

Several minibus taxis run daily to Simunye (and further north to the junction for Mlawula and Mbuluzi) from Manzini (E10, one hour). There's also at least one minibus taxi daily to/from Piggs Peak (E18, 2½ hours).

Hlane Royal National Park

Hlane (the name means 'wilderness') **park** (☎ 528 3943; www.biggameparks.org; admission E25; ☺ 6am-6pm) is near the former royal hunting grounds. It's Swaziland's largest protected area, home to elephants, lions, cheetahs, leopards, white rhinos and many antelope species, and offers wonderfully low-key wildlife-watching.

There are guided walking trails (per person E25), which afford the opportunity to see lions, elephants and rhinos, as well as two-hour wildlife drives (per person E120, minimum two/four for day/night drives) and mountain bike rentals (per hour R55). For more information get a copy of *The History & Significance of Hlane Royal National Park*, which was published to celebrate the return of lions to Swaziland.

Hlane has two good camps. Both can booked through the Royal Swazi Big Game Parks office in Mlilwane Wildlife Sanctuary (p552).

Ndlovu Camp (camp sites per person E40, s/d rondavels from E250/350) is pleasant and rustic, with no electricity, a cooking area, and a restaurant. Accommodation is in self-catering rondavels and cottages. It's just inside the main gate, and near a water hole, which is good for wildlife-watching. Bring whatever food and supplies you'll need with you.

Bhubesi Camp (s/d cottages E250/350) is in a good setting overlooking a river about 10km from Ndlovu. Accommodation is in nice, stone four-person self-catering cottages, and electricity is available.

Minibus taxis to Simunye will drop you at the entrance to Hlane (the gate is about 4km south of Simunye). Once at the park, you can explore most of it with 2WD, with the notable exception of the area where the lions are generally found. Here you'll need a 4WD – either your own or one hired at the park – and a guide. The main road in the park branches off right just before Ndlovu Camp.

Mlawula Nature Reserve

This tranquil **reserve** (☎ 416 1151; www.sntc.org.sz; adult/child E20/10; ☉ 6am-6pm), where the lowveld plains meet the Lebombo Mountains, boasts antelope species and hyenas, among others, plus rewarding bird-watching. Activities include two-hour wildlife drives, night drives, guided bush walks, plus free canoeing and fishing (hire rods for E20). Mountain bikes can also be rented at the reserve.

For accommodation, there's **Sara Camp** (s/d E150/300), with self-catering double safari-style tents, about 3km from the main gate, and **Siphiso camping ground** (camp sites per person E60), where you can pitch your own tent.

Accommodation can be booked through the Ezulwini Tourist Office (p549) or with the National Trust Commission (p545).

The turn-off for the entrance gates to the reserves is about 10km north of Simunye, from where it's another 4km from the main road. Minibus taxis will drop you at the junction (E10, 1¼ hours from Manzini).

Mbuluzi Nature Reserve

Tiny **Mbuluzi Reserve** (☎ 383 8861; www.mbuluzi .co.za; adult/child E20/10) is privately owned and managed by Tambankulu Estates, but comprises part of the larger conservation area that includes Mlawula Nature Reserve and Hlane Royal National Park. The reserve boasts a range of animals, including giraffes, zebras, hippos, antelope species and wildebeests. There have also been over 300 bird species recorded here. Land Rovers are available for wildlife drives (E165 per day, plus E4 per km).

Accommodation here – in a choice of comfortable eight-person or five-person self-catering **cottages** (s/d E300/400) – is more luxurious than at neighbouring Mlawula Nature Reserve, with a price tag to match. There's a minimum E700 per double charge on weekends. **Camp sites** (per person E25) are also possible.

The turn-off for Mbuluzi is the same as that for Mlawula; the reserve entrance is about 600m from the turn-off on the left.

Siteki

Siteki (Marrying Place) is a trading town in the foothills of the Lebombo Mountains about 8km from Lonhlupheko off the MR16. It got its name when Mbandzeni (great-grandfather of the present king) gave his frontier troops permission to marry. Although Siteki isn't really on the way to anywhere, it lies above the surrounding lowveld, with wide views, cooler temperatures and a bustling market.

Stegi Hotel (☎ 343 4126; r per person with half board E180) is a long-standing place with an agreeable ambience, modest, no-frills rooms and good meals.

Mabuda Farm (☎ 343 4124; www.geocities.com /mabudafarm; s/d with breakfast E175/350), a self-catering cottage on a working farm just outside Siteki town, is well recommended.

Minibus taxis from Manzini run several times daily (E9, one hour). There are also one or two minibus taxis daily connecting Siteki with Big Bend (E8, 40 minutes) and Simunye (E6, 45 minutes).

Mkhaya Game Reserve

This top-notch **private reserve** (☎ 528 3943; www.biggameparks.org) is off the Manzini–Big Bend road, near the hamlet of Phuzumoya. It takes its name from the *mkhaya* (or knobthorn) tree, which abounds on the reserve. *Mkhayas* are valued not only for their fruit, from which Swazis brew beer, but for the insect and birdlife they support.

Although small, Mkhaya has a wide range of animals, including white and black rhinos, roan and sable antelopes, and elephants. It's particularly noted for its black rhinos, and boasts that you're more likely to meet one in the wild here than anywhere else in Africa. There are also herds of the indigenous and rare Nguni cattle, which make the reserve economically self-supporting.

Day tours can be arranged, though it's worth staying for at least one night. Note that you can't visit the reserve without booking in advance, and even then you can't drive in alone; you'll be met at Phuzumoya at a specified pick-up time, usually 10am or 4pm.

WHITE-WATER RAFTING

One of the highlights of Swaziland is rafting the Usutu River (which becomes the Lusutfu River). The river is usually sluggish and quite tame, but near Mkhaya Game Reserve it passes through the narrow Bulungu Gorge, which separates the Mabukabuka and Bulunga Mountains, generating rapids.

Swazi Trails (p546) is the best contact to organise a rafting trip. It offers a full-day trip (per person E620, minimum two, including lunch and equipment) involving portaging a 10m waterfall, followed by a sedate trip through scenic country with glimpses of the 'flat dogs' (crocodiles) sunning on the river bank. The crocs haven't devoured anyone recently, hence the claim that rafting here is '...safer than driving through Jo'burg'. In sections, you'll encounter Grade IV rapids, which aren't for the faint-hearted, although even first-timers with a sense of adventure should handle the day easily.

Stone Camp (all-inclusive s/d with full board E960/1650) is reminiscent of a 19th-century hunting camp, with accommodation in rustically luxurious stone and thatch cottages. The price includes wildlife-watching drives and walks and park entry, in addition to full board, and is good value compared to many of the private reserves near Kruger National Park in South Africa.

SOUTHERN SWAZILAND

Southern Swaziland lacks the dramatic scenery of the north and rarely features on tourist itineraries, yet it has several worthwhile attractions. The entire area is quiet and rural, and is a good place to do it to set off on a bike or on foot to discover the 'real' Swaziland. It's also a convenient gateway to/from KwaZulu-Natal, and the base for some good horse riding (near Nsoko).

Big Bend

This sleepy sugar town is appropriately set on a big bend in the Lusutfu River just before it joins the Usutu. The panoramas from the edge of town are picturesque, and if you're here during summer, you can cool off in the pool at the Bend Inn Hotel.

There's an ATM that takes most credit cards at First National Bank on the main street just up from the Bend Inn Hotel.

The **Bend Inn Hotel** (☎ 363 6855; s/d with breakfast E182/268; ☒) is a faded, classic place on a hill just south of town, with good views across the river, acceptable rooms, a restaurant and an outdoor bar.

Lismore Lodge (☎ 363 6613; d E194) has small, comfortable, good-value doubles. It's about 4km south of Big Bend on the MR8. Just next door is the unassuming **Lubombo Lobster** (☎ 363 6308; mains E40-75; ☺ lunch & dinner), where you can get great seafood dishes, including calamari, seafood kebabs and seafood curry.

Riverside Motel (☎ 363 6910; s/d with breakfast E171/262; ☒) is a friendly motel that has decent rooms and a good **restaurant** (mains E35-70; ☺ breakfast, lunch & dinner). It's about 2km further south past Lismore Lodge on the MR8.

GETTING THERE & AWAY

Big Bend makes a convenient stop en route to/from KwaZulu-Natal in South Africa. Minibus taxis go daily to Manzini (E7, one hour) and to Lavumisa border post (E10, one hour).

Nsoko

Nsoko, halfway between Big Bend and the border post of Lavumisa, lies in the heart of sugar-cane country, with the Lebombo Mountains as a backdrop.

Nisela Safaris (☎ 303 0318; www.niselasafaris.co .za; camp sites per person E55, s/d beehive huts per person E90, B&B s/d E205/350, safari-lodge s/d with half board E415/750) is a small private reserve, and is convenient if you're coming into Swaziland from the south. It has various accommodation options, including the rustic 'safari lodge', a pleasant guesthouse and simple beehive huts. The focus is on activities, including game drives (per person E65, minimum two), guided walks (per person E30), canoeing on the Usutu River, fly fishing and visiting some of the reserve's lion cubs. There's also traditional Swazi dancing. Entry to the reserve costs E15 per person.

Nhlangano

Nhlangano is the closest town to the border post at Mahamba, but unless you want to visit the casino, there's no real reason to stop here. There's a well-stocked Spar in the shopping mall in the town centre.

The pleasant **Phumula Farm Guest House** (☎ 207 9099; s/d with breakfast E250/500) is about 3km from the border gate and about 1km off the main road. It's a private house with quiet gardens, pleasant rooms and a braai area. Dinner can also be arranged.

On offer at the **Nhlangano Sun Hotel & Casino** (☎ 207 8211; www.swazisun.sz; s/d E540/620; 🏊) is a grandiose setting and somewhat faded rooms, together with a popular casino. It's 4km southwest of town along the Lavumisa road (MR11).

Phoenix (r E150) is the cheapest place in town, and not appealing except for the price. It's in the town centre, opposite the police station.

Several minibus taxis run daily between Nhlangano and Manzini (E13, 1½ hours), from where you can get another vehicle on to Mbabane. There are also frequent connections to the Mahamba border post (E4), as well as to Piet Retief in South Africa (E15, one hour), though you'll usually need to change vehicles at the border.

Directory

CONTENTS

ACCOMMODATION

South Africa offers a wide selection of good-value accommodation. From backpacker hostels to B&Bs to luxury lodges, you'll find high standards, often for significantly less than you would pay for the equivalent in Europe, Australasia or North America.

At the budget level, the main options are camping, backpackers hostels and self-catering cottages. With just a few exceptions, you can expect clean surroundings and good facilities. The main caveat with places in this price category is that there aren't enough of them; away from tourist

---

PRACTICALITIES

- Use the **metric system** for weights and measures (see the conversion chart inside the front cover).

- Access **electricity** (220–250V AC, 50Hz) with a three-pin adaptor (round pins); they're sometimes sold in camping supply stores.

- Best weekly: *Mail & Guardian*. Best seller: the *Sunday Times*. Worth a look: the *Sunday Independent*. Dailies include the widely read *Sowetan*, the *Star* in Johannesburg and the pin-striped *Business Day*.

- Check out *Getaway* magazine for travel news.

- Tune the TV to the African National Congress–aligned **SABC** in any of South Africa's 11 official languages for the news (SABC3 is mostly English). **e-TV** has a more independent viewpoint. **M-Net** has movies and sports.

- **SABC radio** comes in your choice of 11 languages, and includes the popular Tim Modise talk show on FM. **BBC's World Service** is available on short wave, medium wave and (in and near Lesotho) FM.

---

areas sometimes the only budget option is camping.

Mid-range accommodation is particularly good value. Expect a private bathroom, a clean, comfortable room and – at many of the B&Bs or guesthouses – access to a small garden where you can take in the fresh air and sun (and maybe even enjoy a dip in a pool). The best bargains are found at B&Bs, which generally offer high quality breakfasts and facilities. Self-catering accommodation at national parks – usually priced in the budget to mid-range category– also tends to be very good value.

At the top end, South Africa boasts some of the best wildlife lodges in the region, as well as some classic guesthouses and several superb hotels. In travel magazine polls of

Africa's top hotels and luxury safari lodges, South African establishments are routinely well represented. Places at this level offer all the amenities you would expect from multi-star establishments for prices that are similar to, or slightly less than, those you would pay in Europe or North America. There are also some not-so-superb hotels which can be expensive disappointments, so be selective.

Accommodation in Swaziland is priced similarly to that in South Africa. At the budget level, there are a handful of backpacker hostels, and free-camping is possible in most areas of the country. Lesotho is not known for its high-class hotel accommodation. However, there are several notable exceptions, and camping opportunities abound away from major towns.

Accommodation listings in this book are ordered from budget to mid-range to top end. See inside the front cover for approximate price ranges. Expect to pay somewhat more than this in each category in major tourist areas such as Cape Town (which is one of the most expensive places in the region), and somewhat less in Lesotho.

There are significant seasonal price variations, with rates rising steeply during the December–January school break, and again in the Easter break, when room prices often double, and minimum stays are imposed. Advance bookings are essential during these times. The other school holidays are often classified as high season as well, although it's more common to have 'midseason' pricing. Conversely, you can get some excellent deals during the winter low season, which is also the best time for wildlife-watching. Many places offer discounted midweek or weekend rates, depending on who the majority of their clientele are (business travellers versus tourists). To save money during peak holiday periods, the best bets are camping, backpacker hostels or self-catering places.

B&Bs & Guesthouses

B&Bs and guesthouses (the line between them is often indistinguishable) are two of South Africa's accommodation treats. They're found throughout the country, in cities as well as small towns, and in rural areas you can often stay on farms. Some of the cheapest places aren't much to write home about, but on the whole the standard is high, and rooms are generally excellent

> **ACCOMMODATION PRICES**
>
> Watch out for advertising that boasts room rates that look too good to be true. If a hotel touts rooms costing R190, this usually means R190 *per person* in a twin or double room, with a single room priced, for example, at R290. Prices for double rooms in this book are quoted per room, not per person. Also, all prices in this book refer to rooms with bathroom, excluding breakfast and during the high season, unless otherwise noted. Prices quoted with half board include breakfast and dinner; those quoted with full board include all meals. 'All-inclusive' prices – mainly found in listings for wildlife lodges – generally cover all meals, wildlife drives and sometimes also park entry fees.

value in comparison with their counterparts in the UK, Australia or USA. Unlike British B&Bs, many South African establishments offer much more than someone's spare room, and unlike motels they are individual and often luxurious. Antique furniture, a private veranda, big gardens and a pool are common. In the Winelands north of Cape Town, and in other rural areas, wonderful settings are also part of the deal. Many have separate guest entrances and private bathrooms. Breakfasts are usually large and delectable. Prices start around R300 per double, including breakfast and private bathroom.

In Soweto (p402), Khayelitsha (p145) and other urban areas, you can also stay in township B&Bs, which are an excellent way to get insights into township life. Many owners offer tours of the township, and unparalleled African hospitality at meal times. Expect to pay from R150 per person.

Camping

Camping grounds and caravan parks have long been the accommodation of choice for many South African families. Most towns have an inexpensive municipal camping ground and caravan park, ranging from nice to basic and unappealing. Those near larger towns are often not safe. Much better are privately-run camping grounds, and those in national parks. These are invariably well equipped and pleasant, with ablution blocks,

ONLINE BOOKING

Many regions have B&B organisations and tourist offices that take bookings (see listings in the regional chapters). Another option, if you can't be bothered contacting places individually, is to use one of the many online booking services that cover South Africa. Because most charge listings fees, the cheapest places usually aren't included. Camping grounds (including those with self-catering accommodation) are also not listed, and pickings are slim outside major tourist centres.

www.bookabed.co.za Covers most provinces.
www.bookaholiday.co.za For Cape Town and the Garden Route.
www.farmstay.co.za For farm stays.
www.hostelafrica.com Hostels across Africa; also takes Baz Bus bookings.
www.leisurestay.co.za Upmarket B&Bs and lodges.
www.portfoliocollection.com For upscale B&Bs, private game reserve lodges and boutique hotels.
www.wheretostay.co.za Covers most of the country, and also includes disabled-friendly listings.

power points, cooking areas and water supply. In tourist areas, there are often fancy resorts, complete with swimming pool, restaurant and mini-market. Camping prices are either per person (averaging R40) or per site (averaging R70 for two people, plus R10 per additional person). Camping grounds in popular areas are often booked out during school holidays.

Many caravan parks ban nonporous groundsheets (which are sewn in to most small tents) to protect the grass. If you're only staying a night or two, you can usually convince the manager that your tent won't do any harm. Some caravan parks don't allow tents at all, though if you explain that you're a foreigner without a caravan, it's usually possible to get a site.

In Lesotho and Swaziland, apart from sites in national parks and nature reserves, there are few official camping grounds. However, it's usually possible to free-camp (ie, camp anywhere, not camp for free). Always ask permission from elders in the nearest village before setting up, both out of respect for the local community and to min-

imise any security risks. As a local courtesy, you may be offered a hut for the night; expect to pay about R5 for this. Free-camping isn't recommended in South Africa.

Hostels

South Africa is eminently backpacker-friendly, with a profusion of hostels. However, most of these are clustered in popular areas such as Cape Town and along the Garden Route, so there are still large areas of the country where camping is the only option for shoestringers. Most hostels are of a high standard, with Internet access, self-catering facilities and a travellers bulletin board. Many also offer meals, and all can dispense information on the area and on the best transport connections. Many are also on the Baz Bus route, or willing to collect you at the nearest stop. In addition to dorm beds (which average R60 per night), many hostels also offer private rooms from about R160 per double. Some are willing to let doubles as singles for a bit less. Some hostels also allow you to pitch a tent on their grounds.

In Swaziland, there are backpacker hostels in Mbabane, the Ezulwini Valley and Manzini; in Lesotho, you'll find them in or near Malealea, Semonkong, Mokhotlong and Sani Pass. Prices and facilities are similar to those in South Africa. Many towns in Lesotho also have 'Agricultural Training Centres' or 'Farmers' Training Centres' that accommodate travellers on a space-available basis. Rooms are simple but adequate, with shared bathroom, and rates (R25 per person throughout the country) give one of the best deals going. Most also have a communal kitchen.

The international YHA organisation is represented in South Africa, and known locally as **Hostelling International** (HI; ☎ 021-421 7721; www.hisa.org.za). It has member hostels in most major tourist areas, including one in Swaziland, although there's no noticeable difference between HI hostels and any others. However, a membership card usually pays off, as it entitles you to a 10% discount on accommodation at member hostels, as well as discounts with some bus lines, tour operators, surf shops and more.

Hotels

There are a few decent old-style country hotels, where you can get a double room for about R250, have a meal and catch up on local gossip in the pub. However, most of those in the budget category are too run-down for comfort. The selection is better for mid-range, where you can expect good value and atmospheric surroundings from about R350 per double.

More common are chain hotels, which are found in all major cities and tourist areas. The main ones include:

Formula 1 (☎ 013-741 4490; www.formula1.co.za) The cheapest, with functional but claustrophobic three-person rooms for R199 without breakfast.

City Lodge (☎ 011-884 0660; www.citylodge.co.za) Decent value, with Road Lodges (slightly superior standards to Formula 1, for about R230 per triple); Town Lodges (around R400 per double); City Lodges (quite pleasant for the price, about R600 per double); and Courtyard Hotels (about R840 per double).

Holiday Inn (☎ 0861 447 744, 011-482 3500; www.southernsun.com) No-frills rooms in 'express' hotels; better rooms (with minimal service) at 'Garden Court' hotels; and more comforts at 'Holiday Inn Crowne Plazas'. Ask about special weekend deals.

Southern Sun Group (☎ 461 9744; www.southernsun.com) In addition to running the Holiday Inn chain, it also operates several more-expensive hotels, including those under the InterContinental name.

Protea (☎ 0861 119 000, 021-430 5000; www.proteahotels.com) A network of three- to five-star hotels; Protea's Prokard Club gives a 20% discount to members.

Sun International (☎ 011-780 7800; www.sun-international.co.za) Runs top-end, resort-style hotels in Swaziland and the former Homelands, with casinos attached (left over from the apartheid era, when gambling was illegal in South Africa but legal in the Homelands). Standards are generally high and package deals are available.

Lodges

In and around national parks, especially Kruger National Park, you can relax in luxurious lodges in rustic bush settings. Accommodation is usually in East African–style safari tents, or in a lodge. Expect all

the amenities that you would find in a top-end hotel (including en-suite bathroom with running hot and cold water, comfortable bedding, delicious cuisine etc), although many don't have telephones and televisions. Most luxury lodges charge 'all-inclusive' rates, which include wildlife drives and meals.

Self-Catering Accommodation

This can be excellent value, from around R400 per four-person cottage (also called chalets, cabins and rondavels). Farm cottages are usually the least expensive. Small-town information centres are the best places to find out about these, and in a small community there's a chance that you'll get a ride to the cottage if you don't have transport.

Self-catering chalets or cottages are also often available in caravan parks and camping grounds, both municipal and private, and are common in coastal and tourist areas.

Apart from the occasional run-down place with just a mattress and basin, most self-catering accommodation comes with bedding, towels and a fully equipped kitchen, though confirm what is included in advance. In some farm cottages you'll have to do without electricity, and you might even have to pump water.

The **South African National (SAN) Parks Board** (☎ 012-428 9111; www.parks-sa.co.za; 643 Leyds St, Muckleneuk, Pretoria) has good-value, fully equipped bungalows and cottages. These are aimed at family groups, and start at around R400 for one or two people, plus R90/45 for each additional adult/child. Many parks also have simpler huts, with shared bathrooms and kitchens from around R120 per double.

ACTIVITIES

Thanks to South Africa's diverse terrain and favourable climate, almost anything is possible – from ostrich riding to the world's highest bungee jump. Good facilities and instruction mean that most activities are accessible to anyone, whatever their experience level.

There are dozens of operators. In addition to the ones listed here, ask other travellers and at hostels. Try to book day or overnight trips as close to your destination as possible. For example, if you're in Durban and want to visit a reserve further north, it's better (and usually cheaper) to travel to a hostel closer to the reserve and take a day trip from there, rather than booking a longer trip from Durban.

Aerial Pursuits

Ideal weather conditions and an abundance of high points from which to launch yourself make aerial pursuits highly popular. An added attraction of taking to the South African skies is that it is relatively inexpensive, compared with elsewhere in the world, and conditions are generally favourable year-round. A helpful contact for getting started is the **Aero Club of South Africa** (☎ 011-805 0366; www.aeroclub.org.za).

South Africa is one of the world's top destinations for paragliding, particularly Cape Town's Table Mountain. Although the flying is good year-round, the strongest thermals are from November to April. For experienced pilots, airspace restrictions are minimal and there's great potential for long-distance, cross-country flying. **South African Hang Gliding and Paragliding Association** (☎ 012-668 1219; www.paragliding.co.za) can provide names of operators, and numerous schools offer courses for beginners. In Cape Town, try **Paragliding Cape Town** (☎ 021-554 0592). In Swaziland, **Emoyeni Paragliding School** (☎ 505 7405; airsports@realnet.co.sz) in Manzini has paragliding courses.

Good places to float over the countryside in a hot air balloon include Sabie (p425) and the surrounding Mpumalanga area. Microlight flying is another way to get a bird's eye view on things. Check out www.otto.co.za/micro/ for an overview and a list of airfields.

South Africa boasts the world's highest bungee jump (p223) at Bloukrans River Bridge, between Plettenberg Bay and Storms River. There are several other popular jumps as well, including one at Gouritz Bridge, near Mossel Bay (p190).

Bird-Watching

With its enormous diversity of habitats, South Africa is a paradise for bird-watchers. Top spots include:

Cape Peninsula & West Coast Cape of Good Hope, within Table Mountain National Park (p100), is excellent for seabird-watching, as is West Coast National Park (p210), about 120km to the north.

Kruger National Park (p320) One of the continent's best areas for birding; the south and the far north are considered the best areas, and the park is known particularly for its raptors and migrants.

Northern KwaZulu-Natal Mkhuze Game Reserve (p320) hosts over 400 species within its 36,000 hectares and the Greater St Lucia Wetland Park (p315) protects one of the most significant water bird breeding grounds in Southern Africa.

In Lesotho, good places for twitchers include eyries in Lesotho's Maluti Mountains near the eastern Drakensberg escarpment. Swaziland's Malolotja Nature Reserve (p557) is one of the best birding spots in the country.

There are bird-watching clubs in all major cities in South Africa, and most parks and reserves can provide you with birding lists. Other useful contacts include www.sabirding.co.za (which also covers Lesotho and Swaziland) and www.capebirdingroute.org.

Many parks and reserves have field guides on hand, but it's still worth bringing your own.

Canoeing, Kayaking & Rafting

South Africa has few major rivers, but the ones that do flow year-round offer rewarding canoeing and rafting. Popular destinations include the Blyde and Sabie rivers, both in Mpumalanga province; the waterways around Wilderness (p196) and Wilderness National Park (p197) in the Western Cape; the Orange River, especially through Augrabies Falls National Park (p507); and the Tugela (p289). There's some serene canoeing at the Greater St Lucia Wetland Park (p315). In Swaziland, the classic rafting destination is the Great Usutu River (p560).

Rafting is highly rain-dependent, with the best months in most areas from December/January to April. Good contacts include **Felix Unite** (☎ 021-425 5181; www.felixunite.com), **Hardy Ventures** (☎ 013-751 1693; www.hardyventure.com) and **180° Adventures** (☎ 031-566 4955). In Swaziland, the main operator is **Swazi Trails** (☎ 416 2180; www.swazitrails.co.sz).

For sea kayaking, good contacts include the Cape Town–based **Coastal Kayak** (☎ 021-439 1134; www.kayak.co.za) and the **Sea Kayaking Association of South Africa** (☎ 021-790 5611; www.recskasa.org.za).

Diving

Take the plunge off the southernmost end of the African continent into your choice of oceans. To the west, the main dive sites are

SAFE DIVING

In popular diving areas, including Sodwana Bay, we've had some reports about slipshod diving operations. When choosing an operator, make quality, rather than cost, the priority. Factors to consider include an operator's experience and qualifications; knowledgeableness and seriousness of staff; whether it's a fly-by-night operation or well established; and the type and condition of equipment and frequency of maintenance. Assess whether the overall attitude is serious and professional, and ask about safety considerations – radios, oxygen, emergency evacuation procedures, boat reliability and back-up engines, first-aid kits, safety flares and life jackets. On longer dives, do you get an energising meal, or just tea and biscuits? An advantage of operators offering PADI- or NAUI-certified courses is that you'll have the flexibility to go elsewhere in the world and have what you've already done recognised at other PADI or NAUI dive centres. To check an operator's credentials, contact the **South Africa Underwater Federation** (☎ 021-930 6549; www.sa-underwater.org.za).

around the Cape Peninsula, known in particular for wreck diving, and for diving amid giant kelp forests. To the east, the main area is the KwaZulu-Natal north coast where – particularly around the diver's paradise of Sodwana Bay – there's some excellent warmwater diving with beautiful coral reefs and the chance to see dolphins and sometimes whale sharks. There are several rewarding sites off the Eastern Cape coast near Port Elizabeth, and many resort towns along the Garden Route have diving schools.

Conditions vary widely. The best time to dive the KwaZulu-Natal shoreline is from May through September, when visibility tends to be highest. In the west, along the Atlantic seaboard, the water is cold year-round, but at its most diveable, with many days of high visibility, between November and January/February.

All coastal towns where diving is possible have dive outfitters, and costs are generally lower here than elsewhere in the region. Expect to pay from around R1600 for a four-day open water certification course, and from about R180 for full equipment rental. With the exception of sites around Sodwana Bay during the warmer months (when a 3mm wetsuit will suffice), you'll need at least a 5mm wetsuit for many sites, and a drysuit for some sites to the south and west. Strong currents and often windy conditions mean that advanced divers can find challenges all along the coast. Sodwana Bay is probably the best all-round choice for beginners.

A variant on all this is shark diving, which involves being lowered in a cage and seeing sharks up close without having to worry that you'll become their next meal.

The main place for this is at Gansbaai near Hermanus (p169). Some operators allow snorkellers in the cage, too, if you're not a qualified diver. While shark diving is a good opportunity to get to know these shadows of the deep, there are some ecological downsides. The most obvious problem is that the sharks are baited to draw them close, and so come to associate humans with food.

Fishing

Sea fishing is popular, with a wide range of species in the warm and cold currents that flow past the east and west coasts, respectively. River fishing, especially for introduced trout, is popular in parks and reserves, with some particularly good highland streams in the Drakensberg. Licences are available for a few rand at park offices, and some places rent equipment. Useful websites include **South African Fishing** (www.safishing.co.za), **South African Bass Fishing** (www.bassfishing.co.za) and **Fly Fishing South Africa** (www.flyfisher.co.za).

Lesotho is an insider's tip among trout anglers. The season runs from September through May (same in South Africa), and there is a small licence fee, a size limit and a bag limit of 12 fish. Only rod and line and artificial nonspinning flies may be used. For more information, contact the **Ministry of Agriculture Livestock Division** (☎ 2232 3986; Private Bag A82, Maseru 100). The nearest fishing area to Maseru is the Makhaleng River, 2km downstream from Molimo-Nthuse Lodge (a two-hour drive from Maseru). Other places to fish are the Malibamat'so River near Oxbow; the Mokhotlong River near Mokhotlong in the northeast; and the Thaba-Tseka main dam.

Hiking
SOUTH AFRICA

South Africa is a hiker's paradise, with an excellent system of well-marked trails varied enough suit every ability. Some have accommodation – from camping to simple huts with electricity and running water – and all must be booked well in advance. Many have limits as to how many hikers can be on them at any one time. Most longer trails and wilderness areas require hikers to be in a group of at least three.

Designated wilderness areas, such as Cederberg Wilderness Area (p214), have off-trail hiking only. Little information is available on suggested routes, and it's up to you to survive on your own.

KwaZulu-Natal Nature Conservation (KZN Wildlife; ☎ 033-845 1000; www.kznwildlife.com) controls most trails in KwaZulu-Natal. Elsewhere, most trails are administered by the **SAN Parks Board** (☎ 012-428 9111; www.parks-sa.co.za) or the various Forest Region authorities. To find out about local hiking clubs, contact the **Hiking Federation of Southern Africa** (☎ 012-327 0083; www.linx.co.za/trails/info/hikefed.html).

Shorter hikes – from an hour up to a full day – are possible almost everywhere and require no advance arrangements. Some particularly good areas include Cape Peninsula National Park (especially near Cape Point) and the Drakensberg.

It's also possible to take guided walks in national parks, accompanied by armed

---

SOUTH AFRICA'S TOP HIKES

Following are some of South Africa's top hiking trails and their booking contacts; more details are given in the relevant chapters.

Cape Peninsula & Western Cape

Hoerikwaggo Hiking Trail (p118; Table Mountain National Park; 021-701 8692; www .tmnp.co.za) This trail, which was officially opened in 2004, takes you on a stunningly beautiful five-day hike over Table Mountain and down the Atlantic Coast, culminating at Cape Point.

Outeniqua Trail (p199; Forestry Department; ☎ 044-382 5446, 870 8323) Up to eight days in indigenous forest near Knysna.

Whale Hiking Trail (p173; De Hoop Reservations Office; ☎ 028-425 5020) Five days of hiking along the coastline in De Hoop Nature Reserve, with the added bonus of some prime whale-watching opportunities in season.

Eastern Cape

Otter Trail (p222; SAN Parks Board; ☎ 012-428 9111; www.parks-sa.co.za) Five days on the coast along the Garden Route (note that this trail is nearly always booked out).

Tsitsikamma Trail (p222; Forestry Department; ☎ 012-481 3615) A five-day hike running inland through the forests, parallel to the Otter Trail but hiked in the opposite direction (this trail is rarely booked out).

Amatola Trail (p254; Department of Water Affairs & Forestry; ☎ 043-642 2571, 604 5433; amatolHK@dwaf.co.za) Up to six days in the former Ciskei homelands.

Free State

Rhebok Hiking Trail (p363; SAN Parks Board; ☎ 012-428 9111; www.parks-sa.co.za) Two days in Golden Gate Highlands National Park.

KwaZulu-Natal

Giant's Cup (p334; KZN Wildlife; ☎ 033-845 1000) Up to five days in the southern Drakensberg. There are also wilderness trails and guided walks in Hluhluwe-Imfolozi, Mkhuze and Lake St Lucia parks and reserves.

Limpopo

Hanglip Trail (p465; Komatiland Forests Ecotourism; ☎ 012-481 3615) Up to two days in the verdant Soutpansberg range.

Mpumalanga

Blyderivierspoort Trail (p429; Mpumalanga Parks Board; ☎ 013-759 5432; mpbinfo@cis.co.za) Up to 2½ days in the Blyde River Canyon area.

Kruger National Park (p440; SAN Parks Board; ☎ 012-428 9111; www.parks-sa.co.za) Wilderness trails and guided walks.

Northern Cape

Klipspringer Hiking Trail (p505; Augrabies Falls National Park; ☎ 054-452 9200) Three days of stunning scenery along the banks of the Orange River.

Kodaspiek Trail (p513; Richtersveld National Park; ☎ 027-831 1506) Two days wandering amid incredible mountain desert landscapes.

rangers to ward off stampeding elephants and rambunctious rhinos. You won't cover much distance, but they offer the chance to experience the wild with nothing between you and nature. For more, see p64.

Safety is not a major issue on most trails, although on a few longer trails there have been muggings. Check with the local hiking club and with the Hiking Federation when booking your hike. On longer trails, hike in a group, and limit the valuables you carry.

Hiking is possible year-round, although you'll need to be prepared in summer for extremes of wet and heat. The best time of year is March through October.

Useful books include:

The Guide to Hiking Trails: Exploring Southern Africa on Foot Willie & Sandra Olivier. Out of print, but well worth tracking down.

Complete Guide to Walks & Trails in Southern Africa Jaynee Levy. Too heavy to carry, but good for an overview.

Drakensberg Walks David Bristow

Western Cape Walks David Bristow

LESOTHO

The entire country is ideal for hiking, away from major towns. The eastern highlands and the Drakensberg crown in particular attract serious hikers, with Sehlabathebe (p537) and Ts'ehlenyane (p529) parks, Bokong Nature Reserve (p533) and the area around Sani Top (p531) among the highlights. Malealea (p533) and Semonkong (p533) also make ideal bases. Wherever you are, there are few organised hiking trails as in South Africa – just footpaths – and you can walk about anywhere. You'll need a compass, and the relevant topographical maps (see p522).

In all areas, especially the remote eastern highlands, rugged conditions can make walking dangerous if you aren't experienced and prepared. Temperatures can plummet to near-zero even in summer, and thunderstorms and thick fog are common. Waterproof gear and warm clothes are essential. In summer many rivers flood and fords can become dangerous. Be prepared to change your route or wait until the river subsides. By the end of the dry season, good water can be scarce, especially in higher areas. For more information see the boxed text on p534.

SWAZILAND

The best place for hiking is Malolotja Nature Reserve (p557). Mlawula Nature Reserve (p559) also has good trails. In almost any rural area, you can set out on foot, following the generations-old tracks that crisscross the countryside. Weather conditions aren't as extreme as in Lesotho, but if you're hiking during the summer, be prepared for torrential downpours and hail storms.

Horse Riding & Pony Trekking

Horse riding is popular in South Africa and Swaziland, and it's easy to find rides ranging from several hours to several days, and for all experience levels. Particularly good areas in South Africa include the KwaZulu-Natal Drakensberg (p323), Limpopo's Waterberg range (p462), and the Wild Coast (p263). Riding is also offered in several national parks, including Addo Elephant (p235) and Golden Gate (p363) National Parks. In Swaziland, you can ride at Mlilwane Wildlife Sanctuary (p552), among other places.

Contacts include:

Fynbos Horse Trails (www.fynbostrails.com) Western Cape.

Nyanza Horse Trails (www.iafrica.sz/biz/Nyanza) Swaziland.

Horizon Horseback Adventures (www.ridinginafrica .com) Waterberg.

Equus Horse Safaris (www.equus.co.za) Waterberg.

Wild Coast Trails (www.wildcoast.org.za) Wild Coast.

Khotso Horse Trails (www.khotsotrails.co.za) Drakensberg.

Lesotho has its own version of equestrian enjoyment, with pony trekking on tough Basotho ponies a superb and popular way of seeing the highlands; see p534.

Kloofing (Canyoning)

Kloofing (called canyoning elsewhere, and a mix of climbing, hiking, swimming and some serious jumping) has a small but rapidly growing following in South Africa. Places where you can give things a try include Cape Town (with several nearby possibilities, see p118) and along the Drakensberg Escarpment (p423) in Mpumalanga. Operators who can sort you out include **Adventure Village** (www.adventure-village.co.za) and **Day Trippers** (www.daytrippers.co.za). There's a definite element of risk in the sport, so when hunting for operators, check their credentials carefully before signing up.

Mountain Biking

South Africans have taken to mountain biking in a big way, and you'll find trails almost everywhere. Some suggestions to get you started: the De Hoop Nature Reserve (p173), with overnight and day trails; the ride up (and down) Sani Pass, on the border between South Africa and Lesotho (p531); Citrusdal (p215), with a network of trails; the area around Cederberg Wilderness area (p214); Mountain Zebra National Park (p245); Knysna (p197) and surrounding area, with a good selection of trails; Sabie (p425), with several excellent trails; and Swaziland's Mlilwane Wildlife Sanctuary (p552). Cape Town is something of an unofficial national hub.

Useful sources of information include **SA-MTB** contactable through the South African Cycling Federation (www.sacf.co.za), which can also put you in touch with local mountain biking clubs; **Mountain Bike South Africa e-zine** (www.mtb.org.za); the **Linx Africa trail listing** (www.linx.co.za/trails/lists/bikelist.html); and Paul Leger's *Guide to Mountain Bike Trails in the Western Cape*. The bimonthly *Ride* is the main South African mountain-biking magazine.

Ostrich Riding

For information on ostrich riding – that most arcane and perhaps not the most animal-ethical of activities – see p186.

Rock Climbing

Some of the most challenging climbing is on the close-to-sheer faces of the KwaZulu-Natal Drakensberg. Another of South Africa's top sites is in Mpumalanga at Waterval Boven in Mpumalanga. The **South African Climbing Info Network** (www.saclimb.co.za) has listings and photos of many other climbing and bouldering sites. For information on regional clubs, contact the **Mountain Club of South Africa** (MCSA; ☎ 021-465 3412; www.mcsa.org.za). **Roc-n-Rope** (☎ 013-257 0363; www.rocrope.com) is another useful contact.

Surfing

South Africa has some of the best and least-crowded surfing in the world. Most surfers will have heard of Jeffrey's Bay, but there are myriad alternatives, particularly along the Eastern Cape coast from Port Alfred northwards. The best time of the year for surfing the southern and eastern coasts is autumn and early winter (from about April to July).

Boards and gear can be bought in most of the big coastal cities. New boards cost around US$185 and good-quality second-hand boards around US$100. If you plan to surf Jeffrey's Bay, you'll need a decent-sized board, as it's a fast wave.

For more information see the boxed texts on p189 and p225. Also check out www.wavescape.co.za, and *Zig Zag*, South Africa's biggest surf magazine.

Whale-Watching

South Africa is considered one of the world's best spots to sight these graceful giants from land, without needing to go out in a boat. Southern right and humpback whales are regularly seen offshore between June/July and November, with occasional spottings also of Bryde's and killer whales. Hermanus (p168) – where southern right whales come to calve – is the unofficial whale-watching capital, complete with a whale crier and an annual Whale Festival. At the nearby Walker Bay, whales approach to within 50m of the shoreline. Other favoured spots include the False Bay shoreline, especially between Cape Point and Muizenberg, and from Gordon's Bay southeast; and Mossel (p190) and Plettenberg (p203) Bays. The whales continue their progress around the Cape and up the KwaZulu-Natal coast, although by the time they reach Durban, they're often considerably further out to sea. See the boxed text on p171 for more.

Wildlife-Watching

South Africa is a wildlife-watching destination *par excellence*, and its large animal populations are one of the country's biggest attractions. In comparison with other countries in the region (Botswana and Zambia, for example), wildlife-watching in South Africa tends to be very accessible, with good roads and excellent accommodation for all categories of traveller. It is also comparatively inexpensive, although there are plenty of pricier choices for those seeking a luxury experience in the bush. For more, see the Environment and Kruger National Park chapters (p61 and p440, respectively).

Swaziland also offers some excellent wildlife-watching, in generally low-key surroundings. Among the highlights: Mlilwane Wildlife Sanctuary (p552), Mkhaya Game Reserve (p560) and Hlane Royal National Park (p558).

BUSINESS HOURS

Usual business hours are listed inside the front cover. Exceptions to this have been noted in individual listings in this book. In addition to regular banking hours, many foreign exchange bureaus remain open until 5pm Monday through Friday, and until noon on Saturday. In urban areas, many supermarkets stay open until 6pm or 8pm and are also open 9am to noon on Sundays.

CHILDREN
South Africa

South Africa is an eminently suitable destination if you're travelling with children. With its abundance of national parks, beaches, swimming pools and hiking trails, plus a good collection of museums and a handful of amusement parks, it offers plenty to do for travellers of all ages in a generally hazard-free setting. Most South Africans are welcoming to children, and you should have no shortage of offers for assistance.

PRACTICALITIES

Baby-changing rooms are not common, though clean restrooms abound, and in most you should be able to find a make-shift spot to change a nappy (diaper). Nappies, powdered milk and baby food are widely available, except in very rural areas. It's difficult to find brands of processed baby food without added sugar. These are available at supermarkets in all major towns; always check the security seal on jars. Short-term daycare is becoming more common, and many upscale hotels and resorts in tourist areas can arrange childcare.

Many wildlife lodges have restrictions on children under 12, so in most national parks and reserves, the main accommodation options will be camping or self-catering. Otherwise, family-oriented accommodation, such as triple-bed hotel rooms and four- to six-person self-catering cottages, are common throughout South Africa, and most hotels can provide cots. Many hotels offer children's discounts, averaging 50%. Children under 12 are also usually admitted at discounted rates to parks (free for children under two years of age, discounted for those aged under 16), museums and other places where entry fees are charged.

Most car-rental agencies will provide safety seats, but you'll need to book them in advance, and usually pay extra. When planning your itinerary, try to minimise long distances between stops.

Breast-feeding in public won't raise an eyebrow among Africans, but in other circles it's best to be discreet.

Seek medical advice on malaria prophylactics for children if you'll be in malarial areas (anywhere in the lowveld, including Kruger National Park). Swimming in streams should generally be avoided, due to the risk of bilharzia infection. Otherwise, there are few health problems. Should your child become ill, good-quality medical care is available in all major cities.

Lonely Planet's *Travel with Children* by Cathy Lanigan is full of tips for keeping children and parents happy on the road.

SIGHTS & ACTIVITIES

Botanical gardens, an aquarium, the cable car to Table Mountain, swimming pools, good facilities, and a low-key ambience make Cape Town the best urban destination if you're travelling with children. Among smaller towns, Oudtshoorn (p167) deserves mention because of its ostriches and the nearby Cango Caves.

For seaside relaxation, some of the beaches near Cape Town and along the Garden Route are ideal for families. One to try, because of its calmer waters and sheltered setting, is at Arniston (p172).

For older children, hiking in the Drakensberg is another option.

Wildlife-watching is suitable for older children who have the patience to sit for long periods in a car, but less suitable for younger ones. Addo Elephant National Park is one of the better destinations, in part because it's malaria-free, and in part because of the likelihood of sighting elephants. Kruger National Park is tempting because of its easy accessibility and family-friendly rest camps. However think twice before going, as it's in a malaria area. If you do give in to temptation, visit in the winter when the risk of malaria is lower, and come prepared with nets, repellent and suitable clothing.

Lesotho & Swaziland

Lesotho and Swaziland are also welcoming destinations for children. Swaziland in particular is a good family destination, with a very child-friendly attitude and a relaxed pace. The main caveat is the presence of malaria, which is a real risk in lower-lying areas of the country. There's no malaria in Lesotho, but because of it's more rugged terrain and conditions, it's better suited for older children who would enjoy hiking or pony trekking (note that some pony trekking centres only arrange treks for those over 12 years old).

Numerous hotels in Swaziland offer family-friendly accommodation, and there are amusements such as minigolf to keep children occupied. In Lesotho, everything is a bit rougher around the edges, though if you (and your children) are of an adventurous bent, you'll likely find travel here straightforward and enjoyable. Informal childcare arrangements can be made in both countries; ask at your hotel. Major hotels have western-style bathrooms, but in rural areas often the only choice is a long-drop. Nappies, powdered milk and baby food are available in Mbabane, Manzini and Maseru, with only a limited selection in smaller towns.

There are reasonable medical facilities in Mbabane and Maseru, but for anything serious, you'll need to head to South Africa.

CLIMATE CHARTS

South Africa has been favoured by nature with one of the most temperate climates on the African continent, and plenty of sunny, dry days. The main factors influencing conditions are altitude and the surrounding oceans (see p13 for more). Sample climate charts follow.

COURSES
Language

There are numerous established language schools for learning Xhosa, Zulu and Afrikaans, including:

Interlink Cape Town (☎ 021-439 9834; www.interlink .co.za) Afrikaans, Xhosa.

Inlingua Cape Town (☎ 021-419 0494; www.inlingua .co.za) Afrikaans.

Language Teaching Centre Cape Town (☎ 021-425 3585; www.languageteachingcentre.co.za) Afrikaans, Xhosa.

University of Natal (☎ 031-260 2510; www.nu.ac.za /department/default.asp?dept=zuludund; Durban) Zulu.

University of the Witwatersrand (☎ 011-717 4240; www.wits.ac.za/fac/arts/african_languages/aflghome .htm) Zulu.

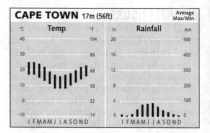

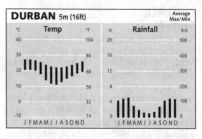

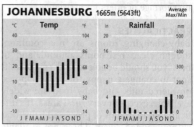

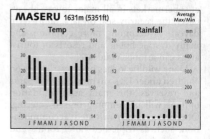

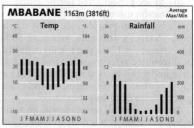

TALK (Transfer of African Language Knowledge; ☎/fax 011-487 1950; www.phaphama.org; PO Box 94144, Yeoville 2143, Jo'burg) organises 'immersion visits' in which you live in a homestay arrangement in either a township or rural area while receiving an hour or so daily of instruction in an African language and getting introduced to local culture. Costs average about R600 per person for a three-night stay. It can also arrange shorter tours of Soweto, focusing on whatever aspects interest you the most.

Wine Tasting

For the ultimate in fine living, ensconce yourself in an atmospheric B&B in the Winelands, and enrol yourself in a wine-tasting course. Useful contacts include: **Cape Wine Academy** (☎ 021-809 7597; www.capewineacademy.co.za), which is based in Stellenbosch and runs courses in both Stellenbosch and Cape Town; and, the Nose Wine Bar (p132) in Cape Town, which runs a four-week course for around R250.

CUSTOMS

You're permitted to bring 1L of spirits, 2L of wine, 400 cigarettes and up to R1250 worth of souvenirs into South Africa without paying duties. For more details, contact the **Department of Customs & Excise** (☎ 0800 002 870; Private Bag X923, Pretoria 0001). The import and export of protected animal products such as ivory is not permitted.

DANGERS & ANNOYANCES
Crime

Crime is the national obsession and, apart from car accidents, it's the major risk that you'll face in South Africa. However, try to keep things in perspective, and remember that despite the statistics and newspaper headlines, the majority of travellers visit the country without incident.

The risks are highest in Jo'burg, followed by some township areas and other urban centres. Daylight muggings are common in certain sections of Jo'burg, and the city's metro train system has had a problem with violent crime. No matter where you are, you can minimise the risks by following basic safety precautions, including the following:

- Never carry anything you can't afford to lose; in particular, don't flash around a camera. Use reliable safes wherever you can find them for storing your documents and valuables.
- Never look as though you might be carrying valuables, and leave watches, necklaces and earrings out of sight; wearing an expensive-looking T-shirt makes you look just as rich as wearing jewellery or a suit does. Completely avoid external money pouches.
- Avoid groups of young men; trust older mixed-sex groups.
- Divide your cash into several stashes, and always have some 'decoy' money or a 'decoy' wallet readily accessible to hand over if you are mugged. Don't keep money in your back pocket.
- Decoy wallet or not, keep a small amount of cash handy and separate from your other money so that you don't need to pull out a large wad of bills for making purchases.
- One of the greatest dangers during muggings or carjackings, especially in Jo'burg, is that your assailants will assume that you are armed, and that you will kill them if you get a chance. Stay calm, and don't resist or give them any reason to think that you will fight back.
- Listen to local advice on unsafe areas.
- Avoid deserted areas day and night, and especially avoid the commercial business district areas of larger cities at night and weekends.
- If you're going to visit a township – and it will certainly be one of the highlights of your visit to South Africa – go with a trusted guide or as part of a tour.
- Try not to look apprehensive or lost.
- Avoid driving at night and, day or night, keep your doors locked and windows up. Especially if you'll be driving alone, it's worth hiring a mobile phone. Leave your car in secure parking at night, and don't leave anything valuable inside.

Crime rates are nowhere near as high in Lesotho and Swaziland as they are in South Africa. Maseru has seen an increase in armed robberies, break-ins and carjackings targeting expatriates (though it's still small-scale compared with South Africa), and street crime is rising in Mbabane and Manzini. As long as you follow the basic precautions, you should be fine. Elsewhere in Lesotho and Swaziland, crime is negligible.

BEATING THE ATM SCAMS

If you are a victim of crime in South Africa, it's most likely to occur at an ATM. There are dozens of scams that involve stealing your cash, your card or your personal identification number (PIN) – usually all three. Thieves are just as likely to operate in Stellenbosch as in downtown Jo'burg and they are almost always well-dressed and well-mannered men.

The ATM scam you're most likely to encounter involves the thief tampering with the machine so your card becomes jammed. By the time you realise this you've entered your PIN. The thief will have seen this, and when you go inside to report that your card has been swallowed, he will take the card and leave you several thousand rand shorter. We make no guarantees, but if you follow the rules listed here you stand a better chance of avoiding this and other scams.

- Avoid ATMs at night and in secluded places. Rows of machines in shopping malls are usually the safest.
- Most ATMs have security guards. If there's no guard around when you're withdrawing cash, watch your back, or get someone else to watch it for you.
- Watch carefully the people using the ATM ahead of you. If they look suspicious, go to another machine.
- Use ATMs during banking hours and if possible take a friend. If your card is jammed in a machine, one person can stay at the ATM while the other seeks assistance from the bank.
- When you put your card into the ATM press cancel immediately. If the card is returned then you know there is no blockage in the machine and it should be safe to proceed.
- Don't hesitate to be rude in refusing any offers of help to complete your transaction.
- If someone does offer, end your transaction immediately and find another machine.
- Carry your bank's emergency phone number and if you do lose your card report it immediately.

Drugs

Dagga or *zol* (marijuana) was an important commodity in the Xhosa's trade with the San. Today it is illegal but widely available. There are heavy penalties for use and possession but many people still use the drug – often quite openly, as you'll discover in some of the backpacker hostels and bars you might frequent. The legal system does not distinguish between soft and hard drugs.

Ecstasy is just as much a part of rave and clubbing culture in South Africa as it is elsewhere. South Africa is also reputed to be the world's major market for the barbiturate Mandrax, which is now banned in many countries (including South Africa) because of its devastating effects. Drugs such as cocaine and heroin are becoming widely available and their use accounts for much property crime.

DISABLED TRAVELLERS

South Africa is a good destination for disabled travellers, with an ever-expanding network of facilities catering to those who are mobility impaired or blind. **SAN Parks** (☎ 012-

428 9111; www.parks-sa.co.za) has an excellent and inspirational summary of accommodation and trail accessibility for the mobility impaired at all its parks, and is the best travel website we have seen anywhere in terms of incorporating disabled access information throughout its pages.

Wheelchairs are sometimes available for visitors at several botanical gardens, including Kirstenbosch (Cape Town), though you should call in advance to confirm. Kirstenbosch and several nature reserves also have Braille or guided trails for the visually impaired. Other destinations with facilities for the disabled have been noted throughout the book.

A helpful initial contact is the **National Council for Persons with Physical Disabilities in South Africa** (☎ 011-726 8040; www.ncppdsa.co.za). Other useful sources of information include:

Access-Able Travel Source (www.access-able.com) Has lists of tour operators offering tours for travellers with disabilities.

Carp Diem Tours (☎ /fax 027-217 1125) Specialises in tours for the physically challenged and the elderly in Western and Northern Capes.

Central Reservations (www.centralres.co.za/disabled .html) A small listing of disabled-friendly accommodation.

Eco-Access (www.eco-access.org) Has an overview of disabled-related initiatives in South Africa.

Epic-Enabled (www.epic-enabled.com) Can help arrange tours, plus Kruger safaris.

Linx Africa (www.linx.co.za/trails/lists/disalist.html) For province-by-province listings of disabled-friendly trails.

South African Tourism (www.southafrica.net) Has informative disability-related links on its website, focusing on disabled facilities in national parks.

DISCOUNT CARDS

A membership card for **Hostelling International** (HI; www.hisa.org.za) or the affiliated International Youth Hostel Association entitles you to discounts on HI-affiliated hostels, as well as on the Baz Bus (5%), Intercape (15%) and more. You can apply through the HI website.

EMBASSIES & CONSULATES
South African Embassies & Consulates

Diplomatic representation abroad includes the following. For a full listing see www.dfa .gov.za/foreign/sa-abroad/index.htm.

Australia (☎ 02-6273 2424; www.rsa.emb.gov.au; Rhodes Pl, Yarralumla, Canberra ACT 2600)

Botswana (☎ 390 4800; sahcgabs@botsnet.bw; 29 Queens Rd, Gaborone)

Canada (☎ 613-744 0330; www.southafrica-canada.com; 15 Sussex Dr, Ottawa, Ontario K1M 1M8)

France (☎ 01 53 59 23 23; www.afriquesud.net; 59 Quai d'Orsay, 75343 Paris, Cedex 07)

Germany (☎ 030-22 0730; www.suedafrika.org; 4th fl, Atrium Bldg, Friedrichstrasse 60, Berlin 101117)

Ireland (☎ 01-661 5553; information@saedublin.com; 2nd fl, Alexandra House, Earlsfort Centre, Earlsfort Tce, Dublin 2)

Israel (☎ 03-525 2566; www.safis.co.il; 16th fl, Top Tower, 50 Dizengoff St, 64332, Tel Aviv)

Kenya (☎ 02-242 664; sahc@africaonline.co.ke; Lonrho House, Standard St, Nairobi)

Malawi (☎ 01-773 722; sahc@malawi.net; 3rd fl, Kang'ombe House, Robert Mugabe Crescent, Lilongwe)

Mozambique (☎ 01-490059, 491614; sahc@tropical .co.mz; Avenida Eduardo Mondlane 41, Maputo)

Namibia (☎ 061-205 7111; sahcwin@iafrica.com.na; RSA House, cnr Jan Jonker St & Nelson Mandela Ave, Windhoek 9000)

Netherlands (☎ 70-392 4501; www.southafrica.nl; Wassenaarseweg 40, the Hague 2596 CJ)

New Zealand Representation accredited from Australia, see above.

UK (☎ 020-7451 7299; www.southafricahouse.com; South Africa House, Trafalgar Sq, London WC2N 5DP)

USA (☎ 202-232 4400; www.saembassy.org; 3051 Massachusetts Ave NW, Washington DC 20008) Also consulates in New York, Chicago and Los Angeles.

Zimbabwe (☎ 04-753147; sahcomm@ecoweb.co.zw; 7 Elcombe St, Belgravia, Harare)

Lesotho Embassies & Consulates

In countries without Lesotho representation, contact the UK representative. Lesotho's diplomatic representations abroad include the following:

Belgium (☎ 02-705 3976; lesothobruemb@skynet.be; Blvd General Wahis 45, 1030 Brussels)

Germany (☎ 030-257 5720; lesoembger@aol.com; Dessauer Strasse 28/29, 10963 Berlin)

Italy (☎ 06-854 2419; les.rome@flashnet.it; Via Serchio 8, 00198 Rome)

UK (☎ 020-7235 5686; lhc@lesotholondon.org.uk; 7 Chesham Pl, Belgravia, London SW1 8HN)

USA (☎ 202-797 5533/4; lesotho@afrika.com; 2511 Massachusetts Ave NW, Washington DC 20008)

Swazi Embassies & Consulates

In countries without Swazi representation, contact the UK representative.

Kenya (☎ 02-339231; 3rd fl, Silopark House, Transnational Plaza, Mama Ngina St, Nairobi)

Mozambique (☎ 493846, 491721; Avenida Kwame Nkrumah, Maputo)

UK (☎ 020-7630 6611; www.swaziland.org.uk; 20 Buckingham Gate, London SW1E 6LB)

USA (☎ 202-234 5002; 1712 New Hampshire Ave, NW, Washington DC 20009)

Embassies & Consulates in South Africa

Most countries have their main embassy in Pretoria, with an office or consulate in Cape Town (which becomes the official embassy during Cape Town's parliamentary sessions). Some countries also maintain consulates in Jo'burg and in Durban.

South Africa is a gold mine for travellers hunting visas for other African countries. As some of these can be difficult to collect as you travel around, it makes sense to get as many as you can here.

The following list includes some of the more important embassies and consulates; most are open in the mornings only for visa services, usually between 9am and noon. For more embassies and consulates, check www.dfa.gov.za/foreign/forrep/index.htm or the phone book.

Australia (Map pp406-7; ☎ 012-342 3740; 292 Orient St, Arcadia, Pretoria)

Botswana High Commission in Pretoria (Map pp406-7; ☎ 012-430 9640; 24 Amos St, Colbyn); Consulate in Cape Town (Map pp102-3; ☎ 021-421 1045; 4th fl, Southern Life Centre, 8 Riebeeck St, City Bowl); Consulate in Jo'burg (Map p380; ☎ 011-403 3748; 2nd fl, Future Bank Bldg, 122 De Korte St, Braamfontein)

Canada High Commission in Pretoria (Map pp406-7; ☎ 012-422 3000; www.canada.co.za; 1103 Arcadia St, Hatfield); Consulate in Cape Town (Map pp102-3; ☎ 021-423 5240; 19th fl, Reserve Bank Bldg, 60 St George's Mall, City Bowl)

France Embassy in Pretoria (Map pp406-7; ☎ 012-429 7000; france@embafrance-za.org; 807 George Rd, Arcadia); Consulate in Cape Town (Map p106; ☎ 021-423 1575; 2 Dean St); Consulate in Jo'burg (Map pp376-7; ☎ 011-778 5600; 3rd fl, Standard Bank Bldg, 191 Jan Smuts Ave, Rosebank)

Germany Embassy in Pretoria (Map pp406-7; ☎ 012-427 8977; 180 Blackwood St); Consulate in Cape Town (Map pp102-3; ☎ 021-424 2410; 825 St Martini Gardens, 74 Queen Victoria St)

Ireland Embassy in Pretoria (Map pp406-7; ☎ 012-342 5062; 1st fl, Southern Life Plaza, 1059 Schoeman St); Consulate in Cape Town (Map pp102-3; ☎ 021-423 0431; 54 Keerom St, City Bowl)

Lesotho (Map pp406-7; ☎ 012-322 6090; lesothoh@global.co.za; 343 Pretorius St, Pretoria)

Mozambique High Commission in Pretoria (Map pp406-7; ☎ 012-401 0300; 529 Edmond St, Arcadia); Consulate in Jo'burg (Map pp376-7; ☎ 011-327 2942, 327 2943; 18 Hurlingham Rd, Illovo); Consulate in Cape Town (Map pp102-3; ☎ 021-426 2944; 3rd fl, Castle Bldg, 45 Castle St); Consulate in Durban (Map pp284-5; ☎ 031-304 0200; Room 520, 320 West St); Consulate in Nelspruit (Map p433; ☎ 013-753 2089, 752 7396; 64 Bester St)

Namibia (Map pp406-7; ☎ 012-481 9100; 197 Blackwood St, Arcadia, Pretoria)

Netherlands Embassy in Pretoria (Map pp406-7; ☎ 012-344 3910; www.dutchembassy.co.za; 825 Arcadia St); Consulate in Cape Town (Map pp102-3; ☎ 021-421 5660; kaa@minbuza.nl; 100 Strand St, City Bowl)

New Zealand (Map pp406-7; ☎ 012-342 8656; Block C, Hatfield Gardens, Pretoria)

Swaziland High Commission in Pretoria (Map pp406-7; ☎ 012-344 1910; 715 Government Ave, Arcadia); Consulate in Jo'burg (Map p380; ☎ 403 7472; 6th fl, Braamfontein Centre, 23 Jorissen St)

UK High Commission in Pretoria (Map pp406-7; ☎ 012-421 7800; 256 Glyn St, Hatfield); Consulate in Cape Town (Map pp102-3; ☎ 021-425 3670; Southern Life Centre, 8 Riebeeck St, City Bowl); Consulate in Durban (Map pp284-5; ☎ 031-305 3041; 22 Gardner St)

USA Embassy in Pretoria (Map pp406-7; ☎ 012-342 1048; 877 Pretorius St, Arcadia); Consulate in Cape Town (Map pp102-3; ☎ 021-421 4280; 4th fl, Broadway Industries Centre, Foreshore); Consulate in Jo'burg (Map pp376-7; ☎ 011-644 8000; 1 River St, Killarney); Consulate in Durban (Map pp284-5; ☎ 031-304 4737; 29th fl, Durban Bay House, 333 Smith St)

Zimbabwe High Commission in Pretoria (Map pp406-7; ☎ 012-342 5125; 798 Merton Ave, Arcadia); Consulate in Cape Town (Map pp102-3; ☎ 021-461 4710; 55 Kuyper St, Zonnebloem); Consulate in Jo'burg (Map p380; ☎ 011-838 2156; 17th fl, 20 Anderson St)

Embassies & Consulates in Lesotho

Canada (Map p523; ☎ 2231 4187, 2231 6435; www .dfait-maeci.gc.ca/southafrica/; 5th fl, LNDC, Block D, Kingsway, Maseru)

France (Map p523; ☎ 2232 5722; alliancefrancaise@ ilesotho.com; Alliance Française Bldg, Kingsway, Maseru)

Germany (☎ 2232 4198; germanembassypretoria@ gonet.co.za; 70C Maluti Rd, Maseru West)

Ireland (Map p523; ☎ 2231 4068; irishcon@lesoff.co.za; Tonakholo Rd, Maseru West)

Netherlands (Map p523; ☎ 2231 2114; www.dutch embassy.co.za/cons_les.htm; Lancer's Inn, Maseru)

South Africa (Map p523; ☎ 2231 5758; sahcls@lesoff .co.za; 10th fl, Lesotho Bank Towers, Kingsway, Maseru)

UK (Map p523; ☎ 2231 3961; www.bhc.org.ls; Linare Rd, Maseru)

USA (Map p523; ☎ 2231 2666; www.usembassy.org.ls; 254 Kingsway, Maseru)

Embassies & Consulates in Swaziland

Mozambique (☎ 404 3700; Mountain Inn Rd, Mbabane)

South Africa (Map p547; ☎ 404 4651; sahc@iafricaon line.sz; 2nd fl, the Mall, Plasmall St, Mbabane)

UK (Map p547; ☎ 404 2581; enquiries.mbabane@fco.gov .uk; 2nd fl, Lilunga House, cnr Gwamile St & Somhlolo Rd, Mbabane)

USA (Map p547; ☎ 404 6441/2; www.usembassy.state.gov /mbabane; 7th fl, Central Bank Bldg, Warner St, Mbabane)

FESTIVALS & EVENTS

South Africa hosts dozens of festivals, and there's always something going on somewhere in the country. Some of the best or most intriguing are listed here (plus a few highlights from Lesotho and Swaziland). For other events, see the destination chapters. **South Africa Tourism** (www.southafrica.net) also has listings of festivals around the country.

JANUARY

Cape Town New Year Karnival (Cape Town Minstrel Carnival) Cape Town's longest-running street party is held 1–2 January, with ribald song and dance parades, colourful costumes and general revelry. It's followed by a Jazzathon at the Waterfront.

FEBRUARY

Kavadi Festival The major Hindu festival, held twice annually (January–February and April–May) in Durban, in honour of the Hindu god Muruga. It's accompanied by the piercing of the body with skewers as a sign of devotion.

MARCH

Cape Argus Cycle Tour (www.cycletour.co.za) Held in the second week of March, this spin around the Cape Peninsula is the largest bicycle race in the world, with over 30,000 entries.

Klein Karoo National Arts Festival (☎ 044-203 8600; www.karoofees.com, in Afrikaans) Enjoy all things Afrikaans at this festival that aims to seek unity between Afrikaans speakers of all races; held in Oudtshoorn (Western Cape) in late March/early April.

APRIL

Old Mutual Two Oceans Marathon (www.twoocean smarathon.org.za) One of the world's most beautiful marathon routes, held around the Cape Peninsula on Easter Saturday.

Rustler's Valley One World Unity Party (www.rust lers.co.za/pages/easterpage.html) An off-beat music-centred party on Easter weekend that's an annual high-light for alternative lifestyle lovers of every sort. Rustler's Valley, Free State.

Splashy Fen Music Festival (www.splashyfen.co.za) Rock, pop and jazz with a fringe; held in late April at Splashy Fen Farm, about 20km north of Underberg in the foothills of the southern Drakensberg.

JUNE

Comrades Marathon (www.comrades.com) This 89km road race – queen of marathons – is run between Durban and Pietermaritzburg, alternating directions each year, mid-June.

JULY

National Arts Festival (www.nafest.co.za) Get in touch with South Africa's creative pulse at the country's largest arts festival, held annually in early July at Grahamstown (Eastern Cape).

AUGUST/SEPTEMBER

Umhlanga (Reed) Dance Swaziland's week-long debutante ball in August/September; young Swazi women journey to Lobamba to help repair the queen mother's home and then dance before the king.

OCTOBER

Morija Arts & Cultural Festival (www.morijafest.com) A celebration of Basotho culture; held in early October in Morija (Lesotho).

NOVEMBER

Diwali The Durban Indian community's three-day Festival of Lights.

DECEMBER

Incwala The sacred rain and harvest festival of the Swazi, held in December/January, depending on the moon.

FOOD

Eating listings in this book are ordered by Budget (roughly R25–35), Mid-Range (R40–70) and Top End (R80 and up). Sit-down meals in restaurants (without getting into *haute cuisine*) consistently cost between R40 and R60 per person (less in pubs), and fresh produce everywhere is good value.

For more on the highs and lows of eating well in South Africa (plus Lesotho and Swaziland), see the Food & Drink chapter.

GAY & LESBIAN TRAVELLERS

South Africa's constitution is one of the few in the world that explicitly prohibits discrimination on the grounds of sexual orientation, and there are active gay and lesbian communities and scenes in Cape Town, Jo'burg, Pretoria and Durban. Cape Town is without doubt the focal point, and the most openly gay city on the continent.

Things have come a long way since 1990, when Jo'burg hosted a **Gay Pride parade** (www.sapride.org) with many supporters wearing brown paper bags over their heads to conceal their identity. The parade, which is held annually in late September, is still going strong. There's also a separate annual gay and lesbian film festival, **Out in Africa** (www.oia.co.za), with a good selection of international and local films in Jo'burg, Pretoria and Cape Town. In December everyone fights for tickets for the popular **Mother City Queer Project party** (www.mcqp.co.za) in Cape Town.

Despite the liberality of the new constitution, it will be a while before the more conservative sections of society begin to accept it. Outside the cities, in both black and white communities, homosexuality remains frowned upon, if not taboo. Even in Cape Town there was a public rumpus when a delegation of overseas gay travel agents came to town in 2001. This prompted the local Christian and Muslim communities to band together to denounce the promotion of the city as a gay destination.

A good contact is the **Lesbian & Gay Equality Project** (☎ 011-487 3810; www.gaysouthafrica.org.za). Cape Town's **Triangle Project** (☎ 021-448 3812; www.triangle.org.za) is one of the leading AIDS support organisations, offering professional counselling, legal advice and education programmes.

The country's longest-running gay newspaper is the monthly *Exit* (www.exit.co .za). The glossy monthly *OUTright* is for gay males; *Womyn* is its lesbian equivalent. Both are available at CNA and other chain bookstores nationwide. The Gauteng-based magazine *Rush* is also worth looking out for; it's often available at gay venues. There's also a gay and lesbian link on the South Africa tourism website (www.south africa.net). For more, see the boxed text on p135, and also p393.

Swaziland is much more conservative than South Africa. Both male homosexual and lesbian activities are officially illegal, and gay sexual relationships are culturally taboo. In Lesotho, there is no official prohibition of homosexual activity, though gay sexual relationships are taboo and open displays of affection – whatever your orientation – are frowned upon.

HOLIDAYS
Public Holidays
After the 1994 elections, public holidays underwent a dramatic shake-up. For example, the Day of the Vow, which celebrated the Boers' victory in the Battle of Blood River, has become the Day of Reconciliation. The officially ignored but widely observed Soweto Day, marking the Soweto uprisings, is now celebrated as Youth Day. Human Rights Day is held on the anniversary of the Sharpeville massacre (see p38).

Current public holidays are:

SOUTH AFRICA
New Year's Day 1 January
Human Rights Day 21 March
Good Friday March/April
Easter Sunday March/April
Easter Monday March/April
Family Day 17 April
Constitution or Freedom Day 27 April
Workers' Day 1 May
Youth Day 16 June
Women's Day 9 August
Heritage Day 24 September

Day of Reconciliation 16 December
Christmas Day 25 December
Day of Goodwill 26 December

LESOTHO
New Year's Day 1 January
Moshoeshoe Day 11 March
Hero's Day 4 April
Good Friday March/April
Easter Monday March/April
Workers' Day 1 May
Ascension Day May
King's Birthday 17 July
Independence Day 4 October
Christmas Day 25 December
Boxing Day 26 December

SWAZILAND
New Year's Day 1 January
Good Friday March/April
Easter Monday March/April
King Mswati III's Birthday 19 April
National Flag Day 25 April
King Sobhuza II's Birthday 22 July
Umhlanga (Reed) Dance August/September
Somhlolo Day 6 September (Independence)
Incwala Ceremony December/January (exact dates vary each year)
Christmas Day 25 December
Boxing Day 26 December

School Holidays
South Africa's major holiday periods are the December–January school holidays as well as the Easter break. Many shops and businesses close, accommodation in national parks and tourist areas is fully booked and peak-season prices are in effect. At the beginning and end of these holiday periods, public transport fills up, as do seats on domestic and international flights, and you'll likely encounter long queues at popular border posts.

The situation is similar during other school holidays, but not as intense. During these times, accommodation prices are often increased, but not by as much.

The provinces stagger their school holidays. They are approximately late March to early April (varying depending when Easter is); late June to mid-July; late September to early October; and early December to mid-January. For exact dates, see www .gov.za/sa_overview/schoolcal06.htm. The main school holiday periods in Lesotho and Swaziland parallel those in South Africa.

INSURANCE

Travel insurance covering theft, loss and medical problems is highly recommended. Before choosing a policy spend time shopping around, as those designed for short package tours in Europe may not be suitable for the South African veld. Also be sure to read the fine print, as some policies specifically exclude 'dangerous activities', which can mean scuba diving, motorcycling, bungee jumping and more. At a minimum, check that the policy covers emergency evacuation at least to Jo'burg and/or an emergency flight home. If you'll be in Lesotho and Swaziland, check to see whether the evacuation plan extends to these countries.

If your policy requires you to pay first and claim later for medical treatment, be sure to keep all documentation. Some policies ask you to call back (reverse charges) to a centre in your home country where an immediate assessment of your problem is made. See p607 for more.

For information about vehicle insurance, see p602; for health insurance see p607.

INTERNET ACCESS

Internet access is widely available in South Africa. Many hostels offer email facilities, and there are Internet cafés in every major town. Costs average R25 per hour. If you're travelling with your own computer, hooking up in hotel rooms is straightforward, requiring only the phone connection jack for your modem. Most top hotels have broadband, and should be able to provide the cable.

In Swaziland, there's Internet access in Mbabane and in a few places in the Ezulwini Valley; elsewhere in the country, connections are few and far between. In Lesotho, you can log on in Maseru.

Lonely Planet's **ekit** (www.ekno.lonelyplanet .com) offers free web-based email. See p16 for helpful websites for planning your Southern Africa travels.

LEGAL MATTERS

If you have the misfortune to be arrested in South Africa, you have the right to keep silent; the right to be released on bail or warning, unless there's a good reason to keep you in jail; the right to a lawyer; and the right to food and decent conditions. Apart from traffic offences such as speeding and drunk driving, the main area to

---

COMING OF AGE

- The legal age for voting in South Africa (and in Lesotho and Swaziland) is 18.

- Driving is legal once you're 18.

- The legal drinking age is 18.

- Heterosexual sex is legal when you turn 16 (18 in Swaziland). In Lesotho the age of consent is 14 for boys and 16 for girls.

- The homosexual age of consent is 19 in South Africa, and undefined in Lesotho and Swaziland.

- Women in Swaziland are considered legal minors, and under Lesotho customary law, women are minors for purposes of land ownership.

---

watch out for is drug use and possession. Despite a relatively open drug culture, use and possession are illegal: arrests happen and penalties are stiff.

MAPS

Good country maps are widely available for all three countries, and a recommended investment if you'll be driving. Some to look for are Map Studio's *Tourist Map* (1:2,500,000) and the Automobile Association of South African (AASA) series of maps covering the country. Michelin maps also cover South Africa, Lesotho and Swaziland. Lonely Planet's *Cape Town City Map* is useful whether you're visiting the city by car or on foot. All of these are readily available in map stores and bookstores in major cities in South Africa. A good place to look is **Map Studio** (www.mapstudio.co.za), with branches in Cape Town, Durban and Jo'burg.

For any hiking done away from established trails, a topographical map is highly recommended. Government maps (except for those covering the Drakensberg area) are available from the **Map Office** (☎ 011-339 4949; www.mapoffice.co.za; ground fl, Standard House, 40 De Korte St, Braamfontein; PO Box 207, Wits 2050, Gauteng; ⏰ 7.30am-4pm Mon-Fri). Drakensberg maps – essential if you plan on hiking – are available from KwaZulu-Natal Nature Conservation (see p63).

In Lesotho, 1:50,000 topographical maps are available from the Department of Land, Surveys & Physical Planning (see p522) for R35 each. It also sells a good 1:250,000 country map (R50, 1994). The AASA puts out the helpful *Motoring in Lesotho*, available at the tourist information office and bookstores in Maseru.

In Swaziland, the tourist office hands out a free country map, with city plans for Mbabane and Manzini on the reverse, though none are particularly accurate. Better is the AASA's *Motoring in the Kingdom of Swaziland* map, which is on sale at the tourist information office in Mbabane (E20), and at bookstores. Topographical maps (1:50,000) are available from the **Ministry of Public Works & Transport Surveyor General's office** (☎ 404 2321; Mhlambanyatsi Rd, Mbabane).

MONEY

South Africa's currency is the rand (R), which is divided into 100 cents. There is no black market. The coins are one, two, five, 10, 20 and 50 cents, and R1, R2 and R5. The notes are R10, R20, R50, R100 and R200. There have been forgeries of the R200 note and some businesses are reluctant to accept them.

In Lesotho, the currency is the loti (plural maloti, M), which is divided into 100 lisente. In Swaziland, it's the lilangeni (plural emalangeni, E). Both the loti and the lilangeni are fixed at a value equal to the South African rand. Rand is accepted everywhere in both Lesotho and Swaziland, though you will invariably be given maloti or emalangeni in change.

The value of the rand has fluctuated wildly in recent years, and is currently on the upswing, which means South Africa is no longer the good value that it recently was, though it's still less expensive than Europe and North America. For exchange rates, see the table inside the front cover. For information on costs, see p14.

The best currencies to bring are US dollars, euros or British pounds in a mixture of travellers cheques and cash, plus a Visa or MasterCard as backup and for withdrawing money from ATMs.

ATMs

There are ATMs in all cities in South Africa, most of which give cash advances against cards belonging to the Cirrus network. For safety precautions, see p574.

In Lesotho there is an ATM in Maseru that accepts international cards. All other

ATMs in Lesotho only work if you have a local bank account.

In Swaziland, there are two ATMs in Mbabane that accept international cards.

Credit Cards

These are widely accepted in South Africa, especially MasterCard and Visa, and can also be used at many ATMs for cash advances. Nedbank is an official Visa agent and Standard Bank is a MasterCard agent – both have branches across the country.

In Lesotho and Swaziland, credit cards are only accepted by the major tourist establishments.

Moneychangers

SOUTH AFRICA

Cash is readily exchanged at banks (First National, Nedbank and Standard Bank are usually the best) and foreign exchange bureaus in all major cities.

Most banks change travellers cheques in major currencies with varying commissions. Nedbank is associated with American Express, and First National Bank and Nedbank are associated with Visa. Thomas Cook has travellers cheques in rand, though it works out best in the end to buy US dollar cheques. If you do buy some rand cheques, do so just before departure to minimise the effects of devaluation.

The Thomas Cook agent in South Africa is Rennies Travel, a large chain of travel agencies, and there are American Express offices in major cities. Neither charges commission for its own travellers checks, though you'll usually get a higher rate of exchange from a bank. Rennies also changes other travellers cheques without fees.

Keep at least some of your exchange receipts as you'll need these to reconvert leftover rand when you leave.

LESOTHO

The only place where you can reliably exchange foreign cash and travellers cheques is in Maseru. Commissions average 2.5% on travellers cheques (minimum M25), and 1.25% on cash (minimum M40). Rand notes are usually available on request.

SWAZILAND

First National and Nedbank change cash and travellers cheques. Rates are similar at both, but commissions vary. Most banks ask to see the purchase receipt when cashing travellers cheques. Standard Bank has branches in Mbabane, Manzini, Nhlangano, Piggs Peak, Simunye, Tshaneni, Matsapha and Big Bend. First National also has branches around the country, while Nedbank is in Mbabane, Manzini and Matsapha.

Taxes & Refunds
SOUTH AFRICA
South Africa has a value-added tax (VAT) of 14%, but departing foreign visitors can reclaim much of this on goods being taken out of the country. To make a claim, the goods must have been bought at a shop participating in the VAT foreign tourist sales scheme, their total value must exceed R250, and you will need a tax invoice for each item. This is usually the receipt, but must include the following:

- the words 'tax invoice'
- the seller's VAT registration number
- the seller's name and address
- a description of the goods purchased
- the cost of the goods and the amount of VAT charged, or a statement that VAT is included in the total cost of the goods
- a tax invoice number
- the date of the transaction.

For purchases over R500, your name and address and the quantity of goods must also appear on the invoice. All invoices must be originals – no photocopies.

At your point of departure, you'll need to fill in a form or two and show the goods to a customs inspector. At airports, make sure you have goods checked by the inspector before you check in your luggage. After going through immigration, make the claim and pick up your refund cheque; at some airports you can cash it immediately at a bank (in any major currency). If your claim comes to more than R3000, your cheque will be mailed to your home address. There's an efficient system in place in the Cape Town Tourism offices, and those of other major cities, enabling you to process the paperwork beforehand.

You can claim at the international airports in Jo'burg, Cape Town and Durban, and at the following local airports: Bloemfontein, Gateway, Lanseria, Mmabatho, Mpumalanga Kruger (Nelspruit), Port Elizabeth and Upington. It's also possible to claim at the Beitbridge (Zimbabwe) and Komatipoort (Mozambique) border crossings and at major harbours.

LESOTHO & SWAZILAND
Both Lesotho and Swaziland have a VAT of 14%, applied similarly to that in South Africa although there are not yet any systems for refunds in place. In both countries, many hotels omit the tax when quoting rates, although we've included it in the listings in this book.

Tipping
Wages are low, and tipping is expected; around 10% to 15% is usual in tourist areas. The main exceptions are in rural parts of Lesotho and Swaziland, where it's more normal to simply round up the bill.

PHOTOGRAPHY & VIDEO
In South Africa, film (slide and print), cameras and accessories are readily available in large towns, and processing, including slide processing, is generally of a high standard. Blank video tapes are available in major cities, although they won't work on North American machines. Film selection is much more limited in Lesotho and Swaziland, with a modest selection of print film available in major towns.

For wildlife photos, a good lightweight 35mm single lens reflex (SLR) automatic camera with a lens between 210mm and 300mm should do the trick. Video cameras with zoom facility may be able to get closer and digital cameras will perform all sorts of magic. An early start to the day is advisable as most wildlife is active during the cooler hours. When photographing animals, take light readings on the subject to avoid underexposure. The first two hours after sunrise and the last two before sunset are the best times of day to take photos on sunny days. In Lesotho and Swaziland, you can often capture some excellent special effects with the sunlight just after a summer storm.

In all three countries, be careful about taking photos of soldiers, police, airports, defence installations and government buildings. It goes without saying that you should always ask permission before taking a photo of anyone, but particularly so if you're in a tribal village.

Lonely Planet's *Travel Photography: A Guide to Taking Better Pictures* by Richard I'Anson will help you do just what the title says.

POST

Post offices are open from 8.30am to 4.30pm Monday to Friday and 8am to noon Saturday. Rates average R1.70 for a domestic letter, and from about R4 for an airmail letter. In South Africa and Swaziland, both domestic and international deliveries are generally reliable, but can be slow. In Lesotho, delivery is slow and unreliable. For mailing anything of value consider using one of the private mail services, such as Postnet. Poste restante is available in all major cities in South Africa, in Maseru in Lesotho, and in Manzini and Mbabane in Swaziland.

SHOPPING
South Africa

Handicrafts of varying quality are sold everywhere – though more expensively here than in Lesotho and Swaziland. Most carvings of animals and people are not traditional, although some are still quite attractive. Items to watch for include Venda pottery and woodcarvings, and Zulu beadwork and basketry. Township-produced crafts, such as wirework, also make great gifts, and are inexpensive and light to carry.

Western consumer goods are readily available in major towns and cities, where you'll invariably find department stores and shopping malls.

Lesotho

The famous Lesotho blanket – the country's all-purpose garment – is usually made outside Lesotho. However some local production remains, and these colourful wool and mohair textiles have been transformed into an art form in the internationally acclaimed wall hangings produced by Moteng weavers.

Other handicrafts include mohair tapestry, and woven-grass products such as mats, baskets and the ubiquitous Basotho hat. Trekking sticks come plain or decorated and can be found everywhere.

Swaziland

Because of the strength of Swaziland's traditional culture, many items here are made for the local market as much as for tourists. Popular items include woven grassware such as *liqhaga* ('bottles' that are so tightly woven that they are used for carrying water) and mats; and wooden items, ranging from bowls to *knobkerries* (traditional Southern African weapons/sticks). Swazi candles – works of art in wax – are also well worth seeking out. Good places to look for crafts include Malkerns, Mbabane and the Ezulwini Valley.

Bargaining

With the exception of the occasional curio stand, bargaining isn't expected in South Africa. In Lesotho and Swaziland, you'll find a mix of fixed-price shops, and curio stands where the vendors are willing to bargain.

SOLO TRAVELLERS

Solo travel in South Africa, Lesotho and Swaziland – whether you're male or female – is straightforward. While you may be a minor curiosity in rural areas, especially solo women travellers, it's likely that in most places no-one will even bat an eye. Times when you'd likely want to find a group to join up with would be for a safari (to cut costs), on hiking trails (many in South Africa have a three-person minimum for safety reasons), and at night. Especially in urban areas and at night, women travelling alone should use caution, and avoid isolating situations. See also p585.

TELEPHONE
South Africa

South Africa has good telephone facilities. Local calls are relatively inexpensive (about R0.75 for three minutes), whereas domestic long-distance calls (from about R1.30 per minute) and international calls (from R5 per minute to Europe) can be pricey. Phonecards are widely available. There are also private phone centres where you can pay cash for your call, but at double the rate of public phones. International calls are cheaper after 8pm on weekdays, and between 8pm Friday and 8am Monday. For reverse-charge calls, dial ☎ 0900.

A good way to avoid high charges when calling home, or to make reverse-charge calls, is to dial your 'Country Direct' number, which puts you through to an operator in your country. Major Country Direct numbers include:

Australia Direct (☎ 0800 990 061)
Belgium Direct (☎ 0800 990 032)
Canada Direct (☎ 0800 990 014)
Denmark Direct (☎ 0800 990 045)
Ireland Direct (☎ 0800 990 353)
Japan Direct (☎ 0800 990 081)
Netherlands Direct (☎ 0800 990 031)
New Zealand Direct (☎ 0800 990 064)
UK Direct – BT (☎ 0800 990 044)
UK Direct – Call UK (☎ 0800 990 544)
USA Direct – AT&T (☎ 0800 990 123)
USA Direct – MCI Call US (☎ 0800 990 011)
USA Direct – Sprint Express (☎ 0800 990 001)

Another good way to cut costs is to use Lonely Planet's **ekit card** (www.ekno.lonelyplanet .com), which provides cheap international calls for travellers. Access numbers from South Africa are ☎ 0800 997 285 or ☎ 0800 992 921.

PHONE CODES
South Africa's country code is ☎ 27. To make an international call from South Africa (including to Lesotho and Swaziland), dial ☎ 09, followed by the country code, local area code (without the initial zero) and telephone number.

Telephone numbers in South Africa are 10 digits, including the local area code, which must always be dialled, unless you are in the same town. South African area codes are given at the start of each section, or with the telephone number. There are also several four-digit nationwide prefixes (for use within South Africa only) followed by six-digit numbers. These prefixes include: ☎ 0800 (toll free), ☎ 0860 (charged as a local call), and ☎ 0861 (flat-rate calls).

MOBILE PHONES
The mobile-phone network covers most of the country, and mobile-phone ownership is widespread. The network operates on the GSM digital system, which you'll need to know if you're thinking of bringing your phone from home.

The three major mobile networks are **Vodacom** (www.vodacom.co.za), **MTN** (www.mtn.co.za) and **Cell C** (www.cellc.co.za). Hiring a mobile phone is relatively inexpensive, but call charges average about R2.50 per minute. Some car-rental firms offer deals on mobile phones. An alternative is to use your own phone (check ahead that it's compatible),

and insert a local prepaid or pay-as-you-go SIM card from one of the three mobile networks. These cards are readily available at shopping malls and shops in all larger cities and towns.

The main codes for mobile phones are: ☎ 082 (Vodacom), ☎ 083 (MTN) and ☎ 084 (Cell C).

Lesotho
Lesotho's telephone system works reasonably well, although you don't have to go far off the beaten track to be away from the telephone system altogether.

The country code is ☎ 266; there are no area codes. To make international calls, including to South Africa, dial ☎ 00, followed by the country code, area code (minus the initial zero) and telephone number. For international reverse charge calls dial ☎ 109.

The main cellphone service is provided by **Vodacom Lesotho** (☎ 212000; www.vodacom.co.ls), based in Maseru. The coverage area extends north to Butha-Buthe, south to Quthing (Moyeni) and east to Mohale Dam. Charges are similar to those in South Africa.

Swaziland
Swaziland also has a reasonably good telephone network. The country code is ☎ 268; there are no area codes. To make international calls, including to South Africa, dial ☎ 00 for international, then the country code and city code. Dial ☎ 94 to make a reverse-charge call.

International calls are expensive, and most easily made using phonecards. You can also make international calls (but not reverse-charge calls) at the Mbabane post office. Outside of major towns, it's necessary to book international calls through an operator (☎ 94).

Mobile-phone services are provided by **MTN** (www.swazimtn.sz) and **Vodacom** (www.voda com.co.za).

TIME
South African Standard Time is two hours ahead of GMT/UTC, seven hours ahead of USA Eastern Standard Time, and eight hours behind Australian Eastern Standard Time. At noon in Jo'burg, it's 10am in London, 5am in New York, and 8pm in Sydney. There is no daylight-saving time. Lesotho and Swaziland are in the same time zone as South Africa.

This is a wide region to be covered by one time zone and the sun rises and sets noticeably earlier in Durban than it does in Cape Town. Most timetables and businesses use the 24-hour clock.

TOILETS

Finding a clean, Western-style toilet in South Africa is usually not a problem. There are few public toilets, but tourist information offices and restaurants are often willing to give you a key to their facilities. In rural areas, and anywhere outside of major towns in Swaziland and Lesotho, long-drops – holes in the ground, sometimes with footrests or makeshift seats – are the norm.

TOURIST INFORMATION
South Africa

The main government tourism organisation is **South African Tourism** (☎ 011-778 8000; www .southafrica.net), which has a helpful website with news of upcoming events and various links.

For more detail on individual provinces, there are provincial tourism organisations, of varying quality. In addition to these, almost every town in the country has at least one tourist office. These are private entities, and depend on commissions (5% is usually built into their hotel rates) for their existence. Also, be aware that many tourist offices will only recommend the services of member organisations (ie those that have paid up) – you may well have to push to find out about all the possible options, especially cheaper accommodation.

Provincial tourist offices include:
Eastern Cape Tourism Board (☎ 043-701 9600; www.ectourism.co.za)
Free State Tourism Board (☎ 051-447 1362; www .dteea.fs.gov.za)
Gauteng Tourism Authority (☎ 011-327 2000; www .gauteng.net)
KwaZulu-Natal Tourism Authority (☎ 031-366 7500; www.kzn.org.za)
Limpopo Tourism Board (☎ 015-295 8262; www .limpopotourism.org.za)
Mpumalanga Tourism Authority (☎ 013-752 7001; www.mpumalanga.com)
North-West Province Parks & Tourism Board (☎ 018-386 1225; www.tourismnorthwest.co.za)
Northern Cape Tourism Authority (☎ 053-832 2657; www.northerncape.org.za)
Western Cape Tourism Board (☎ 021-426 5639; www.capetourism.org)

TOURIST OFFICES ABROAD
South African Tourism offices abroad include the following:
Australia (☎ 02-9261 3424; sydney@southafricantourism .com; level 6, 285 Clarence St, Sydney, NSW 2000)
France (☎ 01 45 61 01 97; paris@southafricantourism .com; 61 Rue La Boëtie, 75008 Paris)
Germany (☎ 069-929 1290; frankfurt@southafricantour ism.com; An der Hauptwache 11, D-60313 Frankfurt)
Japan (☎ 03-3478 7601; tokyo@southafricantourism .com; Akasaka Lions Bldg, 1-1-2 Moto Akasaka, Minato-ku, Tokyo 107-0051)
UK (☎ 0181-971 9350; london@southafricantourism.com; 6 Alt Grove, Wimbledon, London SW19 4DZ)
USA (☎ 212-730 2929; us@southafricantourism.com; 20th fl, 500 Fifth Ave, New York, NY 10110)

Lesotho & Swaziland

The **Lesotho Tourism Board** (☎ 2231 2896; ltbhq@ltb .org.ls; Kingsway) in Maseru can provide general information about the country. Better is the tourism page on the **Lesotho government website** (www.lesotho.gov.ls).

Swaziland isn't well served by official tourist services, either internally or externally. The two main tourist offices are the **tourist office** (☎ 442 4206) at Mantenga Craft Centre in the Ezulwini Valley, and the main **tourist information office** (☎ 404 2531; Swazi Plaza) in Mbabane. Main tourism websites include www.welcometoswaziland.com and www .mintour.gov.sz.

VISAS
South Africa

Visitors on holiday from most Commonwealth countries (including Australia and the UK), most Western European countries, Japan and the USA don't require visas. Instead, you'll be issued with a free entry permit on arrival. These are valid for a stay of up to 90 days. However, if the date of your flight out is sooner than this, the immigration officer will use it as the date of your permit expiry unless you specifically request otherwise.

If you aren't entitled to an entry permit, you'll need to get a visa (also free) before you arrive. These aren't issued at the borders, and must be obtained at a South African embassy or consulate. Allow up to several weeks for processing. South Africa has consular representation in most countries, with a partial listing given on p575. The website of the South African High Commission in

London (www.southafricahouse.com) has a helpful overview of visa requirements, and lists the nationalities that require visas.

If you do need a visa (rather than an entry permit), get a multiple-entry visa if you plan to make a foray into Lesotho, Swaziland or any other neighbouring country. This avoids the hassle of applying for another South African visa in a small town such as Maseru or Mbabane.

For any entry – whether you require a visa or not – you need to have at least two completely blank pages in your passport, excluding the last two pages.

VISA EXTENSIONS

Applications for visa or entry-permit extensions, and for re-entry visas, should be made at the **Department of Home Affairs** (http://home-aff airs.pwv.gov.za), with branches in Cape Town, Durban, Jo'burg and Pretoria. Visa extensions cost about R400.

Lesotho

Citizens of most Western European countries, Japan, Israel, the USA and most Commonwealth countries are granted a free entry permit at the border. The standard permitted stay is two weeks, although if you ask for longer it's often granted. For a lengthier stay, you'll need to apply in advance to the **Director of Immigration & Passport Services** (☎ 2232 3771, 2232 1110; PO Box 363, Maseru 100).

Travellers who require visas can get these in South Africa (see Embassies & Consulates, p575). You'll need one passport photo and R30/50 for single/multiple entry; processing takes 24 hours. If you arrive at the Maseru Bridge border crossing without a visa and with some luck, you'll be issued a temporary entry permit to allow you to get into Maseru, where you can apply for a visa at the Ministry of Immigration. However, don't count on this, as it depends completely on the whim of the border officials.

Swaziland

Most people don't need a visa to visit Swaziland. For those who do (including citizens of Austria and Switzerland), they are available free of charge at border posts and at the airport. In South Africa, you can get them in Pretoria and Jo'burg (see p575). In countries without Swazi diplomatic representation, contact the UK representative.

Anyone staying for more than 60 days must apply for a temporary residence permit from the **Chief Immigration Officer** (☎ 404 2941; PO Box 372, Mbabane).

Visas for Neighbouring Countries

Visas for Namibia are not issued at the border, though many nationalities don't require one. Visas for Zimbabwe and Mozambique are available at the borders. For Mozambique it's cheaper to arrange your visa in advance at the Mozambican High Commission in Mbabane, or in Nelspruit. Both issue express visas in 24 hours.

If you'll be arranging your visa in advance: Zimbabwean visas take at least a week to issue in South Africa; those for Namibia take two to three days; and those for Botswana take between four and 14 days. Nonexpress Mozambique visas take one week.

WOMEN TRAVELLERS
Attitudes Towards Women

Sexism is a common attitude among South African men, regardless of colour. Modern ideas such as equality of the sexes have not filtered through to many people, especially away from the cities. Women are usually called 'ladies' unless they play sport, in which case they are called 'girls'.

Fortunately times are changing and there are plenty of women who don't put up with this, but South African society as a whole is still decades behind most developed countries. Also, ironically, there has been something of an antifeminist backlash without there having been many feminist gains in the first place. The fact that black women were at the forefront in the liberation struggle and that many of them have entered politics may change this, however.

Not surprisingly, there are big differences between the lives of women in the region's various cultures. In traditional black cultures, women often have a very tough time, but this is changing to some extent because a surprising number of girls have the opportunity to stay at school while the boys are sent away to work. In South Africa's white communities, however, the number of girls finishing secondary school is significantly lower than the number of boys, which is against international trends.

The practice of female genital mutilation (female circumcision) is not part of the traditional cultures of South Africa (or Lesotho or Swaziland).

There's a very high level of sexual assault and other violence against women in South Africa, the majority of which occurs in townships and rural areas. Given the extremely high levels of HIV/AIDS in the country, the problem is compounded through the transfer of infection.

A large part of the problem in South Africa is the leniency of the judicial system that repeatedly lets perpetrators of sex offences off with short sentences. This, particularly in recent times, has had women's groups around the country voicing their concerns and demanding that the government step in and take tougher action.

There have been incidents of travellers being raped, but these cases are isolated, and cause outrage in local communities. For most female visitors paternalistic attitudes are the main problem rather than physical assault.

Safety Precautions

Single female travellers have a curiosity value that makes them conspicuous, but it may also bring forth generous offers of assistance and hospitality. It is always difficult to quantify the risk of assault – and there is such a risk – but plenty of women do travel alone safely in South Africa.

Obviously the risk varies depending on where you go and what you do. Hitching alone is extremely foolhardy. What risks there are, however, are significantly reduced if two women travel together or, even better, if a woman travels as part of a mixed-sex couple or group. But while the days of apartheid have long gone, a mixed-race couple will almost certainly attract attention and receive some antagonistic reactions – old attitudes die hard.

However you travel, especially inland and in the more traditional black communities, it's best to behave conservatively. On the coast, casual dress is the norm, but elsewhere dress modestly (full-length clothes that aren't too tight) if you do not wish to draw attention to yourself. Don't go out alone in the evenings on foot – always take a taxi; avoid isolated areas, roadways and beaches during both day and evening hours; avoid hiking alone; and carry a mobile phone if you'll be driving alone.

Although urban attitudes are more liberal, common sense and caution, particularly at night, are essential.

WORK

Unemployment is high in South Africa, and finding work is difficult. There are tough penalties for employers taking on foreigners without work permits, although this doesn't seem to have stopped foreigners getting jobs in restaurants or bars in tourist areas. If you do line something up, you can usually earn from around R15 per hour plus tips (which can be good). The best time to look for work is from October to November, before the high season starts, and before university students begin holidays.

Volunteer work is a more likely possibility, especially if you're interested in teaching or wildlife conservation. A good initial contact is **Volunteer Abroad** (www.volunteerabroad .com), with extensive listings of volunteer opportunities in the country.

Unless you have a UK passport, anyone coming to South Africa to do volunteer work needs to get a work permit. Applications for these should be made through the South African embassy or consulate in your home country; processing usually takes one month.

Transport

> **THINGS CHANGE**
>
> The information in this chapter is particularly vulnerable to change. Check directly with the airline or a travel agent to make sure you understand how a fare (and ticket you may buy) works, and be aware of the security requirements for international travel. Shop carefully. The details given in this chapter should be regarded as pointers and are not a substitute for your own careful, up-to-date research.

GETTING THERE & AWAY

ENTRY REQUIREMENTS
Passports

As long as you have complied with visa and entry permit requirements (see p584), there are no restrictions on any nationalities for entering South Africa, Lesotho or Swaziland.

Entering South Africa

Once you have an entry permit or visa (see p584), South Africa is straightforward and hassle-free to enter. Travellers arriving by air are required to have an onward ticket – preferably an air ticket, though an overland ticket also seems to be acceptable. On arrival you may have to satisfy immigration officials that you have sufficient funds for your stay, so it pays to be neat, clean and polite.

If you're coming to South Africa after travelling through the yellow-fever zone in Africa (which includes most of East, West and Central Africa) or South America, you must have an international vaccination certificate against yellow fever. No other vaccinations are mandatory, although there are some you should consider (607).

Entering Lesotho

Almost everyone enters Lesotho overland from South Africa, although it's also possible to fly from Johannesburg (Jo'burg). Entry permits are easy to get at any of Lesotho's borders and at the airport. If you are a citizen of a country for which a visa is required (see p584), it's best to arrange this in advance. Vaccination certificate requirements are the same as those for South Africa.

Entering Swaziland

Most travellers enter Swaziland overland, although it's also possible to fly in from South Africa and Mozambique. Entry is usually hassle-free. Visas are readily available at the border for those nationalities that require one (see p584), although you'll save yourself queuing time by arranging the visa in advance. Vaccination certificate requirements are the same as for South Africa.

AIR
Airports & Airlines

The major air hub for South Africa, and for the entire surrounding region, is **Johannesburg International Airport** (code JIA or JNB; ☎ 011-921 6911; www.johannesburg-jnb.com). It's had a face-lift, and has a full range of shops, restaurants, Internet access, ATMs, foreign exchange bureaus and mobile-phone rental shops.

Cape Town International Airport (code CPT; ☎ 021-937 1200; www.airports.co.za) receives numerous direct flights from Europe, and is becoming an increasingly important gateway. It has a forex bureau, and mobile-phone rental shops.

The smaller **Durban International Airport** (code DUR; ☎ 031-451 6666; www.airports.co.za) handles several regional flights, as does **Mpumalanga Kruger International Airport** (code MQP; ☎ 013-753 7500) near Nelspruit and Kruger National Park.

Lesotho's **Moshoeshoe International Airport** (code MSU; ☎ 2235 0777), 21km southeast of Maseru, and Swaziland's **Matsapha International Airport** (code MTS; ☎ 84455), 8km west of Manzini, handle regional flights only.

South African Airways (SAA; airline code SA; ☎ 0860 359 722, 011-978 1111; www.flysaa.com; hub JIA) is the national airline, with an excellent route network and safety record. In addition to its international routes, it operates regional flights together with its subsidiaries **South African Airlink** (SAAirlink; ☎ 011-978 1111; www.saairlink.co.za) and **South African Express** (☎ 011-978 5577; www.saexpress.co.za).

Other international carriers flying to/from Jo'burg include:

Air France (airline code AF; ☎ 0860 340 340, Cape Town 021-934 8818; www.airfrance.fr; hub Charles de Gaulle Airport, Paris)

Air Mauritius (airline code MK; Jo'burg ☎ 011-444 4600, Cape Town 021-421 6294; www.airmauritius.com; hub SSR Airport, Mauritius) Also serves Cape Town.

Air Namibia (airline code SW; Jo'burg ☎ 011-390 2876, Cape Town 021-936 2755; www.airnamibia.com.na; hub Chief Hosea Kutako Airport, Windhoek) Also serves Cape Town.

British Airways (airline code BA; Jo'burg ☎ 011-441 8600, Cape Town 021-934 0292; www.britishairways.com; hub Heathrow Airport, London) Also serves Cape Town.

Cathay Pacific (airline code CX; ☎ 011-700 8900; www.cathaypacific.com; hub Hong Kong International Airport)

Comair (airline code MN; ☎ 0860 435 922, Jo'burg 011-921 0222; www.comair.co.za; hub JIA) Operates British Airways flights within Africa.

Egyptair (airline code MS; ☎ 011-390 2202, 880 4126; www.egyptair.com.eg; hub Cairo International Airport)

Emirates Airlines (airline code EK; ☎ 011-883 8420; www.emirates.com; hub Dubai International Airport)

Kenya Airways (airline code KQ; ☎ 011-881 9696, 881 9795; www.kenya-airways.com; hub Jomo Kenyatta International Airport, Nairobi)

KLM (airline code KL; ☎ 0860 247 747, 082-234 5747; www.klm.com; hub Schiphol Airport, Amsterdam) Also serves Cape Town.

LTU International Airways (airline code LT; ☎ 021-936 1190; www.ltu.de; hub Düsseldorf Airport, Düsseldorf)

Lufthansa (airline code LH; ☎ 0861 266 554, Cape Town 021-415 3735; www.lufthansa.com; hub Frankfurt International Airport) Also serves Cape Town.

Malaysia Airlines (airline code MH; Jo'burg ☎ 011-880 1916, Cape Town 021-419 8010; www.malaysiaairlines.com; hub Kuala Lumpur) Also flies to Cape Town.

Qantas (airline code QF; ☎ 011-441 8550; www.qantas.com.au; hub Kingsford Smith Airport, Sydney)

Singapore Airlines (airline code SQ; Jo'burg ☎ 011-880 8560, Cape Town 021-674 0601; www.singaporeair.com; hub Singapore Changi Airport) Also serves Cape Town.

Swiss International Airlines (airline code LX; ☎ 0800 555 777; www.swiss.com; hub Kloten Airport, Zurich)

Virgin Atlantic (airline code VS; Jo'burg ☎ 011-340 3400, Cape Town 021-683 2221; www.virgin-atlantic.com; hub London) Also serves Cape Town.

SAAirlink is the only commercial carrier currently flying into Lesotho. **Swazi Express Airways** (☎ 518 6840; www.swaziexpress.com) and **Swaziland Airlink** (☎ 518 6155; www.saairlink.co.za), both based at Matsapha International Airport, are the main regional carriers servicing Swaziland. Swaziland Airlink is a joint venture between the Swazi government and SAAirlink in South Africa; it has replaced Royal Swazi Airways as the national carrier.

Tickets

South Africa is well served by various European carriers, as well as by direct flights from Australasia and North America. Fares from Europe and North America are usually highest in December and January, and again between July and September. They're lowest in April and May (except for the Easter holiday period) and in November. The rest of the year falls into the shoulder season category, although it's worth hunting for special deals at any time. London is the main hub for discounted fares. It's often slightly cheaper to fly into Jo'burg, than directly to Cape Town. Useful online ticket sellers include:

Cheapflights (www.cheap-flights.co.uk) With links to online travel agents in the UK.

Flight Centre (www.flightcentre.com)

Flights.com (www.eltexpress.com)

Microsoft Expedia (www.expedia.co.uk; www.expedia.ca)

OneTravel.com (www.onetravel.com)

STA Travel (www.statravel.com)

Travel.com.au (www.travel.com.au) Bookings from Australia.
Travelocity (www.travelocity.com)

COURIER FLIGHTS

Courier fares can be a bargain way of getting to South Africa, although you may have to surrender all your baggage allowance, take only carry-on luggage, and have limited or no flexibility with flight dates and times. Most courier flights are into Jo'burg, with some into Cape Town. The **International Association of Air Travel Couriers** (www.aircourier.co.uk), and the **Air Courier Association** (www.aircourier.org), are good places to start looking; for both you'll need to pay a modest membership fee to access their fares. Be aware that many of the advertised courier fares are for one way only.

INTERCONTINENTAL (ROUND-THE-WORLD) TICKETS

Round-the-world (RTW) tickets give you a limited period (usually a year) to circumnavigate the globe. You can go anywhere that the carrying airline and its partners go, as long as you stay within the set mileage or number of stops, and don't backtrack. RTW tickets that include Jo'burg or Cape Town start at around UK£1400 from the UK (about A$2850 from Australia). While it's possible to include both Jo'burg and Cape Town on a RTW itinerary, this usually means flying into one city and out of the other. In between the two cities you'll need to travel overland or arrange a domestic flight.

Travel agents can also put together 'alternative' RTW tickets, which are more expensive, but more flexible, than standard RTW itineraries. If you want a multiple-stop itinerary without the cost of a RTW ticket, consider combining tickets from two low-cost airlines.

Online RTW ticket sellers include:

Airbrokers (www.airbrokers.com) For travel originating in North America.
Airtreks (www.airtreks.com) For travel originating in Canada or the USA.
Oneworld (www.oneworld.com) An airline alliance offering RTW packages.
Roundtheworldflights.com (www.roundtheworld flights.com) For travel originating in the UK.
Star Alliance (www.staralliance.com) An airline alliance offering RTW packages.

DEPARTURE TAX

Airport departure tax is included in ticket prices in South Africa. Departure tax in Lesotho is M20, and in Swaziland it's E20. On flights from Swaziland into South Africa, there is an additional tax of R120.

From Africa

There are good connections between Jo'burg and most major African cities on SAA and on regional airlines. An overview follows.

Antananarivo, Madagascar Air Madagascar (www .airmadagascar.mg) Connections to Mauritius and Réunion.
Bulawayo, Zimbabwe Air Zimbabwe (www.airzim.co.zw)
Dar es Salaam, Tanzania SAA (www.flysaa.com)
Gaborone, Botswana Air Botswana (www.airbotswana .co.bw)
Harare, Zimbabwe Air Zimbabwe, Comair (www.comair .co.za)
Lagos, Nigeria SAA
Maputo, Mozambique SAA, Linhas Aéreas de Moçambique (www.lam.co.mz)
Mauritius Air Mauritius (www.airmauritius.com)
Nairobi, Kenya SAA, Kenya Airways (www.kenya-air ways.com) Kenya Airways also flies between Nairobi and Cape Town.
Victoria Falls, Zimbabwe side Air Zimbabwe, Comair
Windhoek, Namibia Comair, Air Namibia (www.air namibia.com.na) Both also fly between Windhoek and Cape Town.

Most intra-African flights have set pricing, with little of the competition-driven discounting that you'll find in other parts of the world. However, there are sometimes good deals available. For round-trip fares, always ask about excursion rates and student discounts. It's often cheaper to buy a return rather than a one-way fare. Some sample one-way fares/durations: Jo'burg to Maputo (US$130, one hour); Jo'burg to Dar es Salaam (US$500, 3½ hours); Jo'burg to Antananarivo (US$550 to US$750 depending on season, three hours). Discount travel agents in South Africa that handle regional and international flights include:

Flight Centre (☎ 0860 400 727, Jo'burg 011-327 5355, Cape Town 021-939 4280; www.flightcentre.co.za) An international agency with offices in Jo'burg, Cape Town and several other cities; guarantees that it will beat any genuine quoted current price.

TRANSPORT

Rennies Travel (☎ 0861 100 155, Jo'burg 011-407 3211; www.renniestravel.co.za) The Thomas Cook agent, with offices in Jo'burg and throughout South Africa.

STA Travel (Jo'burg ☎ 011-447 5414, Cape Town 021-418 6570; www.statravel.co.za) The queen of student and budget travel agencies, with offices in Jo'burg, Cape Town and elsewhere.

The only commercial flight to/from Lesotho is SAAirlink's three-times daily run between Jo'burg and Moshoeshoe airport (R1079 one way, one hour).

Swaziland Airlink, a division of SAAirlink, flies three times daily between Matsapha and Jo'burg (R1015, one hour). Swazi Express flights link Swaziland's Matsapha airport with Durban (R930, one hour), with a connection on to Maputo, Mozambique, R700, 30 minutes).

From Asia

Direct flights link Jo'burg with Singapore (Singapore Airlines, 10½ hours), Hong Kong (Cathay Pacific, 13 hours) and Kuala Lumpur (Malaysia Airlines, 10½ hours). It's also possible to connect from Asia (Singapore, Hong Kong and Mumbai) to Mauritius on Air Mauritius, and then from there to Jo'burg (four hours between Mauritius and Jo'burg). Singapore, Hong Kong and Bangkok are the best places to shop for discount tickets. Useful ticket discounters include:

Phoenix Services (☎ 2722 7378; Hong Kong)

Shoestring Travel (☎ 2723 2306; Hong Kong)

STA Travel Bangkok (☎ 02-236 0262, ext 211-4; www.statravel.co.th); Singapore (☎ 6737 7188; www .statravel.com.sg)

STIC Travels (☎ 011-2335 7468; www.stictravel.com; New Delhi)

Traveller Services (☎ 2375 2222; www.taketraveller .com; Hong Kong)

Some sample round-trip fares: Jo'burg–Hong Kong US$920; Jo'burg–Singapore US$1100; Jo'burg–Mauritius US$430.

From Australia & New Zealand

There are direct flights from Sydney on Qantas and SAA, and from Perth on SAA, to Jo'burg and Cape Town. Expect to pay from around A$1920/1720 round-trip between Sydney/Perth and Jo'burg (flying time about 14 hours from Sydney, 10½ hours from Perth). Air Mauritius has a few direct flights from Perth to Mauritius with

a stopover, then a direct flight to Jo'burg for around A$1580 return. Alternatively, you can connect on Air Mauritius via Singapore, Hong Kong or Mumbai (Bombay).

Singapore Airlines and Malaysia Airlines are both worth checking for special deals, with return fares between Sydney and Jo'burg/Cape Town starting at about A$1680. Return tickets to/from the UK via Jo'burg and Asia are also worth looking into.

Good places to start your ticket search include:

Flight Centre (☎ 13 16 00 Australia-wide; www.flight centre.com.au) Branches throughout Australia.

STA Travel (☎ 1300-733 035, 03-8417 6911; www.sta travel.com.au) Branches in all major cities and on many university campuses.

There are no direct flights from New Zealand; the best options are going via Australia, Singapore or Malaysia. Expect to pay around NZ$2300 for a return. **Flight Centre** (☎ 09-309 6171; www.flightcentre.com) and **STA Travel** (☎ 0508 782 872; www.statravel.co.nz) both have many branches throughout the country.

From Canada & the USA

SAA flies direct from both New York and Atlanta to Jo'burg (from US$1100 round-trip, 17½ hours), and this is generally one of the least expensive routings.

Otherwise, the best fares are via London, with good deals sometimes available from Amsterdam or other European capitals. The cheapest way to do things is to fly first to London on an inexpensive airline, and then buy a bucket-shop or online ticket from there to South Africa. Expect to pay from US$1300 round-trip for the entire routing.

From the US west coast, you can sometimes get good deals via Asia. Malaysia Airlines flies from Los Angeles to Kuala Lumpur, from where you can connect to Jo'burg and Cape Town.

Discounters include:

Flight Centre (☎ 888-967 5355; www.flightcentre.ca; Canada)

STA Travel (☎ 800-781 4040; www.statravel.com; USA)

Travel CUTS (☎ 800-667 2887; www.travelcuts.com; Canada)

From Continental Europe

You can fly to South Africa from any European capital, with the major hubs Paris, Amsterdam, Frankfurt and, to a lesser extent, Zurich. All are within an approximately nine-hour flight of Jo'burg. All the European airlines listed on p587 fly into Jo'burg, with several, including British Airways, KLM and Lufthansa, also flying into Cape Town. Some will allow you to fly into one city and out of the other for no extra charge. Round-trip fares into Jo'burg start from about €600. Check with the following agencies for discounted fares:

Kilroy Travels Netherlands (☎ 020-524 5100; www.kilroytravels.com); Germany (☎ 030-310 0040)

Nouvelles Frontières (☎ nationwide 08 25 00 08 25, Paris 01 45 68 70 00; www.nouvelles-frontieres.fr; France)

OTU Voyages (☎ 01 40 29 12 12; www.otu.fr; France)

SSR (☎ 01-261 2954; www.ssr.ch; Switzerland)

STA Travel (☎ 01805-456 422, 030-2016 5063; www.statravel.de; Germany)

From the Middle East

The best connections are to Jo'burg from Cairo (Air Kenya, Egypt Air), and from Dubai (Emirates). Expect to pay from US$600. Agencies to try in the region include:

Egypt Panorama Tours (☎ Cairo 02-350 5880; www.eptours.com; Egypt)

Israel Student Travel Association (ISSTA; ☎ Jerusalem 02-625 7257; Israel)

From South America

SAA and **Varig** (www.varig.com.br) link São Paulo and Jo'burg (about nine hours), with connections in South America to Rio de Janeiro, Brasília and various other cities. Malaysia Airlines flies between Cape Town and Buenos Aires. Expect to pay from US$1400 round-trip between the two continents.

From the UK & Ireland

Fares between the UK and South Africa (about 13½ hours flying time) are very competitive, with return tickets to Jo'burg starting from about UK£550. Airlines flying between London and South Africa include British Airways, Virgin Atlantic and SAA. There are no direct flights between Ireland and South Africa. You'll need to connect via London or a continental European capital.

Most British travel agents are registered with the **Association of British Travel Agents** (ABTA; www.abta.com), which will give you some protection if the agent you buy your ticket from goes out of business. Tickets from unregistered bucket shops are riskier but sometimes

cheaper. London is the best place to buy a ticket, but specialist agencies elsewhere in the UK can provide comparable value.

The following companies are considered reliable:

Africa Travel Centre (☎ 020-7387 1211; www.africatravel.co.uk)

Bridge the World (☎ 0870 444 7474; www.b-t-w.co.uk)

North-South Travel (☎ 01245-608291; www.northsouthtravel.co.uk)

STA Travel (☎ 0870 160 0599; www.statravel.co.uk)

Trailfinders (☎ 020-7938 3939; www.trailfinders.com)

Travel Bag (☎ 0870 890 1456; www.travelbag.co.uk)

Also check ads in weekend newspapers, travel magazines and listings in free magazines, especially the *SA Times*, which is aimed at South Africans in the UK.

LAND
Bicycle

There are no restrictions on bringing your own bicycle into South Africa, Lesotho or Swaziland. Two helpful sources of background information are the **International Bicycle Fund** (☎ in the USA 206-767 0848; www.ibike.org) and **SA-Cycling** (www.sa-cycling.com).

Border Crossings
BOTSWANA

There are 15 official South Africa/Botswana border posts. All are open between 8am and 4pm, and many have longer hours. The main ones are at **Ramatlhabama** (☼ 6am-8pm) north of Mafikeng; **Skilpadshek/Pioneer Gate** (☼ 6am-10pm) northwest of Zeerust; and **Kapfontein/Tlokweng Gate** (☼ 6am-10pm) north of Zeerust. Others include **McCarthy's Rust** (☼ 6am-6pm) near Kgalagadi Transfrontier Park; and **Martin's Drift** (☼ 8am-6pm) northwest of Polokwane/Pietersburg. Some of the more remote crossings are impassable to 2WD vehicles, and may be closed completely during periods of high water. Otherwise, the crossings are hassle-free.

LESOTHO

All of landlocked Lesotho's borders (listed next) are with South Africa, and are straightforward to cross. The main crossing is at Maseru Bridge, east of Bloemfontein; queues here are often very long exiting Lesotho, and also sometimes on weekend evenings coming into Lesotho, so use other posts if possible.

TRANSPORT

LESOTHO BORDERS

Border crossing	Opening hours	Nearest Lesotho/South Africa town
Caledonspoort	6am-10pm	Butha-Buthe/Fouriesburg
Ficksburg Bridge	24hr	Maputsoe/Ficksburg
Makhaleng Bridge	8am-6pm Mon-Fri, 8am-4pm Sat & Sun	Mohale's Hoek/Zastron
Maseru Bridge	24hr	Maseru/Ladybrand
Nkonkoana Gate	8am-4pm	Sehlabathebe/Bushman's Nek
Ongeluksnek	8am-4pm	Mphaki/Matatiele
Peka Bridge	8am-4pm	Peka/Clocolan
Qacha's Nek	7am-10pm	Qacha's Nek/Matatiele
Ramatseliso's Gate	7am-5pm	Tsoelike/Matatiele
Sani Pass	8am-4pm	Mokhotlong/Himeville
Sephapo's Gate	8am-4pm	Mafeteng/Boesmanskop
Tele Bridge	8am-10pm	Quthing/Sterkspruit
Van Rooyens Gate	6am-10pm	Mafeteng/Wepener

MOZAMBIQUE
South Africa/Mozambique border posts are at **Komatipoort/Ressano Garcia** (☉ 6am-7pm), east of Nelspruit and heavily travelled; and at **Kosi Bay/Ponta d'Ouro** (☉ 8am-4pm) on the coast, well north of Durban.

NAMIBIA
There are South Africa/Namibia border posts at **Nakop/Ariamsvlei** (☉ 24hr) west of Upington; at **Vioolsdrif/Noordoewer** (☉ 24hr) north of Springbok and en route to/from Cape Town; and at **Rietfontein/Aroab** (☉ 6am-10pm) just south of Kgalagadi Transfrontier Park. It's not possible to cross the border at Kgalagadi Transfrontier Park itself; Rietfontein is the closest crossing. There's also a border post at **Alexander Bay/Oranjemund** (☉ 6am-10pm) on the coast, but public access is usually not permitted. Note that Namibian visas are not available at any of these border posts.

SWAZILAND
There are 12 South Africa/Swaziland border posts, all of which are hassle-free. Note that small posts close at 4pm. The busiest crossing (and a good place to pick up lifts) is at **Oshoek/Ngwenya** (☉ 7am-10pm) about 360km southeast of Pretoria. Others include **Mahamba** (☉ 7am-10pm), which is the best crossing to use from Piet Retief in Mpumalanga; **Josefsdal/Bulembu** (☉ 7am-4pm), along the unpaved road from Piggs Peak to Barberton (Mpumalanga) and tricky in wet weather; **Matsamo/Jeppe's Reef** (☉ 7am-8pm), which is southwest of Malelane and a pos-

sible route to Kruger National Park; **Mananga** (☉ 7am-6pm), southwest of Komatipoort; **Onverwacht/Salitje** (☉ 7am-4pm), north of Pongola in KwaZulu-Natal; and **Golela/Lavumisa** (☉ 7am-10pm), en route between Durban and Swaziland's Ezulwini Valley.

The Swaziland/Mozambique border is at busy **Lomahasha/Namaacha** (☉ 7am-5pm) in the extreme northeast of the country. Another border post with Mozambique, at Goba/Mhlumeni, is scheduled to open soon. Mozambique visas are currently being issued at Lomahasha, but it's better and cheaper to get them in Mbabane.

There's an E5 road tax for vehicles entering Swaziland. If you're continuing from Swaziland into Mozambique, your car must have two red hazard triangles in the boot in case of a breakdown. All of Swaziland's borders can be comfortably crossed in a 2WD, except for Josefsdal/Bulembu, which is possible in a 2WD but smoother with a 4WD.

ZIMBABWE
The only border post between Zimbabwe and South Africa is at **Beitbridge** (☉ 5.30am-10.30pm) on the Limpopo River. There's lots of smuggling, so searches are thorough and queues often long. The closest South African town to the border is Musina (15km south), where you can change money.

Vehicles pay a R130 toll at the border to use the Limpopo Bridge, when entering or leaving South Africa. South Africans need a visa (free) to get into Zimbabwe but can obtain it at the border. Most other nationalities, including Commonwealth and US passport holders, require visas, which are available at the border, payable in US dollars only.

Ignore the touts on the Zimbabwe side trying to 'help' you through Zimbabwe immigration and customs. Despite their insistence, there's no charge for the government forms needed for immigration.

Bus

Numerous buses cross the borders between South Africa and all of its neighbours. These are the most efficient way to travel overland, unless you have your own vehicle. Other than sometimes lengthy queues, there are usually no hassles. At the border, you'll need to disembark to take care of visa formalities, then reboard your same bus and continue on. Visa prices are not included in the ticket price for trans-border routes. Many bus lines offer student discounts, upon presentation of a student ID.

It's also possible to travel to/from all of South Africa's neighbours by local minibus taxi. A few routes go direct, though sometimes it's necessary to walk across the border and change vehicles on the other side.

Car & Motorcycle

If you're arriving in South Africa via car or motorcycle, you'll need the vehicle's registration papers, liability insurance and your licence (see p600). You'll also need a *carnet de passage en douane*, which acts as a temporary waiver of import duty. The carnet – which should be arranged through your local automobile association – should specify any expensive spare parts that you're planning to carry with you, such as a gearbox. South African registered vehicles don't need a carnet to visit any of South Africa's neighbouring countries.

The requirements for entering Swaziland and Lesotho are the same as for South Africa. If you're driving a car rented in South Africa and plan to take it across international borders, including into Lesotho or Swaziland, you'll need to get a permission form from your rental company.

For information on road rules, see p603.

Border posts themselves generally don't have petrol stations or repair shops; you'll need to go to the nearest large town.

From Botswana

BUS

From Jo'burg/Pretoria, **Intercape Mainliner** (☎ 0861 287 287, 021-380 4400; www.intercape.co.za) runs daily buses to Gaborone (R125, six hours). A cheaper but less safe and less comfortable alternative is one of the minibuses that run throughout the day between Jo'burg and Gaborone (R75, six hours) via Mafikeng (North-West Province). In Gaborone, these leave from the northwest corner of the main bus terminal starting at 6am. In Jo'burg, departures are from Park Station. To do the trip in stages, take a City Link bus from Jo'burg to Mafikeng, from where there are direct minibuses over the border to Lobatse (R17, 1½ hours). There are also direct minibuses between Jo'burg and Palapye (Botswana) via Martin's Drift (R80, eight hours).

TRAIN

There are no cross-border trains, but it's possible to travel the Botswana leg of the journey between Francistown, near the border with Zimbabwe, and Lobatse, near the border with South Africa, via Gaborone.

From Lesotho

BUS

A direct bus – currently the Big Sky line – runs Monday to Friday between Bloemfontein and Maseru (R45, three hours). Via minibus taxi, the quickest connections are from Bloemfontein to Botshabelo (Mtabelo; R35, one hour), and then from there to Maseru (R20, 1½ hours). There are also buses and minibus taxis several times weekly between Jo'burg and Maseru (R110, 5½ hours), and daily minibus taxis between Maseru and Ladybrand (16km from the Maseru Bridge border crossing). All these routes will bring you into Maseru coming from South Africa; leaving Maseru, you'll need to go to the South Africa side of Maseru Bridge.

Other useful connections include a daily minibus taxi between Mokhotlong (Lesotho) and Underberg (South Africa) via Sani Pass (see p530); and several taxis daily between Qacha's Nek (Lesotho) and Matatiele (South Africa; R15, 45 minutes). If you're travelling between Jo'burg and northern Lesotho, take a minibus taxi to Ficksburg, cross the border, and then get a minibus taxi on to

Butha-Buthe and points north. There are also sometimes direct taxis between Jo'burg and Butha-Buthe via Caledonspoort border (R100, five hours).

CAR

The easiest entry points for car and motorcycle are on the northern and western sides of the country. Most of the entry points to the south and east are unpaved, though all are possible in a 2WD except Sani Pass. You'll need a 4WD to enter Lesotho via Sani Pass; it's possible to exit via this route with a 2WD with sufficient clearance, but a 4WD is recommended.

It's more economical to rent a car in South Africa than in Lesotho (you'll need the necessary permission papers, see p593). There's a road tax of M5, payable on entering Lesotho.

From Mozambique
BUS

Several large 'luxury' buses run daily between Jo'burg/Pretoria and Maputo via Nelspruit and Komatipoort (US$20, eight hours). These include:

Greyhound (☎ 012-323 1154; www.greyhound.co.za)
Intercape Mainliner (☎ 0861 287 287, 021-380 4400; www.intercape.co.za)
Panthera Azul (☎ 011-337 7438, 333 4249, Maputo 01-302 077, 302 083; panthera@virconn.com)
Translux (☎ 011-774 3333, Maputo 01-300 622; www.translux.co.za)

Translux and Panthera Azul are the most reliable. You can also travel in each direction on these lines between Nelspruit and Maputo, but not between Nelspruit and Jo'burg.

Alternatively, the **Baz Bus** (☎ 021-439 2323; www.bazbus.com) links Jo'burg/Pretoria, Nelspruit and Durban with Manzini (Swaziland), from where you can get a minibus taxi to Maputo. See p598 for more information on Baz Bus.

Panthera Azul has buses three times weekly between Durban and Maputo (US$21, 8½ hours) via Big Bend (Swaziland) and Namaacha.

Minibuses depart Maputo daily in the morning for the Namaacha/Lomahasha border post (US$1.50, 1½ hours) with some continuing on to Manzini (US$4, 3½ hours).

CAR

For travel to/from Mozambique via the Kosi Bay border, you'll need your own vehicle (4WD is necessary on the Mozambique side). Alternatively, most places to stay in Ponta d'Ouro (Mozambique) do transfers for about US$10. Hitching between the border and Ponta d'Ouro is easy on weekends and during South African school holidays.

There's a good tarmac toll road connecting Jo'burg with Maputo via Ressano Garcia, with tolls on the South Africa side between Middelburg and Witbank, at Machadodorp and 45km east of Nelspruit.

From Mozambique to Swaziland via Namaacha, the road is good tarmac the entire way, and easily negotiated with 2WD.

TRAIN

The daily except Saturday *Komati* train operated by Shosholoza Meyl (see p605) links Jo'burg and Maputo via Pretoria, Nelspruit and Komatipoort (1st/2nd/economy class US$25/20/10, 17–19 hours). Because service on the Mozambique side is so slow, it's best to take the train to Komatipoort at the border (1st/2nd/economy class from Jo'burg R185/130/70), and then a minibus from there to Maputo (US$3, 1½ hours). If you take the train the whole way, you'll need to buy the ticket for the Mozambique section at the border. On the Mozambique side, only 2nd and economy class are available.

From Namibia
BUS

Intercape Mainliner (www.intercape.co.za) runs four times weekly between Cape Town and Windhoek via Upington (US$50, 20 hours). It's also possible to travel between Jo'burg and Windhoek with Intercape Mainliner (US$60, 25 hours) on these same days, with a change of buses in Upington.

TRAIN

The **Trans-Namib** (☎ Namibia 061-298 2533; www.transnamib.com.na) 'StarLine' runs twice weekly between Windhoek and Upington (25 hours).

From Swaziland
BUS

The best connections are on the **Baz Bus** (☎ 021-439 2323; www.bazbus.com), which runs from Jo'burg/Pretoria to Manzini (R260 di-

CROSS-BORDER RAIL LINKS

Other than the connections mentioned on p591, there are no regularly scheduled passenger rail services between South Africa and the neighbouring countries. However, some of the special trains listed on p605 do cross-border routes. *Shongololo Express* has South Africa routings that also take in Mbabane (Swaziland), Bulawayo, Great Zimbabwe and Victoria Falls (all Zimbabwe). A 16-day route linking Cape Town with various points in Namibia is planned to start soon. *Rovos Rail* has routes linking Pretoria with Swapkomund (Namibia), and one that passes through Victoria Falls and Bulawayo en route between Cape Town and Dar es Salaam (Tanzania).

rect, R290 hop on/hop off) via Nelspruit, and between Durban and Manzini (R300 direct, R475 hop on/hop off) via the KwaZulu-Natal coast.

Minibus taxis run daily between Jo'burg (Park Station), Mbabane and Manzini (R110, four hours), between Manzini and Durban (R150, eight hours), and between Manzini and Maputo (Mozambique; R20, 2½ hours). For many routes, you'll need to change minibuses at the border. Most long-distance taxis leave early in the morning.

HITCHING

If you're hitching into Swaziland, most South Africans enter through the Oshoek/ Ngwenya border post. The casinos in the north (near the Matsamo/Jeppe's Reef border post) and southwest (near the Mahamba border post) attract traffic, especially on weekends, and are also good places to look for lifts into/out of the country.

From Zimbabwe

BUS

There is a daily service between Jo'burg and Harare via Polokwane (Pietersburg) and Pretoria (R350, 17 hours) on Translux, Greyhound and Intercape Mainliner. Greyhound also has buses six times weekly from Jo'burg/ Pretoria to Bulawayo (R220, 15 hours), as does Translux (R230; night service).

SEA

South Africa is an important stop on world shipping routes. Cape Town in particular is a major port of call for cruise ships. Many cruise ships also stop at Durban, and several freighter lines sailing from Europe have passenger cabins. It's also possible to find both cruise and freighter lines linking South African ports with various points in Mozambique (including the Bazaruto Archipelago), Madagascar and Mauritius.

The thrill of approaching the tip of the continent by sea doesn't come cheap. Even on the freighters, passenger accommodation is usually in comfortable (sometimes even plush) cabins. Expect to pay from about US$2500 per person one way for a 23- to 27-day journey from a UK port to Cape Town, often via the Canary Islands. Fares from South Africa tend to be lower than fares to South Africa. Useful contacts include:

Freighter World Cruises Inc (☎ 800-531 7774, 626-449 3106; www.freighterworld.com) Based in the USA.

Navique (www.tallships.co.za) Has cargo ships between Durban and various Mozambican ports that sometimes take passengers; based in South Africa.

Royal Mail Ship St Helena (☎ 020-7816 4800; www .rms-st-helena.com) Based in the UK.

Safmarine (☎ 021-408 6911; www.safmarine.co.uk) This UK-based company actively seeks passengers for its container ships, which sail to many of the world's major ports; fares are often negotiable.

Starlight Lines (www.starlight.co.za) A good contact for connections to Mozambique, Madagascar and Mauritius; based in South Africa.

Strand Voyages (☎ 020-7836 6363; www.strandtravel .co.uk) Based in the UK.

The Cruise People (☎ 020-7723 2450, 0800 526 313; www.cruisepeople.co.uk) Based in the UK.

Another good source of information about routes and the shipping lines plying them is the *OAG Cruise & Ferry Guide*, published quarterly by the **Reed Travel Group** (☎ 01582-600 111) in the UK. Durban is one of the better places to look for a lift on private yachts sailing up the East African coast.

TOURS

Dozens of tour and safari companies organise package tours to South Africa. As an alternative, if you prefer a more independent approach, you can prebook flights and hotels for the first few nights, then join tours locally (see Tours under Getting

Around, following). Almost all operators include Kruger National Park and Cape Town and the Peninsula in their itineraries. For special interests (bird-watching, flower-watching etc), check the advertisements in specialist magazines. Following is a list of possible tour companies:

Australia
Adventure World (☎ 02-8913 0755; www.adventure world.com.au) Offers a wide range of tours, safaris, car hire and hotel packages in South Africa and neighbouring countries.
African Wildlife Safaris (☎ 03-9696 2899; www.afri canwildlifesafaris.com.au) Sells discounted tickets and designs mainly wildlife safaris in Southern Africa, including South Africa.
Peregrine Travel (☎ 03-9663 8611; www.peregrine .net.au) Caters to all budgets, from overland truck tours to upscale wildlife safaris, with Swaziland included in some itineraries.

France
Makila Voyages (☎ 01 42 96 80 00; www.makila.fr) Upper-end tailored tours in South Africa and Swaziland, plus safaris.

UK
Discover the World (☎ 01737-218 800; www.discover -the-world.co.uk) Exclusive, wildlife-oriented tours to Kruger National Park and a whale-watching excursion to the Cape peninsula.
Dragoman (☎ 0870 499 4475; www.dragoman.co.uk) Overland tours.
Guerba (☎ 01373-826 611; www.guerba.com) Overland tours.
Exodus Expeditions (☎ 020-8675 5550; www.exodus travels.co.uk) Organises a variety of tours, including overland trips, and walking and cycling itineraries.
In the Saddle (☎ 1299-272 997; www.inthesaddle.com) Strictly for horse aficionados, with various rides in South Africa, including in the Western Cape, and in the Greater St Lucia Wetland Park.
Naturetrek (☎ 01962-733 051; www.naturetrek.co.uk) Specialist nature tours, including springtime wildflower itineraries in Namaqualand and a botanically-oriented tour in the Drakensberg and Lesotho.
Temple World (☎ 020-8940 4114; www.templeworld .co.uk) Upper-end luxury 'educational' tours focusing on history, ecology and wildlife.

USA
Adventure Centre (☎ 800-228 2747, 510-654 1879; www.adventurecenter.com) Budget to mid-range tours including a 22-day South Africa circuit that takes in bits of

Swaziland and Lesotho; it's also the US agent for several overland operators.
Africa Adventure Company (☎ 1800-882 9453, 954-491 8877; www.africa-adventure.com) Upper-end wildlife safaris, including the private reserves around Kruger National Park, plus other itineraries in Cape Town and the Garden Route.
Born Free Safaris (☎ 800-472 3274; www.bornfreesaf aris.com) Offers a good range of Cape to Kruger itineraries.
Bushtracks (☎ 1800-995 8689, international calls 650-326 8689; www.bushtracks.com) Private air luxury safaris.
International Expeditions(☎ international 205 428 1700, USA/Canada 800 633 4734; www.ietravel.com) Upper-end, wildlife-oriented safaris taking in Kruger National Park, Cape Town and a taste of Swaziland.
Wilderness Travel (☎ 800-368 2794, 510-558 2488; www.wildernesstravel.com) Runs a two-week Cape Town to Kruger National Park itinerary.

GETTING AROUND

AIR
Airlines in South Africa, Lesotho & Swaziland
In addition to being the international flag carrier, **South African Airways** (SAA; ☎ 0860 359 722, 011-978 1111; www.flysaa.com) is the main domestic carrier, with an extensive and efficient route network to major cities. Its subsidiaries, **SAAirlink** (☎ 011-978 1111; www.saair link.co.za) and **SA Express** (☎ 0800 114 799, 011-978 5577; www.saexpress.co.za), also service domestic routes, and share SAA's excellent safety record.

Domestic fares aren't cheap; if you plan to take some internal flights, check with a travel agent before you leave home for special deals on tickets and air passes. General fare and route information is given in the regional chapters. Other airlines flying domestically, all of which enjoy a good reputation, include:
Comair (☎ 0860 435 922, 011-921 0222; www.comair .co.za) Operates British Airways flights within Africa, and has flights linking Cape Town, Durban, Jo'burg and Port Elizabeth.
Kulula.com (☎ 0861 585 852; www.kulula.com) In partnership with British Airways, operates no-frills flights between Jo'burg, Cape Town, Durban and Port Elizabeth.
National Airlines (☎ 021-934 0350; www.flynal.com) Five flights weekly between Cape Town and Alexander Bay via Kleinsee (Northern Cape) and Springbok.
Nationwide Airlines (☎ 0861 737 737, 011-327 3000; www.nationwideair.co.za) Operates in partnership with

Virgin Atlantic, and has flights linking Jo'burg, Cape Town, Durban, George, Port Elizabeth, Sun City and Nelspruit.
Swazi Express Airways (☎ 518 6840; www.swaziexpress.com) Several flights weekly connecting Manzini with Durban and Maputo (Mozambique); charter service in Swaziland and surrounding region.
Swaziland Airlink (☎ 518 6155; www.saairlink.co.za) Daily flights between Jo'burg and Manzini/Matsapha.

BICYCLE
South Africa
As long as you're fit enough to handle its many hills, South Africa offers some rewarding cycling. It has scenic and diverse terrain, an abundance of camping places, and many good roads, most of which don't carry much traffic (although most don't have any sort of shoulder). The Cape Peninsula and the Winelands of the Western Cape are excellent biking areas. Elsewhere in the country, there are a few places where meandering between small towns is possible (usually with lots of hills), such as in southern Free State. The Wild Coast in the Eastern Cape is also beautiful and challenging, while the northern lowveld offers wide plains.

When planning, it's worth keeping in mind that much of the country (except for Western Cape and the west coast) gets most of its rain in summer (late November to March), in the form of violent thunderstorms. When it isn't raining, summer days can be unpleasantly hot, especially in the steamy lowveld. Distances between major towns are often long but, except in isolated areas such as the Karoo or Limpopo province, you're rarely very far from a village or a farmhouse.

Safety is another consideration. When planning, contact other cyclists through local cycling clubs or bicycle shops to get the most recent information on the routes you're considering. **SA-Cycling** (www.sa-cycling.com) posts cyclists diaries, suggests several routes, and has listings of cycling clubs. Other things to remember are that it's illegal to cycle on highways, and that roads near urban areas are too busy for comfort.

Mixing cycling with public transport doesn't work well, as most bus lines don't want bicycles in their luggage holds, and minibuses don't carry luggage on the roof. In some cases, the only alternative may be to arrange transporting your bicycle with a carrier company.

Mountain bikes and their spare parts are widely available. However, it's often difficult to find specialised parts for touring bikes, especially away from Cape Town and Jo'burg. It's worth establishing a relationship with a good bike shop in a city before you head off into the veld, in case you need something couriered to you. Bring a good lock to counter the ever-present risk of theft, leave the bicycle inside your accommodation (preferably inside your room) and chain it to something solid.

Lesotho & Swaziland
Both Lesotho and Swaziland are excellent cycling destinations, especially Lesotho, although the country's mountainous terrain means that it's only for the fit. You'll need a mountain bike for both countries; stock up on spares in South Africa. The main weather constraints are icy roads in wintertime in Lesotho, and thunderstorms and flooding in both countries during the summer.

The classic mountain-bike route in Lesotho is over the Sani Pass, with almost unlimited other options as well. It's sometimes possible to rent bicycles through some of the lodges on the South Africa side of the Sani Pass.

Swaziland is also ideally suited for cycling, except for main towns and the heavily travelled Ezulwini Valley. Another option is the shorter mountain-bike trails in Hlane Royal National Park and in Mlilwane Wildlife Sanctuary, both of which rent bicycles.

It's not common to transport bicycles on public transport in Lesotho and Swaziland, but you can usually arrange something with the driver.

Hire & Purchase
If you'll be doing extensive cycling, it's best to bring your own bicycle. For day rides, some hostels in South Africa have short-term mountain bike rental. Rentals can also sometimes be arranged through bike shops in Cape Town and other cities, though you'll usually be required to leave a credit card deposit.

There's a good selection of mountain bikes for sale in all larger South African cities, with Cape Town probably the best place to look. For touring bikes, the main markets are Cape Town and Jo'burg. To resell your bicycle at the end of your trip, hostel bulletin boards are good places to advertise.

BOAT

Despite South Africa's long coastline, there are few opportunities to travel by boat. The most likely possibilities are taking a ship between Cape Town and Durban, and between Port Elizabeth and Durban. Useful contacts include the local offices of **Safmarine** (☎ 021-408 6911; www.safmarine.co.uk) and **Navique** (www.tallships.co.za), as well as local yacht clubs. Also check out the informative www.cruiser.co.za, which posts a bulletin board matching up crews with ships.

BUS
South Africa

Buses in South Africa aren't the deal that they are in many other countries. However, together with the less-appealing minibus taxis (see p604), they're the main form of public transport, with a reliable and reasonably comfortable network linking all major cities. Note that many long-distance services run through the night. The main lines include:

Baz Bus (☎ 021-439 2323; www.bazbus.com) Baz Bus caters almost exclusively to backpackers and travellers, and is a good alternative to the major bus lines as well as a good way to meet other travellers. It offers hop-on, hop-off fares and door-to-door service between Cape Town and Jo'burg via the Northern Drakensberg, Durban and the Garden Route. It also has a loop from Durban via Zululand and Swaziland to Jo'burg, passing near Kruger National Park. Point-to-point fares are more expensive than on the other major lines, but can work out more economically if you take advantage of the hop-on/hop-off feature. The Baz Bus drops off and picks up at many hostels along the way, and has transfer arrangements with those off the main routes for a nominal extra charge. You can book directly with Baz Bus, as well as with most hostels.

City to City (☎ 011-773 2762) This line (sometimes known as Transtate) operates in partnership with Translux, with whom it often shares an office, and has taken over the routes that once carried people from the Homelands, Lesotho and Swaziland to and from the big cities during the apartheid regime. Services are less expensive than on the other lines, and still predominantly serve black South Africans – thus going to many off-the-beaten-track places, including townships and mining towns. Destinations from Jo'burg include Umtata, Nelspruit, Hazyview, Beitbridge (for Zimbabwe), Piet Retief, and various towns in KwaZulu-Natal, plus Manzini and Mbabane in Swaziland. Many services originate at Jo'burg's Park Station Transit Centre, where there are booking counters and an information desk.

Greyhound (☎ 012-323 1154; www.greyhound.co.za) Routes and pricing are similar to those for Translux (listing following). Greyhound also has a Jo'burg to Durban route via Zululand and Richards Bay, and offers frequent special deals.

Intercape Mainliner (☎ 0861 287 287, 021-380 4400; www.intercape.co.za) Services primarily the western half of the country, plus Nelspruit (en route to Mozambique). Prices are somewhat less than on Translux and Greyhound.

Translux (☎ 011-774 3333; www.translux.co.za) This is the main long-distance bus operator, with services connecting Cape Town, Knysna, Plettenberg Bay, Durban, Bloemfontein, Port Elizabeth, East London, Umtata, Nelspruit (en route to Mozambique) and various towns along the Garden Route.

There are no class tiers on any of the bus lines, although Translux, Intercape and Greyhound would be the equivalent of 'luxury' lines, with air-con and often video and a toilet. City to City's service is no-frills.

On the three main lines, Greyhound, Intercape Mainliner and Translux, fares are roughly calculated by distance, though short runs are disproportionately expensive. Some sample one-way fares/durations: Jo'burg to Cape Town (R400, 19 hours); Jo'burg to Durban (R185, eight hours); and Cape Town to Knysna (R150, eight hours). Baz Bus one-way fares for hop-on, hop-off service are: Cape Town to Durban via the Garden Route (R1520); Jo'burg–Swaziland–Durban–Drakensberg–Jo'burg loop (R960)

Prices for the three main lines rise during school holidays; all offer student and senior citizen discounts, and Intercape has backpacker discounts. Also inquire about travel passes, if you'll be taking several bus journeys.

For the three main lines, reservations should be made at least 24 hours in advance (72 hours in advance for Intercape Mainliner, and as much in advance as possible for travel during peak periods). It's sometimes possible to get a seat at the last minute, but this shouldn't be counted on.

Lesotho

Lesotho has a good network of buses and minibuses (known locally as 'minibus taxis' or – more commonly – just 'taxis') covering most parts of the country. Buses are slightly cheaper than minibus taxis, and somewhat slower, and service all major towns. Minibus taxis also service the major towns, as well as many smaller towns.

For the larger buses, although you'll be quoted long-distance fares, it's best to just buy a ticket to the next major town. Most of the passengers will get off there anyway, which means you'll likely be stuck waiting for the bus to fill up again while other buses leave first. Buying tickets in stages is only slightly more expensive than buying a direct ticket. Heading northeast from Maseru, you usually need to change at Maputsoe, although this also sometimes happens en route into Maputsoe if your bus meets another coming the other way.

There are no classes, and service is very much no-frills. It's not necessary (or possible) to reserve a seat in advance. Most departures are in the morning (generally, the longer the journey, the earlier the departure).

Swaziland

In Swaziland, there are only a few domestic buses, most of which start and terminate at the main stop in the centre of Mbabane. The main form of public transport is minibus. These run almost everywhere, with frequent stops en route, and cost slightly more than buses. Minibuses leave when full; no reservations are necessary. Sample fares include: Mbabane to Manzini (E5, 35 minutes); Mbabane to Piggs Peak (E7, one hour); Manzini to Big Bend (E7, one hour).

CAR & MOTORCYCLE

South Africa is ideal for driving, and away from the main bus and train routes, having your own wheels is the best way to get around. If you're in a group, it's also often the most economical. Most major roads are in excellent condition, and off the main routes there are interesting back roads to explore.

The country is crossed by many national routes (eg N1). On some sections a toll is payable, based on distance (frequently close to R30). There's always plenty of warning that you're about to enter a toll section (marked by a black 'T' in a yellow circle), and there's always an alternative route (marked by a black 'A' in a yellow circle). On alternative routes, signposting is sparse, generally only directing you to smaller towns or giving route numbers, rather than the direction of the next large city. Smaller roads are numbered (eg, R44), and when you ask directions most people will refer to

> **PARKING**
>
> In Johannesburg and other areas where secure parking is an issue, information is included on parking availability (**P**) in Sleeping listings. In rural areas, and in Lesotho and Swaziland, hotels generally have guarded lots.

these numbers rather than destinations, so it pays to have a good road map (see p579).

Lesotho and Swaziland are also well-suited to driving, though you'll find more gravel and dirt away from major routes. Main routes in Lesotho are numbered beginning with A1 (Main North Road), and side routes branching off from these are given 'B' route numbers. Ice is a major hazard in winter.

Swaziland is crossed roughly from west to east by the MR3, which is a major highway as far east as Manzini. Good tarmac roads also connect other major towns; elsewhere you'll find mostly unpaved roads, most in reasonably good condition, except after heavy rains. For more, see Road Conditions (p599).

Automobile Associations

Automobile Association of South Africa (AASA; ☎ membership 011-799 1000, emergencies 082 16 111; www.aasa.co.za) has a limited vehicle breakdown service that can be useful if you will be driving in the areas it covers. It also has a good supply of maps, available free to members and for sale in many tourist offices and bookstores. For breakdown service, hold onto the window stickers that you get with membership. The initial joining fee is waived for members of many foreign motoring associations, so it's worth bringing your membership details.

In theory, the AASA covers Lesotho and Swaziland, although its towing and breakdown service doesn't extend to these countries. In South Africa, the emergency breakdown service covers Gauteng, Cape Town, Durban, Pietermaritzburg, East London and Port Elizabeth. In Lesotho and Swaziland, you'll need to rely on local repair facilities in the major towns.

Bringing Your Own Vehicle

For requirements on bringing your own vehicle, see left.

Driving Licence

In South Africa, you can use your driving licence from your home country if it carries your photo; otherwise you'll need an international driving permit, obtainable from a motoring organisation in your home country. In Lesotho and Swaziland, licences from most other countries are accepted for stays of less than six months, as long as they are in English, or you have a certified translation.

Fuel & Spare Parts

Petrol costs about R3.80 per litre for leaded or unleaded in all three countries, and must be paid for in cash. There's no self-service. An attendant will always fill up your tank for you, clean your windows and ask if the oil or water needs checking; a 5% to 10% tip is standard practice.

Along main routes in South Africa and Swaziland, there are plenty of petrol stations, many open 24 hours. In rural areas, and in Lesotho, fill up whenever you can, and in Lesotho, carry a jerry can with extra fuel. Unleaded fuel is readily available, except in the more remote areas of Lesotho. There are service stations in all major South African towns. In Lesotho, the main service stations are in Maseru, with limited facilities in other major towns. In Swaziland, Mbabane and Manzini have the best facilities; Manzini is the best place for sourcing spare parts.

Hire

Car rental is relatively inexpensive in South Africa. Most companies have a minimum age requirement of 21 years (23 years in Swaziland). All accept major credit cards. Car-rental rates in Swaziland are similar to those in South Africa. For Lesotho, it usually works out less expensive to rent the vehicle in South Africa and drive it over the border.

Major international car-rental companies are listed below. All the South Africa listings have offices in major cities; in Swaziland, the only agents are in Manzini; in Lesotho, they are in Maseru.

Rates average from about US$30 per day including insurance and 200km free

ROAD DISTANCES (KM)

	Bloemfontein	Cape Town	Durban	East London	George	Graaf-Reinet	Johannesburg	Kimberly	Maseru	Mbabane	Nelspruit	Polokwane (Pietersburg)	Port Elizabeth	Pretoria	Springbok	Upington
Bloemfontein	---															
Cape Town	998	---														
Durban	628	1660	---													
East London	546	1042	667	---												
George	764	436	1240	630	---											
Graaf-Reinet	422	672	945	388	342	---										
Johannesburg	396	1405	598	992	1168	826	---									
Kimberly	175	960	842	722	734	501	467	---								
Maseru	157	1160	590	630	913	519	438	334	---							
Mbabane	677	1680	562	1238	1450	1097	361	833	633	---						
Nelspruit	754	1779	689	1214	1509	1167	358	832	713	173	---					
Polokwane (Pietersburg)	727	1736	929	1323	1595	1595	331	798	769	488	315	---				
Port Elizabeth	676	756	927	300	330	251	1062	763	822	1548	1373	1398	---			
Pretoria	454	1463	656	1050	1226	859	58	525	488	372	328	273	1119	---		
Springbok	975	554	1642	1365	846	911	1274	800	1252	1678	1474	1543	1289	1200	---	
Upington	576	821	1243	958	857	667	875	401	731	1157	1144	1075	902	813	387	---

per day. Rental of a 4WD starts at about US$50, though better deals are often available. For cheaper rates and unlimited mileage deals, it's best to book and prepay through your agent at home before coming to South Africa. You may be charged extra if you nominate more than one driver. If a nonnominated driver has an accident, you won't be covered by insurance.

Avis South Africa (☎ 0861 021 111, 011-923 3660; www .avis.co.za); Swaziland (Matsapha Airport ☎ 518 6226); Lesotho (Moshoeshoe Airport ☎ 2235 0328, Lesotho Sun Hotel 2232 0087)

Budget South Africa (☎ 0861 016 622; www.budget.com); Lesotho (☎ 2231 6344)

Europcar (☎ 0800 011 344, 011-394 8831; www.europ car.co.za; South Africa)

Hertz (☎ 0861 600136, 021-400 9650; www.hertz.co.za; South Africa)

It's also worth checking with **Travelocity** (www.travelocity.com) and the no-frills airline **Ku-lula.com** (www.kulula.com), both of which often have good car-rental deals.

Local car-rental companies are usually less expensive, though they tend to come and go, and some have limits on how far you can take the car from the rental point. Several are listed below, all with agents in major cities; see also p396 and p138. Also check with backpacker hostels; many can arrange better deals, from around US$25 per day or less.

Affordable Car Hire (☎ 404 9136; affordable@posix .co.sz; Swaziland)

Imperial South Africa (☎ 0861 131 000, 011-574 1000; www.imperialcarrental.co.za); Swaziland (☎ 404 0459, 518 4396); Lesotho (☎ 2235 0299)

Tempest (☎ 0860 031 666, 011-396 1080; www.temp estcarhire.co.za; South Africa)

Renting a camper van is another option, although one-way rentals are often not possible, or attract large fees. Some camper-van rentals include camping gear. 'Bakkie' campers, which sleep two in the back of a canopied pick-up, are cheaper. Two places to try, both in Jo'burg, are:

African Leisure Travel (☎ 011-792 1884; www.african leisure.co.za)

Britz 4x4 Rentals (☎ 011-396 1860)

For motorcycle rental, a good contact is **Motozulu** (☎ 039-695 0348; www.motozu.lu.ms) in Port Shepstone (KwaZulu-Natal); see also p138. Mopeds and scooters are available for hire in Cape Town and several other tourist areas.

CHOOSING A DEAL

South Africa is a big country, but unless you're on a tight schedule you probably don't need to pay higher rates for unlimited kilometres. For meandering around, 400km a day should be more than enough, and if you plan to stop for a day here and there 200km a day might be sufficient.

However, if you're renting with an international company and you book through the branch in your home country, you'll probably get unlimited kilometres at no extra cost, except at peak times such as December–January. When getting quotes, be sure that they include the 14% value-added tax (VAT).

One-way rentals are usually possible with larger companies if you are driving between major cities, although there's sometimes a drop-off charge.

Choose a car powerful enough to do the job. The smallest cars are OK for one person but with any more they'll be straining on the hills, which, even on major highways, are steep. Really steep hills may also make automatics unpleasant to drive. If you'll be going into Lesotho, consider a 4WD.

During the summer months, hail damage is a distinct and costly possibility, so see if it's covered before signing the rental agreement. Many contracts used to stipulate that you couldn't enter townships. While this usually isn't the case now, check anyway. If you plan to visit Swaziland, Lesotho or any other country, check that the rental agreement permits this, and make sure you get the standard letter from the rental company granting permission.

Finally, pay attention to the amount of 'excess' (the amount for which you're liable before insurance covers the rest) built into the insurance arrangement. Sometimes you'll have the choice of paying a higher insurance premium to lower or cancel the excess. A few companies offer 100% damage and theft insurance at a higher rate.

Insurance

Insurance for third-party damage and damage to or loss of your vehicle is highly recommended, though not legally required for private-vehicle owners. It can be difficult to arrange by the month. The AASA is a good contact, and may be willing to negotiate payment for a year's worth of insurance with a pro-rata refund when you sell the car. One recommended insurance agency is the Cape Town–based **First Bowring** (☎ 021-425 1460).

Purchase

South Africa is the best place in the region to purchase a vehicle for use on a long South Africa itinerary or on a larger sub-Saharan itinerary. Although prices tend to be cheaper in Jo'burg, most people do their buying in Cape Town – a much nicer place to spend the week or two that it will likely take for the process. Cape Town is also not a bad place to sell, as prices tend to be higher, although the market is small.

Cape Town's main congregation of used-car dealers is on Voortrekker Rd between Maitland and Belleville Sts, where you may also find a dealer willing to agree to a buy-back deal.

Buying privately, you won't have any dealer warranties, but prices will be cheaper. The weekly *Cape Ads* (www.capeads.com) is the best place to look. Also try **Auto Trader** (www.autotrader.co.za), which advertises thousands of cars around the country.

No matter who you buy from, make sure that the car details correspond accurately with the ownership (registration) papers, that there is a current licence disc on the windscreen and that the vehicle has been checked by the **police clearance department** (Cape Town ☎ 021-945 3891). Check the owner's name against their identity document, and check the car's engine and chassis numbers. Consider getting the car tested – in Cape Town, try **Same Garage** (Map pp112-3; ☎ 434 1058; 309 Main Rd, Sea Point). A full test can cost up to R300; less detailed tests are around R150.

Cheap cars will often be sold without a roadworthy certificate. This certificate is required when you register the change-of-ownership form and pay tax for a licence disc. A roadworthy used to be difficult to obtain but some private garages are now allowed to issue them (R220), and some will overlook minor faults.

For something decent, plan on spending at least R25,000. For a 4WD, Series 1, 2 and 3 Land Rovers will cost from R15,000 to R40,000, depending on the condition. A recommended contact in Cape Town is **Graham Duncan Smith** (☎ 021-797 3048), who's a Land Rover expert and has helped people buy a 4WD in the past; he charges a R100 consultation fee and R165 per hour for engineering work.

To register your car, present yourself along with the roadworthy, a current licence, an accurate ownership certificate, a completed change-of-ownership form (signed by the seller), a clear photocopy of your ID (passport) along with the original, and your money to the **City Treasurer's Department, Motor Vehicle Registration Division** (☎ 021-400 2385; ☒ 8am-2pm Mon-Fri) in the Civic Centre, Cash Hall, on the foreshore in Cape Town. Call ahead to check how much cash you'll need, but it will be under R500. You can also get blank change-of-ownership forms here.

Road Conditions
SOUTH AFRICA

Main roads are generally in excellent condition. Outside large cities and towns, you may encounter dirt roads, most of which are regularly graded and reasonably smooth. In the former Homeland areas, beware of dangerous potholes, washed-out roads, unannounced hairpin bends and the like.

LESOTHO

Driving in Lesotho is more challenging, although it's getting easier as new roads are built in conjunction with the Highlands Water Project. The sealed roads in the highlands are good, but very steep in places. Rain will slow you down and ice and snow in winter can make things dangerous. If you're driving an automatic car, you'll be relying heavily on your brakes to get around steep downhill corners. Away from main roads, there are still many places where even a 4WD will get into trouble. Apart from rough roads, river floodings after summer storms present the biggest problem. People and animals on the road can also be a hazard.

There are sometimes army roadblocks, usually searching for stolen cars. If you're driving a car hired from South Africa and get stopped, you'll need to present the letter from the rental agency giving you permission to take the car into Lesotho.

SWAZILAND

Swaziland's road network is quite good, and most major routes are tarred. There are also some satisfyingly rough back roads through the bush. The road between Tshaneni (northwest of Hlane Royal National Park) and Piggs Peak is gravel for most of the way, and slippery when wet.

Malagwane Hill, from Mbabane into the Ezulwini Valley, was once listed in the *Guinness Book of Records* as the most dangerous stretch of road in the world. Although conditions are greatly improved, driving down the Ezulwini Valley in heavy traffic and bad conditions can still be dangerous. Away from the population centres and border crossing areas there is very little traffic.

Road Hazards

South Africa has a horrific road-accident record, with the annual death toll around 10,000. (Some estimates place it at over 15,000.) The N1 between Cape Town and Beaufort West is considered to be the most dangerous stretch of road in the country.

The main hazards are your fellow drivers, with overtaking blind and overtaking with insufficient passing room the major dangers. Drivers of cars coming up behind you will expect you to move into the emergency lane to let them pass, though the emergency lane may already be occupied. Drivers on little-used rural roads often speed and they often assume that there is no other traffic. Watch out especially for oncoming cars at blind corners on these roads. There is alcohol breath-testing in South Africa and in Swaziland, but given the high blood-alcohol level permitted (over 0.08% in South Africa, and 0.15% in Swaziland) drunk drivers remain a danger.

Animals and pedestrians on the roads are another hazard, especially in rural areas. Standard advice is that if you hit an animal in an area in which you're uncertain of your safety, it's best to continue to the nearest police station and report it there. During the rainy season, and especially in higher areas of steamy KwaZulu-Natal, thick fog can slow you to a crawl. In the lowveld, summer hailstorms can damage your car.

In Lesotho, watch out for the steep terrain, hairpin turns, and ice and other inclement weather conditions.

In Swaziland, apart from drunk drivers and wandering cattle, the main danger is speeding minibuses, especially on gravel roads.

CARJACKING

In Jo'burg, and to a lesser extent in the other big cities, carjacking is a problem, though it's more likely if you're driving something flash rather than a standard rental car. The carjackers are almost always armed, and people have been killed for their cars. Stay alert, keep windows wound up and doors locked at night, and keep your taste in cars modest. If you're stopped at a red light and notice anything suspicious, it's standard practice to check that the junction is clear, and run the light. If you do get carjacked, don't resist, just hand over the keys immediately.

Road Rules

In South Africa, Lesotho and Swaziland, driving is on the left-hand side of the road, as in the UK, Japan and Australia. Seatbelts are mandatory for the driver and front-seat passenger in all three countries.

There are a few local variations on road rules. The main one is the 'four-way stop' (crossroad), which can occur even on major roads. All vehicles are required to stop, with those arriving first the first to go (even if they're on a minor cross street). On freeways, faster drivers will expect you to move into the emergency lane to let them pass, and will probably flash their hazard lights as thanks. At roundabouts, vehicles already in the roundabout, and those approaching it from the right, have the right of way.

In Swaziland, if an official or royal motorcade approaches, you're required to pull over and stop.

SPEED LIMITS

In South Africa, the speed limit is 100km/h on open roads, and 120km/h on most major highways, though it's widely ignored. The usual limit in towns is 60km/h.

In Lesotho, the speed limit is 80km/h on main roads, and 50km/h in villages. In Swaziland, it's 80km/h on open roads, and 60km/h in towns.

HITCHING

Hitching is never entirely safe in any country. This is especially true in South Africa, particularly in and near urban areas, and it's not a form of travel we can recommend. However, sometimes in rural areas it may be the only way to get somewhere. If you do decide to hitch, do so in pairs, avoid hitching at night, and let someone know where you are going. It's also advisable to catch public transport well beyond city limits before starting to hitch. Women should never hitch alone.

Hitching is easier and arguably safer in Swaziland and Lesotho, although you should still follow the same precautions. Be prepared to wait a long time for a car on back roads, and for lots of competition from locals.

LOCAL TRANSPORT

For getting around within a city or town (as opposed to intercity travel, which is covered under Buses, p598), the main options are city buses, minibus taxis and regular taxis – either shared or private hire. In a few places, such as Cape Town and Durban, you'll have other options such as the *rikki* (small open vans) and *tuk-tuk* (motorised tricycle), and Cape Town, Jo'burg and Pretoria have metro commuter trains (see p605).

Bus

Cape Town, Jo'burg, Pretoria and several other urban areas have city bus systems. Fares are cheap and routes, which are sign-boarded, are extensive. However, services usually stop running early in the evening, and there aren't many buses on weekends.

Minibus Taxi

Minibus taxis run almost everywhere – within cities, to the suburbs and to neighbouring towns. They leave when full and, happily – especially if you've travelled elsewhere in sub-Saharan Africa – 'full' in South Africa isn't as full as it is in many neighbouring countries. Most accommodate 14 to 16 people, with the slightly larger 'Sprinters' taking about 20.

Minibus taxis have the advantages of an extensive route network and cheap prices. These are outweighed, however, by the fact that driving standards and vehicle conditions often leave a lot to be desired, and there

> **MINIBUS TAXI ETIQUETTE**
>
> - Passengers with lots of luggage should sit in the first row behind the driver.
> - Pay the fare with coins, not notes. Pass the money forward (your fare and those of the people around you) when the taxi is full. Give it to one of the front-seat passengers, not the driver. If you're sitting in the front seat you might have to collect the fares and provide change.
> - If you sit on the folding seat by the door it's your job to open and close the door when other people get out. You'll have to get out of the taxi each time.
> - Say 'Thank you, driver!' when you want to get out, not 'Stop!'

are many accidents. The reputation of minibus taxis has also been tarnished by isolated outbreaks of gangster-style shoot-outs between the various companies competing for business, including incidents where crowded taxis were machine-gunned. Although things have settled down in recent years, minibuses in some areas and on some routes are still considered unsafe, and reports of muggings and other incidents remain a regular feature. In other areas – notably central Cape Town, where they're a handy and popular way to get around – they are fine.

Away from train and main bus routes, minibus taxis may be the only choice for public transport. They're also a good way to get insights into local life. If you want to try one, read the newspapers, ask for local advice on areas to avoid, and don't ride at night. As most minibus taxis don't carry luggage on the roof, stowing backpacks can be a hassle.

Although minibus taxis in Lesotho and Swaziland don't have stellar road safety records either, they have none of the violence that's associated with their South African counterparts, and are widely used, both for short and longer routes.

Private Taxi

Larger cities in all three countries have a private taxi service. (In Lesotho, you'll only find taxis in Maseru.) Occasionally, you'll find a taxi stand, but usually you'll need to telephone for a cab. Numbers are given in the Getting Around sections of the individual cities. Prices average about R7 to R8 per kilometre.

Shared Taxi

In some towns (and on some longer routes), the only transport option is a shared taxi, basically a smaller version of the minibus taxi. They are slightly more expensive than minibus taxis, and comparable in safety.

TOURS

There are dozens of tours available, ranging from budget-oriented overland truck tours to exclusive luxury safaris. The best way to get information on tours geared to budget travellers is from the network of backpacker hostels around the country. Many have travellers bulletin boards, and some are directly affiliated with budget-tour operators.

Some tour operators to try include the following:

African Routes (☎ 031-563 5080; www.africanroutes .co.za) Offers camping and overland itineraries for younger travellers, including a whirlwind one-week trip taking in Kruger National Park, Swaziland and the Drakensberg.

All in Exclusive (☎ 011-764 2722; allintours@worldon line.co.za) Small-scale upper-end tours aimed at senior travellers.

BirdWatch Cape (☎ 021-762 5059; www.birdwatch .co.za) A small outfit for serious twitchers, focusing on Cape Town and surrounding areas.

Bok Bus (☎ 082-320 1979; www.bokbus.com) Five-day budget-oriented tours along the Garden Route.

Bundu Safari Company (☎ 011-675 0767; www .bundusafaris.co.za) Budget-oriented tours ranging from one to several days, focusing on Kruger National Park and the surrounding area.

Connex (☎ 011-884 8110; www.connex.co.za) Similar to Springbok-Atlas (see that listing).

Encompass Africa (☎ 021-434 9932; encompassafrica@yebo.co.za) A backpacker-oriented outfit offering various itineraries based out of Cape Town.

Malealea Lodge (☎ 051-447 3200; www.malealea.co .ls) The main operator for tours in Lesotho, offering everything from cross-country horse treks to 4WD excursions; can also arrange pick-ups from Bloemfontein in South Africa.

Springbok-Atlas (☎ 021-460 4700; www.springbok atlas.com) One of the major coach-tour operators, offering mid-range tours along popular routes, including day tours. Aimed at older tourists.

Swazi Trails (☎ 416 2180 in Swaziland; www.swazi trails.co.sz) Specialises in day or half-day tours around Swaziland, including white-water rafting, cultural tours and hiking.

Thaba Tours (☎ 072-114 1198, Lesotho 2234 0202; www.thabatours.de) Lesotho specialists, and tours combining South Africa and Lesotho.

Thompsons South Africa (☎ 031-250 3100; www .thompsonssa.com) Mid-range and top-end package tours and safaris, including a two-week tour taking in South Africa's main tourist spots.

Wilderness Safaris (☎ 011-807 1800; www.wilderness -safaris.com) Upscale specialist operator offering luxury safaris and special-interest trips, including bird-watching, botanical and short cycling itineraries; also operates several luxury bush camps.

TRAIN

South Africa's Shosholoza Meyl passenger trains are run by **Spoornet** (☎ 011-773 2944; www.spoornet.co.za), and offer regular services connecting major cities on 'name trains' (some of the main routes are listed on p605). These are a good and safe, albeit slow, way to get around, and much more comfortable than taking the bus. The trains are also relatively affordable and, unlike the long-distance buses, fares on short sectors are not inflated.

On overnight journeys, 1st- and 2nd-class fares include a sleeping berth, but there's an additional charge of R20 for bedding hire. Alternatively, you can hire a private compartment (which sleeps four in 1st class and six in 2nd class) or a coupe (which sleeps two in 1st class and three in 2nd class) – these are a good way of travelling more securely. Meals are available in the dining car, or in the comfort of your compartment.

Tickets must be booked at least 24 hours in advance (you can book up to three months in advance). Bookings for anywhere in the country can be done at any individual station, or through the **Shosholoza Meyl Reservations Centre** (☎ 0860 008 888). For an overview of what awaits you on the South African rails, check out **The Man in Seat 61** (www.seat61.com/South%20Africa.htm).

Routes

Main routes include the following:
Algoa Jo'burg–Port Elizabeth via Bloemfontein; daily; 20 hours.
Amatola Jo'burg–East London via Bloemfontein; Sunday to Friday; 20 hours.
Bosvelder Jo'burg–Musina via Makhado; daily; 17 hours.
Diamond Express Jo'burg–Bloemfontein; three times weekly; nine hours.

TRANSPORT

RIDING THE RAILS

Train travel in South Africa has a place of its own, with an eclectic band of devotees. In addition to the routes mentioned under Train – where the emphasis is on functionality and getting from one place to another – there are numerous special lines. Following are some of the possibilities.

Blue Train (☎ 021-449 2672, 012-334 8459; www.bluetrain.co.za) South Africa's most famous train, with such a reputation among rail aficionados that some people come to South Africa just to ride it. Schedules vary, and are now much curtailed from what they once were, but the train usually runs about twice weekly between Pretoria/Jo'burg and Cape Town, with departures on Monday, Wednesday and/or Friday. For 27 hours of luxury, regular deluxe/luxury one-way fares are R18,300/20,430, including all meals and drinks. In addition to the contacts listed here, some travel agents, both in South Africa and in other countries, also take bookings. It's worth inquiring about special packages, including one-way flights from Jo'burg to Cape Town and a night's accommodation. Also inquire about low-season fares if you are thinking about travelling between May and August.

Mike & Rachel Barry (☎ /fax 023-230 0331; www.tulbagh.net/tulbagh_train_packages.htm) Organises an interesting range of upper mid-range one- and two-day package trips by train from Cape Town to Tulbagh, the Klein Cederberg Nature Reserve and Matjiesfontein.

Rovos Rail (☎ 012-315 8242; www.rovos.co.za) Rivals the *Blue Train* as the most luxurious and expensive service in Africa. Regular trips include Pretoria–Cape Town over two nights/three days (as opposed to the *Blue Train*'s one night/two days), with stops at Matjiesfontein and Kimberley; Pretoria–Durban; and Cape Town–George.

Shongololo Express (☎ 011-781 4616; www.shongololo.com) Not quite as luxurious as the other classic trains (though it's still quite acceptable); you travel by night and then disembark for a day's sightseeing – the land-based version of a cruise. Among others, offers a 16-day tour taking in South Africa's major sites.

Union Ltd Steam Rail Tours (☎ 021-449 4391; http://home.intekom.com/bluegrass/sites/steamsa/) Runs re-stored steam trains. The *Union Limited* was the pre-*Blue Train* king of the line in South Africa, running to Cape Town with passengers who were meeting liners to Europe. The train was luxurious in its time and has been meticulously restored. It runs several tours, including the six-day 'Golden Thread' from Cape Town along the coast to Oudtshoorn and back again. Passengers have more room than they once did, with two people now sharing a four-berth compartment and singles in a two-berth compartment.

There are also many less-ritzy steam train trips, including the *Apple Express* from Port Elizabeth (p231), the *Outeniqua Choo-Tjoe* between Knysna and George (p194), and the *Banana Express* along the KwaZulu-Natal south coast from Port Shepstone (p301).

Komati Jo'burg–Komatipoort via Pretoria, Middleburg and Nelspruit; daily; 12 hours; connects to the Komatipoort–Maputo train.

Trans Karoo Pretoria/Jo'burg–Cape Town via Kimberly; daily; 28 hours.

Trans Natal Jo'burg–Durban via Ladysmith and Pieter-maritzburg; five times weekly; 13½ hours.

Trans Oranje Cape Town–Durban via Kimberley, Bloemfontein and Kroonstad; weekly; 31 hours.

Some 1st-/2nd-/economy-class sample fares: Jo'burg–Durban R250/165/100; Cape Town–Pretoria R550/350/230; Jo'burg–

Port Elizabeth R365/245/145. Return fares are double the one-way fares. It's possible to put a vehicle on board the *Trans Karoo* for an extra R1345.

There are no passenger trains in Lesotho or Swaziland.

Metro Trains

There are metro services in Jo'burg, Cape Town and Pretoria. See p398, p140 and p417 for more information. Always check the safety situation before using metro services, as robbery is a problem.

Health

CONTENTS

As long as you stay up to date with your vaccinations and take basic preventive measures, you're unlikely to succumb to most of the health hazards covered in this chapter. While South Africa, Lesotho and Swaziland have an impressive selection of tropical diseases on offer, it's more likely you'll get a bout of diarrhoea or a cold than a more exotic malady. The main exception to this is malaria, which is a real risk in lower-lying areas of Swaziland, and in eastern South Africa.

BEFORE YOU GO

A little predeparture planning will save you trouble later. Get a check-up from your dentist and from your doctor if you have any regular medication or chronic illness, eg high blood pressure and asthma. You should also organise spare contact lenses and glasses (and take your optical prescription with you); get a first aid and medical kit together; and arrange necessary vaccinations.

Travellers can register with the **International Association for Medical Advice to Travellers** (IAMAT; www.iamat.org), which provides directories of certified doctors. If you'll be spending much time in more remote areas, such as parts of Lesotho, consider doing a first aid course (contact the Red Cross or St John's Ambulance), or attending a remote medicine first aid course, such as that offered by the **Royal Geographical Society** (www.wildernessmedicaltraining.co.uk).

If you are bringing medications with you, carry them in their original containers, clearly labelled. A signed and dated letter from your physician describing all medical conditions and medications, including generic names, is also a good idea. If carrying syringes or needles, be sure to have a physician's letter documenting their medical necessity.

INSURANCE

Find out in advance whether your insurance plan will make payments directly to providers, or will reimburse you later for overseas health expenditures. In South Africa, Lesotho and Swaziland, most doctors expect payment in cash. It's vital to ensure that your travel insurance will cover any emergency transport required to get you to a hospital in a major city, or all the way home, by air and with a medical attendant if necessary. Not all insurance covers this, so check the contract carefully. If you need medical help, your insurance company might be able to help locate the nearest hospital or clinic, or you can ask at your hotel. In an emergency, contact your embassy or consulate.

RECOMMENDED VACCINATIONS

The **World Health Organization** (www.who.int/en/) recommends that all travellers be covered for diphtheria, tetanus, measles, mumps, rubella and polio, as well as for hepatitis B, regardless of their destination. The consequences of these diseases can be severe, and outbreaks do occur.

According to the **Centers for Disease Control and Prevention** (www.cdc.gov), the following vaccinations are recommended for South Africa, Lesotho and Swaziland: hepatitis A, hepatitis B, rabies and typhoid, and boosters for tetanus, diphtheria and measles. Yellow fever is not a risk in the region, but the certificate is an entry requirement if travelling from an infected region (see p611).

MEDICAL CHECKLIST

It's a very good idea to carry a medical and first aid kit with you, to help yourself in the case of minor illness or injury. Following is a list of items to consider packing.

- antibiotics (prescription only), eg ciprofloxacin (Ciproxin) or norfloxacin (Utinor)
- antidiarrhoeal drugs (eg loperamide)
- acetaminophen (paracetamol) or aspirin
- anti-inflammatory drugs (eg ibuprofen)
- antihistamines (for hay fever and allergic reactions)
- antibacterial ointment (eg Bactroban) for cuts and abrasions (prescription only)
- antimalaria pills, if you'll be in malarial areas
- bandages, gauze, gauze rolls
- scissors, safety pins, tweezers
- pocket knife
- DEET-containing insect repellent for the skin
- permethrin-containing insect spray for clothing, tents, and bed nets
- sun block
- oral rehydration salts
- iodine tablets (for water purification)
- sterile needles, syringes and fluids if travelling to remote areas

ONLINE RESOURCES

There is a wealth of travel health advice on the Internet. The Lonely Planet website at www.lonelyplanet.com is a good place to start. The World Health Organization publishes the helpful *International Travel and Health*, available free at www.who.int /ith/. Other useful websites include **MD Travel Health** (www.mdtravelhealth.com) and **Fit for Travel** (www.fitfortravel.scot.nhs.uk).

Official government travel health websites include:

Australia www.dfat.gov.au/travel/
Canada www.hc-sc.gc.ca/pphb-dgspsp/tmp-pmv /pub_e.html
UK www.doh.gov.uk/traveladvice/index.htm
USA www.cdc.gov/travel/

FURTHER READING

- *A Comprehensive Guide to Wilderness and Travel Medicine* (1998) Eric A Weiss.
- *Healthy Travel* (1999) Jane Wilson-Howarth.
- *Healthy Travel Africa* (2000) Isabelle Young.
- *How to Stay Healthy Abroad* (2002) Richard Dawood.
- *Travel in Health* (1994) Graham Fry.
- *Travel with Children* (2004) Cathy Lanigan.

IN TRANSIT

DEEP VEIN THROMBOSIS (DVT)

Prolonged immobility during flights can cause deep vein thrombosis (DVT) – the formation of blood clots in the legs. The longer the flight, the greater the risk. Although most blood clots are reabsorbed uneventfully, some might break off and travel through the blood vessels to the lungs, where they could cause life-threatening complications.

The chief symptom is swelling or pain of the foot, ankle or calf, usually but not always on just one side. When a blood clot travels to the lungs, it may cause chest pain and breathing difficulty. Travellers with any of these symptoms should immediately seek medical attention. To prevent DVT walk about the cabin, perform isometric compressions of the leg muscles (ie contract the leg muscles while sitting), drink plenty of fluids and avoid alcohol.

JET LAG

If you're crossing more than five time zones you could suffer jet lag, resulting in insomnia, fatigue, malaise or nausea. To avoid jet lag try drinking plenty of fluids (nonalcoholic) and eating light meals. Upon arrival, get exposure to natural sunlight and readjust your schedule (for meals, sleep, etc) as soon as possible.

IN SOUTH AFRICA, LESOTHO & SWAZILAND

AVAILABILITY & COST OF HEALTH CARE

Good quality health care is available in all of South Africa's major urban areas, and private hospitals are generally of excellent standard. Public hospitals, by contrast are often underfunded and overcrowded, and in off-the-beaten-track areas, such as the former homelands, and in Lesotho and Swaziland, reliable medical facilities are rare.

Prescriptions are generally required in South Africa. Drugs for chronic diseases should be brought from home. There is a high risk of contracting human immuno-deficiency virus (HIV) from infected blood transfusions. The **BloodCare Foundation** (www .bloodcare.org.uk) is a useful source of safe, screened blood, which can be transported to any part of the world within 24 hours.

INFECTIOUS DISEASES

Following are some of the diseases that are found in South Africa, Lesotho and Swaziland, though with a few basic preventative measures, it's unlikely that you'll succumb to any of these.

Cholera

Cholera is caused by a bacteria and spread via contaminated drinking water. In South Africa, the risk to travellers is very low; you're only likely to encounter it in eastern rural areas, where you should avoid tap water and unpeeled or uncooked fruits and vegetables. The main symptom is profuse watery diarrhoea, which causes debilitation if fluids are not replaced quickly. An oral cholera vaccine is available in the USA, but it is not particularly effective. Most cases of cholera can be avoided by close attention to good drinking water and by avoiding potentially contaminated food. Treatment is by fluid replacement (orally or via a drip), but sometimes antibiotics are needed. Self-treatment is not advised.

Dengue Fever (Break-bone Fever)

Dengue fever, spread through the bite of the mosquito, causes a feverish illness with headache and muscle pains similar to those experienced with a bad, prolonged attack of influenza. There might be a rash. Mosquito bites should be avoided whenever possible. It's present in southeastern coastal areas of South Africa, and in Lesotho and Swaziland. Self-treatment: paracetamol and rest.

Filariasis

Filariasis is caused by tiny worms migrating in the lymphatic system, and is spread by the bite from an infected mosquito. Symptoms include localised itching and swelling of the legs and/or genitalia. Treatment is available. Self-treatment: none.

Hepatitis A

Hepatitis A – which occurs in all three countries – is spread through contaminated food (particularly shellfish) and water. It causes jaundice and, although it is rarely fatal, it can cause prolonged lethargy and delayed recovery. If you've had hepatitis A, you shouldn't drink alcohol for up to six months afterwards, but once you've recovered, there won't be any long-term problems. The first symptoms include dark urine and a yellow colour to the whites of the eyes. Sometimes a fever and abdominal pain might be present. Hepatitis A vaccine (Avaxim, VAQTA, Havrix) is given as an injection: a single dose will give protection for up to a year, and a booster after a year gives 10-year protection. Hepatitis A and typhoid vaccines can also be given as a single dose vaccine, hepatyrix or viatim. Self-treatment: none.

Hepatitis B

Hepatitis B – found in all three countries – is spread through infected blood, contaminated needles and sexual intercourse. It can also be spread from an infected mother to the baby during childbirth. It affects the liver, causing jaundice and occasionally liver failure. Most people recover completely, but some people might be chronic carriers of the virus, which could lead eventually to cirrhosis or liver cancer. Those visiting high-risk areas for long periods or those with increased social or occupational risk should be immunised. Many countries now routinely give hepatitis B as part of the childhood vaccination programme. It is given singly or can be given at the same time as hepatitis A (hepatyrix).

A course will give protection for at least five years. It can be given over four weeks or six months. Self-treatment: none.

HIV

HIV, the virus that causes acquired immune deficiency syndrome (AIDS), is an enormous problem in South Africa, Lesotho and Swaziland, with a devastating impact on local health systems and community structures. KwaZulu-Natal has one of the highest rates of infection on the continent, with an HIV-positive incidence of about 35%, and South Africa has more people living with HIV than any country in the world. The statistics are similarly sobering for Lesotho and Swaziland. The virus is spread through

HEALTH

infected blood and blood products, by sexual intercourse with an infected partner and from an infected mother to her baby during childbirth and breastfeeding. It can be spread through 'blood to blood' contacts, such as with contaminated instruments during medical, dental, acupuncture and other body-piercing procedures, and through sharing used intravenous needles. At present there is no cure; medication that might keep the disease under control is available, but these drugs are too expensive, or unavailable, for the overwhelming majority of South Africans. If you think you might have been infected with HIV, a blood test is necessary; a three-month gap after exposure and before testing is required to allow antibodies to appear in the blood. Self-treatment: none.

Malaria

Malaria is mainly confined to the eastern half of South Africa (northern KwaZulu-Natal, Mpumalanga, Limpopo) and to Swaziland, although parts of North-West Province can also be malarial. Apart from road accidents, it's probably the only major health risk that you face travelling in this area, and precautions should be taken. The disease is caused by a parasite in the bloodstream spread via the bite of the female Anopheles mosquito. There are several types of malaria; falciparum malaria is the most dangerous type and the predominant form in South Africa. Infection rates vary with season and climate, so check out the situation before departure. Several different drugs are used to prevent malaria, and new ones are in the pipeline. Up-to-date advice from a travel health clinic is essential as some medication is more suitable for some travellers than others (eg people with epilepsy should avoid mefloquine, and doxycycline should not be taken by pregnant women or children aged under 12).

The early stages of malaria include headaches, fevers, generalised aches and pains, and malaise, which could be mistaken for flu. Other symptoms can include abdominal pain, diarrhoea and a cough. Anyone who develops a fever in a malarial area should assume malarial infection until a blood test proves negative, even if you have been taking antimalarial medication. If not treated, the next stage could develop within 24 hours, particularly if falciparum malaria is the parasite: jaundice, then reduced consciousness and coma (also known as cerebral malaria) followed by death. Treatment in hospital is essential, and the death rate might still be as high as 10% even in the best intensive-care facilities.

Many travellers think that malaria is a mild illness, and that taking antimalarial drugs causes more illness through side effects than actually getting malaria. This is unfortunately not true. If you decide against antimalarial drugs, you must understand the risks, and be obsessive about avoiding mosquito bites. Use nets and insect repellent, and report any fever or flu-like symptoms to a doctor as soon as possible. Some people advocate homeopathic preparations against malaria, such as Demal200, but as yet there is no conclusive evidence that this

---

ANTIMALARIAL A TO D

■ **A** – Awareness of the risk. No medication is totally effective, but protection of up to 95% is achievable with most drugs, as long as other measures have been taken.

■ **B** – Bites – avoid at all costs. Sleep in a screened room, use a mosquito spray or coils, sleep under a permethrin-impregnated net at night. Cover up at night with long trousers and long sleeves, preferably with permethrin-treated clothing. Apply appropriate repellent to all areas of exposed skin in the evenings.

■ **C** – Chemical prevention (ie antimalarial drugs) is usually needed in malarial areas. Expert advice is needed as resistance patterns can change, and new drugs are in development. Not all antimalarial drugs are suitable for everyone. Most antimalarial drugs need to be started at least a week in advance and continued for four weeks after the last possible exposure to malaria.

■ **D** – Diagnosis. If you have a fever or flu-like illness within a year of travel to a malarial area, malaria is a possibility, and immediate medical attention is necessary.

is effective, and many homeopaths do not recommend their use.

Malaria in pregnancy frequently results in miscarriage or premature labour, and the risks to both mother and foetus during pregnancy are considerable. Travel throughout the region when pregnant should be carefully considered. Adults who have survived childhood malaria have developed immunity and usually only develop mild cases of malaria; most Western travellers have no immunity at all. Immunity wanes after 18 months of nonexposure, so even if you have had malaria in the past and used to live in a malaria-prone area, you might no longer be immune.

Rabies

Rabies is spread by receiving bites or licks from an infected animal on broken skin. Few human cases are reported in South Africa, with the risks highest in rural areas. It is always fatal once the clinical symptoms start (which might be up to several months after an infected bite), so post-bite vaccination should be given as soon as possible. Post-bite vaccination (whether or not you've been vaccinated before the bite) prevents the virus from spreading to the central nervous system. Animal handlers should be vaccinated, as should those travelling to remote areas where a reliable source of post-bite vaccine is not available within 24 hours. Three preventive injections are needed over a month. If you have not been vaccinated you'll need a course of five injections starting 24 hours or as soon as possible after the injury. If you have been vaccinated, you'll need fewer post-bite injections, and have more time to seek medical help. Self-treatment: none.

Schistosomiasis (Bilharzia)

This disease is a risk in eastern parts of South Africa, and in Swaziland. (Lesotho, happily, is considered schistosomiasis-free.) It's spread by flukes (minute worms) that are carried by a species of freshwater snail, which then sheds them into slow-moving or still water. The parasites penetrate human skin during swimming and then migrate to the bladder or bowel. They are excreted via stool or urine and could contaminate fresh water, where the cycle starts again. Swimming in suspect freshwater lakes or slow-running

rivers should be avoided. Symptoms range from none, to transient fever and rash, and advanced cases might have blood in the stool or in the urine. A blood test can detect antibodies if you might have been exposed, and treatment is readily available. If not treated the infection can cause kidney failure or permanent bowel damage. It's not possible for you to infect others. Self-treatment: none.

Tuberculosis (TB)

TB is spread through close respiratory contact and occasionally through infected milk or milk products. BCG vaccination is recommended if you'll be mixing closely with the local population, especially on long-term stays, although it gives only moderate protection against TB. TB can be asymptomatic, only being picked up on a routine chest X-ray. Alternatively, it can cause a cough, weight loss or fever, sometimes months or even years after exposure. Self-treatment: none.

Typhoid

This is spread through food or water contaminated by infected human faeces. The first symptom is usually a fever or a pink rash on the abdomen. Sometimes septicaemia (blood poisoning) can occur. A typhoid vaccine (typhim Vi, typherix) will give protection for three years. In some countries, the oral vaccine Vivotif is also available. Antibiotics are usually given as treatment, and death is rare unless septicaemia occurs. Self-treatment: none.

Yellow Fever

Although not a problem within South Africa, Lesotho or Swaziland, you'll need to carry a certificate of vaccination if you'll be arriving in South Africa from an infected country. Infected countries include most of South Africa's neighbours; for a full list see the websites of the **World Health Organization** (www .who.int/wer/) or the **Centers for Disease Control and Prevention** (www.cdc.gov/travel/blusheet.htm).

TRAVELLERS' DIARRHOEA

While less likely in South Africa than elsewhere on the continent, this is a common travel-related illness – sometimes simply due to dietary changes – and it's possible that you'll succumb, especially if you're spending a lot of time in rural areas or eating at inexpensive local food stalls. To avoid diarrhoea, only eat fresh fruits or vegetables if cooked or peeled, and be wary of dairy products that might contain unpasteurised milk. Although freshly cooked food can often be a safe option, plates or serving utensils might be dirty, so be selective when eating food from street vendors (make sure that cooked food is piping hot all the way through). If you develop diarrhoea, be sure to drink plenty of fluids, preferably an oral rehydration solution, containing lots of water and some salt and sugar. A few loose stools don't require treatment but, if you start having more than four or five stools a day, you should start taking an antibiotic (usually a quinoline drug, such as ciprofloxacin or norfloxacin) and an antidiarrhoeal agent (such as loperamide) if you're not within easy reach of a toilet. If diarrhoea is bloody, persists for more than 72 hours or is accompanied by fever, shaking chills or severe abdominal pain, you should seek medical attention.

Amoebic Dysentery

Contracted by eating contaminated food and water, amoebic dysentery causes blood and mucus in the faeces. It can be relatively mild and tends to come on gradually, but seek medical advice if you think you have the illness as it won't clear up without treatment (which is with specific antibiotics).

Giardiasis

This, like amoebic dysentery, is also caused by ingesting contaminated food or water. The illness usually appears a week or more after you have been exposed to the offending parasite. Giardiasis might cause only a short-lived bout of typical travellers' diarrhoea, but it can also cause persistent diarrhoea. Ideally, seek medical advice if you suspect you have giardiasis, but if you are in a remote area you could start a course of antibiotics.

ENVIRONMENTAL HAZARDS
Heat Exhaustion

This condition occurs following heavy sweating and excessive fluid loss with inadequate replacement of fluids and salt, and is primarily a risk in hot climates when taking unaccustomed exercise before full acclimatisation. Symptoms include headache, dizziness and tiredness. Dehydration is already happening by the time you feel thirsty – aim to drink sufficient water to produce pale, diluted urine. Self-treatment: fluid replacement with water and/or fruit juice, and cooling by cold water and fans. The treatment of the salt-loss component consists of consuming salty fluids as in soup, and adding a little more table salt to foods than usual.

Heatstroke

Heat exhaustion is a precursor to the much more serious condition of heatstroke. In this case there is damage to the sweating mechanism, with an excessive rise in body temperature; irrational and hyperactive behaviour; and eventually loss of consciousness and death. Rapid cooling by spraying the body with water and fanning is ideal. Emergency fluid and electrolyte replacement is usually also required by intravenous drip.

Insect Bites & Stings

Mosquitoes might not always carry malaria or dengue fever, but they (and other insects) can cause irritation and infected bites. To avoid these, take the same precautions as you would for avoiding malaria (see p610). Bee and wasp stings cause real problems only to those who have a severe allergy to the stings (anaphylaxis), in which case, carry an adrenaline (epinephrine) injection.

Scorpions are found in arid areas. They can cause a painful bite that is sometimes life-threatening. If bitten by a scorpion, take a painkiller. Medical treatment should be sought if collapse occurs.

Ticks are always a risk away from urban areas. If you get bitten, press down around the tick's head with tweezers, grab the head and gently pull upwards. Avoid pulling the rear of the body as this may squeeze the tick's gut contents through the attached mouth parts into the skin, increasing the risk of infection and disease. Smearing chemicals on the tick will not make it let go and is not recommended.

Snake Bites

Basically, avoid getting bitten! Don't walk barefoot, or stick your hand into holes or cracks. However, 50% of those bitten by venomous snakes are not actually injected with poison (envenomed). If bitten by a snake, do not panic. Immobilise the bitten limb with a splint (such as a stick) and apply a bandage over the site, with firm pressure – similar to bandaging a sprain. Do not apply a tourniquet, or cut or suck the bite. Get medical help as soon as possible.

Water

High-quality water is widely available in South Africa and drinking from taps is fine, except in rural areas. In Lesotho and Swaziland, stick to bottled water, and purify stream water before drinking it.

TRADITIONAL MEDICINE

According to some estimates, as many as 85% of residents of South Africa, Lesotho and Swaziland rely in part, or in whole, on traditional medicine. It's estimated that there are over 200,000 traditional healers in South Africa alone (in comparison with some 20,000 Western medical practitioners). Given the comparatively high costs, and the unavailability of Western medicine in many rural areas, these traditional healers are the first contact for much of the population when they fall ill. The sangoma (traditional healer) and *inyanga* (herbalist) hold revered positions in many communities, and traditional medicinal products are widely available in local markets. On the darker side of things, *muti* killings (in which human body parts are sought for traditional medicinal purposes) are also common – reported approximately monthly – as are abuses in which false claims are made for cures, or in which diseases spread by unsanitary practices.

While there is still no national legislation regulating traditional medicinal practitioners, there are several umbrella groups, including the Traditional Healers' Association of South Africa, and the African Herbal Medicine Association. These aim to raise awareness of and curb abuses in the practice of traditional medicine, but there is a long way to go.

HEALTH

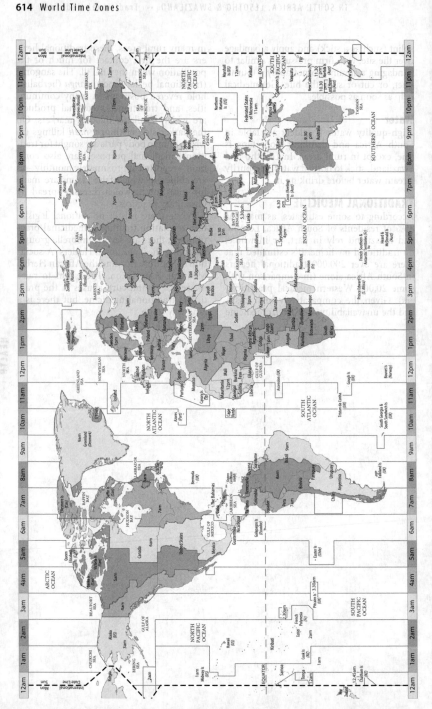

Language

CONTENTS

WHO SPEAKS WHAT WHERE?

South Africa

South Africa's official languages were once only English and Afrikaans, but nine others have since been added to the list. The complete list of official languages is: Zulu (23.8%), Xhosa (17.6%), Afrikaans (13.3%), North Sotho (9.4%), English and Tswana (8.2% each), South Sotho (7.9%), Tsonga (4.4%), Swati (2.7%), Venda (2.3%), Ndebele (1.6%). (The figures in brackets are from the 2001 census and show first language speakers as a percentage of total population.)

Forms, brochures and timetables are usually bilingual (English and Afrikaans) but road signs alternate. Most Afrikaans speakers also speak good English, but this is not always the case in small rural towns and among older people. However, it's not uncommon for Blacks in cities to speak at least six languages; Whites can usually speak two.

In the Cape Town area only three languages are prominent: Afrikaans (spoken by many Whites and Coloureds), English (spoken by nearly everyone) and Xhosa (spoken mainly by Blacks).

Lesotho & Swaziland

The official languages of Lesotho are South Sotho and English.

The official languages of Swaziland are Swati and English. English is the medium of instruction in all schools and is widely understood. Parliamentary proceedings and debates in are held in both languages.

SOUTH AFRICAN ENGLISH

English has undergone some changes during its time in South Africa. Quite a few words have changed meaning, new words have been appropriated and, thanks to the influence of Afrikaans, a distinctive accent has developed. British rather than US practice is followed in grammar and spelling. In some cases British words are preferred to their US equivalents (eg 'lift' not 'elevator', 'petrol' not 'gas'). In African English, repetition for emphasis is common: something that burns you is 'hot hot'; fields after the rains are 'green green'; a crowded minibus with no more room is 'full full', and so on.

AFRIKAANS

Although Afrikaans is closely associated with Afrikaners, it is also the first language of many Coloureds. Ironically, it was probably first used as a common language by the polyglot Coloured community of the Cape, and passed back to Whites by nannies and servants. Around six million people speak the language, roughly half of whom are Afrikaners and half of whom are Coloured.

Afrikaans developed from the High Dutch of the 17th century. It has abandoned the complicated grammar of Dutch and incorporated vocabulary from French, English, indigenous African languages and even Asian languages (as a result of the influence of East Asian slaves). It's inventive, powerful and expressive, but it wasn't recognised as one of the country's official languages until 1925, before which it was officially termed a dialect of Dutch.

Pronunciation

a	as the 'u' in 'pup'
e	when word stress falls on **e**, it's as in 'net'; when unstressed, it's as the 'a' in 'ago'
i	when word stress falls on **i**, it's as in 'hit'; when unstressed, it's as the 'a' in 'ago'

o	as the 'o' in 'fort', but very short
u	as the 'e' in 'angel' with lips pouted
r	a rolled 'rr' sound
aai	as the 'y' sound in 'why'
ae	as 'ah'
ee	as in 'deer'
ei	as the 'ay' in 'play'
oe	as the 'u' in 'put'
oë	as the 'oe' in 'doer'
ooi/oei	as the 'ooey' in 'phooey'
tj	as the 'ch' in 'chunk'

Greetings & Conversation

Hello.	Hallo.
Good morning.	Goeiemôre.
Good afternoon.	Goeiemiddag.
Good evening.	Goeienaand.
Good night.	Goeienag.
How are you?	Hoe gaan dit?
Good, thank you.	Goed dankie.
Please.	Asseblief.
Thank you.	Dankie.
Thank you very much.	Baie dankie.
Pardon.	Ekskuus.
Yes.	Ja.
No.	Nee.
What?	Wat?
How?	Hoe?
How many/much?	Hoeveel?
Where?	Waar?
Isn't that so?	Né?
Do you speak English?	Praat U Engels?
Do you speak Afrikaans?	Praat U Afrikaans?
I only understand a little Afrikaans.	Ek verstaan net 'n bietjie Afrikaans.
Where are you from?	Waarvandaan kom U?
from ...	van ...
overseas	oorsee
son/boy	seun
daughter/girl	dogter
wife	vrou
husband	eggenoot
mother	ma
father	pa
sister	suster
brother	broer
nice/good/pleasant	lekker
bad	sleg
cheap	goedkoop
expensive	duur
party/rage	jol

Shopping & Services

art gallery	kunsgalery
bank	bank
building	gebou
church	kerk
city	stad
city centre	middestad
emergency	nood
enquiries	navrae
exit	uitgang
information	inligting
office	kantoor
pharmacy/chemist	apteek
police	polisie
police station	polisiestasie
post office	poskantoor
rooms	kamers
tourist bureau	toeristeburo
town	dorp

Transport

avenue	laan
car	kar
freeway	vrymaak
highway	snelweg
road	pad, weg
station	stasie
street	straat
track	spoor
traffic light	verkeerslig
utility/pick-up	bakkie
arrival	aankoms
departure	vertrek
one way ticket	enkel kaartjie
return ticket	retoer kaartjie
to	na
from	van
left	links
right	regs
at the corner	op die hoek
travel	reis

In the Country

bay	baai
beach	strand
caravan park	woonwapark
field/plain	veld
ford	drif
game reserve	wildtuin
hiking trail	wandelpad
lake	meer
marsh	vlei
mountain	berg
point	punt
river	rivier

Food & Drinks

barbecue	*braaivleis/braai*
beer	*bier*
bread	*brood*
cheese	*kaas*
chicken	*hoender*
cup of coffee	*koppie koffie*
dried, salted meat	*biltong*
farm sausage	*boerewors*
fish	*vis*
fruit	*vrugte*
glass of milk	*glas melk*
hotel bar	*kroeg*
meat	*vleis*
pork	*varkvlies*
steak	*biefstuk*
tea	*tee*
vegetables	*groente*
water	*water*
wine	*wyn*

Time & Days

When?	*Wanneer?*
am	*vm*
pm	*nm*
soon	*nou-nou*
today	*vandag*
tomorrow	*môre*
yesterday	*gister*
daily	*daagliks*
weekly	*weekblad*
public holiday	*openbare vakansiedag*

Monday	*Maandag (Ma)*
Tuesday	*Dinsdag (Di)*
Wednesday	*Woensdag (Wo)*
Thursday	*Donderdag (Do)*
Friday	*Vrydag (Vr)*
Saturday	*Saterdag (Sa)*
Sunday	*Sondag (So)*

Numbers

1	*een*
2	*twee*
3	*drie*
4	*vier*
5	*vyf*
6	*ses*
7	*sewe*
8	*ag*
9	*nege*
10	*tien*
11	*elf*
12	*twaalf*

13	*dertien*
14	*veertien*
15	*vyftien*
16	*sestien*
17	*sewentien*
18	*agtien*
19	*negentien*
20	*twintig*
21	*een en twintig*
30	*dertig*
40	*veertig*
50	*vyftig*
60	*sestig*
70	*sewentig*
80	*tagtig*
90	*negentig*
100	*honderd*
1000	*duisend*

NDEBELE

Ndebele is spoken as a first language by relatively small percentages of the people in South Africa's northern provinces.

Hello.	*Lotsha.*
Goodbye.	*Khamaba kuhle/Sala kuhle.*
Yes.	*I-ye.*
No.	*Awa.*
Please.	*Ngibawa.*
Thank you.	*Ngiyathokaza.*
What's your name?	*Ungubani ibizo lakho?*
My name is ...	*Ibizo lami ngu ...*
I come from ...	*Ngibuya e ...*

NORTH SOTHO

Most mother-tongue speakers of North Sotho can be found in South Africa's north-eastern provinces, with the vast majority to be found in Limpopo.

Hello.	*Thobela.*
Goodbye.	*Sala gabotse.*
Yes.	*Ee.*
No.	*Aowa.*
Please.	*Ke kgopela.*
Thank you.	*Ke ya leboga.*
What's your name?	*Ke mang lebitso la gago?*
My name is ...	*Lebitso laka ke ...*
I come from ...	*Ke bowa kwa ...*

SOUTH SOTHO

South Sotho is one of two official languages in Lesotho (English being the other), and is also spoken by Basotho people in the Free State, North-West Province and Gauteng in

South Africa. It's useful to know some words and phrases if you're planning to visit Lesotho, especially if you want to trek in remote areas.

Hello.	*Dumela.*
Greetings father.	*Lumela ntate.*
Peace father.	*Khotso ntate.*
Greetings mother.	*Lumela 'me.*
Peace mother.	*Khotso 'me.*
Greetings brother.	*Lumela abuti.*
Peace brother.	*Khotso abuti.*
Greetings sister.	*Lumela ausi.*
Peace sister.	*Khotso ausi.*

There are three commonly used ways of saying 'How are you?':

How are you?	*O kae?* (sg)
	Le kae? (pl)
How do you live?	*O phela joang?* (sg)
	Le phela joang? (pl)
How did you get up?	*O tsohele joang?* (sg)
	Le tsohele joang? (pl)

The responses are:

I'm here.	*Ke teng.* (sg)
	Re teng. (pl)
I live well.	*Ke phela hantle.* (sg)
	Re phela hantle. (pl)
I got up well.	*Ke tsohile hantle.* (sg)
	Re tsohile hantle. (pl)

These questions and answers are quite interchangeable. Someone could ask you *O phela joang?* and you could answer *Ke teng.*

When trekking, people always ask *Lea kae?* (Where are you going?) and *O tsoa kae?* or the plural *Le tsoa kae?* (Where have you come from?). When parting, use the following expressions:

Stay well.	*Sala hantle.* (sg)
	Salang hantle. (pl)
Go well.	*Tsamaea hantle.* (sg)
	Tsamaeang hantle. (pl)

'Thank you' is *kea leboha*, pronounced 'ke·ya le·bo·wa'. The herd boys often ask for *chelete* (money) or *lipompong* (sweets), pronounced 'dee·pom·pong'. If you want to say 'I don't have any', the answer is *ha dio*, pronounced 'ha dee·o'.

SWATI

Swati is one of two official languages in Swaziland (the other is English) and is also widely spoken as a first language in South Africa's Mpumalanga province. It's very similar to Zulu, and the two languages are mutually intelligible.

Hello. (to one person)	*Sawubona.* (lit: 'I see you')
Hello. (to more than one person)	*Sanibonani.*
How are you?	*Kunjani?*
I'm fine.	*Kulungile.*
We're very well.	*Natsi sikhona.*
Goodbye. (if leaving)	*Salakahle.* (lit: 'stay well')
Goodbye. (if staying)	*Hambakahle.* (lit: 'go well')
Please.	*Ngicela.*
I thank you.	*Ngiyabonga.*
We thank you.	*Siyabonga.*
Yes.	*Yebo.* (also a common all purpose greeting)
No.	*Cha.* (pronounced as a click)
Sorry.	*Lucolo.*
What's your name?	*Ngubani libito lakho?*
My name is ...	*Libitolami ngingu ...*
I'm from ...	*Ngingewekubuya e ...*
Do you have?	*Une yini?*
How much?	*Malini?*
Is there a bus to ...?	*Kukhona ibhasi yini leya?*
When does it leave?	*Isuka nini?*
Where is the tourist office?	*Likuphi lihovisi leti vakashi?*

today	*lamuhla*
tomorrow	*kusasa*
yesterday	*itolo*
morning	*ekuseni*
afternoon	*entsambaba*
evening	*kusihlwa*
night	*ebusuku*

TSONGA

Tsonga is spoken as a first language in South Africa's north, predominantly in the provinces of Limpopo and Gauteng, and to a lesser extent in Mpumalanga and North-West Province.

Hello.	*Avusheni.* (morning)
	Inhelekani. (afternoon)
	Riperile. (evening)
Goodbye.	*Salani kahle.*
Yes.	*Hi swona.*
No.	*A hi swona.*

Please.	*Nakombela.*
Thank you.	*I nkomu.*
What's your name?	*U mani vito ra wena?*
My name is ...	*Vito ra mina i ...*
I come from ...	*Ndzihuma e ...*

TSWANA

Tswana is spoken in South Africa as a first language mainly in North-West Province and Gauteng, with lesser numbers of first language speakers in the eastern areas of Northern Cape and the western parts of the Free State.

Hello.	*Dumela.*
Goodbye.	*Sala sentle.*
Yes.	*Ee.*
No.	*Nnya.*
Please.	*Ke a kopa.*
Thank you.	*Ke a leboga.*
What's your name?	*Leina la gago ke mang?*
My name is ...	*Leina la me ke ...*
I come from ...	*Ke tswa ...*

VENDA

Venda is spoken mainly in the northeastern border region of South Africa's Limpopo province.

Hello.	*Ndi matseloni.* (morning)
	Ndi masiari. (afternoon)
	Ndi madekwana. (evening)
Goodbye.	*Kha vha sale zwavhudi.*
Yes.	*Ndi zwone.*
No.	*A si zwone.*
Please.	*Ndikho u humbela.*
Thank you.	*Ndo livhuwa.*
What's your name?	*Zina lavho ndi nnyi?*
My name is ...	*Zina langa ndi ...*
I come from ...	*Ndi bva ...*

XHOSA

Xhosa is the language of the Xhosa people. It's the dominant indigenous language in South Africa's Eastern Cape province, although you'll meet Xhosa speakers throughout the region.

It's worth noting that *bawo* is a term of respect used when addressing an older man.

Good morning.	*Molo.*
Goodnight.	*Rhonanai.*
Do you speak English?	*Uyakwazi ukuthetha siNgesi?*

Are you well?	*Uphilile na namhlanje?*
Yes, I'm well.	*Ewe, ndiphilile kanye.*
Where are you from?	*Uvela phi na okanye ngaphi na?*
I'm from ...	*Ndivela ...*
When will we arrive?	*Siya kufika nini na?*
The road is good.	*Indlela ilungile.*
The road is bad.	*Indlela imbi.*
I'm lost.	*Ndilahlekile.*
Is this the road to ...?	*Yindlela eya ... yini le?*
Would you show me the way to ...?	*Ungandibonisa na indlela eye ...?*
Is it possible to cross the river?	*Kunokwenzeka ukuwela umlambo?*
How much is it?	*Idla ntoni na?*
day	*usuku*
week	*iveki*
month (moon)	*inyanga*
east	*empumalanga*
west	*entshonalanga*

ZULU

Zulu is the language of the people of the same name. In terms of numbers, it is South Africa's predominant first language, with most mother-tongue speakers residing in KwaZulu-Natal.

As with several other Nguni languages, Zulu uses a variety of 'clicks' that take some dedicated practice to master to any degree. Many people don't try, although it's worth the effort, if just to provide amusement for your listeners. To ask a question, add *na* to the end of a sentence.

Hello.	*Sawubona.*
Goodbye.	*Sala kahle.*
Please.	*Jabulisa.*
Thank you.	*Ngiyabonga.*
Yes.	*Yebo.*
No.	*Cha.*
Excuse me.	*Uxolo.*
Where does this road go?	*Iqondaphi lendlela na?*
Which is the road to ...?	*Iphi indlela yokuya ku ...?*
Is it far?	*Kukude yini?*
north	*inyakatho*
south	*iningizimu*
east	*impumalanga*
west	*intshonalanga*
water	*amanzi*
food	*ukudla*
lion	*ibhubesi*
rhino (black)	*ubhejane*
rhino (white)	*umkhombe*

Glossary

For more food and drink terms, see the Food and Drink Menu Decoder (p88) and Food Glossary (p90), and for general terms see the language chapter (p615).

amahiya – traditional Swazi robe

ANC – African National Congress; national democratic organisation formed in 1912 to represent Blacks

AWB – Afrikaner Weerstandsbeweging, Afrikaner Resistance Movement; an Afrikaner extremist right-wing group

bakkie – pick-up truck

balimo – ancestors (Sotho)

Bantu – literally 'people'; during the apartheid era, used derogatorily to refer to Blacks; today, used only in reference to ethnolinguistics – ie Bantu languages, Bantu-speaking peoples

Bantustans – see homelands

BCP – Basotholand Congress Party

bilharzia – another name for schistosomiasis, a disease caused by blood flukes, passed on by freshwater snails

bittereinders – 'bitter enders' in Afrikaans; Boer resistors in the 1899–1902 Anglo-Boer War who fought until the 'bitter end'

BNP – see Basotholand National Party

Boers – see Trekboers

braai – short for braaivleis, a barbecue at which meat is cooked over an open fire (Afrikaans)

Broederbond – secret society open only to Protestant Afrikaner men; was highly influential under National Party rule

bubblegum – a form of township music influenced by Western pop

byala – traditional beer

Coloureds – apartheid-era term used to refer to those of mixed-race descent

dagga – marijuana, also known as *zol*

diamantveld – diamond fields

difaqane – 'forced migration' of many Southern African tribes (Sotho), equivalent to *mfecane* (Zulu)

dorp – small village or rural settlement

drostdy – residence of a Landdrost

free-camp – camping where you want, away from a formal campsite; permission should be sought and money offered

fynbos – literally 'fine-leafed bush', primarily proteas, heaths and ericas

gogo – grandmother (Zulu)

highveld – high-altitude grassland region

homelands – areas established for Blacks under apartheid and considered independent countries by South Africa (never accepted by UN); reabsorbed into South Africa after 1994

IFP – Inkatha Freedom Party; Black political movement, founded around 1975 and lead by Chief Mangosouthu Buthelezi, working against apartheid

igogogo – musical instrument made from an oil can

iGqirha – Xhosa spiritual healer

impi – Zulu warrior

indunas – tribal headmen

inyanga – medicine man and herbalist who also studies patterns of thrown bones

isicathamiya – a soft-shoe-shuffle style of vocal music from KwaZulu-Natal

iXhwele – Xhosa herbalist

jol – party, good time

karamat – tomb of a Muslim saint

Khoikhoi – pastoralist San

Khoisan – collective term referring to the closely related San and Khoikhoi peoples

kloof – ravine

kloofing – canyoning

knobkerry – traditional African weapon; a stick with a round knob at the end, used as a club or missile

kommando – Boer militia unit

kopje – small hill

kraal – a hut village, often with an enclosure for livestock; also a Zulu fortified village

kroeg – bar

kwaito – form of township music; a mix of mbaqanga, jive, hip-hop, house, ragga and other dance styles

kwela – township interpretation of American swing music

Landdrost – an official acting as local administrator, tax collector and magistrate

lapa – a circular building with low walls and a thatched roof, used for cooking, partying etc

LCD – Lesotho Congress for Democracy

lekgotla – place of gathering

lekker – very good, enjoyable or tasty

lekolulo – a flute-like instrument played by herd boys (Sotho)

lesokoana – wooden stick or spoon, traditionally used for stirring mealie pap

liqhaga – 'bottles' that are so tightly woven that they are used for carrying water

lowveld – low-altitude area, having scrub vegetation

maskanda – Zulu form of guitar playing

matjieshuis – Afrikaans term for traditional woven Nama 'mat' huts

mbaqanga – form of township music; literally 'dumpling' in Zulu, combining church choirs, doo-wop and sax jive

mdube – vocal style mixing European and African church choirs

mfecane – see *difaqane*

minwane – dinosaur footprints

Mkhulumnchanti – Swazi deity

mokorotlo – conical hat worn by the Basotho

molianyeoe – see *mokorotlo*

moraba-raba – popular board game played with wooden beads and four rows of hollows; known elsewhere in Africa as *mancala* and *bao*

moroka-pula – rainmaker

mqashiyo – similar vocal style to mbaqanga

muti – traditional medicine

Ncwala – Swazi first fruits ceremony

ndlovukazi – she-elephant, and traditional title of the Swazi royal mother

ngaca – (also *ngaka*) learned man

ngwenyama – lion, and traditional title of the Swazi king

PAC – Pan African Congress; political organisation of Blacks founded in 1959 to work for majority rule and equal rights

piri-piri – hot pepper

pinotage – a type of wine, a cross between Pinot Noir and Hermitage or Shiraz

pont – river ferry

Poqo – armed wing of the PAC

rikki – an open small van used as public transport in Cape Town

rondavel – a round hut with a conical roof

San – nomadic hunter-gatherers who were South Africa's earliest inhabitants

sangoma – traditional healer

sandveld – dry, sandy belt

setolo-tolo – stringed instrument played with the mouth by men (Sotho)

shebeen – drinking establishment in Black township; once illegal, now merely unlicenced

slaghuis – butchery

slenter – fake diamond

snoek – firm-fleshed migratory fish that appears off the Cape in June and July; served smoked, salted or curried

sourveld – a type of grassland

swart gevaar – 'Black threat'; term coined by Afrikaner nationalists during the 1920s

Telkom – government telecommunications company

thkolosi – small, maliciously playful beings (Sotho)

thomo – stringed instrument played by women (Sotho)

thornveld – a vegetation belt dominated by acacia thorn trees and related species

tokoloshe – evil spirits, similar to the Sotho *thkolosi* (Xhosa)

township – planned urban settlement of Blacks and Coloureds, legacy of the apartheid era

Trekboers – the first Dutch who trekked off into the interior of what is now largely Western Cape; later shortened to Boers

trokkie –truck stop

tronk – jail (Afrikaans)

tuk-tuk – motorised tricycle

uitlanders – 'foreigners'; originally the name given by Afrikaners to the immigrants who poured into the Transvaal after the discovery of gold

Umkhonto we Sizwe – armed wing of the ANC

veld – elevated open grassland (pronounced 'felt')

velskoene – handmade leather shoes

VOC – Vereenigde Oost-Indische Compagnie (Dutch East India Company)

volk – collective Afrikaans term for Afrikaners

volkstaal – people's language (Afrikaans)

volkstaat – an independent, racially pure Boer state (Afrikaans)

Voortrekkers – original Afrikaner settlers of Orange Free State and Transvaal who migrated from the Cape Colony in the 1830s in search of greater independence

Behind the Scenes

THIS BOOK

This is the 6th edition of *South Africa, Lesotho & Swaziland*. The 1st edition of this book was researched and written by Richard Everist and John Murray. The 2nd, 3rd and 4th editions were updated by Jon Murray and Jeff Williams. The 5th edition was updated by Simon Richmond, Alan Murphy, Kim Wildman and Andrew Burke. This edition was updated by Mary Fitzpatrick, Becca Blond, Gemma Pitcher, Matt Warren and Simon Richmond. Also contributing were Jane Cornwell, Dr Caroline Evans, Sally Sara, Charlene Smith, David Malherbe, Nic Vorster and Chester Mackley.

THANKS from the Authors

Mary Fitzpatrick My thanks go first and foremost to Rick, for doing most of the driving and for the unflagging support and enthusiasm, and to Christopher, for being so patient and showing me a side of Southern Africa that I hadn't seen before. A big debt of gratitude also to my coauthors, in particular to Simon Richmond, my predecessor as coordinator of this book, for so generously sharing his expertise and for helping with missing pieces of information. Finally, many thanks to the countless other people who helped me in South Africa, Lesotho and Swaziland, both with the research for this book, and during previous forays.

Becca Blond A big thanks to my sister Jessica for travelling around South Africa with me. Thanks to Kim Wildman in Cape Town; John and Andrea Martin in Pretoria; and David Malherbe for helping

update the 'Surfing on the Garden Route' boxed text. Big thanks to Garth and Elly at Wildside Backpackers in Buffalo Bay; Mirjam Elsinger & Leslie Langeler in Plett; Andrew Hockly at the Kalahari Adventure Centre; Eko-Africa for showing me a different side of Knysna; Lisa and Craig at Ashanti Lodge, and Noni and Bob at Oak Lodge, in Cape Town; the guys at Swellendam Backpackers Lodge; and to Elmine Boonzaaier in Hermanus. As always thanks to my family – David, Patricia, Jenny and Vera, and my best friend Lani – for their constant support.

Gemma Pitcher First of all big thanks to all the patient, but nameless, hotel receptionists, tourist board employees and general passers-by who helped me with so much hard-to-find information throughout my research. In the Eastern Cape, special thanks to Sal for being such a great driver and unofficial tour guide in the Transkei, Sean for sending me reams of information, Dave from Bulungula for reminding us all to keep it real, the Pondo Crop boys for taking the time to fill in so much detail, and Mike for stepping in to help with transport in Port St Johns. Thanks also to Craig Llewelyn-Williams in London, Paul and the team from the Mantis Collection, and Jaci from Madikwe – well met by the petrol pumps! Thanks also Kim Wildman for putting me up in Cape Town, and to my new friend Sylvain for making sure it wasn't ALL work while I was there! Lastly, thanks to my family and friends back home, who remain the stoical, if bemused, pillar of support they always have been.

Matt Warren Huge thanks go to Elsabee and Paul at the Johannesburg Development Agency and Mandy at the City of Johannesburg: you made my trip a joy. I am also hugely grateful to Wayne and Wendy in Tugela Mouth for the rafting, the raving and the quiet times; and to Kevin in Durban for his endless energy, tremendous thirst and nose for a good day's fishing. Thanks also to Lisa for keeping a roof over my head and a spring in my step, to Kingsley for seeing me through the Rugby World Cup and Annette for the parties and the late-night city tours.

Simon Richmond A huge round of applause, as always, goes to the dynamic Sheryl Ozinsky and her fabulous staff at Cape Town Tourism. The 'grand dames' Lee and Toni were also their usual hospitable and opinionated selves. Kim Wildman very kindly gave me a great base from which to work. Steve and Jeremy opened up a few doors in the Waterkant as did Brent Meersman into the worlds of the arts and politics. Many thanks to Anne Wallis Brown, Patricia Davidson and Estelle Jacobs for their advice and assistance.

CREDITS

South Africa, Lesotho & Swaziland 6 was commissioned and developed in Lonely Planet's Melbourne office by Hilary Rogers. The manuscript was assessed by Cathy Lanigan and Will Gourlay, who also steered the book through production. Cartography for this book was developed by Shahara Ahmed, Sarah Sloane and James Ellis.

The book was coordinated by Fionnuala Twomey (editorial) and Natasha Velleley (cartography). Susie Ashworth, Emily Coles, Kyla Gillzan, Charlotte Harrison, Victoria Harrison, Brooke Lyons, Linda Suttie and Gina Tsarouhas assisted with editing and proofing. Marion Byass, Chris Crook, Jenny Jones, Julie Sheridan and Chris Thomas assisted with cartography.

Sally Darmody and Vicki Beale laid the book out, with assistance provided by Laura Jane, Margie Jung and Michael Ruff. Pepi Bluck designed the cover and Maria Vallianos supplied the artwork. Emma Koch assisted with layout checking. Quentin Frayne prepared the Language chapter, and Fionnuala Twomey prepared the index.

Overseeing production were Eoin Dunlevy and Celia Wood (Project Managers), Dan Caleo and Martin Heng (Managing Editors), Shahara Ahmed (Managing Cartographer), and Kate McDonald and Adriana Mammarella (Layout Managers).

THANKS from Lonely Planet
Many thanks to the hundreds of travellers who used the last edition and wrote to us with helpful hints, useful advice and interesting anecdotes:
A Gep Aadriaanse, Palmer Acheson, Alasdair Adam, DK & Sue Adams, Maryanne Adams, Matthew Albert, Jessica Aldred, Jeff & Alison Allan, Alison Allgaier, Anne Almlid, Christine Anderson, Steve & Carrie Andersson, Garth Angus, Stephen Anich, Sarah Annetts, Suttipong Aramkun, Silvia Ardesi **B** Jerry Baker, Monica Baker, Bas den Bakker, Lucy Bale, Gary Barnett, Lee Barnsdale, Joerg Bartussek, Gareth Beacham, Emma Bear, Thijs Beckers, Jacqueline Bell, Joop Bemelmans, Michael Bentley, Nick Bercham, Wim Berghius, Megan Berkle, Brodbeck Bermhard, Jenny Berrisford, Amei Binns, Susan Bird, Rolf Bischoff, Marianne Biscoff, Sarah Bisi, Sarah & Gianluca Bisi, Barbara Bittman Worthen, Steve Blair, Peter Bockier, Sarah Boddie, Gerda Bogaards, Valentina Bojanic, Christian Boness, Eileen Booth, Pascal Borriello, Dirk Boye, Theo Brazao, Muck Bremer, Kate Brieley, Christine Britton, Mark Broome, Andre Brown, Anna Brown, Theronda Bruwer, Juergen Buchelt, Paul Bunney, Dean Burgess, Gary & Jo Burgess, Jan Burgess, RG Burgess, Kari Busiahn **C** Deb Cady, Carlos Arturo Camargo, Erika Carlsson, Michaela Carnaffan, Philip Carter, Jennifer Cernades, Tracy Chapman, Kim Chatfield, Cindy Choua, Charlie Clancy, Julia Clark, Mieke Clerx, Andrew Clote, Thomas Coggin, Mike & Jane Cole-Hamilton, Yvonne & Brendan Colley, Rob Collier, Tony Collins, Ben Coogan, Jenny Cook, Rebecca Coolidge, Annette Cooper, Bryan Cooper, Vicky Cosemans, Gerald Coulter, David Covill, Christina Cramer, Marianne Crane, Malcolm Craven,

Richard Crawford, Kirsten Cunningham, Monique Cuthbert, James Cutler **D** Scott Daby, Viviana D'Alto, Rob Davidowitz, Janet Davidson, Sarah Davidson, Julie Davies, Charles Dawson, Tim Day, Vikram Dayal, Fred de Groot, Frouke de Groot, Gere de Jager, Kees de Ruiter, Tom De Schauwer, Warren De Villiers, Emma Dean, Nele Decock, Gérard Decq, Emily Deere, Julia Deere, Ernest DeLeef, Steven Den Hond, Ann Desplenter, Ian C Dickinson, Donald Diedrichs, Francesco Diodato, Rob Dirven, Nancy Dlusztus, Luc & Erna Doesburg, Alison Doherty, Charly Dolman, Albertine Donker, Robbie Donovan, Jan & Karin Doorakkers, G Downman, Ellen Drake, Elizabeth Drew, Lunay Dreyer, Ian Drury, Andre du Plessis, Peter Duifhuizen, Christine Duxbury **E** Cathy Eckhardt, Carla Eddles, Gary Edgar, John & Ailsa Edmonds, Sylvia Edwards, Martina Eggert, Ilya Eigenbrot, Frank Eisenhuth, Mariette Elling, Buzz Ellingworth, Paul Empringham, Pascal Endstra, Jim Evans, Julie Evans, Margaret Evans, Peter Evans **F** Cooley Fales, Casper Fargaze, Mariella Farrugia, Eugen Fehler, Megan Felton, Patrick Fiere, Ralf Figi, Lisa Findley, Hanne Finholt, Pandora Fleming-Smith, Kate Flood, Jill Foster, Eep Francken, Bryan & Sonja Fraser, Frederic A Frech, Mike French, Sascha Frenzel, Michael Freund, Jens Friis, Renee Frouws, Alex Furstenberg **G** Michaela Gabriel, Rolf & Christa Gaebele, Mark Galecki, Chris Gandy, Doug Gandy, Jenny & Oliviero Gardella, Elizabeth Garrett, Dana Garrison, Ewan Gatherer, Stefan Gergely, Anne Gevers, Kosty Gilis, Tom Gilmore, Ben Giola, Maggie Gliksten, Harry & Liz Glover, Jennifer Goldenstede, Peter Goltl, Nicola Goodman, Jack Graham, Mark Graham, Romano Grandis, Peter Graser, Sybille & Klaus Gravius, Vasily V Grebennikov, Jim Green, Val Green, Sarah Greenfield, Guus Greve, Mark & Dorothy Griffiths, Stefan Gutmann **H** Matej Hacin, Ole Peder Hagen, Jitka Hajkova, Hana Hall, Lucy C Hall, Penny Hall, Thomas Hall, Tina Hall, Myriam Hamel, Andrew Hamling, Eva Hammer, Christian Hansen, Angus Hardern, Barbara Harriott, Peter Harris, Ashley Harty, Michelle Harvey, Kate Harvie, Chris Haverly, Helen Hawkings, Joern Hendrichs, Tom E Henkemans, Jennifer Henry, Steve Henry, Stefaan Herbout, Andrew Hill, Peter Hiller, Matti Holmberg, Elizabeth Hope, Reuben Horsley, Sarah Horton, Derek Huby, Glenda Hudson, Max Huggett, David Hulshuis, James & Jane Humphreys, Karen Humphreys, Maureen Hunter, Bonnie S Hyra **I** Peter Isaksson, Alene Ivey **J** Wijnand Jakobs, Steve James, Rory Jenkins, CM Johnson, Rebecca Johnson, Hugh & Maire Jones, Jonathon G Jones, Martin Jones, Stella Jundul, Catherine Junor **K** James Kagambi, Joanne Kaptein, Helen Karavanas, Itamar Katz, Christophe Keckeıs, Ben & Paul Keown, Christine Kerner, Clare Kerr, Steve Ketola, Patti Kidd, Silje Kile, Paul Kilfoil, Leslie King, Tim Kingston, Pat Kinney, Giel Klanker, Christine Knibbs, Joris Koene, Wessel Koornstra, Istvan Kops, Nicky Korunich, Ulf Kotlenga, Klaas Jan Kramer, Goedele Krekels, Uli Kress, Birgit Kroener-Herwig, M Kruger, Mario Kutz **L** Noshir M Lam, Sandy Lam, Radka Langhammerova, Mark Lawford, Marc Le Dilosquer, Helen Leadbitter, Iara Lee, Angela Leeding, Michelle Legault, Chris Lempers, Bruno Lenaerts, Cathy Levesque, Judy Levison, Miltos Liakopoulos, Peter Lie, Frank Liesegang, Ying Ling Lin, Wolfgang Lindbichler, Johan Lindqvist, Mary Lindsey, John Linnemeier, Gaby Lipscomb, Michael Locketz, Angela, Nicola & Jan Lorenz, Marlien Lourens, Henneke Louter, Rosalie Lubbinge, Richard Lucas, Artur

Lueders **M** Morgan Mabaso, Sophie Macgregor, Marian Mackenzie-Ross, Bernard Madigan, Richard Mahoney, Stephan Maier, John Mamone, Melissa & John Mann, Florient Mannaioni, Alan Mansfield, Pat Mansfield, J Marcovecchio, Ilya Marritz, David & Sally Martin, Karl Martin, Shelly Martin, Su Martin, Toby Martin, Clara Mindy Martone-Boyce, Debbie & Nick Maskell, Robyn Mason, Nick Matzke, Beth McCabe, Richard McCarthy, Carolyn McHugh, Sue McKenzie, Nel McLucas, Fiona McPhie, Olga Mears, Maarten Mettrop, Thibault Meyer-Jueres, E Meyrick, Robert Miles, Natasha Milijasevic, Natasha & Paul Pellizzari Milijasevic, Greg Mill, Rob Millar, Keith & Mandy Miller, James Mills, Corina Miltenburg, Barbara Molony, Karin Moor, Mirban Mooyman, Chris & Sandy Morgan, Iwan Morgan, Jonathan Morgan, Karyn Morgan, Lauren Morley, Sarah-Jane Morley, Siiri Morley, Janine Moroni, David Morris, Heather Mothershead, Rolf Muggen, Tim Muirhead, Iain Mulligan, Joanne Munnerley, Susanne Munt, Michel Muylle **N** Giorgia Naccarato, Frick Nadja, Elaine K Napier, Andreas Naujoks, Jacob Nestingen, Neville Newton, Nigel Vere Nicoll, Freerk Nienhuis, Alex Nikolic, Amanda Norman, Sarah Nouwen, Ami Nukada, Pam Nunn **O** Lawrence Oberfeld, Julie Odell, Orla O'Flanagan, Vic Okamoto, John oldham, Soren Olesen, Jarl Olsen, Jacquey & Alfred Oppenheimer, Tracy & Massimo Orione, Paddy Orpen, Jen Osborne, Volker & Rolf Ostheimer, Dan O'Toole, Bianca Oudshoff, Lynne & Wayne Oxenham **P** Vittorio Paielli, Janet Palfrey, Michael Pancoe, Ken Park, Rowena Parry, Kiran & Maya Patel, Daniel Paz, Gavin Pearce, Zdenek Pecka, Bob Perrin, Giorgio Perversi, J Peters, Karen Pickett, Heinie Pieterse, R Pithers, Andrew Plested, Tibor Poelmann, Charlie Pointer, Jan Maarten Pol, Mike Pomfrey, Kathy Posey, Lance Posey, Julie Price, Mike Price, Philippe Priquet **Q** Arnoud Quanjer, Todd Quattro **R** Niels Rameil, Peter Ras, Thomas Rau, Helen & Paul-Olivier Raynaud-Lacroze, Ian Reason, Lawrence Reichard, Lynne Reid Banks, Jacqueline Remmelzwaal, Benoit Renard, Siegbard Reppisch, Inken Resa-Thomas, Meloney Retallack, Heiko Reuper, Nick Reynolds, Thomas Richter, Andrew Ridler, Evan Roberts, Leslie Robin, Malcolm Robinson, Keith Rodwell, Andrea Rogge, M Roskam, Kari Ruitenberg, Vic Russell, Monika Rutishauser, Elizabeth Rutter, David Ryan, John Ryder **S** David Saffery, Stanley & Debbie Sampson, Juliette Sanders, Marian Sansom, Andre Schaapherder, Robert Schmid, Markus Schmidt, Nicholas Schmidt, Reinhild Schmidt, Matthias Schneider, Kilaan Schoeman, Josette Schoenmakers, Debra Scott, Charlene Searle, Chris Seavell, Nick Sebley, Ulrike Seidel, Paul Selinger, Erika Seymour, Olwen Shand, Kim Shockley, Emily Shults, Lawrie Shuttleworth, Tom Siebeling, Luisa Sieveking, Hanna Simson, Eshana Singh, Niko Sklarzik, Boris Skoric, Evan Smith, Fergus Smith, Jonathan Smith, Keith Smith, Tom Smyth, Anthony Snelson, Karin Snelson, Susan Snijders, Gail Snyman, Michael Soier, Martina Soudek, Jens Sprenger, Ervin Staub, Patricia Steele, Guenter Stempfer, Anouhk Sterken, Nicky Stevens, Angus Stewart, Frank Stober, Karlheinz & Elke Stocker, Ruth C Stoky, Katja Stolle, Terrilee Stone, Bill & Ann Stoughton, Ivo Streng, Jordy Sturms, Hoylen Sue **T** Tiawanna Taylor, Sofia Tengvall, R Thackham, Dianne Thomas, Sharon Thomas, Thomas Thomas, Paul Thomson, Kate Thornburg, HB Thorpe, Trond Thue, Alec Tiffin, Jean & Anne Marie Tourneboeuf, Philippe Tran, Luca

Trapani, Karen Treanor, Danielle Tromp, Daniela Truttmann, Jo Turner, Daniel Twentyman **U** Fabio Umehara, Camille Unnerstall, Heike Uphoff, Brett Utian, Rune Utne Reiten **V** Signild Vallgarda, Martin van Buren, Mia van Buul, Joyce van der Heijden, Gerrit van der Staak, Zannie van der Walt, Corne van Dongen, Wilma van Hoeven, Martin van Huijstee, Sofie van Luyck, Teun van Metelen, Caroline van Moorsel, Geogette van Schothorst, Jeanette & Martijn van Werkhoven, Jeffrey van Wylick, Lettie van Zyl, Peter van't Westeinde, Jos Vanwede, SB Vaughan, Annemarie Veenkamp, Marcel Verheijen, Sean Vermooten, Byron Versfeld, Mark Vickerage, Sabine Villmann, Martin Vipond, Esther Visser, Jolanda Vissers, Gerald Vlach, Joost Vollaard, Franco A Volta, Alex von Furstenberg, Craig von Hagen, Esther Vusser **W** Armin Wagner, Jennifer Walker, Sam Wallace, Kevin Walters, Sally Walton, Bill Walworth, Steph Weeks, Sara Wehter, Danielle Welsh, Kerrin Werner, Nick, Lindsay, Thomas & Esther Whitlock; Camilla Wickstrom, Elke Widmayer, Stephan Widmer, Natasja Wientjes, Hennie Wiersma-den Dulk, Eddie Wilde, Aled Williams, Gillian Williams, Paul Williams, Wayne & Pat Williams, Carol Williamson, Sean & Dympna Wilson, Ian Wittet, Katherine Wolf, John Woodland, Ian Wright, Barry Wrightson, Veronica Wrightson **Y** Christina Yee **Z** August Ziegler, Betty Ziegler, Michael Ziemba, Niklas Zimmermann, Mike Zinsley

ACKNOWLEDGMENTS

Many thanks to the following for the use of their content:

Globe on back cover – Mountain High Maps® © 1993 Digital Wisdom, Inc.

Index

INDEX

000 Map pages
000 Location of colour photographs

644

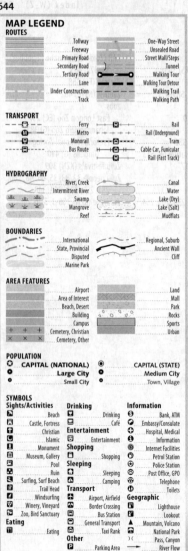
LONELY PLANET OFFICES

Australia
Head Office
Locked Bag 1, Footscray, Victoria 3011
☎ 03 8379 8000, fax 03 8379 8111
talk2us@lonelyplanet.com.au

USA
150 Linden St, Oakland, CA 94607
☎ 510 893 8555, toll free 800 275 8555
fax 510 893 8572, info@lonelyplanet.com

UK
72–82 Rosebery Ave,
Clerkenwell, London EC1R 4RW
☎ 020 7841 9000, fax 020 7841 9001
go@lonelyplanet.co.uk

France
1 rue du Dahomey, 75011 Paris
☎ 01 55 25 33 00, fax 01 55 25 33 01
bip@lonelyplanet.fr, www.lonelyplanet.fr

Published by Lonely Planet Publications Pty Ltd
ABN 36 005 607 983

© Lonely Planet 2004

© photographers as indicated 2004